QUINLAN'S
ILLUSTRATED DIRECTORY OF FILM CHARACTER ACTORS

QUINLAN'S
ILLUSTRATED DIRECTORY OF
FILM CHARACTER ACTORS

DAVID QUINLAN

b

B.T. Batsford Ltd · London

To Peter Brummell, whose continued support and
research has greatly helped in my ambition to make
this book the best of its kind

First published 1985
Reprinted 1989
First paperback edition 1992
New edition 1995

ISBN 0 7134 7040 2

Printed in Great Britain by
The Bath Press, Bath
for the Publisher
B.T. Batsford Ltd
4 Fitzhardinge Street
London W1H 0AH

FOREWORD

THE classic film character actor of yesteryear has almost disappeared from today's screens. Theirs were the faces you almost always recognized, but whose names you rarely knew.

True character actors are few today and their names often appear before the title, unlike their counterparts of the Hollywood studio years. These denizens of our late-night TV screens could count themselves lucky if they were billed in small print following the word 'With' in the credits; for many early films carried no cast lists at all, leaving the audience with only the memory of a familiar face.

And so these people stayed in the shadows, confident only of constant employment, especially if they stuck to the stereotypes in which many found themselves established, be it flapping fusspot, blustering blatherer, tough tomato, cockney char, faded floozie, busybody, nosy neighbour, vicious villain, comic cop, femme fatale, Latin lover, doughty dowager or foreign fiend.

Their names remained a secret between them and their friends, their agents and those producers and directors wise enough to hire these ever-reliables when their image became familiar. Thus, in the boom years of the late 1930s and early 1940s, such actors might run up as many as 20 film credits in a single year. No wonder their faces, bit part by bit part, gradually became more recognizable.

Hard though many fought against it, such 'typing' was part of their attraction. You could rely on well-loved mannerisms, and variations on a familiar performance that could steal a scene from the star at the flick of an eyelid, a clearing of the throat, or the arch of an eyebrow. It was no more possible to see icy Gale Sondergaard as a nice person than it was to visualize twitchy little Elisha Cook as a winner, or to see British films' favourite foreigner Eric Pohlmann as a trusty friend.

And so, although our favourites understandably tried to take on a wider range of roles, their attempts, although interesting within the context of a single film, usually failed to break the pattern that had been set in stone, any more than they met with filmgoers' favour.

In the mind's eye, it's still possible — with the help of these players — to take trips into whole genres of the past — for example, the underworld of Hollywood's *noir* history. Walking perhaps too quickly down these mean streets, one might be tailed by scowling, shadowy Jack Lambert, and have to dodge swiftly into a darkly-lit nightclub, where wheezy Percy Helton would be pinkly polishing glasses at the bar. Sidling past menacing Marc Lawrence, cigarette drooping from lip, at the corner table, one might hurry up the stairs to seek uneasy sanctuary with crooked club owner Laird Cregar, breaking in on his conversation with squirrel-eyed sycophant John Abbott.

Escaping into the night, you could be picked up by cheery cabbie Harry Bellaver and head for the station where dilapidated Houseley Stevenson or bespectacled, less trustworthy Charles Halton might sell you a ticket to a train heading out of town, where you'd be welcomed aboard by chubby conductor Harry Hayden, but tracked by hired killers like lean John Kellogg and swarthy Abner Biberman.

Riding into town in a western could be equally dodgy. There were always mean hombres like Jack

Tim Curry

Elam waiting to shoot you in the back from ambush. Punk kids like Skip Homeier eager to prove their skill in the draw. Gamblers like grimly smiling Victor Jory to outwit. The seemingly benevolent town banker (Edward Andrews) and crocodile-smiling saloon owner (Lyle Bettger) would most likely be behind most of the crooked rackets around. All the while, old-timers like Clem Bevans and Hank Worden kept a low profile in their rocking chairs on the boardwalk while solid citizens like Edgar Buchanan lived longer if they stayed indoors.

In the world of musicals, if the backers of your show included windy Thurston Hall and disapproving Cecil Cunningham, you were in trouble: they and their cash would disappear at the mere whiff of scandal. But there were always such true-blue, rough diamond types like William Demarest and James Gleason to see you through.

In swashbucklers, you would do well to beware the glint in the eyes of such suave villains as Robert Douglas, George Macready, John Sutton and Henry Daniell. These guys were mean mothers with a sword and about as trustworthy as the glacial charms of Binnie Barnes, Frieda Inescort, Hillary Brooke or Isobel Elsom as Milady This-Or-That. You can meet most of these characters again in the pages that follow; the remainder can be found in our companion volume, *Quinlan's Illustrated Directory of Film Stars*.

Simon Callow

EXPLAINING THE CHOICE

Although today's actors largely escape such enjoyable type-casting, it has left a yawning gap in the 1980s and 1990s between character stars, like Dianne Wiest, Forest Whitaker and many others, and the true bit-part player no longer destined to make a mark in film history.

Yet these versatile quasi-stars are also among the true inheritors of the mantle of the character players of days gone by — and you will find an abundance of present-day examples in this book, lodged here not to belittle their star status, but to forge a link between the present and the past.

Meanwhile the relatively few genuine character actors of recent times — such people as M Emmet Walsh, Stephen Tobolowsky, Hector Elizondo, J T Walsh and Robert Prosky — find themselves here too: more typecast, perhaps, than the character stars billed above them, but a nonetheless welcome sight for all that, in almost any movie.

As always, a few possible inclusions have been left by the wayside. With modern stars especially, this is always a contentious and controversial decision-making area. The poor author can rely on a few of those selected amazingly dropping from view, or suddenly deciding to act in the theatre, while a handful of those left out will seemingly take the decision in the mid 1990s to begin to work fiercely in the cinema.

Michael Gambon

In this latter category of missing men, a regretful tip of the hat to mournful, muskrat-like, Irish-born Michael Gambon, who followed his brilliant Maigret on TV with a flurry of film roles in Britain and Hollywood; the goateed, wild-eyed Steve Buscemi of *Reservoir Dogs* fame; curly-haired, chubby-cheeked Colm Meaney, portrayer of wily Irishmen; Tim Curry, a striking eccentric lead now blossoming as unctuously hand-rubbing types; native American Graham Greene of *Dances With Wolves*; cool, calculating black American Samuel L Jackson, the Oscar nominee from *Pulp Fiction*; and dazzling Simon Callow, the waistcoated *bon viveur* from *Four Weddings and a Funeral*. All can at least look forward to inclusion in a third edition if the author and publisher can stand the strain.

With regard to the filmographies that follow the brief career study on each performer, these are as complete as human endeavour can achieve, including every film appearance that could be found, as well as TV movies, short subjects, and narrations, both in fiction and non-fiction; those carried over from the first edition have, in many cases, been substantially expanded, thanks to the researches not only of the author, but of film buffs all over the world, to whom grateful thanks.

Nonetheless, further additions will be more than welcome. One cannot imagine that such in-and-out cough-and-spitters as Hank Worden, Alma Beltran and Britain's Arthur Mullard have yielded up anything like a full credit list yet. As they stand, however, all the entries in this book contain the longest filmographies on their subjects yet published.

References to Academy Awards won and, in most cases, Oscar nominations as well, should be found within the notes on the actor or actress concerned. Any symbols or abbreviations are explained at the foot of the entry, except the single asterisk, which will always indicate a short film, that is one of three reels (about 35 minutes) or less. Photographs are usually taken from a player's most prolific or best-remembered period, unless the choice of picture was restricted by the difficulty in hunting down anything on the subject at all. Dates of death are complete to 1 April 1995, and the earliest date of birth has usually been taken, provided that it has been corroborated by more than one source.

Alphabetical order has again been strictly adhered to in the sequence of entries. Thus once more Le Mesurier follows Lembeck but comes before Leonard, while DeLuise is sandwiched between Dehner and Demarest. Mac and Mc names are not treated as one — so you may need to check in both places. Dates given for films are intended to be the copyright

Steve Buscemi

dates shown on the credit titles of the film. On the rare occasion that a film does not bear a date, the year of earliest showing has been chosen.

The following pages are a tribute to 1110 men and women who have entertained us right royally over the years. But perhaps they would wish no better tribute than that uttered by Sydney Greenstreet in *The Maltese Falcon* when he said 'By gad sir, you are a character — that you are.'

ACKNOWLEDGEMENTS

I would like to thank the scores of correspondents from around the world who have made contributions to this second edition of what I hope is a very special book — among them Bill Ayres, Christopher Glazebrook, Ray Gain, Matthew Wilkinson, Sunil Hiranandani, Henry Rintoul, Allen Dace, Lionel Perry, Alan Frank, Joan Lee, Howard Thomas, Matthew Wilkinson, Paul Hathaway, Gary Nichols, Bill Oughton, M S Eastwood and Richard Webber. My apologies to all the important contributors whose names I have left off this list. My thanks also to the Stills Section of the British Film Institute, without whose files the book would not be nearly as well illustrated. For additional photographs, I am also grateful to Ray Gains, of Vermont, USA, who has generously improved on some existing photographs in the first edition which fell below the overall standard.

My thanks to those actors who found the time to check their own filmographies, and, in a few cases, supplied me with photographs as well. The remainder of the stills in this book not covered by the foregoing notes are from my own collection.

Thanks also to the staff of the Indian Film Archives for checking and verifying the copyright dates for the Hindi films of Saeed Jaffrey.

Almost all the photographs in this book were originally issued to publicize or promote films or TV material made or distributed by the following companies, to whom I gladly offer acknowledgement: Allied Artists, American-International, Anglo-Amalgamated, Artificial Eye, Associated British-Pathé, ATP, ATV, Avco-Embassy, BIP, Brent-Walker, British and Dominions, British United Artists, Cannon-Classic, Carolco, Cinerama, Columbia, Walt Disney/Buena Vista, Eagle-Lion, Ealing Studios, EMI, Enterprise, Entertainment, Filmakers Associates, First Artists, First Independent, First National, Gainsborough, Gala, Gaumont/Gaumont-British, Goldwyn, Granada TV, Grand National, Hammer, Hand-Made, Hemdale, Hollywood Pictures, Lippert, London Films, London Weekend TV, Lorimar, Mainline, Medusa, Metro-Goldwyn-Mayer, Miracle, Monogram, New Line, New World, Orion, Palace Pictures, Paramount, PRC, The Rank Organization, Rediffusion, Republic, RKO/RKO Radio, Hal Roach, Selznick, Touchstone Pictures, 20th Century-Fox, UIP, United Artists, Universal/Universal-International, Vestron, Virgin Films, Warner Brothers and Yorkshire TV.

Whistler. The Crime Doctor's Warning (GB: The Doctor's Warning). 1946: The Notorious Lone Wolf. One More Tomorrow. Bandit of Sherwood Forest. Anna and the King of Siam. Humoresque. 1947: Deception. Navy Bound. The Web. Adventure Island. Time Out of Mind. The Woman in White. 1948: If Winter Comes. Dream Girl. The Return of the Whistler. 1949: Madame Bovary. 1950: Her Wonderful Lie. Sideshow. 1951: Thunder on the Hill (GB: Bonaventure). Crosswinds. Thunder in the East (released 1953). 1952: The Merry Widow. Rogue's March. 1953: The Steel Lady (GB: The Treasure of Kalifa). Sombrero. 1957: Public Pigeon Number One. 1958: Gigi. 1963: Who's Minding the Store? 1965: The Greatest Story Ever Told. 1966: Gambit. 1967: The Jungle Book (voice only). 1968: Three Guns for Texas (originally for TV). 1969: 2,000 Years Later. 1973: The Cat Creature (TV). 1975: The Black Bird. 1976: Sherlock Holmes in New York (TV). 1982: Slapstick (US: Slapstick of Another Kind). 1983: Smorgasbord (completed 1981. Later: Cracking Up). 1985: Lady Jane. 1993: Dragon World.

Fired Wife. *The Last Will and Testament of Tom Smith. 1944: Mr Skeffington. Follow the Boys. An American Romance. The Hitler Gang (narrator only). 1945: The Affairs of Susan. Duffy's Tavern. Kiss and Tell. 1946: The Kid from Brooklyn. 13 Rue Madeleine. 1947: The Fabulous Joe. 1948: Dream Girl. That Lady in Ermine. 1953: Island in the Sky. So This Is Love (GB: The Grace Moore Story). 1954: Night People. 1955: The Indian Fighter. 1956: Sincerely, Willis Wayde (TV). The Steel Jungle. 1957: Bernardine. Raintree County. 1958: Handle With Care. 1964: The Confession (GB: TV as Quick! Let's Get Married). 1965: Mirage. 1971: Zora. 1973: Man Without a Country (TV). Silent Night, Bloody Night (later Death House. GB: Night of the Dark Full Moon). 1984: The Ultimate Solution of Grace Quigley (GB: Grace Quigley).

ABBOTT, John 1905–

Dishevelled British-born actor with basilisk eyes and drooping lower lip, playing eccentric, often untrustworthy characters in Hollywood from 1941. He began his career as a commercial artist, then switched to acting and appeared on the London stage and in a few British films before going permanently to America, where his continental-style features were seen in many roles. Memorable in *Jane Eyre* and *The Woman in White*, he had a leading role in one film: *London Blackout Murders*. He still popped up in occasional film and TV roles into his seventies.

1935: Conquest of the Air (released 1940). 1937: Mademoiselle Docteur. The Return of the Scarlet Pimpernel. 1938: This Man is News. Algiers. 1939: Ten Days in Paris (US: Missing Ten Days). The Saint in London. 1941: The Shanghai Gesture. 1942: They Got Me Covered. Mrs Miniver. London Blackout Murders (GB: Secret Motive). Joan of Paris. Nightmare. Get Hep to Love (GB: She's My Lovely). The Gorilla Man. Rubber Racketeers. This Above All. 1943: Mission to Moscow. Dangerous Blondes. Jane Eyre. 1944: The Mask of Dimitrios. Summer Storm. Cry of the Werewolf. U-Boat Prisoner (GB: Dangerous Mists). Once Upon a Time. End of the Road. Abroad with Two Yanks. The Falcon in Hollywood. The Imposter. Secrets of Scotland Yard. 1945: The Vampire's Ghost. Pursuit to Algiers. Saratoga Trunk. Scotland Yard Investigator. Honeymoon Ahead. A Thousand and One Nights. The Power of the

ABEL, Walter 1898–1987

Stern-looking, often moustachioed, dark-haired American actor, strangely one of Broadway's foremost exponents of farce before embarking seriously on a movie career that saw him much cast as senior officers, lawyers and chiefs of detectives. Played D'Artagnan in his second sound film; otherwise mainly in supporting roles. Latterly frequently seen as a harassed father. Remained a working actor into his eighties.

1918: Out of a Clear Sky. 1920: The North Wind's Malice. 1930: Liliom. 1935: The Three Musketeers. 1936: The Lady Consents. Two in the Dark. The Witness Chair. Fury. We Went to College (GB: The Old School Tie). Second Wife. 1937: Portia on Trial (GB: The Trial of Portia Merriman). Wise Girl. Green Light. 1938: Law of the Underworld. Racket Busters. Men With Wings. 1939: First Offender. King of the Turf. 1940: Miracle on Main Street. Who Killed Aunt Maggie? Dance Girl Dance. Arise, My Love. 1941: Michael Shayne, Private Detective. Hold Back the Dawn. Skylark. Hearts in Springtime/Glamour Boy. 1942: Beyond the Blue Horizon. Star Spangled Rhythm. Holiday Inn. Wake Island. 1943: So Proudly We Hail!

ABRAHAM, F. Murray 1939–

Lean, lithe, dark, frequently moustachioed Texas-born American actor of gaunt features and Syrian/Italian origin, a taller version of Britain's Ben Kingsley. Like Kingsley, Abraham had to wait a long time for his big chance (in Abraham's case, Salieri in *Amadeus*), but then crowned his triumph with an Oscar. He has since done sterling work in the theatre, while remaining difficult to cast in films, where he has appeared increasingly in cameo roles. The F stands for Fahrid.

1971: They Might Be Giants. 1973: Serpico. 1975: The Prisoner of Second Avenue. The Sunshine Boys. 1976: The Ritz. All the President's Men. 1977: Sex and the Married Woman (TV). 1978: Madman/Camp 708. The Big Fix. 1983: Scarface. 1984: Amadeus. 1986: The Name of the Rose. 1987: The Rose of the Names. 1988: Russicum/The Third Solution. The Favorite. 1989: Personal Choice/Beyond the Stars. Slipstream. The Betrothed. An Innocent Man. 1990: Eye of the Widow. The Bonfire of the Vanities. Largo Desolato (TV). The Battle of the Three Kings. 1991: Cadence (GB: Stockade). By the Sword. Mobsters. Helena. Money. The First Circle. 1992: Sweet Killing. Quiet Flows the Don. 1993: Finnegan's Wake. Last Action Hero. Liberazione dozier (TV). National Lampoon's Loaded Weapon 1. La seconda volta. Nostradamus. 1994: Surviving the Game. Un film de fare. La dernière carte. 1995: Dshamilja/Jamila. Sweetheart.

34th Street. Giorgino. Occhiopinocchio. Jacob (TV). 1995: A Kid in King Arthur's Court. Citizen X (TV).

ACOSTA, Rodolfo or Rudy 1920–1974
Dark, moustachioed, hawkishly handsome Mexican actor, in Hollywood from 1950 after acclaim in his native country. In the film capital, however, Acosta found himself mostly confined to playing sneering bandits in huge sombreros. A little cold, perhaps, for bona-fide leading roles, although he was top-billed once, in the minor crime drama *The Tijuana Story*. Then it was back to a whole posse of westerns before his early death. Sometimes also billed as Rudolfo.

ACKLAND, Joss
(Jocelyn Ackland) 1928–
Fair-haired, heavily-built British stage actor hardly seen in films until the 1970s, when he played a string of characters who often hid various shades of wickedness beneath a florid complexion and a beaming smile. But the stage gave him his biggest hit — as Perón in the London production of *Evita*. In the late 1980s and early 1990s, he mixed scene-stealing character roles with some really nasty villains. His hearty tones are frequently used for narrations, voice-overs and commercials.

1950: Seven Days to Noon. 1952: Ghost Ship. 1958: Next to No Time! A Midsummer Night's Dream (dubbed voice only). 1960: Die Brücke (GB and US: The Bridge). 1962: In Search of the Castaways. 1965: Rasputin the Mad Monk. 1966: East West Island (narrator only). 1969: Crescendo. 1970: The House That Dripped Blood. 1971: Villain. Mr Forbush and the Penguins (US: Cry of the Penguins). 1972: England Made Me. The Happiness Cage/The Mind Snatchers. 1973: Hitler: The Last Ten Days. Penny Gold. The Three Musketeers (The Queen's Diamonds). 1974: S*P*Y*S. The Black Windmill. The Little Prince. 1975: Royal Flash. Great Expectations (TV. GB: cinemas). Operation Daybreak. One of Our Dinosaurs is Missing. *The Magic Dream (narrator only). 1976: *World Within a Ring (narrator only). 1977: Silver Bears. 1978: Watership Down (voice only). Who is Killing the Great Chefs of Europe? (GB: Too Many Chefs). 1979: Cuba (voice only). The Love Tapes (narrator only). Saint Jack. 1980: A Nightingale Sang in Berkeley Square/The Biggest Bank Robbery (originally for cinemas, but shown only on TV). Rough Cut. The Apple (GB: Star Rock). Dangerous Davies The Last Detective (TV). 1985: Lady Jane. A Zed and Two Noughts. 1987: The Sicilian. White Mischief. 1988: To Kill a Priest. It Couldn't Happen Here. 1989: Lethal Weapon 2. Jekyll and Hyde (TV). 1990: The Hunt for Red October. To Forget Palermo. The Secret Life of Ian Fleming (TV). Tre colonne in cronaca. 1991: The Object of Beauty. The Princess and the Goblin (voice only). The Bridge. Bill and Ted's Bogus Journey. A Murder of Quality (TV). Once Upon a Crime. Sherlock Holmes and the Incident at Victoria Falls (TV). 1992: The Mighty Ducks (GB: Champions). Project Shadowchaser. Voices in the Garden (TV). 1993: Nowhere to Run. 1994: Raging Earth. Mad Dogs and Englishmen. Miracle on

1946: Rosenda. La malquerida. 1947: The Fugitive. 1949: Salon Mexico. 1950: Victimas del pecado. Pancho Villa Returns. One Way Street. 1951: Victimas del divorcio. The Bullfighter and the Lady. 1952: Llévarme en tus brazos. Horizons West. Yankee Buccaneer. 1953: San Antone. Destination Gobi. Wings of the Hawk. Appointment in Honduras. City of Bad Men. Hondo. 1954: Passion. Drum Beat. Night People. 1955: A Life in the Balance. The Littlest Outlaw. 1956: Bandido! The Proud Ones. La ultimo rebelde (GB and US: The Last Rebel). 1957: The Tijuana Story. Apache Warrior. The Last Stagecoach West. Trooper Hook. 1958: From Hell to Texas (GB: Manhunt). 1960: Flaming Star. Let No Man Write My Epitaph. Walk Like a Dragon. 1961: One-Eyed Jacks. Posse from Hell. The Second Time Around. 1962: How the West Was Won. Savage Sam. 1964: Rio Conchos. 1965: The Sons of Katie Elder. The Reward. The Greatest Story Ever Told. 1966: Return of the Seven. 1967: Valley of Mystery (originally for TV). Stranger on the Run (TV). 1968: Dayton's Devils. Impasse. 1969: Che! Young Billy Young. 1970: Run Simon Run (TV). Flap (GB: The Last Warrior). The Great White Hope. 1971: Legacy of Blood. 1972: The Magnificent Seven Ride!

ADAM, Ronald 1896–1979
Tall, ministerial, balding British actor with eyebrows like woolly earthworms and big, round, smily face. He was mostly seen as bureaucrats and administrators: his authority perhaps stemmed from his days as an officer in World War I (he was a prisoner-of-war) and a wing-commander in World

War II (wangling his way in despite his age). In between, he gave up a career as a chartered accountant to concentrate on the stage. Film character roles became plentiful as he neared middle age. Also a prolific writer and the author of several plays.

1936: Song of Freedom. 1938: The Drum (US: Drums). Strange Boarders. Kate Plus Ten. Inspector Hornleigh. 1939: Q Planes (US: Clouds Over Europe). The Lion Has Wings. The Missing People. Meet Maxwell Archer (US: Maxwell Archer, Detective). Too Dangerous to Live. At the Villa Rose (US: House of Mystery). 1940: Hell's Cargo (US: Dangerous Cargo). 1941: The Big Blockade. 1942: The Foreman Went to France (US: Somewhere in France). The Day Will Dawn (US: The Avengers). The Young Mr Pitt. 1943: Escape to Danger. 1945: Journey Together. Pink String and Sealing Wax. 1946: Green for Danger. 1947: The Phantom Shot. Take My Life. Fame is the Spur. An Ideal Husband. 1948: Bonnie Prince Charlie. The Bad Lord Byron. Counterblast. All Over the Town. Christopher Columbus. The Case of Charles Peace. 1949: Under Capricorn. Black Magic. That Dangerous Age (US: If This Be Sin). Helter Skelter. Diamond City. Obsession (US: The Hidden Room). 1950: My Daughter Joy (US: Operation X). Seven Days to Noon. Shadow of the Past. The Adventurers (US: The Great Adventure). 1951: Hell is Sold Out. The Lavender Hill Mob. Laughter in Paradise. The Late Edwina Black. Mr Denning Drives North. Captain Horatio Hornblower RN (US: Captain Horatio Hornblower). I'll Never Forget You (US: The House in the Square). Angels One Five. Scrooge (US: A Christmas Carol). 1952: Appointment in London. Hindle Wakes (US: Holiday Week). Circumstantial Evidence. Top Secret (US: Mr Potts Goes to Moscow). My Wife's Lodger. 1953: Thought to Kill. Flannelfoot. Stryker of the Yard. The Million Pound Note (US: Man With a Million). The Beachcomber. Malta Story. Front Page Story. Martin Luther. 1954: Escape by Night. Johnny on the Spot. To Dorothy a Son (US: Cash on Delivery). The Black Knight. Seagulls Over Sorrento (US: Crest of the Wave). Forbidden Cargo. 1955: The Man Who Never Was. Private's Progress. 1956: Reach for the Sky. Bhowani Junction. Around the World in 80 Days. Tons of Trouble. Assignment Redhead (US: Requirement for a Redhead). Lust for Life. 1957: Sea Wife. The Surgeon's Knife. Kill Me Tomorrow. Woman and the Hunter (GB:

Triangle on Safari). Carry On Admiral (US: The Ship Was Loaded). The Naked Truth (US: Your Past is Showing!). 1958: The Golden Disc. 1959: Carlton-Browne of the FO (US: Man in a Cocked Hat). The Man Who Could Cheat Death. Please Turn Over. 1960: Snowball. Kidnapped. And the Same to You. 1961: Shoot to Kill. Offbeat. Three on a Spree. Carry On Regardless. 1962: The Golden Rabbit. Postman's Knock. Two-Letter Alibi. Inside Information. Satan Never Sleeps (GB: The Devil Never Sleeps). 1963: Cleopatra. Heavens Above! 1964: The Tomb of Ligeia. 1966: Who Killed the Cat? 1968: Hellboats. 1970: Song of Norway. 1971: Zeppelin. The Ruling Class. 1973: The Zoo Robbery. 1976: The Man from Nowhere. 1978: The Greek Tycoon.

ADAMS, Dorothy 1900–1988
Dark-haired, weepy-eyed, careworn-looking American actress whose characters wore expressions of dismay or concern and were often pioneer women or work-hard-for-the-kids wives, ground down by life and/or the land. Richly described by one 1950s correspondent as 'a human wailing wall'. Married fellow character player Byron Foulger (qv). In the early 1960s, she became a lecturer on theatre arts, and appeared less often in films and television from then on. Mother of character actress Rachel Ames (1931–).

1938: Condemned Women. Crime Ring. Broadway Musketeers. 1939: Career. The Women. Bachelor Mother. Calling Dr Kildare. Disputed Passage. Ninotchka. 1940: A Child is Born. Cross-Country Romance. We Who Are Young. Lucky Partners. Nobody's Children. Untamed. *The Great Meddler. 1941: Flame of New Orleans. One Foot in Heaven. Whistling in the Dark. The Devil Commands. Shepherd of the Hills. Bedtime Story. Affectionately Yours. My Life with Caroline. Penny Serenade. Tobacco Road. 1942: Hi Neighbor! Lady Gangster. The Gay Sisters. Joe Smith – American (GB: Highway to Freedom). Dr Gillespie's New Assistant. 1943: So Proudly We Hail! O My Darling Clementine! 1944: Laura. *Dark Shadows. Since You Went Away. *Mister Co-Ed. Bathing Beauty. 1945: The Falcon in San Francisco. Captain Eddie. Circumstantial Evidence. Keep Your Powder Dry. Fallen Angel. *Phantoms Inc. *Guest Pests. The Trouble with Women (released 1947). 1946: The Best Years of Our Lives. Nocturne. Sentimental Journey. The Gangster. The Inner Circle. Miss Susie Slagle's

(completed 1944). O.S.S. 1947: Unconquered. Will Tomorrow Ever Come? The Foxes of Harrow. That's My Man. 1948: Sitting Pretty. He Walked by Night. 1949: Down to the Sea in Ships. Not Wanted. The Sainted Sisters. Samson and Delilah. Montana. 1950: The Cariboo Trail. The Outriders. Paid in Full. The Jackpot. 1951: The First Legion. 1952: Carrie. Fort Osage. Jet Job. The Winning Team. The Greatest Show on Earth. 1955: The Prodigal. 1956: The Man in the Gray Flannel Suit. Three for Jamie Dawn. These Wilder Years. The Ten Commandments. The Killing. Johnny Concho. The Broken Star. 1957: Buckskin Lady. An Affair to Remember. 1958: Gunman's Walk. Unwed Mother. The Big Country. 1960: From the Terrace. 1969: The Good Guys and the Bad Guys. 1974: The Virginia Hill Story (TV). 1975: Peeper.

ADDY, Wesley 1912–
Tall, slim, white-haired American actor, almost entirely on stage, frequently in production with his wife (since 1961), former Hollywood star Celeste Holm. His few film roles (often in pictures directed by Robert Aldrich) have been as cold, calculating characters, less showy than the main villain, but less likely to pay the price.

1951: The First Legion. Scandal Sheet (GB: The Dark Page). 1952: My Six Convicts. Dreamboat. 1955: Kiss Me Deadly. The Big Knife. Timetable. 1956: The Garment Jungle. 1959: Ten Seconds to Hell. The Nine Lives of Elfego Baca (TV. GB: cinemas). 1962: What Ever Happened to Baby Jane? 1963: Four for Texas. 1964: Hush...Hush. Sweet Charlotte. 1965: Mister Buddwing (GB: Woman Without a Face). 1966: Seconds. 1967: Cosa Nostra: an Arch Enemy of the FBI (TV. GB: cinemas). 1970: Tora! Tora! Tora! 1971: The Grissom Gang. Beware! The Blob (GB: Son of Blob). 1976: Network. 1977: The Love Boat II (TV). Tail Gunner Joe (TV). 1979: The Europeans. 1982: The Verdict. 1984: The Bostonians. 1994: Nick of Time. Mr 247.

ADLER, Luther
(Lutha Adler) 1903–1984
Distinguished American stage player – from a famous acting family – whose squat build, olive complexion and heavy-jowled features consigned him mainly to roles as oily villains

and kings of the underworld. His film appearances were surprisingly few, although he did crop up on TV's Hawaii Five-O in the 1970s with another of his unctuous crime czars. Married (second) to actress Sylvia Sidney (Sophia Koson 1910–) from 1938 to 1946. Played Hitler twice.

1937: Lancer Spy. 1945: Cornered. 1948: Saigon. The Loves of Carmen. Wake of the Red Witch. 1949: House of Strangers. South Sea Sinner (GB: East of Java). D.O.A. 1950: Under My Skin. Kiss Tomorrow Goodbye. 1951: The Desert Fox (GB: Rommel – Desert Fox). M. The Magic Face. 1952: Hoodlum Empire. 1953: The Tall Texan. 1954: The Miami Story. 1955: Crashout. The Girl in the Red Velvet Swing. 1956: Hot Blood. 1958: Last Clear Chance (TV). The Plot to Kill Stalin (TV). 1959: The Last Angry Man. Rank and File (TV). 1965: The Three Sisters. 1966: Cast a Giant Shadow. 1968: Sunshine Patriot (TV). The Brotherhood. 1970: God Bless the Children (TV). 1974: Murph the Surf (GB: Live a Little, Steal a Lot). Crazy Joe. 1975: The Man in the Glass Booth. Mean Johnny Barrows. 1976: Voyage of the Damned. The Three Sisters (and 1965 film). 1981: Absence of Malice.

ADORF, Mario 1930–
Dark-haired, swarthy, husky, often moustachioed Swiss-born actor. As he resembles Mexican actor Pedro Armendariz, it was not surprising that he was first seen by many international filmgoers in an Armendariz-type role as Sergeant Gomez in Major Dundee, by which time he had been busy in

continental (mainly German) films for a decade. Despite a tendency to be typed as a heavy, Adorf has sought a wide variety of roles, and British TV audiences got to know him in the early 1980s through his participation in *Don Camillo* (title role) and *Smiley's People*. He made his initial breakthrough to recognition in Germany as the imbecile murderer in *Nachts, wenn der Teufel kam*, and still works busily on stage and screen all over Europe.

1954: 08/15. 1955: Zweiter Teil 08/15. 08/ 15 in der Heimat. 1956: Mädchen und Männer. Kirschen in Nachbars Garten. Harter Männer — heisse Liebe. Robinson soll nicht sterben (US: The Girl and the Legend). 1957: Nachts, wenn der Teufel kam (US: The Devil Strikes at Night). Der Arzt von Stalingrad. 1958: Das Mädchen Rosemarie (GB: The Girl Rosemarie. US: Rosemary). 1959: Das Totenschiff. Am Tag, als der Regen kam. Bumerang (GB and US: Cry Double Cross). 1960: Schachnovelle (GB: Three Moves to Freedom. US: The Royal Game/Brainwashed). Mein Schulfreund. Qui êtes-vous, Monsieur Sorge? Le goût de la violence. 1961: A cavallo della tigre. Lulu. Strasse der Verheissung. Station Six — Sahara. 1963: Moral 63. La visita. Winnetou, erste Teil (GB: Winnetou the Warrior. US: Apache Gold). Der letzte Ritt nach Santa Cruz (GB: Last Ride to Santa Cruz. US: Last Stage to Santa Cruz). Vorsicht, Mister Dodd. 1964: Major Dundee. Die Goldsucher von Arkansas. Le soldatesse (US: The Camp Followers). That Man in Istanbul. 1965: Die Herren. La guerre secrète (GB and US: The Dirty Game). Ten Little Indians. Tierra del Fuego/Vergeltung in Catano (GB and US: Sunscorched). Io la conoscevo bene. Ganovenehre. 1966: Operazione San Gennaro (GB: Operation San Gennaro. US: Treasure of San Gennaro). Una rosa per tutti (GB and US: A Rose for Everyone). Tendres Requins. 1967: Le dolci signore (US: Anyone Can Play). Zärtliche Haie. 1968: Questi fantasmi (GB and US: Ghosts Italian Style). E per tetto un cielo di stelle. Engelchen macht weiter hoppe-hoppe Reiter. *Massnahmen gegen Fanatiker. 1969: Gli specialisti. The Red Tent. L'uccello dalle piume di cristallo (GB: The Gallery Murders. US: The Bird with the Crystal Plumage). Die Herren mit der weisse Weste. Deadlock (TV). 1970: L'arciere di Sherwood. Cran d'ârret. Un'anguilla da trecento millioni. 1971: L'avventure di Pinocchio (originally for TV). Malastrana/La corte notte delle bambole di vetro. La violenza — quinto potere (GB and US: Sicilian Checkmate). La polizia ringrazia (GB: The Law Enforcers). Milano calibro 9 (GB: The Contract). Quando le donne persero la coda. Herzbube (GB and US: King, Queen, Knave). 1972: La 'mala' ordina (GB: Manhunt in Milan. US: The Italian Connection). Il delitto Matteotti. 1973: Sans sommation/ Without Warning. Die Reise nach Wien. 1974: Processo per direttissima. Il clan del quartiere latino. Der dritte Grad/Der Fehler. Brigitte, Laura, Ursula, Monica, Raquel, Litz, Maria, Florina, Barbara, Claudia e Sofia...le chiamo tutte...anima via. La polizia chiede aiuto (US: The Coed Murders). 1975: Die verlorene Ehre der Katharina Blum (GB and US: The Lost Honour/Honor of Katharina Blum). Cuore di cane. MitGift. La smagliatura. 1976: Bomber

und Paganine. Un anno di scuole. Gefundenes Fressen. 1977: Das letzte Schuljahr (TV). Der Hauptdarsteller. Io ho paura. Difficile morire. Tod oder Freiheit. Taugenichts. 1978: Deutschland im Herbst (GB and US: Germany in Autumn). Fedora. Saladin. 1979: The Tin Drum. Milo Milo. 1980: L'impreinte des géants. 1981: Fitzcarraldo (unfinished version). Lola. La disubbidienza. Marco Polo (shortened version of TV mini-series). 1982: L'invitation au voyage. Côte d'amour. 1983: Klassenverhältnisse. Les tilleuls de Lautenbach (TV). 1984: La vigna di uve nere. Via Mala (TV). Faccia fittasi (TV). 1985: Marie Ward. Coconuts. The Holcroft Covenant. Die Flucht ohne Ende (TV). Olga and Her children (TV). Momo (released 1987). 1986: Mino (TV). The Second Victory. 1987: Des Teufels Paradies. Heimatmuseum (TV). Vado a riprendermi il gatto. Notte Italiana. 1988: La madre. 1989: Francesco. Die Drahtseilbahn. Try This On for Size. The Snare. Quiet Days in Clichy. 1990: Bronsteins Kinder. 1991: Pizza Colonia. Café Europa. Money. 1993: Abissinia. Amigomio. 1994: Felidae (voice only).

ADRIAN, Iris
(I.A. Hostetter) 1912–1994

Fluffy blonde American supporting actress and dancer. A chorus girl (and beauty contest winner) in the late 1920s, Adrian graduated to play dozens of flea-brained, often grumpy-looking floozies and garrulous gold-diggers, progressing to wisecracking matrons in later years. She played her share of tough dames, too, as well as dancing opposite George Raft in a couple of semi-musicals. She turned up in several cameos for the Walt Disney studio from the early 1960s to the late 1970s.

1928: *Chasing Husbands. 1930: Paramount on Parade. Let's Go Native. *The Freshman's Goat. 1932: *If I'm Elected. *College Cuties. 1934: *Raring to Go/ *Tearing to Go. 1935: Rhumba/Rumba. Stolen Harmony. The Gay Deception. Murder at Glen Athol (GB: The Criminal Within). Grand Exit. 1936: A Message to Garcia. One Rainy Afternoon. Lady Luck. Our Relations. Stage Struck. Mister Cinderella. Gold Diggers of 1937. 1937: *Man to Man. 1939: One Third of a Nation. Back Door to Heaven. 1940: Meet the Wildcat. Go West/ Marx Brothers Go West. 1941: Horror Island. The Lady from Cheyenne. Meet the Champ.

Too Many Blondes. Road to Zanzibar. Wild Geese Calling. New York Town. Sing Another Chorus. Hard Guy. Swing It Soldier (GB: Radio Revels of 1942). I Killed That Man. 1942: Roxie Hart. To the Shores of Tripoli. Rings on Her Fingers. Juke Box Jenny. Fingers at the Window. Broadway. Moonlight Masquerade. Orchestra Wives. Highways by Night. The McGuerins from Brooklyn. Calaboose. Thunder Birds. 1943: Ladies' Day. The Crystal Ball. He's My Guy. His Butler's Sister. Taxi, Mister. Lady of Burlesque (GB: Striptease Lady). Action in the North Atlantic. Hers to Hold. Submarine Base. Spotlight Scandals. Career Girl. 1944: Million Dollar Kid. Shake Hands with Murder. Once Upon a Time. Swing Hostess. The Singing Sheriff. The Woman in the Window. Bluebeard. I'm from Arkansas. Alaska. 1945: It's a Pleasure. Road to Alcatraz. Steppin' in Society. Boston Blackie's Rendezvous (GB: Blackie's Rendezvous). The Stork Club. The Trouble with Women (released 1947). 1946: The Bamboo Blonde. Cross My Heart. Vacation in Reno. 1947: Fall Guy. Love and Learn. Philo Vance Returns. The Wistful Widow of Wagon Gap (GB: The Wistful Widow). 1948: *How to Clean House. Out of the Storm. Smart Woman. The Paleface. 1949: Miss Mink of 1949. Flamingo Road. My Dream is Yours. The Lovable Cheat. †Two Knights in Brooklyn/ Two Mugs from Brooklyn. Mighty Joe Young. Sky Dragon. Trail of the Yukon. Tough Assignment. I Married a Communist (GB: The Woman on Pier 13). Always Leave Them Laughing. There's a Girl in My Heart. 1950: Blondie's Hero. Joe Palooka in Humphrey Takes a Chance (GB: Humphrey Takes a Chance). Once a Thief. Sideshow. Hi-Jacked. *Foy Meets Girl. 1951: Stop That Cab. GI Jane. Varieties on Parade. The Racket. My Favorite Spy. 1952: Carson City. The Big Trees. *Heebie Gee Gees. 1953: Take the High Ground. Crime Wave (GB: The City Is Dark). The Misadventures of Buster Keaton (TV. GB: Cinemas). 1954: Highway Dragnet. The Fast and the Furious. *So You Want to Know Your Relatives. 1956: Earth vs the Flying Saucers. *So You Want to be Pretty. 1957: The Helen Morgan Story (GB: Both Ends of the Candle). Carnival Rock. 1958: The Buccaneer. 1961: Blue Hawaii. The Errand Boy. 1964: Fate is the Hunter. That Darn Cat! 1967: The Odd Couple. 1968: The Love Bug. 1970: The Barefoot Executive. 1971: Scandalous John. 1974: The Apple Dumpling Gang. 1976: Freaky Friday. The Shaggy DA. No Deposit, No Return. 1978: Getting Married (TV). 1980: Herbie Goes Bananas. Murder Can Hurt You! (TV). 1981: Paternity.

† Alternative GB titles for combined version of The McGuerins from Brooklyn/Taxi, Mister.

AHN, Philip 1908–1978

A sombre-faced, high-cheekboned, taut-featured, American-born Hollywood oriental actor. Cast from the mid 1930s as an assorted collection of inscrutable types, Ahn's characters were mostly sympathetic until the war years, when his thin, unsmiling expression turned quite readily to nasty ruthlessness. These roles carried bitter irony, as Ahn's father was a Korean diplomat who died in a wartime Japanese prison camp. He found a secure niche in the 1970s with his

running role as the old man in the TV series *Kung Fu*.

1936: Klondike Annie. Anything Goes. The General Died at Dawn. Stowaway. 1937: Tex Rides with the Boy Scouts. Something to Sing About. Daughter of Shanghai (GB: Daughter of the Orient). China Passage. Roaring Timber. The Good Earth. Thank You, Mr Moto. 1938: Red Barry (serial). Hawaii Calls. Charlie Chan in Honolulu. 1939: Island of Lost Men. Barricade. Panama Patrol. Disputed Passage. North of Shanghai. King of Chinatown. 1940: Drums of Fu Manchu (serial). The Shadow (serial). Passage from Hong Kong. 1941: They Met in Bombay. 1942: China Girl. Submarine Raider. We Were Dancing. Ship Ahoy. A Yank on the Burma Road (GB: China Caravan). Across the Pacific. Let's Get Tough. They Got Me Covered. 1943: Around the World. China. Behind the Rising Sun. Scream in the Night/Scream in the Dark. Adventures of the Flying Cadets (serial). Adventures of Smilin' Jack (serial). The Amazing Mrs Holliday. 1944: The Keys of the Kingdom. Forever Yours/They Shall Have Faith (GB: The Right to Live). Dragon Seed. The Story of Dr Wassell. The Purple Heart. 1945. Back to Bataan. They Were Expendable. Blood on the Sun. China's Little Devils. God is My Co-Pilot. Betrayal from the East. China Sky. 1947: Singapore. The Chinese Ring. The Red Hornet. Intrigue. Women in the Night. 1948: The Cobra Strikes. The Miracle of the Bells. Saigon. Rogues' Regiment. The Creeper. 1949: State Department — File 649 (GB: Assignment in China). Boston Blackie's Chinese Venture (GB: Chinese Adventure). Impact. 1950: The Big Hangover. Halls of Montezuma. The Glass Menagerie. 1951: China Corsair. The Sickle or the Cross. Secrets of Monte Carlo. I Was an American Spy. 1952: Japanese War Bride. Macao. Target — Hong Kong. Red Snow. Battle Zone. 1953: China Venture. Battle Circus. His Majesty O'Keefe. Fair Wind to Java. 1954: The Shanghai Story. Hell's Half-Acre. 1955: Love is a Many-splendored Thing. The Left Hand of God. 1956: Around the World in 80 Days. 1957: The Way to the Gold. Battle Hymn. 1958: Hong Kong Confidential. 1959: Never So Few. Yesterday's Enemy. 1960: The Great Impostor. 1961: One-Eyed Jacks. 1962: A Girl Named Tamiko. Confessions of an Opium Eater (GB: Evils of Chinatown). Diamond Head. 1963: Shock Corridor. 1965: Paradise, Hawaiian Style. 1967: Thoroughly Modern Millie. The Karate Killers (TV. GB: cinemas).

1968: Hawaii Five-O (TV). 1971: Voodoo Heartbeat (released 1975). 1972: Kung Fu (TV). 1973: Jonathan Livingstone Seagull (voice only). The World's Greatest Athlete. 1976: The Killer Who Wouldn't Die (TV). 1977: Jimbuck (later Portrait of a Hitman).

AIELLO, Danny 1933–

Thick-set, dark-haired New Yorker with pugnacious, even threatening features who adapts easily to tough, down-to-earth or working class roles. Following long Broadway experience he made a low-key entry into films at the age of 40. Better roles took a while to come, but he had made his bulky presence felt by the 1980s, and was nominated for an Oscar towards the end of the decade for *Do the Right Thing*. He was handed his biggest leading role to date at the age of 58 when cast in *Ruby*, as the man who shot President Kennedy's alleged assassin Lee Harvey Oswald. He won an Emmy in 1981 for his role in the TV movie *Family of Strangers*. His son, Danny Aiello III, has been a leading Hollywood stuntman for more than a decade.

1973: Bang the Drum Slowly. 1974: The Godfather Part II. 1976: The Front. 1977: Fingers. 1978: Lovey: A Circle of Children, Part II (TV). The Last Tenant (TV). Bloodbrothers. Hooch. 1979: Defiance. 1980: Hide in Plain Sight. 1981: Chu Chu and the Philly Flash. Family of Strangers (TV). Fort Apache The Bronx. 1982: A Question of Honor (TV). 1983: Deathmask. Once Upon a Time in America. Blood Feud (TV). 1984: Old Enough. 1985: The Protector. Lady Blue (TV). Key Exchange. The Stuff. The Purple Rose of Cairo. 1987: Daddy (TV). The Pick-Up Artist. Man on Fire. Moonstruck. Radio Days. 1988: White Hot. Alone in the Neon Jungle (TV). Russicum/The Third Solution. The January Man. 1989: Do the Right Thing. The Preppie Murder (TV). Crack in the Mirror. Harlem Nights. Making 'Do the Right Thing'. 1990: The Closer. Jacob's Ladder. Once Around. 1991: Hudson Hawk. 29th Street. 1992: Mistress. Ruby. 1993: The Pickle. The Cemetery Club. Taking Gary Feldman. 1994: Prêt-a-Porter (US: Ready to Wear). Me and the Kid (TV). Léon (US: The Professional). 1995: Power of Attorney. City Hall. Two Much. He Ain't Heavy.

AKED, Muriel 1887–1955

Bony-faced British actress who tended to play sourpusses, easily shocked spinsters, gossipy neighbours and grasping landladies. She hit her stride in British films with the coming of sound, trooping on and off in handfuls of scene-stealing cameos, noticeably in *Rome Express*, *Trouble* and *The Happiest Days of Your Life*. She also played a running role, through 26 years, in the four screen versions of that old comedy chestnut *A Sister to Assist 'Er*.

1922: A Sister to Assist 'Er. 1926: Bindle's Cocktail. 1930: Bed and Breakfast. The Middle Watch. 1931: A Sister to Assist 'Er (remake). 1932: Her First Affaire. Rome Express. Goodnight Vienna (US: Magic Night). The Mayor's Nest. Indiscretions of Eve. 1933: The Good Companions. Friday the Thirteenth. No Funny Business. Yes, Madam. Trouble. 1934: The Queen's Affair (US: Runaway Queen). Evensong. Autumn Crocus. The Night of the Party. Josser on the Farm. 1935: Can You Hear Me Mother? 1936: Don't Rush Me. Fame. Public Nuisance Number One. Royal Eagle. 1937: Mr Stringfellow Says No. 1938: A Sister to Assist 'Er (second remake). 1939: The Girl Who Forgot. A Girl Must Live. The Silent Battle (US: Continental Express). 1941: Cottage to Let (US: Bombsight Stolen). Kipps (US: The Remarkable Mr Kipps). 1942: The Demi-Paradise (US: Adventure for Two). 1943: The Life and Death of Colonel Blimp (US: Colonel Blimp). 1944: 2,000 Women. 1945: The Wicked Lady. They Knew Mr Knight. 1946: The Years Between. 1947: Just William's Luck. 1948: A Sister to Assist 'Er (third remake). So Evil My Love. Another Shore. It's Hard to Be Good. 1949: William Comes to Town. The Blue Lamp. 1950: The Happiest Days of Your Life. 1951: The Wonder Kid. Flesh and Blood. 1953: The Story of Gilbert and Sullivan (US: The Great Gilbert and Sullivan).

AKINS, Claude 1918–1994

A burly, surly-looking American actor in the Ernest Borgnine tradition, with thick dark hair and roundly solid features. After a late start in films, Akins's scowling features almost inevitably found him cast as villains. Just as inevitably, it seemed, his later career brought better and more sympathetic roles, and his by-now cheerful grin was also to be seen in leading roles in TV series. Died from cancer.

1951: *A Place in the Sun.* 1953: *Seminole. From Here to Eternity.* 1954: *The Caine Mutiny. Bitter Creek. Down Three Dark Streets. The Human Jungle. The Raid. Shield for Murder.* 1955: *Man with the Gun* (GB: *The Trouble Shooter*). *The Sea Chase. Battle Stations.* 1956: *The Proud and Profane. Johnny Concho. Hot Summer Night. The Burning Hills. The Sharkfighters.* 1957: *Joe Dakota. The Lonely Man. The Kettles on Old MacDonald's Farm.* 1958: *The Defiant Ones. Onionhead.* 1959: *Porgy and Bess. Don't Give Up the Ship. Yellowstone Kelly. Hound Dog Man. Rio Bravo.* 1960: *Inherit the Wind. Comache Station.* 1961: *Claudelle Inglish* (GB: *Young and Eager*). 1962: *How the West Was Won. Black Gold. Merrill's Marauders.* 1964: *The Killers. A Distant Trumpet.* 1965: *Incident at Phantom Hill.* 1966: *Return of the Seven. Ride Beyond Vengeance.* 1967: *First to Fight. Waterhole Number Three* (GB: *Waterhole Three*). 1968: *The Devil's Brigade.* 1969: *The Great Bank Robbery.* 1970: *River of Mystery* (TV). *Sledge* (GB: *A Man Called Sledge*). *Lock, Stock and Barrel* (TV). *Flap* (GB: *The Last Warrior*). 1971: *The Night Stalker* (TV). 1972: *Skyjacked.* 1973: *The Timber Tramp. Battle for the Planet of the Apes. Death Squad* (TV). *The Norliss Tapes* (TV). 1974: *In Tandem* (TV). *Shadow of Fear* (TV). 1975: *Eric* (TV). *Medical Story* (TV). 1976: *Tentacles. Kiss Me, Kill Me* (TV). 1977: *Yesterday's Child* (TV). 1978: *BJ and the Bear* (TV). *Little Mo* (TV). *The Broken Badge* (TV). *Killer on Board* (TV. *Ebony, Ivory and Jade* (TV). *Murder in Music City* (TV). 1979: *The Concrete Cowboys* (TV). 1980: *Tarantulas: The Deadly Cargo* (TV. Filmed 1977). 1981: *Manhunt for Claude Dallas* (TV). 1983: *Desperate Intruder* (TV). 1984: *The Baron and the Kid* (TV). 1986: *Monster in the Closet.* 1987: *The Farm. If It's Tuesday, It Must Still Be Belgium* (TV). 1989: *Pushed Too Far.* 1991: *Falling from Grace/Souvenirs. Sherlock Holmes and the Incident at Victoria Falls* (TV). 1992: *Trilogy of Fear.*

ALBERNI, Luis 1887–1962
Screw-faced, big-nosed, bulge-eyed, purse-lipped Spanish actor with curly, greasy, slightly thinning black hair that ran to a thick lump at the back. Short of stature but expansive of gesture, he came to Hollywood as a young man and, with the coming of sound, pitched into a whole string of voluble and excitable Latins who alternately annoyed

and baffled the stars. Mostly in comedy cameos, he played some quieter and more dramatic roles in his later years when his features had assumed a kind of wise calm.

1921: *Little Italy.* 1922: *The Man from Beyond.* 1923: *The Valley of Lost Souls. The Bright Shawl.* 1930: *The Santa Fe Trail* (GB: *The Law Rides West*). 1931: **Monkey Business in Africa. *The Great Junction Hotel. Side Show. Manhattan Parade. *Rule 'Em and Weep. Men in Her Life. The Mad Genius. Svengali. The Last Flight. *I Surrender Dear. Sweepstakes. I Like Your Nerve. Children of Dreams. One Heavenly Night. The Tip Off.* 1932: **First in War. The Woman in Room 13. The Cohens and Kellys in Hollywood. Hombres en mi vida. Girl in the Tonneau. Hypnotized. Working*

Wives. Crooner. Guilty or Not Guilty. Week-End Marriage (GB: *Working Wives*). *The Kid from Spain. The Big Stampede. Cock of the Air. High Pressure. A Parisian Romance. Trouble in Paradise.* 1933: **Artists' Muddles. *Sherman Said It. The California Trail. Child of Manhattan. The Last Trail. *California Weather. Topaze. I Love That Man. Men Must Fight. The Sphinx. Trick for Trick. The Man from Monterey. When Ladies Meet. Above the Clouds* (GB: *Winged Devils*). *Flying Down to Rio. Lady Killer.* 1934: *The Black Cat* (GB: *House of Doom*). *The Captain Hates the Sea. Goodbye Love. *When Do We Eat? The Count of Monte Cristo. La buenaventura. La ciudad de Carton. I Believed in You. Glamour. One Night of Love. When Strangers Meet.* 1935: *Bad Boy. Goin' to Town. The Gay Deception. Love Me Forever* (GB: *On Wings of Song*). *Roberta. The Gilded Lily. Let's Live Tonight. The Winning Ticket. Asegure a su mujer. In Caliente. Metropolitan. Music is Magic. Public Opinion. *Ticket or Leave It. Manhattan Moon* (GB: *Sing Me a Love Song*). 1936: *Anthony Adverse. Colleen. The Dancing Pirate. Follow Your Heart. Hats Off. Ticket to Paradise.* 1937: *Manhattan Merry-Go-Round* (GB: *Manhattan Music Box*). *Sing and Be Happy. Two Wise Maids. Under Suspicion. When You're in Love* (GB: *For You Alone*). *Easy Living. The Great Garrick. The*

King and the Chorus Girl (GB: *Romance is Sacred*). *Hitting a New High. Madame X. Love on Toast. Mr Dodd Takes the Air.* 1938: *I'll Give a Million.* 1939: *The Great Man Votes. The Amazing Mr Williams. Let Freedom Ring. The Housekeeper's Daughter. Naughty But Nice. East 20.* 1940: *Enemy Agent* (GB: *Secret Enemy*). *Public Deb No. 1. Scatterbrain. The Lone Wolf Meets a Lady.* 1941: *The Lady Eve. Law of the Tropics. They Met in Argentina. Road to Zanzibar. San Antonio Rose. World Premiere. That Hamilton Woman* (GB: *Lady Hamilton*). *Babes on Broadway. Obliging Young Lady. She Knew All the Answers. They Met in Bombay.* 1942: *I Married an Angel. Mexican Spitfire's Elephant. Two Weeks to Live. Northwest Rangers.* 1943: *Here Comes Elmer. Harvest Melody. Nearly Eighteen. Submarine Base. My Son, the Hero. Here Comes Kelly. Henry Aldrich Plays Cupid* (GB: *Henry Plays Cupid*). *Passport to Heaven. The Conspirators. You're a Lucky Fellow, Mr Smith.* 1944: *In Society. Machine Gun Mama. When the Lights Go On Again. Men on Her Mind. Voice in the Wind. Rainbow Island.* 1945: *A Bell for Adano. Wonder Man. Hit the Hay. Live Wires.* 1946: *In Fast Company.* 1947: *Night Song.* 1949: *Captain Carey, USA* (GB: *After Midnight*). 1950: *When Willie Comes Marching Home.* 1952: *What Price Glory?* 1956: *The Ten Commandments.*

ALBERTSON, Jack 1907–1981
Plum-nosed, sandy-haired American actor, usually cast as grouchy old men. Started as a dancer and straight man to comedians in vaudeville. He won a Best Supporting Actor Academy Award in 1968 for *The Subject is Roses*, although his triumph was barely seen outside the United States. Probably achieved his greatest popularity in old age on television in the comedy series *Chico and the Man*, which won him an Emmy. Died from cancer.

1937: *Rebecca of Sunnybrook Farm.* 1938: *Next Time I Marry.* 1940: *Strike Up the Band.* 1947: *Miracle on 34th Street* (GB: *The Big Heart*). 1952: *Top Banana.* 1955: *Bring Your Smile Along.* 1956: *The Unguarded Moment. Over-Exposed. The Eddy Duchin Story. The Harder They Fall. You Can't Run Away from It.* 1957: *Don't Go Near the Water. Monkey on My Back. Man of a Thousand Faces.* 1958: *Teacher's Pet.* 1959: *The Shaggy Dog. Never*

Steal Anything Small. 1961: Convicts Four (GB: Reprieve!). The George Raft Story (GB: Spin of a Coin). Lover Come Back. Mantrap. 1962: Period of Adjustment. Days of Wine and Roses. Who's Got the Action? 1963: Son of Flubber. A Tiger Walks. 1964: Kissin' Cousins. The Patsy. Roustabout. 1965: How to Murder Your Wife. 1967: The Flim Flam Man (GB: One Born Every Minute). How to Save a Marriage – and Ruin Your Life. 1968: Changes. The Subject Was Roses. 1969: The Monk (TV). Squeeze a Flower. Justine. A Clear and Present Danger (TV). 1970: Rabbit Run. Lock, Stock and Barrel (TV). 1971: Willy Wonka and the Chocolate Factory. The Showdown (TV). A Time to Every Purpose. Congratulations, It's a Boy (TV). 1972: The Late Liz. The Poseidon Adventure. Pick Up on 101 (GB: Echoes of the Road). 1978: The Comedy Company (TV). Charlie's Balloon (TV. GB: Charlie and the Great Balloon Chase). 1979: Valentine (TV). 1980: Marriage is Alive and Well (TV). 1981: The Fox and the Hound (voice only). Dead and Buried. 1982: My Body, My Child (TV). Terror at Alcatraz (TV).

ALEXANDER, Terence 1923–
Round-faced, smoothly-spoken, pushy-looking, London-born actor with dark hair. In repertory at 16, he started a regular film career in the 1950s, usually appearing in light roles – as smooth upper-class charmers, junior ministers, beguiling rogues or amiable oafs. He was a natural for a part in *The League of Gentlemen* – and it was probably his best film role. Still acting, but entirely on stage and TV since 1979.

1947: Comin' Thro' the Rye. 1950: The Elusive Pimpernel (US: The Fighting Pimpernel). The Woman with No Name (US: Her Paneled Door). 1951: Death is a Number. A Tale of Five Cities (US: A Tale of Five Women). 1952: The Gentle Gunman. Top Secret (US: Mr Potts Goes to Moscow). *The First Elizabeth (narrator only). *The Stately Home of Kent (narrator only). *Just a Drop (narrator only). 1953: Glad Tidings. Park Plaza 605 (US: Norman Conquest). 1954: The Runaway Bus. Dangerous Cargo. The Green Scarf. Hands of Destiny. Out of the Clouds. 1955: Portrait of Alison (US: Postmark for Danger). Who Done It? 1956: The Green Man. 1957: The One That Got Away. 1958: The Square Peg. *Death Was a Passenger. Danger Within (US: Breakout).

1959: Breakout (different GB film from preceding entry). Don't Panic Chaps! The Doctor's Dilemma. The Price of Silence. 1960: The League of Gentlemen. The Bulldog Breed. 1961: Carry On Regardless. Man at the Carlton Tower. 1962: The Gentle Terror. She Always Gets Their Man. On the Beat. The Fast Lady. 1963: The Mind Benders. The VIPs. Bitter Harvest. 1964: *All in Good Time. The Intelligence Men. 1965: Judith. 1967: The Long Duel. *The Spare Tyres. 1968: Only When I Larf. 1969: What's Good for the Goose. Run a Crooked Mile (TV). The Magic Christian. All the Way Up. 1970: Waterloo. 1973: Vault of Horror. The Day of the Jackal. 1974: The Internecine Project. 1978: Ike (TV). 1979: The Boy Who Never Was.

ALISON, Dorothy 1925–1992
A cool, capable Australian actress with sympathetic, faintly motherly personality. A doll-like, dark-haired beauty in her early days, she came to England in 1949 and worked as a secretary until acting jobs became more frequent. Her career reached its zenith when she played Nurse Brace in *Reach for the Sky*. Thereafter, it declined somewhat into care-worn roles, but she re-emerged in chirpier cameos in the 1980s. British films never made the use of her that they might have done, and she was back in Australia by the mid 1980s.

1948: Eureka Stockade. 1949: Sons of Matthew (GB and US: The Rugged O'Riordans). 1952: Mandy (US: Crash of Silence). 1953: Turn the Key Softly. 1954: The Maggie (US: High and Dry). The Purple Plain. Child's Play. Companions in Crime. 1956: The Long Arm (US: The Third Key). The Feminine Touch (US: The Gentle Touch). Reach for the Sky. The Silken Affair. 1957: The Scamp. Interpol (US: Pickup Alley). 1958: The Man Upstairs. 1959: The Nun's Story. Life in Emergency Ward 10. 1961: Two Living, One Dead. 1962: The Prince and the Pauper. 1966: Georgy Girl. 1967: Pretty Polly (US: Loss of Innocence). 1971: Blind Terror (US: See No Evil). Doctor Jekyll and Sister Hyde. 1972: Baxter! (US: The Boy). The Amazing Mr Blunden. 1978: En vandring i solen. 1980: *The Errand. 1982: The Return of the Soldier. 1983: Invitation to the Wedding. The Winds of Jarrah. 1984: The Schippan Mystery (TV). 1988: Rikky and Pete. Two Brothers Running. A Cry in the Dark. 1989: Malpractice.

ALLEN, Patrick 1927–
Tall, long-jawed, light-haired, tough-looking, Nyasaland-born, Canadian-raised leading man and (often villainous) character player whose inimitable resonant voice guaranteed him a juicy income from voice-overs in TV commercials after a long and varied career in British television series (most notably *Crane*) and films. Married to actress Sarah Lawson (1928–) since 1956.

1953: World for Ransom. 1954: Dial M for Murder. 1955: Cross Channel. King's Rhapsody. *Dead on Time. 1984. Confession (US: The Deadliest Sin). 1956: Wicked As They Come. 1957: High Tide at Noon. The Long Haul. Accused (US: Mark of the Hawk). 1958: The Man Who Wouldn't Talk. High Hell. Tread Softly, Stranger. Dunkirk. I Was Monty's Double (US: Monty's Double). 1959: Jet Storm. 1960: Never Take Sweets from a Stranger (US: Never Take Candy from a Stranger). 1961: The Sinister Man. 1962: The Traitors. Captain Clegg (US: Night Creatures). Flight from Singapore. 1966: The Night of the Generals. 1967: The Life and Times of John Huston Esquire (narrator only). I'll Never Forget What's 'is Name (voice only). Night of the Big Heat (US: Island of the Burning Damned). 1968: Cream's Last Concert (narrator only). 1969: Carry On Doctor (voice only). The Body Stealers. When Dinosaurs Ruled the Earth. 1970: Puppet on a Chain. The World at Their Feet (narrator only). 1971: Erotic Fantasies (narrator only). The Sword and the Geisha (narrator only). *Winter with Dracula (narrator only). 1972: Diamonds on Wheels. 1973: *Way Out East (narrator only). 1974: Persecution. The Wilby Conspiracy. The Domino Principle (GB: The Domino Killings. Released 1978). The Battle of Billy's Pond (voice only). 1978: The Wild Geese. Caligula (dubbed voice only). 1980: The Sea Wolves. 1981: Murder is Easy (TV). 1982: Who Dares Wins (US: The Final Option). 1987: Roman Holiday (TV). 1992: Fergie & Andrew – Behind the Palace Doors (TV). 1993: Body and Soul (TV).

ALLGOOD, Sara 1883–1950
Dublin-born actress whose memorable sprinkling of mother roles—most of them involved in tragedy of some kind or other—was topped by the one in *How Green Was My Valley*, for which she received an Oscar nomination. She made her first film appear-

ance in Australia, and later worked for Alfred Hitchcock, whom she considered a 'cheap, second-rate director'! In Hollywood from 1940. Died from Bright's Disease.

1918: Just Peggy. 1929: Blackmail. To What Red Hell. 1930: Juno and the Paycock (US: The Shame of Mary Boyle). 1932: The World, the Flesh and the Devil. 1933: The Fortunate Fool. 1934: Lily of Killarney (US: Bride of the Lake). Irish Hearts (US: Norah O'Neale). 1935: Peg of Old Drury. Riders to the Sea. Lazybones. The Passing of the Third Floor Back. 1936: Pot Luck. Sabotage (US: The Woman Alone). It's Love Again. Southern Roses. 1937: Kathleen Mavourneen (US: Kathleen). Storm in a Teacup. The Sky's the Limit. The Londonderry Air. 1938: Sixty Glorious Years (US: Queen of Destiny). 1939: On the Night of the Fire (US: The Fugitive). 1940: That Hamilton Woman (GB: Lady Hamilton). 1941: Dr Jekyll and Mr Hyde. Lydia. How Green Was My Valley. 1942: Roxie Hart. This Above All. It Happened in Flatbush. The War Against Mrs Hadley. Life Begins at 8.30 (GB: The Light of Heart). 1943: Forever and a Day. City Without Men. Jane Eyre. 1944: The Lodger. Between Two Worlds. The Keys of the Kingdom. 1945: The Strange Affair of Uncle Harry (GB: Uncle Harry). Kitty. 1946: The Spiral Staircase. Cluny Brown. 1947: The Fabulous Dorseys. Ivy. Mother Wore Tights. Mourning Becomes Electra. My Wild Irish Rose. 1948: The Girl from Manhattan. One Touch of Venus. The Man from Texas. The Accused. 1949: Challenge to Lassie. 1950: Sierra. Cheaper by the Dozen.

ALLISTER, Claud
(William C. Palmer) 1891–1970
Monocled, long-nosed, weak-chinned British comedy actor with light-brown hair smarmed across, large eyes and asinine smile that showed off his big teeth. His upper-class voice was well in keeping with the 'silly ass' nature of the characters he played, and he remained in demand on both sides of the Atlantic until his retirement in 1955. A former clerk who swapped the Stock Exchange for the stage, he went on to make a splendidly well-cast Algy in several Bulldog Drummond films.

1929: Bulldog Drummond. The Trial of Mary Dugan. Charming Sinners. Three Live Ghosts. 1930: Monte Carlo. The Florodora Girl (GB: The Gay Nineties). The Czar of Broadway.

*Slightly Scarlet. In the Next Room. Such Men Are Dangerous. Murder Will Out. Ladies Love Brutes. Reaching for the Moon. 1931: I Like Your Nerve. Platinum Blonde. *On the Loose. Captain Applejack. Meet the Wife. Papa Loves Mama. *Roughhouse Rhythm. The Sea Ghost. 1932: The Midshipmaid (US: Midshipmaid Gob). Two White Arms (US: Wives Beware). Diamond Cut Diamond (US: Blame the Woman). The Return of Raffles. The Unexpected Father. Medicine Man. 1933: The Private Life of Henry VIII. Excess Baggage. That's My Wife. Sleeping Car. 1934: The Lady is Willing. Those Were the Days. The Return of Bulldog Drummond. The Private Life of Don Juan. 1935: The Dark Angel. Every Night at Eight. Three Live Ghosts (and 1929 film). 1936: Dracula's Daughter. Yellowstone. 1937: Bulldog Drummond at Bay. *Oh What a Knight. The Awful Truth. Let's Make a Night of It. Danger — Love at Work. Radio Parade of 1937. 1938: Men Are Such Fools. Storm over Bengal. Kentucky Moonshine (GB: Three Men and a Girl). The Blonde Cheat. 1939: Arrest Bulldog Drummond! Captain Fury. 1940: Pride and Prejudice. Lillian Russell. 1941: Charley's Aunt. The Reluctant Dragon. Confirm or Deny. A Yank in the RAF. Never Give a Sucker an Even Break (GB: What a Man!). 1943: Forever and a Day. The Hundred Pound Window. 1944: Kiss the Bride Goodbye. 1945: Don Chicago. Dumb Dora Discovers Tobacco (US: Fag End). 1946: Gaiety George. 1948: Quartet. The First Gentleman (US: Affairs of a Rogue). 1949: The Adventures of Ichabod and Mr Toad (voice only). 1951: Hong Kong. 1952: Down Among the Sheltering Palms (filmed 1950). 1953: Kiss Me, Kate! 1954: The Black Shield of Falworth.*

AMBLER, Joss 1900–1959
Stocky little British actor with wispy brown hair and (sometimes) toothbrush moustache, heavily employed by the British cinema from 1937 to 1947. He spent a great deal of his younger days in Australia where he made his screen debut but, on his return to Britain, was soon much in demand for lawyers, doctors and other professional advisers (occasionally even shady businessmen), all of which he bumbled through in his customary buzzy manner. At one time married to American actress June Lang (Winifred J Vlasek. 1915–).

1933: Waltzing Matilda. 1937: Captain's Orders. The Last Curtain. 1938: The Citadel.

Break the News. Premiere (US: One Night in Paris). Keep Smiling. Meet Mr Penny. The Claydon Treasure Mystery. Murder in Soho (US: Murder in the Night). 1939: Secret Journey (US: Among Human Wolves). The Spy in Black (US: U-Boat 29). Come On, George. Black Eyes. Trouble Brewing. 1940: Contraband (US: Blackout). Fingers. The Briggs Family. 1941: Atlantic Ferry (US: Sons of the Sea). Once a Crook. The Black Sheep of Whitehall. Break the News. The Prime Minister. Jeannie.

Penn of Pennsylvania (US: The Courageous Mr Penn). The Big Blockade. 1942: Flying Fortress. Next of Kin. The Peterville Diamond. Much Too Shy. Gert and Daisy Clean Up. 1943: Happidrome. Headline. Rhythm Serenade. The Silver Fleet. Battle for Music. Somewhere in Civvies. 1944: Give Me the Stars. A Canterbury Tale. Candles at Nine. The Halfway House. 1945: They Were Sisters. I'll Be Your Sweetheart. The World Owes Me a Living. The Agitator. Here Comes the Sun. 1946: The Years Between. Under New Management. 1947: Mine Own Executioner. 1948: Behind These Walls (voice only). 1950: The Magnet. Her Favourite Husband (US: The Taming of Dorothy). 1952: Ghost Ship. Who Goes There! (US: The Passionate Sentry). Something Money Can't Buy. 1953: The Captain's Paradise. Background (US: Edge of Divorce). The Triangle. 1954: The Harassed Hero. Aunt Clara. 1955: Miss Tulip Stays the Night. 1956: The Long Arm (US: The Third Key). The Feminine Touch (US: The Gentle Touch). Soho Incident (US: Spin a Dark Web). 1957: Fortune is a Woman (US: She Played with Fire). 1958: Dunkirk. The Big Money (completed 1956).

AMES, Leon
(L Waycoff) 1902–1993
A stocky, moustachioed American actor who began his career in semi-leading roles, but never seemed quite at home in them, and moved from dapper, man-about-town types in the 1930s to good-natured, if faintly harassed fathers in later years. His two most successful television series reflected this: *Life with Father* and *Father of the Bride*. He remained active well into his eighties, having returned from retirement in 1970. He acted as Leon Waycoff in all his early films, up to and including *Reckless* in 1935. Died from complications following a stroke.

1961: *The Absent-Minded Professor.* 1963: *Son of Flubber.* 1964: *The Misadventures of Merlin Jones.* 1966: *The Monkey's Uncle.* 1970: *On a Clear Day You Can See Forever. Tora! Tora! Tora!* 1971: *Toklat. A Capitol Affair (TV).* 1972: *Cool Breeze. Hammersmith is Out. Brother of the Wind* (and narrator). 1973: *The Timber Tramp.* 1974: *The Meal* (filmed 1969). 1976: *Sherlock Holmes in New York (TV).* 1977: *Claws.* 1979: *Just You and Me, Kid. The Best Place to Be (TV).* 1983: *Testament.* 1986: *Jake Speed. Peggy Sue Got Married.*

1931: *Quick Millions. Six Cylinder Love.* 1932: *The Murders in the Rue Morgue. 13 Women. Stowaway. The Famous Ferguson Case. That's My Boy. State's Attorney (GB: Cardigan's Last Case). A Successful Calamity. Silver Dollar. Cannonball Express. Uptown New York.* 1933: *Parachute Jumper. Alimony Madness. The Man Who Dared. Ship of Wanted Man. Forgotten.* 1934: *The Count of Monte Cristo. I'll Tell the World. Now I'll Tell (GB: When New York Sleeps).* 1935: *Rescue Squad. The Crosby Case (GB: The Crosby Murder Case). Reckless. Strangers All. Get That Man. Mutiny Ahead.* 1936: *Stowaway* (and 1932 film of same title). 1937: *Dangerously Yours. Death in the Air. Charlie Chan on Broadway. Murder in Greenwich Village. 45 Fathers.* 1938: *International Settlement. Bluebeard's Eight Wife. Walking Down Broadway. Island in the Sky. Come On Leathernecks. Mysterious Mr Moto. Strange Faces. Cipher Bureau. Suez. Secrets of a Nurse. The Spy Ring/International Spy.* 1939: *Risky Business. I Was a Convict. Pack Up Your Troubles (GB: We're in the Army Now). Mr Moto in Danger Island (GB: Mr Moto on Danger Island). Man of Conquest. Panama Patrol. Fugitive at Large. Code of the Streets. Legion of Lost Flyers. Calling All Marines. Thunder Afloat. *Help Wanted.* 1940: *Marshal of Mesa City. East Side Kids.* 1941: *No Greater Sin (GB: Social Enemy No. 1). Ellery Queen and the Murder Ring (GB: The Murder Ring).* 1943: *The Crime Doctor. The Iron Major. Thirty Seconds Over Tokyo.* 1944: *Meet Me in St Louis. The Thin Man Goes Home.* 1945: *Between Two Women. Son of Lassie. Anchors Aweigh. *Fall Guy. Week-End at the Waldorf. They Were Expendable.* 1946: *The Postman Always Rings Twice. Yolanda and the Thief. Lady in the Lake. No Leave, No Love. The Great Morgan. The Show-Off. The Cockeyed Miracle (GB: Mr Griggs Returns).* 1947: *Undercover Maisie (GB: Undercover Girl). Song of the Thin Man. The Amazing Mr Nordill. Merton of the Movies.* 1948: *Alias a Gentleman. On an Island with You. A Date with Judy. The Velvet Touch.* 1949: *Any Number Can Play. Little Women. Scene of the Crime. Battleground.* 1950: *Ambush. The Big Hangover. Dial 1119 (GB: The Violent Hour). Watch the Birdie. The Skipper Surprised His Wife. The Happy Years. Crisis.* 1951: *Cattle Drive. On Moonlight Bay. It's a Big Country.* 1952: *Angel Face. By the Light of the Silvery Moon.* 1953: *Let's Do It Again. Sabre Jet.* 1957: *Peyton Place.* 1959: *The Raider (TV).* 1960: *From the Terrace.*

ANDERSON, Eddie 'Rochester'
1905–1977
Bronchial-voiced, bulging-eyed, stocky, concerned-looking American comic actor, the son of a minstrel and a high-wire artist. His own career in show business was nothing special until he signed up as radio man-servant to comedian Jack Benny in 1937, a role which gave him his nickname and which he played, on and off, for almost 30 years. He was a popular figure in wartime films, and had the star role in the all-black musical *Cabin in the Sky* in 1943.

1932: *Hat Check Girl (GB: Embassy Girl). What Price Hollywood? False Faces (GB: What Price Beauty?).* 1934: *The Gay Bride. Behold My Wife!* 1935: *Transient Lady (GB: False Witness).* 1936: *Two in a Crowd. Green Pastures. Rainbow on the River. Three Men on a Horse. Show Boat.* 1937: *Melody for Two. Bill Cracks Down (GB: Men of Steel). On Such a Night. Love is News. Public Wedding. Wake Up and Live. White Bondage. Over the Goal. One Mile from Heaven.* 1938: *Kentucky. Reckless Living. You Can't Take It With You. Gold Diggers in Paris (GB: The Great Impostors). Jezebel. Thanks for the Memory. Going Places. Exposed. Strange Faces.* 1939: *Honolulu. You Can't Cheat an Honest Man. Gone With the Wind. Man About Town.* 1940: *Buck Benny Rides Again. Love Thy Neighbor.* 1941: *Topper Returns. Birth of the Blues. Kiss the Boys Goodbye.* 1942: *Tales of Manhattan. Star Spangled Rhythm.* 1943: *The Meanest Man in the World. Cabin in the Sky. What's Buzzin' Cousin?* 1944: *Broadway Rhythm.* 1945: *Brewster's Millions. I Love a Bandleader (GB: Memory for Two).* 1946: *The Show-Off. The Sailor Takes a Wife.* 1957: *Green Pastures (TV remake).* 1963: *It's a Mad, Mad, Mad, Mad World.*

ANDERSON, Jean 1908–
Kindly but resolute-looking, dark-haired British player with prominent nose, small features and smiling mouth, an actress from an early age who did repertory work in Cambridge and Dublin before coming to the London stage. She was almost always seen in sympathetic roles, to which she brought a benevolent force of personality: nurses, policewomen, teachers, social workers and various senior officials. She made fewer films than one imagined, and became entrenched in television from the early 1970s in two long-running series, *The Brothers* and *Tenko*. Still in cameos, as forthright as ever.

1947: *The Mark of Cain.* 1948: *Bond Street.* 1949: *The Romantic Age (US: Naughty Arlette). Elizabeth of Ladymead.* 1950: *The Franchise Affair. Seven Days to Noon.* 1951: *Out of True. Life in Her Hands. White Corridors.* 1952: *Time Bomb (US: Terror on a Train). The Brave Don't Cry.* 1953: *Street Corner (US: Both Sides of the Law). The Weak and the Wicked. The Kidnappers (US: The Little Kidnappers). Johnny on the Run.* 1954: *The Dark Stairway. Lease of Life.* 1956: *Secret Tent. A Town Like Alice.* 1957: *Heart of a Child. Robbery Under Arms. Lucky Jim. The Barretts of Wimpole Street.* 1959: *Solomon and Sheba. SOS Pacific.* 1961: *Spare the Rod.* 1962: *The Inspector (US: Lisa). The Waltz of the Toreadors.* 1963: *The Silent Playground. The Comedy Man. The Three Lives of Thomasina.* 1967: *Half a Sixpence.* 1969: *Country Dance (US: Brotherly Love). Run a Crooked Mile (TV).* 1971: *The Night Digger.* 1979: *The Lady Vanishes.* 1983: *Screamtime (video).* 1987: *Empire of the Sun.* 1988: *Madame Sousatzka.* 1990: *Circles of Deceit (TV). Back Home (TV).* 1991: *The Black Velvet Gown (TV). London Kills Me.* 1992: *The Bogey Man (TV). Leon the Pig Farmer.* 1994: *The Whipping Boy (TV).*

ANDERSON, John 1922–1992
Lean, laconic, lantern-jawed, fair-haired American actor who looked a certainty for fanatical Confederate colonels and powers behind the thrones of western towns. In his early days, he spent more than three years acting on a Mississippi riverboat, only leaving to serve with the Coast Guard during World War II. He appeared fairly regularly in films from the late 1950s, mainly in westerns, but was most prolific on television, where his

running role as the hero's brother in *Wyatt Earp* had first brought him to prominence. Died from a heart attack.

1952: Against All Flags. 1955: Target Zero. 1956: Introduction to Erica (TV. GB: cinemas). 1958: The True Story of Lynn Stuart. 1959: Last Train from Gun Hill. 1960: Psycho. 1961: Ride the High Country (GB: Guns in the Afternoon). 1962: Geronimo. A Walk on the Wild Side. How the West Was Won. 1964: The Satan Bug. 1965: The Hallelujah Trail. 1966: Scalplock (TV: GB: cinemas). Namu the Killer Whale. A Covenant with Death. Welcome to Hard Times (GB: Killer on a Horse). 1968: Massacre Harbor. Five Card Stud. Day of the Evil Gun. A Man Called Gannon. Heaven with a Gun. 1969: Set This Town on Fire (TV. Released 1973). Young Billy Young. The Great Bank Robbery. 1970: Soldier Blue. Cotton Comes to Harlem. The Animals (GB: Five Savage Men). 1971: Hitched (TV. GB: Westward the Wagon). 1972: Man and Boy. Molly and Lawless John. The Stepmother. 1973: Call to Danger (TV). Brock's Last Case (TV). Il consigliore (GB: The Counsellor). Executive Action. 1974: The Dove. Heatwave (TV). Smile Jenny, You're Dead (TV). Manhunter (TV). 1975: Dead Man on the Run (TV). The Specialist. Death Among Friends (TV). 1976: The Dark Side of Innocence (TV). The Hancocks (TV). Bridger: The 40th Day (TV). Once an Eagle (TV). The Quest (TV). 1977: Tail Gunner Joe (TV). Peter Lundy and the Medicine Hat Stallion (TV). The Last Hurrah (TV). The Lincoln Conspiracy. 1978: The Immigrants (TV). Donner Pass: The Road to Survival (TV). The Deerslayer (TV). 1979: Shadow of Fear (TV). 1980: Smokey and the Bandit II (GB: Smokey and the Bandit Ride Again). In Search of Historic Jesus (TV. GB: Jesus). 1981: Zoot Suit. 1982: The First Time (TV). Missing Children: A Mother's Story (TV). 1983: Lone Wolf McQuade. 1986: I-Man (TV). Amerasia. The Summons. Never Too Young to Die. Scorpion. 1987: American Harvest (TV). 1988: Eight Men Out. Regeneration. 1989: Full Exposure: The Sex Tapes Scandal (TV). 1990: Follow Your Heart (TV).

ANDERSON, Dame Judith

(Frances Anderson) 1898–1992
Formidable, dark-haired, strong-featured Australian-born actress who played Mrs Danvers in the 1940 *Rebecca*, a role that brought her an Academy Award nomination, and set her up for a good run of generally malevolent matrons in the *cinema noir* of the 1940s. Perfect casting for Lady Macbeth; a pity she did not play the role until she was 62. Created Dame in 1960. Died from pneumonia after suffering a brain tumour.

1930: *Madame of the Jury. 1932: *Judith Anderson. 1933: Blood Money. 1940: Forty Little Mothers. Rebecca. 1941: Lady Scarface. Free and Easy. 1942: All Through the Night. Kings Row. 1943: Edge of Darkness. Stage Door Canteen. 1944: Laura. 1945: And Then There Were None (GB: Ten Little Niggers). The Diary of a Chambermaid. 1946: The Specter of the Rose. The Strange Love of Martha Ivers. Pursued. 1947: The Red House. Tycoon. 1950: The Furies. 1953: Salome. 1954: Come of Age. 1956: The Ten Commandments. 1957: The Clouded Image (TV). 1958: Cat on a Hot Tin Roof. 1960: To the Sounds of Trumpets (TV). Cinderfella. Macbeth. 1961: Don't Bother to Knock! (US: Why Bother to Knock?). 1970: A Man Called Horse. 1973: The Borrowers (TV). 1974: Inn of the Damned. The Underground Man (TV). 1984: Star Trek III The Search for Spock. 1985: Hitchcock, il brivido del genio. 1986: Impure Thoughts.

ANDERSON, Richard 1926–

Lean-faced, sleekly dark-haired, brainy-looking, slightly diffident American 'second lead'. He found a niche as senior officers and wise counsellors in successful TV series (most notably *The Six Million Dollar Man*) after his days as an MGM contract player were over.

1949: Twelve O'Clock High. 1950: Storm Warning. The Vanishing Westerner. The Magnificent Yankee (GB: The Man with 30 Sons). Payment on Demand. A Life of Her Own. 1951: Cause for Alarm. No Questions Asked. The Unknown Man. Across the Wide Missouri. The People Against O'Hara. Rich, Young and Pretty. 1952: Just This Once. Scaramouche. Holiday for Sinners. Fearless Fagan. I Love Melvin. 1953: Dream Wife. The Story of Three Loves. 1954: Escape from Fort Bravo. Give a Girl a Break. 1955: The Student Prince. Hit the Deck. It's a Dog's Life. 1956: Forbidden Planet. The Search for Bridey Murphy. A Cry in the Night. 1957: Three Brave Men. Paths of Glory. The Buster Keaton Story. 1958: The Gunfight at Dodge City. The Long, Hot Summer. Curse of the Faceless Man. 1959: Compulsion. 1960: The Wackiest Ship in the Army. 1963: Johnny Cool. A Gathering of Eagles. 1964: Seven Days in May. Kitten with a Whip. 1966: The Ride to Hangman's Tree. Seconds. 1969: Along Came a Spider (TV). 1970: Tora! Tora! Tora! Macho Callahan. 1971: The Astronaut (TV). Doctors' Wives. Dead Men Tell No Tales (TV). 1972: Menace on the Mountain (TV. GB: cinemas). The Honkers. The Longest Night (TV). The Night Strangler (TV). Play It As It Lays. Say Goodbye, Maggie Cole (TV). 1973: Black Eye. Jarrett (TV). Partners in Crime (TV). 1978: The Immigrants (TV). 1979: Sharks! Murder by Natural Causes (TV). 1981: Rally. 1985: Perry Mason Returns (TV). 1987: Return of the Six Million Dollar Man and The Bionic Woman (TV). 1988: Stranger on My Land (TV). 1989: The Bionic Showdown (TV). 1992: The Player. 1993: Gettysburg. 1994: The Glass Shield.

ANDERSON, Warner 1911–1976

Dependable, grave-looking American supporting actor who enjoyed a good run of doctors, judges, senior officers and attorneys until the mid 1950s, after which he was lost almost entirely to long-running television series, latterly as editor Matthew Swain in *Peyton Place*. He made one appearance in a silent film as a child, and played in vaudeville and legitimate theatre before coming to the screen.

1916: Sunbeam. 1943: *Oklahoma Outlaws. This Is the Army. 1944: Destination Tokyo (shown in 1943). *Trial by Trigger. 1945: Her Highness and the Bellboy. Objective Burma. Bud Abbott and Lou Costello in Hollywood. My

Reputation. Dangerous Partners. Week-End at the Waldorf. 1946: Bad Bascomb. Three Wise Fools. Faithful in My Fashion. 1947: The Arnelo Affair. Dark Delusion (GB: Cynthia's Secret). The Beginning or the End? Song of the Thin Man. High Wall. 1948: Command Decision. Tenth Avenue Angel. Alias a Gentleman. 1949: The Lucky Stiff. The Doctor and the Girl. 1950: Destination Moon. 1951: Santa Fé. Detective Story. The Blue Veil. Go For Broke. Only the Valiant. *The Guest. Bannerline. 1952: The Star. 1953: A Lion is in the Streets. The Last Posse. 1954: City Story. The Caine Mutiny. Drum Beat. Yellow Tomahawk. 1955: Blackboard Jungle. The Violent Men (GB: Rough Company). A Lawless Street. 1958: The Line-Up. 1961: Armored Command. 1964: Rio Conchos. 1969: Gidget Grows Up (TV).

ANDREWS, Edward 1914–1985

Avuncular, heftily-built American actor whose big, beaming, bespectacled features could adapt just as easily to comic panic or coldly genuine menace. It was in the latter vein that he broke into films (in The Phenix City Story) after years of solid work on Broadway, but he was soon instantly identifiable in a series of characters whose hale-and-hearty exteriors hid a wide variety of characteristics beneath. An incorrigible stealer of the stars' limelight in his peak (1955–66) years. Died from a heart attack.

1955: The Phenix City Story (GB: The Phoenix City Story). 1956: Tea and Sympathy. The Harder They Fall. These Wilder Years. The Unguarded Moment. Tension at Table Rock. 1957: Hot Summer Night. Three Brave Men. The Tattered Dress. Trooper Hook. 1958: The Fiend That Walked the West. 1959: Night of the Quarter Moon. 1960: Elmer Gantry. 1961: The Young Doctors. The Absent-Minded Professor. The Young Savages. Advise and Consent. Love in a Goldfish Bowl. 1962: Son of Flubber. 40 Pounds of Trouble. 1963: The Man from Galveston (TV. GB: cinemas). The Thrill of It All. A Tiger Walks. 1964: The Brass Bottle. Good Neighbor Sam. Kisses for My President. Send Me No Flowers. Youngblood Hawke. 1965: Fluffy. 1966: The Glass Bottom Boat. Birds Do It. 1969: The Over-the-Hill Gang (TV). The Trouble with Girls. 1970: The Intruders (TV). Tora! Tora! Tora! 1971: Million Dollar Duck. How to Frame a Figg. Travis Logan DA (TV). 1972: Now You See Him Now You Don't.

Avanti! 1973: Charley and the Angel. 1975: The Photographer. Swiss Family Robinson (TV). 1976: How to Break Up a Happy Divorce (TV). 1977: Don't Push, I'll Charge When I'm Ready (TV. Filmed in 1969). 1978: Freedom Riders (TV). My Undercover Years with the Ku Klux Klan (TV). The Seniors. Lacy and the Mississippi Queen (TV). 1979: Supertrain (TV. Later: Express to Terror). 1980: The Final Countdown. 1984: Gremlins. Sixteen Candles.

ANDREWS, Harry 1911–1989

Craggy, stern-faced, solid-headed British actor with receding dark hair. After he swapped a largely Shakespearian stage career (begun in 1933) for films, Andrews' jutted jaw and determined expression came much into call for sergeant-majors, martinet figures and similar forbidding roles. He later moved on to fanatics of various shapes and shades, with one or two gentler roles for welcome relief. Died from a viral infection complicated by asthma.

1953: The Red Beret (US: Paratrooper). 1954: The Black Knight. The Man Who Loved Redheads. Helen of Troy. 1956: A Hill in Korea (US: Hell in Korea). Alexander the Great. Moby Dick. 1957: Saint Joan. 1958: I Accuse! Ice-Cold in Alex (US: Desert Attack). 1959: Solomon and Sheba. The Devil's Disciple. A Touch of Larceny. In the Nick. 1960: Circle of Deception. 1961: The Best of Enemies. Barabbas. 1962: Lisa (GB: The Inspector). 55 Days at Peking. Reach for Glory. Nine Hours to Rama. 1963: Cleopatra. The Informers. 1964: Nothing But the Best (shown 1963). The System. The Truth About Spring. 633 Squadron. 1965: The Hill. The Agony and the Ecstasy. Sands of the Kalahari. 1966: The Jokers. Modesty Blaise. The Deadly Affair. The Night of the Generals. 1967: Danger Route. The Long Duel. I'll Never Forget What's 'is Name. 1968: The Charge of the Light Brigade. Play Dirty. The Night They Raided Minsky's. A Dandy in Aspic. 1969: The Sea Gull. A Nice Girl Like Me. Battle of Britain. Too Late the Hero. The Southern Star. Destiny of a Spy/The Gaunt Woman (TV). Country Dance (US: Brotherly Love). 1970: Wuthering Heights. Entertaining Mr Sloane. 1971: Nicholas and Alexandra. Burke and Hare. I Want What I Want. Night Hair Child. The Ruling Class. The Nightcomers. 1972: Man of La Mancha. 1973: Theatre of Blood. The Final Programme (US: The Last Days of Man on

Earth). Man at the Top. The Mackintosh Man. 1974: The Internecine Project. Valley Forge (TV). The Story of Jacob and Joseph (TV). 1976: The Bluebird. The Passover Plot. Sky Riders. 1977: The Prince and the Pauper (US: Crossed Swords). The Medusa Touch. Equus. 1978: The Big Sleep. Death on the Nile. The Four Feathers (TV. GB: cinemas). Watership Down (voice only). Superman. 1979: SOS Titanic. 1980: Never Never Land (made for cinemas, but shown only on TV). Hawk the Slayer. 1984: Mesmerized. 1988: Cause Célèbre (TV).

ANKRUM, Morris
(M. Nussbaum) 1896–1964

Tall, small-eyed, ferret-featured, grey-moustached, slightly stooping American actor who rarely looked happy on screen and played villains in low-budget westerns and townsfolk of one kind or another in bigger films. Originally an economics professor, he became interested in acting while teaching in California, beginning his screen career under the name Stephen Morris. Later he balanced accounts a little by playing judges and officers in 1950s films. Died from trichinosis. His son, David Ankrum (1947–) is also an actor.

1933: †Reunion in Vienna. 1934: †Stand Up and Cheer. 1936: †Hopalong Cassidy Returns. †Trail Dust. †Hills of Old Wyoming. †North of the Rio Grande. †Rustlers' Valley. 1937: †Borderland. 1939: Three Texas Steers (GB: Danger Rides the Range). 1940: The Showdown. Cherokee Strip (GB: Fighting Marshal). Three Men from Texas. Buck Benny Rides Again. Light of Western Stars. Knights of the Range. 1941: This Woman is Mine. The Roundup. Doomed Caravan. In Old Colorado. Pirates on Horseback. Border Vigilantes. Wide Open Town. The Bandit Trail. I Wake Up Screaming (GB: Hot Spot). Road Agent. 1942: Roxie Hart. Ride 'Em Cowboy. Ten Gentlemen from West Point. The Loves of Edgar Allan Poe. Tales of Manhattan. The Omaha Trail. Reunion/Reunion in France (GB: Mademoiselle France). Tennessee Johnson (GB: The Man on America's Conscience). Time to Kill. 1943: Let's Face It. Dixie Dugan. Swing Fever. Whistling in Brooklyn. Cry Havoc. Assignment in Brittany. I Dood It (GB: By Hook or by Crook). The Human Comedy. Best Foot Forward. The Heavenly Body. 1944: Thirty Seconds Over Tokyo. Rationing.

Meet the People. Barbary Coast Gent. Marriage is a Private Affair. The Thin Man Goes Home. Gentle Annie. *Radio Bugs. *Dark Shadows. See Here, Private Hargrove. Return from Nowhere. 1945: The Hidden Eye. Adventure. The Harvey Girls. *The Purity Squad. 1946: Courage of Lassie. Little Mr Jim. The Cockeyed Miracle (GB: Mr Griggs Returns). The Green Years. The Postman Always Rings Twice. Blue Sierra. Undercurrent. Lady in the Lake. The Mighty McGurk. 1947: Undercover Maisie (GB: Undercover Girl). Cynthia (GB: The Rich, Full Life). The Sea of Grass. Song of the Thin Man. Merton of the Movies. Desire Me. High Wall. Good News. 1948: Alias a Gentleman. Joan of Arc. For the Love of Mary. *The Fabulous Fraud. Bad Men of Tombstone. Fighting Back. 1949: We Were Strangers. Colorado Territory. Slattery's Hurricane. The Fountainhead. 1950: In a Lonely Place. Rocketship X-M. The Damned Don't Cry. Chain Lightning. Borderline. Short Grass. The Redhead and the Cowboy. Southside 1—1000 (GB: Forgery). 1951: The Lion Hunters (GB: Bomba and the Lion Hunters). Fighting Coast Guard. Along the Great Divide. My Favorite Spy. Tomorrow is Another Day. Flight to Mars. 1952: Son of Ali Baba. And Now Tomorrow. Red Planet Mars. Mutiny. The Raiders. Hiawatha. The Man Behind the Gun. Fort Osage. 1953: Flight Nurse. Mexican Manhunt. Arena. Invaders from Mars. Devil's Canyon. Fort Vengeance. Sky Commando. The Moonlighter. 1954: Southwest Passage (GB: Camels West). Apache. Vera Cruz. Three Young Texans. Taza, Son of Cochise. Silver Lode. Two Guns and a Badge. Drums Across the River. The Saracen Blade. The Outlaw Stallion. The Steel Cage. Cattle Queen of Montana. 1955: Jupiter's Darling. The Silver Star. Chief Crazy Horse (GB: Valley of Fury). Abbott and Costello Meet the Mummy. The Eternal Sea. Tennessee's Partner. Crashout. No Man's Woman. The Last Command. Jujin Yukiotoko (GB and US: Half Human). 1956: Fury at Gunsight Pass. When Gangland Strikes. The Naked Gun. Earth vs the Flying Saucers. Walk the Proud Land. Death of a Scoundrel. Quincannon, Frontier Scout (GB: Frontier Scout). The Desperadoes Are in Town. 1957: Drango. Zombies of Mora-Tau (GB: The Dead That Walk). The Badge of Marshal Brennan. Kronos. Hell's Crossroads. The Giant Claw. The Beginning of the End. Omar Khayyam. 1958: Badman's Country. Young and Wild. Twilight for the Gods. Tarawa Beachhead. The Saga of Hemp Brown. From the Earth to the Moon. Frontier Gun. How to Make a Monster. Giant from the Unknown. Most Dangerous Man Alive (released 1961). 1960: The Little Shepherd of Kingdom Come. 1963: 'X' — The Man with the X-Ray Eyes (GB: The Man with the X-Ray Eyes). 1964: Guns of Diablo (TV. GB: cinemas).

† As Stephen Morris

ANSARA, Michael 1922–

Back in the 1950s, American-born (of Lebanese ancestry) Ansara vied with the Australian Michael Pate (qv) as the actor most likely to be found in action pictures as Red Indians or ruthless, bearded Middle Eastern despots. Ever ready with a sword or an arrow, his handsome, olive-complexioned,

rather cruel-looking features propelled him into a whole run of powerful villains, and it was no surprise when he turned up as Cochise in a TV series based on the film Broken Arrow. Married to actress Barbara Eden (B. Huffman. 1934–) from 1958 to 1973; earlier married to actress Jean Byron.

1944: Action in Arabia. 1947: Intrigue. 1949: South Sea Sinner (GB: East of Java). 1950: Kim. 1951: My Favorite Spy. Only the Valiant. Soldiers Three. Bannerline. 1952: Yankee Buccaneer. The Golden Hawk. Diplomatic Courier. Brave Warrior. Road to Bali. The Lawless Breed. 1953: White Witch Doctor. Julius Caesar. Serpent of the Nile. The Bandits of Corsica (GB: Return of the Corsican Brothers). The Robe. Slaves of Babylon. The Diamond Queen. 1954: Sign of the Pagan. The Egyptian. Three Young Texans. Princess of the Nile. The Saracen Blade. Bengal Brigade (GB: Bengal Rifles). 1955: Diane. New Orleans Uncensored (GB: Riot on Pier 6). Abbott and Costello Meet the Mummy. Jupiter's Darling. 1956: The Ten Commandments. Pillars of the Sky (GB: The Tomahawk and the Cross). The Ox-Bow Incident (TV. GB: cinemas). The Lone Ranger. Gun Brothers. 1957: Last of the Badmen. The Tall Stranger. The Sad Sack. Quantez. 1959: The Killers of Mussolini (TV). The Comancheros. Voyage to the Bottom of the Sea. 1962: Five Weeks in a Balloon. 1964: A Truce to Terror (TV). The Confession (GB: TV, as Quick! Let's Get Married). 1965: Harum Scarum (GB: Harem Holiday). The Greatest Story Ever Told. 1966: ...And Now Miguel. The Destructors. Texas Across the River. How I Spent My Summer Vacation (TV. GB: cinemas, as Deadly Roulette). 1967: The Pink Jungle. Sol Madrid (GB: The Heroin Gang). 1968: Daring Game. 1969: Guns of the Magnificent Seven. The Last Conquistador. The Phynx. How to Make It (GB: Target Harry). 1971: Powderkeg (TV. GB: cinemas). 1972: Stand Up and Be Counted. 1973: It's Alive! The Doll Squad. Call to Danger (TV). Ordeal (TV). 1974: Shootout in a One-Dog Town (TV). The Bears and I. 1975: Dear Dead Delilah (filmed 1972). Barbary Coast (TV. GB: In Old San Francisco). 1976: Day of the Animals. The Message/Mohammed — Messenger of God. 1977: The Manitou. 1981: The Guns and the Fury. 1982: Bayou Romance (TV). 1983: The Fantastic World of DC Collins (TV). 1984:

Access Code (video). 1985: KGB — The Secret War (later Lethal). 1986: Knights of the City (filmed 1984). 1987: Assassination. 1990: Border Shootout.

ARCHARD, Bernard 1916–

Gaunt, angular-faced, serious-looking, cold-eyed, tight-lipped British actor with high forehead and dark hair who gave incisive performances and was often cast as prosecutors, interrogators and religious fanatics. He was 'about to emigrate to Canada' when given the role that won him his greatest popular success, in the long-running TV series Spycatcher in 1959, and has been busy in all media ever since.

1958: The Secret Man. 1960: Village of the Damned. 1961: Clue of the New Pin. Man Detained. 1962: Flat Two. Two-Letter Alibi. The Password is Courage. *A Woman's Privilege. 1963: The Silent Playground. The List of Adrian Messenger. 1964: Face of a Stranger. 1966: The Spy with a Cold Nose. 1967: Son of the Sahara (serial). 1968: The Mini Affair. File of the Golden Goose. Play Dirty. 1969: Run a Crooked Mile (TV). 1970: Fragment of Fear. The Horror of Frankenstein. Song of Norway. 1971: Macbeth. Dad's Army. 1972: Madigan: The Lisbon Beat (TV). 1973: The Day of the Jackal. 1979: The Purple Twilight (TV). 1980: The Sea Wolves. 1983: Krull. 1985: King Solomon's Mines. 1990: Hidden Agenda.

ARDEN, Eve

(Eunice Quedens) 1912–1990

Sharp-looking, highly-animated, light-haired American actress, a Ziegfeld Follies dancer who became the archetypal wisecracking Hollywood heroine's friend of the 1940s. After playing a fistful of such roles — one of which, in Mildred Pierce, earned her an Academy Award nomination in the Best Supporting Actress category — she enjoyed huge success on television in the 1950s. After an unsuccessful first marriage, she remained married to her second husband, minor actor Brooks West, from 1951 to his death in 1984. She herself died from heart failure after more than a year of suffering from cancer and heart problems. Eve Arden was always cagy about her age which, officially 78 at her death, may have been 82.

1929: †Song of Love. 1933: †Dancing Lady. 1937: Oh, Doctor. Stage Door. 1938: Coconut Grove. Letter of Introduction. Having Wonderful Time. Women in the Wind. 1939: Big Town Czar. The Forgotten Woman. Eternally Yours. At the Circus. 1940: A Child is Born. Slightly Honorable. Comrade X. No, No, Nanette. 1941: Ziegfeld Girl. That Uncertain Feeling. She Couldn't Say No. She Knew All the Answers. San Antonio Rose. Sing for Your Supper. Manpower. Whistling in the Dark. Obliging Young Lady. 1942: Last of the Duanes. Bedtime Story. 1943: Hit Parade of 1943. Let's Face It. 1944: Cover Girl. The Doughgirls. My Reputation (released 1946). 1945: Pan Americana. Earl Carroll's Vanities. Mildred Pierce. Patrick the Great. 1946: The Kid from Brooklyn. Night and Day. 1947: Song of Scheherezade. The Arnelo Affair. The Unfaithful. 1948: The Voice of the Turtle. One Touch of Venus. Whiplash. 1949: My Dream is Yours. The Lady Takes a Sailor. 1950: Paid in Full. Curtain Call at Cactus Creek (GB: Take the Stage). Tea for Two. Three Husbands. 1951: Goodbye, My Fancy. 1952: We're Not Married. 1953: The Lady Wants Mink. 1954: *Hollywood Life. 1956: Our Miss Brooks. 1959: Anatomy of a Murder. 1960: The Dark at the Top of the Stairs. 1965: Sergeant Deadhead. 1969: In Name Only (TV). 1972: A Very Missing Person (TV). All My Darling Daughters (TV). 1973: Mother of the Bride (TV). 1975: The Strongest Man in the World. 1978: A Guide for the Married Woman (TV). Grease. 1980: The Dream Merchants (TV). 1981: Under the Rainbow. Pandemonium/Thursday the 12th. 1982: Grease 2.

† As Eunice Quedens

ARMETTA, Henry 1888–1945

Short, stocky, moustachioed, Italian-born Hollywood actor with slitted eyes and whale-like mouth, who cornered the market in harassed, excitable, voluble foreigners from the beginnings of sound. He also starred in a few short comedy vehicles of his own. His early death from a heart attack robbed him of the well-deserved opportunity of carrying a film-filled career through to the end of the studio era. Stowed away on a ship to come to America in 1902.

1915: The Nigger. 1916: The Marble Heart. 1917: The Eternal Sin. 1918: My Cousin. 1919: The Jungle Trail. 1920: Fantomas (serial). 1923: The Silent Command. 1925: The Desert's Price. 1927: Seventh Heaven. 1928: Street Angel. Love Song. Alias Jimmy Valentine. Homesick. 1929: Lady of the Pavements (GB: Lady of the Night). In Old Arizona. The Trespasser. Sunny Side Up. Love, Live and Laugh. Jazz Heaven. 1930: A Lady to Love. *Society Goes Spaghetti. The Climax. *Razored in Old Kentucky. Ladies Love Brutes. Little Accident. Lovin' the Ladies. *Hey Diddle-Diddle. Romance. *Moonlight and Monkey Business. Sins of the Children (GB: The Richest Man in the World). Sehnsucht jeder Frau. *He Loved Her Not. 1931: Just a Gigolo (GB: The Dancing Partner). Strangers May Kiss. Leftover Ladies (GB: Broken Links). Five and Ten (GB: Daughter of Luxury). A Tailor-Made Man. Hush Money. *The Wife o' Riley. The Unholy Garden. Laughing Sinners. Speak Easy. 1932: Hat Check Girl (GB: Embassy Girl). Scarface (The Shame of a Nation). Arsène Lupin. The Passionate Plumber. High Pressure. The Doomed Battalion. Weekends Only. Central Park. Red-Headed Woman. Cauliflower Alley. Steady Company. Huddle (GB: Impossible Lover). They Just Had to Get Married. Forbidden. Prosperity. A Farewell to Arms. Uptown New York. Okay, America (GB: Penalty of Fame). Men of America (GB: Great Decision). 1933: The Devil's Brother (GB: Fra Diavolo). *Pick Me Up. The Cohens and Kellys in Trouble. Her First Mate.

Too Much Harmony. Laughing at Life. Deception. *The Trial of Vince Barnett. What! No Beer? *Hello Pop. So This is Africa. *Open Sesame. Don't Bet on Love. 1934: The Cat and the Fiddle. Cross Country Cruise. One Night of Love. Viva Villa! The Poor Rich. *Full Coverage. The Hide-Out. Embarrassing Moments. Gift of Gab. *Ceiling Whacks. The Black Cat. Two Heads on a Pillow. Wake Up and Dream. Imitation of Life. The Merry Widow. The Man Who Reclaimed His Head. Kiss and Make Up. Cheating Cheaters. Romance in the Rain. Let's Talk It Over. 1935: Straight from the Heart. Vanessa, Her Love Story. Night Life of the Gods. *Romance of the West. After Office Hours. I've Been Around. Dinky. *Social Splash. Princess O'Hara. Unknown Woman. Three Kids and a Queen (GB: The Baxter Millions). The Show Goes On. *Old Age Pension. Manhattan Moon (GB: Sing Me a Love Song). 1936: Magnificent Obsession. Let's Sing Again. The Crime of Dr Forbes. Poor Little Rich Girl. The Magnificent Brute. Two in a Crowd. 1937: Top of the Town. Make a Wish. Manhattan Merry-Go-Round (GB: Manhattan Music Box). Seventh Heaven. 1938: Everybody Sing. Speed to Burn. Submarine Patrol. Road Demon. *My Pop. 1939: Fisherman's Wharf. The Lady and the Mob. Winner Take All. *Home Cheap Home. I Stole a Million. Rio. 1940: The Outsider. Dust Be My Destiny. Escape. Three Cheers for the Irish. We Who are Young. You're Not So Tough. The Man Who Talked Too Much. 1941: Caught in the Act. The Big Store. *Slick Chick. 1942: Stage Door Canteen. Good Luck Mr Yates. 1943: Thank Your Lucky Stars. 1944: Allergic to Love. Ghost Catchers. Once Upon a Time. 1945: Penthouse Rhythm. A Bell for Adano. Anchors Aweigh. Colonel Effingham's Raid (GB: Man of the Hour).

ARMSTRONG, R.G. 1917–

Big, balding, glowering American supporting actor who became one of Hollywood's few really distinctive character players in the post-1960 era, often in menacing or bigoted roles. A frustrated writer, the 6 foot 3 inch Armstrong turned to acting in 1952, when he enrolled at The Actors' Studio. Entering mainline Hollywood films in 1958, he soon became a man in demand, especially for portraits of mid-west rednecks and religious fanatics. The initials stand for Robert Golden.

1957: The Garden of Eden. 1958: From Hell to Texas (GB: Manhunt). Never Love a Stranger. No Name on the Bullet. 1959: The Fugitive Kind. 1960: Ten Who Dared. 1961: Ride the High Country (GB: Guns in the Afternoon). 1962: Six Gun Law (TV. GB: cinemas). 1963: He Rides Tall. 1964: Major Dundee. 1966: El Dorado. 1968: Tiger by the Tail. 80 Steps to Jonah. 1969: The McMasters...Tougher than the West Itself! 1970: The Ballad of Cable Hogue. The Great White Hope. Angels Die Hard. 1971: The Great Northfield Minnesota Raid. J W Coop. 1972: The Final Comedown. Ulzana's Raid. The Century Turns/Hec Ramsey

(TV). 1973: My Name is Nobody. Deliver Us from Evil (TV. Released 1975). Pat Garrett and Billy the Kid. Running Wild. White Lightning. 1974: Manhunter (TV). Boss Nigger (GB: The Black Bounty Hunter). Reflections of Murder (TV). Who Fears the Devil/The Legend of Hillbilly John (filmed 1972). 1975: White Line Fever. Race with the Devil. Mean Johnny Barrows. 1976: Kingston: The Power Play (TV). Stay Hungry. Dixie Dynamite. Slumber Party '57. 1977: Mr Billion. The Car. The Pack. 1978: Heaven Can Wait. Devil Dog: The Hound of Hell (TV). Fast Charlie — the Moonbeam Rider. The Time Machine (TV). Texas Detour. Good Luck, Miss Wyckoff. 1979: Steel. The Last Ride of the Dalton Gang (TV). The Villain (GB: Cactus Jack). The Legend of the Golden Gun (TV). Dear Detective (TV). 1980: Hammett (released 1982). Where the Buffalo Roam. 1981: Reds. Raggedy Man. The Pursuit of D B Cooper/Pursuit. Evilspeak. 1982: The Beast Within. The Shadow Riders (TV). 1983: Lone Wolf McQuade. 1984: Children of the Corn. 1985: Road Trip. 1986: The Best of Times. Jocks. Oceans of Fire. Red-Headed Stranger. 1987: LBJ: The Early Years (TV). Predator. Independence (TV). Bulletproof. 1988: Trapper County War. 1989: Ghettoblaster. 1990: Dick Tracy. 1992: Crazy Joe. 1993: Warlock: The Armageddon.

ARNATT, John 1917–

Squarely-built British actor with solid, shadowed face and slimline moustache, from underneath which a pipe would project. Most at home in modern dress, he projected the image of discretion, authority and reliability through many post-war British films. Strangely, one of his longest-running roles was as a bad guy in fancy dress, though he never looked entirely comfortable through his four seasons as the Deputy Sheriff of Nottingham in TV's The Adventures of Robin Hood. He was more at home as a detective inspector, narrowing his eyes over the evidence. Making his stage debut at 19, he was twice married, firstly to actress Betty Huntley-Wright (1911–). Still around in theatre and television.

1937: Mademoiselle Docteur. 1948: Dick Barton Strikes Back. 1949: Meet Simon Cherry. 1950: Dick Barton at Bay. Pool of London. 1951: The House in the Square (US: I'll Never Forget You). Mr Denning Drives North. Cry

the Beloved Country. 1952: Circumstantial Evidence. House of Blackmail. 1954: The Village. Forbidden Cargo. 1956: The Passionate Stranger (US: A Novel Affair). Fortune Is a Woman (US: She Played with Fire). 1959: *Learning in Britain (narrator only). 1960: The Pure Hell of St Trinian's. The Bulldog Breed. The Impersonator. No Love for Johnnie. 1961: The Third Alibi. Whistle Down the Wind. 1962: Only Two Can Play. The Set-Up. Dr Crippen. Out of the Fog. Captain Clegg (US: Night Creatures). 1963: Shadow of Fear. Clash by Night (US: Escape by Night). 1964: Hysteria. Runaway Railway. 1965: Licensed to Kill (US: The Second Best Secret Agent in the Whole Wide World). Joey Boy. 1966: Where the Bullets Fly. 1967: Our Mother's House. A Challenge to Robin Hood. 1968: Headline Hunters. 1969: The Breaking of Bumbo. 1971: Crucible of Terror. 1974: Sign It Death (TV). 1979: Licensed to Love and Kill.

ARNE, Peter
(P.A. Albrecht) 1920–1983
Dark, tight-lipped, furtive-looking, narrow-eyed, incisive, Malaya-born British actor who had some good roles as heartless, half-smiling villains in British action films of the 1950s and early 1960s before his career dipped disappointingly into minor supporting parts, sometimes verging on the comic. Perhaps the oiliness was piled on a bit thickly, but he was always good value for money. Believed to have been murdered by a student who subsequently drowned himself.

1944: For Those in Peril. 1948: Saraband for Dead Lovers (US: Saraband). 1953: Front Page Story. You Know What Sailors Are. 1954: Mystery on Bird Island. The Men of Sherwood Forest. The Brain Machine. *Night Plane to Amsterdam. Knights of the Round Table. The Purple Plain. The Dam Busters. 1955: Timeslip (US: The Atomic Man). *Murder Anonymous. Cockleshell Heroes. 1957: High Tide at Noon. Strangers' Meeting. Tarzan and the Lost Safari. The Moonraker. 1958: Ice Cold in Alex (US: Desert Attack). Intent to Kill. 1959: Danger Within (US: Breakout). 1960: Conspiracy of Hearts. Sands of the Desert. A Story of David. Scent of Mystery (GB: Holiday in Spain). 1961: The Hellfire Club. The Treasure of Monte Cristo (GB: The Secret of Monte Cristo). The Pirates of Blood River. 1963: The Victors. Girl in the Headlines (US: The Model Murder Case). The

Mouse on the Moon. 1964: The Black Torment. The Secret of Blood Island. 1966: Khartoum. The Sandwich Man. 1967: Battle Beneath the Earth. 1968: Chitty Chitty Bang Bang. 1969: The Oblong Box. 1970: House of Evil. 1971: When Eight Bells Toll. Nobody Ordered Love. Straw Dogs. Murders in the Rue Morgue. 1972: Antony and Cleopatra. Pope Joan. 1974: The Return of the Pink Panther. 1977: Providence. 1978: The Passage. Agatha. 1982: Victor/Victoria. Trail of the Pink Panther. 1983: Curse of the Pink Panther.

ARNO, Sig
(Siegfried Aron) 1895–1975
German-born comic actor with humorous mouth and rolling eyes, who had both light-weight and dramatic leading roles in German films (in all of which he was billed as Siegfried Arno) before fleeing the country in 1933. Like so many continental refugees, Arno, after travelling (and acting) through several countries, ended up in Hollywood, where he contributed a delightful series of cameos as over-eager men-on-the-make whose fractured English made the hero instantly suspicious. Died from Parkinson's Disease.

1923: Schicksal. 1924: Eine Frau von vierzig Jahren. 1926: Der Panzergewolbe. Manon Lescaut. Schatz mach Kasse. 1927: Die Liebe der Jeanne Ney (GB and US: The Love of Jeanne Ney). Beef und Steak. Moral. Bigoudis. 1928: Sigi, der Matrose. Leise flehen meine Lieder. Der schönste Mann im Staate. Um eine Nasenlänge. Tragödie im Zirkus Royale. Geschichten aus dem Wienerwald. Rutschbahn. Moderne Piraten. 1929: Aufruhr im Junggesellenheim. Die Buchse der Pandora (GB and US: Pandora's Box). Ihr dunkler Punkt. Das Tagebuch einer Verlorenen (GB and US: Diary of a Lost Girl). Wir halten fest und treu zusammen. 1930: Die vom Rummelplatz. Wien du Stadt der Lieder. Heute Nacht — eventuell. 1931: Schuberts Frühlingstraum. Keine Feier ohne Meyer. Schritzenfest im Schilda. Das Geheimnis der roten Katze. Im Kampf mit der Unterwelt. Eine Freundin so goldig wie Du. Schachmatt (GB: Checkmate). Die Nacht ohne Pause (GB: Night Without End). Der Storch streikt. Ein ausgekochter Junge. Mortiz macht sein Glück. Die grosse Attraktion. 1933: Zapfenstreich am Rhein. 1938: Dramatic School. 1939: The Star Maker. The Bridal Suite. The Hunchback of Notre Dame. 1940: Comrade X.

The Mummy's Hand. Diamond Frontier. The Great Dictator. Dark Streets of Cairo. A Little Bit of Heaven. 1941: This Thing Called Love. Ringside Maisie. Raiders of the Desert. Sing for Your Supper. New Wine (GB: The Great Awakening). It Started with Eve. Hellzapoppin. Two Latins from Manhattan. The Chocolate Soldier. Gambling Daughters. 1942: Pardon My Sarong. Juke Box Jenny. I Married an Angel. Two Yanks in Trinidad. Tales of Manhattan. Kid Glove Killer. Highways by Night. The Palm Beach Story. The Devil with Hitler. 1943: The Crystal Ball. Du Barry Was a Lady. Larceny with Music. Taxi, Mister. Thousands Cheer. Passport to Suez. Let's Have Fun. His Butler's Sister. 1944: Once Upon a Time. Up in Arms. Standing Room Only. The Great Moment. And the Angels Sing. Song of the Open Road. 1945: Bring on the Girls. Roughly Speaking. A Song to Remember. 1946: One More Tomorrow. 1947: It Happened on Fifth Avenue. 1949: The Great Lover. Holiday in Havana. 1950: Nancy Goes to Rio. Duchess of Idaho. The Toast of New Orleans. 1951: On Moonlight Bay. 1952: Diplomatic Courier. 1953: Fast Company. The Great Diamond Robbery.

ASKEW, Luke 1937–

Tall, rangy, brown-haired, mean-looking American actor with worried brown eyes. He came to Hollywood after a varied early career – television announcer, manager of a waste-paper plant, off-Broadway acting work – and played mostly unkempt villains, often in westerns. Less often seen in films since the late 1970s.

1966: Hurry Sundown. The Happening. 1967: Cool Hand Luke. Will Penny. 1968: The Green Berets. The Devil's Brigade. 1969: La notte dei serpenti. Easy Rider. Flare-Up. 1970: Angel Unchained. 1971: The Great Northfield Minnesota Raid. 1972: The Glass House (TV. GB: cinemas). The Magnificent Seven Ride! The Culpepper Cattle Co. 1973: Pat Garrett and Billy the Kid. 1974: Slipstream. Manhunter (TV). Night Games (TV). This is the West That Was (TV). 1975: Mackintosh & TJ. Posse. Part 2 Walking Tall (GB: Legend of the Lawman). Attack on Terror: the FBI vs the Ku Klux Klan (TV). 1976: A Matter of Wife...or Death (TV). The Quest (TV). The Invasion of Johnson County (TV). 1977: Rolling Thunder. 1978:

Wanda Nevada. 1982: The Beast Within. 1983: White Star. 1984: The Warrior and the Sorceress. 1985: White Dragon/Legend of the White Horse. 1986: Kung Fu: The Movie (TV. GB: Kung Fu/Kung Fu II). 1987: Bulletproof. 1989: Back to Back. 1993: Through My Ex-Enemy's Eyes.

ASKIN, Leon 1907–

Tubby, swarthy, sometimes moustachioed Austrian actor with receding dark hair and menacing lips who started his career on the German stage, but fled the Nazis in 1933. Coming to New York in 1940, Askin became an American citizen in 1943. From 1952, he began a spasmodic flirtation with the Hollywood and (from 1959) international film scenes, waddling on and off as Slavic villains and eccentrics – occasionally dramatic but more often comic. He also directs, teaches and lectures on drama.

1952: Assignment – Paris! Road to Bali. 1953: Desert Legion. The Robe. The Veils of Bagdad. South Sea Woman. 1954: China Venture. Knock on Wood. Secret of the Incas. Valley of the Kings. 1955: Son of Sinbad. Carolina Cannonball. 1956: Spy Chasers. 1958: My Gun is Quick. The Last Blitzkrieg. 1959: Abschied von den Wolken (GB: Rebel Flight to Cuba). 1961: One, Two, Three. Unter Ausschluss der Öffentlichkeit. 1962: Lulu. The Testament of Dr Mabuse. Sherlock Holmes und das Halsband des Todes (GB and US: Sherlock Holmes and the Deadly Necklace). 1964: John Goldfarb, Please Come Home. 1965: Do Not Disturb. 1966: Carnival of Thieves (US: Caper of the Golden Bulls). What Did You Do in the War, Daddy? 1967: Guns for San Sebastian. Double Trouble. The Perils of Pauline. 1968: Lucrezia Borgia, l'amante del diavolo/Lucrezia. Die funkstreife Gottes. A Fine Pair. The Wicked Dreams of Paula Schultz. 1969: La morte bussa due volta. The Maltese Bippy. 1972: Hammersmith is Out. 1973: Doctor Death: Seeker of Souls. The World's Greatest Athlete. Genesis II (TV). 1974: Young Frankenstein. 1975: Death Knocks Twice. 1979: Going Ape! 1982: Airplane II The Sequel. 1983: Frightmare. 1984: Odd Jobs. 1985: First Strike. Stiffs. Savage Island. 1987: Deshima. 1994: Hohenangst (US: Fear of Heights). Occhiopinocchio.

ASLAN, Gregoire

(Krikor Aslanian) 1908–1982

Alarmed-looking, dark-haired, balding, big-nosed actor with large face and full, usually pursed lips. Born in Istanbul, the bag-eyed Aslan began his career at 18 as a vocalist and drummer with a dance band in Paris. He also did vaudeville and cabaret work and a stint as a comedian before beginning to turn to acting. In post-war years, his thick Gallic accent and double-takes became a familiar part of the film scene in British studios and he tackled both comic and dramatic roles. Billed as Coco Aslan throughout the earlier part of his career, a nickname he gradually discarded after the 1950s. Died from a heart attack.

1938: Feu de joie. 1939: Tourbillon de Paris. 1940: Les surprises de la radio. 1946: En êtes-vous bien sur? 1948: Hans le marin (GB: The Wicked City). Sleeping Car to Trieste. 1949: Occupe-toi d'Amélie. 1950: Les joyeux pèlerins. Last Holiday. Cairo Road. Cage of Gold. The Adventurers (US: The Great Adventure). 1951: L'auberge rouge (GB and US: The Red Inn). Pas de vacances pour Monsieur Le Maire. Un enfant dans la tourneste. 1952: Le secret d'une mère. 1953: Act of Love. Innocents in Paris. Cet homme est dangereux. 1954: Oasis. 1955: Confidential Report (US: Mr Arkadin). Joe Macbeth. 1956: Celui qui doit mourir (US: He Who Must Die). L'homme aux clès d'or. 1957: Les fanatiques/The Fanatics. Windom's Way. 1958: The Snorkel. The Roots of Heaven. Sea Fury. 1959: Killers of Kilimanjaro. Our Man in Havana. The Three Worlds of Gulliver. 1960: Under Ten Flags. The Criminal. Il suffit d'aimer. 1961: The Rebel (US: Call Me Genius). King of Kings. The Devil at Four O'Clock. Invasion Quartet. Village of Daughters. The Happy Thieves. 1963: Cleopatra. Crooks in Cloisters. 1964: The Fabulous Adventures of Marco Polo (US: Marco the Magnificent). Aimez-vous les femmes? (GB: Do You Like Women?). The Main Chance. The Yellow Rolls Royce. Paris When It Sizzles. Une ravissante idiote (GB: A Ravishing Idiot. US: Adorable Idiot). 1965: The High Bright Sun (US: McGuire, Go Home!). Moment to Moment. 1966: Lost Command. Our Man in Marrakesh. A Man Could Get Killed. 1967: The 25th Hour. 1968: Mazel Tov ou le mariage (GB and US: Marry Me! Marry Me!). A Flea in Her Ear. 1969: Twelve Plus One. Les tripes au soleil (US: Checkerboard). 1970: You Can't

Win 'Em All. 1972: Die rote Kapelle (TV). Sex Shop. 1973: The Girl from Hong Kong. The Golden Voyage of Sinbad. 1974: The Girl from Petrovka. The Return of the Pink Panther. QB VII (TV). Bon baisers de Hong Kong. Auf Kreuz gelegt. 1976: The Killer Who Wouldn't Die (TV). 1977: Blood-Relations. 1978: Meetings with Remarkable Men.

ASNER, Ed(ward) 1929–

Thick-set, gruff-voiced, balding, aggressive American actor in Hollywood films, cast as tough characters after long theatre training. His career really took off in the 1970s with his long-running TV portrait of hard-nosed, soft-hearted newspaper editor Lou Grant in a series of that name – a character he had created on another TV series, *The Mary Tyler Moore Show.* But his career received a severe setback in the early 1980s when, as militant president of the Screen Actors' Guild, he clashed showily with President Reagan (himself a former president of SAG). The *Lou Grant* series nosedived in the ratings and was promptly cancelled. In the early 1990s, looking much older, Asner was seen in some solid roles in TV movies.

1962: Kid Galahad. 1964: The Satan Bug. Fanfare for a Death Scene (TV). 1965: The Slender Thread. 1966: The Venetian Affair. The Doomsday Flight (TV. GB: cinemas). 1967: El Dorado. Gunn. 1969: Daughter of the Mind (TV). Change of Habit. 1970: They Call Me MISTER Tibbs! Halls of Anger. The Todd Killings. The House on Greenapple Road (TV). The Old Man Who Cried Wolf (TV). Do Not Throw Cushions in the Ring. 1971: The Last Child (TV). They Call It Murder (TV). Skin Game. 1972: Haunts of the Very Rich (TV). 1973: Police Story (TV. GB: cinemas). The Girl Most Likely To ... (TV). 1974: The Wrestler. 1975: The Imposter (TV). Death Scream (TV). Hey! I'm Alive (TV). 1976: Gus. 1977: The Life and Assassination of the Kingfish (TV). The Gathering (TV). 1979: The Family Man (TV). 1981: Fort Apache the Bronx. O'Hara's Wife. A Small Killing (TV). The Marva Collins Story (TV. Narrator only). 1983: Daniel. 1984: Anatomy of an Illness (TV). 1986: Following the Footsteps (TV). Vital Signs (TV). The Christmas Star (TV). 1987: Pinocchio and the Emperor of the Night (voice only). Cracked Up (TV). 1988: Moon Over Parador. 1990: Happily Ever After (voice only). Good Cops, Bad Cops (TV). 1991: Yes Virginia,

There is a Santa Claus (TV). Silent Motive (TV). 1993: Earth and the American Dream (voice only). Gypsy (TV. GB: cinemas). 1994: Heads (TV). Cats Don't Dance (voice only). *Down on the Waterfront.

ATES, Roscoe 1892–1962

Bug-eyed, sawn-off, jug-eared, scrawny-necked American comedy actor with scruffy hair who often seemed to be wearing funny clothes and hats the wrong way round – and cashed in by re-creating a childhood stutter and making it part of his many nervous characters. Ates escaped being browbeaten by heroes and henpecked by screen wives when he became the comic sidekick of cowboy star Eddie Dean in 15 1940s westerns. He had begun his career as a concert violinist. Four times married, Ates died from lung cancer.

1929: South Sea Rose. 1930: Reducing. The Lone Star Ranger. Caught Short. The Big House. City Girl. Billy the Kid. Love in the Rough. 1931: The Great Lover. Cracked Nuts. The Big Shot (GB: The Optimist). The Champ. A Free Soul. Cimarron. Too Many Cooks. Politics. 1932: *Shampoo the Magician. *Never the Twins Shall Meet. Freaks. Ladies of the Jury. The Rainbow Trail. Young Bride/Love Starved/Veneer. Roadhouse Murder. Hold 'Em, Jail! Come On, Danger. Deported. 1933: Renegades of the West. The Past of Mary Holmes. The Cheyenne Kid. Golden Harvest. Alice in Wonderland. What! No Beer? Scarlet River. Lucky Devils. *Hollywood on Parade B-3. 1934: Woman in the Dark. She Made Her Bed. The Merry Wives of Reno. 1935: The People's Enemy. 1936: God's Country and the Woman. Fair Exchange. 1938: Riders of the Black Hills. The Great Adventures of Wild Bill Hickok (serial). 1939: Three Texas Steers (GB: Danger Rides the Range). Gone With the Wind. Rancho Grande. 1940: Fireman, Save My Choo-Choo. *You're Next. Cowboy from Sundown. Captain Caution. Untamed. I Want a Divorce. Chad Hanna. 1941: I'll Sell My Life. Ziegfeld Girl. *Glove Affair. Birth of the Blues. Mountain Moonlight (GB: Moving in Society). She Knew All the Answers. Sullivan's Travels. Robin Hood of the Pecos. Reg'lar Fellers. Bad Men of Missouri. One Foot in Heaven. 1942: The Palm Beach Story. The Affairs of Jimmy Valentine. 1944: Can't Help Singing. 1946: Colorado Serenade.

Down Missouri Way. Driftin' River. Tumbleweed Trail. Wild West. Stars Over Texas. 1947: Wild Country. Range Beyond the Blue. West to Glory. Black Hills. Shadow Valley. 1948: Check Your Guns. Tornado Range. The Westward Trail. Inner Sanctum. The Hawk of Powder River. Prairie Outlaws. The Tioga Kid. Thunder in the Pines. 1950: The Hills of Oklahoma. Father's Wild Game. 1951: Honeychile. 1952: The Blazing Forest. 1953: Those Redheads from Seattle. The Stranger Wore a Gun. 1955: Lucy Gallant. Abbott and Costello Meet the Keystone Kops. Come Next Spring. 1956: The Birds and the Bees. The Kettles in the Ozarks. Meet Me in Las Vegas (GB: Viva Las Vegas!). 1957: Run of the Arrow. The Big Caper. Short Cut to Hell. 1958: The Sheepman. 1961: The Silent Call. The Errand Boy. The Ladies' Man.

ATWILL, Lionel 1885–1946

Suave, usually moustachioed British-born actor of impeccable diction and an air of faintly seedy sophistication. His characters suppurated corruption under their skins of suavity. He went to Hollywood, where he was soon busy playing dozens of mad professors, crooked lawyers and staring-eyed scientists, but made a memorable Moriarty to Basil Rathbone's Sherlock Holmes. His career survived a rather pofaced scandal in the early 1940s over the showing of 'blue movies' at his home. Died from pneumonia.

1918: Eve's Daughter. For Sale. The Marriage Price. 1921: The Highest Bidder. Indiscretion. 1928: *The White-Faced Fool. *The Actor's Advice to His Son. 1932: The Silent Witness. Doctor X. 1933: The Vampire Bat. Secret of Madame Blanche. The Mystery of the Wax Museum. Murders in the Zoo. The Secret of the Blue Room. Song of Songs. The Sphinx. Solitaire Man. 1934: Nana. Beggars in Ermine. Stamboul Quest. One More River (GB: Over the River). The Age of Innocence. The Firebird. The Man Who Reclaimed His Head. 1935: Mark of the Vampire. The Devil Is a Woman. Murder Man. Rendezvous. Captain Blood. 1936: Lady of Secrets. Till We Meet Again. Absolute Quiet. 1937: The High Command. The Road Back. The Last Train from Madrid. The Wrong Road. Lancer Spy. The Great Garrick. 1938: The Great Waltz. Three Comrades. 1939: Son of Frankenstein. The Three Musketeers. The Hound of the Baskervilles. The Mad Empress (GB: Carlotta, the Mad Empress). The Gorilla. The

Sun Never Sets. Mr Moto Takes a Vacation. The Secret of Dr Kildare. Balalaika. 1940: Johnny Apollo. Charlie Chan in Panama. The Girl in 313. Boom Town. Charlie Chan's Murder Cruise. 1941: The Great Profile. Man Made Monster (GB: The Electric Man). 1942: The Ghost of Frankenstein. Junior G-Men of the Air (serial). The Strange Case of Dr RX. To Be or Not To Be. Pardon My Sarong. Cairo. Night Monster (GB: The Hammond Mystery). The Mad Doctor of Market Street. Sherlock Holmes and the Secret Weapon. 1943: Frankenstein Meets the Wolf Man. Captain America (serial). 1944: Lady in the Death House. Secrets of Scotland Yard. Raiders of Ghost City (serial). House of Frankenstein. 1945: Fog Island. Crime Inc. House of Dracula. 1946: Lost City of the Jungle (serial). Genius at Work.

AUER, Mischa
(M. Ounskowsky) 1905–1967
Pop-eyed, pencil-moustached, anxious-looking Russian-born comedy actor who came to Hollywood with the advent of sound, and stayed to create a memorable gallery of eccentric comic characters, usually flapping over some fresh disaster. He was at his peak in the late 1930s, but continued working until his death, in Italy, from a heart attack. Oscar nominee for My Man Godfrey.

1928: Something Always Happens. The Mighty. Marquis Preferred. 1929: Fame and the Devil. The Studio Murder Mystery. 1930 The Benson Murder Case. Inside the Lines. The Lady from Nowhere. Just Imagine. Women Love Once. Paramount on Parade. The Unholy Garden. 1931: Drums of Jeopardy. The Yellow Ticket (GB: The Yellow Passport). King of the Wild (serial). Delicious. No Limit. The Midnight Patrol. Command Performance. 1932: Last of the Mohicans (serial). The Intruder. Mata Hari. Sinister Hands. Murder at Dawn (GB: The Death Ray). No Greater Love (GB: Divine Love). Drifting Souls. Scarlet Dawn. Arsène Lupin. The Unwritten Law. The Monster Walks. Call Her Savage. Western Code. Beauty Parlor. 1933: Rasputin and the Empress (GB: Rasputin the Mad Monk). Dangerously Yours. Sucker Money (GB: Victims of the Beyond). Tarzan the Fearless (serial). Infernal Machine. Corruption. Gabriel Over the White House. The Flaming Signal. After Tonight (GB: Sealed Lips). Cradle Song. Girl Without a Room. Storm at Daybreak. 1934: Wharf Angel. The Crosby Case (GB: The Crosby Murder Case). Viva Villa!

Bulldog Drummond Strikes Back. Change of Heart. Stamboul Quest. Student Year. Woman Condemned. 1935: Mystery Woman. Lives of a Bengal Lancer. Clive of India. The Adventures of Rex and Rinty (serial). Anna Karenina. Condemned to Live. Biography of a Bachelor Girl. The Crusades. I Dream Too Much. 1936: Murder in the Fleet. The House of 1000 Candles. One Rainy Afternoon. The Princess Comes Across. Winterset. The Gay Desperado. We're Only Human. Here Comes Trouble. Tough Guy. My Man Godfrey. Sons o' Guns. 1937: That Girl from Paris. Three Smart Girls. Top of the Town. We Have Our Moments. Pick a Star. Marry the Girl. Merry-Go-Round. Vogues of 1938. Prescription for Romance. 1938: 100 Men and a Girl. Service de Luxe. It's All Yours. The Rage of Paris. You Can't Take It with You. Little Tough Guys in Society. Sweethearts. 1939: East Side of Heaven. Unexpected Father (GB: Sandy Takes a Bow). Destry Rides Again. *Three and a Day. 1940: Alias the Deacon. Sandy is a Lady. Public Deb Number One. Margie. Spring Parade. Trail of the Vigilantes. Seven Sinners. 1941: Flame of New Orleans. Cracked Nuts. Hold That Ghost! Moonlight in Hawaii. Hellzapoppin. Sing Another Chorus. 1942: Don't Get Personal. Twin Beds. 1943: Around the World. 1944: Lady in the Dark. Up in Mabel's Room. 1945: A Royal Scandal (GB: Czarina). Brewster's Millions. And Then There Were None (GB: Ten Little Niggers). 1946: Sentimental Journey. She Wrote the Book. 1947: For You I Die. 1948: Sofia. 1949: Al diavolo la celebrita. 1951: The Sky is Red. 1952: Song of Paris (US: Bachelor in Paris). 1954: Mr Arkadin (GB: Confidential Report). Escalier de service. 1955: Frou-Frou. Treize à table. L'impossible M. Pipelet. Futures vedettes (GB: Sweet Sixteen). Cette sacrée gamine (GB and US: Mam'zelle Pigalle). 1956: Mannequins de Paris. La polka des menottes. En effeuillant la marguerite (GB: Mam'selle Striptease. US: Please Mr Balzac). 1957: Le tombeur. The Monte Carlo Story. 1958: Nathalie, agent secret (GB and US: The Foxiest Girl in Paris). Tabarin. Sacrée jeunesse. A pied, à cheval et en spoutnik (GB: Hold Tight for the Satellite. US: A Dog, a Mouse and a Sputnik). 1962: We Joined the Navy. Les femmes d'abord (US: Ladies First). *The King's Breakfast. 1964: What Ever Happened to Baby Toto? Queste pazza, pazze, pazze donne. 1966: The Christmas That Almost Wasn't. Par amore . . . par magia. Drop Dead, Darling (US: Arrivederci, Baby).

AYLMER, Sir Felix
(F.A. Jones) 1889–1979
Distinguished, beady-eyed, bald, thin-lipped, sleepy-eyed British actor, adept at fussy or incisive characters, who was for many years president of the British actors' association Equity. At first often seen as minor, mean-minded officials, his characters increased in benevolence in later years, when he was to be spotted as bishops, academics, judges and ministers of the crown. He only had one leading role of importance in the British cinema, in Mr Emmanuel, but produced a typically fine performance for the occasion. He was also amusing in a semi-lead in The Ghosts of Berkeley Square. Knighted in 1965.

1930: Escape. The Temporary Widow. 1932: The Lodger (US: The Phantom Fiend). The World, the Flesh and the Devil. 1933: The Ghost Camera. The Shadow. Home Sweet Home. The Wandering Jew. 1934: Whispering Tongues. Night Club Queen. The Path of Glory. My Old Dutch. Doctor's Orders. The Soul of a Nation (narrator only). Evergreen. The Iron Duke. 1935: The Ace of Spades. Hello Sweetheart. The Divine Spark/Casta Diva. Old Roses. The Price of a Song. Brown on Resolution (later For Ever England. US: Born for Glory). The Clairvoyant. Checkmate. Her Last Affaire. She Shall Have Music. The Improper Duchess. 1936: Jack of All Trades (US: The Two of Us). Rhodes of Africa (US: Rhodes). In the Soup. Tudor Rose (US: Nine Days a Queen). Royal Eagle. Seven Sinners (US: Doomed Cargo). As You Like It. Dusty Ermine (US: Hideout in the Alps). The Man in the Mirror. The Mill on the Floss. Sensation! 1937: Dreaming Lips. The Frog. Glamorous Night. The Vicar of Bray. Action for Slander. Victoria the Great. Dinner at the Ritz. The Live Wire. The Rat. Bank Holiday (US: Three on a Weekend). South Riding. 1938: Just Like a Woman. Kate Plus Ten. Break the News. I've Got a Horse. Sixty Glorious Years (US: Queen of Destiny). The Citadel. 1939: Spies of the Air. Young Man's Fancy. Laugh It Off. Dr O'Dowd. 1940: The Briggs Family. Charley's (Big-Hearted) Aunt. Night Train to Munich (US: Night Train). Saloon Bar. The Case of the Frightened Lady (US: The Frightened Lady). The Girl in the News. Spellbound (US: The Spell of Amy Nugent). 1941: Quiet Wedding. The Ghost of St Michael's. Kipps (US: The Remarkable Mr Kipps). The Saint's Vacation. Major Barbara. Atlantic Ferry (US: Sons of the Sea). This England (Scotland: Our Heritage). Once a Crook. I Thank You. The Seventh Survivor. The Black Sheep of Whitehall. Hi, Gang! South American George. 1942: The Young Mr Pitt. Sabotage at Sea. Uncensored. The Peterville Diamond. Thursday's Child. 1943: The Life and Death of Colonel Blimp (US: Colonel Blimp). Escape to Danger. †Bell Bottom George. *Welcome to Britain. The Demi-Paradise (US: Adventure for Two). Time Flies. 1944: English Without Tears (US: Her Man Gilbey). Mr Emmanuel. Henry V. 1945: *Julius Caesar. The Way to the Stars (US: Johnny in the Clouds). Caesar and Cleopatra. The Wicked Lady. 1946: The Years Between. The Magic Bow. The Laughing Lady. 1947: Green Fingers. The Man Within (US: The Smugglers). A Man About the House.

The October Man. The Ghosts of Berkeley Square. 1948: The Calendar. Escape. Hamlet. Quartet. Alice in Wonderland (voice only). 1949: Prince of Foxes. Edward My Son. Christopher Columbus. 1950: Your Witness (US: Eye Witness). So Long at the Fair. Trio. She Shall Have Murder. 1951: No Highway (US: No Highway in the Sky). The Lady with a Lamp. The House in the Square (US: I'll Never Forget You). 1952: Ivanhoe. The Man Who Watched Trains Go By (US: Paris Express). Quo Vadis? 1953: The Master of Ballantrae. The Triangle. The Love Lottery. Knights of the Round Table. 1954: The Angel Who Pawned Her Harp. 1956: Loser Takes All. Anastasia. 1957: Saint Joan. 1958: Separate Tables. I Accuse! The Two-Headed Spy. 1959: The Doctor's Dilemma. The Mummy. 1960: Never Take Sweets from a Stranger (US: Never Take Candy from a Stranger). The Hands of Orlac. Exodus. From the Terrace. 1961: Macbeth. The Road to Hong Kong. 1962: The Boys. 1963: The Running Man. Becket. 1964: The Chalk Garden. Masquerade. 1968: Decline and Fall . . . of a birdwatcher! Hostile Witness.

† Scenes deleted from final release print

BACKUS, Jim 1913–1989

Well-built, brown-haired, dark-faced American comedy actor, seen either beaming or scowling — there were few half-measures with Backus characters. After military service in World War II, the one-time radio announcer became a familiar part of the cinema scene for 20 years, playing grouchy growlers and over-hearty businessmen. He was also popular as the long-suffering husband of Joan Davis on TV's *I Married Joan*, and as the rasping tones of cartoonland's short-sighted Mr Magoo. Died from Parkinson's Disease and pneumonia.

1942: The Pied Piper. 1949: One Last Fling. The Great Lover. Father Was a Fullback. Easy Living. A Dangerous Profession. Ma and Pa Kettle Go to Town (GB: Going to Town). 1950: Customs Agent. Emergency Wedding (GB: Jealousy). The Hollywood Story. Bright Victory (GB: Lights Out). The Killer That Stalked New York (GB: The Frightened City). 1951: I Want You. Iron Man. Half Angel. The Man with a Cloak. M. His Kind of Woman. I'll See You In My Dreams. 1952: Pat and Mike. Deadline USA (GB: Deadline). Here Come the Nelsons. The Rose Bowl Story. Don't Bother to

Knock. Androcles and the Lion. Above and Beyond. Angel Face. I Love Melvin. 1953: Geraldine. 1954: Deep in My Heart. 1955: Francis in the Navy. Rebel Without a Cause. The Square Jungle. 1956: The Great Man. Meet Me in Las Vegas (GB: Viva Las Vegas!). The Naked Hills. You Can't Run Away from It. The Opposite Sex. The Girl He Left Behind. 1957: Top Secret Affair (GB: Their Secret Affair). Man of a Thousand Faces. Eighteen and Anxious. The Pied Piper of Hamelin (TV. GB: cinemas). 1958: The High Cost of Loving. Free Week-End (TV). Macabre. 1959: The Big Operator. The Wild and the Innocent. 1001 Arabian Nights (voice only). A Private's Affair. Ask Any Girl. 1960: Ice Palace. 1962: The Wonderful World of the Brothers Grimm. The Horizontal Lieutenant. Boys' Night Out. Zotz! Critic's Choice. 1963: Sunday in New York. Johnny Cool. The Wheeler Dealers (GB: Separate Beds). It's Mad, Mad, Mad, Mad World. Operation Bikini. My Six Loves. Advance to the Rear (GB: Company of Cowards) 1964: John Goldfarb, Please Come Home. 1965: Fluffy. Billie. 1966: Hurry Sundown. 1967: Don't Make Waves. 1968: Hello Down There. Where Were You When the Lights Went Out? 1969: The Cockeyed Cowboys of Calico County (GB: TV, as A Woman for Charlie). Wake Me When the War is Over (TV). 1970: Myra Breckinridge. 1971: Getting Away from It All (TV). The Magic Carpet (TV). 1972: Now You See Him Now You Don't. 1973: The Girl Most Likely to (TV). 1974: Miracle on 34th Street (TV). 1975: The Return of Joe Forrester (TV). Friday Foster. Crazy Mama. 1976: The Feather and Father Gang (TV). 1977: Pete's Dragon. 1978: Good Guys Wear Black. Return to Gilligan's Island (TV). 1979: Seven from Heaven. The Rebels (TV). The Castaways on Gilligan's Island (TV). The Gossip Columnist (TV). Chomps. There Goes the Bride. Angel's Brigade. 1981: Jayne Mansfield — An American Tragedy (TV). The Harlem Globetrotters on Gilligan's Island (TV). 1982: Slapstick (US: Slapstick of Another Kind). 1984: Prince Jack.

BACON, Irving 1892–1965

This soft-spoken, open-faced, sandy-haired, genial, guileless-looking American midwesterner was one of the most prolific of all Hollywood's character players. Usually cast as a solid citizen, Bacon could project honesty, friendliness and perplexity with equal ease, and sometimes all three together, as with his long-running characterization of

the mailman in the Blondie comedy films. Sometimes his 'honesty' was turned into gullibility with total conviction. This filmography does not cover fleeting appearances Bacon is said to have made in Sennett shorts in pre-World War I times.

*1923: Anna Christie. 1926: *The Prodigal Bridegroom. 1927: California or Bust. *The Girl from Everywhere. 1928: The Goodbye Kiss. *The Swim Princess. The Head Man. The Three Sinners. 1929: Half Way to Heaven. *The Old Barn. Side Street (GB: Three Brothers). The Saturday Night Kid. All at Sea. China Bound. *Button My Back. The Duke Steps Out. Stark Mad. Hot Stuff. Hard to Get. Two Sisters. 1930: Spring is Here. Wide Open. Free and Easy. Street of Chance. 1931: Her Majesty Love. Alias the Bad Man. Branded Men. Fighting Caravans. Newly Rich. Union Depot (GB: Gentleman for a Day). 1932: File No. 113. This is the Night. Million Dollar Legs. No One Man. Central Park. The Match King. The Big Broadcast. I Am a Fugitive from a Chain Gang. If I Had a Million. Lawyer Man. *Just a Pain in the Parlor. *High Hats and Low Brows. Madame Racketeer (GB: The Sporting Widow). 1933: *Sing, Bing, Sing. The Mind Reader. Central Airport. Lilly Turner. He Learned About Women. Hello, Everybody! Private Detective 62. Big Executive. Lone Cowboy. Laughing at Life. Lady for a Day. I Love That Man. The Bowery. Sitting Pretty. Tillie and Gus. The Keyhole. Ann Vickers. 1934: Miss Fane's Baby is Stolen (GB: Kidnapped). Six of a Kind. The Hell Cat. It Happened One Night. Massacre. Babbitt. No Ransom. By Your Leave. Honor of the Range. Shadows of Sing Sing. You Belong to Me. Hat, Coat and Glove. The Pursuit of Happiness. Ready for Love. Now I'll Tell (GB: When New York Sleeps). George White's Scandals. Broadway Bill (GB: Strictly Confidential). Romance in Manhattan. The House of Mystery. 1935: Here Comes Cookie (GB: The Plot Thickens). Millions in the Air. By Your Leave. West of the Pecos. Powdersmoke Range. Private Worlds. Murder on a Honeymoon. Goin' to Town. The Virginia Judge. The Glass Key. Two Fisted. Ship Café. It's a Small World. Diamond Jim. Manhattan Moon (GB: Sing Me a Love Song). Bright Lights. It's a Great Life. Page Miss Glory. The Farmer Takes a Wife. Men Without Names. Murder Man. She Couldn't Take It (GB: Woman Tamer). Bad Boy. *Tuned Out.*

1936: Love on a Bet. Three Cheers for Love. Murder with Pictures. The Bride Walks Out. The Texas Rangers. Petticoat Fever. Earthworm Tractors (GB: A Natural Born Salesman). The Music Goes Round. The Singing Kid. Rhythm on the Range. Hollywood Boulevard. Drift Fence. Lady, Be Careful. Wives Never Know. Valiant is the Word for Carrie. The Big Broadcast of 1937. Let's Make a Million. Hopalong Cassidy Returns. Arizona Mahoney. San Francisco. Mr Deeds Goes to Town. Timothy's Quest. The Plainsman. Trail of the Lonesome Pine. China Clipper. Big Town Girl. 1937: It's Love I'm After. Internes Can't Take Money (GB: You Can't Take Money). Exclusive. Seventh Heaven. The Big City. True Confession. Topper. Marry the Girl. Angel's Holiday. Sing and Be Happy. A Star is Born. Passport Husband. There Goes My Girl. Vogues of 1938 (GB: Vogues). 1938: Midnight Intruder. Professor Beware! The Cowboy and the Lady. You Can't Take It with You. Exposed. The Big Broadcast of 1938. The First Hundred Years. The Texans. The Chaser. Tip-Off Girls. The Arizona Wildcat. Sing, You Sinners. Spawn of the North. There Goes My Heart. Kentucky Moonshine (GB: Three Men and a Girl). The Amazing Dr Clitterhouse. The Sisters. City Girl. Mr Moto's Gamble. Racket Busters. The Mad Miss Manton. Strange Faces. Swing Your Lady. Hard to Get. Letter of Introduction. Blondie. Sweethearts. Man-Proof. Every Day's a Holiday. 1939: Too Busy to Work. The Adventures of Huckleberry Finn. Tail Spin. Pack Up Your Troubles (GB: You're in the Army Now). On Your Toes. Boy Slaves. Invisible Stripes. The Gracie Allen Murder Case. Lucky Night. Second Fiddle. I Stole a Million. Hollywood Cavalcade. Gone With the Wind. Blondie Takes a Vacation. Rio. The Oklahoma Kid. Blondie Brings Up Baby. The Lady's from Kentucky. Torchy Runs for Mayor. Indianapolis Speedway (GB: Devil on Wheels). Heaven with a Barbed Wire Fence. Lone Wolf Spy Hunt (GB: The Lone Wolf's Daughter). They Made Me a Criminal. Big Town Czar. At the Circus/Marx Brothers at the Circus. You Can't Cheat an Honest Man. Blondie Meets the Boss. The Housekeeper's Daughter. Bachelor Mother. *Hollywood Slaves. 1940: The Grapes of Wrath. The Man Who Wouldn't Talk. Star Dust. You Can't Fool Your Wife. Dr Ehrlich's Magic Bullet (GB: The Story of Dr Ehrlich's Magic Bullet). Young People. Blondie on a Budget. Edison, the Man. Manhattan Heartbeat. The Return of Frank James. Gold Rush Maisie. The Howards of Virginia (GB: The Tree of Liberty). Blondie Has Servant Trouble. Dreaming Out Loud. Lillian Russell. Blondie Plays Cupid. Young People. Brother Rat and a Baby (GB: Baby Be Good). Broadway Melody of 1940. His Girl Friday. The Doctor Takes a Wife. Sailor's Lady. Love, Honor and Oh Baby! Jennie. Western Union. 1941: Michael Shayne, Private Detective. Meet John Doe. Great Guns. Four Mothers. Cadet Girl. Henry Aldrich for President. A Girl, a Guy and a Gob (GB: The Navy Steps Out). Tobacco Road. Blondie Goes Latin (GB: Conga Swing). She Couldn't Say No. Ride On, Vaquero. Caught in the Draft. Accent on Love. Too Many Blondes. Moon Over Her Shoulder. It Started with Eve. Never Give a Sucker an Even Break (GB: What a Man!). Blondie in Society (GB: Henpecked). Remember the Day. The Lone Wolf Takes a Chance.

Barnacle Bill. Skylark. Our Wife. Million Dollar Baby. Back Street. They Died with Their Boots On. Wild Man of Borneo. 1942: The Bashful Bachelor. The Spoilers. Through Different Eyes. Juke Girl. Young America. Pardon My Sarong. Holiday Inn. Footlight Serenade. The Daring Young Man. Give Out, Sisters. Blondie for Victory (GB: Troubles Through Billets). Between Us Girls. Freckles Comes Home. Get Hep to Love (GB: She's My Lovely). Star Spangled Rhythm. The Great Man's Lady. Sweetheart of the Fleet. Lady in a Jam. Blondie's Blessed Event (GB: A Bundle of Trouble). 1943: The Desperados. Dixie Dugan. The Amazing Mrs Holliday. A Stranger in Town. Shadow of a Doubt. Johnny Come Lately (GB: Johnny Vagabond). Hers to Hold. Follow the Band. King of the Cowboys. Two Weeks to Live. Happy Go Lucky. The Good Fellows. So's Your Uncle. In Old Oklahoma (GB: War of the Wildcats). Action in the North Atlantic. Girl Crazy. Gung Ho! It's a Great Life (and 1935 version). Footlight Glamour. This is the Army. What a Woman! (GB: The Beautiful Cheat). A Guy Named Joe. 1944: Pin-Up Girl. Weekend Pass. Wing and a Prayer. Chip Off the Old Block. Her Primitive Man. Since You Went Away. Heavenly Days. The Thin Man Goes Home. Can't Help Singing. The Story of Dr Wassell. Casanova Brown. Knickerbocker Holiday. 1945: Roughly Speaking. Patrick the Great. Out of This World. Guest Wife. Under Western Skies. Hitchhike to Happiness. One Way to Love. Week-End at the Waldorf. Spellbound. 1946: Night Train to Memphis. Wake Up and Dream. My Brother Talks to Horses. 1947: Saddle Pals. Monsieur Verdoux. The Bachelor and the Bobby-Soxer (GB: Bachelor Knight). Dear Ruth. High Wall. 1948: Moonrise. State of the Union (GB: The World and His Wife). Albuquerque (GB: Silver City). The Velvet Touch. Adventures in Silverado. Good Sam. Rocky. Family Honeymoon. Words and Music. Dynamite. 1949: John Loves Mary. Dear Wife. The Green Promise (GB: Raging Waters). Night unto Night. The Big Cat. It's a Great Feeling. Manhandled. Woman in Hiding. Down Memory Lane. 1950: Born to be Bad. Wabash Avenue. Emergency Wedding (GB: Jealousy). Sons of New Mexico (GB: The Brat). Riding High. Never a Dull Moment. Mr Music. 1951: Honeychile. Cause for Alarm. Two Weeks to Live. Katie Did It. Desert of Lost Men. Here Comes the Groom. 1952: O Henry's Full House (GB: Full House). It Grows on Trees. Room for One More. Rose of Cimarron. 1953: Devil's Canyon. Kansas Pacific. Sweethearts on Parade. Fort Ti. The Glenn Miller Story. 1954: Ma and Pa Kettle at Home. Black Horse Canyon. Duffy of San Quentin (GB: Men Behind Bars). A Star is Born. 1955: Run for Cover. At Gunpoint (GB: Gunpoint!). 1956: Hidden Guns. Dakota Incident. 1958: Ambush at Cimarron Pass. Fort Massacre.

BADDELEY, Hermione

(H. Clinton-Baddeley) 1906–1986
Jolly-looking, fair-haired, full-faced British actress, on the London stage at 11 years old. A notable wit − especially in tandem with Hermione Gingold (qv) as 'The Two Hermiones' − she could be both sophisticated and blowzy and contributed a rich

range of characters to the screen after a long stage career. Most of these were 'below stairs' types, but some of them, like the vengeful Ida in Brighton Rock, she turned memorably into semi-leads. The younger sister of stage and TV actress Angela Baddeley (1904–1976), she was nominated for an Oscar in Room at the Top. Died following a stroke.

1926: A Daughter in Revolt. 1927: The Guns of Loos. 1930: Caste. 1934: Love, Life and Laughter. 1935: Royal Cavalcade (US: Regal Cavalcade). 1941: Kipps (US: The Remarkable Mr Kipps). 1947: It Always Rains on Sunday. Brighton Rock. 1948: No Room at the Inn. Quartet. 1949: Passport to Pimlico. Dear Mr Prohack. 1950: The Woman in Question (US: Five Angles on Murder). There is Another Sun (US: Wall of Death). Tom Brown's Schooldays. 1951: Hell is Sold Out. Scrooge (US: A Christmas Carol). 1952: Song of Paris (US: Bachelor in Paris). Time Gentlemen Please! The Pickwick Papers. Cosh Boy (US: The Slasher). 1953: Counterspy (US: Undercover Agent). *The Amazing Mr Canasta. 1954: The Belles of St Trinian's. 1956: Women Without Men (US: Blonde Bait). 1958: Room at the Top. 1959: Jet Storm. Expresso Bongo. 1960: Midnight Lace. Let's Get Married. 1961: Rag Doll. Information Received. 1964: Mary Poppins. The Unsinkable Molly Brown. 1965: Do Not Disturb. Harlow. The Adventures of Bullwhip Griffin. Marriage on the Rocks. 1967: The Happiest Millionaire. 1970: The Aristocats (voice only). 1972: Up the Front. 1974: The Black Windmill. 1979: There Goes the Bride. Chomps. 1982: The Secret of NIMH (voice only). I Take These Men (TV). 1983: This Girl for Hire (TV). 1985: Shadow Chasers (TV).

BAINTER, Fay 1891–1968

Dark-haired, dark-eyed American actress with soothing smile, an expert at motherly types. Her attractively husky voice and sympathetic nature made her a top featured attraction throughout the late 1930s and early 1940s. Her double nomination as Best Actress and Best Supporting Actress in 1938 (she won the latter Oscar for Jezebel) led to a change in the Academy rules. Her other Oscar nomination was for The Children's Hour in 1962.

1934: This Side of Heaven. 1937: The Soldier and the Lady (GB: Michael Strogoff). Quality Street. Make Way for Tomorrow. 1938: Jezebel.

White Banners. Mother Carey's Chickens. The Arkansas Traveller. The Shining Hour. 1939: Yes, My Darling Daughter. The Lady and the Mob. Daughters Courageous. 1940: Our Neighbors, the Carters. Young Tom Edison. Our Town. Maryland. A Bill of Divorcement. 1941: Babes on Broadway. Woman of the Year. 1942: The War Against Mrs Hadley. Journey for Margaret. Mrs Wiggs of the Cabbage Patch. 1943: The Human Comedy. Salute to the Marines. Presenting Lily Mars. Cry Havoc. The Heavenly Body. 1944: Dark Waters. Three is a Family. 1945: State Fair. 1946: The Kid from Brooklyn. The Virginian. 1947: Deep Valley. The Secret Life of Walter Mitty. 1948: Give My Regards to Broadway. June Bride. 1951: Close to My Heart. 1953: The President's Lady. 1962: The Children's Hour (GB: The Loudest Whisper). Bon Voyage!

BAKALYAN, Richard or Dick 1931–
Light-haired, scrunch-faced, weasel-eyed American tough-guy actor with boxer's profile, once described in his younger days as 'the most compulsively watchable juvenile delinquent of them all'. Bakalyan even made his debut in a film called *The Delinquents*, but his hoods remained small-time both on screen and in the scale of the movies. Later he played some friendlier roles and tried some Disney comedy films. But he was always at his sharpest and most convincing as gangsters, whether comic or dramatic. He got his first lead for years in the 1992 film *Billy Royal*, but it's for the parts he played peddling drugs to the kids in the 1950s that he'll be remembered.

1956: The Delinquents. 1957: The Brothers Rico. The Delicate Delinquent. Dino (GB: Killer Dino). Hear Me Good. 1958: The Cool and the Crazy. The Bonnie Parker Story. Hot Car Girl. Juvenile Jungle. 1959: –30– (GB: Deadline Midnight). Up Periscope. Paratroop Command. 1961: The Errand Boy. 1962: Panic in Year Zero. Pressure Point. 1963: Operation Bikini. 1964: The Patsy. Robin and the Seven Hoods. 1965: None But the Brave. Von Ryan's Express. The Greatest Story Ever Told. 1966: Follow Me, Boys! 1967: The Saint Valentine's Day Massacre. Never a Dull Moment. 1969: The Computer Wore Tennis Shoes. *It's Tough To Be a Bird (voice only). 1971: The Animals. 1972: Now You See Him, Now You Don't. 1973: Charley and the Angel. 1974: Chinatown. 1975: The Strongest Man in the World. 1976: The Shaggy D.A. Woman of the Year (TV). 1977: Pine Canyon is Burning (TV). Return from Witch Mountain. 1979: H.O.T.S. The Man with Bogart's Face/Sam Marlow, Private Eye. 1981: The Fox and the Hound (voice only). 1983: Shooting Stars (TV). 1984: Blame It on the Night. 1985: The Heart of a Champion: The Ray Mancini Story (TV). 1992: Billy Royal.

BALDWIN, Walter 1896–1977
Light-haired, open-mouthed, eager-looking American actor, often seen with rimless spectacles. Usually unexcitingly dressed in well-worn clothes, Baldwin played friendly, small-town men — storekeepers, farmers and the like, sometimes oppressed by the bad guys, but more often just a part of a realistic rural background. His characters were sympathetic but had few teeth. Came to Hollywood in early middle age after extensive Broadway experience and stayed for 18 years before becoming busier on TV.

1939: The Secret of Dr Kildare. 1940: Angels Over Broadway. Arizona. 1941: All That Money Can Buy (GB: The Devil and Daniel Webster). They Died with Their Boots On. Harvard, Here I Come (GB: Here I Come). I'm Nobody's Sweetheart Now. *Coffins on Wheels. The Devil Commands. Look Who's Laughing. Miss Polly. Barnacle Bill. Kings Row. 1942: Syncopation. For Me and My Gal (GB: For Me and My Girl). Laugh Your Blues Away. The Man Who Returned to Life. Scattergood Rides High. After Midnight with Boston Blackie (GB: After Midnight). In This Our Life. Tennessee Johnson (GB: The Man on America's Conscience). 1943:

The Kansan (GB: Wagon Wheels). A Stranger in Town. Always a Bridesmaid. Happy Land. 1944: Mr Winkle Goes to War (GB: Arms and the Woman). Since You Went Away. Together Again. Home in Indiana. Dark Mountain. Tall in the Saddle. Louisiana Hayride. I'm from Arkansas. I'll Be Seeing You. You Can't Ration Love. The Reckless Age. 1945: Trail to Vengeance (GB: Vengeance). Bring On the Girls. Murder He Says. Captain Eddie. Roughly Speaking. Rhythm Round-Up (GB: Honest John). State Fair. The Lost Weekend. Girl of the Limberlost. Why Girls Leave Home. Christmas in Connecticut (GB: Indiscretion). Colonel Effingham's Raid (GB: Man of the Hour). Blonde Ransom. Johnny Comes Flying Home. 1946: The Best Years of Our Lives. Young Widow. Sing While You Dance. The Time of Their Lives. To Each His Own. The Bride Wore Boots. Cross My Heart. The Strange Love of Martha Ivers. Dragonwyck. Claudia and David. The Best Years of Our Lives. Our Hearts Were Growing Up. Personality Kid. Sister Kenny. The Perfect Marriage. 1947: The Unsuspected. Unconquered. Mourning Becomes Electra. Framed (GB: Paula). King of the Wild Horses. The Beginning or the End. 1948: Winter Meeting. Hazard. Return of the Bad Men. Rachel and the Stranger. A Miracle Can Happen (later and GB: On Our Merry Way). Cry of the City. Albuquerque (GB: Silver City). The Man from Colorado. 1949: Special Agent. Come to the Stable. Calamity Jane and Sam Bass. Thieves' Highway. On the Town. The Gay Amigo. Flamingo Road. 1950: Cheaper by the Dozen. Stella. Storm Warning. The Jackpot. 1951: Rough Riders of Durango. The Racket. I Want You. A Millionaire for Christy. 1952: Carrie. The Winning Team. Something for the Birds. Scandal at Scourie. 1953: Ride, Vaquero! 1954: The Long, Long Trailer. Living It Up. Destry. 1955: Interrupted Melody. Stranger on Horseback. Glory. The Desperate Hours. 1956: The Fastest Gun Alive. You Can't Run Away from It. 1960: Oklahoma Territory. 1961: Wild in the Country. 1962: Hemingway's Adventures of a Young Man (GB: Adventures of a Young Man). 1964: Cheyenne Autumn. 1968: Rosemary's Baby. 1969: Hail, Hero!

BALFOUR, Michael 1918–
Thick-lipped, pudgy, rosy-cheeked, insolent-looking American-born actor with dark, fluffy hair. Balfour came to a career in British films after varied experience in circuses, burlesque and stock companies. Minor British crime movies kept him very busy and his stocky figure, often clad in dark shirts and light ties or bow-ties, was to be seen as minor crooks, taxi-drivers and slow-witted sidekicks of the hero. Rarely out of the studios from 1947 to 1972, then mainly on TV. He returned to circus work in the mid 1980s, but was still occasionally seen in film 'bits'.

1947: Just William's Luck. 1948: Sleeping Car to Trieste. No Orchids for Miss Blandish. William Comes to Town. The Small Voice (US: Hideout). Obsession (US: The Hidden Room). 1949: Helter Skelter. Stop Press Girl. Don't Ever Leave Me. Melody Club. 1950: Blackout. Her Favourite Husband (US: The Taming of Dorothy). *Help Yourself. Prelude to Fame.

Cage of Gold. 1951: The Quiet Woman. A
Case for PC49. 1952: 13 East Street. Top
Secret (US: Mr Potts Goes to Moscow). Hot Ice.
Venetian Bird (US: The Assassin). 1953: Love
in Pawn. Genevieve. The Red Beret (US: Para-
trooper). Johnny on the Run. Albert RN. The
Captain's Paradise. Moulin Rouge. The Long
Memory. Three's Company. Recoil. Small Town
Story. Park Plaza 605 (US: Norman Conquest).
Black 13. Three Steps to the Gallows (released
1955. US: White Fire). The Steel Key. 1954:
36 Hours (US: Terror Street). The Sea Shall
Not Have Them. The Scarlet Web. River Beat.
Meet Mr Callaghan. Delayed Action. The
Diamond (US: Diamond Wizard). Devil's Point
(US: Devil's Harbor). The Belles of St Trinian's.
One Good Turn. The Million Pound Note (US:
Man with a Million). Track the Man Down.
The Delavine Affair. Secret Venture. 1955:
Dust and Gold. Double Jeopardy. The Reluctant
Bride (US: Two Grooms for a Bride). Gentlemen
Marry Brunettes. Impulse. Barbados Quest
(US: Murder on Approval). 1956: Secret of the
Forest. Breakaway. The Big Money (released
1958). It's a Great Day. Reach for the Sky.
1957: Light Fingers. The Steel Bayonet. Quater-
mass II (US: Enemy from Space). Man from
Tangier. Hour of Decision/Table in the Corner.
1958: Fiend Without a Face. Surprise Package.
1959: Look Back in Anger. The Flesh and the
Fiends (US: Mania). Sink the Bismarck! 1960:
Carry On Constable. Make Mine Mink. Too
Hot to Handle. 1961: The Monster of Highgate
Ponds. The Hellfire Club. Pit of Darkness. The
Treasure of Monte Cristo (US: The Secret of
Monte Cristo). 1962: Design for Loving. She
Always Gets Their Man. The Fast Lady. 1963:
The Rescue Squad. Echo of Diana. A Stitch in
Time. 1964: The Sicilians. Beware of the Dog.
Five Have a Mystery to Solve. 1966: Strangler's
Web. Where the Bullets Fly. Fahrenheit 451.
Kaleidoscope. Press for Time. The Sandwich
Man. 1968: The Fixer. 1969: The Oblong Box.
*The Undertakers. 1970: The Private Life of
Sherlock Holmes. Hoverbug. The Adventurers.
Man of Violence/The Sex Racketeers. 1971:
Macbeth. The Magnificent Six and a Half (third
series). The Canterbury Tales. 1972: Wreck
Raisers. Madigan: The London Beat (TV). 1976:
The 'Copter Kids. Joseph Andrews. 1977:
Candleshoe. Come Play with Me. 1978: The
Stick-Up. The Nativity (TV). 1979: The Pris-
oner of Zenda. *Resting Rough. 1985: The
Holcroft Covenant. 1987: Casanova (TV). 1989:
Batman. 1990: The Krays. 1992: Revenge of
Billy the Kid.

BALL, Vincent 1923–
Cheerful, long-faced Australian actor with
fair, curly hair, who worked his passage to
England as a deck hand on a tramp steamer,
then won a scholarship to RADA. He got
some quite nice supporting roles in British
films, but was a bit colourless when starring
in B features of the early 1960s. In the mid
1970s, Ball returned to Australia, where
he proved, now ruddy-cheeked and distinguished-looking, a reliable character star.

1948: The Blue Lagoon (stunt double only).
Warning to Wantons. 1949: The Interrupted
Journey. Stop Press Girl. 1950: Come Dance
with Me. 1951: Encore. Talk of a Million (US:
You Can't Beat the Irish). London Entertains.
1952: Made in Heaven. 1953: *The Drayton
Case. 1954: *The Dark Stairway. Dangerous
Voyage (US: Terror Ship). Devil's Point (US:
Devil's Harbor). The Black Rider. 1955: John
and Julie. The Big Fish (narrator only). Stolen
Time (US: Blonde Blackmailer). The Blue Peter
(US: Navy Heroes). 1956: The Long Arm (US:
The Third Key). A Town Like Alice. The Baby
and the Battleship. The Secret of the Forest.
1957: Face in the Night (US: Menace in the
Night). The Naked Truth (US: Your Past is
Showing!). Robbery Under Arms. 1958: Blood
of the Vampire. Sea of Sand (US: Desert Patrol).
Danger Within (US: Breakout). 1960: Dentist
in the Chair. Identity Unknown. Dead Lucky.
Summer of the Seventeenth Doll (US: Season of
Passion). 1961: Feet of Clay. Nearly a Nasty
Accident. Very Important Person. Highway to
Battle. The Middle Course. A Matter of WHO.
1962: Carry On Cruising. 1963: Echo of Diana.
The Three Lives of Thomasina. The Mouse on
the Moon. 1967: Follow That Camel. 1968:
Nobody Runs Forever (US: The High Com-
missioner). Where Eagles Dare. 1969: Oh!
What a Lovely War. 1971: Not Tonight Darling!
Clinic Xclusive. 1975: That Lucky Touch.
1976: Deathcheaters. 1977: Demolition (TV).
1978: The Irishman. 1979: Alison's Birthday.
1980: Time Lapse. 'Breaker' Morant. 1981:
Deadline. 1982: Southern Cross (GB: The
Highest Honor). 1983: Phar Lap. 1985: Flight
into Hell. Butterfly Island. 1986: Double Sculls
(TV). 1987: The Year My Voice Broke. 1989:
The Hijacking of the Achille Lauro (TV). 1992:
Frauds. Love in Limbo. 1993: Sirens. 1994:
Muriel's Wedding.

BALSAM, Martin 1919–
Versatile, pug-faced, balding, dark-haired,
concerned-looking American actor originally of 'The Method' school, who first
sprang to prominence as the foreman of the
jury in 12 Angry Men. Although also vividly
remembered as the doomed detective in
Psycho, and in brilliant form opposite Joanne
Woodward in Summer Wishes, Winter Dreams,
this native New Yorker, who switched easily
from character roles to leads and back,
never quite realised his full potential in the
cinema. But he did win an Academy Award
in his forties for A Thousand Clowns. The
father of actress Talia Balsam.

1954: On the Waterfront. 1957: 12 Angry
Men. Time Limit. 1958: Bomber's Moon (TV).
Marjorie Morningstar. 1959: Al Capone. Free
Week-End (TV). Middle of the Night. 1960:
Psycho. Tutti a casa. 1961: Ada. Breakfast at
Tiffany's. 1962: Cape Fear. La citta prigoniera
(GB: The Captive City. US: The Conquered
City). 1963: Who's Been Sleeping in My Bed?
The Carpetbaggers. 1964: Seven Days in May.
Youngblood Hawke. 1965: A Thousand Clowns.
Harlow (Carroll Baker version). The Bedford
Incident. 1966: After the Fox. Hombre. The
Paths to Eden. 1969: Me, Natalie. Trilogy. The
Good Guys and the Bad Guys. 1970: Hunters
Are for Killing (TV). Tora! Tora! Tora! Catch
22. The Old Man Who Cried Wolf (TV). Little
Big Man. 1971: Imputazione di omicidio per
uno studente (US: Suspected of Murder). The
Anderson Tapes. The True and the False. Con-
fessione di un commissario di polizia al procurate
della republica (US: Confessions of a Police
Commissioner). 1972: Eyes Behind the Stars.
The Stone Killer. The Man. Night of Terror
(TV). 1973: Summer Wishes, Winter Dreams.
A Brand New Life (TV). Six Million Dollar
Man (TV). I consiglori (US: Counselor-at-
Crime). Trapped Beneath the Sea (TV). 1974:
The Taking of Pelham One-Two-Three. Murder
on the Orient Express. Miles to Go Before I
Sleep (TV). Corruzione al Palazzo di Giustizia.
1975: Mitchell. Death Among Friends (TV).
Cry Onion. The Time of the Assassin/Il tempo
degli assassini. Cipolla Colt. 1976: All the
President's Men. The Lindbergh Kidnapping Case
(TV). Raid on Entebbe (TV. GB: cinemas). The
Sentinel. Con la rabbia agli occhi (GB: Anger in
His Eyes). Two-Minute Warning. 1977: Silver
Bears. The Storyteller (TV). Contract on Cherry
Street (TV). Shadow of a Killer. Death Rage.
Occhi dalle stelle. 1978: Rainbow (TV).
Diamanti rosso angue. The Millionaire (TV).
Siege (TV). 1979: Gardenia. The House on

Garibaldi Street (originally for TV). Cuba. Aunt Mary (TV). The Seeding of Sarah Burns/ Sanctuary of Fear (TV). There Goes the Bride. 1980: The Love Tapes (TV). 1981: The Salamander. 1982: Little Gloria — Happy at Last (TV). 1983: The Goodbye People. I Want to Live! (TV). The People vs Jean Harris (TV). 1984: Innocent Prey. Fratelli dello spazio. 1985: St Elmo's Fire. Death Wish 3. Grown-Ups (TV). Murder in Space (TV). 1986: The Delta Force. Brothers in Blood. Whatever It Takes. Once Again. Second Serve (TV). Private Investigations. 1987: Dead End. Kids Like These (TV). 1988: The Child Saver (TV). 1989: Two Evil Eyes. 1991: Cape Fear (remake). 1993: Innocent Prey. 1994: The Silence of the Hams.

BANCROFT, George 1882–1956

My favourite American heavy from the days of early sound, Bancroft was also capable of projecting tough, dominant masculinity, notably in his four films for Josef von Sternberg, *Underworld*, *The Docks of New York*, *The Dragnet* and *Thunderbolt*. Now perhaps best remembered as the stage driver in Ford's *Stagecoach*, one of many supporting roles he later played. Received an Oscar nomination for *Thunderbolt*. Began his career singing in black-face minstrel shows. Retired at 60 to run a horse-ranch.

1921: The Journey's End. 1922: Driven. The Prodigal Judge. 1924: The Deadwood Coach. Teeth. 1925: Pony Express. Code of the West. The Rainbow Trail. The Splendid Road. 1926: Old Ironsides (GB: Sons of the Sea). The Enchanted Hill. The Runaway. Sea Horses. 1927: Underworld (GB: Paying the Penalty). White Gold. The Rough Riders (GB: The Trumpet Calls). Too Many Crooks. Tell it to Sweeney. 1928: The Docks of New York. The Dragnet. The Showdown. The Mighty. 1929: Thunderbolt. The Wolf of Wall Street. 1930: Paramount on Parade. Derelict. Ladies Love Brutes. Rich Man's Folly. 1931: The World and the Flesh. Scandal Sheet. 1932: Lady and Gent. 1933: Blood Money. 1934: Elmer and Elsie. 1936: Mr Deeds Goes to Town. Hell-Ship Morgan. Wedding Present. 1937: A Doctor's Diary. John Meade's Woman. Racketeers in Exile. Angels with Dirty Faces. Submarine Patrol. Stagecoach. Each Dawn I Die. Rulers of the Sea. Espionage Agent. 1940: Little Men. Northwest Mounted Police. When the Daltons Rode. Green Hell. 1941: Young Tom Edison. Texas. The Bugle Sounds. 1942: Syncopation. Whistling in Dixie.

BANNER, John
(Johann Banner) 1910–1973

Chubby Austrian actor who led a very spotty Hollywood film career after fleeing from the Nazis in 1938. There were a few heavily-accented bad guys, but Banner was really built for comedy and, from 1965 to 1970, found enormous success on television playing the would-be-menacing but comically hapless Sergeant Schultz in the P-o-W series *Hogan's Heroes*—an act imitated by other comedians for many years. It did not, however, lead to success in films and, on his 63rd birthday, Banner died from an intestinal haemorrhage.

1942: Once Upon a Honeymoon. Seven Miles from Alcatraz. Desperate Journey. The Moon is Down. 1943: Tonight We Raid Calais. The Fallen Sparrow. This Land is Mine! Chetniks. The Immortal Sergeant. They Came to Blow Up America. 1946: Black Angel. Rendezvous. Nocturne. Tangier. 1948: To the Victor. The Argyle Secrets. My Girl Tisa. 1950: Guilty of Treason (GB: Treason). King Solomon's Mines. 1951: Go for Broke. Callaway Went Thataway (GB: The Star Said No). 1953: The Juggler. 1954: Executive Suite. 1955: The Rains of Ranchipur. 1956: Never Say Goodbye. 1958: The Beast of Budapest. The Young Lions. 1959: The Blue Angel. The Wonderful Country. 1960: The Story of Ruth. 1961: 20,000 Eyes. Operation Eichmann. Hitler. 1962: The Interns. 1963: The Yellow Canary. The Prize. 1964: 36 Hours. Bedtime Story. 1968: The Wicked Dreams of Paula Schultz. 1970: Togetherness.

BARBIER, George 1862–1945

Bulky, bespectacled American actor with thinning silver hair who came to Hollywood in his late sixties and played windbags, blowhards and crusty eccentrics there until he died in harness at 83. He trained for the ministry, but was sidetracked into acting after appearing in pageants at theological college, and was soon a Broadway fixture. With the coming of sound to the cinema, Barbier brought his outraged expression, wormlike lips and scenic eyebrows to the screen in a long line of blusterers and table-thumpers (sometimes with hearts of gold) that extended over 100 films. Died from a heart attack.

1924: Monsieur Beaucaire. 1930: The Big Pond. The Sap from Syracuse (GB: The Sap Abroad). 1931: Girls About Town. The Smiling

Lieutenant. Touchdown (GB: Playing the Game). 24 Hours (GB: The Hours Between). 1932: The Big Broadcast. The Broken Wing. Madame Racketeer (GB: The Sporting Widow). Evenings for Sale. No One Man. One Hour with You. Skyscraper Souls. The Strange Case of Clara Deane. Strangers in Love. Million Dollar Legs. The Phantom President. No Man of Her Own. 1933: Hello, Everybody. A Lady's Profession. Love, Honor and Oh, Baby! Mama Loves Papa. Sunset Pass. Turn Back the Clock. This Day and Age. Tillie and Gus. Under the Tonto Rim. 1934: College Rhythm. Elmer and Elsie. The Cat's Paw. Many Happy Returns. The Merry Widow. Journal of a Crime. Miss Fane's Baby is Stolen. The Notorious Sophie Lang. Ladies Should Listen. Many Happy Returns. She Loves Me Not. 1935: The Crusades. Broadway Gondolier. Here Comes Cookie (GB: The Plot Thickens). Hold 'Em, Yale! (GB: Uniform Lovers). McFadden's Flats. Millions in the Air. Old Man Rhythm. Life Begins at Forty. 1936: Early to Bed. The Milky Way. The Preview Murder Mystery. The Princess Comes Across. Spendthrift. Wife vs Secretary. Three Married Men. 1937: A Girl with Ideas. Hotel Haywire. It's Love I'm After. On the Avenue. Waikiki Wedding. 1938: The Adventures of Marco Polo. Hold That Co-Ed (GB: Hold That Girl). My Lucky Star. Hold That Kiss. Straight, Place and Show (GB: They're Off). Little Miss Broadway. Sweethearts. Tarzan's Revenge. Thanks for Everything. 1939: News is Made at Night. Smuggled Cargo. S.O.S.-Tidal Wave (GB: Tidal Wave). Remember? Wife, Husband and Friend. 1940: The Return of Frank James. Village Barn Dance. 1941: Marry the Boss's Daughter. Million Dollar Baby. Sing Another Chorus. The Man Who Came to Dinner. Repent at Leisure. Week-End in Havana. 1942: The Magnificent Dope. Song of the Islands. Thunder Birds. Yankee Doodle Dandy. 1943: Hello, Frisco, Hello. 1944: Weekend Pass. 1945: Blonde Ransom. Her Lucky Night.

BARCROFT, Roy
(Howard Ravenscroft) 1902–1969

The tall, solid, dark-haired, often moustachioed western villain who always looked as if he meant business, Barcroft's florid features were probably punched more often by cowboy heroes, especially in Republic 'B' features of the 1940s, than those of any other actor. After service in World War I, the man from Crab Orchard, Nebraska, or

Weeping Water, Texas (according to which biographer you believe) tried a career as a clarinettist before settling into scores of films. In later years, he grew a bushy white beard for more sympathetic character roles. An infected leg wound led to his death from cancer.

*1931: Mata Hari. 1932: A Woman Commands. 1937: SOS Coastguard (serial). Dick Tracy (serial). Join the Marines. Night Key. Rosalie. 1938: Heroes of the Hills. The Crowd Roars. Blondes at Work. Stranger from Arizona. The Frontiersman. Flaming Frontiers (serial). 1939: Mexicali Rose. Silver on the Sage. Renegade Trail. Yukon Flight. They All Came Out. Crashing Thru. The Phantom Creeps (serial). Daredevils of the Red Circle (serial). Another Thin Man. Man from Texas. Riders of the Frontier. The Oregon Trail (serial). Rancho Grande. 1940: Hidden Gold. Bad Man from Red Butte. Stage to Chino. Winners of the West (serial). Ragtime Cowboy Joe. East of the River. Santa Fé Trail. West of Carson City. Flash Gordon Conquers the Universe (serial). Deadwood Dick (serial). The Green Hornet Strikes Again (serial). Abe Lincoln in Illinois (GB: Spirit of the People). Trailing Double Trouble. The Showdown. 1941: Pals of the Pecos. The Bandit Trail. Wide Open Town. Jesse James at Bay. Outlaws of the Cherokee Trail. The Masked Rider. King of the Texas Rangers (serial). West of Cimarron. Riders of Death Valley (serial). Riders of the Badlands. Sky Raiders (serial). They Died with Their Boots On. White Eagle. Sheriff of Tombstone. 1942: Stardust on the Sage. Romance on the Range. Sunset on the Desert. Pirates of the Prairie. Land of the Open Range. The Lone Rider in Cheyenne. West of the Law. The Valley of Vanishing Men (serial). Dawn on the Great Divide. Nazi Agent. Northwest Rangers. Sunset Serenade. *Cactus Capers. Ridin' Down the Canyon. Below the Border. Tennessee Johnson (GB: The Man on America's Conscience). 1943: The Old Chisholm Trail. Hoppy Serves a Writ. Cheyenne Roundup. Calling Wild Bill Elliott. Carson City Cyclone. The Stranger from Pecos. False Colors. Wagon Tracks West. Bordertown Gun Fighters. Riders of the Rio Grande. The Masked Marvel (serial). Canyon City. Dr Gillespie's Criminal Case (GB: Crazy to Kill). Idaho. Chatterbox. Hands Across the Border. In Old Oklahoma (later and GB: War of the Wildcats). The Man from Music Mountain. Overland Mail Robbery. Raiders of Sunset*

Pass. Sagebrush Law. Six-Gun Gospel. 1944: Call of the South Seas. The Laramie Trail. The Cherokee Flash. Hidden Valley Outlaws. Code of the Prairie. The Girl Who Dared. Lights of Old Santa Fé. Stagecoach to Monterey. Sheriff of Sundown. Firebrands of Arizona. Cheyenne Wildcat. The Big Bonanza. The Fighting Seabees. Haunted Harbor (serial). Man from Frisco. Rosie the Riveter (GB: In Rosie's Room). Storm over Lisbon. Tucson Raiders. 1945: The Vampire's Ghost. Bells of Rosarita. Sunset in El Dorado. Along the Navajo Trail. Dakota. Marshal of Laredo. Manhunt of Mystery Island (serial). Wagon Wheels Westward. The Purple Monster Strikes (serial). Santa Fé Saddlemates. Colorado Pioneers. Trail of Kit Carson. The Lone Texas Ranger. Topeka Terror. Corpus Christi Bandits. 1946: Home on the Range. Daughter of Don Q (serial). Alias Billy the Kid. Sun Valley Cyclone. My Pal Trigger. Night Train to Memphis. Traffic in Crime. The Phantom Rider (serial). Stagecoach to Denver. The Plainsman and the Lady. Crime of the Century (voice only). The Last Frontier Uprising. 1947: Jesse James Rides Again (serial). Oregon Trail Scouts. The Web of Danger. Vigilantes of Boomtown. Rustlers of Devil's Canyon. Spoilers of the North. Springtime in the Sierras. Wyoming. Marshal of Cripple Creek. Blackmail. Along the Oregon Trail. The Wild Frontier. Bandits of Dark Canyon. Son of Zorro (serial). The Fabulous Texan. 1948: The Plunderers. The Bold Frontiersman. Old Los Angeles. G-Men Never Forget (serial). Madonna of the Desert. The Main Street Kid. Lightnin' in the Forest. Oklahoma Badlands. Secret Service Investigator. Trail to Alcatraz. The Timber Trail. Out of the Storm. Eyes of Texas. Sons of Adventure. Grand Canyon Trail. Renegades of Sonora. Marshal of Amarillo. Desperadoes of Dodge City. Sundown in Santa Fé. The Far Frontier. The Gallant Legion. Montana Belle (released 1952). 1949: The Duke of Chicago. The Ghost of Zorro (serial). Hellfire. Sheriff of Wichita. Prince of the Plains. Frontier Investigator. Law of the Golden West. Federal Agents vs Underworld Inc (serial). South of Rio. Down Dakota Way. San Antone Ambush. Ranger of Cherokee Strip. Outcasts of the Trail. Powder River Rustlers. Pioneer Marshal. 1950: Singing Guns (voice only). The James Brothers of Missouri (serial). The Vanishing Westerner. Vigilante Hideout. Desperadoes of the West. The Savage Horde. Federal Agent at Large. Under Mexicali Stars. Salt Lake Raiders. Surrender. Rustlers on Horseback. Gunmen of Abilene. Rock Island Trail (GB: Transcontinental Express). Radar Patrol vs Spy King (serial. Voice only). Woman from Headquarters (voice only). The Arizona Cowboy. Code of the Silver Sage. North of the Great Divide. Tyrant of the Sea. The Missourians. 1951: Wells Fargo Gunmaster. In Old Amarillo. Don Daredevil Rides Again (serial). Insurance Investigator. Night Riders of Montana. The Dakota Kid. Rodeo King and the Senorita. Utah Wagon Train. Fort Dodge Stampede. Arizona Manhunt. Street Bandits. Honeychile. Government Agents vs Phantom Legion (serial. Voice only). Pals of the Golden West. Desert of Lost Men. Rhythm Inn. Flying Disc Men from Mars (serial). 1952: Hoodlum Empire. Oklahoma Annie. Radar Men from the Moon (serial). Border Saddlemates. Wild Horse Ambush. Leadville Gunslinger. Thundering

Caravans. Old Oklahoma Plains. Black Hills Ambush. Ride the Man Down. Desperadoes' Outpost. The WAC from Walla Walla (GB: Army Capers). South Pacific Trail. Captive of Billy the Kid. Tropical Heat Wave. 1953: Marshal of Cedar Rock. Down Laredo Way. Iron Mountain Trail. Bandits of the West. Savage Frontier. Old Overland Trail. El Paso Stampede. Shadows of Tombstone. 1954: Rogue Cop. Man with the Steel Whip (serial). The Desperado. Two Guns and a Badge. 1955: Man Without a Star. Oklahoma! The Spoilers. Carolina Cannonball. The Cobweb. Commando Cody (serial). 1956: Gun Brothers. The Last Hunt. 1957: The Kettles on Old MacDonald's Farm. Gun Duel in Durango. The Domino Kid. Last Stagecoach West. Band of Angels. Gunfire at Indian Gap. 1958: The Plunderers of Painted Flats. 1959: Escort West. 1960: Freckles. Ten Who Dared. 1961: When the Clock Strikes. Six Black Horses. 1964: He Rides Tall. 1965: Billy The Kid vs Dracula. 1966: Destination Inner Space. Gunpoint. Texas Across the River. 1967: The Way West. 1968: Rosemary's Baby. Bandolero! 1969: Gaily, Gaily (GB: Chicago, Chicago). The Reivers. 1970: Monte Walsh.

BARKER, Eric 1912–1990
Small, dark-haired, bespectacled, nervous-looking British radio comedian who, after success in such post-war series as *Merry-Go-Round*, *Waterlogged Spa* and *Just Fancy*, often in partnership with his wife Pearl Hackney, took on a whole new career at 44 as a film character comedian, often playing busybodies or petty officials. Boulting Brothers comedies gave him a good start (he won a British Academy Award in their *Brothers in Law*) and he was a semi-regular in British films for the next 10 years. Catchphrase (and the title of his autobiography): 'Steady, Barker!'

*1936: Carry On London. 1937: West End Frolics. Concert Party. 1938: On Velvet. 1956: Brothers in Law. 1957: Happy is the Bride! 1958: Blue Murder at St Trinian's. Carry on Sergeant. *A Clean Sweep. Bachelor of Hearts. 1959: Left, Right and Centre. 1960: Carry On Constable. Dentist in the Chair. Watch Your Stern. The Pure Hell of St Trinian's. 1961: Dentist on the Job (US: Get On with It!). Nearly a Nasty Accident. Raising the Wind (US: Roommates). On the Fiddle (US: Operation Snafu). 1962: Carry On Cruising. The*

Fast Lady. On the Beat. 1963: The Mouse on the Moon. Heavens Above! Father Came Too. 1964: The Bargee. Carry on Spying. Ferry 'Cross the Mersey. 1965: Three Hats for Lisa. Those Magnificent Men in Their Flying Machines. 1966: Doctor in Clover. The Great St Trinian's Train Robbery. Maroc 7. 1969: Twinky (US: Lola). 1970: There's a Girl in My Soup. Cool It Carol! (US: The Dirtiest Girl I Ever Met). 1972: That's Your Funeral. 1978: The Chiffy Kids (second series). Carry On Emmannuelle.

BARNARD, Ivor 1887–1953
Slightly built, dark-haired (balding) British actor with weasel-like, secretive features that could turn furtive, frightened or plain mean. Ideally cast as Wemmick in *Great Expectations*, he was involved in many of the best British films of the 1938–48 period. Just before his death, John Huston used him as one of his cargo of grotesques—a worthy companion for Peter Lorre and Robert Morley—in *Beat the Devil*.

1920: The Skin Game. 1931: Sally in Our Alley. 1932: Illegal. Blind Spot. 1933: The Good Companions. The Wandering Jew. The Crime at Blossom's. Sleeping Car. The Roof. Waltz Time. 1934: Love, Life and Laughter. Princess Charming. Death at Broadcasting House. Brides to Be. 1935: The Price of Wisdom. The 39 Steps. The Village Squire. Some Day. Foreign Affaires. 1936: Dreams Come True. The House of the Spaniard. The Man Behind the Mask. 1937: What a Man. The Frog. Storm in a Teacup. The Mill on the Floss. Victoria the Great. Farewell to Cinderella. Secret Lives (US: I Married a Spy). Double Exposures. 1938: Pygmalion. Everything Happens to Me. 1939: *Eye Witness *Oh Dear Uncle! Cheer Boys Cheer. Black Eyes. The Stars Look Down. 1940: The House of the Arrow (US: Castle of Crimes). 1941: The Saint's Vacation. Quiet Wedding. 1943: The Silver Fleet. Undercover (US: Underground Guerillas). Escape to Danger. 1944: Hotel Reserve. Don't Take It to Heart. English Without Tears (US: Her Man Gilbey). 1945: Caesar and Cleopatra. The Wicked Lady. Perfect Strangers (US: Vacation from Marriage). Murder in Reverse. Great Day. 1946: Great Expectations. The Grand Escapade. Appointment With Crime. 1947: So Well Remembered. Mrs Fitzherbert. 1948: Oliver Twist. London Belongs to Me (US: Dulcimer Street). Esther Waters. So Evil, My Love. The Queen of Spades. 1949: Paper Orchid. 1950: Madeleine.

1951: Hell is Sold Out. 1952: Hot Ice. The Importance of Being Earnest. Time Gentlemen Please! 1953: Malta Story. Sea Devils. Beat the Devil.

BARNETT, Vince 1902–1977
Short, jaunty, bald, fast-talking American actor with rolling, watery eyes and wispy moustache, who played runts, weasels and whining Runyonesque gangsters, often in comic vein. One of life's losers on screen, but a well-liked and ubiquitous figure off it as an inveterate wisecracker and practical joker. In his twenties, Barnett was an airmail pilot who pioneered trans-American routes.

1929: Wide Open. 1930: Her Man. Night Work. All Quiet on the Western Front. Dancing Sweeties. Queen of Scandal. A Royal Flush. One Heavenly Night. 1931: *Scratch As Catch Can. Side Show. 1932: Tiger Shark. Oh! My Operation. Rackety Rax. Night Mayor. Flesh. The Big Cage. Horse Feathers. The Death Kiss. Scarface – The Shame of a Nation. 1933: *The Trial of Vince Barnett. Made on Broadway (GB: The Girl I Made). The Prizefighter and the Lady (GB: Everywoman's Man). I Cover the Waterfront. Sunset Pass. The Girl in 419. Man of the Forest. Tugboat Annie. Heritage of the Desert. *Rockabye Cowboy. Fast Workers. Madame Spy. 1934: The Cat's Paw. The Ninth Guest. Air Maniacs. *Two Lame Ducks. *Super Stupid. Now I'll Tell (GB: When New York Sleeps). Kansas City Princess. No Ransom (GB: Bonds of Honour). Registered Nurse. Take the Stand (GB: The Great Radio Mystery). The Crimson Romance. Hell in the Heavens. Young and Beautiful. She Loves Me Not. Thirty-Day Princess. The Affairs of Cellini. The Secret Bride (GB: Concealment). 1935: *Just Another Murder. Princess O'Hara. Black Fury. Don't Bet on Blondes. The Silk Hat Kid. Streamline Express. Champagne for Breakfast. Riff Raff. I Live My Life. The Rest Cure. 1936: San Francisco. After the Thin Man. Dancing Feet. Down to the Sea. *Pirate Party on Catalina Isle. Yellow Cargo. *The Brain Busters. Captain Calamity. I Cover Chinatown. 1937: The Woman I Love (GB: The Woman Between). A Star is Born. We're in the Legion Now. Boots of Destiny. Trailing Trouble. The Bank Alarm. 1938: Little Miss Broadway. Water Rustlers. The Headleys at Home (GB: Among Those Present). Ride 'Em Cowgirl. 1939: Exile Express. Overland Mail. The Singing Cowgirl.

1940: East Side Kids. Boys of the City. Seven Sinners. The Ghost Creeps. Heroes of the Saddle. 1941: Gangs Incorporated. Sierra Sue. A Girl, a Guy and a Gob (GB: The Navy Steps Out). A Dangerous Game. Paper Bullets. The Blonde Comet. Blondie in Society (GB: Henpecked). Sunset Murder Case. Jungle Man. *Your Last Act. *Speaky-Spak-Spoke. *What the Country Needs. *Love Turns Winter to Spring. Puddin' Head (GB: Judy Goes to Town). I Killed That Man. 1942: Klondike Fury. Girls' Town. The Corpse Vanishes (GB: The Case of the Missing Brides). My Favorite Spy. Baby Face Morgan. X Marks the Spot. Foreign Agent. Stardust on the Sage. Bowery at Midnight. Prison Girls/ Gallant Lady. Phantom Plainsmen. Queen of Broadway. 1943: Silent Witness (GB: Attorney for the Defence). I Escaped from the Gestapo (GB: No Escape). Cosmo Jones – Crime Smasher (GB: Crime Smasher). Tornado. Kid Dynamite. Danger – Women at Work! High Explosive. Captive Wild Woman. Thundering Trails. Petticoat Larceny. 1944: The Mask of Dimitrios. Leave It to the Irish. Sweethearts of the USA (GB: Sweethearts on Parade). 1945: River Gang (GB: Fairy Tale Murder). High Powered. Thrill of a Romance. 1946: No Leave, No Love. The Virginian. Sensation Hunters. Swell Guy. The Killers. The Falcon's Alibi. Two Sisters from Boston. Bowery Bombshell. 1947: I Cover Big Town. Little Miss Broadway (and 1938 film). Big Town After Dark. The Trespasser. Shoot to Kill. Brute Force. High Wall. Gas House Kids Go West. The Flame. 1948: Big Town Scandal. Joe Palooka in The Knockout. Thunder in the Pines. 1949: *Sweet Cheat. Knock on Any Door. Big Jack. Loaded Pistols. Deputy Marshal. 1950: *Photo Phonies. *International Burlesque. Mule Train. Border Treasure. 1951: On Dangerous Ground. Kentucky Jubilee. I'll See You in My Dreams. 1952: Carson City. Red Planet Mars. Springfield Rifle. 1953: Charade. 1954: The Human Jungle. We're No Angels. 1957: The Quiet Gun. Girl on the Run. Outlaw Queen. 1959: The Rookie. 1965: Zebra in the Kitchen. Dr Goldfoot and the Bikini Machine (GB: Dr G and the Bikini Machine). 1966: The Spy in the Green Hat (TV. GB: cinemas). 1967: The Big Mouth. 1975: Crazy Mama. Summer School Teachers.

BARR, Patrick 1908–1985
Affable, square-built British actor (born in India) who, after more than 20 years of solid

supporting reliability as policemen, service-men, doctors and best friends, suddenly became extremely popular on British television in the mid-fifties. This belated success led to a few leading roles in films, and a deservedly higher rating as an actor. Away on active service from 1940 to 1946.

*1932: Men of Tomorrow. The Merry Men of Sherwood. 1933: Meet My Sister. 1934: Irish Hearts (US: Norah O'Neale). 1935: Gay Old Dog. 1936: Wednesday's Luck. East Meets West. Things to Come. Midnight at Madame Tussaud's (US: Midnight at the Wax Museum). 1937: The Cavalier of the Streets. The Show Goes On. The Return of the Scarlet Pimpernel. Incident in Shanghai. 1938: Sailing Along. Star of the Circus (US: Hidden Menace). Meet Mr Penny. Marigold. The Gaunt Stranger (US: The Phantom Strikes). Yellow Sands. 1939: Let's Be Famous. 1940: Contraband (US: Blackout). The Case of the Frightened Lady (US: The Frightened Lady.) 1949: Man on the Run. Adam and Evelyne. The Blue Lagoon. Golden Arrow (US: Three Men and a Girl). 1951: To Have and to Hold. The Lavender Hill Mob. Death of an Angel. 1952: The Story of Robin Hood and His Merrie Men. King of the Underworld. I vinti. You're Only Young Twice! 1953: Murder at Scotland Yard. *Ghost for Sale. Black Orchid. *Murder at the Grange. Single-Handed (US: Sailor of the King). The Intruder. Black 13. Gilbert Harding Speaking of Murder. Escape by Night. 1954: Duel in the Jungle. Seagulls over Sorrento (US: Crest of the Wave). Time is My Enemy. The Brain Machine. The Dam Busters. 1955: *All Living Things. Room in the House. 1956: It's Never Too Late. 1957: At the Stroke of Nine. Saint Joan. Lady of Vengeance. 1958: Next to No Time! 1960: Urge to Kill. 1961: The Valiant. *Dam the Delta (narrator only). 1962: The Longest Day. *Jam Session. 1963: On the Run. Billy Liar! Ring of Spies. 1968: The Great Pony Raid. 1969: Guns in the Heather. 1972: The Flesh and Blood Show. 1973: The Satanic Rites of Dracula (US: Dracula and his Vampire Bride). 1974: House of Whipcord. The Black Windmill. 1978: The First Great Train Robbery. Home Before Midnight. 1979: The Godsend. 1983: Octopussy.*

BARRAT, Robert 1891–1970

A big, powerful, banana-nosed, sandy-haired, baleful-eyed American actor, often seen as imposing, sometimes harsh figures of authority, but equally at ease as strong, nasty (sometimes foreign) villains, or benign, pipe-smoking officials. Resident at Warners through the 1930s, he had some spectacular fights on screen, notably the one with Joel McCrea in *Union Pacific.*

1915: Her Own Way. 1922: Whispering Shadows. 1933: The Mayor of Hell. Picture Snatcher. The Devil's in Love. Tugboat Annie. Baby Face. King of the Jungle. The Silk Express. Lilly Turner. Captured! Heroes for Sale. Wild Boys of the Road (GB: Dangerous Days). The Kennel Murder Case. I Loved a Woman. From Headquarters. Ann Carver's Profession. The Secret of the Blue Room. 1934: I Sell Anything. Fog Over Frisco. Dames. Dark Hazard. A Very Honorable Guy. Massacre. Wonder Bar. Mid-

night Alibi. Hi, Nellie! Gambling Lady. Upper World. Friends of Mr Sweeney. The Dragon Murder Case. Here Comes the Navy. Housewife. Return of the Terror. Big-Hearted Herbert. The St Louis Kid (GB: A Perfect Weekend). The Fire Bird. I Am a Thief. Bordertown. 1935: The Florentine Dagger. While the Patient Slept. Dressed to Thrill. Captain Blood. Devil Dogs of the Air. Stranded. Special Agent. Dr Socrates. Moonlight on the Prairie. A Village Tale. The Murder Man. 1936: The Country Doctor. Exclusive Story. Trail of the Lonesome Pine. I Married a Doctor. Sons o' Guns. The Last of the Mohicans. Mary of Scotland. Draegerman Courage (GB: The Cave-In). The Charge of the Light Brigade. God's Country and the Woman. Trailin' West (GB: On Secret Service). Black Legion. 1937: The Life of Emile Zola. Souls at Sea. Confession. Love is on the Air (GB: The Radio Murder Mystery). The Barrier. Mountain Justice. Bad Man of Brimstone. 1938: Penitentiary. Forbidden Valley. Marie Antoinette. The Buccaneer. The Texans. Charlie Chan in Honolulu. Breaking the Ice. Shadows over Shanghai. 1939: Colorado Sunset. Allegheny Uprising (GB: The First Rebel). Union Pacific. Bad Lands. Conspiracy. The Cisco Kid and the Lady. Man of Conquest. Heritage of the Desert. Return of the Cisco Kid. 1940: Northwest Passage. Go West/The Marx Brothers Go West. Captain Caution. The Man from Dakota (GB: Arouse and Beware). Fugitive from a Prison Camp. Laddie. 1941: Riders of the Purple Sage. Parachute Battalion. They Met in Argentina. 1942: The Girl from Alaska. American Empire (GB: My Son Alone). Fall In. 1943: They Came to Blow Up America. Bomber's Moon. Johnny Come Lately (GB: Johnny Vagabond). A Stranger in Town. 1944: Enemy of Women. The Adventures of Mark Twain. 1945: Grissly's Millions. They Were Expendable. Road to Utopia. The Great John L (GB: A Man Called Sullivan). Dakota. Strangler of the Swamp. San Antonio. Wanderer of the Wasteland. 1946: Dangerous Millions. Magnificent Doll. Just Before Dawn. The Time of Their Lives. Sunset Pass. 1947: Road to Rio. The Sea of Grass. The Fabulous Texan. 1948: I Love Trouble. Relentless. Bad Men of Tombstone. Joan of Arc. 1949: Canadian Pacific. Song of India. The Lone Wolf and His Lady. Riders of the Range. The Doolins of Oklahoma (GB: The Great Manhunt). The Kid from Texas (GB: Texas Kid—Outlaw). 1950: An American Guerilla in the Philippines (GB: I Shall Return). The Baron of Arizona. Davy Crockett—

Indian Scout. Double Crossbones. 1951: Pride of Maryland. Flight to Mars. Darling, How Could You? (GB: Rendezvous). Distant Drums. 1952: Denver and Rio Grande. Son of Ali Baba. 1953: Cow Country. 1955: Tall Man Riding.

BARTY, Billy 1924–

A near legend in his own lifetime is this long-serving, light-haired Hollywood dwarf actor with the face of an innocent demon. He played babies and children in Warner musicals of the 1930s – notably the 'tot' who offers Dick Powell a can opener to cut into Ruby Keeler's metal suit in *Gold Diggers of 1933* – and has continued to crop up in films down through the years. TV series occupied him in the 1950s while from the mid 1970s his career experienced an unexpected but very welcome resurgence in cinema films that continues to the present day. Besides the list below, Barty played in many of the 'Mickey McGuire' comedy shorts between 1927 and 1934 as Mickey Rooney's younger brother. An active campaigner for the rights of small people in America.

1931: Daddy Long Legs. 1933: Gold Diggers of 1933. Out All Night. Roman Scandals. Footlight Parade. Alice in Wonderland. 1934: Gift of Gab. 1935: A Midsummer Night's Dream. Bride of Frankenstein. 1937: Nothing Sacred. Hollywood Hotel. 1942: Here We Go Again. 1950: Pigmy Island. 1952: The Clown. 1957: The Undead. 1962: Billy Rose's Jumbo (GB: Jumbo). 1964: Roustabout. 1965: Harum Scarum (GB: Harem Holiday). 1970: Pufnstuf. 1973: The Godmothers. 1974: The Day of the Locust. Punch and Jody (TV). 1975: Won Ton Ton, the Dog Who Saved Hollywood. 1976: Twin Detectives (TV). The Amazing Dobermans. W C Fields and Me. 1977: The Happy Hooker Goes to Washington. 1978: Foul Play. Lord of the Rings (voice only). 1979: Firepower. Skatetown USA. 1980: Hardly Working. 1981: Being Different. Under the Rainbow. 1984: Night Patrol. 1985: Legend. 1986: Tough Guys. 1987: Masters of the Universe. Crazylegs (later Off the Mark). Rumpelstiltskin. Body Slam. Snow White. 1988: Willow. 1989: UHF. Lobster Man from Mars. 1990: Wishful Thinking. The Rescuers Down Under (voice only). Diggin' Up Business. 1991: Life Stinks. 1992: The Naked Truth. 1994: The Princess and the Pea. The Legend of D.B. Taggart.

BASS, Alfie 1916–1987

Chunky, diminutive Londoner with juicy lips and distinctively squashed features beneath a mop of black hair. Often seen in cockney and/or Jewish 'cloth cap' roles, he lurked under a cloak of anonymity until his co-starring part as one of *The Lavender Hill Mob* brought his name to the public's attention. Later he tackled weightier roles, although almost always in the same vein as that in which he had started. Less often seen in films after 1958, following his creation of the malingering soldier 'Bootsie' who appeared in two long-running TV series, *The Army Game* and *Bootsie and Snudge*. Died from a heart attack.

1943: The Bells Go Down. 1945: Johnny Frenchman. Perfect Strangers (US: Vacation from Marriage). Brief Encounter. 1947: Holiday Camp. It Always Rains on Sunday. 1948: Vice Versa. The Monkey's Paw. *They Gave Him the Works. Man on the Run. 1949: The Hasty Heart. Boys in Brown. 1950: Stage Fright. Pool of London. 1951: Talk of a Million (US: You Can't Beat the Irish). The Galloping Major. The Lavender Hill Mob. High Treason. Brandy for the Parson. 1952: Treasure Hunt. Derby Day (US: Four Against Fate). The Planter's Wife (US: Outpost in Malaya). Made in Heaven. 1953: Top of the Form. The Square Ring. 1954: To Dorothy a Son (US: Cash on Delivery). The Angel Who Pawned Her Harp. The Passing Stranger. Time is My Enemy. Make Me an Offer. Svengali. 1955: The Night My Number Came Up. Murder by Proxy. A Kid for Two Farthings. *The Bespoke Overcoat. The Ship That Died of Shame (US: PT Raiders). King's Rhapsody. 1956: Jumping for Joy. Tiger in the Smoke. A Child in the House. Behind the Headlines. A Touch of the Sun. Sailor Beware! (US: Panic in the Parlor). No Road Back. 1957: Carry On Admiral (US: The Ship Was Loaded). Hell Drivers. 1958: A Tale of Two Cities. I Was Monty's Double (US: Monty's Double). I Only Arsked! 1960: The Millionairess. 1965: Help! 1966: Doctor in Clover. Alfie. The Sandwich Man. A Funny Thing Happened on the Way to the Forum. 1967: Dance of the Vampires (US: The Fearless Vampire Killers). A Challenge for Robin Hood. Up the Junction. Bindle (One of Them Days). 1968: The Fixer. 1971: The Magnificent Seven Deadly Sins. 1976: The Chiffy Kids (series). 1977: Come Play With Me. 1978: Revenge of the Pink Panther. Death on the Nile. 1979: Moonraker. 1980: High Rise Donkey.

BASSERMAN, Albert 1867–1952

Prominent on the German stage for many years, Basserman became a big star in sombre Teutonic dramas of the early silent days. His appearances became less regular after the mid-twenties, and he ultimately fled the Nazi regime and ended up in Hollywood, where he crammed a large number of films into a few years, mostly as heavy-set avuncular types. Died in an air crash. Basserman spelt with two 'n's in German films. Nominated for an Oscar in *Foreign Correspondent.*

1912: Der Andere. 1913: Der König. Der letzte Tag. 1914: Das Erteil des Arztes. 1917: Der eiserne Wille. Du sollst keine anderen Götte haben. Herr und Diener. 1918: Die Brüder von Zaarden. Dr Schotte. Lorenzo Burghardt. Vater und Sohn. 1919: Das Werk seines Lebens. Der letzte Zeuge. Die Duplizität der Ereignisse. Eine schwache Stunde. Puppen des Todes. 1920: Die Sohne des Grafen Dossy. Die Stimme. Masken. 1921: Das Weib des Pharao (US: Loves of Pharaoh). Die kleine Dagmar. Die Nächte des Cornelis Brouwer. 1922: Christopher Columbus. Frauenopfer. Lucrezia Borgia. Erdgeist. 1924: Helena. 1925: Briefe, die ihn nicht erreichten. Der Herr Generaldirektor. 1926: Wenn des Herz der Jugend spricht. 1929: Fräulein Else. Napoleon auf St Helena. 1930: Alraune. Dreyfus. 1931: Gefahren der Liebe. Kadetten. 1914: Voruntersuchung. Zum goldenen Anker. 1933: Ein gewisser Herr Gran. 1938: Letzte Liebe. 1939: La famille Lefrançais (US: Heroes of the Marne). 1940: Dr Ehrlich's Magic Bullet. Foreign Correspondent. A Dispatch from Reuter's (GB: This Man Reuter). Moon Over Burma. Knute Rockne, All American (GB: A Modern Hero). Escape. 1941: The Shanghai Gesture. A Woman's Face. New Wine. (GB: The Great Awakening). 1942: The Moon and Sixpence. Invisible Agent. Once Upon a Honeymoon. Fly By Night. Reunion in France (GB: Mademoiselle France). 1943: Desperate Journey. Good Luck Mr Yates. Passport to Heaven. 1944: Madame Curie. Since You Went Away. 1945: Rhapsody in Blue. 1946: Strange Holiday. The Searching Wind. 1947: The Private Affairs of Bel Ami. Escape Me Never. 1948: The Red Shoes.

BATES, Florence

(F. Rabe) 1888–1954
Formidable was about the only word for this dominant, galleon-shaped American actress

much in demand in the 1940s: her matrons were meddlesome and her matriarchs monstrous. She was once a lawyer (how the opposition must have suffered), but her Edythe Van Hopper in Alfred Hitchcock's *Rebecca* set her galloping through a gallery of gorgons and gargoyles. Contemporary audiences were said to have cheered when her character was pushed into a pool in 1941's *Love Crazy*. Died from a heart attack.

1937: The Man in Blue. 1940: Rebecca. Calling All Husbands. Son of Monte Cristo. Hudson's Bay. Kitty Foyle. 1941: Road Show. Love Crazy. The Chocolate Soldier. Strange Alibi. 1942: The Devil and Miss Jones. The Tuttles of Tahiti. My Heart Belongs to Daddy. The Moon and Sixpence. We Were Dancing. They Got Me Covered. Mexican Spitfire at Sea. 1943: Slightly Dangerous. His Butler's Sister. Mister Big. Heaven Can Wait. Mr Lucky. 1944: The Mask of Dimitrios. Kismet. Since You Went Away. Belle of the Yukon. The Racket Man. Tahiti Nights. Tonight and Every Night. 1945: Saratoga Trunk. San Antonio. Out of This World. 1946: Claudia and David. The Man I Love. Cluny Brown. The Diary of a Chambermaid. Whistle Stop. The Time, the Place and the Girl. 1947: The Brasher Doubloon (GB: The High Window). Love and Learn. Desire Me. The Secret Life of Walter Mitty. 1948: Texas, Brooklyn and Heaven (GB: The Girl from Texas). Winter Meeting. The Inside Story. River Lady. My Dear Secretary. Portrait of Jennie (GB: Jennie). I Remember Mama. A Letter to Three Wives. 1949: The Judge Steps Out. The Girl from Jones Beach. On the Town. 1950: Belle of Old Mexico. County Fair. The Second Woman (GB: Ellen). 1951: Lullaby of Broadway. The Tall Target. Havana Rose. The Whistle at Eaton Falls (GB: Richer Than the Earth). Father Takes the Air. 1952: The San Francisco Story. Les Misérables. 1953: Paris Model. Main Street to Broadway.

BATES, Kathy

(Kathleen Bates) 1948–
Dumpy, dark-haired, homely, rather pudding-faced American actress with pleasant personality, a highly-respected, award-winning Broadway actress for many years before making any sort of impact on films and TV, where she remained a character player rather than the star she was on stage. Winning an Oscar as the obsessive fan who keeps James Caan prisoner in *Misery*

helped, and there were some semi-leading roles to follow, although she missed out on the film version of her great stage success *Frankie and Johnny (in the Clair de Lune)* when the producers opted for youth and glamour, to the detriment of the story. Married actor Tony Campisi in 1991.

1971: Taking Off. 1977: Straight Time. 1982: Come Back to the 5 & Dime, Jimmy Dean, Jimmy Dean. 1983: Two of a Kind. 1985: Johnny Bull (TV). 1987: Summer Heat. 1988: The Morning After. Arthur 2 On the Rocks. 1989: Roe vs Wade (TV). Signs of Life. Melanie Rose. Men Don't Leave. No Place Like Home (TV). My Best Friend is a Vampire. 1990: White Palace. Dick Tracy. Misery. 1991: The Road to Mecca. Shadows and Fog. At Play in the Fields of the Lord. Fried Green Tomatoes (GB: Fried Green Tomatoes at the Whistle Stop Café). 1992: Prelude to a Kiss. Used People. Hostages (TV). 1993: A Home of Our Own. 1994: North. Curse of the Starving Class. 1995: Dolores Claiborne. Angus.

BAYLDON, Geoffrey 1924–
Tall, fair-haired, scarecrow-like British actor whose name became familiar to the public only after his starring role in the television series *Catweazle* when he was well into his forties. Later, he was also cannily cast as The Crowman in another children's TV series, *Worzel Gummidge*. Extensive stage work, especially in Shakespearian roles, preceded his entry into feature-film parts in 1953, after which he wandered skeletally through some 60 movies – never better cast than as one of the emaciated prisoners-of-war in *King Rat*.

1953: The Beggar's Opera. *The Stranger Left No Card. 1955: Three Cases of Murder. 1958: A Night to Remember. Dracula (US: The Horror of Dracula). The Camp on Blood Island. The Two-Headed Spy. 1959: Whirlpool. Idle on Parade (US: Idol on Parade). Yesterday's Enemy. The Rough and the Smooth (US: Portrait of a Sinner). Libel. 1960: Suspect (US: The Risk). The Day They Robbed the Bank of England. Cone of Silence (US: Trouble in the Sky). Greyfriars Bobby. 1961: Bomb in the High Street. The Webster Boy. 1962: The Prince and the Pauper. The Amorous Prawn. The Longest Day. Jigsaw. 55 Days at Peking. 1963: Becket. 1964: A Jolly Bad Fellow. 1965: King Rat. Dead Man's Chest. Life at the Top. Where the Spies Are. Sky West and Crooked (US: Gypsy Girl). 1966: To Sir, with Love. 1967: Assignment K. Two a Penny. Casino Royale. 1968: A Dandy in Aspic. Inspector Clouseau. The Bush Baby. Otley. 1969: Frankenstein Must Be Destroyed. 1970: The Raging Moon (US: Long Ago Tomorrow). Fade Out. Say Hello to Yesterday. Scrooge. The House That Dripped Blood. 1971: The Magnificent Seven Deadly Sins. 1972: Asylum. Au Pair Girls. Tales from the Crypt. 1973: Gawain and the Green Knight. Steptoe and Son Ride Again. 1974: QB VII (TV). 1976: The Slipper and the Rose. The Pink Panther Strikes Again. Charleston. 1979: Porridge. 1983: Bullshot. 1988: Madame Sousatzka. The Tenth Man (TV). 1991: The Necessary Love.

BEATTY, Ned 1937–
Round-faced, pleasantly portly American actor with wavy brown rumpled hair, usually in sweaty roles: can play comic, dramatic, sympathetic or silly. He gained wide-ranging theatrical experience (he played Big Daddy in a production of *Cat on a Hot Tin Roof* at 21) before heading for Hollywood and landing a good variety of parts following his major-role debut in *Deliverance*. This plumper version of Dick Powell (*qv*) was an Oscar nominee for *Network* and unlucky not to win a second nomination for his engaging performance as the refugee singer in *Hear My Song*.

*1961: The Hustler. 1972: Deliverance. Cancel My Reservation. The Life and Times of Judge Roy Bean. Footsteps (TV). 1973: The Marcus-Nelson Murders (TV). Dying Room Only (TV). The Last American Hero. White Lightning. The Thief Who Came to Dinner. 1974: The Ex-*ecution of Private Slovik (TV). 1975: W W and the Dixie Dancekings. Nashville. Attack on Terror: The FBI versus the Ku Klux Klan (TV). The Deadly Tower (TV). 1976: Mikey and Nicky. Big Henry and the Polka Dot Kid (TV). The Big Bus. All the President's Men. Network. Silver Streak. 1977: Exorcist II: The Heretic. Remember Those Poker-Playing Monkeys? Gray Lady Down. The Great Georgia Bank Hoax/ Shenanigans. Tail Gunner Joe (TV). Lucan (TV). 1978: A Question of Love (TV). Superman. 1979: Promises in the Dark. 1941. Wise Blood. Alambrista! The American Success Company (later Success). Friendly Fire (TV). 1980: Hopscotch. Superman II. Guyana Tragedy: The Story of Jim Jones (TV). All God's Children (TV). 1981: The Violation of Sarah McDavid (TV). The Incredible Shrinking Woman. Pray TV (TV). Splendor in the Grass (TV). 1982: The Toy. The Ballad of Gregorio Cortez. Golda/A Woman Called Golda (TV). 1983: Kentucky Woman (TV). Stroker Ace. Touched. Denmark Vesey (TV). 1984: The Last Days of Pompeii (TV). 1985: Experiment in Freedom (TV). Some Sunny Day. Restless Natives. Trouble at the Royal Rose/Trouble with Spies (released 1987). Alfred Hitchcock Presents (TV). Hostage Flight (TV). 1986: The Big Easy. Back to School. 1987: The Unholy. The Fourth Protocol. Rolling Vengeance. The Haunting of Barney Palmer (TV). Switching Channels. Midnight Crossing. The Passage. 1988: Physical Evidence. Go Toward the Light (TV). After the Rain. Imagination. Purple People Eater. Shadows in the Storm. 1989: African Timber. Captain America. Big Bad John. Chattahoochee. Time Trackers. Spy (TV). Tennessee Nights. Ministry of Vengeance. Tom Alone (TV). Twist of Fate. 1990: Repossessed. Black Creek. A Cry in the Wind. Last Train Home (TV). Dive. Angel Square. Twilight Blue. Back to Hannibal (TV). The Tragedy of Flight 403: The Inside Story (TV). 1991: Hear My Song. 1992: Before Midnight. Illusions. Prelude to a Kiss. Ed and His Dead Mother. Blind Vision. T Bone n Weasel (TV). 1993: Rudy. Earth and the American Dream (voice only). Tuskegee Subject # 626. 1994: Radioland Murders. Bon Appetit Mama. Replikator. The Legend of D.B. Taggart. 1995: Just Cause.*

BEAVERS, Louise 1898–1962
Squarely-built, benign black American actress whose cooks, housekeepers and lady's maids proved a great comfort to movie heroines in times of trouble. Once a member of an all-girl minstrel show, she came to Hollywood in 1924 as a dresser to the stars, but bit parts in silent films soon led to regular featured roles in talkies. Best remembered as Claudette Colbert's servant and confidante in *Imitation of Life* (1934), this most perfect of Hollywood housekeepers in real life hated cooking. Died from heart failure after a long struggle against diabetes.

1923: Gold Diggers. 1927: Uncle Tom's Cabin. 1928: *Election Day. 1929: Barnum Was Right. The Glad Rag Doll. Coquette. Nix on Dames. Wall Street. Gold Diggers of Broadway. 1930: Manslaughter. Our Blushing Brides. Second Choice. True to the Navy. She Couldn't Say No. Wide Open. Back Pay. Recaptured Love. Safety in Numbers. 1931: Party

Husbands. Ladies of the Big House. Millie. Heaven on Earth. Annabelle's Affairs. Up for Murder. Don't Bet on Women. Girls About Town. Sundown Trail. Good Sport. Six Cylinder Love. Reckless Living. 1932: The Expert. *Old Man Minick. *You're Telling Me. Freaks. Night World. It's Tough to be Famous. Midnight Lady (GB: Dream Mother). Young America (GB: We Humans). The Dark Horse. Street of Women. Wild Girl (GB: Salomy Jane). What Price Hollywood? Unashamed. Divorce in the Family. The Strange Love of Molly Louvain. Hell's Highway. Pick Up. Too Busy to Work. 1933: 42nd Street. She Done Him Wrong. Girl Missing. What Price Innocence? *Grin and Bear It. Central Airport. Only Yesterday. A Shriek in the Night. Midnight Mary. Hold Your Man. Her Bodyguard. The Big Cage. Bombshell (GB: Blonde Bombshell). Notorious But Nice. Her Splendid Folly. In the Money. 1934: Glamour. I Believed in You. Palooka (GB: The Great Schnozzle). Bedside. I've Got Your Number. I Give My Love. The Cheaters. Hat, Coat and Glove. The Merry Frinks (GB: The Happy Family). Imitation of Life. West of the Pecos. The Merry Wives of Reno. A Modern Hero. Registered Nurse. Dr Monica. Gambling Lady. 1935: Annapolis Farewell (GB: Gentlemen of the Navy). 1936: General Spanky. Bullets or Ballots. Wives Never Know. Rainbow on the River. The Gorgeous Hussy. 1937: Wings Over Honolulu. Make Way for Tomorrow. Love in a Bungalow. The Last Gangster. 1938: Life Goes On. Scandal Sheet. Brother Rat. The Headleys at Home (GB: Among Those Present). Peck's Bad Boy with the Circus. Reckless Living (remake). 1939: Made for Each Other. The Lady's from Kentucky. Reform School. 1940: Women Without Names. Parole Fixer. I Want a Divorce. No Time for Comedy. 1941: Virginia. Belle Starr. Sign of the Wolf. Shadow of the Thin Man. The Vanishing Virginian. Kisses for Breakfast. 1942: Reap the Wild Wind. Holiday Inn. The Big Street. Seven Sweethearts. Tennessee Johnson (GB: The Man on America's Conscience). Young America (remake). 1943: Good Morning, Judge! All By Myself. Du Barry Was a Lady. Top Man. Jack London. There's Something about a Soldier. 1944: Follow the Boys. Dixie Jamboree. Barbary Coast Gent. South of Dixie. 1945: Delightfully Dangerous. 1946: Lover Come Back. Young Widow. 1947: Banjo. Good Sam. Mr Blandings Builds His Dream House. For the Love of Mary. 1949: Tell It to the Judge. 1950: Girls' School (GB: Dangerous Inheritance). My Blue Heaven.

The Jackie Robinson Story. 1951: Colorado Sundown. 1952: I Dream of Jeanie. Never Wave at a WAC (GB: Army Capers). 1956: Goodbye, My Lady. You Can't Run Away from It. Teenage Rebel. 1957: The Hostess with the Mostest (TV). Tammy and the Bachelor (GB: Tammy). 1958: The Goddess. 1960: The Facts of Life. All the Fine Young Cannibals.

BECKWITH, Reginald 1908–1965
Bumbling, curly-haired, chubby British actor of the 'Oh-dear-what's-to-become-of-us?' school. He started as a successful playwright with acting as the second string to his bow: but, after 1948, these roles began to be reversed (although he continued to write — Boys in Brown was one of his earliest hit plays) and he was to be found wringing his hands in the background of numerous British comedies. He could also tackle comic businessmen and straight dramatic roles with equal conviction. His writing talents led him to try film and theatre criticism and from 1941 to 1945 he was a war correspondent for the BBC.

1940: Freedom Radio (US: A Voice in the Night). 1946: This Man is Mine. 1948: My Brother's Keeper. Scott of the Antarctic. 1949: Miss Pilgrim's Progress. 1950: The Body Said No! Mr Drake's Duck. 1951: Circle of Danger. Another Man's Poison. Brandy for the Parson. 1952: Whispering Smith Hits London (US: Whispering Smith versus Scotland Yard). Penny Princess. You're Only Young Twice! 1953: Genevieve. The Titfield Thunderbolt. Innocents in Paris. Don't Blame the Stork! The Million Pound Note (US: Man with a Million). 1954: Fast and Loose. The Runaway Bus. Lease of Life. Dance Little Lady. Aunt Clara. The Men of Sherwood Forest. 1955: The Lyons in Paris. Break in the Circle. They Can't Hang Me! A Yank in Ermine. Dust and Gold. Charley Moon. 1956: The March Hare. It's a Wonderful World. A Touch of the Sun. Jumping for Joy. 1957: Carry on Admiral (US: The Ship Was Loaded). These Dangerous Years (US: Dangerous Youth). Lucky Jim. Night of the Demon (US: Curse of the Demon). Light Fingers. 1958: Up the Creek. Law and Disorder. Next to No Time! Rockets Galore (US: Mad Little Island). Further Up the Creek. The Captain's Table. 1959: The 39 Steps. The Horse's Mouth. The Ugly Duckling. Upstairs and Downstairs. The Navy Lark. Friends and Neighbours. Desert Mice. Expresso Bongo. Bottoms Up! 1960:

Dentist in the Chair. Doctor in Love. There Was a Crooked Man. The Night We Got the Bird. The Girl on the Boat. 1961: Five Golden Hours. Double Bunk. Dentist on the Job (US: Get on with It!) The Day the Earth Caught Fire. 1962: Night of the Eagle (US: Burn, Witch, Burn). Hair of the Dog. The Prince and the Pauper. The Password is Courage. *The King's Breakfast. Lancelot and Guinevere. 1963: Just for Fun. The VIPs. Doctor in Distress. Never Put It in Writing. 1964: The Yellow Rolls Royce. A Shot in the Dark. Gonks Go Beat. 1965: The Amorous Adventures of Moll Flanders. Thunderball. The Secret of My Success. The Big Job. How to Undress in Public Without Undue Embarrassment. Where the Spies Are. Mister Moses.

BEDDOE, Don 1903–1991
Apple-cheeked, auburn-haired American actor with small, twinkling blue eyes, seen as impish confederates, excitable reporters or defective detectives. Although he was 35 when he came to Hollywood from Broadway, his cherubic, butter-innocent looks allowed him a good variety of middle-range roles before he moved into old codgers and, in one delightful instance, a leprechaun trapped in a bottle. He had the lead in 1961's Saintly Sinners. Married for the second time at the age of 71, Beddoe, a great traveller, was obviously a believer that life begins any time you choose.

1938: There's That Woman Again (GB: What a Woman). 1939: Lone Wolf Spy Hunt (GB: The Lone Wolf's Daughter). Good Girls Go to Paris. Flying G-Men (serial). *Andy Clyde Gets Spring Chicken. Outside These Walls. Mandrake the Magician (serial). Romance of the Redwoods. Golden Boy. Missing Daughters. Taming of the West. The Man They Could Not Hang. Coast Guard. Blondie Meets the Boss. Those High Gray Walls (GB: The Gates of Alcatraz). Beware Spooks! My Son is Guilty (GB: Crime's End). The Amazing Mr Williams. *Three Sappy People. Konga, the Wild Stallion (GB: Konga). 1940: The Doctor Takes a Wife. Texas Stagecoach (GB: Two Roads). Beyond the Sacramento (GB: Power of Justice). The Lone Wolf Strikes. *Mr Clyde Goes to Broadway. *You Nasty Spy. *The Heckler. *The Spook Speaks. Scandal Sheet. Charlie Chan's Murder Cruise. Blondie on a Budget. Men Without Souls. Escape to Glory/Submarine Zone. Island of Doomed Men. The Man from Tumbleweeds.

Manhattan Heartbeat. Girls of the Road. West of Abilene (GB: The Showdown). Before I Hang. Military Academy. This Thing Called Love. The Secret Seven. Glamour for Sale. The Lone Wolf Meets a Lady. 1941: The Lone Wolf Keeps a Date. The Face Behind the Mask. Texas. Unholy Partners. Sing for Your Supper. Under Age. The Big Boss. The Blonde from Singapore. Sweetheart of the Campus (GB: Broadway Ahead). The Lone Wolf Takes a Chance. Two Latins from Manhattan. She Knew All the Answers. This Thing Called Love (GB: Married But Single). The Phantom Submarine. Harvard, Here I Come (GB: Here I Come). 1942: Meet the Stewarts. Shut My Big Mouth. The Talk of the Town. Tales of Manhattan. Sabotage Squad. Blondie for Victory (GB: Troubles Through Billets). Honolulu Lu. Lucky Legs. Junior Army. Not a Ladies' Men. The Boogie Man Will Get You. Smith of Minnesota. 1943: Power of the Press. 1944: Winged Victory. 1945: Getting Gertie's Garter. Crime Inc. Midnight Manhunt. One Exciting Night. 1946: Behind Green Lights. O.S.S. The Well-Groomed Bride. The Notorious Lone Wolf. The Best Years of Our Lives. California. 1947: Buck Privates Come Home (GB: Rookies Come Home). Blaze of Noon. The Farmer's Daughter. Welcome Stranger. They Won't Believe Me. The Bachelor and the Bobby-Soxer (GB: Bachelor Knight). Calcutta. 1948: If You Knew Susie. Another Part of the Forest. An Act of Murder. Black Bart (GB: Black Bart – Highwayman). 1949: Bride of Vengeance. Flame of Youth. Hideout. The Lady Gambles. Once More, My Darling. Easy Living. Dancing in the Dark. Dear Wife. Gun Crazy/Deadly is the Female. Woman in Hiding. The Crime Doctor's Diary. 1950: The Great Rupert. Caged. Young Daniel Boone. Tarnished. Beyond the Purple Hills. Cyrano de Bergerac. Emergency Wedding (GB: Jealousy). Southside 1–1000 (GB: Forgery). The Company She Keeps. Gasoline Alley. The Enforcer (GB: Murder Inc). 1951: The Sword of d'Artagnan. As Young As You Feel. The Racket. Starlift. Three Guys Named Mike. Francis Goes to the Races. Million Dollar Pursuit. Rodeo King and the Senorita. Belle le Grand. Corky of Gasoline Alley (GB: Corky). Man in the Saddle (GB: The Outcast). The Unknown Man. Behave Yourself! Scandal Sheet (And 1940 version. GB: The Dark Page). 1952: The Narrow Margin. Hoodlum Empire. The Big Sky. Carson City. Room for One More. Washington Story (GB: Target for Scandal). Carrie. Don't Bother to Knock. The Iron Mistress. Blue Canadian Rockies. Stop, You're Killing Me! The Clown. 1953: The System. Blades of the Musketeers. Cow Country. 1954: Loophole. A Star is Born. River of No Return. The Steel Cage. Jubilee Trail. 1955: Wyoming Renegades. Tarzan's Hidden Jungle. The Night of the Hunter. 1956: Behind the High Wall. The Rawhide Years. 1957: Shootout at Medicine Bend. 1958: Toughest Gun in Tombstone. Bullwhip! 1959: Warlock. The Joker is Wild. Pillow Talk. 1960: The Wizard of Baghdad. 1961: The Boy Who Caught a Crook. Jack the Giant Killer. Saintly Sinners. 1962: Papa's Delicate Condition. 1965: A Very Special Favor. 1966: Lassie the Voyager (TV). Texas Across the River. 1968: The Impossible Years. 1969: Generation (GB: A Time for Giving). 1970: How Do I Love Thee? 1979: Nickel Mountain (released 1985).

BEERY, Noah Jnr 1913–1994

Stocky, dark-haired American supporting actor with small, round face, slow, lopsided grin and easy-going air, the son of Noah Beery Snr (qv) and nephew of Wallace Beery (1885–1949). He never quite rose to the rank of co-star, but pursued his career with dogged cheeriness, mostly in westerns as sidekicks, good or bad, at first headstrong, later philosophical. In later years, a welcome part of television's The Rockford Files, playing James Garner's father. Married to Maxine, daughter of cowboy star Buck Jones, from 1940 to 1966 (first of two). Died following brain surgery.

1920: The Mark of Zorro. 1922: Penrod. 1923: Penrod and Sam. 1929: Father and Son. 1930: Love Trader. Renegades. 1932: Heroes of the West (serial). The Jungle Mystery (serial). 1933: The Three Mesquiteers (serial). Fighting with Kit Carson (serial). Sunset Pass. Rustlers' Roundup. 1934: The Trail Beyond. Tailspin Tommy (serial). Tailspin Tommy in the Great Air Mystery (serial). 1935: Call of the Savage (serial). Stormy. Five Bad Men. Devil's Canyon. 1936: Parole! Ace Drummond (serial). 1937: The Road Back/Return of the Hero. Some Blondes Are Dangerous. The Mighty Treve. 1938: Girls' School. Trouble at Midnight. Outside the Law. Forbidden Valley. 1939: Only Angels Have Wings. Flight at Midnight. Of Mice and Men. *Glove Slingers. Parents on Trial. Bad Lands. The Strange Case of Dr Meade. 1940: Twenty-Mule Team. A Little Bit of Heaven. The Carson City Kid. The Light of Western Stars. Passport to Alcatraz. 1941: Sergeant York. Tanks a Million. Riders of Death Valley (serial). All-American Co-Ed. Two in a Taxi. 1942: Overland Mail (serial). Dudes Are Pretty People. 'Neath Brooklyn Bridge. Tennessee Johnson (GB: The Man on America's Conscience). Hay Foot. 1943: Calaboose. What a Woman! (GB: The Beautiful Cheat). Prairie Chickens. Allergic to Love. Corvette K-225 (GB: The Nelson Touch). Pardon My Gun. Gung Ho! We've Never Been Licked (GB: Texas to Tokyo). Top Man. *Slick Chick. Frontier Badmen. 1944: See My Lawyer. Follow The Boys. Week-end Pass. Allergic to Love. Hi, Beautiful! (GB: Pass to Romance). 1945: Under Western Skies. Her Lucky Night. The Daltons Ride Again. The Beautiful Cheat (GB: What a Woman! Also 1943 films of reverse titles!). The Crimson Canary. See My Lawyer. 1946: The Cat Creeps. 1948: Red River. Indian Agent. 1949: The Doolins of Oklahoma (GB: The

Great Manhunt). 1950: Two Flags West. Davy Crockett – Indian Scout (GB: Indian Scout). Destination Moon. The Savage Horde. Rocketship X-M. 1951: The Last Outpost. The Texas Rangers. 1952: The Story of Will Rogers. Wagons West. The Cimarron Kid. 1953: Wings of the Hawk. War Arrow. Tropic Zone. 1954: The Black Dakotas. Yellow Tomahawk. 1955: White Feather. Jubal. 1956: The Fastest Gun Alive. 1957: Decision at Sundown. The Spirit of St Louis. 1958: Escort West. 1959: Guns of the Timberland. 1960: Inherit the Wind. 1964: The Seven Faces of Dr Lao. 1965: Incident at Phantom Hill. 1966: Hondo and the Apaches. 1967: Journey to Shiloh. 1969: Heaven With a Gun. The Cockeyed Cowboys of Calico County (GB: TV, as A Woman for Charlie). 1970: Little Fauss and Big Halsy. 1973: The Alpha Caper (TV. GB: cinemas, as Inside Job). The Petty Story/Smash-Up Alley (TV. GB: cinemas). Walking Tall. 1974: Sidekicks (TV). The Spikes Gang. Savages (TV). 1976: Part Two, Walking Tall (GB: Legend of the Lawman). 1977: Francis Gary Powers – The True Story of the U-2 Incident (TV). 1980: The Great American Traffic Jam (TV). 1981: The Capture of Grizzly Adams (TV). 1982: Mysterious Two (TV). The Best Little Whorehouse in Texas. 1983: Waltz Across Texas.

BEERY, Noah Snr 1883–1946

Bluff and burly, often moustachioed American actor of ruddy complexion and stern eyebrows, a rough, tough, swarthy villain of strong personality who was at his best in silent days – even though his crackling tones adapted well to sound. Killed by a heart attack at nearly the same age as his slightly more prestigious brother Wallace, with whom he had worked as a chorus boy in musicals at the turn of the century. Best remembered as the sadistic sergeant in the silent version of Beau Geste.

1916: The Human Orchid. The Social Highwayman. 1917: The Clever Mrs Karfax (GB: The Clever Mrs Carfax). Molly Entangled. The Hostage. The Spirit of 76. The Mormon Maid. Sacrifice. The Chosen Prince. 1918: Hidden Pearls. The White Man's Law. His Robe of Honor. Less Than Kin. Believe Me, Xanthippe. Johnny Get Your Gun. The Whispering Chorus. The Squaw Man. The Source. Social Ambitions. The Goat. Too Many Millions. 1919: In Mizzoura. The Woman Next Door. The Red

Lantern. The Valley of the Giants. Vicky Van. Louisiana. Under the Top. A Very Good Young Man. 1920: The Fighting Shepherdess. Go Get It. The Mark of Zorro. Love Madness. The Mutiny of the Elsinore. Dinty. Everywoman. The Sea Wolf. The Sagebrusher. Why Tell? 1921: Bob Hampton of Placer. The Scoffer. Beach of Dreams. Bits of Life. Lotus Blossom. Call of the North. 1922: Tillie. Belle of Alaska. Wild Honey. Penrod. Good Men and True. I Am the Law. The Lying Truth. Crossroads of New York. The Heart Specialist. Flesh and Blood. The Power of Love. Youth to Youth. Omar the Tentmaker. Ebb Tide. 1923: Storm-swept. The Spider and the Rose. Dangerous Trails. Soul of the Beast. Quicksands. Main Street. Wandering Daughters. The Spoilers. Forbidden Lover. Tipped Off. When Law Comes to Hades. Hollywood. To the Last Man. The Destroying Angel. His Last Race. Stephen Steps Out. The Call of the Canyon. 1924: The Heritage of the Desert. The Fighting Coward. Wanderer of the Wasteland. Lily of the Dust. Female. Welcome, Stranger. North of 36. 1925: East of Suez. The Thundering Herd. The Light of Western Stars. The Spaniard (GB: Spanish Love). Contraband. Old Shoes. Wild Horse Mesa. Lord Jim. The Coming of Amos. The Vanishing American. 1926: The Enchanted Hill. The Crown of Lies. Padlocked. Beau Geste. Paradise. 1927: The Rough Riders (GB: The Trumpet Calls). The Love Mart. Evening Clothes. The Dove. 1928: Noah's Ark. Beau Sabreur. Two Lovers. Hell Ship Bronson. 1929: Passion Song. Linda. Careers. The Isle of Lost Ships. The Four Feathers. Love in the Desert. The Godless Girl. The Show of Shows. Glorifying the American Girl. Two O'Clock in the Morning. False Feathers. 1930: Murder Will Out. Song of the Flame. The Way of All Men (GB: Sin Flood). Golden Dawn. Big Boy. Under a Texas Moon. Isle of Escape. Feet First. The Love Trader. Mammy. Renegades. Tol'able David. Oh Sailor, Behave. Bright Lights. A Soldier's Plaything (GB: A Soldier's Pay). 1931: The Millionaire. Honeymoon Lane. In Line of Duty. Homicide Squad (GB: The Lost Men). Shanghaied Love. Riders of the Purple Sage. 1932: The Drifter. The Kid from Spain. Out of Singapore. Stranger in Town. The Stoker. No Living Witness. The Big Stampede. Cornered. The Devil Horse (serial). 1933: Fighting With Kit Carson (serial). The Flaming Signal. Sunset Pass. To the Last Man. She Done Him Wrong. Laughing at Life. The Woman I Stole. Man of the Forest. Easy Millions. The Thundering Herd (remake). 1934: David Harum. Kentucky Kernels (GB: Triple Trouble). Madame Spy. Mystery Line (GB: The Ghost of John Holling). Cockeyed Cavaliers. Happy Landing. The Trail Beyond. Caravan. 1935: Sweet Adeline. King of the Damned. 1936: The Crimson Circle. Live Again. Someone at the Door. The Avenging Hand. The Marriage of Corbal (US: The Prisoner of Corbal). Strangers on a Honeymoon. 1937: Our Fighting Navy (US: Torpedoed!). The Frog. Glamorous Night. Zorro Rides Again (serial). 1938: Bad Man of Brimstone. The Girl of the Golden West. Panamint's Best Man. 1939: Mexicali Rose. Mutiny on the Blackhawk. 1940: Pioneers of the West. Grandpa Goes to Town. Adventures of Red Ryder (serial). A Little Bit of Heaven. The Tulsa Kid. 1941: A Missouri Outlaw.

1942: Overland Mail (serial). The Devil's Trail. Outlaws of Pine Ridge. The Isle of Missing Men. Tennessee Johnson (GB: The Man on America's Conscience). Pardon My Gun. 1943: Mr Muggs Steps Out. The Clancy Street Boys. Carson City Cyclone. Salute to the Marines. 1944: Block Busters. The Million Dollar Kid. Gentle Annie. Barbary Coast Gent. 1945: This Man's Navy. Sing Me a Song of Texas (GB: Fortune Hunter).

BEGLEY, Ed 1901–1970
Blustering, barrel-like, aggressive American character star who had few peers in the portrayal of tyranny in all its many forms. His best performance was probably in *Patterns* (1956), although he won his Academy Award six years later in *Sweet Bird of Youth*. Died of a heart attack. His son, Ed Begley Jr (*qv*), is also an actor.

1947: Big Town. The Web. Boomerang. 1948: Deep Waters. Sitting Pretty. The Street With No Name. Sorry Wrong Number. 1949. Tulsa. It Happens Every Spring. The Great Gatsby. 1950: Backfire. Stars in My Crown. Wyoming Mail. Convicted. Saddle Tramp. Dark City. You're in the Navy Now (originally: USS Teakettle). 1951: The Lady from Texas. On Dangerous Ground. Boots Malone. 1952: Deadline-USA (GB: Deadline). The Turning Point. What Price Glory? Lone Star. 1956: Patterns (GB: Patterns of Power). 1957: Twelve Angry Men. 1959: Odds Against Tomorrow. 1961: The Green Helmet. 1962: Sweet Bird of Youth. 1964: The Unsinkable Molly Brown. 1966: The Oscar. 1967: Warning Shot. Billion Dollar Brain. Firecreek. 1968: A Time to Sing. Hang 'Em High. 1969: The Monitors. Wild in the Streets. The Violent Enemy. The Dunwich Horror. 1970: The Silent Gun (TV). Road to Salina.

BEGLEY, Ed Jr 1949–
Tall, rangy, amiable American comic actor with floppy blond hair and vacant grin. Totally unlike his big, balding father, who played scowling dramatic characters, the younger Begley, acting from an early age, was seen at first as guileless youths, but soon proved at home in faintly outrageous comedy roles. There have been one or two star parts, but largely he has been at his best stealing the thunder of others in top supporting roles. A regular (as Dr Ehrlich) in the

long-running cult TV series *St Elsewhere*, a programme that won him six successive Emmy nominations. Cinema success has been somewhat more elusive: several promising film projects have turned out, in the end, to be rotten apples in Begley's barrel of fun.

1968: Wild in the Streets. 1969: The Computer Wore Tennis Shoes. 1970: Equinox. 1972: Now You See Him, Now You Don't. Family Flight (TV). 1973: Charley and the Angel. Showdown. 1974: Cockfighter. Superdad. 1976: Stay Hungry. 1977: Citizen's Band. Record City. The One and Only. Dead of Night (TV). 1978: Blue Collar. Goin' South. Battlestar Galactica (TV. GB: cinemas). Hardcore (GB: The Hardcore Life). 1979: The In-Laws. The Concorde — Airport '79 (GB: Airport '80...The Concorde). Hot Rod (TV). Elvis! (TV. GB: cinemas, as Elvis — The Movie). A Shining Season (TV). Amateur Night at the Dixie Bar and Grill (TV). 1980: Private Lessons. 1981: Buddy Buddy. An Officer and a Gentleman. 1982: Eating Raoul. Rascals and Robbers — The Secret Adventures of Tom Sawyer and Huck Finn (TV). Cat People. Not Just Another Affair (TV). The Entity. 1983: An Uncommon Love (TV). Get Crazy. This is Spinal Tap. 1984: Protocol. Streets of Fire. 1985: Transylvania 6–5000. 1986: Amazon Women on the Moon. 1988: The Accidental Tourist. The Absent-Minded Professor (TV). 1989: Scenes from the Class Struggle in Beverly Hills. She Devil. 1991: The Story Lady (TV). Meet the Applegates. Running Mates (TV). 1992: In the Line of Duty: Siege at Marion (TV). Dark Horse. Columbo: Undercover (TV). 1993: Cooperstown (TV). Earth and the American Dream (voice only). Even Cowgirls Get the Blues. 1994: Greedy. Renaissance Man. The Pagemaster. Acting on Impulse. Rave Review. The Shaggy Dog (TV). 1995: Two Much Trouble. Batman Forever.

BELLAVER, Harry 1905–1993
Chubby-faced, concerned-looking, 'average Joe' American actor, often seen polishing the bar, but sometimes as shabby policeman, chatty cab-driver or threadbare minion. Hollywood could have kept him a busy man, but he preferred theatre, drama teaching and television work. In the last-named field, he spent five years with the popular series *Naked City* (as Sergeant Frank Arcaro) in the late 1950s and early 1960s.

1939: *Another Thin Man*. 1945: *The House on 92nd Street*. 1949: *Side Street*. 1950: *No Way Out*. *Stage to Tucson* (GB: *Lost Stage Valley*). *Perfect Strangers* (GB: *Too Dangerous to Love*). 1951: *The Lemon Drop Kid*. *The Tanks Are Coming*. 1952: *Something to Live For*. 1953: *From Here to Eternity*. *The Great Diamond Robbery*. *Miss Sadie Thompson*. 1955: *Love Me or Leave Me*. 1956: *The Birds and the Bees*. *Serenade*. 1957: *Slaughter on 10th Avenue*. *The Brothers Rico*. 1958: *The Old Man and the Sea*. 1960: *A Death of Princes* (TV. GB: cinemas). 1964: *One Potato, Two Potato*. 1966: *A Fine Madness*. 1968: *Madigan*. 1972: *The Hot Rock* (GB: *How to Steal a Diamond in Four Uneasy Lessons*). 1976: *God Told Me To* (GB: *Demon*). 1978: *Blue Collar*. *Murder in Music City* (TV). 1980: *Hero at Large*. 1981: *Rivkin: Bounty Hunter* (TV). 1985: *The Stuff*.

BELTRAN, Alma 1920–

Dark-haired, dark-eyed, downtrodden-looking Hollywood actress of olive complexion, who has been playing peasant-type women for nearly half a century. A sort of Mexican-American equivalent of Jane Darwell (*qv*), she sank herself anonymously into the casts of numerous films as domestics, friends and housewives, almost always of a benevolent if unassertive character. Said *Variety* of an appearance in her 45th year of acting: 'Alma Beltran is a believable neighbor'. She's had plenty of practice.

1945: *Mexicana*. *Pan-Americana*. *Yolanda and the Thief*. 1947: *Honeymoon*. *Carnival in Costa Rica*. 1948: *The Loves of Carmen*. *He Walked by Night*. 1953: *Sombrero*. 1954: *Jubilee Trail*. 1957: *Dragoon Wells Massacre*. 1968: *Blue*. *I Love You, Alice B Toklas*. 1970: *Glass Houses*. 1971: *The Marriage of a Young Stockbroker*. *Red Sky at Morning*. 1972: *They Only Kill Their Masters*. *Firehouse* (TV). 1974: *Candy Stripe Nurses*. 1976: *Marathon Man*. 1977: *Mary Jane Harper Cried Last Night* (TV). *Un autre homme, une autre chance* (GB: *Another Man, Another Woman*. US: *Another Man, Another Chance*). 1978: *House Calls*. *The Deerslayer* (TV). 1980: *Herbie Goes Bananas*. *Oh, God! Book II*. 1981: *Fort Apache The Bronx*. 1982: *Zoot Suit*. 1984: *Dark Mirror* (TV). 1986: *Nobody's Fool*. 1987: *Love Among Thieves* (TV). *Desperate* (TV). 1989: *Trust Me*. *Manhunt: Search for the Night Stalker* (TV). 1990: *Ghost*. 1994: *Someone She Knows* (TV).

BENCHLEY, Robert 1889–1945

One of the great Hollywood wits of the 1920s, 1930s and 1940s, dark-haired, smooth-faced Benchley possessed impeccable comic timing, and his appearances as a supporting actor in feature films, often in the character of a well-meaning busybody, were almost always occasions to savour. He also instigated and presented a brilliant series of comedy shorts, most of which began *How to . . . . .* One of these bumbling diatribes, *How to Sleep* (1935), won an Oscar. Died from a cerebral haemorrhage.

1928: **The Treasurer's Report*. **The Sex Life of the Polyp*. **The Spellbinder*. 1929: **Furnace Trouble*. **Lesson Number One*. **Stewed, Fried and Boiled*. 1932: *The Sport Parade*. 1933: *Headline Shooter* (GB: *Evidence in Camera*). *Rafter Romance*. **Your Technocracy and Mine*. *Dancing Lady*. 1934: *The Social Register*. 1935: *China Seas*. **How to Sleep*. **How to Break 90 at Croquet*. 1936: **How to Behave*. **How to Train a Dog*. **How to Vote*. **How to be a Detective*. *Piccadilly Jim*. 1937: *Live, Love and Learn*. **The Romance of Digestion*. *Broadway Melody of 1938*. **How to Start the Day*. **A Night at the Movies*. 1938: **Music Made Simple*. **How to Figure Income Tax*. **An Evening Alone*. **The Courtship of the Newt*. **Opening Day*. **Mental Poise*. **An Hour for Lunch*. **How to Raise a Baby*. **How to Read*. **How to Watch Football*. **How to Sub-Let*. 1939: **How to Eat*. **Dark Magic*. **Home Early*. **The Day of Rest*. **See Your Doctor*. 1940: **Home Movies*. **That Inferior Feeling*. **The Trouble with Husbands*. *Foreign Correspondent*. *Hired Wife*. 1941: *Bedtime Story*. *Nice Girl?* *The Reluctant Dragon*. *Three Girls about Town*. *You'll Never Get Rich*. **How to Take a Vacation*. **Waiting for Baby*. **Crime Control*. **The Forgotten Man*. 1942: **Nothing But Nerves*. **The Witness*. **Keeping in Shape*. **The Man's Angle*. *I Married a Witch*. *The Major and the Minor*. *Take a Letter, Darling* (GB: *The Green-Eyed Woman*). 1943: *Flesh and Fantasy*. *The Sky's the Limit*. *Song of Russia*. *Young and Willing*. **My Tomato*. **No News is Good News*. 1944: **Important Business*. **The National Barn Dance*. **Why, Daddy?* *Her Primitive Man*. *Janie*. *Practically Yours*. *See Here, Private Hargrove*. *It's in the Bag!* (GB: *The Fifth Chair*). 1945: *Duffy's Tavern*. *Kiss and Tell*. *Pan-American*. *Snafu* (GB: *Welcome Home*). *Week-End at the Waldorf*. **Hollywood Victory Caravan*. **I'm a Civilian Here Myself*. *Road to Utopia*. **Boogie Woogie*. 1946: *Janie Gets Married*. *The Bride Wore Boots*.

BENEDICT, William or Billy 1917–

Long-faced, extremely fair haired, donkey-featured American actor who played not-too-bright youths well into his thirties, being endlessly cast as newsboys, messenger boys or slow-witted sidekicks. A real-life ex-newsboy and plumber's mate, he took acting lessons at 16, phoned a 20th Century-Fox casting director long distance the following year and hitchhiked across America to start a Hollywood career that included a long stint as the lugubrious Whitey in the Bowery Boys comedy films. He was still playing a newsvendor in 1954's *Bride of the Monster*, by which time film jobs had become scarce. As his acting career waned, he became an assistant in making miniature sets for Hollywood films. He married for the first time at the age of 52, and became a born-again Christian in the 1970s.

1935: †*Metropolitan*. *Doubting Thomas*. *$10 Raise* (GB: *Mr Faintheart*). *Welcome Home*. *College Scandal* (GB: *The Clock Strikes Eight*). *Ladies Love Danger*. *The Farmer Takes a Wife*. *Way Down East*. *Silk Hat Kid*. *Three Kids and a Queen* (GB: *The Baxter Millions*). *Show Them No Mercy*. (GB: *Tainted Money*). *Steamboat 'Round the Bend*. *Your Uncle Dudley*. 1936: *Ramona*. *Crack-Up*. *Theodora Goes Wild*. *The Country Doctor*. *Captain January*. *Meet Nero Wolfe*. *Adventure in Manhattan* (GB:

Manhattan Madness). M'Liss. The Witness Chair. Can This Be Dixie? They Wanted to Marry. Crack-Up. After the Thin Man. Libeled Lady. 1937: Tim Tyler's Luck (serial). Jim Hanvey − Detective. That I May Live. Rhythm in the Clouds. Love in a Bungalow. Tramp Trouble. Laughing at Trouble. A Dangerous Adventure. The Last Gangster. The Road Back. 1938: There's Always a Woman. Bringing Up Baby. Walking Down Broadway. Say It in French. King of the Newsboys. Little Tough Guys in Society. I Met My Love Again. Hold That Co-Ed (GB: Hold That Girl). Young Fugitives. 1939: *Hollywood Hobbies. Code of the Streets. Newsboys' Home. Call a Messenger. Pack Up Your Troubles (GB: We're in the Army Now). Timber Stampede. Man of Conquest. 1940: Melody Ranch. Adventures of Red Ryder (serial). My Little Chickadee. The Bowery Boy. Legion of the Lawless. Grand Old Opry. Give Us Wings. Lucky Partners. *Chicken Feed. Rhythm on the River. Adventures of Red Ryder (serial). Second Chorus. Young People. The Mad Doctor (GB: A Date with Destiny). And One Was Beautiful. 1941: The Man Who Lost Himself. The Richest Man in Town. In Old Cheyenne. Jesse James at Bay. Citadel of Crime. Adventures of Captain Marvel (serial). Richest Man in Town. Unholy Partners. Cadet Girl. Dressed to Kill. Great Guns. Time Out for Rhythm. She Knew All the Answers. *Variety Reels. The Great Mr Nobody. Tuxedo Junction (GB: The Gang Made Good). 1942: Home in Wyomin'. Confessions of Boston Blackie (GB: Confessions). Junior G-Men of the Air (serial). Heart of the Golden West. Two Yanks in Trinidad. Valley of Hunted Men. A Tragedy at Midnight. The Talk of the Town. The Glass Key. On the Sunny Side. Perils of Nyoka (serial). Get Hep to Love (GB: She's My Lovely). Lady in a Jam. Rings on Her Fingers. Right to the Heart. Mrs Wiggs of the Cabbage Patch. Almost Married. A Night to Remember. The Affairs of Jimmy Valentine. The Ox-Bow Incident (GB: Strange Incident). Wildcat. 1943: Thank Your Lucky Stars. City Without Men. All by Myself. Aerial Gunner. The Clancy Street Boys. Mr Muggs Steps Out. Adventures of the Flying Cadets (serial). Whispering Footsteps. Hangmen Also Die. Nobody's Darling. Ghosts on the Loose. Moonlight in Vermont. 1944: Million Dollar Kid. *America's Children. Follow the Leader. Janie. Goodnight, Sweetheart. Block Busters. The Lady and the Monster (GB: The Lady and the Doctor). The Merry Monahans. Night Club Girl. They Live in Fear. Cover Girl. That's My Baby. My Gal Loves Music. Follow the Boys. Bowery Champs. The Whistler. Greenwich Village. 1945: The Story of G I Joe/ War Correspondent. Docks of New York. Brenda Starr, Reporter (serial). Mr Muggs Rides Again. Hollywood and Vine (GB: Daisy (the Dog) Goes Hollywood). Come Out Fighting. Patrick the Great. Road to Utopia. 1946: Gay Blades. Live Wires. Without Reservations. In Fast Company. Spook Busters. Bowery Bombshell. No Leave, No Love. Mr Hex. Do You Love Me? One More Tomorrow. The Kid from Brooklyn. A Boy, a Girl and a Dog. Never Say Goodbye. 1947: Hard-Boiled Mahoney. The Hucksters. Merton of the Movies. Bowery Buckaroos. News Hounds. Fun on a Week-End. The Pilgrim Lady. 1948: Angels' Alley. Jinx Money. Trouble Makers. Smugglers' Cove. Secret Service Investigator.

Night Wind. 1949: Master Minds. Hold That Baby. Riders of the Pony Express. Fighting Fools. Angels in Disguise. 1950: Blues Busters. Lucky Losers. Blonde Dynamite. Triple Trouble. 1951: Bowery Battalion. Crazy over Horses. Ghost Chasers. Let's Go Navy. 1953: The Magnetic Monster. 1954: Bride of the Monster. 1956: The Killing. 1958: Rally 'Round the Flag, Boys! 1959: Last Train from Gun Hill. 1961: Lover Come Back. 1965: The Hallelujah Trail. Harlow (Carroll Baker version). Zebra in the Kitchen. 1966: Frankie and Johnny. 1967: What Am I Bid? 1968: Funny Girl. 1969: Hello, Dolly. Big Daddy. 1972: The Dirt Gang. The Adventures of Nick Carter (TV). 1973: The Sting. 1974: Homebodies. The Girl on the Late, Late Show (TV). 1975: Farewell, My Lovely. The Return of Joe Forrester (TV). The Big Rip-Off (TV). The Blue Knight (TV). Won Ton Ton, the Dog Who Saved Hollywood. 1977: The Last Hurrah. 1978: Born Again. 1988: Bonanza − the Next Generation (TV).

† Scenes deleted from release print

BENNETT, Jill

(Nora J. Bennett) 1929–1990

Attractive, fair-haired, Malaya-born British actress with gargoyle-like features. She played one or two unusual heroines in her early days, pixie-like creatures with backbones of steel. Her later characters tended to run to the neurotic, but she never really made her mark in British films, despite some telling performances, and her greatest successes were on stage. Married for some years to the playwright John Osborne, but later divorced. He published a vitriolic memoir of her in 1991. Committed suicide with pills.

1951: The Long Dark Hall. 1952: The Hour of 13. Moulin Rouge. 1953: Hell Below Zero. 1954: Aunt Clara. 1955: *Murder Anonymous, 1956: Lust for Life. The Extra Day. 1960: The Criminal (US: The Concrete Jungle). 1965: The Nanny. The Skull. 1968: Inadmissible Evidence. The Charge of the Light Brigade. 1970: Julius Caesar. 1971: I Want What I Want. 1974: Mister Quilp. 1976: Full Circle (US: The Haunting of Julia). 1981: For Your Eyes Only. 1982: Britannia Hospital. The Aerodrome (TV). 1985: Lady Jane. 1988: Hawks. 1990: The Sheltering Sky.

BENSON, George 1911–1983

Fidgety, apologetic, brown-haired Welsh-born actor in British films, whose characters, like those of America's Elisha Cook Jnr (qv), were life's losers, even if they smiled more often than most. Benson's film people, though, were not mean or vindictive; rather, they were shy, ineffectual or menial, his pleasant features usually taking on a perplexed air at some stage of the film, at which his well-rounded tones would express distress. Trained at RADA, he was playing Shakespeare at 18. For such a familiar and welcome face, he made surprisingly few films.

1932: Holiday Lovers. 1933: The Man from Toronto. 1937: Keep Fit. 1938: Break the News. 1939: Young Man's Fancy. 1940: Convoy. 1947: The October Man. Mine Own Executioner. 1949: Helter Skelter. The Lost People. 1950: The Happiest Days of Your Life. Madeleine. Cage of Gold. Highly Dangerous. Pool of London. 1951: The Man in the White Suit. Appointment with Venus (US: Island Rescue). 1952: Mother Riley Meets the Vampire (US: Vampire Over London). 1953: The Captain's Paradise. The Broken Horseshoe. Three's Company. 1954: Doctor in the House. The Young Lovers (US: Chance Meeting). Aunt Clara. Lilacs in the Spring (US: Let's Make Up). 1955: Value for Money. 1957: The Naked Truth (US: Your Past is Showing!). 1958: Dracula (US: The Horror of Dracula). 1959: Model for Murder. Left, Right and Centre. 1960: The Pure Hell of St Trinian's. 1963: A Jolly Bad Fellow (US: They All Died Laughing). A Home of Your Own. 1966: The Great St Trinian's Train Robbery. 1968: The Strange Affair. 1971: What Became of Jack and Jill? (US: Romeo and Juliet '71). 1972: The Creeping Flesh.

BENSON, Martin 1918–

Smooth and oily big-time crooks were the province of this dark, menacing British actor, one of the prime villains from British 'Bs' of the 1950s. Often moustachioed, his faintly oriental features got their biggest break on the other side of the Atlantic as the chancellor in Yul Brynner's Siamese court in The King and I. Then it was back to lunging sneers as untrustworthy types of all nations for British films, often with one of the excellent foreign accents which were another Benson speciality.

ners and barking voices — but most memorably as the hotel's resident major in the TV comedy series *Fawlty Towers*.

1930: London Melody. The Chinese Bungalow. 1933: Trouble. 1934: White Ensign. 1936: East Meets West. His Lordship (US: Man of Affaires). 1937: The Last Adventurers. Jenifer Hale. 1938: The Outsider. 1939: The Saint in London. Black Eyes. Dead Men Are Dangerous.

1941: Banana Ridge. 1942: Suspected Person. 1943: Undercover. 1946: Othello. 1948: Under Capricorn. The Blind Goddess. But Not in Vain. 1949: Trapped by the Terror. The Adventures of PC 49. 1951: I'll Get You For This (US: Lucky Nick Cain). Night Without Stars. Assassin for Hire. Mystery Junction. The Dark Light. Judgment Deferred. 1952: The Frightened Man. Wide Boy. Ivanhoe. The Gambler and the Lady. 1953: Top of the Form. Black 13. Always a Bride. Wheel of Fate. Recoil. Escape by Night. You Know What Sailors Are. 1954: Knave of Hearts (US: Lovers, Happy Lovers). West of Zanzibar. The Death of Michael Turbin. 1955: Passage Home. Doctor at Sea. 1956: The King and I. 23 Paces to Baker Street. Soho Incident (US: Spin a Dark Web). 1957: The Man from Tangier. Interpol (US: Pickup Alley). Doctor at Large. The Flesh is Weak. Istanbul. The Strange World of Planet X (US: Cosmic Monsters). 1958: Window's Way. The Two-Headed Spy. 1959: Killers of Kilimanjaro. The Three Worlds of Gulliver. Make Mine a Million. 1960: Exodus. Once More with Feeling. Sands of the Desert. Oscar Wilde. The Pure Hell of St Trinian's. The Gentle Trap. 1961: Five Golden Hours. Gorgo. Village of Daughters. 1962: Captain Clegg (US: Night Creatures). The Silent Invasion. The Fur Collar. The Devil Never Sleeps (US: Satan Never Sleeps). A Matter of WHO. The Secret Door (released 1964). 1963: Cleopatra. Behold a Pale Horse. 1964: A Shot in the Dark. Goldfinger. Mozambique. 1965: The Secret of My Success. 1966: A Man Could Get Killed. 1967: The Magnificent Two. Battle Beneath the Earth. 1972: Pope Joan. 1973: Tiffany Jones. 1974: The Next Victim. 1976: The Omen. The Message/Mohammed, Messenger of God. Jesus of Nazareth (TV). 1978: Meetings with Remarkable Men. 1979: The Human Factor. 1980: The Sea Wolves. Sphinx. 1985: Arch of Triumph (TV). 1991: The Year of the Comet.

BERKELEY, Ballard 1904–1988

Tall, rangy, brown-haired, long-lasting, terribly-British actor with twinkling eyes and thrusting chin, handsome in a rather old-fashioned kind of way. He took up acting in his mid twenties and brought his military bearing to films, in leading roles at first, even before stage experience. Later played affable types and dogged investigative policemen. In more recent times seen as randy old men and elderly soldiers with courtly man-

*The Gang's All Here (US: The Amazing Mr Forrest). 1942: In Which We Serve. The Day Will Dawn (US: The Avengers). 1946: Quiet Weekend. 1947: They Made Me a Fugitive (US: I Became a Criminal). 1949: Third Time Lucky. Stage Fright. 1950: Blackmailed. Mr Drake's Duck. 1951: The Frightened Man. The Long Dark Hall. 1952: Circumstantial Evidence. The Night Won't Talk. The Lost Hours (US: The Big Frame). 1953: The Blue Parrot. Operation Diplomat. The Weak and the Wicked. Three Steps to the Gallows (released 1955. US: White Fire). 1954: Forbidden Cargo. Delayed Action. Dangerous Cargo. Child's Play. The Men of Sherwood Forest. 1955: See How They Run. The Stolen Airliner. 1956: My Teenage Daughter (US: Teenage Bad Girl). Passport to Treason. 1957: Yangtse Incident (US: Battle Hell). After the Ball. *Bullet from the Past. Night of the Demon (US: Curse of the Demon). The Betrayal. Just My Luck. The Man Who Wouldn't Talk. 1958: Chain of Events. Life is a Circus. Further Up the Creek. 1960: Cone of Silence (US: Trouble in the Sky). 1963: Impact. A Matter of Choice. 1965: The Murder Game. The Night Caller. 1968: Star! Hostile Witness. 1970: Concerto per pistole solista (GB: Weekend Murders). 1976: Confessions of a Driving Instructor. 1978: The Playbirds. 1979: Confessions from the David Galaxy Affair. Queen of the Blues. 1980: The Wildcats of St Trinian's. Little Lord Fauntleroy. 1983: Bullshot. 1985: National Lampoon's European Vacation. 1989: The B.F.G. (TV. Voice only).*

BERNSEN, Corbin 1953–

Tall, fair-haired, broad-shouldered, tanned-looking American actor with the smile of a wolf about to devour a lamb. He remained almost unknown to TV and cinema audiences until a growing facility with callow charmers got him cast as the womanising divorce lawyer Arnold Becker in the *LA*

Law TV series. He played some top supporting and minor leading roles in films, but has proved less effective outside his accepted image. Son of actress Jeanne Cooper; married to English-born actress Amanda Pays.

1974: Three the Hard Way. 1976: King Kong. Eat My Dust! 1981: S.O.B. 1987: Mace. Hello Again. 1988: Bert Rigby, You're a Fool. 1989: Disorganized Crime. Major League. Breaking Point (TV). 1991: Shattered. Dead on the Money (TV). 1992: Frozen Assets. Black Creek. Love Can Be Murder (TV). 1993: Appointment for a Killing (TV). Grey Night. The Killing Box. Final Mission. A Brilliant Disguise. 1994: Major League II. Radioland Murders. Temptress. The New Age. 1995: Tales from the Hood. Someone to Die For.

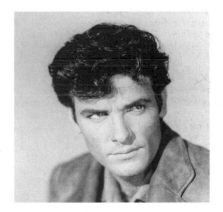

BEST, James 1926–

Tall, taciturn, surly-looking American actor with narrow eyes and a shock of dark, wavy hair. Rangily handsome, he looked the leading man type when Universal-International added him to their rota of rising young stars in 1950. But there was a wildness and unreliability to Best's characters on screen that led to the former male model being confined to colourful, often sulky supporting roles before the studio let him go after four years. Something of a cult favourite, Best continued to crop up over the years, often in westerns as shifty ranchhands: smiles were rare. After a patch of roustabouts and rednecks, Best found a regular niche in his sixties in the TV series *The Dukes of Hazzard*.

1950: *Comanche Territory. Winchester '73. Peggy. Kansas Raiders. Mystery Submarine. 1951: Apache Drums. Target Unknown. Air Cadet (GB: Jet Men of the Air). The Cimarron Kid. 1952: Steel Town. Ma and Pa Kettle at the Fair. Francis Goes to West Point. The Battle at Apache Pass. Flat Top (GB: Eagles of the Fleet). 1953: Seminole. Column South. The President's Lady. City of Bad Men. 1954: The Caine Mutiny. The Raid. They Rode West. Return from the Sea. Riders to the Stars. 1955: Seven Angry Men. Come Next Spring. 1956: Gaby. The Rack. Calling Homicide. When Gangland Strikes. 1957: Last of the Badmen. Hot Summer Night. Man on the Prowl. 1958: The Left-Handed Gun. The Naked and the Dead. Cole Younger, Gunfighter. 1959: Cast a Long Shadow. The Killer Shrews. Ride Lonesome. Verboten! 1960: The Mountain Road. 1963: Black Gold. Shock Corridor. 1964: The Quick Gun. 1965: Shenandoah. Black Spurs. 1966: Three on a Couch. 1967: First to Fight. 1968: Firecreek. 1970: Run, Simon, Run (TV). 1972: Sounder. The Brain Machine. 1974: Savages (TV). 1975: The Runaway Barge (TV). 1976: The Savage Bees (TV. GB: cinemas). Ode to Billy Joe. Nickelodeon. 1977: Rolling Thunder. 1978: Hooper. The End. 1990: B L Stryker: Night Train (TV).

Spanky. The Lady Consents. Down the Stretch. Two in Revolt. 1937: Breezing Home. We Who Are About to Die. The Lady Fights Back. Super Sleuth. You Can't Buy Luck. Meet the Missus. Saturday's Heroes. 1938: Merrily We Live. *Prairie Papas. Youth Takes a Fling. Blondie. Gold is Where You Find It. Spring Madness. Everybody's Doing It. Goodbye Broadway. I'm from the City. Vivacious Lady. 1939: Private Detective. A Miracle on Main Street. The Saint Strikes Back. Mr Moto in Danger Island (GB: Mr Moto on Danger Island). Blackmail. Nancy Drew, Trouble Shooter. At the Circus/Marx Brothers at the Circus. The Covered Trailer. Mr Moto Takes a Vacation. 1940: Blondie on a Budget. I Take This Woman. The Ghost Breakers. Slightly Honorable. Money and the Woman. Who Killed Aunt Maggie? 1941: *West of the Rockies. Road Show. High Sierra. Kisses for Breakfast. The Lady from Cheyenne. Flight from Destiny. Scattergood Baines. The Body Disappears. Highway West. Nothing But the Truth. The Smiling Ghost. 1942: Whispering Ghosts. Juke Girl. A-Haunting We Will Go. Busses Roar. Maisie Gets Her Man (GB: She Got Her Man). The Hidden Hand. Scattergood Survives a Murder. 1943: The Powers Girl (GB: Hi! Beautiful). Cabin in the Sky. Dixie. The Kansan (GB: Wagon Wheels). Thank Your Lucky Stars. Cinderella Swings It. 1944: The Adventures of Mark Twain. The Girl Who Dared. Home in Indiana. Music for Millions. 1945: The Monster and the Ape (serial). Hold That Blonde. Pillow to Post. Red Dragon. 1946: Dangerous Money. The Bride Wore Boots. She Wouldn't Say Yes. The Face of Marble. 1947: Suddenly It's Spring. The Red Stallion. 1948: Smart Woman. Half Past Midnight. The Shanghai Chest. 1949: Jackpot Jitters (GB: Jiggs and Maggie in Jackpot Jitters). *The Hidden Hand. 1950: *High and Dizzy. 1951: South of Caliente.

† As 'Sleep 'n' Eat'.

1950: No Man of Her Own. Union Station. 1951: The First Legion. Dear Brat. 1952: The Greatest Show on Earth. Hurricane Smith. Denver and Rio Grande. 1953: All I Desire. The Vanquished. Forbidden. The Great Sioux Uprising. 1954: Carnival Story. Drums Across the River. Destry. 1955: The Sea Chase. 1956: The Lone Ranger. Explosion (TV. GB: cinemas). Showdown at Abilene. Gunfight at the OK Corral. 1959: Guns of the Timberland. Showdown at Sandoval (TV. GB: cinemas, as Gunfight at Sandoval). 1965: Town Tamer. 1966: Johnny Reno. Nevada Smith. Return of the Gunfighter. The Fastest Guitar Alive. 1968: The Golden Bullet. Impasse. 1970: The Hawaiians (GB: Master of the Islands). 1971: The Seven Minutes.

BEVAN, Billy
(William Bevan Harris) 1887–1957
Few people who watched the fleeting glimpses of this stumpy, cheerful, energetic, moustachioed comic actor in his later career as a small-part player, realised that he had been a leading comedian in Hollywood's silent era. Born in Australia, he arrived in America in 1917 and made his film debut three years later, his diminutive figure quickly moving into star roles in Sennett comedy shorts. With the coming of the 1930s Bevan, his comic star waning, slipped into dozens of 'bit' character roles, typically providing light relief as menials or policemen (an occupation from which his five-feet-two would have barred him in real life) in minor, English-set Hollywood thrillers.

1919: *Salome vs Shenandoah. 1920: *Let 'Er Go. *‡The Quack Doctor. *My Goodness. Love, Honor and Behave. *It's a Boy. *A Fireside Brewer. 1921: *Love and Doughnuts. *Be Reasonable. *By Heck. *A Stray from the Steerage. A Small Town Idol. 1922: *Home-Made Movies. *Gymnasium Jim. *The Duck Hunter. *Oh Daddy. *On Patrol. *Ma and Pa. *When Summer Comes. The Crossroads of New York. 1923: The Extra Girl. *Nip and Tuck. *Inbad the Sailor. 1924: The White Sin. *Wandering Waistlines. *Wall Street Blues. *Lizzies of the Field. *The Cannon Ball Express. *Little Robinson Corkscrew. *One Spooky Night. 1925: *Honeymoon Hardships. *The Lion's Whiskers. *Skinners in Silk. *The Iron Nag. *Butter Fingers. *From Rags to Britches. *Giddap. *Super-Hooper-Dyne Lizzies.

BEST, Willie 1913–1962
Stocky, stoop-shouldered, open-mouthed, rather downcast-looking American performer who became the epitome of the 'Yas, massa' black servant who panicked at the slightest provocation. The image was much castigated in later years but Best, who was initially billed as 'Sleep 'n' Eat', after a character he played, milked it to great effect, especially in comic chillers, where his drooping lower lip quivered in fright at the swish of a curtain. Busy in television after his film career until he became terminally ill with the cancer that killed him at 48.

1930: †Feet First. †Skyline. †Up Pops the Devil. 1932: †The Monster Walks (GB: The Monster Walked). 1934: †Little Miss Marker (GB: Girl in Pawn). †Kentucky Kernels (GB: Triple Trouble). †David Harum. †West of the Pecos. 1935: †Murder on a Honeymoon. The Nitwits. Jalna. Annie Oakley. The Arizonian. The Littlest Rebel. Hot Tip. 1936: The Green Pastures. Murder on a Bridle Path. The Bride Walks Out. Mummy's Boys. Racing Lady. Make Way for a Lady. Thank You, Jeeves. General

BETTGER, Lyle 1915–
Fair-haired actor whose slightly sinister charm won him some good post-war roles on Broadway. On moving into films in 1950, his crooked smile, shifty eyes and husky voice qualified him for a whole range of treacherous villains. In the fifties he went into TV, and sixties film roles proved to be only pale echoes of his meatier parts at Paramount and Universal.

*Sneezing Beezers. *Over There-Abouts. 1926: *Circus Today. *Whispering Whiskers. *Ice Cold Cocos. *Trimmed in Gold. *Wandering Willies. *Fight Night. *Hayfoot, Strawfoot. *Muscle Bound Music. *A Sea Dog's Tale. *Masked Mamas. *Hubby's Quiet Little Game. *Hoboken to Hollywood. *The Divorce Dodger. *Flirty Four-Flushers. 1927: *Peaches and Plumbers. *Should Sleep-walkers Marry? *Easy Pickings. *Gold Digger of Weepah. *The Bull Fighter. *Cured in the Excitement. *The Golf Nut. A Small Town Princess. 1928: Motorboat Mamas. *Motoring Mamas. *Blindfold. *The Best Man. *The Bicycle Flirt. *His Unlucky Night. *Caught in the Kitchen. *Hubby's Latest Alibi. *The Lion's Roar. *The Beach Club. Riley the Cop. *His New Steno. *Hubby's Week-End Trip. 1929: High Voltage. *Foolish Husbands. *Pink Pajamas. *Calling Hubby's Bluff. *Button My Back. *Don't Get Jealous. The Sky Hawks. *The Trespasser. 1930: *Scotch. Journey's End. For the Love o' Lil (GB: For the Love of Lil). Temptation (GB: So Like a Woman). Peacock Alley. For the Defense. Monte Carlo. 1931: Born to Love. Transatlantic. *Ashore from the Steerage. *Bungalow Troubles. 1932: Sky Devils. Me and My Gal (GB: Pier 13). The Silent Witness. Payment Deferred. Vanity Fair. *Honeymoon Beach. *Spot on the Rug. 1933: Looking Forward (GB: Service). *The Big Squeal. Alice in Wonderland. Cavalcade. Luxury Liner. *Uncle Jake. A Study in Scarlet. Midnight Club. Too Much Harmony. The Way to Love. Peg o' My Heart. 1934: Bulldog Drummond Strikes Back. The Lost Patrol. Shock. One More River (GB: Over the River). Caravan. Limehouse Blues. 1935: Black Sheep. A Tale of Two Cities. The Last Outpost. Mystery Woman. Widow from Monte Carlo. 1936: Mr Deeds Goes to Town. The Song and Dance Man. Lloyds of London. Dracula's Daughter. Piccadilly Jim. Private Number (GB: Secret Interlude). God's Country and the Woman. 1937: Slave Ship. Another Dawn. Personal Property (GB: The Man in Possession). The Sheik Steps Out. The Wrong Road. Riding on Air. 1938: Arrest Bulldog Drummond. The Girl of the Golden West. The Young in Heart. Mysterious Mr Moto. Shadows over Shanghai. Blonde Cheat. A Christmas Carol. Bringing Up Baby. 1939: Pack Up Your Troubles (GB: We're in the Army Now). Captain Fury. We Are Not Alone. Let Freedom Ring. Grand Jury Secrets. 1940: The Invisible Man Returns. The Earl of Chicago. The Long Voyage Home. Tin Pan Alley. 1941: One Night in Lisbon. Shining Victory. Dr Jekyll and Mr Hyde. Confirm or Deny. Suspicion. Scotland Yard. Penny Serenade. 1942: This Above All. I Married a Witch. Mrs Miniver. The Man Who Wouldn't Die. Counter Espionage. London Blackout Murders (GB: Secret Motive). 1943: Young and Willing. Holy Matrimony. Forever and a Day. The Return of the Vampire. Jane Eyre. Appointment in Berlin. 1944: Once Upon a Time. The Pearl of Death. The Lodger. National Velvet. The Invisible Man's Revenge. South of Dixie. Tonight and Every Night. 1945: The Picture of Dorian Gray. Hangover Square. The Woman in Green. 1946: Devotion (completed 1943). Cluny Brown. Terror by Night. 1947: Moss Rose. The Swordsman. It Had to Be You. Love from a Stranger (GB: A Stranger Walked In). 1948: The Black Arrow. Let's Live a Little.

1949: The Secret Garden. The Secret of St Ives. Tell It to the Judge. That Forsyte Woman (GB: The Forsyte Saga). 1950: Rogues of Sherwood Forest. The Fortunes of Captain Blood.

† And co-directed

BEVANS, Clem
(C. Blevins) 1879–1963

Gaunt, massively white-bearded (often disguising a surprisingly small chin), beak-nosed and beady-eyed, Bevans, jaws moving up and down from his side-walk rockingchair as he surveyed the newest arrival in town, was one of the most recognizable old-timers in Hollywood films—mostly westerns. 'Discovered' for films at 56, Bevans still managed to creak his grasshopper frame through close to 100 of them before retiring at 77.

1935: Way Down East. 1936: Rhythm on the Range. Come and Get It. The Phantom Rider (serial). 1937: Dangerous Number. Topper. Toast of New York. Idol of the Crowds. Riding on Air. The Big City. 1938: Mr Chump. Of Human Hearts. Valley of the Giants. Young Fugitives. Comet over Broadway. Tom Sawyer, Detective. *Miracle Money. Hold That Co-Ed (GB: Hold That Girl). Boy Meets Girl. 1939: Ambush. Maisie. Zenobia (GB: Elephants Never Forget). *Help Wanted. Hell's Kitchen. Idiot's Delight. Night Work. Outside These Walls. Thunder Afloat. Main Street Lawyer (GB: Small Town Lawyer). Yes, My Darling Daughter. Undercover Doctor. They Made Me a Criminal. Dodge City. Stand Up and Fight. Cowboy Quarterback. The Kid from Kokomo (GB: Orphan of the Ring). King of the Underworld. The Oklahoma Kid. Young Tom Edison. 1940: Abe Lincoln in Illinois. (GB: Spirit of the People). Gold Rush Maisie. Twenty-Mule Team. Go West/The Marx Brothers Go West. The Captain is a Lady. Untamed. The Girl from God's Country. Calling All Husbands. Granny Get Your Gun. Half a Sinner. 1941: Midnight Angel. Sergeant York. Pacific Blackout. She Couldn't Say No. Texas. The Parson of Panamint. The Smiling Ghost. Wyoming (GB: Bad Man of Wyoming). 1942: Saboteur. Tombstone the Town Too Tough to Die. The Forest Rangers. This Gun for Hire. Captains of the Clouds. Mrs Wiggs of the Cabbage Patch. Lucky Jordan. 1943: The Human Comedy. Lady Bodyguard. The Kansan (GB: Wagon Wheels). Happy Go Lucky. The Woman of the Town. 1944: Night Club Girl. Tall in the Saddle. 1945: Grissly's Millions. Captain Eddie. 1946:

The Yearling. Gallant Bess. Wake Up and Dream. 1947: Yankee Fakir. The Millerson Case. Mourning Becomes Electra. 1948: Texas, Brooklyn and Heaven (GB: The Girl from Texas). Portrait of Jennie (GB: Jennie). The Paleface. Moonrise. Relentless. Highway 13. 1949: Loaded Pistols. Big Jack. Streets of Laredo. Rim of the Canyon. Deputy Marshal. The Gal Who Took the West. Tell It to the Judge. 1950: Joe Palooka Meets Humphrey. Harvey. 1951: Gold Raiders (GB: Stooges Go West). Silver City Bonanza. Man in the Saddle (GB: The Outcast). 1952: Wait 'Til the Sun Shines, Nellie. Captive of Billy the Kid. Hangman's Knot. 1953: The Stranger Wore a Gun. 1954: The Boy from Oklahoma. Hurricane at Pilgrim Hill. 1955: Ten Wanted Men. The Twinkle in God's Eye. The Kentuckian. 1956: Davy Crockett and the River Pirates.

BIBERMAN, Abner 1909–1977

Slit-eyed, Polynesian-looking, chunky American actor with dark hair, quizzical eyebrows and set expression. Originally a journalist, he turned to acting in the 1930s, coming to Hollywood in 1939 and soon qualifying for all kinds of foreign menaces. In the 1950s he doubled up as a drama coach at Universal-International (as it then was), the studio that gave him the chance to direct films in 1955, after which he gave up acting. From the end of that decade, Biberman worked solidly in TV, directing episodes of drama series.

1936: Soak the Rich. 1939: The Rains Came. The Magnificent Fraud. Gunga Din. Each Dawn I Die. Panama Patrol. Another Thin Man. The Roaring Twenties. Lady of the Tropics. Panama Lady. Balalaika. 1940: Zanzibar. Ski Patrol. South of Pago-Pago. His Girl Friday. Golden Gloves. The Girl from Havana. Enemy Agent. South to Karanga. 1941: Singapore Woman. South of Tahiti (GB: White Savage). The Monster and the Girl. This Woman is Mine. The Gay Vagabond. The Devil Pays Off. 1942: Beyond the Blue Horizon. Broadway. Whispering Ghosts. Little Tokyo USA (GB: East of Chinatown). King of the Mounties (Serial). 1943: The Leopard Man. Submarine Alert. Behind the Rising Sun. Bombardier. 1944: Dragon Seed. The Bridge of San Luis Rey. The Keys of the Kingdom. Two-Man Submarine. 1945: Back to Bataan. Captain Kidd. Betrayal from the East. Salome, Where She Danced.

1946: *Strange Conquest.* 1950: *Winchester 73.* 1951: *Roaring City.* 1952: *Viva Zapata!* 1954: *Elephant Walk. Knock on Wood. The Golden Mistress.*

As director:
1954: *The Golden Mistress (as Joel Judge).* 1955: *The Looters. Running Wild.* 1956: *The Price of Fear. Behind the High Wall.* 1957: *Gun for a Coward. The Night Runner. Flood Tide (GB: Above All Things).* 1968: †*Hawaii Five-O: Once Upon a Time (TV).* † *Too Many Thieves (TV. GB: cinemas).*

† Co-directed

BIKEL, Theodore 1924–
Swarthy, black-haired, heavy-set, Austrian-born actor and entertainer, a beefier version of Topol. He fled to Palestine before World War II and moved to England in post-war times; where he began his film career, mainly as sweaty, threatening foreigners. Later he could be found in Hollywood, playing characters of more kindly dispositions. Also sings, plays guitar and is keenly interested in (New York) politics. He was nominated for an Oscar as the sheriff in the *The Defiant Ones.*

1951: *The African Queen.* 1952: *Moulin Rouge.* 1953: *Never Let Me Go. Melba. Desperate Moment. A Day to Remember.* 1954: *The Colditz Story. The Love Lottery. The Kidnappers (US: The Little Kidnappers). The Young Lovers (US: Chance Meeting). The Divided Heart. Forbidden Cargo.* 1955: *Above Us the Waves. Flight from Vienna.* 1956: *The Pride and the Passion.* 1957: *The Vintage. The Enemy Below.* 1958: *Word from a Sealed-Off Box (TV). Fraulein. I Want to Live! I Bury the Living. The Defiant Ones.* 1959: *The Blue Angel. A Woman Obsessed. The Angry Hills.* 1960: *A Dog of Flanders.* 1964: *My Fair Lady.* 1965: *Sands of the Kalahari. Who Has Seen the Wind?* 1966: *Mas allá de las montañas. The Russians Are Coming, the Russians Are Coming. The Last Chapter (narrator only).* 1967: *Festival.* 1968: *Sweet November. The Desperate Ones. My Side of the Mountain.* 1970: *Flap (GB: The Last Warrior). Darker than Amber.* 1971: *200 Motels. The Little Ark.* 1972: *Killer by Night (TV).* 1975: *Murder on Flight 502 (TV).* 1976: *Victory at Entebbe (TV. GB: cinemas).* 1978: *Loose Change (TV).* 1984: *Prince*

Jack. 1986: *Very Close Quarters.* 1987: *Dark Tower.* 1988: *See You in the Morning. A Stoning in Fulham County (TV).* 1989: *The Final Days (TV). Christine Cromwell: Things That Go Bump in the Night (TV).* 1991: *Shattered.* 1992: *The Association Game/Red Target/Crisis in the Kremlin.* 1993: *Crime and Punishment. My Family Treasure. Benefit of the Doubt.*

BING, Herman 1889–1947
Bulky, pigeon-cheeked, pursed-lipped, red-nosed German actor with pale, round eyes and unruly curly hair. He came to Hollywood in the 1920s as assistant to the director FW Murnau, but soon became a comedy character relief in dozens of (especially light) films, typically as an easily flustered Viennese shopkeeper or official who minced words in more senses than one. He found work extremely hard to get in wartime, and shot himself at 57.

1927: *Sunrise – A Song of Two Humans (GB: Sunrise).* 1929: *A Song of Kentucky. Married in Hollywood.* 1930: *Menschen hinter Gettern. Anna Christie (German-language version only). Show Girl in Hollywood. The Three Sisters.* 1931: *The Great Lover. The Guardsman. Women Love Once.* 1932: *Westward Passage. The Crash. Three on a Match. Blessed Event. Big City Blues. Murders in the Rue Morgue. The Tenderfoot. Jewel Robbery. Hypnotized. Silver Dollar. Unashamed. Flesh.* 1933: *After Tonight. The Nuisance (GB: Accidents Wanted).* *Fits in a Fiddle.* *The Plumber and the Lady. Lady Killer. Chance at Heaven. The Bowery. Dinner at Eight. My Lips Betray. The Great Jasper. Blood Money. College Coach (GB: Football Coach). Footlight Parade.* 1934: *The Hide-Out. The Black Cat (GB: The House of Doom). Mandalay. Melody in Spring. The Merry Widow. Evelyn Prentice. Manhattan Melodrama. I Sell Anything. One Night of Love. The Cat's Paw. Broadway Bill (GB: Strictly Confidential). Manhattan Love Song. I'll Tell the World. The Mighty Barnum. Embarrassing Moments. Twentieth Century. Love Time. Crimson Romance. The Cat and the Fiddle. When Strangers Meet.* 1935: *Barbary Coast. Vagabond Lady.* *Stage Frights. It Happened in New York. The Great Hotel Murder. Call of the Wild. Redheads on Parade. The Florentine Dagger. Don't Bet on Blondes. Calm Yourself. In Caliente. Three Kids and a Queen (GB: The*

Baxter Millions). Every Night at Eight. His Family Tree. Fighting Youth. $1,000 a Minute. The Night is Young. Hands Across the Table. Thunder in the Night. *The Misses Stooge.* 1936: *Laughing Irish Eyes. Rose Marie. Three Wise Guys.* *Slide, Nelly, Slide! Human Cargo. Dimples. The Great Ziegfeld. The King Steps Out. Adventure in Manhattan (GB: Manhattan Madness). That Girl from Paris. The Music Goes Round. Tango. Come Closer, Folks. The Champagne Waltz.* 1937: *Oh What a Knight. Maytime. Beg, Borrow or Steal.* 1938: *Every Day's a Holiday. Paradise for Three. Vacation from Love. The Great Waltz. Sweethearts. Bluebeard's Eighth Wife. Four's a Crowd.* 1940: *Broadway Melody of 1940. Public Deb No. 1. Bitter Sweet.* 1941: *Dumbo (voice only).* 1942: *The Devil with Hitler.* 1943: *Passport to Heaven.* 1945: *Where Do We Go from Here?* 1946: *Rendezvous 24. Night and Day.* 1947: *Song of Love.*

BINNS, Edward 1916–1990
Everything about this impassive, thin-lipped, light-haired, reliable-looking American actor was square. His build, his shoulders, his face, even his characters. You could rely on a man played by Binns, even if he looked slightly worried most of the time and worn at the edges. At the same time, he could vanish in the crowd, like the policeman on your trail – which he frequently was. In films, he had decent roles, but would often be the first one on the cast not mentioned on the posters. Who now remembers him from among the *12 Angry Men?* TV gave him his finest hour, inevitably as a cop, as the star of the series *Brenner,* which ran on and off from 1959 to 1964. He stayed around to the end, though you might not have noticed: Mr Cellophane, that's him.

1951: *Teresa.* 1952: *Without Warning.* 1953: *Vice Squad (GB: The Girl in Room 17).* 1956: *The Scarlet Hour. Beyond a Reasonable Doubt.* 1957: *12 Angry Men. Portland Exposé. Young and Dangerous.* 1959: *North by Northwest. Compulsion. Man in the Net. Curse of the Undead.* 1960: *Desire in the Dust. Heller in Pink Tights.* 1961: *Judgment at Nuremberg.* 1962: *A Public Affair. Hemingway's Adventures of a Young Man (GB: Adventures of a Young Man).* 1964: *The Americanization of Emily. Fail Safe.* 1966: *The Plainsman.* 1967: *Chubasco.* 1969: *Patton (GB: Patton – Lust for Glory).* 1971: *The Sheriff (TV).* 1972:*

*Fireball Forward (TV). 1973: Hunter (TV).
Lovin' Molly. 1975: Night Moves. 1976: Just
an Old Sweet Song (TV). 1978: Oliver's Story.
1979: The Power Within (TV). The Pilot.
1980: The Murder That Wouldn't Die (TV).
FDR – The Last Year (TV). 1982: The Verdict.
1987: Before God. 1989: After School.*

BIRCH, Paul 1908–1969

Craggy, fair-haired American actor, a sort
of strait-laced version of Jay C Flippen (*qv*).
Almost entirely a Broadway actor until the
1950s, he was kept in routine rugged character roles when he did go to Hollywood –
sheriffs, attorneys and the like – apart from
two fine performances much treasured by
fantasy film fans in the leading roles of *The
Beast with 1,000,000 Eyes* and *Not of This
Earth*, both from the Roger Corman stable.

*1946: Till the End of Time. 1952: Assignment
– Paris! The War of the Worlds. 1953: Ride
Clear of Diablo. 1954: Silver Lode. 1955:
Apache Woman. Five Guns West. Man Without
a Star. The Fighting Chance. Rebel Without a
Cause. Strange Lady in Town. 1956: The
Fastest Gun Alive. The Beast with 1,000,000
Eyes. When Gangland Strikes. The White
Squaw. Everything But the Truth. Not of This
Earth. The Day the World Ended. 1957: Gun
for a Coward. The 27th Day. Joe Dakota. The
Tattered Dress. The Spirit of St Louis. 1958:
The World Was His Jury. Queen of Outer
Space. Gunman's Walk. Wild Heritage. The
Gun Runners. 1959: Gunmen from Laredo.
1960: Too Soon to Love. The Dark at the Top
of the Stairs. Pay or Die! Portrait in Black.
1961: Two Rode Together. 1962: A Public
Affair. The Man Who Shot Liberty Valance.
1963: It's a Mad, Mad, Mad, Mad World. The
Raiders. 1966: Welcome to Hard Times (GB:
Killer on a Horse). A Covenant with Death.*

BIRD, Norman 1920–

Light-haired, doleful-looking, slightly
baggy-eyed British actor with man-in-the-
street air, usually sporting a toothbrush
moustache. Refers to himself as 'the man
with the cardigan' and has played numerous
henpecked, inadequate, interfering or tenta-
tively friendly little men or petty officials.
Busiest in films in the 1960s.

*1954: An Inspector Calls. 1959: The League of
Gentlemen. The Angry Silence. 1961: The Man
in the Moon. Very Important Person (US: A
Coming-Out Party). The Secret Partner.
Whistle down the Wind. Victim. Cash on
Demand. 1962: Night of the Eagle (US: Burn
Witch Burn). Term of Trial. In Search of the
Castaways. Maniac. The Punch and Judy Man.
1963: The Mind Benders. Bitter Harvest.
80,000 Suspects. Hot Enough
for June (US: Agent 8¾). 1964: The Bargee.
First Men in the Moon. The Beauty Jungle
(US: Contest Girl). The Black Torment. 1965:
The Hill. Sky West and Crooked (US: Gypsy
Girl). 1966: The Wrong Box. 1968: A Dandy
in Aspic. The Limbo Line. 1969: Run a Crooked
Mile (TV). All at Sea. 1970: The Rise and Rise
of Michael Rimmer. The Virgin and the Gypsy.
The Raging Moon (US: Long Ago Tomorrow)
1971: Hands of the Ripper. Please Sir! 1972:
Young Winston. Doomwatch. Ooh...You Are
Awful (US: Get Charlie Tully). 1976: The
Slipper and the Rose. The Chiffy Kids (series).
Chimpmates (1st series). 1978: The Medusa
Touch. The Lord of the Rings (voice only).
1981: The Final Conflict (later Omen III The
Final Conflict). 1984: Black Carrion (TV. US:
cinemas). 1993: Shadowlands.*

BISSELL, Whit(ner) 1919–

Fair-haired, pear-faced, inquisitive-looking
American actor who rarely played sympathetic characters, but rather those whose
ostensible interest in the community cloaked
self-enriching schemes. His do-gooders
were no-gooders, his solid citizens usually
revealed a yellow streak and sometimes he

was just the weak victim of his oppressors.
On stage as a child, he briefly started a
Hollywood career before war service intervened. Had one leading role, as a mad
professor in *I Was a Teenage Frankenstein*.

*1942: Ten Gentlemen from West Point. 1943:
Holy Matrimony. Destination Tokyo. 1946: It
Shouldn't Happen to a Dog. Cluny Brown.
Somewhere in the Night. 1947: Gentleman's
Agreement. The Sea of Grass. Night Song.
Brute Force. The Senator Was Indiscreet (GB:
Mr Ashton Was Indiscreet). 1948: A Double
Life. Another Part of the Forest. Canon City.
He Walked by Night. Raw Deal. That Lady in
Ermine. Chicken Every Sunday. 1949: Side
Street. Anna Lucasta. Crime Doctor's Diary.
Tokyo Joe. 1950: Perfect Strangers (GB: Too
Dangerous to Love). When Willie Comes March-
ing Home. The Killer That Stalked New York
(GB: The Frightened City). Convicted. For
Heaven's Sake. Wyoming Mail. The Great
Missouri Raid. A Life of Her Own. 1951: Red
Mountain. The Family Secret. The Sellout.
Night into Morning. Sealed Cargo. The Red
Badge of Courage. Tales of Robin Hood. The
Lost Continent. Boots Malone. 1952: Hoodlum
Empire. The Turning Point. Skirts Ahoy! 1953:
Devil's Canyon. It Should Happen to You.
1954: The Shanghai Story. The Caine Mutiny.
The Cowboy (voice only). Riot in Cell Block 11.
Three Hours to Kill. Target Earth. The Atomic
Kid. The Creature from the Black Lagoon. The
Big Combo. 1955: The Desperate Hours. Not
As a Stranger. The Naked Street. Shack Out on
101. At Gunpoint! (GB: Gunpoint!). 1956:
Miracle on 34th Street (TV. GB: cinemas).
Invasion of the Body Snatchers. The Proud
Ones. Dakota Incident. The Man from Del Rio.
Gunfight at the OK Corral. 1957: The Young
Stranger. Johnny Tremain. I Was a Teen-
age Werewolf. The Wayward Girl. The Tall
Stranger. I Was a Teenage Frankenstein (GB:
Teenage Frankenstein). 1958: Monster on the
Campus. The Defiant Ones. Gang War. No
Name on the Bullet. 1959: The Black Orchid.
Warlock. Never So Few. Beloved Infidel. 1960:
The Time Machine. The Magnificent Seven.
1961: Bird Man of Alcatraz. One Third of
a Man. 1962: The Manchurian Candidate.
Hemingway's Adventures of a Young Man (GB:
Adventures of a Young Man). The Final Hour
(TV. GB: cinemas). Trauma. 1963: Advance to
the Rear (GB: Company of Cowards). Spencer's
Mountain. Hud. 1964: Seven Days in May.
Where Love Has Gone. 1965: Fluffy. The
Hallelujah Trail. 1966: A Covenant with
Death. 1968: Five Card Stud. 1969: ...
And Sudden Death. Airport. Once You Kiss a
Stranger. 1970: City Beneath the Sea (TV.
GB: cinemas, as One Hour to Doomsday). 1971:
A Tattered Web (TV). In Broad Daylight (TV).
1972: The Salzburg Connection. Pete 'n' Tillie.
1973: Soylent Green. Cry Rape! (TV). 1974:
The FBI vs Alvin Karpis, Public Enemy No.
One. (TV). 1975: Nick and Nora (TV). Psychic
Killer. 1976: Flood! (TV. GB: cinemas). 1977:
The Lincoln Conspiracy. Last of the Mohicans
(TV). The Incredible Rocky Mountain Race
(TV). Casey's Shadow. 1978: Donner Pass:
The Road to Survival (TV). The Time Machine
(TV. And cinema version). 1979: Night Rider
(TV). Strangers: The Story of a Mother and
Daughter (TV). 1981: Nine to Five.*

BLACKMER, Sidney 1894–1973

Suave, elegant American actor, good at upper-class sneers and often seen as society crooks with a weakness for women. Began his career in Pearl White serials, then didn't film again for 12 years. He was married to actresses Lenore Ulric (from 1928 to 1939) and Suzanne Kaaren (from 1942 to 1973), both of whom had successful minor careers. Died from cancer.

1914: The Perils of Pauline (serial). 1915: The Romance of Elaine (serial). 1927: Million Dollar Mystery (serial). 1929: A Most Immoral Lady. 1930: The Love Racket (GB: Such Things Happen). Strictly Modern. The Bad Man. Kismet. Little Caesar. Mothers Cry. Sweethearts and Wives. 1931: Woman Hungry (GB: The Challenge). It's a Wise Child. The Lady Who Dared. One Heavenly Night. Daybreak. Once a Sinner. 1933: The Cocktail Hour. The Wrecker. From Hell to Heaven. The Deluge. 1934: Goodbye Love. Transatlantic Merry-Go-Round. This Man is Mine. The Count of Monte Cristo. Down to Their Last Yacht (GB: Hawaiian Nights). 1935: The Great God Gold. The President Vanishes (GB: Strange Conspiracy). A Notorious Gentleman. The Little Colonel. Behind the Green Lights. Streamline Express. Smart Girl. False Pretenses. The Girl Who Came Back. Forced Landing. Fire Trap. 1936: The Florida Special. Missing Girls. The President's Mystery (GB: One for All). Heart of the West. Early to Bed. Woman Trap. 1937: Shadows of the Orient. House of Secrets. A Doctor's Diary. This is My Affair (GB: His Affair). Thank You Mr Moto. Women Men Marry. Girl Overboard. Michael O'Halloran. The Last Gangster. Charlie Chan at Monte Carlo. Wife, Doctor and Nurse. Heidi. John Meade's Woman. 1938: In Old Chicago. Straight, Place and Show (GB: They're Off). Sharpshooters. Speed to Burn. Suez. Orphans of the Storm. Trade Winds. While New York Sleeps. 1939: The Convict's Code. Fast and Loose. It's a Wonderful World. Unmarried (GB: Night Club Hostess). Law of the Pampas. Hotel for Women/Elsa Maxwell's Hotel for Women. Within the Law. Trapped in the Sky. 1940: Maryland. I Want a Divorce. Framed. Third Finger, Left Hand. Dance, Girl, Dance. 1941: Cheers for Miss Bishop. Rookies on Parade. The Great Swindle. Love Crazy. Obliging Young Lady. Ellery Queen and the Perfect Crime (GB: The Perfect Crime). Angels with Broken Wings. Murder Among Friends. Down Mexico Way.

The Feminine Touch. The Officer and the Lady. 1942: Always in My Heart. Nazi Agent. Gallant Lady. Quiet Please Murder. The Panther's Claw. The Sabotage Squad. 1943: I Escaped from the Gestapo (GB: No Escape). Murder in Times Square. In Old Oklahoma (later and GB: War of the Wildcats). 1944: Buffalo Bill. Broadway Rhythm. The Lady and the Monster (GB: The Lady and the Doctor). Wilson. 1946: Duel in the Sun. 1948: My Girl Tisa. A Song is Born (narrator only). 1949: The Hero (narrator only). 1950: Farewell to Yesterday (narrator only). 1951: People Will Talk. Saturday's Hero (GB: Idols in the Dust). 1952: Washington Story (GB: Target for Scandal). The San Francisco Story. 1954: Johnny Dark. The High and the Mighty. 1955: The View from Pompey's Head (GB: Secret Interlude). 1956: High Society. Beyond a Reasonable Doubt. Accused of Murder. 1957: Tammy and the Bachelor (GB: Tammy). 1959: Stampede at Bitter Creek (TV. GB: cinemas). 1965: Joy in the Morning. How to Murder Your Wife. 1966: A Covenant with Death. 1968: Rosemary's Baby. 1970: Do You Take This Stranger? (TV). 1971: Revenge is My Destiny (TV).

BLADES, Rubén 1944–

Stocky, chubby-cheeked, small-nosed, moustachioed Panamanian singer and composer who used his status in salsa music to star in a couple of films vaguely about his own career, then surprised Hollywood by staying on to become a useful character player in pugnacious roles. Now best known to international audiences as one of the few contemporary players whose familiar faces are tantalisingly difficult to add the name to. Ran for the presidency of Panama in 1994.

1983: The Last Fight. 1985: Crossover Dreams. The Return of Rubén Blades. 1987: Fatal Beauty. Critical Condition. 1988: Homeboy. The Milagro Beanfield War. *The Heart of the Deal. Dead Man Walking (TV. US: Dead Man Out). 1989: Disorganized Crime. The Lemon Sisters. 1990: Mo' Better Blues. The Two Jakes. 1991: Predator 2. The Josephine Baker Story (TV). Crazy from the Heart (TV). 1994: The Color of Night. A Million to Juan (GB: TV, as A Million to One).

BLAKELY, Colin 1930–1987

Talented, aggressive British leading character actor with set expression and tightly

curled dark hair. Equally adept at harassed fathers, loyal friends, ruthless gangsters or professional men, he seemed to have a go at almost everything at one time or another. Born in Northern Ireland, Blakely did not make his debut on stage until he was 27; but his abrasive approach soon made him a leading figure in the London theatre world and, despite a number of sterling film performances, he remained best known in that medium. Died from leukemia.

1960: Saturday Night and Sunday Morning. 1961: The Hellions. 1962: The Password is Courage. 1963: This Sporting Life. The Informers. Never Put It in Writing. The Long Ships. 1965: The Legend of Young Dick Turpin. 1966: The Spy with a Cold Nose. A Man for All Seasons. 1967: Charlie Bubbles. The Day the Fish Came Out. 1968: Decline and Fall . . . of a Birdwatcher! The Vengeance of She. 1969: Alfred the Great. 1970: The Private Life of Sherlock Holmes. 1971: Something to Hide. 1972: Young Winston. 1973: The National Health. 1974: Love Among the Ruins (TV). Murder on the Orient Express. Galileo. 1976: The Pink Panther Strikes Again. It Shouldn't Happen to a Vet. 1977: Equus. 1978: The Big Sleep. 1979: Nijinsky. Meetings with Remarkable Men. 1980: The Dogs of War. Little Lord Fauntleroy (TV. GB: cinema). Loophole. 1981: The Day Christ Died (TV). Evil Under the Sun. 1982: Don Camillo. Trail of the Pink Panther. 1983: Red Monarch (TV).

BLANDICK, Clara 1880–1962

Dark-haired, flat-faced, small-mouthed American actress who was often stern and disapproving but will be remembered as that homeliest of guardians – Dorothy's Auntie Em in *The Wizard of Oz*. She was born aboard an American ship anchored in Hong Kong harbour. In her twenties and thirties, she established herself as a Broadway actress, making a few film appearances until sound came along. She retired in 1950, subsequently committing suicide 12 years later.

1908: *When Knights Were Bold. 1911: *The Maid's Double. 1914: *Mrs Black is Back. 1916: The Stolen Triumph. 1929: *Poor Aubrey. Men Are Like That. 1930: Sins of the Children (GB: The Richest Man in the World). Wise Girls. The Girl Said No. Burning Up. Romance. Last of the Duanes. Tom Sawyer.

*1931: Inspiration. Once a Sinner. The Easiest Way. It's a Wise Child. Laughing Sinners. Dance, Fools, Dance. Drums of Jeopardy. Daybreak. I Take This Woman. The New Adventures of Get-Rich-Quick Wallingford. Possessed. Bought. Murder at Midnight. Huckleberry Finn. 1932: The Strange Case of Clara Deane. Shopworn. The Wet Parade. Two Against the World. Life Begins (GB: The Dawn of Life). The Expert. Rockabye. Three on a Match. The Bitter Tea of General Yen. 1933: The Mind Reader. Child of Manhattan. Three-Cornered Moon. One Sunday Afternoon. Turn Back the Clock. Ever in My Heart. Charlie Chan's Greatest Case. 1934: Harold Teen (GB: The Dancing Fool). Broadway Bill (GB: Strictly Confidential). The Show-Off. The Girl from Missouri (GB: 100 Per Cent Pure). Jealousy. As the Earth Turns. Beloved. Sisters Under the Skin. Fugitive Lady. 1935: The President Vanishes (GB: Strange Conspiracy). The Winning Ticket. Princess O'Hara. Straight from the Heart. Party Wire. Transient Lady (GB: False Witness). 1936: Fury. Anthony Adverse. The Trail of the Lonesome Pine. The Case of the Velvet Claws. Hearts Divided. In His Steps. The Gorgeous Hussy. Make Way for a Lady. 1937: Wings Over Honolulu. Small Town Boy. A Star is Born. The Road Back/Return of the Hero. The League of Frightened Men. Her Husband's Secretary. You Can't Have Everything. 1938: My Old Kentucky Home. Swing, Sister, Swing. Professor, Beware! Tom Sawyer, Detective. Crime Ring. I Was a Criminal. 1939: The Adventures of Huckleberry Finn. Drums Along the Mohawk. Swanee River. The Wizard of Oz. The Star Maker. 1940: Youth Will Be Served. *Alice in Movieland. Tomboy. Anne of Windy Poplars (GB: Anne of Windy Willows). Dreaming Out Loud. Northwest Mounted Police. 1941: The Wagons Roll at Night. Enemy Within. The Big Store. Private Nurse. One Foot in Heaven. It Started with Eve. The Nurse's Secret. 1942: Lady in a Jam. Rings on Her Fingers. Gentleman Jim. 1943: Heaven Can Wait. Du Barry Was a Lady. Dixie. 1944: Shadow of Suspicion. Can't Help Singing. 1945: Frontier Gal. People Are Funny. Pillow of Death. 1946: So Goes My Love (GB: A Genius in the Family). She-Wolf of London (GB: The Curse of the Allenbys). Claudia and David. A Stolen Life. 1947: Philo Vance Returns. Life with Father. 1948: The Bride Goes Wild. 1949: Mr Soft Touch (GB: House of Settlement). 1950: Love That Brute. Key to the City.*

BLORE, Eric 1887–1959

Inimitable, unctuous, balding actor-comedian who would have made an ideal Uriah Heep but, after going to Hollywood in the 1920s from his native Britain, settled down to performing invaluable service in the Astaire-Rogers musicals and, later, in the Lone Wolf movies. Probably the cinema's best-known butler (no-one excelled him at the pained look) and capable of giving as good as he got in the wisecrack stakes. Died from a heart attack.

*1920: *A Night Out and a Day In. 1926: The Great Gatsby. 1930: Laughter. My Sin. 1931: Tarnished Lady. 1933: Flying Down to Rio. 1934: The Gay Divorcee (GB: The Gay Divorce). Limehouse Blues. 1935: Behold My Wife. Folies Bergère (GB: The Man from the Folies Bergère). The Casino Murder Case. Top Hat. Diamond Jim. Old Man Rhythm. I Dream Too Much. To Beat the Band. Seven Keys to Baldpate. The Good Fairy. 1936: Two in the Dark. The Ex-Mrs Bradford. Sons o' Guns. Piccadilly Jim. Swing Time. Smartest Girl in Town. Quality Street. 1937: The Soldier and the Lady (GB: Michael Strogoff). Shall We Dance? It's Love I'm After. Hitting a New High. Breakfast for Two. 1938: The Joy of Living. Swiss Miss. A Desperate Adventure (GB: It Happened in Paris). 1939: $1,000 a Touchdown. Island of Lost Men. A Gentleman's Gentleman. 1940: The Man Who Wouldn't Talk. The Lone Wolf Strikes. Music in My Heart. Till We Meet Again. The Boys from Syracuse. The Lone Wolf Meets a Lady. Earl of Puddlestone (GB: Jolly Old Higgins). South of Suez. 1941: The Lone Wolf Keeps a Date. The Lady Eve. The Lone Wolf Takes a Chance. Road to Zanzibar. Red Head. Lady Scarface. New York Town. Three Girls about Town. Confirm or Deny. The Shanghai Gesture. 1942: Sullivan's Travels. Secrets of the Lone Wolf (GB: Secrets). The Moon and Sixpence. Counter-Espionage. 1943: Forever and a Day. *Heavenly Music. Happy Go Lucky. Passport to Heaven. Submarine Base. Holy Matrimony. One Dangerous Night. Passport to Suez. The Sky's the Limit. 1944: San Diego, I Love You. 1945: Penthouse Rhythm. Easy to Look At. Kitty. Men in Her Diary. 1946: Two Sisters from Boston. The Notorious Lone Wolf. Abie's Irish Rose. 1947: The Lone Wolf in Mexico. Winter Wonderland. The Lone Wolf in London. 1948: Romance on the High Seas (GB: It's Magic). 1949: Love Happy (later Kleptomaniacs). Ad-*

ventures of Ichabod and Mr Toad (voice only). 1950: Fancy Pants. 1952: Babes in Baghdad. 1955: Bowery to Baghdad.

BLUE, Ben

(Benjamin Bernstein) 1900–1975

Although mainly a Broadway stage performer, this thin, mournful, Canadian-born indiarubber comedian livened up many a dull film by wandering on, doing a drunk act or a running mime gag, and usually bringing the house down. A cartoon of a man from a vaudeville family, he was on the musical-comedy stage at 15, then starred in some film sound shorts and one or two minor romps before settling for cameo appearances. Notable among these was his apartment dweller trying to complete a shave in the famous New York blackout in *Where Were You When the Lights Went Out?* – his farewell film appearance.

*1927: The Arcadians/Land of Heart's Desire. 1930: *One Big Night. 1932: *Strange Innertube. *What Price Taxi? 1933: *Wreckety Wreck. *Call Her Sausage. 1934: College Rhythm. 1936: Follow Your Heart. College Holiday. 1937: Turn Off the Moon. Top of the Town. High, Wide and Handsome. Artists and Models. Thrill of a Lifetime. 1938: College Swing (GB: Swing, Teacher, Swing). The Big Broadcast of 1938. Cocoanut Grove. 1939: Paris Honeymoon. 1942: Panama Hattie. For Me and My Gal (GB: For Me and My Girl). 1943: Thousands Cheer. 1944: Two Girls and a Sailor. Broadway Rhythm. 1945: *Badminton. 1946: Two Sisters from Boston. Easy to Wed. 1947: My Wild Irish Rose. 1948: One Sunday Afternoon. 1963: It's a Mad, Mad, Mad, Mad World. 1966: The Russians Are Coming, the Russians Are Coming. The Busy Body. 1967: A Guide for the Married Man. 1968: Where Were You When the Lights Went Out?*

BLUE, Monte 1890–1963

Moon-faced American romantic lead with sleek brown hair, popular in silent and early sound light dramas, before moving into scores of character roles until his retirement in 1955, following a brief period working in a circus. Part Cherokee Indian, Blue began his career as a stuntman for director D W Griffith after periods as a cowhand, a timberjack and labouring on the railroad. Died from a coronary attack.

1915: The Birth of a Nation. Ghosts. 1916: Matrimaniac. The Microscope Mystery. Hell-to-Pay Austin. The Man Behind the Curtain. Intolerance. 1917: Wild and Woolly. Jim Bludso. Betsy's Burglar. Hands Up! The Man from Painted Post. The Ship of Doom. Betrayed. 1918: Riders of the Night. The Only Road. The Red, Red Heart. Till I Come Back to You. Hands Up (serial. And 1917 film). The Squaw Man. The Romance of Tarzan. *100 Per Cent American. The Goddess of Lost Lake. Johanna Enlists. M'Liss. 1919: In Mizzoura/In Mizzura. Romance and Arabella. Pettigrew's Girl. Every Woman. Told in the Hills. Rustling a Bride. 1920: Something to Think About. The Thirteenth Commandment. A Cumberland Romance. Too Much Johnson. The Jucklins. 1921: The Kentuckians. Moonlight and Honeysuckle. The Affairs of Amatol. A Perfect Crime. Orphans of the Storm. A Broken Doll. 1922: Peacock Alley. My Old Kentucky Home. Loving Lies. Broadway Rose. 1923: Main Street. Brass. The Tents of Allah. The Purple Highway. Defying Destiny. Lucretia Lombard. 1924: How to Educate a Wife. Daughters of Pleasure. The Marriage Circle. Daddies. Revelation. Mademoiselle Midnight. Her Marriage Vow. The Lover of Camille. Being Respectable. The Dark Swan (GB: The Black Swan). 1925: Red Hot Tires. Hogan's Alley. Kiss Me Again. The Limited Mail. Recompense. 1926: The Man Upstairs. Across the Pacific. So This is Paris. Other Women's Husbands. 1927: Bitter Apples. Wolf's Clothing. Brass Knuckles. The Black Diamond Express. The Brute. The Bush Leaguer. One Round Hogan. *Life in Hollywood. 1928: Across the Atlantic. Perfect Crime. White Shadows in the South Seas. 1929: Conquest. Tiger Rose. From Headquarters. Greyhound Limited. No Defense. Skin Deep. The Show of Shows. 1930: Isle of Escape. Those Who Dance. 1931: The Flood. 1932: The Stoker. The Valley of Adventure. The Thundering Herd. 1933: The Nectors. Her Forgotten Past. The Intruder. Officer 13. 1934: Come On Marines! The Last Round-Up. Student Tour. Wagon Wheels. African Incident. College Rhythm. 1935: The Lives of a Bengal Lancer. Hot Off the Press. The Test. Trails of the Wild. G Men. Nevada. Wanderer of the Wasteland. Social Error. On Probation. 1936: Undersea Kingdom (serial). Prison Shadows. The Lawless Nineties. Mary of Scotland. Ride, Ranger, Ride. Treachery Rides the Range. Song of the Gringo. Desert Gold. 1937: Souls at Sea. A Million to One. Rootin' Tootin' Rhythm (GB: Rhythm on the Ranch). The Outcasts of Poker Flat. Secret Agent X-9 (serial). Amateur Crook. Born to the West. High, Wide and Handsome. Thunder Trail. 1938: Hawk of the Wilderness (serial). Tom Sawyer, Detective. Spawn of the North. The Mysterious Rider. A Million to One. Illegal Traffic. The Great Adventures of Wild Bill Hickok (serial). Rebellious Daughters. Cocoanut Grove. The Big Broadcast of 1938. King of Alcatraz (GB: King of the Alcatraz). 1939: Juarez. Dodge City. Union Pacific. Frontier Pony Express. Geronimo. Days of Jesse James. Port of Hate. Our Leading Citizen. 1940: North West Mounted Police. Mystery Sea Raider. A Little Bit of Heaven. Road to Singapore. Young Bill Hickok. Texas Rangers Ride Again. 1941: Riders of Death Valley (serial). King of the Texas Rangers (serial). Treat 'Em Rough. The Great Train Robbery. Arkansas Judge (GB: False Witness). Law of the Timber. Scattergood Pulls the Strings. New York Town. Sunset in Wyoming. Bad Man of Deadwood. North to the Klondike. Sullivan's Travels. 1942: Across the Pacific (and 1926 film). The Palm Beach Story. Gentleman Jim. Road to Morocco. Secret Enemies. Panama Hattie. Reap the Wild Wind. I Married a Witch. The Great Man's Lady. The Hidden Hand. Klondike Fury. My Favorite Blonde. The Forest Rangers. The Hard Way. The Remarkable Andrew. Casablanca. 1943: Northern Pursuit. Mission to Moscow. Edge of Darkness. Truck Busters. Thank Your Lucky Stars. Thousands Cheer. 1944: Passage to Marseille (GB: Passage to Marseilles). The Mask of Dimitrios. The Conspirators. The Adventures of Mark Twain. Janie. 1945: San Antonio. Escape in the Desert. Saratoga Trunk (completed 1943). Danger Signal. The Horn Blows at Midnight. 1946: Janie Gets Married. Cinderella Jones. Shadow of a Woman. Two Sisters from Boston. Easy to Wed. Humoresque. Never Say Goodbye. A Stolen Life. Two Guys from Milwaukee (GB: Royal Flush). The Man I Love. 1947: Bells of San Fernando. Speed to Spare. Life with Father. Cheyenne. Possessed. My Wild Irish Rose. That Way with Women. The Unfaithful. Stallion Road. 1948: Two Guys from Texas (GB: Two Texas Knights). Silver River. Key Largo. Johnny Belinda. 1949: South of St Louis. Ranger of Cherokee Strip. The Younger Brothers. Flaxy Martin. Homicide. Look for the Silver Lining. Colorado Territory. 1950: Dallas. This Side of the Law. Iroquois Trail (GB: The Tomahawk Trail). The Blonde Bandit. Backfire. Montana. 1951: Warpath. Snake River Desperadoes. Gold Raiders (GB: Stooges Go West). Three Desperate Men. The Sea Hornet. 1952: Rose of Cimarron. The Will Rogers Story (GB: The Story of Will Rogers). Hangman's Knot. 1953: The Last Posse. Ride, Vaquero! 1954: Apache. Border Ambush.

BLYTHE, John 1921–1993

In view of the fact that his screen characters were those most likely to sell you black market goods, it was rather surprising that a lot of this British actor's career in the 1950s was taken up introducing advertising magazines on television. A stagehand at 16, he got going in films in post-war years, at first in minor leads as fast-talking reporters but soon, trilby tipped even further back over those round, butter-wouldn't-melt-in-my-mouth features, as bow-tied smoothies on the make.

1939: Goodbye Mr Chips! 1944: *Bon Voyage. The Way Ahead. This Happy Breed. 1947: Holiday Camp. Easy Money. Dear Murderer. Crime Reporter. 1948: River Patrol. Good Time Girl. Here Come the Huggetts. Portrait from Life (US: The Girl in the Painting). 1949: Vote for Huggett. A Boy, a Girl and a Bike. Diamond City. It's a Wonderful Day. The Huggetts Abroad. Boys in Brown. 1950: Lilli Marlene. 1951: Worm's Eye View. 1952: The Frightened Man. 1953: Out of the Bandbox. The Wedding of Lilli Marlene. It's a Grand Life. Three Steps to the Gallows (released 1955. US: White Fire). 1954: The Gay Dog. Meet Mr Malcolm. 1955: As Long As They're Happy. Cockleshell Heroes. 1956: Doublecross. They Never Learn. 1984. 1960: Foxhole in Cairo. Doctor in Love. 1961: No Love for Johnnie. No, My Darling Daughter. 1962: The Devil's Daffodil (US: The Daffodil Killer). Gaolbreak. On the Beat. 1963: A Stitch in Time. Call Me Bwana. The VIPs. 1969: The Bed Sitting Room. 1974: Love Among the Ruins (TV). 1975: The Ups and Downs of a Handyman. 1976: Keep It Up Downstairs.

BODDEY, Martin 1907–1975

Burly British actor, often moustachioed, with dark hair sleekly brushed across his head and dark, almost choleric complexion. He didn't get into films at all until past 40, then played mostly solid types, like police sergeants and inspectors. Occasionally he let the solidity slip into wronged husbands, or even out-and-out villains – these roles having an intensity missing from his other work. Died from a heart attack.

*1948: A Song for Tomorrow. 1949: Landfall. The Third Man. The Dancing Years. 1950: State Secret (US: The Great Manhunt). Seven Days to Noon. Cage of Gold. The Franchise Affair. No Place for Jennifer. The Adventurers (US: The Great Adventure). Cairo Road. 1951: Laughter in Paradise. A Case for PC 49. No Highway (US: No Highway in the Sky). Valley of Eagles. Appointment with Venus (US: Island Rescue). The Magic Box. Cloudburst. Cry, the Beloved Country. 1952: Top Secret (US: Mr Potts Goes to Moscow). Venetian Bird (US: The Assassin). Folly to be Wise. 1953: The Weak and the Wicked. Single-Handed (US: Sailor of the King). Personal Affair. Park Plaza 605 (US: Norman Conquest). Rob Roy the Highland Rogue. 1954: Doctor in the House. Face the Music (US: The Black Glove). Forbidden Cargo. Up to His Neck. Svengali. Seagulls Over Sorrento (US: Crest of the Wave). The Yellow Robe. Mad about Men. Secret Venture. 1955: You Can't Escape. 1956: *Person Unknown. The Silken Affair. Escape in the Sun. Up in the World. The Iron Petticoat. Eyewitness. The Last Man to Hang? 1957: There's Always a Thursday. Man in the Shadow. How to Murder a Rich Uncle. Not Wanted on Voyage. These Dangerous Years (US: Dangerous Youth). Cat Girl. I Accuse! 1958: Carry On Sergeant. Violent Moment. The Two-Headed Spy. Chain of Events. Indiscreet. I Only Arsked! The Square Peg. The Duke Wore Jeans. No Time to Die! (US: Tank Force). 1959: The Boy and the Bridge. Carry On Nurse. The Siege of Pinchgut (US: Four Desperate Men). Idle on Parade (US: Idol on Parade). Killers of Kilimanjaro. I'm All Right, Jack. 1960: Moment of Danger (US: Malaga). Sands of the Desert. Circle of Deception. Too Hot to Handle (US: Playgirl After Dark). Oscar Wilde. 1961: The Kitchen. The Naked Edge. Gorgo. 1962: The Prince and the Pauper. The Wrong Arm of the Law. The Man Who Finally Died. 1963: Girl in the Headlines (US: The Model Murder Case). *Business Connections. 1966: A Man for All Seasons. 1967: Bedazzled. 1972: Tales from the Crypt. Psychomania (US: The Death Wheelers). 1973: Dark Places. 1975: The Naked Civil Servant (TV).*

BOIS, Curt 1901–1991

Small, elegant, dark-haired German actor, of beaky nose, hooded eyes and darting glances. A major figure in his native Berlin in theatre, variety and cabaret in the 1920s, he also recorded a number of songs and acted and directed in films. The rise of Nazism caused Bois and his wife, actress Hedi Ury (first of two) to flee through Austria, Czechoslovakia, France and England, eventually ending up in Hollywood, where he played a variety of cynical or comic cameos, as foreign nobility, displaced persons, dance-masters, dress designers, world-weary pianists or even (in *Casablanca*) a pickpocket. Returning to East Germany in 1950, and West Germany from 1954, he gradually regained his old standing. Appropriately cast in his last film as the spirit of Berlin.

*1908: *Heinerle-Lied. 1909: *Klebolin klebt alles. *Der kleine Detektiv. *Mutterliebe. 1912: *Des Pfarrers Töchterlein. 1914: Das Geschenk des Inders. 1916: Zeitungsmaxe & Co. *Tante Röschen will heiraten. Streichhölzer, kauft Streichhölzer! 1917: Die Spinne. Bobby als Amor. Das unruhige Hotel. Ehestiftung mit Hindernissen. 1918: Der goldene Pol. *So'n kleiner Schwerenöter. Moderne Frauen oder der Dieb. 1919: Die Austernprinzessin. 1922: Sie und die Drei. 1926: Der goldene Schmetterling. Wehe, wenn sie losgelassen. Der Jüngling aus der Konfektion. Gräfin Plättmamsell. 1927: Der Fürst von Pappenheim. Dr Bessels Verwandlung. 1928: Majestät schneidet Bubiköpfe. 1929: Anschluss um Mitternacht. 1931: Der Schlemihl. 1932: Ein steinreicher Mann. *Scherben bringen Glück (and directed). 1937: Tovarich. Hollywood Hotel. 1938: Romance in the Dark. The Amazing Dr Clitterhouse. Gold Diggers in Paris (GB: The Gay Impostors). Garden of the Moon. Boy Meets Girl. The Great Waltz. 1939: Hotel Imperial. The Hunchback of Notre Dame. 1940: The Lady in Question. Boom Town. He Stayed for Breakfast. Hullabaloo. Bitter Sweet. 1941: That Night in Rio. Hold Back the Dawn. Blue, White and Perfect. 1942: My Gal Sal. The Tuttles of Tahiti. Pacific Rendezvous. Casablanca. Destroyer. 1943: Princess O'Rourke. Paris After Dark. The Desert Song. Swing Fever. 1944: Cover Girl. Gypsy Wildcat. Blonde Fever. *1945: Saratoga Trunk (completed 1943). The Spanish Main. 1947: Jungle Flight. 1948: Arch of Triumph. French Leave (GB: Kilroy on Deck). The Woman from Tangier. Let's Live a Little. Up in Central Park. 1949: Caught. A Kiss in the Dark. The Woman in White. The Lovable Cheat. The Great Sinner. Oh, You Beautiful Doll. 1950: Joe Palooka Meets Humphrey. Vendetta (filmed 1946). Fortunes of Captain Blood. 1955: Ein Polterabend (directed only). Herr Puntila und sein Knecht Matti. 1958: Androcles and the Lion. 1960: Das Spukschloss im Spessart. 1964: Fluchtlingsgespräche (TV). Der eingebildete Kranke (TV). 1966: Die hundertste Nacht (TV). 1969: Amerika oder der Verschollene (TV). 1971: Der Pott (TV). Der Trojanische Sessel (TV). 1977: Das Rentenspiel (TV). 1979: Das Idol von Mordassow (TV). Liebe, Tod und Heringshäppchen (TV). 1980: Die Alten kommen (TV). Der Mond scheint auf Kylenamoe (TV). 1981: Das Boot ist Voll. Flächenbrand (TV). 1983: Auf Leben und Tod (directed only). 1987: Wings of Desire.*

BOLAND, Mary
(Marie Anne Boland) 1880–1965

Round-faced, fair-haired American actress with startled eyebrows and suspicious mouth. Generous of girth and mellifluous of speech (rising easily to a cackle, a giggle or hysteria), she turned from drama on the stage to comedy on the screen, scoring a resounding success opposite Charlie Ruggles (*qv*) in a whole series of films in the 1930s, usually playing his harassed, social-climbing (sometimes domineering) wife. In real life this best-loved of film matriarchs never married.

1915: The Edge of the Abyss. 1916: The Stepping Stone. The Price of Happiness. Big Jim Garrity. 1918: His Temporary Wife. The Prodigal Wife. A Woman's Experience. 1919: The Perfect Lover. 1931: Personal Maid. Secrets of a Secretary. 1932: The Night of June 13th. Trouble in Paradise. Evenings for Sale. If I Had a Million. Night After Night. 1933: Three-Cornered Moon. The Solitaire Man. Mama Loves Papa. 1934: Six of a Kind. Melody in Spring. Four Frightened People. Stingaree. Down to Their Last Yacht (GB: Hawaiian Nights). The Pursuit of Happiness. Here Comes the Groom. 1935: People Will Talk. Two for Tonight. Ruggles of Red Gap. The Big Broadcast of 1936. 1936: Wives Never Know. Early to Bed. College Holiday. A Son Comes Home. 1937: Marry the Girl. Mama Runs Wild. There Goes the Groom. Danger – Love at Work. 1938: Little Tough Guys in Society. Artists and Models Abroad (GB: Stranded in Paris). 1939: The Magnificent Fraud. Boy Trouble. The Women. Night Work. 1940: He Married His Wife. One Night in the Tropics. New Moon. Pride and Prejudice. Hit Parade of 1941. 1944: Nothing But Trouble. In Our Time. Forever Yours. They Shall Have Faith (GB: The Right to Live). 1948: Julia Misbehaves. 1950: Guilty Bystander.

BOND, Ward
(Wardell Bond) 1903–1960

Chunky, aggressive, light-haired American actor with jutting lower lip. At first in small roles (after a youthful career in American football), he was often cast as Irish policemen or boxers, but also employed by director John Ford in progressively juicier parts, usually as rugged, warm-hearted westerners. He was enjoying his greatest success, as the wagonmaster in TV's *Wagon Train*, when a

heart attack in his shower struck him down at 57.

1929: Salute. Words and Music. 1930: The Lone Star Ranger. The Big Trail. Born Reckless. 1931: Arrowsmith. Quick Millions. A Connecticut Yankee (GB: The Yankee at King Arthur's Court). 1932: Virtue. Flesh. Hello, Trouble. Rackety Rax. White Eagle. High Speed. Air Mail. The Trial of Vivienne Ware. 1933: Heroes for Sale. Lady for a Day. Son of a Sailor. Wild Boys of the Road (GB: Dangerous Days). When Strangers Marry. College Coach (GB: Football Coach). The Wrecker. Police Car No. 17. Whirlpool. Lucky Devils. The Sundown Rider. Unknown Valley. Obey the Law. 1934: Straightaway. Most Precious Thing in Life. The Poor Rich. Frontier Marshal. Broadway Bill (GB: Strictly Confidential). It Happened One Night. The Defense Rests. The Fighting Ranger. Death on the Diamond. Here Comes the Groom. Chained. The Affairs of Cellini. The Fighting Code. A Voice in the Night. A Man's Game. The Crime of Helen Stanley. Kid Millions. The Circus Clown. Against the Law. Girl in Danger. The Human Side. Tall Timber. The Crimson Trail. 1935: Western Courage. Devil Dogs of the Air. She Gets Her Man. Grand Old Gal. His Night Out. Black Fury. Strangers All. Fighting Shadows. Little Big Shot. The Last Days of Pompeii. 'G' Men. Go into Your Dance. Calm Yourself. The Informer. Guard That Girl. Times Square Lady. Murder in the Fleet. Waterfront Lady. The Headline Woman. Broadway Hostess. Justice of the Range. Men of the Night. Too Tough to Kill. 1936: Cattle Thief. Muss 'Em Up (GB: House of Fate). The Bride Walks Out. Crash Donovan. They Met in a Taxi. The Legion of Terror. Conflict. The Man Who Lived Twice. Fury. The Leathernecks Have Landed (GB: The Marines Have Landed). Avenging Waters. Boulder Dam. Pride of the Marines. The Big Game. The Gorgeous Hussy. Colleen. Fatal Lady. White Fang. 1937: You Only Live Twice. Topper. The Soldier and the Lady (GB: Michael Strogoff). Souls at Sea. Midnight Madonna. They Gave Him a Gun. Dead End. The Devil's Playground. A Fight to the Finish. The Wildcatter. 23½ Hours' Leave. Escape by Night. Night Key. Park Avenue Logger (GB: Millionaire Playboy). The Go-Getter. Mountain Music. The Singing Marine. Music for Madame. 1938: Born to the Wild. The Law West of Tombstone. Reformatory. Professor Beware. Gun Law. Hawaii Calls. Flight into Nowhere. Mr Moto's Gamble. The Amazing Dr Clitterhouse.

*Over the Wall. Numbered Woman. Prison Break. Bringing Up Baby. You Can't Take It With You. Of Human Hearts. Penitentiary. The Adventures of Marco Polo. Going Places. Fugitives for a Night. Submarine Patrol. 1939: Dodge City. Made for Each Other. Son of Frankenstein. They Made Me a Criminal. Waterfront. Trouble in Sundown. The Return of the Cisco Kid. Gone With the Wind. Young Mr Lincoln. Frontier Marshal. The Kid from Kokomo (GB: The Orphan of the Ring). The Oklahoma Kid. The Girl from Mexico. Drums Along the Mohawk. Dust Be My Destiny. Heaven With a Barbed-Wire Fence. Mr Moto in Danger Island (GB: Mr Moto on Danger Island). Confessions of a Nazi Spy. Pardon Our Nerve. 1940: Santa Fé Trail. Buck Benny Rides Again. Little Old New York. Virginia City. The Cisco Kid and the Lady. The Grapes of Wrath. The Mortal Storm. The Long Voyage Home. Sailor's Lady. Kit Carson. 1941: The Shepherd of the Hills. A Man Betrayed (GB: Citadel of Crime). Tobacco Road. Swamp Water (GB: The Man Who Came Back). Sergeant York. Manpower. Doctors Don't Tell. Wild Bill Hickok Rides. The Maltese Falcon. 1942: In This Our Life. Gentleman Jim. The Falcon Takes Over. Sin Town. Ten Gentlemen from West Point. A Night to Remember. 1943: A Guy Named Joe. They Came to Blow Up America. Hitler — Dead or Alive. Cowboy Commandos. Hello, Frisco, Hello. Slightly Dangerous. 1944: Home in Indiana. The Sullivans. Tall in the Saddle. 1945: Dakota. They Were Expendable. 1946: Canyon Passage. It's a Wonderful Life! My Darling Clementine. 1947: The Fugitive. Unconquered. 1948: Fort Apache. 3 Godfathers. The Time of Your Life. Joan of Arc. Tap Roots. 1950: Wagonmaster. Riding High. Singing Guns. Kiss Tomorrow Goodbye. 1951: The Great Missouri Raid. Operation Pacific. Only the Valiant. On Dangerous Ground. 1952: The Quiet Man. Thunderbirds. Hellgate. 1953: Blowing Wild. The Moonlighter. Hondo. 1954: Gypsy Colt. The Bob Mathias Story (GB: The Flaming Torch). Johnny Guitar. The Long Gray Line. *The Red, White and Blue Line. 1955: Mr Roberts. A Man Alone. 1956: The Searchers. Dakota Incident. Pillars of the Sky (GB: The Tomahawk and the Cross). 1957: The Wings of Eagles. The Halliday Brand. 1958: China Doll. 1959: Rio Bravo. Alias Jesse James.*

BONDI, Beulah
(B. Bondy) 1888–1981

Sharp-faced, dark-featured, penetrating American actress who, after a highly successful stage career, spent almost her whole Hollywood life playing widows, mothers, dowagers and grandmothers—in real life she never married—who were usually practical types. Twice nominated for an Academy Award, she travelled around the world twice after officially 'retiring' in 1962. Died following a severe fall.

1931: Street Scene. Arrowsmith. 1932: Rain. 1933: Christopher Bean (GB: The Late Christopher Bean). The Stranger's Return. Finishing School. 1934: The Painted Veil. Two Alone. Ready for Love. 1935: Registered Nurse. Bad Boy. The Good Fairy. 1936: The Invisible

Ray. Trail of the Lonesome Pine. The Moon's Our Home. The Case Against Mrs Ames. Hearts Divided. The Gorgeous Hussy. 1937: Maid of Salem. Make Way for Tomorrow. 1938: The Buccaneer. Of Human Hearts. Vivacious Lady. The Sisters. 1939: On Borrowed Time. Mr Smith Goes to Washington. The Under-Pup. Remember the Night. 1940: Our Town. The Captain is a Lady. 1941: Penny Serenade. Shepherd of the Hills. One Foot in Heaven. 1943: Watch on the Rhine. Tonight We Raid Calais. 1944: I Love a Soldier. Our Hearts Were Young and Gay. The Very Thought of You. And Now Tomorrow. She's a Soldier, Too. 1945: The Southerner. Back to Bataan. 1946: Breakfast in Hollywood (GB: The Mad Hatter). Sister Kenny. It's a Wonderful Life! 1947: High Conquest. 1948: The Snake Pit. The Sainted Sisters. 1949: So Dear to My Heart. The Life of Riley. Reign of Terror/The Black Book. Mr Soft Touch (GB: House of Settlement). The Baron of Arizona. 1950: The Furies. 1951: Lone Star. 1953: Latin Lovers. 1954: Track of the Cat. 1956: Back from Eternity. 1957: The Unholy Wife. 1959: The Big Fisherman. A Summer Place. 1960: Tomorrow (TV). 1961: Tammy, Tell Me True. 1962: The Wonderful World of the Brothers Grimm. 1963: Tammy and the Doctor. 1971: She Waits (TV). 1976: Crossing Fox River (TV).

BORG, Veda Ann 1915–1973

Fluffy blonde (brunette until 1939) Hollywood actress with a cynical air, who worked hard through the 1930s and 1940s as a succession of sluts, double-crossers, gangsters' molls, blowzy waitresses, faithless wives and generally blondes who had seen better days but were often optimistic of something turning up. Career disrupted in 1939 by a car crash, her injuries from which entailed plastic surgery and 10 operations. Married (second) to director Andrew V. McLaglen from 1946 to 1958.

1936: Three Cheers for Love. The Golden Arrow. 1937: Men in Exile. Kid Galahad. San Quentin. The Case of the Stuttering Bishop. Public Wedding. The Singing Marine. Confession. Back in Circulation. Marry the Girl. It's Love I'm After. Dance, Charlie, Dance. Varsity Show. Submarine D-1. Alcatraz Island. Missing Witness. 1938: She Loved a Fireman. Over the Wall. Café Hostess. 1939: The Law Comes to Texas. 1940: A Miracle on Main

Street. Melody Ranch. I Take This Oath. Dr Christian Meets the Women. The Shadow (serial). Laughing at Danger. Glamour for Sale. Bitter Sweet. Behind the News. 1941: The Arkansas Judge (GB: False Witness). The Penalty. The Pittsburgh Kid. The Getaway. I'll Wait for You. Honky Tonk. Down in San Diego. The Corsican Brothers. 1942: About Face. Duke of the Navy. She's in the Army. Two Yanks in Trinidad. I Married an Angel. Lady in a Jam. 1943: Murder in Times Square. Isle of Forgotten Sins. Revenge of the Zombies (GB: The Corpse Vanished). The Girl from Monterey. The Unknown Guest. False Faces (GB: The Attorney's Dilemma). Something to Shout About. 1944: Smart Guy (GB: You Can't Beat the Law). Standing Room Only. Detective Kitty O'Day. Irish Eyes Are Smiling. Marked Trails. The Girl Who Dared. The Big Noise. The Falcon in Hollywood. 1945: What a Blonde. Fog Island. Jungle Raiders (serial). Rough, Tough and Ready (GB: Men of the Deep). Bring on the Girls. Scared Stiff. Nob Hill. Don Juan Quilligan. Dangerous Intruder. Love, Honor and Goodbye. Mildred Pierce. 1946: Life with Blondie. Avalanche. Wife Wanted (GB: Shadow of Blackmail). Accomplice. The Fabulous Suzanne. *I Love My Husband, But! 1947: The Pilgrim Lady. Big Town. Mother Wore Tights. 1948: The Bachelor and the Bobby Soxer (GB: Bachelor Knight). Blonde Savage. Chicken Every Sunday. Julia Misbehaves. 1949: Mississippi Rhythm. One Last Fling. Forgotten Women. 1950: Rider from Tucson. Kangaroo Kid. 1951: Aaron Slick from Punkin Crick (GB: Marshmallow Moon). 1952: Big Jim McLain. Hold That Line. 1953: A Perilous Journey. Mr Scoutmaster. Hot News. Three Sailors and a Girl. 1954: Bitter Creek. 1955: You're Never Too Young. Guys and Dolls. Love Me Or Leave Me. I'll Cry Tomorrow. 1956: The Naked Gun. Frontier Gambler. 1957: The Wings of Eagles. 1958: The Fearmakers. 1959: Thunder in the Sun. 1960: The Alamo.

BOSCO, Philip 1930–

Genial, tall, sympathetic-looking American actor with inquisitive shoulders. He often took over from Edward Andrews (qv) the mask of genial avuncularity that could hide a devious nature. Bosco's father was a carnival man, but the son became a cryptographer, turning to acting in his thirties and winning acclaim for his performances on the Broadway stage. Films were a rarity

until the 1980s, but he won critical applause for his one leading role, in 1985's *Walls of Glass*, and has been a man in demand ever since.

1962: Requiem for a Heavyweight (GB: Blood Money). 1968: A Lovely Way to Die (GB: A Lovely Way to Go). 1983: Trading Places. 1984: The Pope of Greenwich Village. 1985: Heaven Help Us (GB: Catholic Boys). Walls of Glass/Flanagan. The Money Pit. 1986: Children of a Lesser God. 1987: Suspect. 3 Men and a Baby. 1988: Internal Affairs (TV). The Luckiest Man in the World. Working Girl. Another Woman. 1989: The Dream Team. Blue Steel. 1990: Murder in Black and White (TV). Quick Change. 1991: True Colors. F/X 2: The Deadly Art of Illusion. The Return of Eliot Ness (TV). Shadows and Fog. 1992: Straight Talk. 1994: Angie. Against the Wall (cable TV). Milk Money. Safe Passage. Nobody's Fool.

BOSLEY, Tom 1927–

Jaunty, jovial, chubby-cheeked, not-too-tall American actor with dark hair, cheery grin and knitted eyebrows. Although Bosley has been knocking around the show business scene for close to 50 years now in co-star roles, films have never really claimed him. It was the theatre – the title role in the Broadway production of *Fiorello!* won him all sorts of awards including a Tony – and television that brought him his highest profile. From 1974 to 1984 he was Howard Cunningham, father of the family in the immensely successful 1950s' teenage nostalgia comedy show *Happy Days*. Since 1987,

he has been the sleuthing priest in *The Father Dowling Mysteries*.

1947: Call Northside 777. 1948: The Street with No Name. 1963: Love with the Proper Stranger. 1964: The World of Henry Orient. 1967: Divorce American Style. The Secret War of Harry Frigg. 1968: The Bang Bang Kid. Yours, Mine and Ours. 1969: Night Gallery (TV). Marcus Welby MD (TV). 1970: Vanished (TV). 1971: To Find a Man/Sex and the Teenager. A Step Out of Line (TV). Congratulations, It's a Boy! (TV). Mr and Mrs Bo Jo Jones (TV). 1972: The Streets of San Francisco (TV). No Place to Run (TV). 1973: Miracle on 34th Street (TV). 1974: Death Cruise (TV). Mixed Company. The Girl Who Came Gift-Wrapped (TV). 1975: The Last Survivors (TV). Who is the Black Dahlia? (TV). The Night That Panicked America (TV). 1976: The Love Boat (TV). Gus. 1977: Black Market Baby (TV). 1978: With This Ring (TV). 1979: The Triangle Factory Fire Scandal (TV). The Rebels (TV). The Return of the Mod Squad (TV). 1980: For the Love of It. 1981: O'Hara's Wife. 1984: The Jesse Owens Story (TV). 1985: Private Sessions (TV). 1986: Perry Mason: The Case of the Notorious Nun (TV). 1987: Million Dollar Mystery. Pinocchio and the Emperor of the Night (voice only). Fatal Confession (TV). 1988: Wicked Stepmother. 1989: The Missing Body Mystery (TV). Fire and Rain (TV). The Mafia Priest Mystery (TV).

BOUCHEY, Willis 1895–1977

Solidly built, ambivalent-looking American supporting player with greying brown hair. He left the security of a Broadway career to try his luck in the still film-filled Hollywood of the early 1950s and stayed in steady employ there for the remainder of his career, often in westerns as bankers, ageing sheriffs, judges or town big-shots. Sometimes billed as Willis B. Bouchey.

1951: Elopement. 1952: Red Planet Mars. Carbine Williams. Just for You. Assignment–Paris! Don't Bother to Knock! Million Dollar Mermaid (GB: The One-Piece Bathing Suit). Washington Story (GB: Target for Scandal). Deadline–USA (GB: Deadline). 1953: Gun Belt. The Big Heat. The 'I Don't Care' Girl. The President's Lady. Pick-Up on South Street. From Here to Eternity. Dangerous Crossing. 1954: Battle of Rogue River. The Bridges at Toko-Ri. Suddenly! Drum Beat. Them! The

Long Gray Line. The Violent Men (GB: Rough Company). Executive Suite. Fireman, Save My Child. A Star is Born. 1955: I Cover the Underworld. Battle Cry. The Spoilers. The McConnell Story (GB: Tiger in the Sky). Hell on Frisco Bay. The Man on the Ledge (TV. GB: cinemas). Big House USA. 1956: Pillars of the Sky (GB: The Tomahawk and the Cross). Forever Darling. Johnny Concho. Magnificent Roughnecks. 1957: Mister Cory. The Garment Jungle. The Night Runner. The Wings of Eagles. Last of the Badmen. Beau James. Zero Hour! Last Stagecoach West. Darby's Rangers (GB: The Young Invaders). 1958: The Sheepman. The Last Hurrah. No Name on the Bullet. 1959: The Horse Soldiers. 1960: Sergeant Rutledge. 1961: Saintly Sinners. Five Guns to Tombstone. Two Rode Together. You Have to Run Fast. Man Missing. Pocketful of Miracles. 1962: Incident in an Alley. The Man Who Shot Liberty Valance. Panic in Year Zero! How the West Was Won. 1964: Cheyenne Autumn. Where Love Has Gone. Apache Rifles. 1965: McHale's Navy Joins the Air Force. 1966: Return of the Gunfighter. Follow Me, Boys! 1968: Support Your Local Sheriff! 1969: Young Billy Young. The Love God? 1970: Dirty Dingus Magee. The Intruders (TV). 1971: Support Your Local Gunfighter. Lawman. Shootout.

(US: Colonel Blimp). The Adventures of Tartu (US: Tartu). The Demi-Paradise (US: Adventure for Two). San Demetrio London. 1944: Waterloo Road. The Halfway House. The Way Ahead (US: Immortal Battalion). 1946: *An Englishman's Home. 1947: Take My Life. The October Man. The White Unicorn (US: Bad Sister). The Root of All Evil. 1948: My Brother's Keeper. London Belongs to Me (US: Dulcimer Street). The Blue Lagoon. Man on the Run. Against the Wind. 1949: Don't Ever Leave Me. It's Not Cricket. Stop Press Girl. Marry Me! 1950: Madeleine. Mr Drake's Duck. The Happiest Days of Your Life. Trio. The Woman in Question (US: Five Angles on Murder). Highly Dangerous. Pool of London. 1951: Laughter in Paradise. Encore. 1953: Meet Mr Lucifer. The Red Beret (US: Paratrooper). 1954: Diplomatic Passport. The Dog and the Diamonds. Three Cases of Murder. Secret Venture. 1955: The Ship That Died of Shame (US: PT Raiders). 1956: Brothers in Law. 1957: Undercover Girl. The Bridge on the River Kwai. The Tommy Steele Story (US: Rock Around the World). 1958: Dunkirk. Heart of a Child. 1961: Victim. 1962: Emergency. 1963: Hide and Seek. 1966: *The Haunted Man. 1968: Headline Hunters. Twisted Nerve. 1972: Frenzy. For the Love of Ada. 1982: Gandhi.

Life). F.I.S.T. 1979: Beyond the Poseidon Adventure. The Brink's Job. In God We Trust. 1980: Where the Buffalo Roam. Hammett (released 1982). 1981: Outland. 1983: Yellowbeard. 1984: Johnny Dangerously. 1985: Turk 182! 1987: Surrender. Walker. Conspiracy: The Trial of the Chicago 8 (TV). 1988: Red Heat. Disaster at Silo 7 (TV). The In Crowd. 1989: The Dream Team. Speed Zone. 1990: Men of Respect. Solar Crisis (later Starfire). Challenger (TV). 1991: Rubin & Ed. Nervous Ticks. Kickboxer 2: The Road Back. The Tragedy of Flight 403: The Inside Story (TV). Agaguk/ Shadow of the Wolf. 1992: Honeymoon in Vegas. Malcolm X. 1993: Romeo is Bleeding. Taking the Heat. 1994: Exquisite Tenderness. Royce. The Shadow. Killer. The Santa Clause. 1995: Katie. While You Were Sleeping. Born to be Wild.

BRAMBELL, Wilfrid 1912–1985
Scraggy, Irish-born actor of skeletal aspect, specializing in old codgers with teeth missing, but virtually unknown to the public at large until his gigantic success as the horrendous Albert Steptoe, rag-and-bone merchant, in British TV's Steptoe and Son, in which he alternated between pop-eyed horror, cronish cackling and lascivious leers. The series was unsuccessfully transferred to the cinema screen; a sequel was equally disastrous. Died from cancer.

1935: The 39 Steps. 1946: Odd Man Out. 1948: Another Shore. 1956: Dry Rot. 1957: The Story of Esther Costello (US: Golden Virgin). 1958: The Salvage Gang. 1959: Serious Charge (US: A Touch of Hell). 1960: Urge to Kill. 1961: The Sinister Man. Flame in the Streets. What a Whopper! *The Grand Junction Case. In Search of the Castaways. 1962: The Boys. The Fast Lady. 1963: The Small World of Sammy Lee. Crooks in Cloisters. The Three Lives of Thomasina. Go Kart Go! 1964: A Hard Day's Night. 1965: San Ferry Ann. 1966: Where the Bullets Fly. Mano di velluto. 1968: Witchfinder-General (US: The Conqueror Worm). Lionheart. Cry Wolf. 1969: *The Undertakers. Carry On Again, Doctor. 1970: Some Will, Some Won't. 1972: Steptoe and Son. 1973: Steptoe and Son Ride Again. Holiday on The Buses. 1978: The Adventures of Picasso. 1980: High Rise Donkey. 1981: Island of Adventure. 1983: *Death and Transfiguration. Sword of the Valiant.

BOXER, John
(Cyril J. Boxer) 1909–1982
Squarely built, black-haired, pugnacious-looking British actor who played rural figures of authority – aldermen, squires, country policemen and the like – and almost made an entire career out of the role of Petty Officer Herbert in several stage productions of Seagulls Over Sorrento. He swapped stockbroking for an acting career at 19 and remained largely a man of the theatre, despite a busy period of film activity in the 1940s. Died from a heart attack.

1935: Escape Me Never. Royal Cavalcade (US: Regal Cavalcade). The Crouching Beast. 1939: There Ain't No Justice! 1940: Convoy. George and Margaret. 1941: The Black Sheep of Whitehall. They Flew Alone (US: Wings and the Woman). The Big Blockade. 1942: In Which We Serve. The Foreman Went to France (US: Somewhere in France). The Goose Steps Out. The Day Will Dawn (US: The Avengers). Flying Fortress. 1943: The Flemish Farm. Millions Like Us. The Life and Death of Colonel Blimp

BOYLE, Peter 1933–
Bald, aggressive, thick-set, menacing-looking American actor, whose first starring role, as the foul-mouthed central character of Joe, was far from his own previous life as a monk in the Christian Brothers order. Quickly proving himself capable of a wide range of characterizations, Boyle sustained his rating as a star character actor well into the 1980s. He has reverted to playing largely unpleasant types in more recent times.

1966: The Group. 1968: The Virgin President. Medium Cool. 1969: Joe. 1970: Diary of a Mad Housewife. 1971: T R Baskin (GB: A Date with a Lonely Girl). 1972: Steelyard Blues. The Candidate. 1973: Slither. The Friends of Eddie Coyle. Kid Blue/Dime Box. The Man Who Could Talk to Kids (TV). 1974: Crazy Joe. Ghost in the Noonday Sun. Young Frankenstein. 1976: Swashbuckler (GB: The Scarlet Buccaneer). Taxi Driver. Tail Gunner Joe (TV). 1978: Hardcore (GB: The Hardcore

BRANDON, Henry
(Heinrich von Kleinbach) 1912–1990
Dark-haired, German-born actor in American films, with eternally young, if slightly cruel-looking features. He had a leading role in his first film, a Laurel and Hardy feature comedy, as 'the meanest man in Toyland', but star billing eluded him through 40 years of films until he appeared as the tiger-taming man of the wild in the big money-spinning *When the North Wind Blows* 1974, looking so little older you could barely credit it was the same actor who had threatened Buck Rogers with destruction in the 1930s. Died from a heart attack.

*1934: †Babes in Toyland. 1936: †The Preview Murder Mystery. †Big Brown Eyes. Killer at Large. The Garden of Allah. Black Legion. Trail of the Lonesome Pine. Poker Faces. 1937: Jungle Jim (serial). Secret Agent X-9 (serial). I Promise to Pay. Island Captives. *Our Gang Follies of 1938. The Last Train from Madrid. Conquest (GB: Marie Walewska). Westbound Limited. Wells Fargo. 1938: Spawn of the North. Three Comrades. If I Were King. The Last Warning. 1939: Conspiracy. Buck Rogers (serial). Pirates of the Skies. Nurse Edith Cavell. Beau Geste. Marshal of Mesa City. Geronimo. 1940: Florian. Doomed to Die (GB: The Mystery of the Wentworth Castle). The Ranger and the Lady. Half a Sinner. Under Texas Skies. Ski Patrol. The Son of Monte Cristo. Dark Streets of Cairo. Drums of Fu Manchu (serial). 1941: The Corsican Brothers. Bad Man of Deadwood. Shepherd of the Hills. Underground. Hurricane Smith. Two in a Taxi. 1942: A Night in New Orleans. 1943: Edge of Darkness. Drums of Fu Manchu. 1947: Northwest Outpost (GB: End of the Rainbow). 1948: Old Los Angeles. Canon City. The Paleface. Hollow Triumph (GB: The Scar). Wake of the Red Witch. 1949: The Fighting O'Flynn. Tarzan's Magic Fountain. 1951: Flame of Araby. Cattle Drive. The Golden Horde (GB: The Golden Horde of Genghis Khan). 1952: Harem Girl. Scarlet Angel. Wagons West. Hurricane Smith (and 1941 film). War of the Worlds. 1953: Tarzan and the She-Devil. War Arrow. Pony Express. Raiders of the Seven Seas. Scared Stiff. The Caddy. Casanova's Big Night. 1954: Vera Cruz. Knock on Wood. 1955: Silent Fear. Lady Godiva (GB: Lady Godiva of Coventry). 1956: The Ten Commandments. The Searchers. Comanche. Bandido! 1957: Hell's Crossroads. Omar Khayyam. The Land Unknown. 1958: Auntie Mame. The Buccaneer. 1959: The Big*

Fisherman. Okefenokee (GB: Indian Killer). 1961: Two Rode Together. 1963: Captain Sindbad. 1967: Search for the Evil One. 1973: So Long, Blue Boy. 1974: When the North Wind Blows. 1975: The Manhandlers. 1976: Assault on Precinct 13. Treasure Seekers. 1977: The Thoroughbreds (later Run for the Roses). Kino, the Padre on Horseback. 1981: Evita Peron (TV). 1983: To Be or Not to Be. 1988: Wizards of the Lost Kingdom II.

† As Harry Kleinbach

BRENNAN, Eileen 1935–
Abrasive, light-haired American comedy actress with broad, if somewhat strained smile, high cheekbones and faintly oriental looks, pitched somewhere between Thelma Ritter and Gladys George (both *qv*). She was nominated for a best supporting actress Oscar in *Private Benjamin* (a role she repeated in the subsequent TV series), but her career was disrupted when she was severely injured in a car accident in 1982, spending some time in a wheelchair. She had happily returned to films by 1985, if in less showy roles.

1967: Divorce American Style. 1971: The Last Picture Show. 1972: Playmates (TV). 1973: Scarecrow. The Blue Knight (TV. GB: cinemas). The Sting. 1974: Daisy Miller. My Father's House (TV). Come Die with Me (TV). 1975: At Long Last Love. The Night That Panicked America (TV). Hustle. 1976: Murder by Death. 1977: The Last of the Cowboys (later The Great Smokey Roadblock). The Death of Ritchie (TV). 1978: The Cheap Detective. Black Beauty (TV). FM. 1979: When She Was Bad... (TV). 1980: Private Benjamin. 1981: Incident at Crestridge (TV). When the Circus Comes to Town (TV). Pandemonium/Thursday the 12th. 1982: My Old Man (TV). The Funny Farm. 1985: Clue. The Fourth Wise Man (TV). 1986: Babes in Toyland (TV). 1987: Sticky Fingers. Blood Vows: The Story of a Mafia Wife (TV). 1988: Rented Lips. The New Adventures of Pippi Longstocking. Going to the Chapel (TV). 1989: It Had to be You. 1990: Joey Takes a Cab. Texasville. White Palace. Stella. 1991: Deadly Intentions...Again (TV). I Don't Buy Kisses Anymore. 1993: My Name is Kate (TV). Precious Victims (TV). 1994: Take Me Home Again. 1995: Reckless.

BRENNAN, Michael 1912–1982
Solidly-built, brown-haired, hopeful- but slightly dim-looking London-born actor who played tough mugs both straight and comic. Once John Gielgud's stage manager, Brennan brought his wide-apart eyes and long, grinning mouth into the acting scene in the mid-1930s and, in the post-war years, became a familiar, if sporadic visitor to films, between TV and stage assignments. He enjoyed one of his most effective roles as the inept store detective in Norman Wisdom's *Trouble in Store*. Married actress Mary Hignett (1915–1980).

1947: They Made Me a Fugitive (US: I Became a Criminal). The Brass Monkey/Lucky Mascot. Blanche Fury. Captain Boycott. 1948: Noose (US: The Silk Noose). It's Hard to be Good. Cardboard Cavalier. 1949: For Them That Trespass. The Chiltern Hundreds (US: The Amazing Mr Beecham). 1950: Waterfront (US: Waterfront Women). The Clouded Yellow. Morning Departure (US: Operation Disaster). They Were Not Divided. Blackout. No Trace. Paul Temple's Triumph. Tom Brown's Schooldays. Circle of Danger. 1951: The Lady with a Lamp. 1952: Emergency Call (US: Hundred-Hour Hunt). 13 East Street. Made in Heaven. Ivanhoe. Something Money Can't Buy. 1953: Trouble in Store. Personal Affair. It's a Grand Life. 1954: Up to His Neck. 1955: See How They Run. 1956: Up in the World. The Big Money (released 1958). 1957: Just My Luck. Not Wanted on Voyage. 1958: Law and Disorder. Girls at Sea. Dunkirk. A Tale of Two Cities. 1959: The 39 Steps. 1960: The Day They Robbed the Bank of England. Watch Your Stern. 1961: Johnny Nobody. On the Fiddle (US: Operation Snafu). Ambush in Leopard Street. 1962: The Waltz of the Toreadors. The Devil's Agent. Live Now — Pay Later. 1963: The Girl Hunters. Tom Jones. 1964: Act of Murder. 1965: Three Hats for Lisa. Cuckoo Patrol. The Amorous Adventures of Moll Flanders. Thunderball. 1966: Death is a Woman. The Deadly Affair. Just Like a Woman. 1967: Woman Times Seven. 1968: The Great Pony Raid. 1970: Lust for a Vampire. 1971: Fright. 1972: Doomwatch. The Trouble with 2B (series). Up the Front. Nothing But the Night.

BRENNAN, Walter 1894–1974
This cantankerous-looking American actor was born in a town called Swampscott,

Massachusetts, a name exactly suited to the assortment of veteran westerners for which his career will largely be remembered. Usually seen on screen in clothes as crumpled as his face, Brennan's distinctive voice sounded as though it were issuing through a plug of chaw tobaccy. The man who started in films as an extra and stuntman, then played dozens of tiny roles, went on to win best supporting actor Oscars in 1936 (*Come and Get It*), 1938 (*Kentucky*) and 1940 (*The Westerner*) and was actually nominated again in 1941! Died from emphysema.

1926: Watch Your Wife. 1927: Blake of Scotland Yard (serial). The Ridin' Rowdy. Tearin' into Trouble. 1928: The Ballyhoo Buster. The Lariat Kid. Silks and Saddles (GB: Thoroughbreds). One Hysterical Night. 1929: The Long, Long Trail. The Shannons of Broadway. Smiling Guns. 1930: King of Jazz. *Scratch As Scratch Can. 1931: Heroes of the Flames (serial). Dancing Dynamite. Neck and Neck. 1932: Law and Order. Scandal for Sale. Cornered. Hello Trouble. *Twin Lips and Juleps. Texas Cyclone. Two-Fisted Law. The All-American (GB: Sport of a Nation). Miss Pinkerton. The Airmail Mystery (serial). The Fourth Horseman. Parachute Jumper. *The Iceman's Ball. 1933: One Year Later. Man of Action. The Invisible Man. The Phantom of the Air (serial). Saturday's Millions. The Kiss Before the Mirror. Parachute Jumper. Fighting for Justice. The Keyhole. Baby Face. Lilly Turner. The Big Cage. Female. Sing, Sinner, Sing. From Headquarters. Strange People. Silent Men. 1934: Murder in the Private Car (GB: Murder on the Runaway Train). Tailspin Tommy (serial). *Radio Dough. *Fishing for Trouble. *Hunger Pains. *Bric-a-Brac. The Life of Vergie Winters. Gridiron Flash (GB: Luck of the Game). Whom the Gods Destroy. Death on the Diamond. Rustlers' Roundup. *Woman Haters. Good Dame (GB: Good Girl). Half a Sinner. Desirable. Housewife. Stamboul Quest. Riptide. Fugitive Lovers. The Painted Veil. 1935: Welcome Home. The Wedding Night. *Restless Knights. Lady Tubbs (GB: The Gay Lady). Northern Frontier. The Mystery of Edwin Drood. We're in the Money. Public Hero No. One. Party Wire. The Man on the Flying Trapeze (GB: The Memory Expert). Seven Keys to Baldpate. Bride of Frankenstein. Law Beyond the Range. Metropolitan. 1936:

Three Godfathers. Fury. These Three. Come and Get It. Banjo on My Knee. The Moon's Our Home. The Prescott Kid. 1937: She's Dangerous. When Love is Young. Wild and Woolly. The Affairs of Cappy Ricks. 1938: The Adventures of Tom Sawyer. The Buccaneer. Kentucky. The Texans. Mother Carey's Chickens. The Cowboy and the Lady. 1939: Stanley and Livingstone. The Story of Vernon and Irene Castle. They Shall Have Music (GB: Melody of Youth). Joe and Ethel Turp Call on the President. 1940: The Westerner. Northwest Passage. Maryland. 1941: Meet John Doe. Sergeant York. Swamp Water (GB: The Man Who Came Back). Nice Girl? This Woman is Mine. Rise and Shine. 1942: Pride of the Yankees. Stand By for Action! (GB: Cargo of Innocents). 1943: Slightly Dangerous. Hangmen Also Die. North Star. *The Last Will and Testament of Tom Smith. 1944: The Princess and the Pirate. To Have and Have Not. Home in Indiana. 1945: Dakota. 1946: Nobody Lives Forever. My Darling Clementine. A Stolen Life. Centennial Summer. 1947: Driftwood. 1948: Red River. Scudda Hoo! Scudda Hay! (GB: Summer Lightning). Blood on the Moon. 1949: Brimstone. Task Force. The Great Dan Patch. The Green Promise (GB: Raging Waters). 1950: Singing Guns. Curtain Call at Cactus Creek (GB: Take the Stage). Surrender. A Ticket to Tomahawk. The Showdown. 1951: The Wild Blue Yonder (GB: Thunder Across the Pacific). Along the Great Divide. Best of the Bad Men. 1952: Return of the Texan. Lure of the Wilderness. 1953: Sea of Lost Ships. 1954: Drums Across the River. Four Guns to the Border. Bad Day at Black Rock. The Far Country. 1955: At Gunpoint! (GB: Gunpoint!). Come Next Spring. Goodbye, My Lady. 1956: The Proud Ones. Glory. 1957: Tammy and the Bachelor (GB: Tammy). The Way to the Gold. God is My Partner. 1959: Rio Bravo. 1962: How the West Was Won. 1963: Shoot Out at Big Sag. 1964: Those Calloways. 1966: The Oscar. Who's Minding the Mint? 1967: The Gnome-Mobile. 1968: The One and Only Genuine Original Family Band. Support Your Local Sheriff! 1969: The Over-the-Hill Gang (TV). 1970: The Young Country. The Over-the-Hill Gang Rides Again (TV). 1971: Smoke in the Wind. Two for the Money (TV). 1972: Home for the Holidays (TV).

BRESSART, Felix 1880–1949

Sad-eyed, wild-haired refugee from German films (actually born in what was then East Prussia), whose receding chin and five o'clock shadow emphasized his big nose and made his head seem to nod as he offered fractured advice to his fellows. He came to Hollywood in 1939 and hovered about the fringes of a fistful of films, looking mostly doleful but not tragic, before leukaemia struck him down in 1949.

1928: Liebe im Kuhstall. 1930: Die Drei von der Tankstelle (GB: Three Men and Lillian). 1931: Der wahre Jakob. Das alte Lied. Nie wieder Liebe (US: No More Love). Eine Freundin so goldig wie Du. 1932: Der Schrecken der Garnison. Hirsekorn greift ein. Der Herr Bürovorsteher. 1933: Holzapfel

weiss alles. Drei Tage Mittelarrest. Der Sohn der weissen Berg. 1934: Der Glückzylinder. Und wer küsst mich? 1939: Three Smart Girls Grow Up. Bridal Suite. Swanee River. Ninotchka. 1940: Edison the Man. The Shop around the Corner. It All Came True. Third Finger, Left Hand. Bitter Sweet. Comrade X. Escape. 1941: Ziegfeld Girl. Blossoms in the Dust. Married Bachelor. Kathleen. Mr and Mrs North. 1942: To Be or Not to Be. Crossroads. Iceland (GB: Katina). 1943: Above Suspicion. Song of Russia. Three Hearts for Julia. 1944: The Seventh Cross. Blonde Fever. Greenwich Village. Secrets in the Dark. 1945: Dangerous Partners. Without Love. Ding Dong Williams (GB: Melody Maker). 1946: I've Always Loved You (GB: Concerto). The Thrill of Brazil. Her Sister's Secret. 1948: Portrait of Jennie (GB: Jennie). A Song is Born. 1949: Take One False Step.

BRESLAW, Bernard 1933–1993

Giant-sized British cockney comedy actor specializing in gormless types, who scored an overwhelming personal success in TV's *The Army Game* as a witless, kiss-curled private called Popeye. But subsequent starring roles in films were not well chosen (also his hair was disappearing rapidly) and his career suffered a lull until he became a regular in the 'Carry On' series. Died from a heart attack.

1954: The Men of Sherwood Forest. The Glass Cage (US: The Glass Tomb). 1956: Up in the World. 1957: High Tide at Noon. 1958: Blood of the Vampire. I Only Arsked! 1959: The

Ugly Duckling. Too Many Crooks. 1963: *It's All Happening.* 1965: *Carry On Cowboy. Morgan – a Suitable Case for Treatment.* 1966: **Round the Bend. Carry On Screaming.* 1967: *Follow That Camel. Carry On Doctor.* 1968: *Carry On Up the Khyber.* 1969: *Carry On Camping. Moon Zero Two. Carry On Up the Jungle. Spring and Port Wine.* 1970: *Carry On Loving.* 1971: *Up Pompeii. The Magnificent Seven Deadly Sins. Carry On At Your Convenience. Blinker's Spy Spotter.* 1972: *Carry On Matron. Carry On Abroad.* 1973: *Carry On Girls.* 1974: *Vampira (US: Old Dracula). Carry On Dick.* 1975: *One of Our Dinosaurs is Missing. Carry On Behind.* 1976: *Joseph Andrews.* 1977: *Jabberwocky. Behind the Iron Mask (GB: The Fifth Musketeer).* 1980: *Hawk the Slayer.* 1983: *Krull.* 1992: *Leon the Pig Farmer.*

BRIGGS, Johnny 1935–

London-born actor with light, tufty hair, twinkling eyes and slightly shifty charm. Following training at the Italia Conti stage school, he was in films as a boy, but, after achieving prominence as teenage tearaways, found only supporting roles in the cinema of the 1960s and 1970s. TV gave him constant employment, though – and more worthwhile parts; and he has been entirely lost to that medium since 1977, mainly as Mike Baldwin in the long-running soap opera *Coronation Street.*

1947: *Hue and Cry.* 1948: *Quartet.* 1952: *Cosh Boy (US: The Slasher).* 1957: *Second Fiddle.* 1958: *The Diplomatic Corpse.* 1960: *The Bulldog Breed. Light Up the Sky. The Wind of Change.* 1961: *The Wild and the Willing.* 1962: *HMS Defiant (US: Damn the Defiant!).* 1963: *Doctor in Distress. The Leather Boys. A Stitch in Time.* 1964: *The Devil-Ship Pirates.* 633 *Squadron.* 1965: *The Intelligence Men. Information Received.* 1969: *The Last Escape. *Bachelor of Arts.* 1970: *Perfect Friday.* 1971: *Quest for Love.* 1972: *Au Pair Girls. Bless This House. Mission to Monte Carlo. The Best Pair of Legs in the Business.* 1973: *Naughty Wives. Secrets of a Door-to-Door Salesman.* 1974: *Man about the House. Bedtime with Rosie.* 1975: *Carry On Behind.* 1976: *The Office Party. Carry On England.*

BRIMLEY, (A.) Wilford 1934–

Barrel-like, moustachioed, often bespectacled American actor with blinky eyes who has almost always played characters older than his real age. Brimley was a farm worker and rodeo rider who gained weight and became a blacksmith, then determined to be a film actor and gradually got a toehold after years of extra work. Nowadays giving fine performances in fat (!) character roles as crusty but sympathetic types, although less often seen in recent times.

1968: *Bandolero!* 1969: *True Grit.* 1971: *Lawman.* 1976: *The Oregon Trail (TV).* 1978: *The China Syndrome.* 1979: *The Wild, Wild West Revisited (TV). The Electric Horseman.* 1980: *Brubaker. Borderline. Amber Waves (TV). Roughnecks.* 1981: *Rodeo Girl. Death Valley. Absence of Malice. The Big Black Pill (TV).* 1982: *The Thing. Tender Mercies.* 1983: *Tough Enough/Tough Dreams.* 10 *to Midnight. High Road to China.* 1984: *Harry & Son. The Hotel New Hampshire. Country. The Natural. The Stone Boy.* 1985: *Cocoon. Murder in Space (TV). Remo Williams: The Adventure Begins (GB: Remo – Unarmed and Dangerous). Act of Vengeance (TV). Ewoks: The Battle for Endor (TV).* 1986: *Thompson's Last Run (TV). American Justice.* 1987: *End of the Line. Shadow on the Wall.* 1988: *Cocoon: The Return.* 1989: *Eternity. Billy the Kid (TV).* 1990: *Where the Red Fern Grows.* 1991: *Blood River (TV).* 1992: *Where the Red Fern Grows Part Two.* 1993: *Hard Target. The Firm.* 1994: *Op Center (TV).* 1995: *Bioforce 1. Heaven Sent. The Good Old Boys (TV). Chapter Perfect.*

BROCCO, Peter 1903–1993

Scrawny, sharp-featured, often dishevelled American actor with dark, thinning hair and 'continental villain' looks. After star roles in local repertory, he toured French, Italian, Spanish and Swiss theatre before consolidating a hitherto sporadic Hollywood career in post-war years. From 1946, he started playing vicious or frightened little men regularly in movies, actually appearing once as a character called 'Short and Thin'; although 5 feet 9 inches, his slight build could make him on occasion seem less. Amazingly, he was still around on the acting scene in roles both sizeable and tiny well into his eighties; he had his first film lead at 70 in the 1973 film *Homebodies.* His liberal politics caused him to be briefly blacklisted in the late 1950s. Died from a heart attack.

1932: *Devil and the Deep.* 1942: *Stand By All Networks.* 1946: *The Return of Monte Cristo.* 1947: *The Swordsman. Alias Mr Twilight. The Lone Wolf in Mexico.* 1948: *The Gallant Blade. The Countess of Monte Cristo. The Argyle Secrets. The Vicious Circle. Appointment with Murder. The Boy with Green Hair. The Saxon Charm.* 1949: *Post Office Investigator. The Undercover Man. Flaming Fury. Jolson Sings Again. Beyond These Walls. The Lady Gambles. Tension. Search for Danger. Boston Blackie's Chinese Venture (GB: Chinese Adventure). Prison Warden. Susanna Pass. Miss Grant Takes Richmond (US: Innocence is Bliss). The Reckless Moment.* 1950: *Black Hand. Three Secrets. The Killer That Stalked New York (GB: The Frightened City). Key to the City. House by the River. The Breaking Point. Gunmen of Abilene. Champagne for Caesar. Peggy.* 1951: *Flame of Stamboul. The Great Caruso. Road Block. Sirocco. The Tall Target. Francis Goes to the Races. His Kind of Woman. Drums in the Deep South. The Whip Hand. Too Young to Kiss. The Fat Man. Belle le Grand.* 1952: *Ma and Pa Kettle on Vacation (GB: Ma and Pa Kettle Go to Paris). Harem Girl. Woman in the Dark. Radar Men from the Moon (serial). The Narrow Margin. Actors and Sin. Cripple Creek. The Prisoner of Zenda. Mutiny. The Ring.* 1953: *El Alamein (GB: Desert Patrol). The Bandits of Corsica (GB: Return of the Corsican Brothers). The Story of Three Loves.* 1954: *Duffy of San Quentin (GB: Men Behind Bars). Tobor the Great. Rogue Cop.* 1955: *The Racers (GB: Such Men Are Dangerous). Thrill of the Ring. The Big Knife. I'll Cry Tomorrow.* 1956: *Superman Flies Again (TV. GB: cinemas). He Laughed Last. Hot Blood.* 1957: *Black Patch.* 1959: *Compulsion.* 1960: *Elmer Gantry. Spartacus.* 1961: *Fear No More. Underworld USA.* 1962: *The Three Stooges in Orbit. A Public Affair.* 1963: *The Balcony.* 1964: *The Pleasure Seekers.* 1965: *Dark Intruder. Girl Happy. Our Man Flint.* 1966: *The Russians Are Coming, the Russians Are Coming.* 1967: *Enter Laughing. Games.* 1969: *A Time for Dying. Then Came Bronson (TV. GB: cinemas). The Comic. Gaily, Gaily (GB: Chicago, Chicago). Hail, Hero! Some Kind of Nut.* 1971: *Alias Smith and Jones (TV). Johnny Got His Gun. The Priest Killer (TV). What's the Matter with Helen?* 1972: *Outside In. Fuzz.* 1973: *Homebodies. The Killing Kind.* 1974: *The Family Kovack (TV).* 1975: *One Flew Over the Cuckoo's Nest.* 1976: *Raid on Entebbe (TV. GB: cinemas).* 1977: *The One and Only.* 1979:

Butch and Sundance The Early Days. 1980: Cruising. 1982: Fighting Back (GB: Death Vengeance). 1983: The Twilight Zone (GB: Twilight Zone The Movie). Jekyll and Hyde Together Again. Night Partners (TV). 1984: The Ratings Game (TV). 1987: Throw Momma from the Train. 1989: The War of the Roses.

BROMBERG, J. Edward 1903–1951

Plump-chinned, bespectacled, Hungarian-born actor, in America from childhood. Prematurely-greying hair saw him cast in character roles from his 1936 début, often as doctors and professors, but in a generally satisfying variety of types. His services were less in demand in the post-war years and he was in London when he collapsed and died 'of natural causes' just days short of his 48th birthday.

1936: Sins of Man. The Crime of Dr Forbes. Under Two Flags. Girls' Dormitory. Ladies in Love. Star for a Night. Stowaway. Reunion (GB: Hearts in Reunion). 1937: Fair Warning. Seventh Heaven. Charlie Chan on Broadway. That I May Live. Second Honeymoon. 1938: The Baroness and the Butler. Mr Moto Takes a Chance. Four Men and a Prayer. Suez. Sally, Irene and Mary. Rebecca of Sunnybrook Farm. I'll Give a Million. 1939: Jesse James. Hollywood Cavalcade. Wife, Husband and Friend. Three Sons. 1940: The Mark of Zorro. Strange Cargo. The Return of Frank James. 1941: Dance Hall. The Devil Pays Off. Hurricane Smith. Pacific Blackout. 1942: Invisible Agent. Life Begins at Eight-Thirty (GB: The Light of Heart). Tennessee Johnson (GB: The Man on America's Conscience). Reunion/Reunion in France (GB: Mademoiselle France). Half-Way to Shanghai. 1943: Lady of Burlesque (GB: Striptease Lady). Son of Dracula. Phantom of the Opera. 1944: A Voice in the Wind. Chip Off the Old Block. 1945: Salome, Where She Danced. The Missing Corpse. Easy to Look At. Pillow of Death. 1946: Cloak and Dagger. Tangier. The Walls Game Tumbling Down. Queen of the Amazons. 1948: Arch of Triumph. A Song is Born. 1949: I Shot Jesse James. 1950: Guilty Bystander.

BROMLEY, Sydney 1909–1987

Wiry, gimlet-eyed, quick-moving, ginger-bearded British actor, mostly in very minor film roles (after beginning as over-age school-boys in Will Hay comedies) as toothless

hayseeds or rural sages. In the theatre, however, Bromley built up a very different reputation, as a formidable interpreter of eccentric Shakespearian roles. Always highly distinctive.

1935: Boys Will Be Boys. 1936: As You Like It. 1937: Good Morning Boys! (US: Where There's a Will). 1944: Demobbed. 1945: Brief Encounter. 1946: Loyal Heart. 1947: The Mark of Cain. The Dark Road. 1948: To the Public Danger. 1954: The Love Match. Devil's Point (US: Devil's Harbor). 1955: Stolen Time (US: Blonde Blackmailer). 1957: Saint Joan. 1960: The Criminal (US: The Concrete Jungle). 1961: The Piper's Tune. 1962: Paranoia. Captain Clegg (US: Night Creatures). 1963: Heavens Above! Father Came Too. 1965: Monster of Terror (US: Die, Monster, Die). Carry On Cowboy. 1966: Operation Third Form. The Christmas Tree. Slave Girls (US: Prehistoric Women). Carry On Screaming. 1967: Smashing Time. Dance of the Vampires (US: The Fearless Vampire Killers). 1968: A Little of What You Fancy. Night of the Big Heat (US: Island of the Burning Damned). Half a Sixpence. 1971: Macbeth. 1973: No Sex Please – We're British. Frankenstein and the Monster from Hell. 1974: Professor Popper's Problem (serial). 1975: Robin Hood Junior. 1977: The Prince and the Pauper (US: Crossed Swords). Candleshoe. 1980: Dangerous Davies – The Last Detective (TV). 1981: An American Werewolf in London. Dragonslayer. 1984: The Neverending Story. 1985: Pirates. 1987: Crystalstone.

BROOK-JONES, Elwyn 1911–1962

Chubby British actor with round face, small features and dark, receding hair, often to be found playing blue-jowled, sweaty types, usually on the disreputable side. Born in Sarawak, he studied music as a child and was a concert pianist at 11. After a career in concert-halls and cabaret, he turned to acting in the late 1930s, and played many Shakespearian roles, as well as in a number of films—most notably as Tober in *Odd Man Out*.

1941: Dangerous Moonlight (US: Suicide Squadron). Pimpernel Smith (US: Mister V). 1942: Tomorrow We Live (US: At Dawn We Die). 1943: The Night Invader. 1946: Odd Man Out. 1948: The Three Weird Sisters. Good Time Girl. The Small Back Room (US:

Hour of Glory). Bonnie Prince Charlie. It's Hard to Be Good. 1949: Dear Mr Prohack. 1951: Life in Her Hands. I'll Get You for This (US: Lucky Nick Cain). The Wonder Kid. Judgment Deferred. 1952: The Night Won't Talk. 1953: Three Steps in the Dark. 1954: The Harassed Hero. The Case of the Bogus Count. The Gilded Cage. Beau Brummell. 1956: Assignment Redhead (US: Million Dollar Manhunt). Rogue's Yarn. 1958: The Duke Wore Jeans. 1959: Passport to Shame (US: Room 43). The Ugly Duckling. Mystery in the Mine. 1960: The Pure Hell of St Trinian's.

BROPHY, Edward/Ed 1895–1960

Thick-set, podgy-faced, bald American actor in aggressive parts. His speak-first-think-later roles included several thick detectives who embarrassed their superiors, and a rather bizarre collection of valets, blustering politicians and cheap chisellers. His bald head often concealed under a bowler hat, Brophy remains one of the best examples of the recognizable face to which it is hard to put a name.

1920: Yes or No. 1928: West Point (GB: Eternal Youth). The Cameraman. Spite Marriage. 1930: Doughboys (GB: Forward March). Our Blushing Brides. Remote Control. Paid (GB: Within the Law). Those Three French Girls. Free and Easy. 1931: A Free Soul. Parlor, Bedroom and Bath (GB: Romeo in Pyjamas). The Champ. A Dangerous Affair. The Big Shot (GB: The Optimist). 1932: Skyscraper Souls. Speak Easily. Freaks. Flesh. 1933: Broadway to Hollywood (GB: Ring Up the Curtain). What, No Beer? 1934: Death on

the Diamond. The Thin Man. Paris Interlude. The Hide-Out. I'll Fix It. Evelyn Prentice. 1935: The Whole Town's Talking (GB: Passport to Fame). Naughty Marietta. Shadow of Doubt. Mad Love (GB: The Hands of Orlac). China Seas. People Will Talk. I Live My Life. Remember Last Night? She Gets Her Man. Show Them No Mercy (GB: Tainted Money). $1,000 a Minute. 1936: Strike Me Pink. Woman Trap. Spendthrift. Wedding Present. The Case Against Mrs Ames. Kelly the Second. All-American Chump (GB: Country Bumpkin). Here Comes Trouble. Great Guy. Career Woman. Mr Cinderella. 1937: Varsity Show. The Soldier and the Lady (GB: Michael Strogoff). Hideaway Girl. The Great Gambini. Blossoms on Broadway. Jim Hanvey, Detective. The Hit Parade. Oh, Doctor! The Last Gangster. The Girl Said No. Trapped by G-Men (GB: River of Missing Men). 1938: A Slight Case of Murder. Gambling Ship. Romance on the Run. Hold That Kiss. Passport Husband. Vacation from Love. Come On, Leathernecks. Pardon Our Nerve. Gold Diggers in Paris (GB: The Gay Impostors). 1939: For Love or Money. Society Lawyer. You Can't Cheat an Honest Man. The Amazing Mr Williams. The Kid from Kokomo (GB: The Orphan of the Ring). Kid Nightingale. Golden Boy. 1940: Calling Philo Vance. The Big Guy. A Dangerous Game. Sandy Gets Her Man. Dance, Girl, Dance. The Great Profile. Alias the Deacon. Golden Gloves. 1941: The Invisible Woman. Sleepers West. Dumbo (voice only). Thieves Fall Out. The Bride Came COD. Buy Me That Town. The Gay Falcon. Steel Against the Sky. Nine Lives Are Not Enough. 1942: All Through the Night. Broadway. Larceny Inc. Madame Spy. One Exciting Night. Air Force. 1943: Lady Bodyguard. Destroyer. 1944: A Night of Adventure. It Happened Tomorrow. Cover Girl. The Thin Man Goes Home. 1945: I'll Remember April. Wonder Man. See My Lawyer. Penthouse Rhythm. The Falcon in San Francisco. 1946: Swing Parade of 1946. Sweetheart of Sigma Chi. Girl on the Spot. The Falcon's Adventure. Renegade Girl. 1947: It Happened on Fifth Avenue. 1949: Arson Inc. 1951: Roaring City. Danger Zone. Pier 23. 1956: Bundle of Joy. 1958: The Last Hurrah.

BROUGH, Mary 1863–1934
Probably the first great character actress of British sound films. This fierce, chunky little woman brought her haranguing approach from the stage to screen, most notably

in her last few years, as a formidable adversary for the Aldwych farceurs. You felt that anyone hit by Mary Brough's umbrella would stay hit. Brown-haired and pugnacious, she was a stage actress for more than 50 years. Died from a heart ailment.

1914: The Brass Bottle. *Lawyer Quince. *Beauty and the Barge. *The Bo'sun's Mate. A Christmas Carol. *Mrs Scrubs' Discovery. 1915: His Lordship. 1917: Masks and Faces. 1920: The Amazing Quest of Mr Ernest Bliss (serial). London Pride. Enchantment. Judge Not. The Law Divine. The Fordington Twins. John Forrest Finds Himself. 1921: The Will. The Tainted Venus. The Diamond Necklace. Squibs. Demos (US: Why Men Forget). The Bachelor's Club. All Sorts and Conditions of Men. The Golden Dawn. The Night Hawk. The Adventures of Mr Pickwick. The Old Wives' Tale. 1922: Squibs Wins the Calcutta Sweep. Tit for Tat. A Sister to Assist 'Er. 1923: Lily of the Alley. Lights of London. Married Love. The School for Scandal. 1924: Miriam Rozella. Tons of Money. His Grace Gives Notice. The Passionate Adventure. The Alley of Golden Hearts. Not for Sale. 1925: The Only Way. 1926 *John Henry Calling (series). Safety First. 1927: A Sister to Assist 'Er (and 1922 version). 1928: Dawn. Sailors Don't Care. Wait and See. The Physician. The Passing of Mr Quin. *Nursery Chairs. *The King's Breakfast. 1929: Master and Man. The Broken Melody. 1930: Rookery Nook (US: One Embarrassing Night). On Approval. 1931: Tons of Money (and 1924 version). Plunder. The Chance of a Nighttime. 1932: A Night Like This. Thark. 1933: A Cuckoo in the Nest. Up to the Neck. Turkey Time.

BROWN, Clancy 1947–
Big, tall, shambling American actor with curly brown hair and gimlet eyes, who looks menacing even when he's playing the hero. His interpretation of the Frankenstein monster made him one of the few people to emerge with credit from The Bride, but since then he's played various frightening characters without quite rising above the status of co-star. But he did have the leading role in the 1991 TV mini-series, Love, Lies and Murder.

1983: Bad Boys. 1984: Thunder Alley. The Adventures of Buckaroo Banzai Across the Eighth Dimension. 1985: The Bride. 1986: Extreme Prejudice. Highlander. 1987: The Man Who

Broke 1,000 Chains (cable TV). 1988: Shoot to Kill (GB: Deadly Pursuit). An American Murder. 1989: Season of Fear. Blue Steel. Waiting for the Light. 1990: Johnny Ryan (TV). 1991: Ambition (formerly Mind Game). Past Midnight. Cast a Deadly Spell. 1992: Pet Sematary Two. 1993: Last Light (TV). 1994: The Shawshank Redemption.

BRUCE, Nigel
(William N. Bruce) 1895–1953
British actor (born in Mexico) who carved a whole corner for himself in well-meaning bumbler-fumblers and cuckolded husbands. His Doctor Watson in the Sherlock Holmes films of the thirties and forties, although excellent at first, tended to drift into caricature in later films. In British films from 1929, Hollywood from 1934. Died from a heart attack.

1929: Red Aces. 1930: The Squeaker. Escape. Birds of Prey (US: The Perfect Alibi. 1931: The Calendar (US: Bachelor's Folly). 1932: The Midshipmaid. Lord Camber's Ladies. 1933: I Was a Spy. Channel Crossing. The Lady is Willing. 1934: The Scarlet Pimpernel. Springtime for Henry. Stand Up and Cheer. Coming Out Party. Murder in Trinidad. Treasure Island. 1935: Becky Sharp. Jalna. She. The Man Who Broke the Bank at Monte Carlo. 1936: Thunder in the City. The Trail of the Lonesome Pine. The Charge of the Light Brigade. Under Two Flags. *Florence Nightingale. The White Angel. Make Way for a Lady. Follow Your Heart. The Man I Marry. 1937: The Last of Mrs Cheyney. 1938: The Baroness and the Butler. Kidnapped. Suez. 1939: The Hound of the Baskervilles. The Adventures of Sherlock Holmes (GB: Sherlock Holmes). The Rains Came. 1940: Adventure in Diamonds. Rebecca. The Bluebird. Lillian Russell. Hudson's Bay. Susan and God (GB: The Gay Mrs Trexel). A Dispatch from Reuter's (GB: This Man Reuter). 1941: Playgirl. The Chocolate Soldier. Free and Easy. This Woman is Mine. Suspicion. 1942: Roxie Hart. Eagle Squadron. Sherlock Holmes and the Voice of Terror (GB: The Voice of Terror). This Above All. Journey for Margaret. Sherlock Holmes and the Secret Weapon. 1943: Forever and a Day. Sherlock Holmes in Washington. Sherlock Holmes Faces Death. Crazy House. Lassie Come Home. 1944: Follow the Boys. The Pearl of Death. Gypsy Wildcat. The Scarlet Claw. Frenchman's Creek. Sherlock Holmes and Spider Woman (GB: The Spider Woman). House of Fear. 1945: The Corn is Green. Son of Lassie. The Woman in Green. Pursuit to Algiers. 1946: Terror by Night. Dragonwyck. Dressed to Kill (GB: Sherlock Holmes and the Secret Code). 1947: The Two Mrs Carrolls. The Exile. 1948: Julia Misbehaves. 1950: Vendetta. 1951: Hong Kong. 1952: Limelight. Othello. 1953: Bwana Devil. 1954: World for Ransom.

BRYAN, Dora
(D. Broadbent) 1923—
Fluffy blonde British actress, with pixieish smile, nearly always seen as maids or strumpets. Originally from Lancashire, she could vary her high nasal tones effectively enough to suggest the backstreets of Soho or the sidestreets of Southport. A British Academy Award for her fine performance in *A Taste of Honey* did not produce further leading roles for the cinema; indeed her output diminished considerably thereafter.

1946: Odd Man Out. 1948: The Fallen Idol. No Room at the Inn. 1949: Now Barabbas was a robber... Adam and Evelyne (US: Adam and Evalyn). Once Upon a Dream. Don't Ever Leave Me. The Perfect Woman. The Interrupted Journey. Traveller's Joy (released 1951). The Blue Lamp. The Cure for Love. 1950: No Trace. Something in the City. 1951: Files from Scotland Yard. The Quiet Woman. Circle of Danger. Scarlet Thread. No Highway (US: No Highway in the Sky). High Treason. Lady Godiva Rides Again. Whispering Smith Hits London (US: Whispering Smith versus Scotland Yard). 1952: 13 East Street. Gift Horse (US: Glory at Sea). Time Gentlemen Please! Mother Riley Meets the Vampire (US: Vampire Over London). Made in Heaven. The Ringer. Miss Robin Hood. Women of Twilight (US: Twilight Women). 1953: Street Corner (US: Both Sides of the Law). The Fake. The Intruder. You Know What Sailors Are. 1954: Fast and Loose. The Crowded Day. *Harmony Lane. Mad About Men. 1955: As Long As They're Happy. See How They Run. You Lucky People. Cockleshell Heroes. 1956: The Green Man. Child in the House. 1957: The Man Who Wouldn't Talk. Small Hotel. 1958: Hello London! Carry On Sergeant. 1959: Operation Bullshine. Desert Mice. 1960: Follow That Horse! The Night We Got the Bird. 1961: A Taste of Honey. 1966: The Great St Trinian's Train Robbery. The Sandwich Man. 1968: Two a Penny. 1971:

Hands of the Ripper. 1972: Up the Front. 1983: Screamtime (V). 1988: Apartment Zero.
(V) Video

BUCHANAN, Edgar
(William E. Buchanan) 1902—1979
Light-haired, often bewhiskered American actor of chubby build. Appeared mainly in westerns, as veteran sheriffs, boozy bankers, crooked judges, or just as the hero's sidekick. A former dentist, he started alternating acting with dentistry in the 1930s before becoming a full-time actor and making close to 100 films, his distinctive growling voice matching his round 'country-boy' features. Died following brain surgery.

1939: My Son is Guilty (GB: Crime's End). Tear Gas Squad. 1940: Three Cheers for the Irish. Too Many Husbands. The Doctor Takes a Wife. When the Daltons Rode. Arizona. Escape to Glory. The Sea Hawk. 1941: Penny Serenade. Submarine Zone. Her First Beau. Richest Man in Town. Texas. You Belong to Me (GB: Good Morning, Doctor). 1942: Tombstone, the Town Too Tough to Die. The Talk of the Town. 1943: City Without Men. The Desperadoes. Good Luck, Mr Yates. Destroyer. *Mr Smug. 1944: Buffalo Bill. The Impatient Years. Bride By Mistake. 1945: Strange Affair. The Fighting Guardsman. Abilene Town. 1946: The Bandit of Sherwood Forest. The Walls Came Tumbling Down. Perilous Holiday. If I'm Lucky. Renegades. 1947: The Sea of Grass. Framed (GB: Paula). 1948: The Swordsman. Wreck of the Hesperus. Adventures in Silverado. Best Man Wins. The Black Arrow (GB: The Black Arrow Strikes). The Untamed Breed. Coroner Creek. The Man from Colorado. 1949: The Walking Hills. Red Canyon. Any Number Can Play. Lust for Gold. 1950: Cheaper by the Dozen. Cargo to Capetown. The Big Hangover. Devil's Doorway. 1951: The Great Missouri Raid. Cave of Outlaws. Rawhide (GB: Desperate Siege). Silver City (GB: High Vermilion). 1952: Flaming Feather. The Big Trees. Wild Stallion. Toughest Man in Arizona. 1953: It Happens Every Thursday. Shane. Make Haste to Live. She Couldn't Say No (GB: Beautiful But Dangerous). 1954: Dawn at Socorro. Human Desire. Destry. 1955: Rage at Dawn. Wichita. The Silver Star. The Lonesome Trail. 1956: Come Next Spring. 1957: Spoilers of the Forest. 1958: Day of the Bad Man. The Sheepman. 1959: King of the Wild Stallions. It Started

With a Kiss. Hound Dog Man. Edge of Eternity. 1960: Four Fast Guns. Stump Run. Chartroose Caboose. 1961: Cimarron. The Devil's Partner. Tammy Tell Me True. The Comancheros. Ride the High Country (GB: Guns in the Afternoon). 1963: Donovan's Reef. Move Over, Darling. McLintock! A Ticklish Affair. 1964: The Man from Button Willow (voice only). 1965: The Rounders. 1966: Gunpoint. Welcome to Hard Times (GB: Killer on a Horse). 1969: Angel in My Pocket. Something for a Lonely Man. The Over-the-Hill Gang (TV). 1970: The Over-the-Hill Gang Rides Again (TV). 1971: Yuma (TV). 1974: Benji.

BULL, Peter 1912—1984
Corpulent British actor with frog-like features, a hobgoblin of a man usually cast as arrogant, aristocratic nasties who sometimes came to a sticky end. He also enjoyed himself in snooty comedy roles. In private life the most affable of men, Bull wrote several books, ran an astrological shop and was the world's leading authority on teddy bears. At one time he ran his own repertory company, and won the DSC with the Royal Navy during World War II. A formidable wit and genuine English eccentric, the title of his autobiography would have done for most of the people in this book: *I Know the Face But . . .* Some filmographies credit Bull with *The Silent Voice* in 1934, but it's a title I have been unable to verify.

1936: As You Like It. Sabotage (US: The Woman Alone). 1937: Dreaming Lips. Knight Without Armour. Non-Stop New York. 1938: The Ware Case. Marie Antoinette. 1939: Dead Man's Shoes. Young Man's Fancy. Inspector Hornleigh on Holiday (US: Inspector Hornleigh on Leave). 1940: Contraband (US: Blackout). 1941: Quiet Wedding. 1946: The Grand Escapade. 1947: The Turners of Prospect Road. They Made Me a Fugitive (US: I Became a Criminal). 1948: Woman Hater. Saraband for Dead Lovers (US: Saraband). Oliver Twist. Cardboard Cavalier. 1949: The Lost People. 1950: The Reluctant Widow. 1951: I'll Get You for This (US: Lucky Nick Cain). Salute the Toff. The African Queen. The Six Men. Scrooge (US: A Christmas Carol). The Lavender Hill Mob. 1952: The Second Mrs Tanqueray. 1953: Strange Stories. Malta Story. The Captain's Paradise. Saadia. 1954: Beau Brummell. 1955: Footsteps in the Fog. Who Done It?

1956: *The Green Man.* 1958: *The Horse's Mouth. tom thumb.* 1959: *The Scapegoat. The Three Worlds of Gulliver.* 1960: *The Girl on the Boat.* 1961: *Goodbye Again/Aimez-vous Brahms? Follow That Man. The Rebel (US: Call Me Genius).* 1962: *The Old Dark House.* 1963: *Tom Jones.* 1964: *Dr Strangelove, or: How I Learned to Stop Worrying and Love the Bomb.* 1965: *Licensed to Kill (US: The Second Best Secret Agent in the Whole Wide World). You Must Be Joking! The Intelligence Men.* 1967: *Doctor Dolittle.* 1969: *Lock Up Your Daughters!* 1970: *The Executioner.* 1971: *Girl Stroke Boy.* 1972: *Up the Front. Alice's Adventures in Wonderland. Lady Caroline Lamb.* 1975: *Great Expectations (TV. GB: cinemas).* 1976: *Joseph Andrews.* 1978: *Rosie Dixon Night Nurse. The Brute.* 1979: *The Tempest.* 1980: *The Mirror Crack'd.* 1982: **Dead on Time.* 1983: *Yellowbeard.*

BUONO, Victor 1938–1982

It's a pity Victor Buono pointed his massive, heavyweight frame towards comedy, for he could have been a latter-day Laird Cregar. But there are some reminders of what a good, suave, straight villain he could have made, especially in *What Ever Happened to Baby Jane?* (which brought him an Oscar nomination), *The Strangler* and *Goodnight My Love*, the latter a TV movie in which, as the white-suited gourmet villain, he could well be a younger Sydney Greenstreet.

1962: *What Ever Happened to Baby Jane?* 1963: *Four for Texas. My Six Loves.* 1964: *The Strangler. Robin and the Seven Hoods.* 1965: *Hush . . . Hush, Sweet Charlotte. Asylum for a Spy (TV). Big Daddy (released 1969). The Greatest Story Ever Told. Young Dillinger.* 1966: *The Silencers. Who's Minding the Mint? No Place for the Dead.* 1967: *Is This Trip Really Necessary?* 1968: *In the Name of Our Father.* 1969: *Beneath the Planet of the Apes. How to Make It (later Target Harry). La collina degli stivali (US: Boot Hill).* 1970: *Savage Season.* 1971: *L'Uomo dagli occhi di ghiaccio/ The Man with Ice in His Eyes. Mother.* 1972: *The Wrath of God. Goodnight My Love (TV). The Crime Club (TV). Der Würger kommt auf leisen Socken (US: The Mad Butcher). Northeast to Seoul.* 1973: *Arnold.* 1974: *Moon Child. Brenda Starr, Girl Reporter (TV).* 1976: *High Risk (TV).* 1977: *Savage in the City. Cyclone.* 1978: *The Evil.* 1979: *The Return of the Mod Squad (TV). Better Late Than Never (TV). The Man With Bogart's Face.* 1980:

Murder Can Hurt You! (TV). More Wild, Wild West (TV). 1983: *The Flight of Dragons (TV. voice only).*

BURKE, Alfred 1918–

Lean, brown-haired British actor with world-weary look and faintly desperate and dangerous air. He started in British films as villains, then scored a big personal success as a very down-at-heel detective in the long-running TV series *Public Eye.* Later roles revealed the serious actor behind the grubby raincoat, dark shirts and occasional flourish of a revolver.

1955: *The Constant Husband. Touch and Go (US: The Light Touch).* 1956: *Let's Be Happy.* 1957: *Bitter Victory. Interpol (US: Pickup Alley). Yangtse Incident (US: Battle Hell). The Long Haul.* 1958: *No Time to Die! (US: Tank Force). The Man Inside. The Man Upstairs. Law and Disorder.* 1959: *Operation Amsterdam. Model for Murder. The Angry Silence.* 1960: *Moment of Danger (US: Malaga). The Trials of Oscar Wilde (US: The Man with the Green Carnation). Dead Lucky.* 1961: *She Knows Y'Know. Man at the Carlton Tower.* 1962: *Backfire. Crooks Anonymous. On the Beat. The Pot Carriers. The Man Who Finally Died. Locker 69. Mix Me a Person.* 1963: *The Small World of Sammy Lee. The £20,000 Kiss. Farewell Performance.* 1964: *Children of the Damned.* 1965: *The Nanny. The Night Caller.* 1968: *Guns in the Heather.* 1971: *One Day in the Life of Ivan Denisovitch.* 1979: *The House on Garibaldi Street (TV. GB: cinemas).* 1984: *Kim (TV).*

BURKE, Billie

(Mary William Burke) 1885–1970
Pretty American stage star, a silky blonde (daughter of a circus clown) who had leading roles in a few silents after her marriage to showman Florenz Ziegfeld in 1914 (he died in 1932). After his death, she consolidated the Hollywood comeback she had begun in character roles as nice aunts and fluttery matrons. Probably best remembered today as Mrs Topper in the *Topper* ghost comedies, and as the Blue Fairy in *The Wizard of Oz.* Academy Award nomination for *Merrily We Live*

1915: *Peggy.* 1916: *Gloria's Romance (serial).* 1917: *The Land of Promise. The Mysterious*

Miss Terry. Arms and the Girl. 1918: *Eve's Daughter. In Pursuit of Polly. The Make Believe Wife. Let's Get a Divorce.* 1919: *Good Gracious, Annabelle. The Misleading Widow. Wanted – a Husband.* 1920: *Sadie Love. Away Goes Prudence.* 1921: *The Education of Elizabeth. The Frisky Mrs Johnson.* 1929: *Glorifying the American Girl.* 1930: *Ranch House Blues.* 1932: *A Bill of Divorcement.* 1933: *Christopher Strong. Dinner at Eight. Only Yesterday.* 1934: *Finishing School. Where Sinners Meet (GB: The Dover Road). We're Rich Again. Forsaking All Others. Only Eight Hours.* 1935: *Becky Sharp. Doubting Thomas. A Feather in Her Hat. Society Doctor. She Couldn't Take It (GB: Woman Tamer). Splendor. After Office Hours.* 1936: *Piccadilly Jim. My American Wife. Craig's Wife.* 1937: *Parnell. Navy Blue and Gold. Topper. The Bride Wore Red.* 1938: *Everybody Sing. The Young in Heart. Merrily We Live.* 1939: *Topper Takes a Trip. The Wizard of Oz. The Bridal Suite. Eternally Yours. Remember? Zenobia (GB: Elephants Never Forget).* 1940: *And One Was Beautiful. Irene. Hullabaloo. Dulcy. The Ghost Comes Home. The Captain is a Lady.* 1941: *Topper Returns. One Night in Lisbon. The Man Who Came to Dinner.* 1942: *The Wild Man of Borneo. In This Our Life. What's Cookin'? (GB: Wake Up and Dream). They All Kissed the Bride. Girl Trouble.* 1943: *Hi Diddle Diddle. So's Your Uncle. You're a Lucky Fellow, Mr Smith. Gildersleeve on Broadway.* 1944: *Laramie Trail.* 1945: *Swing Out, Sister. The Cheaters.* 1946: *Breakfast in Hollywood (GB: The Mad Hatter). The Bachelor's Daughters.* 1948: **Silly Billy. *Billie Gets Her Man.* 1949: *The Barkleys of Broadway.* 1940: *And Baby Makes Three. Father of the Bride. Three Husbands. The Boy from Indiana (GB: Blaze of Glory).* 1951: *Father's Little Dividend. Darling, How Could You? (GB: Rendezvous).* 1953: *Small Town Girl.* 1957: *The Star-Wagon (TV).* 1958: *Rumors of Evening (TV).* 1959: *The Young Philadelphians (GB: The City Jungle).* 1960: *Sergeant Rutledge. Pepe.*

BURNETTE, Smiley

(Lester Burnette) 1911–1967
In the days when every 'B' western star had comic-books devoted to their imaginary adventures, only two 'sidekicks' were awarded the accolade of a comic to themselves. One of these was George 'Gabby' Hayes (qv); the other was tubby Smiley Burnette, with

his flapjack black stetson, and manic humour. Living up to his nickname by always grinning, Burnette came on like a chubbier version of Eddie Bracken, coming into films with his friend Gene Autry (whose radio vocals he had backed on guitar). He remained one of the most popular 'B'-westerns, with a number of partners, through the 1930s and 1940s, sticking with the genre until it petered out in 1953. When appearing as a regular on the TV comedy series *Petticoat Junction*, Burnette learned he had leukaemia, the disease that killed him at 55. Also a prolific songwriter.

1934: *In Old Santa Fé. Mystery Mountain (serial). 1935: The Phantom Empire (serial). Tumbling Tumbleweeds. Waterfront Lady. Melody Trail. The Sagebrush Troubadour. The Singing Vagabond. The Adventures of Rex and Rinty (serial). Streamline Express. Harmony Lane. 1936: Hitch Hike Lady (GB: Eventful Journey). Doughnuts and Society (GB: Stepping into Society). Red River Valley. Comin' Round the Mountain. Oh, Susannah! The Singing Cowboy. Guns and Guitars. Ride, Ranger, Ride. The Big Show. The Old Corral (GB: Texas Serenade). Hearts in Bondage. A Man Betrayed. The Border Patrolman. 1937: Round-Up Time in Texas. Rootin' Tootin' Rhythm (GB: Rhythm on the Ranch). Git Along Little Dogies (GB: Serenade of the West). Yodelin' Kid from Pine Ridge (GB: The Hero of Pine Ridge). Public Cowboy No. 1. Boots and Saddles. Manhattan Merry-Go-Round (GB: Manhattan Music Box). Springtime in the Rockies. Larceny on the Air. Dick Tracy (serial). Meet the Boy Friend. 1938: The Old Barn Dance. Gold Mine in the Sky. Man from Music Mountain. Prairie Moon. Rhythm of the Saddle. Western Jamboree. The Hollywood Stadium Mystery. Under Western Skies. Billy the Kid Returns. 1939: Home on the Prairie. Mexicali Rose. Blue Montana Skies. Mountain Rhythm. Colorado Sunset. In Old Monterey. Rovin' Tumbleweeds. South of the Border. 1940: Rancho Grande. Gaucho Serenade. Carolina Moon. Ride, Tenderfoot, Ride. Men with Steel Faces (GB: Couldn't Possibly Happen). 1941: Ridin' on a Rainbow. Back in the Saddle. The Singing Hills. Sunset in Wyoming. Under Fiesta Stars. Down Mexico Way. Sierra Sue. 1942: Cowboy Serenade (GB: Serenade of the West). Heart of the Rio Grande. Home in Wyoming. Stardust on the Sage. Call of the Canyon. Bells of Capistrano. Heart of the Golden West. 1943: Idaho. Beyond the*

Last Frontier. King of the Cowboys. Silver Spurs. 1944: Beneath Western Skies. Call of the Rockies. The Laramie Trail. Code of the Prairie. Pride of the Plains. Bordertown Trail. Firebrands of Arizona. 1946: Roaring Rangers (GB: False Hero). Galloping Thunder (GB: On Boot Hill). Frontier Gun Law (GB: Menacing Shadows). Two-Fisted Stranger. South of the Chisholm Trail. Heading West (GB: The Cheat's Last Throw). Terror Trail (GB: Hands of Menace). Gunning for Vengeance (GB: Jail Break). The Desert Horseman (GB: Checkmate). Landrush (GB: The Claw Strikes). The Fighting Frontiersman (GB: Golden Lady). 1947: The Lone Hand Texan (GB: The Cheat). Prairie Raiders (GB: The Forger). Riders of the Lone Star. The Buckaroo from Powder River. West of Dodge City (GB: The Sea Wall). Law of the Canyon (GB: The Price of Crime). The Stranger from Ponca City. The Last Days of Boot Hill. 1948: Whirlwind Raiders (GB: State Police). Phantom Valley. Blazing Across the Pecos (GB: Under Arrest). El Dorado Pass (GB: Desperate Men). West of Sonora. Six Gun Law. Trail to Laredo (GB: Sign of the Dagger). Quick on the Trigger (GB: Condemned in Error). 1949: Desert Vigilante. Challenge of the Range (GB: Moonlight Raid). Horsemen of the Sierras (GB: Remember Me). Bandits of El Dorado (GB: Tricked). The Blazing Trail (GB: The Forged Will). South of Death Valley (GB: River of Poison). Laramie. Renegades of the Sage (GB: The Fort). 1950: Trail of the Rustlers (GB: Lost River). Streets of Ghost Town. Outcasts of Black Mesa (GB: The Clue). Across the Badlands (GB: The Challenge). Raiders of Tomahawk Creek (GB: Circle of Fear). Texas Dynamo (GB: Suspected). Lightning Guns (GB: Taking Sides). Frontier Outpost. 1951: Whirlwind. Fort Savage Raiders. Prairie Roundup. Bonanza Town (GB: Two-Fisted Agent). The Kid from Amarillo (GB: Silver Chains). Riding the Outlaw Trail. Snake River Desperadoes. Cyclone Fury. Pecos River (GB: Without Risk). 1952: Junction City. Smoky Canyon. The Hawk of Wild River. The Rough, Tough West. Laramie Mountains (GB: Mountain Desperadoes). The Kid from Broken Gun. 1953: Winning of the West. On Top of Old Smoky. Pack Train. Goldtown Ghost Riders. Saginaw Trail. Last of the Pony Riders.*

BUSEY, Gary 1944–

Tall, toothy, gangling, broad-shouldered, fair-haired American actor, a man of many faces (you might be hard put to recognise Busey as himself) who was nominated for an Academy Award for his performance as a legendary figure of rock 'n' roll in *The Buddy Holly Story*. Busey not only looked like Holly (he looks nothing like him in real life), but contrived to sing like him as well. He's been around longer than you might think, and in a wider variety of roles than most other contemporary Hollywood players. Films rather too few until the past decade, when he embraced sympathetic and unsympathetic characters with equal relish and enthusiasm. A musician (played drums) for several years in his twenties.

1971: *Angels Hard As They Come. 1972: Dirty Little Billy. The Magnificent Seven Ride! 1973: Blood Sport (TV). Lolly Madonna XXX*

(GB: *The Lolly Madonna War). The Last American Hero. Hex. 1974: The Execution of Private Slovik (TV). The Law (TV). Thunderbolt and Lightfoot. 1976: The Gumball Rally. A Star is Born. 1977: Straight Time. 1978: Big Wednesday. The Buddy Holly Story. Foolin' Around (released 1980). 1980: Carny. 1982: Barbarosa (completed 1979). 1983: DC Cab (GB: Street Fleet). Didn't You Hear? 1984: The Bear. 1985: Insignificance. Silver Bullet. 1986: Let's Get Harry. Eye of the Tiger. 1987: Lethal Weapon. Bulletproof. 1988: Act of Piracy. 1989: Hider in the House. The Neon Empire. 1990: Predator 2. My Heroes Have Always Been Cowboys. Point Break. Wild Texas Wind (TV). 1992: Canvas (GB: Canvas – The Fine Art of Murder). The Player. Chrome Soldiers (TV). Under Siege. South Beach. 1993: Vengeance/The Set Up. Rookie of the Year. The Firm. Double Suspicion. Fallen Angels 2 (TV). 1994: Surviving the Game. Warriors. Pee Wee Football. Drop Zone. America! Chasers. 1995: Red Palms. Man With a Gun. Acts of Love.*

BUTTERWORTH, Charles 1896–1946

Twittering timidity was doleful-looking Charles Butterworth's stock-in-trade. A former law graduate and reporter, he turned to acting and brought his uniquely nervous manner to films with the coming of sound, together with a perennially dubious expression and a streak of fair hair that threatened to disappear from the top of his head. Often cast as vacillating rich bachelors who didn't get the girl. Killed in a car crash.

1930: *The Life of the Party. Illicit. 1931: Side Show. The Bargain. The Mad Genius. *The*

*Stolen Jools (GB: The Slippery Pearls). 1932: Beauty and the Boss. Love Me Tonight. Manhattan Parade. 1933: The Nuisance (GB: Accidents Wanted). Penthouse (GB: Crooks in Clover). My Weakness. 1934: Student Tour. Hollywood Party. The Cat and the Fiddle. Forsaking All Others. Bulldog Drummond Strikes Back. 1935: Ruggles of Red Gap. The Night is Young. Baby Face Harrington. Orchids to You. Magnificent Obsession. 1936: Half Angel. We Went to College. Rainbow on the River. The Moon's Our Home. 1937: Swing High, Swing Low. Every Day's a Holiday. 1938: Thanks for the Memory. 1939: Let Freedom Ring. 1940: The Boys from Syracuse. Second Chorus. 1941: Road Show. Blonde Inspiration. *There's Nothing to It. Sis Hopkins. 1942: What's Cookin'? (GB: Wake Up and Dream). Night in New Orleans. Give Out, Sisters. 1943: Always a Bridesmaid. The Sultan's Daughter. This is the Army. 1944: Follow the Boys. Bermuda Mystery. Dixie Jamboree.*

*Live Now – Pay Later. Kill or Cure. 1963: The Horse without a Head. The Rescue Squad. Doctor in Distress. 1964: Never Mention Murder. A Home of Your Own. 1965: Carry on Cowboy. The Amorous Adventures of Moll Flanders. 1966: A Funny Thing Happened on the Way to the Forum. Carry On Screaming. 1967: Don't Lose Your Head. Follow That Camel. *Ouch! Danny the Dragon. 1968: Carry On Doctor. Prudence and the Pill. Carry On Up the Khyber. 1970: Carry On Camping. Carry On Again, Doctor. 1970: Carry On Henry. Carry On Loving. 1971: The Magnificent Seven Deadly Sins. 1972: Carry On Abroad. Bless This House. Not Now Darling. 1973: Carry On Girls. 1974: Carry On Dick. 1975: Carry On Behind. 1976: Carry On England. The Ritz. Robin and Marian. 1977: What's Up Nurse? 1978: Carry On Emmannuelle. The First Great Train Robbery (US: The Great Train Robbery).*

Alexander Graham Bell (GB: The Modern Miracle). Everybody's Baby. Quick Millions. Chicken Wagon Family. Too Busy to Work. The Jones Family at the Grand Canyon. 1940: A Child is Born. The Blue Bird. On Their Own. The Ghost Comes Home. My Love Came Back. Lucky Partners. Laddie. Young As You Feel. 1941: Arkansas Judge (GB: False Witness). Meet John Doe. The Devil and Miss Jones. When Ladies Meet. Ellery Queen and the Perfect Crime (GB: The Perfect Crime). The Vanishing Virginian. 1942: Rings on Her Fingers. Roxie Hart. The Affairs of Martha. The War Against Mrs Hadley. Once Upon a Thursday. 1943: Presenting Lily Mars. Heaven Can Wait. The Heavenly Body. 1944: I'll Be Seeing You. 1945: Thrill of a Romance. Captain Eddie. Salty O'Rourke. The Enchanted Cottage. A Letter for Evie. 1946: Dragonwyck. Faithful in My Fashion. Meet Me on Broadway. Little Mr Jim. My Brother Talks to Horses. 1947: Singapore. It Had to Be You. Cynthia (GB: The Rich Full Life). Living in a Big Way. 1948: B.F.'s Daughter (GB: Polly Fulton). 1949: In the Good Old Summertime. The Big Wheel. 1950: Please Believe Me. Devil's Doorway. Louisa. Walk Softly, Stranger. The Reformer and the Redhead (voice only). The Skipper Surprised His Wife. 1951: Angels in the Outfield (GB: Angels and the Pirates). Bannerline. According to Mrs Hoyle. 1952: No Room for the Groom. Because You're Mine. 1954: The Rocket Man. 1960: Please Don't Eat the Daisies.

BUTTERWORTH, Peter 1919–1979
Tubby, brown-haired British light comedian and comic supporting actor, often as querulous incompetents or bungling minor officials. In very minor post-war film roles before bumbling his way to success on children's television, Butterworth was later a valuable member of the 'Carry On' team. He married star impressionist Janet Brown in 1949. Died from a heart attack.

*1948: William Comes to Town. 1949: The Adventures of Jane. Murder at the Windmill (US: Murder at the Burlesque). Miss Pilgrim's Progress. 1950: Circle of Danger. Night and the City. Paul Temple's Triumph. Mr Drake's Duck. The Body Said No! 1951: The Case of the Missing Scene. Old Mother Riley's Jungle Treasure. Appointment with Venus (US: Island Rescue). Saturday Island (US: Island of Desire). 1952: Penny Princess. Is Your Honeymoon Really Necessary? 1953: *Watch Out! *A Good Pull-Up. Will Any Gentleman? 1954: *Five O'Clock Finish. The Gay Dog. 1955: *Playground Express. Fun at St Fanny's. *Black in the Face. *That's an Order. 1958: Blow Your Own Trumpet. tom thumb. 1960: The Spider's Web. Escort for Hire. 1961: The Day the Earth Caught Fire. Murder She Said. 1962: Fate Takes a Hand. The Prince and the Pauper. She'll Have to Go (US: Maid for Murder).*

BYINGTON, Spring 1886–1971
From the moment Spring Byington appeared on screen as Marmee in *Little Women* (1933), there was no competition for the title of Hollywood's favourite mother. That, and her bewitching sense of comedy, kept her in dozens of similar roles from the mid-thirties to the early fifties. Strangely, this queen of homely matriarchs (she began on stage in 1900) was a divorcee who never re-married. Oscar nominee for *You Can't Take It With You.*

*1931: *Papa's Slay Ride. 1933: Little Women. 1935: Werewolf of London. Love Me Forever (GB: On Wings of Song). Orchids to You. Way Down East. Ah, Wilderness! Mutiny on the Bounty. Broadway Hostess. 1936: The Charge of the Light Brigade. The Great Impersonation. Every Saturday Night. The Voice of Bugle Ann. Educating Father. Back to Nature. Palm Springs (GB: Palm Springs Weekend). Stage Struck. The Girl on the Front Page. Dodsworth. Theodora Goes Wild. 1937: The Green Light. Penrod and Sam. Off to the Races. Big Business. Hot Water. Hotel Haywire. The Road Back. Borrowing Trouble. It's Love I'm After. Clarence. A Family Affair. 1938: Love on a Budget. A Trip to Paris. Safety in Numbers. The Buccaneer. Penrod and his Twin Brother. Jezebel. You Can't Take It With You. The Adventures of Tom Sawyer. Down on the Farm. 1939: The Jones Family in Hollywood. The Story of*

BYRNE, Eddie 1911–1981
Open-faced Irish character player with dark, crinkly hair, often seen as figures of some authority, who came to British films after winning attention both as a variety star and a straight actor at the Abbey Theatre, Dublin. He had one or two minor leading roles in the early 1950s, a decade in which he seemed to be turning up in every third British film. He returned to Ireland in the mid 1960s.

1945: The Rake's Progress (US: Notorious Gentleman). 1946: Odd Man Out. I See a Dark Stranger (US: The Adventuress). Hungry Hill. 1947: Captain Boycott. Night Beat. 1949: Saints and Sinners. 1951: Lady Godiva Rides Again. Mr Denning Drives North. 1952: Time Gentlemen Please! The Gentle Gunman. 1953: The Square Ring. Albert R.N. (US: Break to Freedom). 1954: Trouble in the Glen. Happy

*Ever After (US: Tonight's the Night). Beautiful Stranger (US: Twist of Fate). Aunt Clara. The Divided Heart. Children Galore. The Sea Shall Not Have Them. A Kid for Two Farthings. 1955: Three Cases of Murder. Stolen Assignment. One Way Out. 1956: The Extra Day. It's Great to be Young. Reach for the Sky. The Man in the Sky (US: Decision Against Time). Zarak. 1957: Seven Waves Away (US: Abandon Ship!). The Admirable Crichton (US: Paradise Lagoon). Face in the Night (US: Menace in the Night). These Dangerous Years (US: Dangerous Youth). 1958: Rooney. Dunkirk. Wonderful Things! Floods of Fear. 1959: Jack the Ripper. The Bridal Path. The Mummy. The Scapegoat. The Shakedown. 1960: Jackpot. The Bulldog Breed. 1961: Johnny Nobody. The Mark. 1962: The Break. Mutiny on the Bounty. The Pot Carriers. Locker 69. The Punch and Judy Man. 1963: The Running Man. The Cracksman. 1964: Devils of Darkness. 1966: Island of Terror. Vengeance of Fu Manchu. 1967: Mister Ten Per Cent. *Gold is Where You Find It. 1969: Sinful Davey. Where's Jack? Guns in the Heather. I Can't...I Can't (GB: Wedding Night). 1971: All Coppers Are... 1972: Never Mind the Quality Feel the Width. 1973: The Mackintosh Man. 1977: A Portrait of the Artist As a Young Man. Star Wars. 1979: The Outsider.*

*The Spider and the Fly. The Adventures of Jane. 1950: Tony Draws a Horse. Midnight Episode. 1951: Laughter in Paradise. Old Mother Riley's Jungle Treasure. The Wonder Kid. Night Without Stars. 1952: Ivanhoe. Babes in Bagdad. Alf's Baby. 1953: Heights of Danger. The Case of the Marriage Bureau. Destination Milan. The Captain's Paradise. Always a Bride. The Blakes Slept Here. The Love Lottery. The Case of Soho Red. 1954: Romeo and Juliet. I cavalieri della regina/ D'Artagnan and the Three Musketeers/Knights of the Queen. 1955: The Adventures of Quentin Durward (US: Quentin Durward). Kismet. 1956: Rommel's Treasure. Westward Ho! The Wagons. 1957: Johnny Tremain. Black Patch. Omar Khayyam. So Soon to Die (TV). Dragoon Wells Massacre. 1958: Terror in a Texas Town. In Love and War. 1959: Say One for Me. The Angry Hills. 1960: The Time Machine. Seven Thieves. 1963: The Sword in the Stone (voice only). Twice Told Tales. 1965: The Family Jewels. *Winnie the Pooh and the Honey Tree (voice only). 1967: The Jungle Book (voice only). 1968: *Winnie the Pooh and the Blustery Day (voice only). 1969: Foreign Exchange (TV). The Spy Killer (TV). 1974: *Winnie the Pooh and Tigger Too (voice only). Miracle on 34th Street (TV).*

C

CABOT, Sebastian 1918–1977

Beefy, brown-bearded British actor with small, deep-set eyes, good at expressing fake concern. After years of supporting roles in big films, and villains in minor ones, he went to America in 1955 and achieved unexpected success, popularity and recognition there, chiefly on television as pompous but lovable buffoons. Had a leading role (the old Edmund Gwenn part as Kris Kringle) in his last film, a TV remake of *Miracle on 34th Street*. Died after a stroke.

1935: Foreign Affaires. 1936: Secret Agent. The Man Behind the Mask. 1937: Knight Without Armour. The Cotton Queen. 1941: Love on the Dole. Jeannie. Pimpernel Smith (US: Mister V). 1942: Old Mother Riley Detective. 1943: Old Mother Riley Overseas. 1944: The Agitator. 1946: Othello. 1947: Dual Alibi. Teheran (US: The Plot to Kill Roosevelt). They Made Me a Fugitive (US: I Became a Criminal). 1948: Third Time Lucky. 1949: Dick Barton Strikes Back. Old Mother Riley's New Venture.

CADELL, Jean 1884–1967

Red-headed Scottish actress with inquisitive features and piercing blue eyes. She played a few 'wee lassies' in silent films, but her career in movies really got under way with the coming of sound, in numerous roles as housekeepers, busybodies, maids and mothers. The Barbara Mullen of her day,

although perhaps in less good-humoured parts. Her penultimate feature film brought her first starring role.

*1912: David Garrick. 1915: The Man Who Stayed at Home. 1920: Anna the Adventuress. Alf's Button. 1923: The Naked Man. 1930: The Loves of Robert Burns. Escape. 1932: Two White Arms (US: Wives Beware). Fires of Fate. 1933: Timbuctoo. 1934: Little Friend. The Luck of a Sailor. 1935: David Copperfield. 1936: Whom the Gods Love (US: Mozart). Love from a Stranger. 1937: South Riding. 1938: Pygmalion. 1939: Confidential Lady. 1941: Quiet Wedding. 1942: The Young Mr Pitt. 1943: Dear Octopus (US: The Randolph Family). 1944: Soldier, Sailor. 1945: I Know Where I'm Going. 1947: Jassy. 1948: Bond Street. 1949: Marry Me. Whisky Galore! (US: Tight Little Island). That Dangerous Age (US: If This Be Sin). No Place for Jennifer. 1950: Madeleine. The Reluctant Widow. 1951: The Late Edwina Black. 1952: I'm a Stranger. 1953: Meet Mr Lucifer. Three's Company. 1956: Keep It Clean. 1957: Let's Be Happy. The Surgeon's Knife. The Little Hut. 1958: Rockets Galore (US: Mad Little Island). 1959: Upstairs and Downstairs. Serious Charge (US: A Touch of Hell). 1960: A Taste of Money. 1961: *Like Unto You. Very Important Person.*

CALHERN, Louis
(Carl Henry Vogt) 1895–1956

Affable Hollywood character star who moved easily from swindlers and roués to avuncular figures as his hair turned from black to silver. But he had an interesting relapse into villainy in *The Asphalt Jungle* and was an unexpectedly impressive Julius Caesar. Died from a heart attack. Two of his four wives (all divorced) were actresses Ilka Chase and Natalie Schafer. His screen name was an anagram of the first seven letters of his real name.

1921: The Blot. Too Wise Wives. What's Worth While. Woman, Wake Up! 1923: The Last Moment. 1931: Stolen Heaven. Road to Singapore. Blonde Crazy (GB: Larceny Lane). 1932: Okay, America (GB: Penalty of Fame). They Call It Sin (GB: The Way of Life). Night After Night. Afraid to Talk. 1933: 20,000 Years in Sing Sing. Strictly Personal. Frisco Jenny. The Woman Accused. Diplomaniacs. Duck Soup. The World Gone Mad (GB: The Public Be Hanged). 1934: The Affairs of Cellini.

The Count of Monte Cristo. The Man with Two Faces. 1935: The Arizonian. The Last Days of Pompeii. Sweet Adeline. Woman Wanted. 1936: The Gorgeous Hussy. 1937: Her Husband Lies. The Life of Emile Zola. 1938: Fast Company. 1939: Juarez. Fifth Avenue Girl. Charlie McCarthy, Detective. 1940: Doctor Ehrlich's Magic Bullet. I Take This Woman. 1943: Nobody's Darling. Heaven Can Wait. 1944: Up in Arms. The Bridge of San Luis Rey. 1946: Notorious. 1948: Arch of Triumph. 1949: The Red Danube. The Red Pony. 1950: Nancy Goes to Rio. Two Weeks with Love. Annie Get Your Gun. The Asphalt Jungle. A Life of Her Own. Devil's Doorway. 1951: The Man with a Cloak. The Magnificent Yankee (GB: The Man with Thirty Sons). It's a Big Country (narrator only). 1952: Invitation. The Washington Story (GB: Target for Scandal). The Prisoner of Zenda. We're Not Married. The Bad and the Beautiful (voice only). 1953: Confidentially Connie. Julius Caesar. Remains to be Seen. Main Street to Broadway. Latin Lovers. 1954: Rhapsody. Betrayed. Executive Suite. The Student Prince. Men of the Fighting Lady. Athena. 1955: Blackboard Jungle. The Prodigal. 1956: High Society. Forever, Darling.

CALLEIA, Joseph
(J. Spurin-Calleja) 1897–1975
Dark-haired, moustachioed, somewhat shifty-eyed Hollywood actor (and writer), born and raised in Malta (where he also died), who forsook an operatic career to play dozens of swarthy, greasy, smiling and almost always untrustworthy types in gangster films and westerns. His sharp voice was often to be heard in films over a tuxedo, running night-clubs or saloons.

1931: His Woman. 1935: Public Hero No. 1. Riffraff. 1936: Exclusive Story. Sworn Enemy. Tough Guy. His Brother's Wife. Sinner Take All. After the Thin Man. 1937: Man of the People. 1938: Algiers. Marie Antoinette. Four's a Crowd. Bad Man of Brimstone. 1939: Juarez. The Gorilla. Five Game Back. Golden Boy. Full Confession. 1940: My Little Chickadee. Wyoming (GB: Bad Man of Wyoming). 1941: The Monster and the Girl. Sundown. 1942: The Glass Key. Jungle Book. 1943: For Whom the Bell Tolls. The Cross of Lorraine. 1944: The Conspirators. 1946: Gilda. 1947: The Beginning or the End. Lured (GB: Personal Column). Four Faces West (GB: They Passed This Way). 1948: The Noose

Hangs High. Noose (US: The Silk Noose). 1949: Captain Carey USA (GB: After Midnight). 1950: Branded. The Palomino (GB: Hills of the Brave). Vendetta. 1951: Valentino. The Light Touch. 1952: Yankee Buccaneer. The Iron Mistress. When in Rome. 1953: The Caddy. 1955: Underwater. The Treasure of Pancho Villa. 1956: The Littlest Outlaw. Hot Blood. Serenade. 1958: Touch of Evil. The Light in the Forest. 1959: Cry Tough. 1960: The Alamo. 1963: Johnny Cool.

CALTHROP, Donald 1888–1940
Slightly built, fuzzy-haired British actor whose distinctive diction and electrifying presence came into their own with sound, in a vivid selection of men who wouldn't quite meet your gaze: vindictive cowards, uncertain menaces and characters generally living on the edges of their nerves. He was in three Hitchcock films and other big British movies of the early 1930s, but an alcohol problem limited later appearances. Died from a heart attack.

1916: Wanted a Widow. Altar Chains. 1917: Masks and Faces. The Gay Lord Quex. 1918: Goodbye. Nelson. 1925: *Stage Stars Off Stage. 1927: Shooting Stars. 1928: The Flying Squad. 1929: Clue of the New Pin. Blackmail. *Up the Poll. Atlantic. Juno and the Paycock (US: The Shame of Mary Boyle). 1930: *The Cockney Spirit in the War – 1/*All Riot on the Western Front. *The Cockney Spirit in the War – 2. Song of Soho. The Night Porter. *The Cockney Spirit in the War – 3. Loose Ends. Two Worlds. Elstree Calling. Murder! Spanish Eyes. *We Take Off Our Hats. Almost a Honeymoon. *Star Impersonations. Cape Forlorn (US: The Love Storm). 1931: Potiphar's Wife (US: Her Strange Desire). Uneasy Virtue. The Ghost Train. The Bells. Many Waters. Money for Nothing. 1932: Number Seventeen. Fires of Fate. Rome Express. 1933: FP1. Orders is Orders. Early to Bed. I Was a Spy. Sorrell and Son. The Night Watchman's Story. Friday the Thirteenth. This Acting Business. 1934: Red Ensign (US: Strike!). It's a Cop. Nine Forty-Five. The Phantom Light. 1935: The Divine Spark/Casta Diva. The Clairvoyant. Scrooge. Man of the Moment. 1936: The Man Behind the Mask. Broken Blossoms. The Man Who Changed His Mind (US: The Man Who Lived Again). Love from a Stranger. Fire

Over England. Café Colette (US: Danger in Paris). 1937: Dreaming Lips. Cotton Queen. 1938: Shadow of Death. 1939: Band Waggon. *Tommy Atkins. *Tommy Atkins No. 2. *The Sound of Death. 1940: Let George Do It. Charley's (Big-Hearted) Aunt. 1941: Major Barbara.

CAMP, Colleen 1953–
Most of the people in this book are familiar faces to which we have trouble adding the names. This happy-looking American actress is perhaps more of a familiar name to which we have trouble adding the face. Starting out as a child performer at the age of three, she did a lot of television before working as a bird trainer to finance acting lessons, making her adult debut at 20. An actress of many faces who can play anything from sexy to simpering and servile, she has done rather too many indifferent films for comfort and needs some good mainline roles to sustain her career into middle age.

1973: Battle for the Planet of the Apes. 1974: The Swinging Cheerleaders. The Seducers/ Death Game. Smile. 1975: Funny Lady. 1976: Ebony, Ivory and Jade (TV). Amelia Earhart (TV). 1977: Love and the Midnight Auto Supply. 1978: Lady of the House (TV). Game of Death/Bruce Lee's Game of Death. 1979: Who Fell Asleep? Cloud Dancer. Apocalypse Now. 1981: The Seduction. They All Laughed. 1982: Valley Girl. Deadly Games (and 1974 and 1978 films with similar titles!). 1983: The City Girl. Loose Ends. Smokey and the Bandit – Part 3. 1984: Joy of Sex. Doin' Time. 1985: Clue. D.A.R.Y.L. Police Academy 2 – Their First Assignment. The Rosebud Beach Hotel. 1987: Walk Like a Man. Track 29. Screwball Academy. Police Academy 4: Citizens on Patrol. 1988: Illegally Yours. Wicked Stepmother. 1990: My Blue Heaven. 1991: The Vagrant. 1992: Wayne's World. Unbecoming Age. 1993: Sliver. Last Action Hero. 1994: Greedy. 1995: Die Hard – With a Vengeance.

CANNON, Esma 1896–1972
Diminutive Australian-born actress with red-gold hair, narrow eyes and set lips — attributes that frequently saw her cast in spinsterly or busybody roles. Arriving in Britain in the early 1930s, she built a theatrical career there before entering British films in 1937 and contributing dozens of

invaluable cameos as maids, village gossips, maiden aunts and (latterly) strong-minded little old ladies. The 'Carry On' series would probably have kept her busy into her seventies had she not decided to retire in 1963.

1936: Ladies in Love. 1937: The £5 Man. Cotton Queen. The Last Adventurers. 1938: It's in the Air. I See Ice. 1939: Trouble Brewing. Poison Pen. I Met a Murderer. The Spy in Black (US: U-Boat 29). 1940: Contraband (US: Blackout). The Briggs Family. 1941: The Big Blockade. Quiet Wedding. 1942: The Young Mr Pitt. Asking for Trouble. 1943: It's in the Bag. 1944: The Way Ahead (US: Immortal Battalion). English Without Tears (US: Her Man Gilbey). A Canterbury Tale. Don't Take It to Heart. Fanny by Gaslight (US: Man of Evil). 1946: The Years Between. 1947: Jassy. Holiday Camp. 1948: Here Come the Huggetts. Vote for Huggett. 1949: Fools Rush In. Marry Me! Helter Skelter. The Huggetts Abroad. 1950: Guilt is My Shadow. Double Confession. Last Holiday. 1952: Crow Hollow. 1953: The Steel Key. Trouble in Store. Noose for a Lady. The Case of Soho Red. 1954: The Sleeping Tiger. Out of the Clouds. The Dam Busters. 1955: Simon and Laura. 1956: A Touch of the Sun. Sailor Beware! (US: Panic in the Parlor). Three Men in a Boat. 1958: Further Up the Creek. 1959: Jack the Ripper. I'm All Right, Jack. Inn for Trouble. The Flesh and the Fiends (US: Mania). Expresso Bongo. 1960: No Kidding (US: Beware of Children). Carry On Constable. Doctor in Love. 1961: Carry On Regardless. What a Carve Up! (US: No Place Like Homicide). Raising the Wind. Over the Odds. In the Doghouse. 1962: We Joined the Navy. Carry On Cruising. On the Beat. The Fast Lady. 1963: Nurse On Wheels. Hide and Seek. Carry On Cabby.

CANUTT, Yakima
(Enos Canutt) 1895–1986
Swarthy, dark-haired, heavy-browed, hawk-like American actor and stuntman with ferocious scowl. Supposedly of Red Indian heritage, but actually of Scottish-Irish-Dutch-German descent, Canutt was five times world champion rodeo rider before coming to Hollywood as a stuntman in 1922. He soon began taking small roles as well as stunting, which led to his playing villains in many of the westerns starring actors for whom he also doubled, including John Wayne and Gene Autry! He had a hand in the

stories of some of these rousing little films and, from 1939, turned to second-unit direction as well, creating some of the most exciting action sequences ever filmed, becoming a legend in his field. Special Oscar 1966 for achievements as a stuntman and 'for developing safety devices to protect stuntmen everywhere'. The filmography below includes some films in which he appeared both as actor and stuntman, but not his extensive work as stuntman only, topped by his hair-raising stuff in *Stagecoach*.

*1919: Lightning Bryce (serial). 1922: The Heart of a Texan. 1923: The Forbidden Range. 1924: The Days of '49 (serial). The Riddle Rider (serial). The Desert Hawk. Sell 'Em Cowboy (GB: Alias Texas Pete Owens). Ridin' Mad. Branded a Bandit. California in '49 (feature version of serial The Days of '49). 1925: Scar Hanan (GB: The Man With the Scar). The Cactus Cure. Ridin' Comet. Romance and Rustlers. A Two-Fisted Sheriff. Wolves of the Road. White Thunder (GB: The White Rider). The Strange Rider. The Human Tornado. 1926: Desert Greed (GB: Greed of Gold). The Devil Horse. Hellhound of the Plains. The Fighting Stallion. 1927: Open Range. The Outlaw Breaker. 1928: The Vanishing West (serial). 1929: Bad Man's Money. Captain Cowboy. The Three Outcasts. Riders of the Storm. A Texan's Honor. 1930: Bar L Ranch. The Texan (GB: The Big Race). Firebrand Jordan. The Lonesome Trail. Ridin' Law. Canyon Hawks. Westward Bound. 1931: The Fighting Test. Hurricane Horseman (GB: The Mexican). Battling With Buffalo Bill (serial). Pueblo Terror (GB: Paradise Valley). The Vanishing Legion (serial). The Lightning Warrior (serial). 1932: Cheyenne Cyclone (GB: Smashing Through). The Devil Horse. Riders of the Golden Gulch. The Last Frontier (serial). Two-Fisted Justice. The Shadow of the Eagle (serial). The Black Ghost (feature version of The Last Frontier). Hurricane Express (serial). The Last of the Mohicans (serial). Wyoming Whirlwind. 1933: Battling Buckaroo (GB: His Last Adventure). Law and Lawless. Fighting Texans (GB: Randy Strikes Oil). The Telegraph Trail. The Three Musketeers (serial). Via Pony Express. Sagebrush Trail. Scarlet River. Fighting With Kit Carson (serial). The Mystery Squadron (serial). Wolf Dog. 1934: *Carrying the Mail. Burn-Em-Up-Barnes (serial). The Lost Jungle (serial). Devils on Wheels (feature version of Burn-Em-*

*Up-Barnes). Blue Steel. The Lucky Texan. The Man from Utah. Randy Rides Alone. Man from Hell. Fighting Through. The Star Packer. Texas Tornado. West of the Divide. Monte Carlo Nights. Law of the Wild (serial). Mystery Mountain (serial). Neath the Arizona Skies (GB: 'Neath Arizona Skies). *Pals of the West. *The Desert Man. 1935: The Dawn Rider. Circle of Death. The Lawless Frontier. Paradise Canyon. Cyclone of the Saddle. Lawless Range. Westward Ho. Rough Ridin' Ranger (GB: The Secret Stranger). The Phantom Empire (serial). Dante's Inferno. The Farmer Takes a Wife. The Fighting Marines (serial). 1936: King of the Pecos. The Lonely Trail. The Clutching Hand (serial). The Black Coin (serial). The Oregon Trail. Winds of the Wasteland. Ghost Town Gold. Roarin' Lead. San Francisco. Ten Laps to Go. The Trail of the Lonesome Pine. The Vigilantes Are Coming (serial. GB: The Mounties Are Coming). The Lawless Nineties. Wildcat Trooper (GB: Wild Cat). 1937: The Bold Caballero (GB: The Bold Cavalier). Hit the Saddle. In Old Chicago. Come On Cowboys. Gunsmoke Ranch. Riders of the Whistling Skull (GB: The Golden Trail). Trouble in Texas. The Painted Stallion (serial). Range Defenders. Riders of the Rockies. Prairie Thunder. Riders of the Dawn. The Mysterious Pilot (serial). Rootin' Tootin' Rhythm (GB: Rhythm on the Range). S.O.S. Coastguard (serial). Zorro Rides Again (serial). 1938: Dick Tracy Returns (serial). The Secret of Treasure Island (serial). The Lone Ranger (serial). The Girl of the Golden West. Heart of the Rockies. Heroes of the Hills. Overland Stage Raiders. Pals of the Saddle. Santa Fé Stampede. Storm Over Bengal. 1939: Captain Fury. Daredevils of the Red Circle (serial). Cowboys from Texas. The Kansas Terrors. Man of Conquest. Gone With the Wind. Jesse James. The Lone Ranger Rides Again (serial). Dodge City. The Night Riders. The Oregon Trail (serial). The Light That Failed. Wyoming Outlaw. Zorro's Fighting Legion (serial). 1940: Ghost Valley Raiders. Frontier Vengeance. Deadwood Dick (serial). Oklahoma Renegades. Prairie Schooners (GB: Through the Storm). Shooting High. Pioneers of the West. The Ranger and the Lady. Under Texas Skies. Young Bill Hickok. 1941: Bad Man of Deadwood. Jungle Girl (serial). Kansas Cyclone. Prairie Pioneers. Gauchos of Eldorado. The Great Train Robbery. King of the Texas Rangers (serial). Western Union. White Eagle (serial). 1942: Shadows on the Sage. Spy Smasher (serial). 1943: King of the Cowboys. Pride of the Plains. Calling Wild Bill Elliott. For Whom the Bell Tolls. Santa Fe Scouts. Song of Texas. 1944: Hidden Valley Outlaws. 1945: Sunset in El Dorado. 1948: Desert Command (feature version of 1933 serial The Three Musketeers). 1950: Rocky Mountain. The Showdown. 1955: The Far Horizons.*

As director:

1945: Sheriff of Cimarron. †Manhunt of Mystery Island (serial). †Federal Operator 99 (serial). 1947: †G-Men Never Forget (serial). Oklahoma Badlands. Carson City Raiders. †Dangers of the Canadian Mounties (serial). Sons of Adventure. 1949: †Adventures of Frank and Jesse James (serial). 1954: The Lawless Rider.

† Co-directed

CAREY, Harry Jnr 1921–

American actor with gingery fair hair and apple cheeks, the son of western star Harry Carey Snr (1878–1947) and totally unlike his father in looks. He began in semi-leading roles as earnest young soldiers or westerners undergoing ordeals by fire, often in films directed by John Ford, a great friend of his father. But he had moved down to character roles by the early 1950s and was playing western old-timers at a remarkably early age.

1933: Sunset Pass. 1946: Rolling Home. 1947: Pursued. 1948: Red River. Moonrise. So Dear to My Heart. Blood on the Moon. 3 Godfathers. 1949: She Wore a Yellow Ribbon. 1950: Wagonmaster. Rio Grande. Copper Canyon. 1951: Warpath. Cattle Drive. The Wild Blue Yonder (GB: Thunder Across the Pacific). 1952: Monkey Business. 1953: San Antone. Beneath the 12-Mile Reef. Sweethearts on Parade. Island in the Sky. Niagara. Gentlemen Prefer Blondes. 1954: The Outcast (GB: The Fortune Hunter). Silver Lode. The Long Gray Line. 1955: Mister Roberts. House of Bamboo. 1956: The Searchers. The Great Locomotive Chase. 7th Cavalry. Gun the Man Down. 1957: The River's Edge. Kiss Them for Me. 1958: Texas John Slaughter (TV. GB: cinemas). From Hell to Texas (GB: Manhunt). Showdown at Sandoval (TV. GB: cinemas, as Gunfight at Sandoval). 1959: Rio Bravo. Escort West. 1960: Noose for a Gunman. 1961: The Great Impostor. Two Rode Together. Geronimo's Revenge (TV. GB: cinemas). The Comancheros. 1962: A Public Affair. 1964: Cheyenne Autumn. The Raiders. Taggart. 1965: Shenandoah. Billy the Kid vs Dracula. The Rare Breed. 1966: Alvarez Kelly. 1967: The Way West. Cyborg 2087 (GB: Man from Tomorrow). 1968: The Devil's Brigade. Bandolero! The Ballad of Josie. 1969: Ride a Northbound Horse (TV. GB: cinemas). The Undefeated. Death of a Gunfighter. One More Time. 1970: Dirty Dingus Magee. The Moonshine War. 1971: Trinity is Still My Name. Big Jake. Something Big. One More Train to Rob. 1972: Seeta, the Mountain Lion (GB: Run, Cougar, Run). E poi lo chiamarono il Magnifico (GB: Man of the East). 1973: Cahill: United States Marshal (GB: Cahill). 1975: Take a Hard Ride. 1976: Nickelodeon. 1978: Black Beauty (TV). Kate Bliss and the Tickertape Kid (TV). 1980: Wild Times (TV). The Long Riders. 1982: Endangered Species. The Shadow Riders (TV). 1984: Gremlins. Uforia (filmed

1980). 1985: Mask. 1986: Cherry 2000 (released 1988). Crossroads. 1987: The Whales of August. Once Upon a Texas Train (TV). 1988: Illegally Yours. 1989: Breaking In. Bad Jim. 1990: Back to the Future Part III. The Exorcist Part III. 1993: Tombstone. 1994: The Tumbleweed Wagon.

CAREY, Joyce
(J. Lawrence) 1898–1993

Serious-looking, dark-haired British actress, the daughter of Dame Lilian Braithwaite, a distinguished stage player. She made her own start in the theatre at 18, and remained almost entirely in that medium until World War II, after which she began to make occasional film appearances, usually in either shrewish or careworn roles. Remained active in the theatrical and television worlds into her nineties.

1918: God and the Man. Because. 1920: Colonel Newcome the Perfect Gentleman. 1942: In Which We Serve. 1945: Blithe Spirit. The Way to the Stars (US: Johnny in the Clouds). Brief Encounter. 1947: The October Man. 1948: London Belongs to Me (US: Dulcimer Street). It's Hard to be Good. 1949: The Chiltern Hundreds (US: The Amazing Mr Beecham). 1950: The Astonished Heart. Happy Go Lovely. 1951: Cry the Beloved Country (US: African Fury). 1953: Street Corner (US: Both Sides of the Law). 1954: The End of the Affair. 1955: Stolen Assignment. 1956: Loser Takes All. 1958: Alive and Kicking. 1959: Libel. The Rough and the Smooth (US: Portrait of a Sinner). 1960: Let's Get Married. Greyfriars Bobby. 1961: Nearly a Nasty Accident. The Naked Edge. 1963: The VIPs. The Eyes of Annie Jones. A Jolly Bad Fellow (US: They All Died Laughing). 1969: A Nice Girl Like Me. 1972: Father Dear Father. 1974: Only a Scream Away (TV. US: cinemas). The Black Windmill. 1989: Number 27 (TV).

CAREY, Timothy 1924–1994

Dark-haired, bumpy-nosed, shark-like American actor with pallid, dark-eyed, shadowy looks. His characters were usually more dangerous versions of the types played by Harry Dean Stanton (*qv*), spoke through gritted teeth and often looked as though they had had their jaws wired up after some gangster affray. Carey must have played a few nice guys along the way, but it's only the

crazed enforcers that stick in the mind. He was also memorable as the sharpshooter in *The Killing*. Wrote and directed from time to time, and was an acting teacher. Occasionally billed as Tim Carey, or Timothy Agoglia Carey. Died after a stroke.

1952: Hellgate. Bloodhounds of Broadway. 1953: White Witch Doctor. The Wild One. Crime Wave (GB: The City is Dark). 1954: Alaska Seas. East of Eden. 1955: Finger Man. I'll Cry Tomorrow. 1956: Francis in the Haunted House. The Naked Gun. The Last Wagon. The Killing. Flight to Hong Kong. Away All Boats! Rumble on the Docks. 1957: Paths of Glory. Chain of Evidence. Bayou (later Poor White Trash). 1958: Revolt in the Big House. Unwed Mother. 1960: The Boy and the Pirates. 1961: The Second Time Around. One-Eyed Jacks. Convicts Four (GB: Reprieve!). 1962: †The World's Greatest Sinner. The Mermaids of Tiburon (GB: Aquasex). 1963: Shock Treatment. 1964: Bikini Beach. Rio Conchos. 1965: Beach Blanket Bingo. 1967: A Time for Killing (GB: The Long Ride Home). Waterhole Number Three (GB: Waterhole Three). 1968: Head. 1969: Change of Habit. 1971: What's the Matter with Helen? Minnie and Moscowitz. Ransom for a Dead Man (TV. GB: cinemas). 1972: Get to Know Your Rabbit. 1973: The Bait (TV). The Outfit. Dead Weight (TV). Death and the Maiden (TV). 1974: The Conversation. 1975: Chesty Anderson US Navy (later Anderson's Angels). Peeper. 1976: The Killing of a Chinese Bookie. Mean Johnny Barrows. 1977: Speedtrap. 1980: Nightside (TV). 1981: East of Eden (TV. And 1954 film). 1982: Fast-Walking. 1983: D C Cab (GB: Street Fleet). 1985: Echo Park.

† And directed

CARGILL, Patrick 1918–

Aristocratic, sly-looking, grey-haired, narrow-eyed British actor with toothy smile and dry, deliberate speech. A one-time career army officer, he dabbled in acting before World War Two service, then progressed through repertory companies to a succession of West End farces and a sideline career as a playwright. His acting achievements were strictly small time until he hit the big time with the TV series *Father, Dear Father*, which ran for seven years and was turned into a film. One of those intrinsically English actors who seems in recollection to always have been wearing a pinstripe suit.

1953: *The Sword and the Rose.* 1955: *An Alligator Named Daisy.* 1956: *The Extra Day.* *Person Unknown. The Baby and the Battleship. 1958: *Up the Creek.* 1959: *The Night We Dropped a Clanger.* *Carry On Nurse.* *Expresso Bongo.* 1960: *Doctor in Love.* 1961: *Carry On Regardless.* *Clue of the Silver Key.* 1962: *Twice Round the Daffodils.* 1963: *The Hi-Jackers.* *The Cracksman.* *This is My Street.* *Carry On Jack!* (US: *Carry On Venus*). *The Sure Thing* (voice only). *A Stitch in Time.* 1965: *Help!* 1966: *The Wrong Box.* 1967: *A Countess from Hong Kong.* 1968: *Inspector Clouseau.* *Hammerhead.* 1969: *The Magic Christian.* 1970: *Every Home Should Have One* (US: *Think Dirty*). 1971: *Up Pompeii.* 1972: *The Cherry Picker.* 1973: *Father, Dear Father.* 1977: *The Picture Show Man.*

CARNEY, Art 1918–
Square-built, phlegmatic American actor and comedian who after working as a straight man to a string of famous comedians, built himself a big reputation on television. Then, after beating an alcohol problem, he went on to become one of the world's leading character stars in the seventies, following an Oscar for his performance in *Harry and Tonto.*

1941: *Pot o' Gold* (GB: *The Golden Hour*). 1957: *Charley's Aunt* (TV). 1958: *The Fabulous Irishman* (TV). 1959: *The Velvet Alley* (TV). 1964: *The Yellow Rolls Royce.* 1967: *A Guide for the Married Man.* 1972: *The Female Instinct* (TV. GB: *The Snoop Sisters*). 1974:

Harry and Tonto. 1975: *W.W. and the Dixie Dancekings.* *Won Ton Ton the Dog Who Saved Hollywood.* *Death Scream* (TV). *Katherine* (TV). 1976: *Lanigan's Rabbi* (TV). 1977: *The Late Show.* *Scott Joplin — King of Ragtime.* 1978: *The Ravagers.* *Movie Movie.* *House Calls.* 1979: *Defiance.* *Sunburn.* *You Can't Take It with You* (TV). *Going in Style. Letters from Frank. Steel.* 1980: *Roadie. Alcatraz: The Whole Shocking Story* (TV). 1981: *St Helens. Take This Job and Shove It.* 1982: *Ménage à Trois/Summer Lovers* (US: *Better Late Than Never*). *Bitter Harvest* (TV). 1984: *Firestarter. The Naked Face. A Doctor's Story* (TV). *The Muppets Take Manhattan. The Night They Saved Christmas* (TV). *Terrible Joe Moran* (TV). 1985: *The Undergrads/The Undergraduates. Izzy and Mo* (TV). *The Blue Yonder* (TV). 1986: *Time Flyer* (TV). *Miracle of the Heart: a Boys' Town Story* (TV). 1987: *A Cry from the Heart/Night Friend.* 1990: *Where Pigeons Go to Die* (TV). 1993: *Last Action Hero.*

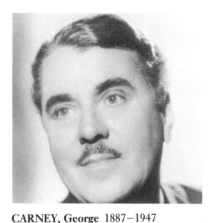

CARNEY, George 1887–1947
Chunky, brown-haired British actor, round of face and short of stature, usually seen in braces and boots as the 'common bloke'. A successful music-hall comedian in his younger days, he proved popular as soon as he entered sound films in 1933 and, a natural, relaxed actor, was often the best thing in some poor films. Probably now best remembered as John Mills's father from *In Which We Serve.*

1916: *Some Waiter!* 1932: *Rome Express.* 1933: *Television Follies. Commissionaire.* 1934: *Say It With Flowers. Night Club Queen. Music Hall. Lest We Forget. Easy Money. A Glimpse of Paradise. Hyde Park. Flood Tide.* 1935: *The Small Man. A Real Bloke. Variety. The City of Beautiful Nonsense. Cock o' the North. Windfall.* 1936: *It's in the Bag. Land Without Music* (US: *Forbidden Music*). *Tomorrow We Live.* 1937: *Beauty and the Barge. Dreaming Lips. Father Steps Out. Little Miss Somebody. Lancashire Luck.* 1938: *Easy Riches. Paid in Error. Kicking the Moon Around* (US: *The Playboy*). *Weddings Are Wonderful. Consider Your Verdict. Miracles Do Happen. The Divorce of Lady X.* 1939: *Where's That Fire? A Window in London* (US: *Lady in Distress*). *Young Man's Fancy. Come on George. The Stars Look Down.* 1940: *Convoy. The Briggs Family.* 1941: *Kipps* (US: *The Remark-*

able Mr Kipps). Love on the Dole. The Common Touch. 1942: *Hard Steel. Thunder Rock. The Day Will Dawn* (US: *The Avengers*). *In Which We Serve. Unpublished Story. Rose of Tralee.* 1943: *The Night Invader. When We Are Married. Schweik's New Adventures.* 1944: *Tawny Pipit. Welcome Mr Washington. Soldier, Sailor. Waterloo Road.* 1945: *The Agitator. I Know Where I'm Going!* 1946: *Spring Song* (US: *Springtime*). *Wanted for Murder. Woman to Woman.* 1947: *The Root of All Evil. The Little Ballerina. Brighton Rock* (US: *Young Scarface*). *Fortune Lane.* 1948: *Good Time Girl.*

CARNOVSKY, Morris 1897–1992
Round-faced American actor of long stage experience and smooth, urbane manner; he was just as likely to be malevolent as benevolent in films and was building up a useful list of credits as a Hollywood character player when his film career was destroyed after he was blacklisted by the House Un-American Activities Committee. Now best remembered as the villain in Bogart's *Dead Reckoning.* A poor man's Luther Adler (*qv*). Died four days short of his 95th birthday.

1937: *The Life of Emile Zola. Tovarich.* 1943: *Edge of Darkness.* 1944: *Address Unknown. The Master Race.* 1945: *Our Vines Have Tender Grapes. Rhapsody in Blue. Cornered.* 1946: *Miss Susie Slagle's* (completed 1944). *Dead Reckoning.* 1947: *Dishonored Lady. Joe Palooka in The Knockout.* 1948: *Saigon. Man-Eater of Kumaon. Siren of Atlantis.* 1949: *Gun Crazy. Thieves' Highway.* 1950: *Western Pacific Agent. Cyrano de Bergerac. The Second Woman* (GB: *Ellen*). 1961: *Vu du pont* (GB and US: *A View from the Bridge*). 1974: *The Gambler.* 1983: *Joe's Barbershop: We Cut Heads.*

CARRADINE, John
(Richmond Carradine) 1906–1988
Tall, dark, cadaverous, thin-lipped American actor with deep, cultured voice. Just as likely to turn up as Arab, westerner or Englishman, he had some good featured roles in the 1930s and 1940s—several of them for John Ford—but later made a great number of cheap horror films. Probably no non-star was so consistently busy from the beginnings of sound to the time of his death. Three of his five sons, David, Keith and Robert,

have followed him profitably into the acting profession. Former sketch artist.

1930: †Tol'able David. 1931: †Bright Lights. †Heaven on Earth. 1932: †Forgotten Commandments. †The Sign of the Cross. 1933: †This Day and Age. †The Invisible Man. †The Story of Temple Drake. †To the Last Man. 1934: †The Black Cat (GB: House of Doom). Cleopatra. †The Meanest Gal in Town. †Of Human Bondage. 1935: The Man Who Broke the Bank at Monte Carlo. Bride of Frankenstein. Les Miserables. She Gets Her Man. Clive of India. Transient Lady (GB: False Witness). Cardinal Richelieu. Alias Mary Dow. Bad Boy. The Crusades. 1936: Anything Goes. Captain January. Winterset. The Garden of Allah. Daniel Boone. Ramona. Under Two Flags. Mary of Scotland. A Message to Garcia (voice only). White Fang. Half Angel. Prisoner of Shark Island. Laughing at Death (GB: Laughing at Trouble). Dimples. 1937: Nancy Steele Is Missing. Ali Baba Goes to Town. Captains Courageous. The Last Gangster. The Hurricane. This Is My Affair (GB: His Affair). Love Under Fire. Danger—Love at Work. Thank You, Mr Moto. 1938: Alexander's Ragtime Band. Of Human Hearts. International Settlement. Four Men and a Prayer. Gateway. Kentucky Moonshine (GB: Four Men and a Girl). I'll Give a Million. Kidnapped. Submarine Patrol. 1939: Drums Along the Mohawk. Frontier Marshal. Stagecoach. Jesse James. The Three Musketeers (GB: The Singing Musketeer). Five Came Back. Mr Moto's Last Warning. The Hound of the Baskervilles. Captain Fury. 1940: Brigham Young—Frontiersman (GB: Brigham Young). The Return of Frank James. The Grapes of Wrath. Chad Hanna. 1941: Western Union. Blood and Sand. Swamp Water (GB: The Man Who Came Back). Man Hunt. King of the Zombies. All That Money Can Buy/The Devil and Daniel Webster/Daniel and the Devil. 1942: Northwest Rangers. Whispering Ghosts. Reunion/Reunion in France (GB: Mademoiselle France). Son of Fury. The Black Swan. 1943: Hitler's Madman. I Escaped from the Gestapo (GB: No Escape). The Isle of Forgotten Sins. Silver Spurs. Gangway for Tomorrow. Revenge of the Zombies. (GB: The Corpse Vanished). Captive Wild Woman. 1944: Bluebeard. The Mummy's Ghost. Barbary Coast Gent. The Adventures of Mark Twain. The Black Parachute. Waterfront. The Invisible Man's Revenge. Alaska. Voodoo Man. The Return of the Ape Man (GB: Lock Your Doors). House of Frankenstein. It's in the Bag!

(GB: The Fifth Chair). 1945: Captain Kidd. House of Dracula. 1946: Fallan Angel. The Face of Marble. Down Missouri Way. 1947: The Private Affairs of Bel Ami. 1949: C-Man. 1953: Casanova's Big Night. 1954: Thunder Pass. The Egyptian. Johnny Guitar. 1955: Desert Sands. The Court Jester. The Kentuckian. Stranger on Horseback. Dark Venture. Half Human. 1956: The Black Sleep. The Female Jungle. The Ten Commandments. Around the World in 80 Days. Hidden Guns. 1957: The True Story of Jesse James (GB: The James Brothers). The Unearthly. Shoes (TV). Hell Ship Mutiny. The Story of Mankind. 1958: The Cosmic Man. The Proud Rebel. The Last Hurrah. Showdown at Boot Hill. 1959: The Oregon Trail. Invisible Invaders. The Incredible Petrified World. 1960: The Adventures of Huckleberry Finn. Tarzan the Magnificent. Sex Kittens Go to College. 1962: Invasion of the Animal People (GB: Terror in the Midnight Sun). The Man Who Shot Liberty Valance. 1964: Curse of the Stone Hand. The Patsy. Cheyenne Autumn. The Wizard of Mars. 1965: Broken Sabre (TV. GB: cinemas). House of the Black Death. Billy the Kid vs Dracula. They Ran for Their Lives (released 1968). 1966: Night of the Beast. Munster Go Home! Night Train to Mundo Fine. 1967: Blood of Dracula's Castle. The Helicopter Spies (TV. GB: cinemas). Hillbillys in the Haunted House. The Hostage. Creatures of the Red Planet. The Fiend with the Electronic Brain. Lonely Man. Dr Terror's Gallery of Horrors. Autopsy of a Ghost. 1968: The Astro Zombies. La senora muerte (GB: The Death Woman. US: Mrs Death). Las vampiras (GB: The Vampires). The Hostage. Genesis (narrator only). The Fakers (later Hell's Bloody Devils). Pact With the Devil. 1969: Smashing the Crime Syndicate (released 1973). Cain's Way. Man with the Synthetic Brain. Blood of the Iron Maiden. Bigfoot. Vampire Men of the Lost Planet. Daughter of the Mind (TV). The Good Guys and the Bad Guys. The Trouble with Girls ... and how to get into it. The McMasters ... Tougher Than The West Itself! 1970: Is This Trip Really Necessary? Crowhaven Farm (TV). Myra Breckinridge. Blood of Frankenstein. Five Bloody Graves. Death Corps (later Shock Waves. GB: Almost Human). Horror of the Blood Monsters (Vampire Men of the Lost Planet with added footage). 1971: Shinbone Alley (voice only). The Seven Minutes. Threshold. Decisions! Decisions! Legacy of Blood. 1972: Blood of Ghastly Horror. The Night Strangler (TV). Boxcar Bertha. House of the Seven Corpses. Red Zone Cuba. Everything You Always Wanted to Know about Sex **But Were Afraid to Ask. Portnoy's Complaint. The Gatling Gun (filmed 1969 as King Gun). Richard. Shadow House. 1973: House of Dracula's Daughter. Superchick. 1,000,000 AD. Bad Charleston Charlie. Hex. Terror in the Wax Museum. Silent Night, Bloody Night (later Death House, and Night of the Dark Full Moon). The Cat Creature (TV). 1974: Moon Child (filmed 1972). Stowaway to the Moon (TV). 1975: Won Ton Ton, the Dog Who Saved Hollywood. Mary, Mary, Bloody Mary. The Killer Inside Me. 1976: Crash. The Last Tycoon. Death at Love House (TV). The Shootist. The Sentinel. 1977: Tail Gunner Joe (TV). The White Buffalo. Golden Rendezvous. The Christmas Coal Mine Miracle (TV). The Mouse

and His Child (voice only). Satan's Cheerleaders. Journey into the Beyond (narrator only). 1978: Missile X. Nocturna. Sunset Cove. Vampire Hookers. The Bees. The Mandate of Heaven. 1979: Monster. The Seekers (TV). Americathon. Teheran Incident/Teheran 1943: The Nesting. 1980: Carradines in Concert. The Long Riders. The Monster Club. Phobia. The Howling. Monstroid. The Boogey Man (GB: The Bogey Man). 1981: Zorro the Gay Blade. Frankenstein Island. The Scarecrow. Dark Eyes (later Satan's Mistress). 1982: The Secret of NIMH (voice only). House of the Long Shadows. 1983: Boogeyman II. Evils of the Night. The Vals (released 1985). 1984: The Ice Pirates. 1985: The Tomb. Reel Horror. Prison Ship 2005 (later Prison Ship Star Slammer). 1986: Monster in the Closet. Revenge. Peggy Sue Got Married. 1987: Evil Spawn. 1988: Buried Alive.

† As John Peter Richmond

CARRILLO, Leo 1880–1961
Plumpish, moustachioed, dark-haired former vaudeville comedian of Spanish-American background who gradually became familiar in Hollywood films for fractured-English character roles. A more benevolent version of Akim Tamiroff (qv); like Tamiroff, he could also give strong performances in minor leading assignments. Latterly played Pancho in the Cisco Kid series that transferred to TV. Died from cancer.

1927: *Italian Humorist. *At the Ball Game. 1928: *The Hell Gate of Soissons. *The Foreigner. The Dove. 1929: Mr Antonio. 1931: Lasca of the Rio Grande. Guilty Generation. Hell Bound. Homicide Squad (GB: The Lost Men). 1932: Broken Wing. Second Fiddle. Cauliflower Alley. Girl of the Rio (GB: The Dove. And 1928 title). Deception. Men Are Such Fools. *Screen Snapshots No. 15. 1933: Parachute Jumper. City Streets. Moonlight and Pretzels (GB: Moonlight and Melody). Obey the Law. Racetrack. Before Morning. 1934: Viva Villa! The Barretts of Wimpole Street. The Gay Bride. Four Frightened People. The Band Plays On. Manhattan Melodrama. 1935: The Winning Ticket. *Star Night at the Coconut Grove. In Caliente. *La Fiesta de Santa Barbara. If You Could Only Cook. Love Me Forever (GB: On Wings of Song). 1936: It Had to Happen. Moonlight Murder. The Gay Desperado. 1937: I Promise to Pay. History is Made at Night. Hotel Haywire. Manhattan Merry-Go-

Round (GB: Manhattan Music Box). 52nd Street. The Barrier. 1938: Arizona Wildcat. Girl of the Golden West. City Streets. Little Miss Roughneck. Too Hot to Handle. Blockade. Flirting With Fate. 1939: The Girl and the Gambler. Society Lawyer. The Chicken Wagon Family. Rio. Fisherman's Wharf. 1940: Twenty-Mule Team. Wyoming (GB: Bad Man of Wyoming). One Night in the Tropics. Lillian Russell. Captain Caution. 1941: Horror Island. Barnacle Bill. Riders of Death Valley (serial). Tight Shoes. The Kid from Kansas. What's Cookin'? (GB: Wake Up and Dream). 1942: Unseen Enemy. Escape from Hong Kong. Men of Texas (GB: Men of Destiny). Top Sergeant. Danger in the Pacific. Timber. Sin Town. American Empire. 1943: Crazy House. *Screen Snapshots No. 105: Frontier Bad Men. Larceny With Music. Follow the Band. Phantom of the Opera. 1944: Babes on Swing Street. Bowery to Broadway. Gypsy Wildcat. Ghost Catchers. Merrily We Sing. Moonlight and Cactus. 1945: Crime Inc. Under Western Skies. Mexicana. 1947: The Fugitive. 1948: The Valiant Hombre. 1949: The Gay Amigo. The Daring Caballero. Satan's Cradle. 1950: The Girl from San Lorenzo. Pancho Villa Returns.

1940: Charlie Chan's Murder Cruise. Waterloo Bridge. Rebecca. 1941: Scotland Yard. Suspicion. Bahama Passage. This Woman Is Mine. 1945: The House on 92nd Street. Spellbound. 1947: Forever Amber. Time Out of Mind. Song of Love. 1948: The Paradine Case. Enchantment. So Evil My Love. 1950: The Happy Years. Father of the Bride. 1951: The First Legion. Strangers on a Train. The Desert Fox (GB: Rommel—Desert Fox). 1952: The Snows of Kilimanjaro. Rogue's March. The Bad and the Beautiful. 1953: Treasure of the Golden Condor. Young Bess. 1954: We're No Angels. 1955: Tarantula! 1956: The Swan. 1959: North by Northwest. 1961: One Plus One (GB: The Kinsey Report). The Parent Trap. 1963: The Prize. 1964: To Trap a Spy (TV. GB: cinemas). The Spy With My Face. 1965: That Funny Feeling. One Spy Too Many (TV. GB: cinemas). 1966: One of Our Spies is Missing! (TV. GB: cinemas). The Spy in the Green Hat (TV. GB: cinemas). 1967: The Karate Killers (TV. GB: cinemas). The Helicopter Spies (TV. GB: cinemas). 1968: How to Steal the World (TV. GB: cinemas). 1969: From Nashville With Music.

to the Waltz. Scrooge. Moscow Nights (US: I Stand Condemned). 1936: Head Office. Secret Agent. Crime Over London. Forget-Me-Not (US: Forever Yours). Talk of the Devil. Tudor Rose (US: Nine Days a Queen). Things to Come. Café Colette (US: Danger in Paris). Le vagabond bien-aimé. Fire Over England. 1937: Secret Lives (US: I Married a Spy). Dark Journey. Victoria the Great. The Frog. Dreaming Lips. Who Killed Fen Markham?/The Angelus. Saturday Night Revue. Old Mother Riley. Knight Without Armour. Glamorous Night. 1938: Sixty Glorious Years (US: Queen of Destiny). Oh Boy. No Parking. We're Going to Be Rich. The Return of the Frog. Strange Boarders. Inspector Hornleigh. 1939: The Saint in London. The Gang's All Here (US: The Amazing Mr Forrest). The Lion Has Wings. Goodbye Mr Chips! Inspector Hornleigh on Holiday (US: Inspector Hornleigh on Leave). 1940: Spare a Copper. 1941: The Common Touch. Penn of Pennsylvania (US: The Courageous Mr Penn). Quiet Wedding. They Flew Alone (US: Wings and the Woman). 1943: Battle for Music. The Adventures of Tartu (US: Tartu). The Dummy Talks. 1945: Pink String and Sealing Wax. 1951: The Lady with a Lamp. Cry, the Beloved Country (US: African Fury). 1952: Moulin Rouge. 1953: The Master of Ballantrae. 1954: The Dam Busters. Beau Brummell. Duel in the Jungle. 1955: An Alligator Named Daisy. 1956: The Silken Affair. Reach for the Sky. Let's Be Happy. 1959: Bobbikins. A Touch of Larceny. 1960: The Trials of Oscar Wilde (US: The Man with the Green Carnation). Sands of the Desert. A Story of David. 1961: Macbeth. 1963: The Three Lives of Thomasina. 1965: Curse of the Fly. 1972: Lady Caroline Lamb.

CARROLL, Leo G. 1892—1972
Beetle-browed, black-haired, English-born (of Irish parents) actor with deep-set eyes and deliberate speech who came to Hollywood via the English stage (debut 1911) and Broadway. He continued to show a preference for the stage, but will be remembered by moviegoers as the villain in Hitchcock's Spellbound and by televiewers as Mr Waverly in the long-running UNCLE series. Was just as likely to be kindly or villainous.

1934: *Mr W's Little Game. What Every Woman Knows. Sadie McKee. Outcast Lady (GB: A Woman of the World). The Barretts of Wimpole Street. Stamboul Quest. 1935: Murder on a Honeymoon. The Right to Live (GB: The Sacred Flame). Clive of India. The Casino Murder Case. 1937: Captains Courageous. London By Night. 1938: A Christmas Carol. 1939: Bulldog Drummond's Secret Police. Charlie Chan in City in Darkness (GB: City in Darkness). Wuthering Heights. The Private Lives of Elizabeth and Essex. Tower of London.

CARSON, Charles 1885—1977
Stern-faced, thin-lipped, sometimes moustachioed, balding British actor who, after deciding to swop civil engineering for an acting career in his early thirties, soon proved himself one of London's most reliable Shakespeare performers of the 1920s. From the mid-1930s onwards, in the cinema, he played a lot of senior officers, solicitors and statesmen, as well as other strong-willed (or self-willed) figures of authority; he was acting regularly on stage and screen until 1961. Directed ENSA plays during World War II.

1931: Dreyfus (US: The Dreyfus Case). Ariane. Many Waters. 1932: Men of Tomorrow. The Chinese Puzzle. Marry Me. Leap Year. There Goes the Bride. 1933: The Blarney Stone (US: The Blarney Kiss). The Shadow. Early to Bed. 1934: Trouble in Store. Whispering Tongues. No Escape. Catherine the Great. Father and Son. The Perfect Flaw. Blossom Time. (US: April Romance). Hyde Park. Blind Justice. The Broken Melody. 1935: D'ye Ken John Peel (US: Captain Moonlight). Sanders of the River (US: Bosambo). Abdul the Damned. Invitation

CARTWRIGHT, Veronica 1949—
Light-haired, thin-faced, British-born actress, in America as a child, but much underused by Hollywood. Beginning as a child and teenage player (like her sister, Angela Cartwright), she developed into a specialist in anguish and anxiety, her highest-profile role coming as the female astronaut who doesn't escape the creature in Alien. She was allowed to show more decisiveness as DA Margaret Flanagan in the TV series L A Law, but even this character proved to have a skeleton in the cupboard that allowed the

Cartwright eyes their familiar red rim before long. She has had short shrift from a cinema that 40 years earlier would have given her meaty roles and lots of them. Married director Richard Compton.

*1958: In Love and War. 1961: The Children's Hour (GB: The Loudest Whisper). 1963: The Birds. Spencer's Mountain. 1964: One Man's Way. 1975: Inserts. 1976: Bernice Bobs Her Hair. 1977: Who Has Seen the Wind. 1978: Goin' South. The Kid from Not-So-Big (TV). Invasion of the Body Snatchers. 1979: Alien. 1980: Guyana Tragedy − The Story of Jim Jones (TV). The Big Black Pill (TV). 1982: Prime Suspect (TV). 1983: Nightmares. The Right Stuff. 1985: My Man Adam. 1986: Flight of the Navigator. Intimate Encounters/ Encounters in the Night (TV). Wisdom. 1987: The Witches of Eastwick. 1988: Valentino Returns. 1989: Desperate for Love (TV). 1990: False Identity. Hitler's Daughter. 1991: *Walking the Dog. Dead in the Water (TV). 1992: Man Trouble. 1993: It's Nothing Personal (TV). 1994: Dead Air (TV). 1995: Candyman Farewell to the Flesh. My Brother's Keeper (TV).*

CARUSO, Anthony 1915–
Tall, solidly built, dark-haired, Italian-looking American actor with scowling, 'mobster'-style handsomeness. After abandoning a career as a singer, he broke into Hollywood films in 1940, but rarely achieved more than gunmen, vengeful rejected suitors and minor hoodlums. He got his first leading role in the 1976 film, *The Zebra Force*, but has been little seen since then.

1940: Johnny Apollo. The Bride Wore Crutches. Northwest Mounted Police. Catman of Paris (released 1946). 1941: Tall, Dark and Handsome. The Bride Came COD. The Corsican Brothers. You're in the Army Now. 1942: Always in My Heart. Sunday Punch. Across the Pacific. Lucky Jordan. 1943: Whistling in Brooklyn. The Ghost and the Guest. Above Suspicion. The Girl from Monterey. Watch on the Rhine. Jitterbugs. 1944: Maisie Goes to Reno (GB: You Can't Do That to Me). The Racket Man. U-Boat Prisoner (GB: Dangerous Mists). And Now Tomorrow. The Conspirators.

*The Story of Dr Wassell. 1945: Don Juan Quilligan. *The Last Installment. *A Gun in His Hand. I Love a Bandleader (GB: Memory for Two). That Night with You. Crime Doctor's Courage (GB: The Doctor's Courage). Pride of the Marines (GB: Forever in Love). Objective Burma! *Isle of Tabu. The Stork Club. *Star in the Night. The Blue Dahlia. 1946: Monsieur Beaucaire. Night Editor (GB: The Trespasser). Tarzan and the Leopard Woman. Don't Gamble with Strangers. The Last Crooked Mile. To Each His Own. Escape Me Never. 1947: News Hounds. Devil Ship. The Trespasser (and 1946 film). Wild Harvest. To the Victor. My Favorite Brunette. The Gangster. They Won't Believe Me. Where There's Life. 1948: The Far Frontier. Incident. The Loves of Carmen. 1949: Song of India. The Undercover Man. Bride of Vengeance. Anna Lucasta. The Threat. Illegal Entry. Scene of the Crime. 1950: Tarzan and the Slave Girl. The Asphalt Jungle. Prisoners in Petticoats. 1951: According to Mrs Hoyle. His Kind of Woman. Pals of the Golden West. Boots Malone. 1952: The Iron Mistress. Blackbeard the Pirate. The Man Behind the Gun. Desert Pursuit. 1953: Raiders of the Seven Seas. Desert Legion. Fighter Attack. The Steel Lady (GB: Treasure of Kalifa). Fort Algiers. 1954: Phantom of the Rue Morgue. The Boy from Oklahoma. Drum Beat. Cattle Queen of Montana. Saskatchewan (GB: O'Rourke of the Royal Mounted). Passion. 1955: Jail Busters. Santa Fé Passage. Thrill of the Ring. City of Shadows. The Magnificent Matador (GB: The Brave and the Beautiful). Tennessee's Partner. The Toughest Man Alive. Hell on Frisco Bay. 1956: A Cry in the Night. Walk the Proud Land. Crashing Las Vegas. When Gangland Strikes. 1957: Baby Face Nelson. The Big Land (GB: Stampeded!). The Lawless Eighties. The Oklahoman. Joe Dakota. 1958: Legion of the Doomed. Most Dangerous Man Alive (released 1961). Fort Massacre. The Badlanders. 1959: Never Steal Anything Small. The Wonderful Country. 1961: Escape from Zahrain. 1964: Where Love Has Gone. 1965: Sylvia. Young Dillinger. 1967: Never a Dull Moment. 1968: Desperate Mission/Joaquin Murieta (shown 1975). 1970: Flap (GB: The Last Warrior). Brother, Cry for Me. 1974: Lenny. The Legend of Earl Durand. 1976: Mean Johnny Barrows. The Zebra Force. 1977: Claws. 1987: Savage Harbor. 1990: The Legend of Grizzly Adams.*

CASSEL, Seymour 1935–
Stocky, twinkle-eyed, plum-nosed, often moustachioed, rather disreputable-looking American actor with straight fair hair, often seen as scruffy rebels in his earlier years, when he was much associated with actor-director John Cassavetes. Following acting studies with Cassavetes. Cassel began playing small roles in his films, sometimes acting in production capacities as well. There was a leading role opposite Gena Rowlands in *Minnie and Moskowitz* and, since the Cassavetes connection ended in the mid 1980s, he has often been showcased as smart-Alec criminals, sometimes with a likeable streak, and with his once long and straggly hair cut down to bushy brevity. Oscar nominee for *Faces*.

1959: Shadows. 1960: Murder Inc. Juke

Box Racket. 1961: Too Late Blues. 1962: The Webster Boy. 1963: The Nutty Professor. 1964: The Hanged Man (TV. GB: cinemas). The Killers (originally for TV). 1968: Faces. Coogan's Bluff. The Sweet Ride. 1970: The Revolutionary. 1971: Minnie and Moskowitz. 1974: Death Game/The Seducers (released 1977). 1976: The Last Tycoon. The Killing of a Chinese Bookie. 1977: Black Oak Conspiracy. Valentino. Scott Joplin. 1978: Convoy. Ravagers. 1979: California Dreaming. Sunburn. 1980: The Mountain Men. Angel on My Shoulder (TV). 1981: King of the Mountain. 1982: Double Exposure. 1983: Blood Feud (TV). I'm Almost Not Crazy. I Want to Live! (TV). 1984: Love Streams. 1986: Beverly Hills Madam (TV). Eye of the Tiger. 1987: Tin Men. Track 29. Survival Game. 1988: Colors. Johnny Be Good. Plain Clothes. Wicked Stepmother. 1990: Dick Tracy. Cold Dog Soup. 1991: White Fang. Dead in the Water. Mobsters (GB: Mobsters: The Evil Empire). 1992: In the Soup. Honeymoon in Vegas. Cold Heaven. 1993: Chain of Desire. Short Cuts. Indecent Proposal. Boiling Point. 1994: When Pigs Fly. Tollbooth. Handgun. Dark Side of Genius. Chasers. It Could Happen to You. The Slaughter of the Cock. There Goes My Baby (filmed 1992). Les Frères Gravel. Imaginary Crimes. 1995: Dead Presidents. Four Rooms. Things to Do in Denver When You're Dead. Things I Never Told You. The Last Home Run. Dream for an Insomniac.

CATLETT, Walter 1889–1960
Flap-eared, light-haired, bulky American character comedian specializing in bespectacled, fussy types whose imperious facade tended to go to pieces under pressure. A child performer, he sang operetta in Australia, became a boxer and developed the famous plum nose, then returned to show business in triumph with the Ziegfeld Follies. Leading roles in Mack Sennett comedy shorts were followed of years of valiant support to the stars (and high living in Hollywood) before starring in feature comedies of small-town life in the late 1940s and early 1950s. Died following a stroke.

*1912: The Leopard Lady. 1924: Second Youth. 1926: Summer Bachelors. 1927: The Music Master. 1929: Why Leave Home?/Imagine My Embarrassment. Married in Hollywood. 1930: The Florodora Girl (GB: The Gay Nineties). The Big Party. The Golden Calf. Happy Days. Let's Go Places. *Aunts in the Pants. *Camping*

Out. 1931: The Front Page. Plantinum Blonde. Palmy Days. The Maker of Men. Yellow. Goldfish Bowl. 1932: *So This is Harris. *Bring 'Em Back Sober. *Oh! My Operation. The Expert. Cock of the Air. Big City Blues. It's Tough to Be Famous. Back Street. Rockabye. Rain. Okay, America (GB: Penalty of Fame). Free, White and 21. Sport Parade. 1933: *The Big Fibber. *Meet the Champ. *Daddy Knows Best. *Dream Stuff. *Husbands' Reunion. *Roadhouse Queen. *One Awful Night. *Private Wives. *Caliente Love. Mama Loves Papa. Only Yesterday. Arizona to Broadway. Private Jones. Olsen's Big Moment. 1934: *Elmer Steps Out. *Get Along Little Hubby. Lightning Strikes Twice. Unknown Blonde. The Captain Hates the Sea. 1935: Every Night at Eight. The Affair of Susan. A Tale of Two Cities. 1936: *Fibbing Fibbers. We Went to College (GB: The Old School Tie). I Loved a Soldier. Follow Your Heart. Sing Me a Love Song. Cain and Mabel. Banjo on My Knee. Mr Deeds Goes to Town. 1937: Four Days' Wonder. On the Avenue. Wake Up and Live. Varsity Show. Love is News. Love Under Fire. Every Day's a Holiday. Danger — Love at Work. Come Up Smiling. 1938: Bringing Up Baby. Going Places. 1939: Kid Nightingale. Zaza. Exile Express. *Static in the Attic. 1940: Pop Always Pays. Li'l Abner (GB: Trouble Chaser). Remedy for Riches. Comin' Round the Mountain. Spring Parade. Half a Sinner. The Quarterback. *You're Next. *Blondes and Blunders. Pinocchio (voice only). 1941: You're the One. Honeymoon for Three. Horror Island. Sing Another Chorus. Wild Bill Hickok Rides. Wild Man of Borneo. Million Dollar Baby. It Started with Eve. Hello Sucker. Manpower. Bad Men of Missouri. Unfinished Business. Steel Against the Sky. 1942: Star Spangled Rhythm. My Gal Sal. They Got Me Covered. Between Us Girls. Maisie Gets Her Man (GB: She Gets Her Man). Yankee Doodle Dandy. Give Out. Sisters. Hearts of the Golden West. 1943: Hit Parade of 1943. West Side Kid. How's About It? Fired Wife. His Butler's Sister. Cowboy in Manhattan. Get Going. 1944: I Love a Soldier. Hat Check Honey. Pardon My Rhythm. Up in Arms. Ghost Catchers. Lady, Let's Dance! Hi, Beautiful (GB: Pass to Romance). My Gal Loves Music. Three is a Family. Her Primitive Man. Lake Placid Serenade. 1945: I Love a Bandleader (GB: Memory for Two). The Man Who Walked Alone. 1946: Riverboat Rhythm. Slightly Scandalous. 1947: I'll Be Yours. 1948: Mr Reckless. Are You With It? The Boy with Green Hair. 1949: Leave It to Henry. Look for the Silver Lining. The Inspector General. Henry the Rainmaker. Dancing in the Dark. 1950: Father's Wild Game. Father Makes Good. 1951: Here Comes the Groom. Honeychile. Father Takes the Air. 1955: Davy Crockett and the River Pirates (originally for TV). 1956: Friendly Persuasion. 1957: Beau James.

CAVANAGH, Paul 1888–1964

Suave, debonair, moustachioed, slightly gaunt British leading man of the 1920s who went to Hollywood and became an equally suave and debonair character player and villain, latterly often in costume. He returned to Britain for a few starring parts in the middle 1930s, but then settled in America for good.

Cavanagh enjoyed his showiest part as Mae West's leading man in *Goin' to Town*, a role in which, as always, he was immaculately dressed and radiated class, Died from a heart attack.

1928: Tesha. Two Little Drummer Boys. 1929: A Woman in the Night (sound remake of Tesha). The Runaway Princess. 1930: Grumpy. The Storm. The Virtuous Sin (GB: Cast Iron). The Devil to Pay. Strictly Unconventional. 1931: Unfaithful. Always Goodbye. Born to Love. The Squaw Man (GB: The White Man). Transgression. Menace. Heartbreak. 1932: The Crash. The Devil's Lottery. A Bill of Divorcement. 1933: Tonight is Ours. In the Money. The Sin of Nora Moran. The Kennel Murder Case. 1934: Shoot the Works (GB: Thank Your Stars). Curtain at Eight. Menace (remake). The Notorious Sophie Lang. Tarzan and His Mate. Uncertain Lady. Escapade. One Exciting Adventure. Wings in the Dark. 1935: Goin' to Town. Without Regret. Thunder in the Night. Splendor. 1936: Champagne Charlie. Crime over London. Café Colette (US: Danger in Paris). 1937: Romance in Flanders (US: Lost on the Western Front). 1939: The Under-Pup. Reno. Within the Law. 1940: I Take This Woman. The Case of the Black Parrot. 1941: Maisie Was a Lady. Shadows on the Stairs. Passage from Hong Kong. 1942: The Strange Case of Dr RX. Captains of the Clouds. Eagle Squadron. Pacific Rendezvous. The Hard Way. The Gorilla Man. 1943: Adventures in Iraq. 1944: Maisie Goes to Reno (GB: You Can't Do That to Me). Marriage is a Private Affair. The Scarlet Claw. The Man in Half-Moon Street. 1945: The House of Fear. The Woman in Green. Club Havana. This Man's Navy. 1946: Night in Paradise. Night and Day. The Verdict. Humoresque. Wife Wanted (GB: Shadow of Blackmail). 1947: Dishonored Lady. Ivy. 1948: The Black Arrow (GB: The Black Arrow Strikes). The Babe Ruth Story. The Secret Beyond the Door. You Gotta Stay Happy. 1949: Madame Bovary. 1950: The Iroquois Trail (GB: The Tomahawk Trail). Rogues of Sherwood Forest. Hit Parade of 1951. Hi-Jacked. 1951: Hollywood Story. The Desert Fox (GB: Rommel — Desert Fox). The Strange Door. The Son of Dr Jekyll. Bride of the Gorilla. All That I Have. The Highwayman. Tales of Robin Hood. 1952: The Golden Hawk. Plymouth Adventure. 1953: Charade. Mississippi Gambler. House of Wax. Port Sinister. The Bandits of Corsica (GB: Return of the Corsican Brothers). Flame of

Calcutta. Blades of the Musketeers. The All-American (GB: The Winning Way). Casanova's Big Night. 1954: Khyber Patrol. The Iron Glove. The Raid. The Law vs Billy the Kid. Magnificent Obsession. 1955: The Purple Mask. Diane. The Prodigal. The Scarlet Coat. The King's Thief. 1956: Francis in the Haunted House. Blonde Bait. 1957: She Devil. God is My Partner. The Man Who Turned to Stone. 1958: In the Money. 1959: The Four Skulls of Jonathan Drake. The Beat Generation.

CAVANAUGH, Hobart 1886–1950

Stocky, balding, brush-moustached American actor whose tiny eyes frequently blinked in bewildered or cowed fashion from behind large spectacles. Almost always cast as the little man done down by life, wife or enemies, Cavanaugh was usually a bank clerk or something similar, forever worried about his own adequacy. One of his first films, a short called *The Poor Fish*, summed up the pattern of his career, although he also (too rarely) played malevolent minions to great effect.

1928: San Francisco Nights. 1929: *Sympathy. 1930: *The Poor Fish. *The Headache Man. 1931: *The Great Junction Hotel. 1932: *Close Friends. 1933: The Devil's Mate (GB: He Knew Too Much). Headline Shooter. Evidence in Camera). Goodbye Again. Mary Stevens MD. Private Detective 62. The Kennel Murder Case. The Mayor of Hell. From Headquarters. Bureau of Missing Persons. I Cover the Waterfront. Broadway Thru a Keyhole. Lilly Turner. Havana Widows. Convention City. No Marriage Ties. My Woman. Footlight Parade. State Fair. A Study in Scarlet. Picture Snatcher. Gold Diggers of 1933: Death Watch. 1934: Now I'll Tell (GB: When New York Sleeps). Wonder Bar. Dark Hazard. Moulin Rouge. Mandalay. Hi, Nellie! Easy to Love. I've Got Your Number. Harold Teen (GB: The Dancing Fool). Jimmy the Gent. The Merry Wives of Reno. The Key. The St Louis Kid (GB: A Perfect Weekend). A Very Honorable Guy. A Modern Hero. The Firebird. I Sell Anything. Housewife. I Am a Thief. Fashions/Fashions of 1934. Madame du Barry. A Lost Lady. Kansas City Princess. Bordertown. 1935: *Broadway Brevities. Wings in the Dark. Captain Blood. While the Patient Slept. Don't Bet on Blondes. We're in the Money. Broadway Gondolier. Page Miss Glory. Dr Socrates. Steamboat 'Round the Bend. A Midsummer Night's Dream. I Live for Love (GB: I Live for You). 1936: Here Comes Carter (GB: The Voice of Scandal). The Lady Consents. Sing, Boy, Sing. Love Letters of a Star. Colleen. Love Begins at Twenty. Hearts Divided. Two Against the World (GB: The Case of Mrs Pembrook). Sing Me a Love Song. Cain and Mabel. The Golden Arrow. Stage Struck. Wife vs Secretary. 1937: The Great O'Malley. Carnival Queen. The Mighty Treve. Mysterious Crossing. Three Smart Girls. Night Key. Girl Overboard. Love in a Bungalow. Reported Missing. That's My Story. 1938: Strange Faces. Cowboy from Brooklyn (GB: Romance and Rhythm). Orphans of the Street. 1939: Rose of Washington Square. Zenobia (GB: Elephants Never Forget). Daughters Courageous. *The Day of Rest. *See Your Doctor. Career. Idiot's Delight. Tell No Tales. Chicken Wagon Family. Reno. Broadway Serenade. Four Wives. The Adventures of Jane Arden. That's Right, You're Wrong. The Covered Trailer. The Honeymoon's Over. I Stole a Million. Never Say Die. Naughty But Nice. 1940: *Home Movies. A Child is Born. You Can't Fool Your Wife. An Angel from Texas. Stage to Chino. Shooting High. Hired Wife. Public Deb No. 1. The Great Plane Robbery. Santa Fé Trail. Charter Pilot. Love, Honor and Oh, Baby! The Ghost Comes Home. Street of Memories. 1941: There's Magic in Music. Reaching for the Sun. Horror Island. Playmates. I Wanted Wings. Thieves Fall Out. Down in San Diego. Meet the Chump. Our Wife. Land of the Open Range. Skylark. 1942: The McGuerins from Brooklyn. A Tragedy at Midnight. My Favorite Spy. Tarzan's New York Adventure. Lady in a Jam. The Magnificent Dope. Jackass Mail. Pittsburgh. Her Cardboard Lover. Whistling in Dixie. Stand By for Action! (GB: Cargo of Innocents). 1943: Pilot No. 5. The Meanest Man in the World. Sweet Rosie O'Grady. Dangerous Blondes. A Scream in the Dark. The Man from Down Under. The Kansan (GB: Wagon Wheels). Gildersleeve on Broadway. Jack London. The Human Comedy. What a Woman! (GB: The Beautiful Cheat). 1944: *The Immortal Blacksmith. San Diego, I Love You. Kismet. Louisiana Hayride. Together Again. 1945: I'll Remember April. Don Juan Quilligan. Roughly Speaking. House of Fear. Lady on a Train. 1946: Black Angel. Margie. Cinderella Jones. Spider Woman Strikes Back. Night and Day. The Hoodlum Saint. Faithful in My Fashion. Easy Come, Easy Go. Little Iodine. 1947: Driftwood. 1948: You Gotta Stay Happy. Best Man Wins. Up in Central Park. The Inside Story. 1949: †Two Knights in Brooklyn/Two Mugs from Brooklyn. A Letter to Three Wives. 1950: Stella.

† Combined GB version of The McGuerins from Brooklyn/Taxi, Mister

CELI, Adolfo 1922–1986

Heftily built, grey-haired, black-eyebrowed, pudgy-faced, Sicilian character actor, popular in international roles after playing Largo (the villain) in the James Bond film Thunderball in 1965. After a promising start in post-war Italian films, he went to South America in 1949, and worked in Argentina and Brazil as a director for the theatre, films and TV. A French film made in Brazil brought him back to Europe and he worked busily there,

mostly as conspirators of one kind or another. He was most occupied on TV from 1977, subsequently gaining a nationwide following in Britain for his performance in The Borgias. Died from a heart attack.

1946: Un Americano in vacanza. 1948: Natale al campo 119 (US: Escape into Dreams). Proibito rubare. 1949: Emigrés/Emigrantes. 1964: L'homme de Rio (GB and US: That Man from Rio). Un monsieur de compagnie. E venne un uomo (GB: A Man Named John. US: And There Came a Man). Tre notti d'amore. 1965: Thunderball. Von Ryan's Express. The Agony and the Ecstasy. Slalom. Rapina al sole. Le belle famiglie. 1966: Das Geheimnis der gelben Monche (GB: Target for Killing). Le roi de coeur (GB and US: King of Hearts). El Greco. Grand Prix. El Yankee. The Honey Pot. Le piacevoli notti. 1967: The Bobo. Grand Slam. Operation Kid Brother. Colpo maestro al servizio di sua maesta Britannica. Ad ogni costo. Tiro a segno per uccidere. Diabolik (GB: and US: Danger: Diabolik). 1968: Il padre di famiglia. U atraco de ita y unetta. Dalle Ardenne all'inferno (GB: From Hell to Glory. US: The Dirty Heroes). Uno scacco tutto matto/Mad Checkmate. Fantabulous. Un condé (GB: Blood on My Hands). Death Sentence. La donna, il sesso e il superuomo. In Search of Gregory. 1969: Midas Run (GB: A Run on Gold). Detective Belli. L'alibi. Sette volte sette/Seven Against Seven. L'arcangelo. Blonde Köder für den Mörder. Io Emanuelle. 1970: Fragment of Fear. Brancaleone alle crociate. The Man from Chicago. Hanna cambiato faccia. Murders in the Rue Morgue. 1971: Apuntamento col dishonore. 1972: Brother Sun, Sister Moon. La 'mala' ordina/The Italian Connection/Mafia Boss/Manhunt in Milan. L'occhio nel labirinto (GB: Blood). Chi l'ha vista morire? Una chica casi decente. Una ragazza tutta nuda assassinata nel parco. Terza ipotesi su un caso di perfetta strategia criminale. 1973: Hitler: The Last 10 Days. Piazza pulita (GB: Pete, Pearl and the Pole). La villeggiatura (GB: Black Holiday). Le mataf. Il sorriso del grande tentatore (GB: The Tempter. US: The Devil is a Woman). 1974: La mano spietata della legge. And Then There Were None (US: Ten Little Indians). Libera amore mio. Le fantôme de la liberté (GB and US: The Phantom of Liberty). 1975: Amici miei. 1976: Le grand escogriffe. Sandokan (originally for TV). Signore e signori – buonanotte. La moglie di mio padre (GB: Confessions

of a Frustrated Housewife). Come una rosa al nase (GB: TV, as Virginity). The Next Man. Uomini si nasce poliziotti si muore (GB: Live Like a Cop, Die Like a Man). 1977: Les passagers (GB: Shattered). Holocaust 2000 (US: The Chosen). 1979: Café Express. 1980: Amici miei II. Car Napping. 1982: Monsignor. 1985: Amici miei III.

As director:

1951: Ciacara. 1952: Aliba. 1953: Tico tico no fuba. 1969: †L'alibi.

† Co-directed.

CHAMBERLAIN, Cyril 1909–1974

Big, tall British actor with distinctive receding dark hair, slightly shifty look, ready scowl and lived-in, 'working class' profile. He began in minor juvenile leads just before war service, but in post-war years settled down to playing a fistful of policemen, fathers and second-string crooks. An aptitude for tongue-in-cheek comedy made him one of the cast in 'Carry On' films from 1958 to 1963. One of his earliest films was The Common Touch: that was something that Chamberlain certainly had.

1938: Crackerjack (US: The Man with a Hundred Faces). Stolen Life. 1939: Dead Men Are Dangerous. Ask a Policeman. Return to Yesterday. This Man in Paris. Poison Pen. Jail Birds. What Would You Do, Chums? 1940: Old Mother Riley in Business. Old Mother Riley in Society. Crook's Tour. Spare a Copper. 1941: *Night Watch. The Common Touch. The Black Sheep of Whitehall. The Big Blockade. 1945: India Strikes (narrator only). 1947: The Dark Road. Dancing with Crime. Night Beat. The Upturned Glass. 1948: London Belongs to Me (US: Dulcimer Street). The Calendar. Here Come the Huggetts. My Brother's Keeper. The Blind Goddess. Quartet. Portrait from Life (US: The Girl in the Painting). It's Not Cricket. Once a Jolly Swagman (US: Maniacs on Wheels). The Bad Lord Byron. 1949: Marry Me! Don't Ever Leave Me. Helter Skelter. Stop Press Girl. Boys in Brown. Whisky Galore! (US: Tight Little Island). The Chiltern Hundreds (US: The Amazing Mr Beecham). Stage Fright. 1950: The Clouded Yellow. Tony Draws a Horse. The Adventurers (US: The Great Adventure). Blackmailed. 1951: Old Mother Riley's

Jungle Treasure. The Lavender Hill Mob. Scarlet Thread. Lady Godiva Rides Again. 1952: Sing Along with Me. Escape Route (US: I'll Get You). Folly to be Wise. 1953: The Net (US: Project M-7). *Out of the Bandbox. Trouble in Store. You Know What Sailors Are. Hell Below Zero. A Day to Remember. 1954: Doctor in the House. The Diamond (US: Diamond Wizard). The Embezzler. Forbidden Cargo. Companions in Crime. 1955: Impulse. Value for Money. An Alligator Named Daisy. Raising a Riot. Man of the Moment. Tiger by the Tail. Windfall. Simon and Laura. Above Us the Waves. Doctor at Sea. Dial 999 (US: The Way Out). Lost (US: Tears for Simon). The Gamma People. 1956: Eyewitness. Up in the World. The Iron Petticoat. *Wall of Death. The Green Man. 1957: Just My Luck. The Prince and the Showgirl. The Tommy Steele Story (US: Rock Around the World). Doctor at Large. After the Ball. No Time for Tears. Blue Murder at St Trinian's. The Man Who Wouldn't Talk. The One That Got Away. 1958: The Duke Wore Jeans. Chain of Events. The Big Money (completed 1956). Carry On Sergeant. A Night to Remember. Wonderful Things! Man with a Gun. 1959: Too Many Crooks. Carry On Nurse. Carry On Teacher. Operation Bullshine. The Ugly Duckling. Upstairs and Downstairs. Please Turn Over. 1960: Carry On Constable. No Kidding (US: Beware of Children). The Bulldog Breed. Doctor in Love. Two-Way Stretch. *The Dover Road Mystery. The Pure Hell of St Trinian's. 1961: A Pair of Briefs. Dentist on the Job (US: Get On with It!). Carry On Regardless. Nearly a Nasty Accident. Raising the Wind (US: Roommates). Flame in the Streets. 1962: Carry On Cruising. On the Beat. The Iron Maiden (US: The Swingin' Maiden). 1963: Carry On Cabby. Two Left Feet. Ring of Spies. A Stitch in Time. 1964: Carry On Spying. 1965: Joey Boy. Sky West and Crooked (US: Gypsy Girl). 1966: The Great St Trinian's Train Robbery. The Yellow Hat.

CHANDLER, George 1898–1985
Oval-faced, unsmiling, brown-haired, olive-complexioned, hound-like American cameo player. Subservient and sometimes sullen, Chandler looked dubious about most things in life, as he came on for fleeting appearances as busboys, clerks, reporters, elevator boys and valets in more than 50 years' worth of films. He started in variety playing the violin over his head ('George Chandler, the

musical nut') and came to Hollywood as a comedian, soon settling into scores of films as a supporting player. Most memorable as Ginger Rogers' disposable husband in Roxie Hart, Chandler was later popular in a gentler role, as Uncle Petrie in TV's Lassie series. Politically busy, this one-time president of the Screen Actors' Guild was also chairman of the Hollywood Overseas Committee during the Vietnam War. Died from complications following cancer surgery.

1927: No Control. 1928: *A Fighting Tenderfoot. *Spats and Spurs. *A Dangerous Dude. *A Clean Sweep. The Cloud Dodger. *Saps and Saddles. *A Tenderfoot Hero. The Kid's Clever. 1929: The Virginian. Vagabond Lover. Black Hills. The Woman from Hell. *A Riding Romeo. *Two Gun Morgan. *Red Romance. *A Thrill Hunter. *A Close Call. *The Go Get 'Em Kid. *A Tenderfoot Terror. *The Lone Rider. 1930: The Florodora Girl (GB: The Gay Nineties). Soup to Nuts. Only Saps Work. The Light of Western Stars. In Gay Madrid. Leathernecking (GB: Present Arms). Manslaughter. The Last Dance. *It Happened in Hollywood. *Pure and Simple. 1931: A Holy Terror. Doctors' Wives. Man of the World. Too Many Crooks. The Woman Between (GB: Madame Julie). Everything's Rosie. *The Great Junction Hotel. *Cowslips. *The Back Page. *Hollywood Girl/The Lure of Hollywood. *Up Pops the Duke. *The Wide Open Spaces. 1932: Beast of the City. Blessed Event. Me and My Gal (GB: Pier 13). Winner Take All. The Famous Ferguson Case. The Strange Love of Molly Louvain. Union Depot (GB: Gentleman for a Day). The Tenderfoot. Afraid to Talk/Merry-Go-Round. The Sport Parade. Is My Face Red? *The Bride's Bereavement, or: The Snake in the Grass. 1933: *The Fatal Glass of Beer. Bureau of Missing Persons. Footlight Parade. Elmer the Great. Picture Snatcher. The White Sister. Lady Killer. Central Airport. The Power and the Glory. She Had to Say Yes. The Life of Jimmy Dolan (GB: The Kid's Last Fight). Son of a Sailor. The Keyhole. The Kennel Murder Case. Parachute Jumper. 1934: Music in the Air. *Rough Necking. Hi, Nellie! †Evelyn Prentice. Dark Hazard. Twenty Million Sweethearts. He Was Her Man. Fog Over Frisco. Big-Hearted Herbert. Happiness Ahead. Six Day Bike Rider. 1935: The Case of the Lucky Legs. Star of Midnight. The Gilded Lily. Front Page Woman. Mary Burns, Fugitive. Murder Man. Stars Over Broadway. The Woman in Red. Welcome Home. While the Patient Slept. Broadway Gondolier. Spring Tonic. 1936: All American Chump (GB: Country Bumpkin). Old Hutch. God's Country and the Woman. Flying Hostess. High Tension. The Accusing Finger. Sing, Baby, Sing. Reunion (GB: Hearts in Reunion). Here Comes Trouble. Fury. The Country Doctor. Libeled Lady. Three Men on a Horse. Pennies from Heaven. Sworn Enemy. The Princess Comes Across. *Neighborhood House (originally feature-length). Women Are Trouble. Speed. 1937: History is Made at Night. Woman Chases Man. *Soak the Poor. Nothing Sacred. A Star is Born. Big Town Girl. Charlie Chan at the Olympics. Maytime. Small Town Boy. Danger! Love at Work. Wake Up and Live. Nancy Steele is Missing. Saratoga. One Mile from Heaven. The Singing Marine. Beg,

Borrow or Steal. They Gave Him a Gun. Dangerous Number. Riding on Air. Love on Toast. Time Out for Romance. Live, Love and Learn. Woman Wise. The Go-Getter. The Jones Family in Hot Water. A Family Affair. Fair Warning. Checkers. Big City. 1938: The Mad Miss Manton. Hard to Get. Men with Wings. Secrets of a Nurse. Gateway. Man-Proof. In Old Chicago. The Shining Hour. Mannequin. Professor, Beware! †Block-Heads. The Cowboy and the Lady. Shopworn Angel. There Goes My Heart. Mr Moto's Gamble. Three Loves Has Nancy. Breaking the Ice. The Last Express. Everybody's Baby. Joy of Living. Three Comrades. Rascals. Valley of the Giants. Vivacious Lady. 1939: Fast and Furious. 20,000 Men a Year. Everything's On Ice. It's a Wonderful World. King of the Turf. Jesse James. I Stole a Million. Second Fiddle. Calling All Marines. Beau Geste. Mr Smith Goes to Washington. Exile Express. Calling Dr Kildare. The Flying Irishman. While New York Sleeps. The Light That Failed. I'm from Missouri. The Jones Family in Hollywood. Made for Each Other. Blondie Meets the Boss. Mr Moto Takes a Vacation. Secret of Dr Kildare. Young Mr Lincoln. St Louis Blues. Boy Slaves. Thou Shalt Not Kill. 1940: Melody Ranch. The Return of Frank James. Broadway Melody of 1940. Manhattan Heartbeat. Abe Lincoln in Illinois. Dr Kildare Goes Home. Charter Pilot. Edison, the Man. Little Old New York. The Man Who Wouldn't Talk. Trail of the Vigilantes. Shooting High. Forgotten Girls. The Mad Doctor (GB: A Date with Destiny). Arizona. 1941: Western Union. Hellzapoppin. Reaching for the Sun. The Gay Vagabond. Broadway Limited. Buy Me That Town. Dance Hall. Tobacco Road. Model Wife. Private Nurse. Obliging Young Lady. Repent at Leisure. Three Sons o' Guns. Mountain Moonlight (GB: Moving in Society). Sleepers West. Remember the Day. Double Date. A Girl, a Guy and a Gob (GB: The Navy Steps Out). †Look Who's Laughing. Men at Large. Design for Scandal. 1942: Here We Go Again. Roxie Hart. Call Out the Marines. That Other Woman. The Great Gildersleeve. Highways by Night. The Forest Rangers. The Great Man's Lady. Isle of Missing Men. Night in New Orleans. Secrets of the Underground. Scattergood Survives a Murder. A Tragedy at Midnight. Private Buckaroo. Thunder Birds. Pardon My Sarong. Castle in the Desert. Are Husbands Necessary? A Night to Remember. The Ox-Bow Incident (GB: Strange Incident). They Got Me Covered. 1943: A Scream in the Dark. The Powers Girl (GB: Hello Beautiful). Hers to Hold. Lady of Burlesque. Swing Fever. Johnny Come Lately (GB: Johnny Vagabond). Sweet Rosie O'Grady. Let's Face It. Never a Dull Moment. City Without Men. Swing Shift Maisie (GB: The Girl in Overalls). Here Comes Elmer. My Kingdom for a Cook. Hi Buddy. 1944: Buffalo Bill. It Happened Tomorrow. Tall in the Saddle. Goin' to Town. Since You Went Away. The Chinese Cat/Charlie Chan in The Chinese Cat. Bride by Mistake. Allergic to Love. Step Lively. Three Men in White. Irish Eyes Are Smiling. Wing and a Prayer. *Community Finance. Hi, Beautiful (GB: Pass to Romance). Johnny Doesn't Live Here Any More. It's in the Bag! (GB: The Fifth Chair). 1945: Strange Confession. This Man's Navy. *Morgan's Folly. The Story of G I Joe/War

Correspondent. Captain Eddie. Colonel Effingham's Raid (GB: Man of the Hour). Lady on a Train. Tell It to a Star. Man from Oklahoma. Without Love. Incendiary Blonde. Pardon My Past. Patrick the Great. See My Lawyer. The Shanghai Cobra. 1946: Little Giant (GB: On the Carpet). So Goes My Love (GB: A Genius in the Family). The Shadow Returns. The Last Crooked Mile. Lover Come Back. A Guy Could Change. Behind the Mask. Because of Him. The French Key. Magnificent Doll. Glass Alibi. Heldorado. The Mask of Diijon. Gallant Journey. The Missing Lady. The Kid from Brooklyn. Strange Impersonation. Rendezvous with Annie. Black Angel. If You Knew Susie. Suspense. *Don't Be a Sucker. The Michigan Kid. Dead Reckoning. 1947: It's a Joke, Son. Magic Town. I'll Be Yours. The Corpse Came COD. Killer McCoy. It Had to be You. Suddenly It's Spring. Reaching from Heaven. Mr District Attorney. Nightmare Alley. The Secret Life of Walter Mitty. Saddle Pals. Road to Rio. Sinbad the Sailor. Night Song. *So You Want to Be in Pictures. The Vigilantes Return. 1948: Alias a Gentleman. Hollow Triumph (GB: The Scar). The Cobra Strikes. The Girl from Manhattan. The Iron Curtain. The Miracle of the Bells. Silver River. Race Street. The Pirate. The Paleface. Sons of Adventure. The Hunted. Lightnin' in the Forest. You Were Meant for Me. The Judge Steps Out (GB: Indian Summer). 1949: *Sweet Cheat. *Knucklehead. Homicide. Canadian Pacific. Once More, My Darling. The House Across the Street. Knock on Any Door. Chicago Deadline. Battleground. Adventure in Baltimore (GB: Bachelor Bait). Ma and Pa Kettle Go to Town (GB: Going to Town). 1950: The Happy Years. Triple Trouble. Perfect Strangers (GB: Too Dangerous to Love). Kansas Raiders. Pretty Baby. The Next Voice You Hear. Singing Guns. 1951: Across the Wide Missouri. Disc Jockey. The Whip Hand. Double Dynamite. Westward the Women. 1952: Woman of the North Country. The Narrow Margin. The WAC from Walla Walla (GB: Army Capers). This Woman is Dangerous. Hans Christian Andersen. And Now Tomorrow. My Man and I. Rose of Cimarron. Target. Somebody Loves Me. Meet Me at the Fair. 1953: Island in the Sky. Marry Me Again. Superman in Exile (TV. GB: cinemas). 1954: Duffy of San Quentin (GB: Men Behind Bars). The High and the Mighty. The Steel Cage. Rails into Laramie. 1955: Apache Ambush. The Girl Rush. Goodbye, My Lady. 1957: Spring Reunion. Gunsight Ridge. 1963: Law of the Lawless. 1964: Dead Ringer (GB: Dead Image). 1965: Black Spurs. 1966: Apache Uprising. The Ghost and Mr Chicken. 1968: Buckskin. 1970: Love, American Style (TV). 1971: One More Train to Rob. 1972: Pickup on 101 (GB: Echoes of the Road). 1974: Escape to Witch Mountain. 1975: Capone. 1976: Griffin and Phoenix (TV. GB, cinemas, as Today is Forever). 1978: Every Which Way But Loose. 1979: The Apple Dumpling Gang Rides Again.

† Scenes deleted from final release print

CHANDLER, John Davis 1937–
Pale-eyed, pale-haired, short, stocky American 'bad guy' actor, who looks like a mole blinking weakly in the sunlight. He whined at a fistful of western heroes and was almost always neurotic and dangerous. He started in modern clothes, though, in the title role of Mad Dog Coll, his snarling, lily-livered style of bravado being exactly right for the part. Failing to find a wider range, he was consequently seen in too few films, although finding richer pastures in TV westerns. Sometimes billed as John Chandler in later roles.

1961: Mad Dog Coll. The Young Savages. Ride the High Country (GB: Guns in the Afternoon). 1962: The Brazen Bell (TV. GB: cinemas). 1964: Those Calloways. Major Dundee. 1965: Once a Thief. 1966: Return of the Gunfighter. 1968: The Hooked Generation. 1969: The Good Guys and the Bad Guys. 1970: Barquero. 1971: Shoot Out. Operation Cobra (TV). Hitched (TV. GB: Westward the Wagon). 1972: Moon of the Wolf (TV). 1973: Pat Garrett and Billy the Kid. Chase (TV). 1974: The Take. The Ultimate Thrill (US: The Ultimate Chase). 1975: Capone. Part 2 Walking Tall (GB: Legend of the Lawman). The Desperate Miles (TV). 1976: The Jaws of Death. Chesty Anderson, US Navy/Anderson's Angels. Scorchy. 1977: Whiskey Mountain. The Shadow of Chikara/Wishbone Cutter. 1980: The Little Dragons. 1982: The Sword and the Sorcerer. 1984: Triumphs of a Man Called Horse. 1987: Love Among Thieves (TV). InnerSpace. Adventures in Babysitting (GB: A Night on the Town). 1990: Crash and Burn. 1991: Only the Lonely. 1993: Phantasm III.

CHAPMAN, Edward 1901–1977
One of Britain's most solid, dependable and prolific leading character actors through several decades. Chapman looked more like a bank manager than an actor and his film career produced a stream of businessmen, mill owners, politicians, shop managers, worried fathers, citizens variously solid and irate and the occasional villain. Died from a heart attack.

1929: Juno and the Paycock (US: The Shame of Mary Boyle). 1930: Murder. Caste. 1931: The Skin Game. Tilly of Bloomsbury. 1932: The Flying Squad. Happy Ever After. 1934: The Queen's Affair (US: Runaway Queen). Guest of Honour. The Church Mouse. Blossom Time (US: April Romance). Girls Will Be Boys. Mister Cinders. 1935: Royal Cavalcade (narrator only. US: Regal Cavalcade). The Divine

Spark. Things to Come. 1936: The Man Who Could Work Miracles. Someone at the Door. Rembrandt. 1937: Who Killed John Savage? 1938: I've Got a Horse. Marigold. Premiere (US: One Night in Paris). The Citadel. 1939: The Nursemaid Who Disappeared. The Four Just Men. X (US: The Secret Four). There Ain't No Justice! Poison Pen. Inspector Hornleigh on Holiday. The Proud Valley. 1940: *Now You're Talking. The Briggs Family. Convoy. Law and Disorder. *Goofer Trouble. 1941: Inspector Hornleigh Goes to It (US: Mail Train). *Eating Out with Tommy. Turned Out Nice Again. Jeannie. Ships with Wings. They Flew Alone (US: Wings and the Woman). 1945: Journey Together. 1947: It Always Rains on Sunday. The October Man. 1948: Mr Perrin and Mr Traill. 1949: The History of Mr Polly. Man on the Run. The Spider and the Fly. Madeleine. 1950: Trio. Night and the City. Gone to Earth (US: The Wild Heart). 1951: The Magic Box. His Excellency. 1952: The Card (US: The Promoter). Mandy. (US: Crash of Silence). The Ringer. Folly to be Wise. 1953: The Intruder. Point of No Return. A Day to Remember. 1954: The End of the Road. The Crowded Day. 1955: The Love Match. A Yank in Ermine. 1956: Bhowani Junction. X the Unknown. Lisbon. 1957: Doctor at Large. Just My Luck. 1958: Innocent Sinners. The Young and the Guilty. The Square Peg. 1959: The Rough and the Smooth (US: Portrait of a Sinner). 1960: School for Scoundrels. Oscar Wilde. The Bulldog Breed. 1963: Hide and Seek. A Stitch in Time. 1965: Joey Boy. The Early Bird. 1970: The Man Who Haunted Himself.

CHAPMAN, Lonny 1920–
Dark-haired, thin-faced, taciturn American actor adept at country cousins, ranchhands, sidekicks and loyal small-town friends. On stage from 1948, he was an occasional visitor to Hollywood from 1954, but never became a really familiar face, and was more gainfully employed by television, where he had his own series, The Investigator, in the late 1950s. Not as regularly in westerns as memory serves, and less often seen in recent times, he has made the stage the major part of his career.

1954: Young at Heart. East of Eden. 1956: Baby Doll. 1963: The Birds. 1965: The Dangerous Days of Kiowa Jones (TV. GB: cinemas). 1966: A Covenant with Death. 1967: Hour of the Gun. 1968: The Stalking Moon. 1969:

The Reivers. Take the Money and Run. 1970: I Walk the Line. 1971: Marriage: Year One (TV). Welcome Home, Soldier Boys. The Cowboys. 1972: The Screaming Woman (TV). The Witch Who Came from The Sea (released 1976). Visions (TV). 1973: Run, Cougar, Run. Hunter (TV). Running Wild. 1974: Where the Red Fern Grows. Big Rose (TV). Hurricane (TV). 1975: The Last Survivors (TV). 1976: Moving Violation. 1977: Alexander: The Other Side of Dawn (TV). 1978: The Bad News Bears Go to Japan. Black Beauty (TV). Terror Out of the Sky (TV). 1979: Hanging by a Thread (TV). Cave-In! (TV). Norma Rae. The Day The World Ended. Running Scared. 1980: The Border. When Time Ran Out ... 1981: Amy. 1986: 52 Pick-Up. 1990: The China Lake Murders (TV).

CHITTY, Erik 1907–1977
Small, shuffling, grey-haired, round-faced, worried-looking, often bespectacled British actor who cornered the market in doddering old fools as soon as he looked old enough, and retained a firm grip on it for 20 years. The main body of his work was for television (more than 200 appearances), especially in the school comedy series *Please Sir!*, but he happily contrived to totter in and out of more than 40 films as well.

1940: Contraband (US: Blackout). 1948: Oliver Twist. All Over the Town. Forbidden. 1950: Your Witness (US: Eye Witness). Chance of a Lifetime. Circle of Danger. 1952: King of the Underworld. 1953: John Wesley. The Saint's Return (US: The Saint's Girl Friday).

*1954: Time is My Enemy. 1955: Footsteps in the Fog. Windfall. *The Stateless Man. Raising a Riot. 1957: The Long Haul. After the Ball. Zoo Baby (released 1960). 1959: Left, Right and Centre. The Devil's Disciple. 1960: The Day They Robbed the Bank of England. 1961: In the Doghouse. Raising the Wind (US: Roommates). 1963: The Horror of it All. 1964: First Men in the Moon. 1965: Doctor Zhivago. 1967: Casino Royale. *Ouch! Bedazzled. 1969: A Nice Girl Like Me. Twinky (US: Lola). Anne of the Thousand Days. 1970: Lust for a Vampire. Song of Norway. The Statue. The Railway Children. 1971: Please Sir! 1972: The Amazing Mr Blunden. 1973: Vault of Horror. 1974: The Flying Sorcerer. 1975: Great Expectations (TV. GB: cinemas). One of Our Dinosaurs is Missing. The Bawdy Adventures of Tom Jones. 1976: The Seven-Per-Cent Solution. 1977: A Bridge Too Far. Jabberwocky. 1978: *Hokusai: An Animated Sketchbook (voice only).*

CHRISTINE, Virginia
(V.C. Kraft) 1917–
Blonde, baby-faced American actress of Swedish extraction, somewhere between Kathleen Freeman (*qv*) and Nancy Olson, and generally seen as maids or downtrodden housewives. There were a few notable exceptions to this, especially an Egyptian princess (in black wig) in *The Mummy's Curse* and a gangster's moll in *The Invisible Wall*. More recently, she spent 11 years advertising coffee (as a character called Mrs Olson) on television. Married from 1940 to fellow character player Fritz Feld (also *qv*).

*1942: *Women at War. 1943: Truck Busters. Action in the North Atlantic. Edge of Darkness. Mission to Moscow. 1944: The Mummy's Curse. The Old Texas Trail (GB: Stagecoach Line). Riders of Ghost City (serial). 1945: Counter-Attack (GB: One Against Seven). Phantom of the Plains. Girls of the Big House. 1946: Idea Girl. The Inner Circle. Murder is My Business. House of Horrors (GB: Joan Bedford is Missing). The Killers. The Scarlet Horseman (serial). The Wife of Monte Cristo. The Mysterious Mr Valentine. 1947: The Gangster. The Invisible Wall. Women in the Night. 1948: Night Wind. 1949: Special Agent. Cover Up. 1950: Cyrano de Bergerac. The Men. 1952: Never Wave at a WAC (GB: The Private Wore Skirts). The First Time. High Noon. 1953: The Woman They Almost Lynched. 1954: Dragnet. 1955: Not As a Stranger. The Cobweb. Good Morning Miss*

Dove. 1956: Invasion of the Body Snatchers. The Killer is Loose. Nightmare. 1957: Three Brave Men. Johnny Tremain. The Careless Years. Spirit of St Louis. 1960: Flaming Star. 1961: Judgment at Nuremberg. 1962: Incident in an Alley. 1963: Cattle King (GB: Guns of Wyoming). Four for Texas. The Prize. 1964: One Man's Way. A Rage to Live. The Killers. 1966: Billy the Kid vs Dracula. 1967: In Enemy Country. Guess Who's Coming to Dinner. 1969: Hail Hero. Daughter of the Mind (TV). 1970: The Old Man Who Cried Wolf (TV). 1976: Woman of the Year (TV).

CHURCHILL, Berton 1876–1940
Hardly anyone today remembers Berton Churchill for anything other than the embezzling banker in the 1939 *Stagecoach*, a memorable performance in the mood of his plumper successor, Sydney Greenstreet. Yet the white-haired, stoat-faced Canadian actor played in dozens of other films as businessmen, judges and fathers, and worked prolifically through the 1930s before uraemic poisoning killed him at 64.

*1919: The Road Called Straight. 1923: Six Cylinder Love. 1924: Tongues of Flame. 1929: Nothing But the Truth. 1930: * Five Minutes from the Station. 1931: Secrets of a Secretary. Air Eagles. A Husband's Holiday. 1932: The Rich Are Always With Us. Cabin in the Cotton. The Dark Horse. Taxi! Impatient Maiden. Two Seconds. Scandal for Sale. Week-Ends Only. American Madness. Madame Butterfly. The Crooked Circle. I Am a Fugitive from a Chain Gang. The Wet Parade. The Mouthpiece. Information Kid/Fast Companions. Faith. If I Had a Million. Common Ground. Forgotten Commandments. False Faces (GB: What Price Beauty). Washington Masquerade (GB: Mad Masquerade). Laughter in Hell. Okay America (GB: Penalty of Fame). It's Tough to be Famous. The Big Stampede. Billion Dollar Scandal. Afraid to Talk. Silver Dollar. 1933: Ladies Must Love. From Hell to Heaven. So This is Africa. Elmer the Great. Private Jones. Hard to Handle. Her First Mate. Only Yesterday. The Little Giant. The Big Brain (GB: Enemies of Society). Heroes for Sale. Golden Harvest. Master of Men. Ladies Must Love. Frisco Jenny. The Avenger. Dr Bull. College Coach (GB: Football Coach). Employees' Entrance. The Mysterious Rider. King of the Ritz. The Girl Is Mine. 1934:*

Judge Priest. Hi, Nellie. Menace. Babbitt. Half a Sinner. Frontier Marshal. Helldorado. Sing Sing Nights (GB: Reprieved!). Strictly Dynamite. Bachelor Brat. Red Head. Murder in the Private Car (GB: Murder on the Runaway Train). Men in White. Let's Be Ritzy (GB: Millionaire for a Day). Dames. Bachelor of Arts. Take the Stand. Friends of Mr Sweeney. Kid Millions. Life is Worth Living. If I Was Rich. Lillies of Broadway. 1935: Ten Dollar Raise (GB: Mr Faintheart). The County Chairman. Steamboat 'Round the Bend. Page Miss Glory. I Live for Love (GB: I Live for You). Vagabond Lady. A Night at the Ritz. Speed Devils. The Rainmakers. The Spanish Cape Mystery. Coronado. 1936: You May Be Next! Colleen. Dizzy Dames. Three of a Kind. Parole! Panic On the Air. Dimples. Under Your Spell. Bunker Bean (GB: His Majesty Bunker Bean). The Dark Hour. 1937: Racing Lady. You Can't Beat Love. Parnell. Wild and Woolly. The Singing Marine. Sing and Be Happy. Public Wedding. Quick Money He Couldn't Say No. 1938: In Old Chicago. Four Men and a Prayer. Kentucky Moonshine (GB: Three Men and a Girl). Meet the Mayor. Wide Open Faces. The Cowboy and the Lady. Sweethearts. Ladies in Distress. Danger On the Air. Down in Arkansas. 1939: Daughters Courageous. Angels Wash Their Faces. Should Husbands Work? Stagecoach. Hero for a Day. On Your Toes. 1940: Brother Rat and a Baby (GB: Baby Be Good). I'm Nobody's Sweetheart Now. Saturday's Children. Twenty Mule Team. Turnabout. The Way of All Flesh. Cross Country Romance. Public Deb No 1. Alias the Deacon.

CIANNELLI, Eduardo 1887–1969
Italian-born character actor who moved from opera singing to acting and became a Hollywood regular from 1937 to 1948, after which he began to commute between America and Italy. His deeply lined features, as menacing as a snake's head, conveyed all kinds of manic masterminds and Mafia mobsters. His sharp and impeccable manners increased the menace beneath. He died from cancer, back in his beloved Rome.

1917: The Food Gamblers. 1933: Reunion in Vienna. 1935: The Scoundrel. 1936: Winterset. 1937: Hitting a New High. Criminal Lawyer. A Night of Mystery. On Such a Night. The Girl from Scotland Yard. The League of Frightened Men. Super-Sleuth. Marked Woman. 1938: Law of the Underworld. Blind Alibi. 1939: Angels Wash Their Faces. Gunga Din. Society Lawyer. Risky Business. Bulldog Drummond's Bride. 1940: Forgotten Girls. Outside the Three-Mile Limit (GB: Mutiny on the Seas). Foreign Correspondent. Zanzibar. Strange Cargo. Mysterious Dr Satan (serial). The Mummy's Hand. Kitty Foyle. 1941: Ellery Queen's Penthouse Mystery. They Met in Bombay. I Was a Prisoner on Devil's Island. Sky Raiders (serial). Paris Calling. 1942: Dr Broadway. You Can't Escape Forever. Cairo. They Got Me Covered. 1943: For Whom the Bell Tolls. Adventures of the Flying Cadets (serial). Flight for Freedom. The Constant Nymph. 1944: The Mask of Dimitrios. Passage to Marseille. Storm Over Lisbon. The Conspirators. Dillinger. 1945: Incendiary Blonde. A Bell for Adano. The Crime Doctor's Warning (GB: The Doctor's Warning). 1946: Gilda. Wife of Monte Cristo. Joe Palooka—Champ. Heartbeat. Perilous Holiday. California. 1947: Seven Keys to Baldpate. Rose of Santa Rosa. The Crime Doctor's Gamble (GB: The Doctor's Gamble). 1948: I Love Trouble. The Lost Moment. To the Victor. The Creeper. A Miracle Can Happen (later On Our Merry Way). Patto con diavolo. 1949: In estase/ Rapture. Fugitive Lady. Volcano. Prince of Foxes. 1950: Gli inesorabili. 1951: E l'amor che mi rovina. The People Against O'Hara. 1952: Lt Giorgio. Sul ponti dei sospiri. I vinti. Prigioniere delle tenebre. I nostri figli. La voce del silenzio. 1953: La nave delle donne maledette (US: Ship of Condemned Women). Attila the Hun. The City Stands Trial. 1954: The Stranger's Hand. Mambo. Helen of Troy. 1955: Proibito. Uomini ombra (US: Shadow Men). 1956: Il riccato di un padre. 1957: Lost Slaves of the Amazon (US: Love Slaves of the Amazon). The Monster from Green Hell. 1958: Houseboat. 1959: The Killers of Mussolini (TV). 1962: 40 Pounds of Trouble. 1963: I pascoli rossi. 1964: The Visit. 1965: The Chase. Massacre at Grand Canyon. 1966: Dr Satan's Robot (feature version of 1940 serial). The Spy in the Green Hat (TV. GB: cinemas). 1968: The Brotherhood. Mackenna's Gold. 1969: The Secret of Santa Vittoria. Stiletto. Colpo rovente. La collina degli stivali (US: Boot Hill). The Syndicate. Mission Impossible Versus the Mob (TV. GB: cinemas).

CLARE, Mary 1894–1970
Gracious, fair-haired British actress of strong and distinctive personality. A much-respected figure on the London stage after a debut there at 16, she became one of the cinema's best villainesses in the 1930s. She possessed a wide range, and was more than capable of carrying a play or film on her own shoulders, as with the title role in Mrs Pym of Scotland Yard.

1920: The Black Spider. The Skin Game. 1922: A Prince of Lovers (US: The Life of Lord Byron). A Gipsy Cavalier (US: My Lady April). Foolish Monte Carlo. 1923: Becket. The Lights of London. 1927: *Packing Up. 1928: The Constant Nymph. The Princes in the Tower. 1929: The Feather. 1931: Hindle Wakes. Many Waters. Keepers of Youth. Bill's Legacy. Gypsy Blood (US: Carmen). Shadows. The Outsider. 1933: The Constant Nymph. 1934: Say it

With Flowers. Jew Süss (US: Power). Night Club Queen. 1935: Lorna Doone. A Real Bloke. The Clairvoyant. The Passing of the Third Floor Back. Line Engaged. The Gun'nor (US: Mister Hobo). 1937: The Mill on the Floss. The Rat. Young and Innocent (US: The Girl Was Young). 1938: Our Royal Heritage. The Challenge. The Lady Vanishes. Climbing High. The Citadel. 1939: A Girl Must Live. There Ain't No Justice! On the Night of the Fire (US: The Fugitive). Mrs Pym of Scotland Yard. 1940: The Briggs Family. *Miss Grant Goes to the Door. Old Bill and Son. 1941: The Big Blockade. *From the Far Corners. The Patient Vanishes (later and US: This Man is Dangerous). 1942: Next of Kin. The Night Has Eyes (US: Terror House). 1943: The Hundred Pound Window. 1944: One Exciting Night (US: You Can't Do Without Love). Fiddlers Three. 1946: London Town (US: My Heart Goes Crazy). 1947: Mrs Fitzherbert. 1948: Oliver Twist. The Three Weird Sisters. My Brother Jonathan. Esther Waters. 1949: Cardboard Cavalier. 1950: Portrait of Clare. The Black Rose. 1952: Penny Princess. Hindle Wakes (remake. US: Holiday Week). Moulin Rouge. 1953: The Beggar's Opera. 1955: Mambo. 1959: The Price of Silence.

CLARENCE, O.B. 1868–1955
Cheerful, round-faced, sturdily-built British actor who, after one or two stronger roles in his earlier days, played genial old buffers from the start of his entry into British sound films — often bespectacled, cloth-capped, working-class types — and went on doing so until he finally retired at 80. Excellent as the

Aged Parent in David Lean's *Great Expectations*. Long stage experience made him one of the most reliable and versatile of supporting players. The 'O' stood for Oliver.

1914: Liberty Hall. 1920: London Pride. The Little Hour of Peter Wells. 1930: The Man from Chicago. 1931: Keepers of Youth. The Bells. 1932: Where is This Lady? The Barton Mystery. The Flag Lieutenant. Jack's the Boy (US: Night and Day). Help Yourself. Goodnight Vienna (US: Magic Night). Perfect Understanding. 1933: Discord. The Only Girl (US: Heart Song). Excess Baggage. Soldiers of the King (US: The Woman in Command). Falling for You. His Grace Gives Notice. A Shot in the Dark. Eyes of Fate. I Adore You. Friday the Thirteenth. Turkey Time. 1934: The Silver Spoon. The Double Event. Song at Eventide. Nell Gwyn. Father and Son. The Great Defender. Lady in Danger. The King of Paris. The Feathered Serpent. The Scarlet Pimpernel. 1935: The Private Secretary. Squibs. Barnacle Bill. Captain Bill. No Monkey Business. 1936: King of Hearts. East Meets West. All In. Seven Sinners (US: Doomed Cargo). The Cardinal. 1937: Dinner at the Ritz. Victoria the Great. Silver Blaze (US: Murder at the Baskervilles). The Return of the Scarlet Pimpernel. The Mill on the Floss. 1938: Old Iron. Pygmalion. It's in the Air (US: George Takes the Air). 1939: Me and My Pal. Jamaica Inn. Black Eyes. Young Man's Fancy. The Dark Eyes of London (US: Human Monster). Probably completed 1936). The Missing People. 1940: Saloon Bar. Return to Yesterday. Spy for a Day. Old Mother Riley in Business. 1941: Dangerous Moonlight (US: Suicide Squadron). Gert and Daisy's Weekend. Inspector Hornleigh Goes to It (US: Mail Train). Quiet Wedding. Turned Out Nice Again. Major Barbara. Old Mother Riley's Circus. Penn of Pennsylvania (US: The Courageous Mr Penn). 1942: Front Line Kids. 1944: On Approval. 1945: A Place of One's Own. The Way to the Stars (US: Johnny in the Clouds). Great Day. 1946: Great Expectations. The Magic Bow. Meet Me at Dawn. While the Sun Shines. School for Secrets (US: Secret Flight). 1947: Uncle Silas (US: The Inheritance). 1948: The Calendar. No Room at the Inn.

CLARK, Ernest 1912–1994

Smooth, aristocratic-looking, brown-haired British actor whose mouth seemed to set naturally in an expression of disapproval and who found himself cast as martinets, civil servants, obstructive officials and strait-laced, humourless, sometimes treacherous types in general. Clark was a reporter on a provincial newspaper at 25 when offered the chance to join a local repertory company; London stage appearances followed from 1939, and films in post-war years. He was well in character as Professor Loftus in the long-running 'Doctor' series on TV. Married (third) actress Julia Lockwood, daughter of Margaret.

1949: Private Angelo. 1950: The Mudlark. Seven Days to Noon. 1952: The Long Memory. 1954: Father Brown (US: The Detective). Doctor in the House. Beau Brummell. The Dam Busters. 1956: Reach for the Sky. Stars in Your Eyes. 1984: The Baby and the Battleship. The Silken

Affair. 1957: Time Without Pity. Man in the Sky (US: Decision Against Time). The Birthday Present. I Accuse! The Safecracker. 1958: A Tale of Two Cities. Woman of Mystery. Blind Spot. 1959: A Touch of Larceny. Sink the Bismarck! 1960: No Love for Johnnie. 1961: The Wild and the Willing. Partners in Crime. Three on a Spree. 1962: Time to Remember. Tomorrow at Ten. A Woman's Privilege. 1963: Master Spy. Billy Liar! Ladies Who Do. *The Invisible Asset. A Stitch in Time. The Devil-Ship Pirates. 1964: *Boy With a Flute. Masquerade. Nothing But the Best. 1965: Cuckoo Patrol. The Secret of My Success. 1966: Finders Keepers. Arabesque. It (US: Return of the Golem). 1967: Attack on the Iron Coast. 1968: Eye of the Devil. Salt and Pepper. 1969: Castle Keep. Run a Crooked Mile (TV). 1970: The Executioner. Song of Norway. 1982: Gandhi. 1983: Memed My Hawk. 1991: The Pope Must Die (US: The Pope Must Diet).

CLARK, Fred 1914–1968

Bald, waspish, apoplectic-mannered American supporting star with coat-hanger shoulders. Usually the victim of the star comedian—or his own nefarious schemes. He only came to films in his thirties, but quickly established himself as a familiar and popular face. Married to actress Benay Venuta from 1952 to 1963, the first of two wives. Died from a liver ailment.

1947: The Unsuspected. Ride the Pink Horse. 1948: Hazard. Fury at Furnace Creek. Cry of the City. Mr Peabody and the Mermaid. Two Guys from Texas (GB: Two Texas Knights).

1949: Flamingo Road. The Younger Brothers. Alias Nick Beal (GB: The Contact Man). The Lady Takes a Sailor. White Heat. Task Force. 1950: Sunset Boulevard. The Eagle and the Hawk. The Jackpot. Dynamite Pass. Mrs O'Malley and Mr Malone. Return of the Frontiersman. 1951: The Lemon Drop Kid. Meet Me After the Show. A Place in the Sun. Hollywood Story. 1952: Dreamboat. Three for Bedroom C. 1953: The Stars Are Singing. The Caddy. How to Marry a Millionaire. Here Come the Girls. 1954: Living It Up. 1955: How to Be Very, Very Popular. Abbott and Costello Meet the Keystone Kops. Daddy Long Legs. The Court-Martial of Billy Mitchell (GB: One Man Mutiny). 1956: The Solid Gold Cadillac. Miracle in the Rain. Back from Eternity. The Birds and the Bees. 1957: Joe Butterfly. The Fuzzy Pink Nightgown. Don't Go Near the Water. 1958: Mardi Gras. Auntie Mame. 1959: The Mating Game. It Started with a Kiss. 1960: Risate di gioia (GB and US: The Passionate Thief). Visit to a Small Planet. Bells Are Ringing. A porte chiuse (GB: Behind Closed Doors). 1962: Zotz! Boys' Night Out. Hemingway's Adventures of a Young Man (GB: Adventures of a Young Man). Les saints nitouches (GB: Wild Living). 1963: Move Over, Darling. 1964: John Goldfarb, Please Come Home. The Curse of the Mummy's Tomb. 1965: Sergeant Deadhead. Dr Goldfoot and the Bikini Machine (GB: Dr G and the Bikini Machine). When the Boys Meet the Girls (GB: When the Girls Meet the Boys). War Italian Style. 1967: I Sailed to Tahiti with an All-Girl Crew. 1968: Skidoo. The Horse in the Gray Flannel Suit.. The Face of Eve (US: Eve).

CLARK, Matt 1936–

Stocky, dark-haired American actor with round, rather sour features, mostly in westerns until the genre pretty much petered out in the 1980s. His dark features and wry mouth were put to good use as storekeepers, clerks, farmers, errant husbands and minor bad guys: smiles were few. Clark, once established in films in his mid thirties, continued to play variations on poor, sometimes devious country boys both in outdoor and city dramas. And, if a western did pop up in later days, the odds were that Clark would be in it somewhere.

1964: Black Like Me. 1967: In the Heat of the Night. Will Penny. 1969: The Bridge at Remagen. 1970: Monte Walsh. Macho Callahan.

1971: The Great Northfield Minnesota Raid. Honky. The Grissom Gang. The Cowboys. Pocket Money. S (GB: The Heist). 1972: The Culpepper Cattle Co. Jeremiah Johnson. The Life and Times of Judge Roy Bean. 1973: Emperor of the North Pole (GB: Emperor of the North). White Lightning. Pat Garrett and Billy the Kid. The Laughing Policeman (GB: An Investigation of Murder). 1974: The Execution of Private Slovik (TV). Melvin Purvis, G-Man (TV. GB: cinemas, as The Legend of Machine-Gun Kelly). This Was the West That Was (TV). The Great Ice Rip-Off (TV). The Terminal Man. 1975: Kansas City Massacre (TV). Hearts of the West (GB: Hollywood Cowboy). 1976: Kid Vengeance. Dynasty (TV). 1977: Outlaw Blues. Dog and Cat (TV). 1978: The Driver (GB: Driver). Lacy and the Mississippi Queen (TV). 1979: Dreamer. The Last Ride of the Dalton Gang (TV). 1980: Brubaker. Ruckus. 1981: Some Kind of Hero. An Eye for an Eye. The Lone Ranger. The Children Nobody Wanted (TV). 1982: Towheads (TV). In the Custody of Strangers (TV). 1983: Love Letters/My Love Letters. Honkytonk Man. 1984: The Adventures of Buckaroo Banzai Across the Eighth Dimension. Country. 1985: Out of the Darkness (TV). Tuff Turf. Love, Mary (TV). Return to Oz. 1986: Let's Get Harry. 1987: The Quick and the Dead (TV). 1988: The Horror Show. 1989: Terror on Highway 91 (TV). Blind Witness (TV). 1990: Back to the Future Part III. Class Action. 1991: A Seduction in Travis County (TV). 1992: Frozen Assets. The Harvest. 1993: Barbarians at the Gate (TV). 1994: Obsession. The Haunted Heart. 1995: Candyman Farewell to the Flesh.

As director:

1988: Da.

CLARKE-SMITH, D. A. 1888–1959

Light-haired, moustachioed, pale-eyed, roguish-looking Scottish actor, often as moustache-twirling lotharios fond of the booze. He brought an infectious sense of humour to many of his stage portrayals from his 1913 debut on and, with sound, found a career in films as well, although he was mainly back on stage after 1939. In private life, this most courtly of screen gentlemen had an unusual hobby: pig-breeding. The 'D' stood for Douglas.

1929: Atlantic. 1931: Shadows. Bracelets. The Old Man. Peace and Quiet. Michael and Mary. 1932: A Letter of Warning. A Voice Said Goodnight. Help Yourself. Illegal. White Face. The Frightened Lady (US: Criminal at Large). 1933: The Laughter of Fools. * Skipper of the Osprey. I'm an Explosive. Friday the Thirteenth. Head of the Family. Mayfair Girl. Sleeping Car. The Good Companions. The Thirteenth Candle. High Finance. Follow the Lady. Smithy. Waltz Time. The Ghoul. Turkey Time. Flat No. 3. 1934: Sabotage (US: When London Sleeps). Warn London! The Man Who Knew Too Much. Keep It Quiet. Designing Woman. A Cup of Kindness. Passing Shadows. The Perfect Flaw. Money Mad. The Feathered Serpent. 1935: Lorna Doone. Key to Harmony. Royal Cavalcade (US: Regal Cavalcade). 1936: The Happy Family. Murder by Rope. Southern Roses. Café Colette (US: Danger in Paris). 1937: Splinters in the Air. Little Miss Somebody. Dangerous Fingers (US: Wanted by Scotland Yard). 1938: Weddings Are Wonderful. I've Got a Horse. 1939: Flying Fifty Five. 1947: Frieda. 1951: Quo Vadis? 1952: Something Money Can't Buy. The Pickwick Papers. 1953: The Sword and the Rose. 1954: Beau Brummell. 1955: The Man Who Never Was. 1956: The Baby and the Battleship.

CLEMENTS, Stanley 1926–1981

Stocky American actor with dark hair, sharp, pointy-chinned features and hunted, aggressive look. He played roles in the Frankie Darro (qv) tradition — punks, street youths and bullying wise guys who whined and snivelled in the end. Associated on and off with the Bowery Boys; replaced Leo Gorcey for their final few comedy films. War service badly hit the progress of his career. Died from emphysema, 11 days after the death of his first wife, actress Gloria Grahame (married 1945–1948).

1941: Accent on Love. Down in San Diego. Nice Girl? Tall, Dark and Handsome. I Wake Up Screaming (GB: Hot Spot). 1942: Right to the Heart. Smart Alecks. On the Sunny Side. 'Neath Brooklyn Bridge. They Got Me Covered. 1943: The More the Merrier. Ghosts on the Loose. Sweet Rosie O'Grady. You're a Lucky Fellow, Mr Smith. Thank Your Lucky Stars. 1944: Girl in the Case (GB: The Silver Key). Going My Way. Cover Girl. 1945: Salty O'Rourke. See My Lawyer. 1947: Variety Girl. 1948: Hazard. Big Town Scandal. Canon City. Joe Palooka in Winner Take All (GB: Winner Take All). The Babe Ruth Story. Racing Luck. 1949: Mr Soft Touch (GB: House of Settlement). Bad Boy. Johnny Holiday. Red Light. 1950: Military Academy With That Tenth Avenue Gang (GB: Sentence Suspended). Destination Murder. 1951: Pride of Maryland. Boots Malone. 1952: Jet Job. Army Bound. Off Limits (GB: Military Policemen). 1953: White Lightning. Hot News. 1954: The Rocket Man. 1955: Air Strike. Robber's Roost. Last of the Desperadoes. Fort Yuma. 1956: Wiretapper. Fighting Trouble. Death of a Scoundrel. Hot Shots. Hold That Hypnotist. 1957: Spook Chasers. Looking for Danger. Up in Smoke. 1958: In the Money. A Nice Little Bank That Should Be Robbed. 1961: Sniper's Ridge. Saintly Sinners. 1963: Tammy and the Doctor. It's a Mad, Mad, Mad World. 1965: That Darn Cat! 1968: Panic in the City. 1973: The Timber Tramp. 1978: Hot Lead and Cold Feet.

CLEVELAND, George 1883–1957

One of the great grandpas of the Hollywood scene. Cleveland's round, twinkling features exuded kindliness and he was very rarely cast as a shady character. Born in Nova Scotia, he began working on stage in 1903 and, when he came to Hollywood in 1934, he was immediately kept frantically busy playing veterans of all descriptions — but mostly in westerns from 1940, where he could be found holding down (never up) the stage line, prospecting for gold, or offering the hero wheezily wise advice. Died from a heart attack during his fourth season with the TV series Lassie.

1934: Monte Carlo Nights. The House of Mystery. The Star Packer. (GB: He Wore a Star). The Man from Utah. Blue Steel. Girl o' My Dreams. School for Girls. City Limits. Mystery Liner (GB: The Ghost of John Holling). 1935: Make Mine a Million. *Do Your Stuff. The Spanish Cape Mystery. She Gets Her Man. Keeper of the Bees. His Night Out. Forced Landing. 1936: Phantom Patrol. *Foolproof. I Conquer the Sea. The Plainsman. Revolt of the Zombies. Robinson Crusoe of Clipper Island (GB: SOS Clipper Island). Flash Gordon (serial). Don't Get Personal. North of Nome. Brilliant Marriage. Rio Grande Romance. Put on the Spot (GB: Framed). 1937: The Man in Blue. Toast of New York. A Girl with Ideas. Breezing Home. Behind the Mike. Night Key. Swing It Professor! (GB: Swing It Buddy). Boy of the Streets. Paradise Express. Trapped by G-Men/River of Missing Men. Prescription for Romance.

Adventure's End. 1938: Rose of the Rio Grande. Under the Big Top (GB: The Circus Comes to Town). The Lone Ranger (serial). Valley of the Giants. Port of Missing Girls. Romance of the Limberlost. Ghost Town Riders. Outlaws of Sonora. 1939: *The Sap Takes a Rap. Streets of New York. Dick Tracy's G-Men (serial). Wolf Call. Stunt Pilot. Home on the Prairie. The Phantom Stage. Mutiny in the Big House. The Strange Case of Dr Meade. Overland Mail. Konga, the Wild Stallion (GB: Konga). 1940: Midnight Limited. West of Abilene (GB: The Showdown). Tomboy. Hidden Enemy. The Haunted House. The Ol' Swimmin' Hole (GB: When Youth Conspires). Pioneers of the West. Drums of Fu Manchu (serial). Blazing Six Shooters (GB: Stolen Wealth). One Man's Law. Chasing Trouble. The Ape. Hi-Yo Silver! (feature version of The Lone Ranger). Queen of the Yukon. 1941: *Sucker List. Nevada City. Wide Open Town. *Forbidden Passage. A Girl, a Guy and a Gob (GB: The Navy Steps Out). All That Money Can Buy/The Devil and Daniel Webster. Sunset in Wyoming. Two in a Taxi. Man at Large. The Obliging Young Lady. Two-faced Woman. Riders of the Purple Sage. Look Who's Laughing. Playmates. 1942: The Big Street. *Hold 'Em Jail. *Mail Trouble. The Spoilers. My Favorite Spy. Joan of Paris. Mexican Spitfire's Elephant. The Falcon Takes Over. Army Surgeon. The Traitor Within. Highways by Night. Powder Town. Seven Miles from Alcatraz. Call Out the Marines. Valley of the Sun. Here We Go Again. 1943: The Woman of the Town. Drums of Fu Manchu. Klondike Kate. Cowboy in Manhattan. Johnny Come Lately. Ladies' Day. The Man from Music Mountain. 1944: Yellow Rose of Texas. Home in Indiana. My Best Gal. It Happened Tomorrow. Man from Frisco. Abroad with Two Yanks. Alaska. When the Lights Go On Again. Can't Help Singing. My Pal Wolf. It's in the Bag! (GB: The Fifth Chair). 1945: God is My Co-Pilot. Song of the Sarong. Dakota. Senorita from the West. Pillow of Death. Sunbonnet Sue. Her Highness and the Bellboy. She Wouldn't Say Yes. 1946: Courage of Lassie. Little Giant (GB: On the Carpet). Wake Up and Dream. The Runaround. Angel on My Shoulder. Blue Sierra. Step by Step. Wild Beauty. Boys' Ranch. The Show-Off. 1947: Mother Wore Tights. I Wonder Who's Kissing Her Now. The Wistful Widow of Wagon Gap (GB: The Wistful Widow). Easy Come, Easy Go. My Wild Irish Rose. 1948: Albuquerque (GB: Silver City). Fury at Furnace Creek. Miraculous Journey. The Plunderers. A Date with Judy. 1949: Home in San Antone (GB: Harmony Inn). Kazan. Miss Grant Takes Richmond (GB: Innocence is Bliss). Rimfire. 1950: Boy from Indiana (GB: Blaze of Glory). Please Believe Me. Frenchie. Trigger Jr. 1951: Fort Defiance. Flaming Feather. 1952: The WAC from Walla Walla (GB: Army Capers). Carson City. Cripple Creek. 1953: San Antone. Affair with a Stranger. Walking My Baby Back Home. 1954: Rails into Laramie. The Outlaw's Daughter. Fireman, Save My Child. Untamed Heiress. Racing Blood. 1955: Goodbye, My Lady.

CLIVE, E.E.

(Edward Clive) 1878–1940

Sturdy, sour-looking, sandy-haired Welsh actor, often cast as spoilsport sobersides or

humourless figure of authority—though he could also be amusing when playing the hero's butler or drily dubious friend. He only spent seven years in Hollywood films, before his death from a heart attack, but in that short span racked up over 80 movies, latterly becoming best known as Bulldog Drummond's manservant Tenny. Clive would certainly have been profitably involved in Universal's Briton-packed Sherlock Holmes series had not early death intervened.

1933: The Invisible Man. Looking Forward (GB: Service). 1934: One More River (GB: Over the River). The Poor Rich. The Gay Divorcee (GB: The Gay Divorce). Tin Pants. Riptide. Bulldog Drummond Strikes Back. Charlie Chan in London. Long Lost Father. 1935: The Mystery of Edwin Drood. A Feather in Her Hat. Bride of Frankenstein. Remember Last Night? We're in the Money. Gold Diggers of 1935. Stars Over Broadway. A Tale of Two Cities. Widow from Monte Carlo. Atlantic Adventure. Page Miss Glory. Captain Blood. Father Brown, Detective. Sylvia Scarlett. Clive of India. The Man Who Broke the Bank at Monte Carlo. 1936: Little Lord Fauntleroy. Love Before Breakfast. The King Steps Out. Dracula's Daughter. All American Chump (GB: Country Bumpkin). Palm Springs (GB: Palm Springs Affair). The Unguarded Hour. Trouble for Two (GB: The Suicide Club). Piccadilly Jim. Libeled Lady. Tarzan Escapes! Camille. The Golden Arrow. The White Angel. The Charge of the Light Brigade. Isle of Fury. Cain and Mabel. Ticket to Paradise. Lloyds of London. The Dark Hour. Show Boat. 1937: They Wanted to Marry. The Great Garrick. Live, Love and Learn. Bulldog Drummond Escapes! Maid of Salem. Ready, Willing and Able. The Road Back/Return of the Hero. Bulldog Drummond's Revenge. It's Love I'm After. On the Avenue. Love Under Fire. Danger—Love at Work. Personal Property. The Emperor's Candlesticks. Night Must Fall. Beg, Borrow or Steal. Bulldog Drummond Comes Back. 1938: Arsene Lupin Returns. Bulldog Drummond's Peril. The First Hundred Years. The Last Warning. Bulldog Drummond in Africa. Kidnapped. Submarine Patrol. Gateway. Arrest Bulldog Drummond! 1939: I'm from Missouri. The Little Princess. Bulldog Drummond's Secret Police. Mr Moto's Last Warning. Man About Town. The Hound of the Baskervilles. Rose of Washington Square. Bulldog Drummond's

Bride. The Adventures of Sherlock Holmes. Bachelor Mother. We Are Not Alone. The Honeymoon's Over. 1939/40: Raffles. 1940: The Earl of Chicago. Congo Maisie. Pride and Prejudice. Foreign Correspondent. Adventure in Diamonds.

CLYDE, Andy 1892–1967

Scraggy, scrunch-faced, brown-haired, lively-eyed, heavily-moustachioed and usually bespectacled Scottish-born character comedian, who ran dual careers in Hollywood as spluttering western sidekicks and the star of minimum-budget two-reel comedies (nearly 150 of them). His characters spun tall tales and usually had an eye for a pretty girl. He left films behind in 1956 and spent the last decade of his life as a regular in such series as The Real McCoys, No Time for Sergeants and Lassie. From a theatrical family, he emigrated to America in 1923.

1924: *One Spooky Night. *Wall Street Blues. *His New Mama. *Little Robinson Corkscrew. *Wandering Waistlines. *Lizzies of the Field. *The Cannon Ball Express. 1925: *Honeymoon Hardships. *Giddap. *The Lion's Whiskers. *From Rags to Britches. *Butter Fingers. *Skinners in Silk. *The Iron Nag. *Sneezing Beezers. *Super-Hooper-Dyne Lizzies. *Over There-Abouts. 1926: *Circus Today. *Whispering Whiskers. *Ice Cold Cocos. *Trimmed in Gold. *Wandering Willies. *Fight Night. *Hayfoot, Strawfoot. *Muscle Bound Music. *A Sea Dog's Tale. *Masked Mamas. *Hubby's Quiet Little Game. *Hoboken to Hollywood. *The Divorce Dodger. *Flirty Four-Flushers. 1927: *Peaches and Plumbers. *Should Sleepwalkers Marry? *Easy Pickings. *Gold Digger of Weepah. *The Bull Fighter. *Cured in the Excitement. *The Golf Nut. 1928: *Branded Man. *The Swim Princess. The Goodbye Kiss. *Blindfold. *Motorboat Mamas. 1929: Midnight Daddies. Should a Girl Marry? Ships of the Night. *The Bride's Relations. *The Old Barn. *Whirls and Girls. *The Bee's Buzz. *The Big Palooka. *Girl Crazy. *The Barber's Daughter. *The Constabule. *The Lunkhead. *The Golfers. *A Hollywood Star. *Clancy at the Bat. *The New Halfback. *Uppercut O'Brien. 1930: *Scotch. *Sugar Plum Papa. *Bulls and Bears. *Match Play. *Radio Kisses. *Fat Wives to Thin. *Campus Crushes. *Goodbye Legs. *The Chumps. *Hello, Television. *Average Husband. *Vacation Loves. *The

Bluffer. *Grandma's Girl. *Take Your Medicine. *Don't Bite Your Dentist. *Racket Cheers. *Bulls and Bears. *No, No, Lady. 1931: *The College Vamp. *The Dog Doctor. *In Conference. *Just a Bear. *The Cow-Catcher's Daughter. *Ghost Parade. *Monkey Business in Africa (GB: Gorilla Love). *Fainting Lover. *Too Many Husbands. *The Cannonball. *Speed. *The Great Pie Mystery. *Taxi Troubles. *All-American Kickback. *Half Holiday. 1932: Million Dollar Legs. *Shopping with Wifie. *Heavens! My Husband. *Speed in the Gay Nineties. *The Boudoir Butler. *Alaska Love. *For the Love of Ludwig. *His Royal Shyness. *The Giddy Age. *Sunkissed Sweeties. *A Fool About Women. *Boy, Oh Boy. 1933: *Artists' Muddles. *Feeling Rosy. *Loose Relations. *The Big Squeal. *Dora's Dunkin' Donuts. *His Weak Moment. *Frozen Assets. *An Old Gypsy Custom. 1934: The Little Minister. *Super Snooper. *Hello, Prosperity. Romance in Manhattan. *Half-Baked Relations. *It's the Cat's. *In the Dog House. 1935: *I'm a Father. Annie Oakley. McFadden's Flats. The Village Tale. *Old Sawbones. *Tramp, Tramp, Tramp. *Alimony Aches. *It Always Happens. *Hot Paprika. 1936: Two in a Crowd. Yellow Dust. Red Lights Ahead. Straight from the Shoulder. *Caught in the Act. *Share the Wealth. *Peppery Salt. *Mister Smarty. *Am I Having Fun! *Love Comes to Mooneyville. *Knee Action. 1937: The Barrier. *Stuck in the Sticks. *My Little Feller. *Lodge Night. *Gracie at the Bat. *He Done His Duty. 1938: *The Old Raid Mule. *Jump, Chump, Jump. *Ankles Away. *Soul of a Heel. *Not Guilty Enough. *Home on the Rage. 1939: It's a Wonderful World. Bad Lands. *Swing, You Swingers. *Boom Goes the Groom. *Now It Can Be Sold. *Trouble Finds Andy Clyde. *All-American Blondes. *Andy Clyde Gets Spring Chicken. 1940: Abe Lincoln in Illinois (GB: Spirit of the People). Cherokee Strip (GB: Fighting Marshal). Three Men from Texas. *Mr Clyde Goes to Broadway. *Money Squawks. Boobs in the Woods. *Fireman, Save My Choo Choo. *A Bundle of Bliss. *The Watchman Takes a Wife. 1941: In Old Colorado. Doomed Caravan. Pirates on Horseback. Border Vigilantes. Wide Open Town. Secrets of the Wasteland. Stick to Your Guns. Twilight on the Trail. Outlaws of the Desert. Riders of the Timberline. *Ring and the Belle. *Yankee Doodle Andy. *Host to a Ghost. *Lovable Trouble. 1942: Undercover Man. Lost Canyon. This Above All. *Sappy Birthday. *How Spry I Am. *All Work and No Pay. *Sappy Pappy. 1943: The Leather Burners. Happy Serves a Writ. Border Patrol. False Colors. Colt Comrades. Bar 20. Riders of the Deadline. *Wolf in Thief's Clothing. *A Maid Made Mad. *Farmer for a Day. *He Was Only Feudin'. 1944: Texas Masquerade. Lumberjack. Forty Thieves. Mystery Man. *His Tale is Told. *You Were Never Uglier. *Gold is Where You Lose It. *Heather and Yon. 1945: Roughly Speaking. Son of the Prairie. *Two Local Yokels. *A Miner Affair. *The Blonde Stayed On. *Spook to Me. 1946: The Devil's Playground. Fool's Gold. The Green Years. Unexpected Guest. Dangerous Venture. The Plainsman and the Lady. That Texas Jamboree (GB: Medicine Man). Throw a Saddle on a Star. *Andy Plays Hooky. 1947: Hoppy's Holiday. The Marauders. *Two Jills and a Jack.

*Wife to Spare. 1948: *Eight-Ball Andy. *Go Chase Yourself. Silent Conflict. The Dead Don't Dream. Strange Gamble. Sinister Journey. False Paradise. Borrowed Trouble. 1949: Crashing Thru. Riders of the Dusk. Shadows of the West. Big Jack. Range Land. Haunted Trails. *Sunk in the Sink. 1950: *Marinated Mariner. *A Blunderful Time. Gunslingers. Arizona Territory. Canyon Raiders. Cherokee Uprising. Fence Riders. Outlaws of Texas. Silver Raiders. 1951: Abilene Trail. *Blonde Atom Bomb. 1952: *A Blissful Blunder. *Hooked and Rooked. *The Fresh Painter. 1953: *Pardon My Wrench. *Love's A-Poppin. *Oh Say, Can You Sue. 1954: *Two April Fools. 1955: *Scratch, Scratch, Scratch. *One Spooky Night. The Road to Denver. Carolina Cannonball. 1956: *Andy Goes Wild. *Pardon My Nightshirt.

COLEMAN, Dabney 1932–
Tall, dark, strongly-spoken, usually moustachioed American actor with wolfish smile and dark, curly, receding hair. Abandoning law studies to become an actor, he only very gradually came through to better roles (notably in the TV series *Buffalo Bill*), with a series of decisive, often neurotically edged performances, frequently in insignificant material. Stalwart in drama, but probably most attractive in comedy, he often plays reprehensible characters.

1965: The Slender Thread. 1966: This Property is Condemned. 1968: The Scalphunters. 1969: The Trouble With Girls . . . and how to get into it. Downhill Racer. 1970: The Brotherhood of the Bell (TV). I Love My Wife. 1973: Cinderella Liberty. Savage (TV). Dying Room Only (TV). The President's Plane is Missing (TV). 1974: The Towering Inferno. Bogard. Bad Ronald (TV). The Dove. 1975: Attack on Terror: The FBI versus the Ku Klux Klan (TV). Returning Home (TV). The Other Side of the Mountain (GB: A Window to the Sky). Bite the Bullet. 1976: Kiss Me, Kill Me (TV). Black Fist/The Black Streetfighter. Midway (GB: Battle of Midway). 1977: Viva Knievel! Rolling Thunder. The Amazing Howard Hughes (TV). 1978: Maneaters Are Loose! (TV). The Other Side of the Mountain Part II. 1979: North Dallas Forty. When She Was Bad (TV). 1980: Nothing Personal. How to Beat the High Cost of Living. Melvin and Howard. Nine to Five. KGOD. 1981: On Golden Pond. Modern

Problems. Callie and Son (TV). 1982: Young Doctors in Love. Tootsie. 1983: WarGames. 1984: Cloak and Dagger. The Muppets Take Manhattan. 1985: Mischief/The Man with One Red Shoe. 1986: Murrow (TV). The Return of Mike Hammer (TV). 1987: Dragnet. The Unholy. Guilty of Innocence: The Lenell Geter Story (TV). Sworn to Silence (TV). Plaza Suite (TV). 1988: Hot to Trot. Maybe Baby (TV). 1989: Where the Heart Is. Short Time. 1990: Meet the Applegates. 1991: Columbo and the Murder of a Rock Star (TV). Clifford. Never Forget (TV). 1992: There Goes the Neighborhood. 1993: Amos & Andrew. The Beverly Hillbillies. 1994: Judicial Consent.

COLLIER, Constance
(Laura C. Hardie) 1875–1955
Impassive British-born stage star who turned to Hollywood in the 1930s (initially as a drama coach) to portray a series of *grandes dames* with varying degrees of eccentricity about them. Her alabaster features could convey every emotion from scorn to sorrow with the minimum of movement. Some filmographies credit her with an appearance in *Our Betters* (1933), but it appears this may be a confusion with Constance Bennett.

1916: Intolerance. The Code of Marcia Gray. Macbeth. Tongues of Men. 1919: The Impossible Woman. 1920: Bleak House. 1922: The Bohemian Girl. 1933: Dinner at Eight. 1934: Peter Ibbetson. 1935: Shadow of Doubt. Anna Karenina. Professional Soldier. 1936: Girls' Dormitory. Little Lord Fauntleroy. Thunder in the City. 1937: Stage Door. A Damsel in Distress. She Got What She Wanted. Wee Willie Winkie. Clothes and the Woman. 1939: Zaza. 1940: Susan and God (GB: The Gay Mrs Trexel). Half a Sinner. 1945: Week-End at the Waldorf. Kitty. 1946: Monsieur Beaucaire. The Dark Corner. 1947: The Perils of Pauline. 1948: Rope. An Ideal Husband. The Girl from Manhattan. 1949: Whirlpool.

COLLINS, Ray 1888–1965
Affable, avuncular type who came to Hollywood in his early fifties as a member of the Orson Welles company, and stayed to exude solid benevolence for nearly 20 years. Universally recognized in the latter stages of his career as the dogged Lieutenant Tragg of the *Perry Mason* series on television. Died from emphysema.

1940: *The Grapes of Wrath*. 1941: *Citizen Kane*. 1942: *The Big Street. Highways by Night. Commandos Strike at Dawn. The Magnificent Ambersons. The Navy Comes Through*. 1943: *The Crime Doctor. Madame Curie* (narrator only). *The Human Comedy. Slightly Dangerous. Salute to the Marines. Whistling in Brooklyn*. 1944: *The Eve of St Mark. See Here, Private Hargrove. Barbary Coast Gent. The Seventh Cross. Can't Help Singing. The Hitler Gang. Shadows in the Night. Miss Susie Slagle's* (released 1946). 1945: *Roughly Speaking. The Hidden Eye. Leave Her to Heaven. Up Goes Maisie* (GB: *Up She Goes*). 1946: *Badman's Territory. Boys' Ranch. Crack-Up. Three Wise Fools. Two Years Before the Mast. The Return of Monte Cristo* (GB: *Monte Cristo's Revenge*). *The Best Years of Our Lives. A Night in Paradise*. 1947: *The Bachelor and the Bobby Soxer* (GB: *Bachelor Knight*). *The Red Stallion. The Swordsman. The Senator Was Indiscreet* (GB: *Mr Ashton Was Indiscreet*). 1948: *Homecoming. Good Sam. The Man from Colorado. A Double Life. Command Decision. For the Love of Mary*. 1949: *Red Stallion in the Rockies. Hideout. It Happens Every Spring. The Fountainhead. Ma and Pa Kettle Go to Town* (GB: *Going to Town*). *The Heiress. Free for All. Francis*. 1950: *Paid in Full. Kill the Umpire. Summer Stock* (GB: *If You Feel Like Singing*). *The Reformer and the Redhead. USS Teakettle* (later *You're in the Navy Now*). 1951: *Ma and Pa Kettle Back on the Farm. I Want You. Reunion in Reno. The Racket. Vengeance Valley*. 1952: *Invitation. Dreamboat. Young Man With Ideas*. 1953: *The Desert Song. Column South. Ma and Pa Kettle at the Fair. Ma and Pa Kettle on Vacation* (GB: *Ma and Pa Kettle Go to Paris*). *Bad for Each Other. The Kid from Left Field*. 1954: *Rose Marie. Athena*. 1955: *The Desperate Hours. Texas Lady*. 1956: *Invitation to a Gunfighter* (TV). *Never Say Goodbye. Gun in His Hand* (TV. GB: cinemas). *The Solid Gold Cadillac*. 1957: *Spoilers of the Forest*. 1958: *Touch of Evil*. 1961: *I'll Give My Life*.

COLONNA, Jerry
(Gerardo Colonna) 1904–1986
Beaming, round-faced, bulge-eyed American musician and comedian who had a black moustache that almost rivalled Groucho Marx's fake one, and an ability to hold a note until it sounded as though it were bouncing around in an echo chamber. He was a trombone player at 14, and later led

his own band, but his raucous voice and sense of ridiculous led him into comedy and, after a regular stint on Bob Hope's radio show, he made engagingly lunatic cameo appearances in film frolics featuring Hope and others. Died from kidney failure.

1937: *52nd Street. Rosalie*. *Swingtime in the Movies*. 1938: *College Swing* (GB: *Swing, Teacher, Swing*). *Little Miss Broadway. Garden of the Moon. Valley of the Giants*. *The Star Reporter No 2*. 1939: *Naughty But Nice. Sweepstakes Winner*. 1940: *Road to Singapore. Comin' Round the Mountain*. 1941: *Melody and Moonlight. You're the One. Sis Hopkins. Ice-Capades*. 1942: *True to the Army. Priorities on Parade. Ice-Capades Revue* (GB: *Rhythm Hits the Ice*). 1943: *Star-Spangled Rhythm*. 1944: *Atlantic City. It's in the Bag!* (GB: *The Fifth Chair*). 1946: *Make Mine Music*. 1947: *Road to Rio*. 1950: *Alice in Wonderland* (voice only). 1951: *Kentucky Jubilee*. 1955: *Meet Me in Las Vegas* (GB: *Viva Las Vegas!*). 1958: *Andy Hardy Comes Home*. 1961: *The Road to Hong Kong*. 1969: *Don't Push, I'll Charge When I'm Ready* (TV).

COLTRANE, Robbie
(Robin Macmillan) 1950–
Outsize, Scottish-born character comedian with rounded features, small, penetrating eyes and floppy black hair. He started out as a comedian on TV alternative comedy shows, but soon showed an impressive range as an actor, whether as snarling, sweating ne'er-do-wells, sharpies on the make, friendly blue-collar workers or, even in one

film, a transvestite night-club queen. Later films brought out the more genial side of a busy man who's also been a hard worker in TV commercials.

1979: *La Mort en direct* (GB: *Death Watch*). *Balham – Gateway to the South*. 1980: *Flash Gordon*. 1981: *Subway Riders*. 1982: *The Ghost Dance. Scrubbers. Britannia Hospital*. 1983: *Krull*. 1984: *Chinese Boxes. Loose Connections*. 1985: *Revolution. National Lampoon's European Vacation. Defence of the Realm. Caravaggio. The Supergrass*. 1986: *Absolute Beginners. Mona Lisa*. 1987: *The Secret Policeman's Third Ball. Eat the Rich*. 1988: *The Fruit Machine. The Strike. Midnight Breaks*. 1989: *Bert Rigby, You're a Fool. Slipstream. Danny, the Champion of the World* (US: TV). *Lenny Live and Unleashed. Let It Ride. Henry V*. 1990: *Nuns on the Run. Perfectly Normal*. 1991: *The Pope Must Die* (US: *The Pope Must Diet*). *Triple Bogey on a Par 5 Hole. Alive and Kicking* (TV). *Comfort Creek*. 1992: *Oh, What a Night*. 1993: *The Adventures of Huck Finn. Cracker – The Mad Woman in the Attic* (TV). 1995: *Goldeneye*.

COMPTON, Joyce
(Eleanor Hunt) 1907–
Fair-haired American actress with twinkling eyes and a cheeky smile who was one of the Wampas Baby Stars in the peak year of 1926, and went on to play zany or scatter-brained blondes for 25 years. She is best recalled as an enchanting female detective called Chris Cross in 1940's *Sky Murder*. Carried on her busy life in the 1950s by combining (mostly television) acting with part-time nursing work.

1925: *The Golden Bed. Sally. What Fools Men. Broadway Lady*. 1926: *Syncopating Sue*. 1927: *Border Cavalier. Ankles Preferred*. 1928: *Soft Living*. 1929: *The Wild Party. Salute. Dangerous Curves. The Sky Hawk*. 1930: *High Society Blues. Three Sisters. Wild Company. Lightnin'*. 1931: *Three Girls Lost. Up Pops the Devil. Women of All Nations. Not Exactly Gentlemen. Good Sport. Annabelle's Affairs*. 1932: *Lena Rivers. Under Eighteen. Westward Passage. Beauty Parlor. Unholy Love. Lady and Gent. False Faces* (GB: *What Price Beauty*). *A Parisian Romance. If I Had a Million. Afraid to Talk. Hat Check Girl* (GB: *Embassy Girl*). 1933: *Clip Joint* (GB: *Sing, Sinner, Sing*).

Fighting for Justice. *Dream Stuff. *Daddy Knows Best. *Knockout Kisses. *The Wrestlers. *The Big Fibber. *Caliente Love. *The Plumber and the Lady. Only Yesterday. *Roadhouse Queen. 1934: The Trumpet Blows. Imitation of Life. *Everything's Ducky. King Kelly of the USA (GB: Irish and Pround Of It). Affairs of a Gentleman. Million Dollar Ransom. The White Parade. 1935: Rustlers of Red Dog (serial). Let 'Em Have It! (GB: False Faces). *Manhattan Monkey Business. Go Into Your Dance (GB: Casino de Paree). Mr Dynamite, *Public Ghost No 1. College Scandal. Magnificent Obsession. 1936: Valley of the Lawless. Love before Breakfast. *Life Hesitates at 40. The Harvester. Under Your Spell. Trapped By Television (GB: Caught By Television). Star for a Night. Ellis Island. Sitting on the Moon. Country Gentleman. Three Smart Girls. Murder with Pictures. 1937: Top of the Town. China Passage. We Have Our Moments. Pick a Star. Wings Over Honolulu. Kid Galahad. Rhythm in the Clouds. The Toast of New York. Small Town Boy. Born Reckless. The Awful Truth. Sea Racketeers. She Asked For It. 1938: You and Me. Love on a Budget. Manproof. The Last Warning. Women Are Like That. Trade Winds. Spring Madness. Going Places. Artists and Models Abroad (GB: Stranded in Paris). *How to Watch Football. 1939: Rose of Washington Square. The Flying Irishman. Reno. Balalaika. Hotel for Women/ Elsa Maxwell's Hotel for Women. 1940: Honeymoon Deferred. Turnabout. Sky Murder. The Villain Still Pursued Her. I Take This Oath. City for Conquest. Who Killed Aunt Maggie? Let's Make Music. They Drive by Night (GB: The Road to Frisco). 1941: Scattergood Meets Broadway. Redtime Story. Moon Over Her Shoulder. Manpower. Blues in the Night. Ziegfeld Girl. 1942: Too Many Women. Thunderbirds. 1943: Silver Skates. Swing Out the Blues. Let's Face It. Silver Spurs. 1945: Hitch-Hike to Happiness. Roughly Speaking. Pillow to Post. Christmas in Connecticut (GB: Indiscretion). Danger Signal. Mildred Pierce. 1946: Behind the Mask. The Best Years of Our Lives. Rendezvous with Annie. Night and Day. Dark Alibi. 1947: Scared to Death. Exposed. Linda Be Good. 1948: A Southern Yankee (GB: My Hero). Incident. Sorry, Wrong Number. 1949: Mighty Joe Young. Grand Canyon. 1950: Jet Pilot (released 1957). 1957: The Persuader. 1958: Girl in the Woods.

CONNOLLY, Walter 1887–1940

Heavyweight American stage actor who came to the screen in the thirties and proved his talent in screwball comedy. Usually with thick, black moustache and pince-nez and at his wits' end, but also a solid performer in dramatic roles. Film-goers would have been happy to see him go on stealing scenes through the 1940s, but a stroke killed him at only 53.

1930: *Many Happy Returns. 1931: Plain-clothes Man. 1932: No More Orchids. Washington Merry-Go-Round (GB: Invisible Power). Man Against Woman. 1933: The Bitter Tea of General Yen. Lady for a Day. Paddy the Next Best Thing. Master of Men. East of Fifth Avenue (GB: Two in a Million). Man's Castle. 1934: Eight Girls in a Boat. It Happened One Night. Once to Every Woman. Twentieth Century.

Whom the Gods Destroy. Servants' Entrance. Lady by Choice. Broadway Bill (GB: Strictly Confidential). The Captain Hates the Sea. White Lies. Many Happy Returns. 1935: Father Brown, Detective. She Couldn't Take It. So Red the Rose. One Way Ticket. 1936: Soak the Rich. The King Steps Out. The Music Goes Round. Libeled Lady. 1937: Nancy Steele is Missing. Let's Get Married. The League of Frightened Men. The Good Earth. First Lady. Nothing Sacred. 1938: Start Cheering. Penitentiary. Four's a Crowd. Too Hot To Handle. 1939: Girl Downstairs. Good Girls Go to Paris. Bridal Suite. Those High Gray Walls (GB: The Gates of Alcatraz). Fifth Avenue Girl. Coastguard. The Great Victor Herbert. The Adventures of Huckleberry Finn.

CONNOR, Kenneth 1916–1993

Wiry little British comedian, a specialist in hurt bewilderment, fierce indignation and, latterly, impotent lechery. His career hardly got started before World War II service but, afterwards, he became radio's man of many comic voices in Peter Sellers' footsteps and, later one of the 'Carry On' gang, to which series of films he returned, with lower billing, after a mid-sixties sabbatical in the theatre. Died from cancer.

1939: Poison Pen. 1949: The Chiltern Hundreds (US: The Amazing Mr Beecham). 1950: Don't Say Die/Never Say Die. 1952: The Beggar's Opera. Elstree Story (voice only). There Was a Young Lady. Miss Robin Hood. 1953: Marilyn (later Roadhouse Girl). 1954: The Black Rider. 1955: The Ladykillers. 1957: Davy. 1958:

Carry on Sergeant. 1959: Make Mine a Million. Carry on Nurse. Carry on Teacher. 1960: Carry on Constable. Dentist in the Chair. Watch Your Stern. His and Hers. 1961: Carry on Regardless. A Weekend with Lulu. Nearly a Nasty Accident. Dentist on the Job (US: Get on with It!). What a Carve Up! (US: Home Sweet Homicide). 1962: Carry on Cruising. 1963: Carry on Cabby. 1964: Gonks Go Beat. Carry on Cleo. 1965: How to Undress in Public without Undue Embarrassment. 1967: Danny the Dragon (serial, voice only). 1968: Captain Nemo and the Underwater City. 1969: Carry on Up the Jungle. 1970: Rhubarb. Carry on Henry. 1972: Carry on Matron. Carry on Abroad. 1973: Carry on Girls. 1974: Carry on Dick. 1975: Carry on Behind. 1976: Carry on England. 1978: Carry on Emmannuelle.

CONRAD, William 1920–1994

Bulky American actor with heavy black moustache and forceful style who changed from writing for radio to playing villains in films. Kept his eye in with an occasional stab at writing and direction before winning world-wide acclaim as television's fat and balding sleuth. Cannon. His beady eyes and inimitable rasping voice (he was also the unseen narrator on the long-running TV series The Fugitive) stole many scenes. Died from a heart attack.

1946: The Killers. 1947: Body and Soul. Four Faces West (GB: They Passed This Way). To the Victor. Sorry, Wrong Number. Joan of Arc. 1948: Arch of Triumph. 1949: Any Number Can Play. Tension. East Side, West Side. 1950: The Milkman. Dial 1119 (GB: The Violent Hour). One Way Street. 1951: Cry Danger. The Sword of Monte Cristo. The Racket. 1952: Lone Star. 1953: Cry of the Hunted. The Desert Song. 1954: The Naked Jungle. 1955: The Cowboy (narrator only). Five Against the House. The Naked Sea (narrator only). 1956: The Conqueror. Johnny Concho. 1957: The Ride Back. 1959: –30– (GB: Deadline Midnight). 1965: Battle of the Bulge. 1970: The Brotherhood of the Bell (TV). The DA: Conspiracy to Kill (TV). 1974: The FBI Story – Alvin Karpis (TV. Narrator only). 1976: Moonshine County Express. 1977: Night Cries. The City (TV. Narrator only). 1978: Keefer (TV). 1980: The Murder That Wouldn't Die (TV). The Return of Frank Cannon (TV). Turnover Smith (TV). 1982: The Mikado (TV). Shock – Trauma (TV). 1985: In Like Flynn (TV). 1986: Killing

Cars. Vengeance: The Story of Tony Cimo (TV). 1987: Jake and the Fatman (TV). 1991: Hudson Hawk (narrator only).

As director:

1963: The Man from Galveston (TV. GB: cinemas). 1965: My Blood Runs Cold. Brainstorm. Two on a Guillotine. 1971: Side Show (TV).

CONRIED, Hans 1917–1982

You might find it hard to put a name to the face, but you really couldn't miss Hans Conried in a film. Lanky and sharp-faced, with startled eyes, this American character comedian was forever popping up in lunatic supporting roles as professors, waiters or photographers, often with nonsensical dialogue that sounded as though he wrote it himself. He might have become a star in The 5,000 Fingers of Dr T, but front-office interference made it a box-office flop. Died from a heart ailment.

1938: Dramatic School. 1939: It's a Wonderful World. On Borrowed Time. Never Say Die. 1940: Dulcy. Bitter Sweet. The Great Dictator. 1941: Maisie Was a Lady. Unexpected Uncle. Blondie in Society (GB: Henpecked). Underground. The Gay Falcon. Weekend for Three. A Date with the Falcon. 1942: Joan of Paris. Saboteur. The Wife Takes a Flyer (GB: A Yank in Dutch). *The Greatest Gift. The Falcon Takes Over. Pacific Rendezvous. Blondie's Blessed Event (GB: A Bundle of Trouble). Journey into Fear. Underground Agent. The Big Street. Once Upon A Honeymoon. Nightmare. 1943: Hostages. Crazy House. Hitler's Children. A Lady Takes a Chance. His Butler's Sister. 1944: Passage to Marseille. Mrs Parkington. 1947: The Senator Was Indiscreet (GB: Mr Ashton Was Indiscreet). 1948: Design for Death (narrator only). 1949: The Barkleys of Broadway. My Friend Irma. Bride for Sale. On the Town. 1950: Jet Pilot (released 1957). Nancy Goes to Rio. Summer Stock (GB: If You Feel Like Singing). 1951: Rich, Young and Pretty. Texas Carnival. The Light Touch. Too Young to Kiss. Behave Yourself! New Mexico. I'll See You in My Dreams. 1952: Three for Bedroom C. The World in His Arms. Big Jim McLain. 1953: Peter Pan (voice only). Siren of Bagdad. The Affairs of Dobie Gillis. The Twonky. The 5,000 Fingers of Dr T. 1954: Davy Crockett, King of the Wild Frontier. 1955: You're Never

Too Young. 1956: The Birds and the Bees. Bus Stop. Miracle on 34th Street (TV. GB: cinemas). 1957: The Monster That Challenged the World. Johnny Tremain. 1958: The Big Beat. Rock-a-Bye Baby. 1959: Juke Box Rhythm. 1001 Arabian Nights (voice only). 1961: Judgment at Nuremberg. 1963: My Six Loves. 1964: Robin and the Seven Hoods. The Patsy. 1968: The Jay Ward Intergalactic Film Festival (voice only). 1969: Wake Me When the War is Over (TV). *Up is Down (narrator only). 1970: The Phantom Tollbooth (voice only). 1973: The Brothers O'Toole (GB: TV). 1976: The Shaggy DA. 1978: The Cat from Outer Space. 1980: Oh, God! Book II. 1981: *Once Upon a Mouse (narrator only). American Dream (TV). Through the Magic Pyramid (TV).

COOK, Elisha Jnr 1903–

The little man with the frightened face who seems to be many people's favourite American character actor, Cook played losers: short, shifty, nervous guys living on life's edge. They made a bluster of bravado, but were always found wanting, or just out of luck. Shot in Shane, knifed in The Black Bird, strangled in Phantom Lady, poisoned in The Big Sleep — Cook Got His in a score of different ways. In Voodoo Island, he was shrunk, and in Hellzapoppin filled full of holes! An assistant stage manager at 17, his film career got going with a vengeance in his thirties, after one or two false starts. It comes as a surprise to find that he made little more than 100 films. Busy in the mid-1980s, as the crime boss Ice Pick in the TV series Magnum. Some sources give his birthdate as 1902, but this seems to be erroneous.

1930: Her Unborn Child. 1936: Two in a Crowd. Pigskin Parade (GB: The Harmony Parade). †Bullets or Ballots. 1937: Wife, Doctor and Nurse. They Won't Forget. The Devil is Driving. Thoroughbreds Don't Cry. Life Begins in College (GB: The Joy Parade). Love is News. Breezing Home. Danger – Love at Work. 1938: Submarine Patrol. Three Blind Mice. My Lucky Star. 1939: Grand Jury Secrets. Newsboys' Home. 1940: Stranger on the Third Floor. He Married His Wife. Public Deb Number One. Tin Pan Alley. 1941: Man at Large. Love Crazy. Sergeant York. The Maltese Falcon. I Wake Up Screaming (GB: Hot Spot). Hellzapoppin. Ball of Fire. 1942: A Gentleman at Heart. In This Our Life. A-Haunting We Will

Go. Sleepytime Gal. Manila Calling. Wildcat. 1943: *Kill or Be Killed. Phantom Lady. 1944: Up in Arms. Casanova Brown. Dark Waters. Dillinger. Dark Mountain. 1945: Why Girls Leave Home. 1946: Blonde Alibi. The Big Sleep. Cinderella Jones. Two Smart People. Joe Palooka – Champ. The Falcon's Alibi. 1947: Born to Kill (GB: Lady of Deceit). The Long Night. The Fall Guy. The Gangster. 1949: Flaxy Martin. The Great Gatsby. 1951: Behave Yourself! 1952: Don't Bother to Knock. Shane. 1953: Thunder Over the Plains. I, the Jury. 1954: Superman's Peril (TV. GB: cinemas). The Outlaw's Daughter. Drum Beat. 1955: Timberjack. The Indian Fighter. Trial. 1956: The Killing. Accused of Murder. 1957: The Lonely Man. Voodoo Island. Plunder Road. Baby Face Nelson. 1958: Chicago Confidential. The House on Haunted Hill. 1959: Day of the Outlaw. 1960: College Confidential. Platinum High School (GB: Rich, Young and Deadly). 1961: One Eyed Jacks. 1962: Papa's Delicate Condition. 1963: Black Zoo. The Haunted Palace. Johnny Cool. 1964: Blood on the Arrow. The Glass Cage. 1966: The Spy in the Green Hat (TV. GB: cinemas). Welcome to Hard Times (GB: Killer on a Horse). 1968: Rosemary's Baby. 1969: The Great Bank Robbery. 1970: El Condor. The Movie Murderer (TV). Night Chase (TV). 1971: The Night Stalker (TV). 1972: Blacula. The Great Northfield Minnesota Raid. Steelyard Blues. 1973: Emperor of the North Pole (GB: Emperor of the North). Electra Glide in Blue. ††Pat Garrett and Billy the Kid. The Outfit. 1974: Messiah of Evil. The Phantom of Hollywood (TV). 1975: The Black Bird. Winterhawk. 1976: St Ives. 1977: Mad Bull (TV). Dead of Night (TV). 1979: Salem's Lot. 1941. The Champ. 1980: Carny. Tom Horn. Harry's War. 1981: National Lampoon's Movie Madness. Leave 'Em Laughing (TV). 1982: Hammett. The Escape Artist. Terror at Alcatraz (TV). 1983: This Girl for Hire (TV). 1984: Off Sides (TV). It Came Upon the Midnight Clear (TV). 1987: The Man Who Broke 1,000 Chains (cable TV).

† Scenes deleted from final release print
†† Scenes deleted but shown in some TV versions

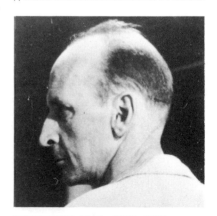

COOLIDGE, Philip 1908–1967

Dark, lanky, stoop-shouldered American actor of hangdog aspect. Only really a visitor to films from television and the stage, he was notable in one or two, especially I Want to Live! and The Tingler, and considerably under-used by Hollywood. Died from cancer.

1947: Boomerang. 1956: The Sharkfighters.
1957: Slander. 1958: I Want to Live! 1959:
The Tingler. It Happened to Jane. The Mating
Game. North by Northwest. 1960: Inherit the
Wind. The Bramble Bush. Because They're
Young. 1962: Bon Voyage! 1964: Hamlet. 1965:
The Greatest Story Ever Told. The Russians
Are Coming, the Russians Are Coming. 1967:
Never a Dull Moment.

COOPER, George A. 1916–
There were few sympathetic roles for this
tough-looking little British actor with snub
nose, small, suspicious eyes and a fuzz of
disappearing hair – a grouchy-looking, wiry
ferret of a man who looked as though he
would tear the throat out of any weak hero,
and nearly did that very thing to Albert
Finney's *Tom Jones*, as the incensed Mr
Fitzpatrick.

1954: The Passing Stranger. 1955: Jumping
for Joy. 1956: Fortune is a Woman (US: She
Played with Fire). Sailor Beware! (US: Panic
in the Parlor). 1957: Miracle in Soho. The
Secret Place. 1958: Violent Playground. A Night
to Remember. 1959: Follow That Horse! Hell is
a City. Our Man in Havana. 1961: In the
Doghouse. 1962: The Wild and the Willing.
Vengeance (US: The Brain). 1963: The Cracks-
man. Tom Jones. Nightmare. 1964: The Bargee.
Ferry 'Cross the Mersey. 1965: Life at the Top.
1967: Smashing Time. 1968: The Strange
Affair. Dracula Has Risen from the Grave.
1969: On Her Majesty's Secret Service. Start
the Revolution Without Me. 1970: The Rise
and Rise of Michael Rimmer. 1971: Diamonds
Are Forever. What Became of Jack and Jill?
(US: Romeo and Juliet '71). 1972: Bless This
House. 1974: The Black Windmill. 1975: Dick
Deadeye, or Duty Done (voice only). 1976:
Chimpmates (1st series). The Chiffy Kids (series).
1982: Red Monarch. 1983: Amy (TV). Nelly's
Version (TV). 1985: Reunion at Fairborough
(TV). 1993: Final Curtain (TV). 1994: Fair
Game (TV).

COOPER, Dame Gladys 1888–1971
Fair-haired, gracious-looking English actress, one of the loveliest leading ladies on
the London stage from the early 1900s on.
She went to Hollywood late in her career
and stayed for many years playing mainly
likeable ladies of the aristocracy. Three times
nominated for an Academy Award: for *Now,*

Voyager (probably her best performance),
The Song of Bernadette and *My Fair Lady.*

1913: The Eleventh Commandment. 1914:
Dandy Donovan, the Gentleman Cracksman.
1916: *The Real Thing at Last. 1917: The
Sorrows of Satan. Masks and Faces. My Lady's
Dress. 1920: Unmarried. 1922: Headin' North.
The Bohemian Girl. 1923: Bonnie Prince
Charlie. 1935: The Iron Duke. 1940: Kitty
Foyle. Rebecca. 1941: That Hamilton Woman
(GB: Lady Hamilton). The Black Cat. The Gay
Falcon. 1942: This Above All. Eagle Squadron.
Now, Voyager. 1943: Forever and a Day.
The Song of Bernadette. Mr Lucky. Princess
O'Rourke. 1944: The White Cliffs of Dover.
Mrs Parkington. 1945: The Valley of Decision.
Love Letters. 1946: The Cockeyed Miracle (GB:
Mr Griggs Returns). The Green Years. 1947:
Beware of Pity. Green Dolphin Street. The
Bishop's Wife. 1948: Homecoming. The Pirate.
1949: The Secret Garden. Madame Bovary.
1951: Thunder on the Hill (GB: Bonaventure).
1952: At Sword's Point (GB: Sons of the
Musketeers). 1955: The Man Who Loved Red-
heads. 1957: Circle of the Day (TV). The
Mystery of 13 (TV). 1958: Separate Tables.
Verdict of Three (TV). 1963: The List of Adrian
Messenger. 1961: My Fair Lady. 1967: The
Happiest Millionaire. 1969: A Nice Girl Like
Me.

COOPER, Melville 1896–1973
Plump-faced, droop-eyed, dark-haired
British actor who went to Hollywood in
1935 and played ineffectual villains pumped
up by their own pomposity. Seemingly ideally

cast as a nose-in-the-air butler, he actually
succeeded in playing a laudable variety of
characters within his range, notably Romney
in *The Scarlet Pimpernel*, the Sheriff of Nottingham in *The Adventures of Robin Hood*, a
con-man in *The Lady Eve* and Mr Collins in
Pride and Prejudice. Died from cancer.

1930: *All Riot on the Western Front. 1931:
Black Coffee. The Calendar (US: Bachelor's
Folly). 1932: Two White Arms (US: Wives
Beware). 1933: Forging Ahead. Leave It to Me.
To Brighton With Gladys. 1934: The Private
Life of Don Juan. The Scarlet Pimpernel. 1935:
The Bishop Misbehaves (GB: The Bishop's
Misadventures). 1936: The Gorgeous Hussy.
1937: The Last of Mrs Cheyney. Thin Ice (GB:
Lovely to Look At). The Great Garrick. Tovarich.
1938: Women Are Like That. The Adventures
of Robin Hood. Hard to Get. Gold Diggers in
Paris (GB: The Gay Imposters). Four's a Crowd.
The Dawn Patrol. Comet Over Broadway.
Dramatic School. The Garden of the Moon.
1939: I'm from Missouri. Two Bright Boys.
The Sun Never Sets. Blind Alley. 1940: Pride
and Prejudice. Too Many Husbands. Rebecca.
Murder Over New York. 1941: Scotland Yard.
Submarine Zone. Flame of New Orleans. The
Lady Eve. You Belong to Me (GB: Good Morn-
ing, Doctor). 1942: This Above All. The Affairs
of Martha (GB: Once Upon a Thursday). Life
Begins at 8:30 (GB: The Light of Heart).
Random Harvest. 1943: Hit Parade of 1943.
The Immortal Sergeant. Holy Matrimony. My
Kingdom for a Cook. 1946: The Imperfect Lady
(GB: Mrs Loring's Secret). Heartbeat. 13 Rue
Madeleine. 1948: Enchantment. 1949: The
Red Danube. And Baby Makes Three. Love
Happy (later Kleptomaniacs). 1950: Father of
the Bride. The Underworld Story. The Petty
Girl (GB: Girl of the Year). Let's Dance. 1953:
It Should Happen to You. The Story of Gilbert
and Sullivan (US: The Great Gilbert and
Sullivan). 1954: Moonfleet. 1955: The King's
Thief. Diane. 1956: Bundle of Joy. Around the
World in 80 Days. 1957: The Story of Mankind.
1958: From the Earth to the Moon.

COOTE, Robert 1909–1982
Plumpish, ruddy-cheeked, moustachioed
English actor largely in Hollywood films
(after screen starts in Britain and Australia),
usually as an affable cove, an RAF officer or
the hero's best friend. He was a real-life
squadron-leader in World War II, with the

Royal Canadian Air Force. After decades of semi-anonymity, he became known worldwide in the 1960s as one of the stars of a television series called *The Rogues*.

1931: Sally in Our Alley. 1933: Loyalties. 1936: Rangle River. 1937: The Thirteenth Chair. The Sheik Steps Out. A Yank at Oxford. 1938: Blonde Cheat. Mr Moto's Last Warning. 1939: Gunga Din. Bad Lands. The House of Fear. Nurse Edith Cavell. The Girl Downstairs. Vigil in the Night. 1940: You Can't Fool Your Wife. 1942: Commandos Strike at Dawn. 1943: Forever and a Day. 1946: A Matter of Life and Death (US: Stairway to Heaven). Cloak and Dagger. 1947: The Ghost and Mrs Muir. Forever Amber. Lured (GB: Personal Column). 1948: The Exile. Macbeth. Bonnie Prince Charlie. Berlin Express. The Three Musketeers. 1949: The Red Danube. 1950: The Elusive Pimpernel (US: The Fighting Pimpernel). 1951: Soldiers Three. The Desert Fox (GB: Rommel—Desert Fox). 1952: Scaramouche. The Prisoner of Zenda. The Merry Widow. 1955: The Constant Husband. Othello. 1956: The Swan. 1958: Merry Andrew. Hello London. The Horse's Mouth. 1959: The League of Gentlemen. 1963: The VIPs. 1964: The Golden Head. 1966: A Man Could Get Killed. The Swinger. 1967: The Cool Ones. 1968: Prudence and the Pill. 1970: Kenner. 1972: Up the Front. 1973: Theatre of Blood. 1975: Target Risk (TV). 1978: Institute for Revenge.

COPLEY, Peter 1915–

One thinks of this British actor — bald, bespectacled and far from benign — as if through a fish-eye lens. As psychiatrists, magistrates and interrogators he displayed a civilized menace to those under his microscope. A stage actor since 1932, when he finally abandoned thoughts of a naval career. Married (first of three) to actress Pamela Brown. Copley was also a legal expert who was called to the bar in 1963: opponents beware! Not many films, but wellremembered from most of them. Still acting, mostly on TV.

*1934: *Tell Me If It Hurts. 1937: Farewell Again (US: Troopship). 1949: Golden Salamander. 1950: The Elusive Pimpernel (US: The Fighting Pimpernel). 1952: The Card (US: The Promoter). The Hour of 13. 1953: The Sword and the Rose. Saadia. The Clue of the Missing Ape. 1956: Peril for the Guy. Foreign Intrigue. 1957: Time Without Pity. Man With-*

out a Body. Just My Luck. The Strange World of Planet X (US: Cosmic Monsters). 1958: Rockets Galore (US: Mad Little Island). 1959: Mystery in the Mine. Follow That Horse! 1961: Victim. 1964: The Third Secret. King and Country. 1965: Help! The Knack...and how to get it. 1966: The Jokers. 1967: Quatermass and the Pit (US: Five Million Miles to Earth). 1968: The Shoes of the Fisherman. Mosquito Squadron. 1969: Frankenstein Must Be Destroyed. All at Sea. Walk a Crooked Path. 1970: The Engagement. Jane Eyre (TV. GB: cinemas). 1971: What Became of Jack and Jill? (US: Romeo and Juliet '71). 1972: That's Your Funeral. 1973: Gawain and the Green Knight. 1975: Hennessey. 1976: Shout at the Devil. 1977: The Black Panther. 1980: Little Lord Fauntleroy (US: TV). 1982: Witness for the Prosecution (TV). 1987: Empire of the Sun. 1993: Second Best.*

CORBY, Ellen
(née Hansen) 1911–

American actress of Scandinavian origins who, after World War II, switched from being a script girl and quickly cornered the market in nosey neighbours, bigoted townswomen, starchy schoolma'ams, repressed spinsters and dowdy servants. Her tight, dark hair and pinched features added character to dozens of films before she turned to television and became Grandma (and sometime scriptwriter) of *The Waltons*, a series for which she took two Emmy Awards to add to her Oscar nomination for *I Remember Mama* in 1948. She was forced to retire in her seventies after a stroke.

1933: Twisted Rails. Little Women. 1941: Twilight on the Trail. 1945: Cornered. 1946: The Dark Corner. It's a Wonderful Life! From This Day Forward. Bedlam. The Locket. In Old Sacramento. The Spiral Staircase. Till the End of Time. The Scarlet Horseman (serial). Cuban Pete (GB: Down Cuba Way). Crack-Up. Sister Kenny. Lover Come Back. The Truth About Murder. 1947: Hal Roach Comedy Carnival/ The Fabulous Joe. Beat the Band. Forever Amber. Railroaded! Born to Kill (GB: Lady of Deceit). They Won't Believe Me. Driftwood. The Bachelor and the Bobby Soxer (GB: Bachelor Knight). 1948: Strike It Rich. I Remember Mama. Fighting Father Dunne. The Dark Past. The Noose Hangs High. If You Knew Susie. 1949: Little Women. Mighty Joe Young. Rusty Saves

a Life. The Judge Steps Out. A Woman's Secret. Madame Bovary. Ma and Pa Kettle Go to Town (GB: Going to Town). Captain China. 1950: The Gunfighter. Caged. Peggy. Edge of Doom (GB: Stronger Than Fear). Harriet Craig. 1951: Goodbye, My Fancy. Angels in the Outfield (GB: Angels and the Pirates). Here Comes the Groom. The Mating Season. The Sea Hornet. The Barefoot Mailman. On Moonlight Bay. 1952: Monsoon. The Big Trees. Shane. Fearless Fagan. 1953: The Woman They Almost Lynched. The Vanquished. A Lion is in the Streets. 1954: About Mrs Leslie. The Bowery Boys Meet the Monsters. Sabrina (GB: Sabrina Fair). Susan Slept Here. Untamed Heiress. 1955: Illegal. 1956: Slightly Scarlet. Stagecoach to Fury. 1957: The Seventh Sin. Night Passage. God is My Partner. Rockabilly Baby. All Mine to Give (GB: The Day They Gave Babies Away). 1958: Macabre. Vertigo. As Young As We Are. 1960: Visit to a Small Planet. 1961: A Pocketful of Miracles. Saintly Sinners. 1963: The Caretakers (GB: Borderlines). Four for Texas. 1964: Hush ... Hush, Sweet Charlotte. The Strangler. 1965: The Family Jewels. The Ghost and Mr Chicken. 1966: The Night of the Grizzly. The Glass Bottom Boat. The Gnome-Mobile. 1968: Ruba al prossimo tuo (GB and US: A Fine Pair). The Legend of Lylah Clare. 1969: A Quiet Couple (TV). Angel in My Pocket. 1971: A Tattered Web (TV). Support Your Local Gunfighter. The Homecoming (TV). 1972: Napoleon and Samantha. 1974: Pretty Boy Floyd (TV). 1982: A Day for Thanks on Waltons' Mountain (TV). 1983: A Wedding on Waltons' Mountain (TV).

COREY, Jeff 1914–

Thin- and bony-faced American actor, with dark eyes and unruly black wavy hair, often seen as men not to be trusted. After quitting his job as a salesman for an acting career, he came to Hollywood in 1940, playing shabbily clothed, sometimes psychotic types. Absent from the screen for 11 years from 1951 after McCarthy blacklisting, Corey established himself as one of Hollywood's leading drama coaches, then returned in much the same (though better dressed) roles as before.

1940: Third Finger, Left Hand. Bitter Sweet. You'll Find Out. 1941: All That Money Can Buy/The Devil and Daniel Webster. The Reluctant Dragon. North to the Klondike. Small Town Deb. Petticoat Politics. Paris Calling.

You Belong to Me (GB: Good Morning, Doctor). 1942: The Man Who Wouldn't Die. Syncopation. Roxie Hart. Tennessee Johnson (GB: The Man on America's Conscience). The Postman Didn't Ring. Girl Trouble. The Moon is Down. 1943: Frankenstein Meets the Wolf Man. My Friend Flicka. 1946: The Killers. Somewhere in the Night. California. Rendezvous with Annie. The Shocking Miss Pilgrim. It Shouldn't Happen to a Dog. 1947: Ramrod. The Gangster. Hoppy's Holiday. Miracle on 34th Street (GB: The Big Heart). Unconquered. Brute Force. The Flame. 1948: The Wreck of the Hesperus. Homecoming. Alias a Gentleman. Cañon City. Let's Live Again. Kidnapped. Wake of the Red Witch. A Southern Yankee (GB: My Hero). Joan of Arc. I, Jane Doe. City Across the River. 1949: Roughshod. Black Shadows (narrator only). Follow Me Quietly. The Hideout. Baghdad. Home of the Brave. 1950: The Outriders. Rock Island Trail (GB: Transcontinental Express). The Nevadan (GB: The Man from Nevada). Singing Guns. The Next Voice You Hear. Bright Leaf. Rawhide/Desperate Siege. The Prince Who Was a Thief. 1951: Red Mountain. Superman and the Mole-Men (GB: Superman and the Strange People). Sirocco. Fourteen Hours. Only the Valiant. New Mexico. Never Trust a Gambler. 1963: The Balcony. The Yellow Canary. 1964: Lady in a Cage. 1965: Once a Thief. The Cincinnati Kid. Mickey One. 1966: Seconds. 1967: In Cold Blood. 1968: The Boston Strangler. Impasse. 1969: True Grit. Butch Cassidy and the Sundance Kid. Set This Town on Fire (TV. Not shown until 1973). Beneath the Planet of the Apes. 1970: Cover Me Babe. The Movie Murderer (TV). A Clear and Present Danger (TV). Getting Straight. They Call Me MISTER Tibbs! Little Big Man. 1971: Shoot-Out. Catlow. Clay Pigeon (GB: Trip to Kill). 1972: Something Evil (TV). High-Flying Spy (TV). 1974: Paper Tiger. The Gun and the Pulpit (TV). 1976: Banjo Hackett: Roamin' Free (TV). The Premonition. The Last Tycoon. 1977: Oh, God! Moonshine Country Express. Curse of the Black Widow (TV). Captains Courageous (TV). 1978: The Pirate (TV). Jennifer (TV). The Wild Geese. 1979: Butch and Sundance The Early Days. 1980: Homeward Bound (TV). Battle Beyond the Stars. 1982: Cry for the Strangers (TV). The Sword and the Sorcerer. 1984: Conan the Destroyer. 1985: Father of Hell Town (TV). Creator. Final Jeopardy (TV). 1986: Second Serve (TV). 1988: Secret Ingredient. Messenger of Death. 1989: A Deadly Silence (TV). 1990: Bird on a Wire. To My Daughter (TV). Up River (completed 1979). 1992: Payoff. 1992: Ruby Cairo. 1993: The Judas Project. Beethoven's 2nd. 1994: Surviving the Game. The Color of Night.

CORRIGAN, Lloyd 1900–1969
Podgy American actor, best remembered from mainly light films in fussy, jovial or panicky roles. An actor until 1925, he worked as a screenwriter from 1926 to 1930 (and occasionally later), a director from 1930 to 1938 and an actor again from 1939 on, working mainly in television from 1955. The son of another popular character star, Lillian Elliott (1875–1959).

1925: The Splendid Crime. 1927: It. 1935: Atlantic Adventure. 1939: The Great Commandment. 1940: High School. The Ghost Breakers. *Jack Pot. Queen of the Mob. Sporting Blood. Captain Caution. The Return of Frank James. Dark Streets of Cairo. The Lady in Question. Two Girls on Broadway. Public Deb No. 1. 1941: Young Tom Edison. Men of Boys' Town. Mexican Spitfire's Baby. North of the Klondike. Whistling in the Dark. Kathleen. A Girl, a Guy and a Gob (GB: The Navy Steps Out). 1942: Confessions of Boston Blackie (GB: Confessions). Tennessee Johnson (GB: The Man on America's Conscience). The London Blackout Murders (GB: Secret Motive). Alias Boston Blackie. Bombay Clipper. Treat 'Em Rough. The Great Man's Lady. The Wife Takes a Flyer. Boston Blackie Goes Hollywood (GB: Blackie Goes Hollywood). The Mystery of Marie Roget. Lucky Jordan. The Mantrap. Maisie Gets Her Man (GB: She Got Her Man). 1943: Captive Wild Woman. Hitler's Children. After Midnight with Boston Blackie (GB: After Midnight). Stage Door Canteen. Nobody's Darling. Tarzan's Desert Mystery. Secrets of the Underworld. King of the Cowboys. Song of Nevada. 1944: Since You Went Away. Rosie the Riveter (GB: In Rosie's Room). Passport to Adventure. Gambler's Choice. Lights of Old Santa Fé. Goodnight, Sweetheart. Reckless Age. The Thin Man Goes Home. 1945: Bring on the Girls. Boston Blackie Booked on Suspicion (GB: Booked on Suspicion). The Fighting Guardsman. Lake Placid Serenade. Crime Doctor's Courage (GB: The Doctor's Courage). 1946: She-Wolf of London (GB: The Curse of the Allenbys). The Bandit of Sherwood Forest. Lady Luck. Two Smart People. The Chase. Alias Mr Twilight. 1947: Blaze of Noon. Stallion Road. The Ghost Goes Wild. Shadowed. 1948: A Date With Judy. Adventures of Casanova. The Return of October (GB: Date With Destiny). Mr Reckless. The Bride Goes Wild. Strike It Rich. The Big Clock. Homicide for Three (GB: An Interrupted Honeymoon). 1949: Blondie Hits the Jackpot (GB: Hitting the Jackpot). Home in San Antone. Dancing in the Dark. The Girl from Jones Beach. 1950: Father is a Bachelor. And Baby Makes Three. My Friend Irma Goes West. Cyrano de Bergerac. When Willie Comes Marching Home. 1951: The Last Outpost. Sierra Passage. Her First Romance (GB: Girls Never Tell). New Mexico. Ghost Chasers. 1952: Rainbow 'Round My Shoulder. Son of Paleface. Sound Off. 1953: Marry Me Again. The Stars Are Singing. 1954: Return from the Sea. The

Bowery Boys Meet the Monsters. 1955: Paris Follies of 1956. 1956: Hidden Guns 1962: The Manchurian Candidate. 1963: It's a Mad, Mad, Mad, Mad World.

As director:
1930: †Follow Thru. †Along Came Youth. 1931: Daughter of the Dragon. The Beloved Bachelor. 1932: The Broken Wing. No One Man. 1933: He Learned about Women. 1934: *La Cucuracha. 1935: Murder on a Honeymoon. 1936: The Dancing Pirate. 1937: Night Key. 1938: Lady Behave.

† Co-directed

COULOURIS, George 1903–1989
British actor with stiff dark hair, staring, baggy eyes and tightly clamped lips, features that got him cast in mean, villainous or even madman roles. He went to America in 1930, but his biggest impact there came 11 years later, as Walter Parks Thatcher in Citizen Kane, a role that set him up for eight years of good character parts, often in eccentric roles. His familiar mournful features, now moustachioed and bald, were back in British films after 1950. He died from a heart attack after suffering from Parkinson's Disease in later years.

1933: Christopher Bean (GB: The Late Christopher Bean). 1940: All This and Heaven Too. The Lady in Question. 1941: Citizen Kane. 1943: Assignment in Brittany. This Land Is Mine. For Whom the Bell Tolls. Watch on the Rhine. 1944: Between Two Worlds. Mr Skeffington. The Master Race. The Conspirators. None But the Lonely Heart. A Song to Remember. 1945: Hotel Berlin. Lady on a Train. Confidential Agent. 1946: Nobody Lives Forever. The Verdict. California. Mr District Attorney. 1947: Where There's Life. 1948: Sleep My Love. Beyond Glory. Joan of Arc. A Southern Yankee (GB: My Hero). 1950: Kill or Be Killed. 1951: Appointment With Venus (US: Island Rescue). Outcast of the Islands. 1952: Venetian Bird (US: The Assassin). 1953: The Heart of the Matter. A Day to Remember. The Dog and the Diamonds. The Runaway Bus. 1954: Doctor in the House. Duel in the Jungle. The Teckman Mystery. Mask of Dust (US: Race for Life). 1955: Private's Progress. Doctor at Sea. 1956: The Big Money (released 1958). 1957: Doctor at Large. The Man Without a Body. Kill Me Tomorrow. Seven Thunders (US: The Beasts of Marseilles). Tarzan and the Lost

Safari. I Accuse! 1958: Spy in the Sky. Woman-eater. No Time to Die! (US: Tank Force). Law and Disorder. Son of Robin Hood. 1960: Conspiracy of Hearts. Bluebeard's 10 Honeymoons. Surprise Package. 1961: King of Kings. Fury at Smuggler's Bay. The Boy Who Stole a Million. 1962: In the Cool of the Day. 1964: The Crooked Road. 1965: The Skull. Too Many Thieves (TV. GB: cinemas). 1966: Arabesque. 1967: Koroshi. 1968: The Assassination Bureau. 1969: Land Raiders. 1970: No Blade of Grass. 1971: Blood from the Mummy's Tomb. 1972: Tower of Evil (US: Horror of Snape Island). The Stranger (TV). 1973: The Suicide Club (TV). The Final Programme (US: The Last Days of Man on Earth). Coffee, Tea or Me? (TV). 1974: Mahler. Papillon. Percy's Progress (US: It's Not the Size That Counts). Murder on the Orient Express. 1976: The Antichrist (US: The Tempter). Shout at the Devil. The Ritz. 1979: The Long Good Friday. 1981: Beyond the Fog.

COWAN, Jerome 1897–1972

Dapper, moustachioed American actor with foxy smile who was nearly 40 when he came to films, but certainly made up for lost time in the next 15 years. His lack of inches confined him to just a few leading roles in the mid-forties, but his character work includes such memorable roles as the doomed Miles Archer in *The Maltese Falcon*, and Dagwood's boss in the later *Blondie* films.

1936: Beloved Enemy. 1937: New Faces of 1937: You Only Live Once. Shall We Dance? The Hurricane. Vogues of 1938. 1938: There's Always a Woman. The Goldwyn Follies. 1939: The Saint Strikes Back. St Louis Blues. The Gracie Allen Murder Case. The Great Victor Herbert. East Side of Heaven. She Married a Cop. The Old Maid. Exile Express. 1940: Wolf of New York. Framed. Castle on the Hudson (GB: Years Without Days). Meet the Wildcat. Ma, He's Making Eyes at Me. Torrid Zone. The Quarterback. City for Conquest. Street of Memories. Victory. Melody Ranch. 1941: High Sierra. Rags to Riches. The Roundup. Affectionately Yours. One Foot in Heaven. Kisses for Breakfast. Kiss the Boys Goodbye. Too Many Blondes. Mr and Mrs North. Singapore Woman. Out of the Fog. The Bugle Sounds. The Maltese Falcon. The Great Lie. 1942: Frisco Lil. The Girl from Alaska. Joan of Ozark (GB: Queen of Spies). Moontide. Thru Different Eyes. Who Done It?

A Gentleman at Heart. Street of Chance. 1943: The Song of Bernadette. Ladies' Day. Hi Ya, Sailor (GB: Everything Happens to Us). The Crime Doctor's Strangest Case (GB: The Strangest Case). Silver Spurs. Mission to Moscow. No Place for a Lady. Find the Blackmailer. 1944: Sing a Jingle (GB: Lucky Days). South of Dixie. Guest in the House. Crime by Night. Mr Skeffington. The Minstrel Man. 1945: Fog Island. Divorce. Getting Gertie's Garter. The Crime Doctor's Courage (GB: The Doctor's Courage). Hitchhike to Happiness. GI Honeymoon. Blonde Ransom. One Way to Love. Behind City Lights. Jungle Captive. 1946: My Reputation. Claudia and David. Murder in the Music Hall. The Kid from Brooklyn. Flight to Nowhere. One Exciting Week. Blondie Knows Best. Mr Ace. Deadline at Dawn. A Night in Paradise. Deadline for Murder. 1947: Blondie's Holiday. Driftwood. The Perfect Marriage. Riffraff. Miracle on 34th Street (GB: The Big Heart). The Unfaithful. Cry Wolf. Dangerous Years. Blondie's Anniversary. Blondie's Big Moment. Blondie in the Dough. 1948: So This is New York. Wallflower. Blondie's Reward. Arthur Takes Over. Night Has a Thousand Eyes. June Bride. 1949: Scene of the Crime. Blondie's Secret. Blondie Hits the Jackpot (GB: Hitting the Jackpot). Blondie's Big Deal (GB: The Big Deal). Always Leave Them Laughing. The Fountainhead. The Girl from Jones Beach. 1950: The West Point Story (GB: Fine and Dandy). Young Man with a Horn (GB: Young Man of Music). The Fuller Brush Girl (GB: The Affairs of Sally). Joe Palooka Meets Humphrey. Peggy. When You're Smiling. Dallas. 1951: Disc Jockey. The Fat Man. Criminal Lawyer. 1952: The Magnificent Adventure. 1953: The System. 1959: Have Rocket, Will Travel. 1960: Visit to a Small Planet. Private Property. 1961: All in a Night's Work. Pocketful of Miracles. 1963: Critic's Choice. Black Zoo. 1964: The Patsy. John Goldfarb, Please Come Home. 1965: Frankie and Johnny. 1966: Penelope. The Gnome-Mobile. 1969: The Comic.

COX, Ronny 1938–

Sandy-haired, pale-eyed American actor of slightful fretful looks and sideways glances. After studying drama at university and building up a substantial range on stage, he entered TV and films as the thinking man's average Joe. There was a sprinkling of leading roles along the way, but he'll be recalled

for his top supporting roles, often as slightly ineffectual, frustrated or treacherous figures of authority. He hasn't made a huge number of films but has been associated with some major box-office hits: probably best-known as the long-suffering Captain Bogomil in the first two *Beverly Hills Cop* films.

1972: The Happiness Cage/The Mind Snatchers. Deliverance. Madigan: The Manhattan Beat (TV). 1973: The Connection (TV). 1974: A Case of Rape (TV). 1975: Hugo the Hippo (voice only). Who is the Black Dahlia? (TV). 1976: Bound for Glory. Having Babies (TV). 1977: The Car. Gray Lady Down. The Girl Called Hatter Fox (TV). 1978: Harper Valley PTA. Lovey: A Circle of Children, Part II (TV). 1979: The Onion Field. Transplant (TV). Kavik the Wolf Dog (GB: The Courage of Kavik the Wolf Dog). When Hell Was in Session (TV). 1980: Fugitive Family (TV). Our Town (TV). The Last Song (TV). Alcatraz: The Whole Shocking Story (TV). One Last Ride. 1981: Fallen Angel (TV). Some Kind of Hero. Taps. 1982: The Beast Within. Two of a Kind (TV). 1983: Tangier. 1984: Beverly Hills Cop. Courage/Raw Courage. 1985: Vision Quest. Reckless Disregard (TV). 1986: Death Stalks the Big Top (TV). Hollywood Vice Squad. 1987: RoboCop. The Abduction of Kari Swenson (TV). Beverly Hills Cop II. Steele Justice. 1988: Target: Favorite Son (TV. Edited version of mini-series). The Comeback (TV). 1989: Loose Cannons. One Man Force. When We Were Young (TV). 1990: Total Recall. Captain America. 1991: Scissors. 1992: Perry Mason: The Case of the Heartbroken Bride (TV). 1993: Second Chances (TV). 1994: A Part of the Family (TV). Hard Evidence. Sweet Justice (TV).

CRAVAT, Nick 1911–1994

Diminutive (five feet two), black-bearded, dark-eyed, narrow-faced, acrobatic American actor, for many years the trapeze partner of Burt Lancaster in an act (Lang and Cravat) that toured circuses, nightclubs and vaudeville. After Lancaster was discovered for films, Cravat also headed for Hollywood, and they devised some swashbuckling stunts together for swashbuckling adventures of the early 1950s. He continued to pop up occasionally in pictures until his retirement in 1977. Often played mutes. Died from lung cancer in the same year as his old partner.

1949: My Friend Irma. 1950: Thelma Jordon (GB: The File on Thelma Jordon). The Flame and the Arrow. 1951: Ten Tall Men. 1952: The Crimson Pirate. 1953: The Veils of Baghdad. 1954: King Richard and the Crusaders. Three-Ring Circus. 1955: Davy Crockett—King of the Wild Frontier. Kiss Me Deadly. 1957: The Story of Mankind. 1958: Run Silent Run Deep. 1965: Cat Ballou. 1967: The Way West. 1968: The Scalphunters. 1970: Valdez is Coming. 1972: Ulzana's Raid. 1974: The Midnight Man. 1977: The Island of Dr Morean.

CRAVEN, Frank 1875–1945

Kindly-looking, apple-cheeked American actor who was a distinguished playwright before becoming a Hollywood character star in late middle age, chiefly as nice old sticks with an effective line in wise philosophy and sometimes as put-upon fathers. While doing this work, he also worked on screenplays and had leading roles in some minor 'family' films. Like the more acerbic Charles Coburn, Craven might well have acted on into his eighties had a heart ailment not intervened.

1928: We Americans (GB: The Heart of a Nation). 1929: The Very Idea. 1932: *The Putter. 1933: State Fair. 1934: That's Gratitude. City Limits. Funny Thing Called Love. He Was Her Man. Let's Talk It Over. 1935: Car 99. Vagabond Lady. Barbary Coast. 1936: Small Town Girl. The Harvester. 1937: Penrod and Sam. Blossoms on Broadway. 1938: You're Only Young Once. Penrod and His Twin Brother. 1939: Miracles for Sale. Our Neighbors, the Carters. 1940: Our Town. City for Conquest. Dreaming Out Loud. 1941: The Lady from Cheyenne. The Richest Man in Town. 1942: In This Our Life. Pittsburgh. Thru Different Eyes. Girl Trouble. Keeper of the Flame. 1943: Son of Dracula. Harrigan's Kid. Jack London. The Human Comedy. Dangerous Blondes. 1944: Destiny. My Best Gal. They Shall Have Faith/ Forever Yours (GB: The Right to Live). 1945: Colonel Effingham's Raid (GB: Man of the Hour).

As director:
1934: That's Gratitude.

CRAWFORD, John 1926–

Powerfully-built, brown-haired American actor of pudgy-faced handsomeness who, despite a not unlimited talent, clung to his

acting career with commendable tenacity, and widened his range in later years. He progressed slowly to minor leading roles in Hollywood by 1957, then crossed to Britain and did some of his best work there, before returning to America in 1964 and taking on some tough, sometimes villainous character parts. He has also written scripts. Not to be confused with actors John Robert Crawford (of Red Line 7000) or Johnny Crawford (of Indian Paint).

1944: Thoroughbreds. 1945: The Phantom of 42nd Street. 1946: The Time of Their Lives. Without Reservations. 1947: G-Men Never Forget (serial). 1948: Adventures of Frank and Jesse James (serial). Dangers of the Canadian Mounted (serial). Sons of Adventure. 1949: Chain Lightning. Ghost of Zorro (serial). 1950: The James Brothers of Missouri (serial). Invisible Monster (serial). Radar Patrol vs Spy King (serial). A Life of Her Own. Mystery Street. Twilight in the Sierras. Union Station. Cyrano de Bergerac. Raton Pass (GB: Canyon Pass). Lonely Hearts Bandits (GB: Lonely Heart Bandits). 1951: Northwest Territory. Honeychile. I Was a Communist for the FBI. 1952: Actors and Sin. Zombies of the Stratosphere (serial). The Greatest Show on Earth. Scaramouche. Stop, You're Killing Me. Old Oklahoma Plains. 1953: Marshal of Cedar Rock. Salome. The Big Heat. Conquest of Cochise. Rebel City. Secret of Outlaw Flats (originally for TV). Serpent of the Nile. Slaves of Babylon. Star of Texas. Man Crazy. Three Sailors and a Girl. 1954: Trader Tom of the China Seas (serial). Battle of Rogue River. Captain Kidd and the Slave Girl. 1956: The Man in the Gray Flannel Suit. 1957: Courage of Black Beauty. 1958: Satan's Satellites. The Space Children. Graft and Corruption. Orders to Kill. The Key. Intent to Kill. Floods of Fear. Blind Spot. 1959: The Devil's Messenger. John Paul Jones. Solomon and Sheba. Hell is a City. The Ghost of Zorro. 1960: Exodus. Piccadilly Third Stop. The Man Who Was Nobody. I Aim at the Stars. 1961: The Impersonator. The Long Shadow. 1962: Come Fly With Me. The 300 Spartans. The Longest Day. The Devil's Messenger. 1963: Jason and the Argonauts. Captain Sindbad. The Victors. 1964: The Americanization of Emily. 1965: Duel at Diablo. The Greatest Story Ever Told. I Saw What You Did. 1966: Return of the Gunfighter. 1967: El Dorado. 1969: La cattura (GB: The Ravine). 1970: Miss Jessica is Pregnant. 1971: J W Coop. 1972: Napoleon

and Samantha. Trouble Man. The Poseidon Adventure. Killer by Night (TV). 1973: Message to My Daughter (TV). The Severed Arm. 1974: The Towering Inferno. Strange Homecoming (TV). 1975: The Swiss Family Robinson (TV). Night Moves. Guilty or Innocent: The Sam Sheppard Murder Case (TV). 1976: The MacAhans (TV). The Enforcer. 1977: Outlaw Blues. 1978: The Two-Five (TV). Desperate Women (TV). Tilt. 1979: Hollywood Knight. Dreamer. The Apple Dumpling Gang Rides Again. 1981: The Boogens. Elvis and the Beauty Queen (TV). The Other Victim (TV). 1985: Jessie (TV).

CRISP, Donald 1880–1974

It's impossible to think of Donald Crisp as anything other than a crusty old shepherd, rancher or patriarch, the collective image from a fistful of 1940s films. But this Scottish-born actor who never lost his burr was a multi-talented man who began his career with D.W. Griffith in the early silent days, and directed many silent films, including some classics from the 1920s, when he also made films in Britain. Won an Oscar in 1941 for How Green Was My Valley and, in his nineties and retired, took to haranguing interviewers with splendidly cantankerous views on 'modern' movies. A grand old man indeed.

1907: *The French Maid. 1909: *Through the Breakers. 1910: *The Two Paths. *Fate's Turning. *Winning Back His Love. *Sunshine Sue. *A Plain Story. *A Child's Stratagem. *Effecting a Cure. *The Golden Supper. 1911: *The Battle. *The Failure. *What Shall We Do With Our Old? *A Wreath of Orange Blossoms. *The Primal Call. *The Diving Girl. *Out from the Shadow. *The Adventures of Billy. *The Poor Sick Man. *The Italian Barber. *In the Days of '49. *Help Wanted. *The White Rose of the Wilds: A Story of the West. *The Miser's Heart. *Heartbeats of Long Ago. *A Decree of Destiny. *Conscience. *Swords and Hearts. *The Squaw's Love. *Her Awakening. *The Making of a Man. *The Long Road. 1912: *When Kings Were the Law. *The Best Man Wins. *The Musketeers of Pig Alley. *The Eternal Mother. 1913: *Pirate Gold. *The Sheriff's Baby. *Drinks Lure. *Two Men of the Desert. *Black and White. *The Daytime Burglar. *The Blue or the Gray. *By Man's Law. *In the Elemental World. *The Mothering

Heart. *Olaf — an Atom. *The Bracelet. 1914: *The Different Man. The Battle of the Sexes. The Escape. Home, Sweet Home. The Mountain Rat. *The Tavern of Tragedy. *The Sisters. *The Mysterious Shot. The Avenging Conscience. *The Newer Woman. *The Warning. The Great Leap. *The Stiletto. *The Miniature Portrait. *Soul of Honor. *Her Birthday Present. On the Brink. *The Weaker Strain. *Down the Hill to Creditville. *The Great God Fear. *His Mother's Trust. *The Niggard. *Another Chance. *A Question of Courage. *Over the Ledge. 1915: *An Old-Fashioned Girl. *How Hazel Got Even. The Birth of a Nation. The Love Route. The Commanding Officer. A Girl of Yesterday. The Foundling. May Blossom. Such a Little Queen. Bred in the Bone. 1916: *By Man's Law. Intolerance. Joan the Woman. Ramona. 1917: The Countess Charming. 1918: One More American. 1919: Broken Blossoms. 1921: Beside the Bonnie Brier Bush (US: The Bonnie Brier Bush). 1925: Don Q Son of Zorro. 1926: The Black Pirate. 1928: The Viking. Stand and Deliver. The River Pirate. 1929: Trent's Last Case. The Pagan. The Return of Sherlock Holmes. 1930: Scotland Yard (GB: Detective Clive, Bart). 1931: Svengali. Kick In. 1932: A Passport to Hell (GB: Burnt Offering). Red Dust. 1933: Broadway Bad (GB: Her Reputation). 1934: The Crime Doctor. The Little Minister. The Key. The Life of Vergie Winters. What Every Woman Knows. 1935: Vanessa. Her Love Story. Laddie. Mutiny on the Bounty. Oil for the Lamps of China. 1936: Mary of Scotland. The Charge of the Light Brigade. The White Angel. A Woman Rebels. The Great O'Malley. Beloved Enemy. 1937: Parnell. The Life of Emile Zola. That Certain Woman. Confession. Sergeant Murphy. 1938: Jezebel. The Amazing Dr Clitterhouse. Valley of the Giants. The Beloved Brat (GB: A Dangerous Age). The Sisters. The Dawn Patrol. Comet over Broadway. 1939: Juarez. The Old Maid. Wuthering Heights. The Oklahoma Kid. Daughters Courageous. The Private Lives of Elizabeth and Essex. 1940: The Story of Dr Ehrlich's Magic Bullet (GB: Dr Ehrlich's Magic Bullet). Brother Orchid. The Sea Hawk. City for Conquest. Knute Rockne—All-American (GB: A Modern Hero). 1941: Dr Jekyll and Mr Hyde. Shining Victory. How Green Was My Valley. 1942: The Gay Sisters. *The Battle of Midway (narrator only). 1943: Forever and a Day. Lassie Come Home. 1944: The Uninvited. The Adventures of Mark Twain. National Velvet. 1945: Son of Lassie. The Valley of Decision. 1947: Ramrod. 1948: Whispering Smith. Hills of Home (GB: Master of Lassie). 1949: Challenge to Lassie. 1950: Bright Leaf. 1951: Home Town Story. 1954: Prince Valiant. The Long Gray Line. *The Red, White and Blue Line. 1955: The Man from Laramie. 1957: Drango. 1958: Saddle the Wind. The Last Hurrah. 1959: The Raider (TV). A Dog of Flanders. 1960: Pollyanna. 1961: Greyfriars Bobby. 1963: Spencer's Mountain.

As director:
1914: *On the Brink. *The Weaker Strain. *The Great God Fear. *The Niggard. *Another Chance. *The Dawn. *The Mysterious Shot. *The Newer Woman. *The Idiot. *The Tavern of Tragedy. *The Milkfed Boy. *Her Father's Silent Partner. *Her Birthday Present. *Their

First Acquaintance. *Her Mother's Necklace. *Down the Hill to Creditville. *The Warning. *His Mother's Trust. *Sands of Fate. *The Availing Prayer. *His Lesson. *Frenchy. 1915: *Paid with Interest. *An Old-Fashioned Girl. 1916: Ramona. 1917: His Sweetheart. The Bond Between. A Roadside Impresario. The Marcellini Millions. The Cook of Canyon Camp. Lost in Transit. The Clever Mrs Carfax. The Countess Charming. 1918: Jules of the Strong Heart. The House of Silence. Less Than Kin. Venus in the East. Under the Top. Believe Me Xanthippe. The Firefly of France. The Goat. The Way of a Man with a Maid. Rimrock Jones. 1919: Johnny Get Your Gun. Poor Boob. Why Smith Left Home. Love Insurance. Too Much Johnson. Something to Do. Putting It Over. A Very Good Young Man. It Pays to Advertise. 1920: The Six Best Cellars. Miss Hobbs. Held by the Enemy. 1921: The Barbarian. Appearances. The Princess of New York. Beside the Bonnie Brier Bush (US: The Bonnie Brier Bush). 1922: Tell Your Children. 1923: Ponjola. 1925: Don Q Son of Zorro. 1926: Young April. Man Bait. Sunny Side Up (GB: Footlights). 1927: Vanity. Dress Parade. Nobody's Widow. The Fighting Eagle (GB: Brigadier Gerard). 1928: The Cop. Stand and Deliver. 1930: The Runaway Bride.

As co-director:
1915: *How Hazel Got Even. 1924: The Navigator.

CRONYN, Hume
(H.C. Blake) 1911–

Short, skinny, waspish Canadian actor with reedy voice, narrow face and frowning brows, often as nosey parkers, henpecked husbands or sadistic pint-size villains. He was little seen in pictures after the 1940s, preferring stage work with his wife Jessica Tandy (married 1942), although he contributed to the scripts of a couple of Hitchcock films in the late 1940s. Never seemed to alter much in aspect on his infrequent appearances thereafter, despite the loss of an eye in 1970. Oscar nomination for *The Seventh Cross. He and his wife made several popular films together in the late 1980s and the early 1990s before her death in 1994.

1943: Shadow of a Doubt. Phantom of the Opera. The Cross of Lorraine. 1944: Lifeboat. The Seventh Cross. Blonde Fever. An American Romance. Main Street After Dark. Ziegfeld

Follies (released 1946). 1945: A Letter for Evie. The Sailor Takes a Wife. 1946: The Green Years. The Postman Always Rings Twice. The Secret Heart (narrator only). 1947: The Beginning or the End? Brute Force. 1948: The Bride Goes Wild. 1949: Top o' the Morning. 1951: People Will Talk. 1956: Crowded Paradise. 1960: Sunrise at Campobello. 1963: Cleopatra. 1964: *Miracle in Minnesota. Hamlet. 1969: The Arrangement. Gaily, Gaily (GB: Chicago, Chicago). 1970: There Was a Crooked Man. 1974: The Parallax View. Conrack. 1981: Honky Tonk Freeway. Roll-Over. 1982: The World According to Garp. 1984: Impulse. 1985: Brewster's Millions. Cocoon. 1987: *Batteries Not Included (the * is part of the title of this film). Foxfire (TV). 1988: Cocoon: The Return. 1989: Age-Old Friends (TV. GB: A Month of Sundays). Day One (TV). 1991: Broadway Bound (TV. GB: cinemas). Christmas on Division Street (TV). 1993: The Pelican Brief. 1994: Camilla. To Dance with the White Dog (TV).

CROSSLEY, Syd 1885–1960
Gangling London-born comic actor, a popular favourite of the British music-halls (where he was billed as 'The Long Comic') who went to America and worked in vaudeville before a brief visit to Hollywood. Back in England from 1929, he slipped quickly into cockney character roles in a fistful of cheap comedies, giving yeoman support to most of the British cinema's comedy stars of the period. Began his stage career as a boy of 14 singing comedy songs.

1925: Keep Smiling. North Star. 1926: The Unknown Soldier. *Mama Behave. The Golden Web. One Hour Married. 1927: The Gorilla. Ain't Love Funny? Jewels of Desire. The Romantic Rogue. Play Safe. The Blood Ship. 1928: Fangs of the Wild. The Circus Kid. *Loud Soup. A Perfect Gentleman. The Cowboy Kid. That Certain Thing. Into No Man's Land (GB: The Secret Lie). 1929: The Younger Generation. The Hate Ship. Atlantic. The Fatal Warning (serial). Pride of Donegal. Just for a Song. 1930: Suspense. The Man from Chicago. *The Musical Beauty Shop. The Middle Watch. 1931: The Flying Fool. Never Trouble Trouble. The Professional Guest. Men Like These (US: Trapped in a Submarine). Tonight's the Night—Pass It On. 1932: The Mayor's Nest. High Society. *On the Air. For the Love of Mike.

Lucky Ladies. The Last Coupon. Here's George. 1933: The King's Cup. Letting in the Sunshine. Leave It to Me. Excess Baggage. The Medicine Man. The Umbrella. Meet My Sister. You Made Me Love You. The Bermondsey Kid. 1934: Master and Man. Night Club Queen. Open All Night. Those Were the Days. Gay Love. It's a Bet. Eighteen Minutes. Dandy Dick. Radio Parade of 1935 (US: Radio Follies). Bagged. Over the Garden Wall. Give Her a Ring. 1935: Me and Marlborough. The Deputy Drummer. Honeymoon for Three. Royal Cavalcade (US: Regal Cavalcade). Jimmy Boy. Music Hath Charms. One Good Turn. The Ghost Goes West. Public Nuisance No. 1. 1936: The Man Behind the Mask. Everything is Rhythm. Cheer Up. Queen of Hearts. Two's Company. Paybox Adventure. Keep Your Seats, Please. The Limping Man. Sporting Love. Double Alibi. Full Speed Ahead. The Man in the Mirror. 1937: Silver Blaze. Sensation. The Gang Show. The Dark Stairway. The Squeaker (US: Murder on Diamond Row). Lucky Jade. Feather Your Nest. Pearls Bring Tears. Boys Will Be Girls. Victoria the Great. There Was a Young Man. Old Mother Riley. Racketeer Rhythm. Cotton Queen. Young and Innocent (US: The Girl Was Young). Sweet Devil. 1938: The Return of Carol Deane. Everything Happens to Me. His Lordship Goes to Press. *Peter's Pence. Save a Little Sunshine. Little Dolly Daydream. We're Going to be Rich. Penny Paradise. 1939: *Oh Dear Uncle. Meet Maxwell Archer (US: Maxwell Archer, Detective). Come On George! 1940: *Open House. 1941: Old Mother Riley's Circus. 1942: Let the People Sing.

CROTHERS, Scatman
(Benjamin Crothers) 1909–1986
Engaging black American musician and spare-time actor of stringy build. A singer-drummer-musician at local speakeasies when only 14, Crothers had formed his own band by the 1930s, and subsequently wrote hundreds of tunes. He briefly visited films in the early 1950s but, after supplying the voice for Scatcat in Disney's cartoon The Aristocats, he brought his infectious grin and husky tones to a good range of screen veteran characterizations. His name derived from the jazz word 'scatting' — improvising nonsense syllables to a melody. Died from lung cancer.

1951: Yes Sir, Mr Bones. 1952: Meet Me at the Fair. 1953: Walking My Baby Back Home.

East of Sumatra. 1954: Johnny Dark. 1956: Between Heaven and Hell. 1958: Tarzan and the Trappers (TV). 1960: The Sins of Rachel Cade. 1963: Lady in a Cage. 1964: The Patsy. 1966: Three on a Couch. 1969: Hello, Dolly! Hook, Line and Sinker. Bloody Mama. 1970: The Aristocats (voice only). The Great White Hope. 1971: Chandler. 1972: Lady Sings the Blues. The King of Marvin Gardens. 1973: Detroit 9000 (GB: Call Detroit 9000). Black Belt Jones. Slaughter's Big Rip-Off. 1974: The Fortune. Truck Turner. Win, Place or Steal/Three for the Money. 1975: Friday Foster. Man on the Outside (TV). Linda Lovelace for President. One Flew Over the Cuckoo's Nest. Coonskin (voice only). 1976: Stay Hungry. Chesty Anderson, US Navy/Anderson's Angels. Silver Streak. The Shootist. 1978: The Cheap Detective. Mean Dog Blues. Vegas (TV). 1979: Scavenger Hunt. 1980: Bronco Billy. The Shining. 1981: The Harlem Globetrotters on Gilligan's Island (TV). Deadly Eyes. 1982: Zapped! Missing Children: A Mother's Story (TV). 1983: Twilight Zone The Movie/The Twilight Zone. Two of a Kind. 1985: The Journey of Natty Gann. 1986: The Transformers — The Movie (voice only). Smart Alec.

CROWDEN, Graham 1922–
Very tall, rangy British actor with disappearing straggly fair hair and gleefully ghoulish grin. An experienced Shakespearian performer, he came to film prominence playing eccentric roles in films directed by Lindsay Anderson. He has been seen as his mournfully mirthful self in too few other films, sometimes as mad professors or priests who should probably be defrocked. Would make a wonderful Marley's Ghost.

1959: The Bridal Path. 1961: Don't Bother to Knock! (US: Why Bother to Knock?). 1964: One Way Pendulum. 1965: Dead Man's Chest. 1966: Morgan — A Suitable Case for Treatment (US: Morgan). 1968: The File of the Golden Goose. If . . . 1969: The Virgin Soldiers. 1970: Leo the Last. The Rise and Rise of Michael Rimmer. 1971: Percy (shown 1970). The Night Digger. Up the Chastity Belt. The Ruling Class. Something to Hide. 1972: The Amazing Mr Blunden. 1973: O Lucky Man! The Final Programme (US: The Last Days of Man on Earth). 1974: The Abdication. The Little Prince. *Romance with a Double Bass. 1976: Star Maidens. 1977: Hardcore (US: Fiona). Jabber-

wocky. 1981: For Your Eyes Only. *Out of Order. 1982: Britannia Hospital. The Missionary. 1984: The Company of Wolves. 1985: Code Name: Emerald. Out of Africa. 1987: Didn't You Kill My Brother? 1990: Kremlin Farewell (TV). 1993: Final Curtain (TV). 1995: The Innocent Sleep.

CRUTCHLEY, Rosalie 1921–
Probably the British actress you would most expect to find behind the creaking door of a haunted house, this slim, black-haired, gloomy-looking lady was a dyed-in-the-wool stage player who made her theatrical debut at 17. She played a violinist who gets bumped off in her first film, a touch of gloom and doom which set the pattern for her movie career. Theatre gave her a better range of roles; it's a medium in which she still remains busy.

1947: Take My Life. 1949: Give Us This Day/Salt to the Devil. 1950: Prelude to Fame. 1951: The Lady With a Lamp. Quo Vadis? 1953: Malta Story. The Sword and the Rose. 1954: Make Me an Offer. Flame and the Flesh. 1956: The Spanish Gardener. The Gamma People. 1957: Miracle in Soho. Seven Thunders (US: The Beasts of Marseilles). No Time for Tears. 1958: A Tale of Two Cities. 1959: Beyond This Place (US: Web of Evidence). The Nun's Story. 1960: Sons and Lovers. Greyfriars Bobby. 1961: *Frederic Chopin. No Love for Johnnie. 1962: Freud (GB: Freud—The Secret Passion). 1963: Girl in the Headlines (US: The Model Murder Case). The Haunting. 1964: Behold a Pale Horse. 1970: Wuthering Heights. 1971: Creatures the World Forgot. Blood from the Mummy's Tomb. Whoever Slew Auntie Roo? (US: Who Slew Auntie Roo?). 1972: Man of La Mancha. Au Pair Girls. 1973: . . . And Now the Screaming Starts. *The Return. The House in Nightmare Park (US: Crazy House). 1974: Mahler. 1976: The Message/Mohammed, Messenger of God. 1982: The Hunchback of Notre Dame (TV). 1983: Memed My Hawk. The Keep. 1985: Eleni. 1987: A World Apart. Little Dorrit I. Little Dorrit II. 1990: The Fool. 1992: God on the Rocks (TV). 1993: Femme Fatale (TV). Four Weddings and a Funeral.

CULVER, Roland 1900–1984
Neat, good-looking, dark-haired English actor with good-natured features that turned owlish in later life. He was usually seen in

drily humorous upper-crust roles. He unspectacularly built up one of the longest careers in the British cinema: a visit to Hollywood from 1946 to 1949 brought a few decent roles, but came too late to make him a star name in America. Died from a heart attack.

*1930: Flat Number Nine. 1931: 77 Park Lane. Fascination. 1932: COD. A Voice Said Goodnight. There Goes the Bride. Love on Wheels. Her First Affaire. Puppets of Fate (US: Wolves of the Underworld). 1933: Head of the Family. Her Imaginary Lover. Mayfair Girl. 1934: Father and Son. Lucky Loser. Two Hearts in Waltztime. The Scoop. Nell Gwyn. Borrow a Million. 1935: Oh, What a Night! 1936: Crime Over London. Accused. 1937: Jump for Glory (US: When Thief Meets Thief). Paradise for Two (US: The Gaiety Girls). 1939: French Without Tears. Blind Folly. 1940: The Girl in the News. *Dangerous Comment. Night Train to Munich (US: Night Train). Fingers. Old Bill and Son. 1941: This England. Quiet Wedding. 1942: One of Our Aircraft is Missing. Unpublished Story. The Day Will Dawn (US: The Avengers). Talk About Jacqueline. The First of the Few (US: Spitfire). Secret Mission. 1943: Dear Octopus (US: The Randolph Family). The Life and Death of Colonel Blimp (US: Colonel Blimp). 1944: On Approval. Give Us the Moon. English Without Tears (US: Her Man Gilbey). 1945: Perfect Strangers (US: Vacation from Marriage). Dead of Night. 1946: Wanted for Murder. To Each His Own. 1947: Down to Earth. Singapore. 1948: The Emperor Waltz. Isn't It Romantic? 1949: The Great Lover. 1950: Trio. 1951: The Late Edwina Black (US: Obsessed). The Magic Box. Encore. Hotel Sahara. 1952: The Holly and the Ivy. The Hour of 13. Folly to be Wise. 1953: Rough Shoot (US: Shoot First). 1954: Betrayed. The Teckman Mystery. The Man Who Loved Redheads. 1955: The Ship That Died of Shame (US: PT Raiders). An Alligator Named Daisy. Touch and Go (US: The Light Touch). 1956: Safari. 1957: The Hypnotist (US: Scotland Yard Dragnet). Light Fingers. The Vicious Circle (US: The Circle). 1958: The Truth About Women. Bonjour Tristesse. Rockets Galore (US: Mad Little Island). Next to No Time! 1961: A Pair of Briefs. 1962: Term of Trial. The Iron Maiden (US: The Swingin' Maiden). 1964: The Yellow Rolls Royce. 1965: Thunderball. 1966: A Man Could Get Killed. 1968: In Search of Gregory. 1969: The Magic Christian.*

1970: The Rise and Rise of Michael Rimmer. Fragment of Fear. 1973: Bequest to a Nation (US: The Nelson Affair). The Legend of Hell House. The Mackintosh Man. 1977: The Uncanny. 1978: The Greek Tycoon. No Longer Alone. 1980: Never Never Land. Rough Cut. 1982: Britannia Hospital. The Missionary. The Hunchback of Notre Dame (TV).

CUNNINGHAM, Cecil 1888–1959
Austere-looking, solidly-built American actress with close-cropped hair, disapproving mouth and hooded eyes. She looked as though she would be easily offended and brook no nonsense, but in fact Cunningham was most at home in comedy, especially as jaded aunts or eccentric secretaries. She did have several stabs at stony-faced villainy, but was less effective and sometimes over the top. Her trademark in comedy was a 'tongue-in-cheek' reaction, one of her many little tics that could convey more than words. Once an opera singer, she came to films with the advent of sound, and stayed until she was 60. Died from arteriosclerosis.

*1929: Their Own Desire. 1930: Paramount on Parade. Anybody's Woman. Playboy of Paris. 1931: Monkey Business. Susan Lenox, Her Fall and Rise (GB: The Rise of Helga). Safe in Hell (GB: The Lost Lady). Mata Hari. Age for Love. 1932: *Never the Twins Shall Meet. *Trouble from Abroad. It's Tough to be Famous. The Impatient Maiden. Love is a Racket. The Wet Parade. The Rich Are Always with Us. Those We Love. If I Had a Million. Blonde Venus. *Just a Pain in the Parlor. Love Me Tonight. *The Candid Camera. 1933: Ladies They Talk About. Baby Face. From Hell to Heaven. *The Druggist's Dilemma. 1934: The Life of Vergie Winters. Manhattan Love Song. We Live Again. People Will Talk. †Bottoms Up. 1935: People Will Talk. 1936: Mr Deeds Goes to Town. Come and Get It. 1937: Swing High – Swing Low. Daughter of Shanghai. Night Club Scandal. The Awful Truth. This Way Please. Artists and Models. King of Gamblers. 1938: Blonde Cheat. College Swing (GB: Swing, Teacher, Swing). Four Men and a Prayer. Girls' School. Kentucky Moonshine (GB: Three Men and a Girl). Marie Antoinette. Scandal Street. Wives Under Suspicion. You and Me. 1939: The Family Next Door. It's a Wonderful World. Lady of the Tropics. Laugh It*

Off. Winter Carnival. 1940: The Captain is a Lady. The Great Profile. Kitty Foyle. Lillian Russell. New Moon. Play Girl. 1941: Back Street. Blossoms in the Dust. Hurry, Charlie, Hurry. Repent at Leisure. 1942: Cairo. Cowboy Serenade (GB: Serenade of the West). Are Husbands Necessary? The Hidden Hand. The Affairs of Martha (GB: Once Upon a Thursday). I Married an Angel. Twin Beds. The Wife Takes a Flyer. 1943: Du Barry Was a Lady. Above Suspicion. In Old Oklahoma (GB: War of the Wildcats). 1945: The Horn Blows at Midnight. †Saratoga Trunk. Wonder Man. 1946: My Reputation. 1948: The Bride Goes Wild.

† Scenes deleted from final release print

CURRIE, Finlay
(F. Jefferson) 1878–1968
Dour, craggy, heavily-built Scottish actor, with powerful, distinctive features, shambling gait and a mass of latterly white hair. A former organist and music-hall singer, he broke into films with the coming of sound, often playing Americans. He continued playing rugged action roles (typically as the convict Magwitch in *Great Expectations*) into his sixties and seventies.

*1931: The Old Man. 1932: The Frightened Lady (US: Criminal at Large). Rome Express. 1933: No Funny Business. It's a Boy. Excess Baggage. Orders is Orders. The Good Companions. 1934: Princess Charming. Little Friend. Mister Cinders. Gay Love. In Town Tonight. My Old Dutch. 1935: The Big Splash. The Improper Duchess. 1936: The Gay Adventure. 1937: Wanted. Catch As Catch Can. Glamorous Night. Command Performance. The Edge of the World. Paradise for Two (US: The Gaiety Girls). 1938: The Claydon Treasure Mystery. Around the Town. Follow Your Star. 1939: *Hospital Hospitality. 1940: Crooks' Tour. 1941: 49th Parallel. Major Barbara. 1942: The Day Will Dawn (US: The Avengers). Thunder Rock. 1943: The Bells Go Down. Undercover (US: Underground Guerillas). Warn That Man. They Met in the Dark. Theatre Royal. The Shipbuilders. 1945: Don Chicago. I Know Where I'm Going! The Trojan Brothers. 1946: Spring Song (US: Springtime). Woman to Woman. Great Expectations. School for Secrets (US: Secret Flight). 1947: The Brothers. 1948: Sleeping Car to Trieste. My Brother Jonathan. So Evil My Love. Mr Perrin and Mr Traill. Bonnie Prince Charlie. 1949: Edward My Son. The History of Mr Polly. Whisky Galore (US:*

Tight Little Island). (narrator only). 1950: The Black Rose. Treasure Island. My Daughter Joy (US: Operation X). Trio. The Mudlark. 1951: People Will Talk. Quo Vadis? 1952: Kangaroo. Stars and Stripes Forever (GB: Marching Along). Ivanhoe. Walk East on Beacon (GB: Crime of the Century). 1953: Rob Roy the Highland Rogue. *Prince Philip (narrator only). Treasure of the Golden Condor. 1954: The End of the Road. Beau Brummell. Captain Lightfoot. Make Me an Offer. 1955: Third Party Risk (US: The Deadly Game). Footsteps in the Fog. King's Rhapsody. 1956: Around the World in 80 Days. Zarak. 1957: The Little Hut. Seven Waves Away (US: Abandon Ship!). Saint Joan. Campbell's Kingdom. Dangerous Exile. 1958: Tempest. The Naked Earth. Six-Five Special. Corridors of Blood. Rockets Galore (US: Mad Little Island) (narrator only). 1959: Ben-Hur. Solomon and Sheba. 1960: Kidnapped. Hand in Hand. The Adventures of Huckleberry Finn. The Angel Wore Red. Giuseppe venduto dai fratelli (GB. Sold into Egypt. US: The Story of Joseph and His Brethren). 1961: Five Golden Hours. Francis of Assisi. Clue of the Silver Key. 1962: Go to Blazes. The Amorous Prawn (US: The Playgirl and the War Minister). The Inspector (US: Lisa). 1963: Billy Liar! The Cracksman. West 11. The Three Lives of Thomasina. The Fall of the Roman Empire. Cleopatra. Murder at the Gallop. 1964: Who Was Maddox? 1965: The Battle of the Villa Fiorita. Bunny Lake is Missing.

CURTIS, Alan
(Harold Neberroth) 1909–1953
Tall, dark-haired, blue-eyed American actor of narrow, chiselled features and vaguely shiftless handsomeness. A former male model, he achieved some prominence in Hollywood in the war years and played B-feature heroes and detectives, but also a number of villains and weak links. Briefly married to actress Ilona Massey (1910–1974), first of two. Died after a kidney operation at 43.

1936: The Smartest Girl in Town. Walking on Air. Winterset. 1937: Bad Gun. China Passage. Don't Tell the Wife. Between Two Women. 1938: The Duke of West Point. Mannequin. Shopworn Angel. Yellow Jack. 1939: Burn 'Em Up O'Connor. Good Girls Go to Paris. Hollywood Cavalcade. Sergeant Madden. 1940: Four Sons. 1941: Come Live With Me. Buck Privates

(GB: Rookies). The Great Awakening. High Sierra. New Wine. We Go Fast. 1942: Remember Pearl Harbor. 1943: Crazy House. Gung Ho. Hitler's Madman. Two Tickets to London. 1944: Destiny. Follow the Boys. Phantom Lady. The Invisible Man's Revenge. 1945: The Daltons Ride Again. Frisco Sal. The Naughty Nineties. See My Lawyer. Shady Lady. 1946: Inside Job. 1947: Flight to Nowhere. Philo Vance's Secret Mission. Renegade Girl. Philo Vance's Gamble. 1948: Enchanted Valley. 1949: The Pirates of Capri/Captain Sirocco (GB: The Masked Pirate). Apache Chief.

CUSACK, Cyril 1910–1993
South African-born, Ireland-bred character star with sandy hair — best-known for fey, whimsical or scruffy roles, but capable of a wide range of characterization. Stocky, thin-lipped and mischievous-looking, he made films all over the world, whether as menace, semi-lead or comic relief, and continued to remain active into his eighties. Father of actresses Sinead, Sorcha, Niamh and Catherine Cusack. Died from motor-neurone disease.

1918: Knocknagow. 1935: Late Extra. The Man Without a Face. 1936: Servants All. 1941: Inspector Hornleigh Goes to It (US: Mail Train). Once a Crook. 1946: Odd Man Out. 1948: Esther Waters. Escape. Once a Jolly Swagman (US: Maniacs on Wheels). The Small Back Room. All Over the Town. 1949: The Blue Lagoon. Christopher Columbus. 1950: Gone to Earth (US: The Wild Heart). The Elusive Pimpernel (US: The Fighting Pimpernel). 1951: Soldiers Three. The Secret of Convict Lake. The Blue Veil. 1953: Saadia. 1954: The Last Moment. Destination Milan. 1955: Passage Home. The Man Who Never Was. 1956: Jacqueline. The Man in the Road. The March Hare. The Spanish Gardener. 1957: Ill-Met by Moonlight (US: Night Ambush). The Rising of the Moon. Miracle in Soho. 1958: Floods of Fear. Gideon's Day (US: Gideon of Scotland Yard). 1959: Shake Hands With the Devil. 1960: A Terrible Beauty (US: Night Fighters). 1961: The Power and the Glory (TV. GB: cinemas). Johnny Nobody. 1962: Waltz of the Torcadors. I Thank a Fool. Lawrence of Arabia. 1963: 80,000 Suspects. 1965: The Spy Who Came in from the Cold. Where the Spies Are. I Was Happy Here (US: Time Lost and Time Remembered). 1966: Fahrenheit 451. The

Taming of the Shrew. 1967: Oedipus the King. 1968: Galileo. 1969: David Copperfield (TV. GB: cinemas). Country Dance (US: Brotherly Love). 1970: King Lear. 1971: Harold and Maude. Tam Lin (GB: The Devil's Widow). Le polizia ringrazia (GB: The Law Enforcers. US: Execution Squad). Sacco and Vanzetti. 1972: The Hands of Cormac Joyce (TV). La 'mala' ordina (GB: Manhunt in Milan). Più forte ragazzi (GB: All the Way, Boys). 1973: Catholics (TV). The Homecoming. La mano spietata delle legge (GB: The Bloody Hands of the Law). 1974: The Abdication. Juggernaut. Run Run Joe. 1975: The Last Circus Show. 1976: Jesus of Nazareth (TV). 1977: Children of Rage. 1978: Les Misérables (TV). Poitín. Cry of the Innocent (TV). 1979: Tristan and Isolt/Lovespell (unreleased). 1981: True Confessions. The Outcasts. 1982: The Kingfisher. 1983: Dr Fischer of Geneva (TV). 1984: 1984. 1986: The Fantasist. 1987: Little Dorrit I. Little Dorrit II. 1988: The Tenth Man (TV). 1989: Danny, the Champion of the World (TV. GB: cinemas). My Left Foot. 1990: The Fool. 1992: Far and Away. Memento Mori (TV). As You Like It.

CUSACK, Joan 1962–
American comic actress of pixie-like prettiness, with sparkling eyes and wild, dark hair. Sometimes seen as the heroine's friend, her characters are often eccentric and usually eye-catching. Became known as a comedienne during a stint on TV's late-night comedy show Saturday Night Live in her early twenties; films have, on the whole, not yet used her talents often enough. Older sister of actor John Cusack. Oscar nominee for Working Girl.

1980: My Bodyguard. 1983: Taps. Class. 1984: Grandview USA. Sixteen Candles. 1987: The Allnighter. Broadcast News. 1988: Working Girl. Stars and Bars. Married to the Mob. 1989: Men Don't Leave. Say Anything. Heart of Midnight. 1990: My Blue Heaven. 1991: The Cabinet of Dr Ramirez. 1992: Hero (GB: Accidental Hero). Toys. 1993: Addams Family Values. 1994: Love Affair. Corrina, Corrina. 1995: Nine Months. Two Much. Mr Wrong.

CUTHBERTSON, Allan 1920–1988
Tall, very fair-haired, moustachioed Australian-born actor of occasional crocodile smile and icily imperious demeanour. Almost

always in unsympathetic roles, whether as coward, traitor, snob, wrong-headed administrator, vindictive officer or killer. It was mostly on television, though, that he revealed the other side of his talent, as a (very) straight-faced foil for some top comedians.

*1953: The Million Pound Note (US: Man with a Million). 1954: Carrington VC (US: Court-Martial). 1955: Portrait of Alison (US: Postmark for Danger). The Man Who Never Was. Cloak Without Dagger (US: Operation Conspiracy). 1956: Anastasia. On Such a Night. *Dick Turpin – Highwayman. Eyewitness. Doublecross. 1957: Barnacle Bill (US: All at Sea). Yangtse Incident (US: Battle Hell). The Passionate Stranger (US: A Novel Affair). 1958: Law and Disorder. Ice Cold in Alex (US: Desert Attack). I Was Monty's Double (US: Monty's Double). Room at the Top. 1959: The Devil's Disciple. The Crowning Touch. Shake Hands With the Devil. The Stranglers of Bombay. Killers of Kilimanjaro. 1960: Tunes of Glory. 1961: The Guns of Navarone. On the Double. The Malpas Mystery. Man at the Carlton Tower. 1962: Freud (GB: Freud – The Secret Passion). The Boys. Solo for Sparrow. The Fast Lady. Term of Trial. Vengeance (US: The Brain). Nine Hours to Rama. 1963: The Informers. Tamahine. Bitter Harvest. The Mouse on the Moon. The Running Man. A Jolly Bad Fellow (US: They All Died Laughing). 1964: The 7th Dawn. 1965: Life at the Top. Cast a Giant Shadow. Operation Crossbow (US: The Great Spy Mission). Game for Three Losers. 1966: Press for Time. 1967: Half a Sixpence. Jules Verne's Rocket to the Moon (US: Those Fantastic Flying Fools). The Trygon Factor. 1968: Captain Nemo and the Underwater City. 1969: Sinful Davey. The Body Stealers (US: Thin Air). 1970: Assault (US: In the Devil's Garden). The Adventurers. The Firechasers. One More Time. Performance. 1971: The Railway Children. 1972: Diamonds on Wheels. 1976: The Chiffy Kids (series). 1979: The Outsider. 1980: Hopscotch. The Sea Wolves. The Mirror Crack'd. 1983: Invitation to the Wedding. 1985: Thirteen at Dinner (TV). 1986: East of Ipswich (TV). 1987: Still Crazy Like a Fox (TV).*

DALBY, Amy 1888–1969

Small, sturdy, sweet-faced, pinch-lipped, light-haired British supporting actress who came to films after a long theatrical career, to play a few spinster aunts and the like. It's almost unbelievable that she wasn't one of Katie Johnson's (qv) gang of little old ladies in *The Ladykillers*; she must have had the flu. In her last film, *Smashing Time*, she played 'demolished old lady'!

1937: South Riding. 1941: Quiet Wedding. Penn of Pennsylvania (US: The Courageous Mr Penn). 1942: The Great Mr Handel. The Night Has Eyes (US: Terror House). 1943: Variety Jubilee. Millions Like Us. The Gentle Sex. Dear Octopus (US: The Randolph Family). 1944: Waterloo Road. Don't Take It to Heart. 1945: The Wicked Lady. Pink String and Sealing Wax. 1947: The White Unicorn (US: Bad Sister). 1948: It's Hard to be Good. My Sister and I. 1949: The Passionate Friends (US: One Woman's Story). 1951: Home to Danger. Brandy for the Parson. 1953: The Straw Man. 1958: Further Up the Creek. The Man Upstairs. Libel! 1962: The Lamp in Assassin Mews. 1963: The Haunting. 1964: Topkapi. 1965: The Intelligence Men. The Secret of My Success. 1966: Doctor in Clover. Fumo di Londra. The Blue Max. The Spy with a Cold Nose. Money-Go-Round. Who Killed the Cat? 1967: Smashing Time.

DALE, Esther 1885–1961

Square-faced, crumple-chinned, light-haired, solidly-built American actress who played characters who never took things at face value. It was difficult to pull the wool over these narrowed eyes, and she was kept very busy in films following a late cinematic debut at almost 50. Mostly seen as crusty types whose hearts of gold were well hidden, she also played nosey neighbours, brisk housekeepers and nurses who would stand no intervention in their patients' care. Married writer-producer Arthur Beckhard who died only a few months before her.

1934: Crime Without Passion. 1935: Curly Top. Mary Burns, Fugitive. The Great Impersonation. I Live My Life. I Dream Too Much. In Old Kentucky. Private Worlds. The Wedding Night. 1936: The Case Against Mrs Ames. Fury. The Farmer in the Dell. Lady of Secrets. Hollywood Boulevard. The Magnificent Brute. Timothy's Quest. 1937: The Awful Truth. Easy Living. Dead End. Damaged Goods (GB: Marriage Forbidden). Outcast. On Such a Night. Wild Money. 1938: Condemned Women. Girls on Probation. Prison Farm. Of Human Hearts. Dramatic School. Stolen Heaven. 1939: Six Thousand Enemies. Bad Little Angel. Broadway Serenade. Big Town Czar. Blackmail. Made for Each Other. Sergeant Madden. Swanee River. Tell No Tales. The Women. 1940: Convicted Woman. A Child is Born. And One Was Beautiful. Blondie Has Servant Trouble. Arise, My Love. Love Thy Neighbor. Opened by Mistake. Laddie. Untamed. Village Barn Dance. Women Without Names. The Mortal Storm. 1941: Aloma of the South Seas. Back Street. All-American Co-Ed. Dangerously They Live. Mr and Mrs Smith. There's Magic in Music. Unfinished Business. 1942: Blondie Goes to College (GB: The Boss Said 'No'). I Married an Angel. Maisie Gets Her Man (GB: She Got Her Man). What's Cookin'? (GB: Wake Up and Dream). Dangerously They Live. Ten Gentleman from West Point. You're Telling Me. Wrecking Crew. 1943: The Amazing Mrs Holliday. Murder in Times Square. The North Star. Hello, Frisco, Hello. Swing Your Partner. 1945: Behind City Lights. Bedside Manner. On Stage, Everybody. Out of this World. 1946: Margie. A Stolen Life. My Reputation. Smoky. 1947: The Egg and I. The Unfinished Dance. 1948: A Song is Born. Ma and Pa Kettle. 1949: Holiday Affair. Ma and Pa Kettle Go to Town (GB: Going to Town). Anna Lucasta. 1950: No Man of Her Own. Walk Softly, Stranger. Surrender. 1951: Too Young to Kiss. On Moonlight Bay. 1952: Monkey Business. Ma and Pa Kettle at the Fair. 1955: Betrayed Women. Ma and Pa Kettle at Waikiki. 1957: The Oklahoman. 1960: North to Alaska.

DALIO, Marcel
(Israel Bleuschild) 1900–1983
Short, dark, dapper, incisive French actor who appeared with distinction in films from many countries. Never quite a star, even in his native France, where he started in revue and music-hall, but a much-respected craftsman who brought all his roles, however small, briskly to life and created instantly identifiable characters. He made his debut in a short film, Les quatres jambes, in 1932.

1933: Mon chapeau. 1934: Les affaires publiques. Turandot. 1935: Une nuit à l'hôtel. 1936: Quand minuit sonnera. Cargaison blanche. L'or. Pépé-le-Moko. Un grand amour de Beethoven. 1937: La grande illusion. Les perles de la Couronne. Gribouille. Alibi. L'homme à abattre. Les pirates du Rail. Naples où baiser de feu. Miarke la fille à l'ours. Marthe Richard. Sarati-le-Terrible. Troïka. 1938: Mollenard. Entrée des artistes (US: The Curtain Rises). Conflit. Chéri-Bibi. La maison du Maltais. 1939: La tradition de minuit. Les quatres jambes. La règle du jeu. L'esclave blanche. Le bois sacré. Tempête sur Paris. Le corsaire. 1941: One Night in Lisbon. The Shanghai Gesture. 1942: Unholy Partners. Joan of Paris. The Pasha's Wives. Flight Lieutenant. Casablanca. The Pied Piper. 1943: Paris After Dark. Tonight We Raid Calais. The Song of Bernadette. The Constant Nymph. 1944: The Conspirators. To Have and Have Not. Pin-Up Girl. Wilson. Action in Arabia. The Desert Song. 1945: The Night is Ending. A Bell for Adano. 1946: Pétrus. Son dernier rôle. Les maudits (GB: The Damned). Le bataillon du ciel. 1947: Dédée d' Anvers. Erreur judiciare. Temptation Harbour. 1948: Snowbound. Hans le marin (GB: The Wicked City). Sombre dimanche. Les amants de Vérone. 1949: Maya. Black Jack. Ménace de mort. Portrait d'un assassin. Aventure à Pigalle. 1950: Porte d'orient. 1951: On the Riviera. Nous irons à Monte Carlo (GB: Monte Carlo Baby). Rich, Young and Pretty. 1952: The Happy Time. Lovely to Look At. The Snows of Kilimanjaro. The Merry Widow. 1953: Scrupule, gangster. Gentlemen Prefer Blondes. Flight to Tangier. 1954: Sabrina (GB: Sabrina

Fair). Lucky Me. Razzia sur la chnouf. La patrouille des Sables. 1955: Les Amants du tage (GB: The Lovers of Lisbon). Jump into Hell. 1956: Hand of Fate (TV. GB: cinemas). Miracle in the Rain. Istanbul. 1957: China Gate. The Sun Also Rises. 10,000 Bedrooms. Tip on a Dead Jockey (GB: Time for Action). 1958: Lafayette Escadrille (GB: Hell Bent for Glory). The Perfect Furlough (GB: Strictly for Pleasure). 1959: Pillow Talk. The Man Who Understood Women. Classé tous risques (GB: The Big Risk). 1960: Can-Can. Song without End. 1961: The Devil at Four O'Clock. Le petit garçon et l'ascenseur. Jessica. 1962: The Devil and the 10 Commandments. Cartouche (GB: Swords of Blood). L'abominable homme des douanes. 1963: Donovan's Reef. The List of Adrian Messenger. A couteaux tirés (US: Daggers Drawn). 1964: Wild and Wonderful. Un monsieur de compagnie. Le monocle rit jaune. 1965: Le dix-septième ciel. Made in Paris. Lady L. 1966: How to Steal a Million. Tendre Voyou (GB: Simon the Swiss. US: Tender Scoundrel). The Oldest Profession. 1967: The 25th Hour. 1968: How Sweet It Is! L'amour c'est gai, l'amour c'est triste. 1969: Justine. 1970: Du blé en liasses. Catch 22. The Great White Hope. 1971: Papa, les petits bâteaux. Les yeux fermés. 1972: Dedée la tendresse. La punition. 1973: Les aventures de Rabbi Jacob (GB and US: The Mad Adventures of "Rabbi" Jacob). Ursule et Grétu. 1974: Trop c'est trop. Que la fête commence. 1975: Le faux cul. The Beast. 1976: L'aile ou la cuisse. Madame Claude. 1977: L'ombre des châteaux. La communion solonelle. Le paradis des riches. L'honorable société. 1978: Une page d'amour. Chausette surprise. 1980: Brigade mondaine. 1981: Vaudou aux Caraïbes.

DALY, Mark 1887–1957
Fair-haired, tubby little Scottish-born actor of ruddy complexion, receding chin, beaky nose and watery eyes, a cheerful character who was once a music-hall comic and member of Fred Karno's troupe. Came to films with sound and soon settled into playing a string of amiable old bumblers. Daly had the leading role in 1953's Alf's Baby and was the old junk shop man who sold Tommy Steele his first guitar in The Tommy Steele Story.

1931: East Lynne on the Western Front. The Beggar Student. 1932: The Third String. 1933: Up for the Derby. Doss House. The Private Life

of Henry VIII. A Cuckoo in the Nest. Say It With Flowers. 1934: The River Wolves. By-Pass to Happiness. Music Hall. There Goes Susie (US: Scandals of Paris). Flood Tide. 1935: That's My Uncle. The Small Man. A Real Bloke. Jubilee Window. The Ghost Goes West. 1936: The Man Who Could Work Miracles. Shipmates o' Mine. Murder at the Cabaret. Hearts of Humanity. The Captain's Table. 1937: Good Morning, Boys (US: Where There's a Will). Wanted! Command Performance. Captain's Orders. Wings of the Morning. Knight Without Armour. 1938: Follow Your Star. Lassie from Lancashire. Break the News. 1939: Q Planes (US: Clouds over Europe). Hoots Mon! Ten Days in Paris (US: Missing Ten Days). 1940: The Farmer's Wife. The Girl in the News. 1941: The Big Blockade. 1942: Next of Kin. 1946: The Voyage of Peter Joe (serial). 1947: Stage Frights. 1948: Bonnie Prince Charlie. 1949: The Romantic Age (US: Naughty Arlette). Three Bags Full. 1953: Alf's Baby. 1954: Don't Blame the Stork! Lease of Life. The Delavine Affair. 1955: Footsteps in the Fog. Keep It Clean. 1956: The Gelignite Gang (US: The Dynamiters). The Feminine Touch (US: The Gentle Touch). You Pay Your Money. 1957: The Shiralee. The Tommy Steele Story (US: Rock Around the World). Soap-Box Derby.

DAMPIER, Claude
(C. Cowan) 1876–1955
Light-haired, bespectacled, idiotically beaming British character comedian who spoke through his buck teeth with a gurgly voice that sounded as though he were operating through a gullet-full of marmalade. A music-hall comedian who made his first two films in Australia, he later proved an enjoyably asinine foil in British films of the 1930s and an ear-stealing part of the post-war Jewel and Warriss radio shows (catchphrase: 'It's me-ee') although he joined them in only one of their (abortive) film forays. Died from pneumonia.

1924: Hello Marmaduke. 1925: The Adventures of Algy. 1930: *Claude Deputises. 1934: Radio Parade of 1935 (US: Radio Follies). 1935: Boys Will Be Boys. So You Won't Talk. White Lilac. She Shall Have Music. No Monkey Business. 1936: King of the Castle. Public Nuisance No. 1. She Knew What She Wanted. Such Is Life. All In. Valiant Is the Word for Carrie. 1937: Wanted! Mr Stringfellow Says No. Sing As You Swing. Riding High. 1940:

*The Backyard Front. 1944: Don't Take It to Heart. 1946: Wot! No Gangsters? 1950: Let's Have a Murder. 1953: Meet Mr Malcolm.

DANIELL, Henry
(Charles H. Daniell) 1894–1963
British-born Hollywood actor with hard, unsmiling face and rat-trap mouth, a villain par excellence, who could also project sympathy in off-beat leading roles. Probably run through by more swashbuckling stars than any other villain except Basil Rathbone.

1929: Jealousy. The Awful Truth. 1930: Last of the Lone Wolf. 1934: The Path of Glory. 1936: The Unguarded Hour. Camille. 1937: The Thirteenth Chair. The Firefly. Madame X. Under Cover of Night. 1938: Holiday. Marie Antoinette. 1939: We Are Not Alone. The Private Lives of Elizabeth and Essex. 1940: The Sea Hawk. The Great Dictator. The Philadelphia Story. All This and Heaven Too. 1941: Four Jacks and a Jill. The Feminine Touch. Dressed to Kill. A Woman's Face. 1942: Sherlock Holmes and the Voice of Terror. Reunion/Reunion in France (GB: Mademoiselle France). Nightmare. Random Harvest. Castle in the Desert. The Great Impersonation. 1943: Mission to Moscow. Sherlock Holmes in Washington. Watch on the Rhine. 1944: Jane Eyre. 1945: The Suspect. Captain Kidd. The Body Snatcher. The Woman in Green. Hotel Berlin. The Chicago Kid. 1946: The Bandit of Sherwood Forest. 1947: The Exile. Song of Love. 1948: Wake of the Red Witch. Siren of Atlantis. 1949: Secret of St Ives. 1950: Buccaneer's Girl. 1954: The Egyptian. 1955: The Prodigal. Diane. 1956: The Man in the Gray Flannel Suit. Lust for Life. Around the World in 80 Days. Confession (TV). 1957: Les Girls. The Sun Also Rises. The Story of Mankind. Mister Cory. Witness for the Prosecution. 1958: From the Earth to the Moon. The Wings of the Dove (TV). 1959: The Four Skulls of Jonathan Drake. 1961: Voyage to the Bottom of the Sea. The Comancheros. The Chapman Report. 1962: The Notorious Landlady. Madison Avenue. Mutiny on the Bounty. Five Weeks in a Balloon. 1964: My Fair Lady.

DANIELS, William 1927–
Waspish, acidulous, dark-haired American actor with slightly testy features, often seen in comedy but equally at home as incisive,

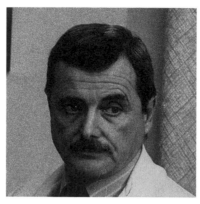

often sneaky types in drama, as well as the occasional offbeat leading role. A major figure on the Broadway stage, Daniels didn't venture into films and TV until the 1960s, but later became a familiar figure in several television series, most notably as Dr Craig in the popular St Elsewhere. Visually a droop-eyed cross between Geoffrey Lewis (qv) and Tony Randall, Daniels has achieved a greater range than either. A credit in some filmographies for an appearance as a young man in Family Honeymoon (1948) seems to be a confusion with the cinematographer William Daniels (1895–1970). Married actress Bonnie Bartlett.

1963: Ladybug, Ladybug. 1965: A Thousand Clowns. 1967: Two for the Road. The President's Analyst. The Graduate. 1969: Marlowe. 1972: 1776. 1973: Murdock's Gang (TV). 1974: The Parallax View. A Case of Rape (TV). 1975: Sarah T – Portrait of a Teenage Alcoholic (TV). One of Our Own (TV). 1976: Black Sunday. A Star is Dead (TV). Francis Gary Powers: The True Story of the U2 Spy Incident (TV). 1977: The One and Only. Oh, God! Killer on Board (TV). The Court-Martial of George Armstrong Custer (TV). 1978: Big Bob Johnson and His Fantastic Speed Circus (TV). Sgt Matlovich vs the US Air Force (TV). 1979: The Million-Dollar Face (TV. Not shown until 1981). Sunburn. The Rebels (TV). 1980: Conquest of the Earth (TV). Damien: The Leper Priest (TV). The Blue Lagoon. City in Fear (TV). 1981: All Night Long. Reds. 1982: Drop-Out Father (TV). Rehearsal for Murder (TV). Rooster (TV). Knight Rider (TV). 1987: The Little Match Girl (TV). Blind Date. 1989: Her Alibi. Howard Beach: Making the Case for Murder (TV). 1991: Clara (TV). 1994: Magic Kid 2.

DANO, Royal 1922–1994
Somehow, this tall, dark, grim-looking American actor always seemed to be playing harbingers of doom in one way or another. His jaws forever clamped tightly together, you felt he would have been happy delivering telegrams of bereavement or finding a nice, damp grave in which to bed down for the night. Sometimes he was a sheriff, sometimes a fire-breathing evangelist, sometimes just the bad guy's henchman: there certainly wasn't much humour in Dano's 42 years of scattered screen roles. Died of a heart attack.

1950: Undercover Girl. Under the Gun. 1951: The Red Badge of Courage. Flame of Araby. 1952: Bend of the River (GB: Where the River Bends). Carrie. 1954: Johnny Guitar. The Far Country. 1955: The Trouble with Harry. Tribute to a Bad Man. 1956: Moby Dick. Santiago (GB: The Gun Runner). Tension at Table Rock. 1957: All Mine To Give (GB: The Day They Gave Babies Away). Man in the Shadow (GB: Pay the Devil). Crime of Passion. Trooper Hook. 1958: Saddle the Wind. Handle with Care. Man of the West. 1959: Never Steal Anything Small. These Thousand Hills. Hound Dog Man. The Boy and the Bridge. Face of Fire. 1960: The Adventures of Huckleberry Finn. Cimarron 1961: King of Kings. Posse from Hell. 1962: The Brazen Bell (TV. GB: cinemas). Savage Sam. 1964: The Seven Faces of Dr Lao. 1965: Gunpoint. The Dangerous Days of Kiowa Jones (TV. GB: cinemas). 1966: Welcome to Hard Times (GB: Killer on a Horse). Backtrack (TV. GB: cinemas). 1967: The Last Challenge (GB: The Pistolero of Red River). 1968: The Manhunter (TV). Day of the Evil Gun. If He Hollers, Let Him Go. 1969: The Undefeated. Death of a Gunfighter. 1970: Run, Simon, Run (TV). Machismo (40 Graves for 40 Guns) (GB: Forty Graves for Forty Guns). 1971: Chandler. Skin Game. The Great Northfield Minnesota Raid. Slingshot. 1972: The Culpepper Cattle Co. Moon of the Wolf (TV). Howzer. 1973: Ace Eli and Rodger of the Skies. Cahill, United States Marshal (GB: Cahill). Electra Glide in Blue. 1974: Big Bad Mama. The Wild Party. Messiah of Evil. 1975: Huckleberry Finn (TV). Capone. The Killer Inside Me. 1976: Drum. Manhunter (TV). The Outlaw Josey Wales. 1977: Hughes and Harlow: Angels in Hell. Bad Georgia Road. Murder in Peyton Place (TV). 1978: One-Man Jury. A Love Affair: The Eleanor and Lou Gehrig Story (TV). Donner Pass: The Road to Survival (TV). 1979: The Last Ride of the Dalton Gang (TV). Strangers: The Story of a Mother and Daughter (TV). 1980: Hammett (released 1982). In Search of Historic Jesus (GB: Jesus). 1981: Take This Job and Shove It. The Big Trade (TV). 1982: Something Wicked This Way Comes. 1983: Murder 1, Dancer 0 (TV). The Right Stuff. Will There Really Be a Morning? (TV). 1984: Teachers. 1985: Angels in Hell. 1986: Cocaine Wars. The Red-Headed Stranger. 1987: House II: The Second Story. LBJ: The Early Years (TV). 1988: Ghoulies II. Killer Klowns from Outer Space. Once Upon a Texas Train (TV). 1990: Spaced Invaders. Joey Takes a Cab. 1991: The Dark Half (released 1993).

DANTINE, Helmut

(H. Guttman) 1917–1982

Tall, dark, smooth-looking Austrian actor with cleanly delineated features. Dantine made no films in his native country, fleeing to Hollywood in 1938, and breaking into movies there three years later. Attracting attention for a while in the absence of many top stars on war service, he found the going tough when hostilities ended, and later moved into production and direction. Later still he took small roles in films with whose production he had been involved. Died 'after a massive coronary'.

1941: International Squadron. 1942: Desperate Journey. To Be Or Not To Be. Mrs Miniver. The Pied Piper. The Navy Comes Through. Casablanca. 1943: Edge of Darkness. Mission to Moscow. Northern Pursuit. 1944: Passage to Marseille (GB: Passage to Marseilles). Hollywood Canteen. 1945: Hotel Berlin. Escape in the Desert. 1946: Shadow of a Woman. 1947: Whispering City. 1952: Guerilla Girl. 1953: Call Me Madam. 1954: Stranger from Venus (US: Immediate Decision). 1956: War and Peace. Alexander the Great. 1957: Clipper Ship (TV). The Story of Mankind. Hell On Devil's Island. 1958: Fräulein. Tempest. 1960: The Hiding Place (TV). 1965: Operation Crossbow (US: The Great Spy Mission). 1974: The Wilby Conspiracy. Bring Me the Head of Alfredo Garcia. 1975: The Killer Elite. 1977: Behind the Iron Mask (GB: The Fifth Musketeer).

As director:
1958: Thundering Jets.

DARRO, Frankie

(F. Johnson) 1917–1976

Slim, whippy, sawn-off, aggressive-looking American actor with a mop of dark, unruly hair. In films from boyhood, often in low-budget westerns, he was the prototype of the Dead End Kids, Stanley Clements (*qv*) and every kid from the wrong side of the tracks who never got the breaks. His best role came early, in *Wild Boys of the Road*. Thereafter, he seemed to be forever playing runts, jockeys and minor leads. It comes as no surprise to find that he actually made a film called *Tough Kid*. Billed as 'Darrow' until 1930, he died from a heart attack.

1923: Judgment of the Storm. 1924: Roaring Rails. The Signal Tower. So Big. Racing for Life. Half-a-Dollar Bill. 1925: Memory Lane.

*Confessions of a Queen. The People versus Nancy Preston. Let's Go Gallagher. The Midnight Flyer. The Phantom Express. Wandering Footsteps. The Wyoming Wildcat. The Cowboy Musketeer. The Fearless Lover. Women and Gold. Fighting the Flames. Bustin' Through (GB: Broke to the Wide). 1926: Kiki. The Cowboy Cop. Flaming Waters. The Carnival Girl. The Arizona Streak. Memory Lane. Mike. Out of the West. Tom and His Pals. Red Hot Hoofs. Wild to Go. The Thrill Hunter. Born to Battle. The Masquerade Bandit. Flesh and the Devil. Hearts and Spangles. Her Husband's Secret. 1927: Long Pants. Lightning Lariats/Laughing Lariats. Cyclone of the Range. Judgment of the Hills. Her Father Said No. The Flying U Ranch. Little Mickey Grogan. Tom's Gang. The Desert Pirate. The Cherokee Kid. Moulders of Men. 1928: The Texas Tornado. Tyrant of Red Gulch (GB: The Sorcerer). When the Law Rides. The Circus Kid. The Avenging Rider. Phantom of the Range. Terror Mountain (GB: Tom's Vacation). Mystery Valley. 1929: The Pride of Pawnee. Trail of the Horse Thieves. The Rainbow Man. Gun Law. The Red Sword. Blaze o' Glory. Idaho Red. 1931: The Mad Genius. The Sin of Madelon Claudet (GB: The Lullaby). The Vanishing Legion (serial). Way Back Home (GB: Old Greatheart). The Public Enemy (GB: Enemies of the Public). 1932: Cheyenne Cyclone. Amateur Daddy. The Lightning Warrior (serial). Three on a Match. 1933: The Big Brain (GB: Enemies of Society). Tugboat Annie. Wild Boys of the Road (GB: Dangerous Days). Laughing at Life. *Hollywood on Parade B-1. The Mayor of Hell. The Wolf Dog (serial). The Big Race (GB: Raising the Wind). 1934: Little Men. The Devil Horse (serial). The Merry Frinks (GB: The Happy Family). No Greater Glory. Broadway Bill (GB: Strictly Confidential). Stranded. Burn 'Em Up Barnes (serial. GB: Devil on Wheels). 1935: Men of Action. Valley of Wanted Men (GB: Wanted Men). The Phantom Empire (serial). Three Kids and a Queen (GB: The Baxter Millions). The Unwelcome Stranger. Red Hot Tires/Racing Luck. The Pay Off. 1936: The Ex Mrs Bradford. Racing Blood. Mind Your Own Business. The Devil Diamond. 1937: Charlie Chan at the Race Track. A Day at the Races. Headline Crasher. Tough to Handle. Saratoga. Anything for a Thrill. Thoroughbreds Don't Cry. Young Dynamite. 1938: Reformatory. Born to Fight. Wanted by the Police. Juvenile Court. 1939: The Great Adventures of Wild Bill Hickok. Tough Kid (GB: The Fifth Round). Boys Reformatory. Irish Luck (GB:*

Amateur Detective). 1940: Chasing Trouble. On the Spot. Pinocchio (voice only). Laughing at Danger. Up in the Air. Men with Steel Faces (GB: Couldn't Possibly Happen). 1941: The Gang's All Here (GB: In the Night). You're Out of Luck. Let's Go Collegiate (GB: Farewell to Fame). Tuxedo Junction (GB: The Gang Made Good). 1942: Junior G-Men of the Air (serial). 1946: Freddie Steps Out. Her Sister's Secret. High School Hero. Junior Prom. 1947: That's My Man (GB: Will Tomorrow Never Come?). Vacation Days. Sarge Goes to College. 1948: Smart Politics. Angels' Alley. Heart of Virginia. Trouble Makers. Hold That Baby! 1949: Fighting Fools. 1950: A Life of Her Own. Riding High. Wyoming Mail. Sons of New Mexico (GB: The Brat). 1951: Pride of Maryland. Across the Wide Missouri. The Sellout. 1952: Pat and Mike. 1953: Two-Gun Marshal. 1954: The Lawless Rider. Living It Up. Racing Blood (and 1936 film of same title). 1956: The Ten Commandments. 1958: The Perfect Furlough (GB: Strictly for Pleasure). 1960: Operation Petticoat. 1964: The Carpetbaggers. 1969: Hook, Line and Sinker. 1974: The Girl on the Late, Late Show (TV).

DARWELL, Jane

(Patti Woodward) 1879–1967

Stout, homely American stage actress who, after a false start in silent films, came back to Hollywood with sound and chalked up a long and impressive portrait gallery of dominating, albeit soft-centred matrons and matriarchs. For one of the most famous, Ma Joad in *The Grapes of Wrath*, she won an Academy Award as Best Supporting Actress. Bid a sentimental farewell to the screen as the old bird-woman in *Mary Poppins*. Died from a heart attack.

*1913: The Capture of Aquinaldo. 1914: Rose of the Rancho. Ready Money. The Only Son. After Five. Master Mind. Brewster's Millions. 1915: The Goose Girl. The Reform Candidate. 1916: The Rug Maker's Daughter. 1920: The Mastermind. 1930: Tom Sawyer. 1931: Huckleberry Finn. Fighting Caravans. Ladies of the Big House. 1932: Back Street. Hot Saturday. Murders in the Zoo. No One Man. 1933: Bondage. Jennie Gerhardt. Bed of Roses. Ann Vickers. Only Yesterday. Air Hostess. One Sunday Afternoon. Before Dawn. *Good Housewrecking. Women Won't Tell. Design for Living. Emergency Call. Child of Manhattan. He Couldn't Take It. The Past of Mary Holmes. Roman*

Scandals. 1934: Once to Every Woman. Finishing School. David Harum. Wake Up and Dream. Desirable. The Scarlet Empress. Heat Lightning. The Firebird. Fashions (GB: Fashion Follies of 1934). Let's Talk It Over. Happiness Ahead. Wonder Bar. Change of Heart. Most Precious Thing in Life. Blind Date. Embarrassing Moments. Journal of a Crime. Gentlemen Are Born. Jimmy the Gent. Million Dollar Ransom. The White Parade. One Night of Love. Bright Eyes. 1935: Beauty's Daughter (later Navy Wife). Life Begins at 40. Paddy O'Day. Curly Top. Tomorrow's Youth. McFadden's Flats. One More Spring. Metropolitan. 1936: Captain January. Little Miss Nobody. The Country Doctor. *Vocalising. White Fang. Ramona. Private Number. Star for a Night. Poor Little Rich Girl. We're Only Human. The First Baby. Craig's Wife. 1937: The Great Hospital Mystery. Dead Yesterday. Dangerously Yours. Wife, Doctor and Nurse. The Singing Marine. Nancy Steele is Missing. Slave Ship. Love Is News. Laughing at Trouble. Fifty Roads to Town. 1938: The Jury's Secret. Five of a Kind. Change of Heart (remake). Time Out for Murder. Little Miss Broadway. Three Blind Mice. Inside Story. Battle of Broadway. Up the River. 1939: Jesse James. Unexpected Father (GB: Sandy Takes a Bow). Zero Hour. The Rains Came. Gone With the Wind. Grand Jury Secrets. 20,000 Men a Year. 1940: The Grapes of Wrath. Chad Hanna. Brigham Young—Frontiersman (GB: Brigham Young). Youth Will Be Served. Untamed. Miracle on Main Street. 1941: The Devil and Daniel Webster/All That Money Can Buy. Here is a Man. Thieves Fall Out. Small Town Deb. Private Nurse. 1942: Young America. The Battle of Midway (narrator only). The Loves of Edgar Allan Poe. Men of Texas (GB: Men of Destiny). It Happened in Flatbush. The Great Gildersleeve. All Through the Night. On the Sunny Side. Highways by Night. The Ox-Bow Incident (GB: Strange Incident). 1943: Battle of Midway. Tender Comrade. Gildersleeve's Bad Day. *A Family Feud. Government Girl. Stage Door Canteen. 1944: Sunday Dinner for a Soldier. She's a Sweetheart. Music in Manhattan. Double Indemnity. Reckless Age. The Impatient Years. 1945: Captain Tugboat Annie. I Live in Grosvenor Square (US: A Yank in London). 1946: Three Wise Fools. My Darling Clementine. Dark Horse. 1947: Red Stallion. Keeper of the Bees. 1948: 3 Godfathers. The Time of Your Life. Train to Alcatraz. 1949: Red Canyon. 1950: Wagonmaster. The Daughter of Rosie O'Grady. Caged. Redwood Forest Trail. Surrender. Three Husbands. The Second Face. Father's Wild Game. 1951: The Lemon Drop Kid. Excuse My Dust. Journey into Light. Fourteen Hours. 1952: We're Not Married. 1953: The Sun Shines Bright. It Happens Every Thursday. Affair With a Stranger. The Bigamist. 1955: Hit the Deck. A Life at Stake. 1956: There's Always Tomorrow. Sincerely, Willis Wayde (TV). Girls in Prison. The Greer Case (TV). 1957: Three Men on a Horse (TV). 1958: The Last Hurrah. 1959: Hound Dog Man. 1964: Mary Poppins.

DA SILVA, Howard

(Harold Silverblatt) 1909–1986
Fair-haired, surly-looking, Broadway-trained American actor, a very useful off-centre

villain whose career was stopped in its tracks by the McCarthy blacklist. He was fired from the film (Slaughter Trail, 1951) on which he was working, and spent 11 years in the wilderness. Unsurprisingly, his film career failed to recover, although he made sporadic returns to movies, mainly in biting cameo roles, from 1962.

1936: Once in a Blue Moon. 1939: Golden Boy. 1940: Abe Lincoln in Illinois (GB: Spirit of the People). I'm Still Alive. *A Day in the Orchard. 1941: The Sea Wolf. Steel Against the Sky. Strange Alibi. Navy Blues. Sergeant York. Bad Men of Missouri. Nine Lives Are Not Enough. Wild Bill Hickok Rides. 1942: Bullet Scars. Native Land. Juke Girl. The Big Shot. Reunion/Reunion in France (GB: Mademoiselle France). The Omaha Trail. Keeper of the Flame. 1943: Tonight We Raid Calais. 1945: Five Were Chosen. Duffy's Tavern. The Lost Weekend. The Blue Dahlia. 1946: Two Years Before the Mast. 1947: Variety Girl. Blaze of Noon. Unconquered. 1949: The Great Gatsby. They Live By Night. Border Incident. 1950: The Underworld Story. Wyoming Mail. Tripoli. 1951: Fourteen Hours. Three Husbands. 1962: David and Lisa. 1963: It's a Mad, Mad, Mad, Mad World. 1964: The Outrage. 1966: Nevada Smith. 1972: 1776. 1974: The Great Gatsby (remake). The Missiles of October (TV). Smile Jenny, You're Dead (TV). 1977: The Private Files of J Edgar Hoover. 1981: Mommie Dearest. 1984: Garbo Talks!

DAVENPORT, Harry 1866–1949

From a long line of actors (his two wives and four children were all in the profession), this tall, distinguished American player brought his own distinctive sense of humour to bear on many of the Hollywood roles he graced. Played Grandpa in 'The Higgins Family' comedy series (1938–1940) and Grandpa again in Meet Me in St Louis. Also directed a few films in the silent era. Died from a heart attack, his last film still to be shown.

1914: Fogg's Millions. *The Accomplished Mrs Thompson. 1915: C.O.D. Father and the Boy. 1916: One Night. The Wheel of the Law. 1917: The False Friend. A Man's Law. The Planter. Sowers and Reapers. 1918: *She's Everywhere. Tony America. 1919: A Girl at Bay. The Unknown Quantity. 1930: Her Unborn Child. 1931: My Sin. His Woman. 1933: Get That Venus. 1934: *Three Cheers for Love.

1935: The Scoundrel. 1936: Three Men on a Horse. The Case of the Black Cat. Legion of Terror. Three Cheers for Love. King of Hockey (GB: King of the Ice Rink). 1937: Fly Away Baby. The Life of Emile Zola. Under Cover of Night. Her Husband's Secretary. White Bondage. They Won't Forget. Four Days' Wonder. Maytime. Radio Patrol (serial). The Great Garrick. Mountain Justice. Mr Dodd Takes the Air. First Lady. The Perfect Specimen. Paradise Express. Wells Fargo. As Good As Married. Armored Car. Fit for a King. 1938: The Sisters. Saleslady. Gold Is Where You Find It. Long Shot. The First Hundred Years. Marie Antoinette. The Cowboy and the Lady. Man Proof. Young Fugitives. The Rage of Paris. Reckless Living. You Can't Take It With You. *Screen Snapshots No 75. The Higgins Family. Tail Spin. 1939: Juarez. Orphans of the Street. My Wife's Relatives. Made for Each Other. Should Husbands Work? The Covered Trailer. Money to Burn. Exile Express. Gone With the Wind. The Story of Alexander Graham Bell (GB: The Modern Miracle). Death of a Champion. The Hunchback of Notre Dame. 1940: Granny Get Your Gun. Too Many Husbands. Grandpa Goes to Town. All This and Heaven Too. Lucky Partners. Foreign Correspondent. Earl of Puddlestone (GB: Jolly Old Higgins). I Want a Divorce. The Story of Dr Ehrlich's Magic Bullet (GB: Dr Ehrlich's Magic Bullet). 1941: That Uncertain Feeling. I Wanted Wings. Hurricane Smith. The Bride Came COD. One Foot in Heaven. Kings Row. Meet John Doe. 1942: Son of Fury. The Ox-Bow Incident (GB: Strange Incident). Larceny Inc. Ten Gentlemen from West Point. Tales of Manhattan. 1943: Shantytown. Headin' for God's Country. We're Never Been Licked (GB: Texas to Tokyo). Jack London. Government Girl. Princess O'Rourke. The Amazing Mrs Holliday. Gangway for Tomorrow. 1944: Meet Me in St Louis. The Impatient Years. The Thin Man Goes Home. Kismet. Music for Millions. 1945: The Enchanted Forest. This Love of Ours. Too Young to Know. Adventure. She Wouldn't Say Yes. A Boy, a Girl and a Dog (GB: Lucky). 1946: Pardon My Past. Courage of Lassie. Blue Skies. Faithful in My Fashion. Three Wise Fools. Claudia and David. Lady Luck. GI War Brides (GB: War Brides). 1947: The Farmer's Daughter. Stallion Road. Keeper of the Bees. The Bachelor and the Bobby-Soxer (GB: Bachelor Knight). That Hagen Girl. Sport of Kings (GB: Heart Royal). The Fabulous Texan. 1948: Three Daring Daughters (GB: The Birds and the Bees). For the Love of Mary.

The Man from Texas. That Lady in Ermine. The Decision of Christopher Blake. 1949: That Forsyte Woman (GB: The Forsyte Saga). Down to the Sea in Ships. Tell It to the Judge. Little Women. 1950: Riding High.

As director:

1915: *Mr Jarr and the Lady Reformer. *Mr Jarr and the Visiting Firemen. *Mr Jarr Brings Home a Turkey. *Mr Jarr Takes a Night Off. *Mr Jarr Visits His Home Town. *Mr Jarr's Big Vacation. *Mr Jarr's Magnetic Friend. *Mrs Jarr and the Beauty Treatment. *Mrs Jarr and the Society Circus. *Mrs Jarr's Auction Bridge. *The Closing of the Circuit. *The Enemies. For a Woman's Fair Name. *The Jarr Family Discover Harlem. *The Jarrs Visit Arcadia. The Island of Regeneration. The Making Over of Geoffrey Manning. *Mr Jarr and Circumstantial Evidence. *Mr Jarr and Gertrude's Beaux. *Mr Jarr and Love's Young Dream. *Mr Jarr and the Captive Maiden. *Mr Jarr and the Dachshund. *Mr Jarr and the Ladies' Cup. 1916: *Myrtle, the Manicurist. *The Resurrection of Hollis. The Supreme Temptation. *The Accusing Voice. 1917: The False Friend. Tillie Wakes Up. The Millionaire's Double. A Son of the Hills. A Man's Law.

DAVI, Robert 1953–
Dark-eyed, dark-haired, straight-staring American actor of long, narrow face and deeply rutted features. He began his entertainment career as an opera singer (a talent later put to use as the singing villain of The Goonies), but went for straight acting after winning a drama scholarship to Hofstra University. Typed as a bad guy for more than a decade, he has only lately been winning a better range of roles, actually getting to play the hero in Maniac Cop 2. His choice of top supporting roles in the past few years has been somewhat shaky, resulting in his participation in several projects of dubious value. His performances, though, continue to be of interest.

1977: Contract on Cherry Street (TV). 1979: And Your Name is Jonah (TV). From Here to Eternity (TV). The Legend of the Golden Gun (TV). 1980: Alcatraz: The Whole Shocking Story (TV). The $5.20 an Hour Dream (TV). Rage (TV). 1984: City Heat. 1985: The Goonies. 1986: Raw Deal. 1987: Wild Thing. Terrorist

on Trial: The United States vs Salim Ajami (TV). 1988: Traxx. Action Jackson. Die Hard. 1989: Licence to Kill. Deceptions (TV). 1990: Maniac Cop 2. Peacemaker. Predator 2. Amazon (released 1992). 1991: The Taking of Beverly Hills. Down and Dirty. White Hot: The Mysterious Murder of Thelma Todd (TV). Under Surveillance/Undercover Assassin. Blue Movie Blue (re-released 1992 as Wild Orchid II: Two Shades of Blue). 1992: S.I.S. Center of the Web. Christopher Columbus The Discovery. Illicit Behavior. Son of the Pink Panther. 1993: Maniac Cop 3: Badge of Silence. Love, Lust and the Electric Chair. They Came from the Darkness. Quick. Cops and Robbersons. Night Trap/Mardi Gras for the Devil. 1994: Dangerous. The November Men. No Contest. The Silencer. Blind Justice. 1995: Showgirls. The Zone.

DAVIES, Betty Ann 1909–1955
Brunette (occasionally blonde) English actress with small, bird-like face and busy acting style, seen mainly as chirpy maids and carefree young heroines until 1941. After a six-year absence, she returned to films in much darker roles, as shrews (notably Miriam in The History of Mr Polly), faithless wives, prostitutes and murder victims. She died at 45 from complications following an operation for appendicitis. One of the original Cochran Young Ladies. Billed in her earliest films as Betty Davies.

1933: Oh! What a Duchess. 1934: Death at Broadcasting House. Youthful Folly. 1935: Joy Ride. Play Up the Band. 1936: She Knew What She Wanted. Excuse My Glove. Chick. Tropical Trouble. Radio Lover. 1937: Lucky Jade. Merry Comes to Town (GB: Merry Comes to Stay). Under a Cloud. Silver Top. 1938: Mountains o' Mourne. 1941: Kipps (US: The Remarkable Mr Kipps). *I Bet. 1947: It Always Rains on Sunday. 1948: Escape. The Passionate Friends (US: One Woman's Story). To the Public Danger. 1949: Now Barabbas was a robber ... (US: Barabbas the Robber). The Man in Black. The Blue Lamp. Which Will You Have? The History of Mr Polly. 1950: Trio. The Woman With No Name (US: Her Paneled Door). 1951: Outcast of the Islands. 1952: Meet Me Tonight. Cosh Boy (US: The Slasher). 1953: Grand National Night (US: Wicked Wife). Gilbert Harding Speaking of Murder. 1954: The Belles of St Trinian's.

Children Galore. 1955: Murder by Proxy (US: Blackout). 1956: *Ring of Greed. Alias John Preston.

DAVIES, Rupert 1916–1976
Burly, affable, crinkly-haired British actor with small features set in a large face. His film career gained momentum in the late 1950s, but almost ground to a halt after he won the title role in the TV series Maigret, continuing as Georges Simenon's pipe-smoking sleuth for several seasons. Most of his remaining film roles were in horror films, usually as comforting peripheral figures; on TV he was a persuasive spokesman for Flora margarine.

1949: Private Angelo. 1955: The Dark Avenger (US: The Warriors). 1957: The Traitor (US: The Accused). 1958: Next to No Time! Sea Fury. The Key. The Man Upstairs. 1959: Sapphire. John Paul Jones. Breakout. Life in Emergency Ward 10. Idle on Parade (US: Idol on Parade). Violent Moment. Devil's Bait. Bobbikins. 1960: The Criminal (US: The Concrete Jungle). Danger Tomorrow. 1965: The Spy Who Came in from the Cold. The Uncle. 1966: Five Golden Dragons. Das Geheimnis der gelben Mönche (GB: Target for Killing). Brides of Fu Manchu. 1967: House of a Thousand Dolls. Submarine X-1. 1968: Curse of the Crimson Altar. Witchfinder-General (US: The Conqueror Worm). Dracula Has Risen from the Grave. 1969: The Oblong Box. 1970: The Firechasers. Waterloo. 1971: Zeppelin. Danger Point! The Night Visitor. 1976: Frightmare.

DAWSON, Anthony 1916–1992
Long, lean, gaunt, dark, moustachioed, sinister British actor who looked as though he would throttle his grandmother for a handful of silver, and slunk famously into film history as the disgraced ex-army officer hired to kill Grace Kelly in Dial M for Murder. Dawson brought his disreputable scowl to a similar part in Midnight Lace, but his other film roles were largely unworthy of his talent. Despite the impeccable accent, he was born in Edinburgh. His work in Italian films from the late 1960s has sometimes led to his credits being confused with those of director Antonio Margheriti, at times credited as Anthony M Dawson. Died from cancer.

1951: The Long Dark Hall. 1952: I Believe in You. Private Information. The Yellow Balloon. Never Look Back. 1953: A Day to Remember. Don't Blame the Stork! 1954: Hobson's Choice. What Every Woman Wants. The Purple Plain. The Happiness of Three Women (US: Wishing Well). 1955: As Long as They're Happy. A Kid for Two Farthings. Doctor at Sea. 1956: The Man Who Knew Too Much. House of Secrets (US: Triple Deception). 1959: Too Many Crooks. Passport to Shame (US: Room 43). The 39 Steps. 1960: The Entertainer. 1961: The Mark. Flame in the Streets. Come September. 1962: A Pair of Briefs. I Thank a Fool. 1963: The Pink Panther. 1967: Pretty Polly (US: A Matter of Innocence).

1939: I Killed the Count (US: Who is Guilty?). 1944: The Way Ahead (US: Immortal Battalion). They Met in the Dark. 1945: The Way to the Stars (US: Johnny in the Clouds). 1946: School for Secrets (US: Secret Flight). Beware of Pity. 1948: The Queen of Spades. 1950: They Were Not Divided. The Woman in Question (US: Five Angles on Murder). The Wooden Horse. 1951: The Long Dark Hall. I'll Get You for This (US: Lucky Nick Cain). Valley of Eagles. 1954: Dial M for Murder. 1955: That Lady. The Man Who Never Was. 1957: Action of the Tiger. Hour of Decision/Table in the Corner. 1958: Grip of the Strangler (US: The Haunted Strangler). 1959: Tiger Bay. Libel. 1960: Midnight Lace. 1961: Curse of the Werewolf. Offbeat. Follow That Man. 1962: Dr No. Seven Seas to Calais. 1964: The Yellow Rolls Royce. 1965: The Amorous Adventures of Moll Flanders. Change Partners. 1966: Kaleidoscope. Triple Cross. 1967: Hell is Empty (completed 1963). L'avventurio (GB and US: The Rover). Operation Kid Brother. Death Rides a Horse/Da uomo a uomo. Dalle Ardenne all' inferno (US: The Dirty Heroes). 1968: E per tutto un cielo di stelle. 1969: Rosolino Palernò, soldato (US: Operation SNAFU). Deadlock. 1970: The Battle of Neretva/The Battle for Neretva. Red Sun. The Valachi Papers. 1972: Cool Million (TV). The Big Game. 1973: Massacre in Rome. 1974: The Count of Monte Cristo (TV. GB: cinemas). 1981: Inchon! 1983: Where is Parsifal? (released 1985). The Jigsaw Man. 1986: Pirates. 1988: Ghoulies II. 1990: Spieler/Gamblers.

DEACON, Richard 1922–1984
Tall, bald-headed, often bespectacled American comic actor who walked as though there were eggs all over the ground and played self-righteous employees eager to shop the hero or heroine to the boss. He became popular in television series (*Mister Ed*, *Leave It to Beaver*, *The Dick Van Dyke Show*, *Mothers-in Law*) and in his fifties started a programme on microwave cookery. Died from a heart attack.

1954: Them! Private Hell 36. Desiree. Rogue Cop. 1955: Abbott and Costello Meet the Mummy. My Sister Eileen. Lay That Rifle Down. Good Morning, Miss Dove. Hot Blood. This Island Earth. Blackboard Jungle. 1956: When Gangland Strikes. Invasion of the Body Snatchers. Francis in the Haunted House. My Man Godfrey. The Kettles in the Ozarks. The

Scarlet Hour. The Proud Ones. The Solid Gold Cadillac. The Power and the Prize. Carousel. 1957: Designing Woman. Kiss Them for Me. The Spirit of St Louis. Affair in Reno. Decision at Sundown. Spring Reunion. 1958: The Last Hurrah. A Nice Little Bank That Should Be Robbed (GB: How to Rob a Bank). 1959: A Summer Place. The Remarkable Mr Pennypacker. The Young Philadelphians (GB: The City Jungle). –30– (GB: Deadline Midnight). 1960: North to Alaska. 1961: Lover Come Back. All in a Night's Work. Everything's Ducky. 1962: That Touch of Mink. 1963: Critic's Choice. The Raiders. Who's Minding the Store? The Birds. 1964: John Goldfarb, Please Come Home. The Patsy. Dear Heart. The Disorderly Orderly. 1965: That Darn Cat! Billie. 1966: Don't Worry, We'll Think of a Title. The Gnome-Mobile. 1967: Blackbeard's Ghost. The King's Pirate. Enter Laughing. 1968: Il sapore della vendetta/The Narco Men. Lady in Cement. The One and Only Genuine Original Family Band. 1978: Piranha. Getting Married (TV). 1980: The Happy Hooker Goes to Hollywood. The Gossip Columnist (TV). Murder Can Hurt You! (TV). 1981: The Man from Clover Grove (completed 1974). 1982: The Awakening of Cassie (TV). 1984: Bad Manners.

DE BANZIE, Brenda 1915–1981
Fair-haired, matronly British actress, mostly seen on stage. After her performance in the 1954 version of *Hobson's Choice*, she became Britain's most unexpected star of the fifties — albeit for only a few years — before moving on to character roles. Died after surgery for a non-malignant tumour.

DeCAMP, Rosemary 1910–
Dark-haired American actress with warm smile and heart-shaped face, whose sympathetic voice matched her screen personality, and had made her a popular actress on radio before she came to Hollywood in 1941. Almost from the very start of her screen career, she appeared in mother roles, having teenage 'daughters' while still in her early thirties. Television work from the 1950s to the 1970s stretched her career as a screen mother over 30 years.

1941: Cheers for Miss Bishop. The Wagons Roll at Night. Hold Back the Dawn. 1942: Jungle Book. Yankee Doodle Dandy. Eyes in the Night. Commandos Strike at Dawn. Smith of Minnesota. 1943: This is the Army. City Without Men. 1944: The Merry Monahans. Bowery to Broadway. Practically Yours. 1945: Pride of the Marines (GB: Forever in Love). Rhapsody in Blue. Danger Signal. Week-End at the Waldorf. Too Young to Know. Blood on the Sun. 1946: From This Day Forward. Two Guys from Milwaukee (GB: Royal Flush). 1947: Nora Prentiss. Night unto Night (released 1949). 1949: The Life of Riley. Look for the Silver Lining. 1950: The Story of Seabiscuit (GB: Pride of Kentucky). The Big Hangover. 1951: On Moonlight Bay. Night into Morning. Scandal Sheet (GB: The Dark Page). 1952: Treasure of Lost Canyon. 1953: So This is Love (GB: The Grace Moore Story). By the Light of the Silvery Moon. Main Street to Broadway. 1955: Many Rivers to Cross. Strategic Air Command. 1960: 13 Ghosts. 1978: The Time Machine (TV). 1981: Saturday the 14th.

DE CASALIS, Jeanne
(J. de Casalis de Pury) 1896–1966
Dark, twittery, pencil-slim, Basutoland-born entertainer in British show business. She began as a straight dramatic ac.ress, but developed into a top music-hall and radio comedienne, inventing the famous gossipy character Mrs Feather and continuing to make eccentric appearances in British films until 1949. At one time married to the actor Colin Clive.

*1925: Settled Out of Court (US: Evidence Enclosed). 1927: The Glad Eye. The Arcadians/ Land of Heart's Desire. 1928: Zero. 1930: Infatuation. Knowing Men. 1932: Nine Till Six. 1933: Radio Parade. Mixed Doubles. 1934: Nell Gwyn. 1938: Just Like a Woman. 1939: Jamaica Inn. The Girl Who Forgot. 1940: Sailors Three (US: Three Cockeyed Sailors). Charley's (Big-Hearted) Aunt. 1941: Cottage To Let (US: Bombsight Stolen). *The Fine Feathers. Pathetone Parade of 1941. 1942: Those Kids from Town. Pathetone Parade of 1942. 1943: They Met in the Dark. 1944: Medal for the General. 1946: This Man Is Mine! 1947: The Turners of Prospect Road. 1948: Woman Hater. 1949: The Twenty Questions Murder Mystery.*

DECKERS, Eugene 1917–1977
Dark-haired, scurrying little French actor with sharp, if screwed-up features, in Britain from World War II times. In post-war years, he became one of the British cinema's regular 'continentals', much in demand for both straight-faced villainy, comic relief and key

character roles. Demands for his services slackened in the late 1950s, as British studio production ground almost to a halt, and he turned to other media.

1946: Woman to Woman. Dual Alibi. 1947: Mrs Fitzherbert. 1948: Sleeping Car to Trieste. Against the Wind. 1949: Golden Salamander. Prince of Foxes. 1950: The Elusive Pimpernel (US: The Fighting Pimpernel). Highly Dangerous. Madeleine. Tony Draws a Horse. So Long at the Fair. 1951: The Lavender Hill Mob. Hotel Sahara. Captain Horatio Hornblower RN. Night Without Stars. 1953: The Love Lottery. 1954: Father Brown (US: The Detective). The Colditz Story. 1955: Doctor at Sea. Man of the Moment. 1956: Port Afrique. Foreign Intrigue. The Iron Petticoat. Women Without Men (US: Blonde Bait). House of Secrets (US: Triple Deception). 1957: Let's Be Happy. Seven Thunders (US: The Beasts of Marseilles). 1959: Northwest Frontier (US: Flame Over India). 1960: Crack in the Mirror. 1961: A Weekend with Lulu. 1962: The Longest Day. 1963: Hell is Empty (released 1967). 1965: Lady L. 1967: The Last Safari. 1968: The Limbo Line. The Assassination Bureau.

DE CORSIA, Ted 1903–1973
Chunky, thick-necked, black-haired American actor from Brooklyn, mostly on radio until he began a belated film career at 45, after which he still managed to scowl and bluster his way through more than 50 films. His raucous voice, set features and slitted eyes made him a favourite for aggressive gangster roles, and he is best remembered as the bad guy who falls from the bridgework in *The Naked City*—his first role in front of the camera.

*1947: *Brooklyn USA (narrator only). 1948: *Brooklyn Makes Capital (narrator only). The Naked City. The Lady from Shanghai. 1949: It Happens Every Spring. Neptune's Daughter. The Life of Riley. Mr Soft Touch (GB: House of Settlement). 1950: The Outriders. Cargo to Capetown. Three Secrets. The Enforcer (GB: Murder Inc.). 1951: Vengeance Valley. New Mexico. Crazy over Horses. Inside the Walls of Folsom Prison. A Place in the Sun. 1952: Captain Pirate (GB: Captain Blood, Fugitive). The Turning Point. The Savage. 1953: Ride Vaquero! Man in the Dark. Hot News. Crime Wave (GB: The City is Dark). 1954: 20,000 Leagues under the Sea. 1955: The Big Combo. The Man With the Gun (GB: The Trouble*

Shooter). *Kismet. 1956: The Kettles in the Ozarks. The Conqueror. The Steel Jungle. Mohawk. The Killing. Showdown at Abilene. Dance with Me, Henry. Slightly Scarlet. Gunfight at the OK Corral. 1957: The Lawless Eighties. The Midnight Story (GB: Appointment with a Shadow). The Joker is Wild. Man on the Prowl. Gun Battle at Monterey. Baby Face Nelson. 1958: Handle with Care. Enchanted Island. Violent Road. The Buccaneer. 1959: South Seas Adventure (narrator only). Inside the Mafia. Noose for a Gunman. Oklahoma Territory. 1960: From the Terrace. Spartacus. 1961: The Crimebusters. 1962: It's Only Money. 1964: Blood on the Arrow. The Quick Gun. 1966: Nevada Smith. 1967: The King's Pirate. 1968: Five Card Stud. 1970: The Delta Factor. 1972: Un homme est mort (US: The Outside Man).*

DEFORE, Don 1913–1993
Cheerful, bluff, hearty, dark-haired American actor with distinctive parting: a likeable part of the Paramount/Warners musical/comedy scene of the late 1940s and early 1950s, as a dumb ox or the amiable suitor who lacked the vital spark to get the girl. Entirely lost to long-running TV series from the 1960s. Name sometimes spelt with a capital F. Best performances on film came when cast against type – as in *Dark City* or *The Facts of Life*. Died from a heart attack.

*1937: Kid Galahad. Submarine D-1. 1938: Brother Rat. Garden of the Moon. Freshman Year. 1941: We Go Fast. 1942: The Male Animal. You Can't Escape Forever. Right to the Heart/Knockout. *Men of the Sky. 1943: The Human Comedy. City Without Men. *Practical Joker. A Guy Named Joe. 1944: Thirty Seconds over Tokyo. And Now Tomorrow. *Return from Nowhere. 1945: The Affairs of Susan. You Came Along. The Stork Club. 1946: Without Reservations. 1947: Ramrod. It Happened on Fifth Avenue. 1948: Romance on the High Seas (GB: It's Magic). One Sunday Afternoon. 1949: Too Late for Tears. My Friend Irma. 1950: Dark City. My Friend Irma Goes West. Southside 1–1000 (GB: Forgery). 1951: The Guy Who Came Back. A Girl in Every Port. *Hollywood on a Sunday Afternoon. 1952: No Room for the Groom. She's Working Her Way Through College. Jumping Jacks. 1957: Battle Hymn. 1958: A Time to Love and a Time to Die. 1960: The Facts of Life. 1981: Carnauba/ A Rare Breed.*

DEHNER, John
(J. Forkum) 1915–1992

Stern-faced, dark-haired, cold-eyed, often moustachioed American actor with skin strung tautly over his features – characteristics which saw him playing sundry martinets, sadistic villains, or humourless upholders of the law. He was often to be found in westerns, sometimes as a crooked town boss or cattleman. He did well in the occasional lead role, too, but probably a lack of warmth held him from becoming a name above the title. Kept busy, though, often in television. Died from emphysema and diabetes.

1941: The Reluctant Dragon. 1944: Thirty Seconds Over Tokyo. Lake Placid Serenade. 1945: Captain Eddie. Twice Blessed. State Fair. Christmas in Connecticut (GB: Indiscretion). Club Havana. She Went to the Races. 1946: O.S.S. Her Kind of Man. Rendezvous 24. Catman of Paris. The Undercover Woman. The Last Crooked Mile. Out California Way. The Searching Wind. 1947: Golden Earrings. Vigilantes of Boomtown. Dream Girl. Blonde Savage. It's a Joke, Son. 1948: Let's Live a Little. He Walked by Night. Prejudice. 1949: The Secret of St Ives. Bandits of El Dorado (GB: Tricked). Tulsa. *Riders of the Pony Express. Horsemen of the Sierras (GB: Remember Me). Feudin' Rhythm (GB: Ace Lucky). Kazan. Mary Ryan, Detective. Barbary Pirate. 1950: Captive Girl. Backfire. Dynamite Pass. David Harding – Counterspy. Rogues of Sherwood Forest. Bodyhold. Destination Murder. Texas Dynamo (GB: Suspected). Last of the Buccaneers. Counterspy Meets Scotland Yard. 1951: Al Jennings of Oklahoma. China Corsair. When the Redskins Rode. Bandits of El Dorado. The Texas Rangers. Lorna Doone. Corky of Gasoline Alley (GB: Corky). Fort Savage Raiders. Hot Lead. Ten Tall Men. 1952: Lady in the Iron Mask. California Conquest. Scaramouche. Aladdin and His Lamp. Cripple Creek. Desert Passage. Harem Girl. Plymouth Adventure. Junction City. Bad Men of Marysville (TV. GB: cinemas). 1953: Man on a Tightrope. Powder River. The Steel Lady (GB: Treasure of Kalifa). Vicki. Gun Belt. Fort Algiers. 1954: Southwest Passage (GB: Camels West). The Bowery Boys Meet the Monsters. Apache. The Cowboy (narrator only). 1955: The Man from Bitter Ridge. The Prodigal. The King's Thief. Tall Man Riding. Duel on the Mississippi. Top Gun. The Scarlet Coat. 1956: A Day of Fury. Carousel. The Fastest Gun Alive. Please Murder Me. Terror at Midnight. Tension at Table Rock. 1957: Revolt at Fort Laramie. The Girl in Black Stockings. Trooper Hook. The Iron Sheriff. 1958: Man of the West. Apache Territory. The Left-Handed Gun. 1959: Cast a Long Shadow. Timbuktu. 1960: The Sign of Zorro. 1961: The Canadians. The Chapman Report. 1963: Critic's Choice. 1964: Youngblood Hawke. 1965: The Hallelujah Trail (narrator only). 1967: The Helicopter Spies (TV. GB: cinemas). Winchester 73 (TV). 1968: Tiger by the Tail. 1969: Stiletto. Something for a Lonely Man. 1970: Dirty Dingus Magee. The Cheyenne Social Club. Quarantined (TV). 1971: Support Your Local Gunfighter. 1972: Slaughterhouse-Five. 1973: The Day of the Dolphin. 1974: Honky Tonk (TV). 1975: The Big Rip-Off (TV). The Killer Inside Me. 1976: Guardian of the Wilderness. Fun With Dick and Jane. The New Daughters of Joshua Cabe (TV). 1977: The Lincoln Conspiracy. Danger in Paradise (TV). 1978: The Boys from Brazil. 1979: The Young Maverick (TV). 1980: Nothing Personal. California Gold Rush (TV). 1982: Bare Essence (TV). Airplane II The Sequel. 1983: The Right Stuff. 1985: Jagged Edge. 1986: Help Wanted: Kids (TV).

DEKKER, Albert
(Albert van Dekker) 1904–1968

Tall, florid, heavy, menacing and moustachioed Hollywood actor of Dutch descent who played mad scientists, rich crooks and sadists in all shades and situations. He was also successful in the occasional leading role (eg The French Key), but from the late forties his cinema career was running downhill. In May 1968 he hanged himself, the coroner recording a verdict of accidental death.

1937: The Great Garrick. 1938: Marie Antoinette. The Last Warning. She Married an Artist. The Lone Wolf in Paris. Extortion. 1939: Paris Honeymoon. Never Say Die. Beau Geste. Hotel Imperial. The Great Commandment. The Man in the Iron Mask. 1940: Strange Cargo. Seven Sinners. Dr Cyclops. 1941: Among the Living. You're the One. Blonde Inspiration. Reaching for the Sun. Buy Me That Town. Honky Tonk. 1942: The Lady Has Plans. The Forest Rangers. Yokel Boy (GB: Hitting the Headlines). In Old California. Star Spangled Rhythm. Once Upon a Honeymoon. Wake Island. A Night in New Orleans. 1943: The Woman of the Town. War of the Wildcats/ In Old Oklahoma. Buckskin Frontier (GB: The Iron Road). The Kansan (GB: Wagon Wheels). 1944: Experiment Perilous. The Hitler Gang (narrator only). 1945: Incendiary Blonde. Salome, Where She Danced. Hold That Blonde. 1946: Two Years Before the Mast. Suspense. The French Key. California. The Killers. 1947: Slave Girl. Gentleman's Agreement. Wyoming. The Pretender. Cass Timberlane. The Fabulous Texan. 1948: Lulu Belle. Fury at Furnace Creek. 1949: Bride of Vengeance. Search for Danger. 1950: Tarzan's Magic Fountain. The Furies. The Kid from Texas (GB: Texas Kid – Outlaw). Destination Murder. 1951: As Young As You Feel. 1952: Wait 'Til the Sun Shines, Nellie. 1954: The Silver Chalice. East of Eden. 1955: Kiss Me Deadly. Illegal. 1957: The She Devil. 1958: Machete. 1959: Suddenly Last Summer. The Sound and the Fury. These Thousand Hills. Middle of the Night. The Wonderful Country. 1965: Gammera the Invincible. 1967: Come Spy with Me. 1969: The Wild Bunch.

DeLUISE, Dom 1933–

Plump, giggling, mischievous (later often bearded) American comedian with round face and disappearing dark hair, who gradually built up a reputation on television, then became a familiar film face through his appearances in films by Mel Brooks and those associated with him. Later he became associated with car-crash comedies and films with Burt Reynolds. At first, DeLuise played dupes and bunglers, but soon diversified to include rogues and charlatans, all in the same broad vein. Later still, his gurgling tones came in handy for voice-overs in several cartoon features. Married actress Carol Arthur.

1963: Diary of a Bachelor. 1964: Fail Safe. The Ordeal of Thomas Moon (unreleased). 1966: The Glass Bottom Boat. The Busy Body. 1968: What's So Bad About Feeling Good? The Twelve Chairs. 1970: Norwood. 1971: Who Is Harry Kellerman and Why is He Saying These Terrible Things About Me? 1972: Every Little Crook and Nanny. Evil Roy Slade (TV). 1974: Only with Married Men (TV). Blazing Saddles. 1975: The Adventure of Sherlock Holmes' Smarter Brother. 1976: Silent Movie. 1977: The World's Greatest Lover. Sextette. 1978: The Cheap Detective. The End. 1979: The Muppet Movie. Hot Stuff (and directed). The Last Married Couple in America. Diary of a Young Comic

(TV). 1980: *Wholly Moses! Smokey and the Bandit II* (GB: *Smokey and the Bandit Ride Again*). *The Cannonball Run. Fatso.* 1981: *History of the World Part I.* 1982: *The Secret of NIMH* (voice only). *The Best Little Whorehouse in Texas.* 1983: *Cannonball Run II. Happy* (TV). 1984: *Johnny Dangerously.* 1986: *Haunted Honeymoon. An American Tail* (voice only). 1987: *Ben, Bonzo, Mo and Big Bad Joe. My African Adventure. Spaceballs* (voice only). *Un tassinaro in New York/Italian Taxi Driver. Going Bananas.* 1988: *Oliver & Company* (voice only). *All Dogs Go to Heaven* (voice only). 1989: *Loose Cannons.* 1990: *The Princess and the Dwarf. Happily Ever After* (voice only). 1991: *Autobahn* (US: *Trabbi Goes to Hollywood*). *An American Tail: Fievel Goes West* (voice only). *Almost Pregnant.* 1992: *Munchie* (voice only). 1993: *Robin Hood: Men in Tights.* 1994: *A Troll in Central Park* (voice only). *The Silence of the Hams. Don't Drink the Water* (TV). 1995: *All Dogs Go to Heaven II* (voice only).

DEMAREST, William 1892–1983

Craggy, grizzled veteran of well over 100 films, who became, from the 1930s to the 1960s, one of Hollywood's best-known and best-loved familiar faces. He began in vaudeville as a song-and-dance act with his brother Rubin (1886–1962), but moved into films right at the beginning of sound and, after a hiatus from 1929 to 1933, established himself with dozens of Brooklynese character studies. Although often a softhearted and slightly dense policeman, he also excelled at brooding suspicion and tightlipped sarcasm. Oscar nomination for *The Jolson Story*.

1926: *When the Wife's Away.* 1927: *A Night at Coffee Dan's. Don't Tell the Wife. Fingerprints. Simple Sis. A Million Bid. In Old San Francisco. The Bush Leaguer. A Sailor's Sweetheart. The Jazz Singer. Matinee Ladies. The Gay Old Bird. What Happened to Father. The Black Diamond Express. The First Auto. A Reno Divorce.* 1928: *Five and Ten Cent Annie* (GB: *Ambitious Annie*). *The Butter and Egg Man* (GB: *Actress and Angel*). *Papa's Vacation. A Girl in Every Port. The Escape. Sharp Shooters. The Crash. Pay As You Enter.* 1932. *The Runaround.* 1934: *White Lies. Circus Clown. Fog Over Frisco. Fugitive Lady. Many Happy Returns.* 1935: *The Murder Man. The Casino Murder Case. After Office Hours.*

Diamond Jim. Bright Lights (GB: *Funny Face*). *Hands Across the Table.* 1936: *The Great Ziegfeld. Love on the Run. Wedding Present. Charlie Chan at the Opera. Mind Your Own Business.* 1937: *Don't Tell Your Wife. The Great Hospital Mystery. The Big City. Rosalie. Blonde Trouble. The Great Gambini. Oh Doctor! The Hit Parade. Easy Living. Time Out for Romance. Wake Up and Live.* 1938: *Rebecca of Sunnybrook Farm. Josette. One Wild Night. While New York Sleeps. Romance on the Run. Peck's Bad Boy With the Circus.* 1939: *King of the Turf. The Gracie Allen Murder Case. Mr Smith Goes to Washington. The Great Man Votes. The Cowboy Quarterback. Miracles for Sale. Laugh It Off* (GB: *Lady Be Gay*). 1940: *Tin Pan Alley. Little Men. Wolf of New York. The Great McGinty* (GB: *Down Went McGinty*). *The Farmer's Daughter. Christmas in July. Comin' Round the Mountain.* 1941: *Ride On, Vaquero. Glamour Boy. Dressed to Kill. Rookies on Parade. The Lady Eve. Country Fair. The Devil and Miss Jones.* 1942: *Pardon My Sarong. Sullivan's Travels. All Through the Night. True to the Army. My Favorite Spy. The Palm Beach Story. Life Begins at 8.30* (GB: *The Light of Heart*). *Behind the Eight Ball* (GB: *Off the Beaten Track*). *Johnny Doughboy.* 1943: *Stage Door Canteen. True to Life. Dangerous Blondes.* 1944: *Hail the Conquering Hero. The Great Moment. Nine Girls. Once Upon a Time. The Miracle of Morgan's Creek.* 1945: *Duffy's Tavern. *Hollywood Victory Caravan. Along Came Jones. Salty O'Rourke. Pardon My Past.* 1946: *Our Hearts Were Growing Up. The Jolson Story.* 1947: *Variety Girl. The Perils of Pauline.* 1948: *The Sainted Sisters. Night Has a Thousand Eyes. A Miracle Can Happen (later On Our Merry Way). Whispering Smith.* 1949: *Jolson Sings Again. Sorrowful Jones. Red, Hot and Blue.* 1950: *Never a Dull Moment. When Willie Comes Marching Home. Riding High. He's a Cockeyed Wonder.* 1951: *The First Legion. Excuse My Dust. The Strip. Behave Yourself!* 1952: *The Blazing Forest. What Price Glory?* 1953: *Dangerous When Wet. Here Come the Girls. The Lady Wants Mink. Escape from Fort Bravo.* 1954: *The Yellow Mountain.* 1955: *Jupiter's Darling. The Far Horizons. The Private War of Major Benson. Lucy Gallant. Sincerely Yours. Hell on Frisco Bay.* 1956: *The Mountain. The Rawhide Years.* 1960: *Pepe.* 1961: *King of the Roaring Twenties* (GB: *The Big Bankroll*). *Twenty Plus Two* (GB: *It Started in Tokyo*). 1962: *Son of Flubber.* 1963: *It's a Mad, Mad, Mad, Mad World.* 1964: *Viva Las Vegas* (GB: *Love in Las Vegas*). *That Darn Cat!* 1973: *Don't Be Afraid of the Dark* (TV). 1975: *The Wild McCullochs. Won Ton Ton—the Dog Who Saved Hollywood.* 1978: *The Millionaire* (TV).

† Scenes deleted from final release print

DENHAM, Maurice 1909–

Quizzical, intelligent-looking, bald British actor who made his name as sundry comic characters in such 1940s radio shows as *ITMA* and *Much-Binding-in-the-Marsh*. His move into films coincided with a shift to more varied character studies, and he remained very busy in that medium until the 1970s, when he became accepted as a penetrating portrayer of heavy personality drama

on television, and a formidable protagonist on stage.

1946: *Home and School. Daybreak.* 1947: *Fame is the Spur. The Man Within* (US: *The Smugglers*). *They Made Me a Fugitive* (US: *I Became a Criminal*). *Take My Life. The Upturned Glass. Holiday Camp. Jassy. Captain Boycott. The End of the River. Easy Money. Dear Murderer. Blanche Fury.* 1948: *Escape. Quartet. Miranda. Oliver Twist. The Peaceful Years* (narrator only). *My Brother's Keeper. London Belongs to Me* (US: *Dulcimer Street*). *The Blind Goddess. Here Come the Huggetts. Look Before You Love. The Bad Lord Byron. The Blue Lagoon.* 1949: *Worth the Risk* (voice only). *It's Not Cricket. Once Upon a Dream. Poet's Pub. A Boy, a Girl and a Bike. Traveller's Joy* (released 1951). *Landfall. Scrapbook for 1933* (voice only). *The Spider and the Fly. Don't Ever Leave Me. Madness of the Heart.* 1951: *No Highway* (US: *No Highway in the Sky*). 1952: *The Net* (US: *Project M-7*). *Time Bomb* (US: *Terror on a Train*). 1953: *Street Corner* (US: *Both Sides of the Law*). *Prince Philip* (narrator only). *Eight O'Clock Walk. The Million Pound Note* (US: *Man with a Million*). *Malta Story* (voice only). 1954: *The Purple Plain. Carrington VC* (US: *Court Martial*). *Animal Farm* (all voices). 1955: *Doctor at Sea. Simon and Laura.* 1956: *23 Paces to Baker Street. Checkpoint.* 1957: *Night of the Demon* (US: *Curse of the Demon*). *Barnacle Bill* (US: *All at Sea*). *Campbell's Kingdom.* 1958: *Man with a Dog. The Captain's Table.* 1959: *Our Man in Havana. Sink the Bismarck!* 1960: *Two Way Stretch. Ali and the Camel* (serial. Voice only). 1961: *The Greengage Summer* (US: *Loss of Innocence*). *Invasion Quartet. For Better . . . For Worse* (narrator only). *The Mark. The Last Rhino* (voice only). 1962: *The Set-Up. HMS Defiant* (US: *Damn the Defiant!*). *The King's Breakfast. Paranoiac.* 1963: *The Very Edge. Downfall. Paranoiac.* 1964: *The 7th Dawn. Hysteria. The Uncle.* 1965: *The Legend of Young Dick Turpin. Those Magnificent Men in Their Flying Machines, or: How I Flew from London to Paris in 11 Hours and 25 Minutes. The Alphabet Murders. The Heroes of Telemark. The Nanny. Operation Crossbow* (US: *The Great Spy Mission*). *The Night Caller* (US: *Blood Beast from Outer Space*). 1966: *After the Fox.* 1967: *Torture Garden. The Long Duel. Danger Route. Attack on the Iron Coast. Jules Verne's Rocket to the Moon* (US: *Those Fantastic Flying Fools* (narrator only). 1968: Negatives. The Best House in London. 1969: A Touch of Love (US: Thank You All Very Much). Some Girls Do. Midas Run (GB: A Run on Gold). 1970: The Virgin and the Gypsy. Countess Dracula. 1971: Sunday, Bloody Sunday. Nicholas and Alexandra. 1973: The Day of the Jackal. Luther. 1976: Shout at the Devil. 1977: Julia. 1979: *Recluse. 1981: From a Far Country. 1985: The Chain. Young Sherlock Holmes. Mr Love. Minder on the Orient Express (TV). 1986: 84 Charing Cross Road. 1988: Tears in the Rain (TV). 1992: Memento Mori (TV).

DENNEHY, Brian 1938–
Thick-necked, hard-driving, fair-haired American actor with curled smile who came to films and TV late in his career, but quickly made his mark with a series of fierce and abrasive performances that augured well for a long stay. He had the lead in the television series *Big Shamus, Little Shamus*, and had bulldozed his way into leading and semi-leading film roles by the late 1980s. The Brian Keith of his day, he has always been convincing as rough diamonds.

1977: Johnny, We Hardly Knew Ye (TV). Semi-Tough. Looking for Mr Goodbar. It Happened at Lakewood Manor (TV. GB: Panic at Lakewood Manor). 1978: Foul Play. F.I.S.T. Ruby and Oswald (TV). A Death in Canaan (TV). A Real American Hero (TV). 1979: Silent Victory: The Kitty O'Neal Story (TV). Dummy (TV). Pearl (TV). Butch and Sundance The Early Days. The Jericho Mile (TV. GB: cinemas). '10'. 1980: Little Miss Marker. The Seduction of Miss Leona (TV). A Rumor of War (TV). 1981: Fly Away Home (TV). Skokie (TV. GB: Once They Marched Through a Thousand Towns). Captured! (later Split Image). 1982: First Blood. I Take These Men (TV). 1983: Never Cry Wolf. Gorky Park. Blood Feud (TV). 1984: Off Sides (TV). Finders Keepers. Hunter (TV). The River Rat. 1985: Cocoon. Silverado. F/X (GB: F/X Murder by Illusion). Annie Oakley (TV). The Check is in the Mail. Twice in a Lifetime. 1986: Legal Eagles. Acceptable Risks (TV). Best Seller. 1987: The Belly of an Architect. The Man from Snowy River II (US: Return to Snowy River). The Lion of Africa (TV). Dear America (voice only). 1988: Cocoon: the Return. A Father's Revenge (TV). Indio (released 1990). Miles from Home. 1989: The Artisan. Day One (TV). Street Legal. Seven Minutes/Georg Elser. Pride and Extreme Prejudice (TV). Perfect Witness (TV). 1990: The Last

of the Finest (GB: Blue Heat). Evidence of Love (TV). Killing in a Small Town (TV). Presumed Innocent. Rising Son (TV). 1991: Gladiator. F/X 2 (GB: F/X 2: The Deadly Art of Illusion. In Broad Daylight (TV). 1992: The Diamond Fleece (TV). Triumph of the Heart. Teamster Boss: The Jackie Presser Story (TV). 1993: Foreign Affairs (TV). Midnight Movie. Murder in the Heartland (cable TV). Jack Reed: Badge of Honor (TV). Lying in Wait/Final Appeal. Prophet of Evil: The Ervil LeBaron Story (TV). 1994: The Stars Fell on Henrietta. Leave of Absence (TV). †Shadow of a Doubt (TV), 1995: Billy the Third. Tommy Boy.

† And directed

DESMONDE, Jerry 1908–1967
Tall, imperious, haughty-looking, crinkly-haired British stage and television personality who became one of entertainment's most skilful comedy 'stooges'. Long music-hall experience led him to becoming straight man to, from 1942, Sid Field, who confounded him with idiocies. After Field's death in 1949, Desmonde found a new zany in Norman Wisdom, who would tug appealingly at his coat-tails after each fresh disaster. Desmonde made several films with both men over a 20-year period, and no-one expressed distaste better.

1946: London Town (US: My Heart Goes Crazy). 1948: Cardboard Cavalier. 1953: Alf's Baby. Trouble in Store. Malta Story. 1954: The Angel Who Pawned Her Harp. 1955: Man of the Moment. Ramsbottom Rides Again. 1956: Up in the World. 1957: A King in New York. 1959: Follow a Star. 1961: Carry On Regardless. 1962: A Kind of Loving. 1963: The Switch. Stolen Hours. A Stitch in Time. 1964: The Beauty Jungle (US: Contest Girl). 1965: The Early Bird. Gonks Go Beat.

DESNY, Ivan
(I. Desnitzky) 1922–
Dark, suave, baby-faced, moustachioed Continental charmer, ideally cast in his first international success as the blackmailing lover in *Madeleine*, but afterwards more often seen in supporting roles. Born in Peking to a Russian father and French mother (refugees from the Russian revolution), he was educated in France, but sent to a German labour camp in 1940. He escaped but was recaptured. Appearing much in European theatres and films from many nations, he is

one of those actors who has cropped up time and again after one had thought his film career might be over.

1947: †La fleur de l'âge. 1948: Le bonheur en location. 1949: Madeleine. 1950: Dangereuse rencontre/Dangerous Mission. † Les trois mousquetaires. 1952: La p ... respectueuse. 1953: Corps sans âme. La signore senze camelia (GB: The Lady Without Camelias). Le bon Dieu sans confession. Weg ohne Umkehr. 1954: Act of Love. Die goldene Pest. Gestädtnis unter vier Augen. Herr über Leben und Tod. 1955: Frou-Frou. Lola Montès. Si Paris nous était conté. André und Ursula. Mädchen ohne Grenzen. Dunja. 1956: Anastasia. Ballerina. OSS 117 n'est pas mort. Club de femmes. Rosen für Bettina. Mannequins de Paris. 1957: Une vie (GB: One Life. US: End of Desire). Is Anna Anderson Anastasia? Wie ein Sturmwind (GB: As the Storm Rages). Donnez-moi ma chance. Alle Sünden dieser Erde. 1958: Der Satan lockt mit Liebe. The Mirror Has Two Faces/Le miroir a deux faces. Petersburger Nächte. La vie à deux (GB: The Two of Us). Was eine Frau im Frühling träumt. Frauensee. 1959: Monsieur Suzuki. 1960: Song Without End. Femme di lusso/Travelling in Luxury. 1961: The Magnificent Rebel. Du quoi tu te mêles, Daniela! 1962: Bon Voyage! L'ammutinamento (GB and US: White Slave Ship). Sherlock Holmes und das Halsband des Todes (GB: Sherlock Holmes and the Deadly Necklace). Number Six. 1963: Der unsichtbare. 1964: I misteri della giungla nera (GB: The Mystery of Thug Island. US: Mysteries of the Black Jungle. 1965: Das Liebeskarussel (GB: Who Wants to Sleep?). 1966: Tendre voyou (GB: Simon the Swiss. US: Tender Scoundrel). Captain from Toledo. Da Berlino l'apocalisse (GB: The Spy Pit). L'affaire Beckett. 1967: I Killed Rasputin. Liebesnächte in der Taiga (GB: Code Name Kill). Der Tod eines Doppelgängers. 1968: Guns for San Sebastian. Mayerling. 1970: The Adventures of Gérard. 1972: Little Mother/ Don't Cry for Me, Little Mother. Nocturno. 1973: Touch Me Not. Das Gewissen. 1974: Paper Tiger. Who? 1975: Faustrecht der Freiheit (GB: Fox. US: Fox and His Friends). Falsche Bewegung (GB: Wrong Movement). 1976: Die Eroberung der Zitadelle. 1977: Halbe-Halbe. 1978: Die Ehe der Maria Braun (GB: The Marriage of Maria Braun). Enigmo rosso (GB: Red Rings of Fear). 1979: Bloodline/Sidney Sheldon's Bloodline. 1980: Malou. Car Napping. La dame sans camélias. 1981: I Hate Blondes!

Lola. 1985: L'avenir d'Emilie (GB: The Future of Emily). Le caviar rouge. 1986: Motten im Licht. Offret/The Sacrifice. 1987: Hotel de France. Un' amore di donna. Escape from the KGB. 1988: Zocker-express. 1989: Quicker Than the Eye. 1991: La désenchantée. Surviving at the Top (TV mini-series shortened for cinemas). J'embrasse pas.

† Unfinished

DEVINE, Andy
(Jeremiah Schwartz) 1905–1977
Jolly, roly-poly American actor with unruly light brown hair and unique, croakingly raucous, high-pitched voice—the comic sidekick of many a western. He got into films through being a college football star, liked it, overcame objections to the effectiveness of his voice in sound films and stayed to cheer up more than 150 of them. Death caused by cardiac arrest.

*1928: We Americans (GB: The Heart of a Nation). Lonesome. Red Lips. 1929: Hot Stuff. Naughty Baby (GB: Reckless Rosie). 1930: The Spirit of Notre Dame (GB: Vigour of Youth). 1931: The Criminal Code. Danger Island (serial). 1932: Law and Order. The Man from Yesterday. The Impatient Maiden. Destry Rides Again. Three Wise Girls. Radio Patrol. Tom Brown of Culver. Fast Companions/Information Kid. The All-American (GB: Sport of a Nation). 1933: Saturday's Millions. The Cohens and Kellys in Trouble. Midnight Mary. Horse Play. Chance at Heaven. Song of the Eagle. The Big Cage. Dr Bull. 1934: The Poor Rich. Let's Talk It Over. Upper World. Gift of Gab. Wake Up and Dream. Million Dollar Ransom. Stingaree. Hell in the Heavens. 1935: *La Fiesta de Santa Barbara. The President Vanishes (GB: Strange Conspiracy). Hold 'Em Yale (GB: Uniform Lovers). Chinatown Squad. Straight from the Heart. The Farmer Takes a Wife. Way Down East. Fighting Youth. Coronado. 1936: Flying Hostess. Romeo and Juliet. The Big Game. Yellowstone. Small Town Girl. 1937: Mysterious Crossing. A Star Is Born. Double or Nothing. You're a Sweetheart. The Road Back. 1938: Yellow Jack. Swing That Cheer. Personal Secretary. Strange Faces. The Storm. Men With Wings. In Old Chicago. Dr Rhythm. 1939: Never Say Die. The Spirit of Culver (GB: Man's Heritage). Mutiny on the Blackhawk. Stagecoach. Tropic Fury. Legion of Lost Flyers. Geronimo. The Man from Montreal. 1940: Little Old New York. Black Diamonds. Hot*
*Steel. Torrid Zone. Margie. Danger on Wheels. The Leather Pushers. When the Daltons Rode. Trail of the Vigilantes. Buck Benny Rides Again. The Devil's Pipeline. 1941: A Dangerous Game. South of Tahiti (GB: White Savage). Lucky Devils. Road Agent. Men of the Timberland. The Kid from Kansas. The Flame of New Orleans. Mutiny in the Arctic. Badlands of Dakota. Raiders of the Desert. 1942: Top Sergeant. North to the Klondike. Timber. Unseen Enemy. Sin Town. *Keeping Fit. Danger in the Pacific. Between Us Girls. Escape from Hong Kong. 1943: Rhythm of the Islands. Frontier Badmen. Corvette K-225 (GB: The Nelson Touch). Crazy House. Ali Baba and the 40 Thieves. 1944: Follow the Boys. Ghost Catchers. Babes on Swing Street. Bowery to Broadway. 1945: Sudan. Frontier Gal (GB: The Bride Wasn't Willing). That's the Spirit. Frisco Sal. 1946: Canyon Passage. 1947: The Michigan Kid. The Vigilantes Return (GB: The Return of the Vigilantes). Bells of San Angelo. Springtime in the Sierras. The Marauders. On the Old Spanish Trail. The Fabulous Texan. Slave Girl. 1948: The Gallant Legion. The Gay Ranchero. Montana Belle (released 1952). Under California Skies. Old Los Angeles. Grand Canyon Trail. The Far Frontier. Eyes of Texas. Nighttime in Nevada. 1949: The Last Bandit. The Traveling Saleswoman. 1950: Never a Dull Moment. 1951: Slaughter Trail. The Red Badge of Courage. †Border City Rustlers (TV). †Two Gun Marshal (TV). †Six Gun Decision (TV). †Arrow in the Dust (TV). †Behind Southern Lines (TV). 1952: †The Ghost of Crossbones Canyon (TV). 1953: Island in the Sky. The Yellow Haired Kid. †Secret of Outlaw Flats (TV). 1954: Thunder Pass. †Marshals in Disguise (TV). †Outlaw's Son (TV). †Titled Tenderfoot (TV). †Timber County Trouble (TV). †Two Gun Teacher (TV). †Phanton Trouble (TV). †Trouble on the Trail (TV). 1955: Pete Kelly's Blues. †The Match Making Marshal (TV). 1956: Around the World in 80 Days. 1960: The Adventures of Huckleberry Finn. 1961: Two Rode Together. 1962: How the West Was Won. The Man Who Shot Liberty Valance. 1963: It's a Mad, Mad, Mad, Mad World. 1965: Zebra in the Kitchen. 1968: The Ballad of Josie. The Road Hustlers. 1969: Ride a Northbound Horse (TV. GB: cinemas). The Over-the-Hill Gang (TV). The Phynx. 1970: Myra Breckinridge. The Over-the-Hill Gang Rides Again (TV). Smoke (TV. GB: cinemas). 1973: Robin Hood (voice only). 1975: Won Ton Ton, the Dog Who Saved Hollywood. 1976: A Whale of a Tale. 1977: The Mouse and His Child (voice only).*

† Released as films in some countries.

DE WOLFE, Billy
(William Jones) 1907–1974
Dark-haired, moustachioed American comedian, much underused by the cinema, but seen to hilarious effect in several Paramount and Warners romps, mainly as prissy suitors destined not to win the heroine. At his best, though, in stage and night-club routines. Spent his early childhood in Wales. Died of lung cancer.

1943: Dixie. 1944: Miss Susie Slagle's (released 1946). 1945: Duffy's Tavern. 1946: Blue Skies. Our Hearts Were Growing Up. 1947: The Perils of Pauline. Dear Ruth. Variety Girl.

1948: Isn't It Romantic? 1949: Dear Wife. 1950: Tea for Two. 1951: Dear Brat. Lullaby of Broadway. 1953: Call Me Madam. 1965: Billie. 1973: The World's Greatest Athlete.

DE WOLFF, Francis 1913–1984
Huge, fearsome, thickly bearded British actor. With his stern expression, fierce eyebrows, charnel-house eyes and immense bulk, he made a formidable villain, but was difficult to cast in a wider variety of roles. He would have made a magnificent Beadle in *Oliver Twist* if Francis L Sullivan (*qv*) hadn't got there first. As it was, his distinctive, RADA-trained tones made his a favourite voice in radio drama.

1935: Sexton Blake and the Mademoiselle. Flame in the Heather. 1936: The Man Behind the Mask. Fire Over England. 1948: It's Hard to be Good. 1949: Adam and Evelyne (US: Adam and Evalyn). Trottie True (US: Gay Lady). Under Capricorn. 1950: Treasure Island. The Naked Heart/Maria Chapdelaine/The Naked Earth. Tom Brown's Schooldays. 1951: Flesh and Blood. Scrooge (US: A Christmas Carol). 1952: Ivanhoe. Miss Robin Hood. Moulin Rouge. 1953: The Master of Ballantrae. The Kidnappers (US: The Little Kidnappers). 1954: The Diamond (US: Diamond Wizard). The Seekers (US: Land of Fury). 1955: Geordie (US: Wee Geordie). King's Rhapsody. 1956: Moby Dick. 1957: The Smallest Show on Earth. Saint Joan. Odongo. 1958: The Roots of Heaven. Sea Fury. Corridors of Blood. 1959: The Hound of the Baskervilles. The Savage Innocents. Tommy the Toreador. The Man Who

Could Cheat Death. 1960: The Two Faces of Dr Jekyll (US: House of Fright). Clue of the Twisted Candle. 1961: The Silent Invasion. Curse of the Werewolf. 1962: The Durant Affair. 1963: The World Ten Times Over (US: Pussycat Alley). Siege of the Saxons. Devil Doll. The Three Lives of Thomasina. From Russia with Love. 1964: The Black Torment. Carry On Cleo. 1965: Licensed to Kill (US: The Second Best Secret Agent in the Whole Wide World). 1966: The Liquidator. Triple Cross. 1967: Questi fantasmi/Ghosts Italian Style. 1968: The Fixer. 1969: Sinful Davey. 1972: Clouds of Witness (TV). 1973: The Three Musketeers (The Queen's Diamonds). 1976: Jesus of Nazareth (TV).

DEXTER, Brad 1917–

Big, muscular, lightish-haired, blue-eyed, square-cut, stiff-moving American actor who looked as though he had wandered in from a Russ Meyer movie, but tended to play grating villains who had as much brain as brawn. A talented amateur boxer, he became more interested in acting and did well for a while in the Hollywood of the early 1950s. Later turned producer, sometimes of films starring Frank Sinatra, a personal friend whose life Dexter once saved in a swimming mishap. The only one of 'The Magnificent Seven' not to become a major star. At one time married to singer Peggy Lee.

1947: Sinbad the Sailor. 1950: The Asphalt Jungle. 1951: Fourteen Hours. 1952: The Las Vegas Story. Macao. 1953: 99 River Street. 1955: Untamed. Violent Saturday. House of Bamboo. 1956: The Bottom of the Bottle (GB: Beyond the River). Between Heaven and Hell. 1957: The Oklahoman. 1958: Run Silent, Run Deep. 1959: Vice Raid. Last Train from Gun Hill. 1960: Thirteen Fighting Men. The Magnificent Seven. 1961: X-15. Twenty Plus Two (GB: It Started in Tokyo). The George Raft Story (GB: Spin of a Coin). 1962: Taras Bulba. 1963: Johnny Cool. Kings of the Sun. 1964: Invitation to a Gunfighter. 1965: Bus Riley's Back in Town. None But the Brave. Von Ryan's Express. 1966: Blindfold. 1972: Jory. 1975: Shampoo. Vigilante Force. 1976: Law and Order (TV). 1977: The Private Files of J Edgar Hoover. Winter Kills (released 1979). 1978: House Calls. 1988: Secret Ingredient.

DIERKES, John 1905–1975
Since this cleft-chinned American actor

always looked a bit like a scarecrow, it was no surprise to find him as The Gaunt Man, looming out of the mist like a phantom in one of his early films, The Red Badge of Courage. Tall (6 ft 4 in), fair-haired and craggy, with coat-hanger shoulders, Dierkes was an economist who worked for the US government before becoming so interested in acting that, in post-war years, he decided to make a career of it. Hollywood welcomed the latecomer, and cast him as detectives, fanatics, prospectors and bandits, to all of which he lent a lived-in look. Died from emphysema.

1948: Macbeth. 1950: Three Husbands. 1951: The Sellout. The Red Badge of Courage. Silver City (GB: High Vermilion). The Thing . . . from another world. 1952: Les Miserables. Plymouth Adventure. Shane. 1953: The Moonlighter. The Vanquished. Abbott and Costello Meet Dr Jekyll and Mr Hyde. A Perilous Journey. 1954: The Naked Jungle. Prince Valiant. Hell's Outpost. Silver Lode. Passion. The Desperado. The Raid. 1955: The Vanishing American. Betrayed Women. Timberjack. The Road to Denver. Not As a Stranger. 1956: Jubal. The Fastest Gun Alive. 1957: Valerie. The Halliday Brand. Buckskin Lady. The Daughter of Dr Jekyll. Duel at Apache Wells. The Guns of Fort Petticoat. 1958: Blood Arrow. Touch of Evil. The Buccaneer. The Left-Handed Gun. The Rawhide Trail. 1959: The Oregon Trail. The Hanging Tree. 1960: The Alamo. 1961: The Comancheros. One-Eyed Jacks. 1962: Convicts Four (GB: Reprieve!). The Premature Burial. 1963: The Cardinal. The Haunted Palace. 'X' – The Man With the X-Ray Eyes (GB: The Man With the X-Ray Eyes). Johnny Cool. 1971: The Omega Man. 1972: Rage. 1973: Oklahoma Crude.

DIFFRING, Anton 1918–1989
Fair-haired, cold-eyed, cruel-looking German actor, who came to Britain after spending four years as an internee in Canada. After playing numerous nasties and Nazis, Diffring almost became a star of the British cinema in the late 1950s, but his lack of warmth did not help him stay in the top rank, and he eventually returned to Germany. Died in France.

1940: Neutral Port. Convoy. Sailors Three (US: Three Cockeyed Sailors). 1950: State Secret (US: The Great Manhunt). Highly

Dangerous. 1951: Hotel Sahara. Appointment with Venus (US: Island Rescue). The Woman's Angle. 1952: Song of Paris (US: Bachelor in Paris). Top Secret (US: Mr Potts Goes to Moscow). 1953: Never Let Me Go. The Red Beret (US: Paratrooper). Albert RN (US: Break to Freedom). Park Plaza 605 (US: Norman Conquest). Operation Diplomat. 1954: Betrayed. The Sea Shall Not Have Them. The Colditz Story. 1955: I Am a Camera. 1956: Doublecross. The Black Tent. House of Secrets (US: Triple Deception). Reach for the Sky. 1957: The Traitors (US: The Accused). The Crooked Sky. Lady of Vengeance. Seven Thunders (US: The Beasts of Marseilles). 1958: A Question of Adultery. Mark of the Phoenix. 1959: The Man Who Could Cheat Death. 1960: Circus of Horrors. 1961: Enter Inspector Duval. 1962: Incident at Midnight. 1964: Vorsicht, Mister Dodd. Liane, Queen of the Amazons. 1965: Operation Crossbow. The Heroes of Telemark. Schüsse im ¾ Takt. 1966: The Blue Max. Fahrenheit 451. 1967: The Double Man. Counterpoint. 1968: Where Eagles Dare. 1969: Michael Kohlhaas. 1971: Zeppelin. L'iguana della lingua di fuoco. The Day the Clown Cried (unfinished). 1972: Der Stoff, aus dem die Träume sind. Don't Cry for Me, Little Mother. Hexen: geschandet und zu Tode gequalt. 1973: Sujetska (GB: The Fifth Offensive). Sieben Tote in der Augen der Katze. Tony Arzenta/Big Guns. Dead Pigeon in Beethoven Street. 1974: The Beast Must Die. Borsalino & Co (GB: Blood on the Streets). Shatter. Der Antwort kennt nur der Wind. 1975: Lehmanns Erzählungen (TV). Mark of the Devil Pt II. Operation Daybreak. The Swiss Conspiracy. 1976: Potato Fritz. Vanessa. Liebesbriefe einer portugiesischen Nonne. Io sono mia. 1977: Valentino. Anna Ferroli. Le mutant. Les Indiens sont encore loin. Waldrausch. 1978: L'imprecateur. Das Einhorn. Hitler's Son. 1979: Tusk. 1981: Escape to Victory (US: Victory). 1982: SAS Malko. SAS San Salvador: 1984: The Masks of Death (TV). 1985: Marie Ward. 1986: Der Sommer des Samurai. Operation Dead End. 1987: Richard and Cosima. Wahnfried. 1988: Faceless!

DIGGES, Dudley 1879–1947
Small, dapper, often moustachioed Irish actor much in demand in the Hollywood of the 1930s. Could be downtrodden, downright evil (as in the 1931 The Maltese Falcon), wise, shifty, dogged or devoted—few escaped typecasting more effectively. Perhaps be-

cause of this, however, his career in films faded by the end of the decade. Died after a stroke.

1929: Condemned (GB: Condemned to Devil's Island). 1930: Outward Bound. Upper Underworld. 1931: Alexander Hamilton. The Maltese Falcon. The Ruling Voice. Devotion. 1932: The Hatchet Man (GB: The Honourable Mr Wong). The First Year. Roar of the Dragon. Tess of the Storm Country. The Strange Case of Clara Deane. 1933: The Narrow Corner. The Mayor of Hell. The King's Vacation. The Emperor Jones. The Invisible Man. The Silk Express. Before Dawn. 1934: Fury of the Jungle (GB: Jury of the Jungle). The World Moves On. Caravan. Massacre. I Am a Thief. What Every Woman Knows. 1935: Notorious Gentleman. China Seas. Mutiny on the Bounty. The Bishop Misbehaves (GB: The Bishop's Misadventures). Three Live Ghosts. Kind Lady (later House of Menace). 1936: The Voice of Bugle Ann. The Unguarded Hour. The General Died at Dawn. Valiant Is the Word for Carrie. 1937: Love Is News. 1939: The Light That Failed. 1939/40: Raffles. 1940: The Fight for Life. 1942: Son of Fury. 1946: The Searching Wind.

to character actress Mona Washbourne (*qv*). Once a lumberjack in Canada.

1951: The Lady with a Lamp. Appointment with Venus (US: Island Rescue). His Excellency. 1952: Hammer the Toff. There Was a Young Lady. 1953: Albert RN (US: Break to Freedom). 1954: Carrington VC (US: Court Martial). 1955: Touch and Go (US: The Light Touch). Port of Escape. The Quatermass Experiment (US: The Creeping Unknown). They Can't Hang Me! The Narrowing Circle. Private's Progress. 1956: The Intimate Stranger (US: Finger of Guilt). The Counterfeit Plan. The Weapon. Reach for the Sky. Brothers in Law. 1957: Three Sundays to Live. Son of a Stranger. Yangtse Incident (US: Battle Hell). Man in the Shadow. The Depraved. You Pay Your Money. I Accuse! 1958: I Only Arsked! Rockets Galore (US: Mad Little Island). The Safecracker. Up the Creek. Carry On Sergeant. Corridors of Blood. Them Nice Americans. The Spaniard's Curse. Carlton-Browne of the FO (US: Man in a Cocked Hat). A Cry from the Streets. Room at the Top. Further Up the Creek. 1959: A Touch of Larceny. Sapphire. I'm All Right, Jack. Devil's Bait. 1960: Sentenced for Life. The Pure Hell of St Trinian's. The Spider's Web. Suspect (US: The Risk). 1961: Gorgo. The Court Martial of Major Keller. The Fourth Square. The Secret Partner. Victim. Life for Ruth (US: Walk in the Shadow). Master Spy. 1963: Ring of Spies. 80,000 Suspects. Heavens Above! 1965: Rotten to the Core. Cuckoo Patrol. Operation Crossbow (US: The Great Spy Mission). Joey Boy. The Amorous Adventures of Moll Flanders. Where the Spies Are. 1966: Naked Evil. The Jokers. 1967: Assignment K. I'll Never Forget What's 'is Name. 1968: Twisted Nerve. 1969: Battle of Britain. Laughter in the Dark. The Games. 1970: The Great White Hope. 10 Rillington Place. There's a Girl in My Soup. Cannon for Cordoba. 1972: Young Winston. 1973: Soft Beds, Hard Battles (US: Undercovers Hero).

remains best-remembered as one of Bette Davis's scheming relatives in *The Little Foxes*.

1939: One Third of a Nation. 1941: Unholy Partners. The Little Foxes. Johnny Eager. 1942: Are Husbands Necessary? Calling Dr Gillespie. Tennessee Johnson (GB: The Man on America's Conscience). Somewhere I'll Find You. George Washington Slept Here. The Talk of the Town. 1943: Lady of Burlesque (GB: Striptease Lady). Someone to Remember. She's for Me. Edge of Darkness. The Song of Bernadette. 1944: National Barn Dance. Home in Indiana. Together Again. 1945: A Song to Remember. A Medal for Benny. Guest Wife. Here Come the Co-Eds. Three's a Crowd. 1946: Sister Kenny. Cinderella Jones. Duel in the Sun. Centennial Summer. Three Wise Fools. Wife of Monte Cristo. The Beast with Five Fingers. 1947: My Favorite Brunette. Welcome Stranger. The Romance of Rosy Ridge. 1948: If You Knew Susie. A Southern Yankee (GB: My Hero). State of the Union (GB: The World and His Wife). 1949: Big Jack. 1952: Never Wave at a WAC. 1953: Half a Hero. The President's Lady. Call Me Madam. 1955: The Court Martial of Billy Mitchell (GB: One Man Mutiny).

DOBKIN, Larry or Lawrence 1919–
Authoritative American actor with deep-set eyes in powerful features, bald from an early age. At first seen as minor villains (after a debut as an extra), his commanding presence soon led to a wider range of roles, while his reassuring tones were often used for narration and voice-overs. Also a writer and producer, Dobkin's extensive work in television before and behind the camera has led to his making fewer film appearances than one remembers.

1947: Kiss of Death. 1949: Not Wanted. 12 O'Clock High. 1950: Whirlpool. Broken Arrow (voice only). Never Fear. Frenchie. 1951: †People Will Talk. Chain of Circumstance. The Day the Earth Stood Still. The Mob (GB: Remember That Face). On the Loose. 1942: Above and Beyond. Angels in the Outfield (GB: Angels and the Pirates). Red Skies of Montana. Diplomatic Courier. Loan Shark. Five Fingers. Deadline – USA (GB: Deadline). Washington Story. Ma and Pa Kettle on Vacation (GB: Ma and Pa Kettle Go to Paris). 1953: The Hindu (later and GB: Sabaka). Julius Caesar. Remains to be Seen. The Robe (voice only). 1954: Riders to the Stars. The Silver Chalice. Knock on Wood (voice only). Them! 1955: Illegal. Kiss of Fire.

DIGNAM, Basil 1905–1979
Round-faced, grey-haired, squarely-built, earnest and slightly worried-looking British actor who played small roles in grade 'A' films and top supporting parts in minor thrillers. In his mid-forties before coming to films after lengthy theatrical experience, he quickly built up a list of credits twice as long as his actor brother Mark Dignam (1909–), who remained busier in the theatre. Married

DINGLE, Charles 1887–1956
Stocky, shambling American actor with a mane of greying hair. A Broadway player who only came to films in his fifties, he often played twinkling-eyed, avuncular sorts who were not as benevolent as they looked. His powerful build also led to his playing some crooked figures of authority. From the late 1940s on, he mixed stage, television and film appearances in equal measure. Probably

The Cowboy (voice only). Jump into Hell. 1956: The 10 Commandments. That Certain Feeling. 1957: Raiders of Old California. The Badge of Marshal Brennan. Sweet Smell of Success. Portland Exposé. 1958: The Defiant Ones. Wild Heritage. 1959: North by Northwest. Tokyo After Dark. The Big Operator. The Gene Krupa Story (GB: Drum Crazy). 1962: The Cabinet of Caligari. Geronimo. 1966: Johnny Yuma. 1969: Patton (GB: Patton: Lust for Glory). 1970: Underground. ‡Tarzan's Deadly Silence (TV. Also shown in cinemas). 1972: The Streets of San Francisco (TV). 1974: The Midnight Man. 1979: In Search of Historic Jesus (GB: Jesus). 1981: Hot Wire. 1990: Curiosity Kills (TV). Rock Hudson (TV).

Also as director:
1972: Like a Crow on a June Bug.

† Most scenes deleted
‡ And directed

In a Lonely Place. Tall Timber (GB: Big Timber). Walk Softly Stranger. The Fuller Brush Girl (GB: The Affairs of Sally). Redwood Forest Trail. 1951: Three Guys Named Mike. 1952: Skirts Ahoy! Thief of Damascus. The First Time. *Mealtime Magic. Because You're Mine. 1953: Flight Nurse. So This Is Love (GB: The Grace Moore Story). The Blue Gardenia. 1954: Massacre Canyon. 1956: Magnificent Roughnecks. Sincerely, Willis Wayde (TV). 1957: The Guns of Fort Petticoat. Destination 60,000. Sweet Smell of Success. My Man Godfrey. 1961: Force of Impulse. Gidget Goes Hawaiian. 1962: The Iron Maiden (US: The Swingin' Maiden). 1963: Gidget Goes to Rome. 1969: The Comic. 1970: Love Hate Love (TV). Tora! Tora! Tora! 1971: Congratulations, It's a Boy (TV). 1972: Stand Up and Be Counted. 1976: McNaughton's Daughter (TV). 1977: Spiderman (TV. GB: cinemas). 1978: Murder by Natural Causes (TV). 1979: Rendezvous Hotel (TV). Portrait of a Stripper (TV).

Girls. A Slight Case of Murder. Annabel Takes a Tour. Army Girl. Personal Secretary. Holiday (GB: Free to Live/Unconventional Linda). 1939: Mr Smith Goes to Washington. The Family Next Door. The Amazing Mr Williams. 1950: My Little Chickadee. Meet the Missus. Scatterbrain. 1941: Model Wife. The Roundup. Sailors on Leave. You Belong to Me (GB: Good Morning, Doctor). Petticoat Politics. Rise and Shine. The Gay Vagabond. 1942: Johnny Doughboy. 1943: Thank Your Lucky Stars. This Is the Army. Sleepy Lagoon. 1945: Pillow to Post. The Bells of St Mary's. 1946: Cross My Heart. Cinderella Jones. In Old Sacramento. 1947: The Fabulous Texan. Little Miss Broadway. The Ghost Goes Wild. Millie's Daughter. 1948: The Snake Pit. Fighting Father Dunne. 1950: Where the Sidewalk Ends. 1951: I'd Climb the Highest Mountain. The Secret of Convict Lake. The Wild Blue Yonder (GB: Thunder Across the Pacific). 1955: A Lawless Street. The Spoilers. 1956: Autumn Leaves. 1957: The Way to the Gold.

DONNELL, Jeff
(Jean Donnell) 1921–1988
Happy-looking, red-haired American actress who played bobby-soxers, kid sisters, prairie flowers, best friends, secretaries, shopgirls and other second-leads for 15 years, only graduating to mothers when she turned 40. Her cheery, chirpy personality was always welcome; in latter days, she was too seldom seen. Married (second of three) to actor Aldo Ray from 1954 to 1956. Died from a heart attack.

1942: My Sister Eileen. The Boogie Man Will Get You. A Night to Remember. 1943: City Without Men. What's Buzzin' Cousin? There's Something About a Soldier. Doughboys in Ireland. *Mr Smug. 1944: She's a Soldier, Too. Nine Girls. Stars on Parade. Carolina Blues. Mr Winkle Goes to War (GB: Arms and the Woman). Cowboy Canteen (GB: Close Harmony). Three Is a Family. Once Upon a Time. 1945: Power of the Whistler. Dancing in Manhattan. Eadie Was a Lady. Song of the Prairie (GB: Sentiment and Song). Over 21. He's My Guy. 1946: Throw a Saddle on a Star. Night Editor (GB: The Trespasser). The Phantom Thief. The Unknown. That Texas Jamboree (GB: Medicine Man). Cowboy Blues (GB: Beneath the Starry Skies). Singing on the Trail (GB: Lookin' for Someone). It's Great To Be Young. Tars and Spars. 1947: Mr District Attorney. *My Pal Ringeye. 1949: Stagecoach Kid. Outcasts of the Trail. Roughshod. Post Office Investigator. Easy Living. 1950: Hoedown.

DONNELLY, Ruth 1896–1982
Light-haired, square-built, sharp-eyed American actress with strong chin. Usually cast as ladies who dished out verbal witticisms to the discomfort of their menfolk; sometimes as dowagers who flirted with gigolos. Soon became the Thelma Ritter of the middle-class bracket, but after the death of her husband in the late 1950s, she left films and turned to song-writing.

1927: Rubber Heels. 1931: Transatlantic. Wicked. The Spider. 1932: Make Me a Star. Blessed Event. The Rainbow Trail. Jewel Robbery. 1933: Ladies They Talk About. Hard to Handle. Lilly Turner. Goodbye Again. Ever in My Heart. Private Detective 62. 42nd Street. Female. Convention City. Bureau of Missing Persons. Sing, Sinner, Sing. Havana Widows. Footlight Parade. Employees' Entrance. 1934: Wonder Bar. Romance in the Rain. Happiness Ahead. Housewife. Heat Lightning. Mandalay. The Merry Wives of Reno. You Belong to Me. 1935: The White Cockatoo. Maybe It's Love. Hands Across the Table. Personal Maid's Secret. Metropolitan. Red Salute (GB: Arms and the Girl). Alibi Ike. Traveling Saleslady. 1936: Mr Deeds Goes to Town. The Song and Dance Man. 13 Hours By Air. Fatal Lady. Cain and Mabel. More Than a Secretary. 1937: Portia on Trial (GB: The Trial of Portia Merriman). Roaring Timber. 1938: The Affairs of Annabel. Meet the

DOOLEY, Paul 1928–
Chunky, florid, versatile American actor with receding dark hair. He originally planned to become a cartoonist, then spent a period as a comedy writer for television. Roles in films by Robert Altman in particular brought him to the fore in his fifties and, although sometimes seen as a father or friend, he has proved himself perfectly capable of handling a leading role, as he proved in A Perfect Couple. Oscar nominee for Breaking Away.

1968: What's So Bad About Feeling Good? 1969: The Out-of-Towners. 1972: Up the Sandbox. 1973: The New York Experience (voices only). 1974: Death Wish. The Dion Brothers (TV. GB: cinemas, as The Gravy Train). 1976: Slap Shot. 1977: Raggedy Ann and Andy (voice only). 1978: A Wedding. 1979: A Perfect Couple. Rich Kids. Breaking Away. Health (shown 1982). 1980: Popeye. 1981: Paternity. 1982: Endangered Species. Kiss Me Goodbye. 1983: Going Berserk! Strange Brew. 1984: Sixteen Candles. Big Trouble. 1986: Monster in the Closet. O C and Stiggs. 1988: Last Rites. Lip Service (TV). 1989: Flashback. When He's Not a Stranger (TV). 1990: Guess Who's Coming for Christmas? The Court-Martial of Jackie Robinson (TV). 1991: White Hot: The Mysterious Murder of Thelma Todd (TV). Shakes the Clown. 1992: Perry Mason: The Case of the Heartbroken Bride (TV). The Player. 1993:

Cooperstown (TV). My Boyfriend's Back. A Dangerous Woman. 1994: State of Emergency (TV). God's Lonely Man. 1995: The Underneath.

DOONAN, Patric 1925–1958
Fair, wavy-haired British actor (son of music-hall comedian George Doonan), with a hunted, shifty look. After numerous roles as secondary crooks, other ranks and the occasional hero's friend, his film career petered out. He might have played hard-nosed police inspectors, but the opportunity seemed to escape him. Committed suicide by gassing himself. Married actress Aud Johansen in 1953.

1940: In the Nick of Time. 1944: Dreaming. 1948: Once a Jolly Swagman (US: Maniacs on Wheels). All Over the Town. 1949: Train of Events. A Run for Your Money. The Blue Lamp. 1950: Blackout. Highly Dangerous. 1951: Appointment with Venus (US: Island Rescue). Calling Bulldog Drummond. The Lavender Hill Mob. The Man in the White Suit. High Treason. 1952: I'm a Stranger. Gift Horse (US: Glory at Sea). The Gentle Gunman. The Net (US: Project M7). 1953: Wheel of Fate. The Red Beret (US: Paratrooper). The Case of Gracie Budd. 1954: What Every Woman Wants. Seagulls Over Sorrento (US: Crest of the Wave). 1955: John and Julie. Cockleshell Heroes.

DORAN, Ann 1911–
Light-haired, rather plain American actress with slightly hunted look. Texas-born Doran has never built up the cult following of some

character players and remained, for almost 50 years, one of the most anonymous supporting people on the Hollywood scene. Often seen as a secretary, friend of the heroine, worried wife or simply frightened female, her leading roles were largely confined to a fistful of two-reel comedies at Columbia. As the epitome of the working woman or average American wife, it wasn't suprising that she appeared in several Frank Capra films of the 1930s and 1940s. He remained her favourite director. Acting since childhood, she has clocked up scores of films plus hundreds of appearances on TV. Perhaps best recalled as James Dean's mother in Rebel Without a Cause.

1922: Robin Hood. 1933: Zoo in Budapest. 1934: Charlie Chan in London. Servants' Entrance. One Exciting Adventure. 1935: Mary Burns, Fugitive. Bad Boy. The Case of the Missing Man. Night Life of the Gods. Way Down East. 1936: Dangerous Intrigue. Let's Sing Again. The Little Red Schoolhouse (GB: Schoolboy Penitentiary). The Man Who Lived Twice. Palm Springs (GB: Palm Springs Affair). Ring Around the Moon. Missing Girls. Mr Deeds Goes to Town. 1937: Devil's Playground. Marry the Girl. Red Lights Ahead. The Go-Getter. Paid to Dance. Stella Dallas. *Gracie at the Bat. The Shadow (GB: The Circus Shadow). When You're in Love (GB: For You Alone). Girls Can Play. Nothing Sacred. 1938: City Streets. Extortion. *The Old Raid Mule. *Ankles Away. Blondie. *Time Out for Trouble. *The Mind Needer. *Many Sappy Returns. *Pie a la Maid. *Half Way to Hollywood. Highway Patrol. The Main Event. Rio Grande. The Lady Objects. She Married an Artist. Start Cheering. *A Doggone Mix-Up. *Sue My Lawyer. *Rattling Romeo. *Skinny the Moocher. The Spider's Web. Penitentiary. Women in Prison. You Can't Take It With You. Blind Alibi. 1939: Coast Guard. The Green Hornet (serial). Flying G-Men (serial). Good Girls Go to Paris. Homicide Bureau. Let Us Live. The Man They Could Not Hang. Mr Smith Goes to Washington. *Three Sappy People. *Trouble Finds Andy Clyde. *Static in the Attic. My Son is a Criminal. Romance of the Redwoods. Rio Grande. Smashing the Spy Ring. A Woman is the Judge. 1940: Girls of the Road. *Cold Turkey. *South of the Border. *Blondes and Blunders. Glamour for Sale. Five Little Peppers at Home. Manhattan Heartbeat. Untamed. 1941: Buy Me That Town. *Half Shot at Sunrise. *Lovable Trouble. Dr Kildare's Wedding Day (GB: Mary Names the Day). Ellery Queen's Penthouse Mystery. Criminals Within. The Kid from Kansas. Blue, White and Perfect. Meet John Doe. Murder Among Friends. New York Town. Penny Serenade. Sun Valley Serenade. Dive Bomber. Sing Another Chorus. 1942: Beyond the Blue Horizon. Mr Wise Guy. My Sister Eileen. The Hard Way. Street of Chance. *Three Blonde Mice. They All Kissed the Bride. Yankee Doodle Dandy. 1943: Gildersleeve on Broadway. The More the Merrier. Air Force. Old Acquaintance. Slightly Dangerous. So Proudly We Hail! True to Life. 1944: Henry Aldrich's Little Secret (GB: Henry's Little Secret). I Love a Soldier. *His Tale is Told. *Doctor, Feel My Pulse. The Story of Dr Wassell. Here Come the Waves. Mr Skeffington. 1945:

Pride of the Marines (GB: Forever in Love). Roughly Speaking. 1946: Our Hearts Were Growing Up. The Perfect Marriage. The Strange Love of Martha Ivers. 1947: Fear in the Night. For the Love of Rusty. The Crimson Key. My Favorite Brunette. Magic Town. Road to the Big House. Second Chance. Reaching from Heaven. Seven Were Saved. The Son of Rusty. Variety Girl. 1948: The Babe Ruth Story. He Walked by Night. Hazard. My Dog Rusty. No Minor Vices. The Accused. Pitfall. The Return of the Whistler. Sealed Verdict. Rusty Leads the Way. The Snake Pit. The Walls of Jericho. 1949: Air Hostess. Big Jack. Calamity Jane and Sam Bass. The Clay Pigeon. Beyond the Forest. The Kid from Cleveland. The Fountainhead. Holiday in Havana. Rusty's Birthday. One Last Fling. Rusty Saves a Life. 1950: Gambling House. Lonely Hearts Bandits (GB: Lonely Heart Bandits). The Rawhide Trail. Never a Dull Moment. The Jackpot. No Sad Songs for Me. Riding High. Tomahawk (GB: Battle of Powder River). 1951: Her First Romance (GB: Girls Never Tell). The Painted Hills. The People Against O'Hara. Here Come the Nelsons. Starlift. Love is Better than Ever (GB: The Light Fantastic). 1952: Rodeo. The Rose Bowl Story. 1953: War Paint. The Eddie Cantor Story. So This is Love (GB: The Grace Moore Story). 1954: The Bob Mathias Story (GB: The Flaming Torch). Them! The High and the Mighty. City Story. 1955: The Desperate Hours. Rebel Without a Cause. My Sister Eileen. The Reluctant Bride (US: Two Grooms for a Bride). 1957: The Man Who Turned to Stone. Band of Angels. Day of the Bad Man. Shoot-Out at Medicine Bend. Young and Dangerous. 1958: The Deep Six. The Female Animal. IT! The Terror from Beyond Space. Joy Ride. Step Down to Terror (GB: The Silent Stranger). Life Begins at 17. The Badlanders. The Rawhide Trail. Violent Road. Voice in the Mirror. 1959: The FBI Story. Cast a Long Shadow. A Summer Place. Riot in Juvenile Prison. Warlock. 1961: The Explosive Generation. One-Eyed Jacks. Barabbas. 1963: Captain Newman MD. The Carpetbaggers. 1964: The Brass Bottle. Kitten with a Whip. Where Love Has Gone. 1965: Mirage. 1966: Not with My Wife, You Don't! Smoky. The Hostage. A Convenant with Death. 1967: Rosie! 1968: Live a Little, Love a Little. Stay Away, Joe! 1969: The Arrangement. Topaz. Once You Kiss a Stranger. 1970: There Was a Crooked Man. Weekend of Terror (TV). 1971: The Hired Hand. The Priest Killer (TV). 1974: The Last Angry Man (TV). The Story of Pretty Boy Floyd (TV). 1975: The Family Nobody Wanted (TV). The MacAhans: How the West Was Won (TV). 1976: Flood! (TV. GB: cinemas). 1977: Peter Lundy and the Medicine Hat Stallion (TV). Dead of Night (TV). 1978: Little Mo (TV). 1981: Crazy Times (TV). First Monday in October. All Night Long. Advice to the Lovelorn (TV). 1985: Wildcats.

DOUCETTE, John 1921–1994
Saturnine American supporting actor of receding dark hair and sour and shifty features. He was usually to be found in minor but well-drawn roles in westerns, as lawmen in the pay of the town boss, or shadowy figures who never quite met your gaze. Reliability was not a notable asset of this actor's

characters, only of his performances in scores of films throughout the 1950s, after which, with the demise of the co-feature, his movie output rapidly dwindled. In more recent times, he lectured on communicating arts, as well as forming a company to promote educational records. Had eight children. Died from cancer.

1943: Two Tickets to London. 1947: The Burning Cross. The Foxes of Harrow. The Road to the Big House. Ride the Pink Horse. 1948: And Baby Makes Three. Cañon City. Criss Cross. For Those Who Dare. The Fountainhead. In This Corner. I Wouldn't Be in Your Shoes. Rogues' Regiment. Station West. Train to Alcatraz. The Walls of Jericho. 1949: The Crooked Way. The Black Book/Reign of Terror. Bandits of El Dorado (GB: Tricked). The Fighting O'Flynn. Red Stallion in the Rockies. Lust for Gold. Adventures of Batman and Robin (serial). 1950: Broken Arrow. Customs Agent. The Breaking Point. Iroquois Trail (GB: The Tomahawk Trail). Convicted. Border Treasure. The Vicious Years. Winchester 73. Radar Patrol vs Spy King (serial). The Fuller Brush Girl (GB: The Affairs of Sally). Gasoline Alley. Counterspy Meets Scotland Yard. Love That Brute. Sierra. Johnny One-Eye. Return of the Frontiersman. 1951: Cavalry Scout. Corky of Gasoline Alley (GB: Corky). Fixed Bayonets! The Lemon Drop Kid. Only the Valiant. Strangers on a Train. Warpath. The Lady Pays Off. Tales of Robin Hood. The Texas Rangers. Thunder in God's Country. Up Front. Woman in the Dark. Yukon Manhunt. 1952: Bugles in the Afternoon. Desert Pursuit. High Noon. Carbine Williams. Deadline – USA (GB: Deadline). The Ghost of Crossbones Canyon. The Pride of St Louis. Rose of Cimarron. The San Francisco Story. Rancho Notorious. Phone Call from a Stranger. The Treasure of Lost Canyon. Toughest Man in Arizona. Woman in the Dark. Off Limits (GB: Military Policemen). 1953: City of Bad Men. Ambush at Tomahawk Gap. All the Brothers Were Valiant. Flight to Tangier. The Big Heat. Goldtown Ghost Riders. Beach-head. Julius Caesar. The Robe. Perils of the Jungle. The Silver Whip. The Wild One. War Paint. Casanova's Big Night. 1954: Cry Vengeance. Executive Suite. River of No Return. The Forty-Niners. The Last Time I Saw Paris. Return from the Sea. There's No Business Like Show Business. Destry. The Far Country. 1955: Annapolis Story (GB: The Blue and The Gold). House of Bamboo. New York Confidential. The Sea Chase. Seven Cities of Gold. Prince of

Players. 1956: The Fastest Gun Alive. The Burning Hills. Quincannon, Frontier Scout (GB: Frontier Scout). The Bottom of the Bottle (GB: Beyond the River). Dakota Incident. Ghost Town. The Maverick Queen. Red Sundown. Thunder Over Arizona. 1957: Bombers B-52 (GB: No Sleep Till Dawn). The Big Land (GB: Stampeded!). Gunfire at Indian Gap. Last of the Badmen. The Lawless Eighties. Phantom Stagecoach. The Crooked Circle. The Lonely Man. Peyton Place. Sabu and the Magic Ring. The True Story of Jesse James (GB: The James Brothers). Kiss Them for Me. 1958: Gang War. A Nice Little Bank That Should Be Robbed (GB: How to Rob a Bank). The Hunters. Too Much, Too Soon. 1959: Here Come the Jets. 1960: The Time Machine. 1963: Cleopatra. 1964: The Seven Faces of Dr Lao. 1965: The Sons of Katie Elder. 1966: Paradise – Hawaiian Style. Nevada Smith. The Fastest Guitar Alive. 1968: Journey to Shiloh. 1969: True Grit. Patton (GB: Patton – Lust for Glory). 1971: Big Jake. One More Train to Rob. 1973: One Little Indian. 1976: Fighting Mad. Panache (TV). 1978: Donner Pass. The Road to Survival (TV). The Time Machine (TV. And 1960 film). 1983: Heart of Steel (TV).

DOUGLAS, Robert

(Robert D. Finlayson) 1909–
Floridly handsome, light-haired, moustachioed British actor who went to Hollywood in 1948, and used his world-class prowess as a swordsman to give himself eight years of swashbuckling villains. Later became a director and worked prolifically in television. At one time married to actress Dorothy Hyson.

1930: PC Josser. 1931: Many Waters. 1933: The Blarney Stone (US: The Blarney Kiss). 1935: Death Drives Through. 1937: Our Fighting Navy (US: Torpedoed!). London Melody (US: Girls in the Street). Over the Moon. 1938: The Challenge. 1939: The Lion Has Wings. Chinese Bungalow (US: Chinese Den). 1947: The End of the River. 1948: Adventures of Don Juan (GB: The New Adventures of Don Juan). The Decision of Christopher Blake. 1949: The Fountainhead. Homicide. The Lady Takes a Sailor. 1950: Barricade. Buccaneer's Girl. This Side of the Law. The Flame and the Arrow. Spy Hunt (GB: Panther's Moon). Kim. Mystery Submarine. 1951: Thunder on the Hill (GB: Bonaventure). Target Unknown. At Sword's Point (GB: Sons of the Musketeers).

1952: Ivanhoe. The Prisoner of Zenda. 1953: The Desert Rats. Fair Wind to Java. Flight to Tangier. 1954: Saskatchewan (GB: O'Rourke of the Royal Mounted). King Richard and the Crusaders. 1955: The Virgin Queen. Helen of Troy. The Scarlet Coat. Good Morning Miss Dove. 1959: The Young Philadelphians (GB: The City Jungle). Tarzan the Ape-Man. 1960: The Lawbreakers (TV. GB: cinemas). 1968: Secret Ceremony (extended TV version only). 1974: The Questor Tapes (TV).

As director:
1964: Night Train to Paris. 1976: Future Cop (TV).

DOURIF, Brad 1950–

Wild-eyed, dark-haired, round-faced, American actor adept at twitching neurotics, whether pitching for sympathy, laughs or chills. He won an Oscar nomination in his second film, as the tormented Billy Bibbitt in *One Flew Over the Cuckoo's Nest*, but proved difficult to cast in leading roles, even if his performances in them were, to say the least, distinctive. He began to work much more prolifically in the cinema in the late 1980s and early 1990s, sometimes in cameo roles, and to attempt a wider range of more general weirdoes. There were some bizarre ventures at this time, but he was still often the best thing in them.

1975: WW and the Dixie Dancekings. One Flew Over the Cuckoo's Nest. Split! (released 1988). 1977: Gruppenbild mit Dame. 1978: Eyes of Laura Mars. Sergeant Matlovich vs the US Air Force (TV). 1979: Studs Lonigan (TV). Wise Blood. 1980: Guyana Tragedy: The Story of Jim Jones (TV). Heaven's Gate. 1981: Ragtime. 1982: I, Desire (TV). 1984: Dune. 1985: Istanbul. 1986: Blue Velvet. Impure Thoughts. Vengeance: The Story of Tony Cimo (TV). 1987: Fatal Beauty. 1988: Child's Play. Mississippi Burning. Terror on Highway 91 (TV). 1989: Medium Rare. Desperado: The Outlaw Wars (TV). Spontaneous Combustion. 1990: Child's Play 2 (voice only). Grim Prairie Tales. Hidden Agenda. The Horseplayer. Sonny Boy. Graveyard Shift. The Exorcist III. 1991: Body Parts. Jungle Fever. Scream of Stone. London Kills Me. Chaindance. 1992: Critters 4. Innocent Blood. The Diary of the Hurdy-Gurdy Man. Dead Certain. 1993: Trauma. Amos & Andrew. 1994: The Color of Night. Death Machine. Murder in the First. 1995: Phoenix.

DOWLING, Joan 1928–1954
Blonde, blue-eyed British actress whose career progressed from cheerful cockney teenagers to put-upon waifs to sluttish other women. Had difficulty finding a good range of adult roles and, at 26, was found dead in a gas-filled room. Married to Harry Fowler (from 1951).

*1947: Hue and Cry. 1948: Bond Street. No Room at the Inn. *Pathe Pictorial No 132. 1949: For Them That Trespass. A Man's Affair. Landfall. Train of Events. 1950: Murder without Crime. 1951: The Magic Box. Pool of London. 1952: 24 Hours in a Woman's Life (US: Affair in Monte Carlo). Women of Twilight (US: Twilight Women). 1953: The Case of Gracie Budd.*

Now, Voyager. Busses Roar. Across the Pacific. The Gay Sisters. Yankee Doodle Dandy. Larceny Inc. Dangerously They Live. 1943: Air Force. 1944: Mr Skeffington. 1945: Conflict. You Came Along. 1946: Whistle Stop. A Night in Casablanca. 1947: Winter Wonderland. The Pretender. 1948: The Tender Years. Bowie Knife. 1949: Johnny Stool Pigeon. Tarzan's Magic Fountain. 1950: I Was a Shoplifter. Comanche Territory. Winchester '73. Peggy. Harvey. 1951: Little Egypt (GB: Chicago Masquerade). Air Cadet (GB: Jet Men of the Air). You Never Can Tell (GB: You Never Know). Treasure of Lost Canyon. 1952: Bonzo Goes to College. Red Ball Express. 1953: Gunsmoke! The Lone Hand. It Came from Outer Space. War Arrow. The Glenn Miller Story. 1954: Tobor the Great. Four Guns to the Border. 1955: Female on the Beach. All That Heaven Allows. To Hell and Back. 1956: Walk the Proud Land. The Price of Fear. The Night Runner. Gun in His Hand (TV. GB: cinemas). 1957: Jeanne Eagels. Until They Sail. 1958: Step Down to Terror (GB: The Silent Stranger). Reunion (TV). No Name on the Bullet. 1961: Tammy Tell Me True. Back Street. 1963: Showdown. 1964: Dear Heart. The Lively Set. 1965: The Third Day. 1967: Valley of the Dolls. The Counterfeit Killer (TV. GB: cinemas). 1968: The Swimmer. The Smugglers (TV). The Money Jungle. 1969: The Arrangement. Hail Hero. 1971: The Seven Minutes. The Screaming Woman (TV). 1973: Partners in Crime (TV). Scream Pretty Peggy (TV). 1975: The Return of Joe Forrester (TV). The Lives of Jenny Dolan (TV).*

Dictator (US: The Loves of a Dictator). Oh Daddy! 1936: Tropical Trouble. The Crimson Circle. Aren't Men Beasts! 1938: A Spot of Bother. 1939: So This Is London. 1941: Banana Ridge. The Big Blockade. 1942: Women Aren't Angels. 1944: Don't Take It to Heart. Halfway House. 1945: They Knew Mr Knight. 1947: Nicholas Nickleby. 1948: Things Happen at Night.*

DRESDEL, Sonia
(Lois Obee, later legally changed)
1909–1976
Stern-looking, dark-haired English actress who made a formidable villainess—the woman you loved to hate. She preferred a stage career but, even so, some of her film roles were so memorable, especially the evil wife in *The Fallen Idol*, that it's amazing her films were so few and far between. In full flight, she would have made a memorable Lady Macbeth.

1944: The World Owes Me a Living. 1947: While I Live. 1948: This Was a Woman. The Fallen Idol. 1950: The Clouded Yellow. 1951: The Third Visitor. 1956: Now and Forever. The Secret Tent. 1957: Death over my Shoulder. 1960: The Trials of Oscar Wilde (US: The Man with the Green Carnation). 1962: The Break. 1972: Lady Caroline Lamb.

DRAKE, Charles
(C. Ruppert) 1914–
Very tall, well-built, mild-mannered American actor with fair, wavy hair and vaguely bemused expression, in very small roles during the war years, then as 'second lead' in films from the mid-1940s to the early 1960s; his best roles came in movies with his real-life friend Audie Murphy. Could be colourless as juvenile lead, much more absorbing as characters with an interest on either side of the fence.

1939: Career. 1941: Affectionately Yours. Nine Lives Are Not Enough. Sergeant York. Navy Blues. Out of the Fog. You're in the Army Now. I Wanted Wings. The Man Who Came to Dinner. The Maltese Falcon. Million Dollar Baby. Dive Bomber. One Foot in Heaven. The Body Disappears. 1942: The Male Animal.

DRAYTON, Alfred
(A. Varick) 1881–1949
Big, broad-shouldered, bald, barnstorming, husky-voiced, often beaming British actor, equally at home in drama or farce. He made his reputation on stage and never deserted the theatre, although a powerful and very popular member of film casts from 1930.

*1915: Iron Justice. 1919: A Little Bit of Fluff. 1920: The Honeypot. The Winning Goal. A Temporary Gentleman. 1921: *A Scandal in Bohemia. Love Maggy. 1930: The 'W' Plan. The Squeaker. 1931: The Calendar (US: Bachelor's Folly). Brown Sugar. 1932: Lord Babs. 1933: The Little Damozel. Friday the Thirteenth. It's a Boy. Falling for You. 1934: Red Ensign (US: Strike!) Jack Ahoy! Lady in Danger. Radio Parade of 1935 (US: Radio Follies). 1935: Look Up and Laugh. Me and Marlborough. First a Girl. The*

DUGGAN, Andrew 1923–1988
Strong-jawed, fair-haired, reliable-looking American actor who frequently made a mockery of such looks by playing villainous or even comic roles. His characters were

usually smartly dressed, and had eyes that looked right through you and a persuasive charm – not always to the hero or heroine's advantage. A prolific TV guest star in dramas and mini-series. Died from cancer.

1956: Patterns (GB: Patterns of Power). 1957: The Money. Three Brave Men. The Domino Kid. Decision at Sundown. 1958: Return to Warbow. The Bravados. 1959: The Taste of Ashes (TV. GB: cinemas). Westbound. 1961: The Chapman Report. 1962: House of Women. Merrill's Marauders. FBI Code 98. 1963: The Incredible Mr Limpet. Palm Springs Weekend. 1964: Seven Days in May. 1965: The Glory Guys. 1967: In Like Flint. The Secret War of Harry Frigg. 1968: Hawaii Five-O (TV). 1970: Loving. 1971: Skin Game. The Forgotten Man (TV). Two on a Bench (TV). The Homecoming (TV). 1972: Jigsaw (TV). The Streets of San Francisco (TV). Bone (GB: Dial Rat for Terror). 1973: It's Alive! Firehouse (TV). 1974: The Last Angry Man (TV). Panic on the 5:22 (TV). The Bears and I. 1975: Collision Course (TV). Attack on Terror: The FBI Versus the Ku Klux Klan (TV). 1977: Tail Gunner Joe (TV). The Private Files of J Edgar Hoover. The Deadliest Season (TV). Pine Canyon is Burning (TV). The Hunted Lady (TV). 1978: It Lives Again. Overboard/The Suicide's Wife (TV). The Time Machine (TV). A Fire in the Sky (TV). 1979: The Incredible Journey of Dr Meg Laurel (TV). 1980: M Station: Hawaii (TV). The Long Days of Summer (TV). One Last Ride. 1981: Frankenstein's Island. 1983: Doctor Detroit. 1987: J Edgar Hoover (TV). Return to Salem's Lot.

DUKAKIS, Olympia 1931–
Spirited, round-faced, brown-haired, wise-looking American actress who was almost unknown to movie audiences until she won an Academy Award as Cher's mother in *Moonstruck*, achieved at the same time as she created a higher show business profile by being the cousin of Presidential hopeful Michael Dukakis. Later played a variety of star-billed, sympathetic top character roles, and gained a small notoriety by going topless at 60 for her role in the Australian enterprise *'Round the Bend*. Was a fencing champion, physical therapist, then drama teacher before taking to the stage.

1963: Twice a Man. 1964: Lilith. 1969: John and Mary. 1971: Made for Each Other. 1974:

Death Wish. Nicky's World (TV). 1979: The Rehearsal. Rich Kids. The Wanderers. 1980: The Idolmaker. 1981: National Lampoon's Movie Madness/National Lampoon Goes to the Movies (released 1983). 1982: The Neighborhood (TV). 1985: Walls of Glass/Flanagan. 1987: Moonstruck. 1988: Working Girl. 1989: Steel Magnolias. Look Who's Talking. Dad. In the Spirit. 1990: Look Who's Talking Too. 1991: Lucky Day (TV). Over the Hill/'Round the Bend. 1992: Fire in the Dark (TV). Ruby Cairo. 1993: The Cemetery Club. Digger. Armistead Maupin's Tales of the City (TV). 1994: Look Who's Talking Now. Dead Badge. Obsession. I Love Trouble. Naked Gun 33⅓: The Final Insult. The Haunted Heart. 1995: Jeffrey. Sweetheart. Mr Holland's Opus.

DUMBRILLE, Douglass 1888–1974
Stiff-necked, eagle-eyed, saturnine, moustachioed Canadian actor whose smile was that of a conspirator, and whose villains could be stuffy or sadistic, farcical or for real. A good foil for the Marx Brothers, Bob Hope and Abbott and Costello, a fine sophisticated menace for a fistful of 'B' feature detectives to overcome. Sometimes billed as 'Douglas' in the 1930s. Died from a heart attack.

*1916: What 80 Million Women Want. 1931: Monkey Business. His Woman. Dirigible. *The Door Knocker. 1932: That's My Boy. The Wiser Sex. Blondie of the Follies. Laughter in Hell. I Am a Fugitive from a Chain Gang. 1933: The Working Man. Female. The World Changes. The Pride of the Legion. Elmer the Great. Smoke Lightning. The Big Brain. The Man Who Dared. Hard to Handle. The Way to Love. Baby Face. Heroes for Sale. Silk Express. Rustlers' Roundup. Convention City. Gambling Ship. Lady Killer. King of the Jungle. Voltaire. 1934: Massacre. Operator 13 (GB: Spy 13). Fog over Frisco. Hide-Out. Treasure Island. Harold Teen (GB: The Dancing Fool). Hi, Nellie! Journal of a Crime. Broadway Bill (GB: Strictly Confidential). Stamboul Quest. The Secret Bride (GB: Concealment). 1935: Lives of a Bengal Lancer. Naughty Marietta. Love Me Forever. Peter Ibbetson. Air Hawks. Cardinal Richelieu. Crime and Punishment. The Public Menace. Unknown Woman. 1936: The Lone Wolf Returns. The Music Goes Round. Mr Deeds Goes to Town. The Calling of Dan Matthews. End of the Trail. You May Be Next!*

(GB: Panic on the Air). M'Liss. The Witness Chair. The Princess Comes Across. 1937: A Day at the Races. The Firefly. Ali Baba Goes to Town. Woman in Distress. Counterfeit Lady. The Emperor's Candlesticks. 1938: The Buccaneer. Storm Over Bengal. Crime Takes a Holiday. Sharpshooters. Fast Company. Stolen Heaven. Kentucky. The Mysterious Rider. 1939: Thunder Afloat. Charlie Chan at Treasure Island. The Three Musketeers (GB: The Singing Musketeer). Tell No Tales. Captain Fury. Rovin' Tumbleweeds. Charlie Chan in City of Darkness. Mr Moto in Danger Island (GB: Mr Moto on Danger Island). 1940: Slightly Honorable. South of Pago Pago. Virginia City. Catman of Paris (released 1946). 1941: Michael Shayne, Private Detective. The Big Store. Ellery Queen and the Perfect Crime (GB: The Perfect Crime). The Roundup. Murder Among Friends. Washington Melodrama. 1942: Stand By for Action! (GB: Cargo of Innocents). Ride 'Em Cowboy. Castle in the Desert. Ten Gentlemen from West Point. A Gentleman After Dark. I Married an Angel. DuBarry Was a Lady. King of the Mounties (serial). 1943: False Colors. 1944: Lumberjack. Uncertain Glory. Lost in a Harem. Jungle Woman. Gypsy Wildcat. Forty Thieves. 1945: Road to Utopia. Jungle Queen (serial). The Frozen Ghost. The Daltons Ride Again. Flame of the West. A Medal for Benny. 1946: The Cat Creeps. Spook Busters. Night in Paradise. Monsieur Beaucaire. Pardon My Past. Under Nevada Skies. 1947: Christmas Eve. It's a Joke, Son! The Fabulous Texan. The Dragnet. Dishonored Lady. Blonde Savage. 1948: Last of the Wild Horses. 1949: Tell It to the Judge. Alimony. Dynamite. Joe Palooka in the Counterpunch. The Lone Wolf and His Lady. Riders of the Whistling Pines. 1950: Buccaneer's Girl. Her Wonderful Lie. The Kangaroo Kid. Abbott and Costello in the Foreign Legion. Riding High. The Savage Horde. Rapture. 1951: A Millionaire for Christy. 1952: Son of Paleface. Apache War Smoke. Sky Full of Moon. Scaramouche. Sound Off. 1953: Julius Caesar. Plunder of the Sun. Captain John Smith and Pocahontas (GB: Burning Arrows). 1954: World for Ransom. Lawless Rider. The Key Man/A Life at Stake. 1955: Jupiter's Darling. Davy Crockett and the River Pirates. 1956: The Ten Commandments. Shake, Rattle and Rock. Mobs Inc. 1958: The Buccaneer (remake). 1960: High Time. 1962: Air Patrol. 1963: Johnny Cool. 1964: Shock Treatment. What a Way to Go!

DUMKE, Ralph 1899–1964
Truculent-looking, heavyweight, brown-haired American supporting actor, a minor-league Sydney Greenstreet. Most often seen in white trilbies and suits, mopping his brow in the approved Greenstreet fashion. He came to Hollywood in middle age after a long stage career, much of it spent singing in light opera, and played almost entirely villains, entrepreneurs and corrupt businessmen. Occasionally allowed to play a blusterer in the Thurston Hall (*qv*) tradition. His voice became well-known in the 1930s on a popular American radio comedy show called *Sisters of the Skillet*.

1942: Lucky Jordan. 1949: All the King's Men. 1950: Where Danger Lives. Mystery Street.

The Fireball. The Breaking Point. 1951: When I Grow Up. The Law and the Lady. The Mob (GB: Remember That Face). Boots Malone. 1952: The San Francisco Story. Carbine Williams. Rancho Notorious. The War of the Worlds. Holiday for Sinners. We're Not Married. Hurricane Smith. 1953: Hannah Lee/Outlaw Territory. Mississippi Gambler. Lili. Count the Hours (GB: Every Minute Counts). It Should Happen to You. Massacre Canyon. The President's Lady. She Couldn't Say No (GB: Beautiful But Dangerous). Alaska Seas. 1954: They Rode West. Rails into Laramie. Daddy Long Legs. 1955: Artists and Models. Violent Saturday. Hell's Island. 1956: When Gangland Strikes. Francis in the Haunted House. Forever Darling. Invasion of the Body Snatchers. The Solid Gold Cadillac. 1957: The Buster Keaton Story. Loving You. 1960: Wake Me When It's Over. 1961: All in a Night's Work.

DUMONT, Margaret
(Daisy Baker) 1889–1965
Tall, stately American actress, built along dowager duchess lines, who started her career as a singer, but became the world's best-loved comedy foil when she started working, at first on stage, then in films, with the Marx Brothers as characters with whom flattery would get you anywhere. Groucho always insisted that she didn't understand the jokes. Died from a heart attack a few days after a TV sketch with Groucho.

1917: A Tale of Two Cities. 1929: The Cocoanuts. 1930: Animal Crackers. 1931: The Girl Habit. 1933: Duck Soup. 1934: Gridiron Flash

(GB: Luck of the Game). Kentucky Kernels (GB: Triple Trouble). Fifteen Wives (GB: The Man with the Electric Voice). 1935: A Night at the Opera. Orchids to You. Rendezvous. After Office Hours. Reckless. 1936: Anything Goes. The Song and Dance Man. 1937: A Day at the Races. Wise Girl. Youth on Parole. High Flyers. The Life of the Party. 1938: Dramatic School. 1939: The Women. At the Circus. 1941: For Beauty's Sake. The Big Store. Never Give a Sucker an Even Break. 1942: Born To Sing. About Face. †Tales of Manhattan. Rhythm Parade. Sing Your Worries Away. 1943: The Dancing Masters. 1944: Seven Days Ashore. Up in Arms. Bathing Beauty. 1945: Sunset in El Dorado. Billy Rose's Diamond Horseshoe (GB: Diamond Horseshoe). The Horn Blows at Midnight. 1946: Little Giant (GB: On the Carpet). Susie Steps Out. 1952: Three for Bedroom C. Stop, You're Killing Me. 1956: Shake, Rattle and Rock. 1958: Auntie Mame. 1962: Zotz! 1964: What a Way To Go!

† Scene deleted from final release print

DUNN, Michael
(Gary Miller) 1934–1973
The most successful dwarf actor in Hollywood's history, Dunn was forced to abandon a career as a concert pianist because of the congenital chondrodystrophy which eventually brought about his death. After being nominated for an Academy Award in Ship of Fools, he tackled an amazing variety of roles, although none so rewarding as the private eye in the TV movie Goodnight My Love.

1960: Pity Me Not. 1961: Without Each Other. 1965: Ship of Fools. 1966: You're a Big Boy Now. 1967: No Way to Treat a Lady. 1968: Madigan. Boom! Kampf um Rom (GB: The Struggle for Rome). 1969: Justine. Kampf um Rom II. Too Small Ticky. 1971: Murders in the Rue Morgue. You Think You've Got Problems (TV). 1972: *The Swan Song. Goodnight My Love (TV). 1973: The Mutations. The Werewolf of Washington. Frankenstein's Castle of Freaks. 1974: La loba y la paloma. The Abdication.

DUNNE, Griffin 1955–
Dark-haired, fresh-faced American actor and producer, a somewhat better-looking and slightly taller version of Britain's Dudley Moore. A light leading man and equally light character actor, Dunne has often played

amiable wimps or hapless victims of circumstance. He has also produced a number of successful independent movies with partner Amy Robinson. The brother of actress Dominique Dunne (the victim of a sensational murder), he married actress Carey Lowell in 1989.

1975: The Other Side of the Mountain (GB: A Window to the Sky). 1979: Head Over Heels. 1981: An American Werewolf in London. The Fan. 1982: The Wall (TV). Chilly Scenes of Winter (revised version of Head Over Heels). 1983: Cold Feet. 1984: Almost You. Johnny Dangerously. 1985: After Hours. 1986: Amazon Women on the Moon. 1987: Who's That Girl. 1988: Me and Him. The Big Blue. Lip Service (TV). 1989: Perugia. 1990: Once Around. Secret Witness (TV). 1991: My Girl. Buying a Landslide (TV). 1992: Straight Talk. Big Girls Don't Cry ... They Get Even (GB: Stepkids). Hotel Room (TV). 1993: The Pickle. 1994: Search and Destroy. I Like It Like That. Quiz Show.

DUNNOCK, Mildred 1900–1991
Black-haired, thin-featured, birdlike American actress, adept at spinsters, whether fey, warm-hearted, waspish or astute. She worked briefly as a teacher before embarking on an acting career, and enjoying years of success on stage. Film appearances were relatively few but often memorable, and she was exceptionally busy on television in the 1950s. Her strong acting style took her to two Oscar nominations, for Death of a Salesman and Baby Doll, and there might well have

been others for *The Corn is Green* (a repeat of her stage role) and *Sweet Bird of Youth*.

1945: The Corn is Green. 1947: Kiss of Death. 1951: I Want You. Death of a Salesman. 1952: The Girl in White (GB: So Bright the Flame). Viva Zapata! 1953: The Jazz Singer. Bad for Each Other. 1954: Hansel and Gretel (voice only). 1955: The Trouble with Harry. 1956: Baby Doll. Love Me Tender. 1957: Peyton Place. Winter Dreams (TV). The Play Room (TV). 1959: The Nun's Story. Diary of a Nurse (TV). The Story on Page One. 1960: Butterfield 8. 1961: Something Wild. The Power and the Glory (TV. GB: cinemas). 1962: Sweet Bird of Youth. 1964: Behold a Pale Horse. Youngblood Hawke. 1965: 7 Women. 1969: Whatever Happened to Aunt Alice? 1972: A Brand New Life (TV). 1973: A Summer Without Boys (TV). 1975: Murder or Mercy? (TV). The Spiral Staircase. One Summer Love/ Dragonfly. 1979: And Baby Makes Six (TV). Arthur Miller on Home Ground. The Best Place to Be (TV). 1981: Miracle of Love (TV). The Patricia Neal Story (TV). 1983: Isabel's Choice (TV). 1987: The Pick-Up Artist.

DURNING, Charles 1933–
Heavily built, big-faced, blink-eyed, amiable-looking American actor who developed into one of the few star character players of the 1970s. The son of an Army officer, and himself a Korean War veteran who won the Silver Star, Durning tried an amazing variety of jobs—boxer, button-factory operator, bouncer, liftman, ballroom-dancing instructor, construction worker, cabbie and waiter, before settling on acting. An experienced Shakespearian by the time he came to the screen, he gradually rose in prominence from the early 1970s, at first in abrasive and often unpleasant parts, but later in a variety of roles, some of which showed off his talent for comedy.

1965: Harvey Middleman. Fireman. 1970: Hi Mom! I Walk the Line. The Pursuit of Happiness. 1971: Dealing: Or, The Berkeley-to-Boston-Forty-Bricks-Lost-Bag Blues. 1972: Sisters (GB: Blood Sisters). Madigan: The Midtown Beat (TV). Deadhead Miles. 1973: Connection (TV. GB: The Connection). The Sting. 1974: The Front Page. 1975: The Rivalry (TV). The Trial of Chaplain Jensen (TV). Queen of the Stardust Ballroom (TV). Switch (TV). Dog Day Afternoon. Breakheart Pass. The

Hindenberg. 1976: Harry and Walter Go to New York. 1977: Twilight's Last Gleaming. The Choirboys. An Enemy of the People. 1978: The Greek Tycoon. The Fury. Tilt. Special Olympics (TV). 1979: North Dallas Forty. Starting Over. When a Stranger Calls. The Muppet Movie. 1980: Die Laughing. Crisis at Central High (TV). Attica: The Story of a Prison Riot (TV). The Final Countdown. A Perfect Match (TV). 1981: The Best Little Girl in the World (TV). Sharky's Machine. True Confessions. Dark Night of the Scarecrow (TV). 1982: Tootsie. The Best Little Whorehouse in Texas. Hadley's Rebellion. 1983: To Be or Not to Be. Two of a Kind. Scarface (voice only). 1984: Mass Appeal. Stick. Mister Roberts (TV). Big Trouble. 1985: Happy New Year (released 1987). The Man With One Red Shoe/Mischief. Stand Alone. Private Conversations. Death of a Salesman (TV). 1986: Lazaro. Tough Guys. Where the River Runs Black. The Rosary Murders. Solarbabies. 1987: Brenda Starr (released 1990). Case Closed (TV). A Tiger's Tale. I Would Be Called John (TV). The Man Who Broke 1,000 Chains (cable TV). Cop. 1988: Far North. Cat Chaser. 1989: Dinner at Eight (TV). Ballerina/Etoile. 1990: No Cause for Alarm. Bloody Murder! Deadfall. Fatal Sky. Dick Tracy. Project Alien. 1991: V.I. Warshawski. The Return of Eliot Ness (TV). The Story Lady (TV). 1992: As Long As You're Alive. The Water Engine (TV). Tales from Hollywood (TV). 1993: The Hudsucker Proxy. The Music of Chance. When a Stranger Calls Back (TV). 1994: Roommates (TV). 1995: The Last Supper. Home for the Holidays.

DWYER, Leslie 1906–1986
Pugnacious, shortish, brown-haired cockney character star in prominent supporting roles and semi-leads in British films throughout the 1940s and 1950s. Stockily built, with a face like the Man in the Moon, he was typically seen as fast-talking, aggressive 'ordinary blokes', mainly in comedy although he could be likeable in drama too, and rarely overplayed his hand. From a theatrical family, he studied at a stage school, took to the boards at 10 and made his film debut at 15. A lifetime cricket enthusiast.

1921: The Fifth Form at St Dominic's. 1932: The Flag Lieutenant. 1934: Badger's Green. It's a Cop. 1935: Some Day. 1938: Housemaster. 1941: The Goose Steps Out. The Flew

*Alone (US: Wings and the Woman). 1942: The Young Mr Pitt. In Which We Serve. 1943: The Lamp Still Burns. The Bells Go Down. The Yellow Canary. 1944: The Way Ahead (US: Immortal Battalion) 1945: Perfect Strangers (US: Vacation from Marriage). Great Day. Night Boat to Dublin. 1946: I See a Dark Stranger (US: The Adventuress). This Man Is Mine! Piccadilly Incident. 1947: The Little Ballerina. It Always Rains on Sunday. When the Bough Breaks. *Christmas Weekend. Temptation Harbour. 1948: Bond Street. The Calendar. The Bad Lord Byron. It's Hard to Be Good. A Boy, a Girl and a Bike. 1949: It's Not Cricket. Poet's Pub. Now Barabbas was a robber . . . 1950: Lilli Marlene. Double Confession. Midnight Episode. 1951: There Is Another Sun (US: Wall of Death). Laughter in Paradise. Smart Alec. Judgment Deferred. 1952: Hindle Wakes (US: Holiday Week). The Hour of Thirteen. My Wife's Lodger. 1953: Marilyn (later Roadhouse Girl). 1954: Act of Love. The Good Die Young. The Black Rider. 1955: Where There's a Will. Not So Dusty. Room in the House. 1956: *Death of a Ham. *The Milkman. Cloak without Dagger (US: Operation Conspiracy). Eyewitness. Face in the Night (US: Menace in the Night). 1958: Stormy Crossing (US: Black Tide). 1959: The 39 Steps. Left, Right and Centre. 1961: Rendezvous. 1964: Seventy Deadly Pills. I've Gotta Horse. 1965: Monster of Terror (US: Die, Monster, Die). 1968: Lionheart. The Bliss of Mrs Blossom. Up in the Air. Crooks and Coronets (US: Sophie's Place). 1970: *A Hole Lot of Trouble. 1975: One of Our Dinosaurs is Missing. 1977: Chimpmates (series). 1978: Dominique.*

DYALL, Valentine 1908–1985
Very dark and tall, cadaverous, disgruntled-looking British actor, vaguely reminiscent in aspect and voice of Raymond Massey. The son of actor Franklin Dyall (1874–1950) and actress Mary Merrall, he was an emaciated black beetle of a man whose early career was sharply divided between plays (1930–41) and the cinema (1942–54), later combining the two. In the 1940s, his dark-brown voice gained him a million fans who listened to him each week on radio as the narrator of a long series of chillers (opening words: 'This is your storyteller — the man in black'). He was less personable than one expected in films, looking as though he would be happier if he could find a nice,

damp crypt to which to slip away. His voice in narrations, however, continued to be as unmistakeable as it was unmatchable.

1942: Much Too Shy. The Day Will Dawn (US: The Avengers). 1943: The Life and Death of Colonel Blimp (US: Colonel Blimp). The Yellow Canary. The Silver Fleet. 1944: Henry V. Hotel Reserve. 1945: Latin Quarter. I Know Where I'm Going! Pink String and Sealing Wax. Caesar and Cleopatra. Night Boat to Dublin. Brief Encounter. 1946: Prisoners of the Tower (narrator only). *The Clock Strikes Eight. *The Gong Cried Murder. *The House in Rue Rapp. 1947: The Dover Road (narrator only). The White Unicorn (US: Bad Sister). 1948: Corridor of Mirrors. The Story of Shirley Yorke. Night Comes Too Soon. Woman Hater. My Brother's Keeper. Man on the Run. Vengeance Is Mine. The Queen of Spades. Christopher Columbus (narrator only). The Case of Charles Peace. 1949: Filming for Fun (narrator only). Helter Skelter. Dr Morelle—The Case of the Missing Heiress. For Them That Trespass. Golden Salamander. Miss Pilgrim's Progress. The Man in Black. 1950: Room to Let. The Body Said No! Stranger at My Door. 1951: Salute the Toff. 1952: Ivanhoe. Hammer the Toff. Paul Temple Returns. 1953: Knights of the Round Table (narrator only). The Final Test. Strange Stories (narrator only). 1954: The Devil's Jest. Johnny on the Spot. 1956: Suspended Alibi. 1959: Night Train for Inverness. 1960: Identity Unknown. City of the Dead (US: Horror Hotel). 1962: We Joined the Navy (voice only). Fate Takes a Hand. 1963: The Haunting. *The Money Makers (narrator only). The Horror of It All. 1964: First Men in the Moon (voice only). 1965: The Naked World of Harrison Marks (narrator only). 1966: Our Incredible World (narrator only). The Wrong Box. 1967: Casino Royale (voice only). Bedazzled (voice only). 1974: The Great McGonagall. 1976: The Slipper and the Rose. 1977: Come Play With Me. 1978: *A Child's Voice (narrator only). 1982: Britannia Hospital.

DYSART, Richard 1929–
Stocky, fretful, concerned-looking, usually unsmiling, often bespectacled American actor with thinning dark hair and stubborn lower lip, a Broadway actor in his twenties whose later film career was almost buried beneath a slew of professional men and incisive figures of authority. Few people knew his name until he was cast as Leland McKenzie,

the father-figure of the long-running TV series *L.A. Law*, a role that won him an Emmy in 1992. Sometimes billed as Richard A. Dysart.

1963: Love with the Proper Stranger. 1967: Petulia. 1969: The Lost Man. 1971: The Hospital. The Sporting Club. 1973: The Autobiography of Miss Jane Pittman (TV). 1974: The Crazy World of Julius Vrooder/Vrooder's Hooch. The Terminal Man. 1975: The Day of the Locust. The Hindenburg. 1976: The Gemini Man (TV. Later: Code Name Minus One). Riding with Death (TV). 1977: It Happened One Christmas (TV). The Court Martial of George Armstrong Custer (TV). 1978: First, You Cry (TV). An Enemy of the People. Meteor. 1979: Prophecy. Churchill and the Generals (TV). Being There. 1980: The Ordeal of Dr Mudd (TV). Bogie (TV). 1981: Bitter Harvest (TV). People vs Jean Harris (TV). 1982: The Thing. Missing Children: A Mother's Story (TV). 1984: Concealed Enemies (TV). 1985: The Falcon and the Snowman. Mask. Pale Rider. Warning Sign. Malice in Wonderland (TV). 1986: The Last Days of Patton (TV). 1987: Moving Target (TV). Six Against the Rock (TV). Wall Street. 1989: Day One (TV). 1990: Back to the Future Part III. 1993: Marilyn and Bobby: Her Final Affair (TV).

DZUNDZA, George 1945–
Pugnacious, piggy-eyed German-born Hollywood actor with thin top lip, puff cheeks and a small topping of light brown hair. Often seen in aggressive, even explosive roles, the bulkily built Dzundza has also displayed a more delicate side to his talents in such films as *The Butcher's Wife*. Dzundza spent part of his post-war childhood in displaced persons' camps before moving to Holland at the age of four. At 11 he came to America, studied speech and theatre in later college life and began making inroads into Broadway acting from his late twenties. In recent times, he has become one of the few genuine character actors of the modern era, whether as disciplinarians chewing out raw recruits or as middle-aged men with a weakness for young girls.

1975: The Happy Hooker. 1976: Law and Order (TV). 1977: Someone is Out There (TV). 1978: The Deer Hunter. The Defection of Simas Kudirka (TV). 1979: Salem's Lot (TV). 1980:

Kenny Rogers As The Gambler (TV). 1981: Honky Tonk Freeway. Skokie (TV. GB: Once They Marched Through a Thousand Towns). A Long Way Home (TV). 1983: Streamers. Act of Passion (TV). The Face of Rage (TV). 1984: The Lost Honor of Kathryn Beck (TV). 1985: Best Defense. Brotherly Love. The Execution of Raymond Graham (TV). The Rape of Richard Beck (TV). 1986: No Way Out. One Police Plaza (TV). No Mercy. 1987: No Man's Land. Glory Years (TV). 1988: We're a Family Again (TV). The Beast. Terror on Highway 91 (TV). 1989: The Ryan White Story (TV). Impulse. Desperado: The Outlaw Wars (TV). 1990: White Hunter, Black Heart. 1991: Basic Instinct. The Butcher's Wife. 1992: What She Doesn't Know . . . (TV). 1994: Shades of Gray. Babymaker: The Dr Cecil Jacobson Story (TV). 1995: Crimson Tide.

EDWARDS, Glynn 1931–
Brawny, Malaya-born British actor with homely face, receding dark hair and deep, rumbling voice. He studied agriculture, then worked in Trinidad managing a sugar plantation before turning to acting. Once married to fellow character star Yootha Joyce (qv; first of three). Success in the TV series *Minder* enabled him to give more time to his hobby: sailing.

1957: The Heart Within. 1960: Tunes of Glory. 1961: A Prize of Arms. 1962: Sparrows Can't Sing. 1963: The Hi-Jackers. 1964: Smokescreen. Zulu. 1965: The Ipcress File. 1967: Robbery. The Blood Beast Terror. 1968: The Bofors Gun. 1970: Get Carter! Fragment

of Fear. 1971: Burke and Hare. Under Milk Wood. All Coppers Are... 1973: Shaft in Africa. 1974: A Place to Die (TV. US: cinemas). 11 Harrowhouse. 1978: The Stick-Up. The Playbirds. 1979: Confessions from the David Galaxy Affair. 1980: Rising Damp. 1982: Red Monarch. 1983: Champions. 1985: Minder on the Orient Express (TV). 1987: Out of Order.

EDWARDS, Meredith 1917–
Balding, wistful-looking, slightly built Welsh actor who formed a drama company for the firm in Wales where he worked, then turned professional and quickly gained radio and theatrical assignments. Came to films through Ealing Studios and played canny Welshmen, kindly policemen and well-meaning advisers throughout the 1950s. A bright and lively part of any film.

1949: A Run for Your Money. The Blue Lamp. 1950: Midnight Episode. The Magnet. 1951: There Is Another Sun (US: Wall of Death). The Lavender Hill Mob. Where No Vultures Fly. 1952: The Last Page (US: Manbait). Girdle of Gold. The Gambler and the Lady. Gift Horse (US: Glory at Sea). 1953: The Cruel Sea. The Great Game. The Conquest of Everest (narrator only). A Day To Remember. 1954: Meet Mr Malcolm. Devil on Horseback. Burnt Evidence. The Red Dress. Final Appointment. Mad About Men. To Dorothy a Son (US: Cash on Delivery). Mask of Dust (US: Race for Life). 1955: Lost (US: Tears for Simon). Who Done It? 1956: The Long Arm (US: The Third Key). Peril for the Guy. Circus Friends. Town on Trial! 1957: Escapement (US: Zex/The Electronic Monster). 1958: Dunkirk. Law and Disorder. The Supreme Secret. 1959: Tiger Bay. 1960: Doctor in Love. The Trials of Oscar Wilde (US: The Man with the Green Carnation). 1961: Flame in the Streets. Only Two Can Play. Mix Me a Person. 1962: Go to Blazes! 1963: This Is My Street. 1966: The Great St Trinian's Train Robbery. 1976: Gulliver's Travels. 1989: Angry Earth. 1992: Eira Cynta'r Gaeaf (TV). 1993: Tan ar y Comin/A Christmas Reunion (TV).

ELAM, Jack 1916–
Dark-haired, scowling American actor with sightless left eye, who gained steady employment in the 1950s (after switching to acting from accountancy) as a mean hombre always ready to shoot the hero in the back. Mainly

seen in westerns, Elam could also play sympathetic characters and comedy, but was later encouraged to guy his own image rather too much. Gained weight dramatically in more recent times.

1949: *Trailin' West. Wild Weed (GB: The Devil's Weed). The Sundowners (GB: Thunder in the Dust). 1950: One Way Street. Quicksand. High Lonesome. Key to the City. An American Guerilla in the Philippines (GB: I Shall Return). Love That Brute. A Ticket to Tomahawk. 1951: Bird of Paradise. Rawhide/Desperate Siege. Finders Keepers. The Frogmen. The Bushwhackers (GB: The Rebel). 1952: Kansas City Confidential (GB: The Secret Four). The Battle at Apache Pass. My Man and I. The Ring. High Noon. Rancho Notorious. Montana Territory. Lure of the Wilderness. 1953: Gun Belt. The Moonlighter. Count the Hours (GB: Every Minute Counts). Ride, Vaquero! Appointment in Honduras. Ride Clear of Diablo. 1954: Jubilee Trail. Princess of the Nile. Vera Cruz. Cattle Queen of Montana. The Far Country. 1955: Moonfleet. Tarzan's Hidden Jungle. The Man from Laramie. Kiss Me Deadly. Wichita. Artists and Models. Man Without a Star. Kismet. 1956: Jubal. Thunder over Arizona. Pardners. Gunfight at the OK Corral. 1957: Dragoon Wells Massacre. Baby Face Nelson. Night Passage. Lure of the Swamp. 1958: The Gun Runners. 1959: Edge of Eternity. The Girl in Lovers' Lane. 1961: The Last Sunset. Pocketful of Miracles. The Comancheros. 1963: Four for Texas. 1965: The Rare Breed. 1966: Night of the Grizzly. 1967: The Last Challenge (GB: The Pistolero of Red River). Never a Dull Moment. The Way West. Firecreek. 1968: Once Upon a Time...in the West. Sonora. Support Your Local Sheriff! 1969: Ride a Northbound Horse (TV. GB: cinemas). The Over-the-Hill Gang (TV). The Cockeyed Cowboys of Calico County (GB: TV, as A Woman for Charlie). 1970: Dirty Dingus Magee. Rio Lobo. The Wild Country. 1971: Support Your Local Gunfighter. Hannie Caulder. The Last Rebel. 1972: The Daughters of Joshua Cabe (TV). 1973: The Red Pony (TV. GB: cinemas). Shootout in a One-Dog Town (TV). Pat Garrett and Billy the Kid. 1974: A Knife for the Ladies. Sidekicks (TV). Huckleberry Finn (TV). 1976: The New Daughters of Joshua Cabe (TV). The Winds of Autumn. Pony Express Rider. The Creature from Black Lake. Hawmps. 1977: Grayeagle. 1978: The Norsemen. Hot Lead and Cold Feet. Lacy and the Mississippi Queen (TV). 1979:

The Villain (GB: Cactus Jack). The Apple Dumpling Gang Rides Again. The Sacketts (TV). 1980: Soggy Bottom USA. 1981: The Cannonball Run. 1982: Jinxed! Sacred Ground (revised version of Grayeagle). The Girl, the Gold Watch and Dynamite (TV). 1983: Silent Sentence. Cannonball Run. II. 1986: Aurora Encounter. Easy Street (TV). 1987: Down the Long Hills (TV). Hawken's Breed (released 1990). Once Upon a Texas Train (TV). 1988: Where the Hell's That Gold?!!! (TV). 1989: Big Bad John. Score. 1991: The Giant of Thunder Mountain. 1992: Shadow Force. 1994: Bonanza: The Return (TV).

ELIZONDO, Hector 1936–
Dark, often moustachioed, squirrel-like American actor with darting eyes and oval face, bald from an early age. A former ballet student, he became a respected Broadway actor, but had to wait until well into his thirties to get his first decent movie break, as one of the subway gang in The Taking of Pelham One-Two-Three. Subsequently, he was seen as Puerto Ricans, Cubans and other ethnic types, although himself a native New Yorker. Acclaimed in Broadway drama, he was less successful in broad comedy, but gave an elegant light comedy performance as the hotel manager in Pretty Woman, a role that raised his movie profile again. Married actress Carolee Campbell.

1969: The Vixens. 1970: The Landlord. Valdez is Coming. 1971: Born to Win. Pocket Money. The Impatient Heart (TV). 1972: Deadhead Miles. Stand Up and Be Counted. 1974: The Taking of Pelham One-Two-Three. Operation Undercover (US: Report to the Commissioner). 1976: Thieves. Wanted: The Sundance Woman (TV). 1978: The Dain Curse (cinema version of TV mini-series). 1979: American Gigolo. Cuba. 1981: The Fan. 1982: Young Doctors in Love. Honeyboy (TV). 1983: Under Fire. Women of San Quentin (TV). 1984: The Flamingo Kid. 1985: Private Resort. Out of the Darkness (TV). Murder: By Reason of Insanity (TV). 1986: Courage (TV). Nothing in Common. Power, Passion and Murder (TV). 1987: Overboard. 1988: *Astronomy. 1989: Leviathan. Your Mother Wears Combat Boots (TV. GB: Mom's Army). Chains of Gold. 1990: Pretty Woman. Dark Avenger (TV). Taking Care of Business (GB: Filofax). 1991: Frankie & Johnny. Final Approach. Samantha. Necessary

Roughness. Triple Play II (TV). Finding the Way Home (TV). 1992: Pay Dirt. There Goes the Neighborhood. 1993: Dead Wrong. Backstreet Justice. 1994: Perfect Alibi. Beverly Hills Cop 3. Being Human. Exit to Eden.

ELLIOTT, Denholm 1922–1992

Gentlemanly British actor who played true-blue fresh young men, often under fire in war, in British films of the fifties. Returned in the sixties in altogether different persona – that of a dog-eared ex-public school type with crumpled face eager to sell his own mother up the river for money or personal advancement. Perfectly cast in his later years in any role calling for boozy cynicism or world-weariness. Married to Virginia McKenna 1954–1956 (first of two). Oscar nominee for *A Room with a View*. Died from AIDS-related tuberculosis.

1949: Dear Mr Prohack. 1952: The Sound Barrier (US: Breaking the Sound Barrier). The Ringer. The Holly and the Ivy. 1953: The Cruel Sea. The Heart of the Matter. 1954: They Who Dare. Lease of Life. The Man Who Loved Redheads. 1955: The Night My Number Came Up. 1956: Pacific Destiny. 1960: Scent of Mystery (GB: Holiday in Spain). 1962: Station Six Sahara. 1963: Nothing But the Best. 1964: The High Bright Sun (US: McGuire Go Home!). 1965: You Must Be Joking! King Rat. 1966: Alfie. The Spy with a Cold Nose. Maroc 7. 1967: Here We Go round the Mulberry Bush. 1968: The Night They Raided Minsky's. 1969: The Sea Gull. Too Late the Hero. 1970: The Rise and Rise of Michael Rimmer. The House That Dripped Blood. Percy. 1971: Quest for Love. Madame Sin (TV. GB: cinemas). 1973: *The Last Chapter. A Doll's House (Garland). Vault of Horror. 1974: Percy's Progress. The Apprenticeship of Duddy Kravitz. 1975: Russian Roulette. 1976: To the Devil a Daughter. Partners. Robin and Marian. Voyage of the Damned. 1977: A Bridge Too Far. The Hound of the Baskervilles. 1978: Sweeney 2. The Little Girl in Blue Velvet. The Boys from Brazil. Watership Down (voice only). 1979: Game for Vultures. Saint Jack. Zulu Dawn. Cuba. 1980: Rising Damp. Les séducteurs/ Sunday Lovers. Bad Timing (US: Bad Timing/ A Sensual Obsession). 1981: Raiders of the Lost Ark. 1982: Brimstone and Treacle. The Missionary. 1983: †The Wicked Lady. The Hound of the Baskervilles (and 1977 film). Trading Places.

1984: A Private Function. Camille (TV). The Razor's Edge. 1985: Underworld. Defence of the Realm. A Room with a View. Hotel du Lac (TV). 1986: The Whoopee Boys. Mrs Delafield Wants to Marry (TV). The Happy Valley (TV. US: cinemas). 1987: Maurice. Scoop (TV). 1988: †Hanna's War. Stealing Heaven. September. 1989: Killing Dad. Return from the River Kwai. 1990: The Love She Sought (TV). 1991: Scorchers. A Murder of Quality (TV). Toy Soldiers. 1992: Noises Off. One Against the Wind (TV).

† Scenes deleted from final release print

ELPHICK, Michael 1946–

Dark-haired, shadow-jowled, round-faced, rough-voiced Londoner with scowling smile, sometimes seen as over-age tearaways. Elphick is one of the few outstanding British character actors to emerge in more recent times, and an embryonic Long John Silver if ever there were one – though he can be just as effective in quieter roles. His career is symptomatic of the virtual demise of the film character player in Britain – a huge part of it spent in the theatre and on television, where for some years he played the motorbike-riding sleuth *Boon*.

1968: Fraulein Doktor. Where's Jack? 1969: Hamlet. 1970: Eyewitness. The Buttercup Chain. Cry of the Banshee. 1971: Blind Terror (US: See No Evil). 1973: O Lucky Man! Footsteps. 1974: Stardust. 1977: Star Wars. 1978: The Odd Job. The First Great Train Robbery (US: The Great Train Robbery). The One and Only Phyllis Dixey (TV). Black Island. 1979: Quadrophenia. 1980: The Elephant Man. Masada (TV mini-series. Shortened for cinemas as The Antagonists). 1982: Privates on Parade. 1983: Curse of the Pink Panther. Memed My Hawk. Gorky Park. Krull. 1984: Oxford Blues. Forbrydelsens Element/The Element of Crime. Ordeal by Innocence. 1985: Arthur's Hallowed Ground (TV. US: cinemas). Hitler's SS: Portrait in Evil (TV. GB: cinemas). Three Up, Two Down. The Supergrass. 1986: Valhalla (voice only). Pirates. 1987: Little Dorrit I. Little Dorrit II. 1988: Withnail and I. 1990: Buddy's Song. The Krays. 1991: 'Let Him Have It'.

ELSOM, Isobel
(I. Reed) 1893–1981
Fair-haired, regal leading lady from the English stage who enjoyed a very good run

in British films of the silent and early sound era, before finding her way to Hollywood where she played self-righteous upper-crust matrons whose pomposity was made to be punctured. Married/divorced British director Maurice Elvey.

1915: A Prehistoric Love Story. 1916: Milestones. The Way of an Eagle. 1918: The Elder Miss Blossom (US: Wanted a Wife). Tinker, Tailor, Soldier, Sailor. Onward Christian Soldiers. God Bless Our Red, White and Blue. The Man Who Won. 1919: Quinney's. Hope/ Sweethearts. In Bondage. Linked by Fate. A Member of Tattersall's. Mrs Thompson. Edge o' Beyond. 1920: Aunt Rachel. Nance. 1921: For Her Father's Sake. 1922: Dick Turpin's Ride to York. A Debt of Honour. The Game of Life. The Harbour Lights. Broken Shadows. 1923: Just a Mother. The Sign of Four. The Wandering Jew. 1924: The Love Story of Aliette Brunton. Who is the Man? 1925: The Last Witness. *Glamis Castle. *The Tower of London. 1926: Human Law. Tragödie einer Ehe. 1927: Dance Magic. 1931: Stranglehold. The Other Woman. 1932: The Crooked Lady. Illegal. 1933: The Thirteenth Candle. 1934: The Primrose Path. 1941: Ladies in Retirement. 1942: Eagle Squadron. The War Against Mrs Hadley. Seven Sweethearts. You Were Never Lovelier. 1943: Forever and a Day. First Comes Courage. My Kingdom for a Cook. 1944: The White Cliffs of Dover. Between Two Worlds. Casanova Brown. 1945: The Unseen. 1946: Of Human Bondage. Two Sisters from Boston. 1947: The Ghost and Mrs Muir. The Two Mrs Carrolls. Ivy. Monsieur Verdoux. Love from a Stranger (GB: A Stranger Walked In). Escape Me Never. The Paradine Case. 1948: Smart Woman. 1949: The Secret Garden. 1950: Her Wonderful Lie. 1954: Desirée. Deep in My Heart. 1955: The King's Thief. Love is a Many-Splendored Thing. 1956: 23 Paces to Baker Street. Lust for Life. Over-Exposed. 1957: The Guns of Fort Petticoat. 1958: Rock-a-Bye Baby. 1959: The Miracle. The Taste of Ashes (TV. GB: cinemas). The Young Philadelphians (GB: The City Jungle). 1960: The Bellboy. 1961: The Second Time Around. 1962: The Errand Boy. 1963: Who's Minding the Store? 1964: My Fair Lady. The Pleasure Seekers.

EMERSON, Hope 1897–1960
You really couldn't miss Hope Emerson in films. About as wide as a barn door and with eagle-like features, she was also 6 ft 2 in tall.

A vaudeville and Broadway star of the 1920s and 1930s, she was commandeered by the cinema in post-war years and sometimes cast as fearless pioneering frontier western women (Indians beware!), but even more effective as the death-dealing masseuse in *Cry of the City* and the pitiless prison matron in *Caged*. She was nominated for an Oscar for this last performance, but ironically lost to *Harvey*'s Josephine Hull, one of the screen's tiniest actresses. Died from a liver ailment.

1932: *Smiling Faces.* 1948: *Cry of the City. That Wonderful Urge.* 1949: *House of Strangers. Dancing in the Dark. Adam's Rib. Roseanna MyCoy. Thieves' Highway.* 1950: *Caged. Copper Canyon. Double Crossbones.* 1951: *Belle le Grand. Westward the Women.* 1953: *The Lady Wants Mink. Champ for a Day. A Perilous Journey. Casanova's Big Night.* 1955: *Untamed.* 1957: *The Guns of Fort Petticoat. All Mine to Give* (GB: *The Day They Gave Babies Away*). 1958: *Rock-a-Bye Baby.*

EMERY, Gilbert
(G. E. Pottle) 1875–1945
American-born, British-raised, well-travelled, very tall actor of shamblingly aristocratic bearing. He acted all over the world before settling in Hollywood with the coming of sound, where (between taking a sabbatical for stage work in 1932 and 1933) he quickly established himself as craggy figures of authority. His juiciest role came with third billing (as Winslow, Mae West's business manager) in *Goin' to Town*. Although it seems

fairly certain that the Australian and American silents listed below are his work and not that of another acting Gilbert Emery (1882–1934), they are included only in square brackets. A poor man's C Aubrey Smith (*qv*), he also wrote screenplays.

[1919: *The Sentimental Bloke.* 1920: *Ginger Mick.* 1921: *Where the Billy Boils. Cousin Kate.* 1922: *Any Wife. A Daughter of Australia. A Rough Passage. Lust for Gold.*] 1929: *Behind That Curtain. The Sky Hawk.* 1930: *A Lady's Morals* (GB: *Jenny Lind*). *Sarah and Son. Let Us Be Gay. The Prince of Diamonds. The Soul Kiss. The Royal Bed* (GB: *The Queen's Husband*). 1931: *Scandal Sheet. The Lady Refuses. Party Husband. The Ruling Voice. Rich Man's Folly. Ladies' Man. Upper Underworld. The Yellow Ticket* (GB: *The Yellow Passport*). 1932: *A Man Called Back. A Farewell to Arms.* 1934: *All of Me. Gallant Lady. Coming-Out Party. The House of Rothschild. Where Sinners Meet. I Believed in You. One More River* (GB: *Over the River*). *Grand Canary. Now and Forever. Whom the Gods Destroy. The Man Who Reclaimed His Head.* 1935: *Clive of India. Night Life of the Gods. Cardinal Richelieu. Goin' to Town. Harmony Lane. Reckless Roads. Let's Live Tonight. Ladies Crave Excitement. Without Regret. Peter Ibbetson. Magnificent Obsession.* 1936: *Girl on the Front Page. Little Lord Fauntleroy. Dracula's Daughter. Wife vs Secretary. Bullets or Ballots.* 1937: *The Great Barrier* (US: *Silent Barriers*). *The Life of Emile Zola. Double or Nothing. Souls at Sea.* 1938: *The House of Mystery. Making the Headlines. The Buccaneer. Lord Jeff* (GB: *The Boy from Barnardo's*). *The Affairs of Annabel. Always Goodbye. A Man to Remember. Storm Over Bengal.* 1939: *The Saint Strikes Back. The Lady's from Kentucky. Juarez. Nurse Edith Cavell.* 1939–40: *Raffles.* 1940: *Anne of Windy Poplars* (GB: *Anne of Windy Willows*). *A Dispatch from Reuter's* (GB: *This Man Reuter*). *The House of the Seven Gables. River's End. South of Suez.* 1941: *That Hamilton Woman* (GB: *Lady Hamilton*). *New Wine* (GB: *The Great Awakening*). *Rage in Heaven. Adam Had Four Sons. Scotland Yard. A Woman's Face. Singapore Woman. Sundown.* 1942: *The Remarkable Andrew. Escape from Hong Kong. King of the Mounties* (serial). *The Loves of Edgar Allan Poe.* 1943: *Sherlock Holmes in Washington. The Return of the Vampire. Appointment in Berlin.* 1944: *Between Two Worlds.* 1945: *The Brighton Strangler.*

EMHARDT, Robert 1916–1994
Versatile, fat, tiny-eyed, droop-cheeked American actor whose sheer bulk and presence joined forces to grab the attention in his every scene. Hollywood made too little use of this one-time understudy to Sydney Greenstreet, especially in view of the fact that he could project villainy, kindliness or just plain eccentricity with equal perception.

1952: *The Iron Mistress.* 1955: *The Big Knife.* 1957: *3:10 to Yuma.* 1958: *The Badlanders.* 1960: *Wake Me When It's Over.* 1961: *Underworld USA. The Intruder* (GB: *The Stranger*). 1962: *The Mooncussers* (TV. GB: cinemas). *Kid Galahad.* 1966: *The Group.* 1967: *Hostile Guns.* 1968: *Where Were You When the Lights*

Went Out? 1969: *Rascal. Change of Habit. Operation Heartbeat* (TV). *Suppose They Gave a War and Nobody Came?* 1970: *Lawman.* 1971: *Lock, Stock and Barrel* (TV). 1972: *Scorpio.* 1973: *The Stone Killer.* 1974: *It's Alive. Night Games* (TV). *The FBI versus Alvin Karpis, Public Enemy No. One* (TV). 1976: *Alex and the Gypsy.* 1977: *Fraternity Row. It Happened One Christmas* (TV). 1978: *Seniors. Die Sister, Die. Pleasure Cove* (TV). 1979: *Institute for Revenge* (TV). *Aunt Mary* (TV). 1982: *Forced Vengeance* (later *Battlerage*).

ERDMAN, Richard
(John R. Erdman) 1925–
Snub-nosed, eager-looking American supporting actor with a shock of fair hair. He proved perfect casting for 'GI Joes' in war films, but, as the 1950s drew to a close, he began to diversify, directing comedy shows for television (including many segments of *The Dick Van Dyke Show*) as well as drama segments and a couple of feature films. Still busy on one thing and another, but these days only rarely seen in front of the camera.

1944: *Hollywood Canteen. The Very Thought of You. Janie. Mr Skeffington.* 1945: **Star in the Night. Danger Signal. Objective Burma! Too Young to Know.* 1946: *Janie Gets Married. *So You Want to Play the Horses. Night and Day. Nobody Lives Forever. Shadow of a Woman.* 1947: *Deception. That Way with Women. Wild Harvest.* 1948: *The Time of Your Life.* 1949: *Easy Living. Four Days' Leave.* 1950: *The Admiral Was a Lady. The Men. USS Teakettle* (later and GB: *You're in* the Navy Now). 1951: Cry Danger. The Wild Blue Yonder (GB: Thunder Across the Pacific). The Stooge. 1952: The San Francisco Story. Aladdin and His Lamp. The Happy Time. Jumping Jacks. Because You're Mine. 1953: Stalag 17. The Blue Gardenia. Mission Over Korea (GB: Eyes of the Skies) The Steel Lady (GB: The Treasure of Kalifa). 1955: Francis in the Navy. Bengazi. 1956: Anything Goes. The Power and the Prize. 1957: Bernardine. 1958: The Rawhide Trail. Saddle the Wind. 1959: Face of Fire. 1963: The Brass Bottle. 1966: Namu the Killer Whale. 1969: The Great Man's Whiskers (TV. Not shown until 1973). Rascal. 1970: Tora! Tora! Tora! 1972: Visions (TV). 1973: The Brothers O'Toole. 1974: Mr Majestyk. 1979: Spider-Man The Dragon's Challenge (TV. GB: cinemas). 1982: Heidi's Song (voice only). 1984: Trancers. 1985: Tomboy. 1987: Stewardess School. Valet Girls. 1988: Jesse (TV).

As director:
1971: Bleep. 1973: The Brothers O'Toole. 1983: Teenage Tease.

ERICKSON, Leif
(William Anderson) 1911–1986
Big, broad, blond, benign American actor who sweated away for years in stiffish 'second lead' roles before finding his niche in the 1960s as the father-figure in the TV western series *High Chaparral*. He began as a band singer and trombonist, but hit more headlines for his stormy marriages to Frances Farmer and Margaret (Maggie) Hayes until TV came along. Later married a nonprofessional; they were still married at the time of his death from cancer. His only son was killed in a car crash in 1971. Sometimes billed as Leif Erikson.

1933: The Sweetheart of Sigma Chi (GB: Girl of My Dreams). 1935: Wanderer of the Wasteland. Nevada. 1936: Desert Gold. Drift Fence. Girl of the Ozarks. College Holiday. 1937: Conquest (GB: Marie Walewska). Waikiki Wedding. The Thrill of a Lifetime. 1938: The Big Broadcast of 1938: Ride a Crooked Mile. 1939: Crisis (narrator only). One Third of a Nation. Escape from Yesterday. 1941: H. M. Pulham Esq. Nothing But the Truth. The Blonde from Singapore (GB: Hot Pearls). 1942: Are Husbands Necessary? The Fleet's In. Night Monster (GB: House of Mystery). Arabian Nights. Eagle Squadron. Pardon My Sarong.

1947: The Gangster. Blonde Savage. 1948: The Gay Intruders. Sorry, Wrong Number. Miss Tatlock's Millions. Joan of Arc. The Snake Pit. 1949: Partners in Crime. Johnny Stool Pigeon. The Lady Gambles. 1950: Stella. Three Secrets. Dallas. Mother Didn't Tell Me. Love That Brute. The Showdown. 1951: The Tall Target. Reunion in Reno. The Cimarron Kid. Sailor Beware! Show Boat. 1952: With a Song in My Heart. Carbine Williams. My Wife's Best Friend. Abbott and Costello Meet Captain Kidd. Never Wave at a WAC (GB: The Private Wore Skirts). 1953: Trouble Along the Way. Fort Algiers. Perilous Journey. Paris Model. Invaders from Mars. Captain Scarface. 1954: On the Waterfront. 1956: Star in the Dust. Tea and Sympathy. The Fastest Gun Alive. 1957: The Vintage. One Coat of White (TV). Istanbul. Kiss Them for Me. Panic Button (TV). 1958: Twilight for the Gods. The Young Lions. Once Upon a Horse. 1959: The Raider (TV). 1960: The Shape of the River (TV). 1962: A Gathering of Eagles. 1963: The Carpetbaggers. 1964: Strait-Jacket. Roustabout. 1965: I Saw What You Did. Mirage. 1971: Terror in the Sky (TV). The Deadly Dream (TV). 1972: Man and Boy. The Family Rico (TV). The Daughters of Joshua Cabe (TV). 1975: Winterhawk. Force Five (TV). Abduction. 1977: Twilight's Last Gleaming. 1981: Hunter's Moon. 1983: Wild Times (TV).

ERWIN, Stuart 1902–1967
Fair-haired American actor with open, puzzled face, the Eddie Bracken of his day in roles of hapless innocence, first as fresh college kids, then as honest Joes. Very successful in television from 1949 onwards, initially in his own show with his wife, actress June Collyer (1907–1968). Oscar nominee for *Pigskin Parade*.

1928: Mother Knows Best. A Pair of Tights. 1929: Speakeasy. Happy Days. The Exalted Flapper. New Year's Eve. Thru Different Eyes. Sweetie. The Cockeyed World. The Trespasser. This Thing Called Love. Dangerous Curves. The Sophomore. 1930: Men without Women. Paramount on Parade. Young Eagles. Dangerous Nan McGrew. Only Saps Work. Playboy of Paris. Love Among the Millionaires. Maybe It's Love. Along Came Youth. 1931: No Limit. Up Pops the Devil. The Magnificent Lie. Dude Ranch. Working Girls. 1932: *Hollywood on Parade No. 2. Two Kinds of Women. Make Me a Star. The Big Broadcast. The Misleading

Lady. Strangers in Love. 1933: Face in the Sky. The Crime of the Century. International House. Hold Your Man. The Stranger's Return. Day of Reckoning. Before Dawn. Going Hollywood. He Learned About Women. Under the Tonto Rim. 1934: Viva Villa! Palooka (GB: The Great Schnozzle). Chained. Have a Heart. Bachelor Bait. The Band Plays On. The Party's Over. 1935: Ceiling Zero. After Office Hours. 1936: Exclusive Story. Absolute Quiet. Women Are Trouble. Pigskin Parade (GB: The Harmony Parade). All American Chump (GB: The Country Bumpkin). 1937: Dance, Charlie, Dance. Second Honeymoon. Slim. I'll Take Romance. Checkers. Small Town Boy. 1938: Three Blind Mice. Mr Boggs Steps Out. Passport Husband. 1939: It Could Happen to You. Back Door to Heaven. Hollywood Cavalcade. The Honeymoon's Over. 1940: When the Daltons Rode. Our Town. Sandy Gets Her Man. A Little Bit of Heaven. 1941: Cracked Nuts. The Bride Came COD. 1942: The Adventures of Martin Eden. Blondie for Victory (GB: Trouble Through Billets). Drums of the Congo. 1943: He Hired the Boss. 1944: The Great Mike. 1945: Pillow to Post. 1947: Killer Dill. Heaven Only Knows. Heading for Heaven. 1948: Strike It Rich. 1950: Father is a Bachelor. 1953: Main Street to Broadway. 1956: †Snow Shoes (TV). 1958: †The Right Hand Man (TV). 1959: †A Diamond is a Boy's Best Friend (TV). 1960: †Wrong Way Mooche (TV). †For the Love of Mike (GB: None But the Brave). 1963: †Son of Flubber. 1964: †The Misadventures of Merlin Jones. 1968: Shadow Over Elveron (TV).

† As Stu Erwin

ESMOND, Carl
(Willy Eichberger) 1905–
Dark, handsome, often moustachioed Austrian who began his career as a bank clerk in Vienna, then switched to acting, but was forced to flee the Nazis in the early 1930s. After one or two films in Britain as a romantic singing lead, he ended up in Hollywood (later becoming an American citizen) where, after the war was over, he had an increasingly sporadic film career, despite quite charismatic performances, sometimes in villainous parts. Much on TV till 1974.

1934: Blossom Time (US: April Romance). Evensong. 1935: Invitation to the Waltz. 1938: The Dawn Patrol. 1939: Little Men. Thunder Afloat. 1940: The Catman of Paris (released 1946). 1941: Sundown. Sergeant York. 1942:

Pacific Rendezvous. Panama Hattie. Seven Sweethearts. The Navy Comes Through. 1943: First Comes Courage. Margin for Error. Ministry of Fear. 1944: Address Unknown. The Story of Dr Wassell. The Master Race. Experiment Perilous. 1945: Without Love. This Love of Ours. Her Highness and the Bellboy. 1946: Lover Come Back. 1947: Smash-Up, the Story of a Woman (GB: A Woman Destroyed). Slave Girl. 1948: Walk a Crooked Mile. 1950: Mystery Submarine. The Desert Hawk. 1952: The World in His Arms. 1955: Lola Montès. The Racers (GB: Such Men Are Dangerous). 1958: From the Earth to the Moon. 1959: Thunder in the Sun. 1961: Hitler. Brushfire! 1962: Kiss of the Vampire (TV version only). 1965: Agent for HARM. Morituri (GB: The Saboteur, Code Name Morituri). 1984: My Wicked, Wicked Ways: The Legend of Errol Flynn (TV).

EVANS, Gene 1922–
Red-haired, blue-eyed, unhandsome, huskily built, hard-driving American actor with gruff voice, usually in tough or brutish roles, but occasionally effective in leads. The cinema underestimated his versatility, but television allowed him to show his more benevolent side in the series *My Friend Flicka*. In later years, he continued to be seen mainly in westerns and outdoor dramas.

1947: Under Colorado Skies. 1948: Assigned to Danger. Criss Cross. Larceny. Berlin Express. 1949: Mother is a Freshman (GB: Mother Knows Best). It Happens Every Spring. 1950: Jet Pilot (released 1957). Never a Dull Moment. Dallas. The Asphalt Jungle. Wyoming Mail. Storm Warning. Armored Car Robbery. 1951: Sugarfoot. Steel Helmet. I Was an American Spy. The Big Carnival (later and GB: Ace in the Hole). Fixed Bayonets! Force of Arms. 1952: Park Row. Thunderbirds. Mutiny. 1953: Donovan's Brain. The Golden Blade. 1954: Cattle Queen of Montana. The Long Wait. Hell and High Water. 1955: Crashout. Wyoming Renegades. 1956: Massacre at Sand Creek (TV). 1957: The Helen Morgan Story (US: Both Ends of the Candle). The Sad Sack. Damn Citizen! 1958: Money, Women and Guns. Revolt in the Big House. Young and Wild. The Bravados. Behemoth the Sea Monster (US: The Giant Behemoth). 1959: The Hangman. Operation Petticoat. 1961: Gold of the Seven Saints. 1963: Shock Corridor. 1965: Apache Uprising.

1966: Nevada Smith. Waco. 1967: The War Wagon. 1968: Support Your Local Sheriff! 1969: Dragnet (TV. GB: The Big Dragnet). 1970: The Ballad of Cable Hogue. The Intruders (TV). There Was a Crooked Man ... 1971: Support Your Local Gunfighter. 1972: The Bounty Man (TV). 1973: Pat Garrett and Billy the Kid. Walking Tall. Camper John. 1974: A Knife for the Ladies. Shootout in a One-Dog Town. Sidekicks. People Toys/Devil Times Five/The Horrible House on the Hill. 1975: The Last Day (TV). Matt Helm (TV). 1976: The MacAhans: How the West Was Won (TV). Sourdough. 1977: Fire! (TV. GB: cinemas). 1978: The Magic of Lassie. Kate Bliss and the Tickertape Kid (TV). Lassie: The New Beginning (TV). 1979: The Concrete Cowboys (TV). The Sacketts (TV). The Last Ride of the Dalton Gang (TV). 1980: Casino (TV). Wild Times (TV). 1981: California Gold Rush (TV). 1982: Travis McGee (TV). The Shadow Riders (TV). 1984: Blame It on the Night. 1987: The Alamo: 13 Days to Glory (TV). The Law and Harry McGraw (TV).

EVEREST, Barbara 1890–1968
Plump-cheeked, kind-eyed, dark-haired British actress who found herself cast as wives, mothers and housekeepers after returning to films to play character roles following a session as a leading lady in silent days. She worked solidly but unobtrusively in British films of the 1930s, then surprisingly went to Hollywood in 1941 and gave some of her most striking performances (especially those in *The Uninvited* and *Jane Eyre*), winning co-star billing. On her return to Britain, she was a magnificent as Eric Portman's domineering mother in *Wanted for Murder*, but then slipped back into smaller roles.

1916: The Hypocrites. Man Without a Soul (US: I Believe). 1919: Whosoever Shall Offend. Not Guilty. The Lady Clare. Till Our Ship Comes In (series). 1920: The Joyous Adventures of Aristide Pujol. Calvary. Testimony. 1921: The Bigamist. 1922: Fox Farm. The Persistent Lovers. A Romance of Old Bagdad. 1932: Lily Christine. There Goes the Bride. The Lodger (US: The Phantom Fiend). The World, the Flesh and the Devil. When London Sleeps. 1933: The Roof. The Umbrella. Love's Old Sweet Song. The Wandering Jew. She Was Only a Village Maiden. The River Wolves.

*Home Sweet Home. The Lost Chord. 1934: Passing Shadows. Song at Eventide. The Warren Case. 1935: Scrooge. The Lad. The Passing of the Third Floor Back. 1936: Love in Exile. Men of Yesterday. The Man Behind the Mask. 1937: Death Croons the Blues. Jump for Glory (US: When Thief Meets Thief). Old Mother Riley. 1939: Discoveries. Inquest. Trunk Crime (US: Design for Murder). Meet Maxwell Archer (US: Maxwell Archer, Detective). 1940: Tilly of Bloomsbury. The Second Mr Bush. *Bringing It Home. 1941: *Telefootlers. The Prime Minister. This Man is Dangerous/The Patient Vanishes. He Found a Star. 1942: Commandos Strike at Dawn. 1943: Phantom of the Opera. Forever and a Day. Mission to Moscow. The Uninvited. Jane Eyre. 1944: Gaslight (GB: The Murder in Thornton Square). 1945: The Fatal Witness. The Valley of Decision. 1946: Wanted for Murder. 1947: Frieda. 1949: Children of Chance. Madeleine. 1950: Tony Draws a Horse. 1954: An Inspector Calls. 1957: The Safecracker. 1959: Upstairs and Downstairs. 1961: The Damned (US: These Are the Damned). Dangerous Afternoon. El Cid. 1962: The Man Who Finally Died. 1963: Nurse on Wheels. 1965: Rotten to the Core. 1967: Franchette.*

FAIRBROTHER, Sydney
(S. Tapping) 1872–1941
Petite, fair-haired British actress, attractive even in old age, who had a strong personality and played mostly indomitable and independent cockney ladies in comedy films, occasionally in leading roles. On stage at 17, she had a few indeterminate character roles in silent films, but came into her own in British films of the 1930s. Her personal popularity boosted several minor comedies and added zest to major ones. Retired in 1938.

1915: Iron Justice. 1916: The Mother of Dartmoor. Frailty/Temptation's Hour. The Game of Liberty (US: Under Suspicion). Me and Me Moke (US: Me and M'Pal). A Mother's Influence. 1917: Auld Lang Syne. 1919: In Bondage. 1920: A Temporary Gentleman. Laddie. The Children of Gibeon. 1921: The Bachelor's Club. The Rotters. The Golden Dawn. 1923: Married Love (US: Maisie's Marriage). Heartstrings. Love, Life and Laughter (US: Tip Toes). The Beloved Vagabond. The Rest Cure. Don Quixote.

Sally Bishop. 1924: Reveille. The Happy Prisoner. *Wanted, a Boy. 1925: *Cats. *Raising the Wind. *A Fowl Proceeding. *Billets. *Spots. *A Friend of Cupid. 1926. Nell Gwynne. *Bindle Introduced. *Bindle in Charge. *Bindle, Millionaire. *Bindle's Cocktail. *Bindle, Matchmaker. *Bindle at the Party. 1927: The Silver Lining. Confetti. My Lord the Chauffeur. 1928: *The Market Square. 1931: The Other Mrs Phipps. Murder on the Second Floor. The Ghost Train. The Temperance Fete. 1932: The Third String. *Postal Orders. A Letter of Warning. Double Dealing. Down Our Street. Insult. Lucky Ladies. The Return of Raffles. 1933: Excess Baggage. Home Sweet Home. *Dora. 1934: *A Touching Story. The Crucifix. Chu Chin Chow. Gay Love. Brewster's Millions. 1935: The Private Secretary. The Last Journey. 1936: Fame. All In. 1937: Dreaming Lips. Rose of Tralee. King Solomon's Mines. Paradise for Two (US: The Gaiety Girls). 1938: Make It Three. Little Dolly Daydream.

FARGAS, Antonio 1946–
Loose-limbed, loose-lipped, tall, stringy black American actor who bears a vague resemblance to Sammy Davis Jr and often plays fey characters with cores of steel. Born in New York City, he was acting from an early age: his first film role was as a 90-year-old witch doctor! Most of his early movies, though, were low-budget or underground projects and he didn't achieve national prominence until his running role as the flamboyant underworld 'snitch', Huggy Bear, in the massively successful TV series Starsky and Hutch. That understandably type-cast

him, but he has worked hard for a good range of roles since. He has an unusual sideline: the restoration and preservation of 18th century colonial homes.

1964: The Cool World. 1968: Sidewalks of New York. 1969: Three. Putney Swope. 1970: Pound. The Great White Hope. 1971: Cisco Pike. Shaft. Believe in Me. 1972: Across 110th Street. 1973: Cleopatra Jones. Busting. 1974: The Gambler. Foxy Brown. Conrack. 1975: Huckleberry Finn (TV). Cornbread, Earl and Me. Next Stop, Greenwich Village. Starsky and Hutch (TV). 1976: Car Wash. 1978: Pretty Baby. 1980: Escape (TV). Nurse (TV). Up the Academy. 1981: The Ambush Murders (TV). 1982: Paper Dolls (TV). 1984: Firestarter. 1985: Streetwalkin'. Crimewave. 1986: Florida Straits. 1987: The Night of the Sharks (released 1990). 1988: Shakedown (GB: Blue Jean Cop). 1989: I'm Gonna Git You, Sucka! The Borrower (released 1991). 1991: Whore. La belle anglaise. Howling VI – The Freaks. 1992: Made for Each Other (TV). 1993: Percy and Thunder (TV).

FARNSWORTH, Richard 1920–
Although many of his 'roles' in films were stuntwork and are not recorded here, this lean, grey, twinkle-eyed, droop-moustached American player deserves his place in this book for sheer durability. An ex-rodeo rider, he was stunting at 16, before becoming regular stunt man for Roy Rogers and an 'occasional' for other cowboy stars. 'I'd go out and drive my head into the ground and get a bigger cheque than they would,' he says. Eventually, he 'just got tired of doing stunt work. The ground was gettin' kinda hard.' Small parts came along ('I'd be drivin' a coach or something that needed lines') and escalated in later years to the point where he was nominated for an Oscar in Comes a Horseman and won a Canadian Oscar for The Grey Fox.

1937: A Day at the Races. 1938: The Adventures of Marco Polo. 1944: This is the Army. 1948: Red River. 1953: Arrowhead. The Wild One. 1957: The Tin Star. 1960: Spartacus. 1961: Six Black Horses. 1965: Duel at Diablo. 1966: Texas Across the River. 1969: The Good Guys and the Bad Guys. 1970: Monte Walsh. 1971: The Cowboys. Pocket Money. 1972: Ulzana's Raid. The Soul of Nigger Charley. The Life and Times of Judge Roy Bean. 1975:

Strange New World (TV). 1976: The Duchess and the Dirtwater Fox. 1977: Un autre homme, une autre chance (GB: Another Man, Another Woman. US: Another Man, Another Chance). 1978: Comes a Horseman. 1980: Tom Horn. Ruckus. Resurrection. 1981: The Legend of the Lone Ranger. A Few Days at Weasel Creek (TV). 1982: Independence Day/Restless. Waltz Across Texas. The Grey Fox. Travis McGee (TV). 1983: Ghost Dancing (TV). 1984: The Natural. Rhinestone. 1985: Sylvester. Chase (TV). The Last Frontier/Trackers 2180 (later Spacerage). Anne of Green Gables (TV). 1986: Wild Horses (TV). 1988: Good Old Boy. 1989: Red Earth, White Earth (TV). Desperado: The Outlaw Wars (TV). 1990: Highway to Hell. Misery. The Two Jakes. Havana. 1993: The Fire Next Time (TV). 1994: The Getaway. Lassie. 1995: The Magic Forest.

FAYLEN, Frank
(F. Ruf) 1905–1985
Thin, wiry, tough-looking American supporting player with a shock of fairish curly hair and a face you couldn't trust, often half-concealed beneath tip-tilted trilby. He had his best roles in the mid-1940s, notably as the male nurse, Bim, in The Lost Weekend. On stage in his parents' vaudeville act at 18 months, he switched from song-and-dance on stage to tough guys on film at 30. Married to actress Carol Hughes (1915–), a one-time heroine of Flash Gordon serials, from 1936. Disappointingly, his film output petered out soon after he had turned 50.

1935: Thanks a Million. 1936: Down the Stretch. King of Hockey (GB: King of the Ice Rink). Bullets or Ballots. The Golden Arrow. Night Waitress. Smart Blonde. China Clipper. Gold Diggers of 1937. Border Flight. 1937: Wine, Women and Horses. The Cherokee Strip (GB: Strange Laws). That Certain Woman. Marked Woman. Kid Galahad. The Go-Getter. Talent Scout. Midnight Court. The Case of the Stuttering Bishop. They Won't Forget. Headin' East. Dance, Charlie, Dance. Mr Dodd Takes the Air. Public Wedding. San Quentin. Ever Since Eve. Back in Circulation. 1938: The Invisible Menace. *Crime Rave. Four's a Crowd. Too Hot to Handle. 1939: Idiot's Delight. Five Came Back. Thunder Afloat. Waterfront. Reno. Nick Carter – Master Detective. No Place to Go. The Star Maker. It's a Wonderful World. Gone With the Wind. Lucky Night. The Story of Vernon and Irene Castle. Women in the Wind. Edison the Man. Invisible Stripes. 1940: Curtain Call. Margie. Married and In Love. No Time for Comedy. East of the River. Saturday's Children. The Grapes of Wrath. The Fighting 69th. Brother Orchid. Castle on the Hudson (GB: Years Without Days). They Drive by Night (GB: The Road to Frisco). Pop Always Pays. 1941: Come Live with Me. Thieves Fall Out. City Limits. Knockout/Right to the Heart. Let's Go Collegiate (GB: Farewell to Fame). Top Sergeant Mulligan. Father Steps Out. No Hands on the Clock. Affectionately Yours. H.M. Pulham Esq. International Squadron. Model Wife. Johnny Eager. Sergeant York. Unholy Partners. Footsteps in the Dark. The Reluctant Dragon. 1942: Pride of the Yankees. Dr Kildare's Victory (GB: The Doctor and the Debutante). Across the Pacific. Star Spangled Rhythm. The Palm Beach Story. Dudes Are Pretty People. Fall In. Maisie Gets Her Man (GB: She Got Her Man). Somewhere I'll Find You. Wake Island. The Hard Way. Yankee Doodle Dandy. About Face. A-Haunting We Will Go. Joe Smith — American (GB: Highway to Freedom). Whispering Ghosts. The McGuerins from Brooklyn. 1943: Thank Your Lucky Stars. Silver Skates. She's for Me. Unknown Guest. Andy Hardy's Blonde Trouble. Taxi, Mister. Mission to Moscow. That Nazty Nuisance. Good Morning, Judge. Yanks Ahoy. Prairie Chickens. Get Going. The Mystery of the 13th Guest. Salute for Three. Three Hearts for Julia. Corvette K-225 (GB: The Nelson Touch). The Gang's All Here (GB: The Girls He Left Behind). Tarzan's Desert Mystery, The Falcon Strikes Back. Follow the Band. A Guy Named Joe. Slightly Dangerous. 1944: The Canterville Ghost. Address Unknown. And the Angels Sing. Standing Room Only. An American Romance. See Here, Private Hargrove. 1945: The Affairs of Susan. Duffy's Tavern. You Came Along. The Lost Weekend. *Boogie Woogie. Bring on the Girls. The Incendiary Blonde. Masquerade in Mexico. The Blue Dahlia. 1946: Our Hearts Were Growing Up. To Each His Own. The Well-Groomed Bride. Blue Skies. It's a Wonderful Life! Two Years Before the Mast. Cross My Heart. California. 1947: Welcome Stranger. Variety Girl. Road to Rio. Easy Come, Easy Go. The Perils of Pauline. Suddenly It's Spring. The Trouble with Women. 1948: Hazard. Race Street. Blood on the Moon. Whispering Smith. 1949: Francis. †Two Mugs from Brooklyn/Two Knights in Brooklyn. 1950: Copper Canyon. The Eagle and the Hawk. Convicted. The Nevadan (GB: The Man from Nevada). 1951: Detective Story. My Favorite Spy. Father's Little Dividend. Fourteen Hours. As You Were. Passage West (GB: High Venture). 1952: The Sniper. The Lusty Men. Hangman's Knot. 1953: 99 River Street. 1954: The Lone Gun. Red Garters. Riot in Cell Block 11. 1955: The Looters. The McConnell Story (GB: Tiger in the Sky). 1956: Away All Boats. 7th Cavalry. Everything But the Truth. Terror at Midnight (GB: And Suddenly You Run). Gunfight at the OK Corral. 1957: Three Brave Men. Dino (GB: Killer Dino). 1960: North to Alaska. 1965: Fluffy. When the Boys Meet the Girls. The Monkey's Uncle. 1968: Funny Girl.

† Combined GB version of 1942/3 films The McGuerins from Brooklyn and Taxi, Mister.

FELD, Fritz 1900—1993
Tall, usually moustachioed, lisping German-born comic actor, in America from 1922 (with the director Max Reinhardt), and soon in sound films as the archetypal, fussy, sardonic head waiter. His leaning stance, foreign accent and the champagne-cork noise he made with his cheek soon made him an unmistakable part of the Hollywood scene. He was busy with stage work and promoting his writing career through most of the 1930s, but from 1937 settled in to provide dozens of amusing cameos for the cinema. Married to equally successful character player Virginia Christine (qv) from 1940. A co-founder of the Hollywood Playhouse.

1920: Der Golem: Wie er in die Welt kam. Dämen der Welt. 1921: Christian Wahnschaffe. 1925: The Swan. 1928: The Dove. *The Sorcerer's Apprentice. The Leopard Lady. The Last Command. A Ship Comes In (GB: His Country). Blindfold. 1929: One Hysterical Night (GB: No, No, Napoleon). The Charlatan. Broadway. Black Magic. 1937: I Met Him in Paris. Expensive Husbands. Hollywood Hotel. Tovarich. True Confession. Lancer Spy. *Swingtime in the Movies. 1938: Go Chase Yourself. Campus Confesions (GB: Fast Play). Romance in the Dark. Bringing Up Baby. The Affairs of Annabel. Artists and Models Abroad (GB: Stranded in Paris). Gold Diggers in Paris (GB: The Gay Impostors). I'll Give a Million. *Out Where the Stars Begin. 1939: Idiot's Delight. At the Circus/Marx Brothers at the Circus. When Tomorrow Comes. Little Accident. *Springtime in the Movies. *Quiet, Please. Everything Happens at Night. 1940: It's a Date. Millionaire Playboy. Victory. Little Old New York. Ma, He's Making Eyes at Me. I Was an Adventuress. Sandy is a Lady. 1941: Four Jacks and a Jill. Come Live with Me. World Premiere. Mexican Spitfire's Baby. Three Sons o' Guns. You Belong to Me (GB: Good Morning, Doctor!). Skylark. 1942: Shut My Big Mouth. Sleepytime Gal. Maisie Gets Her Man (GB: She Gets Her Man). Iceland (GB: Katina). 1943: Henry Aldrich Swings It (GB: Henry Swings It). Phantom of the Opera. Holy Matrimony. 1944: Knickerbocker Holiday. Passport to Adventure. Take It Big. Ever Since Venus. 1945: The Great John L (GB: A Man Called Sullivan). George White's Scandals. Captain Tugboat Annie. 1946: Catman of Paris (filmed 1940). I've Always Loved You. Wife of Monte Cristo. Her Sister's Secret. Gentleman Joe Palooka. 1947: Carnival in Costa Rica.

*Cupid Goes Nuts. The Secret Life of Walter Mitty. Fun on a Weekend. 1948: If You Knew Susie. The Noose Hangs High. Julia Misbehaves. Trouble Makers. My Girl Tisa. You Gotta Stay Happy. Mexican Hayride. 1949: The Lovable Cheat. The Great Lover. Appointment with Danger (released 1951). 1950: The Jackpot. Belle of Old Mexico. Riding High. 1951: Missing Women. Rhythm Inn. Kentucky Jubilee. Sky High. Little Egypt (GB: Chicago Masquerade). My Favorite Spy. *So You Want to Enjoy Life. *So You Want to be a Doctor. Journey into Light. 1952: Aaron Slick from Punkin Crick (GB: Marshmallow Moon). The Star. O. Henry's Full House (GB: Full House). Has Anybody Seen My Gal. 1953: *So You Want to be a Musician. Casanova's Big Night. Call Me Madam. Crime Wave (GB: The City is Dark). The French Line. 1954: Riding Shotgun. Living It Up. Paris Playboys. 1955: Jail Busters. 1956: *So You Want to be Pretty. 1957: Up in Smoke. 1959: Juke Box Rhythm. Don't Give Up the Ship. 1961: Ladies' Man. Pocketful of Miracles: The Errand Boy. 1963: Promises! Promises! Wives and Lovers. Who's Minding the Store? Four for Texas. The Miracle of Santa's White Reindeer. 1964: The Patsy. 1965: Harlow. 1966: Three on a Couch. Penelope. Way . . . Way Out. Made in Paris. Fame is the Name of the Game (TV). 1967: Caprice. Barefoot in the Park. 1968: The Wicked Dreams of Paula Schultz. 1969: The Comic. Hello, Dolly! The Computer Wore Tennis Shoes. The Phynx. 1970: Which Way to the Front? (Ja! Ja! Mein General, But Which Way to the Front?). 1972: Call Her Mom (TV). 1973: Herbie Rides Again. 1974: Only with Married Men (TV). 1975: The Strongest Man in the World. The Sunshine Boys. Won Ton Ton, the Dog Who Saved Hollywood. 1976: Silent Movie. Freaky Friday. 1977: The World's Greatest Lover. 1979: Fun on a Weekend. 1980: Herbie Goes Bananas. 1981: History of the World Part I. † . . . All the Marbles (GB: The California Dolls). 1982: Heidi's Song (voice only). 1983: Last of the Great Survivors (TV). 1986: †A Fine Mess. 1987: Barfly. 1988: Homer & Eddie. 1989: Get Smart, Again (TV). B-Men (TV).

† Scenes deleted from final release print.

FELL, Norman 1924—
Sad-eyed, worried-looking, light-haired American actor who started to mix films with TV and theatre from the late 1950s, and proved as adept with a throwaway gag as a straight dramatic role. Mostly, though (and especially on TV), he played superiors who did the fretting while the hero went his own sweet way. Was an Air Force aerial gunner during World War II.

1959: Pork Chop Hill. 1960: The Rat Race. Inherit the Wind. Ocean's 11. 1962: PT 109. 1963: It's a Mad, Mad, Mad World. Sergeant Ryker (TV. Later issued to cinemas). 1964: The Killers. The Hanged Man (TV. GB: cinemas). Quick, Before It Melts. 1966: The Young Warriors. 1967: The Secret War of Harry Frigg (GB: Fitzwilly Strikes Back). The Movie Maker (TV). The Graduate. 1968: Bullitt. The Young Runaways. 1969: Three's a Crowd (TV). If It's Tuesday, This

Must Be Belgium. 1970: *Rabbit Test. The Boatniks. Catch 22.* 1972: *The Heist (TV. GB: Suspected Person).* 1973: *The Stone Killer. Charley Varrick.* 1974: *Thursday's Game (made for cinemas in 1971, but shown only on TV three years later). Airport 1975.* 1975: *Death Stalk (TV). Cleopatra Jones and the Casino of Gold.* 1976: *Richie Brockelman: The Missing 24 Hours (TV). Guardian of the Wilderness.* 1978: *The End.* 1980: *For the Love of It (TV). This Year's Blonde (TV).* 1981: *Paternity. On the Right Track. Kinky Coaches and the Pom Pom Pussycats.* 1983: *Uncommon Valor (TV).* 1985: *Transylvania 6–5000.* 1986: *Stripped to Kill. You're Driving Me Crazy.* 1989: *C.H.U.D. II (Bud the C.H.U.D.).* 1991: *For the Boys. The Boneyard. Hexed (released 1993).* 1992: *The Naked Truth.* 1994: *Beach House.*

FENEMORE, Hilda 1919–
Dark-haired, British supporting actress of plump-cheeked yet vaguely pinched features, one of the great portrayers of the working classes during the flourishing British studio years of the 1950s. If Marianne Stone (*qv*) was the woman next door, Fenemore epitomised the aproned mum whose son had gone to the bad. It was a role she played several times, but never to better effect than in 1960's *The Wind of Change.* London-born, she also worked prodigiously on TV.

1948: *Esther Waters.* 1950: *Chance of a Lifetime.* 1951: *Saturday Island (US: Island of Desire).* 1952: *The Wallet. Time Bomb (US: Terror on a Train).* 1953: *The Large Rope.* *Bouncer Breaks Up. The Titfield Thunderbolt.*

1954: *Adventure in the Hopfields. Hands of Destiny. The End of the Road.* 1955: *Souls in Conflict. Room in the House.* 1956: *Supersonic Saucer. Johnny You're Wanted. The Secret Place.* 1957: *Treasure at the Mill. The Tommy Steele Story (US: Rock Around the World). Quatermass II (US: Enemy from Space). Black Ice. The Safecracker.* 1958: *The Young and the Guilty. Innocent Sinners. The Strange World of Planet X.* 1959: *Carry On Nurse.* 1960: *Carry On Constable. Feet of Clay. Double Bunk. The Wind of Change.* 1961: *Four Winds Island.* 1962: *The Boys. Out of the Fog. Strongroom.* 1963: *Doctor in Distress. The War Lover. This is My Street. Clash by Night (US: Escape by Night).* 1964: *Witchcraft.* 1965: *Joey Boy.* 1966: *Money-Go-Round.* 1967: *Casino Royale.* 1971: *I Want What I Want.* 1972: *Something Like the Truth (later The Offence).* 1973: *Along the Way. Our Little Lot. Op de Hollandische Toer.* 1974: *The Double Kill (TV. US: cinemas). The Boy with Two Heads (serial).* 1975: *The Bawdy Adventures of Tom Jones.* 1976: *Full Circle (US: The Haunting of Julia).* 1977: *Chimpmates (series).* 1978: *The Stud. Absolution.* 1986: *South of the Border (TV).* 1991: *Broke (TV).* 1992: *Gone to Seed (TV).*

FERGUSON, Frank 1899–1978
Light-haired American actor whose bedraggled toothbrush moustache gave him a faintly gloomy look. Mostly just a townsman in films, but seen down the years in dozens of different kinds of role, although usually a professional man on either side of the law, occasionally a shabby sheriff or a hangdog reporter. He came to Hollywood from Broadway with the shortage of acting talent in the wartime years and stayed for more than two decades, gradually improving the quality of his roles, and later settling into a niche in TV's *Peyton Place* as Eli Carson. He died from cancer.

1940: *Father is a Prince.* *Sockaroo. Gambling on the High Seas.* 1941: *They Died With Their Boots On. Life Begins for Andy Hardy. You'll Never Get Rich. The Body Disappears.* 1942: *Spy Ship. Grand Central Murder. The War Against Mrs Hadley. You Can't Escape Forever. The Spirit of Stanford. You Were Never Lovelier. City of Silent Men. Boss of Big Town. My Gal Sal. Broadway. Reap the Wild Wind. Ten Gentlemen from West Point. This Gun for Hire.* 1943: *Truck Busters. Mission to Moscow. Pilot No. 5. Salute to the Marines.* 1945: *The Dolly Sisters. The Trouble With Women (released 1947). Rhapsody in Blue. Thrill of a Romance.* 1946: *Little Miss Big (GB: The Baxter Millions). Swell Guy. Night and Day. Canyon Passage. Cross My Heart. The Searching Wind. Lady Chaser. Secrets of a Sorority Girl (GB: Secrets of Linda Hamilton). If I'm Lucky. Blonde for a Day. The Perfect Marriage. OSS. The Man I Love. California.* 1947: *They Won't Believe Me. T-Men. Variety Girl. The Beginning or the End? The Farmer's Daughter. The Perils of Pauline. Blaze of Noon. The Fabulous Texan. Cass Timberlane. Welcome Stranger. Road to Rio. Killer at Large.* 1948: *Fort Apache. They Live by Night. Abbott and Costello Meet Frankenstein (GB: Abbott and Costello Meet the Ghosts). The Hunted. Miracle of the Bells. The Vicious Circle. The Bride Goes Wild. The Walls of Jericho. Walk a Crooked Mile. The Inside Story. The Wonderful Urge. Rachel and the Stranger. Fighting Father Dunne.* 1949: *Caught. The Barkleys of Broadway. Follow Me Quietly. Free for All. State Department – File 649 (GB: Assignment in China). Slightly French. Dynamite. Shockproof. Roseanna McCoy. Dancing in the Dark.* 1950: *He's a Cockeyed Wonder. The West Point Story (GB: Fine and Dandy). The Lawless (GB: The Dividing Line). Frenchie. Under Mexicali Skies. Tyrant of the Sea. The Good Humor Man. The Great Missouri Raid. The Furies. Right Cross. Key to the City. Louisa.* 1951: *Thunder in God's Country. Santa Fé. Elopement. Warpath. The People Against O'Hara. On Dangerous Ground. The Barefoot Mailman. The Cimarron Kid. The Model and the Marriage Broker. Boots Malone.* 1952: *Rancho Notorious. Wagons West. The Iron Mistress. Rodeo. It Grows on Trees. The Lone Hand. Bend of the River (GB: Where the River Bends). Has Anybody Seen My Gal. Ma and Pa Kettle at the Fair. The Marrying Kind. Oklahoma Annie. The Winning Team. Rose of Cimarron. Million Dollar Mermaid (GB: The One-Piece Bathing Suit). Stars and Stripes Forever (GB: Marching Along). Models Inc (GB: That Kind of Girl). Room for One More.* 1953: *Main Street to Broadway. City of Bad Men. The Beast from 20,000 Fathoms. Big Leaguer. The Marksman. Star of Texas. The Woman They Almost Lynched. Wicked Woman. Trouble Along the Way. House of Wax. Powder River. Texas Badman. Outlaw Territory/Hannah Lee. The Blue Gardenia.* 1954: *Johnny Guitar. A Star is Born. The Shanghai Story. The Outcast (GB: The Fortune Hunter). Superman and Scotland Yard (TV. GB: cinemas). Young at Heart. Drum Beat. Moonfleet. The Violent Men (GB: Rough Company). Riding Shotgun. Battle Cry.* 1955: *New York Confidential. A Lawless Street. Trial. The Eternal Sea. The McConnell Story (GB: Tiger in the Sky). At Gunpoint! (GB: Gunpoint!). City of Shadows.* 1956: *Tribute to a Bad Man.* 1957: *This Could be the Night. The Phantom Stagecoach. The Iron Sheriff. Gun Duel in Durango. The Lawless Eighties.* 1958: *The Light in the Forest. Cole Younger, Gunfighter. Andy Hardy Comes Home. Terror in a Texas Town. Man of the West.* 1959: *The Big Night.* 1960: *Sunrise at Campobello. Raymie.* 1961: *Pocketful of Miracles. Those Calloways. Hush . . . Hush, Sweet Charlotte. The Quick Gun.* 1965: *The Great Sioux Massacre.* 1969: *Along Came a Spider (TV).*

FERRER, Miguel 1954–

American actor with long, narrow, un-handsome features, receding light-brown hair and faint air of aggressive contempt that got him cast as authoritative slimebags along with a few more sympathetic, but still strong-charactered roles. The son of actor Jose Ferrer and singer/actress Rosemary Clooney, he grew up wanting to be a professional musician, but switched careers from drumming to acting after portraying his father's character as a young man in an episode of the TV series *Magnum* in 1981. After a busy start in films, the theatre took most of his time between 1984 and 1987. Then his portrayal of the conniving executive Morton in *RoboCop* made his face familiar and he grew increasingly well-employed by the cinema in the early 1990s in both dramatic and comic roles.

1982: And They're Off. 1983: The Evil That Men Do. Heartbreaker. Under Pressure. 1984: The Last Horror Film (made 1981). Star Trek III The Search for Spock. Lovelines. Flashpoint. 1985: Kiss of the Spider Woman. 1987: RoboCop. Downpayment on Murder (TV). Valentino Returns. 1988: Cat Squad – Python Wolf (TV). 1989: DeepStar Six. Shannon's Deal (TV). Revenge. 1990: The Guardian. 1991: Murder in High Places (TV). 1992: The Harvest. In the Shadow of a Killer (TV). Twin Peaks: Fire Walk with Me. Scam. 1993: Point of No Return (GB: The Assassin). Hot Shots! Part Deux. Another Stakeout. 1994: Royce. Blank Check (GB: Blank Cheque).

FETCHIT, Stepin

(Lincoln Perry) 1892–1985
Gloomy-looking black actor who, after beginning his career in minstrel shows, had a great film success in 1929 as the slow-moving Gummy in *Hearts of Dixie*, and repeated it over and over again. Although reviled in later years over his 'Yas'm; Iza comin'' image, Fetchit became the first great black Hollywood star, at one time owning six houses and a fleet of limousines (including a pink one) – but went bankrupt in 1945. He tried a comeback in the 1950s, but his image was passé. Died from pneumonia.

1927: In Old Kentucky. 1928: Nameless Men. The Tragedy of Youth. The Devil's Skipper. 1929: Show Boat. Hearts in Dixie. Big Time.

*Salute. Fox Movietone Follies of 1929. Thru Different Eyes, The Kid's Clever. The Ghost Talks. 1930: Cameo Kirby. Swing High. La fuerzer del querer. The Big Fight. A Tough Winter. 1931: Neck and Neck. The Wild Horse. The Prodigal. The Galloping Ghost (serial). 1933: *Slow Poke. 1934: David Harum. The World Moves On. Stand Up and Cheer. Carolina (GB: The House of Connelly). Judge Priest. Bachelor of Arts. Marie Galante. 1935: Helldorado. One More Spring. The Virginia Judge. The County Chairman. Steamboat 'Round the Bend. Charlie Chan in Egypt. 1936: 36 Hours to Kill. Dimples. 1937: On the Avenue. Love is News. Fifty Roads to Town. 1938: His Exciting Night. 1939: Zenobia (GB: Elephants Never Forget). 1946: *Baby, Don't Go 'Way from Me. Broadway and Main. 1947: Miracle in Harlem. Big Timers. 1952: Sudden Fear. Bend of the River (GB: Where the River Bends). 1953: The Sun Shines Bright. 1971: Cutter (TV). 1974: Amazing Grace. 1975: Won Ton Ton, the Dog Who Saved Hollywood.*

FIEDLER, John 1925–

Bald, pink-faced, squeaky-voiced, querulous, stocky, often bespectacled American actor, seen as small-town storekeepers or henpecks whose rebellions were soon squashed. After wartime service in the US navy, Wisconsin-born Fiedler took up an acting career, making the first of many television appearances in 1950. Dramatically, he scored in his first film as one of the *12 Angry Men*. In comedy, his harassed little men were like cartoon characters. In real life, a keen bridge player.

*1957: 12 Angry Men. Stage Struck. 1961: A Raisin in the Sun. 1962: That Touch of Mink. 1964: The World of Henry Orient. Kiss Me, Stupid. Guns of Diablo. 1965: Girl Happy. 1966: A Fine Madness. 1967: The Ballad of Josie. Fitzwilly (GB: Fitzwilly Strikes Back). The Odd Couple. 1968: *Winnie the Pooh and the Blustery Day (voice only). 1969: The Great Bank Robbery. True Grit. Rascal. Suppose They Gave a War and Nobody Came. 1971: A Tattered Web (TV). Cannon (TV). Making It. Honky. 1972: Skyjacked. Deathmaster. 1973: Hitched (TV. GB: Westward the Wagon). Double Indemnity (TV). 1974: * Winnie the Pooh and Tigger Too (voice only). Bad Ronald (TV). The Fortune. 1975: Who is the Black Dahlia? (TV). Woman of the Year (TV). 1976: The Shaggy DA. 1977: The Rescuers (voice only). 1978: Harper Valley PTA. Human Feelings (TV). 1980: The Cannonball Run. The Monkey Mission (TV). 1981: The Fox and the Hound (voice only). Sharky's Machine. 1982: Savannah Smiles. 1983: I Am the Cheese. 1986: Seize the Day (originally for TV).*

FIELDING, Fenella 1932–

Plummy-voiced, doe-eyed, lascivious-looking dark-haired British comedy actress with extravagant figure. After she sprang to fame in West End revue, British films decided she was too good to miss, and they were right. The only trouble was that they never figured out what to do with her. In the mid-1960s they came close, but, alas, she was allowed to go back to the stage.

*1959: Follow a Star. Sapphire. 1960: Doctor in Love. Foxhole in Cairo. No Love for Johnnie. 1961: Carry on Regardless. In the Doghouse. 1962: The Old Dark House. 1963: Doctor in Distress. 1965: How to Undress in Public Without Undue Embarrassment (narrator only). 1966: Doctor in Clover. *Road to St Tropez (narrator only). Carry On Screaming. Drop Dead Darling (US: Arrivederci, Baby!). 1969: Lock Up Your Daughters! 1970: Dougal and the Blue Cat (voice only). 1983: Robin Hood (TV. GB: The Zany Adventures of Robin Hood).*

FINLAYSON, James 1877–1953

Scrawny Scotsman with bald head, walrus moustache and wizened features, imperishably associated with Laurel and Hardy through the 33 shorts and features he made with them, almost entirely with the Hal

Roach studio where Finalyson got his own first starring opportunities in the early 1920s. Although no great actor, Finlayson had an amazing facial range, squeezing one eye almost closed while widening the other, as part of his famous 'double take and fade away'. In 1934/5, he made a series of small comedy features in England, but soon returned to America—and Stan and Ollie. Died from a heart attack.

1919: *Love's False Faces. *Why Beaches Are Popular. 1920: Married Life. *You Wouldn't Believe It. Down on the Farm. 1921: A Small Town Idol. Home Talent. 1922: The Crossroads of New York. *Home Made Movies. *The Counter Jumper. 1923: Hollywood. *White Wings. *Roughest Africa. *Where's My Wandering Boy Tonight? *Pitfalls of a Big City. A Man About Town. *The Soilers. *The Barnyard. *No Wedding Bells. 1924: *Near Dublin. *Wide Open Spaces/Wild Bill Hiccup. *Brothers Under the Chin. *Smithy. *Rupert of Hee-Haw/Rupert of Cole-Slaw. 1925: Welcome Home. *Official Officers. *Mary, Queen of Tots. *Yes, Yes, Nanette. *Unfriendly Enemies. *Moonlight and Noses. *Hard Boiled. Innocent. *Thundering Fleas. *Husbands. *The Caretaker's Daughter. 1926: *Madame Mystery. *Never Too Old. *The Merry Widower. *Wise Guys Prefer Brunettes. *Raggedy Rose. *The Nickel Hopper. 1927: *Seeing the World. *With Love and Hisses. *Love 'Em and Weep. *Do Detectives Think? *Hats Off. *Flying Elephants. *Sugar Daddies. *The Call of the Cuckoos. *The Second Hundred Years. No Man's Law. 1928: Lady Be Good. Ladies' Night in a Turkish Bath (GB: Ladies' Night). Show Girl. Bachelor's Paradise. *Should Tall Men Marry? *Galloping Ghosts. 1929: *Liberty. *Big Business. *Men o' War. *The Hoose Gow. Two Weeks Off. Hard to Get. Wall Street. *Fast Freight. 1930: *Dollar Dizzy. *Night Owls. *Another Fine Mess. For the Defense. Young Eagles. Flight Commander. The Dawn Patrol. 1931: Big Business Girl. *One of the Smiths. *False Roomers. *A Melon-Drama. *Catch As Catch Can. *Oh! Oh! Cleopatra. *Scratch As Catch Can. *Trouble from Abroad. *One Good Turn. *Our Wife. *Chickens Come Home. *The Hasty Marriage. Pardon Us (GB: Jailbirds). *Stout Hearts and Willing Hands. 1932: *The Chimp. *Boy, Oh Boy. †*Any Old Port. *The Iceman's Ball. Pack Up Your Troubles. *So This Is Harris. *Union Wages. *Thru Thin and Thicket, or Who's Zoo in Africa. Thunder

Below. *The Millionaire Cat. *Jitters, the Butler. 1933: The Devil's Brother (GB: Fra Diavolo). *Mush and Milk. *Me and My Pal. *His Silent Racket. *Hokus Fokus. *The Druggist's Dilemma. *The Gay Nighties. The Girl in Possession. Dick Turpin. Strictly in Confidence. 1934: What Happened to Harkness. Oh! No, Doctor. Big Business (and 1929 short). Father and Son. Nine Forty Five. Trouble in Store. 1935: Handle with Care. Who's Your Father? *Thicker Than Water. Bonnie Scotland. *Manhattan Monkey Business. 1936: The Bohemian Girl. Our Relations. *Life Hesitates at 40. 1937: All Over Town. Pick a Star. Way Out West. Toast of New York. Angel. 1938: Carefree. *False Roomers. Block-Heads. Wise Girl. 1939: The Great Victor Herbert. The Flying Deuces. A Small Town Idol (revised sound version of 1921 film). Hollywood Cavalcade. A Chump at Oxford. 1939—40: Raffles. 1940: Foreign Correspondent. Saps at Sea. 1941: Nice Girl? One Night in Lisbon. 1942: To Be or Not To Be. 1943: Yanks Ahoy! 1946: Till the Clouds Roll By. 1947: The Perils of Pauline. Thunder in the Valley (GB: Bob, Son of Battle). 1948: Grand Canyon Trail. Julia Misbehaves. 1950: Royal Wedding (GB: Wedding Bells). 1951: Here Comes the Groom.

† Scenes deleted from final release print.

FITZGERALD, Barry
(William Shields) 1888—1961
Diminutive Irish actor (at the Abbey Theatre from 1915) with rumpled features and twinkling blue eyes, who won an Academy Award as the Catholic priest (in real life he was a Protestant) in Going My Way, and remained Hollywood's favourite Irishman from 1936 to 1952. Died a few weeks after brain surgery.

1929: Juno and the Paycock (US: The Shame of Mary Boyle). 1934: Guests of the Nation. 1936: When Knights Were Bold. The Plough and the Stars. 1937: Ebb Tide. 1938: Pacific Liner. Bringing Up Baby. The Dawn Patrol. Four Men and a Prayer. Marie Antoinette. 1939: The Saint Strikes Back. Full Confession. 1940: The Long Voyage Home. San Francisco Docks. 1941: The Sea Wolf. Tarzan's Secret Treasure. How Green Was My Valley. 1943: Two Tickets to London. The Amazing Mrs Holliday. Corvette K-225 (GB: The Nelson Touch). 1944: Going My Way. None But the Lonely Heart. I Love a Soldier. 1945: And Then There Were None (GB: 10 Little Niggers).

Duffy's Tavern. Incendiary Blonde. The Stork Club. 1946: Two Years Before the Mast. California. 1947: Welcome Stranger. Easy Come, Easy Go. Variety Girl. 1948: The Naked City. The Sainted Sisters. Miss Tatlock's Millions. 1949: Top o' the Morning. 1950: The Story of Seabiscuit (GB: Pride of Kentucky). Union Station. 1951: Silver City (GB: High Vermilion). 1952: The Quiet Man. Il filo d'erba. 1954: Happy Ever After (US: Tonight's the Night). 1956: The Catered Affair (GB: Wedding Breakfast). 1958: Rooney. 1959: The Cradle of Genius. Broth of a Boy.

FITZGERALD, Walter
(W. Bond) 1896—1976
Square-faced, reliable-looking, solidly built British actor who projected honesty and integrity with gritty conviction. He abandoned a career on the Stock Exchange for studies at RADA, made his stage debut at 26 and, after a late start to his cinema career, enjoyed a particularly good run of film roles from 1942 to 1950. Also very busy in the theatre and on TV until his retirement in the late 1960s.

1932: Murder at Covent Garden. 1941: This England. 1942: In Which We Serve. Squadron Leader X. 1943: San Demetrio London. 1944: Strawberry Roan. 1945: Great Day. 1947: Mine Own Executioner. Blanche Fury. 1948: This Was a Woman. The Fallen Idol. The Winslow Boy. The Small Back Room. 1949: Edward My Son. 1950: Treasure Island. 1951: Flesh and Blood. 1952: The Pickwick Papers. The Ringer. The Net (US: Project M7). Appointment in London. 1953: The Cruel Sea. Twice Upon a Time. *Too Many Detectives. Personal Affair. Front Page Story. Our Girl Friday (US: The Adventures of Sadie). 1954: Lease of Life. 1955: The Green Scarf. Cockleshell Heroes. 1956: Around the World in 80 Days. The Man in the Sky (US: Decision Against Time). 1957: The Birthday Present. Something of Value. 1958: The Camp on Blood Island. Darby O'Gill and the Little People. 1959: Third Man on the Mountain. Sapphire. 1962: HMS Defiant (US: Damn the Defiant!). We Joined the Navy. 1963: Incident at Midnight.

FIX, Paul
(P. F. Morrison) 1901—1983
Wry-faced American actor with light brown hair. He only fenced with films until the

1930s when he became a Hollywood fixture, one of many players whose faces were more familiar than their names, at first often in unsympathetic roles such as cowardly crooks. Later Fix film characters pursued a policy of non-aggression and a succession of sheriffs, taxi-drivers, judges, seamen, ranchers and priests established him well on the right side of the law. His mild-mannered, dry-humoured approach made him something of a lesser Barry Fitzgerald (*qv*).

*1920: The Adventuress. 1926: Hoodoo Ranch. 1927: Chicago. 1928: The First Kiss. 1929: Lucky Star. Trial Marriage. 1930: Ladies Love Brutes. Man Trouble. 1931: Bad Girl. Three Girls Lost. The Fighting Sheriff. The Good Bad Girl. 1932: The Last Mile. Dancers in the Dark. Scarface (The Shame of a Nation). Life Begins (GB: The Dawn of Life). * Free Eaters. South of the Rio Grande. Back Street. Fargo Express. The Racing Strain. Sky Devils. 1933: Zoo in Budapest. Hard to Handle. The Sphinx. The Avenger. The Mad Game. Gun Law. Blood Money. Somewhere in Sonora. Emergency Call. The Devil's Mate (GB: He Knew Too Much). 1934: Little Man, What Now? Rocky Rhodes. The Woman Who Dared. Flirtation Walk. Stamboul Quest. The Count of Monte Cristo. 1935: The Desert Trail. The Eagle's Brood. Let 'Em Have It (GB: False Faces). Men Without Names. Bar-20 Rides Again. Miss Pacific Fleet. The Crimson Trail. The World Accuses. His Fighting Blood. The Throwback. Mutiny Ahead. Living on Velvet. Valley of Wanted Men. Bulldog Courage. Millions in the Air. Don't Bet on Blondes. Reckless. 1936: The Road to Glory. Charlie Chan at the Race Track. The Phantom Patrol. Yellowstone. Straight from the Shoulder. Navy Born. The Prisoner of Shark Island. The Ex-Mrs Bradford. Winterset. The Plot Thickens (GB: The Swinging Pearl Mystery). Two in a Crowd. After the Thin Man. The Bridge of Sighs. 1937: Souls at Sea. Western Gold (GB: The Mysterious Stranger). Armored Car. The Big City. Paid to Dance. King of Gamblers. The Game That Kills. Woman in Distress. Daughter of Shanghai. Border Café. On Such a Night. 1938: King of Alcatraz (GB: King of the Alcatraz). Gun Law. The Buccaneer. Mannequin. The Crowd Roars. Penitentiary. When G-Men Step In. Crime Ring. Mr Moto's Gamble. The Saint in New York. Smashing the Rackets. The Night Hawk. Crime Takes a Holiday. 1939: Mutiny on the Blackhawk. Two Thoroughbreds. Disbarred. Wall Street Cowboy. They All Come*

Out. The Girl and the Gambler. News is Made at Night. Heritage of the Desert. Those High Gray Walls (GB: The Gates of Alcatraz). Star Reporter. Behind Prison Gates. Code of the Streets. Undercover Doctor. 1940: The Ghost Breakers. Outside the Three-Mile Limit (GB: Mutiny on the Seas). The Crooked Road. Black Friday. Dr Cyclops. Triple Justice. Black Diamonds. Virginia City. Glamour for Sale. Queen of the Mob. Strange Cargo. The Fargo Kid. Trail of the Vigilantes. The Great Plane Robbery. 1941: A Missouri Outlaw. Citadel of Crime (GB: Outside the Law). Down Mexico Way. H.M. Pulham Esq. Unfinished Business. Public Enemies. Hold That Ghost! Mob Town. The Roar of the Press. 1942: Pittsburgh. Highways by Night. That Other Woman. South of Santa Fé. Sherlock Holmes and the Secret Weapon. Jail House Blues. Escape from Crime. Kid Glove Killer. Youth on Parade. Alias Boston Blackie. Sleepytime Gal. Dr Gillespie's New Assistant. 1943: Hitler—Dead or Alive. Mug Town. Captive Wild Woman. Bombardier. In Old Oklahoma (later War of the Wildcats). The Unknown Guest. 1944: The Fighting Seabees. Tall in the Saddle. 1945: Flame of the Barbary Coast. Grissly's Millions. Back to Bataan. Dakota. 1947: Tycoon. 1948: Wake of the Red Witch. Angel in Exile. Red River. Strange Gamble. Force of Evil. The Plunderers. 1949: The Fighting Kentuckian. She Wore a Yellow Ribbon. Hellfire. Fighting Man of the Plains. 1950: California Passage. Surrender. Jet Pilot (released 1957). The Great Missouri Raid. 1951: Warpath. 1952: What Price Glory? Ride the Man Down. Denver and Rio Grande. 1953: Star of Texas. Fair Wind to Java. Island in the Sky. Devil's Canyon. 1954: Superman's Peril (TV. GB: cinemas). Hondo. Johnny Guitar. Ring of Fear. The High and the Mighty. 1955: Top of the World. The Sea Chase. Blood Alley. 1956: Giant. Santiago (GB: The Gun Runner). Toward the Unknown (GB: Brink of Hell). Man in the Vault. The Bad Seed. Stagecoach to Fury. 1957: Night Passage. The Devil's Hairpin. Man in the Shadow (GB: Pay the Devil). 1958: Guns, Girls and Gangsters. Lafayette Escadrille (GB: Hell Bent for Glory). The Notorious Mr Monks. 1962: To Kill a Mockingbird. 1963: Mail Order Bride (GB: West of Montana). 1964: The Outrage. 1965: Baby, the Rain Must Fall. The Sons of Katie Elder. Shenandoah. 1966: Nevada Smith. An Eye for an Eye. Ride Beyond Vengeance. Incident at Phantom Hill. Welcome to Hard Times (GB: Killer on a Horse). 1967: El Dorado. The Ballad of Josie. Winchester '73 (TV). 1968: The Day of the Evil Gun. 1969: The Undefeated. The Profane Comedy/Set This Town on Fire (TV). Young Billy Young. Zabriskie Point. 1970: Dirty Dingus Magee. The House on Greenapple Road (TV). 1971: Something Big. Shoot Out. 1972: Night of the Lepus. 1973: Cahill, US Marshal (GB: Cahill). Pat Garrett and Billy the Kid. Guilty or Innocent: The Sam Sheppard Murder Case (TV). 1977: Grayeagle. The City (TV). 1978: Just Me and You. Wanda Nevada. 1979: Hanging by a Thread (TV).

FLEMING, Ian 1888–1969
Diffident, dogged, self-effacing, reliable-looking Australian-born actor in British films; his acting career spanned more than 60

years. On stage in Australia at 16, he came to Britain in 1914, then made his name in films at the beginning of sound as an excellent Dr Watson to Arthur Wontner's Sherlock Holmes in several Conan Doyle adventures. After that he was kept busy for 30 years, often as professional men offering level-headed advice. Played so many doctors that he probably had his own black bag.

1926: Second to None. 1928: The Ware Case. 1929: The Devil's Maze. 1930: The School for Scandal. 1931: The Sleeping Cardinal (US: Sherlock Holmes' Fatal Hour). 1932: The Missing Rembrandt. Lucky Girl. After Dark. 1933: Called Back. Paris Plane. 1934: The Third Clue. Passing Shadows. 1935: The Riverside Murder. The Triumph of Sherlock Holmes. School for Stars. Sexton Blake and the Mademoiselle. The Crouching Beast. 1936: 21 Today. Hearts of Humanity. Royal Eagle. Crime Over London. Prison Breaker. 1937: Darby and Joan. Racing Romance. Jump for Glory (US: When Thief Meets Thief). Silver Blaze (US: Murder at the Baskervilles). 1938: Almost a Honeymoon. Ghost Tales Retold. Dial 999. The Claydon Treasure Mystery. Bad Boy (later Branded). The Reverse Be My Lot. Quiet Please. The Return of Carol Deane. Double or Quits. If I Were Boss. 1939: The Nursemaid Who Disappeared. Q Planes (US: Clouds Over Europe). Dead Men Are Dangerous. Me and My Pal. Sons of the Sea. Men Without Honour. Shadowed Eyes. The Lion Has Wings. The Good Old Days. 1940: Gentleman of Venture (US: It Happened to One Man). The Briggs Family. Let George Do It. Three Silent Men. Tilly of Bloomsbury. Night Train to Munich (US: Night Train). 1941: Hatter's Castle. Ships With Wings. Jeannie (US: Girl in Distress). They Flew Alone (US: Wings and the Woman). 1942: Next of Kin. Sabotage at Sea. Let the People Sing. Salute John Citizen. Soldiers Without Uniform. Talk About Jacqueline. 1943: Up with the Lark. They Met in the Dark. We Dive at Dawn. The Life and Death of Colonel Blimp (US: Colonel Blimp). Escape to Danger. Rhythm Serenade. The Yellow Canary. Bell Bottom George. The Butler's Dilemma. 1944: Tawny Pipit. Waterloo Road. He Snoops to Conquer. 1945: I Didn't Do It. They Knew Mr Knight. 1946: George in Civvy Street. Appointment with Crime. 1947: Captain Boycott. Anna Karenina. 1948: Quartet. 1949: For Them That Trespass. What a Carry On. A Matter of Murder. School for Randle. 1950: The Woman

in Question (US: Five Angles on Murder). Shadow of the Past. 1951: Chelsea Story. Laughter in Paradise. Salute the Toff. Outcast of the Islands. 1952: Circumstantial Evidence. Come Back Peter. Hammer the Toff. Wings of Danger (US: Dead on Course). The Black Orchid. Crow Hollow. Deadly Nightshade. The Voice of Merrill (US: Murder Will Out). 1953: Recoil. The Saint's Return (US: The Saint's Girl Friday). It's a Grand Life. Stryker of the Yard. Park Plaza 605 (US: Norman Conquest). 1954: The Seekers (US: Land of Fury). The Embezzler. Delayed Action. Eight O'Clock Walk. Companions in Crime. What Every Woman Wants. 1955: Police Dog. 1956: Guilty? 1957: High Flight. The Birthday Present. 1958: A Woman Possessed. Innocent Meeting. Virgin Island/Our Virgin Island. 1959: Web of Suspicion. Man Accused. Crash Drive. Your Money or Your Wife. The Flesh and the Fiends (US: Mania). 1960: Make Mine Mink. Bluebeard's Ten Honeymoons. The Trials of Oscar Wilde (US: The Man with the Green Carnation). Too Hot to Handle (US: Playgirl After Dark). 1961: No, My Darling Daughter! Return of a Stranger. 1962: The Lamp in Assassin Mews. The Boys. 1963: Tamahine. Crooks in Cloisters. 1964: Seventy Deadly Pills. 1965: The Return of Mr Moto. 1967: River Rivals (serial).

FLEMYNG, Robert 1912–

Elegant, brown-haired British leading man who seems in retrospect to have been in scores of films since his debut as a smooth young foil for Jessie Matthews, but has in fact made comparatively few. Always authoritative and in command of the situation, whether as officer, lawyer, teacher, politician or, latterly, judge. His principal work, to which he has brought commanding presence and ringing tones, has remained for the theatre.

1937: Head over Heels (US: Head over Heels in Love). 1948: Bond Street. The Guinea Pig. 1949: Conspirator. The Blue Lamp. 1950: Blackmailed. 1951: The Magic Box. 1952: The Holly and the Ivy. 1955: Cast a Dark Shadow. The Man Who Never Was. 1956: Funny Face. 1957: Let's Be Happy. Windom's Way. 1959: Blind Date/Chance Meeting. A Touch of Larceny. 1960: Radius. 1962: *The King's Breakfast. L'orribile segreto del Dottor Hichcock (GB: The Terror of Dr Hichcock). US: The Horrible Doctor Hichcock). 1963: Mystery

Submarine (US: Decoy). 1966: The Quiller Memorandum. The Deadly Affair. The Spy with a Cold Nose. 1967: The Blood Beast Terror (US: Deathshead Avenger). 1969: The Body Stealers. Oh! What a Lovely War. Battle of Britain. 1970: The Firechasers. 1971: The Darwin Adventure. Young Winston. 1972: Travels with My Aunt. 1977: The Medusa Touch. Golden Rendezvous. 1978: The Four Feathers (TV. GB: cinemas). The Thirty-Nine Steps. 1980: Rebecca (TV). 1988: Paris by Night. 1992: Memento Mori (TV). Kafka. 1993: Shadowlands.

FLETCHER, Louise 1936–

Tall, square-built, light-haired American actress of stern and forthright manner. Born to deaf parents, she acted steadily in TV series of the late 1950s and early 1960s, but retired to marry in 1964, re-emerging 10 years later with two excellent portrayals of treacherous, unsmiling women in Thieves Like Us and One Flew Over the Cuckoo's Nest, for the second of which she won a Best Actress Oscar. But her height and style possibly limited further appearances, and her profile has been noticeably lower in recent times.

1963: A Gathering of Eagles. 1974: Can Ellen Be Saved? (TV). Thieves Like Us. 1975: One Flew Over the Cuckoo's Nest. Russian Roulette. 1977: Exorcist II: The Heretic. 1978: The Cheap Detective. Thou Shalt Not Commit Adultery (TV). 1979: Natural Enemies. The Magician of Lublin. The Lady in Red. 1980: The Lucky Star. Mama Dracula. 1981: Dead Kids. Brainstorm (released 1983). 1982: Talk to Me. 1983: Strange Invaders. *Overnight Sensation. 1984: Firestarter. 1985: A Summer to Remember (TV). Invaders from Mars. 1986: Nobody's Fool. Second Serve (TV). The Boy Who Could Fly. 1987: Flowers in the Attic. J Edgar Hoover (TV). 1988: Two Moon Junction. 1989: Best of the Best. Shadowzone. Dangerous Pursuit (TV). Final Notice (TV). Blue Steel. 1990: Twilight Blue. Nightmare on the 13th Floor (TV). 1992: The Player. Blind Vision. 1994: A Return to Two Moon Junction. Tollbooth. Tryst. Giorgino. The Haunting of Seacliff Inn (TV). 1995: American Perfect. Virtuosity.

FLIPPEN, Jay C. 1898–1971

Bulldog-faced, craggy, thick-set American actor with thick, grey curly hair and beetle

brows that expressed doubt or incredulity. For years he was a minstrel and comic in travelling shows and made a couple of early two-reeler comedy films. He returned to films in 1947 as a character actor, to play hard eggs who could be comic or genuinely tough, and was much in demand until the end of the fifties. Lost a leg in later years. Died from an aneurysm (swollen artery).

1928: *†The Ham What Am. 1929: *†The Home Edition. 1934: Million Dollar Ransom. Marie Galante. 1947: Brute Force. Intrigue. 1948: They Live By Night. 1949: Down to the Sea in Ships. A Woman's Secret. Oh, You Beautiful Doll. 1950: The Yellow Cab Man. Love That Brute. Winchester '73. Jet Pilot (released 1957). Two Flags West. Buccaneer's Girl. 1951: The Lemon Drop Kid. Flying Leathernecks. The People Against O'Hara. The Lady from Texas. The Model and the Marriage Broker. 1952: Bend of the River (GB: Where the River Bends). The Las Vegas Story. Woman of the North Country. 1953: Thunder Bay. East of Sumatra. Devil's Canyon. The Wild One. 1954: Carnival Story. The Far Country. 1955: Six Bridges to Cross. Man Without a Star. Strategic Air Command. It's Always Fair Weather. Oklahoma! 1956: Kismet. The Killing. The Seventh Cavalry. The King and Four Queens. The Halliday Brand. 1957: Night Passage. Hot Summer Night. Public Pigeon Number One. The Restless Breed. The Deerslayer. The Midnight Story (GB: Appointment With a Shadow). Run of the Arrow. Lure of the Swamp. 1958: Escape from Red Rock. Before I Die (TV). From Hell to Texas (GB: Manhunt). 1960: Wild River. Where the Boys Are. Studs Lonigan. The Plunderers. 1962: Six-Gun Law (TV. GB: cinemas). How the West Was Won. 1964: Looking for Love. 1965: Cat Ballou. 1966: Fame is the Name of the Game (TV). 1967: The Spirit is Willing. Firecreek. 1968: The Sound of Anger (TV). Hellfighters. 1969: Hello, Dolly! 1970: The Old Man Who Cried Wolf (TV). 1971: Sam Hill—Who Killed the Mysterious Mr Foster? (TV). The Seven Minutes.

† As J.C. Flippin

FORD, Paul

(P. F. Weaver) 1901–1976

Lugubrious, balding, bloodhound-jowled American comic actor specializing in outrage and despair. He made his name as the hapless colonel in Phil Silvers' TV 'Bilko'

series *You'll Never Get Rich* in the 1950s. Subsequently Ford, once a puppeteer at the onset of a belated showbusiness career, was a delight in several leading character roles.

1945: The House on 92nd Street. 1948: Naked City. 1949: Lust for Gold. All the King's Men. The Kid from Texas (GB: Texas Kid—Outlaw). 1950: Perfect Strangers (GB: Too Dangerous to Love). 1956: The Teahouse of the August Moon. 1958: The Missouri Traveler. The Matchmaker. 1960: The Right Man (TV). 1961: The Music Man. Advise and Consent. 1962: Who's Got the Action? 1963: It's a Mad, Mad, Mad, Mad World. 1965: Never Too Late. 1966: The Russians Are Coming, the Russians Are Coming. A Big Hand for the Little Lady (GB: Big Deal at Dodge City). The Spy With a Cold Nose. 1967: The Comedians. 1969: In Name Only (TV). Twinky (US: Lola). 1971: Journey Back to Oz (voice only). 1972: Richard.

FORD, Wallace
(Samuel Grundy) 1897–1966

Broad-shouldered, tow-haired, British-born Hollywood actor who played goodhearted, affable types, tough heroes, Irishmen and gangsters with a soft streak. He hit the headlines in the mid-1930s when seeking (and finding) his long-lost parents in England. His acting improved in stocky character roles, after a few leads in the 1930s, and he remained in films and TV until his death from a heart ailment.

1930: *Absent-Minded. *Fore! The Swellhead (GB: Counted Out). 1931: Possessed. Sky-

scraper Souls. X Marks the Spot. *1932: Freaks. Beast of the City. Prosperity. Hypnotized. Central Park. Are You Listening? The Wet Parade. The Big Cage. City Sentinel. 1933: Goodbye Again. East of Fifth Avenue (GB: Two in a Million). Employees' Entrance. Headline Shooter (GB: Evidence in Camera). My Woman. Night of Terror. Three Cornered Moon. She Had to Say Yes. 1934: Money Means Nothing. A Woman's Man. Men in White. The Man Who Reclaimed His Head. I Hate Women. The Lost Patrol. The Whole Town's Talking (GB: Passport to Fame). 1935: Another Face (GB: It Happened in Hollywood). The Nut Farm. *Screen Snapshots No 5. The Informer. Swell Head (and 1930 film). In Spite of Danger. She Couldn't Take It. Men of the Hour. Get That Man. Mary Burns—Fugitive. One Frightened Night. The Mysterious Mr Wong. Sanders of the River. 1936: OHMS (US: You're in the Army Now). Rogues' Tavern. Two in the Dark. Absolute Quiet. A Son Comes Home. 1937: Jericho (US: Dark Sands). Mad About Money (US: He Loved an Actress). Swing It Sailor. Exiled to Shanghai. 1939: Back Door to Heaven. 1940: Isle of Destiny. Two Girls on Broadway (GB: Change Your Partner). Love, Honor and Oh! Baby. Give Us Wings. The Mummy's Hand. Scatterbrain. 1941: A Man Betrayed (GB: Citadel of Crime). The Roar of the Press. Blues in the Night. Murder by Invitation. 1942: Scattergood Survives a Murder. Inside the Law. X Marks the Spot (and earlier version). All Through the Night. Seven Days' Leave. The Mummy's Tomb. 1943: The Marines Come Through. Shadow of a Doubt. The Cross of Lorraine. The Ape Man. 1944: Secret Command. Machine Gun Mama. 1945: The Woman Who Came Back. The Great John L (GB: A Man Called Sullivan). Spellbound. They Were Expendable. Blood on the Sun. On Stage, Everybody. 1946: The Green Years. A Guy Could Change. Rendezvous with Annie. Crack-Up. The Black Angel. Lover Come Back. Dead Reckoning. 1947: Magic Town. T-Men. 1948: Shed No Tears. Coroner Creek. The Man from Texas. Embraceable You. Belle Starr's Daughter. 1949: Red Stallion in the Rockies. The Set-Up. 1950: The Breaking Point. Dakota Lil. The Furies. Harvey. 1951: Warpath. He Ran All the Way. Painting the Clouds with Sunshine. 1952: Flesh and Fury. Rodeo. 1953: She Couldn't Say No (GB: Beautiful But Dangerous). The Nebraskan. The Great Jesse James Raid. 1954: The Boy from Oklahoma. Destry. Three Ring Circus. 1955: The Man from Laramie. The Spoilers. Lucy Gallant. A Lawless Street. Wichita. The Ox-Bow Incident (TV. GB: cinemas). 1956: Johnny Concho. The Maverick Queen. The First Texan. Snow Shoes (TV). Stagecoach to Fury. Thunder Over Arizona. The Rainmaker. 1957: The Last Man (TV). 1958: The Last Hurrah. The Matchmaker. Twilight for the Gods. 1959: Warlock. 1961: Tess of the Storm Country. 1965: A Patch of Blue.*

FOSTER, Barry 1931–

Versatile British actor with fair, curly hair, who looks like a serious Jon Pertwee (*qv*). His most successful work has been for television – especially in years-apart series about the Dutch detective Van der Valk –

and he has made fewer films than one expected, although his contribution as the murderer in Hitchcock's *Frenzy* should not be underestimated.

1956: The Battle of the River Plate (US: Pursuit of the Graf Spee). The Baby and the Battleship. 1957: High Flight. Yangtse Incident (US: Battle Hell). 1958: Sea Fury. Sea of Sand. Dunkirk. 1959: Yesterday's Enemy. 1962: Playback. 1964: King and Country. 1966: The Family Way. 1967: Robbery. 1968: Inspector Clouseau. Twisted Nerve. The Guru. 1969: Battle of Britain. 1970: Ryan's Daughter. 1972: Frenzy. 1974: Quiet Day in Belfast. Der letzte Schrei. 1976: Sweeney! 1978: The Wild Geese. The Three Hostages (TV). 1980: Danger on Dartmoor. 1981: The Bomber. 1982: Heat and Dust. 1984: To Catch a King (TV. GB: cinemas). 1985: Hotel du Lac (TV). 1986: The Whistle Blower. 1987: Three Kinds of Heat. Maurice. 1989: King of the Wind. 1990: Impromptu.

FOSTER, Dudley 1925–1973

Dark, cadaverous English actor with scruffy hair who played scheming and untrustworthy types in British films, alternating leads in second features with character parts in bigger films. He was particularly good in one minor thriller, *Never Mention Murder*, in 1964, but, after four years off screen he was seen in smaller roles and, in January 1973 committed suicide.

1956: No Road Back. 1959: Operation Bullshine. The Two-Headed Spy. 1960: The Man in the Moon. 1962: Term of Trial. 1963:

Ricochet. 1964: Never Mention Murder. 1965: The Little Ones. A Study in Terror (US: Fog). 1969: Where's Jack? Foreign Exchange (TV). Moon Zero Two. 1970: The Rise and Rise of Michael Rimmer. Wuthering Heights. 1971: Quest for Love. Dulcima. Follow Me (US: The Public Eye). 1972: That's Your Funeral. 1973· Mistress Pamela.

FOSTER, Meg 1948–

Tall, open-faced, tawny-haired American actress with unusually striking blue-grey eyes. At her best in offbeat roles, it seemed that the less she had to do in a film, the more effective she was. This capability has led to some vivid semi-cameos in recent times, and she looks set to steal scenes for some years yet to come. She missed a slice of television immortality when, after starring in the pilot to Cagney and Lacey, opposite Tyne Daly, she dropped out of the ensuing series.

1970: Adam at 6 am. The Todd Killings. 1971: The Death of Me Yet (TV). 1972: Thumb Tripping. 1973: Sunshine (TV. GB: cinemas). 1974: Welcome to Arrow Beach. Things in Their Season (TV). 1975: Promise Him Anything (TV). 1976: James Dean (TV). 1977: Sunshine Christmas (TV). Pressure Point (TV). Once in Paris. 1978: A Different Story. 1979: The Legend of Sleepy Hollow. Carny. 1980: Guyana Tragedy: The Story of Jim Jones (TV). 1981: Ticket to Heaven. 1983: Desperate Intruder (TV). The Osterman Weekend. 1985: The Emerald Forest. 1986: The Wind. 1987: Masters of the Universe. Desperate (TV). 1988: They Live! 1989: Best Kept Secrets (TV). Betrayal of Silence (TV). Leviathan. Relentless. Stepfather II. 1990: Jezebel's Kiss. Back Stab. 1991: Prodigy. Relentless II: Dead On. Futurekick. Diplomatic Immunity. 1992: Project Shadowchaser. 1993: Best of the Best II. Hidden Fears. 1994: Oblivion. Shrunken Heads. 1995: Undercover.

FOULGER, Byron 1900–1970

Squat, square-faced, often bespectacled and moustachioed American actor with thinning brown hair, generally seen as furtive, unpleasant characters who might be treacherous, cringing, servile, edgy or all four. Shuffled his way almost apologetically through scores of roles in the 1930s, 1940s and 1950s, his rat-trap jaws almost inevitably coming into demand for TV series after

that, usually as narrow-minded spoilsports. Married to equally prolific character actress Dorothy Adams (qv) and father of actress Rachel Ames, also known as Judith Ames (1931–). Died from a heart condition.

1937: History is Made at Night. True Confession. The Duke Comes Back (GB: The Call of the Ring). Larceny on the Air. A Day at the Races. Dick Tracy (serial). The Prisoner of Zenda. The Awful Truth. Make Way for Tomorrow. The Luck of Roaring Camp. 1938: I Am a Criminal. Lady in the Morgue (GB: The Case of the Missing Blonde). Fools of Desire/ It's All in Your Mind. Crime Ring. Born to be Wild. Tenth Avenue Kid. Delinquent Parents. Tarnished Angel. I Am the Law. You Can't Take It with You. Say It in French. King of the Newsboys. Test Pilot. Gangster's Boy. Listen Darling. The Spider's Web (serial). 1939: At the Circus/Marx Brothers at the Circus. In Name Only. Union Pacific. Let Us Live! Mutiny on the Blackhawk. Exile Express. The Spellbinder. The Girl from Rio. The Man They Could Not Hang. Television Spy. The Secret of Dr Kildare. The Girl from Mexico. Andy Hardy Gets Spring Fever. Mr Smith Goes to Washington. Bad Little Angel. Million Dollar Legs. Some Like It Hot. 1940: Flash Gordon Conquers the Universe (serial). Heroes of the Saddle. The Great McGinty (GB: Down Went McGinty). The Man with Nine Lives (GB: Behind the Door). Edison, the Man. Sky Murder. Ellery Queen, Master Detective. Christmas in July. Arizona. Untamed. Dr Kildare's Crisis. Golden Gloves. Boom Town. I Want a Divorce. Parole Fixer. The Saint's Double Trouble. Abe Lincoln in Illinois (GB: Spirit of the People). Opened by Mistake. *Good Bad Guys. 1941: Man-Made Monster (GB: The Electric Man). Remember the Day. Ridin' on a Rainbow. The Gay Vagabond. Mystery Ship. Sweetheart of the Campus (GB: Broadway Ahead). Dude Cowboy. Sullivan's Travels. Harvard, Here I Come (GB: Here I Come). The Road to Happiness. The Penalty. Sis Hopkins. Meet Boston Blackie. You Belong to Me (GB: Good Morning Doctor). She Knew All the Answers. Bedtime Story. H.M. Pulham Esq. *Helping Hands. *Come Back Miss Pipps. 1942: The Panther's Claw. The Tuttles of Tahiti. Man from Headquarters. Reap the Wild Wind. The Forest Rangers. The Palm Beach Story. Quiet Please Murder. Stand by for Action! (GB: Cargo of Innocents). The Wrecking Crew. Fingers at the Window. The Magnificent Dope. Pacific Rendezvous. The

Sabotage Squad. Miss Annie Rooney. *Keep 'Em Sailing. 1943: The Human Comedy. The Adventures of a Rookie. So Proudly We Hail! Sweet Rosie O'Grady. In Old Oklahoma (later War of the Wildcats). Hi Diddle Diddle. The Kansan (GB: Wagon Wheels). Hoppy Serves a Writ. Dixie Dugan. Coney Island. Silver Spurs. The Black Raven. Hangmen Also Die. The Falcon Strikes Back. What a Woman! (GB: The Beautiful Cheat). Appointment in Berlin. Margin for Error. First Comes Courage. Ministry of Fear. Shantytown. The Power of God. 1944: Enemy of Women. Summer Storm. Roger Touhy – Gangster (GB: The Last Gangster). The Miracle of Morgan's Creek. The Whistler. Henry Aldrich's Little Secret. A Night of Adventure. Since You Went Away. Dark Mountain. Beautiful But Broke. Swing in the Saddle (GB: Swing and Sway). Marriage is a Private Affair. *He Forgot to Remember. Girl Rush. Three Men in White. Maisie Goes to Reno (GB: You Can't Do That to Me). Music for Millions. It's in the Bag! (GB: The Fifth Chair). Casanova Brown. Mrs Parkington. Take It Big. The Great Moment. An American Romance. And Now Tomorrow. Barbary Coast Gent. Ladies of Washington. Music in Manhattan. Ever Since Venus. Lady in the Death House. 1945: The Master Key (serial). Grissly's Millions. Circumstantial Evidence. The Hidden Eye. The Adventures of Kitty O'Day. Arson Squad. The Blonde from Brooklyn. Snafu (GB: Welcome Home). Sensation Hunters. Week-End at the Waldorf. The Lost Weekend. Don Juan Quilligan. Adventure. Nob Hill. Wonder Man. *Purity Squad. The Cheaters. Brewster's Millions. Let's Go Steady. Cornered. Scarlet Street. 1946: Sentimental Journey. Just Before Dawn. The Postman Always Rings Twice. The Mysterious Mr M (serial). Till the Clouds Roll By. The French Key. Dick Tracy vs Cueball. San Quentin. Magnificent Rogue. Secret of the Whistler. Two Sisters from Boston. The Plainsman and the Lady. House of Horrors (GB: Joan Medford is Missing). The Show Off. Courage of Lassie. The Hoodlum Saint. The Magnificent Doll. Suspense. Deadline at Dawn. Blonde Alibi. Dead Reckoning. 1947: The Michigan Kid. Hard-Boiled Mahoney. The Bells of San Fernando. The Adventures of Don Coyote. Too Many Winners. Stallion Road. The Red Hornet. The Chinese Ring. The Trouble with Women. Unconquered. The Long Night. Easy Come, Easy Go. They Won't Believe Me. Song of Love. Linda Be Good. 1948: The Hunted. Arch of Triumph. Out of the Storm. The Return of October (GB: Date with Destiny). I Surrender Dear. The Three Musketeers. Relentless. Best of the Badmen. A Southern Yankee (GB: My Hero). The Kissing Bandit. The Bride Goes Wild. Let's Live a Little. He Walked by Night. They Live By Night. 1949: Samson and Delilah. I Shot Jesse James. Arson, Inc. The Inspector General. The Dalton Gang. Satan's Cradle. Mighty Joe Young. Dancing in the Dark. Red Desert. Streets of Laredo. 1950: The Girl from San Lorenzo. Salt Lake Raiders. The Return of Jesse James. Champagne for Caesar. Experiment Alcatraz. Dark City. Union Station. Riding High. Key to the City. To Please a Lady. 1951: Lightning Strikes Twice. FBI Girl. Footlight Varieties. Gasoline Alley. The Home Town Story. A Millionaire for Christy. The Sea Hornet. Best of the Badmen. Superman and the Mole-Men

(GB: *Superman and the Strange People*). *Hollywood Honeymoon*. 1952: *Apache Country*. *My Six Convicts*. *Cripple Creek*. *The Steel Fist*. *Confidentially Connie*. *Hold That Line*. *We're Not Married*. *Newlyweds Take a Chance*. *Rose of Cimarron*. *Skirts Ahoy*. *The Sniper*. *The Sword of D'Artagnan*. 1953: *Paris Model*. *The Magnetic Monster*. *Cruisin' Down the River*. *Bandits of the West*. *A Perilous Journey*. *Run for the Hills*. 1954: *Cattle Queen of Montana*. *Silver Lode*. 1955: *At Gunpoint* (GB: *Gunpoint!*). *The Scarlet Coat*. *The Spoilers*. 1956: *You Can't Run Away from It*. *The Desperadoes Are in Town*. *The Young Stranger*. 1957: *The River's Edge*. *Sierra Stranger*. *Dino* (GB: *Killer Dino*). *The Buckskin Lady*. *Gun Battle at Monterey*. *Up in Smoke*. *The Young Stranger*. 1958: *Going Steady*. *Man from God's Country*. *The Long, Hot Summer*. *In the Money*. *Onionhead*. 1959: *King of the Wild Stallions*. 1960: *Twelve Hours to Kill*. *Ma Barker's Killer Brood/Bloody Brood*. 1961: *The Devil's Partner*. *Pocketful of Miracles*. *Ride the High Country* (GB: *Guns in the Afternoon*). 1963: *Son of Flubber*. *Who's Minding the Store*? 1964: *Guns of Diablo*. 1965: *Marriage on the Rocks*. 1966: *The Gnome-Mobile*. *The Spirit is Willing*. 1967: *Aliens from Another Planet*. 1969: *Hook, Line and Sinker*. *The Cockeyed Cowboys of Calico Country* (GB: TV, as *A Woman for Charlie*). 1970: *The Love War* (TV). *There Was a Crooked Man . . .*

Barabbas was a robber . . . 1950: *Trio*. *Once a Sinner*. *Dance Hall*. *Mr Drake's Duck*. *She Shall Have Murder*. 1951: *Introducing the New Worker*. *There is Another Sun*. *The Dark Man*. *Scarlet Thread*. *High Treason*. *Madame Louise*. 1952: *A Spot of Bother*. *I Believe in You*. *Food for Thought*. *Angels One Five*. *The Paper Chase*. *The Last Page* (US: *Manbait*). *Height of Ambition*. *The Pickwick Papers*. *Shedding the Load*. *Top of the Form*. *A Sweeping Statement*. 1953: *A Day to Remember*. *Don't Blame the Stork!* 1954: *Conflict of Wings*. *Up to His Neck*. 1955: *Stock Car*. *The Blue Peter* (US: *Navy Heroes*). 1956: *Fire Maidens from Outer Space*. *Behind the Headlines*. *Home and Away*. *Town on Trial!* 1957: *The Supreme Secret*. *West of Suez* (US: *Fighting Wildcats*). *Booby Trap*. *Lucky Jim*. *The Birthday Present*. *Soapbox Deby*. 1958: *I Was Monty's Double* (US: *Monty's Double*). *Diplomatic Corpse*. 1959: *Idle on Parade* (US: *Idol on Parade*). *The Heart of a Man*. *The Dawn Killer* (serial). *Don't Panic Chaps!* 1962: *Lawrence of Arabia*. *The Golliwog*. *Flight from Singapore*. *Crooks Anonymous*. *Tomorrow at Ten*. *The Longest Day*. 1963: *Just for Fun*. *Clash by Night* (US: *Escape by Night*). *Ladies Who Do*. *70 Deadly Pills*. 1965: *Life at the Top*. *Joey Boy*. *The Nanny*. 1966: *Doctor in Clover* (US: *Carnaby MD*). *Secrets of a Windmill Girl*. 1969: *Start the Revolution Without Me*. 1975: *GREAT: Isambard Kingdom Brunel* (voice only). 1977: *The Prince and the Pauper* (US: *Crossed Swords*). 1980: *High Rise Donkey*. *Sir Henry at Rawlinson End*. *George and Mildred*. 1983: *Fanny Hill*. 1989: *Chicago Joe and the Showgirl*.

FOWLER, Harry 1926–
Jaunty British actor with brashly cheerful manner and shovel-shaped face. A former newspaper boy, his distinctive cockney voice got him wartime parts on radio before a film debut in 1942. Enjoyed his finest hour as the leader of the street kids in *Hue and Cry*, after which he was seen in a long series of character roles, from fat to tiny. Moustachioed from 1970, and latterly starring in TV series. Married to actress Joan Dowling (*qv*) from 1951 to her death in 1954.

1942: *Salute John Citizen*. *Those Kids from Town*. *Went the Day Well?* (US: *48 Hours*). 1943: *The Demi-Paradise* (US: *Adventure for Two*). *Bell Bottom George*. *Get Cracking*. 1944: *Give Us the Moon*. *Don't Take It to Heart*. *Champagne Charlie*. 1945: *Painted Boats* (US: *The Girl on the Canal*). 1947: *Hue and Cry*. 1948: *Trouble in the Air*. *A Piece of Cake*. 1949: *Landfall*. *For Them That Trespass*. *Now

FOWLEY, Douglas (V)
(Daniel Fowley) 1911–
Tall, thin-lipped, strong-voiced, dark-eyed American actor who was soon typecast as a villain when he decided to make acting his career after trying various other occupations in the early 1930s. As age tempered his characterizations, they tended to become bemused rather than plain mean; he was notable as the bellowing movie director in *Singin' in the Rain*, and subsequently found ready employers in many TV series.

1933: *The Mad Game*. 1934: *The Gift of Gab*. *Operator 13* (GB: *Spy 13*). *The Thin Man*. *The Woman Who Dared*. *Student Tour*. *I Hate Women*. *Let's Talk It Over*. *The Girl from

Missouri (GB: *100 Per Cent Pure*). 1935: *Miss Pacific Fleet*. *Straight from the Heart*. *Transient Lady* (GB: *False Witness*). *Night Life of the Gods*. *Two for Tonight*. *Old Man Rhythm*. 1936: *Ring Around the Moon*. *Dimples*. *Small Town Girl*. *Big Brown Eyes*. *Navy Born*. *Crash Donovan*. *Sing, Baby, Sing*. *Thirty-Six Hours to Kill*. *15 Maiden Lane*. 1937: *Woman Wise*. *Time Out for Romance*. *On the Avenue*. *Fifty Roads to Town*. *Wake Up and Live*. *This Is My Affair* (GB: *His Affair*). *One Mile from Heaven*. *Wild and Woolly*. *Charlie Chan on Broadway*. *She Had to Eat*. *Love and Hisses*. *City Girl*. *Passport Husband*. 1938: *Mr Moto's Gamble*. *Walking Down Broadway*. *Alexander's Ragtime Band*. *Keep Smiling*. *Time Out for Murder*. *Inside Story*. *Submarine Patrol*. *Arizona Wildcat*. 1939: *Lucky Night*. *Dodge City*. *The Boy Friend*. *It Could Happen to You*. *Charlie Chan at Treasure Island*. *Slightly Honorable*. *Henry Goes Arizona* (GB: *Spats to Spurs*). 1940: *Cafe Hostess*. *Twenty-Mule Team*. *Wagons Westward*. *Pier 13*. *The Leather Pushers*. *Cherokee Strip* (GB: *Fighting Marshal*). *East of the River*. *Ellery Queen, Master Detective*. 1941: *The Great Swindle*. *The Parson of Panamint*. *Tanks a Million*. *Doctors Don't Tell*. *Dangerous Lady*. *Secrets of the Wasteland*. *Mr District Attorney in the Carter Case* (GB: *The Carter Case*). 1942: *Mississippi Gambler*. *For the Common Defense*. *The Devil with Hitler*. *Pittsburgh*. *Sunset on the Desert*. *Somewhere I'll Find You*. *Mr Wise Guy*. *Hay Foot*. *The Gay Sisters*. *Meet the Mob*. *So's Your Aunt Emma*. *I Live on Danger*. *The Man in the Trunk*. *Stand by for Action!* (GB: *Cargo of Innocents*). 1943: *Jitterbugs*. *Johnny Doesn't Live Here Any More*. *Gildersleeve's Bad Day*. *Chance of a Lifetime*. *Bar 20*. *Minesweeper*. *Swing Shift Maisie* (GB: *The Girl in Overalls*). *Colt Comrades*. *The Kansan* (GB: *Wagon Wheels*). *Sleepy Lagoon*. *Riding High* (GB: *Melody Inn*). *Lost Canyon*. 1944: *The Story of Dr Wassell*. *The Racket Man*. *Rationing*. *One Body Too Many*. *See Here, Private Hargrove*. *Shake Hands with Murder*. *And the Angels Sing*. *Detective Kitty O'Day*. *Lady in the Death House*. 1945: *Don't Fence Me In*. *Life with Blondie*. *Behind City Lights*. *Along the Navajo Trail*. 1946: *Chick Carter, Detective* (serial). *'Neath Canadian Skies*. *Her Sister's Secret*. *Driftin' Along*. *In Fast Company*. *The Glass Alibi*. *Rendezvous 24*. *North of the Border*. *Larceny in Her Heart*. *Freddie Steps Out*. *Blonde Alibi*. *High School Hero*. 1947: *Wild Country*. *Undercover Maisie* (GB: *Undercover Girl*). *Backlash*. *Three on a Ticket*. *Key Witness*. *Yankee Fakir*. *The Sea of Grass*. *Jungle Flight*. *Desperate*. *The Hucksters*. *The Trespasser*. *Gas House Kids in Hollywood*. *Fall Guy*. *Scared to Death*. *Ridin' Down the Trail*. *Roses Are Red*. *Merton of the Movies*. *Rose of Santa Rosa*. 1948: *Docks of New Orleans*. *Waterfront at Midnight*. *If You Knew Susie*. *The Dude Goes West*. *Black Bart* (GB: *Black Bart – Highwayman*). *Coroner Creek*. *Joe Palooka in Winner Take All* (GB: *Winner Take All*). *Behind Locked Doors*. *Gun Smugglers*. *So You Want to be a Gambler*. *Renegades of Sonora*. *The Denver Kid*. *Badmen of Tombstone*. 1949: *Flaxy Martin*. *Massacre River*. *Battleground*. *Clunked in the Clink*. *Susanna Pass*. *Arson, Inc.* *Search for Danger*. *Mighty Joe Young*. *Take Me Out to the Ball Game* (GB: *Everybody's Cheering*). *Any Number Can Play*.

Satan's Cradle. Renegades of the Sage. Joe Palooka in the Counter-Punch. 1950: Bunco Squad. Rider from Tucson. Armored Car Robbery. Hoedown. Edge of Doom (GB: Stronger Than Fear). Killer Shark. He's a Cockeyed Wonder. Mrs O'Malley and Mr Malone. Rio Grande Patrol. Stage to Tucson (GB: Lost Stage Valley). Beware of Blondie. 1951: Chain of Circumstance. Tarzan's Peril (GB: Tarzan and the Jungle Queen). Callaway Went Thataway (GB: The Star Said No). Finders Keepers. Across the Wide Missouri. Criminal Lawyer. South of Caliente. 1952: Just This Once. Singin' in the Rain. This Woman is Dangerous. Room for One More. Horizons West. The Man Behind the Gun. 1953: A Slight Case of Larceny. The Band Wagon. Cruisin' Down the River. Red River Shore. Kansas Pacific. Casanova's Big Night. 1954: Deep in My Heart. The Naked Jungle. Southwest Passage (GB: Camels West). Catwomen of the Moon. The Lone Gun. The High and the Mighty. Three Ring Circus. Untamed Heiress. 1955: The Girl Rush. The Lonesome Trail. Texas Lady. 1956: Bandido! The Broken Star. The Man from Del Rio. Rock Pretty Baby. 1957: Bayou. Kelly and Me. The Badge of Marshal Brennan. Raiders of Old California. 1958: A Gift for Heidi. 1959: These Thousand Hills. 1960: Desire in the Dust. 1961: Barabbas. Buffalo Gun. 1962: Miracle of the White Stallions (GB: Flight of the White Stallions). 1963: Who's Been Sleeping in My Bed? Nightmare in the Sun. 1964: The Seven Faces of Dr Lao. Guns of Diablo (TV. GB: cinemas). 1969: The Good Guys and the Bad Guys. 1972: Seeta The Mountain Lion (GB: Run, Cougar, Run). 1973: Walking Tall. Homebodies. 1975: Starsky and Hutch (TV). 1976: Black Oak Conspiracy. 1977: From Noon Till Three. Sunshine Christmas (TV). The White Buffalo. 1978: The North Avenue Irregulars (GB: Hill's Angels).

As director:
1960: Macumba Love.

FRANCEN, Victor
(V. Franssen) 1888–1977
Suave Belgian actor with lined face and heavy eyebrows. He filmed extensively in France before World War II, then fled to Hollywood, where he settled in happily at Warners to play cunning charmers, often effete millionaires with cigarette holder and silk dressing gown. At his best in the mid-1940s.

1921: Crépuscule d'épouvante. 1922: Le logis de l'horreur. 1923: La neige sur les pas. 1924: La doute. 1930: La fin du monde. 1931: Après l'amour. L'aiglon. 1932: Les ailes brisées. 1933: Le voleur. Mélo. 1934: L'aventurier. Ariane, jeune fille Russe. 1935: Le chemineau. Veille d'armes. 1936: L'appel de la vie. La porte du large. Nuits de feu. Le roi. 1937: Double crime sur la Ligne Maginot. Feu! Tamara la Complaisante. Forfaiture. 1938: J'accuse. Sacrifice d'honneur. La vierge folle. 1939: La fin du jour. Entente cordiale. L'homme du Niger. 1940: The Living Corpse. The Open Road. 1941: Hold Back the Dawn. 1942: The Tuttles of Tahiti. Ten Gentlemen from West Point. Tales of Manhattan. 1943: Mission to Moscow. The Desert Song. Madame Curie. Devotion (released 1946). 1944: In Our Time. Passage to Marseille (GB: Passage to Marseilles). The Mask of Dimitrios. Hollywood Canteen. Follow the Boys. The Conspirators. 1945: Confidential Agent. San Antonio. 1946: Night and Day. The Beast With Five Fingers. 1947: The Beginning or the End? La revoltée. To the Victor. 1949: La nuit s'achève. 1950: The Adventures of Captain Fabian. 1954: Hell and High Water. Boulevard de Paris. 1955: Bedevilled. 1957: A Farewell to Arms. 1958: Der Tiger von Eschnapur. Das Indische Grabmal. 1960: Journey to the Lost City (combined US version of preceding two films). 1961: Fanny. 1967: Top Crack.

FRANZ, Eduard 1902–1983
Grey-haired, benevolent-looking American actor who dispensed kindness and wisdom to many a hot-headed young hero during his 37-year tenure of films and television. Played fathers, uncles, counsellors, doctors, elders and psychiatrists and once claimed to have perfected '14 different wise looks'.

1947: Killer at Large. 1948: The Iron Curtain. Hollow Triumph (GB: The Scar). Wake of the Red Witch. 1949: Madame Bovary. The Doctor and the Girl. Outpost in Morocco. Francis. Oh, You Beautiful Doll. Whirlpool. 1950: The Vicious Years (GB: The Gangster We Made). Tarnished. Molly. The Magnificent Yankee (GB: The Man With Thirty Sons). Emergency Wedding (GB: Jealousy). 1951: The Great Caruso. The Thing. . .from another world. The Desert Fox (GB: Rommel—Desert Fox). The Unknown Man. Shadow in the Sky. 1952: Because You're Mine. One Minute to Zero. Everything I Have is Yours. 1953: Dream Wife. Latin Lovers.

Sins of Jezebel. The Jazz Singer. 1954: Sign of the Pagan. Broken Lance. Beachhead. 1955: Lady Godiva (GB: Lady Godiva of Coventry). The Last Command. White Feather. The Indian Fighter. Man on the Ledge (TV. GB: cinemas). 1956: The Ten Commandments. Three for Jamie Dawn. The Burning Hills. 1957: Man Afraid. 1958: Day of the Bad Man. Last of the Fast Guns. A Certain Smile. 1959: The Miracle. The Four Skulls of Jonathan Drake. 1960: The Story of Ruth. 1961: Francis of Assisi. The Fiercest Heart. 1962: Hatari! Beauty and the Beast. 1966: Cyborg 2087. 1967: The President's Analyst. 1970: The Brotherhood of the Bell (TV). 1971: Johnny Got His Gun. 1974: Panic on the 5.22 (TV). The Sex Symbol (TV). 1983: Twilight Zone—The Movie.

FRASER, Bill 1907–1987
Big, balding, bag-eyed British actor, alternately affable or aggressive, but almost always in comedy roles. Born in Scotland, he switched from a banking to a theatrical career at 24 and ran a seaside repertory company through the middle and late 1930s. He tried revue in the war years, but it was his success on television, playing the spluttering Snudge in The Army Game and Bootsie and Snudge, that earned him national popularity. In a career that spanned everything from Shakespeare to pantomime dames, he made fewer films than you'd expect: a fraction over one a year for his 48 years in movies. Died from emphysema.

1940: East of Piccadilly (US: The Strangler). 1941: The Common Touch. 1949: Helter Skelter. 1952: Meet Me Tonight. Lady in the Fog (US: Scotland Yard Inspector). Time Bomb (US: Terror on a Train). The Card (US: The Promoter). 1953: The Captain's Paradise. Meet Mr Lucifer. 1954: Orders Are Orders. Duel in the Jungle. The Barefoot Contessa. 1955: Jumping for Joy. 1956: Charley Moon. Alias John Preston. 1957: Doctor at Large. Second Fiddle. Just My Luck. 1958: The Long Knife. Another Time, Another Place. A Clean Sweep. 1959: The Man Who Liked Funerals. 1960: Doctor in Love. 1962: The Fast Lady. 1963: What a Crazy World. 1964: A Home of Your Own. Masquerade. The Americanization of Emily. 1965: I've Gotta Horse. Joey Boy. 1968: Diamonds for Breakfast. The Best House in London. Captain Nemo and the Underwater

City. 1970: All the Way Up. Up Pompeii. 1971: Up the Chastity Belt. 1972: Up the Front. Ooh . . . You Are Awful (US: Get Charlie Tully). That's Your Funeral. 1973: Love Thy Neighbour. Moments. 1974: Dead Cert. The Amorous Milkman. 1979: Comedians (TV). The Corn is Green (TV). 1981: Eye of the Needle. 1983: Wagner. 1985: Christmas Present. 1986: Pirates. 1987: Little Dorrit I. Little Dorrit II.

FRASER, Ronald 1930–

British character star with rumpled hair, small, piggy features and inimitable breathless delivery. Rarely looking smart on screen, he swiftly made his mark as a specialist in pugnacity and pomposity who could sometimes give remarkably self-effacing portrayals. At his best in the mid-1960s, when he was briefly in leading roles, he is still capable of lifting inferior material and a delight on the stage in restoration comedy.

1957: Black Ice. 1959: Bobbikins. 1960: The Sundowners. There was a Crooked Man. The Girl on the Boat. The Long and the Short and the Tall (US: Jungle Fighters). 1961: The Best of Enemies. Don't Bother to Knock! (US: Why Bother to Knock?). The Hellions. 1962: The Pot Carriers. In Search of the Castaways. Private Potter. The Punch and Judy Man. 1963: The VIPs. Girl in the Headlines (US: The Model Murder Case). Crooks in Cloisters. 1964: The Beauty Jungle (US: Contest Girl). Victim Five (US: Code Seven, Victim Five). Allez France (US: The Counterfeit Constable). Daylight Robbery. 1965: The Flight of the Phoenix. 1966: The Whisperers. 1967: Fathom. Sebastian. 1968: The Killing of Sister George. 1969: Sinful Davey. The Bed Sitting Room. Too Late the Hero. 1970: The Rise and Rise of Michael Rimmer. 1971: The Magnificent Seven Deadly Sins. Rentadick. 1972: Ooh . . . You Are Awful (US: Get Charlie Tully). 1974: Swallows and Amazons. Percy's Progress. Paper Tiger. The Count of Monte Cristo (TV. GB: cinemas). 1977: Hardcore. Come Play with Me. 1978: The Wild Geese. 1982: Trail of the Pink Panther. 1983: Tangier. 1986: Absolute Beginners. 1988: Scandal. 1991: 'Let Him Have It'. 1993: The Mystery of Edwin Drood.

FRASER, Liz
(Elizabeth Winch) 1933–

Big, busty, bouncy British comedy actress who cornered the market in dumb cockney blondes, especially in Peter Sellers comedies and the 'Carry On' series, before showing that she could tackle the odd dramatic role as well. Drifted back into broad film comedies in the 1970s after a long period away; television and the theatre have offered her more rewarding roles in recent times. A prolific worker for charities.

1955: ‡Touch and Go (US: The Light Touch). 1957: †The Smallest Show on Earth. †Not Wanted on Voyage. †Davy. 1958: †Wonderful Things! †Alive and Kicking. 1959: †Top Floor Girl. I'm All Right, Jack. The Night We Dropped a Clanger. Follow a Star. Desert Mice. 1960: Two Way Stretch. Doctor in Love. The Night We Got the Bird. The Pure Hell of St Trinian's. The Bulldog Breed. 1961: The Rebel (US: Call Me Genius). Fury at Smuggler's Bay. Double Bunk. Carry On Regardless. Watch It Sailor! Raising the Wind (US: Roommates). A Pair of Briefs. The Painted Smile. 1962: Carry On Cruising. The Amorous Prawn. Live Now—Pay Later. 1963: Carry On Cabby. 1964: Every Day's a Holiday (US: Seaside Swingers). The Americanization of Emily. 1966: The Family Way. 1967: Up the Junction. 1971: Dad's Army. 1972: Hide and Seek. 1974: Three for All. 1975: Carry On Behind. Adventures of a Taxi Driver. 1976: Confessions of a Driving Instructor. Under the Doctor. 1977: Adventures of a Private Eye. Confessions from a Holiday Camp. 1978: Rosie Dixon Night Nurse. 1979: The Great Rock 'n' Roll Swindle. 1989: The Lady and the Highwayman (TV). Chicago Joe and the Showgirl.

† As Elizabeth Winch
‡ As Elizabeth Fraser

FRAWLEY, William 1887–1966

Lovable, cherubic, balding American character actor who vies with Allen Jenkins and Jesse White in the memory as cigar-chewing gangsters with tough exteriors and soft centres. Overcame an alcohol problem to become a TV star of the early fifties as the irascible Fred Mertz in *I Love Lucy* then, in the sixties, as Bub in another long-running TV series, *My Three Sons*. Died from a heart attack.

*1915: *Cupid Beats Father. 1916: Lord Loveland Discovers America. 1929: *Fancy That. *Turkey for Two. 1931: Surrender. 1933: Hell*

*and High Water (GB: Cap'n Jericho). Moonlight and Pretzels (GB: Moonlight and Melody). 1934: Miss Fane's Baby is Stolen (GB: Kidnapped!). Bolero. Shoot the Works (GB: Thank Your Stars). Here Is My Heart. The Crime Doctor. The Witching Hour. The Lemon Drop Kid. 1935: Ship Café. Car 99. Alibi Ike. Harmony Lane. Welcome Home. Hold 'em, Yale (GB: Uniform Lovers). College Scandal (GB: The Clock Strikes Eight). 1936: Strike Me Pink. The Princess Comes Across. The General Died at Dawn. Three Married Men. Three Cheers for Love. Desire. F-Man. Rose Bowl (GB: O'Riley's Luck). 1937: Blossoms on Broadway. Double or Nothing. Something to Sing about. High, Wide and Handsome. 1938: Mad About Music. Professor, Beware! Crime Takes a Holiday. Sons of the Legion. Touchdown Army (GB: Generals of Tomorrow). 1939: Persons in Hiding. Ambush. St Louis Blues. Grand Jury Secrets. Night Work. Rose of Washington Square. The Adventures of Huckleberry Finn. Ex-Champ. Stop, Look and Love. 1940: Untamed. The Quarterback. Rhythm on the River. Golden Gloves. Opened by Mistake. The Farmer's Daughter. One Night in the Tropics. Those Were the Days. 1941: The Bride Came C.O.D. Dancing on a Dime. Blondie in Society (GB: Henpecked). Cracked Nuts. Six Lessons from Madame La Zonga. Footsteps in the Dark. Public Enemies. 1942: Treat 'em Rough. Roxie Hart. It Happened in Flatbush. Give Out, Sisters. Wildcat. Moonlight in Havana. Gentleman Jim. *The Yankee Doodler. 1943: We've Never Been Licked (GB: Texas to Tokyo). Whistling in Brooklyn. Larceny With Music. 1944: Minstrel Man. Ziegfeld Follies (released 1946). The Fighting Seabees. Going My Way. Lake Placid Serenade. 1945: Flame of the Barbary Coast. Hitchhike to Happiness. Lady on a Train. 1946: The Virginian. Rendezvous With Annie. The Inner Circle. The Crime Doctor's Manhunt. 1947: Miracle on 34th Street (GB: The Big Heart). Down to Earth. I Wonder Who's Kissing Her Now? Monsieur Verdoux. My Wild Irish Rose. Mother Wore Tights. Hit Parade of 1947. Blondie's Anniversary. 1948: Texas, Brooklyn and Heaven (GB: The Girl from Texas). Good Sam. The Babe Ruth Story. Chicken Every Sunday. Joe Palooka in Winner Take All (GB: Winner Take All). The Girl from Manhattan. 1949: The Lady Takes a Sailor. Red Light. Home in San Antone (GB: Harmony Inn). East Side, West Side. The Lone Wolf and His Lady. 1950: Blondie's Hero. Kill the Umpire. Kiss Tomorrow*

Goodbye. Pretty Baby. 1951: The Lemon Drop Kid. Rhubarb. Abbott and Costello Meet the Invisible Man. 1952: Rancho Notorious. 1962: Safe at Home!

FREED, Bert 1919–1994

Of medium height, but heftily built, this thick-necked, crop-haired, tough-looking American actor of Russian parentage, played top sergeants, crooks and policemen. A semi-regular in films from 1950 to 1954 and again from 1963 to 1971, but at other times only a rare migrant from heavy schedules in television and the theatre. His characters licked more than one raw recruit into shape in their time. In private life, this film tough guy was a bridge fanatic!

1946: Boomerang! 1947: Carnegie Hall. 1949: Ma and Pa Kettle Go to Town (GB: Going to Town). 1950: Key to the City. Black Hand. No Way Out. 711 Ocean Drive. Halls of Montezuma. 1951: The Company She Keeps. Where the Sidewalk Ends. Detective Story. Red Mountain. 1952: The Atomic City. The Snows of Kilimanjaro. 1953: Tangier Incident. 1954: Take the High Ground. The Long, Long Trailer. Men of the Fighting Lady. 1955: The Desperate Hours. The Cobweb. 1957: Paths of Glory. 1958: The Goddess. 1959: The Gazebo. 1960: The Subterraneans. Why Must I Die? (GB: 13 Steps to Death). 1962: What Ever Happened to Baby Jane? 1963: Twilight of Honor (GB: The Charge is Murder). 1964: Invitation to a Gunfighter. Shock Treatment. Fate is the Hunter. 1966: Nevada Smith. The Swinger. 1967: PJ (GB: New Face in Hell). Hang 'em High. 1968: Madigan. Wild in the Streets. 1969: Then Came Bronson (TV. GB: cinemas). 1970: There Was a Crooked Man . . . Breakout (TV). Billy Jack. Evel Knievel. Till Death (shown 1977). 1975: Death Scream (TV). 1977: In the Matter of Karen Ann Quinlan (TV). La devoradora des hombres. Love and the Midnight Auto Supply. Barracuda (The Lucifer Project). 1979: Norma Rae. 1980: Skag/The Wildcatters (TV). 1981: Charlie and the Great Balloon Chase (TV).

FREEMAN, Kathleen 1920–

Cheerful, chubby, round-faced, light-haired American supporting actress whose 'farmgirl' features were first seen as bobbysoxers and college girls. She played small roles and occasional minor leads (Lonely Hearts

Bandits) for more than a decade, before her raucous tones, expressive face and now aggressive manner made her an inveterate scene-stealer of the 1960s, especially in Jerry Lewis comedies. A kindlier but indomitable version of Britain's Peggy Mount. Had a rare tough leading part in Wild Harvest (1961).

1948: *Annie Was a Wonder. The Naked City. The Saxon Charm. Casbah. Behind Locked Doors. 1949: Mr Belvedere Goes to College. The House by the River. 1950: A Life of Her Own. Lonely Hearts Bandits (GB: Lonely Heart Bandits). The Reformer and the Redhead. Once a Thief. No Man of her Own. Cry Danger. 1951: Appointment with Danger (filmed 1949). A Place in the Sun. Cause for Alarm. Behave Yourself! The Wild Blue Yonder (GB: Thunder Across the Pacific). Kid Monk Baroni (GB: Young Paul Baroni). The Company She Keeps. Love is Better Than Ever (GB: The Light Fantastic). Let's Make It Legal. 1952: Talk About a Stranger. Singin' in the Rain. The Bad and the Beautiful. O. Henry's Full House (GB: Full House). The Greatest Show on Earth. Wait 'Til the Sun Shines, Nellie. The Prisoner of Zenda. Monkey Business. Bonzo Goes to College. 1953: She's Back on Broadway. The Magnetic Monster. Half a Hero. The Glass Web. The Affairs of Dobie Gillis. Dream Wife. The Glass Wall. A Perilous Journey. 1954: Athena. Three-Ring Circus. The Far Country. 1955: Artists and Models. 1956: Hollywood or Bust. 1957: The Midnight Story (GB: Appointment with a Shadow). Kiss Them for Me. Pawnee (GB: Pale Arrow). 1958: The Fly. Houseboat. Too Much, Too Soon. The Buccaneer. The Missouri Traveler. 1959: Don't Give Up the Ship. 1960: North to Alaska. 1961: The Ladies' Man. The Errand Boy. Wild Harvest. 1962: Madison Avenue. 1963: The Nutty Professor. Mail Order Bride (GB: West of Montana). 1964: The Rounders. The Disorderly Orderly. 1965: Marriage on the Rocks. 1966: Three on a Couch. 1967: Point Blank. The Helicopter Spies (TV. GB: cinemas). 1968: Hook, Line and Sinker. Support Your Local Sheriff! 1969: The Good Guys and the Bad Guys. Death of a Gunfighter. Le sorelle/So Evil My Sister. 1970: But I Don't Want to Get Married (TV). Myra Breckinridge. Hitched (TV. GB: Westward the Wagon). The Ballad of Cable Hogue. Which Way to the Front? (GB: Ja! Ja! Mein General! But Which Way to the Front?). 1971: Head On. Support Your Local Gunfighter. Where Does It Hurt? 1972: Stand Up and Be Counted.

Call Her Mom (TV). 1973: Unholy Rollers. Your Three Minutes Are Up. 1974: The Daughters of Joshua Cabe Return (TV). 1975: The Strongest Man in the World. 1978: The Norseman. 1980: The Blues Brothers. 1981: Heartbeeps. 1986: The Malibu Bikini Shop (completed 1984). The Best of Times. 1987: Innerspace. Teen Wolf Too. In the Mood (later and GB: The Woo Woo Kid). 1988: Glitz (TV). 1989: Chances Are. 1990: Hollywood Chaos. The Princess and the Dwarf. Gremlins 2: The New Batch. Joey Takes a Cab. 1991: Tales from the Crypt (TV). The Willies. Dutch. 1992: FernGully The Last Rainforest (voice only). 1993: Reckless Kelly. Hocus Pocus. 1994: The Naked Gun 33¹/₃: The Final Insult. 1995: Monastery.

FREEMAN, Morgan 1937–

Authoritative, lean-faced black American actor with low, drawling, persuasive voice, a calming influence in many of his film roles. An early ambition to be a jet pilot led to four years in the US Air Force before he began to study acting. The breakthrough to Broadway roles came at 30 and his became a well-known face (and voice) on the children's TV show The Electric Company from 1971 to 1976, as Easy Reader. Film roles were virtually non-existent until 1980, but he has been able to prove his worth in the past 15 years, chalking up three Academy Award nominations (for Street Smart, Driving Miss Daisy and The Shawshank Redemption) and assuming a progressively higher profile in big-budget films.

1971: Who Says I Can't Ride a Rainbow? (GB: TV, as Barney). 1978: Roll of Thunder. Hear My Cry (TV). 1979: Hollow Image (TV). 1980: Attica (TV). Brubaker. 1981: Eyewitness (GB: The Janitor). The Marva Collins Story (TV). 1984: Harry & Son. Teachers. 1985: The Execution of Raymond Graham (TV). Marie – a True Story. That Was Then . . . This is Now. 1986: Resting Place (TV). Street Smart. 1988: Clean and Sober. Blood Money/Clinton and Nadine. 1989: Driving Miss Daisy. Glory. Lean on Me. Phantom of the Mall. 1990: Johnny Handsome. The Bonfire of the Vanities. 1991: Robin Hood – Prince of Thieves. Hit Man. 1992: The Power of One. Unforgiven. 1994: The Shawshank Redemption. 1995: Outbreak. Seven. Moll Flanders.

As director:
1993: Bopha!

FRICKER, Brenda 1947–

Light-haired, dumpling-homely, Dublin-born actress in British (recently international) films, equally effective as weary wives or no-nonsense administrators. Her plain looks and reassuring personality were mainly seen on TV until outstanding success in the British TV series *Casualty*, and an Academy Award for her role in the film *My Left Foot* (as best supporting actress) brought her to the forefront of character stars. She left Britain for Hollywood, which kept her busy in leading character roles in the early 1990s. Briefly returned to Britain in 1993 to play a sleuth in the TV series *Seekers*.

1969: Sinful Davey. 1979: Bloody Kids. Quatermass (TV. US: cinemas, as The Quatermass Conclusion). 1985: Our Exploits at West Poley. 1989: My Left Foot. 1990: The Field. 1992: Hook. Home Alone 2: Lost in New York. UTZ. 1993: Deadly Advice. So I Married an Axe Murderer. 1994: Angels in the Outfield. A Man of No Importance. Out of Ireland (voice only). 1995: Moll Flanders.

FRÖBE, Gert

(Karl-Gerhardte Fröbe) 1912–1988

Squat, thick-set, small-eyed, sandy-haired, menacing German actor who moved from untrustworthy little men to international menaces, when he put on weight and triumphed in the title role of *Goldfinger* (1964). After that he was more selective about his appearances, often appearing as a comic villain in international productions. Died from a heart attack.

1945: Die Kreuzlschreiber. 1948: Berliner Ballade. 1949: Nach Regen scheint Sonne. 1952: Der Tag vor der Hochzeit. 1953: Arlette erobert Paris. Salto mortale. Man on a Tightrope. Ein Herz spielt falsch. Hochzeit auf Reisen. 1954: Mannequins für Rio. Das zweite Leben/ Double destin. Ewiger Walzer. Die kleine Stadt will schlafen gehn. Morgengrauen. Das Kreuz am Jägerstag. 1955: Der Postmeister (GB: Her Crime Was Love). Der dunkle Stern. Vom Himmel Gefallen/Special Delivery. Confidential Report (US: Mr Arkadin). Das Forsthaus in Tirol. The Heroes Are Tired/Les héros sont fatigués. They Were So Young. Ich weiss, wofür ich liebe. Ein Mädchen aus Flandern. 1956: Waldwinter. Ein Herz schlägt für Erika. Celui qui doit mourir. Der tolle Bomberg. Typhoon over Nagasaki. Das Herz von St Pauli. 1957: Robinson soll nicht sterben. El Hakim. Echec au porteur. Charmants garçons. 1958: Grafatigués. I batellieri di Volga (GB: The Boatmen. US: The Volga Boatman). Es geschah am hellichten Tag (GB: Assault in Broad Daylight). The Girl Rosemarie. Nasse Asphalt. Der Pauker. Das Mädchen mit den Katzenaugen. Nick Knattertons Abenteuer. Grabenplatz 17 (US: 17 Sinister Street). 1959: Jons und Erdman. Und ewig singen die Wälder (GB: Vengeance in Timber Valley). Schüsse im Morgengrauen. Douze heures d'horloge. Old Heidelberg. Am Tag, als der Regen kam. Menschen im Hotel. 1960: Le bois des amants (GB: Between Love and Duty). Der Gauner und der lieber Gott. Bis dass das Geld euch scheidet. Der Rächer (US: The Avenger). The 1,000 Eyes of Dr Mabuse. Das kunstseidene Mädchen. Soldatensender Calais. 12 Stunden Angst. 1961: The Green Archer. The Return of Dr Mabuse. Via mada. 1962: Auf Wiedersehen. Heute kündigt mir mein Mann. The Longest Day. Die Rote. The Testament of Dr Mabuse. The Threepenny Opera. 1963: Der Mörder (GB: Enough Rope). Karussell der Leidenschaften. Peau de banane (GB and US: Banana Peel). 1964: Goldfinger. $100,000 au soleil. Tonio Kröger. 1965: Is Paris Burning? Those Magnificent Men in Their Flying Machines. A High Wind in Jamaica. Du Rififi à Paname (GB: Rififi in Paris). Ganoversehre. Eschappement libre (US: Backfire). Das Liebeskarussell (GB and US: Who Wants to Sleep?). 1966: Triple Cross. 1967: Rocket to the Moon (US: Those Fantastic Flying Fools). Caroline Chérie. I Killed Rasputin. 1968: Chitty Chitty Bang Bang. 1969: Monte Carlo or Bust (US: Those Daring Young Men in Their Jaunty Jalopies). 1971: S (GB: The Heist). 1972: Ludwig. 1973: Nuits rouges/ L'homme sans visage (GB: Shadowman). 1974: Der räuber Hotzenplotz. And Then There Were None. 1975: Mein Onkel Theodor. Les magiciens. Dr Justice. Profezia per un delitto. 1977: The Serpent's Egg. Das Gesetz des Clans. Tod oder Freiheit. 1978: Der Tiefstapler. Der Schimmelreiter. 1979: Bloodline/Sidney Sheldon's Bloodline. 1980: Le coup du parapluie. The Falcon. 1981: Daisy Chain.

FRYE, Dwight 1899–1943

Small, dapper American actor whose dark-haired, fresh-faced looks seemed to qualify him for lounge lizards. But there was a hint of anguish about the features that drew directors of horror films and bizarre thrillers

to cast him in featured roles. The grotesques that resulted were often genuinely frightening, and his pathetic, chilling Renfield in the 1930 *Dracula* has never been bettered. Died from a heart attack.

*1927: The Night Bird. 1930: The Doorway to Hell. Man to Man/Barber John's Boy. Dracula. 1931: The Maltese Falcon. The Black Camel. Frankenstein. 1932: A Strange Adventure. Attorney for the Defense. By Whose Hand? The Western Code. 1933: The Invisible Man. The Vampire Bat. The Circus Queen Murder. 1934: King Solomon of Broadway. 1935: Bride of Frankenstein. Atlantic Adventure. The Crime of Dr Crespi. The Great Impersonation. 1936: Florida Special. Alibi for Murder. Beware of Ladies. Tough Guy. 1937: The Man Who Found Himself. Sea Devils. Great Guy (GB: Pluck of the Irish). The Road Back. Something to Sing About. Renfrew of the Royal Mounted. The Shadow. 1938: The Invisible Enemy. *Think It Over. Who Killed Gail Preston? Sinners in Paradise. Fast Company. Adventure in the Sahara. The Night Hawk. 1939: The Man in the Iron Mask. The Cat and the Canary. Son of Frankenstein. Conspiracy. I Take This Woman. 1940: Drums of Fu Manchu (serial). Gangs of Chicago. Phantom Raiders. Son of Monte Cristo. Sky Bandits. 1941: The People Versus Dr Kildare (GB: My Life is Yours). The Blonde from Singapore. The Devil Pays Off. Mystery Ship. 1942: The Ghost of Frankenstein. Danger in the Pacific. Prisoner of Japan. Sleepytime Gal. 1943: Dead Men Walk. Hangmen Also Die. Frankenstein Meets the Wolf Man. Submarine Alert. Dangerous Blondes.*

FURSE, Judith 1912–1974

Gargantuan, circular-faced, dark-haired British supporting actress frequently called upon to express bigotry, ruthlessness or outrage. A formidable matron or school governor. On stage at 12, she was the sister of the lighter-haired Jill Furse, a budding leading lady of the late 1930s who suffered from ill-health and died tragically young. She also directed a number of productions on stage.

1939: Goodbye Mr Chips! 1944: English Without Tears (US: Her Man Gilbey). A Canterbury Tale. 1945: Johnny Frenchman. 1946: Quiet Weekend. While the Sun Shines. 1947: Black Narcissus. 1948: One Night With You. Bond Street. It's Hard to be Good. 1949: Dear Mr Prohack. Helter Skelter. Marry Me! The

enjoyed the better successes of his later years back on stage. The 'Skeets' was a childhood nickname: mosquito, describing the way he zipped around. Died from a heart attack.

Romantic Age (US: Naughty Arlette). 1951: The Browning Version. The Man in the White Suit. I Believe in You. 1952: Mother Riley Meets the Vampire (US: Vampire Over London). 1953: The Heart of the Matter. A Day to Remember. 1954: Mad About Men. 1955: Cockleshell Heroes. 1957: Doctor at Large. 1958: Blue Murder at St Trinian's. Further Up the Creek. 1959: Serious Charge (US: A Touch of Hell). 1960: Scent of Mystery (GB: Holiday in Spain). Sands of the Desert. Not a Hope in Hell. 1961: In the Doghouse. Carry On Regardless. A Weekend With Lulu. 1962: Postman's Knock. The Iron Maiden (US: The Swingin' Maiden). I Thank a Fool. Live Now—Pay Later. 1963: Carry On Cabby. 1964: A Jolly Bad Fellow (shown 1963). Carry On Spying. 1965: The Amorous Adventures of Moll Flanders. Sky West and Crooked (US: Gypsy Girl). 1969: Sinful Davey. Twinky (US: Lola). 1971: Man in the Wilderness. 1972: The Adventures of Barry McKenzie.

1923: The Daring Years. 1927: The Potters. New York. For the Love of Mike. 1928: Stocks and Blondes (GB: Blondes and Bonds). Alex the Great. Three-Ring Marriage. The Racket. 1929: Pointed Heels. Close Harmony. Fast Company. The Dance of Life. 1930: Honey. Paramount on Parade. Her Wedding Night. Love Among the Millionaires. The Social Lion. Let's Go Native. 1931: Possessed. It Pays to Advertise. Up Pops the Devil. Road to Reno. 1932: Merrily We Go to Hell (GB: Merrily We Go to —). The Phantom of Crestwood. The Unwritten Law. Night Club Lady. The Sport Parade. The Conquerors. Bird of Paradise. *Hollywood on Parade. The Trial of Vivienne Ware. 1933: Reform Girl. The Past of Mary Holmes. Too Much Harmony. Easy Millions. Alice in Wonderland. *Private Wives. 1934: The Crosby Case (GB: The Crosby Murder Case). In The Money. Bachelor Bait. The Meanest Gal in Town. Riptide. Woman Unafraid. Lightning Strikes Twice. 1935: The Perfect Clue. 1936: Polo Joe. Yours for the Asking. Hats Off. The Man I Marry. 1937: Espionage. 1938: Danger in the Air. Mr Satan. 1939: Idiot's Delight. 1941: Citadel of Crime (GB: Outside the Law). Zis Boom Bah! 1942: Brooklyn Orchid. 1945: The Duke of Chicago. 1952: Three for Bedroom C.

GARDENIA, Vincent

(Vincente Scognamiglio) 1921–1992

Bulky, full-faced Italian-born actor, in America from childhood and usually seen as the trilbied, forehead-mopping police chief, Mafia boss or city official. First acted at five with his father's Italian theatre in Manhattan, but didn't get a foothold in films until he was nearly 50, around the same time as he received a Tony for *The Prisoner of Second Avenue* on stage, and an Oscar nomination for *Bang the Drum Slowly*. He became known in the 1970s as the detective trying to keep tabs on Charles Bronson in the *Death Wish* films. Second Academy Award nomination for *Moonstruck*. Died from a heart attack.

1945: The House on 92nd Street. 1958: Cop Hater. 1960: Murder Inc. 1961: The Hustler.

Mad Dog Coll. A View from the Bridge. Parrish. 1965: The Third Day. 1969: Jenny. Mission Impossible vs The Mob. 1970: The Pursuit of Happiness. Where's Poppa? Cold Turkey. 1971: Little Murders. 1972: Hickey and Boggs. 1973: Bang the Drum Slowly. Lucky Luciano. 1974: Death Wish. The Front Page. 1975: The Manchu Eagle Murder Caper Mystery. 1976: Il grande rocket. 1977: Fire Sale. Greased Lightning. 1978: Heaven Can Wait. 1979: Firepower. Goldie and the Boxer (TV). Marciano (TV). 1980: Home Movies (shown 1979). The Last Flight of Noah's Ark. 1981: Thornwell (TV). Death Wish II. 1982: Muggable Mary (TV. GB: Street Cop). 1984: Dark Mirror (TV). 1985: Movers and Shakers. Brass (TV). The Odd Squad. 1986: Honor Thy Father. Little Shop of Horrors. A Sicilian in Sicily. 1987. Moonstruck. DeadHeat. Swiss Cheese. 1988: Cavalli si nasce/Born to be Horses. 1989: Skin Deep. Age-Old Friends (TV. GB: A Month of Sundays). The Tragedy of Flight 403: The Inside Story (TV). 1991: The Super.

GALLAGHER, Skeets

(Richard Gallagher) 1891–1955

Round-faced, cheery-looking American song-and-dance man, occasional romantic lead and oft-time quipster from the sidelines, silver-haired from his late thirties. A vaudevillian of long standing, in comedy acts with various female partners, his livewire (occasionally over-the-top) performances made him a popular attraction in Hollywood films from 1929 to 1934. Thereafter his career dipped into smaller roles, and he

GARDINER, Reginald

(William R. Gardiner) 1903–1980

Dark-haired, moustachioed, owlish-looking British comic actor, raconteur and recording artist, chiefly remembered for the 'silly ass' characterizations he created when he went to Hollywood in the mid-thirties, but in fact capable of a much wider range. His record of train noises remains a collector's item: so do some of his performances. Retired in 1965 following injuries sustained in a fall. Died from pneumonia.

*1931: *My Old China. Aroma of the South Seas. *Bull Rushes. The Perfect Lady. 1932: Flat No. 9. Lovelorn Lady. Josser on the River. 1933: Radio Parade. Just Smith (US: Leave It to Smith). 1934: How's Chances? Borrow a Million. Virginia's Husband. 1935: Opening Night. A Little Bit of Bluff. Royal Cavalcade (US: Regal Cavalcade). 1936: Born to Dance. 1937: A Damsel in Distress. 1938: Everybody Sing. Sweethearts. Marie Antoinette. 1939: The Night of Nights. The Flying Deuces. The Girl Downstairs. 1940: The Great Dictator. Dulcy. The Doctor Takes a Wife. 1941: My Life with Caroline. A Yank in the RAF. Sundown. The Man Who Came to Dinner. 1942: Captains of the Clouds. 1943: Forever and a Day. The Immortal Sergeant. Sweet Rosie O'Grady. Claudia. 1944: Molly and Me. 1945: Christmas in Connecticut (US: Indiscretion). The Horn Blows At Midnight. The Dolly Sisters. 1946: Do You Love Me? Cluny Brown. One More Tomorrow. 1947: I Wonder Who's Kissing Her Now. 1948: That Wonderful Urge. Fury at Furnace Creek. That Lady in Ermine. 1950: Wabash Avenue. I'll Get By. Halls of Montezuma. 1951: Elopement. 1952: Androcles and the Lion. 1954: The Barefoot Contessa. Black Widow. 1955: Ain't Misbehavin'. 1956: The Birds and the Bees. Around the World in 80 Days. 1957: The Story of Mankind. 1958: Rock-a-Bye Baby. No Time at All (TV). 1961: Back Street. 1962: Mr Hobbs Takes a Vacation. 1964: What a Way to Go! 1965: Do Not Disturb. Sergeant Deadhead.*

1971: Taking Off. Bananas. Cry Uncle (GB: Super Dick). Believe in Me. You've Got to Walk It Like You Talk It or You'll Lose That Beat. The Organization. 1972: Top of the Heap. Deadhead Miles. Get to Know Your Rabbit. Footsteps (TV). The Candidate. 1973: The Marcus-Nelson Murders (TV). Slither. Busting. 1974: The Good, the Bad and the Beautiful. The Virginia Hill Story (TV). The Conversation. The Front Page. Mother, Jugs and Speed (released 1976). 1975: Nashville. 1976: Serpico: The Deadly Game (TV). Growing Pains: Number One. The Million-Dollar Rip-Off (TV). Gable and Lombard. Paco. 1977: The Stunt Man (released 1980). 1978: Fyre. Sketches of a Strangler. Skateboard. Nowhere to Run (TV). Ring of Passion (TV). †The Brink's Job. 1980: †One Trick Pony. †National Lampoon Goes to the Movies. 1981: †Leave 'Em Laughing. †Continental Divide. †One from the Heart. 1982: †Der Stand der Dinge/The State of Things. 1983: The Black Stallion Returns. Get Crazy. 1984: Teachers. Irreconcilable Differences. The Cotton Club. 1985: Desert Bloom. 1986: Killer in the Mirror (TV). 1987: You Ruined My Life (TV). Beverly Hills Cop II. 1988: Chief Zabu. 1989: Night Visitor/Never Cry Devil. Let It Ride. 1990: Dick Tracy. Club Fed. 1991: Until the End of the World. Family Prayers. 1992: Miracle Beach. Jack and His Friends. 1993: Glass Shadow. 1994: Les patriotes. 1995: Destiny Turns on the Radio.

† As Allen Goorwitz

Headline Shooter (GB: Evidence in Camera). 1934: British Agent. Things Are Looking Up. Four Frightened People. The Line-Up (GB: Identity Parade). Strictly Dynamite. 1935: Black Fury. A Night at the Ritz. Traveling Saleslady. Bright Lights (GB: Funny Face). Don't Bet on Blondes. Broadway Gondolier. 1936: Manhunt. The Sky Parade. Alibi for Murder. Blackmailer. Lucky Corrigan. The Milky Way. Navy Born. Flying Hostess. 1937: Breezing Home. Fury and the Woman. You Only Live Once. Wings over Honolulu. Some Blondes Are Dangerous. Behind the Mike. Reported Missing. She Asked for It. You're a Sweetheart. 1938: The Crowd Roars. The Devil's Party. Personal Secretary. The Crime of Dr Hallet. Women in the Wind. 1939: Within the Law. Broadway Serenade. The Housekeeper's Daughter. Three Sons. House of Fear. Joe and Ethel Turp Call on the President. 1940: Isle of Destiny. They Knew What They Wanted. Turnabout. Star Dust. Sporting Blood. Double Alibi. 1941: Flying Cadets. Sealed Lips. Cheers for Miss Bishop. I Wake Up Screaming (GB: Hot Spot). Keep 'em Flying. 1942: Bombay Clipper. Miss Annie Rooney. A Close Call for Ellery Queen (GB: A Close Call). Who Done It? Enemy Agents Meet Ellery Queen (GB: The Lido Mystery). Destination Unknown. The Mayor of 44th Street. A Desperate Chance for Ellery Queen (GB: A Desperate Chance). 1943: No Place for a Lady. Swing Fever. Harrigan's Kid. The Canterville Ghost. 1945: She Gets Her Man. One Exciting Night. Midnight Manhunt. Song of the Sarong. The Bells of St Mary's. Follow That Woman. Behind Green Lights. 1946: Strange Impersonation. Night Editor (GB: The Trespasser). Murder in the Music Hall. Hot Cargo. Rendezvous 24. Till the End of Time. Swell Guy. 1948: The Argyle Secrets. Waterfront at Midnight. 1949: Dynamite. 1955: Man on the Ledge (TV. GB: cinemas). 1956: Miracle in the Rain. The Rawhide Years.

GARFIELD, Allen
(A. Goorwitz) 1939–
Mournful-looking, dark, balding, plump (until recent times) American actor who played greasy and often obnoxious types during the first decade of his film career. He looked a different kind of character actor when he reappeared, trimmed and toupeed, in the early 1980s. Garfield was a Golden Gloves boxer and a journalist before turning to acting at 26. His first job on the New York stage, as a spear carrier, lasted only a few days—he caught chickenpox! Now plays high-pressure types prone to anxiety attacks.

1968: Greetings. Orgy Girls '69. 1969: Roommates/March of the Spring Hare. Putney Swope. 1970: Hi Mom! The Commitment (released 1975). The Owl and the Pussycat.

GARGAN, William 1905–1979
American actor of Irish extraction, similar in looks to James Dunn, and largely seen in the same sort of roles, persisting as the hero of 'B' features, notably the last few 'Ellery Queens', until the late forties. His voice was reduced to a whisper after an operation for cancer of the larynx in 1960, although he had long become entrenched in television. Died of cancer, but did much good work for the American Cancer Society. Oscar-nominated for *They Knew What They Wanted*.

1917: Mother's Darling. 1929: My Mother's Eyes (later Lucky Boy). 1930: Follow the Leader. 1931: His Woman. 1932: Rain. The Sport Parade. Misleading Lady. The Animal Kingdom (GB: The Woman in His House). 1933: Sweepings. The Story of Temple Drake. Emergency Call. Aggie Appleby — Maker of Men (GB: Cupid in the Rough). Night Flight. Lucky Devils.

GAUGE, Alexander 1914–1960
Corpulent brown-haired British actor usually seen in faintly disreputable roles. His best was probably his first, as the vengeful husband in *The Interrupted Journey*. His film career, largely confined thereafter to petty crooks, practically dried up altogether after he was cast as Friar Tuck in the long-running *Adventures of Robin Hood* series on TV with Richard Greene. Born in Wenchow,

China, Gauge committed suicide with barbiturates.

1949: The Interrupted Journey. 1951: Flesh and Blood. 1952: Murder in the Cathedral. Mother Riley Meets the Vampire (US: Vampire Over London). The Pickwick Papers. Penny Princess). 1953: Counterspy (US: Undercover Agent). Will Any Gentleman?... Martin Luther. House of Blackmail. The Great Game. The Square Ring. 1954: Beau Brummell. Fast and Loose. Double Exposure. Dance Little Lady. The Golden Link. *The Blazing Caravan. Mystery on Bird Island. 1955: Before I Wake (US: Shadow of Fear). Tiger by the Tail (US: Crossup). The Reluctant Bride (US: Two Grooms for a Bride). The Hornet's Nest. Handcuffs, London. No Smoking. 1956: Port of Escape. Breakaway. The Green Man. The Iron Petticoat. The Passionate Stranger (US: A Novel Affair). 1959: Les canailles (GB: Take Me As I Am. US: The Ruffians). 1961: Nothing Barred.

GAWTHORNE, Peter 1884–1962
Heavily built, large-headed, fiercely blustering, silver-haired, Irish-born supporting actor who returned from Hollywood in 1932 to become a stalwart of the British cinema, especially in comedies (several with Will Hay) as pompous officers, minion-hating millionaires or other top-ranking figures of authority doomed to deflation.

1929: Bulldog Drummond. Behind the Curtain. Sunny Side Up. His Glorious Night. 1930: Temple Tower. Those Three French Girls. One Hysterical Night. 1931: Charlie Chan Carries On. The Man Who Came Back. 1932: The Flag Lieutenant. Jack's the Boy (US: Night and Day). C.O.D. His Lordship. The Lodger (US: The Phantom Fiend). Perfect Understanding. 1933: The Blarney Stone (US: The Blarney Kiss). Just Smith (US: Leave It to Smith). Prince of Arcadia. The House of Trent. 1934: Two Hearts in Waltztime. Grand Prix. Girls Please. Something Always Happens. The Camels Are Coming. Money Mad. My Old Dutch. Dirty Work. Murder at Monte Carlo. 1935: The Iron Duke. Boys Will Be Boys. Who's Your Father? Me and Marlborough. Crime Unlimited. Stormy Weather. The Crouching Beast. Man of the Moment. No Limit. 1936: Wolf's Clothing. The Man Behind the Mask. Pot Luck. East Meets West. Crime Over London. Windbag the Sailor. The Amazing Quest of Ernest Bliss (US:

Romance and Riches). A Woman Alone (US: Two Who Dared). Everybody Dance. 1937: The Ticket of Leave Man. Good Morning, Boys! (US: Where There's a Will). Gangway. Mr Stringfellow Says No. Father Steps Out. Brief Ecstasy. Under a Cloud. The Last Adventurers. Riding High. *George Bizet, Composer of Carmen. 1938: Alf's Button Afloat. Easy Riches. Inspector Hornleigh. Convict 99. Scruffy. Hey! Hey! USA. 1939: Dead Men Are Dangerous. Ask a Policeman. Home from Home. Flying Fifty-Five. Sword of Honour. Secret Journey (US: Among Human Wolves). Where's That Fire? What Would You Do Chums? Traitor Spy (US: The Torso Murder Mystery). Goodbye Mr Chips! Laugh It Off. Band Waggon. 1940: Three Silent Men. They Came by Night. Two for Danger. Gasbags. Crooks' Tour. 1941: Inspector Hornleigh Goes to It (US: Mail Train). Cottage to Let (US: Bombsight Stolen). Love on the Dole. Pimpernel Smith (US: Mister V). Old Mother Riley's Ghosts. I Thank You. They Flew Alone (US: Wings and the Woman). 1942: The First of the Few (US: Spitfire). Let the People Sing. Women Aren't Angels. Much Too Shy. 1943: Bell Bottom George. The Hundred Pound Window. 1945: Murder in Reverse. 1946: This Man is Mine! 1948: Nothing Venture. The Case of Charles Peace. 1949: Kind Hearts and Coronets. High Jinks in Society (US: Hi Jinks in Society). 1950: Soho Conspiracy. 1951: Death is a Number. 1952: Paul Temple Returns. 1954: Five Days (US: Paid to Kill). A Tale of Three Women.

GEER, Will
(W. Ghere) 1902–1978
Abrasively distinctive American actor whose career in shifty middle-aged roles was abruptly halted by the McCarthy blacklist. He returned in the 1960s to play a variety of ratty, crafty and lovable old men, culminating in his western patriarch in TV's long-running outdoor soap opera *The Waltons*. Got his first leading role at the age of 75 in *The Billion Dollar Hobo*. Died from a respiratory ailment.

1932: The Misleading Lady. 1934: Spitfire. 1935: Becky Sharp. The Mystery of Edwin Drood. 1940: Fight for Life (narrator only). 1948: Deep Waters. 1949: Anna Lucasta. Lust for Gold. Johnny Allegro (GB: Hounded). Intruder in the Dust. The Kid from Texas (GB: Texas Kid—Outlaw). 1950: It's a Small World.

Convicted. To Please a Lady. Broken Arrow. Winchester 73. Double Crossbones. Comanche Territory. 1951: The Tall Target. The Barefoot Mailman. Bright Victory (GB: Lights Out). 1954: Salt of the Earth. 1955: Mobs Inc. (TV. GB: cinemas). 1962: Advise and Consent. 1964: Black Like Me. 1966: Seconds. 1967: In Cold Blood. The President's Analyst. 1968: Bandolero! 1970: Pieces of Dreams. The Moonshine War. The Reivers. Brother John. 1971: The Brotherhood of the Bell (TV). Sam Hill: Who Killed the Mysterious Mr Foster? (TV). 1972: Napoleon and Samantha. Jeremiah Johnson. The Rowdyman. Dear Dead Delilah. Brock's Last Case (TV). 1973: Executive Action. The Memory of Us. Savage (TV). Isn't It Shocking? (TV). 1974: The Hanged Man (TV). Hurricane (TV). Honky Tonk (TV). 1975: The Silence (TV). The Manchu Eagle Murder Caper Mystery. The Night That Panicked America (TV). 1976: Bound for Glory (voice only). The Blue Bird. Moving Violation. Law and Order (TV). 1977: The Billion Dollar Hobo. 1978: A Woman Called Moses (TV). The Mafu Cage. Unknown Powers.

GEORGE, Chief Dan
(Geswanouth Slaholt) 1899–1981
Aged Canadian Indian who only came to films at 70 (after a TV debut at 62), but showed an amazing aptitude for acting in his few appearances, even upstaging Clint Eastwood in *The Outlaw Josey Wales*. Academy Award nominee for *Little Big Man*. Spent most of his working life as a docker until a serious accident forced him to quit.

1969: Smith! 1970: Little Big Man. 1972: Cancel My Reservation. Cold Journey. *A bon pied, bon oeil. 1973: Alien Thunder (later Dan Candy's Law). 1974: Harry and Tonto. The Bears and I. 1975: The Peach Gang (TV). 1976: The Outlaw Josey Wales. Shadow of the Hawk. 1979: Americathon. Spirit of the Wind.

GEORGE, Gladys
(G. Clare) 1900–1954
From 1936 to 1942 wry-faced Gladys George was the queen of Hollywood's brassy blondes with hearts of gold. They had seen better days and they never got the hero — but they usually stole the picture. Nominated for an Academy Award (and unlucky not to win it) for *Valiant is the Word for Carrie*, she was married and divorced four times, and

suffered from cancer in later years. Died from a brain haemorrhage.

1919: The Oath. 1920: Woman in the Suitcase. Below the Surface. Home Spun Folks. Red Hot Dollars. 1921: The Easy Road. Chickens. The House That Jazz Built. 1934: Straight is the Way. 1936: Valiant is the Word for Carrie. 1937: Stand In. Madame X. They Gave Him a Gun. 1938: Love is a Headache. Marie Antoinette. 1939: I'm from Missouri. Here I am a Stranger. The Roaring Twenties. 1940: A Child is Born. The House Across the Bay. The Way of All Flesh. 1941: The Maltese Falcon. The Lady from Cheyenne. Hit the Road. 1942: The Hard Way. 1943: The Crystal Ball. Nobody's Darling. 1944: Christmas Holiday. Minstrel Man. 1945: Steppin' in Society. 1946: The Best Years of Our Lives. 1947: Millie's Daughter. 1948: Alias a Gentlemen. 1949: Flamingo Road. 1950: Undercover Girl. Bright Leaf. 1951: Detective Story. Lullaby of Broadway. He Ran All the Way. Silver City (GB: High Vermilion). 1953: It Happens Every Thursday.

GEORGE, Muriel 1883–1965

Dumpy, homely, brown-haired British actress, usually seen with shopping basket, heavy coat and old-fashioned hat. Once a character performer in music-hall and variety, her cheerfully tired, round-faced looks slotted well into a whole gallery of lower-class ladies in the British cinema—landladies, mothers, chars, cleaners and maiden aunts. Married/divorced fellow character player Ernest Butcher (1885–1965). Semi-retired in post-war years.

*1932: His Lordship. Yes, Mr Brown. 1933: Cleaning Up. 1934: My Song for You. Something Always Happens. Nell Gwyn. 1935: Wedding Eve. Key to Harmony. Mr What's His Name. Old Faithful. Squibs. 1936: Limelight (US: Backstage). The Happy Family. Whom the Gods Love (US: Mozart). Busman's Holiday. Not So Dusty. King of Hearts. 1937: Song of the Road. Merry Comes to Town (US: Merry Comes to Stay). Dr Syn. Overcoat Sam. Talking Feet. Lancashire Luck. Who's Your Lady Friend? 21 Days (US: 21 Days Together). Bank Holiday. 1938: A Sister to Assist 'Er. Sixty Glorious Years (US: Queen of Destiny). Darts Are Trumps. Crackerjack (US: Man with a Hundred Faces). 1940: Pack Up Your Troubles. The Briggs Family. *Food for Thought. You Will Remember. 1941: Quiet Wedding. Freedom Radio (US: A Voice in the Night). *Lady Be Kind. *Telefootlers. *Mr Proudfoot Shows a Light. South American George. Cottage to Let (US: Bombsight Stolen). Love on the Dole. *Rush Hour. They Flew Alone (US: Wings and the Woman). 1942: The Young Mr Pitt. Unpublished Story. Went the Day Well? (US: 48 Hours). Alibi. 1943: The Bells Go Down. Dear Octopus (US: The Randolph Family). 1944: Kiss the Bride Goodbye. The Man from Scotland Yard. 1945: A Place of One's Own. For You Alone. Perfect Strangers (US: Vacation from Marriage). I'll Be Your Sweetheart. 1946: The Years Between. 1947: Jassy. When the Bough Breaks. 1948: A Sister to Assist 'Er (remake). 1950: The Dancing Years. Last Holiday. 1951: Encore. 1953: The Triangle. 1955: Simon and Laura.*

GERAY, Steven
(Stefan Gyergay) 1899–1973

Born in Uzhgorod, on the Russian-Czech border, the diminutive, dapper, sometimes moustachioed Geray (often billed as Steve) made his name in the Hungarian theatre, and seems to have made no films before coming to London in 1934. He moved to Hollywood in 1940, and quickly entered the most rewarding phase of his career there, sneaking scenes from the stars and playing leading roles in *The Moon and Sixpence* and *So Dark the Night*, the latter a minor but striking psychological thriller that contains his finest work on screen.

1935: Dance Band. The Student's Romance. 1936: A Star Fell from Heaven. 1937: The

High Command. Jump for Glory (US: When Thief Meets Thief). Let's Make a Night of It. 1938: Premiere (US: One Night in Paris). Lightning Conductor. Inspector Hornleigh. 1940: Dark Streets of Cairo. 1941: Blue, White and Perfect. Man at Large. The Shanghai Gesture. 1942: Secret Agent of Japan. Castle in the Desert. A Gentleman at Heart. The Moon and Sixpence. Eyes in the Night. The Wife Takes a Flyer (GB: A Yank in Dutch). 1943: Hostages. *To My Unborn Son. *Heavenly Music. Henry Aldrich Swings It (GB: Henry Swings It). Night Plane from Chungking. Pilot No. 5. The Phantom of the Opera. Above Suspicion. Assignment in Brittany. Background to Danger. Whistling in Brooklyn. Appointment in Berlin. 1944: Meet the People. The Seventh Cross. In Society. The Conspirators. The Mark of Dimitrios. *Easy Life. 1945: Tarzan and the Amazons. Hotel Berlin. Spellbound. Cornered. The Crimson Canary. Mexicana. 1946: Gilda. So Dark the Night. The Return of Monte Cristo (GB: Monte Cristo's Revenge). Deadline at Dawn. Blondie Knows Best. 1947: The Crime Doctor's Gamble (GB: The Doctor's Gamble). Mr District Attorney. Blind Spot. Gunfighters (GB: The Assassin). The Unfaithful. When a Girl's Beautiful. 1948: I Love Trouble. Port Said. 1949: The Dark Past. Ladies of the Chorus. El Paso. Sky Liner. Once More, My Darling. Tell It to the Judge. Holiday in Havana. The Lone Wolf and His Lady. 1950: A Lady Without Passport. Woman on the Run. Harbor of Missing Men. Under My Skin. In a Lonely Place. All About Eve. Pygmy Island. The Second Woman (GB: Ellen). 1951: I Can Get It for You Wholesale (GB: This Is My Affair). Target Unknown. My Favorite Spy. The House on Telegraph Hill. Little Egypt (GB: Chicago Masquerade). Savage Drums. 1952: A Lady Possessed. Bal Tabarin. The Big Sky. Affair in Trinidad. O Henry's Full House (GB: Full House). Night Without Sleep. 1953: Tonight We Sing. Call Me Madam. The Golden Blade. Gentlemen Prefer Blondes. The Great Diamond Robbery. The Story of Three Loves. Royal African Rifles (GB: Storm Over Africa). 1954: Knock on Wood. Tobor the Great. The French Line. Paris Playboys. 1955: A Bullet for Joey. New York Confidential. To Catch a Thief. Daddy Long Legs. Artists and Models. 1956: The Birds and the Bees. Attack! Stagecoach to Fury. 1958: A Certain Smile. 1959: Verboten. Count Your Blessings. 1963: Dime With a Halo. 1964: Wild and Wonderful. 1965: Ship of Fools. Jesse James Meets Frankenstein's Daughter. 1966: The Swinger.*

GIBSON, Wynne
(Winnifred Gibson) 1899–1987

Fair-haired, square-faced American actress (a chorus girl at 15) who started her film career late in life (although studio biographies advanced her date of birth by varying numbers of years), but enjoyed a good run of gold-digging blondes while with Paramount in the early 1930s. Left acting in the 1950s to become an actors' agent for the remainder of her working life. Died following a stroke.

1929: Nothing But the Truth. 1930: Children of Pleasure. The Fall Guy (GB: Trust Your Wife). 1931: June Moon. City Streets. Kick-

In. Ladies of the Big House. Man of the World. The Gang Buster. Road to Reno. 1932: If I Had a Million. Night After Night. Lady and Gent. The Strange Case of Clara Deane. The Devil is Driving. Two Kinds of Women. *The Stolen Jools (GB: The Slippery Pearls). 1933: Aggie Appleby, Maker of Men (GB: Cupid in the Rough). Emergency Call. Her Bodyguard. The Television Follies. Crime of the Century. 1934: Gambling. The Crosby Case (GB: The Crosby Murder Case). Sleepers East. The Captain Hates the Sea. 1935: Admirals All. The Crouching Beast. 1936: Come Closer, Folks! 1937: Michael O'Halloran. Trapped by G-Men. Racketeers in Exile. 1938: Flirting with Fate. Gangs of New York. 1939: My Son is Guilty (GB: Crime's End). 1940: Forgotten Girls. Café Hostess. A Miracle on Main Street. 1941: Double Cross. 1942: A Man's World. 1943: The Falcon Strikes Back. Mystery Broadcast.

GILBERT, Billy 1893–1971
Tall, dark, portly, ruddy-complexioned, usually moustachioed, explosive American comic and 'straight' support, whose frequent cameos filled the screen (he weighed 280 lbs) in more ways than one. Often a pince-nez'd, short-tempered, smartly-dressed businessman confounded by the likes of Laurel and Hardy, the Marx Brothers or, in many shorts, the all-female combination of Thelma Todd and ZaSu Pitts. Sometimes seen as an easily exasperated foreigner, he could also handle a song-and-dance routine and directed productions on Broadway. Died following a stroke. The voice/sneeze of Sneezy in Snow White and the Seven Dwarfs.

1916: Bubbles of Trouble. 1921: Dynamite Allen. 1927: *Smith's Pony. 1929: Noisy Neighbors. Woman from Hell. *The Woman Tamer. 1930: *The Doctor's Wife. *Movie Daze. *The Beauties. 1931: *Dogs is Dogs. *War Mamas. *Shiver My Timbers. *The Panic is On. *The Hasty Marriage. *One Good Turn. *A Melon-Drama. *Catch As Catch Can. *The Pajama Party. Chinatown After Dark. 1932: *Free Eats. *Spanky. *The Tabasco Kid. *What Price Taxi? *Young Ironsides. *Just a Pain in the Parlor. *Strange Inner-Tube. *Never the Twins Shall Meet. Pack Up Your Troubles. *The Nickel Nurser. *In Walked Charley. Blondie of the Follies. Million Dollar Legs. *First in War. *You're Telling Me. *County Hospital. *Their First Mistake. *The Chimp. *Strictly Unreliable. *The Music Box. *Seal Skins. *Sneak Easily. *On the Loose. *Red Noses. *Towed in a Hole. 1933: This Day and Age. *Fallen Arches. *The Big Fibber. *Rummy. *Wreckety Wreck. *Thundering Taxis. *Taxi Barons. *Nothing But the Truth. *Luncheon at Twelve. *Maids à la Mode. *The Bargain of the Century. *Asleep in the Fleet. *One Track Minds. Sons of the Desert (GB: Fraternally Yours. Voice only). 1934: Happy Landing (GB: Air Patrol). Peck's Bad Boy. Eight Girls in a Boat. Cockeyed Cavaliers. The Merry Widow. Evelyn Prentice. *Another Wild Idea (voice only). *The Cracked Iceman. *Them Thar Hills. *Men in Black. *Soup and Fish. *Roaming Vandals. *Tripping Through the Tropics. *Get Along Little Hubby. 1935: A Night at the Opera. Millions in the Air. Mad Love (GB: The Hands of Orlac). Escapade. *Just Another Murder. *Nurse to You. *His Bridal Sweet. *Pardon My Scotch. *His Old Flame. Hail Brother. Here Comes the Band. I Dream Too Much. 1936: Sutter's Gold. Parole! Love on the Run. Three of a Kind. Dangerous Waters. The Bride Walks Out. Grand Jury. The Big Game. Early to Bed. Night Waitress. Kelly the Second. *The Brain Busters. *So and Sew. Hi, Gaucho! Give Us This Night. The First Baby. Poor Little Rich Girl. F-Man. Devil Doll. My American Wife. One Rainy Afternoon. 1937: *Swing Fever. The Man Who Found Himself. The Outcasts of Poker Flat. Live, Love and Learn. Rosalie. We're on the Jury. Sea Devils. Maytime. Music for Madame. China Passage. The Toast of New York. The Life of the Party. The Firefly. On the Avenue. Espionage. Broadway Melody of 1938. One Hundred Men and a Girl. Captains Courageous. Fight for Your Lady. When You're in Love (GB: For You Alone). Snow White and the Seven Dwarfs (voice only). 1938: Mr Doodle Kicks Off. She's Got Everything. My Lucky Star. The Girl Downstairs. Maid's Night Out. Joy of Living. Block-Heads. Angels with Dirty Faces. Happy Landing (and 1934 film of same title). Breaking the Ice. Peck's Bad Boy with the Circus. Army Girl (GB: The Last of the Cavalry). The Great Waltz. 1939: Forged Passport. Destry Rides Again. Rio. The Under-Pup. The Star Maker. Million Dollar Legs. 1940: Sing, Dance, Plenty Hot (GB: Melody Girl). The Great Dictator. His Girl Friday. Women in War. Scatterbrain. Safari. A Night at Earl Carroll's. Sandy is a Lady. Seven Sinners. A Little Bit of Heaven. Queen of the Mob. Cross Country Romance. The Villain Still Pursued Her. Tin Pan Alley. No, No, Nanette. Lucky

Partners. 1941: *Crazy Like a Fox. Reaching for the Sun. New Wine (GB: The Great Awakening). One Night in Lisbon. Angels with Broken Wings. Model Wife. Week-End in Havana. *Meet Roy Rogers. Our City. 1942: Mr Wise Guy. Sleepytime Gal. Valley of the Sun. Song of the Islands. Arabian Nights. 1943: Shantytown. Crazy House. *Shot in the Escape. Spotlight Scandals. Always a Bridesmaid. Stage Door Canteen. 1944: *Ghost Crazy. *Wedded Bliss. Three of a Kind. Ever Since Venus. Three's a Family. Ghost Catchers. Crazy Knights. 1945: Anchors Aweigh. Trouble Chasers. 1947: Fun and Fancy Free (voice only). 1948: The Kissing Bandit. The Counterfeiters. 1949: Bride of Vengeance. 1952: Down Among the Sheltering Palms. 1961: Paradise Alley. 1962: Five Weeks in a Balloon.

GILCHRIST, Connie
(Rose C. Gilchrist) 1901–1985
Fair-haired, formidably-built, strong-featured, Brooklyn-born actress. If you met Connie Gilchrist behind the bar, you knew she'd stand no nonsense. Even her below-stairs characters were inclined to speak their minds. A stage actress from 1917, she was signed by M-G-M in 1940, forming the third point of the triangle in the Marjorie Main-Wallace Beery roughhouse comedies there, and duetting delightfully with Judy Garland in Presenting Lily Mars. Later a match for Robert Newton in his Long John Silver TV series, playing Purity Pinker.

1940: Hullabaloo. 1941: Married Bachelor. Down in San Diego. Dr Kildare's Wedding Day (GB: Mary Names the Day). Whistling in the Dark. H.M. Pulham Esq. Billy the Kid. The Wild Man of Borneo. Two-Faced Woman. Johnny Eager. Barnacle Bill. A Woman's Face. Woman of the Year. 1942: This Time for Keeps. We Were Dancing. Born to Sing. Tortilla Flat. Sunday Punch. The War Against Mrs Hadley. Grand Central Murder. Apache Trail. 1943: Andy Hardy's Blonde Trouble. Swing Shift Maisie (GB: The Girl in Overalls). Presenting Lily Mars. Cry Havoc! The Heavenly Body. Thousands Cheer. The Human Comedy. 1944: Rationing. *Important Business. Music for Millions. See Here, Private Hargrove. Nothing But Trouble. The Seventh Cross. The Thin Man Goes Home. 1945: The Valley of Decision. Junior Miss. Up Goes Maisie (GB: Up She Goes). 1946: Bad Bascomb. Faithful in

My Fashion. Young Widow. Merton of the Movies. Cloak and Dagger. 1947: Good News. Song of the Thin Man. The Hucksters. 1948: Big City. Tenth Avenue Angel. Chicken Every Sunday. An Act of Violence. Luxury Liner. The Bride Goes Wild. A Letter to Three Wives. 1949: Little Women. The Story of Molly X. 1950: Stars in My Crown. A Ticket to Toma-hawk. Buccaneer's Girl. Peggy. Undercover Girl. Tripoli. The Killer That Stalked New York (GB: The Frightened City). Louisa. 1951: Here Comes the Groom. Thunder on the Hill (GB: Bonaventure). Chain of Circumstance. Flesh and Fury. 1952: One Big Affair. Bonzo Goes to College. The Half-Breed. 1953: Houdini. The Great Diamond Robbery. It Should Happen to You. 1954: Long John Silver. The Far Country. Under the Black Flag (TV. GB: cinemas). 1956: The Man in the Gray Flannel Suit. 1958: Auntie Mame. Some Came Running. 1959: Machine Gun Kelly. Say One for Me. 1960: The Schnook (GB: Double Trouble). 1962: The Interns. Swingin' Along (revised version of The Schnook). 1963: A Tiger Walks. 1964: The Misadventures of Merlin Jones. A House is Not a Home. Two on a Guillotine. 1965: Fluffy. The Monkey's Uncle. Sylvia. Tickle Me. 1969: Some Kind of a Nut. 1972: Fuzz.

GILLINGWATER, Claude 1870–1939
Lofty, balding American actor with craggy features and caterpillar eyebrows. He came to Hollywood to play the recalcitrant earl finally converted by *Little Lord Fauntleroy* in the 1921 version, and found himself consistently typed in the same sort of role, his crotchety old codgers several times falling victim to Shirley Temple's wiles in the 1930s. At the age of 69, Gillingwater shot himself.

1921: Little Lord Fauntleroy. My Boy. 1922: The Dust Flower. Fools First. Remembrance. The Stranger's Banquet. 1923: Alice Adams. Three Wise Fools. The Christian. Souls for Sale. Crinoline and Romance. Dulcy. A Chapter in Her Life. Tiger Rose. 1924: Daddies. How to Educate a Wife. Idle Tongues. Madonna of the Streets. 1925: Seven Sinners. Cheaper to Marry. A Thief in Paradise. Winds of Chance. We Moderns. Wages for Wives. 1926: Into Her Kingdom. For Wives Only. That's My Baby. 1927: Barbed Wire. The Gorilla. Fast and Furious. Naughty But Nice. Husbands for Rent. 1928: Women They Talk About. Stark Mad. The Little Shepherd of Kingdom Come. Oh, Kay! Remember? 1929: The Great Divide.

So Long, Letty. Stolen Kisses. A Dangerous Woman. Glad Rag Doll. Smiling Irish Eyes. 1930: The Flirting Widow. Dumbbells in Ermine. Toast of the Legion. 1931: Gold Dust Gertie (GB: Why Change Your Husband?). Illicit. The Conquering Horde. Kiss Me Again. *Wide Open Spaces. Daddy Long Legs. *Oh! Oh! Cleopatra. Compromised (GB: We Three). 1932: Tess of the Storm Country. 1933: Ann Carver's Profession. The Avenger. I Loved a Woman. Ace of Aces. Skyway. Before Midnight. 1934: Broadway Bill (GB: Strictly Confidential). The Show-Off. City Limits. You Can't Buy Everything. The Unknown Blonde. In Love with Life (GB: Re-Union). Green Eyes. The Back Page. The Captain Hates the Sea. 1935: Calm Yourself. Mississippi. Baby Face Harrington. The Woman in Red. A Tale of Two Cities. Strange Wives. 1936: Florida Special. The Prisoner of Shark Island. Poor Little Rich Girl. Ticket to Paradise. Wives Never Know. Can This Be Dixie? Counterfeit. 1937: Conquest (GB: Marie Walewska). Top of the Town. A Yank at Oxford. 1938: Just Around the Corner. There Goes My Heart. Little Miss Broadway. 1939: Café Society.

GINGOLD, Hermione 1897–1987
Rampant, trenchant, cuttingly witty British comic actress with wonderfully unique gurgling tones, adept at dragons, grotesques and eccentric aunts. Remembered by many for her revue roles, especially in tandem with Hermione Baddeley (*qv*) as The Two Hermiones, and for her radio characters including the long-running Mrs Doom. Her two best film roles, in *Gigi* and *Bell, Book and Candle*, came in the same year: 1958. She died from heart disease.

1932: Dance Pretty Lady. 1936: Someone at the Door. Public Nuisance No. 1. 1937: Merry Comes to Town. 1938: Meet Mr Penny. 1943: The Butler's Dilemma. 1952: The Pickwick Papers. Cosh Boy (US: The Slasher). 1953: Our Girl Friday (US: The Adventures of Sadie). 1956: Around the World in 80 Days. 1958: Gigi. Bell, Book and Candle. 1961: The Naked Edge. The Music Man. 1962: Gay Purr-ee (voice only). 1964: I'd Rather Be Rich. 1965: Harvey Middleman, Fireman. Promise Her Anything. 1966: Munster Go Home! 1967: Jules Verne's Rocket to the Moon (US: Those Fantastic Flying Fools). 1971: Banyon (TV). 1976: A Little Night Music. 1984: Garbo Talks!

GIRARDOT, Etienne 1856–1939
Tiny, wizened, hook-nosed, punch-chinned, beady-eyed, fiercely-blinking British actor (of French parentage) often seen as fussy, pernickety characters of minor authority. Despite having lived in California for many years, his film credits are almost all contained in the last seven years of the 1930s. There can't be many actors who started the major part of their film career at 77, but Girardot actually won something of a cult following for himself, especially as the feisty little coroner, Dr Doremus, in the Philo Vance detective mysteries.

1912: The Violin of Monsieur. 1916: Artie, the Millionaire Kid. 1919: The Belle of New York. 1931: Union Depot (GB: Gentleman for a Day). 1933: Blood Money. Advice to the Love-lorn. The Kennel Murder Case. 1934: Mandalay. Twentieth Century. Fashions of 1934 (GB: Fashions). The Dragon Murder Case. Little Man, What Now? The Firebird. Born to be Bad. Return of the Terror. The Whole Town's Talking (GB: Passport to Fame). 1935: Clive of India. Grand Old Girl. Hooray for Love. In Old Kentucky. Curly Top. The Bishop Misbehaves. I Live My Life. Metropolitan. Chasing Yesterday. 1936: College Holiday. The Devil is a Sissy (GB: The Devil Takes the Count). Half Angel. Hearts Divided. The Music Goes 'Round. The Garden Murder Case. The Longest Night. Go West, Young Man. 1937: Wake Up and Live. Danger – Love at Work! The Road Back/Return of the Hero. The Great Garrick. Breakfast for Two. 1938: Port of Seven Seas. Having Wonderful Time. Professor, Beware! Arizona Wildcat. There Goes My Heart. 1939: Fast and Loose. Exile Express. For Love or Money. The Story of Vernon and Irene Castle. Little Accident. Hawaiian Nights. The Hunchback of Notre Dame. 1940: Isle of Destiny.

GLEASON, James 1886–1959
Wiry, thin-faced American actor with pencil moustache, a wisp of hair and rasping Brooklyn accent—a familiar face from the onset of sound in scores of films as policemen, editors, army sergeants, taxi drivers and cynically wisecracking best friends. He never failed to build an identifiable and usually likeable character. He was a long-term sufferer from asthma, eventually the cause of his death at 72. Also wrote—plays for theatre and screenplays for the cinema. Academy

Award nominee for *Here Comes Mr Jordan*. Husband of actress Lucile Gleason (1888–1947). Father of actor Russell Gleason (1908–1947).

*1922: Polly of the Follies. 1928: The Count of Ten. 1929: *The Garden of Eatin'. High Voltage. Oh, Yeah! (GB: No Brakes). The Shannons of Broadway. His First Command. The Broadway Melody. *Fairways and Foul. The Flying Fool. 1930: The Swellhead (GB: Counted Out). *Don't Believe It. Big Money. What a Widow! Dumbbells in Ermine. The Matrimonial Bed (GB: A Matrimonial Problem). *No Brakes (and 1929 feature). Her Man. Puttin' on the Ritz. 1931: A Free Soul. *Where Canaries Sing Bass. Sweepstakes. The Big Gamble. Suicide Fleet. *Slow Poison. *Doomed to Win. It's a Wise Child. Beyond Victory. 1932: *Lights Out. Battle Royal. *High Hats and Low Brows. *Stealin' Home. *Yoo Hoo. The Penguin Pool Murder (GB: The Penguin Pool Mystery). Fast Companions/Information Kid. The Crooked Circle. *Rule 'em and Weep. The All-American (GB: Sport of a Nation). Lady and Gent. Blondie of the Follies. The Devil is Driving. 1933: Orders is Orders. Hoopla. Clear All Wires. Billion Dollar Scandal. *Rockabye Cowboy. *Alias the Professor. *Mister Mugg. *Gleason's New Deal. 1934: Search for Beauty. Murder on the Blackboard. Change of Heart. The Meanest Gal in Town. *Pie for Two. 1935: Helldorado. Murder on a Honeymoon. Hot Tip. West Point of the Air. 1936: Murder on a Bridal Path. The Ex-Mrs Bradford. Don't Turn 'em Loose. The Plot Thickens (GB: The Swinging Pearl Mystery). The Big Game. Yours for the Asking. We're Only Human. 1937: Manhattan Merry-Go-Round (GB: Manhattan Music Box). Forty Naughty Girls. 1938: Army Girl (GB: The Last of the Cavalry). The Higgins Family. 1939: Should Husbands Work? The Covered Trailer. My Wife's Relatives. On Your Toes. 1940: Earl of Puddlestone (GB: Jolly Old Higgins). Grandpa Goes to Town. Money to Burn. 1941: Affectionately Yours. Meet John Doe. Nine Lives Are Not Enough. Here Comes Mr Jordan. Tanks a Million. Babes on Broadway. A Date with the Falcon. 1942: My Gal Sal. Hayfoot. Tales of Manhattan. Footlight Serenade. Manila Calling. The Falcon Takes Over. Tramp, Tramp, Tramp. 1943: Crash Dive. A Guy Named Joe. Arsenic and Old Lace. 1944: The Keys of the Kingdom. Once Upon a Time. 1945: The Clock (GB: Under the Clock). Captain Eddie. A Tree Grows in Brooklyn. This Man's Navy. 1946: The Hoodlum Saint. Lady Luck. The Well-Groomed Bride. Home Sweet Homicide. 1947: Down to Earth. The Homestretch. Tycoon. The Bishop's Wife. 1948: When My Baby Smiles at Me. The Return of October (GB: Date with Destiny). Smart Woman. The Dude Goes West. 1949: The Life of Riley. Bad Boy. Take One False Step. Miss Grant Takes Richmond (GB: Innocence is Bliss). 1950: Riding High. *Screen Snapshots No. 182. The Yellow Cab Man. Key to the City. The Jackpot. Joe Palooka in The Squared Circle (GB: The Squared Circle). 1951: Come Fill the Cup. Joe Palooka in The Triple Cross (GB: The Triple Cross). Two Gals and a Guy. I'll See You in My Dreams. 1952: What Price Glory? We're Not Married. The Story of Will Rogers. 1953: Movie Stuntmen (GB: Hollywood Thrill Makers). Forever Female. 1954: Suddenly! 1955: The Night of the Hunter. The Girl Rush. 1956: Star in the Dust. 1957: Spring Reunion. Loving You. Man in the Shadow (GB: Pay the Devil). 1958: The Female Animal. Once Upon a Horse. Man or Gun. Rock-a-Bye Baby. Money, Women and Guns. The Last Hurrah. The Time of Your Life (TV).*

As co-director.
1929: Oh, Yeah! (GB: No Brakes). 1935: Hot Tip.

GLOVER, Brian 1934–

Chunky, usually unsmiling, often shaven-headed, pugnacious British actor who plays uncouth, drooling, over-age yobboes, or uncaring authoritatarians. Yorkshire born, Glover boasted the contrasting occupations of wrestler and schoolmaster before he entered the acting profession at 34, ironically playing a teacher in his first film. Since then he has played lots of characters who alienate their fellows on stage, screen and TV and his distinctive voice has long been in demand for TV commercial voice-overs. Has also written plays.

1969: Kes. 1973: O Lucky Man! 1974: Mister Quilp. 1975: Brannigan. 1976: Trial by Combat (US: Dirty Knights' Work). Sweeney! 1977: Jabberwocky. Joseph Andrews. 1978: The First Great Train Robbery (US: The Great Train Robbery). Absolution (released 1980). 1981: An American Werewolf in London. 1982: Britannia Hospital. Red Monarch (TV). 1984: The Company of Wolves. Ordeal by Innocence/Agatha Christie's Ordeal by Innocence. Laughterhouse/Singleton's Pluck. *1985: The McGuffin (TV). 1988: To Kill a Priest. 1992: Alien. Leon the Pig Farmer. Kafka. 1994: Prince of Jutland.*

GLOVER, Danny 1947–

Tall, solid, reassuring black American actor who has occasionally deliberately steered himself away from his natural comforting authority to tackle nasty or outrageous characters. After training at the Black Actors' Workshop, the California-born Glover has worked his way through a mixture of leading, co-star and cameo roles, and even built himself a small portion of box-office clout as Mel Gibson's long-suffering (and steady, of course) partner in the *Lethal Weapon* cop thrillers.

*1978: Escape from Alcatraz. 1981: Chu Chu and the Philly Flash. 1982: Out. 1983: Iceman. The Face of Rage (TV). 1984: Witness. Places in the Heart. The Stand-In. 1985: Silverado. 1986: The Color Purple (shown 1985). 1987: Mandela (TV). Lethal Weapon. 1988: Memorial Day (TV). Dead Man Walking (TV. US: Dead Man Out). Bat*21. 1989: Lethal Weapon 2. A Raisin in the Sun (TV). 1990: Predator 2. To Sleep with Anger. Flight of the Intruder. 1991: Grand Canyon. A Rage in Harlem. Pure Luck. 1992: Lethal Weapon 3. 1993: The Saint of Fort Washington. Bopha! 1994: Angels in the Outfield. Maverick. 1995: Operation Dumbo Drop.*

GLOVER, John 1944–

Brown-haired, slim, hyena-like American actor of cutting talent and considerable range. Particularly expert, though, at playing toothy specimens of seedy decadence. Following long stage experience, around the country, off Broadway and in New York, he began to play film roles regularly after appearing as Diane Keaton's foot-fetishist boyfriend in *Annie Hall*. But he soon built up a formidable range of villains: blackmailers, plotters, drug dealers and corrupt bosses, as well as playing one or two offbeat leading roles, always as unconventional figures.

1972: Shamus. 1977: Annie Hall. Julia. 1978: Somebody Killed Her Husband. 1979: Last Embrace. 1980: The American Success Company (later Success). Melvin and Howard. Brubaker.

The Mountain Men. 1981: *The Incredible Shrinking Woman.* 1982: *A Little Sex.* 1983: *The Evil That Men Do.* 1984: *Ernie Kovacs – Between the Laughter* (TV). *A Flash of Green.* 1985: *White Nights. An Early Frost* (TV). *A Killing Affair* (released 1989 as *My Sister's Keeper*). 1986: *52 Pick-Up. Apology/Apology for Murder* (TV). *Willy/Milly* (TV. Later: *Something Special*). *I Was a Teenage Boy.* 1987: *Life on the Edge. Moving Target* (TV). *The Scream* (TV). 1988: *Hot Paint* (TV). *Rocket Gibraltar. Masquerade. The Chocolate War. David* (TV). *Scrooged.* 1989: *Meet the Hollowheads.* **Home. Twist of Fate* (TV). *Traveling Man* (TV). *Breaking Point* (TV). *Michelangelo: A Season of Giants* (TV). 1990: *Gremlins 2: The New Batch. An Enemy of the People* (TV). *Robocop 2. El Diablo* (cable TV). 1991: *What Ever Happened to Baby Jane* (TV). *Drug Wars II: The Cocaine Cartel* (TV). *Dead on the Money* (TV). 1992: *Majority Rule* (TV). *Ed and His Dead Mother.* 1993: *South Beach* (TV). 1994: *Automatic. Bon Appetit Mama.*

GLOVER, Julian 1935–

Tall, languid, fair-haired British actor, a master of the supercilious sneer who has often played cool and calculating villains and arrogant spymasters. A former army officer, he made a belated London stage debut at 26, but the theatre thereafter kept him busy, leaving room for fewer films than his admirers would have liked. Married actresses Eileen Atkins and Isla Blair.

1963: *Tom Jones.* 1964: *Girl with Green Eyes.* 1965: *I Was Happy Here* (US: *Time Lost and*

Time Remembered). *The Alphabet Murders.* 1966: *Theatre of Death.* 1967: *Quatermass and the Pit* (US: *Five Million Miles to Earth*). 1968: *The Magus.* 1969: *The Adding Machine. Alfred the Great* (US: *Grigsby*). 1970: *The Last Grenade* (US: *Grigsby*). *Wuthering Heights. The Rise and Rise of Michael Rimmer.* 1971: *Nicholas and Alexandra. Antony and Cleopatra.* 1973: *Hitler: The Last Ten Days. Luther.* 1974: *The Internecine Project. Juggernaut. Dead Cert. The Story of Jacob and Joseph* (TV). *QB VII* (TV). *Mirror of Deception* (TV. US: cinemas). 1976: *The Brute.* 1977: *Gulliver's Travels.* 1980: *The Empire Strikes Back.* 1981: *For Your Eyes Only. Ivanhoe* (TV). 1982: *Guerre en pays neutre. Heat and Dust.* 1984: *Kim* (TV). 1985: *Tusks* (released 1990). *OSS* (TV. GB: 92 *Grosvenor Street*). 1987: *Cry Freedom. The Fourth Protocol. Hearts of Fire. The Secret Garden* (TV). 1989: *Treasure Island* (TV. GB: cinemas). *Indiana Jones and the Last Crusade.* 1991: *King Ralph.* 1993: *The Chance.* 1994: *In the Mouth of Madness.*

GODDARD, Alf 1897–1981

Big, tough, hearty, brown-haired, hook-nosed British actor, a bargain-basement Victor McLaglen who looked like the ex-boxer he was and got into films via stuntwork in the silent days. Played manual workers, soldiers, crooks and, especially in comedy, anyone not averse to kicking sand in the weakling hero's face.

1923: *The Sign of Four.* 1925: **So This is Jolly Good. Battling Bruisers.* 1926: *Every Mother's Son. White Heat. Mademoiselle from Armentières. Second to None.* 1927: *Downhill* (US: *When Boys Leave Home*). *Hindle Wakes* (US: *Holiday Week*). *Remembrance. A Sister to Assist 'Er. The Flight Commander. Carry On.* 1928: *Sailors Don't Care. Mademoiselle Parley-Voo. What Money Can Buy. Smashing Through. You Know What Sailors Are. Balaclava* (US: *Jaws of Hell*). *The Last Post.* 1929: *Down Channel. High Treason. Rough Seas.* 1930: **The Cockney Spirit in the War No. 2. Alf's Button. The Brat. Bed and Breakfast.* 1931: *Old Soldiers Never Die. East Lynne on the Western Front. The Happy Ending. Splinters in the Navy.* 1932: *The Third String.* 1933: *Too Many Wives. Pride of the Force. Enemy of the Police.* 1934: *Lost in the Legion. Strictly Illegal. 1935: It's a Bet. The Clairvoyant. First a Girl. No Limit.* 1936: *Song of Freedom. The Amazing Quest of Ernest Bliss* (US: *Romance*

and Riches). 1937: *Farewell Again* (US: *Troopship*). *The Squeaker* (US: *Murder on Diamond Row*). *Action for Slander. King Solomon's Mines. Non Stop New York. The Green Cockatoo* (US: *Four Dark Hours*). *Bank Holiday* (US: *Three on a Weekend*). *Owd Bob* (US: *To the Victor*). 1938: *The Drum* (US: *Drums*). *Convict 99. St Martin's Lane* (US: *Sidewalks of London*). *Luck of the Navy* (US: *North Sea Patrol*). *Night Journey. The Ware Case.* 1939: *Murder in Soho* (US: *Murder in the Night*). *Young Man's Fancy. Let's Be Famous. A Window in London* (US: *Lady in Distress*). *Return to Yesterday.* 1940: *Spy for a Day. Convoy.* 1941: *The Saint Meets the Tiger. South American George.* 1942: *The Young Mr Pitt. Much Too Shy.* 1943: *They Met in the Dark. The Butler's Dilemma.* 1944: *The Way Ahead* (US: *Immortal Battalion*). 1945: *The Way to the Stars* (US: *Johnny in the Clouds*). *I'll Be Your Sweetheart. They Knew Mr Knight. Perfect Strangers* (US: *Vacation from Marriage*). 1953: *Innocents in Paris.*

GOMBELL, Minna 1892–1973

The characters of this flinty, pinch-faced, diminutive blonde American actress, who sized up many a taller opponent before cutting her *down* to size, were always ready with a sharp retort. They had seen it, done it and got the scars to prove it. The Maryland-born actress, a doctor's daughter, had tended to play aristocratic ladies in her theatre days but, after, coming to Hollywood to repeat her stage role in *The Great Power*, in 1929, she was soon into a string of saloon keepers, burlesque veterans, nagging wives and tough authoritarians like her asylum nurse in *The Snake Pit*. Earlier in her career she was known as Nancy Garter!

1929: *The Great Power.* 1931: *The Good Sport. Skyline. Sob Sister* (GB: *The Blonde Reporter*). *Bad Girl. Doctors' Wives.* 1932: *Stepping Sisters. The Rainbow Trail. Dance Team. After Tomorrow. Careless Lady. Bachelor's Affairs. The First Year. Wild Girl* (GB: *Salomy Jane*). 1933: *Pleasure Cruise. What Price Innocence?* (GB: *Shall the Children Pay?*). *Hello, Sister!/Walking Down Broadway. The Big Brain* (GB: *Enemies of Society*). *The Way to Love. Wild Boys of the Road* (GB: *Dangerous Days*). *Hoopla.* 1934: *Keep 'Em Rolling. Cross-Country Cruise. Marrying Widows. The Thin Man. No More Women.*

Registered Nurse. Strictly Dynamite. Hell Cat. The Lemon Drop Kid. The Merry Widow. Babbitt. Cheating Cheaters. 1935: Two Sinners (GB: Two Black Sheep). Women Must Dress. The White Cockatoo. Miss Pacific Fleet. 1936: Champagne Charlie. Banjo on My Knee. 1937: Make Way for Tomorrow. Wife, Doctor and Nurse. Slave Ship. 1938: The Great Waltz. Going Places. Block-Heads. Comet Over Broadway. 1939: Second Fiddle. Stop, Look and Love. The Hunchback of Notre Dame. 1940: Boom Town. 1941: Thieves Fall Out. High Sierra. Doomed Caravan. 1942: Cadets on Parade. Mexican Spitfire Sees a Ghost. 1943: Salute for Three. 1944: Chip Off the Old Block. Destiny. The Town Went Wild. Johnny Doesn't Live Here Anymore. Night Club Girl. 1945: Man Alive. Swingin' on a Rainbow. Sunbonnet Sue. Penthouse Rhythm. Swingin' on Broadway. 1946: The Best Years of Our Lives. Perilous Holiday. 1947: Wyoming. 1948: Mr Reckless. The Snake Pit. Return of the Bad Men. 1949: The Last Bandit. 1950: Pagan Love Song. 1951: Here Comes the Groom. I'll See You in My Dreams.

GOMEZ, Thomas
(Sabino Tomas Gomez) 1905–1971
Although well into his thirties before he tried films, this heavy-jowled, scowling American actor whose greasy black hair fitted his oily characters, was soon a staple part of villainy in numerous forties' Hollywood thrillers. The fifties only proved that he was less effective when used as comic relief, and he faded from the scene. Billed as S. Tomas Gomez in some early films. Academy Award nomination for Ride the Pink Horse.

1942: Sherlock Holmes and the Voice of Terror. Arabian Nights. Pittsburgh. Who Done It? 1943: Corvette K-225 (GB: The Nelson Touch). Crazy House. White Savage (GB: White Captive). Frontier Badmen. 1944: The Climax. Phantom Lady. Dead Man's Eyes. In Society. Can't Help Singing. Bowery to Broadway. Follow the Boys. 1945: Patrick the Great. I'll Tell the World. Frisco Sal. The Daltons Ride Again. 1946: A Night in Paradise. Swell Guy. The Dark Mirror. 1947: Singapore. Captain from Castile. Johnny O'Clock. Ride the Pink Horse. 1948: Angel in Exile. Key Largo. Casbah. 1949: Come to the Stable. Force of Evil. That Midnight Kiss. Sorrowful Jones. I

Married a Communist (GB: The Woman on Pier 13). 1950: Kim. The Eagle and the Hawk. The Furies. The Toast of New Orleans. Dynamite Pass. Macao (released 1952). 1951: The Sellout. Anne of the Indies. The Harlem Globetrotters. The Merry Widow. Pony Soldier (GB: MacDonald of the Canadian Mounties). 1953: Sombrero. 1954: The Gambler from Natchez. The Adventures of Hajji Baba. 1955: The Looters. Night Freight. Las Vegas Shakedown. The Magnificent Matador (GB: The Brave and the Beautiful). 1956: Trapeze. The Conqueror. 1958: Sea of Sand (US: Desert Patrol). 1959: John Paul Jones. But Not for Me. 1961: Summer and Smoke. The Power and the Glory (TV. GB: Cinemas). 1968: Stay Away Joe. Shadow over Elveron (TV). 1969: Beneath the Planet of the Apes.

GOODLIFFE, Michael 1914–1976
Thin-faced, very dark-eyed, alert-looking British actor of shadowed aspect and black hair stretching forward from receding temples. A vicar's son, he learned his craft at Stratford's Shakespeare Theatre, but war service (including five years in a POW camp) interrupted his career. He entered films from 1948 in featured roles as policemen, soldiers, relatives or sympathetic figures of authority, often giving better performances than those billed above him. Never quite a star, despite success in a couple of TV series towards the end of his too-short career, he committed suicide (by leaping from a height) while in hospital.

1948: The Small Back Room (US: Hour of Glory). 1949: Stop Press Girl. 1950: The Wooden Horse. *Family Portrait (narrator only). 1951: Captain Horatio Hornblower RN (US: Captain Horatio Hornblower). Cry, the Beloved Country (US: African Fury). 1952: The Hour of 13. Sea Devils. 1953: Rob Roy the Highland Rogue. Front Page Story. 1954: Beau Brummell. The End of the Affair. 1955: The Adventures of Quentin Durward (US: Quentin Durward). Dial 999 (US: The Way Out). Double Jeopardy. 1956: The Battle of the River Plate (US: Pursuit of the Graf Spee). Wicked As They Come. 1957: The One That Got Away. Fortune is a Woman (US: She Played with Fire). 1958: A Night to Remember. The Camp on Blood Island. Carve Her Name with Pride. Up the Creek. Law and Disorder. Further Up the Creek. 1959: The Battle of the Sexes. The White Trap. The

39 Steps. Peeping Tom. Sink the Bismarck! 1960: The Trials of Oscar Wilde (US: The Man with the Green Carnation). Conspiracy of Hearts. 1961: No Love for Johnnie. The Day the Earth Caught Fire. 1962: Number Six. Jigsaw. 1963: 80,000 Suspects. A Stitch in Time. The £20,000 Kiss. 1964: The 7th Dawn. Man in the Middle. Woman of Straw. The Gorgon. Troubled Waters. 633 Squadron. 1965: Von Ryan's Express. 1966: The Night of the Generals. The Jokers. 1969: The Fifth Day of Peace (released 1972). Gott mit Uns. 1970: Cromwell. 1971: The Johnstown Monster. 1972: Henry VIII and His Six Wives. 1973: Hitler: The Last Ten Days. 1974: The Man with the Golden Gun. 1976: To the Devil a Daughter.

GOODWIN, Bill 1910–1958
A rarity: a radio announcer who became a film character player. Genial, good-humoured Goodwin, a chunkily-built Californian with a big smile, short, prominent nose and brown wavy hair slicked back, began as an actor but was already making his voice a familiar one on radio comedy shows at 24. He worked with Eddie Cantor, Bob Hope and Edgar Bergen & Charlie McCarthy, but he was most fondly associated with George Burns and Gracie Allen in a partnership that lasted more than 20 years. His amiable personality made him an integral part of these shows and, from 1940, he began to get film acting roles, usually as the fall guy or hero's friend. The cheery Goodwin was found dead in his car at 47, from a suspected heart attack.

1940: Let's Make Music. 1941: Blondie in Society (GB: Henpecked). 1942: Wake Island. Blondie Goes to College (GB: The Boss Said 'No'). 1943: Riding High (GB: Melody Inn). So Proudly We Hail! Henry Aldrich Gets Glamour (GB: Henry Gets Glamour). No Time for Love. 1944: Bathing Beauty. 1945: Incendiary Blonde. River Gang. The Stork Club. Spellbound. 1946: House of Horrors (GB: Joan Medford is Missing). The Jolson Story. To Each His Own. Earl Carroll Sketchbook (GB: Hats Off to Rhythm). 1947: Hit Parade of 1947. Heaven Only Knows. 1948: Mickey. So This is New York. 1949: It's a Great Feeling. The Life of Riley. Jolson Sings Again. 1950: Tea for Two. Mr Music. 1952: The First Time. 1953:

The Atomic Kid. 1954: Lucky Me. 1956: The Opposite Sex. Bundle of Joy. 1958: The Big Beat. Going Steady.

GOODWIN, Harold 1917–

Yorkshire-born small-part player in British films. After three years in repertory at Liverpool, he used his slight stature and gormless expression to propel himself into dozens of 'innocent' roles of low intelligence – sidekicks, straight men, friends, soldiers and workers in low-paid jobs. One can still see his mournful features and slick of dark hair beneath some enormous flat cap. An early ambition to be a British James Cagney was, of course, stillborn.

*1938: The Ware Case. 1950: Dance Hall. The Happiest Days of Your Life. The Magnet. 1951: Appointment with Venus (US: Island Rescue). The Galloping Major. Lady Godiva Rides Again. The Man in the White Suit. Green Grow the Rushes. Judgment Deferred. 1952: Angels One Five. The Card (US: The Promoter). The Cruel Sea. 1953: Grand National Night (US: Wicked Wife). The Case of Gracie Budd. The Million Pound Note (US: Man with a Million). 1954: The Harassed Hero. One Good Turn. The Gay Dog. The Dam Busters. A Kid for Two Farthings. 1955: The Ship That Died of Shame (US: PT Raiders). The Ladykillers. You Lucky People. Josephine and Men. Who Done It? 1956: Now and Forever. Charley Moon. The Long Arm (US: The Third Key). Zarak. The Last Man to Hang? Three Men in a Boat. 1957: Carry On Admiral (US: The Ship Was Loaded). The Smallest Show on Earth. Barnacle Bill (US: All at Sea). The Prince and the Showgirl. The Bridge on the River Kwai. Seawife. 1958: Girls at Sea. The Square Peg. Law and Disorder. Sea of Sand. The Captain's Table. 1959: The Mummy. The Bandit of Zhobe. The Ugly Duckling. Wrong Number. Sink the Bismarck! 1960: Spartacus. Operation Cupid. The Bulldog Breed. 1961: The Terror of the Tongs. Nearly a Nasty Accident. On The Fiddle (US: Operation Snafu). *The Square Mile Murder. Never Back Losers. 1962: The Traitors. Hair of the Dog. Number Six. Phantom of the Opera. The Longest Day. Crooks Anonymous. The Fast Lady. 1963: The Hi-Jackers. The Comedy Man. 1964: Curse of the Mummy's Tomb. *All in Good Time. 1965: The Saboteur, Code Name Morituri. Monster of Terror (US: Die, Monster,*

Die). 1967: Don't Raise the Bridge, Lower the River. 1968: The Bush Baby. 1969: Frankenstein Must Be Destroyed. Some Will, Some Won't. 1970: Hoverbug. 1971: Quest for Love. 1974: All Creatures Great and Small. 1976: The Chiffy Kids (series). 1977: Jabberwocky.

GORDON, C. Henry
(H. G. Racke) 1883–1940

Dark-haired, often moustachioed, shifty-featured New York-born actor with flickering snake-like eyes. A memorable villain in all kinds of exotica, but especially as the vile khan confronted by Errol Flynn in *The Charge of the Light Brigade*, he menaced heroes in such far-away places as China, Russia, Egypt, Turkey, Morocco and the Sahara Desert; he was devious and treacherous in well over half the many screen roles he packed into his 11 years in films. There would doubtless have been more – especially in Universal extravaganzas of the wartime years – but for his sudden death following a leg amputation.

1930: Renegades. A Devil with Women. 1931: Honor of the Family. A Woman of Experience. The Black Camel. Young As You Feel. Charlie Chan Carries On. Once a Sinner. Hush Money. Berge in Flammen. 1932: The Washington Masquerade (GB: Mad Masquerade). State's Attorney (GB: Cardigan's Last Case). Doomed Battalion. The Strange Love of Molly Louvain. Miss Pinkerton. Roar of the Dragon. Kongo. Hell's Highway. Thirteen Women. Scarlet Dawn. Scarface (The Shame of a Nation). Mata Hari. The Gay Caballero. The Crooked Circle. Jewel Robbery. 1933: Penthouse (GB: Crooks in Clover). Gabriel Over the White House. Secret of Madame Blanche. Whistling in the Dark. Clear All Wires. Made on Broadway (GB: The Girl I Made). Storm at Daybreak. Turn Back the Clock. Night Flight. Stage Mother. The Devil's in Love. The Chief (GB: My Old Man's a Fireman). Advice to the Lovelorn. Broadway Thru a Keyhole. Rasputin and the Empress (GB: Rasputin – The Mad Monk). The Women in His Life. 1934: Hide-Out. Straight is the Way. Death on the Diamond. Fugitive Lovers. This Side of Heaven. Stamboul Quest. Men in White. Lazy River. 1935: The Great Hotel Murder. The Lives of a Bengal Lancer. The Crusades. Pursuit. The Big Broadcast of 1936. 1936: Under Two Flags. Hollywood Boulevard. The Big Game. Love Letters of

*a Star. The Charge of the Light Brigade. 1937: Trouble in Morocco. The River of Missing Men. Charlie Chan at the Olympics. Conquest (GB: Marie Walewska). Trapped by G-Men. Sophie Lang Goes West. Stand-In. 1938: The Black Doll. Yellow Jack. Tarzan's Revenge. The Long Shot. Sharpshooters. Adventure in Sahara. Invisible Enemy. 1939: Man of Conquest. Heritage of the Desert. The Return of the Cisco Kid. Charlie Chan in City of Darkness. Trapped in the Sky. 1940: *Women in Hiding. Passport to Alcatraz (GB: Alien Sabotage). Kit Carson. Charlie Chan at the Wax Museum. *You the People.*

GORDON, Colin 1911–1972

Fair-haired, moustachioed, bespectacled, aristocratic-looking British actor, born in Sri Lanka (then Ceylon). He played characters whose air of cynical and snooty authority could turn to harassed bewilderment – teachers, lawyers and especially civil servants. He made his name in an award-winning stage performance as a teacher, Billings, in *The Happiest Days of Your Life* (strangely Richard Wattis (qv) played the role in the film version) and his acid tones became well-known to radio listeners as George Cole's brother-in-law in the long-running comedy series *A Life of Bliss*. Made his West End stage debut (in 1934) as the hind legs of a horse.

1947: Jim the Penman. 1948: Bond Street. It's Hard to be Good. The Winslow Boy. 1949: Helter Skelter. Traveller's Joy (released 1951). Golden Arrow (US: Three Men and a Girl. Released 1952). Edward My Son. 1951: The Third Visitor. The Long Dark Hall. Green Grow the Rushes. Circle of Danger. Laughter in Paradise. The Man in the White Suit. The Lady with a Lamp. 1952: Folly to be Wise. The Hour of 13. Mandy (US: Crash of Silence). 1953: The Heart of the Matter. Grand National Night (US: Wicked Wife). Innocents in Paris. 1954: Up to His Neck. Escapade. Little Red Monkey (US: The Case of the Red Monkey). 1955: John and Julie. Jumping for Joy. Keep It Clean. 1956: The Extra Day. A Touch of the Sun. Up in the World. The Green Man. 1957: The Key Man. The One That Got Away. The Safecracker. 1958: Alive and Kicking. Virgin Island (US: Our Virgin Island). The Doctor's Dilemma. The Key. The Crowning Touch. 1959:

The Mouse That Roared. Please Turn Over. Bobbikins. 1960: Make Mine Mink. His and Hers. The Big Day. Carry on Constable. The Day They Robbed the Bank of England. 1961: Don't Bother to Knock! (US: Why Bother to Knock?). Three on a Spree. The Horsemasters. House of Mystery. In the Doghouse. Very Important Person (US: A Coming-Out Party). 1962: Night of the Eagle (US: Burn, Witch, Burn). Crooks Anonymous. The Devil's Agent. The Boys. Strongroom. Seven Keys. 1963: Bitter Harvest. The Running Man. Heavens Above! The Pink Panther. 1964: Allez France! (US: The Counterfeit Constable). 1965: The Liquidator. 1966: The Great St Trinian's Train Robbery. The Psychopath. The Family Way. 1967: The Trygon Factor. Casino Royale. 1968: Subterfuge. Don't Raise the Bridge, Lower the River. 1969: Mischief.

GORDON, Don 1926–

Dour, dark, intense, hollow-cheeked American actor with short, dark, wavy, receding hair, seemingly leading man material, but in fact seen only in supporting roles in an 'occasional' film career that has spanned more than 40 years. Probably best recalled by filmgoers as Steve McQueen's sidekick in *Bullitt*, he became familiar to TV viewers in the late 1970s as Prentiss in the series *Lucan*.

1947: The Woman on the Beach. 1949: Once More, My Darling. Roseanna McCoy. 1951: It's a Big Country. Let's Go Navy. When I Grow Up. Force of Arms. 1952: Talk About a Stranger. 1953: Girls in the Night (GB: Life After Dark). Law and Order. 1957: Revolt at Fort Laramie. 1959: Cry Tough. 1961: True Gang Murders. 1965: The Lollipop Cover. 1968: Bullitt. 1969: The Gamblers. 1970: Cannon for Cordoba. WUSA. 1971: Z.P.G. (GB: Zero Population Growth). The Last Movie. Charlie Chan: Happiness is a Warm Clue (TV). 1972: Fuzz. Slaughter. 1973: Papillon. The Mack. 1974: The Towering Inferno. The Education of Sonny Carson. 1976: Street Killing (TV). 1980: Out of the Blue/Cebe (released 1982). Sparrow. 1981: The Final Conflict (later Omen III: The Final Conflict). Enter the Ninja. 1983: Confessions of a Married Man (TV). 1985: Warbus. 1987: Lethal Weapon. 1989: Code Name Vengeance. Skin Deep. The Borrower (released 1991).

GORDON, Hal 1894–1946

Short, thick-set, dark-haired British comic actor with ever-present aggressive leer. A former law clerk, then music-hall performer, he got into British films with the coming of sound. The cheerful, rather dim-witted personality he projected made him the ideal partner for some broad comedians of the 1930s, especially big, bluff Leslie Fuller. From 1939 onwards, Gordon combined acting with running a pub, doubtless always ready with a smile.

*1928: Adam's Apple (US: Honeymoon Ahead). 1929: When Knights Were Bold. 1930: The Windjammer. *The Cockney Spirit in the War No. 2. *The Cockney Spirit in the War No. 3. 1931: Out of the Blue. Old Soldiers Never Die. Poor Old Bill. Up for the Cup. Bill and Coo. Money for Nothing. Creeping Shadows (US: The Limping Man). Tonight's the Night – Pass It On. 1932: Partners Please. Insult. Jack's the Boy (US: Night and Day). The New Hotel. The Strangler. Old Spanish Customers. Help Yourself. The Indiscretions of Eve. The Bad Companions. Brother Alfred. Strip, Strip, Hooray! Lucky Girl. The Last Coupon. Josser in the Army. His Wife's Mother. Money Talks. For the Love of Mike. Sleepless Nights. Lord Camber's Ladies. Let Me Explain, Dear. Down Our Street. 1933: Their Night Out. Hawleys of High Street. Facing the Music. The Pride of the Force. Crime on the Hill. A Southern Maid. 1934: Master and Man. The Great Defender. Those Were the Days. Happy. A Political Party. The Outcast. Sometimes Good. My Song Goes Round the World. Lost in the Legion. Wishes. 1935: Dance Band. Captain Bill. Eighteen Minutes. Dandy Dick. No Monkey Business. Music Hath Charms. Lend Me Your Wife. The Deputy Drummer. Invitation to the Waltz. Play Up the Band. Man of the Moment. 1936: No Escape/No Exit. Queen of Hearts. Sabotage (US: The Woman Alone). OHMS (US: You're in the Army Now). The Man Behind the Mask. One Good Turn. The Amazing Quest of Ernest Bliss (US: Romance and Riches). Keep Your Seats, Please. It's in the Bag. Dusty Ermine (US: Hideout in the Alps). Southern Roses. 1937: Keep Fit. Old Mother Riley. The Divorce of Lady X. Victoria the Great. Action for Slander. East of Ludgate Hill. 1938: Father o' Nine. Hold My Hand. We're Going to Be Rich. It's in the Air (US: George Takes the Air). Dead Men Tell No Tales. Break the News. St Martin's Lane (US: Sidewalks of London).*

*1939: Come on George. Trouble Brewing. 1940: Let George Do It. *Food for Thought. Spare a Copper. 1942: Next of Kin. We'll Smile Again. 1943: Theatre Royal. Old Mother Riley, Detective. Millions Like Us. 1944: Give Me the Stars. Heaven is Round the Corner. Welcome Mr Washington. It Happened One Sunday. Kiss the Bride Goodbye. 1946: I'll Turn to You.*

GORDON, Leo 1922–

One of the few striking Hollywood uglies of the 1950s not to make stardom. In any case, Gordon, a dark-haired, square-faced, mean-looking actor usually cast as sullen, loud-mouthed, aggressive heavies – although he could quite successfully play against this stereotype – has preferred to work on his second-string career as a writer, contributing several screenplays, before returning sporadically to acting in recent times. Sometimes billed as Leo V Gordon.

1953: All the Brothers Were Valiant. Gun Fury. Hondo. City of Bad Men. China Venture. 1954: Riot in Cell Block 11. The Yellow Mountain. Sign of the Pagan. The Bamboo Prison. 1955: Ten Wanted Men. Santa Fé Passage. Seven Angry Men. Soldier of Fortune. Robbers' Roost. The Man With the Gun (GB: The Trouble Shooter). Rin Tin Tin – Hero of the West (TV. GB: cinemas). Tennessee's Partner. 1956: Red Sundown. The Conqueror. Great Day in the Morning. Johnny Concho. The Outlander (TV. GB: cinemas). The Steel Jungle. The Man Who Knew Too Much. Great Day in the Morning. 7th Cavalry. 1957: The Restless Breed. Black Patch. The Lonely Man. Lure of the Swamp. The Tall Stranger. Baby Face Nelson. Man in the Shadow (GB: Pay the Devil). 1958: The Notorious Mr Monks. Quantrill's Raiders. Ride a Crooked Trail. Apache Territory. Cry Baby Killer. Texas John Slaughter (TV. GB: cinemas). 1959: The Big Operator. Escort West. The Jayhawkers. 1960: Noose for a Gunman. 1961: The Intruder (GB: The Stranger). 1962: The Nun and the Sergeant. Tarzan Goes to India. 1963: The Haunted Palace. Kings of the Sun. McLintock! 1964: L'arme à gauche. The Dictator's Guns (GB: Guns for the Dictator). Kitten With a Whip. 1965: Girls on the Beach. 1966: Tobruk. Night of the Grizzly. Beau Geste. 1967: The Devil's Angels. Hostile Guns. The St Valentine's Day Massacre. 1968: Buckskin. 1970: You Can't

Win 'em All. 1971: The Trackers (TV). 1972: Bonnie's Kids. 1973: My Name is Nobody. 1975: Barbary Coast (TV. GB: In Old San Francisco). 1976: Nashville Girl. 1978: Hitler's Son. Bog. 1980: Rage (TV). 1982: Fire and Ice (voice only). 1985: Savage Dawn. 1988: Saturday the 14th Strikes Back. Big Top Pee-wee. 1989: Alienator. 1990: Mob Boss. 1994: Maverick.

GORDON, Mary
(M. Gilmour) 1882–1963

Diminutive but heftily built Scottish-born actress in Hollywood films from 1925 after coming to America with a touring company. She could be kindly, truculent, or down-to-earth, and played scores of small supporting roles as mothers, housekeepers, washer-women and landladies before her bun-like features found their perfect niche as Mrs Hudson, Basil Rathbone's housekeeper, in the Sherlock Holmes films (and on radio). Later played Leo Gorcey's much put-upon mother in one or two Bowery Boys films.

1925: Tessie. The People vs Nancy Preston. The Home Maker. 1926: Black Paradise. 1927: Clancy's Kosher Wedding. Naughty Nanette. 1928: The Pendulum. Our Dancing Daughters. The Old Code. Madame X. Dynamite. The Saturday Kid. One of the Bravest. Sunny Side Up. 1930: Oh, for a Man! *When the Wind Blows. Dance with Me. 1931: The Black Camel. Subway Express. 1932: The Texas Cyclone. Almost Married. Dancers in the Dark. Call Her Savage. Blonde Venus. The Trial of Vivienne Ware. Wild Girl (GB: Salomy Jane). Pack Up Your Troubles. 1933: *Nature in the Wrong. Pilgrimage. My Woman. Design for Living. She Done Him Wrong. The Power and the Glory. The Whirlwind. Lucky Dog. 1934: Cross Streets. The Man from Hell. Beloved. The Little Minister. The Whole Town's Talking (GB: Passport to Fame). 1935: *I'm a Father. Vanessa – Her Love Story. Bonnie Scotland. Bride of Frankenstein. The Irish in Us. Water-front Lady. Mutiny on the Bounty. 1936: *Share the Wealth. Laughing Irish Eyes. Forgotten Faces. Stage Struck. Little Lord Fauntleroy. The Lady Consents. Mary of Scotland. Yellowstone. The Plough and the Stars. After the Thin Man. Bullets or Ballots. 1937: Great Guy (GB: Pluck of the Irish). The Man in Blue. Souls at Sea. Meet the Boy Friend. Nancy Steele is Missing. Pick a Star. One Hundred Men and a Girl. Double Wedding. The Great

O'Malley. A Damsel in Distress. Way Out West. Toast of New York. You Can't Have Everything. One-Man Justice. Married Before Breakfast. 1938: Lady Behave. Kidnapped. Gateway. Angels with Dirty Faces. City Streets. The Cowboy from Brooklyn (GB: Romance and Rhythm). Blonde Cheat. Tail Spin. Thanks for Everything. 1939: The Jones Family in Hollywood. Wings of the Navy. Day Time Wife. My Son is Guilty (GB: Crime's End). The Hound of the Baskervilles. Parents on Trial. Captain Fury. She Married a Cop. The Adventures of Sherlock Holmes (GB: Sherlock Holmes). Rulers of the Sea. Joe and Ethel Turp Call on the President. The Marshal of Mesa City. Code of the Streets. Broadway Serenade. †Mr Smith Goes to Washington. The Night of Nights. The Escape. Off the Record. Tell No Tales. Racketeers of the Range. 1940: My Son, My Son. Tear Gas Squad. The Last Alarm. I Take This Oath. Kitty Foyle. No, No, Nanette. When the Daltons Rode. Queen of the Mob. Nobody's Children. Saps at Sea. The Doctor Takes a Wife. Brother Orchid. Women Without Names. Public Deb No. 1. The Invisible Man Returns. 1941: Pot o' Gold (GB: The Golden Hour). How Green Was My Valley. Blue, White and Perfect. The Invisible Woman. Flight from Destiny. Borrowed Hero. It Started with Eve. Riot Squad. Appointment for Love. Double Cross. Unfinished Business. Sealed Lips. Unexpected Uncle. Four Jacks and a Jill. Bombay Clipper. 1942: Sherlock Holmes and the Voice of Terror. Fly by Night. Dr Broadway. Gentleman Jim. Powder Town. Meet the Stewarts. It Happened in Flatbush. Sherlock Holmes and the Secret Weapon. The Mummy's Tomb. Boss of Big Town. Half-Way to Shanghai. The Strange Case of Dr RX. The Pride of the Yankees. 1943: Sherlock Holmes Faces Death. Two Tickets to London. Forever and a Day. Sweet Rosie O'Grady. Here Comes Kelly. Keep 'em Slugging. Sarong Girl. Sherlock Holmes in Washington. Smart Guy. Whispering Footsteps. You're a Lucky Fellow, Mr Smith. Sherlock Holmes and the Spider Woman (GB: Spider Woman). 1944: Ever Since Venus. Million Dollar Kid. Pearl of Death. The Last Ride. Music for Millions. Follow the Leader. The Hour Before the Dawn. Hollywood Canteen. Hat Check Honey. The Racket Man. Secrets of Scotland Yard. Irish Eyes Are Smiling. The Scarlet Claw. 1945: Divorce. The Woman in Green. Strange Confession. See My Lawyer. Captain Eddie. Kitty. Pillow of Death. Pride of the Marines (GB: Forever in Love). The House of Fear. The Body Snatcher. Pursuit to Algiers (GB: Sherlock Holmes in Pursuit to Algiers). 1946: Little Giant (GB: On the Carpet). Sentimental Journey. The Dark Horse. The Hoodlum Saint. Terror by Night. In Fast Company. Sing While You Dance. Dressed to Kill (GB: Sherlock Holmes and the Secret Code). Shadows Over Chinatown. Sister Kenny. Singin' in the Corn (GB: Give and Take). 1947: The Secret Life of Walter Mitty. Stallion Road. Exposed. The Invisible Wall. The Long Night. Angels' Alley. 1948: The Strange Mrs Crane. The Judge Steps Out (GB: Indian Summer). Highway 13. Fort Apache. 1949: Mighty Joe Young. Deputy Marshal. Shamrock Hill. Haunted Trails. The File on Thelma Jordon (GB: Thelma Jordon). 1950: West of Wyoming.

† Scene deleted from final release print

GORDON, Nora(h) 1894–1970

Pudding-faced British small-part actress with red-gold hair and honest if severe features. She followed her character-actor husband Leonard Sharp (1890–1958) into films and appeared sporadically in mother roles in British films over a 25-year period. Her daughter, Dorothy Gordon (1924–) is also an actress. The spelling of her Christian name varies from film to film.

1941: Danny Boy. Facing the Music. Old Mother Riley's Circus. Sheepdog of the Hills. Gert and Daisy's Weekend. South American George. Somewhere in Camp. 1942: Front Line Kids. Old Mother Riley, Detective. 1947: Death in High Heels. Green Fingers. Journey Ahead. The Mark of Cain. My Brother Jonathan. 1948: The Fallen Idol. Good Time Girl. 1949: Floodtide. 1950: The Woman in Question (US: Five Angles on Murder). Blackmailed. 1951: Happy Go Lovely. Circle of Danger. Night Was Our Friend. The Woman's Angle. 1952: Sing Along with Me. Trent's Last Case. 1953: Murder at 3am. Murder by Proxy (Released 1955. US: Blackout). Twice Upon a Time. 1954: Radio Cab Murder. A Kid for Two Farthings. The Glass Cage (US: The Glass Tomb). 1955: The Constant Husband. Police Dog. 1957: Woman in a Dressing Gown. *Day of Grace. 1958: High Jump. 1959: Horrors of the Black Museum. Sapphire. Sentenced for Life. Top Floor Girl. 1960: Compelled. Sons and Lovers. 1961: *The Silent Weapon. Carry On Regardless. The Grass is Greener. The Rebel (US: Call Me Genius). Victim. The Young Ones. The Piper's Tune. 1962: Twice Round the Daffodils. Postman's Knock. Mrs Gibbons' Boys. 1963: Crooks in Cloisters. Heavens Above! 1964: Carry On Spying. The Curse of the Mummy's Tomb. 1965: The Nanny. The Intelligence Men.

GORDON, Ruth
(Ruth G. Jones) 1896–1985

Tiny, sharp-faced American actress and writer who played a couple of leading roles in silents, mothers in the 1940s and aged eccentrics in more recent times. She turned the early part of her life into a play: it was filmed, as The Actress, in 1953. Long married to writer/director Garson Kanin, with whom she wrote several screenplays for Spencer Tracy and Katharine Hepburn. Academy Award (best supporting actress) in 1968 for

Rosemary's Baby. Oscar nominee for *Inside Daisy Clover*. Died from a stroke in her sleep.

*1915: Camille. The Wheel of Life/The Whirl of Life 1939: *Information Please (series 1, number 8). 1940: Abe Lincoln in Illinois (GB: Spirit of the People). Dr Ehrlich's Magic Bullet (GB: The Story of Dr Ehrlich's Magic Bullet). *Information Please (series 2, number 2). 1941: Two-Faced Woman. 1943: Edge of Darkness. Action in the North Atlantic. 1966: Lord Love a Duck. Inside Daisy Clover. 1968: Rosemary's Baby. 1969: Whatever Happened to Aunt Alice? 1970: Where's Poppa? 1972: Harold and Maude. 1973: Isn't It Shocking? (TV). 1975: The Prince of Central Park (TV). 1976: The Big Bus. 1977: The Great Houdinis (TV). Look What's Happened to Rosemary's Baby (TV). Perfect Gentlemen (TV). 1978: Every Which Way But Loose. 1979: Scavenger Hunt. Boardwalk. 1980: Any Which Way You Can. My Bodyguard. Smokey and the Bandit II (GB: Smokey and the Bandit Ride Again). 1982: Don't Go to Sleep (TV). Jimmy the Kid. 1984: Mugsy's Girls/Delta Pi. The Trouble with Spies. 1985: Voyage of the Rock Aliens. Maxie.*

GORSHIN, Frank 1933–
Fair-haired, ferret-faced, sawn-off, Brooklynesque American actor and entertainer with uneven features and cocky grin. At first cast as delinquents and troublemakers, he found his greatest international fame on TV as The Riddler in the cult success of the late 1960s, *Batman*. More recently, he has been seen as a comedy impressionist in night-clubs, and in a variety of low-budget exploitation movies – much the sort of stuff, beefed up to adult rating, that he was making 35 years ago.

1956: The Proud and Profane. Between Heaven and Hell. The True Story of Jesse James (GB: The James Brothers). Hot Rod Girl. 1957: Invasion of the Saucer Men. Dragstrip Girl. Runaway Daughters. Portland Exposé. 1958: Tank Battalion. 1959: Warlock. Night of the Quarter Moon. 1960: Bells Are Ringing. Studs Lonigan. Where the Boys Are. 1961: The Great Impostor. Ring of Fire. The George Raft Story (GB: Spin of a Coin). Sail a Crooked Ship. 1965: That Darn Cat! Ride Beyond Vengeance. 1966: Batman. 1968: Skidoo. 1975: Sky Heist (TV). 1977: Record City. 1979: Death Car on the Freeway (TV). 1981: Underground Aces. 1982: The Uppercrust. 1984: Hot Resort. 1986: Hollywood Vice Squad. 1988: Midnight. 1989: Beverly Hills Bodysnatchers. 1993: The Meteor Man. 1995: After the Game. Fields of Deception. Cul-de-Sac.

GOSS, Helen 1903–
Pleasantly plump, red-haired, full-faced, high-cheekboned, cheerful-looking British actress who played a few barmaids and servants in between concentrating on her other career as a drama coach, notably in charge of the acting side of the Rank 'Charm School' for starlets in post-war years.

1932: Bachelor's Baby. 1934: Important People. 1936: Hail and Farewell. 1937: The Reverse Be My Lot. 1943: Dear Octopus (US: The Randolph Family). 1944: Fanny by Gaslight (US: Man of Evil). 1945: A Place of One's Own. The Wicked Lady. Pink String and Sealing Wax. They Were Sisters. The Rake's Progress. 1947: The Mark of Cain. 1948: My Sister and I. The Weaker Sex. 1949: Stage Fright. 1950: The Woman in Question (GB: Five Angles on Murder). Blackmailed. 1951: Cheer the Brave. Appointment with Venus (US: Island Rescue). Honeymoon Deferred. 1952: Something Money Can't Buy. The Pickwick Papers (US: Outpost in Malaya). 1953: The Sword and the Rose. 1954: Dance Little Lady. The Stranger's Hand. Three Cornered Fate. 1957: Action of the Tiger. 1958: Gideon's Day (US: Gideon of Scotland Yard). Carry On Sergeant. 1959: The Hound of the Baskervilles. 1960: Moment of Danger (US: Malaga). The Two Faces of Dr Jekyll (US: House of Fright). 1965: The Uncle. 1967: Half a Sixpence. 1970: Jane Eyre (TV. GB: cinemas).

GOSSETT, Lou(is) 1936–
Slim, tall, whippy black American actor, balding, then shaven-headed, who struggled for years to make an impact in worthwhile roles while 'wearing loincloths' in a TV series set in Africa. Notice began to be taken of his powerful presence in the 1970s, and the big breakthrough came when he took the Best Supporting Actor Oscar for 1981's *An Officer and a Gentleman*, in a typically forthright role. Sometimes billed as Lou(is) Gossett Jr, he has more recently been seen as a variety of thinking man's action heroes.

1961: A Raisin in the Sun. 1968: The Bush Baby. Companions in Nightmare (TV). 1970: The Landlord. Leo the Last. W.U.S.A. 1971: Skin Game. 1972: Travels with My Aunt. 1973: The Laughing Policeman (GB: An Investigation of Murder). 1974: The White Dawn. It's Good to be Alive (TV). Sidekicks (TV). 1975: Delancey Street: The Crisis Within (TV). 1976: The River Niger (completed 1972). J.D.'s Revenge. The Lazarus Syndrome (TV). 1977: Little Ladies of the Night (TV). The Deep. The Choirboys. 1978: To Kill a Cop (TV). It Rained All Night the Day I Left. The Critical List (TV). 1979: The Man Who Stands Alone/This Man Stands Alone (TV. GB: Lawman Without a Gun). 1981: Don't Look Back (TV). An Officer and a Gentleman. 1982: Benny's Place (TV). 1983: Jaws 3-D. Sadat (TV). 1984: Finders Keepers. The Guardian (TV). 1985: Enemy Mine. The Iron Eagle. 1986: Firewalker. 1987: The Principal. A Gathering of Old Men (TV). 1988: Goodbye Miss 4th of July (TV. GB: Farewell to Freedom). Roots: The Gift (TV). Iron Eagle II. 1989: The Punisher. Gideon Oliver: Sleep Well, Professor Oliver (TV). 1990: Zora is My Name (TV). The Father Clements Story (TV). Sadie and Simpson (cable TV). El Diablo (cable TV). 1991: Toy Soldiers. Iron Eagle III. Keeper of the City. Cover-Up. The Josephine Baker Story (TV). 1992: Diggstown (GB: Midnight Sting). Carolina Skeletons. Liberators. On the Streets of LA (TV). 1993: Genghis Khan. Monolith. 1994: High Lonesome (TV). Ray Alexander: Murder in Mind (TV). A Good Man in Africa. Curse of the Starving Class. Flashfire. 1995: Iron Eagle IV.

GOTELL, Walter 1924–

Bald, severe-looking British actor with low eyebrows and crooked smile who uniquely found time to combine acting, farming and business careers. Acting was the first of these, and he broke into films (before military service) as a young man straight from repertory, sometimes playing youthful Nazi zealots. Later he returned in more 'senior' roles as figures of authority – headmasters, superintendents and an assortment of martinets, a range which stood him in good stead on television. Also became managing director of a group of engineering companies.

*1942: Tomorrow We Live (US: At Dawn We Die). The Goose Steps Out. Secret Mission. The Day Will Dawn (US: The Avengers). 1943: The Night Invader. We Dive at Dawn. 1944: 2,000 Women. 1950: The Wooden Horse. Lilli Marlene. Cairo Road. 1951: The African Queen. The Man with the Twisted Lip. 1953: Albert RN (US: Break to Freedom). Desperate Moment. The Red Beret (US: Paratrooper). Stryker of the Yard. 1954: Duel in the Jungle. *The Mysterious Bullet. The Death of Michael Turbin. 1955: Dial 999 (US: The Way Out). Above Us the Waves. 1956: The Man Who Knew Too Much. 1958: Ice-Cold in Alex (US: Desert Attack). I Was Monty's Double (US: Monty's Double). No Safety Ahead. The Man Inside. 1959: Solomon and Sheba. The Bandit of Zhobe. The Treasure of San Teresa. Shake Hands with the Devil. Sink the Bismarck! 1960: Conspiracy of Hearts. The Two Faces of Dr Jekyll (US: House of Fright). Moment of Danger (US: Malaga). Circus of Horrors. Circle of Deception. 1961: The Guns of Navarone. The Devil's Daffodil (US: The Daffodil Killers. And German-language version). The Damned (US: These Are the Damned). 1962: 55 Days at Peking. Lancelot and Guinevere (US: Sword of Lancelot). The Road to Hong Kong. The Devil's Agent. 1963: From Russia with Love. The Million Dollar Collar. 1964: Lord Jim. 1965: The Spy Who Came in from the Cold. 1967: Attack on the Iron Coast. 1968: Cry Wolf. 1969: The File of the Golden Goose. 1971: Endless Night. 1972: Our Miss Fred. 1976: Black Sunday. 1977: The Assignment. The Spy Who Loved Me. March or Die. 1978: The Stud. The Boys from Brazil. 1979: Moonraker. The London Connection (US: TV, as The Omega Connection). Cuba. 1980: Cry of the Innocent (TV). 1981: For Your Eyes Only. 1983: Memed My Hawk. Octopussy. The Scar-*

let and the Black (TV). 1985: KGB: The Secret War (later: Lethal). A View to a Kill. Up the Military/Basic Training. 1986: The Shadow of Harry (TV). Liberty (TV). Charley Hannah (TV). 1987: The Living Daylights. 1988: Sleeping Camp 2: Unhappy Campers. 1989: She Knows Too Much. 1990: Wings of Fame. 1991: The Pope Must Die (US: The Pope Must Diet). Puppet Master 3.

GOUGH, Michael 1917–

Thin-lipped, Malaya-born actor of unwavering gaze, in British films from 1947: He moved from dark, sensitive, intense young men in the 1940s to more outright villains, and then along the Peter Cushing trail to leading roles in horror films, mostly as scientists whose creations got the better of them. In smaller roles since the end of the 1960s, notably as Michael Keaton/Val Kilmer's man-servant in the *Batman* films.

1947: Blanche Fury. Anna Karenina. 1948: Bond Street. Saraband for Dead Lovers (US: Saraband). The Small Back Room (US: Hour of Glory). 1950: Blackmailed. Ha'penny Breeze. 1951: No Resting Place. The Man in the White Suit. Night Was Our Friend. 1953: Twice Upon a Time. Rob Roy the Highland Rogue. The Sword and the Rose. 1955: Richard III. 1956: Reach for the Sky. 1957: Ill Met by Moonlight (US: Night Ambush). The House in the Woods. 1958: Dracula (US: The Horror of Dracula). The Horse's Mouth. 1959: Model for Murder. Horrors of the Black Museum. 1961: Konga. Mr Topaze (US: I Like Money). What a Carve-Up! (US: Home Sweet Homicide). 1962: Candidate for Murder. The Phantom of the Opera. 1963: Black Zoo. Tamahine. 1964: Dr Terror's House of Horrors. 1965: Game for Three Losers. The Skull. 1967: They Came from Outer Space. Berserk! 1968: Un soir, un train. Curse of the Crimson Altar (US: Crimson Cult). 1969: Women in Love. A Walk with Love and Death. 1970: Julius Caesar. Trog. The Corpse. 1971: The Go-Between. 1972: Henry VIII and His Six Wives. Vincent the Dutchman. 1973: Horror Hospital. The Legend of Hell House. 1974: Galileo. QB VII (TV). Monet in London (narrator only). 1976: Satan's Slave. 1978: The Boys from Brazil. 1979: L'amour en question. 1981: Venom. 1982: Witness for the Prosecution (TV). 1983: Memed My Hawk. The Dresser. Arthur the King (TV. Released 1985). 1984: A Christmas Carol (TV.

GB: cinemas). Top Secret! Oxford Blues. 1985: Out of Africa. Hard Travelling (TV). Stranger than Fiction (voice only). 1986: Shattered Spirits (TV). Caravaggio. 1987: Maschenka. The Fourth Protocol. 1988: The Serpent and the Rainbow. The Mountain and the Molehill (TV). 1989: Strapless. Batman. 1990: The Shell Seekers (TV). The Garden (narrator only). 1991: 'Let Him Have It'. 1992: Batman Returns. 1993: Wittgenstein. Nostradamus. The Age of Innocence. 1994: Uncovered. 1995: Batman Forever.

GOULD, Harold 1923–

Silver-haired, often moustachioed, roguish-looking, smooth American actor, an avuncular version of Groucho Marx. After an early career (until 1960) as a drama lecturer at a California university, he moved full-time to acting, became a prolific performer on television and proved equally at home in comedy or (tightening the lips and screwing up the eyes) more serious drama. His wolfish smile became familiar to millions of TV viewers with his role as Martin Morgenstern during the five-year run of the series *Rhoda*. Sometimes billed as Harold J Gould.

1961: Two for the Seesaw. 1962: The Couch. 1963: The Yellow Canary. 1964: The Satan Bug. Ready for the People. Marnie. The Spy with My Face. Inside Daisy Clover. 1966: Harper (GB: The Moving Target). An American Dream (GB: See You in Hell, Darling). 1967: Project X. 1969: The Arrangement. He and She. 1970: The Lawyer. 1971: Ransom for a Dead Man (TV. GB: cinemas). Mrs Pollifax – Spy. Where Does It Hurt? A Death of Innocence (TV). 1973: The Sting. Murdock's Gang (TV). 1974: The Front Page. 1975: The Strongest Man in the World. Medical Story (TV). Love and Death. 1976: The Big Bus. How to Break Up a Happy Divorce (TV). Gus. Silent Movie. The Feather and Father Gang (TV). 1977: The One and Only. 1979: 11th Victim (TV). Better Late Than Never (TV). Aunt Mary (TV). The Man in the Santa Claus Suit (TV). 1980: King Crab (TV). Seems Like Old Times. Kenny Rogers as The Gambler (TV). The Scarlett O'Hara War (TV). The Silent Lovers (TV). 1982: Born to be Sold (TV). Help Wanted: Male (TV). 1983: Kenny Rogers as The Gambler – Part II: The Adventure Continues (TV). 1984: The Red-Light Sting (TV). Mrs Delafield Wants to Marry (TV). Playing for

Keeps. The Dream Chasers. 1985: The Fourth Wise Man (TV). 1989: Get Smart, Again (TV). Romero. 1991: Birch Street Gym. 1995: Flesh Suitcase.

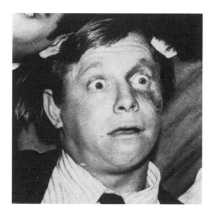

GRABOWSKI, Norman 1933–

Gorilla-like, pale-eyed, snub-nosed American cameo actor with close-cropped fair hair, a former pro football player and creator of customised cars who came to films in the late 1950s and played amiable, sometimes aggressive dimwits in teen exploitation films and Disney comedies. Sometimes billed as Norm Grabowski, or simply Grabowski, or Norman 'Woo Woo' Grabowski.

1958: Darby's Rangers. High School Confidential! 1959: The Beat Generation. Girls' Town. 1960: College Confidential. Sex Kittens Go to College. 1961: The Chapman Report. The Honeymoon Machine. 1963: Son of Flubber. 1964: The Misadventures of Merlin Jones. Roustabout. 1965: Sergeant Deadhead/ Sergeant Deadhead, the Astronut! The Monkey's Uncle. 1966: Out of Sight. 1967: The Gnome-Mobile. The Happiest Millionaire. Blackbeard's Ghost. 1968: The Horse in the Gray Flannel Suit. 1973: Herbie Rides Again. The Naked Ape. 1974: The Towering Inferno. 1978: Hooper. 1981: The Cannonball Run.

GRANT, Richard E 1957–

Tall, long-faced, basilisk-eyed, dark-haired, Swaziland-born actor with high forehead, in Britain since 1982 after education and early acting experience in South Africa. His open-mouthed expression can adapt quickly to contempt, menace, determination or self-satisfaction at the drop of a line and, despite several leading roles, he has proved equally, if not more adept with top featured roles demanding waspish qualities.

1985: Honest, Decent and True (TV). 1986: Withnail and I. 1987: Hidden City. 1988: Warlock. 1989: How to Get Ahead in Advertising. Killing Dad. Thieves in the Night (TV). Mountains of the Moon. 1990: Henry and June. 1991: L.A. Story. Hudson Hawk. 1992: The Player. Bram Stoker's Dracula. 1993: *Franz Kafka's It's a Wonderful Life (TV). Posse. The Age of Innocence. 1994: An Awfully Big Adventure. Prêt-à-Porter. (US: Ready to Wear). 1995: The Cold Light of Day. Jack and Sarah.

GRAPEWIN, Charley 1869–1956

Solidly-built American actor, playwright, composer and author who came to Hollywood when he was past 60, and must have delighted himself, as well as audiences, by prolonging his career for a further 15 years as the prototype of wise, wheezy, elderly relations. Remembered by most as Grandpa Joad in The Grapes of Wrath, but also by series fans as Inspector Queen in the Ellery Queen crime thrillers of the early 1940s.

1902: Above the Limit. 1929: *Ladies' Choice. *That Red-Headed Hussy. The Shannons of Broadway. *Jed's Vacation. 1930: Only Saps Work. 1931: The Millionaire. Gold Dust Gertie (GB: Why Change Your Husband?) 1932: Hell's House. No Man of Her Own. Disorderly Conduct. Lady and Gent. The Woman in Room 13. American Madness. Huddle (GB: Impossible Lover). The Washington Masquerade (GB: Mad Masquerade). The Night of June 13th. Wild Horse Mesa. Big Timer. 1933: Hello, Everybody! The Kiss Before the Mirror. Midnight Mary. Beauty for Sale. Don't Bet on Love. Pilgrimage. Wild Boys of the Road (GB: Dangerous Days). Heroes for Sale. Torch Singer (GB: Broadway Singer). Hell and High Water (GB: Cap'n Jericho). Turn Back the Clock. Female. 1934: Anne of Green Gables. Judge Priest. The Quitter. The Loudspeaker (GB: The Radio Star). Caravan. She Made Her Bed. Two Alone. Return of the Terror. 1935: The President Vanishes (GB: Strange Conspiracy). King Solomon of Broadway. Alice Adams.

Shanghai. Eight Bells. Party Wire. In Spite of Danger. One Frightened Night. Ah, Wilderness! Superspeed. Rendezvous. 1936: The Petrified Forest. Sinner Take All. Small Town Girl. The Voice of Bugle Ann. Libeled Lady. Without Orders. 1937: The Good Earth. A Family Affair. Captains Courageous. Between Two Women. Bad Man of Brimstone. The Big City. Broadway Melody of 1938. Bad Guy. 1938: Three Comrades. Girl of the Golden West. Of Human Hearts. Three Loves Has Nancy. Listen, Darling. Artists and Models Abroad (GB: Stranded in Paris). 1939: Stand Up and Fight. The Wizard of Oz. Burn 'em Up O'Connor. Sabotage (GB: Spies at Work). Hero for a Day. The Man Who Dared. Sudden Money. Dust Be My Destiny. I Am Not Afraid. 1940: Texas Rangers Ride Again. Ellery Queen, Master De-ective. Johnny Apollo. Earthbound. The Grapes of Wrath. Rhythm on the River. 1941: Ellery Queen's Penthouse Mystery. Ellery Queen and the Murder Ring (GB: The Murder Ring). Ellery Queen and the Perfect Crime (GB: The Perfect Crime). They Died with Their Boots On. Tobacco Road. 1942: Enemy Agents Meet Ellery Queen (GB: The Lido Mystery). A Close Call for Ellery Queen (GB: A Close Call). Crash Dive. A Desperate Chance for Ellery Queen (GB: A Desperate Chance). 1944: Follow the Boys. Atlantic City. The Impatient Years. 1947: Gunfighters (GB: The Assassin). 1948: The Enchanted Valley. 1949: Will James' Sand (GB: Sand). 1951: When I Grow Up.

GRAY, Charles

(Donald Gray) 1928–

Fair-haired British actor with large, square head and fruity tones, a dab hand at smug and supercilious characters who sometimes progressed to top-grade villainy (as with his Blofeld in Diamonds Are Forever). Even when he was affable and hearty, you felt he was faking, and the lack of further film roles for his distinctive personality was the cinema's loss. Also the 'voice' for Jack Hawkins in several films after he had lost the use of his own.

1957: I Accuse! 1959: Tommy the Toreador. Follow a Star. The Desperate Man. 1960: The Entertainer. 1961: Man in the Moon. 1965: Masquerade. 1966: The Night of the Generals. 1967: You Only Live Twice. The Man Outside. The Secret War of Harry Frigg. 1968: The Devil Rides Out (US: The Devil's Bride). The

File of the Golden Goose. Mosquito Squadron. 1970: The Excutioner. Cromwell. 1971: Diamonds Are Forever. 1974: The Beast Must Die! 1975: The Rocky Horror Picture Show. 1976: Seven Nights in Japan. The Seven Per Cent Solution. 1977: Silver Bears. 1978: The Legacy. 1979: The House on Garibaldi Street (TV. GB: cinemas). 1980: The Mirror Crack'd. 1981: Shock Treatment. 1982: Charles and Diana, a Royal Love Story (TV). 1983: The Jigsaw Man. 1990: Harry and Harriet.

GREEN, Danny 1903–1973
Thickly-built, balding, tough-looking British actor. Born in the East End of London (within the sound of Bow Bells; a true cockney), he was typecast as hulking thugs and few cinemagoers ever knew his name until, in his early fifties, he was cast as One Round in the famous black comedy *The Ladykillers*. After that, he went back to playing mainly small roles until his retirement in 1968. Spent several years in America as a boy, and is said to have appeared in a couple of silent films there.

1929: Atlantic. The Silent House. The Crooked Billet. 1934: Things Are Looking Up. 1936: Crime Over London. 1937: Gangway. Midnight Menace (US: Bombs Over London). Non-Stop New York. Knight Without Armour. The Squeaker (US: Murder on Diamond Row). Silver Blaze (US: Murder at the Baskervilles). Jericho (US: Dark Sands). 1938: Hey! Hey! USA. 1940: 'Bulldog' Sees It Through. 1944: Fiddlers Three. Welcome Mr Washington. Madonna of the Seven Moons. 1945: The Echo Murders. 1947: Dancing with Crime. The Man Within (US: The Smugglers). 1948: Good Time Girl. No Orchids for Miss Blandish. 1949: Three Bags Full. Helter Skelter. 1950: Someone at the Door. The Lady Craved Excitement. State Secret (US: The Great Manhunt). Her Favourite Husband (US: The Taming of Dorothy). Once a Sinner. Mr Drake's Duck. 1951: A Tale of Five Cities (US: A Tale of Five Women). Whispering Smith Hits London (US: Whispering Smith versus Scotland Yard). 1952: Little Big Shot. 1953: Top of the Form. Laughing Anne. 1954: A Kid for Two Farthings. 1955: Jumping for Joy. The Ladykillers. 1956: Assignment Redhead (US: Requirement for a Redhead). Interpol (US: Pickup Alley). Seven Waves Away (US: Abandon Ship!). 1958: A Tale of Two Cities. The 7th Voyage of Sinbad.

Hidden Homicide. 1959: Beyond This Place (US: Web of Evidence). In the Wake of a Stranger. 1960: Girls of Latin Quarter. Man in the Moon. 1962: The Fast Lady. The Old Dark House. 1963: A Stitch in Time. 1966: Doctor in Clover. 1967: Smashing Time. 1968: The Fixer.

GREEN, Nigel 1924–1972
South Africa-born dark-haired actor of smooth, saturnine, superior features, in British films from the early 1950s after theatrical experience. He began playing much larger roles after *Zulu* (1963), and came close to becoming a star in the late 1960s. Died from an accidental overdose of sleeping pills. Formerly married to actress Patricia Marmont.

1953: Meet Mr Malcolm. 1954: Stranger from Venus (US: Immediate Decision). The Sea Shall Not Have Them. 1955: As Long As They're Happy. 1956: Reach for the Sky. Find the Lady. 1957: Bitter Victory. The Gypsy and the Gentleman. 1958: Corridors of Blood (released 1961). 1959: Witness in the Dark. Beat Girl (US: Wild for Kicks). The League of Gentlemen. 1960: The Criminal (US: The Concrete Jungle). Too Hot to Handle (US: Playgirl After Dark). Sword of Sherwood Forest. Gorgo. The Queen's Guards. 1961: The Man at the Carlton Tower. Pit of Darkness. The Spanish Sword. 1962: The Primitives. The Durant Affair. Mysterious Island. Playback. The Man Who Finally Died. Mystery Submarine (US: Decoy). The Prince and the Pauper. 1963: Jason and the Argonauts. Zulu. Saturday Night Out. 1964: The Masque of the Red Death. 1965: The Ipcress File. The Face of Fu Manchu. The Skull. 1966: Khartoum. Deadlier Than the Male. Let's Kill Uncle. Tobruk. 1967: Africa—Texas Style! 1968: Play Dirty. Fräulein Doktor. The Pink Jungle. The Wrecking Crew. 1969: The Kremlin Letter. 1970: Countess Dracula. 1971: The Ruling Class. 1973: Gawain and the Green Knight.

GREENWOOD, Charlotte
(Frances C. Greenwood) 1890–1978
Tall, horsey-faced but happy-looking American actress and eccentric dancer, with hearty, no-nonsense voice. She played plain Janes in her early days, then moved on to character roles in comedies and musicals and became internationally known for her long-legged, high-kicking dance routines.

At her best while under contract to Fox in the early 1940s, but also notable as Aunt Eller in *Oklahoma!* One could hardly believe her when she boomed 'That's about as far as I can go' at the end of one of her routines.

1915: Jane. 1928: Baby Mine. 1929: So Long, Letty. 1930: *Love Your Neighbor. *Girls Will Be Boys. 1931: Parlor, Bedroom and Bath (GB: Romeo in Pyjamas). Palmy Days. Stepping Out. Flying High (GB: Happy Landing). The Man in Possession. 1932: Cheaters at Play. 1933: Orders is Orders. 1940: Young People. Star Dust. Down Argentine Way. 1941: Moon Over Miami. Tall, Dark and Handsome. 1942: The Perfect Snob. Springtime in the Rockies. 1943: Dixie Dugan. The Gang's All Here (GB: The Girls He Left Behind). 1944: Up In Mabel's Room. Home in Indiana. 1946: Wake Up and Dream. 1947: Driftwood. 1949: The Great Dan Patch. Oh, You Beautiful Doll. 1950: Peggy. 1953: Dangerous When Wet. 1955: Oklahoma! 1956: The Opposite Sex. Glory.

GREGG, Everley 1888–1959
Very dark-haired, moon-faced British actress of strong personality. After long theatrical experience, she made a striking film debut as the nagging Catherine Parr, the king's last wife in *The Private Life of Henry VIII*. Films called her back from time to time, though her raised eyebrows and thin upper lip were progressively seen in more routine roles. But a tally of only 45 feature films in 25 years speaks volumes of her affection for the theatre.

1933: The Private Life of Henry VIII. 1935: The Scoundrel. The Ghost Goes West. 1936: Thunder in the City. 1938: Blondes for Danger. Pygmalion. 1939: Spies of the Air. 1941: Major Barbara. Freedom Radio (US: A Voice in the Night). 1942: Uncensored. In Which We Serve. The First of the Few (US: Spitfire). 1943: The Demi-Paradise (US: Adventure for Two). The Gentle Sex. 1944: *The Two Fathers. This Happy Breed. 1945: Brief Encounter. 1946: Gaiety George (US: Showtime). Great Expectations. I See a Dark Stranger (US: The Adventuress). Piccadilly Incident. 1947: The Woman in the Hall. 1949: Marry Me! The Huggetts Abroad. Stage Fright. 1950: The Astonished Heart. The Woman in Question (US: Five Angles on Murder). The Franchise Affair. 1951: The Magic Box. Worm's Eye View. 1952: Moulin Rouge. Stolen Face. *A Spot of Bother. *The Paper Chase. *A Sweeping Statement. *Shedding the Load *Food for Thought. *Height of Ambition. 1953: Genevieve. The Blakes Slept Here. 1954: The Night of the Full Moon. Father Brown (US: The Detective). 1955: Lost (US: Tears for Simon). The Man Who Never Was. 1956: Brothers in Law. The Hostage. 1957: Carry On Admiral (US: The Ship Was Loaded). *Danger List. 1958: Room at the Top. Bachelor of Hearts. 1959: Deadly Record.

GREGORY, James 1911–
American actor with distinctive, receding dark, wavy hair, slightly reminiscent of Joseph Cotten. His film career was slow to start after he switched from stockbroking to acting in the post-war years, but in latter days he became one of television's most frequent and efficient guest stars in drama series. His gruff voice and soothing manner often concealed villainous instincts, but he also played friendly advisers and unbending superiors. Has made up for his late start by notching up almost 40 years as an actor.

1948: The Naked City. 1951: The Frogmen. 1956: Nightfall. The Scarlet Hour. The Big Caper. 1957: Gun Glory. The Young Stranger. 1958: Underwater Warrior. Onionhead. 1959: Al Capone. Hey Boy! Hey Girl! 1961: X-15. 1962: Two Weeks in Another Town. The Manchurian Candidate. PT 109. 1963: Twilight of Honor (GB: The Charge is Murder). The Great Escape. Captain Newman MD. 1964: A Distant Trumpet. Quick, Before it Melts. A

Rage to Live. 1965: The Sons of Katie Elder. 1966: The Silencers. Murderers' Row. 1967: The Secret War of Harry Frigg. The Ambushers. Clambake. 1968: Hawaii Five-O (TV). 1969: The Love God? Beneath the Planet of the Apes. 1970: The Hawaiians (GB: Master of the Islands). 1971: Shoot Out. Million Dollar Duck. 1972: The Late Liz. A Very Missing Person (TV). The Weekend Nun (TV). 1973: Miracle on 34th Street (TV). 1975: The Strongest Man in the World. The Abduction of Saint Anne/ They've Kidnapped Anne Benedict (TV). 1976: Francis Gary Powers: The True Story of the U-2 Spy Incident (TV). 1979: The Main Event. 1980: The Comeback Kid (TV). The Great American Traffic Jam (TV). 1981: Goldie and the Boxer Go to Hollywood. 1983: Wait 'Til Your Mother Gets Home (TV). The Flight of Dragons (voice only).

GRENFELL, Joyce
(J. Phipps) 1910–1979
Toothy, engaging, dark-haired British monologuist, originally from stage revue. Once described herself as 'about eight feet tall with a face like a reflection in a spoon'. Her crisp, fruity upper-class voice and ability to create a delightful range of ever-so-English characters was much underused by the cinema. Died from cancer.

1941: *A Letter from Home. 1943: The Lamp Still Burns. The Demi-Paradise (US: Adventure for Two). 1946: While the Sun Shines. 1948: *Designing Women. Alice in Wonderland (voice only). 1949: Poet's Pub. Scrapbook for 1933 (voice only). A Run for Your Money. Stage Fright. 1950: The Happiest Days of Your Life. 1951: The Galloping Major. Laughter in Paradise. The Magic Box. 1952: The Pickwick Papers. 1953: Genevieve. The Million Pound Note (US: Man With a Million). 1954: Forbidden Cargo. The Belles of St Trinian's. 1957: The Good Companions. Blue Murder at St Trinian's. 1958: Happy is the Bride! 1960: The Pure Hell of St Trinian's. 1962: The Old Dark House. 1964: The Yellow Rolls Royce. The Americanization of Emily.

GRIFFIES, Ethel
(E. Woods) 1878–1975
Severe-looking, tight-lipped, brown-haired, often bespectacled British actress, mainly in Hollywood since 1924 with sporadic intervals for appearances in British and American

theatres. On stage at two, she was still treading the boards at 87. She could play frail and vulnerable, or fierce and disapproving; made several stage appearances as the ill-fated Mrs Bramson in Night Must Fall, but did not take the role in either film version. Died following a stroke.

1917: The Cost of a Kiss. 1921: Hard Cash. 1930: Old English. Chances/Changes. Stepdaughters. 1931: Manhattan Parade. Once a Lady. The Road to Singapore. Waterloo Bridge. The Millionaire. 1932: Love Me Tonight. The Impatient Maiden. Westward Passage. Are You Listening? Union Depot (GB: Gentleman for a Day). Lovers Courageous. Devil's Lottery. Payment Deferred. 1933: Tonight Is Ours. A Lady's Profession. Alice in Wonderland. Midnight Club. Torch Singer. White Woman. Doctor Bull. Bombshell (GB: Blonde Bombshell). Looking Forward (GB: Service). The House of Rothschild. Horseplay. 1934: Bulldog Drummond Strikes Back. We Live Again. Of Human Bondage. Jane Eyre. Olsen's Big Moment. Sadie McKee. Fog. Four Frightened People. The Painted Veil. Call It Luck. 1935: Vanessa: Her Love Story. Hold 'Em Yale (GB: Uniform Lovers). The Werewolf of London. Anna Karenina. The Return of Peter Grimm. Enchanted April. The Mysterious Mr Davis (US: My Partner, Mr Davis). The Mystery of Edwin Drood. Twice Branded. 1936: Guilty Melody. Not So Dusty. 1937: A Yank at Oxford. Kathleen Mavourneen (US: Kathleen). Over the Moon (released 1940). 1938: Crackerjack (US: The Man With A Hundred Faces). 1939: The Star Maker. I'm from Missouri. We Are Not Alone. 1940: Vigil in the Night. Anne of Windy Poplars (GB: Anne of Windy Willows). The Stranger on the Third Floor. Irene. Waterloo Bridge (and 1931 version). 1941: Great Guns. Dead Men Tell. Time to Kill. A Yank in the RAF. How Green Was My Valley. Billy the Kid. Man at Large. Remember the Day. 1942: Between Us Girls. Mrs Wiggs of the Cabbage Patch. Castle in the Desert. Son of Fury. The Postman Didn't Ring. 1943: Shadow of a Doubt. Forever and a Day. Holy Matrimony. First Comes Courage. Jane Eyre (and 1934 version). 1944: Music for Millions. The White Cliffs of Dover. Pardon My Rhythm. The Keys of the Kingdom. Tonight and Every Night. 1945: The Thrill of a Romance. Molly and Me. The Horn Blows at Midnight. Uncle Harry/The Strange Affair of Uncle Harry. Saratoga Trunk. 1946: Devotion (completed 1943). Sing While You Dance. 1947: Millie's Daughter. The Homestretch. Forever Amber. The Brasher Doubloon (GB: The High Window). 1963: Billy Liar! The Birds. 1965: Bus Riley's Back in Town.

GRIFFITH, Hugh 1912–1980

Fiercely-staring, bushy-browed, chubby-cheeked Welsh actor noted for extravagantly scene-stealing character portraits on both British and international scenes. A former bank clerk, he switched to acting in his middle-twenties. Won an Academy Award (best supporting actor) in 1959 for his portrayal of the Sheikh in Ben-Hur. Also Oscar nominated for Tom Jones.

1940: Neutral Port. 1941: Freedom Radio (US: A Voice in the Night). 1947: The Silver Darlings. 1948: So Evil My Love. The Three Weird Sisters. The First Gentleman (US: Affairs of a Rogue). London Belongs to Me (US: Dulcimer Street). 1949: The Last Days of Dolwyn (US: Woman of Dolwyn). Kind Hearts and Coronets. Dr Morelle – The Case of the Missing Heiress. A Run for Your Money. Scrapbook for 1933 (voice only). 1950: Gone to Earth (US: The Wild Heart). 1951: The Galloping Major. Laughter in Paradise. 1953: The Million Pound Note (US: Man with a Million). The Beggar's Opera. The Titfield Thunderbolt. 1954: The Sleeping Tiger. *Outpost. 1955: Passage Home. 1957: The Good Companions. Lucky Jim. 1959: Ben-Hur. 1960: Exodus. The Story on Page One. The Day They Robbed the Bank of England. 1961: The Counterfeit Traitor. 1962: Mutiny on the Bounty. Term of Trial. The Inspector (US: Lisa). 1963: Hide and Seek. Tom Jones. 1964: The Bargee. 1965: The Amorous Adventures of Moll Flanders. 1966: Dare I Weep, Dare I Mourn. The Evil Eye. How to Steal a Million. Oh Dad, Poor Dad, Mama's Hung You in the Closet and I'm Feeling So Sad. The Poppy Is Also a Flower (GB: Danger Grows Wild). 1967: The Chastity Belt. Sailor from Gibraltar. Il mario è l'ammazzo quando mi pare. 1968: Oliver! The Fixer. 1969: Cry of the Banshee. Start the Revolution without Me. 1970: Wuthering Heights. 1971: The Abominable Dr Phibes. Whoever Slew Auntie Roo? (US: Who Slew Auntie Roo?). The Canterbury Tales. 1972: Dr Phibes Rises Again. What? 1973: Take Me High. Craze. The Final Programme (US: The Last Days of Man on Earth). Crescete e molti-

plicatavi. Luther. The House in Nightmare Park (US: Crazy House). 1974: Legend of the Werewolf. Cugini carnali (GB: The Visitor). 1975: Bridges to Heaven. 1976: Joseph Andrews. The Passover Plot. 1977: The Hound of the Baskervilles. The Last Remake of Beau Geste. Casanova & Co (GB: The Rise and Rise of Casanova). 1978: Grand Slam (TV). 1980: The Biggest Bank Robbery/A Nightingale Sang in Berkeley Square (made for cinemas but shown only on TV).

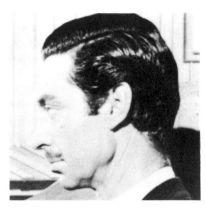

GRIFFITH, James 1916–1993

Lean, laconic, lazy-lidded, slack-jawed, black-haired, drawling American actor who got his best roles in the early 1950s when, playing a series of true-life westerners, he stole scenes from the stars and edged up to third place on the cast list. Griffith's talent was too unusual to succeed on this level for long, however, and he slipped back into smaller roles. A musician with Spike Jones' band in the late forties, he died from cancer.

1944: Pardon My Rhythm. 1948: Blonde Ice. Appointment with Murder. Every Girl Should Be Married. 1949: Search for Danger. Daughter of the West. Fighting Man of the Plains. Oh, You Beautiful Doll! Holiday Affair. Alaska Patrol. Young Man with a Horn (GB: Young Man of Music). 1950: The Breaking Point. The Petty Girl (GB: Girl of the Year). Indian Territory. Bright Leaf. The Cariboo Trail. Double Deal. The Great Missouri Raid. In a Lonely Place. 1951: As Young As You Feel. Apache Drums. The Lady Pays Off. Rhubarb. Drums in the Deep South. Goodbye My Fancy. Payment on Demand. Al Jennings of Oklahoma. Chain of Circumstance. Inside the Walls of Folsom Prison. 1952: Eight Iron Men. Red Skies of Montana. Ma and Pa Kettle at the Fair. Wait 'Til the Sun Shines, Nellie. 1953: No Escape. Powder River. The Kid from Left Field. Botany Bay. Kansas Pacific. A Lion is in the Streets. Ride Clear of Diablo. 1954: The Boy from Oklahoma. Jesse James vs the Daltons. The Black Dakotas. The Law vs Billy the Kid. The Shanghai Story. Masterson of Kansas. Dragnet. Drum Beat. Day of Triumph. Rails into Laramie. 1955: Son of Sinbad. I Cover the Underworld. Apache Ambush. Count Three and Pray. The Kentuckian. Phantom of the Jungle (TV. GB: cinemas). At Gunpoint! (GB: Gunpoint!). 1956: The Killing. Anything Goes. Tribute to a Bad Man. The First Texan. Rebel

in Town. Domino Kid. Overnight Haul (TV. GB: cinemas). 1957: Raintree County. The Guns of Fort Petticoat. The Vampire. Omar Khayyam. 1958: Return to Warbow. The Man from God's Country. Bullwhip. Seven Guns to Mesa. 1959: Frontier Gun. The Big Fisherman. The Amazing Transparent Man. 1960: North to Alaska. Spartacus. 1961: Pocketful of Miracles. 1962: How the West Was Won. 1963: Advance to the Rear (GB: Company of Cowards). 1964: Lorna. 1965: Motor Psycho. 1966: A Big Hand for the Little Lady (GB: Big Deal at Dodge City). 1968: The Face of Eve (US: Eve). Day of the Evil Gun. Heaven with a Gun. 1969: Seven in Darkness (TV). Hail, Hero! 1970: Dial Hot Line (TV). 1971: Vanishing Point. 1974: Seven Alone. Hitchhike! (TV). 1975: Not My Daughter. Babe (TV). 1976: Flood! (TV. GB: cinemas). 1977: Speedtrap. 1978: Dynamo. Desperate Women (TV). 1979: The Main Event. 1980: The Legend of Sleepy Hollow (TV).

GRIFFITH, Kenneth 1921–

Small, dark Welsh actor who has often played weasels, or shiftless young men who coveted the heroine but couldn't have her. He had a series of meaty top supporting roles in the immediate post-war years, but from 1954 was seen in much smaller parts. His characters have remained largely unsympathetic, if more effete, and he has also gained a reputation as a TV historian on famous battles.

1940: *Channel Incident. The Farmer's Wife. 1941: Love on the Dole. Hard Steel. The Black Sheep of Whitehall. 1942: The Great Mr Handel. 1946: The Shop at Sly Corner (US: The Code of Scotland Yard). 1947: Fame is the Spur. 1948: Bond Street. Forbidden. 1949: Blue Scar. Helter Skelter. 1950: Waterfront (US: Waterfront Women). The Starfish. 1951: High Treason. 1954: 36 Hours (US: Terror Street). The Green Buddha. Track the Man Down. 1955: The Prisoner. 1984. Private's Progress. 1956: The Baby and the Battleship. Tiger in the Smoke. Brothers in Law. 1957: Lucky Jim. Blue Murder at St Trinian's. The Naked Truth (US: Your Past is Showing!). 1958: A Night to Remember. The Man Upstairs. Chain of Events. The Two-Headed Spy. 1959: Tiger Bay. Carlton-Browne of the FO (US: Man in a Cocked Hat). I'm All Right, Jack. Libel. Expresso Bongo. 1960: Circus of Horrors. Snowball. A French Mistress. Suspect

(US: *The Risk*). 1961: *Rag Doll. Payroll. The Frightened City. Only Two Can Play. The Painted Smile.* 1962: *We Joined the Navy.* 1963: *Heavens Above!* 1965: *Rotten to the Core.* 1966: *The Whisperers.* 1967: *Great Catherine. The Bobo.* 1968: *Decline and Fall . . . of a Birdwatcher! The Lion in Winter. The Assassination Bureau.* 1969: *The Gamblers.* 1970: *Jane Eyre* (TV. GB: *cinemas*). 1971: *Revenge.* 1973: *The House in Nightmare Park.* 1974: *Callan. S*P*Y*S.* 1976: *Sky Riders. Why Shoot the Teacher?* 1978: *The Wild Geese.* 1980: *The Sea Wolves.* 1981: *Berlin Tunnel 21* (TV). 1982: *Who Dares Wins* (US: *The Final Option*). *Remembrance.* 1983: *The Zany Adventures of Robin Hood* (TV). 1993: *Four Weddings and a Funeral.* 1995: *The Englishman Who Went Up a Hill, But Came Down a Mountain. Hidden Memories.*

GUARDINO, Harry 1925–

Worried-looking, dark-haired American actor whose early career gave him a lot of struggle but few parts. Much busier from 1958 onwards; he hasn't quite made the most of the best opportunities that have come his way, remaining a face to which one may have a little difficulty in putting the name. Heavily employed as TV guest star.

1951: *Purple Heart Diary* (GB: *No Time for Tears*). *Sirocco.* 1952: *Flesh and Fury.* 1955: *The Big Tip-Off. Hold Back Tomorrow.* 1958: *Houseboat.* 1959: *The Five Pennies. The Killers of Mussolini* (TV). *Pork Chop Hill. Made in Japan* (TV). *Five Branded Women.* 1961: *King of Kings. The Pigeon That Took Rome.* 1962: *Hell is for Heroes!* 1964: *Rhino!* 1965: *The Adventures of Bullwhip Griffin.* 1966: *Moving Target* (TV). *Operazione San Gennaro* (US: *The Treasure of San Gennaro*). 1967: *Valley of Mystery.* 1968: *Jigsaw. Madigan. The Hell with Heroes.* 1969: *Lovers and Other Strangers. The Lonely Profession* (TV). 1971: *Red Sky at Morning. Octaman. Dirty Harry. Slingshot. The Last Child* (TV). 1973: *They Only Kill Their Masters.* 1972: *Partners in Crime* (TV). *Police Story* (TV. GB: *cinemas*). 1974: *Get Christie Love!* (TV). *Indict and Convict* (TV). 1975: *Capone. Whiffs* (GB: *C.A.S.H.*). 1976: *St Ives. Having Babies* (TV). *The Enforcer.* 1977: *Contract on Cherry Street* (TV). *Street Killing* (TV). *Rollercoaster.* 1978: *Pleasure Cove* (TV). *Blue Orchids. Matilda. No Margin for Error* (TV). 1979: *Goldengirl.* 1980: *Any Which*

Way You Can. 1983: *The Lonely Guy.* 1989: *The Neon Empire.* 1991: *Under Surveillance.* 1992: *Fist of Honor.*

GUILFOYLE, Paul 1902–1961

Sinewy, dark-haired American actor whose close-set, unfriendly-looking features consigned him to playing whining runts and treacherous, lily-livered hoodlums. Two typical roles at either end of his career were Louie the Weasel in *You Can't Beat Love* and an Indian called Worm in *Chief Crazy Horse*. He came to Hollywood in 1935 after an extensive Broadway career, and had already made more than 50 films before the end of 1950. His son Paul is also an actor.

1935: *Special Agent. The Case of the Missing Man. The Crime of Dr Crespi.* 1936: *Wanted: Jane Turner. Roaming Lady. Winterset. Two-Fisted Gentleman.* 1937: *The Soldier and the Lady* (GB: *Michael Strogoff*). *The Woman I Love* (GB: *The Woman Between*). *Behind the Headlines. Sea Devils. You Can't Buy Luck. You Can't Beat Love. Hideaway. Super-Sleuth. Fight for Your Lady. Flight from Glory. Danger Patrol. Crashing Hollywood.* 1938: **Stage Fright. Double Danger. Law of the Underworld. Quick Money. The Saint in New York. This Marriage Business. I'm from the City. Sky Giant. Blind Alibi. Fugitives for a Night. Tarnished Angel. Maid's Night Out. She's Got Everything. The Mad Miss Manton. The Law West of Tombstone. Pacific Liner.* 1939: **Money to Loan. *The Story of Alfred Nobel. Society Lawyer. Heritage of the Desert. Unexpected Father* (GB: *Sandy Takes a Bow*). *News is Made at Night. Our Leading Citizen. One Hour to Live. Sabotage* (GB: *Spies at Work*). *Boy Slaves. Remember the Night.* 1940: *Thou Shalt Not Kill. The Saint Takes Over. The Grapes of Wrath. East of the River. Brother Orchid. Millionaires in Prison. One Crowded Night. Wildcat Bus.* 1941: *The Saint in Palm Springs.* 1942: **Madero of Mexico. *The Incredible Stranger. Who is Hope Schuyler? Time to Kill. The Man Who Returned to Life.* 1943: *North Star* (later *Armored Attack*). *Petticoat Larceny. White Savage* (GB: *White Captive*). *Three Russian Girls.* 1944: *The Seventh Cross. It Happened Tomorrow. Mark of the Whistler. The Master Race. *Dark Shadows. *Thou Shalt Not Kill* (and 1940 feature). 1945: *The Missing Corpse. Why Girls Leave Home.* 1946: *The Virginian. Sweetheart of Sigma Chi.* 1947:

Sinbad the Sailor. Roses Are Red. The Millerson Case. Second Chance. 1948: *The Judge* (GB: *The Gamblers*). 1949: *Follow Me Quietly. Mighty Joe Young. I Married a Communist* (GB: *The Woman on Pier 13*). *Miss Mink of 1949. There's a Girl in My Heart. A Woman's Secret. Trouble Preferred. White Heat.* 1950: *Messenger of Peace. Davy Crockett – Indian Scout* (GB: *Indian Scout*). *Bomba and the Hidden City.* 1951: *When I Grow Up. Journey into Light. Japanese War Bride.* 1952: *Actors and Sin. Confidence Girl.* 1953: *Julius Caesar. The Diamond Queen. Second Chance. Torch Song.* 1954: *Apache. The Golden Idol. A Life at Stake.* 1955: *Chief Crazy Horse* (GB: *Valley of Fury*). *Trial. Not As a Stranger.* 1960: *The Boy and the Pirates.*

As director:

1953: *Captain Scarface.* 1954: *A Life at Stake.* 1960: *Tess of the Storm Country.*

GULAGER, Clu 1928–

Throatily spoken, prematurely grey-haired, baby-faced American actor from a theatrical background. He attracted some attention with his sporadic film performances (especially those in *The Killers* and *The Last Picture Show*) but has divided his time primarily between television and the theatre. His ambitions to give up acting for direction seem to have fallen by the wayside. His father was the well-known cowboy entertainer John Gulager; appropriately, Clu appeared in 1990 in a film called *My Heroes Have Always Been Cowboys.*

1960: *Temple of the Swinging Doll.* 1962: *The Sam Spicer Story.* 1964: *The Killers.* 1965: *. . .And Now Miguel.* 1967: *Sullivan's Empire.* 1969: *Winning.* 1970: *Company of Killers* (originally for TV). *San Francisco International Airport* (TV). 1971: *The Last Picture Show.* 1972: *Molly and Lawless John. Call to Danger* (TV). *Footsteps* (TV). *The Glass House* (TV. GB: *cinemas*). 1973: *Chant of Silence* (TV). *Gangsterfilmen. In Dracula's Castle* (TV). 1974: *En Främling Steg av Tåget. McQ. Hit Lady* (TV). *Houston, We've Got a Problem* (TV). *Smile Jenny, You're Dead* (TV). *Heart in Hiding* (TV). 1976: *The Killer Who Wouldn't Die* (TV). 1977: *Charlie Cobb: Nice Night for a Hanging* (TV). *The Other Side of Midnight.* 1978: *King* (TV). *A Force of One. A Question of Love* (TV). *Willa* (TV). *Stickin' Together*

(TV). Ski Lift to Death (TV). 1979: This Man Stands Alone/The Man Who Stands Alone (TV. GB: Lawman Without a Gun). Black Beauty (TV). 1980: Touched by Love. Kenny Rogers as The Gambler (TV. GB: The Gambler). Skyward (TV). 1983: Living Proof: The Hank Williams Story (TV). Lies. 1984: Chattanooga Choo Choo. The Initiation. Prime Risk. 1985: Return of the Living Dead. Into the Night. A Nightmare on Elm Street Part 2: Freddy's Revenge. Bridge Across Time (TV). 1986: From a Whisper to a Scream (later The Offspring). Hunter's Blood. 1987: Summer Heat. 1988: Uninvited. The Hidden. Tapeheads. 1989: I'm Gonna Git You, Sucka! Teen Vamp. 1990: The Boneyard. Killing Device. My Heroes Have Always Been Cowboys. 1991: The Willies. 1993: Eddie Presley.

As director:
1969: *A Day With the Boys.

GWYNNE, Fred 1926–1993
Sepulchral-voiced, horse-faced, heavy-headed, slow-moving, dry-humoured, tall American comic actor, a Stateside equivalent of France's Fernandel, though alas too seldom in central roles. New York-born, Harvard-educated, the laconic Gwynne shot to fame in two television series, Car 54, Where Are You? and The Munsters, playing a Frankenstein's monster character in the latter. That took care of the 1960s and it was a decade later before he began to re-emerge in eye-catching character roles for the cinema, a medium which could have done with a greater share of his talent over the years, although he was also busy writing books for children. Died from pancreatic cancer.

1954: On the Waterfront. 1966: Munster Go Home! 1969: The Littlest Angel (TV). 1977: Captains Courageous (TV). 1979: La Luna (US: Luna). Father Brown, Detective/ Sanctuary of Fear (TV). 1980: Simon. 1981: So Fine. Any Friend of Nicholas Nickleby is a Friend of Mine (TV). The Munsters' Revenge (TV). 1982: The Mysterious Stranger. 1984: The Cotton Club. 1985: Water (shown 1984). Off Beat. 1986: The Christmas Star (TV). Vanishing Act (TV). The Boy Who Could Fly. Murder By the Book (TV). 1987: Fatal Attraction. The Secret of My Success. Ironweed. 1989: Pet Sematary. Disorganized Crime. 1991: Shadows and Fog. My Cousin Vinny. Murder in Black and White (TV).

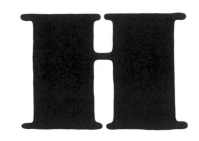

HAADE, William 1903–1966
Tall, tow-haired, tough-looking American actor of ruddy complexion. Visually a cross between Harry Carey and Bruce Cabot, Haade made his debut as the boxing champion managed by Humphrey Bogart in Kid Galahad. After getting himself knocked out by Wayne Morris in the climactic bout, Haade, who was of Dutch extraction, spent the next 20 years being slugged by other movie heroes, mostly in minor westerns, before quitting films for television.

1937: Kid Galahad. Without Warning. Missing Witnesses. He Couldn't Say No. 1938: A Dangerous Adventure. The Invisible Menace. The Stadium Murders/Hollywood Stadium Mystery. My Bill. Boy Meets Girl. The Amazing Dr Clitterhouse. Sing You Sinners. Three Comrades. Down on the Farm. The Texans. If I Were King. Telephone Operator. Shadows Over Shanghai. 1939: The Man They Could Not Hang. Rulers of the Sea. The Gracie Allen Murder Case. Island of Lost Men. Union Pacific. $1,000 a Touchdown. Full Confession. Tom Sawyer, Detective. Unmarried (GB: Night Club Hostess). Night Work. Kid Nightingale. Reno. Geronimo. Invisible Stripes. 1940: North West Mounted Police. Dr Kildare's Crisis. The Man Who Wouldn't Talk. And One Was Beautiful. The Man from Dakota (GB: Arouse and Beware). The Earl of Chicago. Lillian Russell. The Saint's Double Trouble. One Crowded Night. Cherokee Strip (GB: Fighting Marshal). Knute Rockne – All American (GB: A Modern Hero). Bullet Code. Stage to Chino. Flowing Gold. Johnny Apollo. The Grapes of Wrath. Who

Killed Aunt Maggie? They Drive by Night (GB: The Road to Frisco). 1941: Men of Boys' Town. The People Vs Dr Kildare (GB: My Life is Yours). Citadel of Crime (GB: Outside the Law). The Roundup. The Shepherd of the Hills. The Penalty. Honky Tonk. Dance Hall. Sergeant York. Unfinished Business. Sailors on Leave. Rise and Shine. You're in the Army Now. Pirates on Horseback. Knockout/Right to the Heart. Robin Hood of the Pecos. Desert Bandit. Kansas Cyclone. In Old Cheyenne. Man Hunt. Affectionately Yours. 1942: Juke Girl. Jackass Mail. I Married a Witch. Gang Busters (serial). Reap the Wild Wind. Torpedo Boat. The Navy Comes Through. Maisie Gets Her Man (GB: She Gets Her Man). You're Telling Me. To the Shores of Tripoli. Just Off Broadway. Shepherd of the Ozarks (GB: Susanna). Star Spangled Rhythm. Heart of the Rio Grande. Iceland (GB: Katina). Pittsburgh. Hearts of the Golden West. Man from Cheyenne. The Spoilers. A Gentleman After Dark. 1943: The Dancing Masters. Action in the North Atlantic. Hangmen Also Die. Daredevils of the West (serial). Whistling in Brooklyn. She Has What It Takes. Dr Gillespie's Criminal Case (US: Crazy to Kill). Salute to the Marines. Thank Your Lucky Stars. Song of Texas. Scream in the Dark. There's Something About a Sailor. Days of Old Cheyenne. You're a Lucky Fellow, Mr Smith. Sing a Jingle (GB: Lucky Days). 1944: Buffalo Bill. Seven Days Ashore. Here Come the Waves. Timber Queen. Roger Touhy, Gangster (GB: The Last Gangster). Man from Frisco. Three Men in White. The Yellow Rose of Texas. Sheriff of Las Vegas. An American Romance. Bride by Mistake. The Adventures of Mark Twain. 1945: I'll Tell the World. Honeymoon Ahead. The Trouble with Women (released 1947). Nob Hill. Incendiary Blonde. Dakota. Fallen Angel. Pride of the Marines (GB: Forever in Love). Pillow to Post. The Frozen Ghost. The Stork Club. Phantom of the Plains. A Guy Could Change. 1946: Affairs of Geraldine. In Old Sacramento. Renegades. The Well Groomed Bride. Valley of the Zombies. Sentimental Journey. Fallen Angel. My Pal Trigger. The Pilgrim Lady. Lady Chaser. 1947: Where There's Life. Night Unto Night (released 1949). Buck Privates Come Home (GB: Rookies Come Home). The Web. The Secret Life of Walter Mitty. Exposed. Deep Valley. Magic Town. Unconquered. Under Colorado Skies. Big Town After Dark. Down to Earth. It Happened in Brooklyn. Exposed. Four Faces West (GB: They Passed This Way). 1948: The Inside Story. April Showers. Good Sam. Michael O'Halloran. A Song is Born. The Night Has a Thousand Eyes. Shaggy. Tap Roots. Key Largo. Lulu Belle. Strike It Rich. 1949: Scene of the Crime. The Fountainhead. The Wyoming Bandit. I Married a Communist (GB: The Woman on Pier 13). The Bribe. Alaska Patrol. Flamingo Road. The Gal Who Took the West. Night Unto Night. *Prairie Pirates. Malaya (GB: East of the Rising Sun). Last of the Wild Horses. 1950: Rawhide/Desperate Siege. Trial Without Jury. No Man of Her Own. Outcast of Black Mesa (GB: The Clue). The Old Frontier. Buckaroo Sheriff of Texas. Caged. Father of the Bride. The Asphalt Jungle. Joe Palooka in the Squared Circle (GB: The Squared Circle). Copper Canyon. 1951: Leave It to the Marines. Santa Fé. Oh! Susanna. The Sea Hornet. Stop That

Cab. *Three Desperate Men. A Yank in Korea. The Texas Rangers.* 1952: *Skirts Ahoy! Carson City. Here Come the Nelsons. Come Back, Little Sheba. Rancho Notorious. Kansas City Confidential* (GB: *The Secret Four*). 1953: *Red River Shore. Secret of Outlaw Flats* (TV. GB: *cinemas*). 1954: *Untamed Heiress. Silver Lode. Kansas City Confidential* (GB: *The Secret Four*). *Jubilee Trail.* 1955: *Many Rivers to Cross. Abbott and Costello Meet the Keystone Kops. Toughest Man Alive. The Road to Denver.* 1957: *Spoilers of the Forest. The Tall Stranger.*

1944: *Bathing Beauty. Andy Hardy's Blonde Trouble.* 1945: *Our Vines Have Tender Grapes.* 1946: *Bad Bascomb. Mr Ace. Love Laughs at Andy Hardy. She-Wolf of London* (GB: *The Curse of the Allenbys*). *She Wouldn't Say Yes. Our Hearts Were Growing Up. So Goes My Love* (GB: *A Genius in the Family*). 1947: *The Bishop's Wife.* 1948: *Rachel and the Stranger.* 1949: *The Big Cat. Roughshod.* 1950: *A Life of Her Own. The Great Rupert.* 1952: *Wagons West. Rodeo.* 1953: *A Lion Is in the Streets.* 1954: *The Outlaw's Daughter.* 1955: *Betrayed Women.* 1958: *Andy Hardy Comes Home.*

HADEN, Sara 1897–1981

Plain-faced, dark-haired American supporting player, a former child actress who came to Hollywood in her late thirties and played nosey neighbours, spinster aunts, dragon-like secretaries, no-nonsense parole officers and frozen-faced, strait-laced do-gooders in general. Switched to films after a long theatre career, was nasty (on film) to Shirley Temple, then established herself as maiden aunt Milly in the Andy Hardy series.

1934: *Spitfire. The Life of Vergie Winters. Anne of Green Gables. The White Parade. Affairs of a Gentleman. Music in the Air. The Fountain. Finishing School. Hat, Coat and Glove.* 1935: *Mad Love* (GB: *Hands of Orlac*). *O'Shaughnessy's Boy. Way Down East. Magnificent Obsession. Black Fury.* 1936: *Little Miss Nobody. Captain January. Reunion* (GB: *Hearts in Reunion*). *Everybody's Old Man. Half Angel. Can This Be Dixie? Poor Little Rich Girl. The Crime of Dr Forbes.* 1937: *Under Cover of Night. Laughing at Trouble. A Family Affair. First Lady. The Barrier. The Last of Mrs Cheyney.* 1938: *Out West with the Hardys. Four Girls in White. You're Only Young Once. The Hardys Ride High.* 1939: *Tell No Tales. *Think First. *Angel of Mercy. The Secret of Dr Kildare. Andy Hardy Gets Spring Fever. Remember? Judge Hardy and Son.* 1940: *The Shop Around the Corner. Boom Town. Andy Hardy Meets Debutante.* 1941: *Hullabaloo. The Trial of Mary Dugan. Washington Melodrama. Andy Hardy's Private Secretary. Love Crazy. *Come Back, Miss Pipps. Barnacle Bill. Life Begins for Andy Hardy. Keeping Company. H. M. Pulham Esq.* 1942: *The Courtship of Andy Hardy. The Affairs of Martha* (GB: *There's Always a Thursday*). *Andy Hardy's Double Life.* 1943: *Pilot No. 5. The Youngest Profession. Lost Angel. Above Suspicion. Thousands Cheer. Best Foot Forward.*

HALE, Alan

(Rufus A. MacKahn) 1892–1950

Tall, burly American actor with fair, crinkly hair (and sometimes equally fair, crinkly moustache). He played Rochester in a silent *Jane Eyre* at 23, then settled down to 35 years as a top Hollywood character star, mostly in bluff, blustery, likeable, slow-witted roles (his real first name suited him ideally), but occasionally as a strong villain. Early death at 57 (from a liver ailment and virus infection) robbed him of a deserved 300 films before retirement. Also an inventor, he once trained as an opera singer.

1911: *The Cowboy and the Lady.* 1912: *The Drummer.* 1913: *The Prisoner of Zenda. *By Man's Law. *The Courting of David Dunne. *The Children of St Anne. Hearth Lights. *The Madcap of the Hills. *The Master Cracksman. *Dick's Turning. *His Uncle's Heir. *Maria Roma. *The Wager. *Kentucky Foes. *The Silly Sex. *The Smuggler's Sister. *A Hospital Romance. *The Glow Worm. *The Stolen Woman. *His Inspiration.* 1914: *Martin Chuzzlewit. *Masks and Faces. *Strongheart. *Men and Women. *Adam Bede. *The Cricket on the Hearth. *A Scrap of Paper. The Power of the Press. *His Romany Wife. *Woman Against Woman. *Aurora Floyd. *Who's Looney Now? *Gwendolin. *Life's Stream. The Woman in Black. *Ernest Maltravers. *The Closing Net. *On the Heights. *The Ring and the Book.* 1915: *Money. *File No. 113. *Three Hats. *After the Show. Dora Thorne. East Lynne. Jane Eyre. *The Americano. Under Two Flags. *Quicksands of Society. After the Storm. *Captain Fracasse. *His Singular Lesson. *The Smuggler's Ward. *Mrs Randolph's New Secretary. *Among Those Killed. *A Lasting Lesson. *Frederick Holmes' Ward. *The Girl Who

Didn't Forget. *Heart Trouble. *The Wives of Men. *Winning the Widow. *Bad Money. *The Inevitable. *Bob's Love Affair. *The Passing Storm. *Love's Enduring Flame. *His Emergency Wife. *The Man from Town. *Cupid Entangled.* 1916: *Pudd'nhead Wilson. The Purple Lady. Rolling Stones. The Love Thief. The Scarlet Oath. The Woman in the Case. A Woman in Black* (and 1914 film). *The Beast. *A Daughter of Earth. *By Man's Law* (and 1913 film). *Madelaine Morel.* 1917: *The Woman in the Case. The Price She Paid. Life's Whirlpool. One Hour. The Eternal Temptress.* 1918: *Masks and Faces* (remake). *Moral Suicide. The Whirlpool.* 1919: *Love Hunger. The Trap. The Blue Bonnet.* 1920: *The Heart of a Woman.* 1921: *A Wise Fool. The Four Horsemen of the Apocalypse. Over the Wire. The Fox. The Great Impersonation. The Barbarian. A Voice in the Dark.* 1922: *Shirley of the Circus. One Glorious Day. The Dictator. The Trap* (and 1919 film. GB: *Heart of a Wolf*) *Robin Hood. A Doll's House.* 1923: *The Covered Wagon. Cameo Kirby. Hollywood. The Eleventh Hour* (GB: *The Purple Phial*). *Quicksands. Main Street. Long Live the King. The Cricket.* 1924: *Black Oxen. Code of the Wilderness. Girls Men Forget. Troubles of a Bride. One Night in Rome. For Another Woman.* 1925: *Dick Turpin. †The Scarlet Honeymoon. †Braveheart. The Crimson Runner. Flattery. Ranger of the Big Pines. †The Wedding Song. Rolling Stones.* 1926: *†Forbidden Waters. †Risky Business. Hearts and Fists. †The Sporting Lover. Redheads Preferred.* 1927: *†Rubber Tires* (GB: *Ten Thousand Reward*). *Life in Hollywood No 4. Vanity. The Wreck of the Hesperus.* 1928: *The Cop. Oh, Kay! Skyscraper. The Leopard Lady. Sal of Singapore. Power. The Spieler* (GB: *The Spellbinder*). 1929: *Sailor's Holiday. Red Hot Rhythm. The Leatherneck. The Sap.* 1930: *She Got What She Wanted. A Bachelor's Secret. Up and at 'em.* 1931: *Aloha. Susan Lenox, Her Fall and Rise* (GB: *The Rise of Helga*). *Rebound. Night Angel. The Sin of Madelon Claudet* (GB: *The Lullaby*). *The Sea Ghost. Union Depot* (GB: *Gentleman for a Day*). 1932: *So Big. Rebecca of Sunnybrook Farm. The Match King.* 1933: *Picture Brides. What Price Decency? Destination Unknown. The Eleventh Commandment.* 1934: *Of Human Bondage. The Little Minister. Imitation of Life. The Lost Patrol. It Happened One Night. Fog Over Frisco. Great Expectations. Little Man, What Now? Broadway Bill* (GB: *Strictly Confidential*). *Miss Fane's Baby is Stolen* (GB: *Kidnapped*). *The Scarlet Letter. There's Always Tomorrow. Babbitt.* 1935: *Grand Old Girl. The Last Days of Pompeii. The Crusades. The Good Fairy. Another Face* (GB: *It Happened in Hollywood*). 1936: *Two in the Dark. A Message to Garcia. Yellowstone. Our Relations. God's Country and the Woman. Parole! The Country Beyond.* 1937: *Jump for Glory* (US: *When Thief Meets Thief*). *High, Wide and Handsome. Stella Dallas. The Prince and the Pauper. Thin Ice* (GB: *Lovely to Look At*). *Music for Madame.* 1938: *The Adventures of Robin Hood. Algiers. Four Men and a Prayer. Valley of the Giants. Listen, Darling. The Adventures of Marco Polo. The Sisters. Dodge City. The Man in the Iron Mask. Dust Be My Destiny. Pacific Liner. The Private Lives of Elizabeth and Essex. On Your Toes.* 1940: *Virginia City. Three Cheers for the*

Irish. The Fighting 69th. They Drive By Night (GB: The Road to Frisco). Santa Fé Trail. Tugboat Annie Sails Again. The Sea Hawk. Green Hell. 1941: Strawberry Blonde. Manpower. Thieves Fall Out. The Great Mr Nobody. The Smiling Ghost. Footsteps in the Dark. 1942: Juke Girl. Captains of the Clouds. Gentleman Jim. Desperate Journey. 1943: Action in the North Atlantic. Destination Tokyo. Thank Your Lucky Stars. This is the Army. 1944: The Adventures of Mark Twain. Make Your Own Bed. Hollywood Canteen. Janie. 1945: Roughly Speaking. Hotel Berlin. God is My Co-Pilot. Escape in the Desert. 1946: Perilous Holiday. The Time, the Place and the Girl. Night and Day. The Man I Love. Pursued. 1947: Cheyenne. My Wild Irish Rose. That Way with Women. 1948: My Girl Tisa. Whiplash. Adventures of Don Juan (GB: The New Adventures of Don Juan). 1949: South of St Louis. The Younger Brothers. The Inspector General. Always Leave Them Laughing. The House Across the Street. 1950: Colt .45. Stars in My Crown. Rogues of Sherwood Forest.

† And directed

HALE, Alan Jnr
(A. MacKahn) 1918–1990

Beefy, robust, cheerful, fair-haired American actor, the son of Alan Hale. His tousled mop and lopsided grin could be seen in some leading roles – if only in minor features – in the late 1940s, but he did not quite equal his father's standing in the cinema and his greatest success was in such TV series as Casey Jones (a perennial children's favourite) and Gilligan's Island. Died from cancer of the thymus.

1933: Wild Boys of the Road (GB: Dangerous Days). 1938: Dramatic School. 1941: I Wanted Wings. Dive Bomber. All-American Co-Ed. 1942: Top Sergeant. Wake Island. To the Shores of Tripoli. Rubber Racketeers. Eagle Squadron. 1943: Taxi, Mister. No Time for Love. Watch on the Rhine. 1944: And Now Tomorrow. 1946: The Sweetheart of Sigma Chi. Monsieur Beaucaire. 1947: It Happened on Fifth Avenue. Sarge Goes to College. Spirit of West Point. 1948: One Rainy Afternoon. The Music Man. Homecoming. 1949: Rim of the Canyon. Riders in the Sky. The Blazing Trail. It Happens Every Spring. 1950: The Blazing Sun. Kill the Umpire! Short Grass. The Gunfighter. Four Days' Leave. The Underworld

Story. The West Point Story (GB: Fine and Dandy). Sierra Passage. 1951: The Hometown Story. Honeychile. At Sword's Point (GB: Sons of the Musketeers). 1952: Springfield Rifle. Lady in the Iron Mask. The Big Trees. Wait 'Til the Sun Shines, Nellie. Mr Walkie Talkie. Arctic Flight. The Man Behind the Gun. 1953: The Yellow-Haired Kid. The Trail Blazers. Captain John Smith and Pocahontas (GB: Burning Arrows). 1954: Captain Kidd and the Slave Girl. Silver Lode. The Iron Glove. Destry. The Law vs Billy the Kid. Rogue Cop. Young at Heart. 1955: Many Rivers to Cross. The Sea Chase. A Man Alone. Man on the Ledge (TV. GB: cinemas). The Indian Fighter. 1956: All Mine to Give (GB: The Day They Gave Babies Away). The Killer is Loose. Canyon River. The Cruel Tower. The Three Outlaws. Affair in Reno. 1957: Battle Hymn. The True Story of Jesse James (GB: The James Brothers). The Lady Takes a Flyer. 1958: Up Periscope! 1960: Thunder in Carolina. 1961: The Long Rope. 1962: The Iron Maiden (GB: The Swingin' Maiden). 1963: Advance to the Rear (GB: Company of Cowards). The Crawling Hand. 1964: Bullet for a Badman. 1966: Dead Heat on a Merry-Go-Round. 1967: Hang 'Em High. 1968: Tiger by the Tail. 1970: There Was a Crooked Man. 1975: The Giant Spider Invasion. 1977: Behind the Iron Mask (GB: The Fifth Musketeer). 1978: The North Avenue Irregulars (GB: Hill's Angels). Rescue from Gilligan's Island (TV). 1979: The Great Monkey Rip-Off. The Castaways on Gilligan's Island. (TV). Angels' Brigade. 1981: The Harlem Globetrotters on Gilligan's Island (TV). 1983: Hambone and Hillie (GB: The Adventures of Hambone). 1984: Johnny Dangerously. 1985: The Red Fury. 1987: Back to the Beach.

HALE, Jonathan
(J. Hatley) 1891–1966

Tall, skeletal, upright, stern-looking Canadian actor with darkening cheekbones, finely drawn features and greying brown hair. His characters, whether on the right side of the law or the wrong, were never less than civilised, as befitted a former member of the diplomatic service. Turning to acting, a sideline that had always attracted him, Hale arrived in Hollywood in 1934 and ran up scores of film credits over the next 23 years. Sometimes he was a businessman hard on the hero, sometimes a lawyer or doctor or other figure of authority. But he is instantly

recognised by fans of 'B' movie series as Dagwood's boss, Mr Dithers, in the early 'Blondie' films, and as Inspector Fernack, constantly thwarted by the derring-do of The Saint. Left a widower after the death of his wife, Hale shot himself at 74.

1934: Lightning Strikes Twice. 1935: Alice Adams. The Raven. Public Hero No. 1. Navy Wife/Beauty's Daughter. Three Live Ghosts. *Hit and Run Driver. G Men. Page Miss Glory. A Night at the Opera. 1936: The Voice of Bugle Ann. The Devil is a Sissy (GB: The Devil Takes the Count). Fury. China Clipper. Spendthrift. Charlie Chan's Secret. 36 Hours to Kill. Born to Dance. The Singing Kid. The Plainsman. Charlie Chan at the Race Track. Flying Hostess. Happy Go Lucky. After the Thin Man. Educating Father. Too Many Parents. The Case Against Mrs Ames. 1937: John Meade's Woman. Carnival Queen. Midnight Madonna. This is My Affair (GB: His Affair). You Only Live Once. Saratoga. Wings Over Honolulu. Man of the People. Madame X. Outcast. Racketeers in Exile. Sea Devils. Mysterious Crossing. Danger – Love at Work. She's Dangerous. Exiled to Shanghai. A Star is Born. Charlie Chan at the Olympics. League of Frightened Men. Big Town Girl. 1938: Arsene Lupin Returns. Judge Hardy's Children. Blondie. Yellow Jack. There's That Woman Again. Boys' Town. Men with Wings. Road Demon. Her Jungle Love. The Duke of West Point. A Letter of Introduction. Wives Under Suspicion. Over the Wall. The Saint in New York. Breaking the Ice. Fugitives for a Night. Tarnished Angel. Gangs of New York. The First Hundred Years. Tail Spin. Crime Ring. Bringing Up Baby. 1939: Thunder Afloat. Stand Up and Fight. Wings of the Navy. The Saint Strikes Back. In Name Only. Scandal Sheet. Blondie Meets the Boss. The Amazing Mr Williams. Fugitive at Large. Blondie Brings Up Baby. Barricade. In Old Monterey. The Story of Alexander Graham Bell. *One Against the World. 1940: The Big Guy. Blondie Has Servant Trouble. Dulcy. Johnny Apollo. The Saint's Double Trouble. Private Affairs. We Who Are Young. The Saint Takes Over. Blondie Plays Cupid. Melody and Moonlight. 1941: Blondie Goes Latin (GB: Conga Swing). The Bugle Sounds. Flight from Destiny. The Great Swindle. Blondie in Society (GB: Henpecked). Her First Beau. Ringside Maisie (GB: Cash and Carry). The Pittsburgh Kid. Strange Alibi. The Saint in Palm Springs. 1942: Blondie Goes to College (GB: The Boss Said 'No'). Calling Dr Gillespie. Blondie's Blessed Event (GB: A Bundle of Trouble). Joe Smith, American (GB: Highway to Freedom). The Lone Star Ranger. Flight Lieutenant. Miss Annie Rooney. Blondie for Victory (GB: Troubles Through Billets). 1943: The Amazing Mrs Holliday. *Mission 36. The Black Parachute. Hangmen Also Die. Jack London. Sweet Rosie O'Grady. Nobody's Darling. There's Something About a Soldier. Footlight Glamour. It's a Great Life. 1944: And Now Tomorrow. Dead Man's Eyes. The End of the Road. This is the Life. My Buddy. Hollywood Canteen. Since You Went Away. 1945: Leave It to Blondie. Allotment Wives (GB: Woman in the Case). Dakota. GI Honeymoon. Man Alive. The Phantom Speaks. Life with Blondie. Divorce. 1946: Angel on My

Shoulder. *Blondie's Lucky Day. The Cat Creeps. Easy to Wed. Blondie Knows Best. Gay Blades. Riverboat Rhythm. The Strange Mr Gregory. The Walls Came Tumbling Down. Wife Wanted (GB: Shadow of Blackmail). 1947: The Beginning or the End. Her Husband's Affair. The Ghost Goes Wild. High Wall. Rolling Home. The Vigilantes Return. Call Northside 777. 1948: Johnny Belinda. King of the Gamblers. Disaster. Michael O'Halloran. Rocky. Tap Roots. Silver River. The Judge (GB: The Gamblers). 1949: A Dangerous Profession. Rose of the Yukon. Stampede. The Fountainhead. State Department — File 649 (GB: Assignment in China). 1950: Federal Agent at Large. Short Grass. Three Husbands. Triple Trouble. 1951: Insurance Investigator. Let's Go Navy. Rodeo King and the Senorita. Scandal Sheet (And 1939 film of same title. GB: The Dark Page). Strangers on a Train. Sunny Side of the Street. Rhythm Inn. Behind Southern Lines (TV). 1952: The Steel Trap. My Pal Gus. Son of Paleface. 1953: Blueprint for Murder. Kansas Pacific. Taxi. She Couldn't Say No (GB: Beautiful But Dangerous). The Glory Brigade. 1954: Duffy of San Quentin (GB: Men Behind Bars). Woman's World. Men of the Fighting Lady. Riot in Cell Block 11. Superman and Scotland Yard (TV. GB: cinemas). 1955: A Man Called Peter. Illegal. The Night Holds Terror. 1956: Jaguar. The Opposite Sex. Three Outlaws. 1957: Kiss Them for Me. Top Secret Affair (GB: Their Secret Affair). The Way to the Gold. 1963: Four for Texas.*

1937: *Souls at Sea. Make Way for Tomorrow. Wild Money. True Confession. Let's Make a Million. Bulldog Drummond Escapes. King of the Gamblers. Hotel Haywire. This Way, Please. Wells Fargo.* 1938: *Scandal Street. Dangerous to Know. Prison Farm. Stolen Heaven. Bulldog Drummond's Peril. King of Alcatraz (GB: King of the Alcatraz). Tom Sawyer—Detective. The Arkansas Traveler. Men with Wings.* 1939: *Grand Jury Secrets. They Shall Have Music (GB: Melody of Youth). Mr Smith Goes to Washington.* 1940: *His Girl Friday. Arizona. Dark Command. Trail of the Vigilantes.* 1941: *The Parson of Panamint. Mr and Mrs North. Sullivan's Travels.* 1942: *Butch Minds the Baby. The Remarkable Andrew. Tennessee Johnson (GB: The Man on America's Conscience).* 1943: *A Stranger in Town. Woman of the Town. The Desperadoes. The Great Moment.* 1944: *Standing Room Only. Going My Way. The Miracle of Morgan's Creek. Double Indemnity. Mark of the Whistler (GB: The Marked Man).* 1945: *Blood on the Sun. Bring on the Girls. Kiss and Tell. Murder, He Says. Week-End at the Waldorf. Mad Wednesday/The Sin of Harold Diddlebock.* 1947: *Miracle on 34th Street (GB: The Big Heart). Singapore.* 1948: *You Gotta Stay Happy. Unconquered. That Wonderful Urge.* 1949: *Chicken Every Sunday. The Beautiful Blonde from Bashful Bend. Intruder in the Dust.* 1951: *The Big Carnival (GB: Ace in the Hole).* 1952: *Carbine Williams. Holiday for Sinners. The Half-Breed.* 1953: *Vice Squad (GB: The Girl in Room 17). Pony Express.* 1954: *Return to Treasure Island.*

1917: *Cleopatra. The Price Mark. Love Letters.* 1918: *Flare-Up Sal. An Alien Enemy. The Mating of Marcella. The Kaiser's Shadow (GB: The Triple Cross). We Can't Have Everything. The One Woman. The Squaw Man (GB: The White Man). The Midnight Patrol. Tyrant Fear. Brazen Beauty.* 1919: *Who Will Marry Me? The Unpainted Woman. The Exquisite Thief. The Weaker Vessel. The Spitfire of Seville.* 1920: *Empty Hands. The Valley of Dust. The Web of Deceit. The Scarlet Dragon.* 1921: *The Iron Trail. Idle Hands. Mother Eternal.* 1922: *Fair Lady. Wilderness of Youth.* 1923: *The Royal Oak.* 1924: *The Great Well (GB: Neglected Women).* 1930: **Absent Minded.* 1935: *Metropolitan. Crime and Punishment. The Girl Friend. Too Tough to Kill. The Black Room. Love Me Forever (GB: On Wings of Song). Public Menace. Atlantic Adventure. One Way Ticket. The Case of the Missing Man. A Feather in Her Hat. Hooray for Love. Guard That Girl. After the Dance.* 1936: *The Lone Wolf Returns. Theodora Goes Wild. Don't Gamble With Love. The Man Who Lived Twice. Killer at Large. The King Steps Out. The Devil's Squadron. Trapped by Television (GB: Caught by Television). Shakedown. Three Wise Guys. Pride of the Marines. Roaming Lady. Two-Fisted Gentleman. Lady from Nowhere.* 1937: *Penitentiary. Paid to Dance. I Promise to Pay. All American Sweetheart. Women of Glamour. Don't Tell the Wife. Parole Racket. It Can't Last Forever. Venus Makes Trouble. Counsel for Crime. Murder in Greenwich Village. We Have Our Moments. Oh, Doctor.* 1938: *Professor Beware. The Amazing Dr Clitterhouse. No Time to Marry. Women in Prison. The Main Event. There's Always a Woman. Little Miss Roughneck. Extortion. Campus Confessions (GB: Fast Play). The Affairs of Annabel. Women Are Like That. Squadron of Honor. Hard to Get. Fast Company. Going Places. Out West With the Hardys.* 1939: *You Can't Cheat an Honest Man. Each Dawn I Die. Dodge City. Three Smart Girls Grow Up. Stagecoach. First Love. Ex-Champ (GB: Golden Gloves). Our Neighbors—the Carters. Hawaiian Nights. Million Dollar Legs. Mutiny on the Blackhawk. Jeepers Creepers (GB: Money Isn't Everything). The Star Maker. Dancing Co-Ed (GB: Every Other Inch a Lady). The Day the Bookies Wept.* 1940: **Kiddie Cure. The Blue Bird. Money to Burn. City for Conquest. Blondie on a Budget. Sued for Libel. Alias the Deacon. In Old Missouri. The Lone Wolf Meets a Lady. Millionaires in Prison. The Great McGinty (GB: Down Went McGinty). Friendly Neighbors. The Golden Fleecing. Virginia City.* 1941: *The Great Lie. The Lone Wolf Takes a Chance. Where Did You Get That Girl? Washington Melodrama. In the Navy. She Knew All the Answers. Repent at Leisure. Accent on Love. Design for Scandal. Secrets of the Lone Wolf (GB: Secrets). Hold That Ghost! Tuxedo Junction. Pacific Blackout/Midnight Angel. Unexpected Uncle. Four Mothers. Remember the Day. Swing It Soldier (GB: Radio Revels of 1942). The Invisible Woman. Flight from Destiny. The Lone Wolf Keeps a Date. Nine Lives Are Not Enough. Life With Henry.* 1942: *Sleepytime Gal. Counter Espionage. The Night Before the Divorce. The Hard Way. Rings on Her Fingers. Twin Beds. Springtime in the Rockies. Shepherd of the Ozarks (GB: Susanna).*

HALL, Porter

(Clifford P. Hall) 1888–1953

Small, dark-haired, shifty-eyed, moustachioed American actor, the epitome of the double-dealing businessman or (often corrupt) public figure. Following beginnings with a travelling Shakespeare company, he became a considerable figure in the theatrical world before succumbing late in life to the lure of Hollywood. Died from a heart attack.

1931: *Secrets of a Secretary.* 1934: *The Thin Man. Murder in the Private Car (GB: Murder on the Runaway Train).* 1935: *The Case of the Lucky Legs. The Petrified Forest.* 1936: *Too Many Parents. And Sudden Death. The Princess Comes Across. The Story of Louis Pasteur. The General Died at Dawn. Satan Met a Lady. Snowed Under. The Plainsman.*

HALL, Thurston 1882–1958

Large, hearty, generously-built American actor with dark hair and florid complexion. He acted on stages all over the world in his youth, including England, South Africa and New Zealand, before trying his luck in Hollywood, initially as a powerful leading man (his first role was Marc Antony). When he returned as a silver-haired, moustachioed character player in the 1930s, producers soon detected the roguish glint in his eye that caused him to be cast as dozens of smilingly affable, but crooked businessmen, who would wriggle out of a jam and launch some fresh scheme at a bluster of confusion or a clearing of the throat. Died from a heart attack.

The Great Man's Lady. Hello Annapolis (GB: Personal Honour). Call of the Canyon. Her Cardboard Lover. The Great Gildersleeve. We Were Dancing. Crash Dive. 1943: This Land Is Mine! One Dangerous Night. The Youngest Profession. I Dood It (GB: By Hook or By Crook). Footlight Glamour. Sherlock Holmes in Washington. Hoosier Holiday (GB: Farmyard Follies). Here Comes Elmer. He Hired the Boss. 1944: Cover Girl. Wilson. The Adventures of Mark Twain. Goodnight, Sweetheart. The Great Moment. Something for the Boys. In Society. Follow the Girls. Ever Since Venus. Song of Nevada. 1945: Brewster's Millions. Bring on the Girls. The Blonde from Brooklyn. Don Juan Quilligan. The Gay Senorita. Lady on a Train. West of the Pecos. Colonel Effingham's Raid (GB: Man of the Hour). Song of the Prairie (GB: Sentiment and Song). Saratoga Trunk. Thrill of a Romance. 1946: Dangerous Business. One More Tomorrow. Three Little Girls in Blue. She Wrote the Book. Two Sisters from Boston. Without Reservations. 1947: The Secret Life of Walter Mitty. The Farmer's Daughter. Morning Becomes Electra. Swing the Western Way (GB: The Schemer). Son of Rusty. Welcome Stranger. Black Gold. The Unfinished Dance. It Had to Be You. 1948: Three Daring Daughters (GB: The Sun Comes Up). Up in Central Park. King of the Gamblers. Miraculous Journey. Blondie's Secret. Blondie's Reward. 1949: Manhattan Angel. The Fountainhead. The Stagecoach Kid. Rim of the Canyon. Square Dance Jubilee. Bride for Sale. Rusty Saves a Life. Tell It to the Judge. 1950: Girls' School (GB: Dangerous Inheritance). Belle of Old Mexico. Federal Agent at Large. Bright Leaf. Chain Gang. Bandit Queen. 1951: One Too Many (GB: Killer with a Label). Whirlwind. Belle le Grand. Texas Carnival. 1952: One Big Affair. Night Stage to Galveston. Skirts Ahoy! Woman of the North Country. Carson City. The WAC from Walla Walla (GB: Army Capers). It Grows on Trees. 1953: The Band Wagon. 1957: Affair in Reno.

HALLIDAY, John 1880–1947
This native New Yorker, who must have played more cuckolded husbands than most, was a tall, elegant man with neat moustache. He trained as a mining engineer in Scotland, served with the British army in the Boer War, and went to Cambridge, before taking up an engineering career in the Nevada mining territory. Amateur performances

in Gilbert and Sullivan led him to switch careers to acting and he became a respected Broadway figure before trying Hollywood at the beginning of the sound era. Now best remembered as Katharine Hepburn's wayward dad in The Philadelphia Story, he retired to Honolulu, where he died from a heart ailment. He made an isolated debut in the 1916 film The Devil's Toy.

1920: The Woman Gives. The Love Expert. 1929: East Side Sadie. 1930: Father's Son. Recaptured Love. Scarlet Pages. Captain Applejack. 1931: The Ruling Voice. *Chip Shots. *The Spoon. Consolation Marriage (GB: Married in Haste). Fifty Million Frenchmen. Smart Woman. Transatlantic. Millie. The Spy. Once a Sinner. 1932: The Impatient Maiden. Week-Ends Only. Men of Chance. Bird of Paradise. The Age of Consent. The Man Called Back. Perfect Understanding. 1933: The Woman Accused. Terror Aboard. Bed of Roses. The House on 56th Street. 1934: Happiness Ahead. A Woman's Man. Return of the Terror. Housewife. Desirable. Finishing School. The Witching Hour. Registered Nurse. 1935: The Dark Angel. Mystery Woman. Peter Ibbetson. The Melody Lingers On. 1936: Desire. Fatal Lady. Hollywood Boulevard. Three Cheers for Love. 1938: Arsene Lupin Returns. That Certain Age. Blockade. 1939: Elsa Maxwell's Hotel for Women (GB: Hotel for Women). Intermezzo—A Love Story (GB: Escape to Happiness). The Light That Failed. 1940: The Philadelphia Story. Submarine Zone. 1941: Lydia.

HALTON, Charles 1876–1959
Small, sharp-faced American actor with pasted-across grey hair and rimless spectacles: played businessmen, bank managers, doctors and even spies. His characters were suspicious of intentions and generally nobody's fools; you could almost see their noses twitch. A late arrival to the film world, Halton became one of Hollywood's most prolific actors. From 1938 to 1940 alone, he appeared in more than 50 films, often giving incisive cameos; he was at his interfering best in the war years, notably in such films as To Be or Not To Be. Died from hepatitis.

1917: *The Adventurer. 1919: The Climbers. 1930: Laughter. 1931: *The Strange Case. *The Lease Breakers. Honor Among Lovers. 1933: Storm at Daybreak. 1934: Twenty Million Sweethearts. 1936: Sing Me a Love

Song. Stolen Holiday. Come and Get It. Dodsworth. More Than a Secretary. Gold Diggers of 1937. Black Legion. 1937: Penrod and Sam. Ready, Willing and Able. Pick a Star. Woman Chases Man. Blossoms on Broadway. Dead End. The Road Back. The Prisoner of Zenda. Partners in Crime. Talent Scout (GB: Studio Romance). 1938: Penrod's Double Trouble. Bluebeard's Eighth Wife. Stolen Heaven. The Saint in New York. Room Service. The Mad Miss Manton. A Man to Remember. Trouble at Midnight. Penrod and His Twin Brother. I'll Give a Million. I Am the Law. Gold Is Where You Find It. Penitentiary. The Young in Heart. Federal Man Hunt (GB: Flight from Justice). 1939: Nancy Drew—Reporter. Swanee River. No Place to Go. Young Mr Lincoln. Jesse James. Golden Boy. Bachelor Mother. News Is Made at Night. Indianapolis Speedway (GB: Devil on Wheels). I'm from Missouri. Dust Be My Destiny. Lady of the Tropics. Dodge City. Charlie Chan at Treasure Island. Juarez. Sabotage (GB: Spies at Work). They Asked for It. Reno. Sudden Money. They Made Her a Spy. Ex-Champ (GB: Golden Gloves). The Hunchback of Notre Dame. 1940: Stranger on the Third Floor. Behind the News. Gangs of Chicago. The Ghost Comes Home. Foreign Correspondent. Lillian Russell. The Shop Around the Corner. Dr Ehrlich's Magic Bullet (GB: The Story of Dr Ehrlich's Magic Bullet). Dr Cyclops. They Drive by Night (GB: The Road to Frisco). Young People. Twenty-Mule Team. Lucky Partners. The Doctor Takes a Wife. Tugboat Annie Sails Again. I Love You Again. The Westerner. Virginia City. Calling All Husbands. Brigham Young—Frontiersman (GB: Brigham Young). Little Nellie Kelly. 1941: Lady Scarface. Meet the Chump. One Foot in Heaven. Mr District Attorney. Mr and Mrs Smith. I Was a Prisoner on Devil's Island. Tobacco Road. Footlight Fever. Three Girls About Town. A Very Young Lady. H. M. Pulham Esq. Dance Hall. The Smiling Ghost. Million Dollar Baby. Look Who's Laughing. Unholy Partners. Three Sons o' Guns. The Body Disappeared. 1942: Juke Box Jenny. Whispering Ghosts. To Be or Not To Be. The Spoilers. They All Kissed the Bride. In Old California. Tombstone — The Town Too Tough to Die. The Lady Is Willing. Priorities on Parade. There's One Born Every Minute. Across the Pacific. Saboteur. You Can't Escape Forever. That Other Woman. Henry Aldrich, Editor. Captains of the Clouds. 1943: My Kingdom for a Cook. † The Private Life of Dr Paul Joseph Goebbels. Jitterbugs. Lady Bodyguard. Heaven Can Wait. Flesh and Fantasy. Government Girl. Whispering Footsteps. 1944: Shadows in the Night. Address Unknown. Up in Arms. It Happened Tomorrow. Rationing. The Town Went Wild. The Thin Man Goes Home. Enemy of Women. A Tree Grows in Brooklyn. 1945: Rhapsody in Blue. The Fighting Guardsman. She Went to the Races. Mama Loves Papa. One Fascinating Night. Spellbound. Midnight Manhunt. 1946: One Exciting Week. Singin' in the Corn (GB: Give and Take). Because of Him. Three Little Girls in Blue. The Best Years of Our Lives. It's a Wonderful Life! Sister Kenny. 1947: The Ghost Goes Wild. The Bachelor and the Bobby Soxer (GB: Bachelor Knight). 1948: 3 Godfathers. If You Knew Susie. *Bet Your Life. My Dear Secretary. 1949: The Hideout.

The Sickle or the Cross. The Daring Caballero. 1950: The Nevadan (GB: The Man from Nevada). When Willie Comes Marching Home. The Traveling Saleswoman. Stella. Joe Palooka in the Squared Circle (GB: The Squared Circle). 1951: Gasoline Alley. Here Comes the Groom. 1952: Carrie. I Love Melvin. 1953: The Moonlighter. A Slight Case of Larceny. 1954: A Star is Born. 1956: Friendly Persuasion. 1958: High School Confidential!

† Unreleased

Sin of Harold Diddlebock. 1947: Dishonored Lady. *Pet Peeves. Driftwood. Reaching for Heaven. 1948: State of the Union (GB: The World and His Wife). On Our Merry Way (GB: A Miracle Can Happen). Texas, Brooklyn and Heaven (GB: The Girl from Texas) Bungalow 13. 1949: The Red Pony. The Sun Comes Up. The Beautiful Blonde from Bashful Bend. 1950: Wabash Avenue. Riding High. The Great Plane Robbery. 1951: People Will Talk. Comin' Round the Mountain. 1957: Paradise Alley (released 1962). 1959: The Silver Whistle (TV). 1960: 13 Ghosts. 1963: The Cardinal. 1966: The Daydreamer. 1967: Rosie! Ghostbreaker (TV). 1969: Angel in My Pocket. 1970: Brewster McCloud. 1971: The Anderson Tapes. Journey Back to Oz (voice only). 1973: The Night Strangler (TV). 1978: A Last Cry for Help (TV). Donovan's Kid (TV). 1979: Letters from Frank.

on a Dark Street (TV). Murdock's Gang (TV). 1975: Jaws. The Drowning Pool. 1976: Midway (GB: Battle of Midway). 1977: Casey's Shadow. Murder at the World Series (TV). Killer on Board (TV). Damnation Alley. 1978: Jaws 2. 1979: 1941. The Amityville Horror. A Last Cry for Help (TV). 1980: Swan Song (TV). Brubaker. 1982: Mazes and Monsters (TV). Hysterical. 1983: Summer Girl (TV). 1985: Too Scared to Scream. 1986: The Last Days of Patton (TV). Whoops Apocalypse.

HAMILTON, Margaret 1902–1985
Beaky-nosed, beady-eyed, bony-featured American character actress with very dark hair, unforgettable as the Wicked Witch of the West (and Miss Gulch the schoolteacher) in *The Wizard of Oz*. She really was a former teacher who switched to acting and, from 1933, landed scores of roles in Hollywood as nosey neighbours, outraged citizens and members of the local puritan league. She remained very much a working actress into her late seventies, and in private life an avid worker for charity. Died from a heart attack.

1933: Another Language. 1934: Hat, Coat and Glove. There's Always Tomorrow. Broadway Bill (GB: Strictly Confidential). By Your Leave. 1935: The Farmer Takes a Wife. The Wedding Night. Way Down East. People Will Talk. 1936: These Three. Chatterbox. The Trail of the Lonesome Pine. The Witness Chair. The Moon's Our Home. 1937: Laughing at Trouble. When's Your Birthday? You Only Live Once. Nothing Sacred. Mountain Justice. The Good Old Soak. I'll Take Romance. Saratoga. 1938: The Adventures of Tom Sawyer. Mother Carey's Chickens. Four's a Crowd. A Slight Case of Murder. Breaking the Ice. Stablemates. 1939: Angels Wash Their Faces. The Wizard of Oz. Main Street Lawyer (GB: Small Town Lawyer). Babes in Arms. 1940: My Little Chickadee. I'm Nobody's Sweetheart Now. The Villain Still Pursued Her. 1941: Playgirl. The Invisible Woman. The Gay Vagabond. The Shepherd of the Hills. Babes on Broadway. 1942: Twin Beds. Meet the Stewarts. The Affairs of Martha (GB: Once Upon a Thursday). Journey for Margaret. The Ox-Bow Incident (GB: Strange Incident). 1943: City Without Men. Johnny Come Lately (GB: Johnny Vagabond). 1944: Guest in the House. 1945: George White's Scandals. 1946: Janie Gets Married. Faithful in My Fashion. Mad Wednesday/The

HAMILTON, Murray 1923–1986
Tousle-haired, crumple-faced, stockily-built American actor who started his career playing straight-down-the-line types, but, as the lines increased, gained recognition as connivers and men of straw, or officials more concerned with city hall than the people. Notable in this vein were his portraits of the mayor, forever willing to ignore dangers to cram in more tourists, in the *Jaws* films. Died from cancer.

1950: Bright Victory (GB: Lights Out). 1951: The Whistle at Eaton Falls (GB: Richer Than the Earth). 1956: Toward the Unknown (GB: Brink of Hell). The Girl He Left Behind. 1957: Jeanne Eagels. The Spirit of St Louis. Darby's Rangers (GB: The Young Invaders). 1958: Too Much Too Soon. No Time for Sergeants. Houseboat. Girl in the Subway (TV. GB: cinemas). 1959: Anatomy of a Murder. The FBI Story. 1960: Tall Story. 1961: The Hustler. 1962: Papa's Delicate Condition. 1963: The Cardinal. 13 Frightened Girls! Sergeant Ryker (TV. GB: cinemas). 1966: Danger Has Two Faces. An American Dream (GB: See You in Hell, Darling). Seconds. 1967: The Graduate. No Way to Treat a Lady. 1968: The Brotherhood. The Boston Strangler. 1969: If It's Tuesday, This Must Be Belgium. 1971: Vanished (TV). Cannon (TV). A Tattered Web (TV). The Harness (TV). The Failing of Raymond (TV). 1972: Deadly Harvest (TV). Madigan: The Manhattan Beat (TV). 1973: The Way We Were. Incident

HANDL, Irene 1901–1987
Plump-faced British comedy actress with brown, curly hair, plaintive, mewling, ingratiatingly friendly tones and unique way of haranguing her fellow players. She came late to the theatre via an acting course in her early thirties, but was an immediate success as the to-the-rescue maid in *George and Margaret*, a role that also set her up for a film career of mothers, cooks and landladies, to all of which she lent her own touch of eccentricity. After appearing with a number of top comedians, she became a star in her own right in TV series of the 1960s. She also wrote two popular novels. A loveable human puffin.

1937: Missing – Believed Married. The Vulture. 1938: Strange Boarders. The Terror. The Viper. 1939: Mrs Pym of Scotland Yard. On the Night of the Fire (US: The Fugitive). Inspector Hornleigh on Holiday (US: Inspector Hornleigh on Leave). Dr O'Dowd. 1940: The Girl in the News. Night Train to Munich (US: Night Train). George and Margaret. Gasbags. Spellbound (US: The Spell of Amy Nugent). 1941: Pimpernel Smith (US: Mister V). *Mr Proudfoot Shows a Light. 1942: *Partners in Crime. Uncensored. 1943: I'll Walk Beside You. Rhythm Serenade. Get Cracking. The Flemish Farm. Millions Like Us. It's in the Bag. Dear Octopus (US: The Randolph Family). 1944: Welcome Mr Washington. Mr Emmanuel. English Without Tears (US: Her Man Gilbey). Kiss the Bride Goodbye. Give Us the Moon. Medal for the General. 1945: For You Alone. Great Day. Brief Encounter. The Shop at Sly Corner (US: The Code of Scotland Yard). 1946: I'll Turn to You. 1947: Temptation Harbour. The Hills of Donegal. 1948: Woman Hater. Silent Dust. No Orchids for Miss Blandish. The History of Mr Polly. Cardboard Cavalier. 1949. The Fool and the Princess. Adam and Evelyne

(US: Adam and Evalyn). For Them That Trespass. The Perfect Woman. Dark Secret. 1950: Stage Fright. 1951: One Wild Oat. Young Wives' Tale. 1952: Top Secret (US: Mr Potts Goes to Moscow). Treasure Hunt. 1953: The Wedding of Lilli Marlene. Meet Mr Lucifer. The Weak and the Wicked. Stryker of the Yard. The Accused. 1954: Duel in the Jungle. Burnt Evidence. The Case of the Second Shot. The Belles of St Trinian's. Mad About Men. A Kid for Two Farthings. 1955: Now and Forever. Who Done It? 1956: It's Never Too Late. The Silken Affair. Brothers in Law. 1957: Small Hotel. Happy is the Bride! 1958: The Key. Law and Disorder. Carlton-Browne of the F.O. (US: Man in a Cocked Hat). Next to No Time! 1959: The Crowning Touch. Carry On Nurse. Inn for Trouble. I'm All Right, Jack. Desert Mice. Upstairs and Downstairs. The Night We Dropped a Clanger (US: Make Mine a Double). Left, Right and Centre. School for Scoundrels. 1960: Two-Way Stretch. Carry On Constable. Make Mine Mink. Doctor in Love. A French Mistress. The Night We Got the Bird. No Kidding (US: Beware of Children). The Pure Hell of St Trinian's. 1961 Double Bunk. The Rebel (US: Call Me Genius). A Weekend with Lulu. Watch It Sailor! Nothing Barred. 1963: Heavens Above! Just for Fun. 1965: You Must Be Joking! 1966: Morgan — A Suitable Case for Treatment (US: Morgan). The Wrong Box. 1967: Smashing Time. 1968: Lionheart. Wonderwall. 1969: The Italian Job. 1970: Doctor in Trouble. The Private Life of Sherlock Holmes. On a Clear Day You Can See Forever. 1972: For the Love of Ada. Madigan: The London Beat (TV). 1976: Confessions of a Driving Instructor. The Chiffy Kids (series). 1977: Come Play with Me. The Last Remake of Beau Geste. Adventures of a Private Eye. The Hound of the Baskervilles. Stand Up, Virgin Soldiers. 1979: The Great Rock 'n' Roll Swindle. 1980: Riding High. 1985: Hotel du Lac (TV). 1986: Absolute Beginners.

The Private Life of Henry VIII, only one of several important Alexander Korda pictures in which he was cast. Conducted concerts and grand opera in his younger days.

1923: The Pipes of Pan. 1930: Beyond the Cities. 1931: Her Reputation. 1932: That Night in London (US: Overnight). Love on Wheels. There Goes the Bride. Wedding Rehearsal. The Faithful Heart (US: Faithful Hearts). Leap Year. The Man from Toronto. 1933: The Good Companions. The Private Life of Henry VIII. Loyalties. This Week of Grace. *A Dickensian Fantasy. His Grace Gives Notice. 1934: Catherine The Great/The Rise of Catherine the Great. Those Were the Days. What Happened Then? The Great Defender. Chu Chin Chow. Adventure Limited. Easy Money. The Scarlet Pimpernel. Brewster's Millions. Murder at Monte Carlo. 1935: Expert's Opinion. Mimi. Lorna Doone. Street Song. 1936: Whom the Gods Love (US: Mozart). The Lonely Road (US: Scotland Yard Commands). Someone at the Door. As You Like It. The Three Maxims (US: The Show Goes On). Rembrandt. The Man Who Could Work Miracles. Fire Over England. Beloved Imposter. 1937: Dark Journey. Dinner at the Ritz. The Show Goes On (different from 1936 entry). Knight Without Armour. Moonlight Sonata. Knights for a Day. It's Never Too Late to Mend. Action for Slander. Midnight Menace (US: Bombs Over London). The Girl in the Taxi. The Last Chance. Smash and Grab. Over the Moon (released 1940). 21 Days (US: 21 Days Together. Released 1940). 1938: A Royal Divorce. 1939: The Missing People. 1941: Hatter's Castle. The Ghost of St Michael's. Quiet Wedding. Old Mother Riley's Circus. Penn of Pennsylvania (US: The Courageous Mr Penn). 1943: My Learned Friend. 1944: Waterloo Road. Love Story (US: A Lady Surrenders). On Approval. Hotel Reserve. 1947: Nicholas Nickleby. Mine Own Executioner.

1920: The Barton Mystery. A Bachelor Husband. 1922: *Les Misérables (extract). When Knighthood was in Flower. 1924: Yolanda. 1927: Further Adventures of the Flag Lieutenant. Land of Hope and Glory. 1930: Sleeping Partners. 1931: The Speckled Band. 1932: The Barton Mystery (remake). 1933: The Constant Nymph. 1934: The Man Who Changed His Name. Wild Boy. The Lash. 1935: The Triumph of Sherlock Holmes. Escape Me Never. The Invader (US: An Old Spanish Custom). 1936: The Man Who Changed His Mind (US: The Man Who Lived Again). Spy of Napoleon. Fire Over England. Please Teacher. 1937: Underneath the Arches. Knight Without Armour. Silver Blaze (US: Murder at the Baskervilles). The Mutiny of the Elsinore. 1938: The Pearls of the Crown. 1939: The Missing People. Goodbye Mr Chips! 1941: The Prime Minister.

HARDWICKE, Sir Cedric 1893–1964
Scholarly-looking, high-domed English actor with imposing, fruitily booming voice, a former medical student and army officer who took to the London stage in the early thirties and played some choice theatre and film roles. He went to America in 1938, at first with some success as a character star, but then in progressively inferior parts. His last film role, however, was one of his best. Knighted in 1934.

1913: Riches and Rogues. 1926: Nelson. 1931: Dreyfus (US: The Dreyfus Case). 1932: Rome Express. 1933: Orders is Orders. The Ghoul. The Lady is Willing. 1934: Bella Donna. Nell Gwyn. Jew Süss (US: Power). The King of Paris. 1935: Peg of Old Drury. Les Misérables. Becky Sharp. 1936: Things to Come. Laburnum Grove. Tudor Rose (US: Nine Days a Queen). Calling the Tune. 1937: King Solomon's Mines. The Green Light. 1939: On Borrowed Time. The Hunchback of Notre Dame. Stanley and Livingstone. 1940: Tom Brown's Schooldays. The Invisible Man Returns. The Howards of Virginia (GB: The Tree of Liberty). Victory. 1941: Suspicion. Sundown. 1942: The Ghost of Frankenstein. Valley of the Sun. Invisible Agent. The Commandos Strike at Dawn. 1943: The Moon is Down. The Cross of Lorraine. †Forever and a Day. 1944: The Lodger. Wilson. A Wing and a Prayer. The Keys of the Kingdom. 1945: The Picture of Dorian Gray (narrator only). 1946: Beware of Pity. Sentimental Journey. The Imperfect Lady (GB: Mrs Loring's

HANRAY, Lawrence 1874–1947
This slightly-built, wry-faced, balding British purveyor of skeletal skinflints was such an actor of the old school and bore himself with such dignity that you always expected to see him in winged collar and black tie. However, if the characters he played were solicitors, physicians, bankers and noblemen, they were not always sympathetic. He made a first-rate Archbishop Cranmer in

HARDING, Lyn
(David Llewellyn Harding) 1867–1952
Enormous, bushy-browed, Welsh-born actor, equivalent in build to Hollywood's Scottish-born comic heavy Eric Campbell (1879–1917). He made a formidable villain, even well into his sixties, but a sojourn in America, although taking in a couple of film roles, didn't lead to a Hollywood career. Alleged to have made his film debut in 1914.

Secret). 1947: Lured (GB: Personal Column). A Woman's Vengeance. Ivy. Nicholas Nickleby. Tycoon. 1948: Song of My Heart. The Winslow Boy. Rope. I Remember Mama. A Connecticut Yankee in King Arthur's Court (GB: A Yankee in King Arthur's Court). 1949: Now Barabbas was a robber . . . 1950: The White Tower. Mr Imperium (GB: You Belong to My Heart). 1951: The Desert Fox (GB: Rommel − Desert Fox). The Green Glove. 1952: Caribbean (GB: Caribbean Gold). The War of the Worlds (narrator only). *Hollywood Night at 21 Club. 1953: Salome. Botany Bay. 1954: Bait. Helen of Troy. 1955: Richard III. Diane. 1956: Gaby. Mr and Mrs. McAdam (TV). The Vagabond King. The Power and the Prize. The Ten Commandments. Around the World in 80 Days. 1957: Baby Face Nelson. The Story of Mankind. 1961: The Magic Fountain. 1962: Five Weeks in a Balloon. 1964: The Pumpkin Eater.

†Also co-directed

1948: Escape. 1949: Now Barabbas was a robber . . . The Lost People. 1950: Double Confession. 1951: The Dark Man. The Magic Box. 1952: The Holly and the Ivy. The Pickwick Papers. The Ringer. 1953: Will Any Gentleman? 1955: Footsteps in the Fog. Josephine and Men. Private's Progress. 1956: Doublecross. Tons of Trouble. 1957: Yangtse Incident (US: Battle Hell). Date with Disaster. The Hypnotist (US: Scotland Yard Dragnet). Hell Drivers. 1958: On the Run. Carry on Sergeant. 1959: Shake Hands with the Devil. The Mouse That Roared. The Night We Dropped a Clanger (US: Make Mine a Double). Strictly Confidential. The Desperate Man. 1960: And the Same to You. Jackpot. Piccadilly Third Stop. 1962: Tomorrow at Ten. 1963: This Sporting Life. Heavens Above! The World Ten Times Over (US: Pussycat Alley). To Have and to Hold.

† As Billy Hartnell

HARTNELL, William 1908–1975

Voluble, shifty-looking, light-haired British character actor who played brash cockneys in comedies until the tough sergeant of *The Way Ahead* in 1944 typed him in more dramatic roles. Later popular on TV as the first Dr Who. There is some evidence to suggest that he was a crowd player in films of 1931 and 1932. Died following a series of strokes.

1932: Say It with Music. 1933: †I'm an Explosive. †Follow the Lady. †The Lure. 1934: †Seeing is Believing. †The Perfect Flaw. †Swinging the Lead. 1935: †While Parents Sleep. 1936: †Nothing Like Publicity. †Midnight at Madame Tussaud's (US: Midnight at the Wax Museum). 1937: †Farewell Again (US: Troopship). †Too Dangerous to Live. 1938: †They Drive by Night. 1939: †Murder Will Out. 1940: †They Came by Night. 1941: †They Flew Alone (US: Wings and the Woman). †Freedom Radio (US: A Voice in the Night). 1942: †Flying Fortress. †Sabotage at Sea. †Suspected Person. The Goose Steps Out. †The Peterville Diamond. 1943: †The Bells Go Down. †The Dark Tower. †San Demetrio London. †Headline. 1944: †The Way Ahead. †Strawberry Roan. †The Agitator. 1945: †Murder in Reverse. 1946: Appointment with Crime. Odd Man Out. 1947: Temptation Harbour. Brighton Rock (US: Young Scarface).

HARVEY, Paul 1883–1955

Everything about this grey-haired, hearty American actor was large and expansive. He played solid citizens, blustering windbags, comforting fathers, district attorneys who let the hero do the legwork, dyspeptic executives and trilbied authoritarian figures behind desks. After 23 years of such roles, Harvey's long, heavy head, large ears and solid girth were seen in perhaps their best-remembered guise, the Rev Mr Galsworthy in *Father of the Bride* and *Father's Little Dividend*. He was still busily acting at 72 at the time of his death from a coronary thrombosis.

1918: Men Who Have Made Love to Me. 1929: The Awful Truth. 1930: *Strong Arm. 1932: The Wiser Sex. 1933: Advice to the Lovelorn. The House of Rothschild. 1934: The Affairs of Cellini. Broadway Bill (GB: Strictly Confidential). Born to Be Bad. Charlie Chan's Courage. Handy Andy. Hat, Coat and Glove. Kid Millions. She Was a Lady. A Wicked Woman. Looking for Trouble. The Whole Town's Talking (GB: Passport to Fame). 1935: The President Vanishes (US: Strange Conspiracy). Alibi Ike. Four Hours to Kill. Goin' to Town. I'll Love You Always. Broadway Melody of 1936. Thanks a Million. The Petrified Forest. 1936: August Week-End. Black Legion. The General Died at Dawn. Mind Your Own Business. The Plainsman. Rose of the Rancho. The Return of Sophie Lang. Private Number (GB:

Secret Interlude). Three Men on a Horse. The Walking Dead. The Witness Chair. Yellowstone. Postal Inspector. 1937: The Soldier and the Lady (GB: Michael Strogoff). Big City. The Devil is Driving. My Dear Miss Aldrich. High Flyers. On Again, Off Again. 23½ Hours' Leave. 1938: Algiers. Charlie Chan in Honolulu. The Higgins Family. If I Were King. I'll Give a Million. Love on a Budget. The Sisters. A Slight Case of Murder. Rebecca of Sunnybrook Farm. There's That Woman Again. 1939: The Gorilla. Mr Moto in Danger Island (GB: Mr Moto on Danger Island). Forgotten Women. Meet Dr Christian. Never Say Die. News is Made at Night. Stanley and Livingstone. They Shall Have Music. Remember the Night. 1940: Arizona. Behind the News. Dr Ehrlich's Magic Bullet. High School. The Marines Fly High. Sailor's Lady. Brother Rat and a Baby. Manhattan Heartbeat. Maryland. Typhoon. 1941: Great Guns. High Sierra. Remember the Day. Puddin' Head (GB: Judy Goes to Town). Law of the Tropics. Mr District Attorney in the Carter Case (GB: The Carter Case). Ride On, Vaquero. Three Girls About Town. Rise and Shine. Out of the Fog. You Belong to Me (GB: Good Morning, Doctor). You're in the Army Now. 1942: Heart of the Golden West. Blondie's Blessed Event (GB: A Bundle of Trouble). Larceny, Inc. Moonlight Masquerade. The Man Who Wouldn't Die. A Tragedy at Midnight. You Can't Escape Forever. We Were Dancing. 1943: Henry Aldrich Plays Cupid (GB: Henry Plays Cupid). Thank Your Lucky Stars. The Man from Music Mountain. Mystery Broadcast. 1944: Four Jills in a Jeep. Jamboree. In the Meantime, Darling. Two Thoroughbreds. 1945: The Chicago Kid. Don't Fence Me In. The Horn Blows at Midnight. Mama Loves Papa. Pillow to Post. State Fair. Spellbound. The Southerner. Swingin' on a Rainbow. Up Goes Maisie (GB: Up She Goes). 1946: Blondie's Lucky Day. The Bamboo Blonde. Easy to Wed. I've Always Loved You. In Fast Company. Gay Blades. They Made Me a Killer. Heldorado. 1947: The Beginning or the End. Danger Street. The Late George Apley. High Barbaree. Out of the Blue. The Perils of Pauline. When a Girl's Beautiful. Wyoming. Call Northside 777. 1948: Blondie's Reward. Family Honeymoon. Give My Regards to Broadway. Speed to Spare. A Southern Yankee (GB: My Hero). Smuggler's Cove. Waterfront at Midnight. Lightnin' in the Forest. 1949: Duke of Chicago. The Fountainhead. The Girl from Jones Beach. Make-Believe Ballroom. Side Street. Down to the Sea in Ships. John Loves Mary. Mr Belvedere Goes to College. Take One False Step. 1950: The Flying Missile. Father of the Bride. When Willie Comes Marching Home. The Lawless (GB: The Dividing Line). The Milkman. Stella. The Skipper Surprised His Wife. Riding High. Three Little Words. The Yellow Cab Man. Unmasked. A Ticket to Tomahawk. 1951: Excuse My Dust. Father's Little Dividend. Let's Go Navy. The Tall Target. Thunder in God's Country. Up Front. 1952: Dreamboat. April in Paris. Here Come the Nelsons. Has Anybody Seen My Gal. The First Time. Skirts Ahoy! 1953: Remains to be Seen. Calamity Jane. The Girl Who Had Everything. 1954: Sabrina (GB: Sabrina Fair). Three for the Show. 1955: High Society. The Twinkle in God's Eye. 1956: The Ten Commandments.

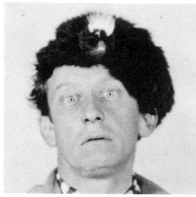

HATTON, Raymond 1887–1971

Cross-looking American actor with unruly dark hair. A leading star of early silents, he formed a comedy team with big Wallace Beery in the late 1920s, Beery's bulk contrasting hilariously with short, skinny Hatton. Despite facial features that seemed to qualify him for villain roles, he got a wide variety of parts before, in the late 1930s, becoming the scruffy sidekick of numerous western stars, latterly Johnny Mack Brown. Died from a heart attack.

1912: *Oh, Those Eyes. 1913: The Squaw Man (GB: The White Man). 1914: The Circus Man. The Making of Bobby Burnit. 1915: The Arab. The Golden Chance. The Woman. The Immigrant (not the Chaplin). Chimmie Fadden. The Warrens of Virginia. Blackbirds. The Unknown. The Wild Goose Chase. The Unafraid. Temptation. The Girl of the Golden West. Armstrong's Wife. Kindling. Chimmie Fadden Out West. 1916: Tennessee's Partner. Oliver Twist. Public Opinion. To Have and to Hold. Easy Money. The Sowers. The Love Mask. The Lash. The Honorable Friend. Joan the Woman. 1917: The Little American. The Woman God Forgot. The American Consul. What Money Can't Buy. The Squaw Man's Son. Hashimura Togo. The Devil Stone. Nan of Music Mountain. Crystal Gazer. Sandy. The Secret Game. Romance of the Redwoods. 1918: The Whispering Chorus. We Can't Have Everything. The Source. Arizona. The Goat. *The Geezer of Berlin. One More American. Johnny Get Your Gun. The Firefly of France. Cruise of the Make-Believe. Less Than Kin. Jules of the Strongheart. 1919: You're Fired! Male and Female (GB: The Admirable Crichton). Everywoman. The Love Burglar. For Better, For Worse. The Dub (GB: The Fool). The Squaw Man (Remake. GB: The White Man). Maggie Pepper. The Wild Goose Chase (different film from 1915). Experimental Marriage. Poor Boob (GB: Poor Fool). Secret Service. The Dancin' Fool. 1920: Jes' Call Me Jim. Officer 666. Stop, Thief! Young Mrs Winthrop. The Sea Wolf. 1921: The Affairs of Anatol. The Ace of Hearts. Doubling for Romeo. Salvage. The Concert. Bunty Pulls the Strings. Peck's Bad Boy. All's Fair in Love. Pilgrims of the Night. 1922: To Have and to Hold. The Hottentot. Pink Gods. Manslaughter. Ebb Tide. His Back Against the Wall. Head Over Heels. 1923: The Virginian. The Barefoot Boy. Java Head. Three Wise Fools. Big Brother. Enemies of Children. The Tie That Binds. A Man of Action. Trimmed in Scarlet. The Hunchback of Notre Dame. 1924: True As Steel. Triumph. Three Women. The Mine with the Iron Door. Half-a-Dollar Bill. The Fighting American. Cornered. 1925: Adventure. Contraband. In the Name of Love. The Devil's Cargo. The Thundering Herd. A Son of His Father. The Top of the World. The Lucky Devil. Tomorrow's Love. 1926: Lord Jim. Behind the Front. Born to the West. Silence. Forlorn River. We're in the Navy Now. 1927: Fashions for Women. Now We're in the Air. Fireman, Save My Child. 1928: Partners in Crime. The Big Killing. Wife Savers. 1929: Her Unborn Child (GB: Her Child). The Office Scandal. Trent's Last Case. Dear Vivien. Hell's Heroes. *When Caesar Ran a Newspaper. The Mighty. 1930: The Silver Horde. Murder on the Roof. Rogue of the Rio Grande. The Road to Paradise. Midnight Mystery. *Pineapples. 1931: The Squaw Man (GB: The White Man). Woman Hungry (GB: The Challenge). Honeymoon Lane. The Lion and the Lamb. *Stung. *Hollywood Halfbacks. Arrowsmith. 1932: Polly of the Circus. The Fourth Horseman. Drifting Souls. Exposed. The Crooked Circle. Law and Order. Uptown New York. Malay Nights (GB: Shadows of Singapore). Stranger in Town. Vanishing Frontier. Alias Mary Smith. Cornered (and 1924 film of same title). Vanity Street. *Divorce à la Mode. *Long Loop Laramie. 1933: Terror Trail. Hidden Gold. The Big Cage. Penthouse (GB: Crooks in Clover). *Rockabye Cowboy. The Three Musketeers (serial). Lady Killer. The Thundering Herd. State Trooper. Under the Tonto Rim. The Women in His Life. Alice in Wonderland. *Tom's in Town. Day of Reckoning. 1934: Lazy River. Fifteen Wives (GB: The Man with the Electric Voice). Straight Is the Way. The Defense Rests. Red Morning. Wagon Wheels. Once to Every Bachelor. 1935: Times Square Lady. Murder in the Fleet. The Daring Young Man. *Desert Death. Wanderer of the Wasteland. Steamboat 'Round the Bend. Nevada. Stormy. Rustlers of Red Gap (serial). Calm Yourself. G-Men. 1936: Arizona Raiders. Desert Gold. Undersea Kingdom (serial). Laughing Irish Eyes. Timothy's Quest. Yellowstone. Fury. The Vigilantes Are Coming (serial). Mad Holiday. Exclusive Story. Women Are Trouble. 1937: Jungle Jim (serial). Marked Woman. San Quentin. Bad Men of Brimstone. Fly-Away Baby. The Adventurous Blonde. Roaring Timber. Public Wedding. Over the Goal. The Missing Witness. Love is On the Air (GB: The Radio Murder Mystery). 1938: Love Finds Andy Hardy. Tom Sawyer, Detective. Touchdown, Army! (GB: Generals of Tomorrow). The Texans. Over the Wall. He Couldn't Say No. Come On, Rangers. I'm from Missouri. Ambush. Wall Street Cowboy. Paris Honeymoon. Undercover Doctor. Six Thousand Enemies. Cowboys from Texas. The New Frontier/Frontier Horizon. Kansas Terror. Career. Frontier Pony Express. Wyoming Outlaw. Rough Riders' Roundup. 1940: Oklahoma Renegades. Kit Carson. Hi Yo Silver! Rocky Mountain Rangers. Covered Wagon Days. Heroes of the Saddle. Queen of the Mob. Pioneers of the West. 1941: Texas. Gunman from Bodie. White Eagle (serial). Arizona Bound. Forbidden Trails. 1942: Down Texas Way. Dawn on the Great Divide. Cadets on Parade. Riders of the West. Ghost Town Law. West of the Law. The Affairs of Martha (GB: Once Upon a Thursday). The Girl from Alaska. Below the Border. Her Cardboard Lover. Reap the Wild Wind. 1943: Outlaws of Stampede Pass. A Stranger in Town. Six Gun Gospel. Stranger from Pecos. Prairie Chickens. The Ghost Rider. The Texas Kid. 1944: Raiders of the Border. Tall in the Saddle. Range Law. West of the Rio Grande. Law of the Valley. Land of the Outlaws. Ghost Guns. Partners of the Trail. Law Men. 1945: Flame of the West. Frontier Flame. Gun Smoke. Navajo Trail. Sunbonnet Sue. Rhythm Roundup (GB: Honest John). The Lost Trail. Frontier Feud. Stranger from Santa Fé. Northwest Trail. 1946: Fool's Gold. Drifting Along. Under Arizona Skies. Border Bandits. Gentleman from Texas. The Haunted Mine. Shadows on the Range. Silver Range. Raiders of the South. Trigger Fingers. Rolling Home. 1947: Trailing Danger. Land of the Lawless. Valley of Fear. Black Gold. Code of the Saddle. The Law Comes to Gunsight. To the Ends of the Earth. Unconquered. Flashing Guns. Prairie Express. Gun Talk. 1948: Back Trail. Overland Trail. Triggerman. Crossed Trails. White Eagle. Frontier Agent. The Sheriff of Medicine Bow. Silver River. The Fighting Ranger. Gunning for Justice. Hidden Danger. 1950: Hostile Country. Fast on the Draw. West of the Brazos. County Fair. Crooked River. Marshal of Heldorado. Operation Haylift. Colorado Ranger. 1951: Skipalong Rosenbloom. Kentucky Jubilee. 1952: The Daltons' Women. †Arrow in the Dust (TV). †Two-Gun Marshal (TV). The Golden Hawk. 1953: Cow Country. 1954: Thunder Pass. 1955: The Twinkle in God's Eye. The Treasure of Ruby Hills. The Day the World Ended. 1956: Dig That Uranium. Flesh and the Spur. Shake, Rattle and Rock. Girls in Prison. 1957: Invasion of the Saucer Men (GB: Invasion of the Hell Creatures). Motorcycle Gang. Pawnee (GB: Pale Arrow). 1959: Alaska Passage. 1964: The Quick Gun. 1965: Requiem for a Gunfighter. 1967: In Cold Blood.

† Shown in cinemas in some countries

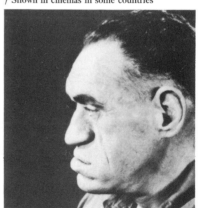

HATTON, Rondo 1894–1946

Thanks to the congenital acromegaly that distorted his body and facial features, this American actor was unmistakeable. It also confined him to playing villainous or horrific roles. But audiences were fascinated by him as a killer called The Creeper in several films, and in 1946, Universal spun an entire film around him, The Brute Man. In the same year, he was dead from a heart attack.

1930: *Hell Harbor.* 1938: *In Old Chicago. Alexander's Ragtime Band.* 1939: *The Hunchback of Notre Dame. Captain Fury. The Big Guy.* 1940: *Chad Hanna. Moon Over Burma.* 1942: *The Cyclone Kid. The Black Swan. The Moon and Sixpence. The Ox-Bow Incident (GB: Strange Incident).* 1943: *Sleepy Lagoon.* 1944: *Raiders of Ghost City (serial). The Pearl of Death. The Princess and the Pirate. Johnny Doesn't Live Here Anymore. Bermuda Mystery.* 1945: *The Royal Mounted Rides Again (serial). Jungle Captive.* 1946: *House of Horrors (GB: Joan Medford is Missing). Spider Woman Strikes Back. The Brute Man.*

HAWTREY, Charles
(George C. Hartree) 1914–1988
Bespectacled, goggle-eyed, thin-lipped, dry-voiced, skinny comic actor who made a whole career out of snooty schoolboys, especially in Will Hay comedies. Dark-haired Hawtrey, from a theatrical family, started in show business as a child: on radio, after brief fame as a boy soprano, he was the voice of Norman Bones, boy detective in children's programmes, for many years. Later one of the 'Carry On' comedy gang. Died from arterial problems following a heart attack

1922: †*Tell Your Children.* 1923: †*This Freedom.* 1932: †*Marry Me.* 1933: †*The Melody Maker.* 1935: **Kiddies on Parade.* 1936: *Sabotage (US: The Woman Alone). Cheer Up! Well Done Henry.* 1937: *Good Morning, Boys! (US: Where There's a Will). The Gap. East of Ludgate Hill.* 1939: *Where's That Fire? Jailbirds.* 1941: *The Ghost of St Michael's. The Black Sheep of Whitehall.* 1942: *Let the People Sing. The Goose Steps Out. Much Too Shy.* 1943: *Bell Bottom George.* 1944: *A Canterbury Tale.* 1946: *Meet Me at Dawn.* 1947: *The End of the River.* 1948: *The Story of Shirley Yorke.* 1949: *Passport to Pimlico. Dark Secret.* 1950: *Room to Let.* 1951: *Smart Alec. The Galloping Major. Brandy for the Parson.* 1952: *Hammer the Toff. You're Only Young Twice!* 1954: *Five Days (US: Paid to Kill).* To Dorothy a Son (US: Cash on Delivery). 1955: *As Long As They're Happy. Man of the Moment. Timeslip (US: The Atomic Man). Simon and Laura. Jumping for Joy. Who Done It?* 1956: *The March Hare.* 1958: *Carry On Sergeant.* 1959: *I Only Arsked! Carry On Nurse. Carry On Teacher. Please Turn Over. Inn for Trouble.* 1960: *Carry On Constable.*

1961: *Carry On Regardless. Dentist on the Job (US: Get On with It!). What a Whopper!* 1963: *Carry On Cabby. Carry On Jack (US: Carry On Venus).* 1964: *Carry On Cleo. Carry On Spying.* 1965: *Carry On Cowboy.* 1966: *Carry On Screaming. Don't Lose Your Head.* 1967: *The Terrornauts. Follow That Camel. Carry On Doctor.* 1968: *Carry On Up the Khyber.* 1969: *Carry On Camping. Carry On Again, Doctor. Zeta One.* 1970: *Carry On Loving. Carry On Up the Jungle. Carry On Henry. Grasshopper Island (TV).* 1971: *Carry On at Your Convenience.* 1972: *Carry On Matron. Carry On Abroad.*

As director:
1945: *What Do We Do Now? Dumb Dora Discovers Tobacco.*

† As Charles Hawtrey Jr

HAYDEN, Harry 1882–1955
Chirpy, chipper, chubby, cheerful chap (born in what was then Oklahoma's Indian Territory) who came to Hollywood at 54 and padded in and out of one-scene roles for nearly 20 years. Usually bespectacled and benign, the little man bowled into a film like a helpful and well-meaning teddy bear, playing clerks, train conductors, detectives, bank tellers and right-minded citizens in general. Hayden's brown hair had long since turned to a sympathetic silver when he rounded out his career with a running role as Harry on the TV series *The Trouble with Father (The New Stu Erwin Show)* in 1954 and 1955.

1936: **Fool Proof. College Holiday. Fury. The Princess Comes Across. Public Enemy's Wife (GB: G-Man's Wife). I Married a Doctor. The Man I Marry. God's Country and the Woman. Killer at Large. Two Against the World (GB: The Case of Mrs Pembrook). The Case of the Black Cat. Black Legion. Three Men on a Horse.* 1937: *Ever Since Eve. Love is on the Air (GB: The Radio Murder Mystery). Love is News. John Meade's Woman. Danger Patrol. Melody for Two. Exclusive. Maytime. Artists and Models.* 1938: *In Old Chicago. Little Tough Guy. Sky Giant. The Law West of Tombstone. Straight, Place and Show (GB: They're Off). Double Danger. Saleslady. Delinquent Parents. I'll Give a Million. *The Wrong Way Out. Four Men and a Prayer. Hold That Co-Ed (GB: Hold That Girl). Angels with Dirty Faces. Kentucky.* 1939: *Hidden Power. The Under-*

Pup. *Wife, Husband and Friend. Society Smugglers. Mr Smith Goes to Washington. Five Little Peppers and How They Grew. House of Fear. The Honeymoon's Over. Invitation to Happiness. The Rains Came. Rose of Washington Square. At the Circus/The Marx Brothers at the Circus. Flight at Midnight. Frontier Marshal. Barricade. Swanee River. The Cisco Kid and the Lady. Here I Am a Stranger.* 1940: *Saps at Sea. The Great McGinty (GB: Down Went McGinty). He Married His Wife. Boom Town. I Want a Divorce. Black Friday. Lillian Russell. I Love You Again. Christmas in July. Manhattan Heartbeat. We Who Are Young. Yesterday's Heroes. The Man Who Wouldn't Talk. The Mad Doctor (GB: A Date with Destiny). Knute Rockne – All American (GB: A Modern Hero). You're Not So Tough.* 1941: *Footsteps in the Dark. A Man Betrayed/Wheel of Fortune (GB: Citadel of Crime). Sleepers West. The Stork Pays Off. Mountain Moonlight (GB: Moving in Society). The Parson of Panamint. The Night of January 16th. Remember the Day. High Sierra. Sullivan's Travels. Hold That Ghost! Last of the Duanes. The Getaway. Week-End in Havana.* 1942: *This Gun for Hire. The Lone Star Ranger. The War Against Mrs Hadley. Calling Dr Gillespie. Careful, Soft Shoulder. Valley of the Sun. We Were Dancing. Yankee Doodle Dandy. You Can't Escape Forever. You're Telling Me. Yokel Boy (GB: Hitting the Headlines). Whispering Ghosts. Rings on Her Fingers. Larceny Inc. Get Hep to Love (GB: She's My Lovely). Joan of Ozark (GB: Queen of Spies). The Magnificent Dope. Tales of Manhattan. The Palm Beach Story. Springtime in the Rockies.* 1943: *How's About It? Hello, Frisco, Hello. Du Barry Was a Lady. Slightly Dangerous. You're a Lucky Fellow, Mr Smith. Youth on Parade. Submarine Alert. She Has What It Takes. The Meanest Man in the World. The Unknown Guest. Salute to the Marines. True to Life. Best Foot Forward. Henry Aldrich Gets Glamour (GB: Henry Gets Glamour). Henry Aldrich Plays Cupid (GB: Henry Plays Cupid).* 1944: *The Great Moment. The Lady and the Monster (GB: The Lady and the Doctor). Thirty Seconds Over Tokyo. Up in Mabel's Room. Barbary Coast Gent. Since You Went Away. The Big Noise. Up in Arms. Weird Woman. The Thin Man Goes Home. Hail the Conquering Hero. The Woman in the Window.* 1945: *Dangerous Partners. Incendiary Blonde. A Medal for Benny. Boston Blackie's Rendezvous (GB: Blackie's Rendezvous). Frisco Sal. The Sailor Takes a Wife. Colonel Effingham's Raid (GB: Man of the Hour). Uncle Harry/The Strange Affair of Uncle Harry. Where Do We Go from Here? Guest Wife. The Blue Dahlia.* 1946: *Ziegfeld Follies (filmed 1944). The Bride Wore Boots. *Maid Trouble. The Hoodlum Saint. The Virginian. Notorious. Two Sisters from Boston. If I'm Lucky. Till the Clouds Roll By. Without Reservations. The Secret Heart. Till the End of Time. My Brother Talks to Horses. The Killers.* 1947: *Easy Come, Easy Go. The Perils of Pauline. Millie's Daughter. Variety Girl. The Unfinished Dance. Key Witness. Merton of the Movies. For the Love of Rusty. Out of the Past (GB: Build My Gallows High).* 1948: *Family Honeymoon. Fighting Father Dunne. Rusty Leads the Way. The Judge Steps Out (GB: Indian Summer). Silver River. The Velvet Touch. Docks of New Orleans. The*

*Dude Goes West. Good Sam. One Touch of Venus. Every Girl Should Be Married. Out of the Storm. Smart Girls Don't Talk. 1949: The Beautiful Blonde from Bashful Bend. Joe Palooka in the Big Fight. Abbott and Costello Meet the Killer, Boris Karloff. Gun Crazy/Deadly is the Female. Intruder in the Dust. The Lone Wolf and His Lady. Prison Warden. Bad Men of Tombstone. *Mr Whitney Had a Notion. Adventure in Baltimore (GB: Bachelor Bait). 1950: The Traveling Saleswoman. Union Station. *Newlyweds' Boarder. 1951: Pier 13. Street Bandits. *Newlyweds' Easy Payments. Double Dynamite. Angels in the Outfield (GB: Angels and the Pirates). *Deal Me In. 1952: When in Rome. *Newlyweds Take a Chance. O Henry's Full House (GB: Full House). Tonight We Sing. And Now Tomorrow. Carrie. Army Bound. 1953: Money from Home. The Last Posse. Hurricane at Pilgrim Hill.*

HAYDN, Richard 1905–1985
Tall, angular, aloof-looking English character actor who cornered the market in prissy professors in the Hollywood of the forties. A former dancer and revue artist, he became an inveterate scene-stealer in comic cameos, and also scored in the occasional serious role, such as his schoolmaster in *The Green Years*. Also a writer (as Edwin Carp) and director.

1941: Charley's Aunt (GB: Charley's American Aunt). Ball of Fire. 1942: Are Husbands Necessary? Thunder Birds. 1943: Forever and a Day. No Time for Love. 1944: Tonight and Every Night. 1945: And Then There Were None (GB: Ten Little Niggers). Adventure. 1946: Cluny Brown. The Green Years. 1947: The Late George Apley. The Beginning or the End? Singapore. Forever Amber. The Foxes of Harrow. 1948: Sitting Pretty. Miss Tatlock's Millions. The Emperor Waltz. 1949: Dear Wife. 1950: Mr Music. 1951: Alice in Wonderland (voice only). 1952: The Merry Widow. 1953: Never Let Me Go. Money from Home. 1954: Her Twelve Men. 1955: Jupiter's Darling. 1956: Toy Tiger. 1958: Twilight for the Gods. 1960: Please Don't Eat the Daisies. The Lost World. 1962: Mutiny on the Bounty. Five Weeks in a Balloon. 1965: The Sound of Music. Clarence the Cross-Eyed Lion. The Adventures of Bullwhip Griffin. 1971: Charlie Chan:

Happiness is a Warm Clue (TV). 1974: Young Frankenstein.

As director:
1948: Miss Tatlock's Millions. 1949: Dear Wife. 1950: Mr Music.

HAYES, George 'Gabby' 1885–1969
Many western heroes had comic sidekicks in the 1930s and 1940s. But bewhiskered (from 1935) George 'Gabby' Hayes was not only about the most popular, but perhaps the only one who was also a star in the public eye. A vaudevillian of long experience, he joined films with the coming of sound, and soon assumed the all-round white whiskers and flapped-back stetson that, together with such expressions as 'Consarn it!' or 'You're durn tootin' built an unforgettable westerner. Died from a heart ailment.

*1923: Why Women Marry. 1929: The Rainbow Man. Smiling Irish Eyes. Big News. 1930: For the Defense. 1931: Nevada Buckaroo. God's Country and the Man. Rose of the Rio Grande. Big Business Girl. Cavalier of the West. Dragnet Patrol (GB: Love Redeemed). 1932: Night Rider. Border Devils. Texas Buddies. From Broadway to Cheyenne (GB: Broadway to Cheyenne). *The Stolen Jools (GB: The Slippery Pearls). Hidden Valley. Winner Take All. Without Honor. Love Me Tonight. Klondike. The Boiling Point. Wild Horse Mesa. The Fighting Champ. The Man from Hell's Edges. Riders of the Desert. Ghost Valley. 1933: The Gallant Fool. Sagebrush Trail. Skyway. The Fugitive. Crashing Broadway. The Sphinx. Galloping Romeo. The Phantom Broadcast (GB: Phantom of the Air). Riders of Destiny. Devil's Mate (GB: He Knew Too Much). Breed of the Border (GB: Speed Brent Wins). The Return of Casey Jones. *Bedlam of Beards. The Ranger's Code. The Fighting Texans (GB: Randy Strikes Oil). Trailing North. Self Defense. West of the Divide. 1934: Monte Carlo Nights. The Star Packer (GB: He Wore a Star). The Man from Utah. In Old Sante Fé. The Lucky Texan. 'Neath Arizona Skies. Blue Steel. Randy Rides Alone. The Man from Hell. Mystery Liner (GB: The Secret of John Holling). The Lost Jungle (serial). House of Mystery. Beggars in Ermine. City Limits. Brand of Hate. 1935: The Throwback. Smokey Smith. Justice of the Range. $1,000 a Minute. Hopalong Cassidy. Texas Terrors. Rainbow Valley. Thunder Mountain.*

*Tumbling Tumbleweeds. The Hoosier Schoolmaster (GB: The Schoolmaster). Tombstone Terror. Bar 20 Rides Again. The Eagle's Brood. Welcome Home. The Outlaw Tamer. Ladies Crave Excitement. Hitchhike Lady. Death Flies East. Lawless Frontier. Honeymoon Limited. Headline Woman. The Lost City (serial). 1936: The Plainsman. Silver Spurs. Song of the Trail. Swifty. Call of the Prairie. Hopalong Cassidy Returns. Valiant is the Word for Carrie. Mr Deeds Goes to Town. The Lawless Nineties. The Bridge of Sighs. Three on the Trail. I Married a Doctor. Hearts in Bondage. The Texas Rangers. Hearts of the West. Trail Dust. Valley of the Lawless. Glory Parade. 1937: Hills of Old Wyoming. Mountain Music. North of the Rio Grande. Rustler's Valley. Borderland. Hopalong Rides Again. Texas Trail. 1938: Forbidden Music. Gold is Where You Find It. Bar 20 Justice. Heart of Arizona. The Frontiersman. In Old Mexico. Pride of the West. Sunset Trail. 1939: In Old Caliente. In Old Monterey. Southward Ho! Man of Conquest. Wall Street Cowboy. Fighting Thoroughbreds. Saga of Death Valley. Days of Jesse James. Renegade Trail. Silver on the Sage. The Arizona Kid. Let Freedom Ring. 1940: Wagons Westward. Young Buffalo Bill. Dark Command. Melody Ranch. Young Bill Hickok. The Carson City Kid. The Ranger and the Lady. Colorado. Border Legion. 1941: In Old Cheyenne. Robin Hood of the Pecos. Nevada City. Sheriff of Tombstone. Jesse James at Bay. Red River Valley. Bad Men of Deadwood. *Meet Roy Rogers. 1942: Man from Cheyenne. Sunset on the Desert. South of Santa Fé. Hearts of the Golden West. Ridin' Down the Canyon. Romance on the Range. Sons of the Pioneers. Sunset Serenade. 1943: Calling Wild Bill Elliott. Bordertown Gunfighters. Death Valley Manhunt. Overland Mail Robbery. Wagon Tracks West. In Old Oklahoma (GB: War of the Wildcats). The Man from Thunder River. 1944: Lights of Old Sante Fé. Tucson Raiders. Mojave Firebrand. The Big Bonanza. Tall in the Saddle. Marshal of Reno. Hidden Valley Outlaws. Leave It to the Irish. 1945: Bells of Rosarita. The Man from Oklahoma. Along the Navajo Trail. Utah. Don't Fence Me In. Sunset in Eldorado. Out California Way. 1946: Home in Oklahoma. My Pal Trigger. Song of Arizona. Badman's Territory. Roll On, Texas Moon. Rainbow over Texas. Under Nevada Skies. Heldorado. 1947: Trail Street. Wyoming. 1948: Albuquerque (GB: Silver City). The Untamed Breed. Return of the Bad Men. 1949: El Paso. 1950: The Cariboo Trail.*

HAYES, Patricia 1909–
Diminutive, brown-haired actress with rather forlorn features, one of Britain's most popular character players, even though she was in relatively few films. Her voice became familiar to young radio fans in the 1940s as that of Henry Bones, *boy* detective, on *Children's Hour*! Later, she made a speciality of disreputable working-class characters and won a British TV Oscar in 1971 for *Edna the Inebriate Woman*. Reckoned to have worked with more top British comedians than any other actress, she is also the mother of actor Richard O'Callaghan.

1936: Broken Blossoms. 1942: Went the Day Well? (US: 48 Hours). 1943: When We Are

Married. The Dummy Talks. 1944: Candles at Nine. Hotel Reserve. 1945: Great Day. 1947: Nicholas Nickleby. 1948: To the Public Danger. 1949: Skimpy in the Navy. Poet's Pub. 1954: The Love Match. 1955: Cloak Without Dagger (US: Operation Conspiracy). The Deep Blue Sea. 1959: The Battle of the Sexes. 1962: Kill or Cure. Reach for Glory. 1963: Heavens Above! Saturday Night Out. 1964: The Bargee. The Sicilians. A Hard Day's Night. 1965: Help! 1967: A Ghost of a Chance. The Terrornauts. 1969: Can Hieronymous Merkin Ever Forget Mercy Humppe and Find True Happiness? Goodbye, Mr Chips. Carry on Again, Doctor. 1970: Grasshopper Island (TV). Fragment of Fear. 1971: Raising the Roof. 1973: Love Thy Neighbour. Servizio di scorta (GB: Blue Movie Blackmail. US: Mafia Junction). 1974: The Best of Benny Hill 1979· *Film. The Corn is Green (TV). 1980: Danger on Dartmoor. 1984: The Neverending Story. 1986: Little Dorrit I. Little Dorrit II. 1988: Willow. A Fish Called Wanda. War Requiem. 1989: The Last Island. 1990: The Fool. 1991: The House of Bernarda Alba (TV). 1993: Crime and Punishment. 1995: The Steal.

HAYTER, James 1907–1983
Short, smily, chubby-cheeked, round-faced, India-born British stalwart, much in demand for supporting roles from the time he decided to try films in 1936. Briefly a star in the early 1950s (at the time he played Friar Tuck and Mr Pickwick), he stayed in good roles for the rest of the decade. Could be comic—or quite touching in more serious

roles. Busy in TV series of the 1970s, a time when he was also a popular voice-over for commercials.

1936: Aren't Men Beasts! Sensation. 1937: Big Fella. 1938: Marigold. Murder in Soho (US: Murder in the Night). 1939: Come On George. Band Waggon. 1940: Sailors Three (US: Three Cockeyed Sailors). 1946: The Laughing Lady. The Captive Heart. School for Secrets (US: Secret Flight). 1947: Nicholas Nickleby. The End of the River. Vice Versa. Captain Boycott. The Ghosts of Berkeley Square. The Mark of Cain. The October Man. My Brother Jonathan. 1948: Quartet. A Song for Tomorrow. The Fallen Idol. Bonnie Prince Charlie. No Room at the Inn. Once a Jolly Swagman (US: Maniacs on Wheels). All Over the Town. Silent Dust. The Blue Lagoon. 1949: For Them That Trespass. Helter Skelter. Don't Ever Leave Me. Scrapbook for 1933 (voice only). Passport to Pimlico. Dear Mr Prohack. The Spider and the Fly. Morning Departure (US: Operation Disaster). 1950: Your Witness (US: Eye Witness). Night and the City. Waterfront (US: Waterfront Women). Trio. The Woman With No Name (US: Her Paneled Door). 1951: Flesh and Blood. Tom Brown's Schooldays. Calling Bulldog Drummond. 1952: The Story of Robin Hood and His Merrie Men. I'm a Stranger. The Crimson Pirate. The Pickwick Papers. The Great Game. 1953: Four-Sided Triangle. Will Any Gentleman? . . . The Triangle. Always a Bride. A Day to Remember. 1954: *The Journey. For Better, For Worse (US: Cocktails in the Kitchen). Beau Brummell. 1955: See How They Run. Touch and Go (US: The Light Touch). Land of the Pharaohs. 1956: Keep It Clean. Port Afrique. It's a Wonderful World. The Big Money (released 1958). 1957: Seven Waves Away (US: Abandon Ship!). The Heart Within. Carry On Admiral (US: The Ship Was Loaded). Sail into Danger. 1958: Gideon's Day (US: Gideon of Scotland Yard). The Key. I Was Monty's Double. The Captain's Table. 1959: The 39 Steps. The Boy and the Bridge. 1961: Go to Blazes. 1962: Out of the Fog. 1967: Stranger in the House (US: Cop-Out). A Challenge for Robin Hood. 1968: Oliver! 1969: David Copperfield (TV. GB: cinemas). 1970: Blood on Satan's Claw. Scramble. The Firechasers. The Horror of Frankenstein. Song of Norway. 1971: Not Tonight Darling! 1975: The Bawdy Adventures of Tom Jones.

HEALEY, Myron 1922–
Big, fair-haired, blue-eyed, mean-looking American actor who mostly played bullying, rarely smiling villains in 'B' westerns, but was also good in some minor leading roles of the 1950s. The son of a prominent Californian proctologist, Healey was a child prodigy who sang on radio and gave violin and piano recitals while still in his early teens. Later he studied acting under Maria Ouspenskaya (qv) and made his film debut in MGM's Crime Does Not Pay two-reel series. After war service as a navigator in the Army Air Corps, Healey clocked up dozens of film credits, also finding time to write a few screenplays. Married (third) actress Adair Jameson in 1971.

1942: *For the Common Defense. *Keep 'Em Sailing. 1943: *Faculty Row. Swing Shift Maisie (GB: The Girl in Overalls). Salute to the Marines. I Dood It (GB: By Hook or By Crook). Thousands Cheer. The Iron Major. 1944: See Here, Private Hargrove. Meet the People. 1946: The Time of Their Lives. Crime Doctor's Man Hunt. Blondie's Big Moment. 1947: The Corpse Came COD. It Had to be You. Buck Privates Come Home (GB: Rookies Come Home). Down to Earth. Millie's Daughter. 1948: Blondie's Reward. The Man from Colorado. Air Hostess. Law of the Barbary Coast. Hidden Danger. Across the Rio Grande. *Silly Billy. Wake of the Red Witch. I, Jane Doe (GB: Diary of a Bride). You Gotta Stay Happy. Ladies of the Chorus. The Return of October (GB: A Date with Destiny). Range Justice. 1949: Trail's End. *The Girl from Gunsight Knock on Any Door. South of Rio. Lawless Code. Haunted Trails. Western Renegades. Gun Law Justice. Riders of the Dusk. Slightly French. Rusty's Birthday. I Was an American Spy. Brand of Fear. Laramie. 1950: Hi-Jacked. No Sad Songs for Me. Salt Lake Raiders. Trail of the Rustlers. Pioneer Marshal. Emergency Wedding. Over the Border. A Woman of Distinction. My Blue Heaven. Abbott and Costello in the Foreign Legion. Johnny One-Eye. The Fuller Brush Girl (GB: The Affairs of Sally). I Killed Geronimo. Outlaw Gold. Between Midnight and Dawn. West of Wyoming. Fence Riders. Law of the Panhandle. Hot Rod. In a Lonely Place. Short Grass. 1951: Colorado Ambush. Montana Desperado. Bonanza Town. The Big Night. The Texas Rangers. Roar of the Iron Horse (serial). The Longhorn. Lorna Doone. Journey into Light. The Hoodlum. Bomba and the Elephant Stampede. *Baby Sitters' Jitters. Silver City (GB: High Vermilion). The Wild Blue Yonder (GB: Thunder Across the Pacific. Voice only). Slaughter Trail. Night Riders of Montana. 1952: The Kid from Broken Gun. Rodeo. Desperadoes' Outpost. West of Wyoming. The Maverick. Fort Osage. Storm Over Tibet. Montana Territory. Apache War Smoke. Monsoon. Fargo. 1953: White Lightning. Vigilante Terror. Texas Bad Man. Kansas Pacific. Private Eyes. The Moonlighter. Saginaw Trail. Son of Belle Starr. Combat Squad. The Fighting Lawman. Hot News. 1954: Cattle Queen of Montana. Silver Lode. Rails into Laramie. 1955: Man Without a Star. Panther Girl of the Kongo (serial). Rage at Dawn. Gang Busters. Ma and Pa Kettle at Waikiki. Yacht on the High Sea (TV. GB: cinemas). Tennessee's Partner.

Jungle Moon Men. African Manhunt. The Man from Bitter Ridge. Count Three and Pray. Guns Don't Argue. 1956: Magnificent Roughnecks. The Claw Monsters (feature version of Panther Girl of the Kongo). Border Showdown (TV. GB: cinemas). Dig That Uranium. Thunder over Sangoland. Slightly Scarlet. The First Texan. The Young Guns. The White Squaw. Calling Homicide. Running Target. 1957: The Restless Breed. Days of the Trumpet. Shoot-Out at Medicine Bend. Hell's Crossroads. Crime Beneath the Sea (GB: Undersea Girl). The Hard Man. The Unearthly. 1958: Quantrill's Raiders. Escape from Red Rock. Cole Younger, Gunfighter. Apache Territory. 1959: Gunfight at Dodge City. Rio Bravo. 1960: The Sign of Zorro. 1961: The George Raft Story (GB: Spin of a Coin). 1962: Convicts Four (GB: Reprieve!). The Final Hour (TV. GB: cinemas). Varan the Unbelievable. 1963: Cavalry Command. 1964: He Rides Tall. 1965: Harlow (Carroll Baker version). Mirage. 1966: Shadow on the Land (TV). 1967: Journey to Shiloh. 1968: The Shakiest Gun in the West. 1969: True Grit. The Over-the-Hill Gang (TV). 1970: The Cheyenne Social Club. Which Way to the Front? (GB: Ja! Ja! Mein General, But Which Way to the Front?). 1975: Goodbye Franklin High. Devil Bear/Claws. Smoke in the Wind. 1977: The Incredible Melting Man. 1978: The Other Side of the Mountain: Part 2. 1979: Spider-Man The Dragon's Challenge (TV. GB: cinemas). 1986: Ghost Fever. 1987: Pulse.

HEATHCOTE, Thomas 1917–1986
Scowling British actor with dark, bequiffed hair and dented cheeks, usually in downbeat or 'countrified' roles, but occasionally as pugnacious criminals. Born in India, he was taken under the wing of Laurence Olivier, who helped him get into films and gave him a small role in one of his earliest, *Hamlet*. Despite a distinctive style, he played only smallish movie parts after that, and gained more popularity and reputation on television and in the theatre.

1947: Night Beat. 1948: Hamlet. 1950: Dance Hall. 1951: Cloudburst. 1953: Malta Story. The Red Beret (US: Paratrooper). The Large Rope. The Sword and the Rose. Blood Orange. 1954: Betrayed. The Seekers (US: Land of Fury). 1955: Above Us the Waves. Doctor at Sea. 1956: The Iron Petticoat. The Last Man

to Hang? Eyewitness. Tiger in the Smoke. 1957: Yangtse Incident/Escape of the Amethyst (US: Battle Hell). 1958: A Night to Remember. Tread Softly, Stranger. 1960: Village of the Damned. 1961: On the Fiddle (US: Operation Snafu). 1962: Billy Budd. 1966: A Man for All Seasons. 1967: Quatermass and the Pit (US: Five Million Miles to Earth). Night of the Big Heat (US: Island of the Burning Damned). 1968: The Fixer. 1970: Julius Caesar. 1971: The Abominable Dr Phibes. Burke and Hare. Demons of the Mind. 1973: Luther. 1976: A Choice of Weapons (later Trial by Combat. US: Dirty Knights' Work). 1983: The Sword of the Valiant. The Jigsaw Man. 1984: The Shooting Party. 1985: Our Exploits at West Poley.

HECKART, Eileen
(Anna Eckart Herbert) 1919–
Thin-faced American actress with dark, tautly curly hair. When she arrived in Hollywood in 1956, after success on Broadway, Heckart looked set to become a regular part of the cinema scene. But she soon returned to stage work, reappearing in 1970s' films only long enough to snatch an Oscar for *Butterflies Are Free*, having already bagged an Emmy in 1967 for *Win Me a Place at Forest Lawn*. Most of her characters were only happy when haranguing their fellows. Also nominated for an Academy Award for *The Bad Seed*.

1956: Miracle in the Rain. The Bad Seed. Bus Stop. Somebody Up There Likes Me. 1958: The Blue Men (TV). Hot Spell. 1959: A Corner of the Garden (TV). 1960: Heller in Pink Tights. 1963: My Six Loves. 1967: Up the Down Staircase. No Way to Treat a Lady. 1969: The Tree. 1972: Butterflies Are Free. The Victim (TV). 1974: Zandy's Bride. The Hiding Place (released 1977). The FBI versus Alvin Karpis, Public Enemy Number One (TV). 1976: Burnt Offerings. 1977: Sunshine Christmas (TV). 1978: Suddenly, Love (TV). 1980: FDR: The Last Year (TV). White Mama (TV). The Big Black Pill (TV). 1982: Games Mother Never Taught You (TV). 1984: Fifty Fifty (TV). 1986: Heartbreak Ridge. Seize the Day (originally for TV). 1989: Stuck with Each Other (TV).

HEGGIE, O. P. 1876–1936
Square-faced, apprehensive-looking, large-eyed, pear-nosed Australian-born actor with a scrap of light-brown hair who was equally

at home with authority, sincerity and querulousness and is undoubtedly best recalled by most nostalgia fans as the blind hermit in *Bride of Frankenstein*. But he was also a resourceful Nayland Smith battling Warner Oland's Fu Manchu in two early sound adventures of the oriental masterfiend. Heggie looked set for a typically busy 1930s' career as a Hollywood character player when a midwinter bout of pneumonia killed him at only 59.

1928: The Actress. The Letter. 1929: The Mysterious Dr Fu Manchu. The Mighty. The Wheel of Life. 1930: The Vagabond King. One Romantic Night. The Return of Dr Fu Manchu. The Bad Man. Playboy of Paris. Sunny. Broken Dishes. 1931: The Woman Between (GB: Madame Julie). East Lynne. Too Young to Marry. Devotion. 1932: Smilin' Through. 1933: The King's Vacation. Zoo in Budapest. 1934: Midnight. Peck's Bad Boy. The Count of Monte Cristo. Anne of Green Gables. 1935: Chasing Yesterday. Bride of Frankenstein. A Dog of Flanders. Ginger. 1936: The Prisoner of Shark Island.

HEINZ, Gerard
(Gerhard Hinze) 1903–1972
Smooth, saturnine German actor in British films, often menacing but occasionally effective in more sympathetic roles. On stage at 18, he led his own travelling company before he was 30, but was thrown into a Nazi concentration camp in 1934, escaping to Czechoslovakia and thence to Switzerland. Arriving in England just before World War

II, he found his film career largely confined to shady foreigners. One source refers to a 1928 'film debut in Berlin' which I have not been able to trace.

*1942: Thunder Rock. Went the Day Well? (US: 48 Hours). 1943: The Adventures of Tartu (US: Tartu). 1944: English Without Tears (US: Her Man Gilbey). 1946: Caravan. 1947: Frieda. Broken Journey. 1948: Portrait from Life (US: The Girl in the Painting). The Fallen Idol. The First Gentleman (US: Affairs of a Rogue). Sleeping Car to Trieste. The Bad Lord Byron. 1949: That Dangerous Age (US: If This Be Sin). Traveller's Joy (released 1951). The Lost People. 1950: State Secret (US: The Great Manhunt). The Clouded Yellow. 1951: White Corridors. His Excellency. 1952: Private Information. Top Secret (US: Mr Potts Goes to Moscow). The Cruel Sea. 1953: Desperate Moment. The Triangle. The Accused. 1954: Lilacs in the Spring (US: Let's Make Up). 1955: Contraband Spain. The Prisoner. 1956: You Pay Your Money. 1957: The Traitor (US: The Accused. And 1953 title). Seven Thunders (US: The Beasts of Marseilles). Accused (and 1953 and 1957 films. US: Mark of the Hawk). The Man Inside. 1959: Carlton-Browne of the F. O. (US: Man in a Cocked Hat). The House of the Seven Hawks. 1960: Offbeat. I Aim at the Stars. 1961: The Guns of Navarone. Highway to Battle. 1962: Operation Snatch. The Password is Courage. Mystery Submarine (US: Decoy). 1963: The Cardinal. 1964: Devils of Darkness. *Boy with a Flute. 1965: The Heroes of Telemark. Operation Crossbow (US: The Great Spy Mission). 1966: Where the Bullets Fly. The Projected Man. The Night of the Generals. 1967: The Dirty Dozen. 1971: Venom.*

squashed by the bad guys. Especially memorable as the creepy guy who lives with scores of cats in *The Crooked Way.*

*1915: The Fairy and the Waif. 1916: The Flower of Faith. 1922: Silver Wings. 1924: The Offenders. 1938: *The Prisoner of Swing. 1947: Miracle on 34th Street (GB: The Big Heart). Call Northside 777. 1948: Hazard. Let's Live Again. Chicken Every Sunday. Larceny. That Wonderful Urge. Criss Cross. 1949: The Crooked Way. The Set Up. Thieves' Highway. Alias Nick Beal (GB: The Contact Man). Free for All. Lust for Gold. Red, Hot and Blue. Abbott and Costello Meet the Killer, Boris Karloff. My Friend Irma. 1950: Copper Canyon. A Life of Her Own. Fancy Pants. Cyrano de Bergerac. Harbor of Missing Men. Riding High. The Sun Sets at Dawn. The Secret Fury. Wabash Avenue. Tyrant of the Sea. Under Mexicali Skies. 1951: Chain of Circumstance. Darling, How Could You? (GB: Rendezvous). The Barefoot Mailman. Night into Morning. Three Guys Named Mike. The Belle of New York. 1952: A Girl in Every Port. I Dream of Jeanie. The Stooge. 1953: Ambush at Tomahawk Gap. Ride, Vaquero! Down Laredo Way. Call Me Madam. She's Back on Broadway. City of Bad Men. The Robe. Scared Stiff. How to Marry a Millionaire. Wicked Woman. 1954: About Mrs Leslie. A Star is Born. Superman in Exile (TV. GB: cinemas). 20,000 Leagues Under the Sea. Lucky Me. White Christmas. 1955: Crashout. Jail Busters. Kiss Me Deadly. Trial. Diane. No Man's Woman. Guns Don't Argue. 1956: Fury at Gunsight Pass. Shake, Rattle and Rock. Terror at Midnight 1957: Jailhouse Rock. Looking for Danger. The Phantom Stagecoach. Spook Chasers. Last Stagecoach West. This Could Be the Night. Rally 'Round the Flag, Boys! 1958: The Sheepman. 1961: The Music Man. Ride the High Country (GB: Guns in the Afternoon). 1963: Four for Texas. The Wheeler Dealers (GB: Separate Beds). 1964: Goodbye Charlie. Hush . . . Hush, Sweet Charlotte. 1965: Zebra in the Kitchen. The Sons of Katie Elder. Dear Brigitte . . . 1966: A Big Hand for a Little Lady (GB: Big Deal at Dodge City). Don't Worry, We'll Think of a Title. 1968: Funny Girl. Head. 1969: Butch Cassidy and the Sundance Kid.*

1971: The Winnipeg Run. 1972: It Ain't Easy. 1973: Emperor of the North Pole (GB: Emperor of the North). The Outfit. 1975: Dog Day Afternoon. Mansion of the Doomed (GB: The Terror of Dr Chaney) 1976: Network. †The Next Man. Return to Earth (TV). 1977: Close Encounters of the Third Kind. 1978: Eyes of Laura Mars. Damien Omen II. 1979: The Visitor. 1980: The Special Edition of Close Encounters of the Third Kind. 1981: Piranha II: Flying Killers/Piranha II: The Spawning. Prince of the City. The Dark End of the Street. 1982: A Question of Honor (TV). 1983: Nightmares. The Right Stuff. Blood Feud (TV). 1984: The Terminator. 1985: Savage Dawn. Jagged Edge. 1986: Choke Canyon. (GB: TV, Dangerous Ground) Aliens. 1987: Near Dark. 1988: Pumpkinhead. Deadly Intent. 1989: The Horror Show. Hit List. Survival Quest. Johnny Handsome. 1990: Tales from the Crypt (cable TV). On Dangerous Ground. Comrades in Arms. 1991: The Brotherhood. The Pit and the Pendulum. Stone Cold. Reason for Living: The Jill Ireland Story (TV). 1992: Delta Heat. Jennifer Eight. Alien 3. Knights. 1993: Hard Target. Man's Best Friend. Super Mario Bros. Excessive Force. The Outfit (and 1973 film). 1994: The Color of Night. Spitfire. Boulevard (cable TV). No Escape. Nature of the Beast/Bad Company. 1995: Street Corner Justice/Street Corner Justus. The Quick and the Dead. Powder.

† As Lance Hendricksen.

HELTON, Percy 1894–1971
Balding, round-faced, piglet-eyed, small, pinkly gasping American actor whose voice ranged from a whisper to a squeak through ever-open mouth. In vaudeville as a child, he grew (though not too much) to become a supporting player who came to the major part of his film career in his fifties, but was always distinctive, no matter how small (and most of them were) the role. He played bartenders, reporters, hangers-on and other peripheral characters whose eager, faintly servile approach was often to be harshly

HENRIKSEN, Lance 1939–
Spare, lean-faced, rather fraught-looking American actor with lined jaw and light, somewhat unruly hair, who often plays characters of sweaty menace. His seaman father took him to live in Borneo for three years as a boy and they travelled around the Pacific before returning to their native New York. Expelled from schools following a stint in a military academy, Henriksen hitchhiked and rode freight trains across America to California, where he eventually enrolled at the Actors' Studio. On stage thereafter, he made no films until 1971, maintaining a low-profile movie career until cast as the astronaut Walter Schirra in *The Right Stuff.* He then twice played the android Bishop in *Alien* films, and has shown up prominently as men with a dangerous edge on either side of the law.

HENSON, Gladys
(née Gunn) 1897–1983
Brown-haired, Ireland-born supporting actress in British films. On stage at 13, she was a Hippodrome chorus girl who grew up

to look plump and motherly with macaw-like features which seemed to suit a lifetime of working-class motherhood. Thus, with only one previous film experience, she came quickly into demand in post-war years, appearing more than once as the wife of Jack Warner, forever doing the washing and cooking the tea. Married to actor-comedian Leslie Henson from 1926 to 1943; never remarried.

1943: *The Demi-Paradise* (US: *Adventure for Two*). 1946: *The Captive Heart*. 1947: *Frieda*. *Temptation Harbour*. *It Always Rains on Sunday*. 1948: *The Weaker Sex*. *Counterblast* (US: *The Devil's Plot*). *London Belongs to Me* (US: *Dulcimer Street*). *The History of Mr Polly*. 1949: *Train of Events*. *The Blue Lamp*. *The Cure for Love*. 1950: *Dance Hall*. *Highly Dangerous*. *The Magnet*. *The Happiest Days of Your Life*. *Cage of Gold*. *Happy Go Lovely*. 1951: *Lady Godiva Rides Again*. *I Believe in You*. 1952: *Derby Day* (US: *Four Against Fate*). 1953: *Those People Next Door*. *Meet Mr Lucifer*. 1955: *Cockleshell Heroes*. 1956: *Stars in Your Eyes*. 1957: *Davy*. *Doctor at Large*. *The Prince and the Showgirl*. 1958: *A Night to Remember*. 1960: *Clue of the Twisted Candle*. *The Trials of Oscar Wilde* (US: *The Man with the Green Carnation*). *Double Bunk*. *Dangerous Afternoon*. *No Love for Johnnie*. 1961: *Stork Talk*. 1962: *Death Trap*. 1963: *The Leather Boys*. 1964: *Go Kart Go! First Men in the Moon*. 1965: *The Legend of Young Dick Turpin*. 1975: *The Bawdy Adventures of Tom Jones*.

HERBERT, Holmes
(Edward Sanger) 1882–1956
Tall, dark, imposing English-born actor with solid features and resounding tones. He made no films in his native country but, once in America, he became a stalwart leading man in silents, often as stern and unrelenting characters. The 'Holmes' in his stage name was taken from Sherlock Holmes, his favourite character. In his younger days, he would have been ideal for the role. As it was, he had to be content with minor roles in the Universal 'Holmes' films of the 1940s, all of which he handled with his customary dignity. Married (second) character actress Beryl Mercer (1882–1939).

1915: **Père Goriot*. *His Wife*. *The Man Without a Country*. 1917: *A Doll's House*. 1918: *The Whirlpool*. *The Death Dance*. 1919: *The White Heather*. *The ABC of Love*. *Other Men's Wives*. *The Divorcee*. *Market of Souls*. 1920: *My Lady's Garter*. *Black Is White*. *His House in Order*. *Lady Rose's Daughter*. *The Right to Love*. *Dead Men Tell No Tales*. 1921: *Heedless Moths*. *The Inner Chamber*. *The Wild Goose*. *The Truth About Husbands*. *Her Lord and Master*. *The Family Closet*. 1922: *Divorce Coupons*. *Evidence*. *Any Wife*. *Moonshine Valley*. *A Woman's Woman*. *A Stage Romance*. 1923: *I Will Repay*. *Swords and the Woman*. *Toilers of the Sea*. 1924: *The Enchanted Cottage*. *Sinners in Heaven*. *Love's Wilderness*. *His Own Free Will*. *Another Scandal*. *Week-End Husbands*. 1925: *Daddy's Gone a-Hunting*. *Wreckage*. *A Woman of the World*. *Wildfire*. *Up the Ladder*. 1926: *Honeymoon Express*. *The Wanderer*. *Josselyn's Wife*. *The Passionate Quest*. *The Fire Brigade*. 1927: *East Side, West Side*. *Mr Wu*. *Lovers? The Heart of Salome*. *The Gay Retreat*. *The Silver Slave*. *The Nest*. *One Increasing Purpose*. *Slaves of Beauty*. *When a Man Loves*. 1928: *The Terror*. *Gentlemen Prefer Blondes*. *The Sporting Age*. *Their Hour*. *Through the Breakers*. *On Trial*. 1929: *The Charlatan*. *Untamed*. *Careers*. *Madame X*. *Her Private Life*. *The Thirteenth Chair*. *Say It with Songs*. *The Kiss*. *The Careless Age*. 1930: *The Ship from Shanghai*. 1931: *The Single Sin*. *The Hot Heiress*. *Broadminded*. *Chances*. *Daughter of the Dragon*. *Dr Jekyll and Mr Hyde*. 1932: *Shop Angel*. *Miss Pinkerton*. *Central Park*. 1933: *Sister to Judas*. *The Mystery of the Wax Museum*. *The Invisible Man*. 1934: *The House of Rothschild*. *The Curtain Falls*. *Beloved*. *One in a Million*. *The Pursuit of Happiness*. *The Count of Monte Cristo*. 1935: *Accent on Youth*. *Sons of Steel*. *Mark of the Vampire*. *Captain Blood*. *The Dark Angel*. *Cardinal Richelieu*. 1936: *The Country Beyond*. *15 Maiden Lane*. *Brilliant Marriage*. *Lloyds of London*. *Gentleman from Louisiana*. *The Charge of the Light Brigade*. *Wife Versus Secretary*. *The Prince and the Pauper*. 1937: *The Girl Said No*. *Slave Ship*. *House of Secrets*. *Love Under Fire*. *The Life of Emile Zola*. *Lancer Spy*. *The Prince and the Pauper*. *Here's Flash Casey*. *The Thirteenth Chair* (remake). 1938: *The Adventures of Robin Hood*. *The Black Doll*. *Mystery of Mr Wong*. *Kidnapped*. *Marie Antoinette*. *The Buccaneer*. *Say It in French*. 1939: *The Little Princess*. *Stanley and Livingstone*. *Everything Happens at Night*. *The Adventures of Sherlock Holmes* (GB: *Sherlock Holmes*). *Juarez*. *Wolf Call*. *Bad Boy* (GB: *Perilous Journey*). *We Are Not Alone*. *Tower of London*. *Trapped in the Sky*. *The Sun Never Sets*. *The Mystery of the White Room*. *Mr Moto's Last Warning*. *Hidden Power*. 1940: *A Dispatch from Reuter's* (GB: *This Man Reuter*). *The Earl of Chicago*. *The Letter*. *Women in War*. *British Intelligence* (GB: *Enemy Agent*). *Foreign Correspondent*. *Boom Town*. *Angel from Texas*. *Phantom Raiders*. *South of Suez*. 1941: *Rage in Heaven*. *Scotland Yard*. *Man Hunt*. *International Squadron*. 1942: *The Ghost of Frankenstein*. *This Above All*. *Danger in the Pacific*. *Invisible Agent*. *Strictly in the Groove*. *Lady in a Jam*. *Sherlock Holmes and the Secret Weapon*. *The Undying Monster* (GB: *The Hammond Mystery*). 1943: *Corvette K-225*

(GB: *The Nelson Touch*). *Sherlock Holmes Faces Death*. *Sherlock Holmes in Washington*. *Two Tickets to London*. *Calling Doctor Death*. 1944: *The Bermuda Mystery*. *The Pearl of Death*. *Our Hearts Were Young and Gay*. *The Uninvited*. *Enter Arsène Lupin*. *The Mummy's Curse*. *House of Fear*. 1945: *Uncle Harry/The Strange Affair of Uncle Harry*. *Confidential Agent*. *Jealousy*. *George White's Scandals*. 1946: *The Verdict*. *Love Laughs at Andy Hardy*. *Three Strangers*. *Cloak and Dagger*. *The Bandit of Sherwood Forest*. *Dressed to Kill* (GB: *Sherlock Holmes and the Secret Code*). 1947: *Over the Santa Fé Trail* (GB: *No Escape*). *Singapore*. *Ivy*. *Bulldog Drummond Strikes Back*. *Bulldog Drummond at Bay*. *This Time for Keeps*. *The Swordsman*. 1948: *Johnny Belinda*. *The Wreck of the Hesperus*. *Jungle Jim*. *Sorry, Wrong Number*. *Command Decision*. *Family Honeymoon*. 1949: *The Stratton Story*. *Barbary Pirate*. *Post Office Investigator*. 1950: *Iroquois Trail* (GB: *The Tomahawk Trail*). 1951: *David and Bathsheba*. *The Unknown Man*. *The Law and the Lady*. *The Magnificent Yankee* (GB: *The Man with 30 Sons*). *The Son of Dr Jekyll*. *Anne of the Indies*. *At Sword's Point* (GB: *Sons of the Musketeers*). 1952: *The Brigand*. *The Wild North*.

HERBERT, Hugh 1887–1952
Black-haired, ruddy-cheeked, cheerful-looking American comic actor, writer and director. From the beginning of sound, he cropped up in dozens of 'excitable' cameo roles, almost all of them characterized by his raising fluttering hands, doing a double-take and crying 'Woo Woo!' Brought a touch of farcical anarchy to nearly everything he tackled. Died from a heart attack.

1927: **Realisation*. **Solomon's Children*. *Husbands for Rent*. 1928: **The Lemon*. **On the Air*. *Lights of New York*. **Mind Your Business*. **The Prediction*. **Miss Information*. *Caught in the Fog*. 1929: **She Went for a Tramp*. 1930: *Danger Lights*. *Hook, Line and Sinker*. *Second Wife*. *The Sin Ship*. 1931: *Traveling Husbands*. *Laugh and Get Rich*. *Cracked Nuts*. *Friends and Lovers*. 1932: *The Lost Squadron*. **Shampoo the Magician*. *Faithless*. *Million Dollar Legs*. 1933: *Goldie Gets Along*. **It's Spring*. *Diplomaniacs*. *Convention City*. *College Coach* (GB: *Football Coach*). *From Headquarters*. *Footlight Parade*. *Bureau of Missing Persons*. *Goodbye Again*. *Strictly Per-*

sonal. *She Had to Say Yes*. 1934: *Easy to Love*. *Dames*. *Fashions of 1934* (GB: *Fashion Follies of 1934*). *Wonder Bar*. *Harold Teen* (GB: *The Dancing Fool*). *Kansas City Princess*. *The Merry Frinks* (GB: *The Happy Family*). *Sweet Adeline*. *The Merry Wives of Reno*. *Fog Over Frisco*. 1935: *Gold Diggers of 1935*. **A Trip Thru a Hollywood Studio*. *The Traveling Saleslady*. *A Midsummer Night's Dream*. *We're in the Money*. *To Beat the Band*. *Miss Pacific Fleet*. 1936: *Colleen*. *Sing Me a Love Song*. *Love Begins at 20* (GB: *All One Night*). *One Rainy Afternoon*. *We Went to College* (GB: *The Old School Tie*). *Mind Your Own Business*. 1937: *Sh! The Octopus*. *That Man's Here Again*. *Marry the Girl*. *The Perfect Specimen*. *Hollywood Hotel*. *Top of the Town*. *The Singing Marine*. 1938: *The Great Waltz*. *Men Are Such Fools*. *Four's a Crowd*. *Gold Diggers in Paris*. 1939: *The Little Accident*. *The Family Next Door*. *Dad for a Day. *Eternally Yours*. *The Lady's from Kentucky*. 1940: *La Conga Nights*. *Slightly Tempted*. *A Little Bit of Heaven*. *Hit Parade of 1941*. *The Villain Still Pursued Her*. *Private Affairs*. 1941: *The Black Cat*. *Hello Sucker*. *Hellzapoppin*. *Meet the Chump*. *Nobody's Fool*. *Badlands of Dakota*. *Mrs Wiggs of the Cabbage Patch*. 1942: *There's One Born Every Minute*. *You're Telling Me*. *Don't Get Personal*. 1943: *It's a Great Life*. **Who's Hugh?* **Pitchin' in the Kitchen*. *Stage Door Canteen*. *Beauty for Sale*. 1944: *Ever Since Venus*. *Music for Millions*. *His Hotel Sweet. **Oh Baby!* *Woo Woo. *Kismet*. 1945: *One Way to Love*. *Wife Decoy. **The Mayor's Husband*. **When the Wife's Away*. *Honeymoon Blues. 1946: **Get Along Little Zombie*. 1947: **Tall, Dark and Gruesome*. *Hot Heir. **Nervous Shakedown*. **Should Husbands Marry?* *Carnegie Hall*. *Blondie in the Dough*. 1948: *A Miracle Can Happen* (later *On Our Merry Way*). *So This Is New York*. *One Touch of Venus*. *A Song Is Born*. *A Punch in Time. *The Girl from Manhattan*. 1949: **Trapped by a Blonde*. *Super Wolf. *The Beautiful Blonde from Bashful Bend*. 1950: **A Slip and a Miss*. **A Knight and a Blonde*. **One Shivery Night*. 1951: *Woo Woo Blues. *Havana Rose*. *Trouble-in-Laws. **The Gink at the Sink*.

HERBERT, Percy 1920–1992

Pugnacious, light-haired, wide-nosed portrayer of cockney characters in British films, a self-confessed 'East End [of London] tearaway' who got into acting via the good offices of Dame Sybil Thorndike, and soon became a staple of the British cinema, whether as soldier, crook, blue-collar worker or comedy relief. Went to America for a while in the late 1960s, incongruously to play a Scot in the TV western series *Cimarron Strip*. Died from a heart attack.

1950: *They Were Not Divided*. 1953: *The Case of Express Delivery*. 1954: *The Young Lovers* (US: *Chance Meeting*). *The Green Buddha*. *One Good Turn*. 1955: *Simba*. *The Gold Express*. *Doctor at Sea*. *The Prisoner*. *Lost* (US: *Tears for Simon*). *The Night My Number Came Up*. *Confession* (US: *The Deadliest Sin*). *Cockleshell Heroes*. 1956: *Child in the House*. *Tiger in the Smoke*. *The Baby and the Battleship*. *A Hill in Korea* (US: *Hell in Korea*). 1957: *Quatermass II* (US: *Enemy from Space*). *The Steel Bayonet*. *Night of the Demon* (US: *Curse of the Demon*). *The Bridge on the River Kwai*. *Barnacle Bill* (US: *All at Sea*). 1958: *The Safecracker*. *Dunkirk*. *No Time to Die!* (US: *Tank Force*). *Sea Fury*. *Sea of Sand* (US: *Desert Patrol*). 1959: *Yesterday's Enemy*. *Serious Charge* (US: *A Touch of Hell*). *Don't Panic Chaps! Deadly Record*. *Idle on Parade* (US: *Idol on Parade*). *A Touch of Larceny*. *The Devil's Disciple*. 1960: *The Challenge*. *There Was a Crooked Man*. *Tunes of Glory*. 1961: *The Guns of Navarone*. *Mysterious Island*. 1962: *Mutiny on the Bounty*. *La citta prigioniera* (GB: *The Captive City*. US: *The Conquered City*). 1963: *The Cracksman*. *Dr Syn Alias the Scarecrow*. *Call Me Bwana*. *Carry On Jack* (US: *Carry On Venus*). *Becket*. 1964: *Guns at Batasi*. *Allez France!* (US: *The Counterfeit Constable*). 1965: *Joey Boy*. *Bunny Lake is Missing*. *Carry On Cowboy*. 1966: *One Million Years BC*. *Tobruk*. 1967: *The Viking Queen*. *Casino Royale*. *Mister Ten Per Cent*. *Night of the Big Heat* (US: *Island of the Burning Damned*). 1969: *Too Late the Hero*. *The Royal Hunt of the Sun*. *One More Time*. 1971: *Captain Apache*. *Man in the Wilderness*. *The Fiend* (US: *Beware My Brethren*). 1972: *Doomwatch*. *Up the Front*. 1973: *The Mackintosh Man*. *Blacksnake* (GB: *Slaves*). *Craze*. 1975: *One of Our Dinosaurs is Missing*. 1977: *Hardcore* (US: *Fiona*). 1978: *The Wild Geese*. 1979: *The London Connection* (US: *The Omega Connection*). 1980: *The Sea Wolves*. 1987: *The Love Child*.

HEYDT, Louis Jean 1905–1960

Stocky, flaxen-haired American supporting actor of Dutch extraction whose hunted, mistrustful look and reliability of performance got him cast in some good thrillers, mostly as little men on the wrong side of the law, or with shady pasts. Also remembered as the barfly to whom Brian Donlevy tells the story in *The Great McGinty* (1940). The quality of his roles diminished after the 1940s—although he had a juicier part in 1957's *The Wings of Eagles*—and he was struck down by a heart attack at 54.

1933: *Before Morning*. 1937: *SOS Coastguard* (serial). *Make Way for Tomorrow*. 1938: *Test Pilot*. *I Am the Law*. **They're Always Caught*. 1939: *Dad for a Day. *Full Confession*. *Let Freedom Ring*. *They Made Her a Spy*. *Charlie Chan at Treasure Island*. *Gone With the Wind*. *Reno*. *Mr Smith Goes to Washington*. *Each*

Dawn I Die. *They Made Me a Criminal*. 1940: *Abe Lincoln in Illinois* (GB: *Spirit of the People*). *The Great McGinty* (GB: *Down Went McGinty*). *A Child is Born*. *Irene*. *The Man Who Talked Too Much*. *Let's Make Music*. *All About Hash. *Santa Fé Trail*. **The Hidden Master*. *Johnny Apollo*. *Joe and Ethel Turp Call on the President*. *Dr Ehrlich's Magic Bullet* (GB: *The Story of Dr Ehrlich's Magic Bullet*). *Pier 13*. 1941: *International Lady*. *Sleepers West*. *High Sierra*. *How Green Was My Valley*. *Power Dive*. *Midnight Angel*. *Dive Bomber*. 1942: *Joe Smith – American* (GB: *Highway to Freedom*). *Dr Kildare's Victory* (GB: *The Doctor and the Debutante*). *A Gentleman After Dark*. *Tortilla Flat*. *Ten Gentlemen from West Point*. *Commandos Strike at Dawn*. *Pacific Blackout*. *Captains of the Clouds*. *Manila Calling*. *Triumph Over Pain*. 1943: *Mission to Moscow*. *Gung Ho! Hostages*. *The Iron Major*. *One Dangerous Night*. *Stage Door Canteen*. *First Comes Courage*. 1944: *The Great Moment*. *The Story of Dr Wassell*. *Her Primitive Man*. *See Here, Private Hargrove*. *Thirty Seconds Over Tokyo*. *Betrayal from the East*. 1945: *They Were Expendable*. *Zombies on Broadway* (GB: *Loonies on Broadway*). *You Came Along*. *Our Vines Have Tender Grapes*. 1946: *Gentleman Joe Palooka*. *The Hoodlum Saint*. *The Big Sleep*. 1947: *Sinbad the Sailor*. *I Cover Big Town*. *Spoilers of the North*. 1948: **California's Golden Beginning*. 1949: *Bad Men of Tombstone*. *Make Believe Ballroom*. *Come to the Stable*. *The Kid from Cleveland*. 1950: *Paid in Full*. *The Furies*. *The Great Missouri Raid*. 1951: *Al Jennings of Oklahoma*. *Rawhide/Desperate Siege*. *Warpath*. *Raton Pass* (GB: *Canyon Pass*). *Drums in the Deep South*. *Two of a Kind*. *Criminal Lawyer*. *Close to My Heart*. *Flesh and Fury*. *Road Block*. *Sailor Beware*. 1952: *Models Inc.* (later *Call Girl*. GB: *That Kind of Girl*). *The Old West*. *Mutiny*. 1953: *Island in the Sky*. *The Vanquished*. 1954: *The Boy from Oklahoma*. *A Star is Born*. 1955: *Ten Wanted Men*. *The Eternal Sea*. *No Man's Woman*. 1956: *The Fastest Gun Alive*. *Stranger at My Door*. *Wetbacks*. 1957: *Raiders of Old California*. *The Wings of Eagles*. 1958: *The Badge of Marshal Brennan*. *The Man Who Died Twice*. 1959: *Inside the Mafia*.

HICKSON, Joan 1906–

Inconspicuous, light-haired British actress with open, hopeful face, in a wide variety of

stage and film roles since her theatrical debut in 1927. Excellent in comedy cameos as middle-class working women or addle-pated relations. In 1983, she completed 50 years in films with her role in *The Wicked Lady* and, at the end of 1984, then became the world's oldest spinster detective as Agatha Christie's Miss Marple in a TV series which ran until 1992.

1933: *Trouble in Store.* 1934: *Widows Might.* 1936: *The Man Who Could Work Miracles. Love from a Stranger.* 1937: *The Lilac Domino.* 1938: *Second Thoughts (US: The Crime of Peter Frame).* 1941: *The Saint Meets the Tiger. Freedom Radio (US: A Voice in the Night).* 1944: *Don't Take It to Heart.* 1945: *The Rake's Progress (US: Notorious Gentleman). I Live in Grosvenor Square (US: A Yank in London). The Trojan Brothers.* 1946: *I See a Dark Stranger (US: The Adventuress).* 1947: *This Was a Woman. Just William's Luck. So Well Remembered.* 1948: *The Guinea Pig (US: The Outsider). Bond Street.* 1949: *Celia. Marry Me!* 1950: *Seven Days to Noon. The Magnet.* 1951: *High Treason. Hell is Sold Out. Hunted (US: The Stranger in Between). The Magic Box. Blind Man's Bluff. Angels One Five.* 1952: *No Haunt for a Gentleman. Tall Headlines. Hindle Wakes (US: Holiday Week). Come Back Peter. The Card (US: The Promoter). Curtain Up.* 1953: *Deadly Nightshade. Love in Pawn. Rough Shoot (US: Shoot First). The Million Pound Note (US: Man with a Million). Single-Handed (US: Sailor of the King).* 1954: *Doctor in the House. Mad About Men. The House Across the Lake. What Every Woman Wants. To Dorothy a Son (US: Cash on Delivery). Dance Little Lady. The Crowded Day.* 1955: *An Alligator Named Daisy. As Long As They're Happy. Doctor at Sea. Value for Money. The Woman for Joe. Simon and Laura. A Time to Kill. Lost (US: Tears for Simon). Jumping for Joy. The Man Who Never Was.* 1956: *The Extra Day. Port of Escape. The Last Man to Hang? Child in the House.* 1957: *Carry On Admiral (US: The Ship Was Loaded). Sea Wife. No Time for Tears. Happy is the Bride! Barnacle Bill (US: All at Sea).* 1958: *Chain of Events. The Horse's Mouth. Behind the Mask.* 1959: *Upstairs and Downstairs. Please Turn Over. The Three Worlds of Gulliver. Carry On Nurse. The 39 Steps.* 1960: *Tunes of Glory. Carry On Constable. No Kidding (US: Beware of Children). Doctor in Love.* 1961: *His and Hers. Carry On Regardless. Raising the Wind*

(US: *Roommates). In the Doghouse. Murder She Said.* 1962: *Crooks Anonymous. I Thank a Fool.* 1963: *Nurse on Wheels. Heavens Above!* 1965: *The Secret of My Success.* 1967: *Casino Royale.* 1968: *Mrs Brown, You've Got a Lovely Daughter.* 1970: *Carry On Loving.* 1971: *Friends. A Day in the Death of Joe Egg.* 1973: *Theatre of Blood. Carry On Girls.* 1974: *Confessions of a Window Cleaner.* 1975: *One of Our Dinosaurs is Missing.* 1978: *Yanks.* 1980: *The Taming of the Shrew (TV).* 1981: *†Time Bandits.* 1983: *The Wicked Lady.* 1985: *Clockwise.* 1989: *King of the Wind.* 1993: *Century.*

† Scenes deleted from final release print

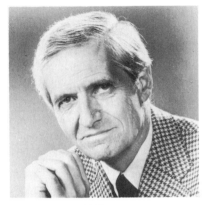

HILL, Arthur 1922–

Soft-spoken, sandy-haired (soon grey), concerned-looking Canadian actor who began in British films, but spent most of his time on stage and television before taking a wide variety of second leads in the cinema from the early 1960s, proving most effective in sympathetic roles although clearly enjoying the occasional corrupt man-at-the-top.

1949: *I Was a Male War Bride (GB: You Can't Sleep Here). Miss Pilgrim's Progress.* 1950: *The Undefeated. The Body Said No!* 1951: *Scarlet Thread. Salute the Toff. Mr Drake's Duck.* 1952: *Paul Temple Returns.* 1953: *A Day to Remember.* 1954: *Life with the Lyons (US: Family Affair). The Crowded Day.* 1955: *The Deep Blue Sea. Raising a Riot.* 1961: *The Young Doctors.* 1962: *The Ugly American. Focus (TV).* 1963: *In the Cool of the Day.* 1965: *Moment to Moment.* 1966: *Harper (GB: The Moving Target).* 1967: *Desperate Hours (TV).* 1968: *Petulia. The Fatal Mistake (TV). Don't Let the Angels Fall.* 1969: *The Chairman (GB: The Most Dangerous Man in the World).* 1970: *Rabbit, Run. The Andromeda Strain. The Pursuit of Happiness. The Other Man (TV).* 1971: *Vanished (TV).* 1971: *Owen Marshall – Counselor at Law (TV).* 1973: *Ordeal (TV).* 1975: *The Killer Elite. The Rivalry (TV).* 1976: *Futureworld. Judge Horton and the Scottsboro Boys (TV). Death Be Not Proud (TV).* 1977: *Tell Me My Name (TV). A Bridge Too Far.* 1978: *The Champ.* 1979: *Butch and Sundance The Early Days. A Little Romance. Hagen (TV).* 1980: *Dirty Tricks. The Ordeal of Dr Mudd (TV). The Return of Frank Cannon (TV). Revenge of the Stepford Wives (TV).* 1981: *Angel Dusted (TV). The*

Amateur. 1982: *Making Love.* 1983: *Miss Lonelyhearts. Something Wicked This Way Comes.* 1984: *The Guardian (TV). Love Leads the Way.* 1985: *A Fine Mess. One Magic Christmas.* 1986: *Perry Mason: The Case of the Notorious Nun (TV). Christmas Eve (TV).*

HILLERMAN, John 1932–

Solid, suave, sardonic, usually immaculately-dressed American actor, seemingly the epitome of nonchalance, with dark hair and carefully groomed moustache. His droll tones are more redolent of an English background than his native Texas at times, and, after a career mainly in TV comedy following studies at the American Theatre Wing, he came much into demand for roles calling for dapper sarcasm. His name was not, however, as well known as it might have been until he became Tom Selleck's co-star in the popular TV series *Magnum PI*, a role which ironically much curtailed his movie work in the 1980s.

1968: *The Birthday Party.* 1970: *Lawman. They Call Me MISTER Tibbs!* 1971: *The Great Man's Whiskers (TV). Sweet, Sweet Rachel (TV). The Last Picture Show.* 1972: *The Carey Treatment. Un homme est mort (GB and US: The Outside Man). What's Up, Doc? Skyjacked. High Plains Drifter.* 1973: *Paper Moon. The Thief Who Came to Dinner.* 1974: *The Nickel Ride. Blazing Saddles. The Last Angry Man (TV). Chinatown. The Law (TV). The Day of the Locust.* 1975: *At Long Last Love. Ellery Queen: Too Many Suspects (TV). Lucky Lady.* 1976: *The Invasion of Johnson County (TV).* 1977: *Audrey Rose. Relentless (TV). Kill Me If You Can (TV).* 1978: *A Guide for the Married Woman (TV). Betrayal (TV).* 1979: *Institute for Revenge (TV. Voice only). Sunburn.* 1980: *The Murder That Wouldn't Die (TV). Marathon (TV).* 1981: *History of the World Part I.* 1982: *Little Gloria . . . Happy at Last (TV).* 1984: *Up the Creek.* 1987: *Assault and Matrimony (TV).* 1988: *Street of Dreams (TV).* 1989: *Real Men Don't Eat Gummy Bears.* 1990: *Hands of a Murderer (TV).*

HINDS, Samuel S. 1875–1948

Although one's abiding memory of this American actor remains an image of him stretched out on the slab beneath Bela Lugosi's pendulum in *The Raven*, in fact he played scores of solid citizens through the

1930s and 1940s. Ironically, fair-haired (turning to silver), affable-looking Hinds was often cast as an attorney—his own profession before turning his hobby of acting into a profitable career in the early 1930s. Occasionally, his honest looks hid a streak of crookedness, a break he no doubt enjoyed after so much kindliness and wisdom.

1932: If I Had a Million. 1933: The Nuisance (GB: Accidents Wanted). The House on 56th Street. Penthouse (GB: Crooks in Clover). The World Changes. The Crime of the Century. Gabriel over the White House. Day of Reckoning. Bed of Roses. Lady for a Day. Berkeley Square. The Deluge. Little Women. One Man's Journey. Hold the Press. This Day and Age. Son of a Sailor. Female. Women in His Life. Convention City. 1934: A Wicked Woman. Operator 13 (GB: Spy 13). Sadie McKee. Fog. The Big Shakedown. Manhattan Melodrama. Most Precious Thing in Life. He Was Her Man. Evelyn Prentice. The Ninth Guest. No Greater Glory. Sisters under the Skin (GB: The Romantic Age). Massacre. Men in White. The Crime Doctor. Straightaway. The Defense Rests. Have a Heart. Sequoia. A Lost Lady (GB: Courageous). Hat, Coat and Glove. The Cat's Paw. 1935: Devil Dogs of the Air. Bordertown. Black Fury. Oil for the Lamps of China. Law Beyond the Range. West Point of the Air. Wings in the Dark. West of the Pecos. Strangers All. She. In Person. College Scandal (GB: The Clock Strikes Eight). Annapolis Farewell (GB: Gentlemen of the Navy). Mills of the Gods. Behind the Evidence. Dr Socrates. Rumba/Rhumba. Private Worlds. Accent on Youth. The Big Broadcast of 1936. The Secret Bride (GB: Concealment). Two-Fisted. Living on Velvet. The Raven. Millions in the Air. Shadow of Doubt. Rendezvous. 1936: Timothy's Quest. Woman Trap. The Trail of the Lonesome Pine. Fatal Lady. Border Flight. Rhythm on the Range. Sworn Enemy. His Brother's Wife. The Gorgeous Hussy. Love Letters of a Star. The Longest Night. Black Legion. 1937: The Mighty Treve. The Lady Fights Back. Top of the Town. Night Key. Wings Over Honolulu. The Road Back. A Girl With Ideas. Prescription for Romance. Double or Nothing. She's Dangerous. Navy Blue and Gold. Stage Door. 1938: Wives Under Suspicion. The Jury's Secret. The Devil's Party. The Rage of Paris. The Road to Reno. Pirates of the Skies. Swing That Cheer. Secrets of a Nurse. The Storm. Test Pilot. You Can't Take It with You. Little Tough Guys in Society.

Double Danger. Forbidden Valley. Young Dr Kildare. Personal Secretary. 1939: Ex-Champ (GB: Golden Gloves). Calling Dr Kildare. Hawaiian Nights. The Under-Pup. Within the Law. Destry Rides Again. One Hour to Live. Newsboys' Home. Career. Charlie McCarthy, Detective. Tropic Fury. Rio. Hero for a Day. First Love. The Secret of Dr Kildare. You're a Sweetheart. No Greater Glory. 1940: Zanzibar. Dr Kildare's Strange Case. It's a Date. Ski Patrol. I'm Nobody's Sweetheart Now. The Boys from Syracuse. Spring Parade. Dr Kildare Goes Home. Seven Sinners. Trail of the Vigilantes. 1941: Adventure in Washington (GB: Female Correspondent). The Lady from Cheyenne. Buck Privates (GB: Rookies). Man-Made Monster (GB: The Electric Man). Back Street. Tight Shoes. Blossoms in the Dust. The Shepherd of the Hills. Dr Kildare's Wedding Day (GB: Mary Names the Day). Unfinished Business. Badlands of Dakota. Keep 'em Flying. Mob Town. Road Agent. 1942: Ride 'em Cowboy. Frisco Lil. Saboteur. Jail House Blues. The Strange Case of Dr RX. Kid Glove Killer. The Spoilers. Lady in a Jam. Grand Central Murder. Pardon My Sarong. Pittsburg. Don Winslow of the Navy (serial). 1943: Mr Big. Top Man. Fired Wife. He's My Guy. Larceny with Music. Keep 'em Slugging. Don Winslow of the Coast Guard (serial). Son of Dracula. It Ain't Hay (GB: Money for Jam). Good Morning, Judge. Hers to Hold. Follow the Band. We've Never Been Licked (GB: Texas to Tokyo). Sing a Jingle (GB: Lucky Days). Hi, Buddy. 1944: The Great Alaskan Mystery (serial). Chip Off the Old Block. Weird Woman. Phantom Lady (voice only). South of Dixie. Jungle Woman. Ladies Courageous. Cobra Woman. The Singing Sheriff. Murder in the Blue Room. Fellow the Boys. 1945: Swing Out, Sister. Frisco Sal. Escape in the Desert. I'll Remember April. Secret Agent X-9 (serial). The Strange Affair of Uncle Harry/Uncle Harry. Week-End at the Waldorf. Lady on a Train. Scarlet Street. Mildred Pierce. Men in Her Diary. 1946: Inside Job. White Tie and Tails. It's a Wonderful Life! Strange Conquest. The Runaround. Little Miss Big (GB: The Baxter Millions). Danger Woman. Blonde Alibi. 1947: The Egg and I. In Self Defense. Time Out of Mind. Slave Girl. Call Northside 777. 1948: Perilous Waters. The Return of October (GB: Date with Destiny). The Boy with Green Hair. 1949: The Bribe.

HINGLE, Pat
(Martin Patterson Hingle) 1923–
Thickly-set, light-haired American actor with natural scowl. A former construction worker, he enrolled at the Actors' Studio and broke into the theatre in 1950, TV and films in 1954. At first cast as surly, edgy types—apart from a role as one of the 'eight new stars' in Fox's No Down Payment—he has taken increasingly sympathetic, if still grouchy parts in recent times, while still never quite finding his niche in the cinema.

1954: On the Waterfront. The Long Gray Line. 1957: The Strange One (GB: End as a Man). No Down Payment. 1960: Wild River (narrator only). 1961: Splendor in the Grass. Black Monday (TV). 1963: The Ugly American. All the Way Home. 1964: Carol for Another Christmas (TV). Invitation to a Gunfighter.

1966: Nevada Smith. 1967: Hang 'em High. Sol Madrid (GB: The Heroin Gang). 1968: Jigsaw (TV. Originally for cinemas). 1969: The Ballad of Andy Crocker (TV). Bloody Mama. Norwood. 1970: A Clear and Present Danger (TV). WUSA. 1971: The City (TV). Sweet Sweet Rachel (TV). If Tomorrow Comes (TV). 1972: The Carey Treatment. Savage (TV). 1973: Happy As the Grass Was Green. Trouble Comes to Town (TV). One Little Indian. The Super Cops. Running Wild. 1974: The Last Angry Man (TV). Deadly Honeymoon. 1975: Deliver Us from Evil (TV). 1976: The Secret Life of John Chapman (TV). *Independence. 1977: Escape from Bogen County (TV). The Gauntlet. Sunshine Christmas (TV). Tarantulas: The Deadly Cargo (TV). 1979: Elvis (TV. GB: cinemas, as Elvis — The Movie). Stone/Killing Stone (TV). Norma Rae. Running Scared. When You Comin' Back, Red Ryder? 1980: Wild Times (TV). The Legend of John Hammer (TV). 1981: Washington Mistress (TV). Of Mice and Men (TV). The Private History of a Campaign That Failed (TV). When Hell was in Session (TV). Off the Minnesota Strip (TV). 1982: The Act. 1983: Running Brave (completed 1980). Sudden Impact. The Fighter. Going Berserk. 1985: The Falcon and the Snowman. Brewster's Millions. Noon Wine (TV). The Lady from Yesterday (TV). The Rape of Richard Beck (TV). 1986: Maximum Overdrive. Casebusters (TV). Manhunt for Claude Dallas (TV). 1987: LBJ: The Early Years (TV). Kojak: The Price of Justice (TV). Baby Boom. 1988: Stranger on My Land (TV). The Town Bully (TV). 1989: Everybody's Baby: The Rescue of Jessica McClure (TV). Batman. 1990: The Grifters. 1991: Not of This World (TV). 1992: Batman Returns. Citizen Cohn (cable TV). 1994: Lightning Jack. Open Season. Truman Capote's One Christmas (TV). Against Her Will: The Carrie Buck Story (TV). 1995: Batman Forever. The Quick and the Dead.

HIRD, Dame Thora 1911–
Slightly built, dynamic British actress with goggle-eyed, purse-lipped looks, ear-crunching voice and personality as bright as her hair. Although from the coast of Lancashire, she proved adept at a variety of terrace-row accents, and played maids, landladies, cleaners, shopwomen and forthright parents. Also popular in TV series, latterly of a religious nature; mother of former child star Janette Scott. Created Dame in 1993.

1940: Spellbound (US: The Spell of Amy Nugent). 1941: The Big Blockade. The Black Sheep of Whitehall. 1942: Next of Kin. Went the Day Well? (US: 48 Hours). The Foreman Went to France (US: Somewhere in France). 1944: 2,000 Women. 1947: The Courtneys of Curzon Street (US: The Courtney Affair). My Brother Jonathan. 1948: Corridor of Mirrors. The Weaker Sex. The Blind Goddess. Portrait from Life (US: The Girl in the Painting). Once a Jolly Swagman (US: Maniacs on Wheels). A Boy, a Girl and a Bike. Fools Rush In. 1949: Madness of the Heart. Maytime in Mayfair. Boys in Brown. Conspirator. The Cure for Love. 1950: The Magnet. Once a Sinner. 1951: The Galloping Major. The Magic Box. 1952: The Frightened Man. Emergency Call (US: Hundred Hour Hunt). Time Gentlemen Please! The Lost Hours (US: The Big Frame). 1953: The Great Game. Background (US: Edge of Divorce). Turn the Key Softly. The Long Memory. Personal Affair. Street Corner (US: Both Sides of the Law). A Day to Remember. 1954: Don't Blame the Stork! For Better, For Worse (US: Cocktails in the Kitchen). The Crowded Day. One Good Turn. The Love Match. 1955: The Quatermass Experiment (US: The Creeping Unknown). Tiger by the Tail (US: Crossup). Simon and Laura. Lost (US: Tears for Simon). 1956: Women without Men (US: Blonde Bait). Sailor Beware! (US: Panic in the Parlor). Home and Away. 1957: The Good Companions. These Dangerous Years (US: Dangerous Youth). 1958: *A Clean Sweep. Further Up the Creek. 1950: The Entertainer. 1961: Over the Odds. 1962: A Kind of Loving. Term of Trial. 1963: Bitter Harvest. 1964: Rattle of a Simple Man. 1970: Some Will, Some Won't. 1971: The Nightcomers. 1985: Uncle of the Bride (TV). 1988: Consuming Passions. 1992: Memento Mori (TV). 1993: Goggle Eyes (TV). Wide Eyed and Legless (TV. US: cinemas, as The Wedding Gift).

HOBART, Rose
(R. Kefer) 1906–
Brown-haired American leading lady with angular features. Called to Hollywood to repeat a stage success (in *Liliom*), she had a few more starring roles in the early 1930s – including Muriel in *Dr Jekyll and Mr Hyde* – then returned in the 1940s to play character roles throughout the decade, often as spiteful, vindictive women, in contrast to her earlier, gentle heroines. A victim of the Hollywood blacklist.

1930: Liliom. A Lady Surrenders. 1931: East of Borneo. Chances. Compromised. Dr Jekyll and Mr Hyde. 1932: Scandal for Sale. 1933: The Shadow Laughs. 1934: Convention Girl (GB: Atlantic City Romance). 1939: Tower of London. 1940: Wolf of New York. Susan and God (GB: The Gay Mrs Trexel). A Night at Earl Carroll's. 1941: Singapore Woman. Lady Be Good. Ziegfeld Girl. I'll Sell My Life. No Hands on the Clock. Mr and Mrs North. Nothing But the Truth. 1942: Adventures of Smilin' Jack (serial). A Gentleman at Heart. Who Is Hope Schuyler? Dr Gillespie's New Assistant. Prison Girls/Gallant Lady. 1943: Swing Shift Maisie (GB: The Girl in Overalls). Salute to the Marines. The Mad Ghoul. Crime Doctor's Strangest Case (GB: The Strangest Case). Air Raid Wardens. 1944: Song of the Open Road. Soul of a Monster. 1945: Conflict. The Brighton Strangler. 1946: The Cat Creeps. Canyon Passage. Claudia and David. 1947: The Farmer's Daughter. The Trouble with Women. Cass Timberlane. 1948: Mickey. 1949: Bride of Vengeance.

HOBBES, Halliwell
(Herbert H. Hobbes) 1877–1962
Big, bald British actor whose strong features and powerful build were belied by a soft voice and gentle manner. He began his career in 1898 on the London stage, but made no films until the sound era in Hollywood (having come to America in 1923). Cast as a butler in one of his earliest films, *Grumpy*, he very soon became one of the film capital's most solid and reliable manservants, most prominently in *The Masquerader*. He also had a keen sense of comedy, used to best advantage as the eccentric De Pinna in *You Can't Take it With You*. Died from a heart attack.

1929: Jealousy. Lucky in Love. 1930: Grumpy. Charley's Aunt. Scotland Yard (GB: 'Detective Clive', Bart). 1931: The Sin of Madelon Claudet (GB: The Lullaby). Five and Ten (GB: Daughter of Luxury). Bachelor Father. Platinum Blonde. The Right of Way. The Woman Between (GB: Madame Julie). Dr Jekyll and Mr Hyde. 1932: The Devil's Lottery. Forbidden. Lovers Courageous. The Menace. Man About Town. Weekends Only. Six Hours to Live. Love Affair. Payment Deferred. 1933: Lady for a Day. Midnight Mary. Looking Forward (GB: Service). If I Were Free. Should Ladies Behave? A Study in Scarlet. Captured! The Masquerader. 1934: I Am Suzanne! All Men Are Enemies. British Agent. Mandalay. We Live Again. The Key. Riptide. Double Door. Menace. Madame Du Barry. Bulldog Drummond Strikes Back. 1935: Folies Bergere (GB: The Man from the Folies Bergere). Captain Blood. Vanessa: Her Love Story. Cardinal Richelieu. The Right to Live (GB: The Sacred Flame). Charlie Chan in Shanghai. The Story of Louis Pasteur. Millions in the Air. Jalna. Father Brown, Detective. Whipsaw. 1936: Rose Marie. Here Comes Trouble. Love Letters of a Star. Dracula's Daughter. The White Angel. Hearts Divided. Give Me Your Heart. Spendthrift. 1937: Varsity Show. Maid of Salem. The Prince and the Pauper. Parnell. Fit for a King. 1938: The Jury's Secret. Service De Luxe. You Can't Take It with You. A Christmas Carol. Kidnapped. Bulldog Drummond's Peril. Storm Over Bengal. 1939: Nurse Edith Cavell. Pacific Liner. Naughty But Nice. Tell No Tales. The Hardys Ride High. Meet Maxwell Archer (US: Maxwell Archer, Detective). The Light That Failed. Remember? 1940: The Earl of Chicago. The Sea Hawk. Third Finger, Left Hand. The Lady with Red Hair. Waterloo Bridge. 1941: That Hamilton Woman (GB: Lady Hamilton). Here Comes Mr Jordan. Dr Kildare's Wedding Day (GB: Mary Names the Day). 1942: To Be or Not to Be. The War Against Mrs Hadley. Journey for Margaret. Son of Fury. The Undying Monster (GB: The Hammond Mystery). 1943: His Butler's Sister. Mr Muggs Steps Out. Sherlock Holmes Faces Death. Forever and a Day. 1944: The Invisible Man's Revenge. Gaslight (GB: The Murder in Thornton Square). Mr Skeffington. Casanova Brown. 1946: Canyon Passage. 1947: If Winter Comes. 1948: You Gotta Stay Happy. The Black Arrow (GB: The Black Arrow Strikes). 1949: That Forsyte Woman (GB: The Forsyte Saga). 1956: Miracle in the Rain. 1957: The Barretts of Wimpole Street.

HOEY, Dennis
(Samuel Hyams) 1893–1960
Dark, taciturn, bulky British actor with increasingly receding hair who often sported moustaches of varying shapes and sizes. After a spotty eight-year slog in British sound films, he went to America in 1940 and created a plank-thick and totally memorable version of Conan Doyle's Inspector Lestrade in the Basil Rathbone

Sherlock Holmes films. Other roles were often much smaller, although he was a Universal regular for most of the war years.

1927: Tiptoes. 1930: The Man from Chicago. 1931: Tell England (US: The Battle of Gallipoli). Never Trouble Trouble. Love Lies. 1932: Verdict of the Sea. Life Goes On. Baroud (US: Love in Morocco). The Maid of the Mountains. 1933: The Good Companions. Maid Happy. Oh What a Duchess! (US: My Old Duchess). I Spy. The Wandering Jew. Facing the Music. 1934: Jew Süss (US: Power). Lily of Killarney (US: Bride of the Lake). Chu Chin Chow. Brewster's Millions. 1935: Maria Marten, or: the Murder in the Red Barn. Immortal Gentleman. Honeymoon for Three. The Mystery of the Marie Celeste (US: Phantom Ship). Did I Betray? 1936: Black Roses. Faust. Uncivilized. 1941: A Yank in the RAF. How Green Was My Valley. Confirm or Deny. 1942: Son of Fury. Cairo. This Above All. Sherlock Holmes and the Secret Weapon. We Were Dancing. 1943: Forever and a Day. They Came to Blow Up America. Bomber's Moon. Sherlock Holmes and the Spider Woman (GB: Spider Woman). Frankenstein Meets the Wolf Man. Sherlock Holmes Faces Death. 1944: The Keys of the Kingdom. Uncertain Glory. The Pearl of Death. National Velvet. House of Fear. 1945: A Thousand and One Nights. 1946: Terror by Night. Roll On, Texas Moon. Kitty. Anna and the King of Siam. She-Wolf of London (GB: The Curse of the Allenbys). The Strange Woman. Tarzan and the Leopard Woman. 1947: Second Chance. The Crimson Key. Where There's Life. Golden Earrings. Christmas Eve. If Winter Comes. The Foxes of Harrow. 1948: Ruthless. Wake of the Red Witch. Joan of Arc. 1949: Bad Men of Tombstone. The Secret Garden. The Kid from Texas (GB: Texas Kid – Outlaw). 1951: David and Bathsheba. 1952: Plymouth Adventure. Caribbean (GB: Caribbean Gold). 1953: Ali Baba Nights.

HOLBROOK, Hal 1925–

Long-faced, dark (now grey) haired American actor with special, wistful qualities and one of the most attractive American speaking voices since Henry Fonda. After a late start, he played a few (often gloomy) leading roles in films, but was always more interesting and incisive in support, especially as 'Deep Throat' in *All the President's Men*. A prolific stage performer, particularly in one-man shows as Mark Twain, and a frequent TV guest star, often as government officials, family advisers or caring men with consciences.

1966: The Group. 1968: Wild in the Streets. 1969: The Whole World is Watching (TV). 1970: A Clear and Present Danger (TV). The Great White Hope. The People Next Door. 1971: Travis Logan DA (TV). Suddenly Single (TV). Goodbye Raggedy Ann (TV). 1972: That Certain Summer (TV). They Only Kill Their Masters. 1973: Magnum Force. Jonathan Livingstone Seagull (voice only). 1974: The Girl from Petrovka. 1976: All the President's Men. Midway (GB: Battle of Midway). 1977: Julia. Capricorn One. 1978: Rituals. 1979: When Hell Was in Session (TV). The Fog. Murder by Natural Causes (TV). The Kidnapping of the President. The Legend of the Golden Gun (TV). Natural Enemies. 1980: Off the Minnesota Strip (TV). The Creeper. The Killing of Randy Webster (TV). Our Town (TV). 1982: Creepshow. Girls' Nite Out. 1983: The Star Chamber. 1984: The Three Wishes of Billy Grier (TV). 1985: OSS (TV). Behind Enemy Lines (TV). 1987: Wall Street. Plaza Suite (TV). The Unholy. 1988: I'll Be Home for Christmas (TV). 1989: Sorry Wrong Number (TV). Fletch Lives. Day One (TV). 1990: Killing in a Small Town (TV) Evidence of Love (TV). 1993: Bonds of Love (TV). The Firm. 1994: Cats Don't Dance (voice). The Case of the Lethal Lifestyle (TV). 1995: Acts of Love.

HOLDEN, Fay
(Dorothy F. Hammerton) 1893–1973
Attractive, brown-haired, round-faced British-born actress, on stage as a child. As an adult, she starred in dramas and musical comedies for theatregoers, then went to America in 1927 and stayed. By the time she came to films in her forties, she had developed careworn-looking, plumpish, matronly looks and seemed perfect casting as the calm and comforting mother of the Hardy family in the famous MGM series which made a star of Mickey Rooney as Andy Hardy. Mrs Hardy remained her favourite role, and she was tempted out of post-1950 film retirement once, to reprise it in 1958. Married fellow character player David Clyde (1885–1945), brother of character comedian Andy Clyde (*qv*). Also acted as Gaby Fay and Dorothy Clyde. Died from cancer.

1936: Polo Joe. I Married a Doctor. White Angel. Wives Never Know. 1937: Double Or Nothing. Exclusive. Guns of the Pecos. Bulldog Drummond Escapes. King of Gamblers. Internes Can't Take Money (GB: You Can't Take Money). Nothing Sacred. Souls at Sea. 1938: You're Only Young Once. The Battle of Broadway. Hold That Kiss. Judge Hardy's Children. Love is a Headache. Love Finds Andy Hardy. Test Pilot. Sweethearts. Out West with the Hardys. 1939: The Hardys Ride High. Judge Hardy and Son. Sergeant Madden. Andy Hardy Gets Spring Fever. 1940: Andy Hardy Meets Debutante. Bitter Sweet. 1941: Blossoms in the Dust. Andy Hardy's Private Secretary. H M Pulham Esq. I'll Wait for You. Life Begins for Andy Hardy. Washington Melodrama. Ziegfeld Girl. 1942: The Courtship of Andy Hardy. Andy Hardy's Double Life. 1944: Andy Hardy's Blonde Trouble. 1946: Canyon Passage. Love Laughs at Andy Hardy. Little Miss Big (GB: The Baxter Millions). 1948: Whispering Smith. 1949: Samson and Delilah. 1950: The Big Hangover. 1958: Andy Hardy Comes Home.

HOLDEN, Gloria 1908–1991
Dark, straight-backed, austere and rather sinister-looking English actress who made an enormous impact in the title role of her first Hollywood film, *Dracula's Daughter*, then waited for offers of other leading roles that never materialized. She returned sporadically in smaller parts from the late 1930s, often proving a formidable adversary for the leading lady. Died from a heart attack.

1930: *The Story Book Parade. 1936: Dracula's Daughter. Wife Versus Secretary. 1937: The Life of Emile Zola. 1938: Test Pilot. Hawaii Calls. Girls' School. 1939: Dodge City. Miracles for Sale. 1940: A Child is Born. 1941: Passage from Hong Kong. This Thing Called Love. The Corsican Brothers. 1942: Miss Annie Rooney. A Gentleman After Dark. Apache Trail. 1943: Behind the Rising Sun. 1945: Having Wonderful Crime. The Adventures of Rusty. Strange Holiday (GB: The Day After Tomorrow). The Girl of the Limberlost. 1946: Hit The Hay. Sister Kenny. 1947: The Hucksters. In Self Defense. Undercover Maisie (GB: Undercover Girl). Killer McCoy. 1948: Perilous Waters. 1949: A Kiss for Corliss. 1951: The Sickle and the Cross. 1952: Has Anybody Seen My Gal. Seeds of Destruction. 1953: Dream Wife. 1956: The Eddy Duchin Story. 1958: This Happy Feeling.

HOLLOWAY, Sterling 1905–1992

Strangely enough, Hollywood's butter-haired, blue-eyed, whisper-voiced, freckle-faced country bumpkin didn't actually make the hundreds of films one imagines. But there was a whole string of yokels and bell-boys – often with some nice one-liners – in the 1930s, and later Holloway was heard as the voices of many Disney characters. His own voice was once described as like a rusty nail being pulled slowly out of a piece of wood. He died from cardiac arrest.

1927: Casey at the Bat. 1928: *The Girl from Nowhere. 1932: American Madness. Blonde Venus. Lawyer Man. Faithless. Rockabye. 1933: Elmer the Great. International House. When Ladies Meet. Hell Below. Gold Diggers of 1933. Dancing Lady. Professional Sweetheart (GB: Imaginary Sweetheart). Blondie Johnson. Wild Boys of the Road (GB: Dangerous Days). Female. Hard to Handle. Picture Snatcher. Going Hollywood. *One Track Minds. Alice in Wonderland. Advice to the Lovelorn. Fast Workers. 1934: The Merry Widow. Gift of Gab. Down to Their Last Yacht (GB: Hawaiian Nights). A Wicked Woman. Adorable. Strictly Dynamite. *Sterling's Rival Romeo. Tomorrow's Children (GB: The Unborn). Back Page. Girl o' My Dreams. *Bring 'em Back A 'Lie. Operator 13 (GB: Spy 13). The Cat and the Fiddle. *My Girl Sally. *Heartburn. *Sterling's Aunts. Murder in the Private Car (GB: Murder on the Runaway Train). The

Whole Town's Talking (GB: Passport to Fame). 1935: 1,000 a Minute. Lottery Lover. I Live My Life. Rendezvous. Life Begins at 40. Doubting Thomas. Steamboat 'Round the Bend. 1936: Avenging Waters. Career Woman. Palm Springs (GB: Palm Springs Affair). 1937: Behind the Mike. Join the Marines. Maid of Salem. The Woman I Love. When Love is Young. Varsity Show. Snow White and the Seven Dwarfs (voice only). 1938: Spring Madness. Dr Rhythm. Professor, Beware! Of Human Hearts. 1939: St Louis Blues. Nick Carter, Master Detective. Remember the Night. 1940: The Blue Bird. Street of Memories. Hit Parade of 1941. Little Men. 1941: Cheers for Miss Bishop. New Wine (GB: The Great Awakening). Top Sergeant Mulligan. Dumbo (voice only). Meet John Doe. Look Who's Laughing. 1942: Don't Get Personal. Iceland (GB: Katina). Bambi (voice only). The Lady is Willing. Star Spangled Rhythm. 1943: Saludos Amigos (voice only). 1944: The Three Caballeros (voice only). 1945: Wildfire (GB: Wildfire: the Story of a Horse). A Walk in the Sun. 1946: Sioux City Sue. *Mr Wright Goes Wrong. *Moron Than Off. Make Mine Music (voice only). Death Valley. 1947: *Scooper Dooper. *Hectic Honeymoon. Saddle Pals. Twilight on the Rio Grande. Robin Hood of Texas. Trail to San Antone. 1948: *Man or Mouse. *Flat Feat. 1949: The Beautiful Blonde from Bashful Bend. 1950: Her Wonderful Lie. Alice in Wonderland (voice only). 1952: Bonzo Goes to College. 1953: *Ben and Me (voice only). 1956: Kentucky Rifle. 1957: Shake, Rattle and Rock! 1960: The Adventures of Huckleberry Finn. 1961: Alakazam the Great (voice only). 1963: My Six Loves. It's a Mad, Mad, Mad, Mad World. 1965: Winnie the Pooh and the Honey Tree (voice only). 1966: Batman. 1967: The Jungle Book (voice only). 1968: Live a Little, Love a Little. Winnie the Pooh and the Blustery Day (voice only). 1970: The Aristocats (voice only). 1975: Won Ton Ton, the Dog Who Saved Hollywood. *Winnie the Pooh and Tigger Too (voice only). 1976: Super Seal. 1977: Thunder on the Highway. Thunder and Lightning.

HOLMES, Taylor 1872–1959

Stocky American actor whose fresh features (dark hair, blue eyes) enabled him to keep going in romantic roles of stage and screen until well into his forties. He played a few indeterminate character parts in the 1930s, then came back to Hollywood in the post-war period to a busy few years of sharply etched studies, notably lawyers and businessmen, both corrupt and incorruptible, having developed baggy eyes that gave him a cunning look. Father of actors Phillips Holmes and Ralph Holmes, both of whom predeceased him, the former in an air crash, the latter a suicide.

1917: Efficiency Edgar's Courtship. Two-Bit Seats. Fools for Luck. Small-Town Guy. Uneasy Money. 1918: A Pair of Sixes. Ruggles of Red Gap. 1919: Taxi. It's a Bear. A Regular Fellow. Upside Down. 1920: Nothing Like Lies. The Very Idea. Nothing But the Truth. 1924: Twenty Dollars a Week. 1925: The Crimson Runner. Borrowed Finery. The Verdict. Her Market Value. 1927: One Hour of Love. 1929: *He Loved the Ladies. *He Did His Best. 1930: *Dad Knows Best. 1931: An American Tragedy. 1933: Before Morning. Dinner at Eight. 1934: Nana. Great Expectations. 1936: The First Baby. The Crime of Dr Forbes. Make Way for a Lady. 1946: Boomerang! 1947: In Self Defense. Kiss of Death. Nightmare Alley. The Egg and I. Time Out of Mind. 1948: Hazard. Smart Woman. Let's Love Again. The Plunderers. An Act of Murder. That Wonderful Urge. Joan of Arc. 1949: Woman in Hiding. Joe Palooka in The Big Fight. Once More, My Darling. Mr Belvedere Goes to College. 1950: Caged. Copper Canyon. Bright Leaf. Double Deal. Father of the Bride. Quicksand. 1951: The First Legion. Rhubarb. Two Tickets to Broadway. Drums in the Deep South. 1952: Hoodlum Empire. Hold That Line. Beware My Lovely. Woman of the North Country. Ride the Man Down. 1953: Gentlemen Prefer Blondes. She's Back on Broadway. 1954: The Outcast (GB: The Fortune Hunter). Tobor the Great. Untamed Heiress. 1955: Hell's Outpost. The Fighting Chance. 1956: The Maverick Queen. The Peacemaker. 1958: Wink of an Eye. Sleeping Beauty (voice only).

HOMEIER, Skip

(George Homeier) 1929–

Fair-haired, long-faced American player, a child actor of the early forties whose stage success as a young Nazi in *Tomorrow the World* started his screen career when he played the same role in the film version. Thereafter, his sullen sallowness propelled him into roles as a variety of mainly vicious or vindictive villains, although he had a brief fling as a leading actor in the mid-fifties.

1944: †Tomorrow the World. 1946: Boys' Ranch. 1948: Mickey. Arthur Takes Over. 1949: The Big Cat. 1950: The Gunfighter. Halls of Montezuma. 1951: Fixed Bayonets! Sealed Cargo. Sailor Beware. 1952: Has Anybody Seen My Gal. 1953: The Last Posse. 1954: The Lone Gun. Beachhead. Black Widow. Dawn at Socorro. Ten Wanted Men. 1955: The Road to Denver. Cry Vengeance. At Gunpoint (GB: Gunpoint!). 1956: The Burning Hills. Between Heaven and Hell. Dakota Incident. No Road Back. Stranger at My Door. Thunder over Arizona. 1957: The Tall T. Lure of the Swamp. Decision at Durango. 1958: Day of the Bad Man. Journey into Darkness. 1959: The Plunderers of Painted Flats. 1960: Comanche Station. 1963: Johnny Shiloh (originally for TV). Showdown. 1964: Bullet for a Badman. Stark Fear. 1966: The Ghost and Mr Chicken. Dead Heat on a Merry-Go-Round. 1968: Tiger by the Tail. 1970: The Challenge (TV). 1971: Two for the Money (TV). 1973: The Voyage of the Yes (TV). 1975: Starbird and Sweet William (cinema film only shown on TV). 1976: Helter Skelter (TV. GB: cinemas). 1977: The Greatest. 1978: Overboard (TV). 1979: The Wild Wild West Revisited (TV). 1982: Quell & Co.

† As Skippy Homeier

HOOTKINS, William 1948–

Bulky, American-born actor with dark, thinning hair and faintly shifty, lip-licking smile, a rare example of a latter-day 'fat man' who revels in sweaty, unsavoury characters. Mostly on television until the late 1970s, he has since appeared in a variety of British, American and international films.

*1973: Billion Dollar Bubble. 1976: The Pink Panther Strikes Again. 1977: Star Wars. Valentino. Twilight's Last Gleaming. 1979: Hanover Street. The Lady Vanishes. Hussy. 1980: Bad Timing (US: Bad Timing – A Sensual Obsession). Flash Gordon. 1981: Raiders of the Lost Ark. Sphinx. 1982: Trail of the Pink Panther. 1983: Bret Maverick (TV). *Out of Order. Curse of the Pink Panther. 1984: Black Carrion (TV. US: cinemas). 1985: Water (shown 1984). Zina. White Nights. DreamChild. 1986: Biggles (US: Biggles – Adventures in Time). Haunted Honeymoon. 1987: The Return of Sherlock Holmes (TV). American Gothic. Waco and Rhinehart (TV).*

1989: Batman. 1990: Hardware. 1991: Hear My Song. 1992: The Princess and the Goblin (voice only). 1993: Dust Devil: The Final Cut. La vida lactea/The Milky Life. 1994: Death Machine.

HOPE, Vida 1918–1962

Strong-looking British actress with rather wild dark hair, often cast in slatternly or vixenish roles, which she took by the scruff of the neck and shook into life. A multi-talented woman—she also directed plays and designed clothes—her careers came to an abrupt end when she was killed in a car crash two days before Christmas. She was married to British film director Derek Twist.

1942: In Which We Serve. 1944: English Without Tears (US: Her Man Gilbey). Champagne Charlie. 1945: The Way to the Stars (US: Johnny in the Clouds). 1946: School for Secrets (US: Secret Flight). While the Sun Shines. Beware of Pity. 1947: Nicholas Nickleby. It Always Rains on Sunday. Hue and Cry. They Made Me a Fugitive (US: I Became a Criminal). 1948: The Mark of Cain. Vice Versa. Woman Hater. 1949: For Them That Trespass. The Interrupted Journey. Paper Orchid. 1950: Double Confession. The Woman in Question (US: Five Angles on Murder). 1951: Cheer the Brave. The Man in the White Suit. Green Grow the Rushes. Angels One Five. 1952: Emergency Call (US: Hundred Hour Hunt). Women of Twilight (US: Twilight Women). The Long Memory. 1953: The Broken Horseshoe. Marilyn (later Roadhouse Girl). 1954: The Case of Diamond Annie. Fast and Loose. Lease of Life. 1956: Charley Moon. 1958: Family Doctor (US: RX Murder). 1961: In the Doghouse.

HOPKINS, Bo 1942–

Rangy, laconic, small-featured American actor with sandy, curly hair, often seen as menacing characters from the southern or south-western states. After a debut in *The Wild Bunch*, the South Carolina-born player became a familiar lean, stetsoned, crunch-faced figure in dozens of westerns and backwoods or small-town action films, often as braggarts bullying the hero or heroine, but only when backed up by half-a-dozen redneck heavies. A James Dean figure gone to the bad.

1969: The Wild Bunch. The Bridge at Remagen. The 1,000 Plane Raid. 1970: The Moonshine War. Monte Walsh. Macho Callahan. 1972: The Only Way Home. The Culpepper Cattle Co. The Getaway. 1973: White Lightning. American Graffiti. The Man Who Loved Cat Dancing. 1974: The Nickel Ride. The Day of the Locust. 1975: The Runaway Barge (TV). Posse. The Kansas City Massacre (TV). The Killer Elite. 1976: Charlie's Angels (TV). The Invasion of Johnson County (TV). A Small Town in Texas. Dawn: Portrait of a Teenage Runaway (TV). Tentacles. 1977: Aspen (TV). Crisis in Sun Valley (TV). 1978: Midnight Express. The Court Martial of Lt William Calley (TV). Thaddeus Rose and Eddie (TV). 1979: More American Graffiti/The Party's Over/ Purple Haze. The Last Ride of the Dalton Gang (TV). Casino/SS Casino (TV). 1980: The Fifth Floor. The Plutonium Incident (TV). Rodeo Girl (TV). 1981: Sweet Sixteen. 1982: Forbidden World. 1983: Ghost Dancing (TV). Mutant/Night Shadows. 1984: Dark Horse (TV). 1985: What Comes Around (TV). 1986: A Smoky Mountain Christmas (TV). Houston: The Legend of Texas (TV). Sex Appeal. 1987: Down the Long Hills (TV). Nightmare at Noon (released 1990). 1988: Trapper County War. The Stalker/The Man from Nowhere. 1989: Triangle of Terror/The Mark of the Beast. Big Bad John. Bounty Hunter. 1990: Final Alliance. 1991: Black Creek. Under Surveillance. 1992: Center of the Web. Terror of Manhattan. The Legend of Wolf Mountain. Inside Monkey Zetterland. 1993: The Ballad of Little Jo. Return to Wolf Mountain. 1994: The Feminine Touch. Texas Payback. Cheyenne Warrior. Riders in the Storm. 1995: Half a Dog's Life.

HOPPER, William 1915–1970

Tall, dark (greying early), clean- and sympathetic-looking American actor, the son of actress-columnist Hedda Hopper (Elda Furry, 1890–1966) and stage actor William DeWolf Hopper (1868–1935). He played many very small roles before war service from 1944 to 1946, always listed (when billed) as DeWolf Hopper. Then, after stage experience, he returned to the cinema as William Hopper, and enjoyed better roles than before, becoming a national figure as Paul Drake in the long-running *Perry Mason* series of the 1950s and 1960s. Died, like his mother, from pneumonia.

1916: Sunshine Dad. Casey at the Bat. Don Quixote. Mr Goode, the Samaritan. Stranded. 1936: Sissy. Murder with Pictures. The Big Broadcast of 1937. 1937: Larceny on the Air. Over the Goal. Mr Dodd Takes the Air. Public Wedding. Back in Circulation. The Adventurous Blonde/Torchy Blane the Adventurous Blonde. Footloose Heiress. Love is in the Air (GB: The Radio Murder Mystery). Mr Dodd Takes the Air. Women Are Like That. 1938: Mystery House. The Patient in Room 18. Daredevil Drivers. 1939: Angels Wash Their Faces. Espionage Agent. The Old Maid. Midnight. Dust Be Your Destiny. On Your Toes. Stagecoach. Nancy Drew and the Hidden Staircase. Pride of the Blue Grass. The Return of Dr X. The Cowboy Quarterback. Invisible Stripes. 1940: A Child is Born. No Time for Comedy. *Pony Express Days. Always a Bride. Money and the Woman. Knute Rockne – All American (GB: A Modern Hero). The Lady with Red Hair. The Fighting Sixty-Ninth. Castle on the Hudson (GB: Years Without Days). Ladies Must Live. Till We Meet Again. The Man Who Talked Too Much. Tear Gas Squad. Gambling on the High Seas. Brother Orchid. Flight Angels. *Sockaroo. Santa Fé Trail. Calling Philo Vance. Always a Bride. Virginia City. 1941: Flight from Destiny. Dive Bomber. Footsteps in the Dark. The Maltese Falcon. High Sierra. Navy Blues. They Died With Their Boots On. Manpower. Affectionately Yours. Blues in the Night. Highway West. You're in the Army Now. The Bride Came C.O.D. Here Comes Happiness. International Squadron. The Body Disappears. Bullets for O'Hara. Right to the Heart (GB: Knockout). Pride of the Blue Grass. 1942: The Big Shot. Lady Gangster. Desperate Journey. All Through the Night. Gentleman Jim. Secret Enemies. Juke Girl. Larceny Inc. The Male Animal. Across the Pacific. Yankee Doodle Dandy. The Hard Way. 1943: Murder on the Waterfront. The Mysterious Doctor. Air Force. 1944: The Last Ride. 1954: Track of the Cat. The High and the Mighty. This is My Love. Sitting Bull. 1955: Conquest of Space. One Desire. One Life (TV. GB: cinemas). Robbers' Roost. Rebel Without a Cause. Goodbye, My Lady. 1956: The First Texan. The Bad Seed. 1957: The Deadly Mantis. Slim Carter. 20,000,000 Miles to Earth. 1970: Myra Breckinridge.

HORDERN, Sir Michael 1911–

Balding, long-faced British actor who gave up teaching for acting and, after World War

II service, became one of Britain's most reliable film players. His resonant tones, mournful expression and watery eyes brought life to a series of harassed officials, both comic and serious, although he was also seen in a wide variety of other parts. His roles grew justifiably larger in the 1960s, while the 1970s saw perhaps his best film part, the seedy reporter in England Made Me. Also the narrator on some of the Scales of Justice shorts from the 1960s, he was knighted in 1983. Although 1939's A Girl Must Live is often listed as his first film, Sir Michael denies he was in it.

1940: The Girl in the News. 1946: The Years Between. A Girl in a Million. Great Expectations. School for Secrets (US: Secret Flight). 1947: Mine Own Executioner. 1948: Third Time Lucky. †Night Beat. Portrait from Life (GB: The Girl in the Painting). The Small Voice (US: Hideout). Good Time Girl. 1949: Train of Events. Passport to Pimlico. 1950: The Astonished Heart. Trio. Highly Dangerous. Tom Brown's Schooldays. 1951: Flesh and Blood. The Magic Box. Scrooge (US: A Christmas Carol). 1952: The Card (US: The Promoter). The Story of Robin Hood and His Merrie Men. The Hour of 13. 1953: Street Corner (US: Both Sides of the Law). Grand National Night (US: Wicked Woman). The Heart of the Matter. Personal Affair. You Know What Sailors Are. 1954: The Beachcomber. Forbidden Cargo. Svengali. 1955: The Night My Number Came Up. The Constant Husband. The Dark Avenger (US: The Warriors). Storm Over the Nile. 1956: Alexander the Great. The Man Who Never Was. Pacific Destiny. The Baby and the Battleship. The Spanish Gardener. 1957: No Time for Tears. I Accuse! Windom's Way. 1958: The Spaniard's Curse. I Was Monty's Double (US: Monty's Double). Girls at Sea. 1959: Sink the Bismarck! 1960: Moment of Danger (US: Malaga). The Man in the Moon. 1961: El Cid. Macbeth. First Left Past Aden (narrator only). 1963: *Position of Trust (narrator only). *The Invisible Asset (narrator only). Cleopatra. The VIPs. Dr Syn Alias the Scarecrow. 1964: The Yellow Rolls Royce. 1965: The Spy Who Came in from the Cold. Genghis Khan. Cast a Giant Shadow. 1966: Khartoum. The Taming of the Shrew. A Funny Thing Happened on the Way to the Forum. The Jokers. 1967: How I Won the War. I'll Never Forget What's 'is Name . . . 1968: Prudence and the Pill. Where Eagles Dare. 1969: The Bed Sitting Room.

1970: Futtock's End. Anne of the Thousand Days. Some Will, Some Won't. *A Christmas Carol (voice only). 1971: Up Pompeii. Girl Stroke Boy. The Pied Piper. The Possession of Joel Delaney. Demons of the Mind. 1972: Alice's Adventures in Wonderland. England Made Me. 1973: Theatre of Blood. The Mackintosh Man. 1974: Juggernaut. Mister Quilp. 1975: Royal Flash. Barry Lyndon (narrator only). Lucky Lady. 1976: The Slipper and the Rose. Joseph Andrews. 1977: *Mr Brit – the Man Who Made Miracles (narrator only). 1978: The Medusa Touch. Watership Down (voice only). Gauguin – the Savage. 1980: The Wildcats of St Trinian's. Shogun (TV. GB: cinemas, in abridged version). 1981: The Missionary. 1982: Gandhi. Oliver Twist (TV. GB: cinemas). 1983: Yellowbeard. Robin Hood (TV. GB: The Zany Adventures of Robin Hood). 1984: Boxer (narrator only). The Trouble with Spies/Trouble at the Royal Rose (released 1987). 1985: Lady Jane. Young Sherlock Holmes. 1986: Labyrinth (voice only). Comrades. 1987: Scoop (TV). The Secret Garden (TV). 1988: Suspicion (TV). 1989: Diamond Skulls (US: Dark Obsession). Danny, the Champion of the World (TV. GB: cinemas). 1990: The Fool. 1992: Freddie as F R O 7 (voice only). Memento Mori (TV).

† Scenes deleted from release print

HORNE, David 1898–1970

Rotund, balding British actor with genial, upper-crust voice, skilful at unctuous self-importance. A Grenadier Guards officer who turned to acting in his late twenties, he found himself cast largely as officers, noblemen and, latterly, senior clubmen, although the cinema gave him a wider variety of parts, sometimes as ruthless figures of authority.

1933: Lord of the Manor. General John Regan. 1934: Badger's Green. The Case for the Crown. 1935: That's My Uncle. The Village Squire. Late Extra. Gentleman's Agreement. 1936: It's Love Again. Under Proof. Seven Sinners (US: Doomed Cargo). The Cardinal. A Touch of the Moon. Conquest of the Air (released 1940). Accused. Debt of Honour. Interrupted Honeymoon. The House of the Spaniard. The Mill on the Floss. 1937: 21 Days (US: 21 Days Together. Released 1940). Farewell Again (US: Troopship). The Green Cockatoo (US: Four Dark Hours). 1938: The Wrecker. 1939: Blind

Folly. The Stars Look Down. Return to Yesterday. 1940: Crimes at the Dark House. The Door with Seven Locks (US: Chamber of Horrors). Night Train to Munich (US: Night Train). 1941: Breach of Promise (US: Adventure in Blackmail). Inspector Hornleigh Goes to It (US: Mail Train). They Flew Alone (US: Wings and the Woman). 1942: The Young Mr Pitt. The First of the Few (US: Spitfire). The Day Will Dawn (US: The Avengers). 1943: San Demetrio London. I Want to be an Actress. The Yellow Canary. The Hundred Pound Window. 1944: Don't Take It to Heart. 1945: The Seventh Veil. The Rake's Progress (US: Notorious Gentleman). I Live in Grosvenor Square (US: A Yank in London). The Wicked Lady. They Were Sisters. The Man from Morocco. 1946: Spring Song (US: Spring Time). Men of Two Worlds (US: Kisenga—Man of Africa). Gaiety George (US: Showtime). Caravan. The Magic Bow. 1947: The Man Within (US: The Smugglers). Easy Money. 1948: It's Hard to be Good. The Winslow Boy. Saraband for Dead Lovers (US: Saraband). Once Upon a Dream. The History of Mr Polly. 1949: Madeleine. 1950: Cage of Gold. 1951: Appointment with Venus (US: Island Rescue). 1953: Spaceways. Thought to Kill. Street Corner (US: Both Sides of the Law). The Intruder. Martin Luther. 1954: A Tale of Three Women. Beau Brummell. 1955: Three Cases of Murder. 1956: Lust for Life. The Last Man to Hang? 1957: The Prince and the Showgirl. The Safecracker. 1958: The Sheriff of Fractured Jaw. 1959: The Devil's Disciple. Operation Bullshine. 1961: Goodbye Again/Aimez-vous Brahms? Dentist on the Job (US: Get on with It!). Clue of the New Pin. 1963: Nurse on Wheels. 1965: The Big Job. 1968: Diamonds for Breakfast. A Flea in Her Ear.

HORSLEY, John 1920–
Sympathetic-looking, heftily-built British actor with large, kindly features and fair, thinning hair. A light leading man, especially on television, a medium in which he worked prodigiously through the 1950s, he later switched from playing police sergeants, inspectors and superintendents (progressively, he says) to doctors, lawyers and other senior professional men, looking dubiously at clients over the tops of their spectacles.

1950: Blackmailed. Highly Dangerous. The Quiet Woman. 1951: Appointment with Venus (US: Island Rescue). Encore. 1952: The

Crimson Pirate. The Lost Hours (US: The Big Frame). The Frightened Man. Deadly Nightshade. The Long Memory. Time Bomb (US: Terror on a Train). 1953: Recoil. Single-Handed (US: Sailor of the King). Wheel of Fate. The 'Maggie' (US: High and Dry). 1954: Meet Mr Malcolm. The Runaway Bus. Delayed Action. Forbidden Cargo. Destination Milan. Mad About Men. Seagulls Over Sorrento (US: Crest of a Wave). The Brain Machine. Father Brown (US: The Detective). Night People. Double Exposure. Little Red Monkey (US: The Case of the Little Red Monkey). 1955: Above Us the Waves. Impulse. Barbados Quest. A Time to Kill. They Can't Hang Me. 1956: The Weapon. Breakaway. Circus Friends. Bond of Fear. 1957: Stranger in Town. Hell Drivers. Man in the Shadow. Yangtse Incident (US: Battle Hell). Barnacle Bill (US: All at Sea). 1958: Operation Amsterdam. Dunkirk. Stormy Crossing (US: Black Tide). 1959: Carry On Nurse. Ben-Hur. Wrong Number. A Touch of Larceny. Sink the Bismarck! 1960: Let's Get Married. 1961: The Sinister Man. The Secret Ways. 1962: Seven Keys. Tiara Tahiti. Jigsaw. Night of the Prowler. Serena. 1963: The Comedy Man. Return to Sender. Panic. 1965: *Material Witness. Rotten to the Core. 1966: Where the Bullets Fly. The Jokers. 1968: The Limbo Line. Hostile Witness. 1983: Secrets (TV). 1985: The Doctor and the Devils. 1987: The Fourth Protocol. 1988: The Woman He Loved (TV).

HORTON, Edward Everett 1886–1970
Tall, dapper, stooping American comic actor who took his worried penguin act through scores of films spanning three decades. His crooked, uncertain leer and crackling delivery created a series of characters (from all walks of life) so liable to flap and fluster that one could imagine them, like Woody Allen, 'at home, having an anxiety attack on the floor'. He proved especially memorable, and valuable, in the Astaire-Rogers musicals of the 1930s. Just before he died (from cancer) he told an interviewer: 'I've had a grand time'. So did his audiences.

1920: Leave It to Me. 1922: The Ladder Jinx. Too Much Business. A Front Page Story. 1923: Ruggles of Red Gap. To the Ladies. Try and Get It. 1924: Flapper Wives. The Man Who Fights Alone. Helen's Babies. 1925: Marry Me. The Business of Love. Beggar on Horseback. The Nut-Cracker (GB: You Can't Fool Your Wife).

1926: The Whole Town's Talking. Poker Faces. La Bohème. 1927: Taxi! Taxi! *No Publicity. *Find the King. *Dad's Choice. 1928: *Miss Information. *Behind the Counter. Horse Shy. *Vacation Wives. *Call Again. *Scrambled Weddings. The Terror. 1929: Sonny Boy. The Hottentot. The Sap. The Aviator. *Trusting Wives. *Ask Dad. *Prince Gabby. *The Eligible Mr Bangs. *Good Medicine. 1930: *The Right Bed. Take the Heir. Wide Open. Holiday. Once a Gentleman. 1931: *The Great Junction Hotel. Reaching for the Moon. Lonely Wives. The Age for Love. Kiss Me Again (GB: Toast of the Legion). Six Cylinder Love. Smart Woman. The Front Page. 1932: Trouble in Paradise. But the Flesh is Weak. Roar of the Dragon. 1933: Soldiers of the King (US: The Woman in Command). It's a Boy! A Bedtime Story. The Way to Love. Design for Living. Alice in Wonderland. 1934: The Gay Divorcee (GB: The Gay Divorce). The Poor Rich. Ladies Should Listen. The Merry Widow. Kiss and Make Up. Easy to Love. Success at Any Price. Uncertain Lady. Sing and Like it. Smarty (GB: Hit Me Again). 1935: The Night is Young. In Caliente. Biography of a Bachelor Girl. Top Hat. $10 Raise (GB: Mr Faintheart). The Devil is a Woman. Going Highbrow. Little Big Shot. The Private Secretary. His Night Out. All the King's Horses. Your Uncle Dudley. 1936: The Man in the Mirror. The Singing Kid. Her Master's Voice. Hearts Divided. Nobody's Fool. 1937: Let's Make a Million. The King and the Chorus Girl (GB: Romance is Sacred). Lost Horizon. Shall We Dance? The Great Garrick. Hitting a New High. Wild Money. Oh, Doctor! Angel. The Perfect Specimen. Danger — Love at Work. 1938: Holiday/Unconventional Linda (GB: Free to Live). College Swing (GB: Swing, Teacher, Swing). Bluebeard's Eighth Wife. Little Tough Guys in Society. 1939: The Gang's All Here (US: The Amazing Mr Forrest). That's Right — You're Wrong. Paris Honeymoon. 1941: Ziegfeld Girl. You're the One. Bachelor Daddy/Sandy Steps Out. Here Comes Mr Jordan. Sunny. Week-End for Three. The Body Disappears. 1942: I Married an Angel. The Magnificent Dope. Springtime in the Rockies. 1943: Forever and a Day. Thank Your Lucky Stars. The Gang's All Here (GB: The Girls He Left Behind). Arsenic and Old Lace. 1944: Her Primitive Man. Summer Storm. San Diego, I Love You. The Town Went Wild. Brazil. 1945: Steppin' in Society. Lady on a Train. 1946: Cinderella Jones. Faithful in My Fashion. Earl Carroll Sketchbook (GB: Hats Off to Rhythm). 1947: The Ghost Goes Wild. Down to Earth. Her Husband's Affairs. 1948: All My Sons. 1957: The Story of Mankind. Three Men on a Horse (TV). 1961: Pocketful of Miracles. 1963: It's a Mad, Mad, Mad, Mad World. 1964: Sex and the Single Girl. 1967: The Perils of Pauline. 1969: 2000 Years Later. 1970: Cold Turkey.

HOUSMAN, Arthur 1888–1942
One of Hollywood's most engaging 'drunks'; in real life, like his only challenger Jack Norton (qv), short, florid, darkly moustachioed Housman never took a drop. He was encountered from time to time by Laurel and Hardy, most notably in Scram! and Our Relations, and could always be relied upon to ruin the best-laid plans at the drop

of a cork. He would probably have carried on tottering into the 1950s but in the winter of 1941/2 he contracted the pneumonia that killed him at only 53.

1912: What Happened to Mary (serial). *How a Horseshoe Upset a Happy Family. 1913: *When the Right Man Comes Along. *The Two Merchants. 1914: *On the Lazy Line (and other one-reelers in the 'Waddy and Arty' series). *Seth's Sweetheart. 1915: *The Champion Process Server. *A Spiritual Elopement. The Apaches of Paris. 1917: Red, White and Blue Blood. Her Good Name. Persuasive Peggy. The Cloud. A Mother's Ordeal. 1918: With Neatness and Dispatch. All Woman. Back to the Woods. 1919: The Bondage of Barbara. Toby's Bow. 1920: The Blooming Angel. A Fool and His Money. The Road of Ambition. The Flapper. 1921: Clay Dollars. The Way of a Maid. Room and Board. Worlds Apart. The Fighter. Is Life Worth Living? 1922: *The Snitching Hour. Man Wanted. Love's Masquerade. Destiny's Isle. Shadows of the Sea. The Prophet's Paradise. Why Announce Your Marriage? 1923: Under the Red Robe. Wife in Name Only. Male Wanted. 1924: Nellie (the Beautiful Cloak Model). Manhandled. 1925: Thunder Mountain. A Man Must Live. The Necessary Evil. The Coast of Folly. The Desert's Price. Night Life of New York. 1926: Braveheart. Whispering Wires. The Bat. The Midnight Kiss. Early to Wed. 1927: Publicity Madness. Bertha the Sewing Machine Girl. Rough House Rosie. Sunrise − A Song of Two Humans (GB: Sunrise). The Spotlight. Love Makes 'Em Wild. 1928: The Singing Fool. Happiness Ahead. Partners in Crime. Fools for Luck. Sins of the Fathers. 1929: Side Street (GB: Three Brothers). Queen of the Night Clubs. Broadway. Times Square (GB: The Street of Jazz). Fast Company. The Song of Love. 1930: Officer O'Brien. The Squealer. Feet First. Girl of the Golden West. Alias French Gertie (GB: Love Finds a Way). 1931: Five and Ten (GB: Daughter of Luxury). Anybody's Blonde (GB: When Blonde Meets Blonde). Bachelor Girl. Night Life in Reno. Caught Plastered. Bachelor Apartment. 1932: Hat Check Girl (GB: Embassy Girl). No More Orchids. Movie Crazy. *Parlor, Bedroom and Wrath. Afraid to Talk. *Scram! *Any Old Port. 1933: She Done Him Wrong. The Intruder. Her Bodyguard. *Sing, Sinner, Sing. *Daddy Knows Best. The Way to Love. *Roadhouse Queen. *Good Housewrecking. 1934: Mrs Wiggs of the Cabbage

Patch. Here is My Heart. *Elmer Steps Out. Success at Any Price. Kansas City Princess. 365 Nights in Hollywood. The Merry Widow. Gridiron Flash (GB: Luck of the Game). *The Chases of Pimple Street. *Something Simple. *The Live Ghost. *Babes in the Goods. *Done in Oil. *Punch Drunks. La veuve joyeuse. 1935: Woman Wanted. Public Hero Number One. Call of the Wild. *It Always Happens. *The Captain Hits the Ceiling. Hold 'Em Yale (GB: Uniform Lovers). Riffraff. Paris in Spring (GB: Paris Love Song). Here Comes Cookie (GB: The Plot Thickens). *The Fixer-Uppers. Diamond Jim. Two for Tonight. The Fire Trap. *Treasure Blues. *Sing, Sister, Sing. 1936: Tough Guy. Our Relations. After the Thin Man. Wives Never Know. Show Boat. With Love and Kisses. Racing Blood. *Am I Having Fun! 1937: Double or Nothing. Step Lively, Jeeves. A Family Affair. 1938: Man-Proof. Secrets of an Actress. Where the West Begins. Hard to Get. 1939: Navy Secrets. They Made Me a Criminal. Broadway Serenade. Blondie Takes a Vacation. 1940: Go West (GB: The Marx Brothers Go West). No Time for Comedy. 1941: Public Enemies. Billy the Kid.

HOUSTON, Glyn 1926−

Taciturn, dark-haired, self-effacing Welsh actor whose cosmopolitan image gave him a much wider variety of parts in British films than his more famous older brother Donald (1923−1991). Glyn progressed gradually to semi-leading roles by the early 1960s, but was thereafter more seen in theatre and TV. With his solid, low-key approach, it seemed he might make an ideal police inspector in a TV series; instead he popped up in another series, proving very effective as detective Lord Peter Wimsey's manservant.

1949: The Blue Lamp. 1950: The Adventurers (US: The Great Adventure). The Clouded Yellow. Trio. 1951: Home to Danger. I Believe in You. 1952: Girdle of Gold. Wide Boy (US: The Slasher). Gift Horse (US: Glory at Sea). The Great Game. The Cruel Sea. 1953: Hell Below Zero. Turn the Key Softly. Stryker of the Yard. The Rainbow Jacket. River Beat. The Sea Shall Not Have Them. The Sleeping Tiger. The Happiness of Three Women. Betrayed. 1955: The Night My Number Came Up. Passage Home. Lost (US: Tears for Simon). Who Done It? Private's Progress. 1956: The Long Arm (US: The Third Key). 1957: The Birthday Present. High Flight. The One That

Got Away. *The Case of the Smiling Widow. 1958: A Night to Remember. Nowhere to Go. A Cry from the Streets. 1959: Battle of the Sexes. Follow a Star. Tiger Bay. Jet Storm. Sink the Bismarck! 1960: The Bulldog Breed. Circus of Horrors. There Was a Crooked Man. The Wind of Change. 1961: Payroll. The Green Helmet. Flame in the Streets. Mix Me a Person. 1962: Phantom of the Opera. Emergency. Solo for Sparrow. 1963: Panic. A Stitch in Time. 1964: One Way Pendulum. 1965: The Brigand of Kandahar. The Secret of Blood Island. 1966: Invasion. 1968: Headline Hunters. 1973: Clouds of Witness (TV). 1977: Are You Being Served? 1980: The Sea Wolves. 1989: Face of the Earth (TV). Conspiracy. 1991: Old Scores (TV). 1993: The Mystery of Edwin Drood.

HOWARD, Arthur
(A. Stainer) 1910−

Lugubrious, donkey-faced, bald British actor with a fine line in dithering, handwringing panic which completely broke up his normal dignity. The 20-years-younger brother of acting superstar Leslie Howard (1890−1943), Arthur was always the journeyman actor of the Howard clan but was only really seized by the British cinema in post-war years. At the same time, he assumed his best-remembered role, at first on TV, then on radio and in a film − that of Pettigrew, the deputy headmaster to 'Professor' Jimmy Edwards' rascally and incompetent headmaster in the Whack-O! series. Later in smaller cameos, but still busy into his seventies.

1933: The Private Life of Henry VIII. The Lady is Willing. 1934: The Scarlet Pimpernel. 1938: Pygmalion. 1947: Frieda. So Well Remembered. The Mark of Cain. 1948: London Belongs to Me (US: Dulcimer Street). The Passionate Friends (US: One Woman's Story). Passport to Pimlico. 1949: Private Angelo. Stage Fright. 1950: The Happiest Days of Your Life. Dick Barton at Bay. State Secret (US: The Great Manhunt). Last Holiday. Cage of Gold. The Undefeated. 1951: The Man in the White Suit. Calling Bulldog Drummond. Lady Godiva Rides Again. Laughter in Paradise. 1952: Never Look Back. Cosh Boy (US: The Slasher). Moulin Rouge. 1953: Glad Tidings. The Story of Gilbert and Sullivan (US: The Great Gilbert and Sullivan). The Intruder. Grand National Night (US: Wicked Wife). Will Any Gentleman?... *Albert RN.* 1954: *The Rainbow Jacket. The Dam Busters. The Belles of St Trinian's. Knave of Hearts (US: Lovers, Happy Lovers). Out of the Clouds.* 1955: *Footsteps in the Fog. The Adventures of Quentin Durward (US: Quentin Durward). The Constant Husband. The Glass Cage (US: The Glass Tomb). One Way Out. Touch and Go (US: The Light Touch).* 1956: *One Wish Too Many. Paradiso. Guilty?* 1957: *I Accuse!* 1958: *Nowhere to Go. I Only Arsked! Law and Disorder. Rockets Galore (US: Mad Little Island).* 1959: *Desert Mice. The Siege of Pinchgut (US: Four Desperate Men). Libel. Friends and Neighbours. Bottoms Up!* 1961: *Watch It Sailor!* 1962: *Kill or Cure.* 1963: *The VIPs. Ladies Who Do.* 1964: *Les félins (GB: The Love Cage. US: Joy House).* 1965: *Lady L.* 1966: *The Ghost Goes Gear. Grand Prix.* 1968: *The Shoes of the Fisherman. The Best House in London.* 1969: *My Lover, My Son.* 1970: *Jane Eyre (TV. GB: cinemas). Hoverbug.* 1971: *Zeppelin. The Magnificent Seven Deadly Sins. Blinker's Spy Spotter.* 1972: *Steptoe and Son.* 1975: *One of Our Dinosaurs is Missing. The Bawdy Adventures of Tom Jones.* 1976: *Full Circle (US: The Haunting of Julia).* 1977: *Hardcore (US: Fiona).* 1979: *The Prisoner of Zenda. Moonraker.* 1981: *The Missionary.* 1982: *Trail of the Pink Panther.* 1983: *Curse of the Pink Panther.* 1984: *Another Country.* 1989: *Conspiracy.*

HOWARD, Shemp

(Shmuel Horowitz) 1891–1955

Squat, solid, chimplike, ever-grinning American comic character actor with flattened dark hair whose career in comedy cameos was somewhat foreshortened when he slightly reluctantly joined his brother Moe at the end of 1946 as one of The Three Stooges. They had first teamed at the time of World War I, doing a blackface comedy act in minstrel shows and on vaudeville. Later they formed part of a comedy act called The Racketeers which supported comic Ted Healy when he broke into films. Shemp had left the act by 1932 and gradually forged a career as a Hollywood cameo player, often as friendly menials or behind-the-counter men, notably the bartender at The Black Pussy Cat cafe in W C Fields' *The Bank Dick*. Shemp replaced his ailing brother Curly in the Stooges' lineup but himself died in the winter of 1955 from a coronary occlusion suffered on the way home from a boxing match.

1930: *Hollywood on Parade.* †*Soup to Nuts.* 1933: †*In the Dough.* 1934: †*Convention Girl (GB: Atlantic City Romance). Art Trouble.* 1936: †*Three of a Kind. For the Love of Pete.* **Joe Palooka.* 1937: †*Headin' East.* †*Hollywood Round-Up.* 1938: *Home on the Range. Not Guilty Enough.* 1939: *Glove Slingers.* †*Another Thin Man.* 1940: †*Road Show. Pleased to Mitt You. Boobs in the Woods. Money Squawks.* †*Millionaires in Prison.* †*Give Us Wings.* †*The Bank Dick (GB: The Bank Detective).* †*The Leather Pushers.* †*Murder over New York.* 1941: †*Buck Privates (GB: Rookies).* †*The Invisible Woman.* †*Cracked Nuts.* †*Meet the Chump.* †*Mr Dynamite.* †*Tight Shoes.* †*Hold That*

Ghost. †*Too Many Blondes.* †*Hellzapoppin.* †*The Flame of New Orleans.* †*Six Lessons from Madame La Zonga.* †*In the Navy.* †*San Antonio Rose.* †*Hit the Road.* 1942: †*Mississippi Gambler.* †*The Strange Case of Dr RX.* †*Private Buckaroo.* /*Arabian Nights.* †*Butch Minds the Baby.* †*Pittsburgh.* †*Who Done It?* 1943: †*It Ain't Hay (GB: Money for Jam). Farmer for a Day.* †*How's About It?* †*Crazy House.* †*Strictly in the Groove.* †*Keep 'Em Slugging* 1944: †*Three of a Kind.* †*Strange Affair.* †*Moonlight and Cactus.* †*Crazy Knights. Pick a Peck of Plumbers. Open Season for Saps.* 1945: *Off Again, On Again. Where the Pest Begins. A Hit with a Miss.* †*Trouble Chasers.* 1946: †*The Gentleman Misbehaves.* †*Blondie Knows Best.* †*Swing Parade of 1946.* †*Dangerous Business.* †*One Exciting Week. Mr Noisy. Jiggers, My Wife. Society Mugs.* 1947: *Bride and Gloom. Out West. Half Wits' Holiday. Brideless Groom. All Gummed Up. Fright Night. Hold That Lion. Sing Me a Song of Six Pants.* 1948: *Squareheads of the Round Table. Shivering Sherlocks. Heavenly Daze. I'm a Monkey's Uncle. Crime on Their Hands. Pardon My Clutch. Fiddlers Three. Hot Scots. Mummy's Dummies.* 1949: *The Ghost Talks.* †*Africa Screams. Hocus Pokus. Who Done It? Fuelin' Around. Vagabond Loafers. Malice in the Palace. Dunked in the Deep.* 1950: *Dopey Dicks. Punchy Cowpunchers. Love at First Bite. Three Hams on Rye. Slap Happy Sleuths. Hugs and Mugs. Self Made Maids. Studio Stoops. A Snitch in Time.* 1951: †*Gold Raiders (GB: Stooges Go West). Don't Throw That Knife. Three Arabian Nuts. Merry Mavericks. Hula La-La. Baby Sitters' Jitters. Scrambled Brains. The Tooth Will Out. The Pest Man Wins.* 1952: *Corny Casanovas. Gents in a Jam. Cuckoo on a Choo-Choo. Three Dark Horses. He Cooked His Goose. Listen, Judge. A Missed Fortune.* 1953: *Loose Loot. Up in Daisy's Penthouse. Spooks. Rip, Sew and Stitch. Goof on the Roof. Booty and the Beast. Tricky Dicks. Pardon My Backfire. Bubble Trouble.* 1954: *Pals and Gals. Income Tax Sappy. Shot in the Frontier. Knutzy Knights. Scotched in Scotland. Musty Musketeers.* 1955: *Gypped in the Penthouse. Fling in the Ring. Stone Age Romeos. Hot Ice. Of Cash and Hash. Bedlam in Paradise. Wham-Bam-Slam. Blunder Boys.* 1956: *Flagpole Sitters. Husbands Beware. Rumpus in the Harem. Scheming Schemers. Creeps. For Crimin' Out Loud. Hot Stuff. Commotion on the Ocean.*

All shorts except † features

HOWLETT, Noel 1901–1984

Alphabetical order places close together Britain's two most prominent portrayers of querulous, pupil-beset schoolteachers. The studious-looking Howlett was in real life a schoolmaster who wavered between teaching and acting in his twenties before deciding on the latter career. Although mostly a man of the theatre (he was major-in-charge of ENSA shows in World War II), he made quite a number of minor film appearances as teachers, doctors, solicitors and company executives before winning national recognition as testy headmaster Cromwell in the popular TV series *Please, Sir!*

1936: *Men Are Not Gods. Such Men Are Dangerous.* 1937: *A Yank at Oxford.* 1939: *The Proud Valley.* 1940: *George and Margaret.* 1947: *When the Bough Breaks. Fortune Lane. This Was a Woman. The White Unicorn (US: Bad Sister). Jassy. Corridor of Mirrors. The Mark of Cain.* 1948: *The Calendar. Scott of the Antarctic. Good Time Girl. The Blind Goddess. The Winslow Boy. Saraband for Dead Lovers (US: Saraband). Once Upon a Dream.* 1949: *The Perfect Woman.* 1950: *Your Witness (US: Eye Witness). So Long at the Fair. The Reluctant Widow.* 1951: *Laughter in Paradise. Scrooge (US: A Christmas Carol). Cloudburst.* 1954: *Father Brown (US: The Detective). One Good Turn.* 1955: *Handcuffs, London.* 1956: *Soho Incident (US: Spin a Dark Web). Lust for Life.* 1958: *Nowhere to Go. The Scapegoat.* 1959: *Battle of the Sexes. Serious Charge (US: A Touch of Hell). You'll Never See Me Again.* 1960: *Let's Get Married.* 1961: *Victim. Mary Had a Little. ...* 1962: *Kiss of the Vampire (US: Kiss of Evil). Tomorrow at Ten. Lawrence of Arabia.* 1963: *Murder at the Gallop.* 1964: *Woman of Straw.* 1965: *The Amorous Adventures of Moll Flanders.* 1967: *Quatermass and the Pit (US: Five Million Miles to Earth).* 1968: *The Bush Baby.* 1969: *Some Will, Some Won't.* 1971: *Please, Sir!* 1978: *Mr Selkie.*

HOYT, John

(J. Hoysradt) 1904–1991

Tall, gaunt-faced, light-haired American actor, a former historian and drama teacher who became an entertainer singing in the chorus of the Ziegfeld Follies, before turning full-time to dramatic acting following World War II. Then he proceeded apace to play scientists, period aristocrats, Nazi officers,

prison wardens and upper-class crooks, as well as a few mad professors in horror films. He also tried his hand at impressions in night-clubs. Died from lung cancer.

1946: OSS. 1947: My Favorite Brunette. Brute Force. The Unfaithful. 1948: Winter Meeting. To the Ends of the Earth. Sealed Verdict. The Decision of Christopher Blake. 1949: Trapped. The Bribe. The Great Dan Patch. The Lady Gambles. Everybody Does It. 1950: The Lawless (GB: The Dividing Line). The Company She Keeps. Outside the Wall. 1951: Quebec. Inside Straight. New Mexico. The Lost Continent. When Worlds Collide. The Desert Fox (GB: Rommel − Desert Fox). 1952: Loan Shark. The Black Castle. Androcles and the Lion. 1953: Julius Caesar. Sins of Jezebel. Casanova's Big Night. 1954: The Student Prince. Moonfleet. Desiree. The Big Combo. 1955: Blackboard Jungle. The Purple Mask. The Girl in the Red Velvet Swing. Trial. 1956: The Conqueror. Forever, Darling. The Come-On. Mohawk. Death of a Scoundrel. Wetbacks. 1957: Sierra Stranger. God is My Partner. Baby-Face Nelson. Fighting Trouble. The Beast of Budapest. 1958: Attack of the Puppet People (GB: Six Inches Tall). 1959: Never So Few. Riot in Juvenile Prison. Curse of the Undead. 1960: Spartacus. 1962: Merrill's Marauders. 1963: Cleopatra. X − The Man with X-Ray Eyes (GB: The Man With the X-Ray Eyes). 1964: The Glass Cage. The Time Travelers. Two on a Guillotine. Young Dillinger. 1965: Duel at Diablo. Operation CIA. 1966: Gunpoint. Fame is the Name of the Game (TV). 1967: Winchester '73 (TV). 1968: Panic in the City. 1970: The Intruders (TV). 1972: Welcome Home, Johnny Bristol (TV). 1974: Flesh Gordon. 1975: The Turning Point of Jim Malloy (TV). 1977: Nero Wolfe (TV). 1978: The Winds of Kitty Hawk (TV). 1980: In Search of Historic Jesus (GB: Jesus). 1985: Desperately Seeking Susan. 1987: Forty Days of Musa Dagh.

HUBER, Harold 1904−1959

With his dark, slick hair, swarthily ruddy complexion, trim moustache and white-toothed smile, this American actor was something of a cut-price Cesar Romero. Typed in villainous roles, as crooked night-club owners and the like, in the early part of his film career, he was later much on the side of the law, especially in Mr Moto and

Charlie Chan thrillers, where he played sharpish inspectors. The war changed the direction of his career and he virtually quit films in post-war years after return from service abroad. In 1950, he became a TV regular in the series *I Cover Times Square* (which he also produced) and continued working steadily in the medium up to his early death. Started as an attorney.

1932: The Match King. Central Park. Lawyer Man. 1933: Frisco Jenny. Parachute Jumper. 20,000 Years in Sing Sing. Girl Missing. Central Airport. Midnight Mary. Ladies They Talk About. The Life of Jimmy Dolan (GB: The Kid's Last Fight). The Silk Express. The Mayor of Hell. Mary Stevens MD. The Bowery. Police Car 17. 1934: Hi, Nellie! No More Women. Forsaking All Others. The Cat's Paw. The Crosby Case (GB: The Crosby Murder Case). The Line-Up. A Very Honorable Guy. Fury of the Jungle. He Was Her Man. The Thin Man. Hide-Out. The Defense Rests. Cheating Cheaters. Port of Lost Dreams. The Merry Frinks (GB: The Happy Family). 1935: Mad Love (GB: The Hands of Orlac). One New York Night (GB: The Trunk Mystery). Naughty Marietta. Port of Lost Dreams. Reckless. The World Accuses. Pursuit. G Men. 1936: The Devil Is a Sissy (GB: The Devil Takes the Count). Kelly the Second. Muss 'Em Up (GB: House of Fate). We're Only Human. San Francisco. Women Are Trouble. The Gay Desperado. Klondike Annie. 1937: The Good Earth. Midnight Taxi. Trouble in Morocco. Angel's Holiday. You Can't Beat Love. Charlie Chan at Monte Carlo. Outlaws of the Orient. Charlie Chan on Broadway. Love Under Fire. 1938: International Settlement. Mr Moto's Gamble. A Slight Case of Murder. The Adventures of Marco Polo. Gangs of New York. Passport Husband. Going Places. A Trip to Paris. Mysterious Mr Moto. Little Tough Guys in Society. While New York Sleeps. 1939: Mr Moto in Danger Island (GB: Mr Moto on Danger Island). You Can't Get Away with Murder. King of the Turf. Chasing Danger. 60,000 Enemies. The Lady and the Mob. Main Street Lawyer (GB: Small Town Lawyer). Beau Geste. Charlie Chan in City in Darkness. Charlie McCarthy, Detective. 1940: The Ghost Comes Home. Dance, Girl, Dance. Kit Carson. 1941: A Man Betrayed (GB: Citadel of Crime). Country Fair. Charlie Chan in Rio. Down Mexico Way. 1942: Pardon My Stripes. A Gentleman After Dark. Sleepytime Gal. Little

Tokyo USA. Manila Calling. The Lady from Chungking. Ice Capades Revue (GB: Rhythm Hits the Ice). 1943: The Crime Doctor. 1950: My Friend Irma Goes West. Let's Dance. 1957: The Joker is Wild.

HUDDLESTON, David 1930−

Hale, hearty, barrel-shaped, ruddy-cheeked American actor who has mixed comforting, avuncular types with suited rascals and rogues. The Virginia-born actor started in stage in Broadway musicals, before beginning a sporadic film career in 1963. After a couple of crusty police lieutenants in TV crime series, he created his most memorable − and certainly cuddliest − character with the title role in *Santa Claus* in 1985.

1963: All the Way Home. 1964: Black Like Me. 1968: A Lovely Way to Die (GB: A Lovely Way to Go). 1969: Slaves. 1970: Norwood. Rio Lobo. 1971: Fools' Parade (GB: Dynamite Man from Glory Jail). Something Big. Sarge: The Badge or the Cross (TV). The Priest Killer (TV). Suddenly Single (TV). Brian's Song (TV). The Homecoming (TV). 1972: Bad Company. Country Blue (released 1975). Brock's Last Case (TV). 1973: Tenafly (TV). Hawkins on Murder (TV). Billy Two Hats. 1974: McQ. Deadly Honeymoon. Blazing Saddles. The Gun and the Pulpit (TV). The Klansman. Heatwave! (TV). 1975: Breakheart Pass. 1976: Crime Busters. The Oregon Trail (TV). Sherlock Holmes in New York (TV). Shark Kill (TV). 1977: The Final Eye (TV). The World's Greatest Lover. The Greatest. 1978: Kate Bliss and the Ticker Tape Kid (TV). Capricorn One. 1979: Gorp. 1980: Smokey and the Bandit II (GB: Smokey and the Bandit Have a Baby). 1981: The Oklahoma City Dolls (TV). Family Reunion (TV). 1983: MADD: Mothers Against Drunk Drivers (TV). 1984: Finnegan Begin Again (cable TV). The Act. 1985: Santa Claus. Blacke's Magic (TV). 1986: Spot Marks the X (TV). When the Bough Breaks (TV). 1987: Frantic. 1988: The Tracker (TV). Dead or Alive. 1989: Margaret Bourke White/Double Exposure (TV).

HUGHES, Roddy 1891−1970

Roly-poly, balding Welsh actor who looked like the man in the moon. A fine singer, he began in musical comedy when first on the London stage during World War I, but soon came into demand for straight character

roles. Theatrical commitments continued to limit his film appearances, but he was never better cast than as Mr Fezziwig in the 1951 *Scrooge*; with his pudgy but mobile features, few players could better express extremes of joy and sorrow without recourse to words.

1932: Reunion. 1933: It's a Boy. Say It With Flowers. 1934: Music Hall. How's Chances? (US: The Diplomatic Lover). A Glimpse of Paradise. Kentucky Minstrels. Lest We Forget. The Old Curiosity Shop. 1935: Breakers Ahead. The Small Man. The Mad Hatters. A Real Bloke. Honeymoon for Three. The Clairvoyant. Sweeney Todd the Demon Barber of Fleet Street. Cock o' the North. The River House Mystery. 1936: The Crimes of Stephen Hawke. Men of Yesterday. Cheer Up. Twelve Good Men. 1937: The House of Silence. Captain's Orders. La mort du Sphinx. Little Miss Somebody. Make Up. 1938: *Confidence Tricksters. *In Your Garden. Convict 99. Hold My Hand. 1939: The Gang's All Here (US: The Amazing Mr Forrest). The Proud Valley. The Stars Look Down. Poison Pen. 1940: Saloon Bar. *Dangerous Comment. The Girl in the News. Old Mother Riley in Business. Under Your Hat. 1941: Pimpernel Smith (US: Mister V). The Saint's Vacation. The Black Sheep of Whitehall. Cottage to Let (US: Bombsight Stolen). The Ghost of St Michael's. South American George. Atlantic Ferry (US: Sons of the Sea). Hatter's Castle. Quiet Wedding. Hard Steel. 1942: In Which We Serve. 1944: Meet Sexton Blake. 1945: Here Comes the Sun. 1946: George in Civvy Street. 1947: Nicholas Nickleby. Green Fingers. The Silver Darlings. So Well Remembered. Fame is the Spur. 1948: The Dark Road. The Small Back Room (US: Hour of Glory). Mr Perrin and Mr Traill. Blanche Fury. Obsession (US: The Hidden Room). 1949: The Last Days of Dolwyn (US: Woman of Dolwyn). Poet's Pub. The Passionate Friends (US: One Woman's Story). 1950: The Reluctant Widow. 1951: The Man in the White Suit. Old Mother Riley's Jungle Treasure. Scrooge (US: A Christmas Carol). Salute the Toff. 1952: The Great Game. Hammer the Toff. Escape Route (US: I'll Get You). 1953: Alf's Baby. Meet Mr Lucifer. Trouble in Store. The Million Pound Note (US: Man with a Million). The Final Test. 1954: The Lark Still Sings. Mystery on Bird Island. 1955: One Jump Ahead. See How They Run. 1956: Around the World in 80 Days. Not So Dusty. 1957: Sea Wife. 1958: The Spaniard's Curse.

Corridors of Blood (released 1961). 1960: The House on Marsh Road. 1961: Greyfriars Bobby.

HULL, Henry 1890–1977

Dark, gauntly handsome American actor, a thin-faced Henry Fonda in his youth who strayed all too rarely from the stage in silent days and was well into his forties before becoming a regular cinema performer. After a couple of leads, including a haunting portrayal of *The Werewolf of London*, he settled into character roles as crusty types with barking voices, often in period drama, and just as likely to pop up on one side of the law as the other. Once a mining engineer in Canada in his early twenties. Also a talented writer who had one or two plays produced on Broadway, Hull made his film debut in the 1916 film *The Little Rebel*.

1916: The Man Who Came Back. 1917: The Family Honor. Rasputin, the Black Monk. A Square Deal. The Volunteer. 1919: Little Women. 1922: One Exciting Night. 1923: The Last Moment. A Bride for a Knight. 1924: The Hoosier School Master (GB: The School Master). For Women's Favor. Roulette. 1925: The Wrong-doers. Wasted Lives. 1928: Matinee Idol. 1931: The Man Who Came Back. 1933: The Story of Temple Drake. 1934: Great Expectations. Midnight. 1935: The Werewolf of London. Transient Lady (GB: False Witness). 1938: Yellow Jack. Boys' Town. Three Comrades. Paradise for Three (GB: Romance for Three). The Great Waltz. 1939: Judge Hardy and Son. Babes in Arms. Spirit of Culver (GB: Man's Heritage). Bad Little Angel. Stanley and Livingstone. The Return of the Cisco Kid. Miracles for Sale. Nick Carter, Master Detective. Jesse James. 1940: The Return of Frank James. The Ape. My Son, My Son. 1941: High Sierra. 1942: The Big Shot. Queen of Broadway. 1943: What a Man. The Woman of the Town. *Seeds of Freedom. The West Side Kid. 1944: Lifeboat. Goodnight, Sweetheart. Voodoo Man. 1945: Objective, Burma! 1947: High Barbaree. Deep Valley. Mourning Becomes Electra. 1948: Scudda Hoo! Scudda Hay! (GB: Summer Lightning). The Walls of Jericho. Belle Starr's Daughter. Portrait of Jennie (GB: Jennie). Fighter Squadron. 1949: Song of Surrender. El Paso. The Fountainhead. Rimfire. The Great Dan Patch. Colorado Territory. The Great Gatsby. 1950: The Return of Jesse James. The Hollywood Story. 1951: The Treasure of Lost

Canyon. 1952: The Mad Monster. 1953: The Last Posse. Inferno. Thunder Over the Plains. 1955: The Man With the Gun (GB: The Trouble Shooter). 1956: Kentucky Rifle. 1957: The Buckskin Lady. 1958: The Sheriff of Fractured Jaw. The Buccaneer. Face of a Hero (TV). The Proud Rebel. 1959: The Oregon Trail. 1961: Master of the World. 1965: The Fool Killer. 1966: The Chase. A Covenant With Death.

HUNNICUTT, Arthur 1911–1979

It seems appropriate that Hunnicutt should have been born in a town called Gravelly. For the gruff, 'countrified' voice and bearded features of this distinctive American player, a sort of backwoods Walter Brennan who chewed dialogue rather than spoke it, were seen in many a western, through the forties, fifties and sixties. In the middle of this period he was a top character star billed above the title. Nominated for an Oscar in *The Big Sky*. Died from cancer.

1940: Northwest Passage. 1942: Wildcat. Silver Queen. Pardon My Gun. Hay Foot. Fall In. Riding Thro' Nevada. 1943: Fighting Buckaroo. Frontier Fury. Johnny Come Lately (GB: Johnny Vagabond). Chance of a Lifetime. Law of the Northwest. Robin Hood of the Range. Hail to the Rangers (GB: Illegal Rights). 1944: Murder, He Says. Abroad with Two Yanks. Riding West (GB: Fugitive from Time). 1949: Lust for Gold. The Great Dan Patch. Pinky. Border Incident. 1950: Stars in My Crown. A Ticket to Tomahawk. The Furies. Two Flags West. Broken Arrow. 1951: Passage West (GB: High Venture). Sugarfoot. The Red Badge of Courage. Distant Drums. 1952: The Big Sky. The Lusty Men. 1953: Split Second. Devil's Canyon. She Couldn't Say No (GB: Beautiful But Dangerous). The French Line. 1955: The Last Command. 1956: The Kettles in the Ozarks. 1957: The Tall T. 1959: Born Reckless. 1963: The Cardinal. A Tiger Walks. 1965: Cat Ballou. The Adventures of Bullwhip Griffin. 1966: Apache Uprising. 1967: El Dorado. 1971: The Trackers (TV). Million Dollar Duck. 1972: The Revengers. Climb an Angry Mountain (TV). The Bounty Man (TV). 1973: Shoot-Out. Mrs Sundance (TV). 1974: The Spikes Gang. Harry and Tonto. The Daughters of Joshua Cabe Return (TV). 1975: Moonrunners. Winterhawk.

HUNT, Linda 1945–

Tiny, dark-haired, solidly built American actress with unusual, almost oriental features. After a previous career insignificant in film terms, she stunned the movie world in 1982 by playing a male Indonesian photographer in *The Year of Living Dangerously*, and winning an Academy Award. Not surprisingly suitable subsequent roles proved difficult to find, and none of them has been particularly rewarding.

1980: Popeye. 1982: The Year of Living Dangerously. 1984: The Bostonians. Dune. 1985: Eleni. Silverado. 1987: Waiting for the Moon. The Room Upstairs (TV). 1989: She-Devil. 1990: Kindergarten Cop. 1991: If Looks Could Kill (GB: Teen Agent). 1992: Third Stone from the Sun (voice only). 1993: Younger and Younger. Twenty Bucks. 1994: Prêt-à-Porter (US: Ready to Wear) 1995: Pocahontas (voice only).

HUNT, Martita 1900–1969

Formidable Argentine-born actress with rich voice who made her name on the British stage and screen and used her horsey features and dominant plainness to create a colourful gallery of villainesses and (later) eccentric dowagers. Perhaps most memorable as Miss Havisham in the 1946 *Great Expectations*.

1920: A Rank Outsider. 1931: Service for Ladies (US: Reserved for Ladies). 1932: Love on Wheels. 1933: I Was a Spy. Friday the Thirteenth. 1934: Too Many Millions. 1935: King of the Damned. The Case of Gabriel Perry. First a Girl. Mr What's-His-Name. 1936: When Knights Were Bold. Pot Luck, Tudor Rose (US: Nine Days a Queen). Sabotage (US: The Woman Alone). Good Morning, Boys (US: Where There's a Will). The Interrupted Honeymoon. The Mill on the Floss. 1937: Farewell Again (US: Troopship). Second Best Bed. 1938: Prison Without Bars. Strange Boarders. Everything Happens to Me. 1939: Trouble Brewing. A Girl Must Live. Goodbye Mr Chips! The Nursemaid Who Disappeared. The Good Old Days. At the Villa Rose (US: House of Mystery). Young Man's Fancy. The Middle Watch. Old Mother Riley Joins Up. 1940: *Miss Grant Goes to the Door. Spare a Copper. Tilly of Bloomsbury. East of Piccadilly (US: The Strangler). 1941: Freedom Radio (US: A Voice in the Night). Quiet Wedding. The Seventh Survivor. They Flew Alone (US: Wings and the Woman). 1942: Lady from Lisbon. Sabotage at Sea. Talk About Jacqueline. 1943: The Man in Grey. 1944: Welcome Mr Washington. 1945: The Wicked Lady. 1946: Great Expectations. 1947: The Little Ballerina. The Ghosts of Berkeley Square. 1948: So Evil My Love. Anna Karenina. My Sister and I. 1949: The Fan (GB: Lady Windermere's Fan). 1952: The Story of Robin Hood and His Merrie Men. Treasure Hunt. Meet Me Tonight. It Started in Paradise. Folly to be Wise. 1953: Melba. 1955: King's Rhapsody. 1956: The March Hare. Three Men in a Boat. Anastasia. 1957: Les Espions. The Admirable Crichton (US: Paradise Lagoon). Dangerous Exile. The Prince and the Showgirl. 1958: Me and the Colonel. La prima notte/Les noces Venetiennes. Bonjour Tristesse. 1959: Bottoms Up! 1960: The Brides of Dracula. Song Without End. 1961: Mr Topaze (US: I Like Money). 1962: The Wonderful World of the Brothers Grimm. 1963: Becket. 1964: The Unsinkable Molly Brown. 1965: Bunny Lake is Missing. 1968: The Best House in London.

HUNTLEY, Raymond 1904–1990

Slight, round-faced, narrow-eyed British actor with dark hair and moustache and indifferent, faintly imperious air. In his earlier days, he was often cast as vicious, underhand villains and, with the war years, sneaky, evil Nazis. As he grew older, the features turned from sinister to cynical, and he enjoyed a good run as pompous civil servants and other supercilious types in British comedies of the 1950s and 1960s.

1934: What Happened Then? 1935: Can You Hear Me, Mother? 1936: Rembrandt. Whom the Gods Love (US: Mozart). 1937: Dinner at the Ritz. Knight Without Armour. 1940: Bulldog Sees It Through. Night Train to Munich (US: Night Train). 1941: The Ghost Train. Inspector Hornleigh Goes to It (US: Mail Train). Once a Crook. Pimpernel Smith (US: Mister V). Freedom Radio (US: A Voice in the Night). The Ghost of St Michael's. 1942: The Day Will Dawn (US: The Avengers). 1943: When We Are Married. 1944: The Way Ahead (US: Immortal Battalion). They Came to a City. 1946: I See a Dark Stranger (US: The Adventuress). School for Secrets (US: Secret Flight). 1947: Broken Journey. 1948: *They Gave Him the Works. Mr Perrin and Mr Traill. So Evil My Love. It's Hard to be Good. 1949: Passport to Pimlico. 1950: Trio. 1951: The Long Dark Hall. The House in the Square (US: I'll Never Forget You). Mr Denning Drives North. 1952: The Last Page (US: Manbait). 1953: Laxdale Hall (US: Scotch on the Rocks). Meet Mr Lucifer. Glad Tidings. 1954: The Teckman Mystery. Aunt Clara. Orders Are Orders. Hobson's Choice. The Dam Busters. 1955: The Constant Husband. Doctor at Sea. The Prisoner. Geordie (US: Wee Geordie). 1956: The Green Man. The Last Man to Hang? Town on Trial! Brothers in Law. 1958: Next to No Time. Room at the Top. Carlton-Browne of the FO (US: Man in a Cocked Hat). 1959: Innocent Meeting. The Mummy. I'm All Right, Jack. Our Man in Havana. Bottoms Up! 1960: Make Mine Mink. Follow That Horse! Sands of the Desert. A French Mistress. Suspect (US: The Risk). The Pure Hell of St Trinian's. 1961: Only Two Can Play. 1962: Waltz of the Toreadors. Crooks Anonymous. On the Beat. Nurse on Wheels. 1963: The Yellow Teddybears. Father Came Too. 1964: The Black Torment. 1965: Rotten to the Core. 1966: The Great St Trinian's Train Robbery. 1968: Hostile Witness. Hot Millions. 1969: The Adding Machine. Destiny of a Spy/The Gaunt Woman (TV). Arthur, Arthur. 1971: Young Winston. 1972: That's Your Funeral. 1974: Symptoms.

HURST, Paul 1888–1953

Big, tough-looking American actor with slow smile and Irish features, including red hair and twinkling eyes. He played breezy but none-too-bright characters on screen, but was nothing like that in real life, starting as an innovative star of early silent serials who sometimes directed material he had written himself. His cowboys then were rather in the Guinn 'Big Boy' Williams (qv) tradition but, with the coming of sound, Hurst settled in to countless cameos, many of them as thick-skulled cops ready to step in and arrest the framed hero before their superiors could advise caution. He made more than 250 films, one of the longest lists in this book, before committing suicide in 1953.

1912: *Red Wing and the Paleface. *The Stolen Invention. *Driver of the Deadwood Coach (GB: Deadwood Stage Driver). *The Mayor's Crusade. *When Youth Meets Youth. 1913: *The Skeleton in the Closet. *The Invaders. *The Big Horn Massacre/The Little Big Horn Massacre. *The Last Blockhouse. *Redemption. *On the Brink of Ruin. *The Struggle. Daughter of the Underworld. 1914: *The Death Sign of High Noon. *The Prison Stain. *The Fatal Opal. *In the Days of the Thundering Herd. *The Smugglers of Lone Isle. *Why the Sheriff is a Bachelor. *The Rajah's Vow. *The Barrier of Ignorance. The Invisible Power. 1915: Whispering Smith. Social Pirates (serial). The Pitfall. The Parasite. *The Corsican Sisters. *The Tragedy of Bear Mountain. *The Figure in Black. *The Vivisectionist. *When Thieves Fall Out. Stingaree (serial). The Man in Irons. The Further Adventures of Stingaree (and directed). *Old Isaacson's Diamonds. 1916: The Manager of the B & A. Lass of the Lumberland (serial). Medicine Bend. The Missing Millionaire. The Moth and the Star. A Voice in the Wilderness. To the Vile Dust. The Millionaire Plunger. Judith of the Cumberlands. The Diamond Runners. The Black Hole of Glenranald. 1917: A Race for a Fortune (serial). The Railroad Riders (serial). The Jackaroo. A Champion of the Law. The Tracking of Stingaree. 1918: Smashing Through. Rimrock Jones. The Tiger's Trail (serial. And co-directed). Play Straight or Fight. 1919: Lightning Bryce (serial. And co-directed). 1920: Shadows of the West. 1921: The Black Sheep. The Crow's Nest. 1922: The Heart of a Texan. Rangeland. The King Fischer's Roost. Table Top Ranch. 1923: Golden Silence. 1924: Branded a Bandit. The Courageous Coward. The Passing of Wolf MacLean. Battling Bunyan. 1925: The Fighting Cub. 1926: The High Hand. The Outlaw Express. The Fighting Ranger. Battling Kid. Son of a Gun. Blue Streak O'Neil. 1927: Rider of the Law. Outlaw's Paradise. Smoking Guns. The Valley of the Giants. Buttons. The Man from Hard Pan. The Red Raiders. The Devil's Saddle. Overland Stage. The Range Raiders. 1928: Lilac Time (GB: Love Never Dies). The Cossacks. 1929: Oh, Yeah! (GB: No Brakes). His First Command. The California Mail. The Lawless Legion. The Rainbow. The Racketeer (GB: Love's Conquest). Tide of Empire. Sailor's Holiday. 1930: The Swellhead (GB: Counted Out). Mountain Justice. Borrowed Wives. Hot Curves. Lucky Larkin. The Lottery Bride. Officer O'Brien. The Runaway Bride. Paradise Island. Shadow of the Law. His First Command. The Third Alarm. 1931: The Public Defender. *De Woild's Champion. The Single Sin. The Secret Six. Kick In. Sweepstakes. Secret Witness. Bad Company. 1932: The Phantom President. Panama Flo. The Thirteenth Guest. Dancers in the Dark. The Big Stampede. Hold 'Em Jail.

My Pal, the King. Island of Lost Souls. 1933: Hold Your Man. Men Are Such Fools. Terror Aboard. Tugboat Annie. Day of Reckoning. The Sphinx. Queen Christina. Grand Slam. Out All Night. Saturday's Millions. Women in His Life. The Big Race (GB: Raising the Wind). Scarlet River. 1934: Take the Stand (GB: The Great Radio Mystery). Midnight Alibi. The Line-Up. Among the Missing. A Very Honorable Guy. Sequoia. *There Ain't No Justice. 1935: Tomorrow's Youth. Wilderness Mail. Romance in Manhattan. Shadow of Doubt. Mississippi. Star of Midnight. Public Hero No. 1. Calm Yourself. Carnival (GB: Carnival Nights). The Gay Deception. Riffraff. The Case of the Curious Bride. 1936: Mr Deeds Goes to Town. San Francisco. The Blackmailer. Robin Hood of Eldorado. The Gay Desperado. I'd Give My Life. To Mary — With Love. It Had to Happen. North of Nome (GB: The Lawless North). We Who Are About to Die. 1937: Fifty Roads to Town. You Can't Beat Love. The Legion of Missing Men. Trouble in Morocco. The Lady Fights Back. Wake Up and Live. Angel's Holiday. This is My Affair (GB: His Affair). Super-Sleuth. Slave Ship. She's No Lady. Wife, Doctor and Nurse. Small Town Boy. Danger — Love at Work. Ali Baba Goes to Town. Second Honeymoon. You Can't Have Everything. 1938: Rebecca of Sunnybrook Farm. In Old Chicago. No Time to Marry. *The Wrong Way Out. Josette. Alexander's Ragtime Band. Island in the Sky. Prison Break. My Lucky Star. The Last Express. Hold That Co-Ed (GB: Hold That Girl). Secrets of a Nurse. Thanks for Everything. 1939: Topper Takes a Trip. Café Society. Broadway Serenade. It Could Happen to You. Each Dawn I Die. Remember? The Kid from Kokomo (GB: The Orphan of the Ring). Quick Millions. Bad Lands. Gone With the Wind. *Glove Slingers. On Your Toes. Heaven with a Barbed-Wire Fence. 1940: Edison, the Man. Torrid Zone. South to Karanga. The Westerner. Tugboat Annie Sails Again. They Drive by Night (GB: The Road to Frisco). Star Dust. Men Against the Sky. *Goin' Fishing. 1941: *Fresh As a Freshman. *Glove Affair. Tall, Dark and Handsome. Petticoat Politics. Virginia. Bowery Boy. The Parson of Panamint. Caught in the Draft. Ellery Queen and the Murder Ring (GB: The Murder Ring). This Woman is Mine. The Great Mr Nobody. 1942: Dudes Are Pretty People. A Night in New Orleans. Sundown Jim. Pardon My Stripes. The Ox-Bow Incident (GB: Strange Incident). Hi'Ya Chum (GB: Everything Happens to Us). 1943: Calaboose. Jack London. Coney Island. Young and Willing. The Sky's the Limit. 1944: Barbary Coast Gent. The Ghost That Walks Alone. Girl Rush. Summer Storm. Greenwich Village. Something for the Boys. 1945: One Exciting Night. The Big Show-Off. Dakota. The Dolly Sisters. Penthouse Rhythm. Her Lucky Night. Nob Hill. Midnight Manhunt. Scared Stiff. Steppin' in Society. 1946: In Old Sacramento. Death Valley. Murder in the Music Hall. The Virginian. The Plainsman and the Lady. Angel and the Badman. 1947: Under Colorado Skies. 1948: The Arizona Ranger. Heart of Virginia. Son of God's Country. Gun Smugglers. California Firebrand. Who Killed 'Doc' Robbin? (GB: Sinister House). Yellow Sky. On Our Merry Way/A Miracle Can Happen. Old Los Angeles.

Madonna of the Desert. 1949: Law of the Golden West. Prince of the Plains. Outcasts of the Trail. South of Rio. Ranger of Cherokee Strip. San Antone Ambush. 1950: Pioneer Marshal. The Vanishing Westerner. The Missourians. The Old Frontier. 1951: Million Dollar Pursuit. 1952: Big Jim McLain. Toughest Man in Arizona. 1953: The Sun Shines Bright.

Also as director:

1921: The Black Sheep. The Crow's Nest. 1922: The Heart of a Texan. Table Top Ranch. 1923: Golden Silence. 1925: The Fighting Ranger. The Son of Sontag. A Western Engagement. The Rattler. 1926: Roaring Road. Son of a Gun. Battling Kid. Shadows of Chinatown. Blue Streak O'Neil. 1927: The Range Raiders. Rider of the Law. Outlaw's Paradise. Smoking Guns.

HUTCHESON, David 1905–1976
Cheerful, sleekly brown-haired, Scottish-born actor of the 'I say, old chap' school, with long, equine features and sunny nature. He played a few dashing heroes in minor films of the 1930s, then settled down to portraits of asinine friends, mostly in comedy. Predominantly on stage after 1952, Hutcheson made something of a habit of playing Colonel Pickering in My Fair Lady in numerous touring performances of the 1960s.

1930: Fast and Loose. 1934: Romance in Rhythm. 1935: The Love Test. 1936: Wedding Group (US: Wrath of Jealousy). This'll Make You Whistle. 1937: The Sky's the Limit. 1939: A Gentleman's Gentleman. She Couldn't Say No. Lucky to Me. The Middle Watch. 1940: 'Bulldog' Sees It Through. Convoy. 1942: Next of Kin. Sabotage at Sea. 1943: The Life and Death of Colonel Blimp (US: Colonel Blimp). Theatre Royal. The Hundred Pound Window. 1944: The Way Ahead (US: Immortal Battalion). 1945: The Trojan Brothers. 1946: School for Secrets (US: Secret Flight). 1947: Vice Versa. 1948: The Small Back Room (US: Hour of Glory). Woman Hater. Sleeping Car to Trieste. 1949: Madness of the Heart. 1950: My Daughter Joy (US: Operation X). The Elusive Pimpernel (US: The Fighting Pimpernel). 1951: Circle of Danger. No Highway (US: No Highway in the Sky). Encore. 1952: Something Money Can't Buy. 1953:

The Blakes Slept Here. 1956: The Big Money (released 1958). 1957: The Birthday Present. 1958: Law and Disorder. 1964: The Evil of Frankenstein. 1965: The Amorous Adventures of Moll Flanders. 1966: Triple Cross. 1969: The Magic Christian. 1970: Every Home Should Have One (US: Think Dirty). 1971: Follow Me (US: The Public Eye). The Abominable Dr Phibes. 1973: The National Health.

HYDE WHITE, Wilfrid 1903–1991

Roguishly avuncular British actor, with spade-shaped face and inimitable sly, drawling tones. Almost always cast as affable upper-class coves, but sometimes with a cunning streak. He shuffled his way with deceptive casualness through 50 years of films. Billed in some of his 1930s' films simply as 'Hyde White'. Bedridden in his last years, he died in Los Angeles from congestive heart failure.

1934: Josser on the Farm. 1935: Admirals All. Night Mail. Alibi Inn. Smith's Wives. 1936: Murder By Rope. Rembrandt. Servants All. The Scarab Murder Case. 1937: Over the Moon (released 1940). Elephant Boy. Bulldog Drummond at Bay. Change for a Sovereign. 1938: Keep Smiling. Just Like a Woman. Meet Mr Penny. I've Got a Horse. 1939: The Lambeth Walk. Poison Pen. The Face at the Window. 1941: Turned Out Nice Again. 1942: Lady from Lisbon. Back Room Boy. Asking for Trouble. 1943: The Butler's Dilemma. The Demi-Paradise (US: Adventure for Two). 1945: Night Boat to Dublin. 1946: Appointment with Crime. While the Sun Shines. Wanted for Murder. 1947: Meet Me at Dawn. The Ghosts of Berkeley Square. My Brother Jonathan. 1948: My Brother's Keeper. Quartet. The Winslow Boy. The Passionate Friends (US: One Woman's Story). Bond Street. The Bad Lord Byron. 1949: Britannia Mews (US: Forbidden Street). The Man on the Eiffel Tower. Adam and Evelyne (US: Adam and Evalyn). That Dangerous Age (US: If This Be Sin). Helter Skelter. The Third Man. Conspirator. Golden Salamander. 1950: Last Holiday. Trio. The Angel with the Trumpet (and German version). Midnight Episode. Highly Dangerous. The Mudlark. Mr Drake's Duck. Blackmailed. 1951: No Highway (US: No Highway in the Sky). The Browning Version. Mr Denning Drives North. Outcast of the Islands. 1952: The Card (US: The Promoter). Top Secret (US:

*Mr Potts Goes to Moscow). 1953: The Story of Gilbert and Sullivan (US: The Great Gilbert and Sullivan). The Triangle. The Million Pound Note (US: Man with a Million). 1954: The Rainbow Jacket. Duel in the Jungle. Betrayed. To Dorothy a Son (US: Cash on Delivery). *The Journey. 1955: John and Julie. See How They Run. The Adventures of Quentin Durward (US: Quentin Durward). 1956: The March Hare. My Teenage Daughter (US: Teenage Bad Girl). The Silken Affair. That Woman Opposite (US: City After Midnight). The Vicious Circle (US: The Circle). Tarzan and the Lost Safari. The Truth about Women. 1958: Wonderful Things! Up the Creek. 1959: Life in Emergency Ward 10. Carry On Nurse. The Lady is a Square. Libel. North West Frontier (US: Flame over India). 1960: Two Way Stretch. Let's Make Love. His and Hers. 1961: On the Fiddle (US: Operation Snafu). On the Double. Ada. 1962: The Prince and the Pauper. Aliki. In Search of the Castaways. Crooks Anonymous. 1963: A Jolly Bad Fellow. 1964: John Goldfarb, Please Come Home. My Fair Lady. 1965: Ten Little Indians. The Liquidator. You Must Be Joking! 1966: Our Man in Marrakesh (US: Bang Bang You're Dead). The Sandwich Man. Chamber of Horrors. 1967: Sumuru (US: The 1,000,000 Eyes of Sumuru). P.J. (US: New Face in Hell). 1968: Sunshine Patriot (TV). 1969: Run a Crooked Mile (TV). The Magic Christian. Skullduggery. Gaily, Gaily (GB: Chicago Chicago). Fear No Evil (TV). Ritual of Evil (TV). 1970: Fragment of Fear. 1972: The Cherry Picker. A Brand New Life (TV). 1977: The Great Houdini (TV). 1978: No Longer Alone. King Solomon's Treasure. The Cat and the Canary. Battlestar Galactica (TV. GB: cinemas). 1979: In God We Trust. The Rebels (TV). 1980: Dick Turpin (TV. US: cinemas). Xanadu (voice only). Damien, the Leper Priest (TV). Oh, God! Book II. Scout's Honor (TV). 1981: Tarzan the Ape-Man. The Letter (TV). 1982: The Toy. 1983: Fanny Hill.*

HYMER, Warren 1906–1948

Snub-nosed, square-chinned, dark-haired New Yorker kept very busy in Hollywood from 1929 to 1942, his close-set eyes and fast delivery of a line lending themselves ideally to dim-witted but generally good-natured characters on either side of the law. The demand for 'big palookas', however, decreased in post-war years and ill-health

also hit his career. He died in hospital 'after a long illness' at only 42. Son of the playwright John B. Hymer.

*1929: The Far Call. Fox Movietone Follies of 1929. Frozen Justice. The Girl from Havana. Speak-Easy. The Cockeyed World. 1930: The Lone Star Ranger. Born Reckless. Men without Women. Oh, for a Man! Up the River. Sinners' Holiday. Men on Call. 1931: The Seas Beneath. Goldie. Charlie Chan Carries On. The Spider. Men Call It Love. The Unholy Garden. 1932: Hold 'Em, Jail! One Way Passage. The Night Mayor. Madison Square Garden. Love is a Racket. 1933: My Woman. Her First Mate. I Love That Man. Midnight Mary. 20,000 Years in Sing Sing. The Billion Dollar Scandal. A Lady's Profession. In the Money. The Mysterious Rider. 1934: Woman Unafraid. *The Gold Ghost. George White's Scandals. The Cat's Paw. She Loves Me Not. Young and Beautiful. Kid Millions. King for a Night. The Crosby Case (GB: The Crosby Murder Case). Belle of the Nineties. One is Guilty. Little Miss Marker (GB: Girl in Pawn). 1935: Hold 'Em Yale (GB: Uniform Lovers). Straight from the Heart. Our Little Girl. The Daring Young Man. The Silk Hat Kid. Navy Wife. Hong Kong Nights. The Gilded Lily. The Case of the Curious Bride. She Gets Her Man. Confidential. Show Them No Mercy (GB: Tainted Money). 1936: Hitch Hike Lady (GB: Eventful Journey). Tango. The Widow from Monte Carlo. The Leavenworth Case. Desert Justice. Laughing Irish Eyes. A Message to Garcia. Everybody's Old Man. Mr Deeds Goes to Town. San Francisco. Rhythm on the Range. Nobody's Fool. Love Letters of a Star. Thirty-Six Hours to Kill. 1937: Join the Marines. You Only Live Once. We Have Our Moments. Meet the Boy Friend. Navy Blues. Sea Racketeers. Wake Up and Live. Ali Baba Goes to Town. Bad Guy. Married Before Breakfast. She's Dangerous. 1938: Arson Gang Busters. Lady Behave. Joy of Living. Submarine Patrol. Gateway. Telephone Operator. Thanks for Everything. You and Me. Bluebeard's Eighth Wife. 1939: The Boy Friend. The Lady and the Mob. Coast Guard. Calling All Marines. Charlie McCarthy, Detective. Mr Moto in Danger Island (GB: Mr Moto on Danger Island). Destry Rides Again. 1940: I Can't Give You Anything But Love, Baby. Love, Honor and Oh, Baby! 1941: Buy Me That Town. Meet John Doe. Birth of the Blues. Skylark. 1942: Mr Wise Guy. Henry and Dizzy. Jail House Blues. Girls' Town. Dr Broadway. So's Your Aunt Emma. One Thrilling Night. Lure of the Islands. Baby Face Morgan. Police Bullets. Phantom Killer. She's in the Army. 1943: Hitler — Dead or Alive. Spy Train. Government Girl. Danger — Women at Work. Gangway for Tomorrow. 1944: Since You Went Away. Three is a Family. 1945: The Affairs of Susan. 1946: Gentleman Joe Palooka. Joe Palooka — Champ.*

HYTTEN, Olaf 1888–1955

Small, dumpy, cherubic, dimple-cheeked, stoat-eyed, hand-rubbing, Scottish-born (but very English) actor with disappearing dark hair. He first came into demand in British silent films of the 1920s, sometimes as tipsy aristocrats, a characterisation that

threaded itself through his busy career when he went to America in 1925 and, in between return visits to Britain, took key cameo roles in Hollywood for nearly 30 years. A cross between Eric Blore (*qv*) and Cecil Parker, Hytten had roles in almost all the Basil Rathbone Sherlock Holmes films of the war years. He died from a heart attack.

1921: *Demos* (US: *Why Men Forget*). *The Knave of Diamonds*. *The Girl Who Came Back*. *Sonia*. *Money*. *Miss Charity*. 1922: *The Knight Errant*. *Trapped by the Mormons*. *The Stockbroker's Clerk*. *The Wonderful Story*. *The Bride of Lammermoor*. *The Crimson Circle*. *His Wife's Husband*. *The Missioner*. *Sir Rupert's Wife*. 1923: *The Cause of All the Trouble*. *Out to Win*. *The Little Door into the World*. *A Gamble with Hearts*. *Chu Chin Chow*. *The Reverse of the Medal*. 1924: *The White Shadow* (US: *White Shadows*). *It is the Law*. 1925: *The Salvation Hunters*. 1928: *Old Age Handicap*. 1929: *Kitty*. *Master and Man*. *City of Play*. 1930: *Grumpy*. *Playboy of Paris*. 1931: *Born to Love*. *Daughter of the Dragon*. *Platinum Blonde*. 1932: *Night Club Lady*. 1933: *Design for Living*. *Berkeley Square*. *The Eagle and the Hawk*. *Blind Adventure*. *Lady Killer*. *A Study in Scarlet*. *Lost in Limehouse, or: Lady Esmeralda's Predicament*. 1934: *Jimmy the Gent*. *Journal of a Crime*. *The Key*. *Mandalay*. *The Mystery of Mr X*. *The Painted Veil*. *British Agent*. *Shock*. *The Moonstone*. *Bulldog Drummond Strikes Back*. *One Night of Love*. *Mystery Liner* (GB: *The Ghost of John Holling*). *Glamour*. *The Richest Girl in the World*. *Jane Eyre*. *Money Means Nothing*. 1935: *Anna Karenina*. *Becky Sharp*. *The Dark Angel*. *The Last Outpost*. *Clive of India*. *A Feather in Her Hat*. *Going Highbrow*. *I Found Stella Parish*. *Living on Velvet*. *Red Morning*. *Secret of the Chateau*. *Strange Wives*. *She Couldn't Take It*. *Two Sinners*. *Thanks a Million*. *Bonnie Scotland*. *Les Miserables*. *The Spanish Cape Mystery*. *Atlantic Adventure*. 1936: *Camille*. *The Last of the Mohicans*. *House of a Thousand Candles*. *Lloyds of London*. *And So They Were Married*. *Doughnuts and Society* (GB: *Stepping into Society*). *Libeled Lady*. *The Lone Wolf Returns*. *Two Black Sheep*. *Sons o' Guns*. *Sylvia Scarlett*. *White Hunter*. *The Widow from Monte Carlo*. *Trouble for Two* (GB: *The Suicide Club*). 1937: *California Straight Ahead*. *We Have Our Moments*. *The Great Garrick*. *Double or Nothing*. *The Emperor's Candlesticks*. *Angel*. *Souls at Sea*. *Dangerous Holiday*. *Easy Living*.

Ebb Tide. *First Lady*. *The Good Earth*. *I Cover the War*. *With Love and Kisses*. *Lancer Spy*. 1938: *The Adventures of Robin Hood*. *Blonde Cheat*. *A Christmas Carol*. *Arrest Bulldog Drummond!* *The Lone Wolf in Paris*. *Marie Antoinette*. *Bluebeard's Eighth Wife*. *Youth Takes a Fling*. 1939: *Allegheny Uprising* (GB: *The First Rebel*). *Television Spy*. *Andy Hardy Gets Spring Fever*. *We Are Not Alone*. *Zaza*. *The Little Princess*. *Our Leading Citizen*. *Little Accident*. *Our Neighbors — The Carters*. *Rulers of the Sea*. 1939–40: *Raffles*. 1940: *Drums of Fu Manchu* (serial). *Gaucho Serenade*. *Arise My Love*. *No Time for Comedy*. *Parole Fixer*. *The Howards of Virginia* (GB: *The Tree of Liberty*). *Captain Caution*. *The Earl of Chicago*. *Escape to Glory*. 1941: *All the World's a Stooge*. *For Beauty's Sake*. *Footsteps in the Dark*. *A Rage in Heaven*. *Nine Lives Are Not Enough*. *The Great Commandment*. *Man Hunt*. *That Hamilton Woman* (GB: *Lady Hamilton*). *The Wolf Man*. *Submarine Zone*. *When Ladies Meet*. *Washington Melodrama*. 1942: *Destination Unknown*. *The Ghost of Frankenstein*. *The Black Swan*. *Bedtime Story*. *Eagle Squadron*. *Seven Days' Leave*. *Journey for Margaret*. *Lucky Jordan*. *Son of Fury*. *The Great Impersonation*. *You're Telling Me*. *Sherlock Holmes and the Voice of Terror*. *This Above All*. *To Be Or Not to Be*. *Spy Ship*. *Casablanca*. 1943: *Sherlock Holmes Faces Death*. *Flesh and Fantasy*. *Happy Go Lucky*. *Holy Matrimony*. *Hit Parade of 1943*. *Mission to Moscow*. *The Return of the Vampire*. *Ministry of Fear*. 1944: *The Lodger*. *Detective Kitty O'Day*. *Leave It to the Irish*. *National Velvet*. *Oh! What a Night*. *The Scarlet Claw*. *Our Hearts Were Young and Gay*. *House of Frankenstein*. 1945: *Hold That Blonde*. *Confidential Agent*. *Pursuit to Algiers/Sherlock Holmes in Pursuit to Algiers*. *Christmas in Connecticut* (GB: *Indiscretion*). *My Name is Julia Ross*. *Babes on Swing Street*. *The Woman in Green*. 1946: *Dressed to Kill* (GB: *Sherlock Holmes and the Secret Code*). *Black Beauty*. *The Notorious Lone Wolf*. *She-Wolf of London* (GB: *The Curse of the Allenbys*). *Magnificent Doll*. *Holiday in Mexico*. *Three Strangers*. *The Verdict*. *Alias Mr Twilight*. 1947: *Bells of San Angelo*. *The Imperfect Lady*. *The Private Affairs of Bel Ami*. *That Way with Women* (completed 1945). *Unconquered*. *If Winter Comes*. 1948: *Kidnapped*. *The Shanghai Chest*. 1949: *That Forsyte Woman* (GB: *The Forsyte Saga*). 1950: *Fancy Pants*. *Kim*. *Rogues of Sherwood Forest*. 1951: *Anne of the Indies*. *The Son of Dr Jekyll*. 1952: *Against All Flags*. *Les Miserables*. 1953: *Perils of the Jungle*. 1955: *The Scarlet Coat*. *The Virgin Queen*.

ILLING, Peter 1899–1966

Stocky, staring-eyed Austrian actor (of Turkish parentage) of rather dangerous appearance, with receding, unruly dark hair, often moustachioed. He appeared on the Berlin stage for 13 years before fleeing to Britain in 1937. In World War II his became known as the German-speaking voice that translated Sir Winston Churchill's speeches for broadcast overseas; but, with peace, the heroic image vanished, and he played mainly unkempt and sometimes powerful villains in British films; on occasion his foreigners were less evil but no less irascible.

1940: *Gaslight* (US: *Angel Street*). 1947: *The Silver Darlings*. *The End of the River*. 1948: *Eureka Stockade* (US: *Massacre Hill*). *Against the Wind*. 1949: *Madness of the Heart*. *The Huggetts Abroad*. *Floodtide*. *Children of Chance*. *Traveller's Joy* (released 1951). 1950: *State Secret* (US: *The Great Manhunt*). *My Daughter Joy* (US: *Operation X*). *Her Favourite Husband*. *The Taming of Dorothy*). 1951: *I'll Get You For This* (US: *Lucky Nick Cain*). *Outcast of the Islands*. 1952: *The Woman's Angle*. *24 Hours of a Woman's Life* (US: *Affair in Monte Carlo*). 1953: *Never Let Me Go*. *Innocents in Paris*. 1954: *West of Zanzibar*. *The House Across the Lake* (US: *Heatwave*). *Flame and the Flesh*. *Mask of Dust* (US: *Race for Life*). *The Glass Slipper*. *The Young Lovers* (US: *Chance Meeting*). *Svengali*. 1955: *That Lady*. *As Long As They're Happy*. *Born for Trouble*. 1956: *It's Never Too Late*. *Bhowani Junction*. *The Battle of the River Plate* (US:

Pursuit of the Graf Spee). Zarak. Passport to Treason. Loser Takes All. 1957: Man in the Shadow (US: Violent Stranger). Miracle in Soho. Interpol (US: Pickup Alley). Fire Down Below. A Farewell to Arms. Manuela (US: Stowaway Girl). Campbell's Kingdom. I Accuse! Escapement (US: Zex/The Electronic Monster). 1959: The Angry Hills. Jet Storm. The Wreck of the Mary Deare. Friends and Neighbours. Whirlpool. 1960: Moment of Danger (US: Malaga). Sands of the Desert. Bluebeard's Ten Honeymoons. Operation Stogie. 1961: The Middle Course. The Secret Partner. The Happy Thieves. Village of Daughters. 1962: The Devil's Daffodil (US: The Daffodil Killer). The Secret Door (released 1964). Nine Hours to Rama. 1963: Echo of Diana. The VIPs. 1964: Devils of Darkness. 1965: A Man Could Get Killed. 1967: The 25th Hour.

INESCORT, Frieda
(F. Wightman) 1900–1976
Tall, dark, Scottish-born actress with faintly forbidding good looks. The daughter of actress Elaine Inescort (only film: 1933's Rolling in Money), she began her film career in America, where she had lived and worked – first as a secretary, then as a stage actress – since 1921. In the 1930s, she appeared as society wives, scheming women and aristocratic cousins. After a break of five years, she played out the remainder of her career in older character roles. Died from multiple sclerosis.

1935: The Dark Angel. If You Could Only Cook. 1936: Hollywood Boulevard. The King Steps Out. Give Me Your Heart. The Garden Murder Case. Mary of Scotland. 1937: Portia on Trial (GB: The Trial of Portia Merriman). The Great O'Malley. Another Dawn. Call It a Day. 1938: Beauty for the Asking. 1939: Zero Hour. Woman Doctor. Tarzan Finds a Son! A Woman Is the Judge. 1940: Pride and Prejudice. Convicted Woman. The Letter. 1941: The Trial of Mary Dugan. Sunny. Father's Son. You'll Never Get Rich. Remember the Day. Shadows on the Stairs. 1942: It Comes Up Love (GB: A Date with an Angel). The Courtship of Andy Hardy. Street of Chance. Sweater Girl. 1943: The Amazing Mrs Holliday. Mission to Moscow. The Return of the Vampire. 1944: Heavenly Days. 1945: *Young and Beautiful. 1948: The Judge Steps Out (GB: Indian Summer). 1950: The Underworld Story.

1951: A Place in the Sun. 1952: Never Wave at a WAC (GB: The Private Wore Skirts). 1953: Casanova's Big Night. 1955: Foxfire. Flame of the Islands. 1956: The Eddy Duchin Story. The She-Creature. 1957: Darby's Rangers (GB: The Young Invaders). 1958: Senior Prom. 1959: The Alligator People. Juke Box Rhythm. 1960: The Crowded Sky.

INGRAM, Rex 1895–1969
Formidable black American actor with powerful features, born on a riverboat but later an honours medical graduate. He succumbed to the lure of an acting career soon afterwards, but it was years before he gained recognition in films, with his starring performance as De Lawd in Green Pastures. He was also impressive as the genie in the 1940 version of The Thief of Bagdad (having had a very minor assignment in the silent version), but most of his other roles were unworthy of his talents. He died from a heart attack. Not to be confused with the great silent films actor-director Rex Ingram (Reginald Hitchcock) 1892–1950.

1918: Salome. Tarzan of the Apes. 1923: Scaramouche. The Ten Commandments. 1924: Thief of Bagdad. 1925: The Wanderer. The Big Parade. 1926: Lord Jim. Beau Geste. 1927: King of Kings. 1928: The Four Feathers. 1929: Hearts in Dixie. 1932: The Sign of the Cross. 1933: King Kong. The Emperor Jones. Love in Morocco. 1934: Harlem After Midnight. 1935: Captain Blood. 1936: Green Pastures. 1939: The Adventures of Huckleberry Finn. 1940: The Thief of Bagdad. 1942: The Talk of the Town. 1943: Cabin in the Sky. Sahara. Fired Wife. 1944: Dark Waters. 1945: A Thousand and One Nights. Adventure. 1948: Moonrise. 1950: King Solomon's Mines. 1955: Tarzan's Hidden Jungle. 1956: The Ten Commandments (and earlier film). Congo Crossing. 1957: Hell on Devil's Island. 1958: Anna Lucasta. God's Little Acre. 1959: Escort West. Watusi. 1960: Elmer Gantry. Desire in the Dust. 1964: Your Cheatin' Heart. 1966: Hurry Sundown. 1967: Journey to Shiloh. How to Succeed in Business Without Really Trying.

IRONSIDE, Michael 1950–
Steely-eyed, strongly built, dangerous-looking Canadian actor with receding fair hair and solid features, a film and media

student who started by making his own movie, but soon revealed a talent for frightening audiences with powerful portraits of psychos and criminal masterminds, usually in science-fiction or adult-rated thrillers. Very prolific from the late 1980s onwards, a period in which his best remembered role remains the ferocious villain of Arnold Schwarzenegger's Total Recall, which almost (but not quite) eclipsed the memory of the man who makes heads explode in Scanners.

1975: *Down Where the Lights Are (and directed). 1977: Outrageous. 1978: I, Maureen. 1980: Scanners. Suzanne. 1981: Visiting Hours. Surfacing. 1983: Spacehunter: Adventures in the Forbidden Zone. Best Revenge. Cross Country. The Sins of Dorian Gray (TV). 1984: The Surrogate. American Nightmare. Coming Out Alive. 1985: Off Your Rocker. Murder in Space (TV). 1986: Top Gun. Feel the Heart. Extreme Prejudice. Office Party. Jo Jo Dancer, Your Life is Calling. 1987: Hello, Mary Lou: Prom Night II. Nowhere to Hide. 1988: Hostile Take Over. Watchers. Destiny to Order. 1989: Thunderground. Murder By Night (TV). Mind Field. 1990: Total Recall. Payback. Highlander II: The Quickening. 1991: McBain. Café Romeo. Neon City. Picture Perfect. The Vagrant. Drop Dead Gorgeous (TV). Deadly Surveillance. Chaindance/Common Bonds. Killer Image. 1992: Sweet Killing. Guncrazy. Black Ice. A Passion for Murder (TV). 1993: Free Willy. In Too Deep/Spanish Rose. Save Me. Forced to Kill. Night Trap/Mardi Gras for the Devil. Red Sun Rising. 1994: The Glass Shield. Father Hood. Sleepless. The Killing Machine. Mortelle Affaire. Red Scorpion 2. The Next Karate Kid. Tokyo Cowboy. Probable Cause (TV). 1995: American Perfect. Bolt. Major Payne.

IVAN, Rosalind 1881–1959
Though in real life a bright, amusing, charming, multi-talented person, this red-haired English-born actress's disagreeable-looking facial features clearly doomed her to playing shrikes and shrews in drama, which she did to great effect. Dubbed 'Ivan the Terrible' by some after her performance as the termagant wife of Charles Laughton in The Suspect, she returned to the stage in the late 1940s and to a career as an acting coach. Died from heart failure.

1916: Arms and the Woman. 1936: The Garden Murder Case. 1941: Paris Calling. It Started

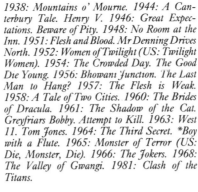

with Eve. 1944: None But the Lonely Heart. 1945: The Suspect. The Corn is Green. Pursuit to Algiers. Scarlet Street. Pillow of Death. 1946: That Brennan Girl. Three Strangers. The Verdict Alias Mr Twilight 1947: Ivy 1948: Johnny Belinda. 1953: The Robe. 1954: Elephant Walk.

1938: Mountains o' Mourne. 1944: A Canterbury Tale. Henry V. 1946: Great Expectations. Beware of Pity. 1948: No Room at the Inn. 1951: Flesh and Blood. Mr Denning Drives North. 1952: Women of Twilight (US: Twilight Women). 1954: The Crowded Day. The Good Die Young. 1956: Bhowani Junction. The Last Man to Hang? 1957: The Flesh is Weak. 1958: A Tale of Two Cities. 1960: The Brides of Dracula. 1961: The Shadow of the Cat. Greyfriars Bobby. Attempt to Kill. 1963: West 11. Tom Jones. 1964: The Third Secret. *Boy with a Flute. 1965: Monster of Terror (US: Die, Monster, Die). 1966: The Jokers. 1968: The Valley of Gwangi. 1981: Clash of the Titans.

JACKSON, Selmer 1888–1971

Kindliness and sincerity oozed from every pore of this silver-haired, slimly-built American actor who spent more than 30 years dispensing wise advice as judges, doctors, bankers, attorneys (both at law and district) and concerned fathers. Possibly Hollywood's most prolific actor during the World War II years, a period in which he racked up well over 100 film credits, often doing just one or two scenes. Television audiences saw him in the 1950s as Mayor Hoover in the popular Wyatt Earp series. Died from heart disease.

1921: The Supreme Passion. 1929: Thru Different Eyes. Why Bring That Up? 1930: Lovin' the Ladies. 1931: Leftover Ladies (GB: Broken Links). Subway Express. Dirigible. The Secret Call. 1932: You Said a Mouthful. Doctor X. Big City Blues. Three on a Match. The Mouthpiece. Winner Take All. 1933: Hell and High Water (GB: Cap'n Jericho). Forgotten. After Tonight. The Working Man. The Little Giant (voice only). Picture Snatcher. 1934: Sisters Under the Skin (GB: The Romantic Age). I've Got Your Number. Let's Fall in Love. Bright Eyes. Jealousy. The Witching Hour. I'll Fix It. The Defense Rests. Now I'll Tell (GB: When New York Sleeps). The Richest Girl in the World. Sadie McKee. Murder in the Clouds. Fog Over Frisco. Stand Up and Cheer. The Secret Bride (GB: Concealment). 1935: Alibi Ike. Red Salute (GB: Arms and the Girl). Page Miss Glory. Devil Dogs of the Air. Living on Velvet. Broadway Gondolier. A Night at the Opera. Carnival. Public Hero No.1. Traveling Saleslady. Front Page Woman. Paddy O'Day. Black Fury. This is the Life. Grand Exit. Don't

JACKSON, Freda 1908–1990

Forbidding-faced, dark-haired British character actress who created some memorably grim portraits, women that made her the Sonia Dresdel (qv) of the lower classes. Started as a singer, but turned to acting in her middle twenties. Film appearances are fewer than one would have liked, but she was really too ferocious for supporting roles.

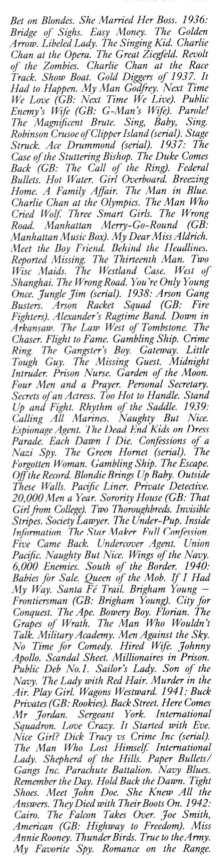

Bet on Blondes. She Married Her Boss. 1936: Bridge of Sighs. Easy Money. The Golden Arrow. Libeled Lady. The Singing Kid. Charlie Chan at the Opera. The Great Ziegfeld. Revolt of the Zombies. Charlie Chan at the Race Track. Show Boat. Gold Diggers of 1937. It Had to Happen. My Man Godfrey. Next Time We Love (GB: Next Time We Live). Public Enemy's Wife (GB: G-Man's Wife). Parole! The Magnificent Brute. Sing, Baby, Sing. Robinson Crusoe of Clipper Island (serial). Stage Struck. Ace Drummond (serial). 1937: The Case of the Stuttering Bishop. The Duke Comes Back (GB: The Call of the Ring). Federal Bullets. Hot Water. Girl Overboard. Breezing Home. A Family Affair. The Man in Blue. Charlie Chan at the Olympics. The Man Who Cried Wolf. Three Smart Girls. The Wrong Road. Manhattan Merry-Go-Round (GB: Manhattan Music Box). My Dear Miss Aldrich. Meet the Boy Friend. Behind the Headlines. Reported Missing. The Thirteenth Man. Two Wise Maids. The Westland Case. West of Shanghai. The Wrong Road. You're Only Young Once. Jungle Jim (serial). 1938: Arson Gang Busters. Arson Racket Squad (GB: Fire Fighters). Alexander's Ragtime Band. Down in Arkansaw. The Law West of Tombstone. The Chaser. Flight to Fame. Gambling Ship. Crime Ring. The Gangster's Boy. Gateway. Little Tough Guy. The Missing Guest. Midnight Intruder. Prison Nurse. Garden of the Moon. Four Men and a Prayer. Personal Secretary. Secrets of an Actress. Too Hot to Handle. Stand Up and Fight. Rhythm of the Saddle. 1939: Calling All Marines. Naughty But Nice. Espionage Agent. The Dead End Kids on Dress Parade. Each Dawn I Die. Confessions of a Nazi Spy. The Green Hornet (serial). The Forgotten Woman. Gambling Ship. The Escape. Off the Record. Blondie Brings Up Baby. Outside These Walls. Pacific Liner. Private Detective. 20,000 Men a Year. Sorority House (GB: That Girl from College). Two Thoroughbreds. Invisible Stripes. Society Lawyer. The Under-Pup. Inside Information. The Star Maker. Full Confession. Five Came Back. Undercover Agent. Union Pacific. Naughty But Nice. Wings of the Navy. 6,000 Enemies. South of the Border. 1940: Babies for Sale. Queen of the Mob. If I Had My Way. Santa Fé Trail. Brigham Young – Frontiersman (GB: Brigham Young). City for Conquest. The Ape. Bowery Boy. Florian. The Grapes of Wrath. The Man Who Wouldn't Talk. Military Academy. Men Against the Sky. No Time for Comedy. Hired Wife. Johnny Apollo. Scandal Sheet. Millionaires in Prison. Public Deb No.1. Sailor's Lady. Son of the Navy. The Lady with Red Hair. Murder in the Air. Play Girl. Wagons Westward. 1941: Buck Privates (GB: Rookies). Back Street. Here Comes Mr Jordan. Sergeant York. International Squadron. Love Crazy. It Started with Eve. Nice Girl? Dick Tracy vs Crime Inc (serial). The Man Who Lost Himself. International Lady. Shepherd of the Hills. Paper Bullets/ Gangs Inc. Parachute Battalion. Navy Blues. Remember the Day. Hold Back the Dawn. Tight Shoes. Meet John Doe. She Knew All the Answers. They Died with Their Boots On. 1942: Cairo. The Falcon Takes Over. Joe Smith, American (GB: Highway to Freedom). Miss Annie Rooney. Thunder Birds. True to the Army. My Favorite Spy. Romance on the Range.

Powder Town. Road to Happiness. Madame Spy. Secret Agent of Japan. Saboteur. Dr Kildare's Wedding Day (GB: Mary Names the Day). The Secret Code (serial). Thru Different Eyes (and 1929 film). Ten Gentlemen from West Point. A Date with the Falcon. 1943: Adventures of the Flying Cadets (serial). Harrigan's Kid. Honeymoon Lodge. Guadalcanal Diary. It Ain't Hay (GB: Money for Jam). Around the World. Margin for Error. Someone to Remember. What a Woman! (GB: The Beautiful Cheat). You Can't Beat the Law. 1944: The Big Noise. Since You Went Away. Hey, Rookie! Destiny. Heavenly Days. Wing and a Prayer. Marine Raiders. Roger Touhy – Gangster (GB: The Last Gangster). Stars on Parade. Sheriff of Las Vegas. The Sullivans. They Shall Have Faith/Forever Yours (GB: The Right to Live). 1945: Black Market Babies. Allotment Wives (GB: Woman in the Case). *Purity Squad. The Caribbean Mystery. Dakota. Dillinger. Circumstantial Evidence. A Sporting Chance. First Yank into Tokyo (GB: Mask of Fury). This Love of Ours. Thrill of a Romance. Out of the This World. The Royal Mounted Rides Again (serial). 1946: Boston Blackie and the Law (GB: Blackie and the Law). San Quentin. Dangerous Money. Child of Divorce. Girl on the Spot. The French Key. She Wrote the Book. The Glass Alibi. Johnny Comes Flying Home. Shock. The Time of Their Lives. Wife Wanted (GB: Shadow of Blackmail). 1947: Headin' for Heaven. Key Witness. Her Husband's Affairs. Dream Girl. The Fabulous Texan. Cass Timberlane. The 13th Hour. Magic Town. The Pretender. Sarge Goes to College. The High Wall. Stepchild. 1948: The Fuller Brush Man (GB: That Mad Mr Jones). King of the Gamblers. Every Girl Should Be Married. Sealed Verdict. The Gentlemen from Nowhere. The Girl from Manhattan. Pitfall. Stage Struck (and 1936 version). 1949: The Crime Doctor's Diary. Alaska Patrol. Forgotten Women. Mighty Joe Young. The Fountainhead. Sorrowful Jones. Tulsa. Renegades of the Sage (GB: The Fort). 1950: Buckaroo Sheriff of Texas. Gunmen of Abilene. The Magnificent Yankee (GB: The Man with 30 Sons). Mark of the Gorilla. No Man of Her Own. Lucky Losers. 1951: Bowery Battalion. Elopement. Purple Heart Diary (GB: No Time for Tears). That's My Boy. 1952: We're Not Married. Sudden Fear. Young Man with Ideas. Deadline – U.S.A. (GB: Deadline). 1953: Rebel City. Sky Commando. Jack McCall – Desperado. The President's Lady. 1954: Demetrius and the Gladiators. Superman Flies Again (TV. GB: cinemas). 1955: Devil Goddess. 1956: Autumn Leaves. 1957: Hellcats of the Navy. Three Brave Men. 1958: The Lost Missile. 1959: The Atomic Submarine. 1960: The Gallant Hours.

JACQUES, Hattie
(Josephine Jacques) 1924–1980
Tall, plumply beaming, dark-haired British character actress, in vivid supporting roles from her early twenties. A radio comedienne from 1947, but did not get into her film comedy stride until the 'Carry On' series came along. Later a notable foil for Eric Sykes in his long-running television show. Married to actor John le Mesurier (qv) from 1949 to 1965. Died from a heart attack.

1946: Green for Danger. 1947: Nicholas Nickleby. 1948: Oliver Twist. 1949: Trottie True (US: Gay Lady). The Spider and the Fly. 1950: Waterfront (US: Waterfront Women). Chance of a Lifetime. 1951: Scrooge (US: A Christmas Carol). 1952: No Haunt for a Gentleman. Mother Riley Meets the Vampire (US: Vampire Over London). The Pickwick Papers. 1953: Our Girl Friday (US: The Adventures of Sadie). All Hallowe'en. 1954: The Love Lottery. Up to His Neck. 1955: As Long As They're Happy. Now and Forever. 1958: Carry On Sergeant. The Square Peg. 1959: Carry On Nurse. Carry On Teacher. Left, Right and Centre. The Night We Dropped a Clanger. The Navy Lark. Follow a Star. School for Scoundrels. 1960: Carry On Constable. Make Mine Mink. Watch Your Stern. 1961: Carry On Regardless. In the Doghouse. 1962: She'll Have to Go (US: Maid for Murder). The Punch and Judy Man. 1963: Carry On Cabby. 1967: The Bobo. The Plank. Carry On Doctor. 1968: Crooks and Coronets (US: Sophy's Place). 1969: Carry On Again, Doctor. The Magic Christian. Carry On Camping. Monte Carlo or Bust (US: Those Daring Young Men in Their Jaunty Jalopies). 1970: Carry On Loving. Rhubarb. 1971: Danger Point. Carry On at Your Convenience. 1972: Carry On Matron. Carry On Abroad. 1974: Three for All. Carry On Dick.

JAECKEL, Richard 1926–
Sturdy American actor with baby face and shock of fair hair who was plucked from the 20th Century-Fox mail room to portray a teenage soldier in *Guadalcanal Diary* and,

apart from serving in the US Navy from mid-1944 to mid-1948, has been playing little tough guys ever since. Star roles between 1952 and 1954 should perhaps have led to something better, but he has been largely confined to soldiers and outlaws since then. Never seems to age. Nominated for an Oscar in *Sometimes a Great Notion*.

1943: Guadalcanal Diary. 1944: Wing and a Prayer. 1948: Jungle Patrol. 1949: City Across the River. Sands of Iwo Jima. Battleground. 1950: The Gunfighter. Wyoming Mail. 1951: Fighting Coast Guard. The Sea Hornet. 1952: Hoodlum Empire. My Son John. Come Back, Little Sheba. 1953: The Big Leaguer. Sea of Lost Ships. 1954: The Shanghai Story. The Violent Men (GB: Rough Company). 1955: Apache Ambush. 1956: Attack! Smoke Jumpers (TV). 1957: 3:10 to Yuma. Ain't No Time for Glory (TV). 1958: Cowboy. The Line-Up. The Naked and the Dead. When Hell Broke Loose. The Gun Runners. 1960: The Gallant Hours. Platinum High School (GB: Rich, Young and deadly). Flaming Star. 1961: Town Without Pity. 1963: The Young and the Brave. Four for Texas. Nightmare in the Sun. 1965: Town Tamer. 1966: Once Before I Die. 1967: The Dirty Dozen. 1968: The Devil's Brigade. The Green Slime. 1969: Latitude Zero. 1970: Gold Seekers. Chisum. 1971: Sometimes a Great Notion (GB: Never Give an Inch). The Deadly Dream (TV) 1972: Ulzana's Raid. 1973: †The Red Pony (TV. GB: cinemas in abridged version). Firehouse (TV). Partners in Crime (TV). Pat Garrett and Billy the Kid. The Outfit. 1974: Chosen Survivors. Born Innocent (TV). 1975: The Last Day (TV). The Drowning Pool. Part Two Walking Tall (GB: Legend of the Lawman). 1976: Delta Fox. The Jaws of Death. Day of the Animals. Grizzly. 1977: Twilight's Last Gleaming. Speedtrap. Assault on Paradise (GB: Maniac). 1978: Champions, a Love Story (TV). The Falcon's Ultimatum. Go West, Young Girl (TV). The Dark. 1979: Salvage (TV. GB: Salvage One). Cold River (released 1982). 1980: Herbie Goes Bananas. Reward (TV). The $5.20 an Hour Dream (TV). 1981: The Awakening of Candra (TV. Not shown until 1983). All the Marbles. . . . (GB: The California Dolls). The Amazing Mr No Legs. 1982: Blood Song. Airplane II The Sequel. 1984: Starman. 1985: The Dirty Dozen: Next Mission (TV). Pacific Inferno (filmed 1977). Black Moon Rising. Spencer: For Hire (TV). The Fix (filmed 1983 as The Agitators). 1986: Killing Machine (filmed 1983). The Kill. 1988: Supercarrier (TV). 1989: Ghettoblaster. Baywatch: Panic at Malibu Pier (TV). 1990: The King of the Kickboxers. Delta Force 2: The Colombian Crackdown. 1991: Baywatch: Nightmare Bay (TV). 1993: Martial Outlaw.

† Scenes deleted from final release print

JAFFE, Sam
(Shalom Jaffe) 1891–1984
Talented little American actor who looked wizened even in early middle age, and specialized in obscure foreign characterizations: Tibetan, Indian, Russian, Israeli and Mexican were only a few. Film appearances were limited by his prolific stage work, but they have often been memorable, notably his native water-carrier in *Gunga Din* and

his High Lama in *Lost Horizon*. Married to actress Bettye Ackerman (1928–) from 1955; she appeared with him during his years as Dr Zorba in television's *Ben Casey*. Died from cancer. Nominated for an Oscar in *The Asphalt Jungle*.

1934: *We Live Again. The Scarlet Empress.* 1937: *Lost Horizon.* 1939: *Gunga Din.* 1943: *Stage Door Canteen.* 1946: *13 Rue Madeleine.* 1947: *Gentleman's Agreement.* 1948: *The Accused.* 1949: *Rope of Sand.* 1950: *Under the Gun. The Asphalt Jungle.* 1951: *I Can Get It for You Wholesale (GB: This is My Affair). The Day the Earth Stood Still.* 1956: *All Mine to Give (GB: The Day They Gave Babies Away).* 1957: *Les espions.* 1958: *The Barbarian and the Geisha.* 1959: *Ben-Hur. The Dingaling Girl (TV).* 1960: *The Sound of Trumpets (TV). In the Presence of Mine Enemies (TV).* 1967: *A Guide for the Married Man. Guns for San Sebastian.* 1969: *The Great Bank Robbery. Night Gallery (TV).* 1970: *The Dunwich Horror. Quarantined (TV). The Old Man Who Cried Wolf (TV).* 1971: *Bedknobs and Broomsticks. *The Tell-Tale Heart. Sam Hill – Who Killed the Mysterious Mr Foster? (TV).* 1974: *QB VII (TV).* 1978: *†The End.* 1980: *Battle Beyond the Stars. Gideon's Trumpet (TV).* 1981: *Jayne Mansfield – An American Tragedy (TV).* 1984: *Nothing Lasts Forever. On the Line.*

† Scenes deleted from final release print

JAFFREY, Saeed 1923–
Burly, dark, plump-cheeked, bushily moustached, roguishly twinkling, beaknosed Indian actor, prolific on radio, TV, films and the stage alike. After starting his own English theatre company in Delhi, he left India for America in the late 1950s, but has been resident in Britain since the late 1960s, when he belatedly started a cinema career which has since run up more than 80 credits, many as enjoyably rascally Hindis, but sometimes in sympathetic or even extravagant roles. His appearances as the suave Rafiq in the cult TV series *Gangsters* (1976/7) made his features familiar, and he has also been prominent in such small-screen series as *The Far Pavilions* and *The Jewel in the Crown*. Since 1983, he has appeared regularly in Hindi and Urdu-speaking films. First wife was actress/cookery writer Madhur Jaffrey. Now married to actress Jennifer Jaffrey.

1969: **The Perfumed Garden. The Guru.* 1970: *The Horsemen.* 1972: *Le soleil se lève à l'est.* 1974: *The Wilby Conspiracy.* 1975: *The Man Who Would Be King.* 1977: *Shatranj ke Khilari/The Chess Players. Asambhava.* 1978: *Hullabaloo Over Georgie and Bonnie's Pictures.* 1979: *The Last Giraffe (TV).* 1980: *Staying On (TV). Sphinx. Ek Baar Phir.* 1981: *Chasme Buddoor (GB: Knock on Wood).* 1982: *Gandhi. Poison. '82 Star. Courtesans of Bombay.* 1983: *Under Fire. Mandi. Kissi se na Kehna. Masoom. Romance.* 1984: *Aagaman. Mahsaal. Ek Din Bahu Ka. A Passage to India. The Razor's Edge. Bhavna.* 1985: *My Beautiful Laundrette. Phir Aayee Barsat. Karishma Kudrat Ka. Ram Teri Ganga Maili. Cricketer. Jaanoo. Saagar.* 1986: *Kala Dhanda Goray Log.* 1987: *Sammy and Rosie Get Laid. Partition (TV). Khudgraz. Jalwa. Aulad.* 1988: *Just Ask for Diamond. Vijay. Hero Hiralal. The Deceivers.* 1989: *Khoon Bari Mang. Eashwar. Hisaab Knooh Ka. Aakhri Gulam. Daata. Ram Lakhan. Manika: The Girl Who Lived Twice (released 1994). Chaalbaaz.* 1990: *Kishen Kanahiya. Dil. Ghar ho to Aisa. Aandhiyan. Masala (released 1992). After Midnight (TV).* 1991: *Heena (GB: Henna). Gunaghar Kaun. Patthar ke Insaan. Yara Dildaara. Ajooba. Afsana Piyar Ka. Indrajeet.* 1992: *Balmaa. Laat Saab. Nishchay. Vansh. Surya Vanshi.* 1993: *Aashiq Awaara. Aaina. Jail Kali.* 1994: *Bollywood.*

JAGGER, Dean 1903–1991
Noble-looking, light-haired American actor of intelligent, deep-set features whose career came in waves. After one false start, he came to Hollywood in the thirties and played supporting roles, returning in 1940 in near-star parts after his portrayal of Brigham Young. In 1949 he revealed himself as a balding character star and promptly won an Academy Award for *12 O'Clock High*. Died following an attack of influenza.

1928: *Handcuffed.* 1929: *The Woman from Hell.* 1930: *Whoopee!* 1934: *College Rhythm. You Belong to Me. Behold My Wife.* 1935: *Home on the Range. Wanderer of the Wasteland. Car 99. Wings in the Dark. Men without Names. People Will Talk.* 1936: *Woman Trap. Thirteen Hours by Air. Revolt of the Zombies. Star for a Night. Pepper.* 1937: *Woman in Distress. Song to the City. Under Cover of Night. Dangerous Number. Escape by Night. Exiled to Shanghai.* 1938: *Having Wonderful*

Time. 1940: *Brigham Young – Frontiersman (GB: Brigham Young).* 1941: *The Men in Her Life. Western Union.* 1942: *Valley of the Sun. The Omaha Trail.* 1943: *North Star (later Armored Attack). I Escaped from the Gestapo (GB: No Escape).* 1944: *Alaska. When Strangers Marry.* 1945: *I Live in Grosvenor Square (US: A Yank in London).* 1946: *Sister Kenny. Pursued.* 1947: *Driftwood.* 1949: *12 O'Clock High. C-Man.* 1950: *Sierra. Dark City.* 1951: *Rawhide. Warpath.* 1952: *My Son John. Denver and Rio Grande. It Grows on Trees.* 1953: *The Robe.* 1954: *Executive Suite. Private Hell 36. White Christmas. Bad Day at Black Rock.* 1955: *The Eternal Sea. It's a Dog's Life.* 1956: *Red Sundown. On the Threshold of Space. Smoke Jumpers (TV). X the Unknown. The Great Man.* 1957: *The Dark Side of the Earth (TV). Three Brave Men. 10 Guns. Bernardine.* 1958: *The Proud Rebel. King Creole. The Nun's Story.* 1959: *Cash McCall.* 1960: *Elmer Gantry.* 1961: *Parrish. The Honeymoon Machine.* 1962: *Jumbo/Billy Rose's Jumbo.* 1967: *First to Fight. Firecreek.* 1968: *Tiger by the Tail. Day of the Evil Gun.* 1969: *Smith! The Lonely Profession (TV). The Kremlin Letter.* 1970: *Remember (TV). Incident in San Francisco (TV).* 1971: *The Brotherhood of the Bell (TV). Vanishing Point.* 1972: *The Delphi Bureau (TV). The Stranger (TV). The Glass House (TV. GB: cinemas).* 1974: *The Great Lester Boggs. So Sad About Gloria. The Hanged Man (TV).* 1976: *God Bless Dr Shagetz. The Lindbergh Kidnapping Case (TV).* 1977: *End of the World.* 1978: *Game of Death (US: Bruce Lee's Game of Death).* 1980: *Alligator. Gideon's Trumpet (TV). Haywire.*

JAMES, Brion 1940–
Bony-bodied, open-mouthed, hook-nosed American actor and entertainer with thinning gingery hair. The son of a man who ran his own cinema business, James started his show business career in Los Angeles as a stand-up comedian. Films seized on the oafish aspects of his make-up and cast him as a series of dangerous, demented or deranged, slobby, yobbish-looking, usually shabbily dressed bad guys. His character in the TV movie *Killing at Hell's Gate*, Turkey Jones, summed up these roles. More recently, as with his studio boss in Robert Altman's *The Player*, he has made some attempt to break away from the familiar mould.

1975: The Kansas City Massacre (TV). 1976: Bound for Glory. Nickelodeon. Harry and Walter Go to New York. The Invasion of Johnson County (TV). 1977: Blue Sunshine. 1978: Corvette Summer (GB: The Hot One). Flying High (TV). KISS Meets the Phantom of the Park (TV). 1979: Wholly Moses! 1980: The Jazz Singer. Trouble in High Timber Country (TV). 1981: Southern Comfort. The Postman Always Rings Twice. Killing at Hell's Gate (TV). 1982: Blade Runner. 48 Hrs. Hear No Evil (TV). 1983: The Ballad of Gregorio Cortez. 1984: A Breed Apart/Carnauba. 1985: Silverado. Crimewave. Enemy Mine. Flesh and Blood. 1986: Armed and Dangerous. Cherry 2000 (released 1988). The Annihilator (TV). 1987: DOA. Nightmare at Noon (released 1990). Steel Dawn (filmed 1985 as Desert Warrior). Love Among Thieves (TV). Kenny Rogers as The Gambler, Part III – The Legend Continues (TV). 1988: Red Heat. The Horror Show. The Wrong Guys. Dead Man Walking (TV. US: Dead Man Out). Red Scorpion. 1989: Mom. Time of the Beast. Tango & Cash. Squad. The Horror Show. Desperado: The Outlaw Wars (TV). Enid is Sleeping (GB: Over Her Dead Body). 1990: The Johnson County Invasion (TV). The Trial of General Yamashito (TV). Street Asylum. Another 48 Hrs. 1991: Hell Comes to Frogtown II. Silhouette. Ultimate Desires. Mutator. 1992: In Exile. The Player. Overkill: The Aileen Wuornos Story (TV). Blade Runner The Director's Cut. Wishman. Black Magic (cable TV). Time Runner. 1993: Full Combat. Nemesis. Scanner Cop. Cabin Boy. Johnny Bago (TV). Future Shock. Brain Smasher: A Love Story. Rio Diablo (TV). The Dark. Striking Distance. Precious Victims. 1994: Radioland Murders. Pterodactyl Women from Beverly Hills. Hong Kong '97. Dominion. Bad Company. F. T. W. Steel Frontier. Art Deco Detective. 1995: From the Edge. Sketch Artist II: Hands That See (TV). Evil Obsession.

JAMES, Clifton 1921–

Fat, pink-faced, throaty-toned, bullfrog-mouthed American actor, popular for a while in the mid 1970s (after a hard climb up the acting ladder) as redneck, cigar-chewing sheriffs and villains who unavailingly tried to stand in the hero's way. Less frequently seen in films since 1977. Another graduate of the Actors' Studio.

1954: On the Waterfront. 1957: The Strange One (GB: End As a Man). 1958: The Last Mile. 1961: Something Wild. 1962: Experiment in Terror (GB: The Grip of Fear). David and Lisa. 1964: Black Like Me. Invitation to a Gunfighter. 1965: The Chase. 1966: The Happening. The Caper of the Golden Bulls (GB: Carnival of Thieves). 1967: Cool Hand Luke. Will Penny. 1969: The Reivers. ... tick ... tick ... tick. 1970: WUSA. 1971: The Biscuit Eater. 1972: The New Centurions (GB: Precinct 45 – Los Angeles Police). 1973: Kid Blue/Dime Box. The Iceman Cometh. The Laughing Policeman (GB: An Investigation of Murder). The Last Detail. The Werewolf of Washington. Live and Let Die. Buster and Billie. 1974: Bank Shot. Bon baisers de Hong Kong. Juggernaut. The Man with the Golden Gun. Rancho de Luxe. 1975: The Deadly Tower (TV). Friendly Persuasion (TV). The Runaway Barge (TV). 1976: Silver Streak. The November Plan (originally for TV). 1977: Little Ladies of the Night (TV). The Bad News Bears in Breaking Training. 1979: Hart to Hart (TV). CaboBlanco. My Undercover Years with the KKK (TV). 1980: Guyana Tragedy: The Story of Jim Jones (TV). Superman II. 1985: Where Are the Children? 1986: Whoops Apocalypse. 1988: Eight Men Out. 1990: The Bonfire of the Vanities.

JAMESON, Joyce 1932–1987

Glamorous, buxom American blonde actress with wide mouth and corncrake voice. She played mostly dames and broads in comedy roles; at her best in two Gothic horror films of the early 1960s when she showed she could be just as effective playing for chuckles and chills. Otherwise mainly on television and in shamefully small roles in films.

1951: The Strip. Show Boat. The Son of Dr Jekyll. 1953: Veils of Bagdad. Problem Girls. The French Line. 1954: Phffft! Son of Sinbad. 1955: Gang Busters. 1956: Crime Against Joe. 1957: Tip on a Dead Jockey (GB: Time for Action). 1960: The Apartment. 1962: Poe's Tales of Terror (GB: Tales of Terror). 1963: The Balcony. Comedy of Terrors. 1964: Good Neighbor Sam. 1966: Boy, Did I Get a Wrong Number! 1968: The Split. 1970: Company of Killers. Run, Simon, Run (TV). 1971): Crosscurrent (TV). 1972: Women in Chains (TV). 1975: Death Race 2000. The First 36 Hours of Dr Durant (TV). Promise Him Anything (TV). 1976: The Outlaw Josey Wales. The Love Boat (TV). Scorchy. 1978: Crash (TV). Every Which Way But Loose. 1979: The Wild, Wild West Revisited (TV). Leo and Loree. 1983: The Man Who Loved Women. 1984: Hardbodies.

JEAYES, Allan 1885–1963

Solidly-built, dark-haired, sometimes moustachioed British actor who tackled a good range of aggressive semi-leads when he came to films at the beginning of sound, then settled down with Korda's London Films to play inspectors, judges and even the occasional oriental. His splendid, resonant voice was used to good effect as the storyteller in *The Thief of Bagdad*. Retired in 1950, but came back for a couple of 'old man' roles just before his death from a heart attack.

1918: Nelson: The Story of England's Immortal Hero. 1921: A Gentleman of France. The Solitary Cyclist. 1922: The Hound of the Baskervilles. The Missioner. 1925: Bulldog Drummond's Third Round (US: The Third Round). 1929: The Hate Ship. 1931: The Ghost Train. Stranglehold. 1932: Above Rubies. The Impassive Footman (US: Woman in Bondage/Woman in Chains). 1933: Anne One Hundred. Little Napoleon. Purse Strings. Paris Plane. Ask Beccles. Song of the Plough. Eyes of Fate. Colonel Blood. 1934: Red Ensign (US: Strike!). Catherine the Great/The Rise of Catherine the Great. The Scarlet Pimpernel. The Camels Are Coming. 1935: Koenigsmark. Sanders of the River (US: Bosambo). Drake of England (US: Drake the Pirate). King of the Damned. 1936: His Lordship (US: Man of Affaires). Forget-Me-Not (US: Forever Yours). Things to Come. Seven Sinners (US: Doomed Cargo). Rembrandt. The House of the Spaniard.

Crown v Stevens. Public Nuisance. Tudor Rose (US: Nine Days a Queen). 1937: Elephant Boy. The High Command. Knight without Armour. Action for Slander. The Squeaker (US: Murder on Diamond Row). The Green Cockatoo (US: Four Dark Hours). 1938: The Return of the Scarlet Pimpernel. A Royal Divorce. Everything Happens to Me. They Drive by Night. Thirteen Men and a Gun. Dangerous Medicine. 1939: The Good Old Days. The Spider. The Four Feathers. The Stars Look Down. A Window in London (US: Girl in Distress). The Proud Valley. 1940: The Thief of Bagdad. Spy for a Day. Sailors Three (US: Three Cockeyed Sailors). Convoy. You Will Remember. Inspector Hornleigh Goes to It (US: Mail Train). The Girl in the News. The Flying Squad. Old Bill and Son. 1941: Pimpernel Smith (US: Mister V). 1942: Tomorrow We Live (US: At Dawn We Die). Uncensored. Talk about Jacqueline. 1943: The Shipbuilders. 1945: Perfect Strangers (US: Vacation from Marriage). Dead of Night. 1946: Lisbon Story. 1947: The Man Within (US: The Smugglers). Blanche Fury. 1948: Saraband for Dead Lovers (US: Saraband). Obsession (US: The Hidden Room). An Ideal Husband. Bonnie Prince Charlie. 1950: Waterfront (US: Waterfront Women). The Reluctant Widow. 1961: Attempt to Kill. 1962: Reach for Glory.

JEFFRIES, Lionel 1926–
Bewhiskered British comedy actor, bald since his twenties. He began as nosey types and men in the street, progressed to inept, would-be malevolent figures of authority and finally put on a little weight to arrive at eccentric blunderers and benevolent benefactors. Jeffries became a force in the British cinema of the early 1970s for his direction of children, but later ventures behind the camera were less successful. An inveterate scene-stealer in his peak period of comic invention.

1949: Stage Fright. 1953: Will Any Gentleman . . .? 1954: The Colditz Story. The Black Rider. 1955: Windfall. No Smoking. The Quatermass Experiment (US: The Creeping Unknown). All for Mary. 1956: Jumping for Joy. Eyewitness. Bhowani Junction. Lust for Life. The Baby and the Battleship. Up in the World. The High Terrace. The Man in the Sky (US: Decision Against Time). 1957: The Vicious Circle (US: The Circle). Hour of Decision. Doctor at Large. Barnacle Bill (US:

All at Sea). Blue Murder at St Trinian's. 1958: Law and Disorder. Dunkirk. Orders to Kill. Up the Creek. The Revenge of Frankenstein. Girls at Sea. The Nun's Story. Behind the Mask. Nowhere to Go. Life is a Circus. Further Up the Creek. 1959: Idle on Parade (US: Idol on Parade). Please Turn Over. Bobbikins. 1960: Two Way Stretch. The Trials of Oscar Wilde (US: The Man in the Green Carnation). Jazzboat. Let's Get Married. Tarzan the Magnificent. 1961: The Hellions. Fanny. 1962: Operation Snatch. Mrs Gibbons' Boys. Kill or Cure. The Notorious Landlady. The Wrong Arm of the Law. 1963: Call Me Bwana. The Scarlet Blade (US: The Crimson Blade). The Long Ships. 1964: First Men in the Moon. The Truth about Spring. Murder Ahoy. 1965: You Must Be Joking! The Secret of My Success. 1966: Drop Dead, Darling (US: Arrivederci Baby!). Oh Dad, Poor Dad, Mama's Hung You in the Closet and I'm Feeling So Sad. The Spy with a Cold Nose. 1967: Jules Verne's Rocket to the Moon (US: Those Fantastic Flying Fools). Camelot. 1968: Chitty Chitty Bang Bang. 1969: Twinky (US: Lola). Twelve Plus One/ The Twelve Chairs. 1970: Eyewitness (and 1956 film. US: Sudden Terror). 1971: Whoever Slew Auntie Roo? (US: Who Slew Auntie Roo?). 1974: Royal Flash. What Changed Charley Farthing. 1977: Wombling Free (voice only). 1978: The Water Babies (voice only). The Prisoner of Zenda. 1982: Ménage à Trois/Better Late Than Never. 1988: A Chorus of Disapproval. 1989: Danny, the Champion of the World (TV. GB: cinemas). Jekyll and Hyde (TV).

As director:
1970: The Railway Children. 1972: The Amazing Mr Blunden. Baxter! 1977: Wombling Free. 1978: The Water Babies.

JENKINS, Allen
(Alfred McGonegal) 1890–1974
Brown-haired, bag-eyed, hook-nosed American actor whose ugly mug might have come straight from a Damon Runyan story, and proved to be his fortune. In the 1930s and 1940s, matchstick often dangling from a drooping lower lip, he was ever ready with a leering remark and played dozens of dim-witted but by and large friendly penny-ante crooks and ne'er-do-wells. Largely retired after 1957, but still played a few cameo roles in his last years, and supplied the voice of officer Dibble in the *Top Cat* cartoons on

TV. Died from complications following surgery.

1931: Straight and Narrow. The Girl Habit. 1932: Rackety Rax. Blessed Event. I Am a Fugitive from a Chain Gang. Three on a Match. *The Stolen Jools (GB: The Slippery Pearls). Lawyer Man. 1933: 42nd Street. Ladies They Talk About. The Mayor of Hell. Employees' Entrance. The Keyhole. Tomorrow at Seven. Professional Sweetheart (GB: Imaginary Sweetheart). The Mind Reader. Havana Widows. Hard to Handle. The Silk Express. Bureau of Missing Persons. Blondie Johnson. 1934: I've Got Your Number. Twenty Million Sweethearts. Happiness Ahead. The Merry Frinks (GB: The Happy Family). The St Louis Kid (GB: A Perfect Weekend). The Case of the Howling Dog. Bedside. The Big Shakedown. Whirlpool. Jimmy the Gent. 1935: A Night at the Ritz. Miss Pacific Fleet. The Case of the Curious Bride. Page Miss Glory. The Irish in Us. Sweet Music. While the Patient Slept. The Case of the Lucky Legs. Broadway Hostess. I Live for Love (GB: I Live for You). 1936: The Singing Kid. Sing Me a Love Song. Three Men on a Horse. Sins of Man. Cain and Mabel. 1937: There Goes My Girl. Dance, Charlie, Dance. The Singing Marine. Marry the Girl. Dead End. Talent Scout. Ready, Willing and Able. Marked Woman. Ever Since Eve. The Perfect Specimen. Sh! The Octopus. 1938: A Slight Case of Murder. Swing Your Lady. Racket Busters. Heart of the North. Going Places. Gold Diggers in Paris (GB: The Gay Imposters). The Amazing Dr Clitterhouse. Hard to Get. Fools for Scandal. *For Auld Lang Syne. 1939: Sweepstakes Winner. Five Came Back. Torchy Plays with Dynamite. Naughty But Nice. Destry Rides Again. 1940: Oh, Johnny, How You Can Love. Meet the Wildcat. Brother Orchid. Margie. Tin Pan Alley. 1941: The Gay Falcon. Time Out for Rhythm. Footsteps in the Dark. Dive Bomber. Ball of Fire. Go West, Young Lady. A Date with the Falcon. 1942: Maisie Gets Her Man (GB: She Got Her Man). The Falcon Takes Over. Tortilla Flat. Eyes in the Night. They All Kissed the Bride. 1943: Stage Door Canteen. 1945: Wonder Man. Lady on a Train. 1946: Singin' in the Corn (GB: Give and Take). The Dark House. Meet Me on Broadway. 1947: The Case of the Babysitter. Fun on a Week-End. Easy Come, Easy Go. Wild Harvest. The Senator Was Indiscreet (GB: Mr Ashton Was Indiscreet). The Hat Box Mystery. 1948: The Inside Story. 1949: The Big Wheel. 1950: Bodyhold. 1951: Let's Go Navy. Crazy Over Horses. Behave Yourself! 1952: The WAC from Walla Walla (GB: Army Capers). Oklahoma Annie. 1957: Three Men on a Horse (remake. TV). 1959: Pillow Talk. Chained for Life. 1963: It's a Mad, Mad, Mad, Mad World. 1964: I'd Rather Be Rich. Robin and the Seven Hoods. For Those Who Think Young. The Spy in the Green Hat (TV. GB: cinemas). 1967: Doctor, You've Got to Be Kidding! 1971: Getting Away from It All (TV). 1974: The Front Page.

JENKINS, Megs 1917–
Prettily plump, round-faced, dark-haired, kind-looking British actress who moved swiftly from sisters to mothers, via a couple of interesting leading roles, in the British

cinema of the immediate post-war years. Memorable as a nurse in *Green for Danger* and as the 'plump woman' in *The History of Mr Polly*. Since in a variety of concerned, motherly or worried parts and active into her seventies in television and on the stage.

1937: *Dr Syn*. 1939: *Inspector Hornleigh on Holiday* (US: *Inspector Hornleigh on Leave*). *The Silent Battle* (US: *Continental Express*). *Poison Pen*. 1943: *Millions Like Us*. *The Lamp Still Burns*. *It's in the Bag*. 1945: *29 Acacia Avenue* (US: *The Facts of Love*). *Painted Boats* (US: *The Girl on the Canal*). 1946: *Green for Danger*. 1947: *The Brothers*. 1948: *Saraband for Dead Lovers* (US: *Saraband*). *The Monkey's Paw*. 1949: *The History of Mr Polly*. *A Boy, a Girl and a Bike*. *No Place for Jennifer*. 1951: *White Corridors*. 1952: *Ivanhoe*. *Secret People*. *The Cruel Sea*. 1953: *Rough Shoot* (US: *Shoot First*). *Trouble in Store*. *Personal Affair*. 1954: *The Gay Dog*. 1955: *Out of the Clouds*. *Ring of Greed*. *John and Julie*. 1956: *The Man in the Sky* (US: *Decision Against Time*). 1957: *The Passionate Stranger*. *The Story of Esther Costello* (US: *Golden Virgin*). 1958: *Indiscreet*. 1959: *Tiger Bay*. *Jet Storm*. *Friends and Neighbours*. 1960: *Conspiracy of Hearts*. 1961: *The Green Helmet*. *Macbeth*. *The Innocents*. *The Barber of Stamford Hill*. 1962: *Life for Ruth* (US: *Walk in the Shadow*). *The Wild and the Willing*. 1964: *Murder Most Foul*. 1965: *Bunny Lake is Missing*. 1967: *Stranger in the House* (US: *Cop-out*). 1968: *Oliver!* 1969: *The Smashing Bird I Used to Know*. *David Copperfield* (TV. GB: cinemas). 1972: *Asylum*. 1974: *The Amorous Milkman*. *The Turn of the Screw* (TV).

JENSON, Roy 1935–

Thuggish-looking, heavily-built but agile, this fair-haired Canadian stuntman turned actor was in films as a teenager. Hollywood kept him working soldily as minor, menacing villains who threatened the direst of bodily harm to the hero, in nearly 100 roles between 1957 and 1981, his busiest film period. His characters could almost always be depended upon to come to a sticky and violent end. He played his first leading role, in *Osceola Sheriff's Office*, as late as 1992. Sometimes billed as Roy C Jenson, Roy Jensen or Roy C Jensen.

1952: *Operation Secret*. 1957: *The Missouri Traveler*. *Hell on Devil's Island*. 1958:

Buchanan Rides Alone. 1959: *Ride Lonesome*. *The Rise and Fall of Legs Diamond*. 1960: *Let No Man Write My Epitaph*. *North to Alaska*. 1961: *Atlantis, the Lost Continent*. *The George Raft Story* (GB: *Spin of a Coin*). *Marines, Let's Go*. *The Fiercest Heart*. 1962: *Two Weeks in a Balloon*. *How the West Was Won*. *Confessions of an Opium Eater* (GB: *Evils of Chinatown*). 1963: *Law of the Lawless*. 1964: *Stage to Thunder Rock*. *36 Hours*. 1965: *Baby, the Rain Must Fall*. 1966: *Harper* (GB: *The Moving Target*). *Daniel Boone — Frontier Trail Rider*. *Apache Uprising*. *Los bandidos*. *Un extrano en la casa*. 1967: *Red Tomahawk*. *The Helicopter Spies* (TV. GB: cinemas). *Waterhole No.3* (GB: *Waterhole 3*). *Hostile Guns*. *The Ambushers*. *Will Penny*. 1968: *Five Card Stud*. *Jigsaw*. *The Thomas Crown Affair*. 1969: *Paint Your Wagon*. *Number One*. *Halls of Anger*. 1970: *Fools*. 1971: *A Tattered Web* (TV). *Sometimes a Great Notion* (GB: *Never Give an Inch*). *Big Jake*. *Powderkeg* (TV. GB: cinemas). 1972: *Journey Through Rosebud*. *The Life and Times of Judge Roy Bean*. *Count Your Bullets*. *Face to the Wind*. *Kung Fu* (TV). *The Glass House* (TV. GB: cinemas). 1973: *Dillinger*. *The Outfit*. *Soylent Green*. *Call to Danger* (TV). *The Way We Were*. *The Red Pony* (TV. GB: cinemas). *Nightmare Honeymoon*. 1974: *Hit Lady* (TV). *Chinatown*. *The Abduction of Saint Anne/They've Kidnapped Anne Benedict* (TV). *Thunderbolt and Lightfoot*. *99 and 44-100ths % Dead* (GB: *Call Harry Crown*). 1975: *Breakout*. *Force Five* (TV). *Framed*. *The Wind and the Lion*. *Breakheart Pass*. 1976: *Helter Skelter* (TV. GB: cinemas). *The Car*. *The Duchess and the Dirtwater Fox*. 1977: *The Gauntlet*. *Telefon*. 1978: *Every Which Way But Loose*. 1980: *The Mountain Men*. *Nightside*. *Any Which Way You Can*. *Tom Horn*. *Foolin' Around*. 1981: *Demonoid*. *Bustin' Loose*. 1982: *Honkytonk Man*. 1983: *Kenny Rogers as The Gambler, Part II — The Adventure Continues* (TV). 1984: *Last of the Great Survivors* (TV). *Red Dawn*. 1986: *Kung Fu — The Movie* (TV). 1990: *The Watch Commander* (TV). 1992: *Osceola Sheriff's Office*.

JEWELL, Isabel 1909–1972

Petite American platinum blonde actress who never quite made it as a star name after coming to Hollywood from Broadway success in 1932. Later played hard-bitten or world-weary dames before falling on hard times when acting roles dried up. There

were several brushes with the law before her death 'from natural causes' at 62. Best remembered as Gloria Stone (who decides to stay in Shangri-La) in the 1937 *Lost Horizon*.

1932: *Blessed Event*. 1933: *Bombshell* (GB: *Blonde Bombshell*). *Bondage*. *Design for Living*. *Counsellor-at-Law*. *Day of Reckoning*. *Advice to the Lovelorn*. *The Women in His Life*. 1934: *Evelyn Prentice*. *She Had to Choose*. *Manhattan Melodrama*. *Here Comes the Groom*. *Let's Be Ritzy*. 1935: *Times Square Lady*. *Shadow of Doubt*. *Mad Love* (GB: *The Hands of Orlac*). *The Casino Murder Case*. *I've Been Around*. *A Tale of Two Cities*. *Ceiling Zero*. 1936: *The Leathernecks Have Landed* (GB: *The Marines Have Landed*). *Valiant is the Word for Carrie*. *Small Town Girl*. *Big Brown Eyes*. *The Man Who Lived Twice*. *Go West Young Man*. *Dancing Feet*. *Career Woman*. *Thirty-Six Hours to Kill*. 1937: *Marked Woman*. *Swing It, Sailor*. *Lost Horizon*. 1938: *The Crowd Roars*. *Love on Toast*. 1939: *They Asked for It*. *Missing Daughters*. *Gone With the Wind*. 1940: *Scatterbrain*. *Oh, Johnny, How You Can Love*. *Northwest Passage*. *Marked Men*. *Babies for Sale*. *Little Men*. *Irene*. 1941: *High Sierra*. *For Beauty's Sake*. 1943: *Danger — Women at Work!* *The Falcon and the Co-Eds*. *The Leopard Man*. *Calling Doctor Death*. *The Seventh Victim*. 1944: *The Merry Monaghans*. 1945: *Steppin' in Society*. 1946: *Sensation Hunters*. *Badman's Territory*. 1947: *Born to Kill* (GB: *Lady of Deceit*). *The Bishop's Wife*. 1948: *Michael O'Halloran*. *The Snake Pit*. *Unfaithfully Yours*. *Belle Starr's Daughter*. 1949: *The Story of Molly X*. 1954: *Drum Beat*. *The Man in the Attic*. 1957: *Bernadine*. 1969: *Ciao, Manhattan*. 1971: *The Arousers* (GB: *Sweet Kill*).

JOHNS, Stratford

(Alan S. Johns) 1925–

Portly South Africa-born actor with large, round face, small features and distinctive 'half head' of dark hair. He seemed destined to play sweaty, unsavoury minor characters until cast as a police inspector in British TV's *Z Cars*; this catapulted him to national stardom and led to another series, *Softly Softly*, with Johns's character promoted to superintendent. After this was over, his bulky figure proved difficult to cast, but he has latterly won some interesting roles on stage.

1954: Burnt Evidence. Hands of Destiny. 1955: The Ladykillers. The Night My Number Came Up. The Dark Avenger (US: The Warriors). The Ship That Died of Shame (US: PT Raiders). Who Done It? 1956: Eyewitness. The Long Arm (US: The Third Key). Tiger in the Smoke. 1957: Across the Bridge. The One That Got Away. 1958: Law and Disorder. No Trees in the Street (US: No Tree in the Street). Indiscreet. Violent Playground. A Night to Remember. 1960: The Professionals. Hand in Hand. 1961: The Naked Edge. The Valiant. The Young Ones. 1962: Two-Letter Alibi. 1966: The Great St Trinian's Train Robbery. 1967: Jules Verne's Rocket to the Moon (US: Those Fantastic Flying Fools). The Plank. 1970: Cromwell. 1980: George and Mildred. The Fiendish Plot of Dr Fu Manchu. 1984: Dance with a Stranger. 1985: Wild Geese II. Hitler's S.S. Portrait in Evil (TV. GB: cinemas). Car Trouble. 1986: Foreign Body. 1987: Brond (TV). 1988: Salome's Last Dance. The Lair of the White Worm. 1990: The Fool. 1991: A Demon in My View. 1993: Splitting Heirs.

JOHNSON, Katie
(Katherine Johnson) 1878–1957
In her latter days seen almost entirely as sweet little old ladies, this British actress with the kindly, rather noble (prominent nose, narrow forehead) features slaved away at minor roles for almost her entire career until given the leading role of Mrs Wilberforce, the landlady who accidentally confounds a gang of robbers and would-be murderers in Ealing Studios' The Ladykillers. For it, she won a British Oscar as best actress, and a second plum role, in How to

Murder a Rich Uncle: her last.

1932: After Office Hours. 1933: Strictly in Confidence. 1934: A Glimpse of Paradise. 1936: Laburnum Grove. Dusty Ermine (US: Hideout in the Alps). Hail and Farewell. 1937: Farewell Again (US: Troopship). The Last Adventurers. The Dark Stairway. Sunset in Vienna (US: Suicide Legion). The Rat. 1938: Marigold. 1939: Inspector Hornleigh on Holiday (US: Inspector Hornleigh on Leave). 1940: Gaslight (US: Angel Street). Two for Danger. 1941: The Black Sheep of Whitehall. Jeannie (US: Girl in Distress). Freedom Radio (US: A Voice in the Night). 1942: Talk about Jacqueline. 1944: He Snoops to Conquer. Tawny Pipit. 1946: The Years Between. The Shop at Sly Corner (US: The Code of Scotland Yard). Meet Me at Dawn. I See a Dark Stranger (US: The Adventuress). 1951: I Believe in You. Death of an Angel. 1952: Lady in the Fog (US: Scotland Yard Inspector). 1953: Three Steps in the Dark. The Large Rope. 1954: The Delavine Affair. The Rainbow Jacket. Out of the Clouds. 1955: John and Julie. The Ladykillers. 1956: How to Murder a Rich Uncle.

JOHNSON, Tor
(T. Johansson) 1903–1971
Massive, shaven-headed, outraged-looking Swedish ex-wrestler with pouched cheeks and deep-set eyes who brought his chilling and sometimes ghoulish appearance to occasional Hollywood films from 1934, many of them horror cheapies. Remembered especially as the police inspector turned into a zombie in the ghastly Plan 9 from Outer Space; as an actor, he was no Mike Mazurki (qv), but was nonetheless unmistakeable whenever he appeared. Died from a heart condition.

1934: Kid Millions. 1935: Man on the Flying Trapeze (GB: The Memory Expert). 1936: Under Two Flags. 1941: Shadow of the Thin Man. 1943: Swing Out the Blues. 1944: The Canterville Ghost. Lost in a Harem. Ghost Catchers. 1945: Sudan. 1947: Road to Rio. 1948: State of the Union (GB: The World and His Wife). Behind Locked Doors. 1949: Alias the Champ. 1950: Abbott and Costello in the Foreign Legion. The Reformer and the Redhead. 1951: Dear Brat. The Lemon Drop Kid. 1952: The San Francisco Story. Lady in the Iron Mask. Houdini. 1954: Bride of the Monster. 1956: Carousel. The Black Sleep. 1957: The Unearthly. Journey to Freedom. 1958: Plan 9

from Outer Space. 1959: Night of the Ghouls (GB: Revenge of the Dead). 1961: The Beast of Yucca Flats.

JOHNSTON, Oliver 1888–1966
Diffident, apologetic, small-faced, frog-mouthed, latterly white-haired British actor who, at the age when most people are thinking of slipping into retirement, started a busy film and television career. By the age of 76, he had progressed to fourth billing, with a prime role in The Tomb of Ligeia!

1938: Kate Plus Ten. Stolen Life. 1950: Night and the City. Highly Dangerous. 1953: *The Silent Witness. The Good Beginning. 1954: Dangerous Voyage (US: Terror Ship). A Tale of Three Women. 1955: Room in the House You Can't Escape. 1956: The Girl in the Picture. Circus Friends. 1957: A King in New York. The Story of Esther Costello (US: Golden Virgin). The Hypnotist (US: Scotland Yard Dragnet). 1958: Nowhere to Go. Bachelor of Hearts. Hello London. Son of Robin Hood. Indiscreet. 1959: Beyond This Place (US: Web of Evidence). A Touch of Larceny. Kidnapped. The Night We Dropped a Clanger (US: Make Mine a Double). The Three Worlds of Gulliver. 1961: Francis of Assisi. Raising the Wind. 1962: Dr Crippen. The Fast Lady. Backfire. 1963: Cleopatra. The Three Lives of Thomasina. Island of Love. 1964: The Tomb of Ligeia. 1965: You Must Be Joking! 1966: It (US: Return of the Golem). A Countess from Hong Kong.

JOLLEY, I. Stanford 1900–1978
On the whole, there was nothing very jolly about most of the scores of roles taken by this tall, dark, moustachioed, slightly sinister-looking American actor who played all kinds of second-line villains over four decades, but concentrated largely on dozens of minor westerns, a field in which he was equally likely to show up as bad guy, rancher, gambler, or (latterly) old-timer in the saloon. His unreliable good looks and florid complexion were probably punched out by more 'B' western heroes than anyone, other than that other double-dyed movie westerner Roy Barcroft (qv). Almost always worked for minor studios.

1923: Luck. 1936: The Big Show. Ghost Town Gold. The Gentleman from Louisiana. The Old Corral (GB: Texas Serenade). 1937: Boy of the

Streets. A Bride for Henry. Dick Tracy (serial). Kid Galahad. A Star is Born. They Won't Forget. 1938: A Christmas Carol. Kentucky. Over the Wall. Woman Against Woman. 1939: The Lone Wolf Spy Hunt (GB: The Lone Wolf's Daughter). The Mystery of Mr Wong. The Private Lives of Elizabeth and Essex. Mr Wong in Chinatown. S.O.S. Tidal Wave (GB: Tidal Wave). Street of Missing Men. 1940: Chasing Trouble. The Ape. The Fatal Hour (GB: Mr Wong at Headquarters). Hidden Enemy. Midnight Limited. Queen of the Yukon. Rollin' Home to Texas. 1941: Arizona Bound. Criminals Within. Desperate Cargo. Emergency Landing. Gentleman from Dixie. Trail of the Silver Spurs. 1942: Arizona Roundup. Black Dragons. Boot Hill Bandits. Border Roundup. Dawn on the Great Divide. Perils of the Royal Mounted (serial). Outlaws of Boulder Pass. The Sombrero Kid. The Valley of Vanishing Men (serial). The Rangers Take Over. Road to Happiness. Prairie Pals. 1943: Bad Men of Thunder Gap. The Black Raven. Corregidor. Blazing Frontier. Death Rides the Plains. Frontier Fury. Batman (serial). The Kid Rides Again. Isle of Forgotten Sins/Monsoon. Man from Music Mountain. The Phantom (serial). The Return of the Rangers. Wild Horse Stampede. Wolves of the Range. Trail of Terror. What a Man! Frontier Law. 1944: Black Arrow (serial). Brand of the Devil. Call of the Jungle. The Chinese Cat/Charlie Chan in The Chinese Cat. Cyclone Prairie Rangers. The Desert Hawk (serial). Gangsters of the Frontier. Outlaw Roundup. Oklahoma Raiders. Shake Hands With Murder. Swing, Cowboy, Swing (GB: Bad Man from Big Bend). The Whispering Skull. 1945: Flaming Bullets. Fighting Bill Carson. Frontier Fugitives. The Fighting Guardsman. Gangsters' Den. Mr Muggs Rides Again. The Power of the Whistler. Crime, Inc. Outlaws of the Rockies. Jungle Raiders (serial). Prairie Rustlers. Secret Agent X-9 (serial). The Scarlet Clue. The Navajo Kid. Stagecoach Outlaws. Springtime in Texas. 1946: Ambush Trail. The Crimson Ghost (serial). Border Bandits. Daughter of Don Q (serial). Lightning Raiders. 'Neath Canadian Skies. North of the Border. Son of the Guardsman (serial). Six Gun Man. Silver Range. Swamp Fire. Terrors on Horseback. Two-Fisted Stranger. 1947: Land of the Lawless. The Black Widow (serial). Prairie Express. The Romance of Rosy Ridge. West of Dodge City (GB: The Sea Wall). Wild Country. 1948: Adventures of Frank and Jesse James (serial). Check Your Guns. Congo Bill (serial).

Dangers of the Canadian Mounted (serial). Feudin' Fussin' and A-Fightin'. The Fighting Ranger. Gunning for Justice. Joan of Arc. Oklahoma Blues. Tex Granger (serial). The Prince of Thieves. Whiplash. 1949: Bandit King of Texas. Desert Vigilante. King of the Rocket Men (serial). Calamity Jane and Sam Bass. Gun Law Justice. Haunted Trails. Curtain Call at Cactus Creek (GB: Take the Stage). Ghost of Zorro (serial). Bodyhold. Roll, Thunder, Roll! Sands of Iwo Jima. Son of Billy the Kid. Stampede. Rimfire. Trouble at Melody Mesa. 1950: Colorado Ranger/Guns of Justice. California Passage. Comanche Territory. The Baron of Arizona. Desperadoes of the West (serial). Fast on the Draw. Hostile Country. Pirates of the High Seas (serial). The Return of Jesse James. Rock Island Trail (GB: Transcontinent Express). Sierra. Trigger Jr. Cattle Queen (GB: Queen of the West). 1951: Captain Video (serial). Don Daredevil Rides Again (serial). Canyon Raiders. Nevada Badmen. I Want You. The Longhorn. Oklahoma Justice. Lawless Cowboys. The Red Badge of Courage. Stage to Blue River. Texas Lawman. The Thundering Trail. Whistling Hills. Westward the Women. Texans Never Cry. 1952: Dead Man's Trail. Fargo. Fort Osage. The Gunman. Hired Gun. Kansas Territory. Leadville Gunslinger. Man from the Black Hills. Rodeo. The Raiders/Riders of Vengeance. Rancho Notorious. The Lawless Breed. Waco (GB: The Outlaw and the Lady). Wagons West. Wild Stallion. Wyoming Roundup. Yukon Gold. 1953: Count the Hours. City of Bad Men. Calamity Jane. The Marksman. Rebel City. Son of Belle Starr. Kansas Pacific. Topeka. Tumbleweed. Vigilante Terror. 1954: The Forty-Niners. The Desperado. Man With the Steel Whip (serial). Seven Brides for Seven Brothers. Silver Lode. Two Guns and a Badge. White Christmas. 1955: Seven Angry Men. Wichita. 1956: Backlash. Perils of the Wilderness (serial). Kentucky Rifle. I Killed Wild Bill Hickok. Fury at Gunsight Pass. The Proud Ones. The Rawhide Years. Outlaw Queen. Three for Jamie Dawn. The Violent Years. The Wild Dakotas. The Young Guns. 1957: Gun Battle at Monterey. Gunsight Ridge. The Halliday Brand. The Iron Sheriff. The Oklahoman. The Storm Rider. 1958: Day of the Bad Man. Gunsmoke in Tucson. The Long, Hot Summer. Man from God's Country. The Saga of Hemp Brown. 1959: Alias Jesse James. Here Come the Jets. Lone Texan. The Rebel Set. The Miracle of the Hills. 1960: Ice Palace. One Foot in Hell. The Story of Ruth. Thirteen Fighting Men. 1961: Atlantis the Lost Continent. The Little Shepherd of Kingdom Come. Posse from Hell. Valley of the Dragons. 1962: The Firebrand. Terror at Black Falls. 1963: The Haunted Palace. 1965: The Bounty Killer. The Restless Ones. 1968: The Shakiest Gun in the West. 1969: The Phynx. 1972: Night of the Lepus.

JONES, Barry 1893–1981

Bald British character actor, often seen looking harassed or dishevelled, who suddenly found himself in leading roles, and even making a run of films in Hollywood, after his eye-catching performance, at the age of 57, as the demented scientist in *Seven Days to Noon*. Born in Guernsey, he had a few mild leading roles in British films of the 1930s.

1932: Women Who Play. Number Seventeen. Arms and the Man. 1936: The Gay Adventure. 1938: Murder in the Family. 1942: Squadron Leader X. 1947: Dancing with Crime. Frieda. 1948: The Calendar. Uneasy Terms. The Bad Lord Byron. 1949: That Dangerous Age (US: If This Be Sin). Madeleine. 1950: Seven Days to Noon. The Clouded Yellow. The Mudlark. 1951: White Corridors. The Magic Box. Appointment With Venus (US: Island Rescue). 1952: Return to Paradise. Plymouth Adventure. 1954: Prince Valiant. Demetrius and the Gladiators. Brigadoon. The Glass Slipper. 1956: Alexander the Great. War and Peace. 1957: Saint Joan. The Safecracker. 1959: The 39 Steps. 1965: The Heroes of Telemark. A Study in Terror (US: Fog).

JONES, Freddie 1927–

One of the few British character players to come to prominence in more recent times, the crafty-looking Jones, with rolling eyes and wildly unruly (disappearing) hair, began life as a laboratory technician, but a belated drama scholarship set him on the path to an acting career. He quickly cornered the British market in twitching, volatile eccentrics and was the best 'monster' since Boris Karloff, in *Frankenstein Must Be Destroyed*. Won numerous awards for his performance as Claudius in the TV series *The Caesars*.

1966: The Persecution and Assassination of Jean Paul Marat ... (The Marat/Sade). 1967: Accident. Far from the Madding Crowd. Deadfall. 1968: The Bliss of Mrs Blossom. Otley. 1969: Frankenstein Must Be Destroyed.

1970: *Assault (US: In the Devil's Garden).
The Man Who Haunted Himself. Doctor in
Trouble. Goodbye Gemini. 1971: Kidnapped.
Mr Horatio Knibbles. Antony and Cleopatra.
1972: Sitting Target. 1973: The Satanic Rites
of Dracula (US: Dracula and His Vampire
Bride). Gollocks! There's Plenty of Room in
New Zealand. 1974: All Creatures Great
and Small. Juggernaut. Vampira (US: Old
Dracula). Son of Dracula/Count Downe.
Romance with a Double-Bass. 1975: Appoint-
ment with a Killer (TV). Never Too Young To
Rock. 1978: The Nativity (TV). 1979: Zulu
Dawn. 1980: The Elephant Man. 1981:
Murder is Easy (TV). 1982: Captain Stirrick.
Firefox. 1983: Krull. E la nave va/And the
Ship Sails On ... 1984: Firestarter. Dune.
1985: Young Sherlock Holmes. Eleanor, First
Lady of the World (TV). The Black Cauldron
(voice only). Lost in London (TV). Time
After Time (TV). 1986: Comrades. 1987:
Maschenka. 1988: Consuming Passions. 1989:
Erik the Viking. S.P.O.O.K.S. 1990: The
Kremlin Farewell (TV). Wild at Heart. Dark
River. The Last Butterfly. 1992: Hotel Room
(TV). 1993: The Mystery of Edwin Drood.
1994: Prince of Jutland. The Neverending Story
III: Escape from Fantasia.*

Angel in My Pocket. 1970: Rabbit Run. The
Movie Murderer (TV). Love Hate Love (TV).
Dirty Dingus Magee. 1971: Skin Game.
Support Your Local Gunfighter. 1972:
Napoleon and Samantha. The Daughters of
Joshua Cabe (TV). The Letters (TV). Pete 'n'
Tillie. 1973: Tom Sawyer. The Outfit. Shootout
in a One-Dog Town (TV). Letters from Three
Lovers (TV). 1974: Roll, Freddy, Roll (TV).
1975: Please Call It Murder (TV). Who is the
Black Dahlia? (TV). 1977: Tail Gunner Joe
(TV). 1980: Nine to Five. California Gold
Rush (TV). 1982: Deathtrap. 1985: Code-
name: Foxfire − Slay It Again Sam. 1986:
Balboa. The Leftovers (TV). 1989: Nowhere to
Run. 1990: Dick Tracy. Arachnophobia. Enid
is Sleeping (GB: Over Her Dead Body). The
Grifters.*

JONES, James Earl 1931−

Authoritative, deep-voiced black actor with
natural, slightly sardonic smile and solid,
heavy build. The son of a boxer who turned
actor, he himself became a star by portraying
a boxer, Jack Johnson, in the Broadway
show *The Great White Hope* (1966–68), a
role that won him an Academy Award
nomination when he repeated it on screen.
Following early struggles, including doing
menial work while seeking a breakthrough,
he was seen on Broadway from 1957 and
TV from 1963. After he had established
himself in films, his resonant tones were
heard as the voice of Darth Vader in the
Star Wars films.

*1964: Dr Strangelove, or: How I Learned to
Stop Worrying and Love the Bomb. 1967: The
Comedians. 1970: The Great White Hope. The
End of the Road. King: A Filmed Record ...
Montgomery to Memphis. 1972: Malcolm X
(narrator only). The Man. 1973: Claudine.
1975: The River Niger. The U.F.O. Incident
(TV). 1976: The Bingo Long Traveling All-
Stars and Motor Kings. Deadly Hero. Swash-
buckler (GB: The Scarlet Buccaneer). Jesus of
Nazareth (TV). 1977: The Greatest. Star Wars
(voice only). Exorcist II: The Heretic. The Last
Remake of Beau Geste. A Piece of the Action.
The Greatest Thing That Almost Happened
(TV). 1978: The Bushido Blade (released
1982). 1979: Guyana Tragedy: The Story of
Jim Jones (TV). 1980: The Red Tide (released
1984 as Bloodtide). The Empire Strikes Back
(voice only). The Golden Moment (TV). 1981:
Conan the Barbarian. 1982: The Flight of*

*Dragons (voice only). 1983: Return of the Jedi
(voice only). 1984: The Vegas Strip Wars (TV).
1985: City Limits. 1986: My Little Girl. Soul
Man. Allan Quatermain and the Lost City of
Gold. 1987: Gardens of Stone. Pinocchio and
the Emperor of the Night (voice only). Matewan.
1988: *Teach 109. Coming to America. 1989:
Best of the Best. Three Fugitives. Field of
Dreams. Bailey's Bridge (TV). Into Thin Air.
Grand Tour (TV). 1990: The Last Elephant
(TV). The Hunt for Red October. The Ambu-
lance. Grim Prairie Tales. Scorchers. Convicts
(released 1991). Last Flight Out (TV). By
Dawn's Early Light (TV). Heat Wave (TV).
1991: True Identity. 1992: Patriot Games.
1993: The Meteor Man. Sommersby. Con-
fessions: Two Faces of Evil (TV). Excessive
Force. The Lion King (voice only). Percy and
Thunder (TV). Hallelujah (TV). The Sandlot
(GB: The Sandlot Kids). 1994: Clean Slate.
Clear and Present Danger. Twilight Zone: Rod
Serling's Lost Classics (TV). Houseguest. Naked
Gun 33⅓. The Final Insult. 1995: Cry, The
Beloved Country (TV). The Ox and the Eye.
Jefferson in Paris. Lone Star.*

JONES, Henry 1912−

Short, roly-poly, round-faced, weak-
chinned, smily American actor who could
just as easily be meek or malevolent, henpecked or horrible. Often, though, he was
the little man who felt the wrath of more
powerful men around him. He would have
made a perfect Mole in a film adaptation of
The Wind in the Willows; as it was, he had to
content himself with stealing scenes in a
variety of colourful supporting roles through
five decades.

*1943: This is the Army. 1951: The Lady Says
No! 1956: The Bad Seed. The Girl He Left
Behind. The Girl Can't Help It. 1957: Will
Success Spoil Rock Hunter? (GB: Oh! For a
Man!). The Mystery of 13 (TV). 3:10 to Yuma.
1958: Vertigo. 1959: The Sounds of Eden
(TV). 1960: Cash McCall. The Bramble Bush.
Angel Baby. 1965: Never Too Late. 1966: Le
scandale/The Champagne Murders. 1967:
Project X. 1968: Something for a Lonely Man
(TV). Support Your Local Sheriff! Stay Away
Joe. 1969: Butch Cassidy and the Sundance
Kid. The Cockeyed Cowboys of Calico County
(GB: TV, as A Woman for Charlie). Rascal.*

JONES, Jeffrey 1947−

Eagle-eyed, fair-haired, slightly maniacal-
looking American whose sporadic film
career has usually found him cast as hyper-
active comic villains. Abandoning medicine
for acting in the late 1960s, Jones spent time
in South America and England (where he
studied acting at LAMDA) before a long
period on the Canadian and Broadway
stages. His film parts were few, but his face
began to be better known after his portrayal
of the mad king in *Amadeus*, and there were
rather more of his off-centre and largely
unsympathetic characters on the big screen
in the 1980s and 1990s.

*1970: Underground. The Revolutionary. 1978:
A Wedding. 1982: The Soldier. 1983: Easy
Money. 1984: Amadeus. 1985: Transylvania
6−5000. 1986: Howard the Duck (GB:
Howard: A New Breed of Hero). Ferris Bueller's
Day Off. 1987: The Hanoi Hilton. Kenny
Rogers as The Gambler, Part III − The Legend
Continues (TV). 1988: Without a Clue. Beetle-
juice. 1989: Valmont. Who's Harry Crumb?
1990: The Hunt for Red October. Enid is
Sleeping (GB: Over Her Dead Body). 1991:
Angel Square. 1992: Mom and Dad Save the
World. Stay Tuned. Welcome to Buzzsaw/Out
on a Limb. 1994: Ed Wood. Houseguest.*

JONES, L.Q.
(Justice McQueen) 1927–

Tall, fair-haired American actor with lived-in face and coat-hanger shoulders, a former horse- and cattle-rancher brought to Hollywood in 1954; he took his screen name from the character he played in his first film. In later years also made forays into production and direction. His powerful, rangy figure was generally seen as an assortment of hardened and/or unkempt westerners.

1954: *Battle Cry*. 1955: *Target Zero. Annapolis Story* (GB: *The Blue and the Gold*). 1956: *Santiago* (GB: *The Gun Runner*). *Toward the Unknown* (GB: *Brink of Hell*). *Between Heaven and Hell. Love Me Tender*. 1957: *Men in War. Operation Mad Ball*. 1958: *Border Showdown* (TV. GB: cinemas). *The Young Lions. Mountain Fortress* (TV. GB: cinemas). *The Naked and the Dead. Buchanan Rides Alone. Julesberg* (TV. GB: cinemas). *Torpedo Run*. 1959: *Warlock. Hound Dog Man. Battle of the Coral Sea*. 1960: *Ten Who Dared. Cimarron. Flaming Star*. 1961: *Ride the High Country* (GB: *Guns in the Afternoon*). 1962: *The Deadly Companions. Hell Is for Heroes!* 1963: *Showdown. The Lady Is My Wife* (TV). 1964: *Apache Rifles. Major Dundee. Iron Angel*. 1966: *Noon Wine* (TV). 1967: *Hang 'em High*. 1968: *Backtrack* (TV). *The Counterfeit Killer* (TV. GB: cinemas). *Stay Away Joe*. 1969: *The Wild Bunch*. 1970: *The Ballad of Cable Hogue. The McMasters ... tougher than the west itself! The Brotherhood of Satan*. 1971: *The Hunting Party*. 1972: *Fireball Forward* (TV). *The Bravos* (TV). 1973: *Pat Garrett and Billy the Kid. The Petty Story/73: The Petty Story/Smash-Up Alley* (TV. GB: cinemas). 1974: *Mrs Sundance* (TV). *Manhunter* (TV). *Mother, Jugs and Speed* (released 1976). *The Strange and Deadly Occurrence* (TV). 1975: *White Line Fever. Winterhawk. Attack on Terror: The FBI Versus the Ku Klux Klan* (TV). *Winner Take All* (TV). 1976: *Banjo Hackett – Roamin' Free* (TV). 1977: *Grayeagle. The Hunting Party*. 1978: *Fast Charlie – The Moonbeam Rider. Standing Tall* (TV). 1979: *The Sacketts* (TV). 1982: *The Beast Within. Timerider – The Adventure of Lyle Swann. Melanie. Sacred Ground* (revised version of *Grayeagle*). 1983: *Lone Wolf McQuade*. 1987: *Bulletproof*. 1988: *Red River* (TV). 1989: *River of Death*. 1990: *The Legend of Grizzly Adams*. 1994: *Lightning Jack*. 1995: *Casino*.

As director:
1964: *The Devil's Bedroom*. 1974: *A Boy and His Dog*.

JONES, Peter 1920–

Tall, often bespectacled, brown-haired, affable-looking British actor and playwright with easy-going air and a whimsical line in humour. In his comedy cameos for films, his liquidly cultivated tones have specialized in men from the ministry, civil servants and any bumblers subject to benevolent bewilderment. His somewhat highbrow radio comedy series with Peter Ustinov, *In all Directions*, gained a cult following during its several seasons in the early Fifties; more recently in the same medium, he has for many years been a popular panellist on the comedy programme *Just a Minute*. The Peter Jones in *The Blue Lagoon* (1948) is a child player.

1944: *Fanny by Gaslight* (US: *Man of Evil*). 1945: *Dead of Night*. 1946: *I See a Dark Stranger* (US: *The Adventuress*). 1947: *Vice Versa*. 1948: *Forbidden*. 1949: *Private Angelo*. 1950: *Cairo Road. Last Holiday. Chance of a Lifetime. The Franchise Affair*. 1951: *High Treason. Home to Danger. The Magic Box. The Browning Version*. 1952: *Miss Robin Hood. Time Gentlemen Please! 24 Hours of a Woman's Life* (US: *Affair in Monte Carlo*). *Angels One Five. Elstree Story. The Yellow Balloon. The Long Memory*. 1953: *Albert RN* (US: *Break to Freedom*). *Always a Bride. Innocents in Paris. The Good Beginning. A Day to Remember*. 1954: *The Red Dress. Forbidden Cargo. For Better, For Worse* (US: *Cocktails in the Kitchen*). 1955: *On Such a Night. John and Julie. Private's Progress*. 1956: *Charley Moon*. 1957: *Blue Murder at St Trinian's*. 1958: *Danger Within* (US: *Breakout*). 1959: *Operation Bullshine. School for Scoundrels*. 1960: *Never Let Go. The Bulldog Breed*. 1961: *Nearly a Nasty Accident. Romanoff and Juliet*. 1963: *A Stitch in Time. Father Came Too*. 1966: *Press for Time. Just Like a Woman. The Sandwich Man*. 1967: *Smashing Time. Carry On Doctor*. 1968: *Hot Millions*. 1974: *The Return of the Pink Panther*. 1975: *Confessions of a Pop Performer*. 1976: *Carry On England. Seven Nights in Japan*. 1977: **Marcia*. 1986: *The Children of Dynmouth* (TV). *Whoops Apocalypse*.

JORY, Victor 1902–1982

Tall, dark, Alaska-born Hollywood actor. If you needed a villain from 1932 to 1957, all you had to do was get out the black jacket and floral waistcoat and call for Victor Jory. Grim-faced Jory's bad guys looked as if they would brook very little mercy and he menaced most of the screen's cowboy heroes. Also a very sinister Oberon in *A Midsummer Night's Dream*. Died from a heart attack. His harsh tones were heard again in the compilation film *The Puppetoon Movie*, released in 1987.

1930: *Renegades*. 1932: *The Pride of the Legion. Second Hand Wife* (GB: *The Illegal Divorce*). 1933: *Handle with Care. Infernal Machine. State Fair. Broadway Bad* (GB: *Her Reputation*). *Sailor's Luck. Trick for Trick. I Loved You Wednesday. The Devil's in Love. My Woman. Smoky*. 1934: *He Was Her Man. I Believed in You. Pursued. Madame Du Barry. Murder in Trinidad. White Lies*. 1935: *Mills of the Gods. Too Tough to Kill. Escape from Devil's Island. Streamline Express. Party Wire. A Midsummer Night's Dream*. 1936: *Hell Ship Morgan. The King Steps Out. Meet Nero Wolfe. Rangle River*. 1937: *Glamorous Night. Bulldog Drummond at Bay. First Lady*. 1938: *The Adventures of Tom Sawyer*. 1939: *Dodge City. Man of Conquest. Women in the Wind. Wings of the Navy. Each Dawn I Die. Susannah of the Mounties. *Men with Whips. I Stole a Million. Gone with the Wind. Call a Messenger. Blackwell's Island*. 1940: *Cherokee Strip* (GB: *Fighting Marshal*). *Knights of the Range. The Green Archer* (serial). *The Light of Western Stars. The Lone Wolf Meets a Lady. River's End. The Girl from Havana. Lady with Red Hair. Give Us Wings. The Shadow* (serial). 1941: *Charlie Chan in Rio. Border Vigilantes. Wide Open Town. Bad Men of Missouri. Riders of the Timberline. Secrets of the Lone Wolf* (GB: *Secrets*). *The Stork Pays Off*. 1942: *Tombstone, the Town Too Tough to Die. Shut My Big Mouth*. 1943: *The Kansan* (GB: *Wagon Wheels*). *Hoppy Serves a Writ. Buckskin Frontier* (GB: *The Iron Road*). *Bar 20. The Unknown Guest. Colt Comrades. The Leather Burners. Power of the Press*. 1947: *A Voice is Born: the Story of Niklos Grafni* (voice only). 1948: *The Loves of Carmen. The Gallant Blade*. 1949: *A Woman's Secret. South of St Louis. Canadian Pacific. Fighting Man of the Plains*. 1950: *The Capture. The Cariboo Trail*. 1951: *Cave of Outlaws. Flaming Feather. The High-*

wayman. 1952: Toughest Man in Arizona. Son of Ali Baba. 1953: The Hindu (GB: Sabaka). Cat Women of the Moon. The Man from the Alamo. 1954: Valley of the Kings. 1956: Introduction to Erica. Lady in Fear (TV. GB: cinemas). Manfish (GB: Calypso). Death of a Scoundrel. Mr and Mrs McAdam (TV). Blackjack Ketchum, Desperado. 1957: Diary of a Nurse (TV). The Man Who Turned to Stone. Last Stagecoach West. 1960: The Fugitive Kind. 1962: The Miracle Worker. 1964: Cheyenne Autumn. 1965: Who Has Seen the Wind (TV). 1967: Ride the Wind (TV. GB: cinemas). 1968: Jigsaw (TV). 1969: Mackenna's Gold (narrator only). A Time for Dying. Perilous Voyage (TV). 1970: Flap (GB: The Last Warrior). The Trail of the Hunter. 1974: Papillon. Frasier the Sensuous Lion. 1976: Perilous Voyage (TV). 1977: Kino, the Padre on Horseback. 1978: Devil Dog – the Hound of Hell (TV). 1980: The Mountain Men.

JOSLYN, Allyn 1901–1981
Light-haired, moustachioed, pawky American actor with distinctive grey-green eyes. His round, indiarubber features could express handsomeness, prissiness, or pompousness, as the role required, but rather too often he was slated to play the suitor who was only in the film as a chopping-block for the hero. His sharply distinctive voice was also heard in thousands of radio programmes over a period of 40 years. Died from cardiac failure.

1937: They Won't Forget. Expensive Husbands. Hollywood Hotel. 1938: The Shining Hour. Sweethearts. 1939: Café Society. Only Angels Have Wings. Fast and Furious. 1940: If I Had My Way. The Great McGinty (GB: Down Went McGinty). Spring Parade. No Time for Comedy. 1941: This Thing Called Love. Bedtime Story. Hot Spot (GB: I Wake Up Screaming). 1942: The Wife Takes a Flyer (GB: A Yank in Dutch). My Sister Eileen. The Affairs of Martha (GB: Once Upon a Thursday). 1943: Young Ideas. The Immortal Sergeant. Heaven Can Wait. Dangerous Blondes. 1944: Bride by Mistake. Sweet and Low Down. The Imposter. Strange Affair. 1945: The Horn Blows at Midnight. Junior Miss. Colonel Effingham's Raid (GB: Man of the Hour). 1946: It Shouldn't Happen to a Dog. Thrill of Brazil. The Shocking Miss Pilgrim. 1948: If You Knew Susie. Moonrise. 1949: The Lady Takes a

Sailor. 1950: Harriet Craig. 1951: As Young As You Feel. 1952: I Love Melvin. 1953: Island in the Sky. Titanic. The Jazz Singer. 1956: The Fastest Gun Alive. You Can't Run Away from It. 1957: Public Pigeon No. One. 1963: Nightmare in the Sun. 1972: The Brothers O'Toole.

JOYCE, Yootha 1927–1980
Toothy blonde British actress with raucous tones and predatory look. She contributed a number of acerbic cameos, both nasty and nice, to British films of the 1960s, usually as working-class women with pretensions. Soon, though, she became a comedy star in the Peggy Mount tradition with her creation of an amorous ogress called Mildred on British television. At one time married (divorced 1968) to actor Glynn Edwards (q.v.). Died from cirrhosis of the liver.

1962: Sparrows Can't Sing. 1963: A Place to Go. 1964: Fanatic (US: Die, Die, My Darling). The Pumpkin Eater. 1965: Catch Us If You Can (US: Having a Wild Weekend). 1966: Kaleidoscope. A Man for All Seasons. 1967: Our Mother's House. Stranger in the House (US: Cop-Out). Charlie Bubbles. †Casino Royale. 1968: *Twenty Nine. 1969: All the Right Noises. 1970: Fragment of Fear. 1971: Burke and Hare. The Night Digger. 1972: Nearest and Dearest. Never Mind the Quality, Feel the Width. 1973: Frankenstein: the True Story (TV: GB: cinemas in abbreviated version). Steptoe and Son Ride Again. 1974: Man About The House. 1980: George and Mildred.

† Scenes deleted from final release print.

JULIA, Raul
(R. Julia y Arcelos) 1940–1994
Hollow-eyed, dark-haired, solidly-built, debonair if rather melancholy-looking Puerto Rican actor in Hollywood films, often as sardonic, dominant characters, or detectives who made their suspects feel distinctly uncomfortable. As well as providing somewhat larger-than-life back-up for stars, since his rise to prominence in the 1980s, Julia also tackled such disparate leading roles as the archbishop in Romero, the dissident bisexual in Kiss of the Spider Woman and the master of the house in The Addams Family. The son of a restaurant owner, he was also a formidable singer, four times Tony-

nominated in Broadway musicals. Most references give his date of birth as 1940, but the actor himself always insisted it was 1944. Died following a stroke.

1969: Stiletto. 1970: McCloud: Who Killed Miss USA? (TV). 1971: The Organization. The Panic in Needle Park. Been Down So Long It Looks Like Up to Me. 1975: Death Scream (TV). 1976: The Gumball Rally. 1978: Eyes of Laura Mars. A Life of Sin. 1981: Strong Medicine (TV). One from the Heart. 1982: The Escape Artist. Tempest. 1983: Overdrawn at the Memory Bank (TV). 1985: Compromising Positions. Kiss of the Spider Woman. 1986: The Penitent (released 1988). The Morning After. Florida Straits. 1987: La gran fiesta. The Alamo: 13 Days to Glory (TV). 1988: Tango Bar. Trading Hearts. Tequila Sunrise. Moon Over Parador. 1989: Mack the Knife. Romero. 1990: Frankenstein Unbound. Presumed Innocent. So Help Me God! The Rookie. Havana. 1991: Best Interests. The Addams Family. 1992: The Plague. 1993: Addams Family Values 1994: One Glorious Summer. Street-fighter.

JUNKIN, John 1930–
Dark-haired, balding British writer and comic actor, with thick London accent and 'ordinary bloke' looks. He began his career as a schoolteacher until scriptwriting took over his life and gradually led him into acting, at first with Joan Littlewood's Theatre Workshop. Subsequently he wrote hundreds of comedy scripts for TV and had his own series as well. Film appearances

usually minor cameos. In private life a great Scrabble enthusiast.

*1962: Sparrows Can't Sing. The Wrong Arm of the Law. The Break. Vengeance (US: The Brain). 1963: Heavens Above! The Primitives. Hot Enough for June (US: Agent 8¾). 1964: A Hard Day's Night. The Pumpkin Eater. 1966: The Wrong Box. Doctor in Clover. The Sandwich Man. Kaleidoscope. 1967: The Plank. How I Won the War. 1970: *Simon, Simon. 1972: Madigan: The London Beat (TV). 1973: Man at the Top. 1976: Confessions of a Driving Instructor. 1977: Confessions from a Holiday Camp. *Marcia. Wombling Free. 1978: Rosie Dixon Night Nurse. Brass Target. 1979: That Summer! Licensed to Love and Kill. 1988: A Handful of Dust. 1989: Chicago Joe and the Showgirl.*

JUSTICE, James Robertson 1905–1975
Glowering, red-bearded, large Scottish actor who was a naturalist and journalist before turning full-time actor in the 1940s and quickly becoming an essential part of the British cinema scene. He made several figures of history, including Henry VIII, larger than life, enlivening dozens of films before his retirement in 1970 – but never more so than as the irascible Sir Lancelot Spratt in the 'Doctor' comedies.

*1944: †Champagne Charlie. †Fiddlers Three. †For Those in Peril. 1946: †Hungry Hill. †Appointment With Crime. 1947: Vice Versa. My Brother Jonathan. 1948: Against the Wind. Quartet. Scott of the Antarctic. Whisky Galore! (US: Tight Little Island). 1949: Christopher Columbus. Stop Press Girl. Poet's Pub. Private Angelo. 1950: Prelude to Fame. My Daughter Joy (US: Operation X). The Magnet. The Black Rose. Blackmailed. 1951: Pool of London. David and Bathsheba. Anne of the Indies. The Lady Says No! Captain Horatio Hornblower RN. Circle of Danger. 1952: The Story of Robin Hood and His Merrie Men. Miss Robin Hood. The Voice of Merrill (US: Murder Will Out). Les Miserables. 1953: The Sword and the Rose. Rob Roy the Highland Rogue. 1954: Doctor in the House. 1955: Out of the Clouds. *Challenge of the North (narrator only). Above Us the Waves. Doctor at Sea. Land of the Pharaohs. An Alligator Named Daisy. Storm Over the Nile. 1956: The Living Idol. The Iron Petticoat. Moby Dick. Checkpoint. 1957: Doctor at Large. Souvenir d'Italie/It Happened in* Rome. Seven Thunders (US: The Beasts of Marseilles). Campbell's Kingdom. Thérèse Etienne. 1958: Orders to Kill. The Revenge of Frankenstein. 1959: Upstairs and Downstairs. 1960: Doctor in Love. Die Botschafterin. A French Mistress. Foxhole in Cairo. 1961: Very Important Person (US: A Coming-Out Party). The Guns of Navarone. Murder She Said. Raising the Wind (US: Roommates). 1962: A Pair of Briefs. Crooks Anonymous. Guns of Darkness. Dr Crippen. Le repos du guerrier (GB: Warrior's Rest). Mystery Submarine. The Fast Lady. 1963: Father Came Too. Das Feuerschiff. Doctor in Distress. Hell Is Empty (released 1967). 1965: You Must Be Joking! The Face of Fu Manchu. Up from the Beach. Those Magnificent Men in Their Flying Machines (narrator only). 1966: Doctor in Clover. 1967: The Trygon Factor. Two Weeks in September. Histoires extraordinares (GB: Tales of Mystery). Lange Beine, lange Finger. 1968: Chitty Chitty Bang Bang, Mayerling. 1969: Zeta One. 1970: Some Will, Some Won't Doctor in Trouble.*

† As James Robertson
‡ As Seamus Mor Na Feasag

KAHN, Madeline 1942–
Big-chinned, purse-lipped American comic actress with copper-coloured hair and a unique way of chewing round a line before spitting it out. She was popular for a while in escapist satires of the 1970s, notably those of Mel Brooks. Trained as an opera singer and started her career in the chorus of *Kiss Me Kate* on stage in the mid-1960s. In 1983 she started her own television show. Nominated for best supporting actress Oscars in *Paper Moon* and *Blazing Saddles*. More often seen on television than in films in recent years.

*1968: *The Dove. 1972: What's Up, Doc? 1973: Paper Moon. From the Mixed-Up Files of Mrs Basil E Frankweiler (GB: The Hideaways). 1974: Blazing Saddles. Young Frankenstein. 1975: At Long Last Love. Won Ton Ton, the Dog Who Saved Hollywood. The Adventure of Sherlock Holmes' Smarter Brother. 1977: High Anxiety. 1978: The Cheap Detective. 1979: The Muppet Movie. Simon. 1980: Happy Birthday, Gemini. Wholly Moses! First Family (GB: TV). 1981: History of the World* Part I. *1982: Slapstick (US: Slapstick of Another Kind). 1983: Yellowbeard. 1984: City Heat. 1985: Clue. 1986: An American Tail (voice only). My Little Pony (voice only). 1990: Betsy's Wedding. 1992: For Richer, For Poorer (TV). 1994: Mixed Nuts.*

KARLIN, Miriam
(M. Samuels) 1925–
Thin, plain-looking, corncrake-voiced British actress with dark hair, wide smile and strong personality. She started her career entertaining wartime troops in ENSA shows, then brought her talents to stage revue, films and television, where she became a nationally known figure as the militant shop steward in *The Rag Trade* comedy series. Films never really made the most of her, and she later toured in one-woman shows.

1952: The Holly and the Ivy. Down Among the Z Men. 1955: The Deep Blue Sea. The Woman for Joe. Fun at St Fanny's. 1956: The Big Money (released 1958). A Touch of the Sun. 1957: The Flesh is Weak. 1958: Room at the Top. Carve Her Name with Pride. 1960: The Entertainer. Hand in Hand. Crossroads to Crime. 1961: Watch It Sailor! On the Fiddle (US: Operation Snafu). 1962: The Phantom of the Opera. I Thank a Fool. 1963: The Small World of Sammy Lee. Heavens Above! Ladies Who Do. 1964: The Bargee. 1966: Just Like a Woman. 1971: A Clockwork Orange. 1975: Barry Lyndon. Mahler. Dick Deadeye (voice only). 1987: The Attic: The Hiding of Anne Frank (TV). 1989: Jekyll & Hyde (TV). 1992: UTZ.

KARNS, Roscoe 1893–1970

Red-haired light relief of dozens of Hollywood films of the 1930s and 1940s — a sort of straighter Red Skelton. Of Irish heritage, Karns took to the stage at 15, coming to films in silent days to play characters who looked on the brighter side of life. Sometimes he was a sidekick of the hero, at others a fast-talking reporter. He left films in the post-war years, working steadily in television until 1961. His son, Todd Karns (Roscoe Karns Jr), much more ruggedly handsome than his father, also appeared in pictures.

1913: A Western Governor's Humanity. 1919: Poor Relations. *Virtuous Husbands. 1920: The Life of the Party. The Family Honor. 1921: The Man Turner. Too Much Married. 1922: Conquering the Woman. Her Own Money. Afraid to Fight. The Trooper. 1923: Other Men's Daughters. 1924: Bluff (GB: The Four Flusher). The Midnight Express. The Foolish Virgin. 1925: Dollar Down. Headlines. Overland Limited. 1926: Ritzy. 1927: Ten Modern Commandments. Wings. The Jazz Singer. 1928: Beggars of Life. Jazz Mad. Beau Sabreur. Object — Alimony. Win That Girl. Warming Up. The Desert Bride. Moran of the Marines. Something Always Happens. 1929: This Thing Called Love. New York Nights. Shopworn Angel. 1930: Man Trouble. Troopers Three. Safety in Numbers. The Costello Case (GB: The Costello Murder Case). Little Accident. Lights of New York. 1931: Laughing Sinners. Leftover Ladies (GB: Broken Links). The Gorilla. Dirigible. Many a Slip. 1932: Ladies of the Big House. Pleasure. Rockabye. Week-End Marriage (GB: Working Wives). Lawyer Man. Night After Night. I Am a Fugitive from a Chain Gang. Two against the World. Roadhouse Murder. The Crooked Circle. One Way Passage. If I Had a Million. Undercover Man. The Stowaway. 1933: One Sunday Afternoon. Today We Live. Gambling Ship. Alice in Wonderland. A Lady's Profession. 20,000 Years in Sing Sing. 1934: Come on, Marines. Search for Beauty. Shoot the Works (GB: Thank Your Lucky Stars). Elmer and Elsie. I Sell Anything. Twentieth Century. It Happened One Night. The Women in His Life. 1935: Red Hot Tires (GB: Racing Luck). Two-Fisted. Stolen Harmony. Four Hours to Kill. Wings in the Dark. Alibi Ike. Front Page Woman. 1936: Border Flight. Woman Trap. Three Cheers for Love. Three Married Men. Cain and Mabel. 1937: Murder Goes to College.

Clarence. A Night of Mystery. On Such a Night. Partners in Crime. 1938: Tip-Off Girls. You and Me. Scandal Street. Dangerous to Know. Thanks for the Memory. 1939: Everything's on Ice. That's Right — You're Wrong. King of Chinatown. Dancing Co-Ed (GB: Every Other Inch a Lady). 1940: Double Alibi. His Girl Friday. Ladies Must Live. Saturday's Children. Meet the Missus. They Drive by Night (GB: The Road to Frisco). 1941: Footsteps in the Dark. Petticoat Politics. The Gay Vagabond. *Black Eyes and Blue. *Half Shot at Sunrise. Woman of the Year. 1942: The Road to Happiness. A Tragedy at Midnight. Yokel Boy (GB: Hitting the Headlines). You Can't Escape Forever. 1943: His Butler's Sister. Stage Door Canteen. Old Acquaintance. My Son, the Hero. 1944: The Navy Way. Minstrel Man. Hi, Good Lookin'. 1945: I Ring Doorbells. One Way to Love. 1946: The Kid from Brooklyn. It's a Wonderful Life! Avalanche. Down Missouri Way. 1947: That's My Man. Vigilantes of Boomtown. Will Tomorrow Ever Come? 1948: Texas, Brooklyn and Heaven (GB: The Girl from Texas). The Devil's Cargo. The Inside Story. Speed to Spare. 1958: Onionhead. 1963: Man's Favorite Sport?

KASKET, Harold 1926–

Chubby British actor with thick black moustache, plus hair and horn-rimmed glasses to match. Originally a comedy impressionist, he came to British films in post-war years and was almost always seen as unctuous foreigners, rubbing their hands, beaming an oily beam, and giving out with such familiar lines as 'You like the English girl, sir? She weel be on again after the next show!' Busy in films until 1961, but much more often seen on TV from then on.

1948: No Orchids for Miss Blandish. 1949: Children of Chance. 1951: Hotel Sahara. 1952: Made in Heaven. Moulin Rouge. 1953: Saadia. The House of the Arrow. 1954: Up to His Neck. One Good Turn. Beau Brummell. Out of the Clouds. A Kid for Two Farthings. 1955: The Dark Avenger (US: The Warriors). Doctor at Sea. Born for Trouble. Dust and Gold. Man of the Moment. 1956: Bhowani Junction. The Man Who Knew Too Much. 1957: Interpol (US: Pickup Alley). The Key Man. Manuela (US: Stowaway Girl). Naked Earth. 1958: Life is a Circus. The Lady is a

Square. Wonderful Things! The Scapegoat. The 7th Voyage of Sinbad. 1959: Carlton-Browne of the FO (US: Man in a Cocked Hat). SOS Pacific. Whirlpool. The Mouse That Roared. The Heart of a Man. Tommy the Toreador. The Navy Lark. 1960: Sands of the Desert. 1961: The Boy Who Stole a Million. The Green Helmet. A Weekend with Lulu. The Greengage Summer (US: Loss of Innocence). The Roman Spring of Mrs Stone. Village of Daughters. The Fourth Square. 1962: Nine Hours to Rama. 1964: The Yellow Rolls Royce. 1965: The Return of Mr Moto. 1966: Arabesque. Doctor in Clover. 1967: Follow That Camel. 1969: Where's Jack? 1982: Trail of the Pink Panther. 1983: Curse of the Pink Panther.

KASZNAR, Kurt

(K. Serwischer) 1912–1979

Plumpish, flat-faced Austrian-born actor with strikingly dark hair and eyes, around on the Hollywood (mostly M-G-M) scene quite a bit in the 1950s, following long stage experience in Europe and (from 1936) America. He ambled amiably through a succession of sub-S. Z. Sakall (qv) roles in musicals, comedies and adventures, providing some attractively fractured English. Married/divorced actress Leora Dana, second of two. Made film debut as a child. Died from cancer.

1924: Max, King of the Circus. 1951: The Light Touch. 1952: Glory Alley. The Happy Time. Anything Can Happen. Lovely to Look At. Talk about a Stranger. 1953: Give a Girl a Break. Sombrero. Ride, Vaquero! Lili. All the Brothers Were Valiant. The Great Diamond Robbery. Kiss Me Kate. 1954: Valley of the Kings. The Last Time I Saw Paris. 1955: Jump Into Hell. My Sister Eileen. Flame of the Islands. 1956: Fanny. The Man Who Knew Too Much. Anything Goes. 1957: Legend of the Lost. The Customs of the Country (TV). A Farewell to Arms. 1958: The Journey. The Bridge of San Luis Rey (TV). 1959: For the First Time. Thieves' Carnival (TV). 1960: Volpone (TV). 1961: Waiting for Godot (TV). 1962: Helden (US: Arms and the Man). 55 Days at Peking. 1963: The Thrill of It All. 1967: Code Name: Heraclitus (TV). Casino Royale. The Perils of Pauline. The Ambushers. The King's Pirate. 1968: The Smugglers (TV). 1971: Once Upon a Dead Man (TV). 1972: The Female Instinct (TV. GB: The Snoop Sisters). 1978: Suddenly, Love.

KATCH, Kurt
(Isser Kac) 1896–1958

This Polish-born actor was a shavenheaded gremlin who was handy to have around in evil-cohort roles of Hollywood's wartime years, following his flight from the Nazis in 1937. His little eyes plotted all kinds of dire deeds then, but he found film work hard to get in the post-war years. His career picked up a bit in the 1950s, but at 62 he died during an operation for cancer.

1938: Tkies khaf/The Vow. 1940: The Mortal Storm. 1941: Don Winslow of the Navy (serial). Man at Large. The Wolf-Man. 1942: Counter Espionage. They Came to Blow Up America. Desperate Journey. Secret Agent of Japan. The Wife Takes a Flyer. Quiet Please Murder. Berlin Correspondent. Edge of Darkness. 1943: Mission to Moscow. Background to Danger. The Strange Death of Adolf Hitler. Watch on the Rhine. Secret Service in Darkest Africa (serial. GB: Desert Agent). Ali Baba and the 40 Thieves. The Purple V. 1944: Make Your Own Bed. The Conspirators. The Purple Heart. The Mask of Dimitrios. The Seventh Cross. The Mummy's Curse. 1945: Salome, Where She Danced. 1946: Angel on My Shoulder. Rendezvous 24. 1947: Strange Journey. Song of Love. 1954: Secret of the Incas. The Adventures of Hajji Baba. 1955: Abbott and Costello Meet the Keystone Kops. Abbott and Costello Meet the Mummy. 1956: Hot Cars. Never Say Goodbye. 1957: The Girl in the Kremlin. The Beast of Budapest. The Pharaoh's Curse. 1958: The Young Lions. The Gift of Love.

KAYE, Stubby
(Bernard Kotzin) 1918–

Roly-poly American comedian, singer, actor and entertainer with easy-going personality, in vaudeville after winning a talent contest at 21, and in the theatre from 1950 when he created Nicely-Nicely Johnson in *Guys and Dolls*, a role he would later repeat for his screen musical debut. His hit song from that show, 'Sit Down You're Rockin' the Boat', remains his best-remembered number, but the cinema has made only infrequent use of his throaty-voiced talents.

1953: Taxi. 1955: Guys and Dolls. 1956: You Can't Run Away from It. 1959: Li'l Abner. 1962: 40 Pounds of Trouble. 1963: The Cool Mikado. 1964: Sex and the Single Girl. 1965: Cat Ballou. 1967: The Way West. 1968: Sweet

Charity. Can Hieronymous Merkin Ever Forget Mercy Humppe and Find True Happiness? 1969: The Cockeyed Cowboys of Calico County (GB: TV, as A Woman for Charlie). The Monitors. 1970: Cool It Carol! (US: The Dirtiest Girl I Ever Met). 1975: Six Pack Annie. 1981: Goldie and the Boxer Go to Hollywood (TV). 1984: Ellis Island (TV miniseries shortened for cinemas). 1988: Who Framed Roger Rabbit. The Big Knife (TV).

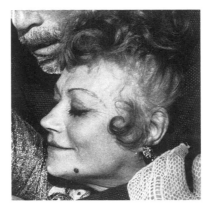

KEDROVA, Lila 1918–

Small, dark-haired, sharp-faced, voracious Russian-born actress, a French resident from the age of 10. In films from her mid thirties, she was hardly known at all on the international scene before her Academy Award-winning portrayal of the pathetic, ageing prostitute in *Zorba the Greek*. Her profile was never as high again, but she has frequently beguiled us in film ventures all over the world, despite remaining firmly based in Paris.

1953: Weg ohne Umkehr (GB and US: No Way Back). Le defroqué. 1954: Futures vedettes (GB: Sweet Sixteen). Razzia sur la chnouff. Les impures. 1955: Des gens sans importance. 1956: Calle mayor (US: The Lovemaker). Jusqu'au dernier. 1957: Montparnasse 19 (GB: The Lovers of Montparnasse. US: Modigliani of Montparnasse). Fino all'ultimo. 1958: La femme et le pantin (GB: A Woman Like Satan). 1959: Mon pôte le gitan. 1964: Zorba the Greek. 1965: A High Wind in Jamaica. 1966: Torn Curtain. Penelope. 1968: Tenderly (GB: The Girl Who Couldn't Say No). The Run-

around. 1969: The Kremlin Letter. 1971: Time for Loving. 1972: Cool Million (TV). Escape to the Sun. 1973: Soft Beds, Hard Battles (US: Undercovers Hero). 1974: Perchè?! 1975: Eliza's Horoscope (released 1977). 1976: The Tenant. 1977: †March or Die. Widow's Nest. Moi, fleur bleue (US: Stop Calling Me Baby!). 1979: Les égouts du paradis. Le cavaleur. Clair de femme. 1980: Tell Me a Riddle. The Red Tide (released 1984 as Bloodtide). 1983: Testament. Sword of the Valiant. 1988: Some Girls (GB: Sisters). 1993: La prossima volta il fuoco. 1995: Getting Away with Murder.

† Scenes deleted from final release print

KEEN, Geoffrey 1916–

Adaptable, tetchy-looking British player with receding dark hair and cultured, deliberate speech guaranteed to annoy subordinates of the characters he played. At first in helpful roles, but later as grouchy bosses – he would have made a good 'M' in the Bond films if Bernard Lee (*qv*) hadn't got the job first, and indeed eventually assumed Lee's mantle after his death. Son of distinguished stage player Malcolm Keen (1887–1970), who also played some film roles.

*1946: Riders of the New Forest. Odd Man Out. 1948: The Fallen Idol. The Small Back Room (US: Hour of Glory). It's Hard to be Good. 1949: The Third Man. *Call-Up. 1950: Treasure Island. Seven Days to Noon. The Clouded Yellow. 1951: Chance of a Lifetime. Cheer the Brave. High Treason. Green Grow the Rushes. His Excellency. Cry the Beloved Country (US: African Fury). 1952: Hunted (US: The Stranger in Between). Lady in the Fog (US: Scotland Yard Inspector). Angels One Five. The Long Memory. 1953: Rob Roy the Highland Rogue. Malta Story. Meet Mr Lucifer. Genevieve. Turn the Key Softly. The 'Maggie' (US: High and Dry). 1954: Face the Music (US: The Black Glove). Doctor in the House. The Divided Heart. Carrington VC (US: Court-Martial). The Glass Cage (US: The Glass Tomb). 1955: Passage Home. Doctor at Sea. Portrait of Alison (US: Postmark for Danger). Storm Over the Nile. The Man Who Never Was. 1956: A Town Like Alice. Smiley. The Long Arm (US: The Third Key). House of Secrets (US: Triple Deception). Yield to the Night (US: Blonde Sinner). Loser Takes All. Zarak. The Spanish Gardener. Sailor Beware! (US: Panic in the Parlor). Town on Trial!*

Fortune Is a Woman (US: She Played with Fire). 1957: The Scamp. The Birthday Present. Doctor at Large. The Secret Place. 1958: Nowhere to Go. Carve Her Name with Pride (voice only). The Scapegoat. 1959: Horrors of the Black Museum. Beyond This Place (US: Web of Evidence). Devil's Bait. The Boy and the Bridge. Deadly Record. Sink the Bismarck! The Angry Silence. 1960: *The Dover Road Mystery. 1961: No Love for Johnnie. Spare the Rod. *The Silent Weapon. The Malpas Mystery. Raising the Wind (US: Roommates). 1962: The Spiral Road. Live Now – Pay Later. A Matter of WHO. The Inspector (US: Lisa). The Prince and the Pauper. The Mind Benders. Torpedo Bay/Finche dura la tempesta. 1963: The Cracksman. Return to Sender. Dr Syn Alias the Scarecrow. 1965: Doctor Zhivago. The Heroes of Telemark. 1966: Born Free. 1967: Berserk! 1968: Thunderbird 6 (voice only). 1970: Cromwell. Taste the Blood of Dracula. 1971: Sacco and Vanzetti. 1972: Living Free. Doomwatch. 1974: QB VII (TV). 1977: The Spy Who Loved Me. Holocaust 2000 (US: The Chosen). No. 1 of the Secret Service. 1979: Licensed to Love and Kill. Moonraker. 1980: The Rise and Fall of Idi Amin. 1981: For Your Eyes Only. 1983: Octopussy. 1985: A View to a Kill. 1987: The Living Daylights.

KEIR, Andrew 1926–

Big, bluff, often bearded Scottish actor whose early films included whimsical comedies but who, from the late 1950s on, both in the cinema and TV, was almost always seen as towers of strength. Seemingly a certainty for the role of Little John in Robin Hood, he somehow managed to steer clear of it, but there were an awful lot of costume dramas as professional soldiers and the like, plus success in a couple of television series in the 1970s.

1950: The Lady Craved Excitement. The Gorbals Story. 1952: The Brave Don't Cry. Laxdale Hall (US: Scotch on the Rocks). 1953: The 'Maggie' (US: High and Dry). 1956: Suspended Alibi (US: Suspected Alibi). 1958: Heart of a Child. High Flight. A Night to Remember. Tread Softly, Stranger. 1960: Tunes of Glory. The Day They Robbed the Bank of England. 1961: Greyfriars Bobby. The Pirates of Blood River. 1962: Torpedo Bay/Finche dura la tempesta. 1963: The Fall of the Roman Empire. Cleopatra. The Devil-Ship Pirates.

1964: Lord Jim. 1966: Dracula Prince of Darkness. Daleks Invasion Earth 2150 AD. The Fighting Prince of Donegal. 1967: The Long Duel. The Viking Queen. Quatermass and the Pit (US: Five Million Miles to Earth). Attack on the Iron Coast. 1969: Adam's Woman. The Royal Hunt of the Sun. 1970: The Last Grenade (US: Grigsby). 1971: Zeppelin. Blood from the Mummy's Tomb. The Night Visitor. Mary Queen of Scots. 1973: Catholics (TV). 1978: Meetings with Remarkable Men. The Thirty-Nine Steps. Absolution. 1980: Lion of the Desert/Omar Mukhtar, Lion of the Desert. 1984: Hunters of the Deep. 1990: The Shell Seekers (TV). 1993: Dragon World. 1995: Rob Roy.

KEITH, Ian
See Yurka, Blanche

KEITH, Robert 1896–1966

Worried-looking, darting-eyed, skull-faced American supporting actor with receding brown hair. He began his career as a singer, then took up straight acting roles; but his main occupation in pre-war years was writing, penning the occasional play in between working as a dialogue writer for Universal and Columbia Studios. In postwar years, he made quick strides towards the top of cast lists, often in tense, nervous roles. Father of film star Brian Keith.

1924: The Other Kind of Love. 1930: Just Imagine. 1931: Bad Company. 1939: Spirit of Culver (GB: Man's Heritage). Destry Rides Again. 1947: Boomerang! Kiss of Death. 1949: My Foolish Heart. 1950: Edge of Doom (GB: Stronger Than Fear). Woman on the Run. Branded. The Reformer and the Redhead. 1951: Fourteen Hours. Here Comes the Groom. I Want You. 1952: Just Across the Street. Somebody Loves Me. 1953: Battle Circus. The Wild One. Small Town Girl. Devil's Canyon. 1954: Drum Beat. Young at Heart. 1955: Underwater! Guys and Dolls. Love Me or Leave Me. 1956: Ransom! Written on the Wind. Between Heaven and Hell. 1957: Men in War. My Man Godfrey. 1958: The Lineup. Tempest. 1959: They Came to Cordura. 1960: Cimarron. 1961: Posse from Hell. Duel of Champions.

KELLAWAY, Cecil 1891–1973

Jolly, round-faced, plump-cheeked, stocky Hollywood actor with silvery hair. Although born in South Africa, initiating his acting

career in Australia and not all that short of stature, he soon became Hollywood's favorite leprechaun. His characters were often wise, sometimes mischievous (notably as the centuries-old warlock in I Married a Witch) and occasionally magic. Went on acting until illness forced his retirement in 1970. Oscar nominee for The Luck of the Irish and Guess Who's Coming to Dinner.

1933: The Hayseeds. 1936: It Isn't Done. 1938: Mr Chedworth Steps Out. Double Danger. Everybody's Doing It. Annabel Takes a Tour. Law of the Underworld. This Marriage Business. Maid's Night Out. Night Spot. Wise Girl. Blonde Cheat. Tarnished Angel. 1939: We Are Not Alone. The Sun Never Sets. Intermezzo (GB: Escape to Happiness). Wuthering Heights. Gunga Din. The Under-Pup. 1940: Mexican Spitfire. The Invisible Man Returns. Adventure in Diamonds. Phantom Raiders. Brother Orchid. The Mummy's Hand. The House of the Seven Gables. Mexican Spitfire Out West. The Letter. South of Suez. Diamond Frontier. The Lady With Red Hair. 1941: West Point Widow. The Night of January 16th. A Very Young Lady. Birth of the Blues. New York Town. Burma Convoy. Small Town Deb. Bahama Passage. Appointment for Love. 1942: The Lady Has Plans. Take a Letter, Darling (GB: The Green-Eyed Woman). I Married a Witch. Are Husbands Necessary? Star-Spangled Rhythm. My Heart Belongs to Daddy. Night in New Orleans. 1943: The Crystal Ball. Forever and a Day. It Ain't Hay (GB: Money for Jam). The Good Fellows. 1944: Frenchman's Creek. Mrs Parkington. And Now Tomorrow. Practically Yours. 1945: Bring on the Girls. Love Letters. Kitty. 1946: Monsieur Beaucaire. The Cockeyed Miracle (GB: Mr Griggs Returns). The Postman Always Rings Twice. Easy to Wed. 1947: Unconquered. Variety Girl. Always Together. 1948: The Decision of Christopher Blake. The Luck of the Irish. Joan of Arc. Portrait of Jennie (GB: Jennie). 1949: Down to the Sea in Ships. 1950: The Reformer and the Redhead. Kim. 1951: Harvey. Half Angel. Francis Goes to the Races. The Highwayman. Katie Did It. Thunder in the East. 1952: Just Across the Street. My Wife's Best Friend. 1953: Young Bess. Cruisin' Down the River. The Beast from 20,000 Fathoms. Paris Model. Hurricane at Pilgrim Hill. 1955: Interrupted Melody. Female on the Beach. The Prodigal. 1956: Toy Tiger. 1957: Johnny Trouble. 1958: The Proud Rebel. Verdict of Three (TV). 1959:

The Shaggy Dog. 1960: The Private Lives of Adam and Eve. Cage of Evil. 1961: Tammy Tell Me True. Francis of Assisi. 1962: Zotz! 1963: The Cardinal. 1964: Hush ... Hush, Sweet Charlotte. The Confession (GB: TV, as Quick! Let's Get Married). 1965: The Adventures of Bullwhip Griffin 1966: Spinout (GB: California Holiday). 1967: Fitzwilly (GB: Fitzwilly Strikes Back). Guess Who's Coming to Dinner. 1968: A Garden of Cucumbers. 1970: The Wacky Zoo of Morgan City (TV). Getting Straight.

KELLEY, Barry
(Edward Kelley) 1908–1991
Expansive (6 ft 2 in, 230 lb), brown-haired (with distinctive 'space' in the centre), deep-voiced, potato-faced, tight-lipped American actor, an ace at corrupt figures in high places. Born in Chicago of Irish parents, he made his theatrical debut in 1930, and remained in that medium until 1947, when brought to Hollywood by director Elia Kazan for a role in Boomerang! He subsequently stayed to play grafters, judges and tough policemen until his early retirement in 1968. Died from congestive heart failure.

1947: Boomerang! 1948: Force of Evil. Ma and Pa Kettle. 1949: Mr Belvedere Goes to College. Red, Hot and Blue. Fighting Man of the Plains. Too Late for Tears. Knock on Any Door. The Undercover Man. Johnny Stool Pigeon. Thelma Jordon (GB: The File on Thelma Jordon). There's a Girl in My Heart. 1950: The Killer That Stalked New York (GB: The Frightened City). The Asphalt Jungle. 711 Ocean Drive. Southside 1–1000 (GB: Forgery). Love That Brute. The Capture. Black Hand. Wabash Avenue. Right Cross. The Great Missouri Raid. Singing Guns. 1951: Flying Leathernecks. Francis Goes to the Races. 1952: Carrie. The Well. Back at the Front (GB: Willie and Joe in Tokyo). Woman of the North Country. 1953: Law and Order. Remains to be Seen. South Sea Woman. Champ for a Day. Vice Squad (GB: The Girl in Room 17). 1954: The Shanghai Story. The Long Wait. 1955: Women's Prison. New York Confidential. 1956: Accused of Murder. 1957: The Wings of Eagles. Monkey on My Back. The Tall Stranger. Gunfire at Indian Gap. 1958: The Buccaneer. Buchanan Rides Alone. 1960: The Police Dog Story. Elmer Gantry. Ice Palace. 1961: Secret of Deep

Harbor. The Clown and the Kid. Jack the Giant Killer. 1962: The Manchurian Candidate. 1964: Rio Conchos. Robin and the Seven Hoods. 1968: The Extraordinary Seaman. The Love Bug.

KELLEY, DeForest 1920–
Dark-haired, open-eyed, wry-mouthed American actor whose precise features could almost in their younger days have belonged to the hero of a puppet series. The son of a Baptist minister from Atlanta, Georgia, Kelley went to California as a teenager, obtaining minor theatre and radio work as an actor and singer (he can supposedly be spotted as one of the chorus of 'stout-hearted men' in MGM's New Moon) and working as a lift-man to make ends meet. Roles in naval training films led to work in films in post-war years; he was briefly in leading roles, but his career was going nowhere as impassive gunmen in westerns when he signed on as TV's Doc 'Bones' McCoy in Star Trek, a role which kept him busy on and off for almost 30 years.

1940: New Moon. 1947: Fear in the Night. Variety Girl. 1948: Canon City. 1949: The Duke of Chicago. Malaya (GB: East of the Rising Sun). 1950: The Men. 1953: Taxi. 1955: House of Bamboo. The View from Pompey's Head (GB: Secret Interlude). Illegal. 1956: Tension at Table Rock. The Man in the Gray Flannel Suit. Gunfight at the OK Corral. 1957: The Velvet Alley (TV). Raintree County. 1958: The Law and Jake Wade. 1959: Warlock. 1963: Gunfight at Comanche Creek. 1964: Where Love Has Gone. Black Spurs. 1965: Marriage on the Rocks. Town Tamer. 1966: Apache Uprising. Johnny Reno. Waco. 1972: Night of the Lepus. 1979: Star Trek: The Motion Picture. 1982: Star Trek II: The Wrath of Khan. 1984: Star Trek III: The Search for Spock. 1986: The Voyage Home: Star Trek IV. 1989: Star Trek V: The Final Frontier. 1991: Star Trek VI: The Undiscovered Country.

KELLOGG, John 1916–
Stocky, whippet-like American actor with dark, tightly wavy hair and sharp, furtive features. After some success in the theatre, he made a few film appearances in the early 1940s before war service in the US Marine

Corps interrupted his career. Film appearances after that continued to be sporadic, usually in modern dress, and often as fast-talking minor gangsters who were soon outwitted by the hero. Sometimes Kellogg would doff his suit and flashy tie in favour of leather jerkins or, occasionally, service uniform, in which his plucky, pugnacious characters belied his shady other half. Television and the theatre dominated his time after 1954, the former medium giving him a running role as Jack Chandler in the popular Peyton Place. Sometimes billed as John Kellog or John G Kellog.

1940: High School. Sailor's Lady. 1941: Among the Living. *Glove Affair. Young Tom Edison. Knockout/Right to the Heart. Mob Town. 1942: Pride of the Yankees. To Be or Not to Be. 1944: Thirty Seconds Over Tokyo. Wing and a Prayer. Miss Susie Slagle's (released 1946). 1945: The Crimson Canary. What Next, Corporal Hargrove? This Man's Navy. A Walk in the Sun. 1946: Mr District Attorney. Because of Him. Without Reservations. Somewhere in the Night. The Strange Love of Martha Ivers. Suddenly It's Spring. 1947: Killer McCoy. The Gangster. Johnny O'Clock. King of the Wild Horses. The Thirteenth Hour. Robin Hood of Texas. Out of the Past (GB: Build My Gallows High). 1948: Station West. Borrowed Trouble. Fighting Back. Secret Service Investigator. Sinister Journey. 1949: House of Strangers. Bad Men of Tombstone. Hold That Baby! Port of New York. Samson and Delilah. Twelve O'Clock High. 1950: Bunco Squad. Hunt the Man Down. Kansas Raiders. The Enforcer (GB: Murder Inc). 1951: Elephant Stampede (GB: Bomba and the Elephant Stampede). Come Fill the Cup. Tomorrow is Another Day. 1952: Rancho Notorious. The Raiders/Riders of Vengeance. The Greatest Show on Earth. Jet Job. 1953: The Fighting Lawman. The Silver Whip. Those Redheads from Seattle. 1954: Gorilla at Large. African Manhunt. 1956: Edge of the City (GB: A Man is Ten Feet Tall). 1961: Go Naked in the World. Convicts Four (GB: Reprieve!). 1966: The Doomsday Flight (TV. GB: cinemas). 1968: Judd for the Defense: Fall of a Skylark (TV). 1970: Night Slaves (TV). 1972: The Bravos (TV). 1973: A Knife for the Ladies. 1975: The Silence (TV). 1981: Raggedy Man. Kent State (TV). 1986: Blind Justice (TV). 1987: Orphans. 1989: Jacob I Have Loved (TV).

KELLY, Patsy
(Sarah Kelly) 1910–1981
Dynamic little dark-haired, plump-jowled American actress who forsook a career as a dancing teacher to come to Hollywood as star comedienne in two-reelers, and play supporting roles in features, often as wise-cracking maids, or gutsy, lower-class girl-friends. She left show business in the wartime years, but returned in 1960 for some welcome cameo roles. Died from cancer. Never married.

*1929: A Single Man. 1931: *The Grand Dame. 1933: Going Hollywood. *Beauty and the Bus. *Air Fright. *Backs to Nature. 1934: *Maid in Hollywood. *Soup and Fish. The Countess of Monte Cristo. The Party's Over. *Babes in the Goods. *I'll Be Suing You. *Roaming Vandals. The Girl from Missouri (GB: 100 Per Cent Pure). *Three Chumps Ahead. Transatlantic Merry-Go-Round. *Opened by Mistake. *One Horse Farmers. *Done in Oil. *Bum Voyage (GB: Bon Voyage). 1935: *Treasure Blues. *The Tin Man. *Sing, Sister, Sing. Go into Your Dance (GB: Casino de Paree). Every Night at Eight. Page Miss Glory. Thanks a Million. *The Misses Stooge. *Slightly Static. *Top Flat. *Hot Money. *Twin Triplets. *All American Toothache. 1936: Private Number. Kelly the Second. Sing, Baby, Sing. Pigskin Parade (GB: Harmony Parade). *Pan Handlers. *Hill-Tillies. *At Sea Ashore. 1937: Nobody's Baby. Wake Up and Live. Pick a Star. Ever Since Eve. 1938: Merrily We Live. There Goes My Heart. The Cowboy and the Lady. 1939: The Gorilla. 1940: Hit Parade of 1941. *The Happiest Man on Earth. Road Show. 1941: Topper Returns. Broadway Limited. 1942: Playmates. Sing Your Worries Away. In Old California. *Screen Snapshots No. 99. 1943: My Son, the Hero. Ladies' Day. Danger! Women at Work. 1947: *Babies, They're Wonderful. 1960: Please Don't Eat the Daisies. The Crowded Sky. 1964: The Naked Kiss. 1966: Ghost in the Invisible Bikini. 1967: C'mon, Let's Live a Little. 1968: Rosemary's Baby. 1969: The Pigeon (TV). The Phynx. 1976: Freaky Friday. 1978: North Avenue Irregulars (GB: Hill's Angels).*

KEMP, Jeremy
(Edmund Walker) 1934–
Scottish actor of red-gold hair and florid features who achieved his first big success in the TV series *Z Cars*, then went into

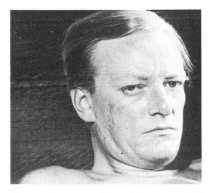

films, taking a number of character lead roles by the scruff of the neck and visibly shaking them around. He has kept featured billing but despite one or two eye-catching performances did not become a box-office star.

1963: Cleopatra. 1964: Dr Terror's House of Horrors. Face of a Stranger. 1965: Operation Crossbow (US: The Great Spy Mission). Cast a Giant Shadow. 1966: The Blue Max. 1967: A Twist of Sand. Assignment K. 1968: The Strange Affair. The Games. 1969: Darling Lili. 1970: Eyewitness. 1972: Pope Joan. 1973: The Belstone Fox. The Blockhouse. 1976: The Seven-Per-Cent Solution. East of Elephant Rock. Queen of Diamonds. 1977: The Thoroughbreds (later Treasure Seekers). A Bridge Too Far. Leopard in the Snow. 1978: Keefer (TV). 1979: The Prisoner of Zenda. Caravans. 1982: The Return of the Soldier. Phantom of the Opera (TV). 1983: Uncommon Valor. 1984: Top Secret! 1988: When the Whales Came. Duel of Hearts (TV). Reasonable Force (TV). 1991: Prisoner of Honor. 1993: Four Weddings and a Funeral.

KENNEDY, Douglas 1915–1973
A rarity: a character actor with leading-man looks. Perhaps, not quite. There was some-thing naggingly unreliable about the genial grin set in the swarthy good looks beneath tight dark curls that got Kennedy cast as friends who turned out to be treacherous or (occasionally) bad guys who revealed a decent streak at the end. Distinguished war service with the Signal Corps, the OSS and Army

Intelligence interrupted the tall New Yorker's film career for six years, before Warners took on his crocodile smile for a while and set it in their post-war night-time world. Later he drifted off into westerns – usually gun-running to the Indians – and even played a TV western hero in *Steve Donovan – Western Marshal*. He died in Hawaii from cancer at 57. Billed in some of his earlier films as Keith Douglas.

1940: Opened by Mistake. Northwest Mounted Police. Arise My Love. Those Were the Days (GB: Good Old School Days). The Ghost Breakers. Women Without Names. The Way of All Flesh. The Mad Doctor (GB: A Date with Destiny). 1941: The Round-Up. The Great Mr Nobody. †Affectionately Yours. †The Bride Came COD. †The Nurse's Secret. †Passage from Hong Kong. 1947: Deep Valley. Always Together. Life with Father. Dark Passage. Stallion Road. Nora Prentiss. Possessed. That Hagen Girl. The Unfaithful. The Voice of the Turtle. The Unsuspected. 1948: Romance on the High Seas (GB: It's Magic). The Decision of Christopher Blake. Embraceable You. One Sunday Afternoon. To the Victor. Whiplash. Johnny Belinda. The Big Punch. 1949: East Side, West Side. Adventures of Don Juan (GB: The New Adventures of Don Juan). Fighting Man of the Plains. The Fountainhead. John Loves Mary. Flaxy Martin. Look for the Silver Lining. One Last Fling. South of Rio. Ranger of Cherokee Strip. South of St Louis. Whirlpool. 1950: Chain Gang. Revenue Agent. The Cariboo Trail. Montana. Convicted. 1951: I Was an American Spy. China Corsair. Indian Uprising. Lion Hunters (GB: Bomba and the Lion Hunters). The Texas Rangers. Callaway Went Thataway (GB: The Star Said No!). Oh, Susanna! For Men Only/The Tall Lie. 1952: Hoodlum Empire. Ride the Man Down. Last Train from Bombay. Fort Osage. The Next Voice You Hear. 1953: Safari Drums (GB: Bomba and the Safari Drums). The All-American (GB: The Winning Way). Gun Belt. Jack McCall, Desperado. Mexican Manhunt. San Antone. Torpedo Alley. War Paint. Sea of Lost Ships. 1954: The Big Chase. Cry Vengeance! Ketchikian (unreleased). The Lone Gun. Sitting Bull. Massacre Canyon. Rails into Laramie. 1955: The Eternal Sea. Wyoming Renegades. Strange Lady in Town. 1956: The Last Wagon. Wiretapper. Strange Intruder. 1957: Hell's Crossroads. Chicago Confidential. Rockabilly Baby. Last of the Badmen. The Land Unknown. 1958: The Bonnie Parker Story. The Lone Ranger and the Lost City of Gold. 1959: The Lone Texan. The Alligator People. 1960: The Amazing Transparent Man. 1961: Flight of the Lost Balloon. 1966: The Fastest Guitar Alive. 1967: Valley of Mystery. 1968: The Destructors.

† As Keith Douglas

KERR, Bill 1922–
Deadpan, dark-haired, slightly gloomy-looking entertainer, born in South Africa. Moving with his show business parents to Australia, he became a child actor there, then stand-up comedian, at which he was a great success in post-war Britain, with such catchphrases as 'Don't wanna worry yer' and 'I've only got four minutes'. Acting

roles, both comic and dramatic, came either side of an extended radio and TV association with Tony Hancock, before Kerr returned to Australia — as a character actor — in the late 1970s.

1933: †Harmony Row. 1934: †The Silence of Dean Maitland. 1951: Penny Points to Paradise. 1952: My Death is a Mockery. Appointment in London. 1953: You Know What Sailors Are. 1954: The Dam Busters. 1955: The Night My Number Came Up. Port of Escape. 1957: The Shiralee. 1958: The Captain's Table. 1960: The Sundowners. 1961: A Pair of Briefs. 1962: The Wrong Arm of the Law. 1963: Doctor in Distress. 1966: Doctor in Clover (US: Carnaby MD). A Funny Thing Happened on the Way to the Forum. 1973: Ghost in the Noonday Sun (unreleased). Tiffany Jones. 1975: Girls Come First. House of Mortal Sin (US: The Confessional). 1981: Deadline. Save the Lady. Gallipoli. 1982: The Pirate Movie. The Year of Living Dangerously. 1983: The Beautiful End of This World. The Settlement. Platypus Cove. Razorback. Great Expectations (voice only). 1984: White Man's Legend (TV). The Glitter Dome. Dusty. Vigil. The Coca Cola Kid. 1985: Relatives. 1986: A Fortunate Life. Double Sculls (TV). 1987: The Lighthorsemen. Running from the Guns. Bushfire Moon/Christmas Visitor. 1988: Kokoda Crescent. 1989: Confidence/Sweet Talker (released 1991). 1991: Over the Hill.

† As Billy Kerr

KIBBEE, Guy 1882–1956

Bald-headed, beaming, pink-cheeked American actor. He started his film career as a ruthless killer (in *City Streets*), but soon developed into a kind of benevolent W. C. Fields, and he was in great demand for character roles throughout the 1930s. Later still he starred in the low-budget 'Scattergood Baines' comedy series as a do-gooding small-town busybody. Died from Parkinson's Disease.

*1931: City Streets. Man of the World. Blonde Crazy (GB: Larceny Lane). Flying High (GB: Happy Landing). *Position and Backswing. Laughing Sinners. Side Show. Stolen Heaven. Union Depot (GB: Gentleman for a Day). The New Adventures of Get-Rich-Quick Wallingford. 1932: Fireman, Save My Child. Taxi! The Strange Love of Molly Louvain. Crooner. Central Park. Week-End Marriage*

(GB: Working Wives). The Mouthpiece. High Pressure. Play Girl. The Crowd Roars. Two Seconds. Man Wanted. So Big. Winner Take All. The Dark Horse. Big City Blues. Rain. Scarlet Dawn. The Conquerors. 1933: 42nd Street. Gold Diggers of 1933. They Just Had to Get Married. The Life of Jimmy Dolan (GB: The Kid's Last Fight). Lady for a Day. The World Changes. Convention City. Girl Missing. Lilly Turner. The Silk Express. Footlight Parade. Havana Widows. 1934: Harold Teen (GB: The Dancing Fool). Big-Hearted Herbert. The Merry Wives of Reno. Babbitt. The Merry Frinks (GB: The Happy Family). Wonder Bar. Dames. Easy to Love. 1935; Mary Jane's Pa (GB: Wanderlust). While the Patient Slept. Don't Bet on Blondes. Going Highbrow. I Live for Love (GB: I Live for You). Captain Blood. Crashing Society. 1936: Captain January. Earthworm Tractors (GB: A Natural Born Salesman). Three Men on a Horse. M'Liss. Little Lord Fauntleroy. I Married a Doctor. The Big Noise (GB: Modern Madness). 1937: Mama Steps Out. Riding on Air. Jim Hanvey, Detective. Bad Man from Brimstone. The Captain's Kid. Don't Tell the Wife. The Big Shot. Mountain Justice. 1938: Three Comrades. Of Human Hearts. Rich Man, Poor Girl. Three Loves Has Nancy. Joy of Living. 1939: It's a Wonderful World. Bad Little Angel. Mr Smith Goes to Washington. Babes in Arms. Let Freedom Ring. Henry Goes Arizona (GB: Spats to Spurs). 1940: Our Town. Chad Hanna. Street of Memories. Scattergood Baines. 1941: It Started With Eve. Design for Scandal. Scattergood Pulls the Strings. Scattergood Meets Broadway. 1942: Sunday Punch. Scattergood Rides High. Tish. Whistling in Dixie. Scattergood Survives a Murder. Miss Annie Rooney. This Time for Keeps. 1943: Girl Crazy. Cinderella Swings It. Power of the Press. White Savage (GB: White Captive). 1944: Dixie Jamboree. 1945: White Pongo (GB: Adventure Unlimited). The Horn Blows at Midnight. 1946: Singing on the Trail (GB: Lookin' for Someone). Cowboy Blues (GB: Beneath the Starry Skies). Gentleman Joe Palooka. Lone Star Moonlight (GB: Amongst the Thieves). 1947: Over the Santa Fé Trail (GB: No Escape). The Romance of Rosy Ridge. Red Stallion. 1948: Fort Apache. 3 Godfathers.*

KIEL, Richard 1939–

Fearsome 7 ft. 2 in. American actor with light-coloured hair, handsome in a thick-

featured way, but confined for many years to lumbering around as giants and monsters. After one or two minor leading roles in the mid-1970s, he hit pay dirt when cast as the villainous, steel-toothed killer Jaws in *The Spy Who Loved Me*, proving so popular that the character was reprised (as a semi-goodie) in another James Bond adventure *Moonraker*. By the 1990s, however, he had returned to giants and bogeymen.

1961: The Phantom Planet. 1962: The Magic Sword. 1963: Eegah! Lassie's Great Adventure (TV. GB: cinemas, as Lassie's Greatest Adventure). House of the Damned. The Nutty Professor. 1964: To Trap a Spy (TV. GB: cinemas). Roustabout. The Human Duplicators. Nasty Rabbit. 1965: Brainstorm. 1966: Las Vegas Hillbillys. Lassie: The Voyager (TV). 1967: A Man Called Dagger. 1968: Now You See It, Now You Don't (TV). Skidoo. 1970: The Boy Who Stole the Elephants (TV). 1974: The Longest Yard (GB: The Mean Machine). 1975: Barbary Coast (TV. GB: In Old San Francisco). Shadow in the Streets (TV). 1976: Silver Streak. Flash and the Firecat. 1977: The Spy Who Loved Me. 1978: They Went That-a-Way and That-a-Way. The Phoenix. Force Ten from Navarone. 1979: Moonraker. The Humanoid. 1981: So Fine. 1982: Hysterical. 1983: Cannonball Run II. War of the Wizards. 1984: The Racketeers. 1985: Pale Rider. The Mob Busters. 1990: Think Big! The Princess and the Dwarf. 1991: The Giant of Thunder Mountain.

KILBRIDE, Percy 1888–1964

Thin, slightly stooping, flat-haired, tight-mouthed, gloomy-looking American actor, who came to Hollywood in middle age and made sporadic appearances there in cameos between stage engagements, mostly as rustics who were a good deal more calculating than they looked. He found a niche as Pa Kettle in the Universal-International comedy series opposite Marjorie Main, which he left to retire in 1955. Died from brain injuries sustained in a car accident.

1933: White Woman. 1936: Soak the Rich. 1942: Keeper of the Flame. George Washington Slept Here. 1943: Crazy House. The Woman of the Town. 1944: The Adventures of Mark Twain. Guest in the House. Knickerbocker Holiday. 1945: State Fair. She Wouldn't Say Yes. Fallen Angel. 1946: The Well Groomed

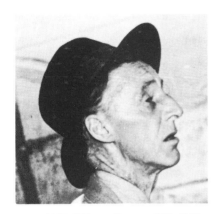

Bride. 1947: Welcome Stranger. Riffraff. The Egg and I. 1948: You Gotta Stay Happy. You Were Meant for Me. Black Bart (GB: Black Bart – Highwayman). Feudin', Fussin' and A-Fightin'. 1949: Ma and Pa Kettle. Mr Soft Touch (GB: House of Settlement). Free for All. The Sun Comes Up. Ma and Pa Kettle Go to Town (GB: Goin' to Town). 1950: Riding High. 1951: Ma and Pa Kettle Back on the Farm. 1952: Ma and Pa Kettle on Vacation (GB: Ma and Pa Kettle Go to Paris). Ma and Pa Kettle at the Fair. 1954: Ma and Pa Kettle at Home. 1955: Ma and Pa Kettle at Waikiki.

down. The Lady from Nowhere. The Road to Glory. Banjo on My Knee. Ramona. 1937: Seventh Heaven. It Happened in Hollywood. The League of Frightened Men. Tovarich. It's All Yours. 1938: The Adventures of Tom Sawyer. Marie Antoinette. Orphans of the Street. Prison Break. Boys' Town. *Miracle Money. Gold Diggers in Paris (GB: The Gay Imposters). 1939: Paris Honeymoon. Fighting Thoroughbreds. St Louis Blues. The Adventures of Huckleberry Finn. The Return of the Cisco Kid. Only Angels Have Wings. Never Say Die. Dust Be My Destiny. Blackmail. *The Story That Couldn't Be Printed. Invisible Stripes. 1940: Florian. Virginia City. My Favorite Wife. Dr Cyclops. The Mark of Zorro. Little Old New York. Till We Meet Again. King of the Lumberjacks. Gold Rush Maisie. All This and Heaven Too. The Return of Frank James. Torrid Zone. Barnyard Follies. Out West With the Peppers. They Knew What They Wanted. Tugboat Annie Sails Again. Chad Hanna. Santa Fe Trail. 1941: Young Tom Edison. Western Union. Mob Town. I Was a Prisoner on Devil's Island. Blood and Sand. Secrets of the Lone Wolf (GB: Secrets). A Date with the Falcon. Sergeant York. 1942: Reap the Wild Wind. This Gun for Hire. Atlantic Convoy. The Ox-Bow Incident (GB: Strange Incident). 1943: Bomber's Moon. Hitler's Madman. Johnny Come Lately (GB: Johnny Vagabond). The Iron Major. 1944: Belle of the Yukon. The Adventures of Mark Twain. Uncertain Glory. Kismet. Barbary Coast Gent. Dangerous Passage. Meet Me in St Louis. 1945: Behind City Lights. Dillinger. Escape in the Desert. The Spanish Main. Spellbound. The Fighting Guardsman. 1946: Little Giant (GB: On the Carpet). Smoky. The Yearling. Duel in the Sun. 1947: Gentleman's Agreement. 1948: Yellow Sky. Northwest Stampede. 1949: Madame Bovary. I Shot Jesse James. Rimfire. Colorado Territory. Wyoming Bandit. 1950: The Old Frontier. The Showdown. The Return of Jesse James. The Bandit Queen. No Way Out. The Flame and the Arrow. 1951. The Tall Target. One Too Many (GB: Killer with a Label). The Lemon Drop Kid. Passage West. Unknown World. 1952: Face to Face.

timing was under-valued and, with the right director, he could be consistently funny. Several of his TV series, too, were considerable personal successes. Married to former actress Carmel Cryan, he died following a fall from a horse while filming *The Return of the Musketeers.*

1960: The Millionairess. 1962: Tiara Tahiti. The Boys. Sparrows Can't Sing. 1963: The Small World of Sammy Lee. A Place to Go. The Informers. Heavens Above! 1964: French Dressing. 1965: The Hill. Help! 1966: The Deadly Affair. A Funny Thing Happened on the Way to the Forum. 1967: How I Won the War. *Albert Carter Q.O.S.O. 1968: The Mini Affair. 1969: Lock Up Your Daughters! The Bed Sitting Room. 1970: Taste the Blood of Dracula. Scrooge. Egghead's Robot. The Firechasers. On a Clear Day You Can See Forever. 1971: Melody (Later SWALK). Willy Wonka and the Chocolate Factory. Madame Sin (TV. GB: cinemas). The Pied Piper. Raising the Roof. 1972: The Alf Garnett Saga. Alice's Adventures in Wonderland. That's Your Funeral. 1973: The Three Musketeers – The Queen's Diamonds. *The Cobblers of Umbrage. 1974: Juggernaut. Eskimo Nell. The Four Musketeers – The Revenge of Milady. The Amorous Milkman. Barry McKenzie Holds His Own. Three for All. 1975: Royal Flash. One of Our Dinosaurs, is Missing. The Adventure of Sherlock Holmes' Smarter Brother. 1976: Not Now, Comrade. 1977: The Last Remake of Beau Geste. The Hound of the Baskervilles. Chimpmates (2nd series). Herbie Goes to Monte Carlo. 1978: Watership Down (voice only). 1979: The London Connection (US: The Omega Connection). *Mad Dogs and Cricketers. 1980: High Rise Donkey. *A Fair Way to Play. Hawk the Slayer. Dick Turpin (GB: TV). 1981: Hammett. 1982: *Two Too Many. 1983: The Boys in Blue. Pavlova – A Woman for All Time. Robin Hood (TV. GB: The Zany Adventures of Robin Hood). 1985: Squaring the Circle. 1986: Pirates. 1987: Casanova (TV). 1988: Just Ask for Diamond. A Man for All Seasons (TV). 1989: The Return of the Musketeers.

KILIAN, Victor 1891–1979

Hulkingly gaunt, arrow-nosed, cavern-cheeked, brown-haired, sometimes bearded American actor who looked perfect casting for Abraham Lincoln, and finally did get to play the role in 1940's *Virginia City.* Not too dissimilar to John Dierkes (*qv*), he was often cast as woodsmen, prospectors, sheriffs and fire-breathing preachers until he became a victim of the McCarthy blacklist. At 85, he began a whole new career as the 'flashing' grandfather in the TV comedy show *Mary Hartman, Mary Hartman* but, sadly, three years later he was killed by burglars at his Hollywood apartment.

1929: Valley Forge. Gentlemen of the Press. 1932: The Wiser Sex. *Artistic Temper. 1935: Bad Boy. Air Hawks. After the Dance. Public Menace. Atlantic Adventure. The Girl Friend. Riffraff. 1936: I Loved a Soldier. The Music Goes 'Round. Adventure in Manhattan (GB: Manhattan Madness). Fair Warning. Shake-

KINNEAR, Roy 1934–1988

Plump, florid, wheezy, wispy-haired British comic character actor and television satirist, from the Theatre Workshop. Although his performances seemed rather unvarying, his

KINSKEY, Leonid 1903–

Lanky Russian eccentric comic actor with long, angular features, thick lips, low forehead, stick-out hair and wonderful fractured English. In numerous cameos from 1932 to 1944, Kinskey, who started out in grand opera in Russia, seemed all arms and legs as he capered on and off the screen as a quasi-mad music teacher or the like. Seen only sporadically in post-war years, he made his latter-day living by staging industrial shows.

1932: The Big Broadcast. Trouble in Paradise. *1933:* Storm at Daybreak. Three Cornered Moon. Duck Soup. Girl Without a Room. *1934:* Change of Heart. Manhattan Melodrama. Goin' to Town. Hollywood Party. We Live Again. The Cat and the Fiddle. The Merry Widow. Fugitive Road. *1935:* The Gilded Lily. Lives of a Bengal Lancer. I Live My Life. Les Misérables. Peter Ibbetson. *1936:* The Garden of Allah. Love on the Run. Next Time We Love (*GB:* Next Time We Live). Rhythm on the Range. The Road to Glory. The Big Broadcast of 1937. Three Godfathers. The General Died at Dawn. *1937:* Married Before Breakfast. *Candid Cameramaniacs. Nothing Sacred. Maytime. Make a Wish. We're on the Jury. Espionage. My Dear Miss Aldrich. Café Metropole. Meet the Boy Friend. The Sheik Steps Out. 100 Men and a Girl. Wise Girl. *1938:* The Big Broadcast of 1938. Outside of Paradise. The Great Waltz. Algiers. A Trip to Paris. Three Blind Mice. Flirting With Fate. Professor, Beware! *1939:* The Story of Vernon and Irene Castle. Day-Time Wife. Exile Express. On Your Toes. Everything Happens at Night. The Spellbinder. *1940:* Down Argentine Way. He Stayed for Breakfast. *1941:* Ball of Fire. Broadway Limited. Lady for a Night. So Ends Our Night. That Night in Rio. Week-End in Havana. *1942:* Brooklyn Orchid. I Married an Angel. The Talk of the Town. Cinderella Swings It. *1943:* Gildersleeve on Broadway. Let's Have Fun. Presenting Lily Mars. *1944:* Can't Help Singing. The Fighting Seabees. That's My Baby. *1946:* Monsieur Beaucaire. *1949:* The Great Sinner. Alimony. *1950:* Nancy Goes to Rio. *1951:* Honeychile. *1952:* Gobs and Gals (*GB:* Cruising Casanovas). *1955:* The Man With the Golden Arm. *1956:* Glory.

KINSKI, Klaus

(Nikolaus Nakszynski) 1926–1991
Stocky, fair-haired, blue-eyed actor born in Danzig (now in Poland), with carved lips, Frankenstein eyebrows and the kind of strained baby-face looks that peppered his early career with sadistic villains. An undisciplined talent in these days, he was already a great scene-stealer; too much so, it seems, for most directors, as he toured nightclubs with a one-man show before becoming a regular in West German (and soon international) films from the early 1960s. Later he mixed fanatics and bizarre guest roles with impressive leading parts for director Werner Herzog. Something of a latter-day Peter Lorre, he was the father of actress Nastassja Kinski. Three times married, he died from bronchial pneumonia.

1948: Morituri. *1951:* Decision Before Dawn. *1954:* Kinder, Mütter und ein General. Ludwig II. *1955:* Um Thron und Liebe Sarajewo. Hanussen. *1956:* Waldwinter. Liebe Corinna. *1957:* A Time to Love and a Time to Die. *1960:* Der Rächer. *1961:* Die toten Augen von London (and English-language version: Dead Eyes of London). Bankraub in der Rue Latour.

Die seltsame Gräfin. The Counterfeit Traitor. Das Rätsel der roten Orchidee (and English-language version: The Puzzle of the Red Orchid). *1962:* The Devil's Daffodil (*US:* Daffodil Killer). Der rote Rausch. Die Tür mit den sieben Schlössern. Das Gasthaus an der Themse. *1963:* The Black Abbot. Der Zinker (*US:* The Squeaker). Scotland Yard jagt Doktor Mabuse (*US:* Dr Mabuse vs Scotland Yard). Die schwartze Kobra. Das indische Tuch. Das Geheimnis der schwarzen Witwe (*US:* Secret of the Black Widow). Piccadilly null Uhr zwölf. Kali-Yug, Goddess of Vengeance. Kali-Yug: The Mystery of the Indian Tomb (combined version shown in GB under former title). *1964:* Last Stage to Santa Cruz. Estambul 65/That Man in Istanbul. Winnetou II (*GB and US:* Last of the Renegades). Die Gruft mit dem Rätselschloss. Wartezimmer zum Jenseits. Das Geheimnis der chinesischen Nelke. *1965:* Traitor's Gate. The Pleasure Girls. The Dirty Game. Doctor Zhivago. For a Few Dollars More. Neues vom Hexer. *1966:* Our Man in Marrakesh (*US:* Bang! Bang! You're Dead). Circus of Fear (*US:* Psycho-Circus). Quien sabe? (*GB and US:* A Bullet for the General). I bastardi (*GB:* Sons of Satan). Carnival of Killers. Das Geheimnis der gelben Mönche (*GB:* Target for Killing). *1967:* Die blaue Hand (*US:* Creature with the Blue Hand). Sumuru (*US:* The 1,000,000 Eyes of Su-Muru). Coplan sauve sa peau (*GB:* Devil's Garden). Five Golden Dragons. Grand Slam. Carmen, Baby. L'uomo, l'orgoglio, la vendetta. ‡Jules Verne's Rocket to the Moon (*US:* Those Fantastic Flying Fools). Sigpress contro Scotland Yard. *1968:* Cinque per l'inferno (*GB:* Five for Hell. *US:* Five into Hell). Marquis de Sade: Justine (*GB:* Justine and Juliet). Sam Cooper's Gold (*US:* The Ruthless Four). Sartana. Vatican Story. Due volte Giuda. Il grande silenzio. *1969:* La peau de torpédo (*GB:* Pill of Death. *US:* Children of Mata Hari). Paroxismus (*GB:* Black Angel. *US:* Venus in Furs). Il dito nella piaga (*US:* The Dirty Two). Quintero. A Doppia Faccia (*US:* Puzzle of Horrors). I'll Dig Your Grave. E Dio disse a Caino . . . (*GB:* And God Said to Cain). Sono Sartana, il vostro becchino. *1970:* How Did a Nice Girl Like You Get into This Business? I leopardi di Churchill (*GB:* Commando Attack). El Conde Dracula (*GB:* Bram Stoker's Dracula. *US:* Count Dracula). Per una bara piena di dollari/Adios Compañeros! La belva. Prega il morte e ammazza il vivo. Giù le mani . . . carogna. The Night of the Assassins.

1971: The Crucified Girls of San Ramon. Dracula im Schloss des Schreckens (*US:* Web of the Spider). L'occhio del ragno (*US:* Eye of the Spider). La bestia uccide a sangue freddo (*GB:* Cold-Blooded Beast. *US:* Slaughter Hotel). Lo chiamavano King (*US:* The Man Called King). Black Killer. Vengeance Trail. Il venditore di morte. *1972:* Aguirre, Wrath of God. The Price of Death. Doppia taglia per Minnesota Stinky. Il ritorno di Clint il solitario. *1973:* Il mio nome è Shanghai Joe (*GB:* To Kill or to Die. *US:* Shanghai Joe). La mano spietata della legge (*GB:* The Bloody Hands of the Law). La mano che nutre la morte. Sette strani cadaveri. La morte ha sorriso all'assassino. Imperativo categorio: contro il crimine con rabbia. *1974:* L'important c'est d'aimer (*US:* That Most Important Thing: Love). Footprints. Le amanti del mostro. Who Stole the Shah's Jewels? La creatura del demonio. *1975:* Lifespan. Un genio, due compari, un pollo (*US:* Nobody's the Greatest). Das Netz (*US:* The Web). Crash che botte. *1976:* Les Marches du Palais. De peur de mourir, idiot. Jack the Ripper. Madame Claude (*US:* The French Woman). *1977:* Entebbe: Operation Thunderbolt. Nuit d'or. Mort d'un pourri. *1978:* Die Song of Roland. Zoo Zéro. *1979:* Nosferatu: Phantom der Nacht (*GB and US:* Nosferatu the Vampyre). Woyzeck. Haine/Hatred/Traquenard. *1980:* Schizoid. La femme-enfant. Love and Money. *1981:* Les fruits de la passion. Venom. Buddy Buddy. *1982:* Fitzcarraldo. Burden of Dreams. Android. The Soldier (*GB:* Codename: The Soldier). *1983:* Der Schatten des Wolfes (made in 1980). The Secret Diary of Sigmund Freud. *1984:* Codename Wildgeese. The Little Drummer Girl. *1985:* El caballero del dragon (*US:* Star Knight). The Hitchhiker. Commando Leopard. Titan Find/Creature. *1986:* Crawlspace. Deadly Sanctuary. Timestalkers (TV). Last of the Templars. Revenge of the Stolen Stars. *1987:* Nosferatu in Venice/Vampires in Venice. Cobra Verde. The Great Hunter. San Francisco Bridge. *1989:* †Paganini. *1990:* Il grande cacciatore.

† And directed
‡ Scenes deleted from final release print

KIRBY, Bruno

(Bruce Kirby Jr) 1950–
Short, jack-in-the-box American actor with receding dark curly hair, excitable voice and (latterly) moustache. The son of another character actor, Bruce Kirby (1925–), the younger Kirby studied with Stella Adler and

Peggy Fleury and has maintained a somewhat higher profile than his father. Since his portrayal of the young Clemenza in *The Godfather Part II*, Kirby has been seen most often in high-billed roles in comedy, providing straight-faced support for the stars in such successes as *Good Morning, Vietnam* and *City Slickers*. Film appearances, though, total fewer than you'd expect.

1971: †The Young Graduates. 1972: †All My Darling Daughters (TV). 1973: †A Summer Without Boys. †The Harrad Experiment. ‡Cinderella Liberty. 1974: †The Godfather Part II. †Superdad. 1976: ‡Baby Blue Marine. 1977: Between the Lines. 1978: Almost Summer. 1979: Some Kind of Miracle (TV). 1980: Borderline. Where the Buffalo Roam. 1981: Million Dollar Infield (TV). Modern Romance. 1982: Kiss My Grits. 1983: This is Spinal Tap. 1984: Birdy. 1985: Flesh and Blood. 1987: Tin Men. Good Morning, Vietnam. 1988: The 'In' Crowd. Bert Rigby, You're a Fool. 1989: When Harry Met Sally... We're No Angels. 1990: The Freshman. 1991: City Slickers. 1993: Golden Gate. Fallen Angels (TV). 1994: The Wildebeest Company. 1995: The Basketball Diaries. Acting on Impulse.

† As B Kirby Jr
‡ As Bruce Kirby

KIRKLAND, Sally 1944–
Voluptuous blonde American actress with aggressive acting style, a maverick sex symbol for 25 years who proved herself an actress of merit at 43 with a virtuoso performance that won an Academy Award nomination. The daughter of a woman who was editor of *Life* magazine for 25 years, Kirkland was with the Actors' Studio at 17, became an associate of Andy Warhol, did countless avant-garde stage shows and became known for her uninhibited nude scenes on both stage and screen. In 1983, she founded the Sally Kirkland Acting Workshop: it kept her off screen for several years before she returned to take that Oscar nod for *Anna*, and followed it with a busy period which contained some bizarre roles in exploitative material which she tackled in her own eye-catching fashion.

1964: The Thirteen Most Beautiful Women. 1968: Blue. Fade-In. 1969: Coming Apart. Futz. 1970: Brand X. 1971: Going Home. 1972: The Young Nurses. 1973: The Way We

Were. The Sting. Cinderella Liberty. 1974: Big Bad Mama. 1975: The Noah. Bite the Bullet. Crazy Mama. The Kansas City Massacre (TV). Death Scream (TV). Breakheart Pass. 1976: Tracks. Pipe Dreams. A Star is Born. Griffin and Phoenix: A Love Story (TV. GB: Tomorrow is Forever). 1977: Stonestreet: Who Killed the Centerfold Model? (TV). 1978: Hometown USA. 1980: Private Benjamin. The Georgia Peaches (TV). 1981: Ladies in Waiting (TV). The Incredible Shrinking Woman. 1982: Human Highway. Double Exposure. 1983: Love Letters/My Love Letters. The Killing Touch. Fatal Games. 1987: Anna. In Self Defense (TV). Addicted to His Love (TV). Hollow Point (TV). Talking Walls (completed 1983). 1988: Melanie Rose/High Stakes. Crack in the Mirror/Do It Up/White Hot. Paint It Black. Cold Feet. 1989: Best of the Best. Revenge. Two Evil Eyes. Superstar. 1990: Bullseye! Heat Wave (TV). The Haunted (TV). Willow B – Women in Prison. Largo Desolata (TV). 1991: Heat of Passion. JFK. 1992: Primary Motive. Hit the Dutchman. Double Threat. Forever/Hollywoodland. Blast 'Em. Our Hollywood Education. 1993: Paper Hearts. No Goodbyes. Flexing with Monty. I Married My Mom. Eye of the Stranger. Schneeweiss-Rosenrot. The Woman Who Loved Elvis (TV). Stringer. Gunmen. 1994: Double Deception/Behind the Truth (TV).*

KISER, Terry 1939–
Brown-haired, moustachioed, dark-complexioned, jackal-like American actor mostly seen as fast-talking men on the make who con the gullible. Despite leading roles on TV in the late 1970s in *The Rollergirls* and the unsuccessful pilot *Benny and Barney: Las Vegas Undercover*, Kiser was a latecomer to TV and films who remained undeservedly unrecognised even as a familiar face until his amazing film performance as the dead Bernie in *Weekend at Bernie's*, confirming that he was most effective in comedy roles.

1968: Rachel, Rachel. 1977: Benny and Barney: Las Vegas Undercover (TV). 1978: The Cops and Robin (TV). 1979: The Last Ride of the Dalton Gang (TV). Rich Kids. Steven. Fast Charlie... The Moonbeam Rider. Steel. 1981: All Night Long. Looker. An Eye for an Eye. 1982: Prime Suspect (TV). Making Love. Six Pack. Starflight One (TV. GB: cinemas). 1983: Your Place... Or Mine? (TV). Surf II. 1986: From a Whisper to a

Scream (later The Offspring). 1988: Friday the 13th, Part VII: The New Blood. 1989: Weekend at Bernie's. 1991: Mannequin on the Move. Into the Sun. 1993: Weekend at Bernie's II.

KLEMPERER, Werner 1919–
Big, smooth German actor, shiningly bald from an early age, who moved to America in 1933 with his father, conductor Otto Klemperer; he became an actor in post-war years, coming to Hollywood to play villains in smart suits. From 1965, he became involved with villainy of a comic kind with his six-year stint as the camp commandant in *Hogan's Heroes*, a portrayal which won him two Emmy awards.

1956: Five Steps to Danger. The Wrong Man. Flight to Hong Kong. Death of a Scoundrel. 1957: Istanbul. Kiss Them for Me. 1958: Houseboat. The High Cost of Loving. The Goddess. 1961: Operation Eichmann. Judgment at Nuremberg. 1962: Tunnel 28 (GB and US: Escape from East Berlin). 1964: Youngblood Hawke. 1965: Dark Intruder. Ship of Fools. 1968: The Wicked Dreams of Paula Schultz. 1969: Wake Me When the War is Over (TV). 1972: Assignment Munich (TV). 1977: The Rhinemann Exchange (TV). 1981: The Return of the Beverly Hillbillies (TV). 1991: The Cabinet of Dr Ramirez.

KLUGMAN, Jack 1922–
Dour-looking, watery-eyed, brown-haired American actor, in surprisingly few films, although enormously productive on television, and popular in two long-running

series, *The Odd Couple* (for which he won two Emmys) and *Quincy*. His glum growl can be sinister, weak, cynical or wryly comic.

1955: Timetable. 1956: Invasion of the Body Snatchers. 1957: 12 Angry Men. The Thundering Wave (TV). 1958: Cry Terror! The Time of Your Life (TV). 1959: The Velvet Alley (TV). 1961: The Million Dollar Incident (TV). 1962: Days of Wine and Roses. I Could Go On Singing. 1963: The Yellow Canary. Act One. 1965: Hail Mafia! 1966: Fame is the Name of the Game (TV). 1968: The Detective. The Split. 1969: Goodbye Columbus, 1971: Who Says I Can't Ride a Rainbow? (later Barney). 1972: Poor Devil (TV). 1974: The Underground Man (TV). 1975: One of My Wives is Missing (TV). 1976: Two-Minute Warning. 1994: Parallel Lives (TV).

KORMAN, Harvey 1927–

Tall, dark-haired, leering, sharklike American comic actor of shambling gait. His talent for impersonation and disguise and his waspish delivery of a sardonically funny line have chiefly been put to use on television, where he has enjoyed long-running stints with *The Danny Kaye Show* and *The Carol Burnett Show*. In films, some of his best opportunities have come in the films of Mel Brooks, although he has also stolen the show as sharpsters in such movies as *Huckleberry Finn*. The larger-than-life characters he creates have perhaps also limited the number of film appearances he's made to date.

1961: Living Venus. 1962: Gypsy. 1963: Son of Flubber. 1965: Lord Love a Duck. 1966: The Man Called Flintstone (voice only). The Last of the Secret Agents? Three Bites of the Apple. 1967: Don't Just Stand There! 1969: The April Fools. Three's a Crowd (TV). 1971: Suddenly Single (TV). 1974: Blazing Saddles. Huckleberry Finn. 1976: The Love Boat (TV). 1977: High Anxiety. 1978: Bud and Lou (TV). 1979: Americathon. 1980: Herbie Goes Bananas. First Family. 1981: History of the World Part I. 1982: Trail of the Pink Panther. 1983: Curse of the Pink Panther. The Invisible Woman (TV). Carpool (TV). 1984: Gone Are the Days (cable TV). 1985: The Long Shot. 1987: Munchies. 1994: Radioland Murders. The Flintstones (voice only).

KOSLECK, Martin

(Nicolai Yoshkin) 1904–1994

German actor who fled to America in 1933, but hardly got a nibble at Hollywood films until World War II loomed. Suddenly Kosleck, with his sleek, dark evil looks, and narrow face and eyes, found himself in demand to portray Nazis and sinister villains generally – quite an irony for a Jewish player. Portrayed Goebbels ('like he was, without a single redeeming feature') several times. Demands for his services slackened after 1946.

1927: Der Fahnentrager von Sedan. 1930: Alraune. Der singende Stadt. 1931: Napoleon auf St Helena. 1933: Fashions of 1934 (GB: Fashions). 1939: Confessions of a Nazi Spy. Nurse Edith Cavell. Nick Carter, Master Detective. Espionage Agent. 1940: Calling Philo Vance. The Mad Doctor (GB: A Date with Destiny). Foreign Correspondent. 1941: International Lady. The Devil Pays Off. Underground. 1942: All Through the Night. Nazi Agent. Berlin Correspondent. Manila Calling. Fly by Night. 1943: Chetniks. North Star. Bombers' Moon. 1944: Secrets of Scotland Yard. The Hitler Gang. The Mummy's Curse. The Great Alaskan Mystery (serial). 1945: Pursuit to Algiers. Gangs of the Waterfront. The Spider. The Frozen Ghost. Strange Holiday (GB: The Day After Tomorrow). 1946: House of Horrors (GB: Joan Medford is Missing). Just Before Dawn. Crime of the Century. The Wife of Monte Cristo. She-Wolf of London (GB: The Curse of the Allenbys). 1947: The Beginning or the End? 1948: Half Past Midnight. Smuggler's Cove. Assigned to Danger. 1961: Hitler. Something Wild. 1964: 36 Hours. 1965: Morituri (GB: The Saboteur, Code Name Morituri). 1966: Agent for HARM. 1967: The Flesh Eaters. 1969: Wake Me When the War is Over (TV). 1970: Which Way to the Front (GB: Ja! Ja! Mein General, But Which Way to the Front?). 1971: Longstreet (TV). 1973: A Day at the White House. 1979: The Man with Bogart's Face.

KOSLO, Paul 1944–

One biography of this baby-faced performer with light, fluffy hair states 'Canadian actor of the seventies'. That's a description that's difficult to dispute, as almost all of Koslo's best-known work comes from that decade, and most of his subsequent film appearances

seem to have sped fast to video. It was in the 1970s that he made a name for himself as deadly, unsmiling villains in action films; subsequent roles have been more sympathetic but less well seen.

1970: The Losers. 1971: The Omega Man. Scandalous John. Vanishing Point. The Birdmen (TV. GB: cinemas, as Escape of the Birdmen). Flux. Welcome Home, Soldier Boys. 1972: Joe Kidd. The Daughters of Joshua Cabe (TV). 1973: Cleopatra Jones. The Laughing Policeman (GB: An Investigation of Murder). Lolly Madonna XXX (GB: The Lolly Madonna War). The Stone Killer. 1974: Mr Majestyk. Bootleggers. Freebie and the Bean. 1975: The Drowning Pool. Rooster Cogburn. 1976: Scott Free (TV). Voyage of the Damned. 1977: Maniac!/Ransom. Tomorrow Never Comes. 1979: Love and Bullets. The Sacketts (TV). 1980: Heaven's Gate. Rape and Marriage – The Rideout Case (TV). 1981: Inmates – A Love Story (TV). 1983: Kenny Rogers as The Gambler Part II – The Adventure Continues (TV). 1984: The Glitter Dome (TV). Hambone and Hillie (GB: The Adventures of Hambone). 1987: A Night in the Life of Jimmy Reardon (GB: Jimmy Reardon). 1989: Loose Cannons (released 1992). The Outsiders (TV). 1990: Robot Jox. 1991: Conagher (TV). Xtro II. Drive Like Lightning. 1992: Project: Shadowchaser. 1993: Chained Heat II.

KOSSOFF, David 1919–

Small, dapper, moustachioed British actor, a former draughtsman and interior designer who became a skilled, multi-voiced radio actor before coming to films in wise, often Jewish-slanted roles. Later he co-starred with Peggy Mount in an enormously popular TV series, *The Larkins* (which led to a film) and became famous for his readings of Bible stories on television. Often played older than his real age.

*1953: The Good Beginning. 1954: The Young Lovers (US: Chance Meeting). The Angel Who Pawned Her Harp. Svengali. A Kid for Two Farthings. 1955: *The Bespoke Overcoat. The Woman for Joe. 1984: Who Done It? 1956: Now and Forever. House of Secrets (US: Triple Deception). Wicked As They Come. The Iron Petticoat. 1958: Innocent Sinners. Count Five and Die. Indiscreet. 1959: Jet Storm. The House of the Seven Hawks. The Journey. The Mouse That Roared. Inn for Trouble. 1960:*

Conspiracy of Hearts. The Two Faces of Dr Jekyll (US: House of Fright). 1962: Freud/ Freud – the Secret Passion. 1963: The Mouse on the Moon. Summer Holiday. Ring of Spies. 1970: The Private Life of Sherlock Holmes. 1974: Three for All. 1979: The London Connection (US: The Omega Connection). 1983: *The Sands of Time (narrator only). 1993: Staggered.

KOTTO, Yaphet 1937–

Rock-like black American actor in aggressive, hard-man characters. After a tough climb to decent roles, he began to get continuous work in films and television from 1967 and burst through to top supporting parts following his assignment as the villain in the James Bond film Live and Let Die. The private Kotto is far from the tough public image: he's a lay reader with the Self Realization Fellowship, a Hindu sect.

1963: Four for Texas. 1964: Nothing But a Man. 1968: Five Card Stud. The Thomas Crown Affair. 1969: The Liberation of L.B. Jones. 1970: Night Chase (TV). 1972: Man and Boy. †The Limit/Speed Limit 65. Bone (GB: Dial Rat for Terror). Across 110th Street. 1973: Live and Let Die. 1974: Truck Turner. Sharks' Treasure. 1975: Report to the Commissioner (GB: Operation Undercover). Friday Foster. 1976: Drum. Monkey Hustle. Raid on Entebbe (TV. GB: cinemas). 1978: Blue Collar. 1979: Alien. 1980: Brubaker. Rage (TV). 1982: Fighting Back (GB: Death Vengeance). 1983: The Star Chamber. Women of San Quentin (TV). 1985: Playing with Fire (TV). The Park is Mine (TV). Warning Sign. 1986:

Badge of the Assassin (TV). Eye of the Tiger. 1987: The Running Man. Desperado (TV). PrettyKill. In Self Defense (TV). Perry Mason: The Case of the Scandalous Scoundrel (TV). 1988: Nightmares of the Devil. The Jigsaw Murders. Terminal Entry. Midnight Run. 1989: A Whisper to a Scream. Black Snow. Ministry of Vengeance. Tripwire. 1990: After the Shock (TV). 1991: Freddy's Dead: The Final Nightmare. Hangfire. 1992: Almost Blue. Chrome Soldiers (TV). Intent to Kill. 1993: It's Nothing Personal (TV). S.I.S. The American Clock (TV). 1994: Dead Badge. Out of Sync. The Puppet Masters.

KOVE, Kenneth 1893–1968

Monocled, moon-faced, long-nosed 'silly ass'-style British comic actor whose profitable stage career (from 1913) was interrupted by the cinema from 1930 to 1936 when he dashed from one film to another during the 'quota' years. After that, he went back to the theatre, with barely a handful of additional film appearances (and some TV with Tony Hancock) before his retirement in the 1960s. His son, John Kove (1921–) was briefly a child actor in the early 1930s.

1930: Murder! The Great Game. 1931: Chance of a Night Time. Down River. The Man at Six (US: The Gables Mystery). Fascination. Almost a Divorce. Out of the Blue. M'Blimey (unreleased). Mischief. 1932: Bachelor's Baby. Two White Arms (US: Wives Beware). Help Yourself. Diamond Cut Diamond (US: Blame the Woman). Pyjamas Preferred. Her First Affaire. The Man from Toronto. 1933: Dora. Send 'Em Back Half Dead. Crime on the Hill. Song of the Plough (US: County Fair). 1934: The Crimson Candle. The Life of the Party. Crazy People. Youthful Folly. Leave It to Blanche. The Scarlet Pimpernel. 1935: Radio Pirates. Marry the Girl. Look Up and Laugh. 1936: Don't Rush Me. Cheer Up! The Bank Messenger Mystery. 1937: Talking Feet. 1939: Black Eyes. 1942: Asking for Trouble. 1945: They Knew Mr Knight. 1949: Stage Fright. 1952: Golden Arrow/Three Men and a Girl (US: The Gay Adventure. Completed 1949). Treasure Hunt. 1953: Innocents in Paris. The Saint's Return (US: The Saint's Girl Friday). 1954: Out of the Clouds. 1956: Charley Moon. 1957: The Naked Truth (US: Your Past is Showing!). 1959: Too Many Crooks. 1962: I compagni (US: The Organizer). 1964: Dr Terror's House of Horrors.

KRABBÉ, Jeroen 1944–

Brown-haired Dutch actor with hook nose, handsome but heavy features and calculating gaze. After founding a touring theatre company in his native Holland and making something of a reputation in translating plays into Dutch, he came to acting prominence in such films by director Paul Verhoeven as Soldier of Orange, Spetters and The Fourth War. In subsequent international films, he has often been cast as a sophisticated and deceptively affable villain – although he has also proved himself capable of quiet underplaying in more sympathetic roles. Also a costume designer, painter and gourmet cook: author of The Economy Cookbook. He was set to direct his first cinema film, Twee Koffers Vol, in 1995.

1963: Fietsen naar de Maan. Holland Off Guard. 1969: Professor Columbus. 1972: The Little Ark. 1974: Alicia. 1977: Soldier of Orange. 1978: Martijn en de Magiër. 1979: Een pak Slaag. Uitgestelde Vragen. Voedsel. 1980: Spetters. 1981: A Flight of Rainbirds. 1982: Het Verleden. De vierde Man/The Fourth Man. 1984: William of Orange (TV). 1985: In de Schaduw de Overwinning/ Shadow of Victory/In the Shadow of Victory. Turtle Diary. †The Diary of Anne Frank (TV). 1986: Jumpin' Jack Flash. No Mercy. 1987: One for the Dancer (TV). The Living Daylights. After the War (TV). Her Secret Life (TV). 1988: A World Apart. Crossing Delancey. Jan Cox: A Painter's Odyssey. Shadowman. 1989: The Punisher. Melancholia. Scandal. 1990: Secret Weapon (TV). Murder East, Murder West (TV). Family of Spies (TV). 1991: Till There Was You. Robin Hood (TV. GB: cinemas). The Prince of Tides. Sahara Sandwich. 1992: Kafka. Stalin (TV). Vor een verlorenen Soldat/ For a Lost Soldier. 1993: King of the Hill. Oeroeg/Going Home. The Fugitive. 1994: The Young Poisoner's Handbook. Immortal Beloved. Farinelli il castrato.

† And directed

KREUGER, Kurt 1916–

Blond Swiss-German actor with the handsomeness of a male model. He came to America in 1937 as a skiing instructor and broke into films in the war years, playing Nazi officers and playboy romeos. Too stiff to stay on the Hollywood scene for long, he drifted away from films after the 1950s,

and went into business buying homes and remodelling them for rent. Later Kreuger wrote a book about his experiences entitled *Hollywood Landlord*, and made a couple of small film appearances in the 1960s, his last to date. He bears a close resemblance to the slightly younger American actor Peter Graves.

1941: A Yank in the RAF. 1942: Joe Smith – American (GB: Highway to Freedom). The Moon is Down. 1943: Edge of Darkness. The Strange Death of Adolf Hitler. Background to Danger. Hangmen Also Die. Secret Service in Darkest Africa (serial. GB: Desert Agent). Sahara. The Purple V. 1944: None Shall Escape. The Hitler Gang. Mademoiselle Fifi (later The Silent Bell). 1945: Hotel Berlin. Escape in the Desert. Paris Underground (GB: Madame Pimpernel). The Spider. 1946: Sentimental Journey. The Dark Corner. 1948: Unfaithfully Yours. 1950: Spy Hunt (GB: Panther's Moon). 1954: La paura/Angst/Fear. 1957: The Enemy Below. 1958: Legion of the Doomed. Dossier (TV. GB: cinemas). 1966: What Did You Do in the War, Daddy? 1967: The St Valentine's Day Massacre. 1968: To Die in Paris (TV).

KROEGER, Berry 1912–1991
Thick-lipped, evil-looking American actor with dark, receding, smarmed-across hair, whose speciality was villains so repulsive they deserved to be wiped from the face of the earth. Redeeming qualities were not in the Kroeger armoury, the grey bags under his eyes heightening the likeness to an eminently hissable silent villain. Such undiluted vitriol was too much, it seemed, to admit him to many films but, after a start in post-war years, his characters continued to surface, like scum on the water, until his retirement in the late 1970s. Died from kidney failure.

1941: Tom, Dick and Harry. 1948: The Iron Curtain. Cry of the City. The Dark Past. An Act of Murder. Act of Violence. 1949: Chicago Deadline. Gun Crazy. Black Magic. Fighting Man of the Plains. Down to the Sea in Ships. 1950: Guilty of Treason (GB: Treason). 1951: The Sword of Monte Cristo. 1953: Battles of Chief Pontiac. 1955: Yellowneck. Blood Alley. 1956: Man in the Vault. 1960: Seven Thieves. The Story of Ruth. The Walking Target. 1961: Atlantis, the Lost Continent. Hitler. Womanhunt. 1963: Youngblood Hawke. 1966: Chamber of Horrors. Monster of the Wax Museum (GB: Nightmare in Wax). 1970: The Incredible Two-Headed Transplant. The Wild Scene. 1971: The Mephisto Waltz. The Seven Minutes. 1973: Pets (GB: Submission). 1975: The Man in the Glass Booth. 1977: Demon Seed.

KRUGER, Otto 1885–1974
This long-faced, pale-eyed, most civilized and courteous of American actors was almost entirely a stage star until his late forties, when he came to the screen to play lawyers, lovers, doctors, politicians both crooked and straight and, in the end, kindly uncles. Even his villains were always immaculately dressed and that deep, metallic voice exuded class. Died on his 89th birthday following a stroke. Filmed in Britain in the late 1930s.

*1915: When the Call Came. The Runaway Wife. A Mother's Confession. 1923: Under the Red Robe. 1928: *The Home Girl. 1929: *Mr Intruder. 1933: Beauty for Sale (GB: Beauty). Ever in My Heart. Gallant Lady. The Prizefighter and the Lady (GB: Everywoman's Man). The Women in His Life. Turn Back the Clock. 1934: Treasure Island. Chained. Springtime for Henry. The Crime Doctor. Men in White. Paris Interlude. 1935: Two Sinners. Vanessa – Her Love Story. *Screen Snapshots No 5. 1936: Dracula's Daughter. Living Dangerously. Lady of Secrets. 1937: Glamorous Night. Counsel for Crime. They Won't Forget. The Barrier. 1938: Housemaster. Star of the Circus (US: Hidden Menace). I Am the Law.*

Thanks for the Memory. Exposed. 1939: Black Eyes. The Gang's All Here (US: The Amazing Mr Forrest). Another Thin Man. Zero Hour. A Woman Is the Judge. Disbarred. 1940: A Dispatch from Reuter's (GB: This Man Reuter). Dr Ehrlich's Magic Bullet (GB: The Story of Dr Ehrlich's Magic Bullet). Scandal Sheet. Seventeen. The Man I Married. 1941: The Men in Her Life. The Big Boss. Mercy Island. 1942: Friendly Enemies (released 1946). Saboteur. 1943: Hitler's Children. Secrets of a Co-Ed (GB: Silent Witness). Corregidor. Tarzan's Desert Mystery. Stage Door Canteen. Night Plane from Chungking. 1944: Cover Girl. Knickerbocker Holiday. Storm Over Lisbon. They Live in Fear. 1945: On Stage, Everybody! Murder, My Sweet (GB: Farewell, My Lovely). The Great John L (GB: A Man Called Sullivan). The Woman Who Came Back. Jungle Captive. The Chicago Kid. Wonder Man. Escape in the Fog. Allotment Wives (GB: Woman in the Case). Earl Carroll's Vanities. 1946: The Fabulous Suzanne. Duel in the Sun. 1947: Love and Learn. 1948: Lulu Belle. Smart Woman. 1950: 711 Ocean Drive. 1951: Payment on Demand. Valentino. 1952: High Noon. 1954: Magnificent Obsession. Black Widow. 1955: The Last Command. 1958: The Colossus of New York. 1959: Della (TV). The Young Philadelphians (GB: The City Jungle). Cash McCall. 1962: The Wonderful World of the Brothers Grimm. 1964: Sex and the Single Girl.

KRUSCHEN, Jack 1922–
Canadian actor of burly build, with chubby face, black (later grey) hair and equally bushy brows. Mostly in comic supporting parts, such as eccentric, explosive professors, he's also a sturdy and sometimes stern dramatic player when the occasion demands. Nominated for a best supporting actor Academy Award in *The Apartment*. Started acting on radio at 16.

1949: Young Man with a Horn (GB: Young Man of Music). Red, Hot and Blue. 1950: Gambling House. Woman from Headquarters. No Way Out. Where Danger Lives. 1951: Cuban Fireball. The People against O'Hara. Comin' Round the Mountain. Meet Danny Wilson. 1952: Tropical Heatwave. Confidence Girl. Just Across the Street. Ma and Pa Kettle on Vacation (GB: Ma and Pa Kettle Go to

Paris). *1953*: The War of the Worlds. Blueprint for Murder. Money from Home. It Should Happen to You. Abbott and Costello Go to Mars. *1954*: Untamed Heiress. Tennessee Champ. The Long, Long Trailer. *1955*: Dial Red O. Carolina Cannonball. Soldier of Fortune. The Night Holds Terror. *1956*: Outside the Law. Julie. The Steel Jungle. *1957*: Badlands of Montana. Reform School Girl. *1958*: The Buccaneer. Cry Terror! Fraulein. The Decks Ran Red. *1960*: The Apartment. The Last Voyage. The Angry Red Planet. Studs Lonigan. Seven Ways from Sundown. *1961*: The Ladies' Man. Where the Boys Are. Lover Come Back. Cape Fear. *1962*: Convicts Four (GB: Reprieve!). Follow That Dream. *1963*: McLintock! *1964*: The Unsinkable Molly Brown. *1965*: Harlow (Carol Lynley version). Dear Brigitte . . . *1966*: Caprice. The Happening. *1968*: Istanbul Express (TV. GB: cinemas). *1971*: Million Dollar Duck. *1972*: Emergency (TV). Deadly Harvest (TV). *1974*: Freebie and the Bean. *1975*: Nick and Nora (TV). The Log of the Black Pearl (TV). *1976*: The November Plan. Guardian of the Wilderness. *1977*: Satan's Cheerleaders. The Incredible Rocky Mountain Race (TV). *1978*: The Time Machine (TV). *1979*: Sunburn. *1981*: Legend of the Wild. Under the Rainbow. Money to Burn. *1984*: Dark Mirror (TV). Cheaters. *1990*: Penny Ante. *1993*: The American Clock (TV).

Fountain. Mighty Joe Young. The Red Danube. Bandits of El Dorado (GB: Tricked). South Sea Sinner (GB: East of Java). Take Me Out to the Ball Game (GB: Everybody's Cheering). *Super-Wolf. Alias the Champ. *1950*: Jackpot Jitters (GB: Jiggs and Maggie in Jackpot Jitters). Wabash Avenue. *A Snitch in Time. Bodyhold. Jiggs and Maggie Out West. *1951*: *Chinatown Chump. The Kid from Amarillo (GB: Silver Chains). The Guy Who Came Back. Love Nest. You Never Can Tell (GB: You Never Know). Fixed Bayonets! Force of Arms. *1952*: Gobs and Gals (GB: Cruising Casanovas). The World in His Arms. No Holds Barred. My Wife's Best Friend. Red Skies of Montana. *Aim, Fire, Scoot. What Price Glory? Target — Hong Kong. Down Among the Sheltering Palms. *1953*: The Glory Brigade. Clipped Wings. Powder River. The Robe. The 5,000 Fingers of Dr T. The Charge at Feather River. *1954*: A Star is Born. Hell and High Water. Fireman, Save My Child. Yukon Vengeance. Tobor the Great. The Human Jungle. The Steel Cage. *1955*: Prince of Players New York Confidential. Abbott and Costello Meet the Keystone Kops. To Hell and Back. Jail Busters. Illegal. Finger Man. The Girl in the Red Velvet Swing. I'll Cry Tomorrow. Love Me or Leave Me. *1956*: The Girl Can't Help it. *Army Daze. *1957*: Bombers B-52 (GB: No Sleep Till Dawn). Sierra Stranger. *1959*: Up Periscope. The Gunfight at Dodge City. Guns of the Timberland. Compulsion. *1962*: All Fall Down. *1963*: A Global Affair.

Peking. The War Lover. The Devil Never Sleeps (US: Satan Never Sleeps). *1963*: The Cool Mikado. *1964*: A Shot in the Dark. Goldfinger. *1965*: The Curse of the Fly. *1966*: Lost Command. The Sandwich Man. The Brides of Fu Manchu. Our Man in Marrakesh (US: Bang! Bang! You're Dead). *1967*: Casino Royale. The Vengeance of Fu Manchu. You Only Live Twice. *1968*: Nobody Runs Forever (US: The High Commissioner). The Shoes of the Fisherman. *1969*: The Most Dangerous Man in the World (US: The Chairman). *1970*: Deep End. *1971*: Madame Sin (TV. GB: cinemas). *1974*: The Return of the Pink Panther. *1975*: Girls Come First. Rollerball. *1976*: The Pink Panther Strikes Again. *1977*: The Last Remake of Beau Geste. The Strange Case of the End of Civilization As We Know It (TV). *1978*: The Revenge of the Pink Panther. *1980*: The Fiendish Plot of Dr Fu Manchu. *1982*: Trail of the Pink Panther. *1983*: Curse of the Pink Panther. *1985*: Plenty. *1987*: Empire of the Sun. *1989*: I Bought a Vampire Motor Cycle. Race for Glory. *1990*: Air America. *1992*: Carry On Columbus. Leon the Pig Farmer. Shooting Elizabeth. *1993*: Son of the Pink Panther.

KULKY, Henry
(H. Kulkavich) 1911–1965

Squat, hairy, dark-haired, flat-nosed, cigar-chewing American actor whose battered features bore mute witness to scores of boxing and wrestling bouts as 'Bomber Kulkavich'. At one time, he was judo champion of South America, but in post-war years fellow ex-wrestler Mike Mazurki (*qv*) introduced him to films, where he played tough minor heavies, and equally tough good-hearted sergeants of army and cavalry alike. Profitably occupied on television from 1956, he died from a heart attack on the set of the *Voyage to the Bottom of the Sea* series in which he was a regular. He used to joke that his wrestling days had taught him all he ever needed to know about acting!

1947: A Likely Story. Northwest Outpost (GB: End of the Rainbow). Call Northside 777. *1949*: *Groan and Grunt. Tarzan's Magic

KWOUK, Burt 1930–

Britain's busiest 'oriental' actor from the past three decades, Manchester-born, Shanghai-raised Kwouk has rarely been off cinema and (mainly) television screens since his film debut in 1957. Best remembered as Peter Sellers' maniacal houseboy Cato in the *Pink Panther* films, he has also become a familiar figure (and voice) in TV commercials and as the Japanese commandant in the long-running *Tenko* series on TV. An unmistakeable character with his attractively harsh tones and impassive stare, he continues to play unblinking cameos.

1957: Windom's Way. *1958*: The Inn of the Sixth Happiness. *1959*: Once More with Feeling. Yesterday's Enemy. Upstairs and Downstairs. Expresso Bongo. *1960*: Visa to Canton (US: Passport to China). *1961*: The Terror of the Tongs. The Sinister Man. *1962*: 55 Days to

KYDD, Sam 1915–1982

Slightly built, but craggy-faced, Irish-born portrayer of resilient cockney types in British films. Just as likely to be friendly or antagonistic, straight or crooked. Before service in World War II, his show-business experience was mainly limited to a period as emcee for a dance band. Interned in a Polish P-o-W camp from 1941 to 1946, he quickly picked up his career in post-war years, appearing in scores of films and a popular TV series, *Crane*. A perfectly cast Sam Weller in a TV version of *The Pickwick Papers*. Died from a respiratory ailment. His son, Jonathan Kydd, is also an actor.

1940: They Came by Night. *1941*: Penn of Pennsylvania (US: The Courageous Mr Penn). *1946*: The Captive Heart. *1947*: Fortune Lane. They Made Me a Fugitive (US: I Became a Criminal). Colonel Bogey. *1948*: Trouble in the Air. It's Hard to be Good. Scott of the Antarctic. Portrait from Life (US: The Girl in the Painting). Fly Away Peter. Love in Waiting. A Song for Tomorrow. To the Public Danger. A Piece of Cake. Passport to Pimlico. Badger's Green. The Small Back Room (US: Hour of

Glory). Vengeance is Mine. Once a Jolly Swagman (US: Maniacs on Wheels). Forbidden. Obsession (US: The Hidden Room). 1949: Movie-Go-Round. Floodtide. Poet's Pub. Stop Press Girl. Saints and Sinners. Madness of the Heart. The Cure for Love. Trottie True (US: Gay Lady). The Blue Lamp. The Hasty Heart. 1950: Blackout. Treasure Island. Cage of Gold. Chance of a Lifetime. The Dark Man. Mr Drake's Duck. No Trace. Seven Days to Noon. The Magnet. The Second Mate. The Clouded Yellow. Pool of London. 1951: High Treason. Captain Horatio Hornblower RN (US: Captain Horatio Hornblower). Cheer the Brave. The Galloping Major. Hell is Sold Out. Mr Denning Drives North. Penny Points to Paradise. Assassin for Hire. Secret People. Angels One Five. Brandy for the Parson. Judgment Deferred. 1952: Hunted (US: The Stranger in Between). Sing Along with Me. Curtain Up! The Voice of Merrill (US: Murder Will Out). The Pickwick Papers. Trent's Last Case. Derby Day (US: Four Against Fate). The Brave Don't Cry. Hot Ice. The Lost Hours (US: The Big Frame). Appointment in London. The Hour of 13. The Cruel Sea. Time Bomb (US: Terror on a Train). 1953: The Runaway Bus. Death Goes to School. The Saint's Return (US: The Saint's Girl Friday). Love in Pawn. The Master of Ballantrae. Single-Handed (US: Sailor of the King). They Who Dare. Malta Story. The Titfield Thunderbolt. The Steel Key. 1954: Lilacs in the Spring (US: Let's Make Up). Devil on Horseback. Radio Cab Murder. Final Appointment. Father Brown (US: The Detective). The Rainbow Jacket. The Embezzler. The End of the Road. Impulse. Cockleshell Heroes. A Kid for Two Farthings. 1955: The Ladykillers. The Glass Cage (US: The Glass Tomb). One Way Out. The Gold Express. Storm Over the Nile. The Dark Avenger (US: The Warriors). The Quatermass Experiment (US: The Creeping Unknown). Portrait of Alison (US: Postmark for Danger). The Constant Husband. Raising a Riot. Where There's a Will. Passage Home. You Can't Escape. Josephine and Men. 1956: A Town Like Alice. The Long Arm (US: The Third Key). Tiger in the Smoke. Soho Incident (US: Spin a Dark Web). The Hideout. Reach for the Sky. Circus Friends. Jacqueline. Ramsbottom Rides Again. The Baby and the Battleship. It's a Wonderful World. Home and Away. 1957: Yangtse Incident (US: Battle Hell). The Scamp. The Smallest Show on Earth. Barnacle Bill (US: All at Sea). Happy is the Bride! Carry On Admiral (US: The Ship Was Loaded). Just My Luck. Dangerous Exile. The Safecracker. 1958: A Tale of Two Cities. Up the Creek. Orders to Kill. I Was Monty's Double (US: Monty's Double). Life is a Circus. Carlton-Browne of the FO (US: Man in a Cocked Hat). Law and Disorder. The Captain's Table. Further Up the Creek. 1959: Too Many Crooks. The Hound of the Baskervilles. The Thirty Nine Steps. Libel. The Price of Silence. I'm All Right, Jack. Follow That Horse! Upstairs and Downstairs. Make Mine a Million. Sink the Bismarck! The Angry Silence. 1960: Dead Lucky. The House in Marsh Road. Suspect (US: The Risk). There Was a Crooked Man. 1961: The Treasure of Monte Cristo (US: The Secret of Monte Cristo). Clue of the Silver Key. 1962: The Iron Maiden (US: The Swingin' Maiden). 1963: Doctor in Distress. The Young

Detectives (serial). 1964: Smokescreen. 1966: Island of Terror. The Projected Man. 1967: Smashing Time. 1968: *Gold is Where You Find It. The Killing of Sister George. 1969: Submarine X1. Till Death Us Do Part. Moon Zero Two. The Magnificent Six and ½ (second series). Too Late the Hero. 1970: The Last Grenade (US: Grigsby). 10 Rillington Place. 1971: Dad's Army. Quest for Love. The Magnificent Six and ½ (third series). Up the Chastity Belt. 1972: The Alf Garnett Saga. 1973: Steptoe and Son Ride Again. 1974: The Amorous Milkman. Confessions of a Window Cleaner. The Fire Fighters. 1975: Great Expectations (TV. GB: cinemas). 1976: The Chiffy Kids (series). 1978: Chimpmates (third series). 1979: Yesterday's Hero. The Shillingbury Blowers (TV). 1980: Danger on Dartmoor. High Rise Donkey. The Mirror Crack'd. 1981: Eye of the Needle.

Vampires (US: The Fearless Vampire Killers). 1968: Otley. 1969: Take a Girl Like You. 1970: Say Hello to Yesterday. 1971: Crucible of Terror. 1972: The Adventures of Don Quixote (TV). 1973: Gawain and the Green Knight. The Final Programme (US: The Last Days of Man on Earth). 1974: The Next Victim (TV. US: cinemas). Mister Quilp. 1976: The Likely Lads. 1977: The Prince and the Pauper (US: Crossed Swords). 1978: Charleston. 1979: Zulu Dawn. 1980: Nijinsky. 1981: Raiders of the Lost Ark. 1982: Firefox. Trenchcoat. 1983: Tangier. The Rothko Conspiracy (TV). Yellowbeard. Invitation to the Wedding. Sahara. Sword of the Valiant. The Hound of the Baskervilles (TV). 1984: Making the Grade. The Adventures of Buckaroo Banzai Across the Eighth Dimension. 1985: Flesh and Blood. The Bengal Lancers (unfinished). Red Sonja. Minder on the Orient Express (TV). 1986: Gunbus. Sky Bandits. 1987: The Sign of Four (TV). 1988: The Lone Runner (filmed 1986). The Avalon Awakening. Manifesto. The Great Escape: The Untold Story (TV). 1989: White Cobra Express. Valmont. 1990: Indiana Jones and the Last Crusade. Face to Face (TV). 1991: Stalingrad.

LACEY, Ronald 1935–1991
Squat, dishevelled, gremlin-like British actor with round face and floppy brown hair. His sarcastic leer took him all the way from young tearaways to faintly decadent second-line villains in such expensive epics as *Raiders of the Lost Ark*. Also a stage director and drama teacher, he died from cancer.

1962: The Boys. 1963: The Comedy Man. Doctor in Distress. Becket. 1964: Of Human Bondage. 1965: Catch Us If You Can (US: Having a Wild Weekend). 1966: The White Bus. 1967: How I Won the War. Dance of the

LADD, Diane
(Rose D. Ladnier) 1939–
Blonde American actress of full-blown attractiveness who can play tarty or dowdy and most shades in between. Trained for the stage, she worked as a model and a Copacabana nightclub dancer before getting a job with a touring company at 18. She was well into her twenties before gaining a toehold in films (on one of her early ones, *The Wild Angels*, she met her first husband, Bruce Dern. Actress Laura Dern is their daughter) and remained a sporadic cinema performer until recent busier days. Nominated (as was Laura) for an Academy Award in *Rambling Rose*, making them the first mother and daughter to be Oscar-nominated in the same year. Also an Oscar nominee for *Alice Doesn't Live Here Anymore*. Billed in some early roles as Diane Lad.

1961: Something Wild. 1962: 40 Pounds of Trouble. 1966: The Wild Angels. 1967: Rebel Rousers (released 1969). 1969: The Reivers. 1970: Macho Callahan. WUSA. 1971: The Steagle. 1972: The Devil's Daughter (TV). 1973: White Lightning. 1974: Alice Doesn't Live Here Anymore. Chinatown. 1976: Embryo. The November Plan. 1978:

Thaddeus Rose and Eddie (TV). Black Beauty (TV). 1979: Willa (TV). 1980: Guyana Tragedy: The Story of Jim Jones (TV). Cattle Annie and Little Britches. 1981: All Night Long. 1982: Desperate Lives (TV). 1983: The Grace Kelly Story (TV). Something Wicked This Way Comes. 1984: I Married a Centerfold (TV). 1985: Crime of Innocence (TV). Smooth Talk. 1987: Black Widow. 1988: Plain Clothes. S.P.O.O.K.S. 1989: National Lampoon's Christmas Vacation (GB: National Lampoon's Winter Holiday). Code Name: Chaos. 1990: Wild at Heart. A Kiss Before Dying. The Look-alike (cable TV). Rock Hudson (TV). 1991: Rambling Rose. Shadow of a Doubt (TV). 1992: Hold Me, Thrill Me, Kiss Me/Forever. Dr Quinn, Medicine Woman (TV). 1993: The Cemetery Club. Hush Little Baby (TV). Carnosaur. 1994: Father Hood. The Spirit Realm. Obsession. The Haunted Heart. 1995: Nixon.

LAHR, Bert
(Irving Lahrheim) 1895–1967

The Cowardly Lion in *The Wizard of Oz*, of course. Apart from that landmark, however, Hollywood hardly made the most of this moon-faced, brown-haired, ever-beaming vaudevillian, a popular figure with audiences and colleagues alike. Alas, his india rubber features and gurgling laugh enlivened too few films, following long musical comedy experience. Died from an internal haemorrhage.

*1929: *Faint Heart. 1931: Flying High (GB: Happy Landing). 1933: Mr Broadway. 1934: *Hizzoner. 1936: *Gold Bricks. 1937: Merry-Go-Round of 1938. Love and Hisses. 1938: Just Around the Corner. Josette. 1939: Zaza. The Wizard of Oz. 1942: Sing Your Worries Away. Ship Ahoy. 1944: Meet the People. 1949: Always Leave Them Laughing. 1951: Mr Universe. 1954: Rose Marie. 1955: The Great Waltz (TV). The Second Greatest Sex. 1962: Ten Girls Ago. 1965: The Fantasticks (voice only). 1966: Thompson's Ghost (TV). 1968: The Night They Raided Minsky's.*

LAMBERT, Jack 1899–1976

Long-faced, sleepy-eyed, severe-looking, often moustachioed Scottish actor, a former boxer who spent ten years on the amateur stage before deciding to turn professional in 1930. He played in several good Ealing

films of the 1940s, enjoying his finest hour as the tough sergeant in *Nine Men*. He could have had a Hollywood contract in the early 1930s, but preferred to work in Britain, where he continued to appear spasmodically in films until the early 1970s.

*1931: A Honeymoon Adventure (US: Footsteps in the Night). 1933: Sorrell and Son. 1934: Red Ensign (US: Strike!). 1935: The Ghost Goes West. 1936: House Broken. 1937: The Last Adventurers. 1938: Première (US: One Night in Paris). Thistledown. The Terror. Marigold. 1939: The Spider. Goodbye Mr Chips! The Outsider. 1943: Nine Men. 1946: The Captive Heart. 1947: Hue and Cry. The Brothers. Dear Murderer. 1948: Eureka Stockade (US: Massacre Hill). 1949: Floodtide. 1952: Hunted (US: The Stranger in Between). The Lost Hours (US: The Big Frame). The Great Game. 1953: The Master of Ballantrae. Front Page Story. Twice Upon a Time. *The Candlelight Murder. 1954: The Sea Shall Not Have Them. Track the Man Down. Companions in Crime. Out of the Clouds. Three Cases of Murder. 1955: Storm Over the Nile. The Dark Avenger (US: The Warriors). Cross Channel. Jumping for Joy. Lost (US: Tears for Simon). 1956: The Last Man to Hang? Reach for the Sky. X the Unknown. 1957: The Little Hut. 1958: Son of Robin Hood. Family Doctor (US: RX Murder). 1959: The Bridal Path. The Shakedown. The Devil's Disciple. 1960: Greyfriars Bobby. 1961: Francis of Assisi. On the Fiddle (US: Operation Snafu). 1963: Bomb in the High Street (shown 1961). 1964: A Shot in the Dark. 1965: Cuckoo Patrol. Dracula – Prince of Darkness. 1966: Modesty Blaise. *Miss Mactaggart Won't Lie Down. 1967: They Came from Beyond Space. 1971: Kidnapped. 1972: Neither the Sea Nor the Sand.*

LAMBERT, Jack (2) 1920–

Fair, surly-looking, strawberry-nosed American actor with curly, receding hair and 'bad guy' looks. Lambert studied to be an English professor but, after gaining his degree, took himself off to Hollywood in the war years and played some really nasty villains in dark clothes, often with a psychopathic streak, and not usually with too much brain. He was a man you loved to see bite the dust but, failing to get a wider range of roles, Lambert drifted away from films after 1963. Also first mate aboard the *Riverboat* in the successful TV series of 1959–61.

*1941: Reaching from Heaven. 1942: About Face. 1943: Swing Fever. Follies Girl. The Lost Angel. Bomber's Moon. The Cross of Lorraine. 1944: The Canterville Ghost. *Tomorrow's Harvest. 1945: Duffy's Tavern. The Hidden Eye. The Harvey Girls. Abilene Town. 1946: Specter of the Rose. The Hoodlum Saint. The Killers. The Plainsman and the Lady. 1947: The Vigilantes Return. Dick Tracy's Dilemma (GB: Mark of the Claw). The Unsuspected. 1948: Force of Evil. Belle Starr's Daughter. River Lady. Disaster. 1949: The Great Gatsby. Border Incident. Big Jack. Brimstone. 1950: Stars in My Crown. Dakota Lil. North of the Great Divide. The Enforcer (GB: Murder Inc). 1951: Montana Belle (completed 1948). The Secret of Convict Lake. 1952: Bend of the River (US: Where the River Bends). Blackbeard the Pirate. 1953: Scared Stiff. 99 River Street. 1954: Vera Cruz. 1955: Run for Cover. Kiss Me Deadly. At Gunpoint! (GB: Gunpoint!). 1956: Backlash. Canyon River. 1957: Chicago Confidential. 1958: Hot Car Girl. Machine Gun Kelly. Party Girl. 1959: Day of the Outlaw. Alias Jesse James. 1960: Freckles. 1961: The George Raft Story (GB: Spin of a Coin). 1962: How the West Was Won. 1963: Four for Texas. 1967: Winchester '73 (TV).*

LAMBLE, Lloyd 1914–

Sandy-haired Australian actor of quiet authority, in Britain from 1951, and quickly building up a gallery there of officers, inspectors, civil servants, concerned parents and the occasional highly placed, cultivated crook. Like so many of his contemporaries, Lamble found the cinema's requirements for his services consistently heavy throughout the 1950s. After 1962, he turned to TV and the theatre, becoming well-known as Mr Eliot in TV's *Crossroads*.

1949: *Strong is the Seed* (GB: *The Farrer Story*). 1951: *Saturday Island* (US: *Island of Desire*). 1952: *Lady in the Fog* (US: *Scotland Yard Inspector*). *Come Back Peter*. *Curtain Up*. *Appointment in London*. 1953: **The Silent Witness*. *The Story of Gilbert and Sullivan* (US: *The Great Gilbert and Sullivan*). *Background* (US: *Edge of Divorce*). *Street Corner* (US: *Both Sides of the Law*). *Mantrap* (US: *Woman in Hiding*). *Three Steps to the Gallows* (released 1955. US: *White Fire*). *The Straw Man*. *Melba*. 1954: *Profile*. *Forbidden Cargo*. *Eight O'Clock Walk*. *The Red Dress*. **The Mirror and Markheim*. *The Green Buddha*. *Out of the Clouds*. *The Dam Busters*. *The Belles of St Trinian's*. *Track the Man Down*. **Fatal Journey*. 1955: *The Blue Peter* (US: *Navy Heroes*). *Contraband Spain*. *The Man Who Never Was*. *Private's Progress*. 1956: *The Gelignite Gang* (US: *The Dynamiters*). *The Girl in the Picture*. *The Man Who Knew Too Much*. **Person Unknown*. *The Good Companions*. *Suspended Alibi* (US: *Suspected Alibi*). 1957: *Night of the Demon* (US: *Curse of the Demon*). *These Dangerous Years* (US: *Dangerous Youth*). *Quatermass II* (US: *Enemy from Space*). *Barnacle Bill* (US: *All at Sea*). *Sea Wife*. *There's Always a Thursday*. *Blue Murder at St Trinian's*. 1958: *Dunkirk*. **Print of Death*. *The Two-Headed Spy*. *No Trees in the Street* (US: *No Tree in the Street*). *The Man Who Wouldn't Talk*. *The Bank Raiders*. 1959: *The Heart of a Man*. *Our Man in Havana*. *The Challenge*. *Breakout*. *Expresso Bongo*. *Behemoth the Sea Monster* (US: *The Giant Behemoth*). 1960: *The Pure Hell of St Trinian's*. *The Trials of Oscar Wilde* (US: *The Man with the Green Carnation*). 1962: *Tiara Tahiti*. *Term of Trial*. *The Boys*. 1965: *Joey Boy*. 1973: *... And Now the Screaming Starts!* *No Sex, Please — We're British*. *On the Game*. 1974: *Eskimo Nell*. 1975: *The Naked Civil Servant* (TV). 1980: *Very Like a Whale* (TV). 1984: *A Christmas Carol* (TV. GB: cinemas).

busy from 1950 on, mostly in support, but occasionally in minor leads. Memorable as the villain in *The Adventures of Quentin Durward*, battling it out in a bell-tower with Robert Taylor. Long married to actress Patricia Driscoll.

1950: *Waterfront* (US: *Waterfront Women*). *The Woman in Question* (US: *Five Angles on Murder*). *She Shall Have Murder*. 1951. *The Galloping Major*. *The Man in the White Suit*. *Night Without Stars*. 1952: *Emergency Call* (US: *100 Hour Hunt*). *The Brave Don't Cry*. *The Lost Hours* (US: *The Big Frame*). *La carrozza d'oro* (GB: *The Golden Coach*). *The Night Won't Talk*. *Song of Paris* (US: *Bachelor in Paris*). 1953: *The Final Test*. *The Intruder*. *Meet Mr Malcolm*. 1954: *Burnt Evidence*. *Time Is My Enemy*. *The End of the Road*. *The Teckman Mystery*. *The Passing Stranger*. 1955: *Passage Home*. *The Adventures of Quentin Durward* (US: *Quentin Durward*). *The Quatermass Experiment*. 1956: *The Baby and the Battleship*. 1957: *High Flight*. 1958: *A Tale of Two Cities*. *I Was Monty's Double* (US: *Monty's Double*). 1959: *The 39 Steps*. *Ben-Hur*. *A Touch of Larceny*. 1960: *Circle of Deception*. *The Queen's Guards*. 1961: *Macbeth*. 1962: *Mutiny on the Bounty*. 1963: *Murder at the Gallop*. *The Scarlet Blade* (US: *The Crimson Blade*). *Panic*. *The Devil-Ship Pirates*. 1964: *The Evil of Frankenstein*. 1965: *The Brigand of Kandahar*. *The Murder Game*. 1966: *Arabesque*. *The Witches* (US: *The Devil's Own*). 1967: *Frankenstein Created Woman*. *Quatermass and the Pit* (US: *5,000,000 Miles to Earth*). 1968: *Decline and Fall ... of a birdwatcher!* *Dr Jekyll and Mr Hyde* (TV). 1969: *Battle of Britain*. 1971: *Burke and Hare*. *Mary Queen of Scots*. 1972: *Pope Joan*. *Nothing But the Night*. *The Creeping Flesh*. 1976: *Escape from the Dark* (US: *The Littlest Horse Thieves*).

and *Witness for the Prosecution*. Died from bronchial pneumonia.

1927: *One of the Best*. *The Constant Nymph*. 1928: **Bluebottles*. **The Tonic*. **Daydreams*. 1929: **Comets*. **Mr Smith Wakes Up*. 1930: **Ashes*. *The Love Habit*. 1931: *The Stronger Sex*. *Potiphar's Wife* (US: *Her Strange Desire*). *The Officer's Mess*. 1933: *The Private Life of Henry VIII*. 1934: *The Private Life of Don Juan*. 1935: *David Copperfield*. *Bride of Frankenstein*. *Naughty Marietta*. **Miss Bracegirdle Does Her Duty*. *The Ghost Goes West*. 1936: *Rembrandt*. 1938: *Vessel of Wrath* (US: *The Beachcomber*). 1941: *Ladies in Retirement*. 1942: *Son of Fury*. *Tales of Manhattan*. 1943: *Forever and a Day*. *Thumbs Up*. *Lassie Come Home*. 1944: *Passport to Adventure*. 1945: *The Spiral Staircase*. 1946: *The Razor's Edge*. 1947: *Northwest Outpost* (GB: *End of the Rainbow*). *The Bishop's Wife*. 1948: *The Big Clock*. 1949: *The Inspector-General*. *The Secret Garden*. *Come to the Stable*. 1950: *Buccaneer's Girl*. *Mystery Street*. *The Petty Girl* (GB: *Girl of the Year*). *Frenchie*. 1951: *Young Man with Ideas*. 1952: *Androcles and the Lion*. *Dreamboat*. *Les Miserables*. 1953: *The Girls of Pleasure Island*. 1954: *Hell's Half Acre*. *Three Ring Circus*. *The Glass Slipper*. 1956: *Stranger in the Night* (TV). 1957: *Witness for the Prosecution*. 1958: *Bell, Book and Candle*. **Fabulous Hollywood*. 1964: *Honeymoon Hotel*. *Mary Poppins*. *Pajama Party*. 1965: *That Darn Cat!* 1966: *Easy Come, Easy Go*. 1967: *Blackbeard's Ghost*. 1969: *Me, Natalie*. *My Dog, the Thief* (TV. GB: cinemas). *In Name Only* (TV). *Rascal*. 1971: *Willard*. 1973: *Arnold*. *Terror in the Wax Museum*. 1976: *Murder by Death*. 1980: *Die Laughing*. 1993: *Turn About: The Story of the Yale Puppeteers* (archive footage).

LAMONT, Duncan 1918–
Born in Portugal and raised in Scotland, this lowering, rugged actor with tousled brown hair and jutting lower lip was just as easily cast as gentle giant or cruel villain. He came to films from repertory and was kept

LANCHESTER, Elsa
(Elizabeth Sullivan) 1902–1986
Bright, bird-like, chestnut-haired British leading lady whose heroines tended to be eccentric; later she became an attention-grabbing character actress after moving to Hollywood. In show business from 16 and originally a singer, she married Charles Laughton in 1929. Probably best remembered now as the creature's mate in *Bride of Frankenstein*. Twice nominated for an Academy Award, in *Come to the Stable*

LANDAU, Martin 1928–
Spare, tall, sharp-faced, dark-haired (now silver) American actor, reminiscent of Raymond Massey, but with a more desperate look. He seemed set for a prolific film career after his second-lead villain in Hitchcock's *North by Northwest*, but then made relatively few films until the 1980s, getting tied up in the television series *Mission Impossible* and *Space 1999*, in both of which he appeared with his wife Barbara Bain. Nominated for an Academy Award in *Tucker: The Man and His Dream* and in *Crimes and Misdemeanors*,

he finally won the Oscar for his portrayal of horror star Bela Lugosi in *Ed Wood*.

1959: Pork Chop Hill. North by Northwest. The Sounds of Eden (TV). The Gazebo. 1962: Stagecoach to Dancer's Rock. 1963: Cleopatra. Decision at Midnight. 1965: The Hallelujah Trail. The Greatest Story Ever Told. 1966: Nevada Smith. 1969: Mission Impossible Versus the Mob (TV. GB: cinemas). 1970: Operation S.N.A.F.U. They Call Me MISTER Tibbs! 1971: Welcome Home Johnny Bristol (TV). A Town Called Bastard (US: A Town Called Hell). 1972: Black Gunn. 1976: Tony Saitta/Tough Tony. Blazing Magnum/Strange Shadows in an Empty Room. 1979: The Fall of the House of Usher. Meteor. The Last Word. 1980: The Death of Ocean View Park (TV). Earthright. Without Warning (GB: The Warning). Operation Moonbase Alpha. 1981: Easter Sunday. The Return. 1982: Alone in the Dark. 1983: The Being (Revised version of Easter Sunday). Trial by Terror (TV). 1984: Access Code. 1986: Treasure Island (released 1991). Kung Fu: The Movie (TV). Sweet Revenge. W.A.R: Women Against Rape. 1987: Cyclone. Empire State. Discovery Bay. Run If You Can. Return of the Six Million Dollar Man and the Bionic Woman (TV). La chouette aveugle. 1988: Paint It Black. Tucker: The Man and His Dream. 1989: The Neon Empire (TV). Max and Helen (TV). Crimes and Misdemeanors. Trust Me. 1990: Firehead. By Dawn's Early Light (cable TV). Real Bullets. 1991: The Color of Evening. No Place to Hide. Eye of the Widow (completed 1989). 1992: Mistress. Something to Live for: The Allison Gertz Story (TV). Legacy of Lies (TV). Tipperary. 1993: Finnegan's Wake. Time is Money. Manhattan Murder Mystery. Frame by Frame. Eye of the Stranger. Intersection. Sliver. 1994: Ed Wood. The Gold Cup. 1995: City Hall. 1996: Pinocchio.

LANDIS, Jessie Royce
(J. R. Medbury) 1904–1972
Dark-haired American stage actress who came to her busiest time in films in her middle forties and played matrons both caustic and dizzy. Her most notable screen appearance was probably as Grace Kelly's mother in *To Catch a Thief*, when she stubs out her cigarette in a soft-boiled egg. Died from cancer.

1930: Derelict. 1937: Oh! Doctor. 1939: First Love. 1949: My Foolish Heart. Mr Belvedere

Goes to College. It Happens Every Spring. 1950: Mother Didn't Tell Me. 1952: Meet Me Tonight. 1953: She Couldn't Say No (GB: Beautiful But Dangerous). 1955: To Catch a Thief. 1956: The Girl He Left Behind. The Swan. 1957: My Man Godfrey. 1958: I Married a Woman. 1959: North by Northwest. A Private's Affair. 1961: Aimez-vous Brahms? (GB: Goodbye Again). 1962: Bon Voyage! Boys' Night Out. 1963: Critics' Choice. Gidget Goes to Rome. 1969: Airport. 1971: Mr and Mrs Bo Jo Jones (TV).

LANE, Charles
(C. Levison) 1905–
Thin, scoop-nosed, long-faced, brown-haired, snoopy-looking American actor of average height. One could think of no better choice to play the kind of 'peeper' a husband would hire to trail his wife with a view to grounds for divorce. Consequently, he was cast as bailiffs, reporters, tax inspectors, debt collectors and various shady characters in pin-stripe suits, trilby hats and (often) rimless spectacles, from behind which beady eyes fastened on their victim. Still acting into his eighties, 'though there aren't many roles for old goats like me'.

1931: †Smart Money. †Road to Singapore. †Blonde Crazy (GB: Larceny Lane). †Union Depot (GB: Gentleman for a Day). 1932: †Manhattan Parade. †The Mouthpiece. †Blessed Event. 1933: †Central Airport. †Employees' Entrance. †The King's Vacation. †Blondie Johnson. †The Silk Express. †Private Detective 62. †Gold Diggers of 1933: †42nd Street. †My Woman. †The Bowery. †Mr Skitch. †Footlight Parade. †Advice to the Lovelorn. †Grand Slam. †She Had to Say Yes. 1934: †The Show-Off. †Twenty Million Sweethearts. †Looking for Trouble. †Twentieth Century. †Broadway Bill (GB: Strictly Confidential). †I'll Fix It. †The Band Plays On. †A Wicked Woman. †Let's Talk It Over. 1935: †Ginger. †One More Spring. †I Live My Life. †Here Comes the Band. The Florentine Dagger. †Princess O'Hara. †Two for Tonight. †Woman Wanted. 1936: †The Milky Way. †Mr Deeds Goes to Town. †Neighbourhood House (later cut to two-reeler). Band of Outlaws. The Crime of Dr Forbes. Born to Dance. The Bride Walks Out. Come Closer, Folks. Easy to Take. It Had to Happen. Lady Luck. Three Men on a Horse. Thirty-Six Hours to Kill. Ticket to Paradise. Two-Fisted Gentleman. 1937: Ali Baba Goes

*to Town. Bad Guy. Born Reckless. Criminal Lawyer. City Girl. Danger, Love at Work. Broadway Melody of 1938: Fit for a King. Internes Can't Take Money (GB: You Can't Take Money). The Jones Family in Hot Water. The Jones Family in Big Business. Sea Devils. Nothing Sacred. River of Missing Men. Partners in Crime. Trapped by G-Men. We're on the Jury. Venus Makes Trouble. One Mile from Heaven. 1938: Always in Trouble. Cocoanut Grove. Having Wonderful Time. Joy of Living. Blondie. In Old Chicago. Inside Story. Kentucky. Professor, Beware! The Rage of Paris. Thanks for Everything. Three Loves Has Nancy. You Can't Take It with You. 1939: Another Thin Man. Beware, Spooks! Charlie McCarthy, Detective. Fifth Avenue Girl. The Flying Irishman. Boy Slaves. The Cat and the Canary. Golden Boy. The Honeymoon's Over. Let Us Live. The Jones Family in Hollywood. News is Made at Night. Rose of Washington Square. Lucky Night. Mr Smith Goes to Washington. Second Fiddle. They All Come Out. *Think It Over. Made for Each Other. Thunder Afloat. Unexpected Father (GB: Sandy Takes a Bow). Miracles for Sale. Honeymoon in Bali (GB: Husbands or Lovers). Ice Follies of 1939. Television Spy. 1940: Alias the Deacon. The Crooked Road. The Doctor Takes a Wife. Dancing on a Dime. Edison, the Man. Buck Benny Rides Again. Blondie Plays Cupid. City for Conquest. Ellery Queen, Master Detective. *The Flag Speaks. A Little Bit of Heaven. The Primrose Path. On Their Own. Sandy is a Lady. It's a Date. Johnny Apollo. The Great Profile. Queen of the Mob. The Leather Pushers. Rhythm on the River. We Who Are Young. You Can't Fool Your Wife. I Can't Give You Anything But Love, Baby. Parole Fixer. Texas Rangers Ride Again. Young As You Feel. 1941: Ball of Fire. Barnacle Bill. Blondie in Society (GB: Henpecked). Buy Me That Town. Ellery Queen's Penthouse Mystery. Appointment for Love. Footlight Fever. Birth of the Blues. Confirm or Deny. Hot Spot (GB: I Wake Up Screaming). Meet John Doe. Back Street. The Big Store. The Crooked Road. The Invisible Woman. Obliging Young Lady. Repent at Leisure. The Invisible Woman. Ride 'Em Cowboy. Ellery Queen and the Perfect Crime (GB: The Perfect Crime). Sealed Lips. Sing Another Chorus. Sis Hopkins. Three Girls About Town. Look Who's Laughing. She Knew All the Answers. You're the One. ‡New York Town. 1942: Are Husbands Necessary? About Face. Broadway. Dudes Are Pretty People. Friendly Enemies. The Adventures of Martin Eden. Born to Sing. Enemy Agents Meet Ellery Queen (GB: The Lido Mystery). A Gentleman at Heart. Home in Wyomin'. The Lady is Willing. Flying Tigers. Pardon My Sarong. The Great Man's Lady. The Mad Martindales. Lady in a Jam. Tarzan's New York Adventure. Thru Different Eyes. They All Kissed the Bride. What's Cookin'? (GB: Wake Up and Dream). Yokel Boy (GB: Hitting the Headlines). 1943: Mr Lucky. Arsenic and Old Lace. 1946: A Close Call for Boston Blackie (GB: Lady of Mystery). The Invisible Informer. Just Before Dawn. The Show-Off (and 1934 film of same title). It's a Wonderful Life! Swell Guy. 1947: Bury Me Dead. The Farmer's Daughter. I Cover Big Town. Intrigue. Louisiana. It Happened on Fifth Avenue. Roses Are Red. Call Northside*

777. *1948: Apartment for Peggy. The Gentle-man from Nowhere. Out of the Storm. Race Street. State of the Union (GB: The World and His Wife). Moonrise. Smart Woman. 1949: The House Across the Street. Mighty Joe Young. Miss Grant Takes Richmond (GB: Innocence is Bliss). Mother is a Freshman (GB: Mother Knows Best). You're My Everything. Streets of San Francisco. 1950: For Heaven's Sake. Bannerline. Love That Brute. Riding High. Rookie Fireman. Watch the Birdie. The Yellow Cab Man. Backfire. 1951: I Can Get It for You Wholesale (GB: This is My Affair). Here Comes the Groom. Criminal Lawyer. 1952: The DuPont Story. The Sniper. Three for Bedroom C. Remains to be Seen. 1953: The Affairs of Dobie Gillis. The Juggler. 1956: The Birds and the Bees. 1957: Top Secret Affair (GB: Their Secret Affair). God is My Partner. 1958: Teacher's Pet. 1959: The Mating Game. The Thirty-Foot Bride of Candy Rock. But Not for Me. 1961: The Music Man. 1962: Papa's Delicate Condition. Alcatraz Express (TV). 1963: It's a Mad, Mad, Mad, Mad World. The Wheeler Dealers (GB: Separate Beds). The Carpetbaggers. 1964: Good Neighbor Sam. Looking for Love. The New Interns. John Goldfarb, Please Come Home. 1965: Billie. 1966: The Ugly Dachshund. The Ghost and Mr Chicken. 1967: The Gnome-Mobile. Eight on the Lam (GB: Eight on the Run). 1968: Did You Hear the One About the Traveling Sales-lady? What's So Bad About Feeling Good? 1970: Get to Know Your Rabbit. The Aristocats (voice only). 1971: The Great Man's Whiskers (TV). Hitched (TV. GB: Westward the Wagon). 1976: Sybil (TV. GB: cinemas). 1978: Movie Movie. Every Which Way But Loose. 1980: The Little Dragons. 1981: Dead Kids. The Return of the Beverly Hillbillies (TV). Strange Behavior (TV). 1983: Sunset Limousine (TV). Strange Invaders. 1985: Murphy's Romance. 1986: When the Bough Breaks (TV). 1987: Date with an Angel. 1995: The Computer Wore Tennis Shoes (TV).*

† As Charles Levison
‡ Scenes deleted from final release print

LANG, Harold 1923–1970
Fair-haired, slim-faced, shady-looking British actor who, in dark shirt and light tie, leeringly menaced many a British 'B' hero of the 1950s before perhaps deciding that such conduct was unbecoming to a RADA gold medalist and concentrating on a stage career, notably touring a record number

of countries, including Sweden, Italy, Germany, Switzerland, Turkey, Portugal, Sri Lanka, Pakistan and Egypt, where he died.

1949: Floodtide. The Spider and the Fly. 1950: Cairo Road. The Franchise Affair. 1951: Calling Bulldog Drummond. Cloudburst. 1952: So Little Time. Wings of Danger (US: Dead on Course). It Started in Paradise. Folly to be Wise. The Long Memory. 1953: Counterspy (US: Undercover Agent). The Saint's Return (US: The Saint's Girl Friday). Laughing Anne. The Story of Gilbert and Sullivan (US: The Great Gilbert and Sullivan). Street Corner (US: Both Sides of the Law). The Intruder. Star of My Night. A Day to Remember. 1954: The Case of the Bogus Count. Adventure in the Hopfields. Dance Little Lady. The Case of Diamond Annie. 36 Hours (US: Terror Street). The Passing Stranger. The Men of Sherwood Forest. 1955: Murder by Proxy (completed 1953. US: Blackout). The Quatermass Experiment (US: The Creeping Unknown). 1956: It's a Wonderful World! The Hideout. 1957: The Flesh is Weak. 1958: Chain of Events. Man with a Gun. A Night to Remember. The Betrayal. Links of Justice. Carve Her Name with Pride. 1959: Ben-Hur. 1962: Paranoiac. 1963: West 11. 1964: Dr Terror's House of Horrors. 1965: The Nanny. He Who Rides a Tiger. 1966: The Psychopath. 1968: Two Gentlemen Sharing.

LANSING, Joi
(Joyce Wassmansdoff) 1928–1972
Buxom American blonde with attractive looks and silky hair, a minor-league Jayne Mansfield, but hotter on the wisecracks. She probably had more talent than most of her rivals on the sexpot scene, but lacked an aura of innocence. She had one or two B-movie leads (the last as late as 1969), but was mostly confined to cameos and minor roles. Began as a singer. Actor Lance Fuller (1928–) was the first (1951–3) of her three husbands. Cancer killed her at 44.

*1947: ‡When a Girl's Beautiful. 1948: †Blondie's Secret. †Julia Misbehaves. †The Counterfeiters. †Easter Parade. 1949: †*Super Cue Men. †The Girl from Jones Beach. †Neptune's Daughter. †Take Me Out to the Ball Game (GB: Everybody's Cheering). 1950: Holiday Rhythm. 1951: On the Riviera. Two Tickets to Broadway. Pier 23. FBI Girl. 1952:*

The Merry Widow. Singin' in the Rain. 1953: The French Line. 1954: *So You Want to Go to a Nightclub. *So You're Taking in a Roomer. 1955: *So You Want to be on a Jury. *So You Want to be a VP. *So You Want to be a Policeman. Fingerman. Son of Sinbad. The Kentuckian. 1956: *The Fountain of Youth. *So You Think the Grass is Greener. Hot Cars. The Brave One. Hot Shots. 1958: Touch of Evil. 1959: But Not for Me. Atomic Submarine. A Hole in the Head. It Started with a Kiss. Who Was That Lady? 1960: Cinderfella. 1965: Marriage on the Rocks. 1967: Hillbillys in a Haunted House. 1969: Bigfoot.*

‡ As Joy Loveland
† As Joyce Lansing

LARCH, John 1924–
Light-haired, light-eyed, tall, cynical-looking American actor with splendidly scornful sneer. He came to Hollywood at 30 and played largely friendly types who couldn't be trusted; then he drifted off into television in the early 1960s, returning later for a few crooked businessmen and others who wore a crooked smile and didn't quite meet your gaze. Married actress Vivi Janiss; her death at 64 left him a widower in 1988.

1954: Bitter Creek. 1955: The Phoenix City Story (GB: The Phenix City Story). Tight Spot. 1956: Man from Del Rio. The Killer is Loose. Written on the Wind. Behind the High Wall. Seven Men from Now. 1957: Gun for a Coward. Man in the Shadow (GB: Pay the Devil). The Careless Years. Quantez. 1958: The Saga of Hemp Brown. From Hell to Texas (GB: Manhunt). 1959: Stampede at Bitter Creek (TV. GB: cinemas). 1960: Hell to Eternity. 1962: Miracle of the White Stallions (GB: The Flight of the White Stallions). How the West Was Won. 1968: The Wrecking Crew. The House of Seven Joys. 1969: The Great Bank Robbery. Hail, Hero! 1970: Move. Cannon for Cordoba. 1971: The Magic Carpet (TV). Women in Chains (TV). Dirty Harry. The City (TV). Play Misty for Me. 1972: Santee. Madigan: The Park Avenue Beat (TV). 1974: The Chadwick Family (TV). Winterkill (TV). Bad Ronald (TV). Framed. 1975: Collision Course (TV). The Desperate Miles (TV). Ellery Queen: Too Many Suspects (TV). 1976: Future Cop (TV). 1978: A Fire in the Sky (TV). The Critical List (TV). 1979: The Amityville Horror. 1982: Airplane II The Sequel.

LaRUE, Jack
(Gaspare Biondolillo) 1900–1984
Flat-faced, sad-eyed, sometimes moustachioed American gangster actor with dark,
wavy hair. Of Italian parentage, he quickly
gained popularity in the early 1930s as a
particularly grim and humourless type of
criminal with few redeeming qualities. His
talent for portaying viciousness propelled
him into a few semi-leading roles, too,
notably (at either end of the main body of
his film career) in *The Story of Temple Drake*
and *No Orchids for Miss Blandish*. In later
years, when acting jobs grew more scarce,
he became a restaurateur. Died from a heart
attack.

1930: *Follow the Leader*. 1932: *Radio Patrol.
Virtue. While Paris Sleeps. The All-American
(GB: Sport of a Nation). The Mouthpiece. A
Farewell to Arms. Blessed Event. Three on a
Match. I Am a Fugitive from a Chain Gang.
Man Against Woman. Lawyer Man.* 1933:
*The Woman Accused. 42nd Street. Terror
Aboard. The Girl in 419. To the Last Man.
The Kennel Murder Case. Christopher Strong.
The Story of Temple Drake. Gambling Ship.
Headline Shooter (GB: Evidence in Camera).*
1934: *The Fighting Rookie (GB: Dangerous
Enemy). Good Dame (GB: Good Girl). Miss
Fane's Baby is Stolen. No Ransom. Straight is
the Way. Take the Stand. Secret of the Chateau.*
1935: *Calling All Cars. Under the Pampas
Moon. The Headline Woman (GB: The Woman
in the Case). Little Big Shot. Times Square
Lady. Remember Last Night? After the Dance.
The Daring Young Man. Men of the Hour.
The Spanish Cape Mystery. Waterfront Lady.
Special Agent. His Night Out. Hot Off the
Press.* 1936: *The Dancing Pirate. Yellow Cargo.
Mind Your Own Business. Bridge of Sighs. Ellis
Island. In Paris AWOL (GB: Let's Pretend
We're Sweethearts). Strike Me Pink. It Couldn't
Have Happened. Go West, Young Man. Born
to Fight.* 1937: *That I May Live. Captains
Courageous. Trapped by G-Men. A Tenderfoot
Goes West. Dangerous Holiday. Her Husband
Lies.* 1938: *Arson Gang Busters. Valley of the
Giants. Under the Big Top (GB: The Circus
Comes to Town). I Demand Payment. Arson
Racket Squad. Murder in Soho (US: Murder
in the Night).* 1939: *The Gang's All Here (US:
The Amazing Mr Forrest). Big Town Czar. In
Old Caliente.* 1940: *Charlie Chan in Panama.
Enemy Agent (GB: Secret Enemy). Forgotten
Girls. East of the River. Fugitive from a Prison*

Camp. *The Sea Hawk.* 1941: *Footsteps in the
Dark. The Gentleman from Dixie. Hard Guy
(GB: Professional Bride). Paper Bullets. Ring-
side Maisie (GB: Cash and Carry). Swamp
Woman.* 1942: *A Desperate Chance for Ellery
Queen (GB: A Desperate Chance). American
Empire (GB: My Son Alone). Highways by
Night. The Pay-Off. Pardon My Sarong. X
Marks the Spot.* 1943: *The Desert Song. The
Girl from Monterey. The Law Rides Again.
Never a Dull Moment. A Gentle Gangster.
Pistol Packin' Mama. Smart Guy (GB: You
Can't Beat the Law). The Sultan's Daughter.
Scream in the Dark. Secret Service in Darkest
Africa (serial).* 1944: *Dangerous Passage.
Follow the Leader. Leave It to the Irish. Machine
Gun Mama. The Last Ride.* 1945: *Dakota.
Cornered. Road to Utopia. Steppin' in Society.
The Spanish Main.* 1946: *In Old Sacramento.
Murder in the Music Hall.* 1947: *Bush Pilot.
Santa Fé Uprising. My Favorite Brunette. Robin
Hood of Monterey.* 1948: *No Orchids for Miss
Blandish.* 1950: *For Heaven's Sake.* 1952:
Ride the Man Down. 1957: *Slaughter on 10th
Avenue.* 1962: *40 Pounds of Trouble.* 1964:
*Robin and the Seven Hoods. For Those Who
Think Young.* 1966: *The Spy in the Green Hat
(TV. GB: cinemas).* 1975: *Won Ton Ton, the
Dog Who Saved Hollywood.*

LAURIE, John 1897–1980
Thin-headed, wild-eyed, frizzy-haired,
bushy-browed, (very) Scottish actor, frequently seen in fanatical or eccentric roles.
Although the earlier characters he created
were often surrounded by gloom and doom,
he also had a dry, faintly maniacal sense of
humour, seen to good effect in his later
years as one of the denizens of TV's *Dad's
Army*. Originally planned to become an
architect, but switched to an acting course
in his early twenties.

1929: *Juno and the Paycock (US: The Shame
of Mary Boyle).* 1934: *Red Ensign (US:
Strike!).* 1935: *Her Last Affaire. The 39 Steps.*
1936: *Tudor Rose (US: Nine Days a Queen).
As You Like It. East Meet West. Born That
Way.* 1937: *The Edge of the World. Farewell
Again (US: Troopship). The Windmill. Jericho
(US: Dark Sands). There Was a Young Man.*
1938: *A Royal Divorce. The Claydon Treasure
Mystery.* 1939: *The Ware Case. The Four
Feathers. Q Planes (US: Clouds Over Europe).*
1940: *Convoy. Laugh It Off. Sailors Three*

(US: *Three Cockeyed Sailors*). 1941: *Dangerous
Moonlight (US: Suicide Squadron). Old Mother
Riley's Ghosts. The Ghost of St Michael's.
Ships with Wings. Old Mother Riley Cleans
Up.* 1943: *The Demi-Paradise (US: Adventure
for Two). The Lamp Still Burns. The Gentle
Sex. The Life and Death of Colonel Blimp (US:
Colonel Blimp).* 1944: *Fanny by Gaslight (US:
Man of Evil). Medal for the General. The Way
Ahead (US: Immortal Battalion). Henry V.*
1945: *I Know Where I'm Going! The Agitator.
Great Day. Caesar and Cleopatra. The World
Owes Me a Living.* 1946: *School for Secrets
(US: Secret Flight). Gaiety George (US: Show-
time).* 1947: *Jassy. The Brothers. Uncle Silas
(US: The Inheritance). Mine Own Executioner.*
1948: *Bonnie Prince Charlie. Hamlet.* 1949:
Floodtide. Madeleine. 1950: *No Trace. Treasure
Island. Trio. Happy Go Lovely. Pandora and
the Flying Dutchman.* 1951: *Laughter in
Paradise. Encore. Saturday Island (US: Island
of Desire).* 1952: **Potter of the Yard. There's a
Way. Tread Softly. The Great Game.* *Rig 20
(narrator only).* 1953: *The Fake. Too Many
Detectives. Love in Pawn. Mr Beamish Goes
South. Strange Stories. Johnny on the Run.*
1954: *Destination Milan. Devil Girl from
Mars. Hobson's Choice. The Black Knight.*
1955: *Richard III.* 1957: **Day of Grace.
Campbell's Kingdom. Murder Reported.* 1958:
*Rockets Galore! (US: Mad Little Island). Next
to No Time!* 1959: *Kidnapped.* 1961: *Don't
Bother to Knock! (US: Why Bother to Knock?).*
1963: *Ladies Who Do. Siege of the Saxons.*
1964: *Eagle Rock (voice only).* 1966: *Mr Ten
Per Cent. The Reptile.* 1971: *Dad's Army. The
Abominable Dr Phibes.* 1975: *One of Our
Dinosaurs is Missing.* 1976: *Pure S.* 1978:
Return to the Edge of the World. 1979: *The
Prisoner of Zenda.*

LAUTER, Ed 1940–
Bald, tall, leering, long-jawed, villainous-
looking American actor, sometimes seen as
toughies whose yellow streak was revealed
in the final reel. A former English graduate
and stand-up comic, he came to films in his
early thirties and was soon one of the few
familiar character faces of the 1970s and
beyond. He acquitted himself more than
adequately as a private eye in the leading
role of a TV movie, but was of more value in
the supporting cast and has lodged at around
fifth billing ever since. Has tackled more
comedy in recent years.

1970: *Maybe I'll Come Home in the Spring (TV). 1971: Hickey & Boggs. 1972: Dirty Little Billy. Rage. The Magnificent Seven Ride! The New Centurions (GB: Precinct 45 — Los Angeles Police). Bad Company. 1973: The Last American Hero. Executive Action. Lolly Madonna XXX (GB: The Lolly Madonna War). Class of '63 (TV). 1974: The Longest Yard (GB: The Mean Machine). The Midnight Man. French Connection II (GB: French Connection No. 2). The Migrants (TV). The Godchild (TV). 1975: Satan's Triangle (TV). A Shadow in the Streets (TV). Breakheart Pass. Last Hours Before Morning (TV). 1976: King Kong. Family Plot. 1977: The Chicken Chronicles. The White Buffalo. My Undercover Years with the Ku Klux Klan/Undercover with the KKK/The Freedom Riders (TV). The Clone Master (TV). Magic. 1979: Love's Savage Fury (TV). The Jericho Mile (TV. GB: cinemas). Nickel Mountain (released 1985). Coming Attractions. 1980: Death Hunt. The Boy Who Drank Too Much (TV). Alcatraz: the Whole Shocking Story (TV). 1981: Loose Shoes. The Amateur. 1982: In the Custody of Strangers (TV). Timerider: The Adventure of Lyle Swann. Rooster (TV). 1983: Cujo. Hardcastle and McCormick (TV). Lassiter. The Big Score. Manimal (TV). 1984: The Seduction of Gina (TV). Finders Keepers. The Cartier Affair (TV). 1985: Youngblood. 3:15. Real Genius. Girls Just Want to Have Fun. Death Wish 3. 1986: The Last Days of Patton (TV). Raw Deal. Double Image (TV). Yuri Nosenko KGB (TV). Firefighter (TV). The Thanksgiving Promise (TV). 1987: Chief Zabu. Revenge of the Nerds II: Nerds in Paradise. 1988: Gleaming the Cube. Goodbye Miss 4th of July (TV. GB: Farewell Miss Freedom). Judgment. 1989: Tennessee Nights. †Fat Man and Little Boy (GB: Shadow Makers). 1991: The Rocketeer. Stephen King's 'Golden Years' (TV). 1992: Calendar Girl, Cop Killer?: The Bambi Bembenek Story (TV). School Ties. 1993: S.I.S./Extreme Justice. 1994: Secret Sins of the Father (TV). Raven Hawk. Digital Man. Trial by Jury. Wagons East./Girl in the Cadillac. Mulholland Falls. 1995: Crash.*

† Scenes deleted from final release print

LAUTER, Harry 1914–1990

Tall, fair-haired, blue-eyed, glum-looking American actor who played villains in serials, westerns and all kinds of low-budget adventure films, and had the height and looks to appear genuinely threatening. He actually

got to play heroes in three mid-1950s serials, but the genre was a dying breed, and he returned to secondary bad guys in minor movies and very small roles in major ones. Took an early retirement from villainy in the early 1970s to concentrate on running an art and antique gallery, and on his own secondary career as a painter. Died from heart failure.

1948: *Moonrise. Incident. Indian Agent. Jungle Patrol. The Gay Intruders. A Foreign Affair. 1949: I Was a Male War Bride (GB: You Can't Sleep Here). Frontier Marshal/Frontier Investigator. Prince of the Plains. Alimony. Bandit King of Texas. Without Honor. The Great Dan Patch. Twelve O'Clock High. Slattery's Hurricane. Tucson. White Heat. Zamba (GB: Zamba the Gorilla). 1950: Blue Grass of Kentucky. Experiment Alcatraz. Between Midnight and Dawn. The Great Jewel Robbery. No Way Out. I'll Get By. *Ready to Ride. 1951: Bowery Battalion. Call Me Mister. According to Mrs Hoyle. I Want You. Hills of Utah. The Kid from Amarillo. Lorna Doone. Operation Pacific. Roadblock. Silver City Bonanza. Let's Go Navy. Thunder in God's Country. Flying Leathernecks. Flying Disc Man from Mars (serial). The Mob (GB: Remember That Face). Whirlwind. The Day the Earth Stood Still. Valley of Fire. The Racket. 1952: Androcles and the Lion. Bugles in the Afternoon. Apache Country. Night Stage to Galveston. Red Ball Express. The Sea Tiger. The Steel Fist. This Woman is Dangerous. Talk About a Stranger. Yukon Gold. 1953: Canadian Mounties vs Atomic Invaders (serial). The Big Heat. Fighter Attack. Flight Nurse. The Fighting Lawman. The Marshal's Daughter. Prince of Pirates. Forbidden. Pack Train. Topeka. Crime Wave (GB: The City is Dark). 1954: The Boy from Oklahoma. The Bob Mathias Story (GB: The Flaming Torch). Dragnet. Dragonfly Squadron. The Forty-Niners. Trader Tom of the China Seas (serial). Return to Treasure Island. Yankee Pasha. 1955: Apache Ambush. It Came from Beneath the Sea. King of the Carnival (serial). The Creature with the Atom Brain. The Crooked Web. At Gunpoint! (GB: Gunpoint!). Lord of the Jungle. Outlaw Treasure. 1956: Blonde Bait. Earth vs the Flying Saucers. Dig That Uranium. The Man in the Gray Flannel Suit. Miami Exposé. Tension at Table Rock. The Werewolf. The Women of Pitcairn Island. 1957: The Badge of Marshal Brennan. Girl on the Run. Death in Small Doses. Hellcats of the Navy. The Oklahoman. Raiders of Old California. Shoot Out at Medicine Bend. 1958: The Cry Baby Killer. Good Day for a Hanging. The Last Hurrah. Missile Monsters. Return to Warbow. Toughest Gun in Tombstone. Tarzan's Fight for Life. 1959: A Date with Death. The Gunfight at Dodge City. Louisiana Hussy (GB: Bad Girl) 1961: Buffalo Gun. Posse from Hell. 1962: The Wild Westerners. Lonely Are the Brave. 1963: Showdown. It's a Mad, Mad, Mad, Mad World. 1964: Bullet for a Badman. The Satan Bug. 1965: Fort Courageous. Convict Stage. 1966: Ambush Bay. Fort Utah. For Pete's Sake! 1967: Tarzan's Jungle Rebellion (TV. Released to cinemas 1970). 1968: More Dead Than Alive. Massacre Harbor. 1969: Barquero. Superbeast (released 1972). 1970:*

Maybe I'll Come Home in the Spring (TV). Zig Zag (GB: False Witness). 1971: The Todd Killings. Escape from the Planet of the Apes.

LAWRENCE, Marc
(Max Goldsmith) 1910–

Dark-haired Italianate Hollywood actor, a former singer and stage actor who devoted himself almost exclusively to films from 1936. With his narrow head, hooded eyes and tight, humourless smile, Lawrence was a natural for gangsters—and very efficient at it too. As he grew older, his pock-marked face took on a mottled appearance, making him look like an ancient, but still very deadly cobra.

1932: *If I Had a Million. 1933: Gambling Ship. White Woman. Lady for a Day. 1934: Death on the Diamond. 1935: Little Big Shot. Dr Socrates. Men of the Hour. G-Men. Don't Bet on Blondes. Strangers All. Go Into Your Dance (GB: Casino de Paree). 1936: Trapped by Television (GB: Caught by Television). Counterfeit. Road Gang. Night Waitress. The Final Hour. Love on a Bet. Under Two Flags. Desire. The Cowboy Star. 1937: I Promise to Pay. Racketeers in Exile. San Quentin. Counsel for Crime. Murder in Greenwich Village. The Shadow (GB: The Circus Shadow). Charlie Chan on Broadway. A Dangerous Adventure. Criminals of the Air. Motor Madness. What Price Vengeance? (GB: Vengeance). 1938: Penitentiary. Convicted. Adventure in Sahara. The Spider's Web (serial). There's That Woman Again (GB: What a Woman!). Charlie Chan in Honolulu. Who Killed Gail Preston? I Am the Law. Squadron of Honor. While New York Sleeps. 1939: Romance of the Redwoods. Blind Alley. The Housekeeper's Daughter. Beware, Spooks! Homicide Bureau. SOS Tidal Wave (GB: Tidal Wave). Sergeant Madden. Ex-Champ (GB: Golden Gloves). The Lone Wolf Spy Hunt (GB: The Lone Wolf's Daughter). *Think First. Code of the Streets. Dust Be My Destiny. Invisible Stripes. 1940: Charlie Chan at the Wax Museum. Brigham Young—Frontiersman (GB: Brigham Young). Love, Honor and Oh, Baby! The Man Who Talked Too Much. Johnny Apollo. The Golden Fleecing. The Great Profile. 1941: A Dangerous Game. The Man Who Lost Himself. Lady Scarface. The Shepherd of the Hills. Public Enemies. The Monster and the Girl. Tall, Dark and Handsome. Blossoms in the Dust. Sundown.*

Hold That Ghost! 1942: Yokel Boy (GB: Hitting the Headlines). Call of the Canyon. This Gun for Hire. Nazi Agent. 'Neath Brooklyn Bridge. The Ox-Bow Incident (GB: Strange Incident). 1943: Hit the Ice. Calaboose. Submarine Alert. Eyes of the Underworld. 1944: Rainbow Island. Tampico. Dillinger. The Princess and the Pirate. 1945: Don't Fence Me In. Flame of the Barbary Coast. Club Havana. Life with Blondie. 1946: Blonde Alibi. The Virginian. Cloak and Dagger. The Big Sleep. 1947: I Walk Alone. Yankee Fakir. Unconquered. Captain from Castile. Joe Palooka in the Knock-Out. 1948: Out of the Storm. Key Largo. 1949: Jigsaw. Tough Assignment. Calamity Jane and Sam Bass. 1950: The Black Hand. Abbott and Costello in the Foreign Legion. The Asphalt Jungle. The Desert Hawk. 1951: Hurricane Island. My Favorite Spy. Vacanze col gangster (GB: Gun Moll). Foreign Legion/Legione straniera. 1952: I tre corsari. Noi peccatore/Noi peccatini. La tratta della bianchi (GB: Girls Marked Danger). 1953: Il piu comico spettacolo del mondo. Fratelli d'Italia. Jolanda, la figlia del corsaro nero. 1954: Ballata tragica/Love Without Tomorrow. Helen of Troy. 1956: Suor Maria. 1957: Kill Her Gently. 1962: Recoil (TV. GB: cinemas). 1963: Johnny Cool. †Nightmare in the Sun. 1964: Due mafiosi contro Al Capone. 1966: Savage Pampas. Johnny Tiger. Deux tueurs. Custer of the West. 1968: Eve, the Savage Venus. Krakatoa – East of Java. 1969: The Five Man Army. The Kremlin Letter. 1971: Diamonds Are Forever. 1973: Frasier, the Sensuous Lion. Honor Thy Father (TV. GB: cinemas). 1974: The Man with the Golden Gun. 1976: Marathon Man. 1977: A Piece of the Action. 1978: Foul Play. King of Kong Island. 1979: Hot Stuff. Goin' Coconuts. Swap Meet. 1980: Supersnooper (US: Super Fuzz). 1982: †Pigs (later Daddy's Darling. Filmed 1972). Cataclysm. Terror at Alcatraz (TV). 1985: Night Train to Terror. 1987: The Big Easy. 1990: Donor (TV). 1992: Newsies (GB: The Newsboys). Ruby.

† Also directed

featured (and sometimes starring) roles in many TV movies of the 1970s and 1980s, and as star of the series. *Phyllis.*

1955: Kiss Me Deadly. 1956: The Rack. 1961: The Chapman Report. 1969: Butch Cassidy and the Sundance Kid. Silent Night, Lonely Night (TV). 1970: The People Next Door. WUSA. Lovers and Other Strangers. 1971: The Steagle. The Last Picture Show. Suddenly Single (TV). 1972: Haunts of the Very Rich (TV). Of Thee I Sing (TV). Of Men and Women (TV). A Brand New Life (TV). Crime Club (TV). 1973: Dying Room Only (TV). Dillinger. Charley and the Angel. Run, Stranger, Run/Happy Mother's Day . . . Love George. 1974: Hitchhike! (TV). Daisy Miller. Death Sentence (TV). Young Frankenstein. The Migrants (TV). A Girl Named Sooner (TV). Thursday's Game (TV). 1975: Death Scream (TV). Someone I Touched (TV). Crazy Mama. The New Original Wonder Woman (TV). 1976: The Love Boat (TV). 1977: It Happened One Christmas (TV). High Anxiety. The Mouse and His Child (voice only). 1978: The Muppet Movie. The North Avenue Irregulars (GB: Hill's Angels). Foolin' Around (released 1980). Willa (TV). Long Journey Back (TV). 1979: SOS Titanic (TV. GB: cinemas). Mrs R's Daughter (TV). This Time Forever. Scavenger Hunt. 1980: Scoring. Yesterday. The Oldest Living Graduate (TV). The Acorn People (TV). Herbie Goes Bananas. 1981: History of the World Part I. Advice to the Lovelorn (TV). 1982: Miss All-American Beauty (TV). 1983: The Woman Who Willed a Miracle (TV). DIXIE: Changing Habits (TV). The Demon Murder Case (TV). Ernie Kovacs: Between the Laughter (TV). 1985: Love is Never Silent (TV). 1986: Bobo. My Little Pony (voice only). Shadow Play. 1987: The Facts of Life Down Under (TV). 1988: Going to the Chapel (TV). 1989: Love Hurts. Prancer. 1990: Texasville. Fine Things (TV). 1993: A Troll in Central Park (voice only). Miracle Child (TV). The Beverly Hillbillies. My Boyfriend's Back. Falsely Accused (TV). 1995: The Gaslight Addition.

par excellence after beginning his career in German and French films. This king of screen co-respondents did not enlarge his range, however, and in post-war years drifted away from the cinema. Died from a heart attack.

*1923: Friedericus Rex. 1924: La mort fortunée. L'âme d'un artiste. 600,000 francs par mois. Le prince charmant. 1925: Les doigts brûlés. 1926: The Sorrows of Satan. 1927: The Love of Sunya. The Angel of Broadway. The Forbidden Woman. Let 'Er Go Gallegher (GB: Gallegher). 1928: Walking Back. Sin Town. 1929: The Veiled Woman. Street Girl. They Had to See Paris. 1930: Half Shot at Sunrise. The Cuckoos. The Midnight Mystery. The Conspiracy. 1931: Bachelor Apartment. Deceit. Woman Pursued. The Lady Refuses. The Gay Diplomat. 1932: *Hollywood on Parade. *The Hollywood Handicap. Unholy Love. 1933: Bombshell (GB: Blonde Bombshell). Made on Broadway (GB: The Girl I Made). Laughing at Life. Sweepings. 1934: Kansas City Princess. The Merry Frinks (GB: The Happy Family). The Merry Widow. Moulin Rouge. 1935: China Seas. Strange Wives. She Couldn't Take It (GB: Woman Tamer). Goin' to Town. Sweepstake Annie (GB: Annie Doesn't Live Here). 1936: The Golden Arrow. Pepper. Love on the Run. 1937: Fair Warning. Conquest (GB: Marie Walewska). History is Made at Night. Maytime. Atlantic Flight. Mama Steps Out. Angel. 1938: Straight, Place and Show (GB: They're Off!). Wise Girl. 1939: You Can't Cheat an Honest Man. Trapped in the Sky. The Mystery of Mr Wong. Elsa Maxwell's Hotel for Women/Hotel for Women. 1940: Public Deb No. 1. Passport to Alcatraz (GB: Alien Sabotage). 1941: The Shanghai Gesture. Blue, White and Perfect. 1942: Foreign Agent. Journey into Fear. Lure of the Islands. 1943: Mission to Moscow. Around the World. 1944: Oh, What a Night! Are These Our Parents (GB: They Are Guilty). 1945: Rhapsody in Blue. 1952: California Conquest. The Snows of Kilimanjo. 1953: The War of the Worlds.*

LEACHMAN, Cloris 1926–
Thin-faced blonde American actress, mostly in anguished roles, but no slouch in screwball comedy. Tremendously busy in television from the late 1940s, but hardly seen in the cinema at all until an Academy Award for *The Last Picture Show* brought her wider recognition. Television called her back for

LEBEDEFF, Ivan 1894–1953
This brown-haired, pencil-moustached, Lithuanian-born actor (an ex-office in the Czar's army) was, in films, a real smoothie. A cigarette, a tan and a dazzling smile usually accompanied his romantic advances; for a few years, he became a Hollywood lothario

LEE, Bernard 1908–1981
Brown-haired British actor with large, honest, friendly face, a screen portrayer of solid, pleasant, dependable types. Never a star, but in demand for reliable character roles for 40 years—only effectively cast against type in 1963's *Ring of Spies*. Pro-

longed his screen presence past retirement with his long-running portrayal of James Bond's affable, humourless boss, 'M', an extension of his many film policemen. Died from cancer.

1934: The Double Event. 1935: The River House Mystery. 1936: Rhodes of Africa (US: Rhodes) 1937: The Black Tulip. 1938: The Terror. Murder in Soho (US: Murder in the Night). 1939: Frozen Limits. The Outsider. 1940: Let George Do it. Spare a Copper. 1941: Once a Crook. 1946: This Man is Mine. 1947: Dusty Bates (serial). The Courtneys of Curzon Street (US: The Courtney Affair). 1948: The Fallen Idol. Quartet. Elizabeth of Ladymead. 1949: The Third Man. The Blue Lamp. 1950: Morning Departure (US: Operation Disaster). Odette. Last Holiday. Cage of Gold. The Adventurers (US: The Great Adventure). 1951: Calling Bulldog Drummond. White Corridors. Appointment with Venus (US: Island Rescue). Mr Denning Drives North. 1952: Gift Horse (US: Glory at Sea). The Yellow Balloon. 1953: Single-Handed (US: Sailor of the King). Beat the Devil. 1954: Father Brown (US: The Detective). Seagulls over Sorrento (US: Crest of the Wave). The Rainbow Jacket. The Purple Plain. 1955: Out of the Clouds. The Ship That Died of Shame (US: PT Raiders). 1956: The Battle of the River Plate (US: Pursuit of the Graf Spee). The Spanish Gardener. 1957: Fire Down Below. Across the Bridge. High Flight. Interpol (US: Pick-up Alley). 1958: Dunkirk. The Key. Nowhere to Go. The Man Upstairs. Danger Within (US: Breakout). 1959: Beyond This Place (US: Web of Evidence). Kidnapped. The Angry Silence. 1960: Cone of Silence (US: Trouble in the Sky). Clue of the Twisted Candle. 1961: Partners in Crime. Clue of the Silver Key. Fury at Smuggler's Bay. The Secret Partner. Whistle down the Wind. 1962: The Share Out. The L-Shaped Room. Dr No. Vengeance (US: The Brain). Two Left Feet. 1963: From Russia with Love. A Place to Go. Ring of Spies. Saturday Night Out. 1964: Who Was Maddox? Gold-finger. Dr Terror's House of Horrors. 1965: The Legend of Young Dick Turpin. Thunderball. The Amorous Adventures of Moll Flanders. The Spy Who Came in from the Cold. 1967: You Only Live Twice. Operation Kid Brother. 1969: Crossplot. On Her Majesty's Secret Service. 1970: 10 Rillington Place. The Man Who Died Twice (TV). The Raging Moon (US: Long Ago Tomorrow). 1971: Danger Point. Diamonds Are Forever. Dulcima. 1973: Live and Let Die. Frankenstein and the Monster from Hell. 1974: Percy's Progress. The Man with the Golden Gun. 1976: Beauty and the Beast. 1977: The Spy Who Loved Me. 1979: Moonraker. 1980: Dangerous Davies—The Last Detective (TV).

LEECH, Richard
(R. McClelland) 1922–

Flat-faced, snub-nosed, chunkily built, Irish-born actor with dark, crinkly hair and rich, fruity voice. His slightly self-satisfied looks often had him cast in British films as unsympathetic officers and gentlemen, or other men trying to woo the heroine from her husband. He had studied (successfully) to be a doctor, but practised for only a year before opting for an acting career. The first

stage appearance of this most cultivated of actors was as a Nubian slave! He has an actress daughter, Eliza McClelland.

*1948: The Small Voice (US: Hideout). 1949: The Temptress. Morning Departure (US: Operation Disaster). 1952: Little Big Shot. Treasure Hunt. 1953: The Red Dress. 1954: Lease of Life. Children Galore. The Dam Busters. 1955: The Prisoner. 1956: It's Never Too Late. The Long Arm (US: The Third Key). The Feminine Touch (US: The Gentle Touch). The Iron Petticoat. The Good Companions. 1957: Yangtse Incident (US: Battle Hell). Night of the Demon (US: Curse of the Demon). These Dangerous Years (US: Dangerous Youth). The Birthday Present. Time Without Pity. The Moonraker. 1958: Dublin Nightmare. A Lady Mislaid. Gideon's Day (US: Gideon of Scotland Yard). Ice Cold in Alex (US: Desert Attack). A Night to Remember. The Horse's Mouth. The Wind Cannot Read. 1960: Tunes of Glory. Doctor in Love. 1961: The Terror of the Tongs. The Wild and the Willing. 1962: The War Lover. I Thank a Fool. 1963: Ricochet. Walk a Tightrope. The Cracksman. 1965: Life at the Top. 1966: The Fighting Prince of Donegal. 1967: *Promenade. 1971: Young Winston. 1973: *The Laughing Girl Murder. 1974: Got it Made/Sweet Virgin (shown 1978). 1980: The Mirror Crack'd. 1982: Gandhi. 1983: Champions. 1984: The Shooting Party. 1985: Florence Nightingale (TV).*

LEIBER, Fritz 1882–1949

American Shakespearian actor with 'noble Roman' profile, very dark hair and piercing gaze. He played one or two distinguished roles in silents (including Julius Caesar in *Cleopatra*), then went back to the stage. He returned to Hollywood in 1935, whitehaired but with profile intact, for 15 years of austere character roles as abbots, doctors, and assorted saintly characters east and west, with so many wise aphorisms to hand that it hurt. Died from a heart attack.

1916: Romeo and Juliet. 1917: The Primitive Call. Cleopatra. 1920: If I Were King. The Song of the Soul. 1921: The Queen of Sheba. 1935: A Tale of Two Cities. The Story of Louis Pasteur. 1936: Under Two Flags. Down to the Sea. Hearts in Bondage. Sins of Man. Anthony Adverse. Camille. 1937: Champagne Waltz. The Prince and the Pauper. The Great Garrick. 1938: Gateway. If I Were King (and earlier

version). The Jury's Secret. Flight into Nowhere. 1939: Nurse Edith Cavell. Pack Up Your Troubles. They Made Her a Spy. The Hunchback of Notre Dame. 1940: All This and Heaven Too. The Sea Hawk. The Way of All Flesh. The Lady with Red Hair. The Mortal Storm. 1941: Aloma of the South Seas. 1942: Crossroads. 1943: First Comes Courage. The Phantom of the Opera. The Desert Song. 1944: Are These Our Parents? (GB: They Are Guilty). The Imposter. Cry of the Werewolf. 1945: The Cisco Kid Returns. The Spanish Main. This Love of Ours. Son of Lassie. 1946: Angel on My Shoulder. Humoresque. Thieves' Holiday (later and GB: A Scandal in Paris). Strange Journey. 1947: High Conquest. Bells of San Angelo. Monsieur Verdoux. Dangerous Venture. The Web. 1948: To the Ends of the Earth. Adventures of Casanova. Another Part of the Forest. Inner Sanctum. 1949: Bagdad. Bride of Vengeance. Samson and Delilah. Song of India. 1950: Devil's Doorway.

LEMBECK, Harvey 1923–1982

Shortish, bulky, black-haired, Brooklynese American actor, in good parts almost right away from 1950 after radio work, and at his most popular in the early 1950s, when he played with Tom Ewell in the 'Willie and Joe' army comedies; he had another good featured role in *Stalag 17*. Semi-leading roles in more dramatic vein were somewhat less successful, but Lembeck was in any case soon entrenched on TV as Rocco, Sergeant Bilko's sidekick, in the long-running comedy series *You'll Never Get Rich*. In later years, he ran The Comedy Workshop before his early death from a heart attack. His son Michael is also an actor.

1950: USS Teakettle (later You're in the Navy Now). 1951: The Frogmen. Finders Keepers. Fourteen Hours. 1952: Back at the Front (GB: Willie and Joe in Tokyo). Just Across the Street. 1953: Girls in the Night (GB: Life After Dark). Stalag 17. Mission over Korea (GB: Eyes of the Skies). 1954: The Command. 1956: Between Heaven and Hell. 1961: Sail a Crooked Ship. A View from the Bridge. The Last Time I Saw Archie. 1963: Beach Party. 1964: Bikini Beach. The Unsinkable Molly Brown. Love With the Proper Stranger. Pajama Party. Sergeant Deadhead. 1965: How to Stuff a Wild Bikini. Beach Blanket Bingo. Dr Goldfoot and the Bikini Machine (GB: Dr G and the Bikini Machine). 1966: Fireball 500. The Spirit is Willing. The Ghost in the Invisible Bikini. 1968: Hello Down There. Lola in Lipstick (TV). 1976: There Is No 13. Raid on Entebbe (TV. GB: cinemas). 1980: The Gong Show Movie.

Le MESURIER, John 1912–1983

Brow-mopping, fretful-looking, (very) British actor, with long, equine features wryly resigned to disaster. He played dramatic roles at first, although his characters were equally as harassed as those in the comic gloom-and-doom which enveloped him from the mid-1950s on, when he became an ostensibly bewildered foil for some of Britain's best comedians. Later popular in the TV series *Dad's Army*. Married to Hattie Jacques (first of two—*qv*) from 1949 to 1965: he left an obituary at the time of his death from an abdominal illness, saying that he had 'conked out'. A human Eeyore.

1948: Death in the Hand. Escape from Broadmoor. 1949: A Matter of Murder. Old Mother Riley's New Venture. 1950: Dark Interval. 1951: Never Take No for an Answer. Blind Man's Bluff. 1952: Mother Riley Meets the Vampire (US: Vampire Over London). 1953: House of Blackmail (voice only). *The Drayton Case. The Blue Parrot. Black 13. The Pleasure Garden. 1954: Dangerous Cargo. Stranger from Venus (US: Immediate Delivery). Beautiful Stranger (US: Twist of Fate). 1955: Police Dog. Josephine and Men. A Time to Kill. Private's Progress. 1956: The Battle of the River Plate (US: Pursuit of the Graf Spee). The

Baby and the Battleship. Brothers in Law. The Good Companions. 1957: Happy is the Bride! These Dangerous Years (US: Dangerous Youth). High Flight. The Admirable Crichton (US: Paradise Lagoon). The Moonraker. The Man Who Wouldn't Talk. 1958: Law and Disorder. Another Time, Another Place. I Was Monty's Double (GB: Monty's Double). Gideon's Day (US: Gideon of Scotland Yard). Blind Spot. Man with a Gun. The Captain's Table. Blood of the Vampire. Too Many Crooks. Carlton-Browne of the FO (US: Man in a Cocked Hat). 1959: Operation Amsterdam. The Lady is a Square. Ben-Hur. A Touch of Larceny. I'm All Right, Jack. The Wreck of the Mary Deare. The Hound of the Baskervilles. Our Man in Havana. Shake Hands with the Devil. Follow a Star. Desert Mice. School for Scoundrels. 1960: Jack the Ripper. The Day They Robbed the Bank of England. Let's Get Married. Never Let Go. Dead Lucky. Doctor in Love. The Night We Got the Bird. The Pure Hell of St Trinians. Bulldog Breed. 1961: Five Golden Hours. The Rebel (US: Call Me Genius). Very Important Person (US: A Coming Out Party). Don't Bother to Knock! (US: Why Bother to Knock?). Invasion Quartet. On the Fiddle (US: Operation Snafu). Village of Daughters. Mr Topaze (US: I Like Money). 1962: Hair of the Dog. Go to Blazes. Jigsaw. Flat Two. The Waltz of the Toreadors. Mrs Gibbons' Boys. Only Two Can Play. The Wrong Arm of the Law. We Joined the Navy. The Punch and Judy Man. 1963: The Pink Panther. In the Cool of the Day. Never Put It in Writing. Hot Enough for June (US: Agent 8¾). The Mouse on the Moon. The Main Attraction. 1964: The Moon-Spinners. 1965: The Early Bird. City Under the Sea (US: War Gods of the Deep). Cuckoo Patrol. Masquerade. Where the Spies Are. Those Magnificent Men in Their Flying Machines. The Liquidator. 1966: The Sandwich Man. Eye of the Devil. Finders Keepers. The Wrong Box. Our Man in Marrakesh (US: Bang! Bang! You're Dead). 1967: *The Inn Way Out. The 25th Hour. Casino Royale. 1968: Salt and Pepper. 1969: *The Undertakers. The Italian Job. Midas Run (US: A Run on Gold). The Magic Christian. 1970: Doctor in Trouble. On a Clear Day You Can See Forever. 1971: Dad's Army. 1972: The Alf Garnett Saga. Au Pair Girls. 1974: Confessions of a Window Cleaner. Barry McKenzie Holds His Own. Three for All. Brief Encounter (TV). 1975: The Adventure of Sherlock Holmes' Smarter Brother. 1977: Stand Up, Virgin Soldiers. Jabberwocky. What's Up Nurse? 1978: Who is Killing the Great Chefs of Europe? (GB: Too Many Chefs). Rosie Dixon Night Nurse. 1979: The Spaceman and King Arthur (US: Unidentified Flying Oddball). 1980: The Fiendish Plot of Dr Fu Manchu. *Late Flowering Love. The Shillingbury Blowers (TV).

LEONARD, Sheldon

(S. L. Barshad) 1907–

Invaluable dark-haired American actor of vaguely shifty looks, a Macdonald Carey from the other side of the tracks and one of the cinema's shadiest characters. Rarely seen without a trilby, his Brooklynesque gangsters were equally divided between the comic and the serious. Left acting all too

soon to turn to production, but was seen in the late 1970s in a few cameo roles.

1934: Ouanga. 1939: Another Thin Man. 1941: Tall, Dark and Handsome. Buy Me That Town. Married Bachelor. Rise and Shine. Week-End in Havana. Private Nurse. 1942: Born to Sing. Tortilla Flat. Lucky Jordan. Pierre of the Plains. Tennessee Johnson (GB: The Man on America's Conscience). The McGuerins from Brooklyn. Street of Chance. 1943: Hit the Ice. Klondike Kate. City Without Men. Taxi, Mister. Passport to Suez. Harvest Melody. 1944: Uncertain Glory. To Have and Have Not. Timber Queen. The Falcon in Hollywood. Gambler's Choice. Trocadero. 1945: Why Girls Leave Home. Zombies on Broadway (GB: Loonies on Broadway). Shadow of Terror. Frontier Gal (GB: The Bride Wasn't Willing). Radio Stars on Parade. Captain Kidd. River Gang. Crime Inc. 1946: Decoy. Bowery Bombshell. The Last Crooked Mile. Somewhere in the Night. The Gentleman Misbehaves. It's a Wonderful Life! Her Kind of Man. Rainbow over Texas. 1947: Sinbad the Sailor. The Fabulous Joe. Violence. The Gangster. 1948: If You Knew Susie. Open Secret. Jinx Money. Joe Palooka in Winner Take All (GB: Winner Take All). Madonna of the Desert. Alias a Gentleman. Shep Comes Home. 1949: Take One False Step. My Dream is Yours. Daughter of the Jungle. †Two Knights in Brooklyn/Two Mugs from Brooklyn. 1950: The Iroquois Trail (GB: The Tomahawk Trail). 1951: Abbott and Costello Meet the Invisible Man. Behave Yourself! Come Fill the Cup. Young Man with Ideas. 1952: Here Come the Nelsons. Breakdown. Stop, You're Killing Me! 1953: Money from Home. Diamond Queen. 1955: Guys and Dolls. 1961: Pocketful of Miracles. 1978: The Brink's Job. The Islander (TV). Top Secret (TV).

† Combined GB version of *The McGuerins from Brooklyn* and *Taxi, Mister*

LERNER, Michael 1937–

Well-upholstered, chunkily-cheeked, cigar-chewing American actor who plays hearty backslappers adept at pulling the wool over your eyes. Forsook a career as a professor of dramatic literature to become an actor in his late twenties, scurrying eagerly through scenes that stole attention from the stars. Academy Award nominee for his portrait of an unctuous studio boss in *Barton Fink*.

1967: *Yoko Ono Number 4/Bottoms (and narrator). 1969: Three's a Crowd (TV). Daughter of the Mind (TV). 1970: Alex in Wonderland. 1971: What's a Nice Girl Like You . . .? (TV). The Ski Bum. Thief (TV). Marriage: Year One (TV). 1972: Magic Carpet (TV). The Candidate. 1973: Firehouse (TV). Reflections of Murder (TV). Busting. 1974: Newman's Law. The Rockford Files (TV). Hangup. 1975: Sarah T: Portrait of a Teenage Alcoholic (TV). The Dream Makers (TV). A Cry for Help (TV). Starsky and Hutch (TV). 1976: F Scott Fitzgerald in Hollywood (TV). St Ives. Scott Free (TV). Dark Victory (TV). 1977: Outlaw Blues. Killer on Board (TV). The Other Side of Midnight. 1978: Ruby and Oswald/Four Days in Dallas (TV). The Passage. Vegas (TV). A Love Affair: The Eleanor and Lou Gehrig Story (TV). 1979: Goldengirl. Hart to Hart (TV). 1980: Coast to Coast. The Baltimore Bullet. Borderline. This Year's Blonde (TV). Threshold. Gridlock (TV. GB: The Great American Traffic Jam). 1981: The Postman Always Rings Twice. 1982: National Lampoon's Class Reunion. 1983: Blood Feud (TV). Rita Hayworth: The Love Goddess (TV). Strange Invaders. 1984: The Execution. 1985: Movers and Shakers. This Child is Mine (TV). 1986: That Secret Sunday/Betrayal of Trust (TV). 1987: The King of Love (TV). Hands of a Stranger (TV). 1988: Eight Men Out. Anguish. Vibes. 1989: Harlem Nights. 1990: The Closer. Maniac Cop 2. Framed (cable TV). Any Man's Death. 1991: Omen IV: The Awakening (TV). Barton Fink. 1992: Newsies (GB: The News Boys). The Comrades of Summer (cable TV). 1993: Amos & Andrew. No Escape/The Penal Colony. 1994: Blank Check (GB: Blank Cheque). The Road to Wellville. Radioland Murders. A Pyromaniac's Love Story. 1995: Girl in the Cadillac.*

LEVANT, Oscar 1906–1972

Shambling, worried-looking, thick-lipped American humorist and pianist who brightened up a number of films at Warners, Paramount, MGM and Fox in the forties and fifties. His subsequent TV show proved a treasury of insult as Oscar got the guests, describing himself as a verbal vampire. Died from a heart attack.

1929: *The Dance of Life. 1935: In Person. 1940: Rhythm on the River. *Information,*

Please (series). Kiss the Boys Goodbye. 1945: Rhapsody in Blue. 1946: Humoresque. 1948: Romance on the High Seas (GB: It's Magic). You Were Meant for Me. 1949: The Barkleys of Broadway. 1951: An American in Paris. 1952: O. Henry's Full House (GB: Full House). 1953: The 'I Don't Care' Girl. The Band Wagon. 1955: The Cobweb.

LEVENE, Sam 1905–1980

Thin, sardonic, whippy, moustachioed Brooklynesque American character actor, typically as sharpsters and not-too-menacing criminals, familiar in trilby and pin-stripe suit. Occasionally, as in *Crossfire* and *Boomerang*, in much more serious roles within social conscience thrillers. Stayed a working actor until his death from a heart attack.

1936: *After the Thin Man. Three Men on a Horse. 1938: Yellow Jack. The Shopworn Angel. The Mad Miss Manton. 1939: Golden Boy. 1941: Married Bachelor. Shadow of the Thin Man. 1942: Sing Your Worries Away. Sunday Punch. Grand Central Murder. The Big Street. Destination Unknown. 1943: I Dood It (GB: By Hook or By Crook). Action in the North Atlantic. Whistling in Brooklyn. Gung Ho! 1944: The Purple Heart. 1946: The Killers. 1947: Boomerang! Brute Force. Crossfire. A Likely Story. Killer McCoy. 1948: Leather Gloves (GB: Loser Take All). The Babe Ruth Story. 1950: Dial 1119 (GB: The Violent Hour). Guilty Bystander. 1953: Three Sailors and a Girl. 1956: The Opposite Sex. 1957: Designing Woman. Sweet Smell of Success. Slaughter on 10th Avenue. A Farewell to Arms.*

1958: *Kathy O. 1963: Act One. 1969: A Dream of Kings. 1972: Such Good Friends. 1976: The Money. Demon/God Told Me To. 1979: Last Embrace . . .And Justice for All.*

LEWIS, Geoffrey 1935–

Sour-mouthed, creaking-voiced, dark-complexioned American actor of medium build who came lamentably late to films, but was soon clocking up three movies a year. Usually plays wrong-headed moaners who look as though they have swallowed a jar of pickles, or pains-in-the-neck who are hard to get rid of, and appeared to great effect in several of Clint Eastwood's more light-hearted romps. Seen in fewer high-profile films, though, since 1980. Father of actress Juliette Lewis.

1963: *The Fat Black Pussycat 1970: The Todd Killings. 1971: Welcome Home Johnny Bristol (TV). Welcome Home, Soldier Boys. 1972: High Plains Drifter. Moon of the Wolf (TV). The Culpepper Cattle Co. Bad Company. 1973: Macon County Line. Dillinger. My Name is Nobody. 1974: Honky Tonk (TV). Thunderbolt and Lightfoot. The Gun and the Pulpit (TV). The Great Waldo Pepper. The Great Ice Rip-Off (TV). Smile. 1975: The Wind and the Lion. Attack on Terror: The FBI versus the Ku Klux Klan (TV). Lucky Lady. 1976: The Return of a Man Called Horse. The New Daughters of Joshua Cabe (TV). The Great Houdinis (TV). 1977: The Deadly Triangle (TV). The Hunted Lady (TV). 1978: Every Which Way But Loose. Tilt. When Every Day Was the Fourth of July (TV). 1979: Salem's Lot (TV). Human Experiments. The Jericho Mile (TV. GB: cinemas). Samurai (TV). 1980: Tom Horn. Bronco Billy. Belle Starr (TV). Any Which Way You Can. Heaven's Gate. 1981: I, The Jury. Shoot the Sun Down. 1982: Life of the Party: The Story of Beatrice (TV). The Shadow Riders (TV). 1983: Return of the Man from UNCLE (TV). September Gun (TV). 10 to Midnight. Travis McGee (TV). 1984: Lust in the Dust. Night of the Comet. Maximum Security. 1985: Stormin' Home (TV). Spenser: For Hire (TV). Stitches. 1986: Dallas: The Early Years (TV). The Annihilator (TV). Spot Marks the X (TV). 1987: Time Out. 1988: Out of the Dark. Desert Rats (TV). Pancho Barnes (TV). Wipeout. The Johnsons Are Home (TV). 1989: Catch Me If You Can. Pink Cadillac. Desperado: The Outlaw Wars (TV). Tango &*

Cash. Fletch Lives. 1990: Gunsmoke: The Last Apache (TV). Disturbed. Matters of the Heart (TV). 1991: Double Impact. 1992: Wishman. The Lawnmower Man. 1993: The Joshua Tree. The Man Without a Face. Only the Strong. Point of No Return (GB: The Assassin). 1994: Bohemia Descending. White Fang II: The Myth of the White Wolf. The Dragon Gate. Maverick.

LEXY, Edward
(E. Gerald Little) 1897–
Stocky, barrel-chested, tight-lipped, brown-haired, moustachioed, aggressive-looking British actor who made his name in the immediate pre-war cinema playing sergeant-majors, as well as bustling policemen. Near the top of the cast from his 1937 debut until 1940; in smaller roles in postwar years, and progressively less often seen towards the end of the 1950s.

1937: The Divorce of Lady X. The Green Cockatoo (US: Four Dark Hours). Action for Slander. Knight Without Armour. Farewell Again (US: Troopship). Smash and Grab. Mademoiselle Docteur. 1938: The Drum (US: Drums). The Terror. South Riding. This Man is News. Kate Plus Ten. Second Best Bed. Sixty Glorious Years (US: Queen of Destiny). St Martin's Lane (US: Sidewalks of London). Many Tanks Mr Atkins. Night Journey. 1939: The Gang's All Here (US: The Amazing Mr Forrest). Too Dangerous to Live. The Outsider. This Man in Paris. Mrs Pym of Scotland Yard. The Spider. Traitor Spy (US: The Torso Murder Mystery). The Proud Valley. 1940: Laugh It Off. Spare a Copper. *Larceny Street. *Dangerous Comment. Convoy. 1944: Medal for the General. 1946: A Girl in a Million. Piccadilly Incident. School for Secrets (US: Secret Flight). 1947: While I Live. Captain Boycott. Temptation Harbour. The Ghosts of Berkeley Square. Good Time Girl. Blanche Fury. 1948: The Mark of Cain. The Winslow Boy. Bonnie Prince Charlie. It's Not Cricket. 1949: For Them That Trespass. Children of Chance. 1950: The Twenty Questions Murder Mystery. 1951: Cloudburst. The Lady With a Lamp. Smart Alec. Night Was Our Friend. 1952: Golden Arrow/Three Men and a Girl (US: The Gay Adventure. Completed 1949). The Happy Family (US: Mr Lord Says No). You're Only Young Twice! Miss Robin Hood. 1954: The Golden Link. Orders Are Orders. 1955: Captain Lightfoot. Where There's a Will.

1956: Up in the World. 1957: The Rising of the Moon. The Man Who Wouldn't Talk. The Story of Esther Costello (US: Golden Virgin).

LITEL, John 1892–1972
Sturdy, dark-haired, softly-spoken, reliable-looking American six-footer with careworn eyes. Employed in the occasional minor lead after making his home in Hollywood from 1936 (chiefly at Warner Brothers), he was more often to be seen as thoughtful, determined (but never aggressive) figures of authority — fathers, attorneys, military officers and other men under pressure. He took up acting after a distinguished military career during which he served with the French forces in World War I and was twice decorated for bravery.

1929: *The Sleeping Porch. 1930: On the Border. Don't Believe It. 1932: Wayward. 1936: Black Legion. 1937: Back in Circulation. Fugitive in the Sky. The Life of Emile Zola. Marked Woman. Alcatraz Island. Midnight Court. Slim. Missing Witness. 1938: The Amazing Dr Clitterhouse. Broadway Musketeers. Gold is Where You Find It. Comet Over Broadway. Jezebel. Little Miss Thoroughbred. Love, Honor and Behave. My Bill. Nancy Drew, Detective. Over the Wall. A Slight Case of Murder. Valley of the Giants. 1939: The Dead End Kids On Dress Parade. Nancy Drew, Trouble Shooter. Dodge City. Dust Be My Destiny. A Child is Born. Nancy Drew and the Hidden Staircase. One Hour to Live. On Trial. The Return of Dr X. Secret Service of the Air. Nancy Drew — Reporter. Wings of the Navy. You Can't Get Away with Murder. 1940: Castle on the Hudson (GB: Years Without Days). The Fighting 69th. An Angel from Texas. It All Came True. Knute Rockne — All American (GB: A Modern Hero). The Man Who Talked Too Much. Money and the Woman. Murder in the Air. Santa Fé Trail. Father is a Prince. Flight Angels. Gambling on the High Seas. They Drive by Night (GB: The Road to Frisco). Virginia City. The Lady With Red Hair. Men Without Souls. 1941: The Big Boss. Don Winslow of the Navy (serial). Father's Son. The Great Mr Nobody. Henry Aldrich for President. Sealed Lips. The Trial of Mary Dugan. Thieves Fall Out. They Died With Their Boots On. 1942: Henry and Dizzy. Boss of Big Town. Madame Spy. Invisible Agent. Men of Texas (GB: Men of Destiny). Henry Aldrich, Editor.

Kid Glove Killer. Mississippi Gambler. The Mystery of Marie Roget. A Desperate Chance for Ellery Queen (GB: A Desperate Chance). 1943: Crime Doctor. Henry Aldrich Swings It (GB: Henry Swings It). *Dangerous Age. Henry Aldrich Haunts a House (GB: Henry Haunts a House). So Proudly We Hail! Murder in Times Square. Henry Aldrich Gets Glamour (GB: Henry Gets Glamour). Where Are Your Children? Henry Aldrich Plays Cupid (GB: Henry Plays Cupid). Submarine Base. 1944: Faces in the Fog. Henry Aldrich — Boy Scout (GB: Henry — Boy Scout). Lake Placid Serenade. Henry Aldrich's Little Secret (GB: Henry's Little Secret). My Buddy. Murder in the Blue Room. 1945: Brewster's Millions. The Crimson Canary. Rhapsody in Blue. The Daltons Ride Again. The Enchanted Forest. Northwest Trail. San Antonio. Salome, Where She Danced. The Crime Doctor's Warning (GB: The Doctor's Warning). 1946: The Madonna's Secret. A Night in Paradise. The Return of Rusty. She Wrote the Book. Sister Kenny. Smooth as Silk. Swell Guy. 1947: The Beginning or the End? Cass Timberlane. Lighthouse. Easy Come, Easy Go. The Guilty. Christmas Eve. Heaven Only Knows. 1948: My Dog Rusty. I, Jane Doe (GB: Diary of a Bride). Pitfall. Rusty Leads the Way. Smart Woman. The Valiant Hombre. Triple Threat. 1949: Rusty Saves a Life. The Gal Who Took the West. Outpost in Morocco. Shamrock Hill. The Sundowners (GB: Thunder in the Dust). Rusty's Birthday. Woman in Hiding. 1950: The Fuller Brush Girl (GB: The Affairs of Sally). Mary Ryan, Detective. Kiss Tomorrow Goodbye. 1951: Little Egypt (GB: Chicago Masquerade). Cuban Fireball. The Groom Wore Spurs. Flight to Mars. Montana Belle (completed 1948). Take Care of My Little Girl. Two Dollar Bettor (GB: Beginner's Luck). The Texas Rangers. 1952: Jet Job. Scaramouche. 1953: Jack Slade (GB: Slade). 1954: Sitting Bull. 1955: Double Jeopardy (GB: Crooked Ring). The Kentuckian. Texas Lady. 1956: The Wild Dakotas. Comanche. 1957: Decision at Sundown. Runaway Daughters. The Hired Gun. 1958: Houseboat. 1961: Lover Come Back. Pocketful of Miracles. Voyage to the Bottom of the Sea. 1963: The Gun Hawk. 1965: The Sons of Katie Elder. 1966: Nevada Smith.

LITHGOW, John 1945–
Big (6th 4 in), puffy-faced, small-eyed, mean-mouthed American actor with thinning hair. He progressed only slowly to top supporting parts, but then worked briskly by modern standards, demonstrating considerable versatility. He can play broad or sensitive as the occasion demands, and has been nominated for Academy Awards in The World According to Garp and Terms of Endearment, fearlessly taking on the portrayal of a transvestite in the former and creating a believable and sympathetic character. Recently playing psychotic villains.

1971: Dealing; or, the Berkeley-to-Boston-Forty-Bricks-Lost-Bag Blues. 1976: Obsession. 1978: The Big Fix. 1979: Rich Kids. All That Jazz. 1980: Mom, the Wolfman and Me (TV). 1981: Big Blonde (TV). Blow Out. 1982: The World According to Garp. I'm Dancing as Fast as I Can. Not in Front of the Children (TV).

1983: The Twilight Zone (GB: Twilight Zone The Movie). Terms of Endearment. The Day After (TV). The Glitter Dome (cable TV. GB: cinemas). 1984: Footloose. 2010. The Adventures of Buckaroo Banzai: Across the Eighth Dimension. Mesmerized. 1985: Santa Claus. 1986: The Manhattan Project (GB: Deadly Game). Resting Place (TV). 1987: Harry and the Hendersons (GB: Bigfoot and the Hendersons). 1988: Distant Thunder. Out Cold. 1989: The Traveling Man (TV). 1990: The Last Elephant (TV). Memphis Belle. The Guys. 1991: At Play in the Fields of the Lord. †L.A. Story. Ricochet. 1992: Raising Cain. 1993: Love, Cheat and Steal (released 1994). Cliffhanger. The Wrong Man. The Pelican Brief. 1994: A Good Man in Africa. Princess Caraboo. Redwood Curtain (TV). My Brother's Keeper (TV). Silent Fall.

† Scene deleted from final release print

LITTLEFIELD, Lucien 1895–1960

Bald, apologetic-looking, watery-eyed American portrayer of the meek and mild who came to Hollywood in early silent days and stayed for 45 years. Taller than one remembers (it must have been all those cringing roles that makes him seem short), he was educated at a military academy, but was already winning film roles at 18 and soon began playing characters many years older than his own age, usually subservient and timid, but sometimes interfering, short-tempered and self-opinionated. Considered a great make-up wizard in silent days, he was also a talented writer who contributed occasionally to screenplays. His middle name was Rameses.

1913: Rose of the Range. 1914: The Ghost Breaker. 1915: Mr Grex of Monte Carlo. A Gentleman of Leisure. The Marriage of Kitty. The Unknown. The Warrens of Virginia. The Wild Goose Chase. 1916: The Blacklist. A Gutter Magdalene. The Love Mask. To Have and to Hold. Temptation. 1917: The Cost of Hatred. The Hostage. The Golden Fetter. On Record. Joan the Woman. The Squaw Man's Son. 1919: The Wild Goose Chase (and 1915 film). 1920: Everywoman. Double Speed. The 14th Man. Eyes of the Heart. Her First Elopement. Jackstraw. The Sins of St Anthony. Sick-a-Bed. The Round-Up. Why Change Your Wife? 1921: Crazy to Marry. The Hell Diggers. The Affairs of Anatol. The Little Clown. The Sheik. Too Much Speed. 1922: Across the Continent. Manslaughter. Her Husband's Trademark. Our Leading Citizen. Rent Free. The Siren Call. To Have and to Hold (and 1916 film). Tillie. 1923: The French Doll. In the Palace of the King. Mr Billings Spends His Dime. The Rendezvous. The Tiger's Claw. Three Wise Fools. 1924: Babbitt. Gerald Cranston's Lady. Gold Heels. Never Say Die. The Painted Lady. Teeth. Name the Man. True as Steel. A Woman Who Sinned. The Deadwood Coach. 1925: Charley's Aunt. Gold and the Girl. Hearts and Spurs. The Rainbow Trail. Tumbleweeds. Soul Mates. *What Price Goofy. 1926: Bachelor Brides. Brooding Eyes. *Innocent Husbands. Twinkletoes. Take It from Me. Tony Runs Wild. The Torrent. 1927: The Cat and the Canary. Cheating Cheaters. The Small Bachelor. My Best Girl. A Texas Steer. Taxi! Taxi! Uncle Tom's Cabin. 1928: Harold Teen. Heart to Heart. The Head Man. Do Your Duty. Mother Knows Best. The Man in Hobbles. A Ship Comes In. A Blonde for a Night. 1929: Drag (GB: Parasites). Clear the Decks. Dark Streets. Girl in the Glass Cage. Making the Grade. Seven Keys to Baldpate. Saturday's Children. This is Heaven. Wall Street. 1930: *Getting a Raise. *The Potters At Home. *The Potters Done in Oil. *His Big Ambition. *Pa Gets a Vacation. *The Potters Out for Game. Big Money. Captain of the Guard. The Great Divide. High Society Blues. Clancy in Wall Street. No, No, Nanette. She's My Weakness. *The Great Junction Hotel. Tom Sawyer. 1931: *Queen of Main Street. *Trouble from Abroad. It Pays to Advertise. Misbehaving Ladies. Reducing. Scandal Sheet. Young As You Feel. 1932: Broken Lullaby (GB: The Man I Killed). *Jimmy's New Yacht. *The Loudmouth. Downstairs. Evenings for Sale. Pride of the Legion (GB: The Big Pay-Off). If I Had a Million. Miss Pinkerton. Devil and the Deep. High Pressure. Shopworn. Jazz Babies. Strangers in Love. Speed Madness. Strangers of the Evening. That's My Boy. 1933: Alice in Wonderland. The Bitter Tea of General Yen. Rasputin and the Empress (GB: Rasputin – The Mad Monk). East of Fifth Avenue (GB: Two in a Million). Chance at Heaven. The Big Payoff. Professional Sweetheart (GB: Imaginary Sweetheart). Rainbow Over Broadway. The Big Brain (GB: Enemies of Society). Sailor's Luck. Skyway. Sons of the Desert (GB: Fraternally Yours). Sweepings. *Dirty Work. 1934: Gridiron Flash (GB: Luck of the Game). Kiss and Make Up. Love Time. Mandalay. Marrying Widows. Stand Up and Cheer. Thirty Day Princess. When Strangers Meet. 1935: Cappy Ricks

Returns (GB: The Return of Cappy Ricks). Man on the Flying Trapeze (GB: The Memory Expert). The Murder Man. One Frightened Night. Ruggles of Red Gap. She Gets Her Man. The Return of Peter Grimm. Sweepstake Annie (GB: Annie Doesn't Live Here). I Dream Too Much. Magnificent Obsession. 1936: Early to Bed. Let's Sing Again. The Moon's Our Home. Rose-Marie. 1937: Bulldog Drummond's Revenge. Born to the West/Hell Town. High, Wide and Handsome. Hotel Haywire. Partners in Crime. Souls at Sea. Wells Fargo. Thunder Trail. Wild Money. 1938: The Gladiator. I Am the Law. Hollywood Stadium Mystery. Reckless Living. The Night Hawk. Scandal Street. Wide Open Faces. 1939: Jeepers Creepers (GB: Money Isn't Everything). Mystery Plane. Pirates of the Skies. Money to Burn. Sabotage (GB: Spies at Work). Unmarried (GB: Night Club Hostess). What a Life! Tumbleweeds (revised sound version of 1925 film). 1940: The Westerner. Those Were the Days (GB: Good Old School Days). L'il Abner (GB: Trouble Chaser). 1941: The Great American Broadcast. Henry Aldrich for President. The Little Foxes. Man at Large. Mr and Mrs North. Murder Among Friends. Life with Henry. 1942: Bells of Capistrano. Castle in the Desert. The Great Man's Lady. Hillbilly Blitzkrieg. Larceny Inc. Whistling in Dixie. 1943: Henry Aldrich Haunts a House (GB: Henry Haunts a House). Silent Witness (GB: Attorney for the Defence). Johnny Come Lately (GB: Johnny Vagabond). Henry Aldrich Gets Glamour (GB: Henry Gets Glamour). 1944: Casanova in Burlesque. The Cowboy and the Senorita. Goodnight, Sweetheart. Lights of Old Santa Fé. Lady, Let's Dance. One Body Too Many. When the Lights Go On Again. Zorro's Black Whip (serial). 1945: The Caribbean Mystery. Detour. Scared Stiff. 1946: In Old Sacramento. Rendezvous with Annie. That Brennan Girl. Love Laughs at Andy Hardy. 1947: The Fabulous Joe. Down to Earth. Sweet Genevieve. 1948: Bad Men of Tombstone. Let's Live a Little. Jinx Money. Lightnin' in the Forest. Hollow Triumph (GB: The Scar). 1949: Susanna Pass. 1951: At Sword's Point (GB: Sons of the Musketeers). 1953: Roar of the Crowd. Casanova's Big Night. 1955: Sudden Danger. 1957: Bop Girl Goes Calypso/Bop Girl. 1958: Wink of an Eye. The High Cost of Loving.

LLOYD, Christopher 1938–

Tall, wide-shouldered, wild-eyed, tautly amiable American actor with scruffy dark hair and features that seemed to qualify him for a gallery of oddballs and grotesques once he had embarked on a belated cinema career in his late thirties following much off-Broadway experience. Best known as the time-travelling Doc Brown in the Back to the Future trilogy, he has also made his mark in the world of black fantasy comedy as the dastardly Judge Doom in Who Framed Roger Rabbit and as the bald, bag-eyed, grinning, gremlin-like Fester in The Addams Family and its sequel. A latter-day career in elderly eccentrics beckons.

1975: One Summer Love/Dragonfly. One Flew Over the Cuckoo's Nest. 1977: Three Warriors. 1978: Goin' South. Midnight Express. Lacy and the Mississippi Queen (TV). 1979: Stunt

Seven (TV). The Lady in Red. The Onion Field. Butch and Sundance The Early Days. 1980: The Black Marble. Pilgrim, Farewell (TV). Schizoid. 1981: The Postman Always Rings Twice. The Legend of the Lone Ranger. National Lampoon Goes to the Movies (released 1983). 1982: Money on the Side (TV). 1983: To Be or Not to Be. Mr Mom (GB: Mr Mum). September Gun (TV). 1984: Street Hawk (TV). The Cowboy and the Ballerina (TV). Joy of Sex. Star Trek III: The Search for Spock. The Adventures of Buckaroo Banzai: Across the Eighth Dimension. 1985: White Dragon/Legend of the White Horse. Clue. Back to the Future. 1986: Miracles. 1987: Amazing Stories. Walk Like a Man. 1988: Track 29. Eight Men Out. Who Framed Roger Rabbit. 1989: Back to the Future Part II. The Dream Team. Un plan d'enfer. Why Me? 1990: Back to the Future Part III. Duck Tales. The Movie — Treasure of the Lost Lamp (voice only). 1991: The Addams Family. Suburban Commando. 1992: Disaster at Valdez (TV. US: Dead Ahead: The Exxon Valdez Disaster). T Bone n Weasel (TV). 1993: Dennis the Menace (GB: Dennis). Twenty Bucks. Addams Family Values. 1994: The Pagemaster. Angels in the Outfield. Camp Nowhere. Radioland Murders. 1995: Things to Do in Denver When You're Dead.

LLOYD, Norman 1914–
Narrow-featured American actor with receding fair hair and a hunted look. He is probably still best remembered for his debut role—the spy who fell from the Statue of Liberty at the end of Hitchcock's Saboteur. Lloyd dropped out of acting in 1952 to

become a producer (notably for Hitchcock himself on many of his TV shows) and sometime director, but returned to play a few cameo roles from the end of the 1960s onwards, including a running role in the TV series St Elsewhere. A vaudevillian at the age of five.

1942: Saboteur. 1945: The Unseen. Within These Walls. The Southerner. A Walk in the Sun. 1946: A Letter for Evie. Spellbound. The Green Years. Young Widow. 1947: The Beginning or the End? 1948: No Minor Vices. 1949: Scene of the Crime. Calamity Jane and Sam Bass. Reign of Terror/The Black Book. 1950: Buccaneer's Girl. The Flame and the Arrow. 1951: The Light Touch. M. Flame of Stamboul. He Ran All the Way. Limelight. 1977: Audrey Rose. 1978: F.M. The Dark Secret of Harvest Home (TV). 1979: King Cobra (later Jaws of Satan). 1980: The Nude Bomb. 1989: Dead Poets Society. Amityville: The Evil Escapes (TV). 1991: Shogun Mayeda/Journey of Honor. 1993: The Age of Innocence.

LOCKE, Harry 1913–1987
Cheery, bustling, bouncy British actor of round face, dark hair and chunky build, a purveyor of 'lower rank' cameos—batmen, orderlies, porters, warders, cab-drivers and the like; in the immediate post-war period, he was also a popular stand-up comedian who told jokes about immigrants on buses getting themselves and the conductor hopelessly confused. A repertory actor at 16, he returned to the stage after the 1960s to round out his career.

1946: Piccadilly Incident. George in Civvy Street. 1948: *A Home of Your Own. Passport to Pimlico. Panic at Madame Tussaud's. No Room at the Inn. 1949: Private Angelo. 1950: The Naked Heart (Maria Chapdelaine/The Naked Earth). The Undefeated. Treasure Island. 1951: Judgment Deferred. Angels One Five. 1952: Father's Doing Fine. Tread Softly. Time Bomb (US: Terror on a Train). 1953: The Red Beret (US: Paratrooper). 1954: The Teckman Mystery. Doctor in the House. Devil on Horseback. A Kid for Two Farthings. 1955: A Yank in Ermine. 1956: Yield to the Night (US: Blonde Sinner). Reach for the Sky. The Baby and the Battleship. The Long Arm (US: The Third Key). Town on Trial! The Silken Affair. 1957: Doctor at Large. Woman in a Dressing-

Gown. Barnacle Bill (US: All at Sea). 1958: Nowhere to Go. The Captain's Table. Carlton-Browne of the F O (US: Man in a Cocked Hat). 1959: Serious Charge (US: A Touch of Hell). Upstairs and Downstairs. I'm All Right, Jack. Carry On Nurse. Sink the Bismarck! 1960: Light Up the Sky. Clue of the Twisted Candle. The Girl on the Boat. 1961: The Man in the Back Seat. Never Back Losers. In the Doghouse. Two and Two Make Six. On the Fiddle (US: Operation Snafu). Watch It Sailor! She'll Have to Go (US: Maid for Murder). The Wild and the Willing. 1962: Tiara Tahiti. Crooks Anonymous. Play It Cool. The Amorous Prawn. The L-Shaped Room. Kill or Cure. 1963: The Small World of Sammy Lee. Heavens Above! What a Crazy World. 1964: Go Kart Go! The Devil-Ship Pirates. A Home of Your Own. 1965: *The Material Witness. The Legend of Young Dick Turpin. The Early Bird. 1966: Alfie. The Family Way. Arabesque. 1967: The Sky Bike. Mr Ten Per Cent. Half a Sixpence. 1968: Carry on Doctor. Subterfuge. 1969: Carry on Again, Doctor. On the Run. Oh! What a Lovely War. 1972: Tales from the Crypt. The Creeping Flesh.

LOCKHART, Gene
(Eugene Lockhart) 1891–1957
Light-haired, short, chubby-faced Canadian-born actor, somewhere between Charles Coburn and Cecil Kellaway, and one of Hollywood's most valuable character players from the 1930s to the 1950s. He started his career as a singer and songwriter, beginning his films in sly crookedness which, by the end of his career, had all but evaporated into crusty benevolence. Oscar nomination for his performance in Algiers. Died from a coronary thrombosis. His wife Kathleen (1881–1978) and daughter June (1925–) have also made many appearances in films.

1922: Smilin' Through. 1934: By Your Leave. The Gay Bride. Star of Midnight. 1935: Ah, Wilderness! Captain Hurricane. Thunder in the Night. Crime and Punishment. I've Been Around. Storm over the Andes. 1936: Brides Are Like That. Earthworm Tractors (GB: A Natural Born Salesman). Career Woman. The Gorgeous Hussy. Wedding Present. Come Closer, Folks. Times Square Playboy (GB: His Best Man). The First Baby. The Garden Murder Case. The Devil is a Sissy (GB: The Devil Takes the Count). Mind Your Own Business.

1937: *Mama Steps Out. Make Way for Tomorrow. Something to Sing About. Too Many Wives. The Sheik Steps Out. 1938: Of Human Hearts. A Christmas Carol. *Stocks and Blondes. Listen, Darling. Sweethearts. Men are Such Fools. Algiers. Meet the Girls. Penrod's Double Trouble. Blondie. Sinners in Paradise. 1939: I'm from Missouri. Our Leading Citizen. Tell No Tales. Blackmail. The Story of Alexander Graham Bell (GB: The Modern Miracle). Hotel Imperial. Geronimo. Bridal Suite. 1940: Edison the Man. We Who Are Young. South of Pago Pago. His Girl Friday. Abe Lincoln in Illinois (GB: Spirit of the People). Dr Kildare Goes Home. A Dispatch from Reuter's (GB: This Man Reuter). 1941: Billy the Kid. Meet John Doe. All That Money Can Buy/The Devil and Daniel Webster. Steel Against the Sky. They Died with Their Boots On. Keeping Company. The Sea Wolf. One Foot in Heaven. International Lady. 1942: The Gay Sisters. Juke Girl. You Can't Escape Forever. 1943: Hangmen Also Die! Find the Blackmailer. Madame Curie. Forever and a Day. Mission to Moscow. The Desert Song. Northern Pursuit. 1944: The White Cliffs of Dover. Action in Arabia. Going My Way. The Man from Frisco. 1945: The House on 92nd Street. That's the Spirit. Leave Her to Heaven. 1946: Meet Me on Broadway. Thieves' Holiday (GB: A Scandal in Paris). The Strange Woman. She-Wolf of London (GB: The Curse of the Allenbys). The Shocking Miss Pilgrim. 1947: The Foxes of Harrow. Cynthia (GB: The Rich, Full Life). Miracle on 34th Street (GB: The Big Heart). Honeymoon (GB: Two Men and a Girl). Her Husband's Affairs. 1948: The Inside Story. Joan of Arc. I, Jane Doe (GB: Diary of a Bride). That Wonderful Urge. Apartment for Peggy. 1949: Down to the Sea in Ships. Madame Bovary. The Inspector-General. The Red Light. 1950: The Big Hangover. Riding High. 1951: Hill Number One. The Sickle and the Cross. Seeds of Destruction. Rhubarb. I'd Climb the Highest Mountain. The Lady from Texas. 1952: Hoodlum Empire. A Girl in Every Port. Bonzo Goes to College. Face to Face. Androcles and the Lion. Apache War Smoke. 1953: Down Among the Sheltering Palms. The Lady Wants Mink. Francis Covers the Big Town. Confidentially Connie. 1954: World for Ransom. The Vanishing American. 1955: The Late Christopher Bean (TV. GB: cinemas). 1956: Carousel. The Man in the Gray Flannel Suit. 1957: Jeanne Eagels.*

LODGE, David 1921–

Tough-looking, moustachioed, well-built British actor with dark, wavy hair whose aggressive Londoners were usually leavened with humour. After varied experience in Gang Shows, a circus and music-hall, he moved into cinema character roles and, following an apprenticeship as tough, back-street types, soon showed a penchant for comedy, making notable contributions to several Peter Sellers films. Broader comedy roles in later days were on the whole less successful, but he remained busy in movies until the early 1980s and proved a prodigious worker for charity.

1954: †Orders Are Orders. 1955: Cockleshell Heroes. Private's Progress. 1956: The Long

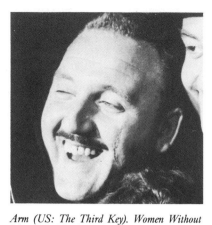

*Arm (US: The Third Key). Women Without Men (US: Blonde Bait). The Battle of the River Plate (US: Pursuit of the Graf Spee). The Intimate Stranger (US: Finger of Guilt). The Counterfeit Plan. 1957: Strangers' Meeting. These Dangerous Years (US: Dangerous Youth). The Naked Truth (US: Your Past is Showing!). The Safecracker. 1958: Up the Creek. No Time to Die! (US: Tank Force). The Silent Enemy. I Was Monty's Double (US: Monty's Double). Ice Cold in Alex (US: Desert Attack). *The Crossroads Gallows. I Only Arsked! Further Up the Creek. Girls at Sea. 1959: Life in Emergency Ward 10. Bobbikins. Idle on Parade (US: Idol on Parade). I'm All Right, Jack. Yesterday's Enemy. The Ugly Duckling. The League of Gentlemen. 1960: Jazzboat. Two Way Stretch. *The Running, Jumping and Standing Still Film. Watch Your Stern. The Bulldog Breed. Never Let Go. 1961: The Hellfire Club. No, My Darling Daughter! Raising the Wind (US: Roommates). Carry On Regardless. The Pirates of Blood River. 1962: Go to Blazes. Mrs Gibbons' Boys. The Dock Brief (US: Trial and Error). Captain Clegg (US: Night Creatures). Time to Remember. The Boys. On the Beat. Kill or Cure. 1963: Two Left Feet. 1964: The Long Ships. A Shot in the Dark. Guns at Batasi. Saturday Night Out. 1965: The Intelligence Men. The Amorous Adventures of Moll Flanders. Cup Fever. The Early Bird. San Ferry Ann. Catch Us If You Can (US: Having a Wild Weekend). The Alphabet Murders/The ABC Murders. 1966: The Sandwich Man. Press for Time. After the Fox. 1967: Casino Royale. Smashing Time. Corruption (released 1969). 1968: The Fixer. Only When I Larf. Headline Hunters. 1969: Crooks and Coronets (US: Sophie's Place). The Smashing Bird I Used to Know (US: Hell House Girls). What's Good for the Goose. The Magic Christian. *Bachelor of Arts (US: Durti Weekend). Oh! What a Lovely War. Scream and Scream Again. 1970: Eyewitness (US: Sudden Terror). Incense for the Damned. Scramble. Toomorrow. Crime Doesn't Pay. Hoffman. The Railway Children. 1971: Raising the Roof. On the Buses. Mr Horatio Knibbles. The Fiend (US: Beware My Brethren). Nobody Ordered Love. The Magnificent Seven Deadly Sins. 1972: Go for a Take. The Amazing Mr Blunden. Some Kind of Hero. Hide and Seek. *Always on Saturday. 1973: Carry On Girls. Charley One-Eye. 1974: Return of the Pink Panther. Ghost in the Noonday Sun. QB VII (TV). Carry On Dick. 1975: Carry On Behind. 1976: Carry On*

England. 1978: *Revenge of the Pink Panther. 1979: The Fiendish Plot of Dr Fu Manchu. 1983: Sahara. Bloodbath at the House of Death. 1989: Edge of Sanity.*

† Scene deleted from final release print

LOGGIA, Robert 1930–

Abrasive, gruff-voiced, dark-haired, twinkling-eyed New Yorker who usually plays rough diamond types, though their hearts may be either of gold or ice. After studying journalism at university, he opted for an acting career, trained at the Actors' Studio, and broke into films and TV playing Mexican bandits or Italianate gangsters, roles that called on him to flash a smile or snarl with equal ease. He starred in a popular TV series, *T.H.E. Cat*, then, after several years away on stage, returned to films and TV as a crusty and trusty character player, mostly as self-made rogues who called a spade a spade. Academy Award nominee for his run-down private eye in *Jagged Edge*.

1956: Somebody Up There Likes Me. 1957: The Garment Jungle. 1958: The Lost Missile. Cop Hater. 1959: The Nine Lives of Elfego Baca (TV. GB: cinemas). 1962: Six Gun Law (TV. GB: cinemas). 1963: Cattle King (GB: Guns of Wyoming). 1964: The Three Sisters. 1965: The Greatest Story Ever Told. 1969: Che! 1976: Street Killing (TV). Mallory: Circumstantial Evidence (TV). Scott Free (TV). 1977: Speedtrap. First Love. Raid on Entebbe (TV. GB: cinemas). 1978: Revenge of the Pink Panther. The Sea Gypsies (GB: Shipwreck!). 1979: No Other Love (TV). Casino/S S Casino (TV). The Ninth Configuration/Twinkle, Twinkle, Killer Kane. The People versus Inez Garcia (TV). 1981: S.O.B. An Officer and a Gentleman. 1982: Trail of the Pink Panther. A Woman Called Golda (TV). 1983: Psycho II. Curse of the Pink Panther. Scarface. 1984: A Touch of Scandal (TV). 1985: Jagged Edge. Prizzi's Honor. Streets of Justice (TV). 1986: "That's Life!". Over the Top. Armed and Dangerous. 1987: Hot Pursuit. The Believers. Conspiracy: The Trial of the Chicago 8 (TV). Gaby: A True Story. 1988: Big. Intrigue (cable TV). Target: Favorite Son (Video. Edited version of TV mini-series Favorite Son). The O'Connors (TV). Oliver and Company (voice only). 1989: Dream Breakers (TV). Code Name: Chaos. Relentless. Two Women/Running Away (TV).

Triumph of the Spirit. White Hot. 1990: Opportunity Knocks. 1991: The Marrying Man (GB: Too Hot to Handle). Necessary Roughness. First Force. The Gladiator. 1992: Afterburn (cable TV). Innocent Blood. 1993: Nurses on the Line (TV). Lifepod (TV). Mercy Mission: The Rescue of Flight 771 (TV). Taking Liberties. 1994: White Mule. The Last Tattoo. I Love Trouble. 1995: Coldblooded.

LÖHR, Marie 1890–1975

Although one remembers this puffy-faced, brown-haired Australian-born actress for her dragons and dowagers, she was on stage at four in her native Sydney and a London stage regular at 11, eventually running up one of the longest lists of credits ever recorded in the British theatre. Film appearances were understandably spasmodic, but hers were always performances to be reckoned with and she was still in leading character roles well into her sixties.

*1916: *The Real Thing at Last. 1918: Victory and Peace. 1932: Aren't We All? 1934: Road House. My Heart Is Calling. Lady in Danger. 1935: Oh Daddy! Royal Cavalcade (US: Regal Cavalcade). Foreign Affaires. Fighting Stock. Cock o' the North. 1936: Whom the Gods Love (US: Mozart). It's You I Want. Dreams Come True. Reasonable Doubt. 1938: South Riding. Pygmalion. 1939: A Gentleman's Gentleman. 1940: George and Margaret. 1941: Major Barbara. 1942: Went the Day Well? (US: 48 Hours). 1944: Twilight Hour. Kiss the Bride Goodbye. 1945: The Rake's Progress (US: Notorious Gentleman). 1946: The Magic Bow. 1947: The Ghosts of Berkeley Square. 1948: Counterblast. Anna Karenina. The Winslow Boy. Silent Dust. 1952: Little Big Shot. Treasure Hunt. 1953: Always a Bride. 1954: Out of the Clouds. 1955: Escapade. On Such a Night. 1956: A Town Like Alice. 1957: Seven Waves Away (US: Abandon Ship!). Small Hotel. 1958: Carlton-Browne of the F O (US: Man in a Cocked Hat). 1967: Great Catherine.*

LOMAS, Herbert 1887–1961

Dour, grim-looking British actor with light brown hair, twisted expression and sepulchral tones, frequently cast as a prophet of doom. Had it not been for the slightness of his stature, he might have made a good Scrooge. Retired in 1952 and went to live in the Devon countryside, where he died.

*1931: Hobson's Choice. Many Waters. 1932: Frail Women. The Sign of Four. When London Sleeps. The Missing Rembrandt. The Man from Toronto. 1933: Daughters of Today. I Was a Spy. 1934: Java Head. The Phantom Light. Lorna Doone. 1935: Fighting Stock. The Black Mask. The Ghost Goes West. 1936: Fame. Fire Over England. Rembrandt. 1937: Knight Without Armour. Over the Moon (released 1940). South Riding. 1939: Inquest. Jamaica Inn. Q Planes (US: Clouds Over Europe). The Lion Has Wings. Ask a Policeman. 1940: *Mr Borland Thinks Again. 1941: The Ghost Train. South American George. Penn of Pennsylvania (US: The Courageous Mr Penn). 1943: They Met in the Dark. Undercover (US: Underground Guerrillas). 1944: Welcome Mr Washington. 1945: I Know Where I'm Going! 1946: The Man Within (US: The Smugglers). 1947: Master of Bankdam. 1948: The Guinea Pig. Bonnie Prince Charlie. 1951: The Magic Box. 1952: The Net (US: Project M7).*

LONG, Walter 1879–1952

Bull-necked, barrel-chested, crop-haired, fiercely scowling American tough-guy actor, who took over from the equally fearsome Noah Young whenever Laurel and Hardy needed an awesome opponent to threaten them with dire physical improbabilities. After blacking up for his first major film, *The Birth of a Nation*, Long was almost always a villain, most notably as Stan

Laurel's (cheating) opponent in *Any Old Port*. More or less retired after 1942: died from a heart attack.

*1913: Traffic in Souls. 1914: The Escape. Home Sweet Home. 1915: The Birth of a Nation. Out of Bondage. Victorine. Martyrs of the Alamo. Jordan is a Hard Road. 1916: Intolerance. Unprotected. Years of the Locust. Daphne and the Pirate. Let Kathy Do It. Sold for Marriage. Joan the Woman. 1917: The Golden Fetter. A Romance of the Redwoods. The Woman God Forgot. The Winning of Sally Temple. The Evil Eye. The Little American. The Cost of Hatred. Hashimura Togo. 1918: The Queen of the Sea. *The Highbenders. 1919: The Mother and the Law. An Adventure in Hearts. The Poppy Girl's Husband. Scarlet Days. 1920: The Sea Wolf. Excuse My Dust. The Fighting Shepherdess. Held in Trust. What Women Love. Go and Get It. 1921: The Fire Cat. Tiger True. A Giant of His Race. The Sheik. White and Unmarried. 1922: Moran of the Lady Letty. Blood and Sand. Across the Continent. The Dictator. The Beautiful and the Damned. Omar the Tent-Maker. My American Wife. To Have and to Hold. Shadows. South of Suva. 1923: Kick In. Desire. The Broken Wing. The Call of the Wild. His Great Chance. The Last Hour. Little Church Around the Corner. The Isle of Lost Ships. The Shock. A Shot in the Night. The Huntress. Quicksands. 1924: The Ridin' Kid from Powder River. Daring Love. Yankee Madness. White Man. Wine. Missing Daughters. 1925: Bobbed Hair. Soul-Fire. Raffles, the Amateur Cracksman. The Reckless Sex. The Verdict. The Lady. The Shock Punch. The Road to Yesterday. 1926: Red Dice. Eve's Leaves. The Highbinders. Steel Preferred. West of Broadway. 1927: White Pants Willie. The Yankee Clipper. Back to God's Country. Jim the Conqueror. Jewels of Desire. 1928: Forbidden Grass. The Thunder God. Gang War. Me, Gangster. 1929: The Black Watch (GB: King of the Khyber Rifles). Black Cargoes of the South Seas. 1930: Beau Bandit. Conspiracy. Moby Dick. 1931: Larceny Lane/The Steel Highway. The Maltese Falcon. Dragnet Patrol (GB: Love Redeemed). Sea Devils. Pardon Us (GB: Jailbirds). *Taxi Troubles. Other Men's Women. Soul of the Slums (GB: The Samaritan). 1932: Cornered. *Any Old Port. *Hawkins & Watkins Inc. Escapade (GB: Dangerous Ground). I Am a Fugitive from a Chain Gang. Silver Dollar. 1933: The House of Rothschild. Easy Millions. Women Won't Tell. Dark Endeavour. 1934: Lightning Strikes Twice. *Three Little Pigskins. *The Live Ghost. *Going Bye Bye. Operator 13 (GB: Spy 13). Six of a Kind. Lazy River. The Thin Man. The Whole Town's Talking (GB: Passport to Fame). 1935: Naughty Marietta. Frisco Kid. 1936: Drift Fence. Wedding Present. The Beloved Rogue. The Glory Trail. 1937: Pick a Star. The Bold Caballero (GB: The Bold Cavalier). North of the Rio Grande. Flaming Lead. Dick Tracy (serial). 1938: The Painted Trail. Six-Shootin' Sheriff. Man's Country. Bar 20 Justice. 1939: Wild Horse Canyon. Fighting Mad. Union Pacific. Honor of the West. 1940: Silver Stallion. When the Daltons Rode. Hidden Gold. 1941: Ridin' on a Rainbow. City of Missing Girls. 1944: Broadway Rhythm. 1948: *No More Relatives. 1950: Wabash Avenue.*

LONSDALE, Michel or Michael 1931–
Sturdy, dark-haired French actor of
cherubic features and chubby build, often
moustachioed and bearded. Of mixed
French and English parentage, his early
years were spent partly in England and
partly in Morocco. Although he was acting
on radio as a teenager, he remained almost
unknown as a film actor outside the Continent until his performance as the man
pursuing Edward Fox in *The Day of the
Jackal* in 1973. After that he performed in
several international films, billed willy-nilly
as Michel or Michael, although his choice
of roles did not always seem wise, and he
has been seen less frequently in more recent
times.

1956: *C'est arrivé à Aden.* 1957: *La main
chaude (released 1959).* 1958: *Une balle dans
le canon.* 1960: *Les portes claquent.* 1961:
*Adorable menteuse. Les snobs. La dénonciation
(US: The Immoral Moment). Le rendez-vous
de minuit. *Nom d'une pipe.* 1962: *The Trial.
Le crime ne paie pas.* 1963: *Tous les enfants du
monde (unfinished).* 1964: *Behold a Pale Horse.
Les copains. Jaloux comme un tigre. *Le loup et
le chien.* 1965: *Je vous salue, Mafia (GB and
US: Hail! Mafia). La bourse et la vie. Is Paris
Burning?* 1966: *Le fer à repasser. *Comédie.
Les compagnons de la marguerite. Le Judoka
agent secret.* 1967: *L'homme à la Buick.
L'authentique procès de Carl-Emmanuel Jung.
La mariée était en noir (GB: and US: The
Bride Wore Black). *Méli-mélodrame.* 1968:
*La pince à ongles (GB: The Nail Clippers).
Baisers volés (GB and US: Stolen Kisses). La
grande lessive.* 1969: *Hibernatus. Détruire, dit-
elle (US: Destroy, She Said). L'hiver. Le jeu
de la puce. *Projet Orfée.* 1970: *L'étalon. Le
printemps. La rose et le revolver. *Un troisième.
1971: Out One (unreleased). Le souffle au coeur
(GB: Dearest Love. US: Murmur of the Heart).
Les assassins de l'ordre. Jaune le soleil. La
vieille fille. Papa, les petits bâteaux. L'automne.
*Station service. *La Poule. *Boris et Pierre.
1972: Il était une fois un flic. The Lumière
Years (narrator only). Chut! La grande Paulette.
*Les musiciens du culte. La raison du plus fou.
1973: La fille au violoncelle. The Day of the
Jackal. Glissements progressifs du plaisir. Les
grands sentiments font les bons gueuletons. Out
One: Spectre. *Le jeu des preuves. *Duo.* 1974:
Stavisky. . . Le fantôme de la liberté (GB and
US: The Phantom of Liberty). Galileo. Une
baleine qui avait mal aux dents. Aloïse. Un*

*linceul n'a pas de poches. Caravan to Vaccares.
Sérieux comme le plaisir. Les suspects. India
Song. La vérité sur l'imaginaire passion d'un
inconnu.* 1975: *The Romantic Englishwoman.
La téléphone rose (GB: The Pink Telephone).
Section spéciale. Folle à tuer (GB: TV, as The
Evil Trap). NE. Les rideaux déchirés. La choisie.
Les oeufs brouillés.* 1976: *Le traqué. Mr Klein.
L'Eden Palace.* 1977: *Le diable dans la boîte.
Die linkshändige Frau (GB and US: The Left-
Handed Woman). L'imprécateur. L'aïdeu nu.
Une sale histoire. Aurais dû faire gaffe, le
choc est terrible.* 1978: *The Passage.* 1979:
*Moonraker. Le rose et le blanc. *Samedi-
Dimanche.* 1980: *Les jeux de la Comtesse
Dolingen de Gratz. The Bunker (TV).* 1981:
*Chariots of Fire. Seuls. *La leçon de chant.
1982: Enigma. Douce enquête sur la violence.
1983: Erendira. Une jeunesse. Chronopolis.
1984: Le bon roi Dagobert. Le juge.* 1985: *The
Holcroft Covenant. L'eveillé du Pont d'Alma
(US: The Insomniac on the Bridge). Canevas la
ville. Cinécalligramme.* 1986: *The Name of the
Rose. Billy-ze-Kick.* 1987: *Operation Madonna.
The Rose of the Names. Souvenir.* 1988: *Les
tribulations heroïque de Balthazar Kober. The
Madonna Man.* 1991: *Ma vie est un enfer.
1993: The Remains of the Day.* 1995: *Jefferson
in Paris.*

LOO, Richard 1903–1983
Hawaiian actor of Chinese parentage, who
graduated from the University of California
in business studies, and became an importer.
When his business was hit by the Depression,
he turned to acting. His roles in the 1930s
were predictable and relatively few but, with
the coming of World War II, he screwed his
pleasant features into a merciless, humourless expression and played some memorable
Japanese tormentors, especially in *The Purple
Heart, China Sky* and, in post-war years,
I Was an American Spy.

1931: *Dirigible.* 1932: *War Correspondent
(GB: Soldiers of Fortune). Secrets of Wu Sin
(GB: Secrets of Chinatown). The Bitter Tea of
General Yen.* 1934: *Now and Forever.* 1935:
Stranded. East of Java (GB: Java Seas). 1936:
*After the Thin Man. Shadow of Chinatown
(serial).* 1937: *The Good Earth. Lost Horizon.
The Singing Marine. That Certain Woman.
Thank You, Mr Moto. West of Shanghai/War
Lord.* 1938: *Shadows Over Shanghai. Too Hot
to Handle. Blondes at Work.* 1939: *Daughter of
the Tong. Island of Lost Men. Mr Wong in*

*Chinatown. Miracles for Sale. Panama Patrol.
North of Shanghai. Lady of the Tropics.* 1940:
*The Fatal Hour. Doomed to Die (GB: The
Mystery of the Wentworth Castle).* 1941: *Secrets
of the Wasteland. They Met in Bombay.* 1942:
*Across the Pacific. Bombs Over Burma. Flying
Tigers. Little Tokyo USA. Road to Morocco.
Star-Spangled Rhythm. Manila Calling. Sub-
marine Raider. Wake Island. A Yank on the
Burma Road (GB: China Caravan). Remember
Pearl Harbor.* 1943: *Behind the Rising Sun.
China. Flight for Freedom. The Falcon Strikes
Back. Jack London. The Amazing Mrs Holliday.
Yanks Ahoy!* 1944: *The Keys of the Kingdom.
The Story of Dr Wassell. The Purple Heart.
1945: Back to Bataan. Betrayal from the East.
China Sky. God is My Co-Pilot. First Yank
into Tokyo (GB: Mask of Fury). Prison Ship.
Tokyo Rose.* 1947: *Seven Were Saved. To the
Ends of the Earth. Web of Danger. Women in
the Night. The Beginning or the End?* 1948:
*The Cobra Strikes. Half Past Midnight. The
Mystery of the Golden Eye. Rogues' Regiment.
1949: The Clay Pigeon. State Department –
File 649 (GB: Assignment in China). Malaya
(GB: East of the Rising Sun).* 1950: *The Steel
Helmet. *Chinatown Chump.* 1951: *Operation
Pacific. I Was an American Spy.* 1952: *Five
Fingers.* 1953: *China Venture. Target Hong
Kong.* 1954: *Hell and High Water. The
Shanghai Story. Living It Up. The Bamboo
Prison.* 1955: *Soldier of Fortune. Love is a
Many-Splendored Thing.* 1956: *The Con-
queror. Around the World in 80 Days. Battle
Hymn.* 1958: *The Quiet American. Hong Kong
Affair.* 1961: *Seven Women from Hell.* 1962:
*Confessions of an Opium Eater (GB: Evils of
Chinatown). A Girl Named Tamiko.* 1966:
The Sand Pebbles. 1969: *A Matter of Humani-
ties (TV).* 1970: *Which Way to the Front?
(GB: Ja! Ja! Mein General! But Which Way to
the Front?).* 1971: *One More Train to Rob.
Chandler.* 1972: *Kung Fu (TV).* 1974: *The
Man With the Golden Gun.* 1975: *Collision
Course (TV).*

LOVE, Montagu 1877–1943
Hefty, square-faced, chunk-nosed British
actor with thinning light-brown hair, in
Hollywood from 1915 (after an early career
as a newspaper cartoonist). Once into his
stride, Love proved himself a thoroughly
hissable villain, starring as Rasputin and
other sinister historical figures. With the
coming of sound, his unyielding features

were seen in lesser, though still striking roles, often in period costume.

1914: The Suicide Club. 1915: The Face in the Moonlight. The Antique Dealer. Hearts in Exile. A Royal Family. The Greater Will. A Woman's Way. Sunday. 1916: Friday the Thirteenth. Husband and Wife. The Scarlet Oath. The Gilded Cage. Bought and Paid For. The Devil's Toy. The Hidden Scar. The Man She Married. The Challenge. 1917: Rasputin The Black Monk. Hands Up! The Brand of Satan. The Dancer's Peril. Forget Me Not. Yankee Pluck. The Guardian. The Dormant Power. 1918: The Awakening. The Cross-Bearer. The Grouch. Broken Ties. The Cabaret. The Good For Nothing. Stolen Orders. Vengeance. *She's Everywhere. 1919: A Broadway Saint. The Hand Invisible. To Him That Hath. Three Green Eyes. Rough Neck. Through the Toils. The Quickening Flame. The Steel King. 1920: Place of Honeymoons. Man's Plaything. The Riddle Woman. The World and His Wife. 1921: Shams of Society. The Wrong Woman. Forever (GB: Peter Ibbetson). The Case of Becky. Love's Redemption. 1922: The Beauty Shop. Streets of Paris/Secrets of Paris. The Darling of the Rich. What's Wrong with Women? 1923: The Leopardess. The Eternal City. 1924: Roulette. A Son of the Sahara. Sinners in Heaven. Love of Women. Restless Wives. Who's Cheating? Week-End Husbands. 1925: The Desert's Price. The Ancient Highway. The Mad Marriage. 1926: Out of the Storm. The Social Highwayman. Brooding Eyes. Don Juan. The Silent Lover. Hands Up! (and 1917 film). The Son of the Sheik. 1927: The Night of Love. The King of Kings. Good Time Charley. The Haunted Ship. Jesse James. One Hour of Love. Rose of the Golden West. The Tender Hour. 1928: The Noose. The Devil's Skipper. The Hawk's Nest. The Haunted House. *Character Studies. The Wind. Silks and Saddles (GB: Thoroughbreds). 1929: The Divine Lady. Synthetic Sin. The Last Warning. Her Private Life. Bulldog Drummond. Charming Sinners. Midstream. The Mysterious Island. The Voice Within. A Most Immoral Lady. 1930: A Notorious Affair. Double Cross Roads. Back Pay. Kismet. The Cat Creeps. Inside the Lines. Reno. Love Comes Along. Outward Bound. The Furies. 1931: Alexander Hamilton. The Lion and the Lamb. 1932: Silver Lining. Stowaway. Vanity Fair. Love Bound. Riding Tornado. Midnight Lady (GB: Dream Mother). Out of Singapore. Broadway Tornado. *The Bride's Bereavement or Snake in the Grass. 1933: His Double Life. 1934: Limehouse Blues. Menace. 1935: Hi Gaucho. The Man Who Broke the Bank at Monte Carlo. Clive of India. The Crusades. 1936: The Country Doctor. Sutter's Gold. Sing, Baby, Sing. Reunion (GB: Hearts in Reunion). Lloyds of London. One in a Million. The White Angel. Champagne Charlie. 1937: The Prince and the Pauper. Parnell. The Life of Emile Zola. Tovarich. The Prisoner of Zenda. London by Night. A Damsel in Distress. Adventure's End. 1938: Professor, Beware! The Buccaneer. If I Were King. Kidnapped. Fighting Devil Dogs. Murder on the High Seas. The Adventures of Robin Hood. 1939: Gunga Din. Juarez. Rulers of the Sea. The Man in the Iron Mask. We Are Not Alone. 1940: Northwest Passage. The Son of Monte Cristo. All This and

Heaven Too. The Sea Hawk. A Dispatch from Reuter's (GB: This Man Reuter). Dr Ehrlich's Magic Bullet (GB: The Story of Dr Ehrlich's Magic Bullet). The Lone Wolf Strikes. Private Affairs. North West Mounted Police. The Mark of Zorro. Hudson's Bay. 1941: The Devil and Miss Jones. Shining Victory. Lady for a Night. 1942: The Remarkable Andrew. Sherlock Holmes and the Voice of Terror. Tennessee Johnson (GB: The Man on America's Conscience). 1943: Forever and a Day. The Constant Nymph. Devotion (released 1946). Holy Matrimony. 1946: Thieves' Holiday (GB: A Scandal in Paris. Filmed 1943).

LOVELL, Raymond 1900–1953

Portly Canadian actor, long in Britain, where he married actress Tamara Desni. He seemed to be forever playing plump princes and ranting regents, although his florid features could also convey a very smooth brand of villainy indeed. Also directed stage plays.

1931: Love, Life and Laughter. The Third Clue. Warn London! 1935: Some Day. The Case of Gabriel Perry. Crime Unlimited. Sexton Blake and the Mademoiselle. King of the Damned. 1936: Not So Dusty. Gaolbreak. Troubled Waters. Gypsy Melody. Fair Exchange. 1937: Glamorous Night. Secret Lives (US: I Married a Spy). Behind Your Back. Midnight Menace (US: Bombs over London). Mademoiselle Docteur. 1938: Murder Tomorrow. 1939: Q Planes (US: Clouds over Europe). 1940: Contraband (US: Blackout). 1941: He Found a Star. 49th Parallel (US: The Invaders). The Common Touch. 1942: The Young Mr Pitt. The Goose Steps Out. Uncensored. Alibi. 1943: Candlelight in Algeria. Warn That Man. The Man in Grey. 1944: Hotel Reserve. The Way Ahead. 1945: Caesar and Cleopatra. Night Boat to Dublin. 1946: Appointment with Crime. 1947: Edge of the River. Easy Money. 1948: Who Killed Van Loon? The Three Weird Sisters. Quartet. The Blind Goddess. But Not in Vain. My Brother's Keeper. The Calendar. Snowbound. So Evil My Love. The Bad Lord Byron. 1949: The Romantic Age (US: Naughty Arlette). Madness of the Heart. Once Upon a Dream. Fools Rush In. 1950: The Mudlark. 1952: Time Gentlemen Please! The Pickwick Papers. 1953: The Steel Key.

LOWE, Arthur 1914–1982

Perceptive, stoutly built British actor who became a character star (via several television series) in his fifties: a supreme example of how even brilliant players can spend a lifetime wasting away in bit parts. But his bumbling, roly-poly characters with thoughts and emotions deeper than their outward pomposity would indicate deservedly brought him leading roles; and he subsequently enriched almost any assignment he was given. Died following a stroke.

1948: London Belongs to Me (US: Dulcimer Street). 1949: Kind Hearts and Coronets. Stop Press Girl. Floodtide. The Spider and the Fly. Poet's Pub. 1950: Cage of Gold. 1953: Gilbert Harding Speaking of Murder. *The Mirror and Markheim. 1954: Final Appointment. 1955: The Reluctant Bride (US: Two Grooms for a Bride). Windfall. One Way Out. The Woman for Joe. Who Done It? 1956: Breakaway. The High Terrace. The Green Man. 1957: Table in the Corner/Hour of Decision. Stranger in Town. 1958: Blind Spot. Stormy Crossing (US: Black Tide). 1959: The Boy and the Bridge. The Day They Robbed the Bank of England. 1960: Follow That Horse! 1961: Go to Blazes. 1962: Murder on Cloud Seven. This Sporting Life. 1965: You Must Be Joking! The White Bus (released 1967). 1968: If . . . 1969: *It All Goes to Show. The Bed Sitting Room. Spring and Port Wine. 1970: Some Will, Some Won't. The Rise and Rise of Michael Rimmer. *A Hole Lot of Trouble. *William Webb Ellis, Are You Mad? Fragment of Fear. 1971: Dad's Army. The Ruling Class. 1972: Adolf Hitler—My Part in His Downfall. 1973: O Lucky Man! Theatre of Blood. No Sex Please—We're British. 1974: Man About the House. 1975: Royal Flash. The Bawdy Adventures of Tom Jones. 1977: The Strange Case of the End of Civilization As We Know It (TV). 1979: The Lady Vanishes. The Lion, the Witch and the Wardrobe (TV. Voice only). Sweet William. 1982: Wagner (TV). Britannia Hospital.

LUKE, Keye 1904–1991

Slightly built Hollywood oriental actor, born in China but raised in America, After studying architecture at university, he became a commercial artist with the RKO studio, and thence to small roles in films. The cinema kept him busy from 1933 as assorted easterners, including two popular series characters – Charlie Chan's Number One

son in the detective thrillers about the proverb-spouting sleuth, and Dr Lee Won How in MGM's Dr Gillespie hospital dramas. He returned to films in 1968, after a 10-year break. as aged but wily orientals. Died after a stroke.

1933: *Kickin' the Crown Around. *Hold Your Temper. *Poor Fish. *Three Little Swigs. 1934: The Painted Veil. Charlie Chan in Paris. 1935: Oil for the Lamps of China. Mad Love (GB: Hands of Orlac). King of Burlesque. Here's to Romance. Charlie Chan in Shanghai. Murder in the Fleet. Shanghai. Charlie Chan in Egypt. Eight Bells. The Casino Murder Case. 1936: Charlie Chan at the Circus. Charlie Chan at the Race Track. Anything Goes. Charlie Chan at the Opera. 1937: Charlie Chan on Broadway. The Good Earth. Charlie Chan at the Olympics. Charlie Chan at Monte Carlo. 1938: International Settlement. Mr Moto's Gamble. 1939: Barricade. Disputed Passage. North of Shanghai. 1940: Phantom of Chinatown. Comrade X. The Green Hornet (serial). No, No, Nanette. Sued for Libel. The Green Hornet Strikes Again (serial). 1941: The Gang's All Here. Bowery Blitzkrieg (GB: Stand and Deliver). Let's Go Collegiate (GB: Farewell to Fame). Mr and Mrs North. No Hands on the Clock. They Met in Bombay. Burma Convoy. Passage from Hong Kong. 1942: A Yank on the Burma Road (GB: China Caravan). Somewhere I'll Find You. Across the Pacific. North to the Klondike. The Falcon's Brother. Dr Gillespie's New Assistant. Adventures of Smilin' Jack (serial). Destination Unknown. Invisible Agent. Journey for Margaret. Mexican Spitfire's Elephant. Spy Ship. A Tragedy at Midnight. 1943: Dr Gillespie's Criminal Case (GB: Crazy to Kill). Salute to the Marines. 1944: Andy Hardy's Blonde Trouble. Three Men in White. 1945: Between Two Women. First Yank into Tokyo (GB: Mask of Fury). How Do You Do? Tokyo Rose. Secret Agent X-9 (serial). 1946: Lost City of the Jungle (serial). 1947: Intrigue. Dark Delusion (GB: Cynthia's Secret). 1948: Sleep My Love. Waterfront at Midnight. The Feathered Serpent. 1949: Sky Dragon. Manhandled. Young Man With a Horn (GB: Young Man of Music). 1953: South Sea Woman. Fair Wind to Java. 1954: Hell's Half Acre. World for Ransom. Bamboo Prison. 1955: Love is a Many-Splendored Thing. 1956: Around the World in 80 Days. 1957: Yangtse Incident (US: Battle Hell). 1958: The Hunters. 1968: Nobody's Perfect. 1969: The Chairman (GB:

The Most Dangerous Man in the World). Project X. 1970: The Hawaiians (GB: Master of the Islands). 1971: Noon Sunday. 1972: Kung Fu (TV). 1973: The Cat Creature (TV). 1974: Judge Dee and the Monastery Murders (TV). 1975: Won Ton Ton, the Dog Who Saved Hollywood. 1977: The Amsterdam Kill. 1979: Just You and Me, Kid. 1981: Fly Away Home (TV). 1982: They Call Me Bruce. 1983: Cocaine and Blue Eyes (TV). 1984: Gremlins. 1985: Blade in Hong Kong (TV). 1986: Kung Fu: The Movie (TV. GB: Kung Fu II). A Fine Mess. The Last Electric Knight (TV). Blood Sport (TV). 1988: Dead Heat. The Mighty Quinn. 1990: Gremlins 2: The New Batch. Alice.

LYNCH, Richard 1942–

Fair-haired, hollow-eyed, sandpaper-faced, muscular American actor of rather forbidding handsomeness, who plays really ferocious villains. Although classically trained, with experience in Shakespeare and Chekhov and with a well-modulated speaking voice, Lynch soon found himself cast, after entering films in his early thirties, as ruthless bad guys who aimed to do unspeakable things to the hero. When he wasn't being a venomous vampire, or the leader of a coven of witches, it seemed he was a power-hungry maniac trying to take over the world. Unfortunately, the exploitation films he's made to date are mostly the sort that go quickly to video.

1973: Scarecrow. The Seven-Ups. 1974: Open Season. 1975: The Happy Hooker. Starsky and Hutch (TV). 1976: Demon/God Told Me To. Delta Fox. The Premonition. 1977: Stunts. Roger and Harry: The Mitera Target (TV). Dog and Cat (TV). Good Against Evil (TV). 1978: Deathsport. 1979: Vampire (TV). Nightmare in Hawaii (TV). Steel. The Ninth Configuration/Twinkle, Twinkle, Killer Kane. 1980: The Conquest of the Earth (TV). The Formula. Alcatraz: The Whole Shocking Story (TV). 1981: Sizzle (TV). 1982: White Water Rebels (TV). The Sword and the Sorcerer. 1983: The Last Ninja (TV). 1984: Savage Dawn. 1985: Invasion USA. Cut and Run. 1986: Night Force. 1987: Little Nikita (GB: TV, as The Sleepers). The Barbarians. 1988: Melanie Rose/High Stakes. Bad Dreams. Spirit. One-Man Force. 1989: Aftershock. Return to Justice. Kojak: Flowers for Matty (TV). 1990: The

Forbidden Dance. Lockdown. 1991: Alligator II: The Mutation. Trancers 2. Maximum Force. Puppet Master III: Toulon's Revenge. 1992: October 32nd. Terror of Manhattan. Merlin. Double Twist/Double Threat. Shirmist. 1993: Scanner Cop. Midnight Confessions. Necronomicon. 1994: Death Match. Tough Guy. 1995: Destination Vegas.

M

MacBRIDE, Donald 1889–1957

Stocky, brown-haired, tight-lipped, full-faced, dogged-looking American actor, often seen as truculent policemen, exasperated editors or bamboozled store managers. Born in Brooklyn, he was a teenage singer in vaudeville, before coming to Hollywood to make silent comedies. He made his career in the theatre for more than 20 years after 1917, until the re-creation of his part as the hotel manager in Room Service, in the Marx Brothers' film version of the stage play, brought him back to films for a trip that lasted 15 years.

1915–1917: *'Mr and Mrs Sidney Drew' comedies. 1916: Hesper of the Mountains. 1917: The Fettered Woman. 1931: His Woman. 1932: The Misleading Lady. 1933: Get That Venus. 1935: *The Old Grey Mayor. *The Chemist. 1938: Room Service. Annabel Takes a Tour. The Amazing Mr Williams. 1939: The Girl and the Gambler. The Flying Irishman. Charlie Chan at Treasure Island. The Girl from Mexico. Blondie Takes a Vacation. The Great Man Votes. The Gracie Allen Murder

Case. Twelve Crowded Hours. The Story of Vernon and Irene Castle. 1940: Curtain Call. Wyoming (GB: Bad Man of Wyoming). Michael Shayne, Private Detective. My Favorite Wife. Murder Over New York. The Saint's Double Trouble. Northwest Passage. Hit Parade of 1941. 1941: Here Comes Mr Jordan. Footlight Fever. The Invisible Woman. High Sierra. Love Crazy. Louisiana Purchase. Topper Returns. You'll Never Get Rich. You're in the Army Now. Rise and Shine. 1942: Juke Girl. Lady Bodyguard. Two Yanks in Trinidad. The Glass Key. My Sister Eileen. Mexican Spitfire Sees a Ghost. A Night to Remember. 1943: They Got Me Covered. Best Foot Forward. A Stranger in Town. 1944: Practically Yours. The Thin Man Goes Home. The Doughgirls. 1945: Bud Abbott and Lou Costello in Hollywood. Hold That Blonde. Penthouse Rhythm. Out of This World. She Gets Her Man. 1946: Doll Face (GB: Come Back to Me). Girl on the Spot. The Dark Horse. Blonde Alibi. The Brute Man. Little Giant (GB: On the Carpet). The Killers. The Dark Corner. The Time of Their Lives. 1947: The Fabulous Joe. Beat the Band. The Egg and I. Buck Privates Come Home (GB: Rookies Come Home). Good News. 1948: Jinx Money. Campus Sleuth. Smart Politics. 1949: The Story of Seabiscuit (GB: Pride of Kentucky). Challenge to Lassie. 1950: Joe Palooka Meets Humphrey. Holiday Rhythm. 1951: Bowery Battalion. Cuban Fireball. Sailor Beware. Rhubarb. Texas Carnival. Two Tickets to Broadway. Meet Danny Wilson. 1952: Gobs and Gals (GB: Cruising Casanovas). The Stooge. 1955: The Seven Year Itch.

MacDONALD, J. Farrell
(John F. MacDonald) 1875–1952

Burly (later positively portly), jovial, bull-necked, bald American actor, who was a singer in stage productions, then tried direction in early silents (among them a couple of Harold Lloyd comedies), before settling down to playing scores of tough but affable character roles, many of them for director John Ford. He was equally happy with cops and prison wardens or outdoor types. His characters were sometimes thick-skulled, but more often resolute and tinged with Irish humour. Worked hard to the end.

1911: *The Lighthouse Keeper. *'Tween Two Loves. *The Scarlet Letter. *The Old Folks' Christmas. *The Piece of String. 1913: *On Burning Sands. *The Female of the Species. *The Dread Inheritance. 1914: *For the Freedom of Cuba. *The Mexican's Last Raid. The Patchwork Girl of Oz. The Last Egyptian. *The Option. *The Gambler's Oath. 1915: Rags. The Heart of Maryland. 1916: The Price of Power. 1917: *Her Heart's Desire. *The Victor of the Plot. 1918: $5,000 Reward. Fair Enough. Three Mounted Men. 1919: Molly of the Follies. A Fight for Love. Riders of Vengeance. Charge it to Me. Roped. Trixie from Broadway. This Hero Stuff. A Sporting Chance. The Outcasts of Poker Flat. Marked Men. 1920: *Two from Texas. *The Boss of Copperhead. *Under Sentence. Bullet Proof. The Path She Chose. Hitchin' Posts. 1921: The Freeze Out. The Wallop. Action. Desperate Youth. Bucking the Line. Trailin'. Little Miss Hawkshaw. Riding with Death. Sky High. 1922: The Bachelor Daddy. Manslaughter. The Bonded Woman. Tracks. The Young Rajah. Come On Over. The Ghost Breaker. Over the Border. 1923: While Paris Sleeps. The Age of Desire. Quicksands. Drifting. Racing Hearts. Fashionable Fakers. 1924: The Brass Bowl. The Storm Daughter. Western Luck. Fair Week. The Signal Tower. Mademoiselle Midnight. Gerald Cranston's Lady. The Iron Horse. 1925: The Scarlet Honeymoon. The Fighting Heart. Thank You. Kentucky Pride. Let Women Alone. Lightnin'. The Lucky Horseshoe. 1926: A Trip to Chinatown. The Dixie Merchant. Bertha, the Sewing Machine Girl. The Shamrock Handicap. The Family Upstairs. The First Year. Three Bad Men. The Country Beyond. The Last Frontier. 1927: Ankles Preferred. The Cradle Snatchers. East Side, West Side. Love Makes 'Em Wild. Paid To Love. Rich But Honest. Colleen. Sunrise—A Song of Two Humans (GB: Sunrise). 1928: Bringing Up Father. The Cohens and Kellys in Paris. Abie's Irish Rose. Riley the Cop. None But the Brave. Phantom City. 1929: Masked Emotions. In Old Arizona. The Four Devils. South Sea Rose. Strong Boy. Masquerade. Happy Days. 1930: Broken Dishes. Men Without Women. The Royal Family of Broadway. Song o' My Heart. Girl of the Golden West. Painted Angel. The Truth About Youth. Born Reckless. Woman Hungry (GB: The Challenge). 1931: River's End. Left-over Ladies (GB: Broken Links). The Painted Desert. The Easiest Way. The Maltese Falcon. The Millionaire. Steel Highway. Other Men's Women. The Squaw Man (GB: The White Man). Too Young to Marry. The Brat. Spirit of Notre Dame (GB: Vigour of Youth). *The Stolen Jools (GB: The Slippery Pearls). Touchdown (GB: Playing the Game). Sporting Blood. 1932: Hotel Continental. Under Eighteen. The Phantom Express. Discarded Lovers. Scandal for Sale. Probation. Week-End Marriage (GB: Working Wives). 70,000 Witnesses. The Thirteenth Guest. Me and My Gal. Steady Company. The Racing Strain. No Man of Her Own. Pride of the Legion (GB: The Big Pay-Off). The Vanishing Frontier. Hearts of Humanity. This Sporting Age. 1933: The Working Man. Laughing at Life. Peg o' My Heart. The Power and the Glory. I Loved a Woman. The Iron Master. Myrt and Marge (GB: Laughter in the Air). Heritage of the Desert. Under Secret Orders. The Fighting Parson. 1934: Romance in Manhattan. Murder on the Campus (GB: At the Stroke of Nine). The Crime Doctor. Man of Two Worlds. Once to Every Woman. The Crosby Case (GB: The Crosby Murder Case). The Cat's Paw. Beggar's Holiday. The Whole Town's Talking (GB: Passport to Fame). 1935: The Square Shooter. Northern Frontier. Let 'Em Have It (GB: False Faces). Star of Midnight. The Best Man Wins. The Healer. The Farmer Takes a Wife. Swell Head. Maybe It's Love. Captain Hurricane. Our Little Girl. The Irish in Us. Front Page Woman. Danger Ahead. Fighting Youth. Stormy. Waterfront Lady. Riffraff. The Arizonian. 1936: Hitch Hike Lady (GB: Eventful Journey). Florida Special. Exclusive Story. Showboat. 1937: The Great Barrier (US: Silent Barriers). Shadows of the Orient. Maid of Salem. Mysterious Crossing. Roaring Timber. Slim. My Dear Miss Aldrich. The Hit Parade. Parnell. County Fair. Slave Ship. Topper. The Game That Kills. Courage of the West. 1938: My Old Kentucky Home. Numbered Woman. State Police. Gang Bullets. Flying Fists. There Goes My Heart. Extortion. White Banners. Come On, Rangers. Little Orphan Annie. The Crowd Roars. Submarine Patrol. 1939: They Shall Have Music. Susannah of the Mounties. Zenobia (GB: Elephants Never Forget). Mickey the Kid. The Housekeeper's Daughter. East Side of Heaven. Full Confession. Conspiracy. The Gentleman from Arizona. The Lone Ranger Rides Again (serial). Coast Guard. 1940: The Light of Western Stars. Knights of the Range. Dark Command. I Take This Oath. Prairie Law. The Last Alarm. *Pony Express Days. Untamed. Stagecoach War. Friendly Neighbors. 1941: In Old Cheyenne. Meet John Doe. Wild Bill Hickok Rides. Law of the Timber. The Great Lie. Broadway Limited. Riders of the Timberline. Sullivan's Travels. 1942: One Thrilling Night. Snuffy Smith – Yard Bird (GB: Snuffy Smith). Reap the Wild Wind. Phantom Killer. The Living Ghost. The Palm Beach Story. Bowery at Midnight. Little Tokyo USA. Captains of the Clouds. 1943: The Ape Man. The Great Moment. Clancy Street Boys. True to Life. Tiger Fangs. *Wedtime Stories. 1944: The Miracle of Morgan's Creek. Irish Eyes Are Smiling. Greenwich Village. Texas Masquerade. Pin-Up Girl. Follow the Boys. Hail the Conquering Hero. Shadow of Suspicion. A Tree Grows in Brooklyn. Ladies of Washington. Follow the Leader. 1945: Nob Hill. Johnny Angel. Pillow of Death. A Tree Grows in Brooklyn. The Dolly Sisters. Hangover Square. The Woman Who Came Back. Pardon My Past. Fallen Angel. 1946: Joe Palooka – Champ. Behind Green Lights. Smoky. My Darling Clementine. My Dog Shep. The Sin of Harold Diddlebock (later and GB: Mad Wednesday!). It's a Wonderful Life! 1947: Web of Danger. Thunder in the Valley (GB: Bob, Son of Battle). Keeper of the Bees. The Bachelor and the Bobby-Soxer (GB: Bachelor Knight). 1948: Fury at Furnace Creek. If You Knew Susie. Unfaithfully Yours. Whispering Smith. Panhandle. Shep Comes Home. Belle Starr's Daughter. The Luck of the Irish. When My Baby Smiles at Me. The Walls of Jericho. Sitting Pretty. 1949: Streets of San Francisco. The Beautiful Blonde from Bashful Bend. Law of the Barbary Coast. You're My Everything. The Dalton Gang. Tough Assignment. Fighting Man of the Plains. 1950: Dakota Lil. Hostile Country. The Daltons' Women. When Willie

Comes Marching Home. Woman on the Run. 1951: Here Comes the Groom. Elopement. Mr Belvedere Rings the Bell. Superman and the Mole Men (GB: Superman and the Strange People). Golden Girl.

As director:

1913: *On Burning Sands. *Jepthah's Daughter. 1914: His Majesty, the Scarecrow of Oz. The Patchwork Girl of Oz. And She Never Knew. *Bill Tell, Pawnbroker. *By the Old Dead Tree. *A Daughter of Earth. Samson. Children of Destiny. *The Magic Cloak of Oz. *The Backslider. *The Tides of Sorrow. *Blacksmith Ben. The Last Egyptian. *The Bond Sinister. 1915: *Lonesome Luke. *Lonesome Luke, Social Gangster. *The Smuggler's Ward. *The Wives of Men. *The Law of Love. *Reapers of the Whirlwind. *The Rehearsal. *Ashes of Inspiration. *His Hand and Seal. *His Wife's Story. *The Chief Inspector. *The Laurel of Tears. *A Woman Without Soul. *The Tides of Retribution. 1916: *Iron Will. *The Guilt of Stephen Eldridge. *The Battle of Truth. *The Mystery of Percival. *Paths That Crossed. *Stronger Than Woman's Will. 1917: *The Mad Stampede.

MacGINNIS, Niall 1913–
Burly, round-faced Irish character actor with a wild mop of dark curly hair, which disappeared in the fifties, giving him a professorial look. Largely a support for the stars in literate action roles, with an occasional villain or semi-lead thrown in. In British films from the mid-thirties, he remained in demand for 35 years.

1935: Turn of the Tide. Hello Sweetheart. The Luck of the Irish. 1936: Ourselves Alone (US: River of Unrest). The Crimson Circle. Debt of Honour. 1937: The Edge of the World. The Last Adventurers. 1938: Mountains o' Mourne. 1940: East of Piccadilly (US: The Strangler). 1941: 49th Parallel (US: The Invaders). 1942: The Day Will Dawn (US: The Avengers). 1943: We Dive at Dawn. Undercover (US: Underground Guerillas). The Hundred Pound Window. 1944: Tawny Pipit. Henry V. 1947: Captain Boycott. Anna Karenina. 1948: Hamlet. No Room at the Inn. 1949: Christopher Columbus. Down to the Sea in Ships. Which Will You Have? (US: Barabbas the Robber). Diamond City. 1950: Chance of a Lifetime. 1951: No Highway (US: No Highway in the

Sky). Talk of a Million (US: You Can't Beat the Irish). 1952: Murder in the Cathedral. 1953: Hell Below Zero. 1954: Conflict of Wings. Martin Luther. Knights of the Round Table. Betrayed. Helen of Troy. 1955: Vom Himmel gefallen/Special Delivery. Alexander the Great. 1956: The Battle of the River Plate (US: Pursuit of the Graf Spee). Lust for Life. 1957: The Shiralee. Night of the Demon (US: Curse of the Demon). 1958: She Didn't Say No! Behind the Mask. The Nun's Story. 1959: Shake Hands with the Devil. Tarzan's Greatest Adventure. This Other Eden. 1960: Never Take Sweets from a Stranger. Kidnapped. A Terrible Beauty (US: The Night Fighters). Foxhole in Cairo. Sword of Sherwood Forest. In the Nick. 1961: Johnny Nobody. 1962: The Prince and the Pauper. The Webster Boy. The Playboy of the Western World. Billy Budd. A Face in the Rain. The Devil's Agent. The Man Who Finally Died. 1963: Jason and the Argonauts. Becket. 1964: The Truth About Spring. 1965: The Spy Who Came in from the Cold. The War Lord. 1966: Island of Terror. A Man Could Get Killed. 1967: The Viking Queen. Torture Garden. 1968: The Shoes of the Fisherman. Krakatoa—East of Java. 1969: Darling Lili. Sinful Davey. River of Mystery (TV). The Kremlin Letter. 1973: The Mackintosh Man. 1978: Crisis at Sun Valley (TV). 1980: Masada (TV. Shortened for cinemas as The Antagonists).

MacGOWRAN, Jack 1916–1973
Sharp-faced, ferret-like, Irish (very Irish), dark-haired purveyor of memorable character studies in British films—usually providing a malicious element in one way or another. His leprechauns looked harmless, and were sometimes comic too, but occasionally insidiously deadly. He began in small roles and worked his way up in films, without ever really deserting the stage. Died from complications following influenza. Father of actress Tara MacGowran.

1951: No Resting Place. 1952: The Quiet Man. The Gentle Gunman. The Titfield Thunderbolt. 1954: The Young Lovers (US: Chance Meeting). 1955: Dust and Gold. 1956: Raiders of the River (serial). Jacqueline. Sailor Beware! (US: Panic in the Parlor). 1957: The Rising of the Moon. Manuela (US: Stowaway Girl). 1958: Darby O'Gill and the Little People. She Didn't Say No! Rooney. 1959: The Boy and the Bridge. Blind Date. Behemoth the

Sea Monster (US: The Giant Behemoth). 1961: Two and Two Make Six. Mix Me a Person. 1962: Vengeance (US: The Brain). Captain Clegg (US: Night Creatures). 1963: Tom Jones. The Ceremony. 1964: Young Cassidy. Lord Jim. 1965: Doctor Zhivago. 1966: Cul-de-Sac. 1967: *The Inn Way Out. Dance of the Vampires (US: The Fearless Vampire Killers). How I Won the War. 1968: *Faithful Departed (narrator only). Wonderwall. 1969: Age of Consent. Start the Revolution Without Me. 1970: King Lear. A Day at the Beach. 1973: The Exorcist.

MACKAY, Fulton 1920–1987
Acidulous, slightly built, wry-mouthed, latterly moustachioed Scottish actor who played everything from ruthless detectives to whisky priests and was also a talented playwright. Somehow, Ealing Studios failed to pick up the ex-quantity surveyor and ex-soldier for their regional comedies and in consequence he made too few films. Enormous personal success did come on television, however, especially through the series Special Branch and Porridge.

1952: I'm a Stranger. The Brave Don't Cry. Laxdale Hall (US: Scotch on the Rocks). 1954: The Last Moment. 1960: Tunes of Glory. 1961: A Prize of Arms. Don't Bother to Knock (US: Why Bother to Knock?). 1962: Mystery Submarine (US: Decoy). 1971: Gumshoe. 1972: Nothing But the Night. 1974: †The Wilby Conspiracy. 1976: The Master of Ballantrae (TV). 1979: Porridge. 1982: Britannia Hospital. 1983: Ill Fares the Land (TV). Local Hero. 1984: To Catch a King (TV). 1985: Water. Defence of the Realm. Dream Child.

† Scene deleted from final release print

MacLANE, Barton 1900–1969
Big, burly, pudgy-faced, red-haired American actor (and ex-football star) who played tough guys with gruff voices at Warners from 1935 to 1942, a time when he was quite near the top of the tree. Insufficient variety in characterizations eventually sent him further down the cast list, although he continued to be busy. Born on Christmas Day, died on New Year's Day (of double pneumonia).

1926: The Quarterback. 1929: The Cocoanuts. 1931: His Woman. 1933: To the Last Man.

Miller Story. Jubilee Trail. Rails into Laramie. 1955: Foxfire. The Silver Star. Jail Busters. Hell's Outpost. Last of the Desperadoes. The Treasure of Ruby Hills. 1956: Backlash. Jaguar. The Man is Armed. Three Violent People. The Naked Gun. Wetbacks. 1957: Sierra Stranger. The Storm Rider. Hell's Crossroads. Naked in the Sun. 1958: The Girl in the Woods. Frontier Gun. The Geisha Boy. 1960: Noose for a Gunman. Gunfighters of Abilene. 1961: Pocketful of Miracles. 1963: Law of the Lawless. 1965: The Rounders. Town Tamer. 1968: Buckskin. Arizona Bushwhackers.

The Thundering Herd. *Let's Dance. Man of the Forest. The Torch Singer. Tillie and Gus. Hell and High Water (GB: Cap'n Jericho). Big Executive. 1934: The Last Round-Up. Lone Cowboy. 1935: The Case of the Curious Bride. Page Miss Glory. I Found Stella Parish. G-Men. Man of Iron. The Case of the Lucky Legs. Go into Your Dance (GB: Casino de Paree). Black Fury. Stranded. Dr Socrates. Ceiling Zero. The Frisco Kid. 1936: The Walking Dead. Jail Break (GB: Murder in the Big House). Bengal Tiger. God's Country and the Woman. Times Square Playboy (GB: His Best Man). Bullets or Ballots. Smart Blonde. Draegerman Courage (GB: The Cave-In). 1937: Wine, Women and Horses. You Only Live Once. San Quentin. Born Reckless. Fly-Away Baby (GB: Crime in the Clouds). The Adventurous Blonde/Torchy Blane, the Adventurous Blonde. The Prince and the Pauper. Ever Since Eve. The Kid Comes Back (GB: Don't Pull Your Punches). 1938: Torchy Gets Her Man. Gold Is Where You Find It. Prison Break. You and Me. Blondes at Work. The Storm. 1939: Stand Up and Fight. Big Town Czar. Mutiny in the Big House. Torchy Blane in Chinatown. I Was a Convict. Torchy Runs for Mayor. 1940: The Secret Seven. Men without Souls. Melody Ranch. Gangs of Chicago. 1941: Western Union. Come Live with Me. Barnacle Bill. The Maltese Falcon. Hit the Road. High Sierra. Manpower. Dr Jekyll and Mr Hyde. Wild Geese Calling. Hit the Road. 1942: All Through the Night. Highways by Night. The Big Street. In This Our Life. 1943: Song of Texas. Man of Courage. Crime Doctor's Strangest Case (GB: The Strangest Case). A Gentle Gangster. The Underdog. Bombardier. 1944: Cry of the Werewolf. The Mummy's Ghost. Gentle Annie. Secret Command. Marine Raiders. Nabonga (GB: The Jungle Woman). 1945: Scared Stiff. The Spanish Main. Tarzan and the Amazons. 1946: The Mysterious Intruder. Santa Fé Uprising. San Quentin. 1947: Tarzan and the Huntress. Cheyenne. Jungle Flight. 1948: Treasure of the Sierra Madre. Relentless. The Dude Goes West. Unknown Island. Silver River. Angel in Exile. The Walls of Jericho. 1949: Red Light. 1950: Kiss Tomorrow Goodbye. The Bandit Queen. Let's Dance. Rookie Fireman. 1951: Best of the Badmen. Drums in the Deep South. 1952: Bugles in the Afternoon. The Half Breed. Thunderbirds. 1953: Cow Country. Kansas Pacific. Sea of Lost Ships. Jack Slade (GB: Slade). Captain Scarface. 1954: The Glenn

MacMAHON, Aline 1899–1991

Distinguished, dark-haired, tall American stage actress originally intended for stardom by Warners when they brought her to the screen. But her horsey, mournful face was obviously destined for more interesting things than straight leads, and she proved as adept with wisecracks as with wisdom. When her studio contract was over, she again devoted the majority of her time to the theatre. Nominated for an Academy Award for Dragon Seed.

1931: Five Star Final. The Mouthpiece. 1932: Heart of New York. Life Begins (GB: The Dawn of Life). The Sign of the Cross. One-Way Passage. Week-End Marriage (GB: Working Wives). Once in a Lifetime. Silver Dollar. 1933: Heroes for Sale. Gold Diggers of 1933. The World Changes. The Life of Jimmy Dolan (GB: The Kid's Last Fight). 1934: Big-Hearted Herbert. Heat Lightning. The Merry Frinks (GB: The Happy Family). Babbitt. Side Streets (GB: Woman in Her Thirties). 1935: I Live My Life. While the Patient Slept. Ah, Wilderness! Mary Jane's Pa (GB: Wanderlust). Kind Lady (GB: House of Menace). 1937: When You're in Love (GB: For You Alone). 1939: Back Door to Heaven. 1941: Out of the Fog. 1942: Tish. The Lady is Willing. 1943: Stage Door Canteen. Seeds of Freedom (narrator only). 1944: Guest in the House. Dragon Seed. *Reward Unlimited. 1946: The Mighty McGurk. 1948: The Search. 1949: Roseanna McCoy. 1950: The Flame and the Arrow. 1953: The Eddie Cantor Story. 1955: The Man from Laramie. 1960: Cimarron. 1961: The Young Doctors. 1962: I Could Go On Singing. Diamond Head. 1963: All the Way Home.

MACRAE, Duncan

(John D. Macrae) 1905–1967

Gaunt, craggy, long-chinned Scottish actor who was a teacher for 20 years before switching careers during World War II. His cadaverous shape loomed memorably in a few films, almost all with a heavy Scottish slant. He was also chairman of the Scottish branch of Equity, the actors' union, and got too few chances at his favourite parts—'dignified fools'.

1947: The Brothers. 1948: Whisky Galore! (US: Tight Little Island). 1950: The Woman in Question (US: Five Angles on Murder). 1952: You're Only Young Twice! 1953: The Kidnappers (US: The Little Kidnappers). The 'Maggie' (US: High and Dry). 1955: Geordie (US: Wee Geordie). 1957: Rockets Galore (US: Mad Little Island). 1958: The Bridal Path. 1959: Kidnapped. Our Man in Havana. 1960: Tunes of Glory. Greyfriars Bobby. 1961: The Best of Enemies. 1963: Girl in the Headlines (US: The Model Murder Case). A Jolly Bad Fellow (US: They All Died Laughing). 1967: Casino Royale. 30 is a Dangerous Age, Cynthia.

MACREADY, George 1899–1973

One of America's most distinctive villains: a blond, blue-eyed death's head of a man with an aristocratic sneer on the upper lip, and skin drawn pellucidly over the features—a face that somehow went with his having run an art gallery before giving into the acting urge in the 1940s. Created a whole range of distinguished nasties and sadists, nearly all with a civilized veneer. An emphysema killed him just after retirement.

1942: Commandos Strike at Dawn. 1943: Ali Baba and the 40 Thieves. 1944: The Seventh Cross. The Story of Dr Wassell. Follow the Boys. Soul of a Monster. Wilson. The Conspirators. 1945: Don Juan Quilligan. The Missing Juror. I Love a Mystery. The Monster and the Ape (serial). A Song to Remember. The Fighting Guardsman. Counter-Attack (GB: One Against Seven). My Name is Julia Ross. 1946: The Man Who Dared. The Walls Came Tumbling Down. Gilda. Two Years Before the Mast. The Bandit of Sherwood Forest. The Return of Monte Cristo (GB: Monte Cristo's Revenge). 1947: The Swordsman. Down to Earth. 1948: The Big Clock. The Black Arrow (GB: The Black Arrow Strikes). The Gallant Blade. Coroner Creek. Beyond Glory. Alias Nick Beal (GB: The Contact Man). 1949: Johnny Allegro (GB: Hounded). The Doolins of Oklahoma (GB: The Great Manhunt). Knock on Any Door. 1950: The Nevadan (GB: The Man from Nevada). Fortunes of Captain Blood. A Lady Without Passport. Rogues of Sherwood Forest. The Desert Hawk. 1951: Tarzan's Peril (GB: Tarzan and the Jungle Queen). Detective Story. The Golden Horde (GB: The Golden Horde of Genghis Khan). The Green Glove. The Desert Fox (GB: Rommel—Desert Fox). 1953: Treasure of the Golden Condor. The Golden Blade. The Stranger Wore a Gun. Julius Caesar. 1954: Duffy of San Quentin (GB: Men Behind Bars). Vera Cruz. 1956: A Kiss Before Dying. Thunder Over Arizona. 1957: Paths of Glory. Gunfire at Indian Gap. The Abductors. 1958: Plunderers of Painted Flats. 1959: Jet over the Atlantic. The Alligator People. 1960: In the Presence of Mine Enemies (TV). Two Weeks in Another Town. Taras Bulba. 1964: Seven Days in May. Dead Ringer (GB: Dead Image). Where Love Has Gone. 1965: The Great Race. The Human Duplicators. 1966: Fame is the Name of the Game (TV). 1967: Asylum for a Spy (TV). 1969: The Young Lawyers (TV). Daughter of the Mind (TV). Night Gallery (TV). 1970: Tora! Tora! Tora! 1971: The Return of Count Yorga.

MADDEN, Peter 1904–1976

Thin, hollow-cheeked, slit-eyed British actor of menacing presence. Born in Malaya, he was, at 16, 'assistant to a drunken magician', later a racing driver and stand-up comic before bringing his grim expression and deep bass voice to film (and later TV) character roles. He once said: 'I'm generally cast as a baddie because I've got such a miserable bloody face. Thank God I never wanted to be a star'. Also a memorable Inspector Lestrade in a TV 'Sherlock Holmes' series of the mid 1960s.

1938: Hey! Hey! USA. 1943: Rhythm Serenade. 1945: The Wicked Lady. 1947: Penny and the Pownall Case. 1948: Counterblast (US: The Devil's Plot). 1949: A Matter of Murder. 1950: The Quiet Woman. Tom Brown's Schooldays. 1958: Battle of the VI (US: VI/Unseen Heroes). Fiend Without a Face. Floods of Fear. 1959: Hell is a City. 1960: Saturday Night and Sunday Morning. Exodus. 1961: The Road to Hong Kong. 1962: The Loneliness of the Long Distance Runner. A Kind of Loving. The Very Edge. 1963: From Russia with Love. Nothing But the Best. 1964: Dr Terror's House of Horrors. Woman of Straw. 1965: Doctor Zhivago. 1966: He Who Rides a Tiger. 1967: The Magnificent Six and a Half (first series). Frankenstein Created Woman. 1969: The Violent Enemy. 1970: The Private Life of Sherlock Holmes. 1971: On the Buses. 1972: Henry VIII and His Six Wives. Nearest and Dearest. 1974: Frankenstein and the Monster from Hell. 1975: One of Our Dinosaurs is Missing. 1976: The Message/Mohammed, Messenger of God.

MADDERN, Victor 1926–1993

Lively, stocky, dark-haired, jut-jawed British actor with expressive features and ready scowl. He made his debut as a cockney private soldier and took a good living from the part for the next 10 years. Maddern could just as easily play jaunty, shifty or sympathetic, which made for one or two interesting variations in his roles when not in uniform. His film output slackened from the early 1970s, after which he was more often seen in theatre and TV productions. A diligent worker for religion-slanted charities, he also ran a public speaking school. Some film buffs reckon they can spot Maddern in It Always Rains on Sunday (1947), a time when he was still at RADA. Died from a brain tumour.

1950: Seven Days to Noon. Morning Departure (US: Operation Disaster). Pool of London. Highly Dangerous. 1951: High Treason. His Excellency. The Franchise Affair. The House in the Square (US: I'll Never Forget You). Angels One Five. 1952: The Planter's Wife (US: Outpost in Malaya). Top Secret (US: Mr Potts Goes to Moscow). Time Bomb (US: Terror on a Train). 1953: Malta Story. Street of Shadows (US: Shadow Man). Single-Handed (US: Sailor of the King). The Good Beginning. 1954: The Young Lovers (US: Chance Meeting). Carrington VC (US: Court-Martial). Fabian of the Yard. Raising a Riot. The Sea Shall Not Have Them. The End of the Affair. 1955: The Night My Number Came Up. Footsteps in the Fog. Josephine and Men. Cockleshell Heroes. It's a Great Day. Private's Progress. 1956: Child in the House. The Last Man to Hang? A Hill in Korea (US: Hell in Korea). The Man in the Sky (US: Decision Against Time). 1957: Seven Waves Away (US: Abandon Ship!). Face in the Night. Saint Joan. Strangers' Meeting. Barnacle Bill (US: All at Sea). Happy is the Bride! Son of a Stranger. The Safecracker. 1958: The Square Peg. Blood of the Vampire. Behind the Mask. Dunkirk. Cat and Mouse/The Desperate Men. I Was Monty's Double (US: Monty's Double). Carve Her Name with Pride. 1959: I'm All Right, Jack. The Siege of Pinchgut (US: Four Desperate Men). Please Turn Over. Sink the Bismarck! 1960: Let's Get Married. Light Up the Sky. Carry On Constable. Exodus. Watch Your Stern. Crossroads to Crime. 1961: Carry On Regardless. Raising the Wind (US: Roommates). On the Fiddle (US: Operation Snafu). Petticoat Pirates. 1962: HMS Defiant (US: Damn the Defiant!). The Longest Day. 1963: Carry On Spying. 1964: Carry On Cleo. 1965: Rotten to the Core. Bunny Lake is Missing. Cuckoo Patrol. Circus of Fear (US: Psycho-Circus). 1966: Run Like a Thief. 1967: The Magnificent Two. *Talk of the Devil. 1968: The Bush Baby. The Lost Continent. Decline and Fall . . . of a birdwatcher! Chitty Chitty Bang Bang. 1969: The Magic Christian. 1970: *A Hole Lot of Trouble. Cromwell. 1971: The Magnificent Six and a Half (third series). *That's All We Need. 1972: Steptoe and Son. 1973: Digby — the Biggest Dog in the World. 1978: Carry On Emmanuelle. Death on the Nile. 1985: The Moving Finger. 1992: Freddie as F.R.O.7 (voice only).

MADISON, Noel

(Nathaniel Moscovitch) 1898–1975
Very dark, sullen-looking American actor who almost always played a bad guy—often one who turned yellow in the end. The son of another character actor, Russian-born Maurice Moscovitch (1871–1940), he was billed in the theatre as Nat Madison, then came to Hollywood with the beginnings of sound. Fleeing from a run of evil gangsters, he made several films in Britain in the late 1930s, including three with Jessie Matthews.

1930: The Doorway to Hell (GB: Handful of Clouds). Sinner's Holiday. Little Caesar. 1931: The Star Witness. 1932: The Hatchet Man (GB: The Honourable Mr Wong). Hat Check Girl (GB: Embassy Girl). Me and My Gal (GB: Pier 13). Play Girl. Symphony of Six Million. Man About Town. The Trial of Vivienne Ware. The Last Mile. Laughter in Hell. 1933: Humanity. Destination Unknown. The House of Rothschild. West of Singapore. Important Witness. 1934: I Like It That Way.

Manhattan Melodrama. Journal of a Crime. Four Hours to Kill. 1935: The Morals of Marcus. G Men. What Price Crime? The Girl Who Came Back. Three Kids and a Queen (GB: The Baxter Millions). My Marriage. Murder at Glen Athol. Woman Wanted. 1936: Muss 'Em Up (GB: House of Fate). Our Relations. Champagne Charlie. Straight from the Shoulder. Easy Money. Missing Girls. The Criminal Within. 1937: House of Secrets. Man of the People. Nation Aflame. Gangway. 1938: Sailing Along. Crackerjack (US: The Man with a Hundred Faces). Climbing High. Kate Plus Ten (US: Queen of Crime). Anything to Declare? Missing Evidence. 1939: Charlie Chan in City of Darkness. 1940: *Know Your Money. The Great Plane Robbery. 1941: Ellery Queen's Penthouse Mystery. *Sucker List. Footsteps in the Dark. Highway West. A Shot in the Dark. 1942: Bombs Over Burma. Secret Agent of Japan. Joe Smith, American (GB: Highway to Freedom). 1943: Miss V from Moscow. Jitterbugs. Shantytown. Forever and a Day. The Black Raven. 1948: The Gentleman from Nowhere.

MADSEN, Michael 1958–

Broad-shouldered, growly, aggressive-looking, heftily built, gruff-voiced American actor with short, fair, wavy hair, a contemporary combination of William Bendix and Kirk Douglas. The son of Emmy Award-winning writer Elaine Madsen (and brother of actress Virginia Madsen), he began a film career in his mid twenties, mainly in fiercely monolithic roles. But his was never quite a name the public could put

a face to until his appearance as one of the *Reservoir Dogs.* He has since taken on one or two leading roles in lesser action films, but remains more full-blooded value for money as a top supporting player. According to Madsen, he has, in addition to the filmography that follows, made a film called *One Point of View:* I have not been able to trace this.

1983: WarGames. Special Bulletin (TV). Blind Alley/Perfect Strangers. 1984: Racing with the Moon. The Natural. 1988: Shadows in the Storm. Blood Red. Iguana. Kill Me Again. 1989: Sea of Love. 1990: The Doors. 1991: Thelma & Louise. To Kill For. 1992: Reservoir Dogs. Double Cross. Trouble Bound. Straight Talk. Fatal Instinct. Baby Snatcher (TV). 1993: Free Willy. Lights Out. A House in the Hills. Final Combination. Fixing the Shadow. Money for Nothing. 1994: The Getaway. Wyatt Earp. Blue Tiger. Almost Blue (TV). Seasons of Change. 1995: Willy II: The Adventure Home. Species. Man With a Gun. Mulholland Falls.

MAGEE, Patrick 1923–1982

Stooped, stocky, intense-looking Irish actor with unkempt silver hair, often in horror films, and almost always the man to send a shiver down your spine with his off-centre presence. Like most 'frighteners', Magee was the very opposite in real life. 'Even a person in a film standing in a high place' he once said 'gives me the shivers'. His anguished eyes and silken voice made numerous appearances in radio, theatre and TV in the works of Samuel Beckett.

1951: Flesh and Blood. 1960: The Criminal (US: The Concrete Jungle). Rag Doll (US: Young, Willing and Eager). 1961: Never Back Losers. A Prize of Arms. 1962: The Boys. The Very Edge. 1963: The Servant. Dementia 13 (GB: The Haunted and the Hunted). The Young Racers. Ricochet. Zulu. Operation Titian (US: Portrait in Terror). 1964: The Masque of the Red Death. Seance on a Wet Afternoon. 1965: The Skull. Monster of Terror (US: Die, Monster, Die). Blood Bath (revised version of Operation Titian). 1966: The Persecution and Assassination of Jean Paul Marat . . . (The Marat/Sade). 1968: The Battle for Anzio (US: Anzio). Decline and Fall . . . of a birdwatcher! The Birthday Party. 1969: Hard Contract. Destiny of a Spy (TV). King Lear. 1970: Cromwell. You Can't Win 'Em All. 1971: The

Fiend (US: Beware My Brethren). A Clockwork Orange. The Trojan Women. Young Winston. 1972: Tales from the Crypt. Pope Joan. Asylum. 1973: Lady Ice. . . . And Now the Screaming Starts! Simona. The Final Programme (US: The Last Days of Man on Earth). Luther. 1974: Demons of the Mind (completed 1971). Galileo. 1975: Barry Lyndon. 1977: Telefon. 1978: Les soeurs Brontë. 1980: Rough Cut. The Black Cat. Sir Henry at Rawlinson End. Hawk the Slayer. The Monster Club. 1981: Chariots of Fire. Dr Jekyll and the Women (GB: The Blood of Dr Jekyll).

MAHONEY, John 1940–

Affable, square-faced, brown-haired, concerned-looking, British-born Hollywood actor who usually plays reliable types but has also been seen as men with guilty secrets. Born in Manchester, he turned to acting at 35 after a career editing medical journals, although he had been a member of the Stratford Children's Theatre for four years as a boy. Very busy in major Hollywood movies from 1987 to 1989 (especially as the professor in *Moonstruck* and the over-protective father in *Say Anything*), he has been somewhat less prominent in the 1990s.

1981: Chicago Story (TV). 1982: Mission Hill. 1983: Listen to Your Heart (TV). 1984: The Killing Floor (TV). 1985: Code of Silence. Lady Blue (TV). First Steps (TV). 1986: The Manhattan Project. Trapped in Silence (TV). Streets of Gold. 1987: Tin Men. Suspect. Moonstruck. 1988: Eight Men Out. Frantic. Betrayed. Target: Favorite Son (TV. Edited version of mini-series). 1989: Say Anything. Love Hurts. The Image (TV). Dinner at Eight (TV). 1990: The Russia House. H.E.L.P. (TV). One False Move (released 1992). 1991: The 10 Million Dollar Getaway (TV). Barton Fink. Article 99. 1992: The Secret Passion of Robert Clayton (TV). The Water Engine (TV). 1993: The Hudsucker Proxy. In the Line of Fire. Striking Distance. 1994: Reality Bites. 1995: The American President.

MAIN, Marjorie
(Mary Tomlinson) 1890–1975
Unique, crow-voiced American actress with bundled-up nest of dark hair and sack-of-potatoes figure who became a film regular after the early death of her husband and delighted audiences with a great series of

haranguing harridans both comic and tragic; most memorably in partnership with Wallace Beery and, later, in the Ma and Pa Kettle series. Oscar-nominated for *The Egg and I*. Died from cancer.

*1932: Hot Saturday. A House Divided. 1933: Take a Chance. 1934: Music in the Air. *New Deal Rhythm. Crime without Passion. 1935: Naughty Marietta. 1937: Dead End. City Girl. Boy of the Streets. Love in a Bungalow. The Shadow (GB: The Circus Shadow). The Man Who Cried Wolf. Stella Dallas. The Wrong Road. 1938: Penitentiary. Girls' School. Romance of the Limberlost. Under the Big Top (GB: The Circus Comes to Town). King of the Newsboys. Too Hot to Handle. Little Tough Guy. Three Comrades. Test Pilot. Prison Farm. There Goes My Heart. 1939: Angels Wash Their Faces. Another Thin Man. Lucky Night. They Shall Have Music (GB: Melody of Youth). The Women. Two Thoroughbreds. 1940: Women without Names. Dark Command. Turnabout. Susan and God (GB: The Gay Mrs Trexel). Wyoming (GB: Bad Man of Wyoming). I Take This Woman. The Captain is a Lady. 1941: The Wild Man of Borneo. The Trial of Mary Dugan. Honky Tonk. A Woman's Face. The Bugle Sounds. Shepherd of the Hills. Barnacle Bill. 1942: Tish. The Affairs of Martha (GB: Once Upon a Thursday). Jackass Mail. Tennessee Johnson (GB: The Man on America's Conscience). We Were Dancing. 1943: Heaven Can Wait. Woman of the Town. Johnny Come Lately (GB: Johnny Vagabond). 1944: Rationing. Meet Me in St Louis. Gentle Annie. 1945: Murder, He Says. The Harvey Girls. 1946: The Show-off. Bad Bascomb. Undercurrent. 1947: The Egg and I. The Wistful Widow of Wagon Gap (GB: The Wistful Widow). 1948: Feudin', Fussin' and a-Fightin'. Ma and Pa Kettle. 1949: Big Jack. Ma and Pa Kettle Go to Town (GB: Going to Town). 1950: Summer Stock (GB: If You Feel Like Singing). Mrs O'Malley and Mr Malone. Mr Imperium (GB: You Belong to My Heart). 1951: It's a Big Country. The Law and the Lady. Ma and Pa Kettle Back on the Farm. 1952: Belle of New York. Ma and Pa Kettle on Vacation (GB: Ma and Pa Kettle Go to Paris). Ma and Pa Kettle at the Fair. 1953: Fast Company. 1954: Ricochet Romance. Ma and Pa Kettle at Home. The Long, Long Trailer. Rose Marie. 1955: Ma and Pa Kettle at Waikiki. 1956: The Kettles in the Ozarks. Friendly Persuasion. 1957: The Kettles on Old MacDonald's Farm.*

MAITLAND, Marne 1920–1991

Dusky, hook-nosed, shady-looking Anglo-Indian actor, much in demand for shifty middle easterners in British films, from the moment he made his first major appearance, appropriately in *Cairo Road*. After that, his characters were to be discovered peddling drugs, smuggling diamonds, pinching curios, involved with refugees and generally making money from every dubious racket going. He lived in Rome for most of the last two decades of his life.

1948: Another Shore. 1950: Cairo Road. 1951: The Lady with a Lamp. His Excellency. Outcast of the Islands. 1952: South of Algiers (US: The Golden Mask). Deadly Nightshade. 1953: Beat the Devil. Saadia. 1954: Father Brown (US: The Detective). Flame and the Flesh. Svengali. Diplomatic Passport. 1955: John and Julie. Break in the Circle. Dust and Gold. 1956: Bhowani Junction. Ramsbottom Rides Again. 1957: Hour of Decision/Table in the Corner. Interpol (US: Pickup Alley). Seven Thunders (US: The Beasts of Marseilles). Accused (US: Mark of the Hawk). Windom's Way. 1958: I Was Monty's Double (US: Monty's Double). I Only Arsked! The Camp on Blood Island. The Wind Cannot Read. Carlton-Browne of the F O (US: Man in a Cocked Hat). 1959: Tiger Bay. The Stranglers of Bombay. I'm All Right, Jack. 1960: Visa to Canton (US: Passport to China). Cone of Silence (US: Trouble in the Sky). Sands of the Desert. 1961: The Middle Course. Three on a Spree. The Terror of the Tongs. 1962: Sammy Going South (US: A Boy Ten Feet Tall). The Phantom of the Opera. Nine Hours to Rama. 1963: Cleopatra. Master Spy. Panic. 1964: First Men in the Moon. Lord Jim. 1965: The Return of Mr Moto. The Reptile. 1966: Khartoum. 1967: The Bobo. 1968: Duffy. Decline and Fall . . . of a birdwatcher! The Bush Baby. The Shoes of the Fisherman. 1969: Anne of the Thousand Days. 1970: The Statue. 1972: Roma (GB: Fellini's Roma). Man of La Mancha. 1973: Shaft in Africa. Massacre in Rome. Il cittadino si ribella. 1974: The Man with the Golden Gun. 1976: The Pink Panther Strikes Again. The Anonymous Avenger. 1977: March or Die. 1979: Ashanti. The Black Stallion. 1980: The Day Christ Died (TV). 1982: Trail of the Pink Panther. 1983: The Scarlet and the Black (TV). Memed My Hawk. 1984: The Assisi Underground. 1985: Broken Melody/Tomorrow. 1987: And the Violins Stopped Playing. 1988: Appointment in Liverpool.

MAKEHAM, Eliot 1882–1956

Brown-haired, inoffensive-looking British actor of small stature, often seen, bespectacled, in apologetic or downtrodden roles, sometimes as little men who triumphed in the end over nagging wives or bullying bosses. He played a few leading roles in the 1930s and made the most of them; otherwise in dozens of minor cameos, as clerks, shopkeepers, auditors and the like. Known to his friends as Billy. Married (third of three) to fellow character player Betty Shale.

*1932: Jack's the Boy. Rome Express. 1933: I Was a Spy. Friday the Thirteenth. Forging Ahead. I'm an Explosive. Princess Charming. Orders is Orders. Britannia of Billingsgate. I Lived with You. The Lost Chord. Little Napoleon. Home Sweet Home. The Laughter of Fools. The Roof. 1934: By-Pass to Happiness. The Unfinished Symphony. The Crimson Candle. Lorna Doone. Once in a New Moon. 1935: The Clairvoyant. The Last Journey. Peg of Old Drury. Two Hearts in Harmony. Her Last Affaire. 1936: To Catch a Thief. A Star Fell from Heaven. The Brown Wallet. Born That Way. Calling the Tune. Someone at the Door. All That Glitters. East Meets West. Tomorrow We Live. The Mill on the Floss. 1937: Take My Tip. Racing Romance. East of Ludgate Hill. Dark Journey. Farewell Again (US: Troopship). Our Island Nation. Head Over Heels (US: Head Over Heels in Love). Storm in a Teacup. A Yank at Oxford. 1938: Coming of Age. Vessel of Wrath (US: The Beachcomber). Darts Are Trumps. Merely Mr Hawkins. Bedtime Story. You're the Doctor. Anything to Declare? The Citadel. Everything Happens to Me. It's in the Air (US: George Takes the Air). Inspector Hornleigh. 1939: What Men Live By. The Four Just Men (US: The Secret Four). The Nursemaid Who Disappeared. Young Man's Fancy. Just William. A Window in London (US: Lady in Distress). Me and My Pal. Return to Yesterday. Spy for a Day. 1940: Saloon Bar. Spare a Copper. Night Train to Munich (US: Night Train). Busman's Honeymoon (US: Haunted Honeymoon). Pastor Hall. *All Hands. *Food for Thought. John Smith Wakes Up. 1941: The Common Touch. Gert and Daisy's Weekend. Hatter's Castle. Facing the Music. They Flew Alone (US: Wings and the Woman). 1942: Went the Day Well? (US: 48 Hours). The Missing Million. Let the People Sing. Suspected Person. Uncensored. 1943: The Adventures of Tartu (US: Tartu).*

Bell Bottom George. The Yellow Canary. 1944: A Canterbury Tale. Don't Take It to Heart. Champagne Charlie. The Halfway House. Madonna of the Seven Moons. Candles at Nine. Give Us the Moon. 1945: I'll Be Your Sweetheart. Perfect Strangers (US: Vacation from Marriage). 1946: Daybreak. The Shop at Sly Corner (US: Code of Scotland Yard). London Town (US: My Heart Goes Crazy). The Magic Bow. 1947: Frieda. The Little Ballerina. Jassy. Nicholas Nickleby. Call of the Blood. 1948: Love in Waiting. No Room at the Inn. Vote for Huggett. Behind These Walls (voice only). So Evil My Love. Forbidden. 1949: Murder at the Windmill (US: Murder at the Burlesque). Children of Chance. 1950: Trio. The Clouded Yellow. Night and the City. The Miniver Story. 1951: Green Grow the Rushes. Scrooge (US: A Christmas Carol). Scarlet Thread. 1952: Decameron Nights. The Yellow Balloon. The Crimson Pirate. 1953: The Fake. Always a Bride. Meet Mr Lucifer. Stryker of the Yard. The Million Pound Note (US: Man With a Million). The Weak and the Wicked. 1954: Doctor in the House. Fast and Loose. The Rainbow Jacket. Companions in Crime. 1956: Sailor Beware! (US: Panic in the Parlor).

MALANDRINOS, Andrea 1896–1970
Short, thick-set, hog-necked, dark-haired, bushily-moustached, bag-eyed, Greek-born portrayer of foreign sorts in British films. A former music-hall entertainer and singer of operatic arias (billed as 'Malandrinos'), he became a supporting player in films in the boom years of the early 1930s, and stayed to play dozens of waiters, hoteliers, curio shop owners and other huffly-snuffly foreigners, forever rubbing his hands together in anticipation, but mostly on the up and up. Generally seemed to be billed as 'Andreas' from 1961. Remained busy to the end.

1930: Raise the Roof. 1932: The Lodger (US: The Phantom Fiend). 1933: Say It with Flowers. The Medicine Man. The Golden Cage. Two Wives for Henry. Send 'Em Back Half Dead. 1934: Broken Melody. How's Chances? The Admiral's Secret. Virginia's Husband. 1935: Midshipman Easy (US: Men of the Sea). King of the Damned. Vintage Wine. The Invader (US: An Old Spanish Custom). Play Up the Band. Limelight (US: Backstage). Late Extra. The Improper Duchess. 1936: Under

Proof. Prison Breaker.The Secret of Stamboul. Dusty Ermine (US: Hideout in the Alps). Land Without Music (US: Forbidden Music). His Lordship (US: Man of Affaires). The Gay Adventure. The Amazing Quest of Ernest Bliss (US: Romance and Riches). Secret Agent. Tropical Trouble. 1937: The Price of Folly. The Show Goes On. Gypsy. A Romance in Flanders (US: Lost on the Western Front). Midnight Menace (US: Bombs Over London). Command Performance. The Sky's the Limit. Non Stop New York. Mad About Money (US: He Loved an Actress). 1938: The Last Barricade. *Take Cover. I See Ice. Crackerjack (US: The Man with a Hundred Faces). Sexton Blake and the Hooded Terror. 1939: Two Days to Live. What Would You Do Chums? 1940: Crooks Tour. Room for Two. 1941: The Big Blockade. Jeannie (US: Girl in Distress). 1942: Flying Fortress. We'll Smile Again. Thunder Rock. 1943: Candlelight in Algeria. The Bells Go Down. 1944: English Without Tears (US: Her Man Gilbey). Champagne Charlie. The Way Ahead (US: Immortal Battalion). 1946: While the Sun Shines. 1947: The End of the River. Frieda. A Man About the House. My Brother Jonathan. 1948: Sleeping Car to Trieste. Forbidden. 1949: The Spider and the Fly. 1950: Cairo Road. Her Favorite Husband (US: The Taming of Dorothy). 1951: Captain Horatio Hornblower RN (US: Captain Horatio Hornblower). Chelsea Story. Salute the Toff. Night Without Stars. The Lavender Hill Mob. 1952: Paul Temple Returns. 13 East Street. Hammer the Toff. 1953: The Captain's Paradise. Innocents in Paris. Gilbert Harding Speaking of Murder. You Know What Sailors Are. A Day to Remember. 1954: The Love Lottery. The Teckman Mystery. Beautiful Stranger (US: Twist of Fate). *Night Plane to Amsterdam. Alive on Saturday (released 1957). 1955: Portrait of Alison (US: Postmark for Danger). Double Jeopardy. Dust and Gold. Cockleshell Heroes. Stolen Time (US: Blonde Blackmailer). 1956: Checkpoint. Port Afrique. Ill-Met by Moonlight (US: Night Ambush). 1957: The Prince and the Showgirl. Just My Luck. There's Always a Thursday. Seven Thunders (US: The Beasts of Marseilles). 1958: The Big Money (completed 1956). Orders to Kill. Links of Justice. No Time to Die! (US: Tank Force). 1959: Beyond This Place (US: Web of Evidence). The Angry Hills. Tommy the Toreador. The Boy and the Bridge. 1960: Sands of the Desert. Make Mine Mink. 1961: Tarnished Heroes. A Weekend with Lulu. The Boy Who Stole a Million. 1962: In the Cool of the Day. Lawrence of Arabia. In Search of the Castaways. Come Fly with Me. 1964: The Yellow Rolls Royce. 1965: Help! San Ferry Ann. Joey Boy. 1966: The Mummy's Shroud. 1967: The Magnificent Two. Dance of the Vampires (US: The Fearless Vampire Killers). 1968: Mosquito Squadron. The Magus. Hammerhead. 1969: Moon Zero Two. Hell Boats. 1970: Man of Violence/The Sex Racketeers. Underground.

MALLALIEU, Aubrey 1873–1948
Sleepy-looking, bespectacled, strongly-built British actor with thinning, pasted-across hair. Said to have played supporting roles in some silent films, he had a long theatrical career before embarking on sound film

character roles in his sixties, and playing more than 100 of them as solicitors, vicars, school governors, judges and assorted senior citizens of some fussiness and dignity.

1934: What Happened to Harkness? 1935: Sweeney Todd The Demon Barber of Fleet Street. Cross Currents. The Last Journey. Music Hath Charms. The Riverside Murder. 1936: Nothing Like Publicity. Prison Breaker. A Touch of the Moon. Not So Dusty. His Lordship (US: Man of Affaires). Love at Sea. Such is Life. All That Glitters. Once in a Million (US: Weekend Millionaire). A Star Fell from Heaven. The Tenth Man. Talk of the Devil. 1937: Over She Goes. The Black Tulip. Holiday's End. The Last Chance. Silver Blaze (US: Murder at the Baskervilles). Mayfair Melody. The Rat. Patricia Gets Her Man. Pearls Bring Tears. When the Devil Was Well. Keep Fit. The Strange Adventures of Mr Smith. Fifty Shilling Boxer. Change for a Sovereign. East of Ludgate Hill. The Frog. The Man Who Made Diamonds. Victoria the Great. 21 Days (released 1940. US: 21 Days Together). 1938: His Lordship Regrets. Thank Evans. Easy Riches. The Reverse Be My Lot. Paid in Error. Simply Terrific. Coming of Age. The Claydon Treasure Mystery. Dangerous Medicine. Sixty Glorious Years (US: Queen of Destiny). Almost a Honeymoon. The Gables Mystery. The Return of Carol Deane. Miracles Do Happen. Save a Little Sunshine. The Return of the Frog. You're the Doctor. His Lordship Goes to Press. 1939: So This is London. Me and My Pal. Murder Will Out. Dead Men Are Dangerous. The Face at the Window. I Killed the Count (US: Who is Guilty?). All at Sea. The Stars Look Down. 1940: The Briggs Family. 'Bulldog' Sees It Through. The Girl in the News. Busman's Honeymoon (US: Haunted Honeymoon). The Door with Seven Locks (US: Chamber of Horrors). Let George Do It. *Salvage with a Smile. Spare a Copper. 1941: *Mr Proudfoot Shows a Light. Atlantic Ferry (US: Sons of the Sea). Facing the Music. *The Fine Feathers. Turned Out Nice Again. The Black Sheep of Whitehall. Gert and Daisy's Weekend. Breach of Promise (US: Adventure in Blackmail). Hatter's Castle. They Flew Alone (US: Wings and the Woman). Penn of Pennsylvania (US: The Courageous Mr Penn). Pimpernel Smith (US: Mister V). 1942: The Young Mr Pitt. Uncensored. Unpublished Story. Let the People Sing. We'll Meet Again. Squadron Leader X. Back Room Boy. It's That Man Again. The

Goose Steps Out. Asking for Trouble. 1943: The Adventures of Tartu (US: Tartu). Theatre Royal. The Lamp Still Burns. My Learned Friend. The Yellow Canary. The Demi-Paradise (US: Adventure for Two). Rhythm Serenade. 1944: Kiss the Bride Goodbye. He Snoops to Conquer. Champagne Charlie. 1945: I'll Be Your Sweetheart. The Wicked Lady. I Live in Grosvenor Square (US: A Yank in London). 29 Acacia Avenue (US: The Facts of Love). A Place of One's Own. For You Alone. Murder in Reverse. 1946: Under New Management. Meet Me at Dawn. A Girl in a Million. Bedelia. School for Secrets (US: Secret Flight). I'll Turn to You. While the Sun Shines. 1947: Frieda. Master of Bankdam. The Ghosts of Berkeley Square. 1948: Counterblast. The Fatal Night. The Queen of Spades. The Winslow Boy. Calling Paul Temple. The Bad Lord Byron. Saraband for Dead Lovers (US: Saraband). Bond Street.

MALLESON, Miles
(William M. Malleson) 1888–1969
Round-faced, fish-mouthed, jolly-looking, lovable British actor, a playwright (from 1913) and screenplay writer (1930–1944), who started by playing cameo roles in films that he had written. His stubby figure, double-jowls and tousled (disappearing) hair soon became an indispensable part of the British cinema. Only failing sight forced him to retire.

1921: The Headmaster. 1930: The Yellow Mask. City of Song (US: Farewell to Love). 1931: Frail Women. 1932: The Sign of Four. The Love Contract. The Mayor's Nest. Love on Wheels. Money Means Nothing. Perfect Understanding. 1933: Summer Lightning. Bitter Sweet. 1934: The Queen's Affair (US: Runaway Queen). Evergreen. Nell Gwyn. Lazybones. 1935: Vintage Wine. Peg of Old Drury. The Thirty Nine Steps. 1936: Tudor Rose (US: Nine Days a Queen). Secret Agent. 1937: The Rat. Victoria the Great. Knight Without Armour. 1938: Sixty Glorious Years (US: Queen of Destiny). 1939: Q Planes (US: Clouds Over Europe). 1940: The Thief of Bagdad. Spellbound (US: The Spell of Amy Nugent). 1941: Major Barbara. This Was Paris. They Flew Alone (US: Wings and the Woman). 1942: Unpublished Story. Thunder Rock. The Foot of the Few (US: Spitfire). 1943: The Demi-Paradise (US: Adventure for Two). The Gentle Sex. I Want to Be an Actress.

Adventures of Tartu (US: Tartu). The Yellow Canary. 1945: Dead of Night. Journey Together. 1946: While the Sun Shines. Beware of Pity. Land of Promise (voice only). 1947: The Mark of Cain. 1948: One Night with You. Idol of Paris. Saraband for Dead Lovers (US: Saraband). Woman Hater. Bond Street. 1949: The History of Mr Polly. Cardboard Cavalier. The Perfect Woman. The Queen of Spades. Kind Hearts and Coronets. Adam and Evelyne. Train of Events. 1950: Golden Salamander. Stage Fright. 1951: The Magic Box. Scrooge. The Man in the White Suit. The Woman's Angle. 1952: The Happy Family (US: Mr Lord Says No). Treasure Hunt. Venetian Bird (US: The Assassin). The Importance of Being Earnest. Folly to Be Wise. Trent's Last Case. 1953: The Captain's Paradise. 1955: Geordie (US: Wee Geordie). King's Rhapsody. Private's Progress. 1956: The Man Who Never Was. The Silken Affair. Three Men in a Boat. Dry Rot. Brothers in Law. 1957: Campbell's Kingdom. The Admirable Crichton (US: Paradise Lagoon). The Naked Truth (US: Your Past is Showing). Barnacle Bill (US: All at Sea). Happy is the Bride. 1958: Dracula (US: The Horror of Dracula). Bachelor of Hearts. Behind the Mask. Gideon's Day (US: Gideon of Scotland Yard). The Captain's Table. 1959: Carlton-Browne of the FO (US: Man in a Cocked Hat). I'm All Right, Jack. Peeping Tom. The Hound of the Baskervilles. Kidnapped. 1960: And the Same to You. The Day They Robbed the Bank of England. The Brides of Dracula. 1961: Fury at Smuggler's Bay. The Hellfire Club. Double Bunk. 1962: Postman's Knock. Go to Blazes. The Phantom of the Opera. Vengeance (US: The Brain). 1963: Heavens Above! A Jolly Bad Fellow. 1964: First Men in the Moon. Circus World (GB: The Magnificent Showman). Murder Ahoy. 1965: You Must Be Joking!

MALTBY, H. F. 1880–1963
Stout, puff-cheecked British actor, a prolific screenplay writer who also played comedy character roles from 1933 up to his retirement in 1945. As well as appearing as self-inflated judges, magistrates, politicians and military men, he still found time to write for the theatre and radio as well. The 'H' stood for Henry. Made 21 films in 1937 alone.

1921: The Rotters. 1933: Facing the Music. I Spy. Home Sweet Home. A Political Party.

1934: Luck of a Sailor. Those Were the Days. Freedom of the Seas. Over the Garden Wall. Josser on the Farm. Falling in Love (US: Trouble Ahead). Lost in the Legion. Girls Will Be Boys. 1935: A Little Bit of Bluff. The Right Age to Marry. It Happened in Paris. The Morals of Marcus. Emil and the Detectives (US: Emil). King of the Castle. Vanity. 1936: Queen of Hearts. Jack of All Trades (US: The Two of Us). Not So Dusty. A Touch of the Moon. Trouble Ahead. Sweeney Todd the Demon Barber of Fleet Street. Two's Company. Fame. The Howard Case. The Crimes of Stephen Hawke. Calling the Tune. Everything Is Thunder. Nothing Like Publicity. To Catch a Thief. Where There's a Will. Busman's Holiday. Head Office. The Heirloom Mystery. Everything in Life. Secret Agent. Reasonable Doubt. 1937: Pearls Bring Tears. Song of the Road. Never Too Late to Mend. Wake Up Famous. Farewell to Cinderella. O Kay for Sound. Take My Tip. The Strange Adventures of Mr Smith. Paradise for Two (US: The Gaiety Girls). Young and Innocent (US: The Girl Was Young). Boys Will Be Girls. Why Pick on Me? Mr Smith Carries On. Sing As You Swing. Song of the Road. Live Wire. The Sky's the Limit. Captain's Orders. What a Man! Owd Bob (US: To the Victor). A Yank at Oxford. 1938: Paid in Error. Darts are Trumps. His Lordship Regrets. Pygmalion. Weddings Are Wonderful. You're the Doctor. Everything Happens to Me. His Lordship Goes to Press. 1939: The Good Old Days. Return to Yesterday. The Gang's All Here (US: The Amazing Mr Forrest). Old Mother Riley Joins Up. 1940: Garrison Follies. Under Your Hat. Facing the Music (and 1933 film). 1941: Bob's Your Uncle. 1942: The Great Mr Handel. 1943: Old Mother Riley Detective. Somewhere in Civvies. 1944: A Canterbury Tale. Medal for the General. 1945: Home Sweet Home. Caesar and Cleopatra. The Trojan Brothers.

MALYON, Eily
(E. Lees-Craston) 1879–1961
Fair-haired, gloomy-looking British actress of strong features and ghoulish grin who came to Hollywood in the early 1930s, her almost weatherbeaten face and sharp delivery qualifying the stage veteran for severe, sour, be-stern-with-the-children roles. She was still glooming about as Mrs Sketcher in 1943's Jane Eyre and only retired at 70.

1931: Born to Love. 1932: Night Court (GB: Justice for Sale). The Wet Parade. Lovers Courageous. 1933: Looking Forward (GB: Service). Today We Live. 1934: The Little Minister. Romance in Manhattan. Forsaking All Others. His Greatest Gamble. Nana. Limehouse Blues. Great Expectations. 1935: Clive of India. The Florentine Dagger. The Flame Within. The Melody Lingers On. A Tale of Two Cities. The Widow from Monte Carlo. Ah, Wilderness. Les Misérables. Mark of the Vampire. Stranded. Kind Lady (GB: House of Menace). 1936: Little Lord Fauntleroy. One Rainy Afternoon. Dracula's Daughter. The White Angel. A Woman Rebels. The Devil-Doll. Anthony Adverse. Three Men on a Horse. Camille. Angel of Mercy. Cain and Mabel. Career Woman. God's Country and the Woman. 1937: Night Must Fall. Parnell. Another Dawn. 1938: Rebecca of Sunnybrook Farm. Kidnapped. The Young in Heart. 1939: On Borrowed Time. The Little Princess. The Hound of the Baskervilles. We Are Not Alone. Confessions of a Nazi Spy. Barricade. 1940: Untamed. Foreign Correspondent. Young Tom Edison. 1941: Man Hunt. Hit the Road. Reaching for the Sun. Arkansas Judge (GB: False Witness). 1942: The Man in the Trunk. Scattergood Survives a Murder. I Married a Witch. You're Telling Me. The Undying Monster (GB: The Hammond Mystery). 1943: Above Suspicion. Shadow of a Doubt. Jane Eyre. 1944: Going My Way. The Seventh Cross. 1945: Scared Stiff. Roughly Speaking. Grissly's Millions. She Wouldn't Say Yes. Paris Underground (GB: Madame Pimpernel). Son of Lassie. 1946: The Secret Heart. Devotion (completed 1943). She Wolf of London (GB: The Curse of the Allenbys). 1948: The Challenge.

MANDER, Miles
(Lionel Mander) 1888–1946
Stocky, light-haired British actor-manager with military bark, plus moustache and bearing to match. Entered films after World War I (he was an aviator), often playing moustache-twirling villains—appropriately billed as Luther Miles. He became a jack of all trades in the 1920s, acting, writing, producing and directing. Mander went to Hollywood in 1935, and was heavily in demand for foxy character parts, mostly in second-feature thrillers, when a heart attack killed him at 57.

1918: †Once Upon a Time. 1920: †The Old Arm Chair. †Testimony. †The Children of Gideon. †A Rank Outsider. 1921: †Place of Honour. †The Road to London. *The Temporary Lady. 1922: Half a Truth. Open Country. 1924: Lovers in Araby. The Prude's Fall. 1925: *The Painted Lady. *The Lady in Furs. *Riding for a King. 1926: The Pleasure Garden (and German version). London Love. *Castles in the Air. 1927: *As We Lie. Tiptoes. The Fake. 1928: The Physician. The First Born. Balaclava (US: Jaws of Hell). Women of Paris. Dr Monnier und die Frauen. Der Faschingskönig. 1929: Meineid. The Crooked Billet. 1930: Loose Ends. Murder! 1931: Frail Women. 1932: The Missing Rembrandt. Lily Christine. *Lost: One Wife. That Night in London (US: Overnight). The Lodger (US: The Phantom Fiend). 1933: Don Quixote. Matinee Idol. Loyalties. The Private Life of Henry VIII. Bitter Sweet. 1934: Four Masked Men. The Case for the Crown. The Battle (US: Thunder in the East). 1935: Death Drives Through. Cardinal Richelieu. The Three Musketeers. Here's to Romance. 1936: Lloyd's of London. 1937: Slave Ship. Youth on Parole. Wake Up and Live. 1938: Kidnapped. Suez. The Mad Miss Manton. 1939: The Three Musketeers (GB: The Singing Musketeer). Stanley and Livingstone. The Little Princess. Tower of London. The Man in the Iron Mask. Wuthering Heights. Daredevils of the Red Circle (serial). 1940: The Primrose Path. Road to Singapore. The House of Seven Gables. Captain Caution. Babies for Sale. Laddie. South of Suez. The Earl of Chicago. 1941: Dr Kildare's Wedding Day (GB: Mary Names the Day). Shadows on the Stairs. That Hamilton Woman (GB: Lady Hamilton). They Met in Bombay. 1942: Mrs Miniver (voice only). Fly By Night. Captains of the Clouds. A Tragedy at Midnight. Fingers at the Window. To Be or Not to Be. Somewhere I'll Find You. Lucky Jordan. A Yank on the Burma Road (GB: China Caravan). Journey for Margaret. Apache Trail. Tarzan's New York Adventure. This Above All. The War Against Mrs Hadley. You're Telling Me. 1943: The Fallen Sparrow. Assignment in Brittany. Five Graves to Cairo. Secrets of the Underground. Phantom of the Opera. Guadalcanal Diary. First Comes Courage. Madame Curie. The Return of the Vampire. 1944: The Pearl of Death. Four Jills in a Jeep. Enter Arsène Lupin. The Scarlet Claw. The White Cliffs of Dover. The Story of Dr Wassell. 1945: Murder, My Sweet (GB: Farewell, My Lovely). The Brighton Strangler. Week-End at the Waldorf. Confidential Agent. The Picture of Dorian Gray. The Crime Doctor's Warning (GB: The Doctor's Warning). Captain Kidd. 1946: The Bandit of Sherwood Forest. The Walls Came Tumbling Down. The Imperfect Lady (GB: Mrs Loring's Secret).

As director:
1926: *The Fair Maid of Perth. *The Whistler. *The Sheik of Araby. *Knee Deep in Daisies. 1927: *As We Lie. *The Sentence of Death. *Packing Up. *False Colours. 1928: The First Born. 1930: The Woman Between (US: The Woman Decides). 1934: Youthful Folly. 1935: The Morals of Marcus. 1936: The Flying Doctor.

† As Luther Miles

MANTEGNA, Joe 1947–
Florid, saturnine, dark-haired, very dark-eyed, hawk-nosed, thick-browed Chicago-born actor often in supporting cameos as gangsters, but equally at home in leading roles, which have given him more variety of characterization. The solidly-built Mantegna was long a man of the stage, often in productions by director-writer David Mamet. He began to appear more frequently in films from the mid 1980s, most notably in one of the leading roles of Mamet's House of Games. Has won Emmy, Tony and Venice Film Festival awards and has also written for the stage.

1978: Towing. 1979: Elvis! (TV. GB: cinemas, as Elvis – The Movie). 1982: Second Thoughts. 1984: The Outlaws (TV). 1985: Compromising Positions. The Money Pit. 1986: Off Beat. Three Amigos! Critical Condition. 1987: House of Games. Weeds. Suspect. 1988: Things Change. 1989: Wait Until Spring, Bandini. 1990: Queens Logic. Alice. The Godfather Part III. 1991: Homicide. Bugsy. 1992: The Water Engine (TV). The Whole World is Watching. Family Prayers. Body of Evidence. The Comrades of Summer (TV). 1993: Searching for Bobby Fischer (GB: Innocent Moves). Two Deaths. 1994: Airheads. Baby's Day Out. State of Emergency (TV). Stranger Things. Above Suspicion. 1995: Forget Paris. Captain Nuke & the Bomber Boys. Up Close and Personal.

MARION CRAWFORD, Howard
1914–1969
Burly, pale-eyed British actor with bristling moustache and ruddy complexion, usually in stolid roles as upper-crust officer types who could be affable or dyspeptic. His hearty but mellow tones made his a popular and prolific voice on radio productions, and he was nudging middle age before he entered the major part of his film career as a character player. Also a notable Dr Watson in a TV 'Sherlock Holmes' series. Died from an overdose of sleeping pills.

1935: The Guv'nor (US: Mister Hobo). Music Hath Charms. †Brown on Resolution (later For Ever England. US: Born for Glory). 1936: Secret Agent. 1938: 13 Men and a Gun. 1940: *Torpedo Raider. 1941: Freedom Radio (US: A Voice in the Night). 1945: The Rake's Progress (US: Notorious Gentleman). 1947: The Phantom Shot. 1948: Man on the Run.

1949: The Hasty Heart. Stage Fright. 1950: Mr Drake's Duck. 1951: The Man in the White Suit. His Excellency. 1952: Where's Charley? Top of the Form. Rose of Baghdad (narrator only). 1953: Star of India. Gilbert Harding Speaking of Murder. Don't Blame the Stork! 1954: West of Zanzibar. The Rainbow Jacket. *Elizabethan Express (narrator only). Knights of the Round Table. Five Days (US: Paid to Kill). 1956: The Silken Affair. Reach for the Sky. The Man in the Sky (US: Decision Against Time). 1957: Don Kikhot (dubbed voice only). The Birthday Present. *Tyburn Case. 1958: Nowhere to Go. The Silent Enemy. Virgin Island (US: Our Virgin Island). Gideon's Day (US: Gideon of Scotland Yard). Next to No Time! 1959: North West Frontier (US: Flame Over India). *The Last Train. Model for Murder. Life in Danger. 1960: Othello. Foxhole in Cairo. Two-Way Stretch (voice only). 1961: Carry On Regardless. 1962: Lawrence of Arabia. 1963: Tamahine. Man in the Middle. 1965: The Face of Fu Manchu. 1966: The Brides of Fu Manchu. The Singing Princess (voice only). Secrets of a Windmill Girl. 1967: Smashing Time. The Vengeance of Fu Manchu. 1968: Blood of Fu Manchu (US: Kiss and Kill). The Charge of the Light Brigade. The Castle of Fu Manchu.

† As Marion Crawford

MARLEY, John 1906–1984
Grey-haired, wise-looking American actor, a rather more handsome equivalent of Eduard Franz (qv) and in films occasionally from 1942. He was scarcely noticed by the paying public until nominated for an Oscar

in 1970's Love Story, even though he had previously won the best actor award at the Venice Film Festival for his work in Faces. Marley started his show business career as half of a comedy team; strangely, there was very little comedy in most of his film roles, which were usually as senior sobersides. Died following open heart surgery.

1942: Native Land. 1947: Kiss of Death. 1948: The Naked City. 1951: The Mob (GB: Remember That Face). 1952: My Six Convicts. 1953: The Joe Louis Story. 1955: The Square Jungle. Timetable. 1957: Flood Tide (GB: Above All Things). 1958: I Want to Live! 1960: Pay or Die! 1962: A Child is Waiting. 1963: America, America (GB: The Anatolian Smile). The Wheeler Dealers (GB: Separate Beds). 1964: Nightmare in the Sun. 1965: Cat Ballou. The Lollipop Cover. 1966: The Etruscans. 1967: In Enemy Country. 1968: Faces. Istanbul Express (TV. GB: cinemas). To Die in Paris (TV). 1970: Sledge/A Man Called Sledge. Love Story. 1971: Incident in San Francisco (TV). L'etrusco uccide ancora. The Godfather. Clay Pigeon (GB: Trip to Kill), The Sheriff (TV). In Broad Daylight (TV). 1972: Images. Dead of Night. The Family Rico (TV). Jory. Deathdream. 1973: Blade. The Alpha Caper (TV. GB: cinemas, as Inside Job). 1974: Framed. 1975: The Dead Are Alive (filmed 1972). 1976: W.C. Fields and Me. 1977: The Greatest. Telethon (TV). The Car. The Private Files of J Edgar Hoover. Kid Vengeance. 1978: Hooper. It Lives Again. 1980: Tribute. 1981: Threshold. Utilities. The Amateur. 1982: Mother Lode. 1983: Falcon's Gold (TV). Robbers of the Sacred Mountain. The Glitter Dome (cable TV. GB: cinemas). 1984: Over the Edge.

MARMONT, Percy 1883–1977
Lean, suave, weathered-looking, cultured British romantic lead—moustachioed in his latter days as a character player—with one of the longest careers in the business. He made his stage debut at 17 and his first film in Australia, on his way to Hollywood, where the fair-haired Marmont proved himself a smooth, versatile leading man, soon in calm, pipe-smoking roles before his return to Britain in 1928 to play neckerchiefed charmers in early middle age. Largely returned to the theatre from 1933 on, giving his last film performance at 85. Actress Patricia Marmont is his daughter.

1917: The Monk and the Woman. 1918: Rose of the World. The Lie. In the Hollow of Her Hand. Turn of the Wheel. 1919: The Winchester Woman. Three Men and a Girl. The Vengeance of Durand. The Climbers. 1920: Dead Men Tell No Tales. Away Goes Prudence. Slaves of Pride. The Sporting Duchess. The Branded Woman. 1921: What's Your Reputation Worth? Love's Penalty. Wife Against Wife. 1922: The First Woman. Married People. 1923: Broadway Broke. The Midnight Alarm. If Winter Comes. The Man Life Passed By. You Can't Get Away with It. The Light That Failed. 1924: The Enemy Sex. The Shooting of Dan McGrew. The Marriage Cheat. When a Girl Loves. Winning a Continent. The Clean Heart. The Legend of Hollywood. K the Unknown. Broken Laws. Idle Tongues. 1925: Daddy's Gone A Hunting. The Shining Adventure. A Woman's Faith. Street of Forgotten Men. Lord Jim. Fine Clothes. Just a Woman. Infatuation. 1926: The Miracle of Life. Mantrap. Fascinating Youth. Aloma of the South Seas. 1927: The Stronger Will. 1928: Sir or Madam. San Francisco Nights (GB: Divorce). The Warning. Yellow Stockings. The Lady of the Lake. 1929: The Silver King. 1930: The Squeaker. Cross Roads. 1931: The Loves of Ariane (US: Ariane). The Written Law. Rich and Strange (US: East of Shanghai). 1932: The Silver Greyhound. Blind Spot. Say it with Music. 1933: Her Imaginary Lover. 1935: White Lilac. Vanity. 1936: David Livingstone. The Captain's Table. Secret Agent. Conquest of the Air (released 1940). 1937: Young and Innocent (US: The Girl Was Young). Action for Slander. Les perles de la couronne (GB and US: Pearls of the Crown). 1940: *Bringing It Home. 1941: Penn of Pennsylvania (US: The Courageous Mr Penn). 1942: Those Kids from Town. 1943: I'll Walk Beside You. 1946: Loyal Heart. 1947: Swiss Honeymoon. 1948: No Orchids for Miss Blandish. 1949: Dark Secret. 1952: The Gambler and the Lady. 1953: Four-Sided Triangle. Thought to Kill. 1954: Knave of Hearts (US: Lovers, Happy Lovers). 1955: Footsteps in the Fog. 1956: Lisbon. 1960: The Trials of Oscar Wilde (US: Man with the Green Carnation). 1968: Hostile Witness.

MARRIOTT, Moore
(George Moore-Marriott) 1885–1949
Short, wiry British actor, from theatrical background. He was a star of the early British cinema before moving into disgruntled roles; but, while still in his forties, he began playing garrulous, sometimes toothless, but usually lovable old codgers and, had he lived longer, would have probably carried on doing so into his eighties. Chiefly now remembered as old Harbottle in the Will Hay comedies.

1906: *Dick Turpin's Ride to York. 1912: A Maid of the Alps. 1914: His Sister's Honour. 1915: By the Shortest of Heads. 1920: The Grip of Iron. Mary Latimer, Nun. The Winding Road. 1921: Four Men in a Van. 1922: The Head of the Family. The Skipper's Wedding. 1923: The Monkey's Paw. *An Odd Freak. *Lawyer Quince. *Dixon's Return. 1924: The Affair at the Novelty Theatre. The Conspirators. *The Clicking of Cuthbert. *The Long Hole. The Mating of Marcus. *Ordeal by Golf. Not

for Sale. 1925: There's Many a Slip. King of the Castle. The Qualified Adventurer. *The Only Man. The Gold Cure. Every Mother's Son. *A Madonna of the Cells. Afraid of Love. 1926: *The Happy Rascals. London Love. *Regaining the Wind. *Goose and Stuffing. *Mined and Counter-Mined. *The Little Shop in Fore Street. *Second to None. *Cash on Delivery. *The Greater War. The Conspirators (and 1924 film). 1927: Passion Island. The Silver Lining. Huntingtower. Carry On! 1928: Victory. Widdecombe Fair. *The Burglar and the Girl. Toni. *The King's Breakfast. Kitty. Sweeney Todd. 1929: *Mr Smith Wakes Up. The Flying Scotsman. Lady from the Sea. Kitty (sound version). 1930: Kissing Cup's Race. Peace on the Western Front. 1931: Aroma of the South Seas. The Lyons Mail. Up for the Cup. 1932: Dance Pretty Lady. The Water Gipsies. Mr Bill the Conqueror (US: The Man Who Won). The Crooked Lady. Nine Till Six. Heroes of the Mine. The Little Waitress. The Wonderful Story. 1933: Money for Speed. A Moorland Tragedy. Dora. Lucky Blaze. A Political Party. The Crime at Blossoms. Hawleys of High Street. Love's Old Sweet Song. The House of Trent. Faces. The Song of the Plough. 1934: *The Black Skull. *The Unknown Warrior. Girls Please. The Scoop (US: A Political Scoop). Nell Gwyn. The Feathered Serpent. 1935: Dandy Dick. Drake of England (US: Drake the Pirate). Peg of Old Drury. *His Apologies. *The Half-Day Excursion. The Man Without a Face. Gay Old Dog. Turn of the Tide. 1936: Strange Cargo. What the Puppy Said. The Amazing Quest of Ernest Bliss (GB: Romance and Riches). Luck of the Turf. When Knights Were Bold. Windbag the Sailor. Wednesday's Luck. Accused. Talk of the Devil. As You Like It. 1937: Feather Your Nest. Fifty Shilling Boxer. The Fatal Hour. Night Ride. Oh, Mr Porter! Victoria the Great. Intimate Relations. Owd Bob (US: To the Victor). Dreaming Lips. 1938: Convict 99. Old Bones of the River. 1939: Ask a Policeman. Where's That Fire? The Frozen Limits. A Girl Must Live. Cheer Boys Cheer. The Band Waggon. 1940: Charley's (Big-Hearted) Aunt. Gasbags. 1941: I Thank You. Hi Gang! 1942: Back Room Boy. 1943: Millions Like Us. Time Flies. 1944: It Happened on Sunday. The Agitator. Don't Take It to Heart. 1945: A Place of One's Own. I'll Be Your Sweetheart. 1946: Green for Danger. 1947: Green Fingers. Jassy. The Root of All Evil. The Hills of Donegal. 1949: The History of Mr Polly. High Jinks in Society.

MARSH, Garry

(Leslie March Geraghty) 1902–1981

Alphabetical order places two of the most prolific figures in British cinema next to each other. Garry Marsh was a big, burly, bustling, blustering character actor with beaming smile and a fine array of harassed looks that made him the forerunner of America's Fred Clark (qv) in exasperation, if not in waspish humour. Played some star roles in comedy-thrillers of the early thirties before giving up the battle with his receding hairline and settling down to dozens of frustrated figures of authority.

1930: Night Birds. PC Josser. 1931: The Eternal Feminine/The Eternal Flame. Uneasy Virtue. Dreyfus (US: The Dreyfus Case). The Man They Could Not Arrest. Stranglehold. The Star Reporter. Third Time Lucky. Keepers of Youth. The Professional Guest. Stamboul. 1932: After Office Hours. COD. Fires of Fate. Don't Be a Dummy. *Postal Orders. Number Seventeen. Maid of the Mountains. 1933: The Lost Chord. Falling for You. Taxi to Paradise. That's a Good Girl. Two Wives for Henry. Forging Ahead. The Love Nest. Ask Beccles. The Silver Spoon. 1934: It's a Cop. Warn London. Money Mad. Josser on the Farm. Rolling in Money. Gay Love. The Green Pack. Lord Edgware Dies. Bella Donna. Are You a Mason? 1935: Widow's Might. Three Witnesses. Mr What's-his-Name. Night Mail. Charing Cross Road. A Wife or Two. Death on the Set (US: Murder on the Set). Inside the Room. Full Circle. Bargain Basement (later Department Store). Scrooge. 1936: When Knights Were Bold. The Man in the Mirror. All In. The Amazing Quest of Ernest Bliss (US: Romance and Riches). Debt of Honour. 1937: It's a Grand Old World. Leave It to Me. Melody and Romance. The Vicar of Bray. A Romance in Flanders (US: Lost on the Western Front). Intimate Relations. The Dark Stairway. Bank Holiday (US: Three on a Week-End). Who Killed Fen Markham?/The Angelus. Meet Mr Penny. 1938: I See Ice. Break the News. The Claydon Treasure Mystery. Convict 99. This Man is News. It's in the Air (US: George Takes the Air). 1939: Let's Be Famous. The Four Just Men (US: The Secret Four). Old Mother Riley Joins Up. Return to Yesterday. Trouble Brewing. This Man in Paris. Hoots Mon! 1940: Let George Do It. 1945: I'll Be Your Sweetheart. Dead of Night. Pink String and Sealing Wax. The Rake's Progress (US:

Notorious Gentleman). 1946: I See a Dark Stranger (US: The Adventuress). The Shop at Sly Corner (US: The Code of Scotland Yard). A Girl in a Million. While the Sun Shines. 1947: Dancing with Crime. Frieda. Just William's Luck. 1948: Good Time Girl. Things Happen at Night. My Brother's Keeper. Badger's Green. William Comes to Town. Forbidden. 1949: Murder at the Windmill (US: Murder at the Burlesque). Paper Orchid. Miss Pilgrim's Progress. 1950: Someone at the Door. Something in the City. Mr Drake's Duck. 1951: Worm's Eye View. Old Mother Riley's Jungle Treasure. Madame Louise. The Magic Box. 1952: The Lost Hours (US: The Big Frame). The Voice of Merrill (US: Murder Will Out). Those People Next Door. 1954: Double Exposure. Aunt Clara. 1955: Man of the Moment. Johnny You're Wanted. Who Done It? 1960: Trouble with Eve. 1963: Ring of Spies. 1966: Where the Bullets Fly. 1967: *Ouch! Camelot.

MARSHALL, E. G.

(Everett Marshall) 1910–

Dark-haired American character star who looks like a serious Bob Hope. From 1930 to 1950 the bulk of his work was in the theatre. From 1950 on he began to tackle TV. He has only flirted with films, although he made quite a name for himself in realist successes of the late fifties, which pushed him into better roles and nearer the top of the cast list.

1945: †The House on 92nd Street. 1946: †13 Rue Madeleine. 1947: †Untamed Fury. †Call Northside 777. 1952: Diplomatic Courier. 1954: The Caine Mutiny. Pushover. Broken Lance. The Silver Chalice. The Bamboo Prison. 1955: The Left Hand of God. The Ox-Bow Incident (TV. GB: cinemas). 1956: The Scarlet Hour. The Mountain. 1957: Clash by Night (TV). Twelve Angry Men. The Bachelor Party. Man on Fire. 1958: The Buccaneer. The Plot to Kill Stalin (TV). The Journey. 1959: A Quiet Game of Cards (TV). Made in Japan (TV). Compulsion. Cash McCall. 1961: Town without Pity. 1965: Is Paris Burning? 1966: The Poppy is Also a Flower (TV. GB: cinemas as Danger Grows Wild). The Chase. 1968: A Case of Libel (TV). The Bridge at Remagen. 1969: A Clear and Present Danger (TV). The Littlest Angel (TV). 1970: Vanished (TV). Tora! Tora! Tora! 1971: The City (TV). Ellery Queen: Don't Look

Behind You (TV). The Pursuit of Happiness. 1972: Look Homeward, Angel (TV). Pursuit (TV). 1974: The Abduction of St Anne (TV). Money to Burn (TV). 1976: Collision Course (TV). *Independence (narrator only). 1977: The Private Files of J. Edgar Hoover. Billy Jack Goes to Washington. 1978: Interiors. 1979: Vampire (TV). 1980: Superman II. 1981: The Phoenix (TV). 1982: Creepshow. 1983: Kennedy (TV). Saigon — Year of the Cat (TV). The Winter of Our Discontent (TV). 1985: Power. My Chauffeur. 1986: Under Siege (TV). 1987: La gran fiesta. 1989: National Lampoon's Christmas Vacation (GB: National Lampoon's Winter Holiday). Two Evil Eyes. 1991: Ironclads (TV). 1992: Consenting Adults. 1993: Russian Holiday. Earth and the American Dream (voice only). 1995: Nixon.

† As Everett Marshall

MARSHALL, Tully
(William Phillips) 1864–1943

Dour, dark-complexioned, grouchy-looking American actor with straggly brown hair, a fine purveyor of dissipated evil and something of a rival to Lon Chaney in silent days as Hollywood's man of many faces. Originally intending to be a lawyer, he started acting on stage at 19 and played a wide variety of roles on Broadway from 1887. Marshall came to Hollywood at 50 and stayed for the remaining three decades of his life, his Fagin in Oliver Twist and high priest in Intolerance (both 1916) setting him up for a whole run of sometimes quite frightening deviants in silent films, culminating in his shuddery portrait of Gloria Swanson's lecherous uncle in Queen Kelly. He was often reduced to grizzled old-timers in sound films, but produced another memorable portrait at 78 as the fifth columnist Brewster in This Gun for Hire. Died from heart and lung problems.

1914: Paid in Full. 1915: The Sable Lorcha. The Painted Soul. Let Katie Do it. 1916: Martha's Vindication. A Child of the Paris Streets. The Devil's Needle. Intolerance. Oliver Twist. Joan the Woman. 1917: The Golden Fetter. A Romance of the Redwoods. A Modern Musketeer. The Countess Charming. Unconquered. We Can't Have Everything. The Devil Stone. 1918: Arizona. Bound in Morocco. M'Liss. A Modern Musketeer. Old Wives for New. The Squaw Man (GB: The White Man).

The Things We Love. Too Many Millions. The Whispering Chorus. The Man from Funeral Range. 1919: Cheating Cheaters. The Crimson Gardenia. Daughter of Mine. Everywoman. The Grim Game. The Girl Who Stayed Home. The Lady of Red Butte. Her Kingdom of Dreams. The Life Line. The Lottery Man. Maggie Pepper. Hawthorne of the USA. The Fall of Babylon (expanded version of section of 1916 film Intolerance). 1920: The Dancin' Fool. Double Speed. Excuse My Dust. The Gift Supreme. Honest Hutch. Sick Abed. The Slim Princess. 1921: The Cup of Life. Hail the Woman. Her Beloved Villain. The Little 'Fraid Lady. Lotus Blossom. Silent Years. The Three Musketeers. What Happened to Rosa? 1922: Any Night. The Beautiful and Damned. Deserted at the Altar. Fools of Fortune. Good Men and True. Is Matrimony a Failure? The Ladder Jinx. The Marriage Chance. The Super Sex. Too Much Business. The Village Blacksmith. Without Compromise. The Lying Truth. 1923: The Barefoot Boy. The Brass Bottle. The Covered Wagon. Broken Hearts of Broadway. The Dangerous Maid. Fools and Riches. Dangerous Trails. Defying Destiny. Temporary Marriage/Her Temporary Husband. His Last Race. Only a Shop Girl. Penrod. The Hunchback of Notre Dame. Ponjola. The Law of the Lawless. Let's Go. Richard the Lion-Hearted. Temporary Marriage. Thundergate. 1924: Along Came Ruth. He Who Gets Slapped. Hold Your Breath. For Sale. Pagan Passions. The Ridin' Kid from Powder River. The Right of the Strongest. Passion's Pathway. Reckless Romance. Smouldering Fires. The Stranger. 1925: Anything Once. Clothes Make the Pirate. The Half-Way Girl. The Merry Widow. The Pace That Thrills. The Talker. 1926: Her Big Night. Old Loves and New. Twinkletoes. The Torrent. 1927: Beware of Widows. The Cat and the Canary. The Gorilla. Jim, the Conqueror. 1928: Conquest. Alias Jimmy Valentine. Drums of Love. The Mad Hour. The Perfect Crime. The Trail of '98. Queen Kelly. 1929: The Bridge of San Luis Rey. The Mysterious Dr Fu Manchu. Redskin. The Show of Shows. Skin Deep. Thunderbolt. Tiger Rose. 1930: The Big Trail. Burning Up. Dancing Sweeties. Common Clay. One Night at Susie's. Mammy. Numbered Men. She Couldn't Say No. Redemption. Tom Sawyer. Under a Texas Moon. Murder Will Out. 1931: Fighting Caravans. The Millionaire. The Unholy Garden. The Virtuous Husband. 1932: Broken Lullaby (GB: The Man I Killed). Arsene Lupin. The Beast of the City. Exposure. Grand Hotel. Klondike (GB: The Doctor's Sacrifice). Night Court. The Hatchet Man (GB: The Honourable Mr Wong). *City Sentinels. Scandal for Sale. Scarface (The Shame of a Nation). Strangers of the Evening. Afraid to Talk. Cabin in the Cotton. Red Dust. The Hurricane Express (serial). Two Fisted Law. 1933: Corruption. Laughing at Life. Night of Terror. Fighting with Kit Carson (serial). 1934: Massacre. Murder on the Blackboard. 1935: Black Fury. Diamond Jim. A Tale of Two Cities. 1937: California Straight Ahead. Behind Prison Bars. Mr Boggs Steps Out. She Asked for It. Stand-In. Hold 'Em Navy. Souls at Sea. A Yank at Oxford. 1938: Arsene Lupin Returns. College Swing (GB: Swing, Teacher, Swing). House of Mystery. Making the Headlines. 1939: Blue

Montana Skies. The Kid from Texas. Invisible Stripes. 1940: Chad Hanna. Brigham Young — Frontiersman (GB: Brigham Young). Go West/The Marx Brothers Go West. Youth Will Be Served. 1941: Ball of Fire. Sergeant York. For Beauty's Sake. 1942: Moontide. Ten Gentlemen from West Point. This Gun for Hire. 1943: Behind Prison Walls. Hitler's Madman.

MARTIN, Edie 1880–1964

Beak-nosed, sharp-chinned, bespectacled, shrilly spoken British actress usually seen in roles almost as tiny as herself, but so distinctive she could be picked out in a second. On stage at six, she remained busy in that medium throughout her working life, which went on into her eighties — although she did find time for more than 60 cameos in films, mostly as maids or frail but fierce old ladies.

1936: Educated Evans. Broken Blossoms. Servants All. The Big Noise. 1937: Action for Slander. Under the Red Robe. Farewell Again (GB: Troopship). The Squeaker (US: Murder on Diamond Row). Return of a Stranger (US: The Face Behind the Scar). 1938: Bad Boy (later reissued as Branded). A Spot of Bother. St Martin's Lane (US: Sidewalks of London). 1939: Old Mother Riley MP. 1940: Old Mother Riley in Business. Busman's Honeymoon (US: Haunted Honeymoon). 1942: Unpublished Story. 1943: The Demi-Paradise (US: Adventure for Two). It's in the Bag. 1944: Don't Take it to Heart. 1945: A Place of One's Own. They Were Sisters. Here Comes the Sun. 1946: Great Expectations. 1947: It Always Rains on Sunday. The Courtneys of Curzon Street (US: The Courtney Affair). When the Bough Breaks. 1948: Another Shore. Oliver Twist. My Brother's Keeper. Elizabeth of Ladymead. Cardboard Cavalier. The History of Mr Polly. 1949: Adam and Evelyne (US: Adam and Evalyn). 1950: Blackmailed. 1951: The Lady With a Lamp. The Galloping Major. The Lavender Hill Mob. The Man in the White Suit. Night Was Our Friend. 1952: Time Gentlemen Please! 1953: Genevieve. The Titfield Thunderbolt. Meet Mr Lucifer. Hobson's Choice. 1954: The Black Rider. Lease of Life. The End of the Road. *The Mysterious Bullet. 1955: The Ladykillers. As Long As They're Happy. Room in the House. An Alligator Named Daisy. Lost (US: Tears for Simon). 1956:

Ramsbottom Rides Again. My Teenage Daughter (US: Teenage Bad Girl). Sailor Beware! (US: Panic in the Parlor). 1957: The Naked Truth (US: Your Past is Showing!). 1958: Too Many Crooks. 1959: Follow a Star. Kidnapped. I'm All Right, Jack. 1961: A Weekend with Lulu. 1962: Sparrows Can't Sing.

MARTIN, Strother 1919–1980

A rare latter-day character star in the best Hollywood tradition, at a time when there weren't too many around. Round-faced, fair-haired Martin first came to Hollywood as a swimming coach (he was a national junior diving champion) but subsequently spent 20 years in small roles — often as cunning countrified whiners — before shuffling his way into a couple of leading parts. But he was still better employed in bolstering the supporting cast.

1950: The Damned Don't Cry. The Asphalt Jungle. 1951: The People Against O'Hara. Rhubarb. 1952: Storm over Tibet. 1953: The Magnetic Monster. South Sea Woman. 1954: A Star is Born. Drum Beat. 1955: The Big Knife. Cowboy. Strategic Air Command. Kiss Me Deadly. Target Zero! 1956: Johnny Concho. The Black Whip. Attack! 1957: Copper Sky. Black Patch. 1959: The Shaggy Dog. The Wild and the Innocent. The Horse Soldiers. 1961: Sanctuary. The Deadly Companions. 1962: The Man Who Shot Liberty Valance. 1963: McLintock! Showdown. 1964: Invitation to a Gunfighter. 1965: Brainstorm. Shenandoah. The Sons of Katie Elder. 1966: Nevada Smith. Harper (GB: The Moving Target). An Eye for an Eye. 1967: The Flim Flam Man (GB: One Born Every Minute). Cool Hand Luke. 1969: True Grit. Butch Cassidy and the Sundance Kid. The Wild Bunch. 1970: The Brotherhood of Satan. The Ballad of Cable Hogue. Red Sky at Morning. 1971: Fool's Parade (GB: Dynamite Man from Glory Jail). Pocket Money. Hannie Caulder. 1973: Ssssssss (GB: Sssnake). The Boy and the Bronc Buster (TV). 1975: Rooster Cogburn. Hard Times (GB: The Street-fighter). One of Our Own (TV). 1976: The Great Scout and Cathouse Thursday. 1977: Slap Shot. 1978: Up in Smoke. The Champ. Steel Cowboy (TV). Love and Bullets. The End. 1979: Nightwing. The Villain (GB: Cactus Jack). Better Late Than Never (TV). 1980: Hotwire. The Secret of Nikola Tesla.

MASSEY, Anna 1937–

Narrow-faced, fair-haired, pencil-slim British actress with shadowed eyes. She had pinched, piquant, highly distinctive features in her younger days that gave her an unconventional attractiveness and a talent that shot her to stage stardom in *The Reluctant Debutante* in 1955. Films reached out, and she did make a mark in *Peeping Tom*, but, unable to pigeonhole her, the cinema seemed to give up on her as a star early on. After a sporadic mid-career as victims and oddballs, she assumed a gaunt, slightly sinister aspect in middle age that got her cast effectively as Mrs Danvers in a TV adaptation of *Rebecca* in 1979 and caused the cinema to call again. Now firmly established as a telling character star. Daughter of actors Raymond Massey and Adrianne Allen, she was married to, and divorced from actor Jeremy Brett. Sister of Daniel Massey.

1958: Gideon's Day (US: Gideon of Scotland Yard). 1960: Peeping Tom. 1965: Bunny Lake is Missing. 1966: The Persecution and Assassination of Jean-Paul Marat . . . (The Marat/Sade). 1969: David Copperfield (TV. GB: cinemas). The Looking Glass War. 1972: Frenzy. 1973: A Doll's House (Patrick Garland). Vault of Horror. 1979: A Little Romance. The Corn is Green (TV). Sweet William. 1981: Five Days One Summer. 1984: Another Country. Sakharov. The Little Drummer Girl. Sacred Hearts. The Chain. 1985: Anna Karenina (TV). Hotel du Lac (TV). The McGuffin (TV). 1986: Foreign Body. 1987: Day After the Fair (TV). A Hazard of Hearts (TV). 1988: Le couleur du vent. 1989: Killing Dad. The Tall Guy. Mountains of the Moon. 1990: Impromptu. 1992: Emily's Ghost. 1995: Haunted. The Grotesque.

MASUR, Richard 1948–

Tall, shambling, benign American actor with open face, wide shoulders and a mass of dark, curly hair. His comforting personality and bristling moustache were seen in a variety of non-aggressive roles for films, after he had come to prominence as the harassed manager of *Hot L Baltimore* on TV in the early 1970s. Latter-day roles have been of the fatherly kind, although it is disappointing that he has not been able to pursue his ambitions to direct in films, despite two encouraging short subjects in 1987, one of

which, *Love Struck*, was nominated for an Academy Award.

1975: Whiffs (GB: C*A*S*H). 1976: Bitter-sweet Love. Having Babies (TV). 1977: Semi-Tough. 1978: Who'll Stop the Rain? (GB: Dog Soldiers). Betrayal (TV). 1979: Hanover Street. Walking Through the Fire (TV). Mr Horn (TV). Scavenger Hunt. 1980: Heaven's Gate. 1981: Fallen Angel (TV). East of Eden (TV). I'm Dancing As Fast As I Can. 1982: The Thing. Invasion of Privacy (TV). Under Fire. Money on the Side (TV). Timerider — The Adventure of Lyle Swann. 1983: Nightmares. Adam (TV). Risky Business. The Demon Murder Case (TV). An Invasion of Privacy (TV). The Winter of Our Discontent (TV). 1984: Flight 90: Disaster on the Potomac (TV). The Burning Bed (TV). 1985: Obsessed with a Married Woman (TV). The Mean Season. Embassy (TV). Wild Horses (TV). My Science Project. Head Office. 1986: Mr Boogedy (TV). When the Bough Breaks (TV). Heartburn. Adam: His Song Continues (TV). The George McKenna Story (TV). 1987: The Believers. Rent-a-Cop. Walker. Bride of Boogedy (TV). 1988: Higher Ground (TV). Shoot to Kill (GB: Deadly Pursuit). License to Drive. 1989: Vietnam, Texas. Far from Home. Third Degree Burn (TV). Settle the Score (TV). Cast the First Stone (TV). 1990: Out of Sight, Out of Mind. Flashback. 1991: The Strong Lady (TV). Going Under. 1992: Encino Man (GB: California Man). My Girl. 1993: The Man Without a Face. And the Band Played On. Six Degrees of Separation. 1994: My Girl 2. Les Patriotes. Search for Grace (TV). 1995: Forget Paris. My Brother's Keeper (TV).

As director:
1987: *Thought to Kill. *Love Struck.

MATTHEWS, A.E. 1869–1960

Round-faced, owl-eyed, affectionately regarded British actor who moved from smooth leading men to character roles on stage, then enjoyed 20 years of fame in his last two decades as the British cinema's most famous crotchety and sometimes rascally old man. For many years Britain's oldest working actor, known to his friends as 'Matty'.

1914: A Highwayman's Honour. 1916: Wanted a Widow. *The Real Thing at Last. The Lifeguardsman. 1918: Once Upon a Time. 1919: The Lackey and the Lady. Castle of

Dreams. 1934: The Iron Duke. 1936: Men Are Not Gods. 1941: Pimpernel Smith (US: Mister V). Quiet Wedding. This England. *Surprise Broadcast. 1942: The Great Mr Handel. Thunder Rock. 1943: The Life and Death of Colonel Blimp (US: Colonel Blimp). Escape to Danger. The Man in Grey. 1944: The Way Ahead (US: Immortal Battalion). They Came to a City. Love Story (US: A Lady Surrenders). Flight from Folly. Twilight Hour. 1946: Piccadilly Incident. 1947: The Ghosts of Berkeley Square. Just William's Luck. 1948: William Comes to Town. 1949: Britannia Mews (US: Forbidden Street). Whisky Galore! (US: Tight Little Island). Edward My Son. The Chiltern Hundreds (US: The Amazing Mr Beecham). Landfall. 1950: Mr Drake's Duck. 1951: The Galloping Major. Laughter in Paradise. The Magic Box. 1952: Penny Princess. Who Goes There! (US: The Passionate Sentry). Castle in the Air. Something Money Can't Buy. Made in Heaven. Skid Kids. 1953: The Million Pound Note (US: Man with a Million). The Weak and the Wicked. 1954: Happy Ever After (US: Tonight's the Night/O'Leary Night). Aunt Clara. 1955: Miss Tulip Stays the Night. 1956: Jumping for Joy. Loser Takes All. Three Men in a Boat. Around the World in 80 Days. 1957: Doctor at Large. Carry on Admiral (US: The Ship Was Loaded). 1960: Inn for Trouble.

MATTHEWS, Lester 1900–1975
Tall, dark, saturnine British actor with receding hairline, slightly stooping gait, dashing moustache and faintly bad-tempered countenance. These attributes combined to have him cast as double-shaded

characters in his days (1931–1934) as a popular leading man of early British sound films, before he went to Hollywood with his then-wife, actress Anne Grey. Here there were a couple of minor leads, but he always looked a little more than his real age, and soon buckled down to dozens of character parts, largely as military men or villains.

1929: *Shivering Shocks. 1931: *The Lame Duck. Creeping Shadows (US: The Limping Man). The Man at Six (US: The Gables Mystery). The Wickham Mystery. Gypsy Blood (US: Carmen). The Old Man. 1932: Her Night Out. The Indiscretions of Eve. Fires of Fate. 1933: The Stolen Necklace. Called Back. On Secret Service (US: Secret Agent). House of Dreams. Their Night Out. Out of the Past. She Was Only a Village Maiden. The Melody Maker. Facing the Music. The Song You Gave Me. 1934: Borrowed Clothes. Boomerang. Song at Eventide. Blossom Time (US: April Romance). Irish Hearts (US: Norah O'Neale). The Poisoned Diamond. 1935: The Werewolf of London. The Raven. 1936: Thank You, Jeeves. Professional Soldier. Spy 77. Song and Dance Man. 15 Maiden Lane. Lloyds of London. Too Many Parents. Tugboat Princess. Crack-Up. 1937: Lancer Spy. The Prince and the Pauper. 1938: There's Always a Woman. Three Loves Has Nancy. Mysterious Mr Moto. If I Were King. Time Out for Murder. The Adventures of Robin Hood. *Think It Over. I Am a Criminal. 1939: The Three Musketeers (GB: The Singing Musketeer). Susannah of the Mounties. Should a Girl Marry? Conspiracy. Mr Moto in Danger Island (GB: Mr Moto on Danger Island). Rulers of the Sea. Everything Happens at Night. 1940: Northwest Passage. British Intelligence (GB: Enemy Agent). The Sea Hawk. Gaucho Serenade. The Biscuit Eater. Women in War. Sing, Dance, Plenty Hot (GB: Melody Girl). 1941: Man Hunt. A Yank in the RAF. The Lone Wolf Keeps a Date. Life Begins for Andy Hardy. Scotland Yard. 1942: Son of Fury. Now, Voyager. The Pied Piper. Across the Pacific. Sunday Punch. Desperate Journey. Manila Calling. London Blackout Murders (GB: Secret Motive). 1943: The Mysterious Doctor. Northern Pursuit. Appointment in Berlin. Ministry of Fear. Two Tickets to London. Corvette K-225 (GB: The Nelson Touch). Tonight We Raid Calais. 1944: Nine Girls. Between Two Worlds. Four Jills in a Jeep. The Invisible Man's Revenge. Gaslight (GB: The Murder in Thornton Square). The Story of Dr Wassell. Shadows in the Night. A Wing and a Prayer. 1945: The Beautiful Cheat (GB: What a Woman!). I Love a Mystery. Son of Lassie. Jungle Queen (serial). Objective Burma! Salty O'Rourke. Two O'Clock Courage. 1946: Three Strangers. 1947: Dark Delusion (GB: Cynthia's Secret). The Paradine Case. Bulldog Drummond at Bay. The Exile. 1948: Fighting Father Dunne. 1949: Free for All. I Married a Communist (GB: The Woman on Pier 13). 1950: Tyrant of the Sea. Her Wonderful Lie. Montana. Rogues of Sherwood Forest. 1951: Anne of the Indies. Corky of Gasoline Alley (GB: Corky). The Desert Fox (GB: Rommel — Desert Fox). The Lady and the Bandit (GB: Dick Turpin's Ride). Lorna Doone. The Son of Dr Jekyll. Tales of Robin Hood. 1952: The Brigand. Against All Flags. Five Fingers.

Captain Pirate (GB: Captain Blood, Fugitive). Jungle Jim in the Forbidden Land. Lady in the Iron Mask. Les Misérables. Savage Mutiny. Stars and Stripes Forever (GB: Marching Along). 1953: Bad for Each Other. Jamaica Run. Fort Ti. Niagara. Trouble Along the Way. Rogue's March. Sangaree. Young Bess. Charge of the Lancers. 1954: Desiree. The Far Horizons. Jungle Man-Eaters. King Richard and the Crusaders. Man in the Attic. Moonfleet. 1955: Ten Wanted Men. The Seven Little Foys. Flame of the Islands. 1957: Something of Value. 1958: Hearts and Hands. 1959: The Miracle. 1960: Song Without End. 1963: A Global Affair. The Prize. 1964: Mary Poppins. 1966: Assault on a Queen. The Scorpio Letters (TV. GB: cinemas). 1968: Star! 1970: Comeback (later Hollywood Horror House).

MAYNE, Ferdy
(Ferdinand Mayer-Börckel) 1916–
Dark-haired (now grey), lantern-faced, sardonic-looking German actor of sinister charm who came to British films via radio and, from 1948 to 1963 in particular, must have menaced more British second-feature heroes than any other actor. His villains had a touch of class and exuded suave decadence. Billed as Ferdi on his first four British films, Ferdinand in the 1980s and beyond when he became a movie wanderer across America and Europe, otherwise as Ferdy throughout the major part of his movie career. Also recently seen in such TV mini-series and series as Evita Perón, Sadat and The Winds of War.

1943: Old Mother Riley Overseas. The Yellow Canary. Warn That Man. The Life and Death of Colonel Blimp (US: Colonel Blimp). 1944: Meet Sexton Blake. English Without Tears (US: Her Man Gilbey). 1945: The Echo Murders. Waltz Time. 1947: Broken Journey. 1949: Vote for Huggett. The Huggetts Abroad. Celia. The Temptress. 1950: State Secret (US: The Great Manhunt). Prelude to Fame. Cairo Road. Night and the City. 1951: Hotel Sahara. Encore. 1952: Venetian Bird (US: The Assassin). The Man Who Watched Trains Go By (US: Paris Express). Made in Heaven. 1953: The Captain's Paradise. The Case of the Second Shot. Desperate Moment. The Broken Horseshoe. All Hallowe'en. The Blue Parrot. Marilyn (later Roadhouse Girl). Three Steps to the Gallows (US: White Fire. Released 1955).

You Know What Sailors Are. 1954: Malaga (US: Fire Over Africa). Beautiful Stranger (US: Twist of Fate). The Divided Heart. Betrayed. Third Party Risk (US: The Deadly Game). 1955: *Crossroads. Storm Over the Nile. Dust and Gold. Value for Money. The Glass Cage (US: The Glass Tomb). 1956: The Narrowing Circle. Gentlemen Marry Brunettes. Find the Lady. *The Magic Carpet. The Big Money (released 1958). The Baby and the Battleship. 1957: You Pay Your Money. The Big Chance. The End of the Line. Three Sundays to Live. Blue Murder at St Trinian's. Seven Waves Away (US: Abandon Ship). The Safecracker. 1958: A Woman of Mystery. Next to No Time! 1959: Ben-Hur. Deadly Record. Third Man on the Mountain. Tommy the Toreador. Our Man in Havana. 1960: Crossroads to Crime. The Spider's Web. 1961: *Frederic Chopin. The Green Helmet. Highway to Battle. 1962: Three Spare Wives. The Password is Courage. Masters of Venus (serial). Freud (GB: Freud – the Secret Passion). The Story of Private Pooley. 1963: Shadow of Treason. 1964: Allez France (US: The Counterfeit Constable). 1965: Those Magnificent Men in Their Flying Machines. Operation Crossbow (US: The Great Spy Mission). Promise Her Anything. 1967: Dance of the Vampires (US: The Fearless Vampire Killers). The Bobo. 1968: Gates to Paradise. The Limbo Line. Where Eagles Dare. The Best House in London. 1969: The Magic Christian. 1970: Eagle in a Cage. The Walking Stick. The Vampire Lovers. The Adventurers. 1971: When Eight Bells Toll. Vampire Happening. Jo. Les grandes vacances. The Blonde in the Blue Movie. Von Richthofen and Brown (GB: The Red Baron). 1972: Au Pair Girls. Innocent Bystanders. Il vichingo venuto del sud. Il terna di Marco. 1973: Idoo Mark Belehnung. 1974: Die Ameisen kommen/The Ants Are Coming. Journey to Vienna. 1975: Barry Lyndon. Floris. Call of Gold (TV). Das Schweigen im Walde/ The Silent Forest. 1976: *Red. The Eagle Has Landed. 1977: L'aube/The Dawn. Les aventuriers américains/The Pawn. 1978: Revenge of the Pink Panther. Fedora. The Pirate (TV). 1979: Freundschaft wider Willen (TV). The Music Machine. A Man Called Intrepid (TV). 1980: Hawk the Slayer. The Formula. 1981: The Levkas Man. Death of a Centerfold (TV). 1982: The Horror Star. 1983: The Secret Diary of Sigmund Freud. The Black Stallion Returns. Yellowbeard. 1984: Conan the Destroyer. 1985: Hot Chili. Night Train to Terror. Howling II: Your Sister is a Werewolf. Lime Street (TV). 1986: Habana Cabana. Frankenstein's Aunt. Pirates. 1988: A Friendship in Vienna (TV). Chief Zabú. The Choice. 1989: Magdalene. My Lovely Monster (released 1991). 1990: River of Diamonds. 1991: Knight Moves. 1992: The Tigress.

MAZURKI, Mike

(Mikhail Mazurski) 1907–1990
Hulking, craggy, fearsomely-featured, dark-haired Austrian-born actor. In America from an early age, he was a professional footballer and wrestler before taking his huge frame to Hollywood to play hoodlums' henchmen. Dim-looking (but actually well-educated), with hook nose, open mouth and aggressive,

small-eyed stare, he would have done any Damon Runyon story proud, and became the definitive Moose Malloy in the 1945 version of Raymond Chandler's Farewell, My Lovely.

1934: Belle of the Nineties. 1935: Black Fury. 1938: Mr Moto's Gamble. 1939: Invisible Stripes. 1941: The Shanghai Gesture. 1942: Gentleman Jim. About Face. That Other Woman. The McGuerins from Brooklyn. Dr Renault's Secret. 1943: Henry Aldrich Haunts a House (GB: Henry Haunts a House). Whistling in Brooklyn. Prairie Chickens. Thank Your Lucky Stars. Taxi, Mister. Swing Fever. Lost Angel. It Ain't Hay (GB: Money for Jam). Mission to Moscow. Behind the Rising Sun. Bomber's Moon. 1944: The Missing Juror. Summer Storm. The Canterville Ghost. The Thin Man Comes Home. The Princess and the Pirate. Shine On, Harvest Moon. 1945: Bud Abbott and Lou Costello in Hollywood. Nob Hill. Murder, My Sweet (GB: Farewell, My Lovely). *The Jury Goes Round 'n' Round. Dick Tracy (GB: Splitface). Dakota. The Spanish Main. The Horn Blows at Midnight. 1946: Live Wires. Mysterious Intruder. The French Key. 1947: Sinbad the Sailor. Unconquered. Nightmare Alley. Killer Dill. I Walk Alone. 1948: The Noose Hangs High. Relentless. 1949: Come to the Stable. Abandoned. The Devil's Henchman. Neptune's Daughter. Rope of Sand. Samson and Delilah. Two Knights in Brooklyn/Two Mugs from Brooklyn (combined GB version of The McGuerins from Brooklyn/Taxi, Mister). 1950: Dark City. He's a Cockeyed Wonder. Night and the City. 1951: Criminal Lawyer. My Favorite Spy. The Light Touch. Pier 23. Ten Tall Men. 1954: The Egyptian. Davy Crockett – King of the Wild Frontier. 1955: Blood Alley. Kismet. The Man from Laramie. New York Confidential. New Orleans Uncensored (GB: Riot on Pier 6). 1956: Around the World in 80 Days. Comanche. Man in the Vault. 1957: Hell Ship Mutiny. 1958: The Buccaneer. The Man Who Died Twice. 1959: Alias Jesse James. Some Like It Hot. 1960: The Facts of Life. The Schnook (GB: Double Trouble). 1961: The Errand Boy. Pocketful of Miracles. 1962: Zotz! Swingin' Along (revised version of The Schnook). Five Weeks in a Balloon. 1963: Donovan's Reef. Four for Texas. It's a Mad, Mad, Mad, Mad World. 1964: The Disorderly Orderly. Cheyenne Autumn. 1965: The Adventures of Bullwhip Griffin. Requiem for a Gunfighter. 1966: 7 Women. 1970: Which Way to

the Front? (Ja! Ja! Mein General, But Which Way to the Front?). 1972: Challenge to be Free. 1974: Centerfold Girls. 1975: Won Ton Ton, the Dog Who Saved Hollywood. The Wild McCullochs. 1977: The Incredible Rocky Mountain Race (TV). One Man Jury. Mad Bull (TV). 1978: The Magic of Lassie. 1979: Gas Pump Girls. The Man with Bogart's Face. 1980: Alligator. All the Marbles . . . (GB: The California Dolls). The Adventures of Huckleberry Finn (TV). 1985: Doin' Time. 1986: Amazon Women on the Moon. 1990: Mob Boss. Dick Tracy.

McANALLY, Ray 1926–1989

Burly, brown-haired, bejowled, soft-spoken Irish actor, often in aggressive roles. Mainly a star of the Irish theatre until the 1980s, McAnally played more than 150 roles at Dublin's Abbey theatre, where he was a life member and worked permanently from 1947 to 1961. Despite giving him the leading role in his first film, the cinema didn't really get a grasp on McAnally until the last decade of his life, when he made his mark with such roles as the papal envoy in The Mission and Christy Brown's father in My Left Foot.

1957: Professor Tim. 1958: Sea of Sand (US: Desert Attack). She Didn't Say No! 1959: Shake Hands with the Devil. 1961: Murder in Eden. The Naked Edge. 1962: Billy Budd. 1966: He Who Rides a Tiger. 1969: The Looking Glass War. 1971: Quest for Love. 1972: Fear is the Key. 1979: The Outsider. 1982: Angel (US: Danny Boy). 1984: Cal. 1986: No Surrender. The Mission. 1987: The Sicilian. Empire State. White Mischief. The Fourth Protocol. 1988: Taffin. High Spirits. 1989: My Left Foot. Jack the Ripper (TV). Venus Peter. We're No Angels.

McCAMBRIDGE, Mercedes

(Carlotta M. McCambridge) 1918–
Dark, heavy-set, gloweringly menacing American actress, usually in unpleasant roles. After an Academy Award in her first film, All the King's Men, she proved difficult to cast and was seen only now and again when the right part could be found. Her power diminished somewhat in the sixties, and she accepted lesser roles. Additional Oscar nomination for Giant. Married/divorced (2nd) director Fletcher Markle. Her son Jon shot himself and his family in 1987.

1949: All the King's Men. 1951: Inside Straight. Lightning Strikes Twice. The Scarf. 1954: Johnny Guitar. 1956: Giant. 1957: A Farewell to Arms. 1958: Touch of Evil. 1959: Suddenly Last Summer. 1960: Cimarron. Angel Baby. 1966: Run Home Slow. 1968: Justine and Juliet. 99 Women (US: Island of Despair). The Counterfeit Killer (TV. GB: cinemas). 1969: Der heisse Tod. 1971: A Capitol Affair (TV). Killer by Night (TV). Two for the Money (TV). The Last Generation. The President's Plane is Missing (TV). 1973: Sixteen. The Girls of Huntingdon House (TV). The Exorcist (voice only). 1974: Like a Crow on a June Bug. 1975: Who is the Black Dahlia? (TV). 1976: Thieves. 1979: The Concorde – Airport '79 (GB: Airport '80 . . . the Concorde). The Sacketts (TV). 1980: Echoes. 1983: Lyman H Lowe's High Class Moving Pictures (narrator only).

McCARTHY, Neil 1933–
Tough-looking British actor whose jagged facial features and unruly, wispy dark hair confined him largely in films to thick-skulled minor heavies. Like so many film hard men, McCarthy, the son of a dentist and once a teacher, is the quiet type in real life, listing his hobbies as the piano and study of foreign languages. If he had been 10 years younger and entered films in the post-war period, McCarthy would doubtless have built up a formidable gallery of aggressors. As it is, TV and the classical theatre have given him more rewarding roles.

1958: The Whole Truth. 1959: Breakout. 1960: The Criminal (US: The Concrete

Jungle). Sands of the Desert. 1961: Offbeat. 1962: We Joined the Navy. Solo for Sparrow. The Pot Carriers. 1963: The Young Detectives (serial). Two Left Feet. The Cracksman. Zulu. 1965: The Hill. Cuckoo Patrol. 1967: Where Eagles Dare. Woman Times Seven. 1968: Project Z (serial). 1971: Follow Me! (US: The Public Eye). Steptoe and Son. 1973: The Zoo Robbery. Steptoe and Son Ride Again. 1974: The Nine Tailors (TV). 1975: Operation Daybreak. Side by Side. 1976: Trial by Combat (US: Dirty Knights' Work). The Incredible Sarah. Fern the Red Deer. 1978: The Thief of Baghdad. 1980: The Monster Club. Shogun (TV. GB: cinemas, in abbreviated version). George and Mildred. 1981: Clash of the Titans. Time Bandits. 1989: Ten Little Indians. Time of the Beast. 1991: Mutator.

McCOWEN, Alec
(Alexander McCowen) 1925–
Light-haired British actor with thin smile. His immense talent for sardonic humour was little used on screen, a medium in which his stocky stature kept him in star character roles. His dramatic characterizations in films — Frenzy apart — have seemed rather bloodless, but he has shone in witty cameos. The bulk of his work has been in the British theatre, where his reputation is justly high.

1952: The Cruel Sea. 1953: *A Midsummer Night's Dream. 1954: The Divided Heart. 1955: The Deep Blue Sea. 1956: The Long Arm (US: The Third Key). Town on Trial! 1957: The Good Companions. Time Without Pity. The One That Got Away. 1958: The Silent Enemy. A Night to Remember. A Midsummer Night's Dream (dubbed voice). 1959: The Doctor's Dilemma. 1962: The Loneliness of the Long Distance Runner. In the Cool of the Day. 1965: The Agony and the Ecstasy. 1966: The Witches (US: The Devil's Own). 1970: The Hawaiians (GB: Master of the Islands). 1972: Frenzy. Travels with My Aunt. 1978: Stevie. 1979: Hanover Street. 1983: Never Say Never Again. Forever Young. 1985: The Assam Garden. 1986: Personal Services. 1987: Cry Freedom. 1989: Henry V. 1992: Maria's Child (TV). 1993: The Age of Innocence.

McDANIEL, Hattie 1895–1952
Big, beaming, much-loved American actress with searching gaze who became the

archetypal black lady's-maid in Hollywood films of the 1930s and 1940s. Her mother was a famous singer of spirituals (father was a Baptist preacher) and Hattie, despite winning a drama medal at 15, initially became a vocalist with a dance band (she was the first black woman to sing on American radio) before taking up acting again in her thirties. She won an Academy Award as best supporting actress for Gone With the Wind, and was a delight singing and dancing Ice Cold Katie in Thank Your Lucky Stars, but retired in 1948 because of ill-health. Sister of actress Etta McDaniel (1890–1946) and actor Sam McDaniel (1886–1962), she died from breast cancer.

1932: The Boiling Point. Hypnotized. The Washington Masquerade (GB: Mad Masquerade). Blonde Venus. The Golden West. 1933: The Story of Temple Drake. I'm No Angel. *Knee Deep in Music. Hello Sister/ Walking Down Broadway. 1934: Operator 13 (GB: Spy 13). Lost in the Stratosphere. Judge Priest. Babbitt. Little Men. *The Chases of Pimple Street. *Fate's Fathead. Imitation of Life. King Kelly of the USA. 1935: Music is Magic. Harmony Lane. Alice Adams. Traveling Saleslady. The Little Colonel. Another Face. *Anniversary Trouble. *Four Star Boarder. Okay Toots! Murder by Television. China Seas. 1936: Gentle Julia. Next Time We Love (GB: Next Time We Live). Show Boat. High Tension. The Postal Inspector. The Singing Kid. Reunion (GB: Hearts in Reunion). Libeled Lady. The First Baby. Hearts Divided. Star for a Night. The Bride Walks Out. Valiant is the Word for Carrie. Can This Be Dixie? *Arbor Day. *Big Time Vaudeville. 1937: Racing Lady. The Crime Nobody Saw. Saratoga. True Confession. 45 Fathers. Nothing Sacred. The Wildcatter. Over the Goal. Don't Tell the Wife. Merry-Go-Round of 1938. 1938: Vivacious Lady. Quick Money. Battle of Broadway. The Shining Hour. The Mad Miss Manton. Carefree. The Shopworn Angel. 1939: Zenobia (GB: Elephants Never Forget). Gone With the Wind. Everybody's Baby. 1940: Maryland. 1941: Affectionately Yours. The Great Lie. They Died With Their Boots On. 1942: The Male Animal. Reap the Wild Wind. In This Our Life. George Washington Slept Here. 1943: Johnny Come Lately (GB: Johnny Vagabond). Thank Your Lucky Stars. 1944: Since You Went Away. Three is a Family. Janie. Hi, Beautiful (GB: Pass to Romance). 1946: Janie Gets Married. Margie. Song of the

South. *Never Say Goodbye.* 1947: *The Flame.* 1948: *Mickey. Family Honeymoon.* 1949: *The Big Wheel.*

McGIVER, John
(George Morris) 1913–1975

American character actor who came to films in his forties and quickly proved a treasure. Instantly identifiable with his pinkly plump features, bald head, tiny eyes and lips pursed in anticipation of some new problem, he was one of the most astute scene-stealers around in the late fifties and early sixties. Died from a heart attack.

1956: *L'homme à l'imperméable.* 1957: *Love in the Afternoon.* 1958: *I Married a Woman. Once upon a Horse.* 1959: *The Gazebo.* 1960: *Love in a Goldfish Bowl.* 1961: *Bachelor in Paradise. Breakfast at Tiffany's.* 1962: *Period of Adjustment. Mr Hobbs Takes a Vacation. The Manchurian Candidate. Who's Got the Action?* 1963: *Take Her, She's Mine. Johnny Cool. Who's Minding the Store? A Global Affair. My Six Loves.* 1964: *Man's Favorite Sport?* 1965: *Marriage on the Rocks. Made in Paris.* 1966: *The Glass Bottom Boat.* 1967: *Fitzwilly (GB: Fitzwilly Strikes Back). The Spirit is Willing. The Pill Caper (TV).* 1969: *Midnight Cowboy.* 1970: *The Feminist and the Fuzz (TV). Lawman.* 1971: *Sam Hill: Who Killed the Mysterious Mr Foster? (TV). The Great Man's Whiskers (TV).* 1973: *Arnold. Mame.* 1974: *The Apple Dumpling Gang.* 1975: *Tom Sawyer (TV).*

McHUGH, Frank
(Francis McHugh) 1898–1981

Cuddly, small-eyed, large-headed American actor of Irish extraction, with light wavy hair and an almost permanent look of amiable bafflement on his face. The son of actors, McHugh played his first stage roles with his parents' stock company. When sound films arrived, however, he left the theatre to become a regular member of the Warner Brothers repertory company from 1930 to 1942, usually as the not-so-bright but true-blue loyal friend of the intrepid hero. Best-remembered for a hyena-like laugh, which could be hilarious or annoying according to taste.

1926: *Mademoiselle Modiste.* 1928: **If Men Played Cards As Women Do.* 1930: *College*

Lovers. The Dawn Patrol. Top Speed. Bright Lights. Little Caesar. The Widow from Chicago. 1931: *Corsair. *The Big Scoop. *That's News to Me. *The Hot Spot. Traveling Husbands. *The Great Junction Hotel. *Wide Open Spaces. Going Wild. Bad Company. Up for Murder. The Front Page. Fires of Youth. Millie. Men of the Sky. Kiss Me Again (GB: The Toast of the Legion).* 1932: *One Way Passage. Blessed Event. *The News Hound. *Pete Burke, Reporter. *Extra, Extra. High Pressure. Union Depot (GB: Gentleman for a Day). The Strange Love of Molly Louvain. Life Begins (GB: The Dawn of Life). The Dark Horse. The Crowd Roars.* 1933: *Parachute Jumper. The Mystery of the Wax Museum. Grand Slam. Private Jones. Telegraph Trail. Convention City. Lilly Turner. Footlight Parade. Professional Sweetheart (GB: Imaginary Sweetheart). Hold Me Tight. The House on 56th Street. Elmer the Great. Son of a Sailor. Havana Widows. Tomorrow at Seven. The Mad Game. Ex-Lady. 42nd Street.* 1934: *Maybe It's Love. Fashions of 1934. Heat Lightning. Here Comes the Navy. Return of the Terror. Happiness Ahead. Merry Wives of Reno. Smarty (GB: Hit Me Again). Let's Be Ritzy (GB: Millionaire for a Day). Six Day Bike Rider. *Not Tonight, Josephine.* 1935: *A Midsummer Night's Dream. Stars over Broadway. The Irish in Us. Page Miss Glory. Devil Dogs of the Air. Gold Diggers of 1935. Three Kids and a Queen (GB: The Baxter Millions).* 1936: *Snowed Under. Freshman Love (GB: Rhythm on the River). Stage Struck. Moonlight Murder. Three Men on a Horse. Bullets or Ballots.* 1937: *Mr Dodd Takes the Air. Marry the Girl. Ever Since Eve. Submarine D-1.* 1938: *Little Miss Thoroughbred. Swing Your Lady. Four Daughters. He Couldn't Say No. Boy Meets Girl. Valley of the Giants.* 1939: *Indianapolis Speedway (GB: Devil on Wheels). Dust Be My Destiny. Daughters Courageous. Four Wives. Dodge City. The Roaring Twenties. On Your Toes.* 1940: *Saturday's Children. The Fighting 69th. 'Til We Meet Again. City for Conquest. Virginia City.* 1941: *Four Mothers. Back Street. Manpower. I Love You Again.* 1942: *Her Cardboard Lover. All Through the Night.* 1944: *Marine Raiders. Bowery to Broadway. Going My Way.* 1945: *A Medal for Benny. State Fair.* 1946: *Deadline for Murder. Little Miss Big (GB: Baxter's Millions). The Hoodlum Saint. The Runaround.* 1947: *Easy Come, Easy Go. Carnegie Hall.* 1948: *The Velvet Touch.* 1949: *Mighty Joe Young. Miss Grant Takes Richmond*

(GB: *Innocence is Bliss*). 1950: *Paid in Full. The Tougher They Come.* 1952: *My Son John. The Pace That Thrills.* 1953: *A Lion is in the Streets. It Happens Every Thursday.* 1954: *There's No Business Like Show Business.* 1957: *Three Men on a Horse (TV).* 1958: *The Last Hurrah.* 1959: *Career. Say One for Me.* 1963: *A Tiger Walks.* 1967: *Easy Come, Easy Go.*

McINTIRE, John 1907–1991

Dark-haired American actor with tightly concentrated features, a taller, thinner-faced version of Barry Fitzgerald. He looked as if he ought to be wearing rimless spectacles even when he wasn't and could play wily villains and caring professional men with equal facility. McIntire often didn't get the billing he deserved during his 1950s stay in Hollywood, and was largely lost to long-running western series on TV after 1961. Married to actress Jeanette Nolan (1911–). Actor Tim McIntire (1943–1986) was their son. Died from cancer.

1947: *Call Northside 777.* 1948: *Black Bart (GB: Black Bart—Highwayman). River Lady. An Act of Murder. The Street with No Name. Command Decision.* 1949: *Down to the Sea in Ships. Ambush. Red Canyon. Johnny Stoolpigeon. Top of the Morning. Francis. Scene of the Crime.* 1950: *The Asphalt Jungle. No Sad Songs for Me. Walk Softly Stranger. Shadow on the Wall. Winchester 73. Saddle Tramp. Under the Gun. USS Teakettle (later You're in the Navy Now).* 1951: *The Raging Tide. That's My Boy. Westward the Women.* 1952: *The World in His Arms. Glory Alley. Horizons West. Sally and Saint Anne. The Lawless Breed.* 1953: *The President's Lady. Mississippi Gambler. A Lion is in the Streets. War Arrow.* 1954: *The Far Country. The Yellow Mountain. Four Guns to the Border. There's No Business Like Show Business. Apache.* 1955: *Stranger on Horseback. The Kentuckian. The Phenix City Story (GB: The Phoenix City Story). The Scarlet Coat. To Hell and Back (narrator only). The Spoilers.* 1956: *World in My Corner. Away All Boats. Backlash. I've Lived Before.* 1957: *The Tin Star.* 1958: *Sing, Boy, Sing. Mark of the Hawk/Accused. The Light in the Forest. The Gunfight at Dodge City.* 1959: *Who Was That Lady?* 1960: *Psycho. Elmer Gantry. Seven Ways From Sundown. Flaming Star.* 1961: *Two Rode Together. Summer and Smoke.* 1967: *Rough Night in Jericho,* 1970:

Longstreet (TV). Powderkeg (TV. GB: cinemas). 1971: Bayou Boy. 1973: Linda (TV). Herbie Rides Again. 1974: The Healers (TV). 1975: Rooster Cogburn. 1976: The New Daughters of Joshua Cabe (TV). 1977: Aspen (TV. GB: The Crisis at Sun Valley). The Rescuers (voice only). 1978: Lassie: The New Beginning (TV). The Jordan Chance (TV). 1979: Mrs R's Daughter (TV). 1981: American Dream (TV). The Fox and the Hound (voice only). 1983: Honkytonk Man. 1984: Cloak and Dagger. 1989: Dream Breakers (TV). Turner & Hooch.

McKERN, Leo
(Reginald McKern) 1920–
Rotund, florid, dark-haired Australian—an engineer turned commercial artist turned actor. Brought his distinctive throaty tones and aggressive approach to Britain in 1946, and was briefly in star roles in the early sixties. Had great personal success in the seventies and beyond in the long-lasting TV comedy-drama series *Rumpole of the Bailey.*

*1952: Murder in the Cathedral. 1955: All for Mary. 1956: X the Unknown. 1957: Time Without Pity. A Tale of Two Cities. 1959: Beyond This Place (US: Web of Evidence). The Mouse That Roared. Yesterday's Enemy. 1960: Jazzboat. Mikhali (narrator only). Scent of Mystery (GB: Holiday in Spain). *The Running, Jumping and Standing Still Film. 1961: The Day the Earth Caught Fire. Mr Topaze (US: I Like Money). 1962: The Inspector (US: Lisa) The Horse Without a Head (US: TV). 1963: Doctor in Distress. A Jolly Bad Fellow (US: They All Died Laughing). Hot Enough for June (US: Agent 8¾). 1964: King and Country. 1965: Help. The Amorous Adventures of Moll Flanders. 1966: A Man for All Seasons. 1967: Assignment K. 1968: Nobody Runs Forever. The Shoes of the Fisherman. Decline and Fall ... of a Birdwatcher! 1970: Ryan's Daughter. 1973: Massacre in Rome. 1975: The Adventure of Sherlock Holmes' Smarter Brother. 1976: The Omen. 1977: Candleshoe. 1978: Damien—Omen II. The Nativity (TV). 1979: The House on Garibaldi Street (TV. GB: cinemas). The Last Tasmanian (narrator only). The Lion, the Witch and the Wardrobe (TV. Voice only). 1980: The Blue Lagoon. 1981: The French Lieutenant's Woman. 1984: Ladyhawke. The Voyage of Bounty's Child (Narrator only). 1985: The Chain. Murder With Mirrors (TV). 1986: Travelling North. 1993: A Foreign Field. 1994: Good King Wenceslas (TV). 1995: On Our Selection.*

McLAUGHLIN, Gibb 1884–1960
Thin, haggard-looking British actor, often with more wrinkles than a prune in his later roles. In his earlier days a gloomy comic monologuist on stage, he came to films to lend his own touch of gleeful ghoulishness and mastery of disguise to everything from ancient retainers to oriental fiends – plus a notable leading role as Edgar Wallace's detective Mr J G Reeder. The cinema seized his unusual talents to keep him frantically busy, especially in the 1930s; by the time he reached his sixties, he could easily have passed for the world's oldest man.

1920: Beyond the Dreams of Avarice. 1921: Carnival. The Road to London. 1922: A Lowland Cinderella. The Bohemian Girl. The Pointing Finger. 1923: Three to One Against. Constant Hot Water. 1924: Claude Duval. Odd Tricks. 1925: The Only Way. Somebody's Darling. Mr Preedy and the Countess. 1926: Nell Gwyn. London. The House of Marney. 1927: Madame Pompadour. The Arcadians/Land of Heart's Desire. Poppies of Flanders. 1928: The White Sheik. The Farmer's Wife. Glorious Youth/Eileen of the Trees. The Price of Divorce. Not Quite a Lady. 1929: Kitty. The Silent House. Power Over Men. The Woman from China. 1930: The 'W' Plan. The Brat/The Nipper. Such is the Law. The School for Scandal. 1931: Third Time Lucky. Potiphar's Wife (US: Her Strange Desire). Sally in Our Alley. Lloyd of the CID (serial. US: Detective Lloyd). My Old China. Jealousy. The Temperance Fête. Congress Dances. 1932: The Love Contract. Goodnight Vienna (US: Magic Night). Whiteface. Money Means Nothing. Where is This Lady? The First Mrs Fraser. Atlantide. 1933: The Thirteenth Candle. King of the Ritz. No Funny Business. High Finance. Britannia of Billingsgate. The Private Life of Henry VIII. Bitter Sweet. Dick Turpin. Friday the Thirteenth. 1934: Catherine the Great/The Rise of Catherine the Great. The Church Mouse. Chu-Chin-Chow. Blossom Time (US: April Romance). Little Friend. The Queen's Affair (US: Runaway Queen). Jew Süss (US: Power). There Goes Susie (US: Scandals of Paris). The Old Curiosity Shop. The Scarlet Pimpernel. 1935: The Love Affair of the Dictator (US: The Loves of a Dictator). The Iron Duke. Swinging the Lead. Bulldog Jack (US: Alias Bulldog Drummond). Drake of England (US: Drake the Pirate). Me and Marlborough. I Give My Heart. Hyde Park Corner. 1936: Two's

Company. Where There's a Will. Broken Blossoms. All In. Juggernaut. Irish for Luck. 1937: You Live and Learn. 1938: Hey! Hey! USA (shown 1937). Almost a Gentleman. Break the News. Mr Reeder in Room 13 (US: Mystery of Room 13). Hold My Hand. Thirteen Men and a Gun. The Loves of Madame DuBarry. Inspector Hornleigh. 1939: Come on George. Confidential Lady. Spy for a Day. 1940: Spellbound (US: The Spell of Amy Nugent). That's the Ticket. 1941: Freedom Radio (US: A Voice in the Night). Penn of Pennsylvania (US: The Courageous Mr Penn). 1942: The Young Mr Pitt. Much Too Shy. Tomorrow We Live (US: At Dawn We Die). 1943: My Learned Friend. 1944: Champagne Charlie. Give Us the Moon. 1945: Caesar and Cleopatra. 1947: Jassy. 1948: Oliver Twist. No Orchids for Miss Blandish. The Queen of Spades. Once Upon a Dream. 1950: Night and the City. The Black Rose. 1951: The Lavender Hill Mob. The House in the Square (US: I'll Never Forget You). 1952: The Card (US: The Promoter). Top Secret (US: Mr Potts Goes to Moscow). The Sound Barrier (US: Breaking the Sound Barrier). The Oracle (US: The Horse's Mouth). The Pickwick Papers. The Man Who Watched Trains Go By (US: Paris Express). 1953: The Million Pound Note (US: Man With a Million). Ali Baba Nights. Grand National Night (US: Wicked Wife). Hobson's Choice. 1954: Mad About Men. The Brain Machine. 1955: The Deep Blue Sea. The Man Who Never Was. Who Done It? 1957: Sea Wife.

McLEOD, Gordon 1889–1961
Dark-haired, stern-looking, moustachioed British actor who came from repertory work in his native Devon to become a character star of the London stage. Regular film work, too, came along in the 1930s, usually in humourless, villainous or exasperated roles. Balding and bespectacled from this period onwards, he was at his best as Alastair Sim's cigar-chewing editor in *The Squeaker* in 1937, but the quality of his roles declined from the 1940s onwards, and he retired in 1954.

*1911: *The Parson Puts His Foot in It. 1919: A Smart Set. 1925: The Only Way. 1928: David Garrick. 1930: The Virtuous Sin (GB: Cast Iron). 1931: The Devil to Pay. 1932: 1933: Chelsea Life. Mixed Doubles. 1934: Lucky Loser. Death at Broadcasting House. The*

Primrose Path. Brides to Be. The Case for the Crown. Borrow a Million. 1935: The Silent Passenger. 1936: To Catch a Thief. The Crimson Circle. Nothing Like Publicity. Not Wanted on Voyage (US: Treachery on the High Seas). Talk of the Devil. 1937: The Show Goes On. Knight Without Armour. The Squeaker (US: Murder on Diamond Row). The Frog. Victoria the Great. The Rat. 1938: Sixty Glorious Years (US: Queen of Destiny). Thistledown. The Drum (US: Drums). I See Ice. Double or Quits. Dangerous Medicine. 1939: Confidential Lady. Q Planes (US: Clouds Over Europe). The Saint in London. Hoots Mon! 1940: Crooks' Tour. That's the Ticket. The Girl in the News. Two for Danger. 1941: The Patient Vanishes/This Man is Dangerous. The Saint's Vacation. The Prime Minister. Facing the Music. The Saint Meets the Tiger. Banana Ridge. Hatter's Castle. 1942: The Balloon Goes Up. The First of the Few (US: Spitfire). We'll Smile Again. 1943: The Yellow Canary. 1944: Tawny Pipit. Meet Sexton Blake. He Snoops to Conquer. 1945: I Didn't Do It. Night Boat to Dublin. 1946: Under New Management. 1947: Easy Money. 1948: Corridor of Mirrors. The Winslow Boy. 1949: Floodtide. The Twenty Questions Murder Mystery. 1950: Chance of a Lifetime. Once a Sinner. 1951: Flesh and Blood. The Galloping Major. A Case for PC 49. Four Days. 1953: The Triangle. The Million Pound Note (US: Man With a Million). Johnny on the Run. 1954: The Diamond (US: Diamond Wizard). A Tale of Three Women. The House Across the Lake (US: Heatwave). 1955: The Man Who Loved Redheads.

McMAHON, Horace 1906–1971
Flat-nosed, wry-mouthed, dark-haired American actor whose frankly homely features were seen as a variety of chisellers and sharpies until stage and film success as the hard-pressed police lieutenant in *Detective Story* left him equally typed as the hard-nosed but basically sympathetic sergeant or senior detective, a role he also played with great success in the TV series *Naked City*. Long married to lovely red-haired actress Louise Campbell (L. Weisbecker 1915–) from the *Bulldog Drummond* films — a true mating of Beauty and the Beast. Died from a heart ailment.

1937: The Wrong Road. Bad Guy. Navy Blues. Exclusive. A Girl with Ideas. Double Wedding.

Paid to Dance. The Last Gangster. They Gave Him a Gun. Kid Galahad. 1938: Tenth Avenue Kid. When G-Men Step In. I Am the Law. Fast Company. Ladies in Distress. King of the Newsboys. Secrets of a Nurse. The Crowd Roars. Broadway Musketeers. Pride of the Navy. Alexander's Ragtime Band. Gangs of New York. Marie Antoinette. Federal Man Hunt (GB: Flight from Justice). 1939: Rose of Washington Square. Sergeant Madden. The Gracie Allen Murder Case. I Was a Convict. Big Town Czar. Laugh It Off (GB: Lady Be Gay). Quick Millions. Sabotage (GB: Spies at Work). She Married a Cop. For Love or Money (GB: Tomorrow at Midnight). That's Right—You're Wrong. Newsboys' Home. Pirates of the Skies. Another Thin Man. 60,000 Enemies. Calling Dr Kildare. 1940: Gangs of Chicago. Dr Kildare's Crisis. The Marines Fly High. I Can't Give You Anything But Love, Baby. Margie. Millionaires in Prison. Oh Johnny, How You Can Love. Dr Kildare's Strangest Case. The Ghost Comes Home. The Leather Pushers. Melody Ranch. We Who Are Young. Dr Kildare Goes Home. My Favourite Wife. 1941: Come Live with Me. Dangerous Blondes. Rookies on Parade. Lady Scarface. Dr Kildare's Wedding Day (GB: Mary Names the Day). The Bride Wore Crutches. Birth of the Blues. The Stork Pays Off. Buy Me That Town. 1942: Jail House Blues. 1944: The Navy Way. Timber Queen. Roger Touhy, Gangster (GB: The Last Gangster). 1946: 13 Rue Madeleine. 1948: Fighting Mad (GB: Joe Palooka in Fighting Mad). The Return of October (GB: Date with Destiny). Smart Woman. Waterfront at Midnight. 1951: Detective Story. 1953: Abbott and Costello Go to Mars. Fast Company. Champ for a Day. Man in the Dark. 1954: Duffy of San Quentin (GB: Men Behind Bars). Susan Slept Here. 1955: My Sister Eileen. Blackboard Jungle. Texas Lady. 1957: Beau James. The Delicate Delinquent. 1959: Never Steal Anything Small. 1966: The Swinger. 1968: The Detective.

McMILLAN, Kenneth 1932–1989
Rotund, crinkly-haired, ruby-cheeked, round-faced, dyspeptic-looking New Yorker who came to acting at 30 after working for years as floor superintendent, then manager at a large department store. After extensive work in daytime soap operas on TV, McMillan came to films at 41, huffing and puffing his way through dozens of roles as

editors, police chiefs, fire chiefs and other blue-collar executives, often with aggressive qualities. He also scored in quieter roles, as concerned fathers, and especially as the dotty vet who treats wounded Nick Nolte as though he were a dog in *Three Fugitives*, McMillan's last cinema film, made shortly before his death from liver disease at 56. Furiously busy in the early 1980s.

1973: Serpico. 1974: The Stepford Wives. The Taking of Pelham One-Two-Three. 1977: Johnny, We Hardly Knew Ye (TV). 1978: Bloodbrothers. Breaking Up (TV). A Death in Canaan (TV). Oliver's Story. Girlfriends. 1979: Chilly Scenes of Winter. Salem's Lot (TV). Manhattan. Carny. Head Over Heels. 1980: Hide in Plain Sight. Little Miss Marker. Borderline. The Hustler of Muscle Beach (TV). 1981: Eyewitness (GB: The Janitor). Ragtime. Whose Life is it, Anyway? Heartbeeps. True Confessions. 1982: Partners. In the Custody of Strangers (TV). 1983: Dixie: Changing Habits (TV). Blue Skies Again. Murder 1, Dancer 0 (TV). Packin' It In (TV). 1984: The Killing Hour (shot 1982). Reckless. When She Says No (TV). Protocol. Cat's Eye. Concrete Beat (TV). Dune. 1985: The Pope of Greenwich Village. Runaway Train. 1986: Armed and Dangerous. Acceptable Risks (TV). 1987: Malone. 1989: Three Fugitives. Top of the Hill (TV).

McNAUGHTON, Gus
(Augustus Howard) 1884–1969
Hollywood had dozens of drily comic sidekicks and fast-talking reporters. But McNaughton was one of the few British character men who fitted into those categories. Originally a stand-up music hall comic, he could do a double-take with the best of them. Small-chinned, large-nosed, thin-lipped and wrinkle-browed, he talked the comedy hero out of more than one tight situation (and, on occasions, into them) and was an enjoyable foil in several George Formby comedies.

1929: Comets. 1930: Murder. Children of Chance. 1932: The Last Coupon. Lucky Girl. Money Talks. Maid of the Mountains. His Wife's Mother. 1933: Radio Parade. Their Night Out. Leave It to Me. Heads We Go (US: The Charming Deceiver). The Love Nest. Song Birds. Crime on the Hill. 1934: Happy. Bagged. Master and Man. Seeing is Believing. Luck of a

Sailor. Wishes. There Goes Susie (US: Scandals of Paris). Crazy People. Spring in the Air. Barnacle Bill. 1935: Royal Cavalcade (US: Regal Cavalcade). The 39 Steps. Joy Ride. Music Hath Charms. Invitation to the Waltz. The Crouching Beast. 1936: Not So Dusty. Keep Your Seats Please. Southern Roses. The Heirloom Mystery. Busman's Holiday. You Must Get Married. 1937: The Strange Adventures of Mr Smith. Storm in a Teacup. Action for Slander. Keep Fit. South Riding. 1938: The Divorce of Lady X. We're Going to be Rich. St Martin's Lane (US: Sidewalks of London). You're the Doctor. Keep Smiling (US: Smiling Along). Easy Riches. 1939: All at Sea. What Would You Do Chums? Blind Folly. Q Planes (US: Clouds over Europe). Trouble Brewing. I Killed the Count (US: Who is Guilty?). There Ain't No Justice! 1940: Two for Danger. George and Margaret. That's the Ticket. Old Bill and Son. 1941: Facing the Music. Jeannie (US: Girl in Distress). South American George. Penn of Pennsylvania (US: The Courageous Mr Penn). 1942: Let the People Sing. Much Too Shy. Rose of Tralee. The Day Will Dawn (US: The Avengers). 1943: The Shipbuilders. 1944: Demobbed. 1945: A Place of One's Own. Here Comes the Sun. The Trojan Brothers. 1947: The Turners of Prospect Road. 1948: This Was a Woman. Lucky Mascot/Brass Monkey.

Helter Skelter. 1950: Someone at the Door. Trio. Shadow of the Past. Four in a Jeep. The Lady Craved Excitement. 1951: The Long Dark Hall. 1952: Hindle Wakes (US: Holiday Week). Curtain Up. Top Secret (US: Mr Potts Goes to Moscow). Love's a Luxury (US: The Caretaker's Daughter). Miss Robin Hood. The Oracle (US: The Horse's Mouth). 1953: Genevieve. Street Corner. Malta Story. Spaceways. The Intruder. 1954: Bang! You're Dead (US: Game of Danger). The Green Scarf. The Teckman Mystery. The Harassed Hero. 1955: Above Us the Waves. Doctor at Sea. 1956: *A Man on the Beach. Charley Moon. A Hill in Korea (US: Hell in Korea). Checkpoint. The Man in the Road. 1957: The Steel Bayonet. Doctor at Large. 1958: The Duke Wore Jeans. The Wind Cannot Read. I Only Arsked! 1959: Carry on Nurse. Heart of a Man. 1962: The Longest Day. Crooks Anonymous. 1963: It's All Happening. Night Must Fall. Kali-Yug—Goddess of Vengeance. Kali-Yug: the Mystery of the Indian Tomb. 1964: Rattle of a Simple Man. I've Gotta Horse. 1965: 24 Hours to Kill. 1966: The Sandwich Man. A Countess from Hong Kong. 1969: Spring and Port Wine. The Engagement. Scrooge. 1973: O Lucky Man! 1974: Law and Disorder. 1980: The Sea Wolves. 1982: Britannia Hospital. 1983: Never Say Never Again. 1984: The Jigsaw Man. 1986: Hotel du Paradis. 1988: Just Ask for Diamond. 1989: The Endless Game (TV). 1990: The Fool. 1993: Staggered.

Heart. Love, Honor and Oh! Baby. 1934: The Defense Rests. Romance in Manhattan. Bedside. Mrs Wiggs of the Cabbage Patch. Hi, Nellie! Murder at the Vanities. What Every Woman Knows. The Captain Hates the Sea. The Last Gentleman. The Merry Widow. Only Eight Hours. The Whole Town's Talking (GB: Passport to Fame). 1935: Biography of a Bachelor Girl. The Return of Peter Grimm. Village Tale. Old Man Rhythm. Accent on Youth. Society Doctor. Baby Face Harrington. Barbary Coast. Captain Blood. Peter Ibbetson. China Seas. Happiness COD. Top Hat. The Informer. The Gilded Lily. The Bride Comes Home. Mark of the Vampire. Kind Lady (GB: House of Menace). She Couldn't Take It. 1936: Pennies from Heaven. Everybody's Old Man. Three Wise Guys. Love on the Run. Two in a Crowd. And So They Were Married. One Rainy Afternoon. Old Hutch. Three Married Men. 1937: Artists and Models. Maid of Salem. Double Wedding. Behind the Headlines. Make a Wish. You're a Sweetheart. Parnell. Three Legionnaires. The Toast of New York. Breakfast for Two. 1938: Adventures of Tom Sawyer. Double Danger. Little Miss Broadway. You Can't Take It with You. Hold That Co-Ed (GB: Hold That Girl). Having Wonderful Time. Goodbye Broadway. 1939: Hollywood Cavalcade. Jesse James. Stagecoach. Blondie Takes a Vacation. The Housekeeper's Daughter. Young Mr Lincoln. Nick Carter, Master Detective. 1940: Dr Ehrlich's Magic Bullet (GB: The Story of Dr Ehrlich's Magic Bullet). The Man from Dakota (GB: Arouse and Beware). The Ghost Comes Home. Phantom Raiders. Third Finger, Left Hand. Turnabout. Star Dust. Hullabaloo. Sky Murder. The Return of Frank James. My Little Chickadee. Oh Johnny, How You Can Love. 1941: A Woman's Face. Design for Scandal. Blonde Inspiration. Rise and Shine. The Feminine Touch. Wild Man of Borneo. Come Live with Me. Babes on Broadway. Barnacle Bill. 1942: Seven Sweethearts. Tortilla Flat. The Omaha Trail. Maisie Gets Her Man (GB: She Got Her Man). Keeper of the Flame. They Got Me Covered. 1943: Air Raid Wardens. DuBarry Was a Lady. Lost Angel. 1944: Maisie Goes to Reno (GB: You Can't Do That to Me). Rationing. Bathing Beauty. Two Girls and a Sailor. The Thin Man Goes Home. Barbary Coast Gent. 1945: State Fair. Colonel Effingham's Raid (GB: Man of the Hour). 1946: Janie Gets Married. Affairs of Geraldine. Because of Him. 1947: The Fabulous Joe. Magic Town.

MEDWIN, Michael 1923–

Cheery-looking, sandy-haired British actor of youthful aspect and pronounced lower lip. Usually seen as brash young men, cockney crooks or soldiers up to all the dodges, he sprinkled these characterizations later with a few lounge-suited wiseacres. Rattled up nearly 70 films before becoming a successful producer. Now only occasionally seen as an actor, although he made a welcome reappearance in a running role in the TV series Shoestring in the early 1980s.

1946: Piccadilly Incident. The Root of All Evil. 1947: Just William's Luck. The Courtneys of Curzon Street (US: The Courtney Affair). Black Memory. An Ideal Husband. 1948: Call of the Blood. Anna Karenina. William Comes to Town. Night Beat. Woman Hater. My Sister and I. Another Shore. Look Before You Love. Operation Diamond. Forbidden. 1949: The Queen of Spades. For Them That Trespass. Trottie True (US: Gay Lady). Boys in Brown.

MEEK, Donald 1880–1946

Dumpy, bald, Scottish-born actor in Hollywood films. With sad eyes, long, thin mouth petering out in the folds of his chubby cheeks, little nose and blinky gaze, he was constantly in employment from the coming of sound until his death, almost always in roles that matched his name—although he could play a nice variety of tunes on the one fiddle. Died from leukaemia.

1923: Six Cylinder Love. 1929: The Hole in the Wall. 1930: The Love Kiss. 1931: Personal Maid. The Girl Habit. *The Clyde Mystery. *The Wall Street Mystery. *The Weekend Mystery. 1932: *The Babbling Book. *The Symphony Murder Mystery. *The Skull Murder Mystery. *Murder in the Pullman. *The Side Show Mystery. *The Crane Poison Case. *The Campus Mystery. Wayward. 1933: College Coach (GB: Football Coach). Ever in My

MEILLON, John 1933–1989

Fair-haired, plump-cheeked Australian actor who came to Britain for a few years in the early 1960s to play scruffy servicemen and slightly down-at-heel figures in crime stories, then returned 'down under' to play ruddy-cheeked, hard-drinking, trilby-hatted businessmen, most notably in the two Crocodile Dundee films. His son John Meillon Jr is also a film actor.

1959: On the Beach. 1960: The Sundowners. Offbeat. The Long and the Short and the Tall. 1961: Watch It Sailor! The Valiant. 1962: Operation Snatch. Billy Budd. Death Trap. The Longest Day. 1963: Cairo. The Running Man. 1964: 633 Squadron. Guns at Batasi.

1965: Dead Man's Chest. 1966: They're a Weird Mob. 1970: Outback. Walkabout. 1972: Sunstruck. 1974: The Cars That Ate Paris. Sidecar Racers. The Dove. Inn of the Damned. 1975: Ride a Wild Pony. 1977: Shimmering Light/Something Light. The Picture Show Man. Born to Run. 1978: The Fourth Wish (TV). 1980: Timelapse. 1981: Heatwave. 1983: The Dismissal. The Wild Duck. 1984: The Camel Boy (voice only). 1985: The Man in the Iron Mask (TV). 1986: Blue Lightning. Frenchman's Farm. Bullseye. 'Crocodile' Dundee (GB and US: Crocodile Dundee). 1987: The Everlasting Secret Family. 1988: Outback Bound (TV). Crocodile Dundee II.

MELVIN, Murray 1932–
Long-faced, snooty-looking, dark-haired, at times sensitive British actor who scored as the sympathetic young homosexual in *A Taste of Honey*, but has since been less successfully cast in more extravagant roles, doing his best work in other media.

1960: Suspect (US: The Risk). The Criminal (US: The Concrete Jungle). 1961: A Taste of Honey. Petticoat Pirates. 1962: HMS Defiant (US: Damn the Defiant!). Solo for Sparrow. Sparrows Can't Sing. 1963: The Ceremony. 1966: Alfie. Kaleidoscope. 1967: Smashing Time. 1968: The Fixer. Nobody Runs Forever (US: The High Commissioner). 1969: Start the Revolution Without Me. 1971: The Devils. The Boy Friend. A Day in the Death of Joe Egg. 1973: Ghost in the Noonday Sun (unreleased). Gawain and the Green Knight. 1974: Ghost Story. 1975: Lisztomania. Barry Lyndon. The Bawdy Adventures of Tom Jones. 1976: Shout

at the Devil. Joseph Andrews. Gulliver's Travels (voice only). 1977: The Prince and the Pauper (US: Crossed Swords). 1979: Stories from a Flying Trunk. 1982: Nutcracker. 1985: Sacred Hearts. 1986: Comrades. 1987: Testimony. Little Dorrit I. Little Dorrit II. 1989: Slipstream. 1990: The Krays. The Fool. 1991: Prisoners of Honor. 'Let Him Have It'. 1992: As You Like It. 1994: Princess Caraboo.

MERCER, Beryl
See Herbert, Holmes

MERKEL, Una 1903–1986
Prettily pixieish American actress with dimpled cheeks and red-gold hair, sometimes in leading roles in the thirties, but more often as the heroine's wisecracking friend or characters called Tootsie, Trixie and the like. In post-war years, looking more sprite-like than ever, she turned up as maiden aunts and sassy spinsters. Oscar nominee for *Summer and Smoke*.

1920: Way Down East. 1923: The White Rose. 1924: †World Shadows. *Love's Old Sweet Song. The Fifth Horseman. 1930: Abraham Lincoln. The Bat Whispers. Eyes of the World. 1931: Six Cylinder Love. The Maltese Falcon. Command Performance. Wicked. Secret Witness/Terror by Night. Don't Bet on Women. Daddy Long Legs. The Bargain. Private Lives. 1932: Red-Headed Woman. She Wanted a Millionaire. Man Wanted. They Call It Sin (GB: The Way of Life). Huddle (GB: Impossible Lover). Impatient Maiden. Men Are Such Fools. 1933: Reunion in Vienna. Whistling in the Dark. Beauty for Sale (GB: Beauty). Her First Mate. Bombshell. The Women in His Life. 42nd Street. Midnight Mary. Broadway to Hollywood (GB: Ring Up the Curtain). Day of Reckoning. Clear All Wires. The Secret of Madame Blanche. 1934: Paris Interlude. This Side of Heaven. Murder in the Private Car (GB: Murder on the Runaway Train). The Cat's Paw. The Merry Widow. Bulldog Drummond Strikes Back. Have a Heart. Evelyn Prentice. 1935: Biography of a Bachelor Girl. One New York Night (GB: The Trunk Mystery). Murder in the Fleet. Baby Face Harrington. It's in the Air. Riffraff. The Night is Young. Broadway Melody of 1936. Speed. We Went to College (GB: The Old School Tie). *How to Stuff a Goose. Born to Dance. 1937: Don't Tell the Wife. Saratoga. Good Old Soak. True Confession. Checkers. 1938: Test Pilot. 1939:

Four Girls in White. On Borrowed Time. Destry Rides Again. Some Like It Hot. 1940: Saturday's Children. Comin' Round the Mountain. The Bank Dick (GB: The Bank Detective). Sandy Gets Her Man. 1941: Cracked Nuts. Double Date. Road to Zanzibar. 1942: Twin Beds. The Mad Doctor of Market Street. 1943: This is the Army. *Quack Service. 1944: *To Heir is Human. *Bachelor Daze. Sweethearts of the USA (GB: Sweethearts on Parade). 1947: It's a Joke, Son. 1948: The Bride Goes Wild. The Man from Texas. 1950: Kill the Umpire. My Blue Heaven. Emergency Wedding (GB: Jealousy). 1951: Rich, Young and Pretty. Golden Girl. A Millionaire for Christy. 1952: With a Song in My Heart. The Merry Widow (remake). I Love Melvin. 1955: The Kentuckian. 1956: Bundle of Joy. The Kettles in the Ozarks. 1957: The Greer Case (TV). The Fuzzy Pink Nightgown. The Girl Most Likely. 1959: The Mating Game. 1961: Summer and Smoke. The Parent Trap. 1963: Summer Magic. A Tiger Walks. 1966: Spinout (GB: California Holiday).

† Unfinished.

MERLIN, Jan 1924–
Fair-haired, lean-jawed American actor with mean eyes and hyena smile. Good-looking in a threatening sort of way, the New Yorker enrolled in theatrical school as a teenager, but struggled along in stock before TV success in *Tom Corbett, Space Cadet*; he was the wisecracking cadet whose catchphrase 'Go blow your jets' became a watchword for American children while the series ran from 1950 to 1955. When he won praise for a Broadway performance of *Rope*, a film contract with Universal-International followed. Despite effective appearances as blond menaces, Merlin didn't quite make the front rank there, and his best work continued to be for the theatre; film appearances have become more sporadic with the passing years.

1955: Six Bridges to Cross. Running Wild. Illegal. 1956: Screaming Eagles. A Strange Adventure. A Day of Fury. The Peacemaker. 1957: Woman and the Hunter (GB: Triangle on Safari). 1958: Cole Younger, Gunfighter. 1959: The Travels of Jaimie McPheeters (TV). 1960: Hell Bent for Leather. 1963: Gunfight at Comanche Creek. 1964: Guns of Diablo. 1967: The St Valentine's Day Massacre. 1968: Strategy of Terror. 1969: Take the Money and

Run. 1972: Twilight People. 1973: I Escaped from Devil's Island. The Slams. 1975: The Hindenburg. 1986: The Gladiator (TV). 1990: Buried Alive (TV). Sweet 15 (TV). 1991: Silk 2 (made 1989).

MERRITT, George 1890–1977

Solid, dependable, fair-haired British actor, on the short side but built like a barn door, who maximized his long career with nearly 80 London theatrical appearances, more than 100 films, and translations and adaptations of several European plays for the London stage. He first trod the boards at 19, but had the misfortune to be studying theatre in Germany at the outbreak of World War I and was interned for the next four years in a prisoner-of-war camp. In films he usually played upholders of the law who were often by no means as dense as they seemed.

1930: Thread o' Scarlet. The 'W' Plan. 1931: A Gentleman of Paris. Bracelets. Dreyfus (US: The Dreyfus Case). 1932: The Blind Spot. The Lodger (US: The Phantom Fiend). Little Fella. 1933: FP 1. White Face. Mr Quincy of Monte Carlo. I Was a Spy. Double Bluff. Going Straight. The Fire Raisers. The Ghost Camera. Crime on the Hill. Turkey Time. 1934: Jew Süss (US: Power). No Escape. My Song for You. Love, Life and Laughter. The Silver Spoon. Nine Forty-Five. 1935: The Clairvoyant. Emil and the Detectives (US: Emil). Jubilee Window. Mr Cohen Takes a Walk. Brown on Resolution (later For Ever England. US: Born for Glory). Ten Minute Alibi. Me and Marlborough. Drake of England (US: Drake the Pirate). Crime Unlimited. Line Engaged. Ticket of Leave. 1936: Rembrandt. Windbag the Sailor. Everything is Thunder. Spy of Napoleon. Dusty Ermine (US: Hideout in the Alps). Prison Breaker. The Man Behind the Mask. Educated Evans. Love at Sea. 1937: Dr Syn. Young and Innocent (US: The Girl Was Young). The Rat. The Vicar of Bray. The Compulsory Wife. The Vulture. Wife of General Ling. Dangerous Fingers (US: Wanted by Scotland Yard). The Return of the Scarlet Pimpernel. 1938: Convict 99. They Drive by Night. The Gaunt Stranger (US: The Phantom Strikes). Mr Reeder in Room 13 (US: Mystery of Room 13). No Parking. 1939: All at Sea. Q Planes (US: Clouds Over Europe). A Window in London (US: Lady in Distress). Young Man's

Fancy. Meet Maxwell Archer (US: Maxwell Archer, Detective). The Proud Valley. The Four Just Men (US: The Secret Four). 1940: The Case of the Frightened Lady (US: The Frightened Lady). Two for Danger. They Came by Night. Spare a Copper. Gasbags. 1941: Ships with Wings. The Big Blockade. Breach of Promise (US: Adventure in Blackmail). The Ghost Train. He Found a Star. The Black Sheep of Whitehall. Hatter's Castle. They Flew Alone (US: Wings and the Woman). 1942: The Day Will Dawn (US: The Avengers). Back Room Boy. Let the People Sing. Women Aren't Angels. Asking for Trouble. We'll Smile Again. 1943: The Adventures of Tartu (US: Tartu). Variety Jubilee. The Yellow Canary. Undercover (US: Underground Guerillas). Escape to Danger. 1944: Love Story (US: A Lady Surrenders). The Way Ahead (US: Immortal Battalion). A Canterbury Tale. Demobbed. Don't Take It to Heart. Waterloo Road. Give Me the Stars. 1945: For You Alone. Don Chicago. Home Sweet Home. The Voice Within. I'll Be Your Sweetheart. 1946: Daybreak. I'll Turn to You. Quiet Weekend. 1947: The Man Within (US: The Smugglers). Nicholas Nickleby. The Root of All Evil. The Upturned Glass. Daughter of Darkness. 1948: Bonnie Prince Charlie. Love in Waiting. Good Time Girl. My Brother's Keeper. Calling Paul Temple. Quartet. 1949: Marry Me! Dark Secret. 1950: Something in the City. Mr Drake's Duck. Pool of London. 1953: Small Town Story. Noose for a Lady. 1954: Night of the Full Moon. The Green Scarf. The End of the Road. 1957: Quatermass II (US: Enemy from Space). 1958: Dracula (US: The Horror of Dracula). Tread Softly, Stranger. 1960: The Full Treatment (US: Stop Me Before I Kill). The Hands of Orlac. The Day the Earth Caught Fire. 1962: What Every Woman Wants. 1968: Crooks and Coronets (US: Sophie's Place).

MERVYN, William
(W. M. Pickwood) 1912–1976

Generously girthed, double-chinned, balding, hail-fellow-well-met British actor whose portentously plummy voice made him a favourite on radio before and during World War II. Film roles were very few and far between in those days, but he became immensely popular in television series

(latterly perfectly cast as a bishop in All Gas and Gaiters) as well as working prodigiously in the theatre. Born in Nairobi, Kenya.

1947: The Loves of Joanna Godden. The Mark of Cain. 1949: That Dangerous Age (US: If This Be Sin). Stop Press Girl. Marry Me! Helter Skelter. The Blue Lamp. 1954: Conflict of Wings (US: Fuss Over Feathers). 1956: Tons of Trouble. The Long Arm (US: The Third Key). 1957: The Admirable Crichton (US: Paradise Lagoon). Barnacle Bill (US: All at Sea). 1958: Carve Her Name with Pride. Dunkirk. 1959: Upstairs and Downstairs. The Battle of the Sexes. A Touch of Larceny. 1960: Circus of Horrors. No Love for Johnnie. 1961: Invasion Quartet. Watch It, Sailor! 1963: Tamahine. Hot Enough for June (US: Agent 8¾). 1964: Murder Ahoy. 1965: The Legend of Young Dick Turpin. Operation Crossbow (US: The Great Spy Mission). Up Jumped a Swagman. 1966: The Jokers. 1967: Deadlier Than the Male. Follow That Camel. 1968: Salt and Pepper. Hammerhead. Hot Millions. The Best House in London. 1969: Carry On Again, Doctor. 1970: Incense for the Damned/Doctors Wear Scarlet. Carry On Henry. The Railway Children. 1971: The Ruling Class. The Magnificent Six and ½ (third series). 1972: Up the Front. 1973: Charley One-Eye. 1975: The Bawdy Adventures of Tom Jones. 1976: Chimpmates (first series).

MEYER, Emile 1908–1987

It's always something of a shock to realize that someone you thought had appeared in hundreds of films didn't make anywhere near that number. And, even though this big, burly, disgruntled-looking American actor, who always looked about 48, did make just over 50, that's fewer than one had imagined. His drawn-back dark hair and furrowed brows were seen as prison wardens, sheriffs, fight managers and cops and administrators both crooked and straight. Began acting in repertory, but films drew him in from 1950 and he also did much character work on TV. Died from Alzheimer's disease.

1950: Panic in the Streets. Cattle Queen (GB: Queen of the West). 1951: The Big Night. The Guy Who Came Back. The People Against O'Hara. The Mob (GB: Remember That Face). 1952: Bloodhounds of Broadway. Carbine

Williams. *The Wild North. Hurricane Smith. We're Not Married.* 1953: *Shane. Girls in the Night* (GB: *Life After Dark*). *The Farmer Takes a Wife.* 1954: *Drums Across the River. Shield for Murder. Silver Lode. Riot in Cell Block 11. The Human Jungle.* 1955: *Blackboard Jungle. Stranger on Horseback. White Feather. The Man with the Gun* (GB: *The Trouble Shooter*). *The Girl in the Red Velvet Swing. The Man with the Golden Arm. The Tall Men.* 1956: *The Maverick Queen. Raw Edge. Gun the Man Down.* 1957: *Sweet Smell of Success. Baby Face Nelson. Paths of Glory. The Delicate Delinquent. Badlands of Montana.* 1958: *Good Day for a Hanging. The Case Against Brooklyn. The Fiend Who Walked the West. The Lineup. Revolt in the Big House.* 1959: *The Girl in Lovers' Lane. King of the Wild Stallions.* 1960: *The Threat. Young Jesse James.* 1963: *Move Over, Darling.* 1964: *Taggart.* 1965: *Young Dillinger.* 1967: *Hostile Guns. A Time for Killing* (GB: *The Long Ride Home*). 1968: *Buckskin. More Dead Than Alive.* 1969: *A Time for Dying.* 1973: *The Blue Knight* (TV. GB: cinemas [abridged]). *The Outfit. Macon County Line.* 1977: *The Legend of Frank Woods.*

MIDDLETON, Charles 1878–1949
American actor with black hair, reptilian eyes and cruel, shifty looks — a perfect murder case suspect, in fact, or out-and-out villain, most memorably as Ming the Merciless in the three *Flash Gordon* serials. In his youth a circus ringmaster, then vaudevillian, he came to Hollywood at 50, although he never looked his age, and racked up almost 150 films in the 20 years remaining to him. Also notable as the harsh fort commandant in both Laurel and Hardy's Foreign Legion films. He married Leora Spellman, an actress 13 years his junior, but she died from a heart attack at 54.

1928: **A Man of Peace. The Farmer's Daughter.* 1929: *The Bellamy Trial. The Far Call. Welcome Danger.* 1930: *East Is West. *The Frame. Beau Bandit. Way Out West. *Christmas Knight. *More Sinned Against Than Usual. Framed.* 1931: *An American Tragedy. Full of Notions. Ship of Hate. Beau Hunks* (GB: *Beau Chumps*). *Safe in Hell* (GB: *The Lost Lady*). *Caught Plastered. The Miracle Woman. Palmy Days. Alexander Hamilton. Sob

Sister* (GB: *The Blonde Reporter*). *A Dangerous Affair.* 1932: *The Hatchet Man* (GB: *The Honourable Mr Wong*). *High Pressure. A House Divided. Manhattan Parade. The Sign of the Cross. I Am a Fugitive from a Chain Gang. The Strange Love of Molly Louvain. Pack Up Your Troubles. Hell's Highway. Mystery Ranch. Kongo. The Phantom President. Silver Dollar. Breach of Promise. Rockabye. Tomorrow at Seven.* 1933: *Pickup. Sunset Pass. Destination Unknown. Disgraced. The Bowery. The World Changes. Mr Skitch. This Day and Age. Big Executive. Duck Soup. White Woman. Lone Cowboy.* 1934: *When Strangers Meet. Nana. The Last Round Up. Murder at the Vanities. Behold My Wife! Whom the Gods Destroy. We Live Again. David Harum. Broadway Bill* (GB: *Strictly Confidential*). *Mrs Wiggs of the Cabbage Patch. Massacre. Red Morning.* 1935: *Special Agent. Steamboat 'Round the Bend. *The Fixer-Uppers. The Frisco Kid. The County Chairman. Hop-a-Long Cassidy. The Square Shooter. In Spite of Danger. The Virginia Judge. Reckless. The Miracle Rider* (serial). 1936: *Flash Gordon* (serial). *Trail of the Lonesome Pine. Road Gang. Empty Saddles. Sunset of Power. Showboat. Wedding Present. Jailbreak. Song of the Saddle. A Son Comes Home. The Texas Rangers. Space Soldiers. Ramona. Career Woman.* 1937: *John Meade's Woman. Last Train from Madrid. We're on the Jury. Two-Gun Law. Slave Ship. Hollywood Cowboy/Wings Over Wyoming. Souls at Sea. The Good Earth. The Yodelin' Kid from Pine Ridge* (GB: *The Hero of Pine Ridge*). *Stand In.* 1938: *Dick Tracy Returns* (serial). *Outside the Law. Flaming Frontiers* (serial). *Strange Faces. Flash Gordon's Trip to Mars* (serial). *Kentucky. Law West of Tombstone.* 1939: *Captain Fury. Jesse James. Blackmail. Daredevils of the Red Circle* (serial). *The Oklahoma Kid. Allegheny Uprising* (GB: *The First Rebel*). *Wyoming Outlaw. Cowboys from Texas. Juarez. The Flying Deuces. $1,000 a Touchdown. Way Down South. *One Against the World.* 1940: *Chad Hanna. Abe Lincoln in Illinois* (GB: *Spirit of the People*). *Thou Shalt Not Kill. The Grapes of Wrath. Rangers of Fortune. Flash Gordon Conquers the Universe* (serial). *Shooting High. Charlie Chan's Murder Cruise. Virginia City. Brigham Young—Frontiersman* (GB: *Brigham Young*). *Santa Fé Trail. Island of Doomed Men.* 1941: *Wild Geese Calling. Sergeant York. Bad Men of Missouri. Shepherd of the Hills. Western Union. Belle Starr. Jungle Man. Wild Bill Hickok Rides.* 1942: *The Mystery of Marie Roget. Tombstone—the Town Too Tough to Die. Men of San Quentin. Perils of Nyoka* (serial). 1943: *Two Weeks To Live. The Black Raven. Hangmen Also Die. *Spook Louder. *Boobs in the Night. *Oklahoma Outlaws. Batman* (serial). **Wagon Wheels West. The Black Arrow* (serial). 1944: *The Town Went Wild. Kismet.* 1945: *Captain Kidd. How Do You Do? Hollywood and Vine* (GB: *Daisy (the Dog) Goes Hollywood*). *Our Vines Have Tender Grapes. Strangler of the Swamp. Northwest Trail. Who's Guilty?* 1946: *Spook Busters. The Killers.* 1947: *The Pretender. Welcome, Stranger. Road to Rio. Jack Armstrong* (serial). *Wyoming. Unconquered. Sea of Grass. Here Comes Trouble. Gunfighters.* 1948: *Station West. Jiggs and Maggie in Court. The Black Arrow* (GB: *The Black Arrow Strikes*. And 1943 serial).

Mr Blandings Builds His Dream House. Feudin', Fussin' and A-Fightin'. 1949: *The Last Bandit.*

MIDDLETON, Guy
(G. Middleton-Powell) 1906–1973
Brown-haired British actor with RAF-style moustache. Came late to acting after a stock exchange career, but soon became one of the cinema's most familiar faces—initially as the most hissable villain, comic or serious, in British films. Subsequently spent a fruitful 25 years playing cads, bounders, officer-types and men-from-the-ministry, with an occasional leading role thrown in. A lifelong cricket fan.

1935: *Jimmy Boy. Trust the Navy. Two Hearts in Harmony.* 1936: *Under Proof. The Gay Adventure. A Woman Alone* (US: *Two Who Dared*). *Take a Chance. The Mysterious Mr Davis. Fame.* 1937: *Keep Fit.* 1938: *Break the News.* 1939: *Goodbye Mr Chips! French Without Tears.* 1940: *For Freedom.* 1941: *Dangerous Moonlight* (US: *Suicide Squadron*). 1942: *Talk about Jacqueline.* 1943: *The Demi-Paradise* (US: *Adventure for Two*). 1944: *Halfway House. English Without Tears* (US: *Her Man Gilbey*). *Champagne Charlie.* 1945: *29 Acacia Avenue* (US: *The Facts of Love*). *The Rake's Progress* (US: *Notorious Gentleman*). *Night Boat to Dublin.* 1946: *The Captive Heart.* 1947: *The White Unicorn* (US: *Bad Sister*). *A Man About the House.* 1948: *Snowbound. One Night with You.* 1949: *Once Upon a Dream. Marry Me. No Place for Jennifer.* 1950: *The Happiest Days of Your Life.* 1951: *The Third Visitor. Laughter in Paradise. Young Wives' Tale.* 1952: *Never Look Back.* 1953: *The Fake. Albert RN* (US: *Break to Freedom*). *Front Page Story.* 1954: *The Harassed Hero. Conflict of Wings. Malaga* (US: *Fire Over Africa*). *The Belles of St Trinian's. Make Me an Offer. The Sea Shall Not Have Them. Alive on Saturday* (released 1957). 1955: *Break in the Circle. A Yank in Ermine. Gentlemen Marry Brunettes.* 1956: *Now and Forever.* 1957: *Doctor at Large. Let's Be Happy. Light Fingers.* 1958: *The Passionate Summer.* 1960: *Escort for Hire.* 1962: *Waltz of the Toreadors. What Every Woman Wants. The Fur Collar.* 1965: *Lady L.* 1969: *Oh! What a Lovely War. The Magic Christian.*

MIDDLETON, Robert

(Samuel Messer) 1911–1977

Glowering, hulking (20 stone), balding, beetle-browed American portrayer of oily villains. He studied music at college, but became a radio announcer, only quitting that job in his late thirties to try the stage. He only had around 10 fruitful years in the cinema, but they were memorable ones, as he ran up as repulsive a gallery of nasties as you could wish to relish. Middleton could play comedy, too, though, and many people remember him best as the lumbering Sir Griswold, trying to remember if the pellet with the poison was in the flagon with the dragon, in Danny Kaye's *The Court Jester*.

1954: The Silver Chalice. The Big Combo. 1955: The Desperate Hours. The Court Jester. Trial. 1956: Red Sundown. Friendly Persuasion. The Proud Ones. Love Me Tender. 1957: The Lonely Man. The Tarnished Angels. 1958: Texas John Slaughter (TV. GB: cinemas). Day of the Bad Man. No Place to Land (GB: Man Mad). The Law and Jake Wade. 1959: Don't Give Up the Ship. Career. 1960: Hell Bent for Leather. 1961: Gold of the Seven Saints. The Great Imposter. 1963: Cattle King (GB: Guns of Wyoming). 1964: For Those Who Think Young. 1966: A Big Hand for the Little Lady (GB: Big Deal at Dodge City). 1970: Company of Killers. Which Way to the Front? (GB: Ja, Ja, Mein General, But Which Way to the Front?). The Cheyenne Social Club. 1973: The Harrad Experiment. Anche gli angeli mangiano fagioli. 1974: The Mark of Zorro (TV). Remember When (TV). 1977: The Lincoln Conspiracy.

MILES, Sir Bernard

(Lord Miles) 1907–1991

Dark-haired, oval-faced British character-creator with distinctive scowling smile. On stage since 1930, he played supporting roles in films from 1933—but gained his real fame as a comic monologuist, portraying knowing rustics. In films, he was mainly cast as simple folk, but he was always well in character in Dickensian parts and, after he became passionately involved with his own London theatre (the Mermaid), it was inevitable that he should move on to a ripe Long John Silver. Knighted in 1969. Created Lord Miles in 1978. Almost blind and confined to a wheelchair in his last years.

*1933: Channel Crossing. 1934: The Love Test. 1935: Late Extra. 1936: Twelve Good Men. Crown v Stevens. Midnight at Madame Tussaud's (US: Midnight at the Wax Museum). 1937: Kew Gardens (narrator only). 1938: The Citadel. The Challenge. Convict 99. 13 Men and a Gun. They Drive by Night. Strange Boarders. The Rebel Son/Taras Bulba. Alf's Button Afloat. 1939: Q Planes (US: Clouds Over Europe). The Four Feathers. Jamaica Inn. The Spy in Black (US: U-Boat 29). The Lion Has Wings. Band Waggon. The Stars Look Down. 1940: Pastor Hall. *Dawn Guard. *Sea Cadets (narrator only). Contraband (US: Blackout). 1941: Freedom Radio (US: A Voice in the Night). This Was Paris. Quiet Wedding. *Home Guard. The Common Touch. The Big Blockade. 1942: One of Our Aircraft Is Missing. The Day Will Dawn (US: The Avengers). In Which We Serve. The First of the Few (US: Spitfire). 1943: Tunisian Victory (voice only). 1944: †Tawny Pipit. *The Two Fathers. 1946: Carnival. Great Expectations. 1947: Nicholas Nickleby. Fame is the Spur. 1948: The Guinea Pig. 1949: *Bernard Miles on Gun Dogs. 1950: †Chance of a Lifetime. 1951: The Magic Box. 1953: *River Ships (narrator only). Never Let Me Go. 1956: Moby Dick. Tiger in the Smoke. Zarak. The Man Who Knew Too Much. 1957: Doctor at Large. Fortune is a Woman (US: She Played with Fire). The Smallest Show on Earth. Saint Joan. 1958: *The Vision of William Blake (narrator only). tom thumb. 1959: Sapphire. 1961: *A Flourish of Tubes (narrator only). 1963: Heavens Above! 1965: *The Specialist. 1968: Baby Love. 1969: Run Wild, Run Free. 1983: Treasure Island—the Musical (TV). 1989: The Lady and the Highwayman (TV).*

† And co-directed

MILJAN, John 1892–1960

Appropriate that John Miljan and Charles Middleton should be close together in this book — as two of the slimiest villains that ever graced the screen. Miljan's villains were perhaps more dangerous, since he also had, under that curly hair and smooth moustache, a wolfish smile that oozed charm over many a poor, unfortunate heroine. He had some memorable exchanges with Mae West in *Belle of the Nineties*, and was still being principal nasty as late as 1955 in *Pirates of Tripoli*.

*1923: Love Letters. 1924: Lone Chance. The Painted Lady. On the Stroke of Three. The Lone Fighter/The Lone Wolf. Empty Hearts. Romance Ranch. 1925: The Unnamed Woman. Sackcloth and Scarlet. †The Phantom of the Opera. Wreckage. The Unholy Three. Overland Limited. Silent Sanderson. Flaming Waters. Morals for Men. The Unchastened Woman. Sealed Lips. 1926: The Devil's Circus. My Official Wife. Brooding Eyes. Unknown Treasures. Race Wild. Footloose Widows. The Amateur Gentleman. Devil's Island. Almost a Lady. 1927: Wolf's Clothing. The Clown. Husbands for Rent. Sailor Izzy Murphy. Final Extra. What Happened to Father? Quarantined Rivals. The Satin Woman. Lovers? Paying the Price. Rough House Rosie. The Ladybird. The Silver Slave. Stranded. Desired Woman. A Sailor's Sweetheart. The Slaver. Ham and Eggs at the Front (GB: Ham and Eggs). Framed. The Yankee Clipper. In Old San Francisco. 1928: Tenderloin. The Little Snob. The Crimson City. Lady Be Good. Glorious Betsy. Women They Talk About. The Terror. Land of the Silver Fox. The Home Towners. *The Beast. *His Night Out. Devil-May-Care. 1929: Innocents of Paris. Fashions in Love. Queen of the Night Clubs. Times Square (GB: The Street of Jazz). The Desert Song. Hard-Boiled Rose. Speedway. The Voice of the City. Stark Mad. Eternal Woman. Untamed. The Unholy Night. *Gossip. 1930: The Unholy Three. The Sea Bat. The Woman Racket. Show Girl in Hollywood. War Nurse. Our Blushing Brides. Paid (GB: Within the Law). His Night Out. Remote Control. Not So Dumb. Free and Easy. Lights and Shadows. 1931: Politics. Inspiration. Iron Man. The Secret Six. A Gentleman's Fate. Son of India. The Great Meadow. Hell Divers. Susan Lenox, Her Fall and Rise (GB: The Rise of Helga). Possessed. The Green Meadow. War Nurse. 1932: Emma. Sky Devils. West of Broadway. Beast of the City. Arsène Lupin. The Wet Parade. Are You Listening? Grand Hotel. The Rich Are Always with Us. Flesh. Night Court (GB: Justice for Sale). Prosperity. The Kid from Spain. The Nuisance (GB: Accidents Wanted). Unashamed. 1933: What! No Beer? King for a Night. Blind Adventure. The Way to Love. Whistling in the Dark. The Sin of Nora Moran. The Mad Game. 1934: The Line-Up (GB: Identity Parade). Unknown Blonde. The Poor Rich. Madame Spy. Whirlpool. Belle of the Nineties. Young and Beautiful. The Ghost Walks. Twin Husbands. 1935: Under the Pampas Moon. Tomorrow's Youth. Mississippi.*

Charlie Chan in Paris. Murder at Glen Athol (GB: The Criminal Within). Three Kids and a Queen (GB: The Baxter Millions). 1936: North of Nome. Sutter's Gold. Private Number. The Gentleman from Louisiana. The Plainsman. Arizona Mahoney. 1938: Border G-Man. Pardon Our Nerve. Man-Proof. Ride a Crooked Mile. If I Were King. *Miracle Money. 1939: Juarez. The Oklahoma Kid. Torchy Runs for Mayor. Fast and Furious. Emergency Squad. 1940: Queen of the Mob. New Moon. Women Without Names. Young Bill Hickok. Texas Rangers Ride Again. 1941: The Cowboy and the Blonde. The Deadly Game. Forced Landing. Riot Squad. Double Cross. 1942: True to the Army. The Big Street. Scattergood Survives a Murder. Boss of Big Town. Criminal Investigator. North of the Rockies. 1943: Bombardier. The Fallen Sparrow. Submarine Alert. The Iron Major. 1944: Bride By Mistake. I Accuse My Parents. The Merry Monahans. It's in the Bag! (GB: The Fifth Chair). 1945: Wildfire. Back to Bataan. 1946: The Last Crooked Mile. White Tie and Tails. The Killers. 1947: Sinbad the Sailor. Unconquered. In Self Defense. Queen of the Amazons. That's My Man (GB: Will Tomorrow Ever Come?). The Flame. 1948: Perilous Waters. 1949: Stampede. Mrs Mike. Adventure in Baltimore (GB: Bachelor Bait). Samson and Delilah 1950: Mule Train. 1951: M. 1952: The Savage. Bonzo Goes to College. 1955: Pirates of Tripoli. Run for Cover. 1956: The Ten Commandments. The Wild Dakotas. The Gentle Stranger (TV). 1957: Apache Warrior. 1958: The Lone Ranger and the Lost City of Gold.

† Scenes deleted from final release print.

MILLER, Dick (Richard) 1928–
Tough-looking, jut-jawed, black-haired, not-too-tall New Yorker with 'street corner' good looks and beefy build. He looked as though he would be more at home in boiler suit and tin helmet than on a film set and was, in his younger days, boxing champion, commercial artist, semi-pro footballer, psychologist and disc jockey before turning to acting. After starring as Brooklynese leads in Z-grade horrors and teenpix – one of them was the now-legendary Walter Paisley in *A Bucket of Blood*, a role he has reprised in other movies – he proved something of a good luck charm for the Roger Corman American International/New World dynasty, appearing in a good percentage of

their exploitation films, latterly in (largely comic) cameos. Billed as Richard in some early roles.

1955: Apache Woman. The Oklahoma Woman. 1956: Gunslinger. It Conquered the World. The Undead. Attack of the Crab Monsters. 1957: Not of This Earth. Rock All Night. Naked Paradise/Thunder Over Hawaii. The Undead. Sorority Girl (GB: The Bad One). Carnival Rock. 1958: War of the Satellites. 1959: A Bucket of Blood. 1960: Last Woman on Earth. The Little Shop of Horrors. 1961: Spy Squad. The Intruder (GB: The Stranger). 1962: The Premature Burial. 1963: The Terror. 'X' – The Man With the X-Ray Eyes (GB: The Man With the X-Ray Eyes). Four for Texas. 1965: Beach Ball. Girls on the Beach. Ski Party. 1966: The Wild Angels. Wild, Wild Winter. 1967: The St Valentine's Day Massacre. The Trip. A Time for Killing (GB: The Long Ride Home). 1968: The Wild Racers. The Legend of Lylah Clare. 1969: TNT Jackson (released 1974). Four Rode Out. 1970: Which Way to the Front? (GB: Ja! Ja! Mein General, But Which Way to the Front?). 1971: The Grissom Gang. 1972: The Young Nurses (GB: Games That Nurses Play). Fly Me. Night Call Nurses. 1973: Executive Action. The Slams. The Student Teachers (GB: Intimate Confessions of the Student Teachers). 1974: Big Bad Mama. Candy Stripe Nurses. Truck Turner. 1975: Hustle. White Line Fever. Capone. Vigilante Force. Summer School Teachers. Dark Town Strutters. 1976: Cannonball (GB: Carquake). Moving Violation. Hollywood Boulevard. 1977: Mr Billion. Grand Theft Auto. Game Show Models. 1978: I Wanna Hold Your Hand. New York, New York. Piranha. Starhops. Corvette Summer (GB: The Hot One). 1979: 11th Victim (TV). '1941'. The Lady in Red. Rock 'n' Roll High School. 1980: The Howling. Dr Heckyl and Mr Hype. Used Cars. The Happy Hooker Goes Hollywood. 1981: Heartbeeps. National Lampoon's Movie Madness. Smokey Bites the Dust. 1982: White Dog. 1983: Get Crazy. The Twilight Zone (GB: Twilight Zone The Movie). Heart Like a Wheel. Lies. All the Right Moves. Space Raiders/Star Child. 1984: The Terminator. Gremlins. 1985: Explorers. After Hours. 1986: Night of the Creeps. Killbots (later Chopping Mall). Jade Jungle (later Armed Response). Amazon Women on the Moon. 1987: InnerSpace. Project X. 1988: Dead Heat. Angel III: The Final Chapter. Under the Boardwalk. 1989: Far from Home. Ghost Writer. The 'burbs. 1990: Gremlins 2: The New Batch. 1991: Evil Toons. Mob Boss. 1992: Unlawful Entry. Matinee. 1993: Fallen Angels. Fallen Angels 2 (TV). Batman: Mask of the Phantasm (voice only). 1994: Mona Must Die. Tales from the Crypt: Demon Knight. Pulp Fiction.

MILLER, Martin
(Rudolf Müller) 1899–1969
Short, studious-looking, bespectacled, jutting-lipped, latterly white-haired Czechoslovakian-born actor in British films, often as professors, technicians, chemists and benevolent old buffers with attractively fractured English. He fled from Berlin to Britain in 1939, founding the Little

Viennese Theatre there. In the early 1950s, he played in more than 1000 performances of the record-breaking whodunnit *The Mousetrap*. Died while filming *The Last Valley* in Austria.

1942: Squadron Leader X. 1943: The Adventures of Tartu (GB: Tartu). 1944: Hotel Reserve. English Without Tears (US: Her Man Gilbey). 1945: Latin Quarter. Night Boat to Dublin. 1946: Woman to Woman. 1947: Frieda. The Ghosts of Berkeley Square. Mine Own Executioner. 1948: Counterblast. The Blind Goddess. Bond Street. Bonnie Prince Charlie. Man on the Run. 1949: The Huggetts Abroad. The Third Man. Helter Skelter. I Was a Male War Bride (GB: You Can't Sleep Here). Don't Ever Leave Me. 1951: Encore. I'll Get You for This (US: Lucky Nick Cain). 1952: Where's Charley? 1953: Twice Upon a Time. Front Page Story. The Genie. You Know What Sailors Are. 1954: To Dorothy a Son (US: Cash on Delivery). Mad About Men. 1955: The Woman for Joe. An Alligator Named Daisy. Man of the Moment. The Gamma People. 1956: A Child in the House. The Baby and the Battleship. 1957: Seven Thunders (US: The Beasts of Marseilles). 1958: Mark of the Phoenix. 1959: Violent Moment. The Rough and the Smooth. Libel. Expresso Bongo. Peeping Tom. 1960: Exodus. 1962: The Phantom of the Opera. 55 Days at Peking. The Fast Lady. 1963: Incident at Midnight. The VIPs. The Pink Panther. 1964: The Yellow Rolls-Royce. Children of the Damned. 1965: Up Jumped a Swagman. 1968: Assignment to Kill.

MILLICAN, James 1910–1955
Relaxed-looking American actor who could play both affable types and shifty-eyed villains. Sandy-haired Millican's laconic line in villainy really should have brought him to the fore earlier, but he became bogged down in small roles after several efforts to break into Hollywood films of the early 1930s ended in failure. He acted at the University of Southern California, but it was Broadway experience that got him regular work in movies from the late 1930s on. He was just moving into a better class of roles at the time of his early death. Once managed a rodeo with fellow film star 'Wild Bill' Elliott.

1932: The Sign of the Cross. 1935: Mills of the Gods. Too Tough to Kill. Atlantic Adventure. 1936: Mr Deeds Goes to Town. The Case of the Black Cat. Panic on the Air. 1937: SOS Coastguard (serial). The Devil is Driving. 1938: You Can't Take It With You. I Am the Law. Annabel Takes a Tour. Who Killed Gail Preston? 1939: Honolulu. Dad for a Day. Mr Smith Goes to Washington. *The Sap Takes a Rap. The Lone Wolf Spy Hunt (GB: The Lone Wolf's Daughter). Only Angels Have Wings. Society Lawyer. Coastguard. A Chump at Oxford. 1940: Golden Gloves. The Phantom Submarine. The Mortal Storm. 1941: Barnacle Bill. The Bugle Sounds. Love Crazy. You'll Never Get Rich. *Coffins on Wheels. Among the Living. I Wanted Wings. Meet John Doe. Down in San Diego. Here Comes Mr Jordan. 1942: The Remarkable Andrew. A Man's World. Star Spangled Rhythm. A Gentleman After Dark. The Glass Key. The Wife Takes a Flyer (GB: A Yank in Dutch). Take a Letter, Darling (GB: Green-Eyed Woman). My Favorite Blonde. Tramp, Tramp, Tramp. Nazi Agent. 1943: So Proudly We Hail! Thousands Cheer. Air Force. A Guy Named Joe. Northern Pursuit. 1944: The Miracle of Morgan's Creek. The Story of Dr Wassell. The Sign of the Cross (revised version of 1932 film). Practically Yours. I Love a Soldier. 1945: Bring On the Girls. Tokyo Rose. The Affairs of Susan. Love Letters. Duffy's Tavern. Incendiary Blonde. The Lost Weekend. The Trouble with Women (released 1947). The Blue Dahlia. 1946: The Searching Wind. Stepchild. Rendezvous With Annie. To Each His Own. The Well-Groomed Bride. Our Hearts Were Growing Up. The Bride Wore Boots. 1947: The Tender Years. Spoilers of the North. Suddenly It's Spring. 1948: Mr Reckless. Hazard. Let's Live Again. Disaster. The Man from Colorado. The Return of Wildfire (GB: Black Stallion). Adventures of Gallant Bess. Rogues' Regiment. In This Corner. Last of the Wild Horses. Command Decision. 1949: The Dalton Gang. Fighting Man of the Plains. The Gal Who Took the West. Grand Canyon. Rimfire. The Stratton Story. 1950: Beyond the Purple Hills. Devil's Doorway. The Gunfighter. Military Academy With That 10th Avenue Gang (GB: Sentence Suspended). Mister 880. Everybody's Dancing. Winchester '73. Convicted. 1951: Al Jennings of Oklahoma. Cavalry Scout. Fourteen Hours. The Great Missouri Raid. I Was a Communist for the FBI. Missing Women. Rawhide/Desperate Siege. Warpath. Scandal Sheet (GB: The Dark Page). 1952:

High Noon. Bugles in the Afternoon. Carson City. Diplomatic Courier. Springfield Rifle. The Winning Team. Torpedo Alley. 1953: Cow Country. Gun Belt. The Silver Whip. A Lion is in the Streets. Crazylegs, All American. The Stranger Wore a Gun. 1954: Dawn at Socorro. 1955: Las Vegas Shakedown. Top Gun. The Vanishing American. Strategic Air Command. The Man from Laramie. The Big Tip Off. Chief Crazy Horse (GB: Valley of Fury). I Died a Thousand Times. 1956: Red Sundown. The Fastest Gun Alive.

MILNER, Martin 1927–

Fresh-faced, cherub-cheeked, blond, bland American actor who played clean-cut young sons, boy friends, college kids and servicemen without ever becoming a name most people would recognize. From 1953 he became involved in several long-running television programmes, almost one on top of another. The last of these, *Adam 12*, finished in 1975 and Milner has been less regularly seen since 1980.

1947: Life With Father. 1948: The Wreck of the Hesperus. 1949: Sands of Iwo Jima. 1950: Louisa. Halls of Montezuma. Cheaper by the Dozen. Our Very Own. 1951: Fighting Coast Guard. Smuggler's Island. I Want You. Operation Pacific. 1952: Belles on Their Toes. The Captive City. My Wife's Best Friend. Springfield Rifle. Battle Zone. Last of the Comanches (GB: The Sabre and the Arrow). 1953: Destination Gobi. 1954: The Long Gray Line. 1955: Francis in the Navy. Pete Kelly's Blues. Mister Roberts. 1956: On the Threshold of Space. Screaming Eagles. Pillars of the Sky (GB: The Tomahawk and the Cross). Gunfight at the OK Corral. 1957: Sweet Smell of Success. Man Afraid. 1958: Marjorie Morningstar. Too Much, Too Soon. 1959: Compulsion. 1960: 13 Ghosts. Sex Kittens Go to College. The Private Lives of Adam and Eve. 1965: Zebra in the Kitchen. 1967: Sullivan's Empire (TV. GB: cinemas). Valley of the Dolls. 1968: Three Guns for Texas (TV. GB: cinemas). 1969: Ski Fever. 1972: Emergency (TV). 1973: Runaway (GB: TV, as The Runaway Train). 1974: Hurricane (TV). 1975: Swiss Family Robinson (TV). 1976: Flood (TV. GB: cinemas). 1977: SST Death Flight (TV. GB: Death Flight). 1978: Black Beauty (TV). Little Mo (TV). 1979: Crisis in Mid Air (TV). The Seekers (TV). 1981: The Ordeal of Bill Carney (TV). 1989: Nashville Beat (TV).

MITCHELL, Grant 1874–1957

Small, pale-faced, fair-haired American actor with very tiny eyes and mouth, square face and little neck. He often played meek and henpecked types who were suckers for the attentions of vamps and golddiggers, but could also project malevolence with some force and was occasionally the unexpected villain of the piece in a whodunnit. Died following a series of strokes.

1923: Radio Mania. 1930: Man to Man. 1931: The Star Witness. 1932: Three on a Match. The Famous Ferguson Case. Big City Blues. No Man of Her Own. A Successful Calamity. Week-End Marriage. 20,000 Years in Sing Sing. 1933: He Learned About Women. Central Airport. Lilly Turner. I Love That Man. Heroes for Sale. Dinner at Eight. The Stranger's Return. Tomorrow at Seven. Saturday's Millions. Dancing Lady. King for a Night. Wild Boys of the Road (GB: Dangerous Days). Our Betters. Convention City. Shadows of Sing Sing. 1934: The Poor Rich. The Show-Off. Gridiron Flash (GB: Luck of the Game). Twenty Million Sweethearts. We're Rich Again. The Secret Bride (GB: Concealment). The Cat's Paw. The Case of the Howling Dog. 365 Nights in Hollywood. One Exciting Adventure. 1935: One More Spring. Travelling Saleslady. Gold Diggers of 1935. Men Without Names. Straight from the Heart. Broadway Gondolier. In Person. A Midsummer Night's Dream. It's in the Air. Seven Keys to Baldpate. 1936: The Garden Murder Case. Next Time We Love (GB: Next Time We Live). Moonlight Murder. Piccadilly Jim. The Devil Is a Sissy (GB: The Devil Takes the Count). Her Master's Voice. Parole! My American Wife. The Ex-Mrs Bradford. 1937: The Life of Emile Zola. First Lady. The Last Gangster. Music for Madame. Hollywood Hotel. Lady Behave. 1938: Women Are Like That. The Headleys at Home (GB: Among Those Present). Peck's Bad Boy with the Circus. Reformatory. Youth Takes a Fling. That Certain Age. 1939: 6,000 Enemies. Juarez. Hell's Kitchen. Mr Smith Goes to Washington. On Borrowed Time. The Secret of Dr Kildare. 1940: The Grapes of Wrath. It All Came True. Edison, the Man. New Moon. My Love Came Back. Castle on the Hudson (GB: Years Without Days). Father Is a Prince. We Who Are Young. 1941: The Bride Wore Crutches. Tobacco Road. One Foot in Heaven. Skylark. The Feminine Touch. Nothing But the Truth. Footsteps in the Dark. The Penalty. The Great Lie. The Man

Who Came to Dinner. 1942: Larceny Inc. Meet the Stewarts. The Gay Sisters. My Sister Eileen. Cairo. Orchestra Wives. 1943: The Amazing Mrs Holliday. Dixie. All by Myself. *The Gold Tower. Arsenic and Old Lace. 1944: Laura. Step Lively. See Here, Private Hargrove. And Now Tomorrow. When the Lights Go On Again. The Impatient Years. 1945: Bedside Manner. A Medal for Benny. Crime Inc. Conflict. Guest Wife. Bring on the Girls. Leave Her to Heaven. Colonel Effingham's Raid (GB: Man of the Hour). 1946: Easy to Wed. Cinderella Jones. 1947: Blondie's Holiday. Blondie's Anniversary. Honeymoon. It Happened on Fifth Avenue. The Corpse Came C.O.D. 1948: Who Killed Doc Robbin? (GB: Sinister House).

Theodora Goes Wild. 1937: Lost Horizon. Man of the People. When You're in Love (GB: For You Alone). I Promise to Pay. The Hurricane. Make Way for Tomorrow. 1938: Love, Honor and Behave. Trade Winds. 1939: Mr Smith Goes to Washington. Only Angels Have Wings. Gone with the Wind. The Hunchback of Notre Dame. Stagecoach. 1940: Our Town. Swiss Family Robinson. Angels over Broadway. The Long Voyage Home. Three Cheers for the Irish. 1941: Out of the Fog. Flight from Destiny. *Cavalcade of the Academy Awards. 1942: This Above All. Moontide. The Black Swan. Tales of Manhattan. Joan of Paris. Song of the Islands. 1943: The Immortal Sergeant. Bataan. The Outlaw. Flesh and Fantasy. 1944: Dark Waters. The Sullivans. The Keys of the Kingdom. Wilson. Buffalo Bill. 1945: Within These Walls. Captain Eddie. Adventure. 1946: Three Wise Fools. The Dark Mirror. It's a Wonderful Life! Swell Guy. 1947: High Barbaree. The Romance of Rosy Ridge. 1948: Silver River. Alias Nick Beal (GB: The Contact Man). 1949: The Big Wheel. 1951: Journey into Light. 1952: High Noon. 1953: Tumbleweed. 1954: Secret of the Incas. Destry. 1956: Miracle on 34th Street (TV. GB: cinemas). While the City Sleeps. 1958: Natchez (TV). Handle with Care. 1959: Too Young to Love. 1960: The Right Man (TV). 1961: Pocketful of Miracles. By Love Possessed.

MITCHELL, Millard 1900–1953
Rasp-voiced, short-haired Cuban-born American actor with sharp, rat-trap, cynical-looking facial features. His image as an acid, but likeable world-weary type had taken him into top featured film roles (such as the producer in Singin' in the Rain) at the time of his death from lung cancer.

1931: Secrets of a Secretary. *Singapore Sue. 1938: Dynamite Delaney. 1940: Mr and Mrs North. 1941: Mr and Mrs Smith. 1942: Grand Central Murder. Little Tokyo USA. Get Hep to Love (GB: She's My Lovely). The Mayor of 44th Street. The Big Street. 1943: Slightly Dangerous. 1946: Swell Guy. 1947: Kiss of Death. A Double Life. 1948: A Foreign Affair. 1949: Twelve O'Clock High. Everybody Does It. Thieves' Highway. 1950: The Gunfighter. Mr 880. Winchester '73. Convicted. USS Teakettle (later You're in the Navy Now). 1951: Strictly Dishonorable. 1952: My Six Convicts. Singin' in the Rain. 1953: The Naked Spur. Here Come the Girls.

MITCHELL, Thomas 1892–1962
Stubby, fleshy-faced, small-eyed, brown-haired American actor who gave deeply-thought, richly enjoyable, often Irish-tinged performances, and was for many years one of Hollywood's best actors and top character stars. Took an Academy Award as best supporting actor in Stagecoach. Also wrote several plays. Died from cancer.

1923: Six Cylinder Love. 1934: *Cloudy with Showers. 1936: Craig's Wife. Adventure in Manhattan (GB: Manhattan Madness).

MITCHELL, Warren 1926–
Balding British actor who, once started in films in earnest at 31, busily built up a formidable list of Jewish cockneys and other ethnic types, before creating a series of suburban monsters that culminated in the long-running, multi-prejudiced Alf Garnett of the TV series Till Death Us Do Part, the forerunner of America's All in the Family. After 1980, he divided his time between stage and screen.

1954: The Passing Stranger. 1957: Manuela (US: Stowaway Girl). Barnacle Bill (US: All at Sea). 1958: Girls at Sea. The Trollenberg Terror (US: The Crawling Eye). Man With a Gun. Three Crooked Men. 1959: Tommy the Toreador. Hell Is a City. 1960: Surprise Package. Two-Way Stretch. The Pure Hell of St Trinians. Doctor in Love. 1961: The Boy who Stole a Million. The Curse of the Werewolf. Don't Bother to Knock! (US: Why Bother to Knock?). The Silent Invasion (released 1967). Postman's Knock. Village of Daughters. The Roman Spring of Mrs Stone. 1962: Incident at Midnight. *The King's Breakfast. We Joined the Navy. The Main Attraction. Operation Snatch. 1963: The Small World of Sammy Lee. Calculated Risk. Unearthly Stranger. 70 Deadly Pills. 1964: Where Has Poor Mickey Gone? The Sicilians. Carry On Cleo. The Intelligence Men. 1965: San Ferry Ann. The Spy Who Came In from the Cold. Help! Promise Her Anything. The Night Caller (US: Blood Beast from Outer Space). 1966: The Sandwich Man. The Jokers. Drop Dead Darling (US: Arrivederci, Baby!). 1967: Dance of the Vampires (US: The Fearless Vampire Killers. Voice only). 1968: Diamonds for Breakfast. Till Death Us Do Part. The Assassination Bureau. The Best House in London. 1969: Moon Zero Two. All the Way Up. 1972: The Alf Garnett Saga. Innocent Bystanders. 1974: What Changed Charley Farthing? 1977: Jabberwocky. Stand Up Virgin Soldiers. 1978: Meetings with Remarkable Men. 1982: Norman Loves Rose. The Plague Dogs (voice only). 1984: Man of Letters (TV). 1985: The Chain. Knights and Emeralds. 1986: Foreign Body. 1987: The Secret Policeman's Third Ball. 1988: Kokoda Crescent.

MOFFATT, Graham 1919–1965
Insolence was in the very bearing of this roly-poly British actor's film fat boys. Not much of an actor, he only had one role, but it dovetailed perfectly with those of Will Hay (dithering incompetence) and Moore Marriott (bewhiskered cunning) in a memorable series of comedy films in the

late thirties. When Hay decided to go solo, Moffatt and Marriott made a few films with other comedians, then Moffatt left films to run a pub. Died from a heart attack.

1934: A Cup of Kindness. 1935: Stormy Weather. The Clairvoyant. 1936: It's Love Again. All In. Where There's a Will. Windbag the Sailor. Good Morning, Boys. 1937: Okay for Sound. Dr Syn. Gangway. Oh, Mr Porter! Owd Bob (US: To the Victor). 1938: Convict 99. The Drum (US: Drums). Old Bones of the River. 1939: Ask a Policeman. Cheer Boys Cheer. Where's That Fire? 1940: Charley's (Big-Hearted) Aunt. 1941: I Thank You. Hi Gang! 1942: Back Room Boy. 1943: Dear Octopus (US: The Randolph Family). 1944: Time Flies. Welcome Mr Washington. A Canterbury Tale. 1945: I Know Where I'm Going! 1946: The Voyage of Peter Joe (serial). 1947: Stage Frights. 1948: Woman Hater. 1949: Three Bags Full (serial). 1950: The Dragon of Pendragon Castle. The Second Mate. 1952: Mother Riley Meets the Vampire (US: Vampire over London). 1960: Inn for Trouble. 1963: 80,000 Suspects.

MOHR, Gerald 1914–1968

Slim, dark, swarthy, treacherous-looking American actor with narrowed eyes, close-cropped hair and wolfish smile. His laconic voice made him an ideal choice to portray Chandler's Philip Marlowe on radio, but he played mostly charming villains in (largely co-feature) films, apart from a stint as the gentleman crook, The Lone Wolf, in the 1940s. Died from a heart attack while in Sweden.

1939: Panama Patrol. Love Affair. Charlie Chan at Treasure Island. 1940: The Sea Hawk. Catman of Paris (released 1946). 1941: We Go Fast. The Monster and the Girl. Jungle Girl (serial). The Reluctant Dragon. Adventures of Captain Marvel (serial. Voice only). Woman of the Year (voice only). 1942: The Lady Has Plans. 1943: Murder in Times Square. Lady of Burlesque (GB: Striptease Lady). One Danger-ous Night. The Desert Song. King of the Cowboys. Redhead from Manhattan. 1945: A Guy Could Change. 1946: Gilda. The Notori-ous Lone Wolf. Passkey to Danger. Dangerous Business. Young Widow. The Truth About Murder (GB: The Lie Detector). The Invisible Informer. 1947: The Lone Wolf in Mexico. The Magnificent Rogue. Heaven Only Knows. The

Lone Wolf in London. 1948: The Emperor Waltz. Two Guys from Texas (GB: Two Texas Knights). 1949: The Blonde Bandit. 1950: Hunt the Man Down. Undercover Girl. 1951: Sirocco. Detective Story. Ten Tall Men. 1952: The Duel at Silver Creek. Son of Ali Baba. The Sniper. The Ring. 1953: Raiders of the Seven Seas. Invasion USA. The Eddie Cantor Story. Money from Home. 1954: Dragonfly Squadron. 1957: The Buckskin Lady. A Question of Loyalty (TV. GB: cinemas). 1958: Guns, Girls and Gangsters. My World Dies Screaming (GB: Terror in the Haunted House). 1959: A Date With Death. The Angry Red Planet. 1960: This Rebel Breed. 1964: Wild West Story. 1968: Funny Girl.

MOODY, Ron

(Ronald Moodnick) 1924–

Mournful-looking British tragi-comedian with deep-set eyes and receding dark hair. He looks perfect casting for the clown who cried, and indeed has played Grimaldi (a pet role) on stage. Unlike Sir Alec Guinness, who won stardom with the kind of star character roles at which Moody, too, excelled, Moody never found his niche in the cinema, although he did repeat his great personal stage success as Fagin in *Oliver!* (ironically, also a Guinness role) in the musical film version – and it won him an Academy Award nomination.

1957: Davy. 1959: Follow a Star. 1960: Make Mine Mink. 1961: Five Golden Hours. A Pair of Briefs. 1962: Summer Holiday. 1963: The Mouse on the Moon. Ladies Who Do. 1964: Murder Most Foul. Every Day's a Holiday (US: Seaside Swingers). 1965: San Ferry Ann. 1966: The Sandwich Man. 1968: Oliver! 1969: The Bed Sitting Room. David Copperfield (TV. GB: cinemas). 1970: The Twelve Chairs. 1971: Flight of the Doves. 1974: Legend of the Werewolf. Dogpound Shuffle (GB: Spot). 1978: Dominique. 1979: The Spaceman and King Arthur (US: Unidentified Flying Oddball). 1981: Dial M for Murder (TV). 1982: Wrong is Right (GB: The Man with the Deadly Lens). Tales of the Golden Monkey (TV). 1984: Where is Parsifal?

MOORE, Alvy 1925–

Skinny, crew-cut, light-haired American actor who was briefly popular, mainly in fast-talking comic roles, in the early 1950s.

From the mid 1960s, he became increasingly interested in production, forming a company with fellow character actor L.Q. Jones (*qv*) and returning to acting in comedy roles in several 'in-house' productions on which he customarily also acted as executive producer. Played brash, bright young types in his earlier days; latterly seen as befuddled codgers.

1952: Okinawa. The War of the Worlds. You for Me. 1953: The Glory Brigade. Destination Gobi. China Venture. The Wild One. Gentlemen Prefer Blondes. Susan Slept Here. 1954: Riot in Cell Block 11. Return from the Sea. There's No Business Like Show Business. Secret of the Incas. 1955: Annapolis Story (GB: The Blue and the Gold). Five Against the House. 1956: Screaming Eagles. 1957: Designing Woman. The Persuader. 1958: The Perfect Furlough (GB: Strictly for Pleasure). 1960: The Wackiest Ship in the Army. 1961: Everything's Ducky. Twist Around the Clock. 1963: For Love or Money. Move Over, Darling. 1964: The Devil's Bedroom. Three Nuts in Search of a Bolt. 1965: Love and Kisses. A Very Special Favor. 1966: The Gnome-Mobile. 1967: One Way Wahini. 1969: The Witchmaker. 1970: The Brotherhood of Satan. 1971: The Late Liz. 1973: Herbie Rides Again. 1974: A Boy and His Dog. 1975: The Specialist. Dr Minx. Smokey and the Hot Wire Gang. 1978: Lacy and the Mississippi Queen (TV). 1979: Cotton Candy (TV). 1980: Ms 45 (GB: Angel of Vengeance). 1983: Mortuary. 1984: They're Playing with Fire. 1985: Here Come the Littles (voice only). Scream (filmed 1981). 1988: Intruder. 1989: The Horror Show. 1990: A Ghost in Monte Carlo (TV). Return to Green Acres (TV).

MOORE, Ida 1883–1964

Of all the many scene-stealers who appear in this book, this tiny American actress with the 'pixilated' features was one of the most incorrigible. A dear little old lady who played dear little old ladies, she appeared as a comedienne on Broadway in her younger days, when she also made a couple of silents. Nearly always peddled sweetness and light, and could get away with murder; clearly relished her role as Needle Nellie in 1951's *Scandal Sheet.*

*1925: Thank You. The Merry Widow. 1943: *Cutie on Duty. 1944: The Uninvited. The Soul of a Monster. Reckless Age. Riders of the*

Santa Fé (GB: Mile a Minute). Hi, Beautiful (GB: Pass to Romance). The Ghost That Walks Alone. Once Upon a Time. She's a Soldier, Too. 1945: Girls of the Big House. Rough, Tough and Ready (GB: Men of the Deep). Her Lucky Night. Eadie Was a Lady. She Wouldn't Say Yes. Easy to Look At. I'll Tell the World. 1946: Cross My Heart. To Each His Own. Talk About a Lady. The Show-Off. I'll Be Yours. From This Day Forward. The Bride Wore Boots. The Dark Mirror. 1947: *Host to a Ghost. Easy Come, Easy Go. It's a Joke, Son. Dream Girl. The Egg and I. High Barbaree. The Long Night. 1948: Money Madness. Good Sam. Johnny Belinda. Return of the Bad Men. Rusty Leads the Way. 1949: Dear Wife. Manhattan Angel. Roseanna McCoy. Ma and Pa Kettle. Hold That Baby. Rope of Sand. Leave It to Henry. The Inspector General/Happytimes. The Sun Comes Up. 1950: Paid in Full. Mother Didn't Tell Me. Harvey. Backfire. Mr Music. Let's Dance. Fancy Pants. 1951: The Lemon Drop Kid. Comin' Round the Mountain. Double Dynamite. Show Boat. Leave It to the Marines. Honeychile. Scandal Sheet (GB: The Dark Page). 1952: Rainbow 'Round My Shoulder. Just This Once. Scandal at Scourie. Something to Live For. The First Time. Carson City. 1953: A Slight Case of Larceny. 1954: The Country Girl. The Long, Long Trailer. 1955: Ma and Pa Kettle at Waikiki. 1957: Desk Set (GB: His Other Woman). 1958: Rock-a-Bye Baby.

MOOREHEAD, Agnes 1900–1974
Doughty red-haired American actress who came to the screen with Orson Welles' Mercury Players, and proceeded to play stern figures of power—not always with a heart of gold either. Memorable as the sophisticated murderess in Dark Passage, and four times nominated for an Academy Award, her distinctively strong face cropped up in later years as pioneers, harridans, witches and even nuns. Died from cancer.

1941: Citizen Kane. 1942: The Magnificent Ambersons. The Big Street. Journey into Fear. 1943: Government Girl. The Youngest Profession. Jane Eyre. 1944: Since You Went Away. The Seventh Cross. Dragon Seed. Tomorrow the World. Mrs Parkington. 1945: Keep Your Powder Dry. Her Highness and the Bellboy. Our Vines Have Tender Grapes. *Victory in Europe. 1946: Summer Holiday (released 1948). 1947: The Beginning or the

End? The Lost Moment. Dark Passage. The Woman in White. 1948: Johnny Belinda. Station West. 1949: Without Honor. The Great Sinner. The Stratton Story. 1950: Caged. Blackjack (US: Captain Blackjack). Adventures of Captain Fabian. 1951: The Blue Veil. Show Boat. Fourteen Hours. 1952: Scandal at Scourie. The Blazing Forest. 1953: The Story of Three Loves. Main Street to Broadway. Those Redheads from Seattle. 1954: Magnificent Obsession. 1955: Untamed. The Left Hand of God. 1956: All That Heaven Allows. Meet Me in Las Vegas (GB: Viva Las Vegas!). The Revolt of Mamie Stover. The Swan. The Conqueror. Pardners. The Opposite Sex. 1957: The True Story of Jesse James (GB: The James Brothers). Raintree County. Jeanne Eagels. The Story of Mankind. 1958: The Dungeon (TV). Tempest. 1959: The Bat. Night of the Quarter Moon. 1960: Pollyanna. 1961: Bachelor in Paradise. Twenty Plus Two (GB: It Started in Tokyo). Jessica. 1962: How the West Was Won. 1963: Who's Minding the Store? 1964: Hush . . . Hush, Sweet Charlotte. 1966: The Singing Nun. 1969: The Ballad of Andy Crocker (TV). 1970: Marriage: Year One (TV). 1971: Suddenly Single (TV). Dear Dead Delilah. Charlotte's Web (voice only). 1973: Frankenstein: The True Story (TV. GB: cinemas). 1974: Three Faces of Love (TV).

MORELAND, Mantan 1901–1973
Solidly built, balding American actor who ran away to join a circus at 12, then spent many years in vaudeville before coming to Hollywood to star in black-only films, also

appearing in a stream of mainline studio films as the archetypal panicky manservant who found everything but his eyes transfixed in times of terror ('Feet—do your thing!'). The ongoing role of Birmingham Brown, Charlie Chan's chauffeur in the Monogram series of the 1940s, allowed the Moreland sense of (dry) humour often to peep through.

1936: Lucky Ghost. 1937: Shall We Dance? Spirit of Youth. Two-Gun Man from Harlem. Gang Smashers. 1938: Harlem on the Prairie. Gun Moll. Next Time I Marry. Frontier Scout. There's That Woman Again. 1939: One Dark Night. Tell No Tales. Irish Luck (GB: Amateur Detective). Riders of the Frontier. 1940: Chasing Trouble. Pier 13. Millionaire Playboy. The City of Chance. Four Shall Die. While Thousands Cheer. Lady Luck. Mr Washington Goes to Town. Professor Creeps (shown 1942). The Girl in 313. Star Dust. The Man Who Wouldn't Talk. Viva Cisco Kid. On the Spot. Condemned Men. The Bowery Boy. Maryland. Laughing at Danger. Drums of the Desert. 1941: Four Jacks and a Jill. Marry the Boss's Daughter. Up Jumped the Devil. Birth of the Blues. King of the Zombies. Ellery Queen's Penthouse Mystery. Cracked Nuts. Bachelor Daddy. It Started With Eve. Up in the Air. Accent on Love. King of the Zombies. The Gang's All Here. Hello, Sucker. Dressed to Kill. Footlight Fever. You're Out of Luck. Sign of the Wolf. Sleepers West. Let's Go Collegiate (GB: Farewell to Fame). World Premiere. 1942: A-Haunting We Will Go. Freckles Comes Home. Andy Hardy's Double Life. The Strange Case of Dr RX. The Palm Beach Story. Treat 'Em Rough. Professor Creeps. Law of the Jungle. The Daring Young Man. Mexican Spitfire Sees a Ghost. Footlight Serenade. The Phantom Killer. Eyes in the Night. Tarzan's New York Adventure. Girl Trouble. It Comes Up Love (GB: A Date with an Angel). 1943: Hit the Ice. Sarong Girl. Cabin in the Sky. Revenge of the Zombies (GB: The Corpse Vanished). Cosmo Jones—Crime Smasher (GB: Crime Smasher). Melody Parade. She's for Me. He Hired the Boss. My Kingdom for a Cook. *Right About Face. Hi'Ya, Sailor. Melody Parade. Slightly Dangerous. Swing Fever. You're a Lucky Fellow, Mr Smith. We've Never Been Licked (GB: Texas to Tokyo). 1944: The Mystery of the River Boat (serial). This Is the Life. The Chinese Cat. Moon Over Las Vegas. Chip Off the Old Block. Pin-Up Girl. South of Dixie. Black Magic. Bowery to Broadway. Charlie Chan in the Secret Service. See Here, Private Hargrove. 1945: The Scarlet Clue. She Wouldn't Say Yes. The Jade Mask. The Shanghai Cobra. The Spider. Captain Tugboat Annie. 1946: Mantan Messes Up. Dark Alibi. Shadows Over Chinatown. Mantan Runs for Mayor. Riverboat Rhythm. Tall, Tan and Terrific. The Trap (GB: Murder at Malibu Beach). What a Guy. 1947: The Red Hornet. Ebony Parade. Juke Joint. The Chinese Ring. 1948: The Mystery of the Golden Eye. Docks of New Orleans. The Feathered Serpent. The Shanghai Chest. Come on, Cowboy. Best Man Wins. The Dreamer. She's Too Mean to Me. Return of Mandy's Husband. 1949: Sky Dragon. 1956: Rockin' the Blues. Rock 'n' Roll Revue. 1957: Rock 'n' Roll Jamboree. 1964: The Patsy. 1965: Spider Baby/Cannibal Orgy. 1966: Alvarez Kelly. 1967: Enter Laughing.

1969: *The Comic.* 1970: *Watermelon Man.*
1971: *Marriage: Year One (TV).* 1972: *The Biscuit Eater.* 1973: *The Young Nurses.*

MORGAN, Frank

(Francis Wupperman) 1890–1949
Had this square-faced, crusty-looking—somewhere between Will Hay and Adolphe Menjou — light-haired American character star not saddened Hollywood by dying in his sleep at 59, there is little doubt that he would have served 20 years at MGM, seen the downfall of the studio system, and gracefully retired. Although his performances were unvarying, mostly as blustering buffoons, and sometimes seem rushed, he carved his own niche of immortality by playing the title role in *The Wizard of Oz.* Oscar nominee for *Tortilla Flat.*

1916: *The Suspect.* 1917: *A Modern Cinderella. The Daring of Diana. Who's Your Neighbor? Baby Mine. Light in the Darkness. The Girl Phillippa. A Child of the Wild. Raffles, the Amateur Cracksman.* 1918: *At the Mercy of Men. The Knife.* 1919: *The Golden Shower. The Gray Towers Mystery.* 1924: *Born Rich. Manhandled.* 1925: *The Scarlet Saint. The Crowded Hour. The Man Who Found Himself.* 1927: *Love's Greatest Mistake.* 1929: **Belle of the Night. Laughter. Dangerous Nan McGrew. Fast and Loose. Queen High.* 1932: *Secrets of the French Police. The Half-Naked Truth.* 1933: *Luxury Liner. Hallelujah, I'm a Bum (GB: Hallelujah, I'm a Tramp). Reunion in Vienna. The Kiss Before the Mirror. The Best of Enemies. Bombshell (GB: Blonde Bombshell). Billion Dollar Scandal. When Ladies Meet. The Nuisance (GB: Accidents Wanted). Broadway to Hollywood (GB: Ring Up the Curtain).* 1934: *Affairs of Cellini. The Cat and the Fiddle. A Lost Lady (GB: Courageous). There's Always Tomorrow. Sisters Under the Skin. Success at Any Price. By Your Leave. The Mighty Barnum.* 1935: *Enchanted April. Naughty Marietta. The Perfect Gentleman. The Good Fairy. Escapade. I Live My Life.* 1936: *Trouble for Two (GB: The Suicide Club). Piccadilly Jim. The Great Ziegfeld. Dimples. The Dancing Pirate.* 1937: *The Last of Mrs Cheyney. Beg, Borrow or Steal. Saratoga. The Emperor's Candlesticks. Rosalie.* 1938: *Port of Seven Seas. Paradise for Three (GB: Romance for Three). Sweethearts. The Crowd Roars.* 1939: *Balalaika. Broadway Serenade. The*

Wizard of Oz. Henry Goes Arizona (GB: Spats to Spurs). 1940: *The Shop Around the Corner. Hullabaloo. Boom Town. The Mortal Storm. Broadway Melody of 1940. The Ghost Comes Home.* 1941: *Keeping Company. The Vanishing Virginian. Washington Melodrama. Honky Tonk. Wild Man of Borneo.* 1942: *White Cargo. Tortilla Flat.* 1943: *A Stranger in Town. Thousands Cheer. The Human Comedy.* 1944: *The White Cliffs of Dover. Casanova Brown.* 1945: *Yolanda and the Thief.* 1946: *The Great Morgan. The Cockeyed Miracle (GB: Mr Griggs Returns). Courage of Lassie. Lady Luck. Summer Holiday (released 1948).* 1947: *Green Dolphin Street.* 1948: *The Three Musketeers.* 1949: *Any Number Can Play. The Great Sinner. The Stratton Story.* 1950: *Key to the City.*

MORGAN, Henry 'Harry'

(Harry Bratsburg) 1915–
Small, weasel-faced, light-haired American character actor who through the forties and early fifties played bad guys, losers and worms that sometimes turned. His prominent performance in *The Glenn Miller Story* changed the course of his career, and his characters became much more likeable. From the mid 1960s, he was seen in considerably broader comic roles. Billed as 'Harry' from 1958.

1942: *The Loves of Edgar Allan Poe. The Omaha Trail. To the Shores of Tripoli. Orchestra Wives. Crash Dive. The Ox-Bow Incident (GB: Strange Incident). A-Haunting We Will Go.* 1943: *Happy Land.* 1944: *Wing and a Prayer. Roger Touhy—Gangster (GB: The Last Gangster). The Eve of St Mark. Gentle Annie.* 1945: *A Bell for Adano. State Fair. The Horn Blows at Midnight.* 1946: *It Shouldn't Happen to a Dog. Dragonwyck. Johnny Comes Flying Home. Somewhere in the Night. From This Day Forward.* 1947: *The Gangster.* 1948: *Race Street. The Big Clock. The Saxon Charm. All My Sons. Yellow Sky. Moonrise.* 1949: *Red Light. Down to the Sea in Ships. Strange Bargain. Holiday Affair. Madame Bovary.* 1950: *Outside the Wall. The Showdown. Dark City.* 1951: *Appointment with Danger. The Blue Veil. Belle le Grand. When I Grow Up. The Well. The Highwayman. Scandal Sheet (GB: The Dark Page).* 1952: *My Six Convicts. Boots Malone. Bend of the River (GB: Where the River Bends). High*

Noon. What Price Glory? Apache War Smoke. Stop, You're Killing Me. Toughest Man in Arizona. 1953: *Thunder Bay. Torch Song. Arena. Champ for a Day. The Glenn Miller Story.* 1954: *The Forty-Niners. The Far Country. About Mrs Leslie. Prisoner of War.* 1955: *Not As a Stranger. Strategic Air Command.* 1956: *The Bottom of the Bottle (GB: Beyond the River). Backlash. The Teahouse of the August Moon.* 1957: *Under Fire.* 1959: *It Started with a Kiss.* 1960: *Murder Inc. Cimarron. Inherit the Wind. The Mountain Road.* 1962: *How the West Was Won.* 1964: *John Goldfarb, Please Come Home.* 1966: *Frankie and Johnny. What Did You Do in the War, Daddy?* 1967: *The Flim Flam Man (GB: One Born Every Minute).* 1968: *Support Your Local Sheriff!* 1969: *Dragnet (TV. GB: The Big Dragnet).* 1970: *But I Don't Want to Get Married (TV). Viva Max! The Feminist and the Fuzz (TV).* 1971: *The Barefoot Executive. Support Your Local Gunfighter. Scandalous John. Ellery Queen: Don't Look Behind You (TV).* 1972: *Jeremiah Johnson. Hec Ramsey/ The Century Turns (TV).* 1973: *Snowball Express. Charley and the Angel.* 1974: *The Apple Dumpling Gang. Sidekicks (TV).* 1975: *The Last Day (TV).* 1976: *The Shootist (TV).* 1977: *The Magnificent Magical Magnet of Santa Mesa/Adventures of Freddie (TV). Exo-Man (TV).* 1978: *The Cat from Outer Space. Kate Bliss and the Ticker Tape Kid (TV). Maneaters Are Loose! (TV). Murder at the Mardi Gras (TV).* 1979: *Better Late Than Never (TV). You Can't Take It With You (TV). The Apple Dumpling Gang Ride Again. The Wild Wild West Revisited (TV).* 1980: *Scout's Honor (TV). More Wild, Wild West (TV). Roughnecks (TV).* 1981: *Rivkin: Bounty Hunter (TV).* 1983: *Sparkling Cyanide/ Agatha Christie's Sparkling Cyanide (TV). The Flight of Dragons (TV. Voice only).* 1985: *Blacke's Magic (TV).* 1987: *Dragnet.* 1988: *41 Going on 30 (TV).* 1989: *The Incident (TV).* 1993: *Incident in a Small Town (TV).*

MORGAN, Ralph

(Raphael Wuppermann) 1883–1956
Recognizably the brother of Frank Morgan (qv), but quieter and more introspective in performance, this short, sturdy, moustachioed American actor with light-brown hair had squarely handsome features but shifty eyes that often caused him to be cast as suspects in cinematic murder cases.

A former lawyer, he could bring great strength to less usual roles, such as the czar in *Rasputin and the Empress*, which combined the sinister and avuncular sides of his personality. Played a few old codgers, too, in his twilight years.

*1915: The Master of the House. 1916: Madame X. 1917: The Penny Philanthropist. 1925: The Man Who Found Himself. 1930: *Excuse the Pardon. 1931: Honor Among Lovers. Charlie Chan's Chance. 1932: Strange Interlude (GB: Strange Interval). Dance Team. Cheaters at Play. Disorderly Conduct. The Son-Daughter. The Devil's Lottery. 1933: Humanity. Rasputin and the Empress (GB: Rasputin—the Mad Monk). The Power and the Glory. Trick for Trick. Shanghai Madness. Walls of Gold. The Mad Game. The Kennel Murder Case. Dr Bull. 1934: Transatlantic Merry-Go-Round. The Last Gentleman. Hell in the Heavens. Their Big Moment (GB: Afterwards). No Greater Glory. Orient Express. Little Men. Stand Up and Cheer. Girl of the Limberlost. She Was a Lady. The Cat and the Fiddle. 1935: Condemned to Live. Star of Midnight. Unwelcome Stranger. Calm Yourself. I've Been Around. Magnificent Obsession. 1936: Muss 'Em Up (GB: House of Fate). Little Miss Nobody. Yellowstone. Human Cargo. Speed. General Spanky. The Ex-Mrs Bradford. Anthony Adverse. Crack-Up. 1937: The Life of Emile Zola. Exclusive. Wells Fargo. The Man in Blue. Behind Prison Bars. Orphans of the Street. The Outer Gate. 1938: Out West With the Hardys. Army Girl (GB: The Last of the Cavalry). Love is a Headache. Wives Under Suspicion. Mother Carey's Chickens. Shadows Over Shanghai. That's My Story. Barefoot Boy. Mannequin. 1939: Fast and Loose. Man of Conquest. Off the Record. Way down South. Smuggled Cargo. Trapped in the Sky. The Lone Wolf Spy Hunt (GB: The Lone Wolf's Daughter). Geronimo. 1940: Forty Little Mothers. I'm Still Alive. *Soak the Old. Wagons Westward. The Mad Doctor (GB: A Date With Destiny). 1941: Dick Tracy vs Crime Inc (serial). Adventure in Washington (GB: Female Correspondent). 1942: Gang Busters (serial). A Close Call for Ellery Queen (GB: A Close Call). Klondike Fury. The Traitor Within. Night Monster (GB: House of Mystery). 1943: Hitler's Madman. Jack London. Stage Door Canteen. 1944: Double Furlough. The Monster Maker. I'll Be Seeing You. Weird Woman. Trocadero. The Impostor. The Great Alaskan Mystery (serial). 1945: Black Market Babies. This Love of Ours. Hollywood and Vine (GB: Daisy (the Dog) Goes Hollywood). The Monster and the Ape. 1947: Mr District Attorney. The Last Roundup. Song of the Thin Man. 1948: Sleep My Love. Sword of the Avenger. The Creeper. 1950: Blue Grass of Kentucky. 1951: Heart of the Rockies. 1953: Gold Fever.*

MORITA, Noriyuki 'Pat' 1928–

Small, compact, round-faced, enigmatic-looking, placid Japanese-American actor with thinning light-brown hair, whose film career was insignificant until cast as Mr Miyagi in the 'Karate Kid' films. Dispensing wit, wisdom and aphorisms with the aplomb of Charlie Chan, Morita soon proved himself an indispensible part of the character acting scene. Frequently in long-running TV series (notably two stints in *Happy Days*), Morita had a long career as a nightclub entertainer before venturing into films and TV. He also wrote the screenplay for his 1987 movie *Captive Hearts*.

1967: Thoroughly Modern Millie. 1968: The Shakiest Gun in the West. 1972: Every Little Crook and Nanny. Cancel My Reservation. Evil Roy Slade (TV). Where Does It Hurt? A Very Missing Person (TV). 1973: Brock's Last Case (TV). 1974: Punch and Jody (TV). 1976: Farewell to Manzanar (TV). Midway (GB: Battle of Midway). 1978: Human Feelings (TV). 1979: The Day the World Ended. 1980: For the Love of It (TV). When Time Ran Out . . . 1981: Full Moon High. 1982: Slapstick (US: Slapstick of Another Kind). Jimmy the Kid. Savannah Smiles. 1984: Night Patrol. The Karate Kid. 1985: Amos (TV). 1986: Karate Kid II. Babes in Toyland (TV). 1987: Captive Hearts. 1989: The Karate Kid Part III. 1990: Hiroshima: Out of the Ashes (TV). Collison Course. 1991: Auntie Lee's Meat Pies. Do Or Die. Miracle Beach. Lena's Holiday. 1992: Goodbye Paradise. Honeymoon in Vegas. 1993: Xianu. Even Cowgirls Get the Blues. Greyhounds (TV). Genghis Khan. 1994: The Next Karate Kid. Timemaster. 1995: American Ninja 5.

MORSE, Barry 1918–

Tall, saturnine, long-faced, dark-haired, balding British actor who, after a low-key British stage and screen career in the 1930s and 1940s went to Canada and America, achieving immortality in the 1950s for TV buffs as the dogged Lt Gerard, forever pursuing David Janssen in *The Fugitive*, a tremendously successful series that ran for five years. His profile was never as high after the series ended in 1967, although he continued to work steadily, mostly on TV. His children Hayward and Melanie both became actors.

1942: The Goose Steps Out. Thunder Rock. 1943: When We Are Married. There's a Future in It. The Dummy Talks. 1946: This Man is Mine. Late at Night. 1947: Mrs Fitzherbert. 1948: Daughter of Darkness. 1950: No Trace. 1963: Kings of the Sun. 1969: Justine. 1970: Puzzle of a Downfall Child. 1971: The Telephone Book. 1972: Running Scared.

Asylum. 1977: Welcome to Blood City. Coup d'état. Power Play (released 1978). Love at First Sight. 1978: To Kill the King. The Shape of Things to Come. 1979: Klondike Fever. One Man. The Changeling. 1980: A Tale of Two Cities (TV). Murder by Phone. The Hounds of Notre Dame. 1982: Funeral Home/Crimes in the Night (made 1980). 1983: The Rothko Conspiracy (TV). 1985: Reunion at Fairborough (TV). Covenant. 1986: Running Scared (and 1972 film of same title). 1987: The Return of Sherlock Holmes (TV). 1994: Tekwar (TV).

MORTON, Clive 1904–1975

Dark-haired, oval-headed, aristocratic British actor often seen in arrogant or supercilious roles. In business with the East India dock company for four years before switching to an acting career. Popular on TV in postwar years, but rarely played more than 'clubman'-type cameos in films. Married to actresses Joan Harben (1909–1962) and Fanny Rowe.

1932: Fires of Fate. The Last Coupon. 1933: The Blarney Stone (US: The Blarney Kiss). 1934: The Great Defender. Evergreen. 1935: The Clairvoyant. Squibs. She Shall Have Music. Scrooge. 1936: Dusty Ermine (US: Hideout in the Alps). The Man Who Changed His Mind (US: The Man Who Lived Again). 1937: Dinner at the Ritz. 1938: Dead Men Tell No Tales. 1942: Uncensored. 1946: While the Sun Shines. 1947: Jassy. This Was a Woman. Mine Own Executioner. 1948: Here Come the Huggetts. Bond Street. The Blind Goddess. Scott of the Antarctic. Quartet. Vote for Huggett. 1949: Kind Hearts and Coronets. A Run for Your Money. Christopher Columbus. The Blue Lamp. Traveller's Joy (released 1951). 1950: Trio. 1951: His Excellency. The Lavender Hill Mob. Night Without Stars. 1952: Castle in the Air. 1953: Turn the Key Softly. All Hallowe'en. 1954: The Harassed Hero. Orders Are Orders. Carrington VC (US: Court Martial). 1955: Richard III. 1956: Beyond Mombasa. 1957: Seven Waves Away (US: Abandon Ship!). Lucky Jim. After the Ball. The Safecracker. The Moonraker. 1958: The Duke Wore Jeans. Next to No Time! 1959: Shake Hands With the Devil. The Navy Lark. Make Mine a Million. 1960: The Pure Hell of St Trinian's. 1961: Clue of the New Pin. 1962: Lawrence of Arabia. A Matter of WHO. I Thank a Fool. 1964: *All in Good Time. 1965: The Alphabet Murders/The ABC Murders. 1967: Stranger in the House (US: Cop-Out). 1968: Star! 1969: Lock Up Your Daughters! Goodbye Mr Chips. 1970: Jane Eyre (TV. GB: cinemas). 1971: Zeppelin. Young Winston. 1972: *The Man and the Snake. 1974: 11 Harrowhouse.

MOWBRAY, Alan 1893–1969
Dark-haired, heavy-set British actor, good-looking despite a large nose and ruddy complexion, who went to America in 1923, arrived in Hollywood in 1931, and found himself typecast in pompous or lofty roles with an occasional break as a strong, under-standing confidant. His imperious style and 'distinguished' manner soon steered him into butler roles, and he became one of the screen's most peerless manservants from the mid-1930s on. Died from a heart attack.

1931: Leftover Ladies (GB: Broken Links). Guilty Hands. God's Gift to Women. Alexander Hamilton. The Honor of the Family. The Man in Possession. 1932: Lovers Courageous. The Silent Witness. Nice Women. Ladies Courageous. The World and the Flesh. *Two Lips and Juleps. *Snake in the Grass. Man about Town. Winner Take All. Jewel Robbery. The Man Called Back. Two Against the World. Sherlock Holmes. Hotel Continental. The Man from Yesterday. The Phantom President. 1933: Berkeley Square. The World Changes. Peg o' My Heart. A Study in Scarlet. Voltaire. Midnight Club. Roman Scandals. Our Betters. Her Secret. 1934: Long Lost Father. Where Sinners Meet (GB: The Dover Road). The Girl from

Missouri (GB: 100 Per Cent Pure). Charlie Chan in London. The House of Rothschild. Cheaters. Little Man, What Now? One More River (GB: Over the River). Embarrassing Moments. 1935: Lady Tubbs (GB: The Gay Lady). Becky Sharp. Night Life of the Gods. The Gay Deception. In Person. She Couldn't Take It. 1936: Rose Marie. Muss 'Em Up (GB: House of Fate). Rainbow on the River. Ladies in Love. Mary of Scotland. Desire. Give Us This Night. The Case Against Mrs Ames. Fatal Lady. My Man Godfrey. 1937: As Good as Married. Topper. Four Days' Wonder. Stand-In. On Such a Night. Music for Madame. Vogues of 1938. On the Avenue. The King and the Chorus Girl (GB: Romance is Sacred). Marry the Girl. Hollywood Hotel. 1938: Merrily We Live. There Goes My Heart. 1939: Topper Takes a Trip. The Llano Kid. Never Say Die. Way Down South. 1940: The Villain Still Pursued Her. Music in My Heart. Curtain Call. The Quarterback. The Boys from Syracuse. Scatterbrain. 1941: Ice-Capades. The Perfect Snob. I Wake Up Screaming (GB: Hot Spot). That Hamilton Woman (GB: Lady Hamilton). That Uncertain Feeling. Footlight Fever. The Cowboy and the Blonde. Moon Over Her Shoulder. 1942: A Yank at Eton. *Three Blonde Mice. We Were Dancing. Panama Hattie. Isle of Missing Men. So This is Washington. Yokel Boy (GB: Hitting the Headlines). The Devil With Hitler. The Mad Martindales. 1943: The Powers Girl (GB: Hello! Beautiful). Slightly Dangerous. His Butler's Sister. Holy Matri-mony. Stage Door Canteen. *Screen Snapshots No 108. 1944: The Doughgirls. My Gal Loves Music. Ever Since Venus. The Devil Checks Up. 1945: The Phantom of 42nd Street. Bring on the Girls. Men in Her Diary. Earl Carroll Vanities. Sunbonnet Sue. Tell It to a Star. Where Do We Go from Here? 1946: Idea Girl. Terror by Night. My Darling Clementine. 1947: The Pilgrim Lady. Lured (GB: Personal Column). Merton of the Movies. Man About Town. Captain from Castile. 1948: The Main Street Kid. My Dear Secretary. Prince of Thieves. Don't Trust Your Husband/An Innocent Affair. Every Girl Should Be Married. 1949: You're My Everything. The Lovable Cheat. The Lone Wolf and His Lady. Abbott and Costello Meet the Killer Boris Karloff. 1950: Wagonmaster. The Jackpot. 1951: The Lady and the Bandit (GB: Dick Turpin's Ride). Crosswinds. 1952: Androcles and the Lion. Blackbeard the Pirate. 1954: Ma and Pa Kettle At Home. The Steel Cage. 1955: The King's Thief. 1956: The King and I. Around the World in 80 Days. The Man Who Knew Too Much. 1961: A Majority of One.

MULLARD, Arthur 1910–
Raucous-voiced, gap-toothed, ever-smiling, dark-haired British cockney player, whose round and battered features bear witness to his bouts as a boxer. Mullard was also a bouncer and a rag-and-bone merchant before getting into pre-war films as an extra and stuntman. In the 1970s his roly-poly figure and rough-and-ready delivery broke into more prominent comedy roles on tele-vision. Says he has been in more than 100 films, which could leave the following list a few dozen short!

1938: Inspector Hornleigh. 1945: I'll Be Your Sweetheart. 1946: The Captive Heart. School for Secrets (US: Secret Flight). 1948: Oliver Twist. Bonnie Prince Charlie. Operation Diamond. The Case of Charles Peace. 1949: Skimpy in the Navy. 1950: There is Another Sun (US: Wall of Death). Happy Go Lovely. Pool of London. 1951: The Man in the White Suit. The Lavender Hill Mob. 1952: Whisper-ing Smith Hits London (US: Whispering Smith versus Scotland Yard). The Man Who Watched Trains Go By (US: Paris Express). The Long Memory. The Pickwick Papers. Women of Twi-light (US: Twilight Women). 1953: Front Page Story. The Master of Ballantrae. Rob Roy the Highland Rogue. Life With the Lyons (US: A Family Affair). 1954: One Good Turn. The Belles of St Trinian's. Radio Cab Murder. Dangerous Cargo. The Diamond (US: Diamond Wizard). The Colditz Story. 1955: As Long As They're Happy. Jumping for Joy. The Lady-killers. My Teenage Daughter (US: Teenage Bad Girl). 1956: Moby Dick. Charley Moon. The Extra Day. Brothers in Law. 1957: The Long Haul. Happy is the Bride! 1958: Grip of the Strangler (US: The Haunted Strangler). The Man Who Liked Funerals. The Bank Raiders. 1959: And the Same to You. 1960: Two-Way Stretch. 1961: It's Trad, Dad (US: Ring-a-Ding Rhythm). Dentist on the Job (US: Get On With It!). On the Fiddle (US: Operation Snafu). 1962: The Wrong Arm of the Law. Postman's Knock. Sparrows Can't Sing. Band of Thieves. Crooks Anonymous. The Loneliness of the Long-Distance Runner. 1963: Carry On Spying. Ladies Who Do. Father Came Too. Heavens Above! 1964: Allez France (US: The Counterfeit Constable). 1965: Cuckoo Patrol. 1966: Morgan – A Suitable Case for Treatment (US: Morgan). The Great St Trinian's Train Robbery. *Fish and Milligan. 1967: Smashing Time. Casino Royale. 1968: Chitty Chitty Bang Bang. 1969: Lock Up Your Daughters! Crooks and Coronets (US: Sophie's Place). 1971: On the Buses. 1972: Steptoe and Son. 1973: Vault of Horror. Holiday on the Buses. 1974: Three for All. 1978: Adventures of a Plumber's Mate.

MULLIGAN, Richard 1932–
Tall, light-haired, narrow-eyed tele-vision star and occasional migrant to the cinema as a character player. The brother of director Robert Mulligan, he was around for years before the role of Bert in the TV comedy series Soap made his name. Always

seen in faintly hysterical roles or as off-centre characters who set their fellows on edge, he faded from prominence after the mid 1980s. It's hard to imagine him in anything but comedy, especially with those fruity tones, but he did do a few straight roles in his early years. Married (second of three) actress Joan Hackett.

*1963: Love With the Proper Stranger. 1964: One Potato, Two Potato. Baby, the Rain Must Fall. 1966: The Group. 1969: The Undefeated. 1970: Little Big Man. *Arthur Penn – The Director. 1972: Irish Whiskey Rebellion. 1973: From the Mixed-Up Files of Mrs Basil E Frankweiler (GB: The Hideaways). 1974: Visit to a Chief's Son. 1976: The Big Bus. 1978: Having Babies III (TV). 1979: Scavenger Hunt. 1980: SOB. 1982: Trail of the Pink Panther. 1983: Jealousy (TV). 1984: Teachers. Meatballs Part II. 1985: The Heavenly Kid. Quicksilver. Micki + Maude. Doin' Time. 1986: A Fine Mess. Babes in Toyland (TV). 1987: Poker Alice (TV). 1988: Oliver & Company (voice only). 1991: UFO Café.*

MUNDIN, Herbert 1898–1939
Short, dumpy, dark-haired, often moustachioed British actor with the common touch, facially not unlike the present-day British comedian Ronnie Corbett. A concert-party and music-hall comedian, he soon won popularity in early British talkies and decided to go to Hollywood, which kept him equally busy, most notably as the man-servant in *Cavalcade*, Barkis in *David Copperfield* and the chirpy Much the Miller

in *The Adventures of Robin Hood*. Killed in a car crash.

*1930: *Ashes. Enter the Queen. 1931: Immediate Possession. The Wrong Mr Perkins. We Dine at Seven. Peace and Quiet. East Lynne on the Western Front. 1932: The Devil's Lottery. Life Begins (GB: The Dawn of Life). The Trial of Vivienne Ware. The Silent Witness. Love Me Tonight. Almost Married. Bachelor's Affairs. One Way Passage. Chandu the Magician. Sherlock Holmes. 1933: Cavalcade. Dangerously Yours. Pleasure Cruise. Adorable. It's Great to be Alive. Arizona to Broadway. The Devil's in Love. Shanghai Madness. Hoop-La. 1934: Such Women Are Dangerous. Call It Luck. Ever Since Eve. Hell in the Heavens. Orient Express. Bottoms Up. All Men Are Enemies. Springtime for Henry. Love Time. 1935: David Copperfield. The Widow from Monte Carlo. Mutiny on the Bounty. Ladies Love Danger. The Perfect Gentleman. Black Sheep. King of Burlesque. 1936: A Message to Garcia. Under Two Flags. Charlie Chan's Secret. Champagne Charlie. Tarzan Escapes! 1937: You Can't Beat Love. Angel. Another Dawn. 1938: Invisible Enemy. Exposed. Lord Jeff (GB: The Boy from Barnardo's). The Adventures of Robin Hood. 1939: Society Lawyer.*

MUNSHIN, Jules 1915–1970
Dark-haired, long-faced, tall, indiarubber-limbed American comedian and dancer with moony smile – the sailor who *wasn't* Gene Kelly or Frank Sinatra in *On the Town*. Worked his way up from small-town nightclubs and vaudeville to Broadway success, but only made a few films for MGM before returning to the stage. Died from a heart attack at 54.

1948: Easter Parade. 1949: Take Me Out to the Ball Game (GB: Everybody's Cheering). On the Town. That Midnight Kiss. 1951: Nous irons à Monte Carlo (GB and US: Monte Carlo Baby). 1957: Silk Stockings. Ten Thousand Bedrooms. 1963: Wild and Wonderful. 1966: Monkeys, Go Home! 1976: Mastermind (filmed 1969).

MURTON, Lionel 1915–
London-born, Canada-raised, long-headed actor and entertainer with throaty tones and receding dark hair, whose eyebrow-raising

expression of cheerful surprise had him cast almost constantly in comedy. He came into prominence with the Canadian navy show, *Meet the Navy* during World War II, and was seen from time to time in post-war British films playing light roles as affable but none-too-bright officials or friends. Also played one or two leading roles in minor films.

1946: Meet the Navy. 1948: Brass Monkey/Lucky Mascot. Trouble in the Air. 1949: I Was a Male War Bride (GB: You Can't Sleep Here). 1950: The Girl is Mine. Dangerous Assignment. 1951: The Long Dark Hall. 1952: The Pickwick Papers. Down Among the Z Men. 1953: Our Girl Friday (US: The Adventures of Sadie). The Runaway Bus. 1954: Night People. 1955: Raising a Riot. 1956: The Battle of the River Plate (US: Pursuit of the Graf Spee). The Baby and the Battleship (narrator only). 1957: Interpol (US: Pickup Alley). Fire Down Below. Carry On Admiral (US: The Ship Was Loaded). 1958: Virgin Island/Our Virgin Island. Up the Creek. The Captain's Table. Further Up the Creek. 1959: The Mouse That Roared. Northwest Frontier (US: Flame Over India). A Touch of Larceny. Make Mine a Million. Our Man in Havana. 1960: Surprise Package. 1961: Petticoat Pirates. Hamilton in the Music Festival (narrator only). 1962: On the Beat. The Main Attraction. Summer Holiday. 1963: Man in the Middle. 1965: The Truth About Spring. Carry On Cowboy. 1966: Doctor in Clover. 1967: The Dirty Dozen. 1968: The Last Shot You Hear. Nobody Runs Forever (US: The High Commissioner). 1969: Patton (GB: Patton: Lust for Glory). 1970: Zeta One. The Revolutionary. Cannon for Cordoba. Welcome to the Club. 1974: Confessions of a Window Cleaner. 1976: Seven Nights in Japan. 1977: Twilight's Last Gleaming. 1979: The London Connection (US: The Omega Connection).

MUSE, Clarence 1889–1979
Pleasant black American actor who found himself typecast as a handyman or other menial, although he was a law graduate who later moved to acting, writing and composing. The role of Jim in the 1931 version of *Huckleberry Finn* established him in Hollywood, and he made films there for 50 years, as well as founding, or co-founding black theatre groups in New York. His star

roles were confined to all-black productions, although he was delightful singing the Oscar-winning *Sunshine Cake* with Bing Crosby and Coleen Gray in *Riding High*. Died from a cerebral haemorrhage.

*1928: *Election Day. 1929: Hearts in Dixie. 1930: A Royal Romance. Guilty? Rain or Shine. 1931: Safe in Hell (GB: The Lost Lady). Dirigible. The Last Parade. The Fighting Sheriff. Huckleberry Finn. Secret Witness/ Terror by Night. Secret Service. 1932: Lena Rivers. The Woman from Monte Carlo. Prestige. Night World. The Wet Parade. Winner Take All. Attorney for the Defense. Is My Face Red? Big City Blues. *Hollywood on Parade A-12. White Zombie. Hell's Highway. Cabin in the Cotton. Washington Merry-Go-Round (GB: Invisible Power). Laughter in Hell. Man Against Woman. 1933: From Hell to Heaven. The Mind Reader. Flying Down to Rio. The Wrecker. Fury of the Jungle (GB: Jury of the Jungle). 1934: Massacre. Broadway Bill (GB: Strictly Confidential). Black Moon. Kid Millions. The Personality Kid. The Count of Monte Cristo. 1935: Alias Mary Dow. O'Shaughnessy's Boy. So Red the Rose. East of Java. Harmony Lane. 1936: *Fibbing Fibbers. Muss 'Em Up (GB: House of Fate). Laughing Irish Eyes. Follow Your Heart. Daniel Boone. Showboat. Spendthrift. 1937: Spirit of Youth. Mysterious Crossing. 1938: The Toy Wife (GB: Frou Frou). Secrets of a Nurse. Prison Train. 1939: Broken Earth. Way Down South. 1940: Zanzibar. Sporting Blood. That Gang of Mine. Murder Over New York. Broken Strings. Maryland. Chad Hanna. 1941: Flame of New Orleans. Adam Had Four Sons. The Invisible Ghost. Love Crazy. Gentleman from Dixie. Among the Living. Belle Starr. Kisses for Breakfast. 1942: The Talk of the Town. Sin Town. The Black Swan. Sherlock Holmes in Washington. Tales of Manhattan. 1943: Watch on the Rhine. Shadow of a Doubt. Heaven Can Wait. Honeymoon Lodge. Flesh and Fantasy. Johnny Come Lately (GB: Johnny Vagabond). The Sky's the Limit. 1944: In the Meantime, Darling. The Soul of a Monster. Follow the Boys. The Racket Man. The Thin Man Goes Home. Jam Session. Double Indemnity. San Diego, I Love You. Calling All Stars. 1945: Scarlet Street. The Lost Weekend. Without Love. God is My Co-Pilot. Boston Blackie's Rendezvous (GB: Blackie's Rendezvous). 1946: She Wouldn't Say Yes. Two Smart People. Night and Day. 1947: Joe Palooka in The*

Knock-Out. A Likely Story. Unconquered. Welcome, Stranger. My Favorite Brunette. 1948: An Act of Murder. King of the Gamblers. Act of Violence. 1949: The Great Dan Patch. 1950: Riding High. County Fair. 1951: My Forbidden Past. Apache Drums. 1952: Caribbean (GB: Caribbean Gold). The Las Vegas Story. 1953: Jamaica Run. The Sun Shines Bright. She Couldn't Say No (GB: Beautiful But Dangerous). 1956: The First Traveling Saleslady. 1959: Porgy and Bess. 1971: Buck and the Preacher. 1973: The World's Greatest Athlete. A Dream for Christmas (TV). 1976: Car Wash. 1977: Passing Through. Ciao, male/Bye Bye Monkey. 1979: The Black Stallion.

MUSTIN, Burt

(Burton Mustin) 1882–1977

Tall, spare, permanently-wizened, beak-nosed, small-eyed, bald, parrot-like American actor who embarked on an acting career at 59 after retiring from his previous profession: car salesman. An enthusiastic lifetime amateur actor and singer (barber shop quartet singing remained an abiding hobby), Mustin must have often been hired just for his amazing face, but ran up dozens of film and scores of TV credits as cranky old codgers in the last 26 years of his life, becoming a national figure in the 1970s as the 'adopted' grandfather with a sideline in song-and-dance in the top TV show *All in the Family*. He drove a car until he was 92 and died a few days short of his 95th birthday: a barber shop quartet sang at the funeral.

1951: The Last Outpost. Detective Story. The Sellout. 1952: Just Across the Street. The Lusty Men. Talk About a Stranger. †We're Not Married. 1953: Half a Hero. A Lion is in the Streets. The Moonlighter. One Girl's Confession. The Silver Whip. Vicki. 1954: Cattle Queen of Montana. Day of Triumph. †Executive Suite. Gypsy Colt. †River of No Return. She Couldn't Say No. Silver Lode. Witness to Murder. 1955: The Desperate Hours. The Kentuckian. The Man with the Gun (GB: The Trouble Shooter). The Return of Jack Slade (GB: Texas Rose). †Prince of Players. 1956: Edge of Hell. Great Day in the Morning. Storm Center. These Wilder Years. 1957: Raintree County. 1958: The Sheepman. Rally 'Round the Flag, Boys! The Big Country. 1959: The

FBI Story. 1960: The Adventures of Huckleberry Finn. Home from the Hill. 1961: Snow White and the Three Stooges (GB: Snow White and the Three Clowns). 1962: Hemingway's Adventures of a Young Man (GB: Adventures of a Young Man). All Fall Down. 1963: Son of Flubber. The Thrill of It All. Twilight of Honor (GB: The Charge is Murder). 1964: The Killers. The Misadventures of Merlin Jones. What a Way to Go! Sex and the Single Girl. 1965: The Adventures of Bullwhip Griffin (released 1967). Cat Ballou. The Cincinnati Kid. 1966: Dead Heat on a Merry-Go-Round. The Ghost and Mr Chicken. 1967: The Reluctant Astronaut. 1968: †The Shakiest Gun in the West. Speedway. 1969: †The Great Bank Robbery. The Love Bug. The Witchmaker. Hail, Hero! The Over-the-Hill Gang (TV). A Time for Dying. 1970: The Over-the-Hill Gang Rides Again (TV). Tiger by the Tail. 1971: Skin Game. Operation Cobra (TV). 1973: Miracle on 34th Street (TV). 1974: Big Rose (TV). 1975: Mobile Two (TV). The Strongest Man in the World. Train Ride to Hollywood. 1976: Baker's Hawk.

† Scenes deleted from final release print

NAISH, J. Carrol

(Joseph C. Naish) 1897–1973

You could never tell what this swarthy, black-haired American actor would turn up as next. He played Italians, Indians, Red Indians, Orientals, Spaniards, Greeks, Mexicans and dozens of others, besides apemen, hunchbacks and various fiends (or comic characters) of vague foreign backgrounds. Almost always hidden beneath make-up; people would have been hard-put to recognize Naish as himself. Virtually lost to films after starting to play Charlie Chan on TV in 1958. Oscar nominations for *Sahara* and *A Medal for Benny*. Although of distinguished Irish descent, Naish never played an Irishman in films!

1926: What Price Glory? 1930: Cheer Up and Smile. Good Intentions. Scotland Yard (GB: 'Detective Clive', Bart). Double Crossroads. 1931: Tonight or Never. Homicide Squad (GB: The Lost Men). Gun Smoke. Kick In. Ladies of the Big House. The Royal Bed (GB: The Queen's Husband). 1932: The Mouthpiece. Week-End Marriage (GB: Working Wives). The Conquerors. The Kid from Spain. Big City Blues.

Two Seconds. Tiger Shark. Washington Merry-Go-Round (GB: Mad Masquerade). The Hatchet Man (GB: The Honourable Mr Wong). Cabin in the Cotton. Beast of the City. It's Tough to be Famous. The Famous Ferguson Case. Crooner. No Living Witness. 1933: The Mystery Squadron (serial). The Devil's in Love. Elmer the Great. Arizona to Broadway. The Whirlwind. Notorious But Nice. Captured. Frisco Jenny. Ann Vickers. Central Airport. The Mad Game. The World Gone Mad (GB: The Public Be Hanged). The Past of Mary Holmes. The Avenger. Silent Men. No Other Woman. The Big Chance. The Infernal Machine. The Last Trail. 1934: Murder in Trinidad. What's Your Racket? The Hell Cat. Return of the Terror. British Agent. The Defense Rests. Marie Galante. Upper World. One Is Guilty. Sleepers East. Bachelor of Arts. Girl in Danger. Hell in the Heavens. 1935: Behind Green Lights. The President Vanishes (GB: Strange Conspiracy). *Spilled Salt. Black Fury. Under the Pampas Moon. Little Big Shot. The Crusades. The Lives of a Bengal Lancer. Captain Blood. Confidential. Front Page Woman. Special Agent. 1936: We Who Are About to Die. Two in the Dark. The Return of Jimmy Valentine. Robin Hood of El Dorado. Absolute Quiet. Ramona. The Charge of the Light Brigade. Special Investigator. Exclusive Story. The Leathernecks Have Landed (GB: The Marines Have Landed). Moonlight Murder. Charlie Chan at the Circus. Anthony Adverse. Crack-Up. 1937: Border Café. Think Fast, Mr Moto. Sea Racketeers. Thunder Trail. Daughter of Shanghai (GB: Daughter of the Orient). Song of the City. Hideaway. Bulldog Drummond Comes Back. Night Club Scandal. 1938: Hunted Men. Tip-Off Girls. Bulldog Drummond in Africa. Illegal Traffic. King of Alcatraz (GB: King of the Alcatraz). Her Jungle Love. Prison Farm. Persons in Hiding. 1939: Undercover Doctor. Beau Geste. Hotel Imperial. King of Chinatown. Island of Lost Men. 1940: Golden Gloves. Typhoon. Down Argentine Way. A Night at Earl Carroll's. Queen of the Mob. 1941: Blood and Sand. That Night in Rio. Forced Landing. The Corsican Brothers. Mr Dynamite. Accent on Love. Birth of the Blues. 1942: Jackass Mail. A Gentleman at Heart. Tales of Manhattan. Dr Renault's Secret. Dr Broadway. The Pied Piper. The Man in the Trunk. Sunday Punch. 1943: Batman (serial). Harrigan's Kid. Sahara. Calling Dr Death. Good Morning, Judge. Behind the Rising Sun. Gung Ho! 1944: Waterfront. The Monster Maker. Two-Man Submarine.

Nabonga (GB: The Jungle Woman). Enter Arsène Lupin. The Whistler. Voice in the Wind. Dragon Seed. House of Frankenstein. Mark of the Whistler (GB: The Marked Man). 1945: *Star in the Night. Strange Confession. The Southerner. A Medal for Benny. Getting Gertie's Garter. 1946: Bad Bascomb. Humoresque. The Beast With Five Fingers. 1947: The Fugitive. Carnival in Costa Rica. Road to Rio. 1948: Joan of Arc. The Kissing Bandit. 1949: That Midnight Kiss. Canadian Pacific. 1950: Rio Grande. The Toast of New Orleans. Annie Get Your Gun. The Black Hand. Please Believe Me. 1951: Across the Wide Missouri. Mark of the Renegade. Bannerline. 1952: Clash by Night. Woman of the North Country. Denver and Rio Grande. Ride the Man Down. 1953: Beneath the 12-Mile Reef. Fighter Attack. 1954: Saskatchewan (GB: O'Rourke of the Royal Mounted). Sitting Bull. 1955: New York Confidential. Violent Saturday. Hit the Deck. The Last Command. Rage at Dawn. Desert Sands. 1956: Yaqui Drums. Rebel in Town. 1957: The Young Don't Cry. This Could Be the Night. 1961: Force of Impulse. 1964: The Hanged Man (TV. GB: cinemas). 1970: Blood of Frankenstein (GB: Dracula vs Frankenstein). Cutter's Trail (TV).

NAISMITH, Laurence
(Lawrence Johnson) 1908–1992
Big, benign, thick-necked British actor with thinning cotton-wool hair; he played clerics, administrators and sympathetic senior citizens. A merchant seaman in his younger days, he joined Bristol Repertory Company in 1930. World War II (he served for seven years in the Royal Artillery) changed the pattern of his career and he became a welcome and reliable film performer in post-war years; despite his turned-down mouth his characters were usually kindly and rarely on the wrong side of the law.

1948: Trouble in the Air. A Piece of Cake. Badger's Green. 1949: Dark Secret. Train of Events. Room to Let. Kind Hearts and Coronets. The Chiltern Hundreds (US: The Amazing Mr Beecham). 1951: High Treason. Chelsea Story. Hell is Sold Out. Calling Bulldog

Drummond. His Excellency. I Believe in You. Whispering Smith Hits London (US: Whispering Smith Versus Scotland Yard). 1952: A Killer Walks. Mother Riley Meets the Vampire (US: Vampire Over London). Penny Princess. The Happy Family (US: Mr Lord Says No). Rough Shoot (US: Shoot First). The Beggar's Opera. Cosh Boy (US: The Slasher). The Long Memory. 1953: Love in Pawn. The Flanagan Boy (US: Bad Blonde). Gilbert Harding Speaking of Murder. Mogambo. The Million Pound Note (US: Man With a Million). 1954: The Black Knight. The Dam Busters. Carrington VC (US: Court Martial). 1955: The Final Column. Josephine and Men. Richard III. The Man Who Never Was. 1956: Tiger in the Smoke. The Weapon. The Extra Day. Lust for Life. The Barretts of Wimpole Street. 1957: Seven Waves Away (US: Abandon Ship!). Boy on a Dolphin. Robbery Under Arms. I Accuse! The Gypsy and the Gentleman. 1958: The Two-Headed Spy. Gideon's Day (US: Gideon of Scotland Yard). The Naked Earth. A Night to Remember. Tempest. 1959: Sink the Bismarck! Third Man on the Mountain. Solomon and Sheba. The Angry Silence. 1960: The Singer Not the Song. The Criminal (US: The Concrete Jungle). The Trials of Oscar Wilde (US: The Man with the Green Carnation). The World of Suzie Wong. Village of the Damned. 1961: Greyfriars Bobby. The Valiant. 1962: The 300 Spartans. We Joined the Navy. I Thank a Fool. The Prince and the Pauper. 1963: Cleopatra. Jason and the Argonauts. The Three Lives of Thomasina. 1965: Sky West and Crooked (US: Gypsy Girl). 1966: The Scorpio Letters (TV. GB: cinemas). Deadlier Than the Male. 1967: Camelot. Fitzwilly (GB: Fitzwilly Strikes Back). The Long Duel. 1968: The Bushbaby. 1969: The Valley of Gwangi. Eye of the Cat. Run a Crooked Mile (TV). 1970: Scrooge. 1971: Quest for Love. Diamonds Are Forever. Young Winston. 1972: The Amazing Mr Blunden. 1981: Mission: Monte Carlo.

NAPIER, Alan
(A. Napier-Clavering) 1903–1988
Extremely tall, distinguished-looking, somewhat gaunt, moustachioed performer of very British aspect. Born in Birmingham, he was mainly a stage player until going to Hollywood in 1939, where he played noblemen, butlers, senior officers and aristocrats. In the 1960s he became familiar as Alfred, the manservant in television's Batman series. Died following a stroke.

1930: Caste. 1931: Stamboul. 1932: In a Monastery Garden. 1933: Loyalties. Bitter Sweet. 1936: Wings Over Africa. 1937: For Valour. 1938: Wife of General Ling. 1939: The Four Just Men (US: The Secret Four). We Are Not Alone. 1940: The Invisible Man Returns. The House of the Seven Gables. 1941: Confirm or Deny. 1942: We Were Dancing. A Yank at Eton. Random Harvest. Cat People. Eagle Squadron. 1943: Lassie Come Home. The Song of Bernadette. Madame Curie. Assignment in Brittany. The Ministry of Fear. Appointment in Berlin. The Uninvited. 1944: Lost Angel. Action in Arabia. The Hairy Ape. Thirty Seconds Over Tokyo. Dark Waters. 1945: Mademoiselle Fifi. Hangover Square. Isle of the Dead. 1946: A Scandal in Paris. Three Strangers. High Conquest. House of Horrors (GB: Joan Medford is Missing). The Strange Woman. 1947: Driftwood. Adventure Island. The Lone Wolf in London. Lured (GB: Personal Column). Sinbad the Sailor. Forever Amber. Ivy. Fiesta. Unconquered. 1948: Joan of Arc. Hills of Home (GB: Master of Lassie). Macbeth. Johnny Belinda. 1949: Criss Cross. The Red Danube. Tarzan's Magic Fountain. My Own True Love. A Connecticut Yankee in King Arthur's Court (GB: A Yankee in King Arthur's Court). Manhandled. Master Minds. 1950: Double Crossbones. Challenge to Lassie. Tripoli. 1951: Tarzan's Peril (GB: Tarzan and the Jungle Queen). The Great Caruso. Across the Wide Missouri. The Blue Veil. The Strange Door. The Highwayman. 1952: Big Jim McLain. 1953: Young Bess. Julius Caesar. 1954: Desiree. Moonfleet. 1955: The Court Jester. 1956: Miami Exposé. The Mole People. 1957: Until They Sail. 1959: Journey to the Center of the Earth. Island of Lost Women. 1961: Wild in the Country. Tender is the Night. 1962: The Premature Burial. 1963: The Sword in the Stone (voice only). 1964: My Fair Lady. Marnie. 36 Hours. Signpost to Murder. 1965: The Loved One. 1966: Batman. 1973: The Paper Chase. Crime Club (TV). 1974: QB VII (TV). 1981: The Monkey Mission (TV).

looked as though he had burst from the pages of a comic book, as some granite hero. But when he broke into mainstream film acting in his early forties, there was something about the set of his eyes that caused producers to cast him as lily-livered villains, or heroes with feet of clay. He's been in several films for director Jonathan Demme, for whom he seems something of a lucky mascot, and tangled with Sylvester Stallone in two of the 'Rambo' films. Also a songwriter.

1965: Love and Kisses. 1968: The Hanging of Jake Ellis. 1969: The House Near the Prado. Cherry, Harry and Raquel! 1970: Moonfire. Beyond the Valley of the Dolls. 1971: The Seven Minutes. 1975: The Super Vixens. 1977: Citizens Band. Thunder and Lightning. Ransom for Alice! (TV). 1978: Big Bob Johnson and His Fantastic Speed Circus (TV). 1979: Last Embrace. 1980: Melvin and Howard. Gridlock/ The Great American Traffic Jam (TV). The Blues Brothers. 1982: First Blood. 1983: Wacko. 1984: The Outlaws (TV). Target Witness. Swing Shift. The Cartier Affair (TV). In Search of a Golden Sky. 1985: Rambo: First Blood Part II. The Night Stalker. 1986: Instant Justice/Marine Issue. Death Stalks the Big Top (TV). Something Wild. 1987: Kidnapped. Deep Space. 1988: The Incredible Hulk Returns (TV). Married to the Mob. One Man Force. 1989: Hit List. Miami Blues. The Trackers. 1990: Ernest Goes to Jail. Future Zone. The Grifters. The Silence of the Lambs. 1991: Indio 2 – The Revolt. Soldier's Fortune. Condor. Under Surveillance. 1992: Hell Comes to Frogtown II. Treacherous Crossing (TV). Skeeter. Center of the Web. 1993: To Die, to Sleep. National Lampoon's Loaded Weapon 1. Body Bags (TV). Philadelphia. Eye of the Beholder. 1994: Shadow of the Serpent. Fatal Pursuit. Dying for Love. Texas Payback. 1995: Hard Justice. 3 Ninjas Knuckle Up. Jury Duty.

1947: The End of the River. 1951: Green Grow the Rushes. Blind Man's Bluff. Death of an Angel. 1952: Stolen Face. 1953: Black Orchid. The Saint's Return (US: The Saint's Girl Friday). *The Dark Stairway. 1954: Conflict of Wings (US: Fuss Over Feathers). Companions in Crime. The Stranger Came Home (US: The Unholy Four). *The Strange Case of Blondie. The Brain Machine. Little Red Monkey (US: The Case of the Little Red Monkey). 36 Hours (US: Terror Street). 1955: A Time to Kill. Out of the Clouds. The Blue Peter. 1956: The Narrowing Circle. The Man in the Road. *Destination Death. Guilty? The Last Man to Hang? *Distant Neighbours (narrator only). A Town Like Alice. *Person Unknown. *The Lonely House. 1957: *The Case of the Smiling Widow. The Shiralee. *The White Cliffs Mystery. Robbery Under Arms. *Night Crossing. 1958: Tread Softly, Stranger. *Crime of Honour. A Night To Remember. Son of Robin Hood. 1959: *The Unseeing Eye. The Witness. *The Ghost Train Murder. Hell is a City. The Angry Silence. Sink the Bismarck! *The Last Train. 1960: *Evidence in Concrete. 1961: The Mark. *The Grand Junction Case. Francis of Assisi. *The Never Never Murder. Barabbas. 1962: Mix Me a Person. HMS Defiant (US: Damn the Defiant!). *Fire Below. 1963: Man in the Middle. 1966: It (US: Return of the Golem). 1967: The Blood Beast Terror. 1968: Nobody Runs Forever. Twisted Nerve. 1974: The Black Windmill.

NASH, Mary
(M. Ryan) 1885–1976
Dark-haired, tight-lipped, stern-looking American actress of upright bearing and reproving gaze. She interrupted her long stage career just long enough to run in two dozen film credits between 1934 and 1946 and be absolutely beastly twice to Shirley Temple. She was also memorable as Katharine Hepburn's mother in The Philadelphia Story, but, after 1940, the quality of her roles declined and she returned to the stage from 1947 to the end of her career.

1916: Arms and the Woman. 1934: Uncertain Lady. 1935: College Scandal (GB: The Clock Strikes Eight). 1936: Come and Get It. 1937: Easy Living. Heidi. The King and the Chorus Girl (GB: Romance is Sacred). Wells Fargo.

NAPIER, Russell 1910–1974
Hook-nosed, intense-looking Australian actor who struggled at first on coming to Britain, then found a running role as the dogged, authoritative, raincoated policeman (usually called Duggan) in charge of numerous cases in the 30-minute series of 'Scotland Yard' featurettes, in which he could be seen, on and off, from 1953 to 1962.

NAPIER, Charles 1935–
Craggy, fair-haired, small-eyed, almost impossibly good-looking American actor with rock-like chin. After working as a male model, he broke into films as brainless sex symbols in sexploitation films by director Russ Meyer. In his younger days, Napier

1939: The Little Princess. The Rains Came. 1940: Charlie Chan in Panama. Gold Rush Maisie. The Philadelphia Story. Sailor's Lady. 1941: Men of Boys' Town. 1942: Calling Dr Gillespie. 1943: The Human Comedy. 1944: Cobra Woman. The Lady and the Monster (GB: The Lady and the Doctor). In the Meantime, Darling. 1945: Yolanda and the Thief. 1946: Monsieur Beaucaire. Swell Guy. Till the Clouds Roll By.

NATWICK, Mildred 1905–1994

One look at this sharp-faced, dark-haired American actress of set expression, and you knew that here was a lady with a sense of humour – but one that would stand no nonsense. In character roles on stage from an early age, she usually played bird-like eccentrics in films, but could also be very droll – especially as Jane Fonda's mother in Barefoot in the Park, a role which saw her nominated for an Academy Award. Also very enjoyable in harness with Helen Hayes as TV's spinster sleuths The Snoop Sisters, and as the witch Griselda in The Court Jester.

1940: The Long Voyage Home. 1945: The Enchanted Cottage. Yolanda and the Thief. 1946: The Late George Apley. 1947: A Woman's Vengeance. 1948: The Kissing Bandit. 3 Godfathers. 1949: She Wore a Yellow Ribbon. 1950: Cheaper by the Dozen. 1952: Against All Flags. The Quiet Man. 1955: Christopher Bean (TV. GB: cinemas). The Court Jester. The Trouble with Harry. 1956: Eloise (TV). Teenage Rebel. 1957: Tammy and the Bachelor (GB: Tammy). 1967: Barefoot in the Park. 1969: If It's Tuesday, This Must Be Belgium. The Maltese Bippy. Trilogy. 1971: Do Not Fold, Spindle or Mutilate (TV). 1972: The Female Instinct (TV. GB: The Snoop Sisters). The House Without a Christmas Tree (TV). A Thanksgiving Treasure (TV). 1974: Money to Burn (TV). Daisy Miller. 1975: At Long Last Love. The Easter Promise (TV). 1976: Addie and the King of Hearts (TV). 1979: You Can't Take It with You (TV). 1982: Maid in America (TV). Kiss Me Goodbye. 1988: Dangerous Liaisons.

NEDELL, Bernard 1898–1972

Dark, dapper, smooth, moustachioed American actor whose suavely crooked countenance had him type-cast as charming gangsters, even in British films, where he spent a long sojourn from 1929 to 1938. Hollywood called him back, but his roles there, though no less shady, were not so interesting and his film career had all but petered out by the late 1940s. Married to actress Olive Blakeney (1903–1963) who left him a widower. A second marriage ended in divorce.

1916: The Serpent. 1929: Eine Nacht in London/A Knight in London. The Silver King. The Return of the Rat. 1930: The Call of the Sea. The Man from Chicago. 1931: Shadows. 1932: Innocents of Chicago (US: Why Saps Leave Home). 1933: Her Imaginary Lover. 1934: The Girl in Possession. 1935: Lazybones. Heat Wave. 1936: Dusty Ermine (US: Hideout in the Alps). The Man Who Could Work Miracles. First Offence/Bad Blood. Terror on Tiptoe. 1937: The Live Wire (US: Plunder in the Air). Pick a Star. The Shadow Man. 1938: Oh Boy! Mr Moto's Gamble. *Come Across. Exposed. 1939: Secret Service of the Air. Lucky Night. Angels Wash Their Faces. They All Come Out. Those High Gray Walls (GB: The Gates of Alcatraz). Some Like It Hot. Fast and Furious. Slightly Honorable. 1940: Rangers of Fortune. Strange Cargo. So You Won't Talk. 1941: The Feminine Touch. Ziegfeld Girl. 1942: Ship Ahoy. 1943: The Desperadoes. Northern Pursuit. 1944: Maisie Goes to Reno (GB: You Can't Do That To Me). One Body Too Many. *Lucky Cowboy. 1945: Allotment Wives. 1946: Crime Doctor's Man Hunt. Behind Green Lights. 1947: Monsieur Verdoux. The Lone Wolf in Mexico. 1948: Albuquerque (GB: Silver City). The Loves of Carmen. 1960: Heller in Pink Tights. 1972: Hickey and Boggs.

NESBITT, Derren 1935–

British actor with thick lips, fair, curly hair and square face. Usually cast in aggressive roles, as small-time crook, smiling two-timer or sadistic villain. Married to Anne Aubrey from 1961 to 1973; the violent repercussions of their subsequent break-up probably harmed his career. Also directs.

1958: A Night to Remember. Room at the Top. The Silent Enemy. 1959: Life in Danger. Behemoth the Sea Monster (US: The Giant Behemoth). In the Nick. 1960: Sword of Sherwood Forest. Carolina. 1961: The Man in the Back Seat. Victim. 1962: Strongroom. Kill or Cure. Term of Trial. 1963: The Informers. 1965: The Amorous Adventures of Moll

Flanders. 1966: Operation Third Form. The Blue Max. 1967: The Naked Runner. 1968: Nobody Runs Forever. Where Eagles Dare. 1969: Monte Carlo or Bust! (US: Those Daring Young Men in Their Jaunty Jalopies). 1970: Berlin Affair (TV). 1971: Burke and Hare. 1972: Innocent Bystanders. Ooh ... You Are Awful (US: Get Charlie Tully). Not Now Darling. 1974: †The Amorous Milkman. 1976: Spy Story. 1978: Give Us Tomorrow. The Playbirds. 1979: The House on Garibaldi Street (TV. GB: cinemas). 1981: The Guns and the Fury. 1982: Funny Money. 1987: Eat the Rich. 1990: Bullseye! Fatal Sky. 1992: Double X – The Name of the Game.

† And directed

NETTLETON, Lois 1929–

Light-haired American actress of sunny features and warm personality, on the tall side perhaps for romantic roles, but very effective in the earlier part of her career before too many film misfires put a stopper on her Hollywood upsurge. Not the kind of actress that the present-day cinema knows what to do with, she has recently been stealing scenes in character roles. Also very busy on TV from 1955, a medium in which she has won two Emmys.

1956: Rendezvous (TV). 1959: Meet Me in St Louis (TV). 1962: Period of Adjustment. Come Fly with Me. 1963: Mail Order Bride (GB: West of Montana). 1967: Valley of Mystery. 1968: The Bamboo Saucer/Collision Course. 1969: The Good Guys and the Bad Guys. Any Second Now (TV). 1970: Weekend *of Terror (TV). Dirty Dingus Magee. The Sidelong Glances of a Pigeon Kicker. 1971: The Forgotten Man (TV). Terror in the Sky (TV). 1972: The Honkers. 1975: Fear on Trial (TV). Echoes of a Summer. 1979: Tourist (TV). 1980: Soggy Bottom USA. 1981: Butterfly. Deadly Blessing. 1982: The Best Little Whorehouse in Texas. 1985: Brass (TV). 1986: Manhunt for Claude Dallas (TV). 1994: The Feminine Touch.*

NICHOLS, Barbara

(B. Nickerauer) 1929–1976

This tall, blonde American actress with the 'Watch it, buster' face seems to be many people's favourite film floozie, and she certainly made her presence felt in most of her roles. A pity that her later life was dogged by illness; she was little seen, even on TV, after the late 1960s, and died following a long coma after liver complications. A striptease girl before she started an acting career.

1954: River of No Return. 1955: Miracle in the Rain. 1956: Manfish (GB: Calypso). Beyond a Reasonable Doubt. The King and Four Queens. The Wild Party. 1957: Sweet Smell of Success. The Pajama Game. Pal Joey. 1958: Ten North Frederick. The Naked and the Dead. 1959: Woman Obsessed. That Kind of Woman. The Scarface Mob (TV. GB: cinemas). Who Was That Lady? 1960: Where the Boys Are. 1961: The George Raft Story (GB: Spin of a Coin). 1962: House of Women. 1963: Looking for Love. 1964: Dear Heart. The Disorderly Orderly. 1965: The Loved One. The Human Duplicators. 1966: The Swinger. 1967: The Power. 1968: Sette uomini e un cervello. 1973: Charley and the Angel. 1975: Won Ton Ton, the Dog Who Saved Hollywood. The Photographer.

NICHOLS, Dandy

(Daisy Nichols) 1907–1986

Dark-haired, pudge-faced British actress whose apologetic manner turned to truculence with the passing of the years as her characters began to stand up for themselves. She started off as maids, chars and housewives that you could almost see tugging their forelocks, but her image changed from philosophical to pugnacious, especially with her long-running TV role as Else, the 'silly old moo' wife of the monstrous Alf Garnett in *Till Death Us Do Part*, and she was allowed

some abrasive dialogue and more interesting roles in her declining years. Died following a fall.

1947: Hue and Cry. Nicholas Nickleby. 1948: Portrait from Life (US: The Girl in the Painting). Woman Hater. The Winslow Boy. The Fallen Idol. Here Come the Huggetts. Scott of the Antarctic. The History of Mr Polly. 1949: Don't Ever Leave Me. Now Barabbas Was a Robber... 1950: Dance Hall. Tony Draws a Horse. The Clouded Yellow. 1951: High Treason. White Corridors. 1952: The Holly and the Ivy. The Happy Family (US: Mr Lord Says No). Mother Riley Meets the Vampire (US: Vampire Over London). Emergency Call (US: Hundred Hour Hunt). The Pickwick Papers. Women of Twilight (US: Twilight Women). 1953: Street Corner (US: Both Sides of the Law). The Wedding of Lilli Marlene. Meet Mr Lucifer. The Intruder. 1954: Time is My Enemy. The Crowded Sky. Mad About Men. 1955: Where There's a Will. The Deep Blue Sea. A Time to Kill. Lost (US: Tears for Simon). 1956: Tiger in the Smoke. Town on Trial! Not So Dusty. The Feminine Touch (US: The Gentle Touch). Yield to the Night (US: Blonde Sinner). 1957: Doctor at Large. The Strange World of Planet X (US: Cosmic Monsters). 1958: The Vikings. Carry On Sergeant. A Cry from the Streets. 1962: Crooks Anonymous. Don't Talk to Strange Men. 1963: Ladies Who Do. The Leather Boys. 1964: Act of Murder. 1965: Help! The Amorous Adventures of Moll Flanders. The Knack ... and how to get it. The Early Bird. Rotten to the Core. 1966: Doctor in Clover. Georgy Girl. 1967: How I Won the War. 1968: The Birthday Party. Carry On Doctor. Till Death Us Do Part. 1969: The Bed Sitting Room. 1972: The Alf Garnett Saga. 1973: O Lucky Man! 1974: Confessions of a Window Cleaner. Three for All. 1982: The Plague Dogs (voice only). Britannia Hospital.

NIMMO, Derek 1931–

Tall, dark, neat British comic actor with mouth as round as his eyes and plummy, upper-class tones; an entertainer born out of his time. Thirty years earlier, he would have been snapped up for leading roles in 'silly ass' comedies. As it was, he only decorated the fringes of a few 1960s' offerings before devoting the major part of his energies to radio (where he became an

expert in panel games), TV (especially in the series *All Gas and Gaiters*) and farces in the theatre. Famous for comic clerics.

*1960: The Millionairess. 1961: Go to Blazes. It's Trad, Dad! 1962: (US: Ring-a-Ding Rhythm). The Amorous Prawn (US: The Amorous Mr Prawn). 1963: Tamahine. Hot Enough for June (US: Agent 8¾). The Small World of Sammy Lee. Heavens Above! 1964: A Hard Day's Night. The System (US: The Girl-Getters). The Bargee. Murder Ahoy! Coast of Skeletons. 1965: Joey Boy. *The Hidden Face. The Liquidator. 1966: The Yellow Hat. Mister Ten Per Cent. 1967: Casino Royale. 1969: A Talent For Loving. 1972: Sunstruck. 1975: One of Our Dinosaurs is Missing.*

NIMOY, Leonard 1931–

Dark-haired, sternly handsome, rarely smiling, tall American actor whose career was mainly in supporting roles until, at 35, he landed the co-starring role of the pixie-eared, half-Vulcan Mr Spock in the TV series *Star Trek*. This unemotional character soon attracted a following of millions worldwide, and, although the series was cancelled after three seasons, he was able to repeat the role in a series of big-screen *Star Trek* films that began in 1979. He directed two of these as well, but his most successful foray into direction to date has undoubtedly been the massive comedy hit *3 Men and a Baby*.

1951: Queen for a Day. Rhubarb. 1952: Francis Goes to West Point. Kid Monk Baroni (GB: Young Paul Baroni). Zombies of the

Stratosphere (serial). 1953: Old Overland Trail. 1954: Them! 1958: The Brain Eaters. Satan's Satellites (feature version of 1952 serial). 1963: The Balcony. 1964: Seven Days in May. 1966: Deathwatch. 1967: Valley of Mystery (TV. GB: cinemas). 1970: Assault on the Wayne (TV). 1971: Catlow. 1972: Baffled! 1973: The Alpha Caper (TV. GB: cinemas, as Inside Job). 1975: The Missing Are Deadly (TV). 1978: Invasion of the Body Snatchers. 1979: Star Trek the Motion Picture. 1980: Seizure – The Story of Kathy Morris (TV). 1982: A Woman Called Golda (TV). Star Trek II: The Wrath of Khan. Marco Polo (TV). 1984: Star Trek III: The Search for Spock. 1986: Transformers – The Movie (voice only). The Voyage Home Star Trek IV. 1988: Just One Step: The Great Peace March. 1989: Star Trek V: The Final Frontier. 1991: Never Forget (TV). Star Trek VI: The Undiscovered Country. 1994: The Pagemaster (voice only). Destiny in Space (narrator only).

As director:
1984: Star Trek III: The Search for Spock. 1986: The Voyage Home: Star Trek IV. 1987: 3 Men and a Baby. 1988: The Good Mother/The Price of Passion. 1990: Funny About Love. 1994: Holy Matrimony.

NOIRET, Philippe 1930–
Dark-haired (now grey), droop-eyed, lap-chinned, houndlike French actor whose lugubrious features can project weariness and integrity with seamless conviction, sometimes within one character. He began acting in his teens, but only really came into his own as a character star in the 1970s, especially in films directed by Bertrand Tavernier, for whom he was memorable as L'horloger de Saint-Paul and several subsequent roles. He also displayed a deft line in dog-eared policemen of a certain grubby integrity, but has proved himself a versatile player who will tackle almost anything; another big personal (and international) hit came with his endearing projectionist in Nuovo Cinema Paradiso. Married to actress Monique Chomette since 1962. A great dog-lover (hardly surprising perhaps) in private life. César (French Oscar) for Le vieux fusil in 1975.

1949: Gigi. 1950: Olivia. 1951: Agence matrimoniale. 1954: La Pointe-Courte. 1960: Ravissante. Zazie dans le métro. 1961: le capitaine Fracasse (US: The Captain). Amours célèbres. Rendez-vous. Tout l'or du monde (GB and US: All the Gold in the World). 1962: Ballade pour un voyou. Comme un poisson dans l'eau. Le crime ne paie pas (US: Crime Does Not Pay). Clémentine chérie. Le massaggiatrici. Thérèse Desqueyroux/Thérèse. 1963: Cyrano et d'Artagnan. Mort où est ta victoire? 1964: Les copains. Monsieur. 1965: *Un autre monde (narrator only). Lady L (voice dubbed by Peter Ustinov). La vie de château. 1966: The Night of the Generals. Who Are You, Polly Maggoo? Les sultans. Tendre voyou (US: Tender Scoundrel). Le voyage du père. 1967: Alexandre, le bien-heureux (US: Very Happy Alexander). L'une et l'autre. Woman Times Seven. *Callot Fécit (narrator only). 1968: Adolphe ou L'âge tendre. The Assassination Bureau. Breughel (narrator only). Mister Freedom. The Immortal Story (voice only, French language version). 1969: Clérambard. Justine. Topaz. Les caprices de Marie (US: Give Her the Moon). 1970: Murphy's War. L'étalon. 1971: Les aveux les plus doux. La vieille fille. La mandarine. Time for Loving. 1972: L'attentat (GB: Plot. US: The French Conspiracy). Siamo tutti in libertà provvisoria. Le trèfle a cinq feuilles. 1973: L'horloger de Saint-Paul (GB: The Watchmaker of Saint Paul. US: The Clockmaker of Saint Paul). La grande bouffe. Les Gaspards. The Serpent. Poil de Carotte. Touche pas à la femme blanche. Un nuage entre les dents. Le mano spietata della legge (US: The Left Hand of the Law). 1974: Le secret (GB and US: The Secret). Que le fête commence (US: Let Joy Reign Supreme). Le jeu avec le feu. 1975: Amici miei. Il commune senso del pudore. Le juge et l'assassin (US: The Judge and His Hangman). Monsieur Albert. Le vieux fusil. 1976: Une femme à sa fenêtre. Le desert des Tartares. 1977: Purple Taxi/Un taxi mauve. Tendre poulet (GB: Dear Detective. US: Dear Inspector). La barricade du point du jour. Coup de foudre (unfinished). 1978: Le témoin. Who is Killing the Great Chefs of Europe? (GB: Too Many Chefs). 1979: On a volé la cuisse de Jupiter. Due pezzi di pane. Rue de Pied-de-Grue. 1980: Pile ou face. Tre fratelli. Une semaine de vacances. Coup de torchon (GB and US: Clean Slate). Il faut tuer Birgitt Haas. 1982: L'étoile du Nord. Amici miei II. 1983: L'Africain. L'ami de Vincent. La grand carnaval. 1984: Aurora (US: TV). Fort Saganne. Souvenirs, souvenirs. Les ripoux (GB: Le Cop). L'été prochain. 1985: Le quatrième pouvoir. Les rois du gag. 1986: Speriamo che sia femmina (US: Let's Hope It's a Girl). *La harka. La femme secrète. Twist Again à Moscou. 'Round Midnight. 1987: Chouans! La famiglia. Masques. Gli occhiali d'oro. Noyade interdite (US: No Drowning Allowed). 1988: Nuovo Cinema Paradiso (GB: New Cinema Paradise. US: Cinema Paradiso). Il frullo del passero. Rosso Veneziano. Young Toscanini. 1989: The Return of the Musketeers. La vie et rien d'autre (US: Life and Nothing But...). Dimenticare Palermo (GB and US: To Forget Palermo). 1990: Faux et usage de faux. Ripoux contre ripoux (GB: Le Cop II). Uranus. 1991: La domenica specialmente. J'embrasse pas/I Don't Kiss. Zuppa di pesce. Trente films contre l'oubli/Contre l'oubli. 1992: Nous deux. Max et Jeremie. 1993: Tango. Tirano banderos. La fille de D'Artagnan (GB: D'Artagnan's Daughter). 1994: For Love, Only for Love. Grosse fatigue. Il postino/Le facteur. Le roi de Paris.

NOONAN, Tommy
(T. Noon) 1921–1968
Dark-haired, breezy, bespectacled American comedian usually as the young man shy about girls. A former teenage player, he broke through from small parts to top featured roles in Gentleman Prefer Blondes. Later there were two or three comedies in harness with Peter Marshall, with whom Noonan had already appeared in Starlift, before Noonan revealed the voyeur beneath the glasses by directing two sexploitation comedies. Half-brother of actor John Ireland. Died from a brain tumour.

1938: Boys' Town. 1945: *Double Honeymoon. *The Big Beef. *Beware of Redheads. *What, No Cigarettes? George White's Scandals. Ding Dong Williams (GB: Melody Maker). Dick Tracy (GB: Split Face). 1946: The Bamboo Blonde. Criminal Court. The Truth About Murder (GB: The Lie Detector). Step by Step. The Big Fix. Crack-Up. From This Day Forward. 1947: The Fabulous Joe. Riff Raff. Born to Kill (GB: Lady of Deceit). A Likely Story. 1948: Open Secret. Jungle Patrol. 1949: Trapped. I Shot Jesse James. I Cheated the Law. Adam's Rib. Battleground. The Set Up. 1950: Holiday Rhythm. The Return of Jesse James. 1951: FBI Girl. Starlift. The Model and the Marriage Broker. 1953: Gentlemen Prefer Blondes. 1954: A Star is Born. 1955: Violent Saturday. How to be Very, Very Popular. 1956: The Ambassador's Daughter. The Best Things in Life Are Free. Bundle of Joy. 1957: The Girl Most Likely. 1959: The Rookie. 1960: The Schnook (GB: Double Trouble). 1962: Swingin' Along (revised version of The Schnook). 1963: †Promises! Promises! 1964: †Three Nuts in Search of a Bolt. 1967: Cotton Pickin Chickenpickers.

† Also directed

NORTON, Jack
(Mortimer J. Naughton) 1889–1958
This affectionately regarded American ex-vaudevillian with dark, crinkly hair and uptilted pencil moustache staggered in a state of blissful screen inebriation through

more than 100 film roles as amiable alcoholics before disappearing to (in real life, teetotal) early retirement at 60. With Arthur Housman (*qv*), he was one of Hollywood's two busiest film 'drunks', and a perfect member for Preston Sturges' 'Ale and Quail Club' in *The Palm Beach Story*. Died from a respiratory ailment.

1934: *The Girl from Missouri (GB: One Hundred Per Cent Pure). *Perfectly Mismated. Cockeyed Cavaliers. *Fixing a Stew. *Super Snooper. *One Too Many. One Hour Late. *Woman Haters. *Counsel on De Fence. Death on the Diamond. Sweet Music. Now I'll Tell (GB: When New York Sleeps). Bordertown. 1935: One Hour Late. Go into Your Dance (GB: Casino de Paree). She Gets Her Man. Calling All Cars. The Golden Lily. Dante's Inferno. Front Page Woman. Stolen Harmony. Page Miss Glory. One More Spring. Doctor Socrates. The Girl from 10th Avenue (GB: Men on Her Mind). Alibi Ike. Going Highbrow. Don't Bet on Blondes. Miss Pacific Fleet. His Night Out. Broadway Gondolier. Ship Cafe. Ruggles of Red Gap. 1936: The Moon's Our Home. *Down the Ribber. After the Thin Man. The Preview Murder Mystery. Gold Diggers of 1937. Too Many Parents. Anything Goes. 1937: Marked Woman. Time Out for Romance. The Great Garrick. Pick a Star. Thoroughbreds Don't Cry. A Day at the Races. My Dear Miss Aldrich. Married Before Breakfast. Meet the Missus. *Swing Fever. 1938: *The Awful Tooth. Man Proof. Arsène Lupin Returns. Kentucky Moonshine (GB: Four Men and a Girl). Strange Faces. Meet the Girls. Jezebel. Hold That Kiss. Love is a Headache. Thanks for the Memory. King of Alcatraz (GB: King of the Alcatraz). 1939: Grand Jury Secrets. Joe and Ethel Turp Call on the President. The Roaring Twenties. Laugh It Off (GB: Lady Be Gay). Society Smugglers. The Lone Wolf Spy Hunt (GB: The Lone Wolf's Daughter). It's a Wonderful World. 1940: The Farmer's Daughter. The Villain Still Pursued Her. Opened by Mistake. Let's Make Music. A Night at Earl Carroll's. The Bank Dick (GB: The Bank Detective). The Ghost Breakers. Road Show. 1941: You Belong to Me (GB: Good Morning, Doctor). Down in San Diego. The Feminine Touch. No Greater Sin (GB: Social Enemy No. 1). *Crazy Like a Fox. *Ready, Willing, But Unable. Louisiana Purchase. No Hands on the Clock. Ride On, Vaquero. 1942: The Spoilers. Ice-Capades Revue (GB: Rhythm Hits the Ice). Moonlight in Havana. Dr Renault's Secret. The Palm Beach Story. My Favorite Spy. Tennessee Johnson (GB: The Man on America's Conscience). The Fleet's In. Roxie Hart. Brooklyn Orchid. The McGuerins from Brooklyn. 1943: Taxi, Mister. Assignment in Brittany. It Ain't Hay (GB: Money for Jam). So's Your Uncle. Thank Your Lucky Stars. The Kansan (GB: Wagon Wheels). The Falcon Strikes Back. Gildersleeve on Broadway. Lady Bodyguard. Prairie Chickens. 1944: *His Tale is Told. Ghost Catchers. Once Upon a Time. The Story of Dr Wassell. Here Come the Waves. The Chinese Cat/Charlie Chan in The Chinese Cat. *His Hotel Sweet. *Doctor, Feel My Pulse! *Heather and Yon. The Miracle of Morgan's Creek. Cover Girl. And the Angels Sing. Shine On Harvest Moon. Hail the Conquering Hero. Make Your Own Bed. The Big Noise. Barbary Coast Gent. Going My Way. 1945: Hold That Blonde. Her Highness and the Bellboy. Wonder Man. Fashion Model. The Naughty Nineties. The Scarlet Clue. Flame of the Barbary Coast. The Horn Blows at Midnight. Man Alive. Strange Confession. Lady on a Train. Two O'Clock Courage. Captain Tugboat Annie. A Guy, a Gal, a Pal. *Dance, Dance, Dance. Double Honeymoon. 1946: *Rhythm and Weep. The Strange Mr Gregory. No Leave, No Love. Blue Skies. Lady Luck. The Hoodlum Saint. Nocturne. The Sin of Harold Diddlebock (later and GB: Mad Wednesday!). The Kid from Brooklyn. Rendezvous 24. Shadows Over Chinatown. Bringing Up Father. 1947: Linda Be Good. Down to Earth. Variety Girl. *The Hired Husband. 1948: Variety Time. Alias a Gentleman. 1949: ††Two Knights in Brooklyn/Two Mugs from Brooklyn.

†† Combined GB version of *The McGuerins from Brooklyn/Taxi, Mister*.

NOVELLO, Jay 1904–1982
Dark, scurrying, rodent-like, usually moustachioed little American actor, just as likely to be a dapper small-time crook or the unkempt Arab in the market-place trying to sell you his wares. Played many nationalities in his time — occasionally even his own! Fairly busy in films until 1966 (although almost always in small roles), and then increasingly tied up in television to the end of his career. Died from cancer.

1938: *Boys' Town. Tenth Avenue Kid. Flirting with Fate. 1939: Calling All Marines. The Girl from Havana. The Border Legion. 1940: *Bandits and Ballads. Colorado. Outside the 3-Mile Limit (GB: Mutiny on the Seas). The Sea Hawk. 1941: Bad Man of Deadwood. Citadel of Crime (GB: Outside the Law). The Great Train Robbery. Robin Hood of the Pecos. Two-Gun Sheriff. Unholy Partners. Sheriff of Tombstone. They Met in Bombay. 1942: Bells of Capistrano. Cairo. Junior G-Men of the Air (serial). King of the Mounties (serial). Dr Broadway. Sleepytime Gal. Swamp Woman. 1943: The Adventures of Smilin' Jack (serial). The Man from Music Mountain. Passport to Suez. Sleepy Lagoon. Phantom Lady. 1944: Captain America (serial). The Great Alaskan Mystery (serial). Can't Help Singing. The Conspirators. Dragon Seed. Mystery of the River Boat (serial). 1945: The Bullfighters. The Chicago Kid. Federal Operator 99 (serial). Hotel Berlin. Passport to Suez. Rhapsody in Blue. 1946: Behind City Lights. Perilous Holiday. 1948: Kiss the Blood Off My Hands (GB: Blood on My Hands). Port Said. 1949: Tell It to the Judge. 1951: Smuggler's Island. Sirocco. 1952: Captain Pirate (GB: Captain Blood, Fugitive). The Iron Mistress. Cattle Town. The Miracle of Our Lady of Fatima (GB: The Miracle of Fatima). Operation Secret. The Sniper. Ma and Pa Kettle On Vacation (GB: Ma and Pa Kettle Go to Paris). 1953: Diamond Queen. Beneath the 12-Mile Reef. The Hindu (GB: Sabaka). The Robe. Crime Wave (GB: The City is Dark). 1954: The Gambler from Natchez. The Mad Magician. 1955: The Prodigal. Bengazi. Son of Sinbad. 1956: Jaguar. Lisbon. The Pride and the Passion. 1957: Execution Night (TV. GB: cinemas). 1958: The Perfect Furlough (GB: Strictly for Pleasure). Most Dangerous Man Alive (released 1961). 1959: The Wonderful Country. 1960: Zorro the Avenger (TV. GB: cinemas). This Rebel Breed. The Lost World. 1961: Atlantis the Lost Continent. Pocketful of Miracles. Escape from Zahrain. 1962: The Sutton Story. 1963: The Man from the Diners' Club. 1965: The Art of Love. Harum Scarum (GB: Harem Holiday). Sylvia. A Very Special Favor. Zebra in the Kitchen. 1966: What Did You Do in the War, Daddy? The Caper of the Golden Bulls (GB: Carnival of Thieves). 1969: The Comic. 1971: Powderkeg (TV. GB: cinemas). 1976: The Domino Principle (GB: The Domino Killings. Released 1978).

O'BRIEN, Virginia 1921–

Dark-haired, deadpan singer and comedienne who joined MGM after Broadway success, but never proved more than an added attraction in several of their musicals, most notably *The Harvey Girls*. Married (first of two) to actor Kirk Alyn, one of the screen portrayers of Superman, from 1942 to 1955. Niece of film director Lloyd Bacon.

*1940: Hullabaloo. Sky Murder. 1941: Ringside Maisie. Lady Be Good. The Big Store. 1942: Ship Ahoy! Panama Hattie. 1943: Du Barry Was a Lady. Thousands Cheer. 1944: Two Girls and a Sailor, Meet the People. Ziegfeld Follies (released 1946). 1945: The Harvey Girls. 1946: The Show-Off. Till the Clouds Roll By. The Great Morgan. 1947: Merton of the Movies. 1948: *Martin Block's Musical Merry-Go-Round. 1955: Francis in the Navy.*

OAKLAND, Simon 1922–1983

Thick-faced, black-haired, gravel-voiced, square-built American actor with Edward G Robinson lips, usually seen as cigar-puffing crook or politician, his sharkish grin marking him out as 'up to no good'. Started his career as a violinist, then moved to an acting career, in films from 1958 after one brief early appearance. His first roles were as co-star, but he soon moved weightily into well-dressed character parts. TV almost completely took over his acting output after 1973. Died from cancer.

1947: T-Men. 1958: The Brothers Karamazov. I Want to Live! 1959: Who Was That Lady? The Rise and Fall of Legs Diamond. 1960: Psycho. Murder Inc. 1961: West Side Story. 1962: Hemingway's Adventures of a Young Man (GB: Adventures of a Young Man). Follow That Dream. One Third of a Man. 1963: Wall of Noise. 1964: The Raiders. Ready for the People. The Satan Bug. 1965: Who Has Seen the Wind? 1966: The Plainsman. The Sand Pebbles. 1967: Tony Rome. Chubasco. 1968: Bullitt. 1970: On a Clear Day You Can See Forever. 1971: Crosscurrent/The Cable Car Murder (TV). The Hunting Party. Scandalous John. The Night Stalker (TV). Chato's Land. 1972: Key West (TV). The Night Strangler (TV). Toma (TV. GB: Man of Many Faces). The Scorpio Scarab. 1973: Emperor of the North Pole (GB: Emperor of the North). Happy Mother's Day ... Love George/Run, Stranger, Run. 1974: Crackle of Death. 1977: Young Joe, The Forgotten Kennedy (TV). 1978: Evening in Byzantium (TV).

O'CONNELL, Arthur 1908–1981

American actor with tousled light-brown hair, owlish, worried-looking face and fluffy, drooping moustache. He got nowhere very fast in films until he received a showy role in *Picnic* (1955), grabbed the chance with both hands, and suddenly became a man in demand, working steadily for 20 years. Film debut in Britain. Oscar-nominated for *Picnic* and *Anatomy of a Murder*. Died from a brain disease.

*1938: Murder in Soho (US: Murder in the Night). Freshman Year. 1940: And One Was Beautiful. *Taint Legal. Dr Kildare Goes*

*Home. Two Girls on Broadway (GB: Choose Your Partner). The Leather Pushers. *Bested by a Beard. *He Asked for It. 1941: Citizen Kane. Lucky Devils. 1942: Blondie's Blessed Event (GB: A Bundle of Trouble). Man from Headquarters. Fingers at the Window. Canal Zone. Shepherd of the Ozarks (GB: Susanna). Yokel Boy (GB: Hitting the Headlines). Law of the Jungle. 1944: It Happened Tomorrow. 1948: The Naked City. State of the Union (GB: The World and His Wife). One Touch of Venus. Homecoming. Open Secret. Force of Evil. Countess of Monte Cristo. 1950: Love That Brute. 1951: The Whistle at Eaton Falls (GB: Richer Than the Earth). 1955: Picnic. 1956: The Proud Ones. The Solid Gold Cadillac. The Man in the Gray Flannel Suit. Bus Stop. The Monte Carlo Story. 1957: April Love. Operation Mad Ball. The Violators. 1958: Man of the West. Voice in the Mirror. 1959: Hound Dog Man. Gidget. Anatomy of a Murder. Operation Petticoat. 1960: Cimarron. The Great Imposter. 1961: Pocketful of Miracles. A Thunder of Drums. Misty. 1962: Follow That Dream. 1963: Nightmare in the Sun. 1964: The Third Secret. Kissin' Cousins. The Seven Faces of Dr Lao. Your Cheatin' Heart. 1965: The Monkey's Uncle. The Third Day. The Great Race. 1966: Ride Beyond Vengeance. Birds Do It. The Silencers. Fantastic Voyage. A Covenant With Death. 1967: The Reluctant Astronaut. The Power. 1968: If He Hollers, Let Him Go! 1969: Seven in Darkness (TV). 1970: The Last Valley. Do Not Throw Cushions into the Ring. There Was a Crooked Man. Suppose They Gave a War and Nobody Came? 1971: A Taste of Evil (TV). 1972: Ben. The Poseidon Adventure. They Only Kill Their Masters. 1973: Shootout in a One-Dog Town (TV). Wicked, Wicked. 1974: Huckleberry Finn (TV). The Hiding Place (released 1977).*

O'CONNOR, Carroll 1922–

Round-faced, curly-haired American actor of Irish extraction who began his acting career in Ireland. Returning to America, he began playing in films and TV from 1960, usually as blustering, apoplectic, bull-at-a-gate types, but his film career as a character star was all but wiped out by his role as Archie Bunker (based on Britain's Alf Garnett) which ran on television from 1971 to 1982, winning O'Connor four Emmy awards. Underwent heart bypass surgery in 1989, but has continued to act.

1945: *Johnny Frenchman.* 1960: *Sacco and Vanzetti (TV). A Fever in the Blood.* 1961: *By Love Possessed. Parrish. Lad: a Dog.* 1962: *Lonely Are the Brave. Belle Sommers.* 1963: *Cleopatra.* 1965: *In Harm's Way.* 1966: *What Did You Do in the War, Daddy? Not With My Wife, You Don't! Hawaii. Warning Shot.* 1967: *Waterhole Number 3 (GB: Waterhole 3). Point Blank.* 1968: *The Devil's Brigade. For Love of Ivy. A Walk in the Night (TV).* 1969: *Fear No Evil (TV). Ride a Northbound Horse (TV. GB: cinemas). Death of a Gunfighter. Marlowe.* 1970: *Kelly's Heroes. Doctors' Wives.* 1974: *Law and Disorder.* 1977: *The Last Hurrah (TV).* 1985: *Brass (TV).* 1987: *The Father Clements Story (TV).* 1988. *Heat of the Night (TV).*

O'CONNOR, Una

(Agnes McGlade) 1880–1959

Twittering, pinch-featured, black-haired Irish actress of pale complexion, darting eyes and birdlike movements. Starting in British films (after an early career with the Abbey Theatre, Dublin), she moved to Hollywood to recreate her stage role (Ellen Bridges) in *Cavalcade*, and was soon launched into a succession of maids, crones, chaperones and nagging wives — mostly less warm-hearted versions of characters played in Britain by Kathleen Harrison. Could be depended on to cry 'Lawks a mussy!' at the drop of a plate.

1929: *Dark Red Roses.* 1930: *Murder! To Oblige a Lady. Timbuctoo.* 1933: *Cavalcade. The Invisible Man. Mary Stevens MD. Pleasure Cruise.* 1934: *The Poor Rich. The Barretts of Wimpole Street. Stingaree. All Men Are Enemies. Orient Express. Chained. *Horse Play.* 1935: *David Copperfield. Father Brown, Detective. The Informer. Bride of Frankenstein. Thunder in the Night. The Perfect Gentleman.* 1936: *The Plough and the Stars. Rose Marie. Little Lord Fauntleroy. Suzy. Lloyds of London.* 1937: *Personal Property. Call It A Day.* 1938: *The Return of the Frog. The Adventures of Robin Hood.* 1939: *We Are Not Alone. All Women Have Secrets.* 1940: *It All Came True. The Sea Hawk. Lillian Russell. He Stayed for Breakfast. Kisses for Breakfast.* 1941: *The Strawberry Blonde. How Green Was My Valley. Her First Beau. Three Girls About Town.* 1942: *Always in My Heart. Random Harvest. My Favorite Spy. This Land is Mine!* 1943: *Forever and a Day. Holy Matrimony. Government Girl.* 1944: *The Canterville Ghost. My Pal Wolf.* 1945: **Whispering Walls. Christmas in Connecticut. The Bells of St Mary's.* 1946: *The Return of Monte Cristo (GB: Monte Cristo's Revenge). Banjo. Child of Divorce. Cluny Brown. Of Human Bondage. Unexpected Guest.* 1947: *Ivy. Lost Honeymoon. The Corpse Came COD.* 1948: *Fighting Father Dunne.* 1949: *The Adventures of Don Juan (GB: The New Adventures of Don Juan).* 1957: *Witness for the Prosecution.*

O'HANLON, George 1912–1989

Rubber-faced, darkly tousle-haired, stocky American dancer, actor and light comedian with distinctive voice and 'honest Joe' features. A bit player and chorus boy at Warners through the 1930s, he could turn up as cabby, reporter, college man or man in the street as well as dancer. He began getting roles with dialogue at the end of the decade, but the 1940s brought his real fame for film buffs, when he played Joe McDoakes, the hapless 'Man behind the 8-ball' in 63 short comedies at the studio that all began with the words *So You . . .* When the series ended in 1956, he played some supporting roles, made a couple of TV series and supplied the voice of George Jetson in *The Jetsons*, a TV cartoon hit that ran for more than a decade from 1962. He died after a stroke. His son, George O'Hanlon Jr, also became an actor.

1932: *The Death Kiss (as extra. And many more).* 1934: *Marrying Widows.* 1937: *Hollywood Hotel.* 1938: *Brother Rat. Jezebel.* 1939: *Hell's Kitchen. Dust Be My Destiny. Daughters Courageous. Women in the Wind.* 1940: *The Fighting 69th. Saturday's Children. Knute Rockne – All American (GB: A Modern Hero). City for Conquest. Sailor's Lady. A Child is Born.* 1941: *Navy Blues. New Wine (GB: The Great Awakening).* 1942: *The Man from Headquarters. Ladies' Day. *So You Want to Give Up Smoking. *So You Think You Need Glasses. Criminal Investigator. A Gentleman After Dark.* 1943: *Nearly Eighteen. Corvette K-225 (GB: The Nelson Touch). Hers to Hold. All by Myself.* 1945: **So You Think You're Allergic.* 1946: **So You Want to Play the Horses. *So You Want to Keep Your Hair. *So You Think You're a Nervous Wreck.* 1947: *The Hucksters. Headin' for Heaven. Spirit of West Point. *So You're Going to be a Father. *So You Want to be in Pictures. *So You're Going on a Vacation. *So You Want to be a Salesman. *So You Want to Hold Your Wife. *So You Want an Apartment.* 1948: *Are You With It? June Bride. *So You Want to be a Gambler. *So You Want to Build a House. *So You Want to be a Detective. *So You Want to be in Politics. *So You Want to be on the Radio. *So You Want to be a Baby-Sitter. The Counterfeiters.* 1949: *Joe Palooka in The Big Fight. Zamba (GB: Zamba the Gorilla). *So You Want to be Popular. *So You Want to be a Muscleman. *So You're Having In-Law Trouble. *So You Want to Get Rich Quick. *So You Want to be an Actor.* 1950: **So You Want to Throw a Party. *So You Think You're Not Guilty. *So You Want to Hold Your Husband. *So You Want to Move. *So You Want a Raise. *So You're Going to Have an Operation. *So You Want to be a Handyman.* 1951: *The Tanks Are Coming. Joe Palooka in The Triple Cross (GB: The Triple Cross). *So You Want to be a Cowboy. *So You Want to be a Paperhanger. *So You Want to Buy a Used Car. *So You Want to be a Bachelor. *So You Want to be a Plumber. *So You Want to Get It Wholesale.* 1952: *Park Row. The Lion and the Horse. Cattle Town. *So You Want to Enjoy Life. *So You're Going to a Convention. *So You Never Tell a Lie. *So You're Going to the Dentist. *So You Want to Wear the Pants. *So You Want to be a Musician.* 1953: **So You Want to Learn to Dance. *So You Want a Television Set. *So You Love Your Dog. *So You Think You Can't Sleep. *So You Want to be an Heir.* 1954: **So You're Having Neighbor Trouble. *So You Want to be Your Own Boss. *So You Want to Go to a Nightclub. *So You're Taking in a Roomer. *So You Want to Know Your Relatives.* 1955: **So You Don't Trust Your Wife. *So You Want to be a Gladiator. *So You Want to be on a Jury. *So You Want to Build a Model Railroad. *So You Want to be a VP. *So You Want to be a Policeman.* 1956: *Battle Stations. *So You Think the Grass is Greener. *So You Want to be Pretty. *So You Want to Play the Piano. *So Your Wife Wants to Work.* 1957: *Bop Girl Goes Calypso. Kronos.* 1959: *†The Rookie.* 1964: *For Those Who Think Young.* 1968: *I Sailed to Tahiti with an All-Girl Crew.* 1971: *Million Dollar Duck.* 1972: *Now You See Him, Now You Don't.* 1973: *Charley and the Angel. The World's Greatest Athlete.* 1976: *Rocky.* 1990: *Jetsons: The Movie (voice only).*

† And directed

O'HERLIHY, Dan 1919–

Tall, taciturn, soft-spoken Irish actor, not unlike Louis Hayward in features. Began in British films, but unexpectedly got his breakthrough to more prominent roles in Mexico, from his leading performance in Bunuel's Robinson Crusoe film. Hollywood seemed to see him mainly as a smiling villain in costume adventures and after a series of unworthy roles he has worked principally for American television. Oscar nomination for *The Adventures of Robinson Crusoe.* Latterly the power-hungry 'Old Man' in the *RoboCop* films. Brother of director Michael O'Herlihy.

1946: Odd Man Out. Hungry Hill. 1948: Macbeth. Kidnapped. Larceny. 1950: Iroquois Trail (GB: The Tomahawk Trail). 1951: The Desert Fox (GB: Rommel − Desert Fox). Soldiers Three. The Highwayman. At Sword's Point (GB: Sons of the Musketeers. Completed 1949). The Blue Veil. 1952: Actors and Sin. Operation Secret. Sword of Venus (GB: Island of Monte Cristo). The Adventures of Robinson Crusoe. 1953: Invasion USA. 1954: Bengal Brigade (GB: Bengal Rifles). The Black Shield of Falworth. 1955: The Purple Mask. The Virgin Queen. 1956: That Woman Opposite (US: City After Midnight). 1957: The Blackwell Story (TV. GB: cinemas). 1958: Home Before Dark. 1959: Imitation of Life. The Young Land. 1960: One Foot in Hell. A Terrible Beauty (US: The Night Fighters). To the Sounds of Trumpets (TV). 1961: King of the Roaring Twenties (GB: The Big Bankroll). Port of Revenge. 1962: The Cabinet of Caligari. 1964: Fail Safe. 1968: How to Steal the World (TV. GB: cinemas). 1969: 100 Rifles. The Big Cube. 1970: Waterloo. 1971: The People (TV). 1972: The Carey Treatment. 1974: QB VII (TV). The Tamarind Seed. 1976: Banjo Hackett − Roamin' Free (TV). 1977: Good Against Evil (TV). 1978: MacArthur (GB: MacArthur the Rebel General). Deadly Game (TV). The Girl in the Empty Grave (TV). 1979: TR Sloane of the Secret Service (TV). 1983: Halloween III: Season of the Witch. 1984: The Last Starfighter. 1986: The Whoopee Boys. Dark Mansions (TV). 1987: RoboCop. The Dead. John Huston and the Dubliners. 1990: RoboCop 2. 1993: Love, Cheat and Steal.

OLIVER, Edna May
(E.M. Nutter, later legally changed) 1883−1942
One of Hollywood's invaluable horse-faced character actresses: Edna May Oliver's characters possessed arched eyebrows, a purposeful stare and a disapproving sniff, and stood no nonsense from anyone. A delight as a spinster schoolteacher sleuth in three mid-thirties whodunnits. Died from an intestinal disorder on her 59th birthday. Oscar nominee for Drums Along the Mohawk.

1923: Wife in Name Only. Three O'Clock in the Morning. Icebound. Restless Wives. 1924: Manhattan. 1925: Lovers in Quarantine. The Lady Who Lied. The Lucky Devil. 1926: The American Venus. Let's Get Married. 1929: The Saturday Night Kid. 1930: Half Shot at Sunrise. Hook, Line and Sinker. 1931: Fanny Foley Herself (GB: Top of the Bill). Newly Rich (GB: Forbidden Adventure). Cimarron. Cracked Nuts. Laugh and Get Rich. 1932: Hold 'em Jail. Lost Squadron. The Conquerors. Ladies of the Jury. Penguin Pool Murder (GB: The Penguin Pool Mystery). 1933: It's Great to be Alive. The Great Jasper. Only Yesterday. Little Women. Alice in Wonderland. Ann Vickers. Strawberry Roan (GB: Flying Fury). Meet the Baron. 1934: We're Rich Again. The Poor Rich. Murder on the Blackboard. The Last Gentleman. 1935: David Copperfield. A Tale of Two Cities. No More Ladies. Murder on a Honeymoon. 1936: Romeo and Juliet. 1937: My Dear Miss Aldrich. Parnell. Rosalie. 1938: Little Miss Broadway. Paradise for Three (GB: Romance for Three). 1939: The Story of Vernon and Irene Castle. Drums Along the Mohawk. Second Fiddle. Nurse Edith Cavell. 1940: Pride and Prejudice. 1941: Lydia.

OLMOS, Edward James 1947−
Dark-haired, wide-mouthed, Los Angeles-born actor of Mexican-American parentage, with deeply-pitted and slightly owlish handsomeness. He started his career as a rock singer and transferred his talents to the musical stage with award-winning results. He soon began to make his presence felt in films and on TV as a resourceful and versatile character star, particularly as the down-to-earth police chief in the hit TV series Miami Vice, which ran from 1984 to 1989. He was deservedly nominated for an Academy Award for his inspired performance as an innovative, real-life maths teacher in Stand and Deliver, but subsequent ventures with Olmos at their centre have been less successful, and his future may lie as top support to the stars in mainline features and leading player in offbeat dramas. Married to actress Lorraine Bracco.

1975: Aloha, Bobby and Rose (as Eddie Olmos). 1977: Alambrista! 1978: Evening in Byzantium (TV). 1980: Fukkatsu no hi/Virus/ Resurrection Day. 1981: Wolfen. Three Hundred Miles for Stephanie (TV). Zoot Suit. 1982: Blade Runner. Seguin (TV). 1983: The Ballad of Gregorio Cortez. 1985: Saving Grace. 1988: Stand and Deliver. 1989: Triumph of the Spirit. 1990: Maria's Story. 1991: Talent for the Game. 1992: American Me. 1993: Blade Runner The Director's Cut. Roosters. Even Cowgirls Get the Blues. 1994: Deadly Games (TV). Mi Familia. A Million to Juan (GB: TV as A Million to One). Slave of Dreams. 1995: Smoke. Lorca. Mirage.

OLSEN, Moroni 1889−1954
Big, bluff, balding, often moustachioed American actor of immense experience with touring companies, heading his own playhouse until lured to Hollywood in 1935. Here he played dominant, larger-than-life characters (Robert E. Lee, Sam Houston, Porthos − twice − and Buffalo Bill included), as well as governors, inspectors, generals and no-nonsense fathers. In his last film, he played a pope.

1935: The Three Musketeers. Annie Oakley. Seven Keys to Baldpate. 1936: We're Only Human. The Farmer in His Dell. Yellow Dust. Two in the Dark. Mary of Scotland. The Witness Chair. Two in Revolt. The Plough and the Stars. Mummy's Boys. Grand Jury. M'Liss. 1937: Adventure's End. The Life of Emile Zola. The Last Gangster. Snow White and the Seven Dwarfs (voice only). Manhattan Merry-Go-Round (GB: Manhattan Music Box). 1938: Gold Is Where You Find It. Kentucky. Kidnapped. Submarine Patrol. Marie Antoinette. There Goes My Heart. 1939: Rose of Washington Square. The Three Musketeers (GB: The Singing Musketeer). Code of the Secret Service. Homicide Bureau. Allegheny Uprising (GB: The First Rebel). Susannah of the Mounties. Barricade. That's Right, You're Wrong. Dust Be My Destiny. Invisible Stripes. 1940: Brother Rat and a Baby (GB: Baby Be Good). East of the River. If I Had My Way.

Brigham Young — Frontiersman (GB: Brigham Young). Santa Fé Trail. Virginia City. 1941: One Foot in Heaven. Three Sons o' Guns. Dive Bomber. Life with Henry. Dangerously They Live. Ship Ahoy! 1942: Sundown Jim. Reunion/Reunion in France (GB: Mademoiselle France). Nazi Agent. My Favorite Spy. Mrs Wiggs of the Cabbage Patch. The Glass Key. 1943: Mission to Moscow. The Song of Bernadette. We've Never Been Licked (GB: Texas to Tokyo). Madame Curie. Air Force. Ali Baba and the 40 Thieves. 1944: Roger Touhy, Gangster (GB: The Last Gangster). Thirty Seconds Over Tokyo. Buffalo Bill. Cobra Woman. 1945: Week-End at the Waldorf. Pride of the Marines (GB: Forever in Love). Don't Fence Me In. Mildred Pierce. Behind City Lights. 1946: A Night in Paradise. Boys' Ranch. The Walls Came Tumbling Down. Notorious. From This Day Forward. The Strange Woman. 1947: The Beginning or the End? That Hagen Girl. Possessed. Life With Father. Black Gold. High Wall. The Long Night. Call Northside 777. 1948: Up in Central Park. Command Decision. 1949: The Fountainhead. Samson and Delilah. Task Force. 1950: Father of the Bride. 1951: No Questions Asked. Father's Little Dividend. Payment on Demand. Submarine Command. At Sword's Point (GB: Sons of the Musketeers). 1952: The Washington Story (GB: Target for Scandal). Lone Star. 1953: Marry Me Again. So This Is Love (GB: The Grace Moore Story). 1954: The Long, Long Trailer. Sign of the Pagan.

O'NEAL, Patrick 1927–1994

Cruel-looking, lithe American actor with equine features and prematurely grey hair. Looked as though he would follow a familiar route from villains to tough heroes, but he did not assert himself at the head of star casts, and remained most interesting in top supporting roles, or evil leading characters, such as his maniac killer in *Chamber of Horrors*. With his wife and brother, he also owned several restaurants. Died from respiratory failure after suffering from tuberculosis.

1954: The Mad Magician. The Black Shield of Falworth. 1960: From the Terrace. De Sista Stegen (GB and US: A Matter of Morals). 1963: The Cardinal. 1965: King Rat. In Harm's Way. 1966: Alvarez Kelly. A Fine Madness. Matchless. Chamber of Horrors. A

Big Hand for the Little Lady (GB: Big Deal at Dodge City). 1967: Assignment to Kill. 1968: Companions in Nightmare (TV). Where Were You When the Lights Went Out? The Secret Life of an American Wife. 1969: Stiletto. Castle Keep. The Kremlin Letter. 1970: El Condor. 1971: Corky. Zora. 1973: The Other Man (TV). Silent Night Bloody Night. The Way We Were. 1974: The Stepford Wives. 1975: Crossfire (TV). 1976: *Independence. The Killer Who Wouldn't Die (TV). Twin Detectives (TV). 1977: The Deadliest Season (TV). 1978: Sharon: Portrait of a Mistress (TV). To Kill the King (TV). Streets of Fear (TV). The Last Hurrah (TV). Like Mom, Like Me (TV). 1980: Make Me an Offer (TV). Studio Murders (TV). 1984: Spraggue (TV). 1985: The Stuff. 1986: The Return of Perry Mason (TV). 1987: Like Father, Like Son. 1988: Maigret (TV). 1989: New York Stories. 1990: Q & A. Alice. 1992: The Diary of the Hurdy-Gurdy Man. For the Boys. Under Siege.

O'NEILL, Henry 1891–1961

Playing figures of authority must have come as second nature to this distinguished, thoughtful-looking American actor whose fair hair went grey early in his career. After 20 years of playing judges, lawyers, officers and doctors in more than 150 films, he probably found it quite a relief to play the occasional murder suspect or villain. But his quiet dignity usually decreed he would be on the right side of the law.

1930: *The Strong Arm. 1933: The World Changes. I Loved a Woman. Lady Killer. Ever in My Heart. The Kennel Murder Case. From Headquarters. Son of a Sailor. The House on 56th Street. Footlight Parade. 1934: Side Streets (GB: Woman in Her Thirties). Fog Over Frisco. Murder in the Clouds. The Key. Wonder Bar. Journal of a Crime. Twenty Million Sweethearts. Upper World. The Personality Kid/Information, Please. The Big Shakedown. The Man With Two Faces. Gentlemen Are Born. The Secret Bride (GB: Concealment). Fashions/Fashions of 1934. 1934: Flirtation Walk. Massacre. Bedside. I've Got Your Number. The Big Shakedown. Now I'll Tell (GB: While New York Sleeps). Madame Du Barry. Midnight Alibi. Big-Hearted Herbert. Midnight. 1935: The Florentine Dagger. Living on Velvet. The Man Who Reclaimed His Head. While the Patient Slept. Dinky. Alias Mary Dow. Oil for

the Lamps of China. The Case of the Lucky Legs. Dr Socrates. Sweet Music. Bordertown. The Great Hotel Murder. Black Fury. Bright Lights (GB: Funny Face). Stranded. We're in the Money. Special Agent. 1936: The Story of Louis Pasteur. Freshman Love (GB: Rhythm on the River). The Walking Dead. Two Against the World (GB: The Case of Mrs Pembrook). The Golden Arrow. The White Angel. Rainbow on the River. Boulder Dam. Road Gang (GB: Injustice). Bullets or Ballots. The Big Noise (GB: Modern Madness). Anthony Adverse. Draegerman Courage (GB: The Cave-In). 1937: The Go-Getter. The Great O'Malley. Mr Dodd Takes the Air. First Lady. Wells Fargo. Marked Woman. The Green Light. The Life of Emile Zola. The Singing Marine. The Great Garrick. Submarine D-1. 1938: Jezebel. The Amazing Dr Clitterhouse. Yellow Jack. The Chaser. Brother Rat. Racket Busters. Gold Is Where You Find It. White Banners. Girls on Probation. 1939: Confessions of a Nazi Spy. Torchy Blane in Chinatown. Lucky Night. Angels Wash Their Faces. Dodge City. Juarez. Four Wives. Wings of the Navy. *Young America Flies. The Man Who Dared. Everybody's Hobby. Invisible Stripes. 1940: A Child Is Born. Calling Philo Vance. Castle on the Hudson (GB: Years Without Days). 'Til We Meet Again. Santa Fé Trail. Knute Rockne — All American (GB: A Modern Hero). They Drive by Night (GB: The Road to Frisco). Dr Ehrlich's Magic Bullet (GB: The Story of Dr Ehrlich's Magic Bullet). The Fighting 69th. Money and the Woman. 1941: The Bugle Sounds. Honky Tonk. Men of Boys' Town. Blossoms in the Dust. Down in San Diego. Shadow of the Thin Man. Billy The Kid. The Trial of Mary Dugan. The Get-Away. Whistling in the Dark. Johnny Eager. 1942: White Cargo. Tortilla Flat. This Time for Keeps. Stand By for Action! (GB: Cargo of Innocents). Born to Sing. 1943: Dr Gillespie's Criminal Case (GB: Crazy to Kill). Whistling in Brooklyn. Air Raid Wardens. The Human Comedy. Best Foot Forward. Girl Crazy. The Heavenly Body. Lost Angel. A Guy Named Joe. 1944: Barbary Coast Gent. *Dark Shadows. Airship Squadron No. 4. Rationing. Two Girls and a Sailor. Nothing But Trouble. 1945: This Man's Navy. Keep Your Powder Dry. Dangerous Partners. Between Two Women. Anchors Aweigh. 1946: Three Wise Fools. The Virginian. Little Mr Jim. The Green Years. Bad Bascomb. The Hoodlum Saint. 1947: The Beginning or the End? This Time for Keeps. 1948: The Return of October (GB: A Date With Destiny). Leather Gloves (GB: Loser Takes All). Alias Nick Beal (GB: The Contact Man). Holiday Affair. You're My Everything. Strange Bargain. The Reckless Moment. 1950: The Flying Missile. Convicted. The Second Woman (GB: Ellen). No Man of Her Own. The Milkman. 1951: The People Against O'Hara. The Family Secret. Scandal Sheet (GB: The Dark Page). 1952: Scarlet Angel. 1953: The Sun Shines Bright. 1955: Untamed. 1957: The Wings of Eagles.

O'QUINN, Terry

(Terrance O'Quinn) 1948–

Balding, often moustachioed, dark-haired, friendly-looking American actor, with 'ordinary' oval-faced features. After years as a struggling actor in New York City and off-

Broadway productions, O'Quinn used his 'man next door' appearance to chilling effect in the 'sleeper' hit *The Stepfather*, as a traveller who marries, then murders families. After that he settled into a variety of genres as a versatile character star, extremely busy in the early 1990s. Always seen as city-dwellers in films, he's the outdoor type in real life, married to a Maryland horse trainer.

1980: *Heaven's Gate. FDR: The Last Year* (TV). 1983: *Without a Trace. Jacobo Timmerman – Prisoner Without a Name, Cell Without a Number* (TV). 1984: *All the Right Moves. Places in the Heart. Mrs Soffel. Mischief. Unfinished Business.* 1985: *Silver Bullet. An Early Frost* (TV). *Right to Kill?* (TV). 1986: *Women of Valor* (TV). *Between Two Women* (TV). *SpaceCamp.* 1987: *Black Widow. The Stepfather.* **The Jogger. Stranger on My Land* (TV). *When the Time Comes* (TV). 1988: *Young Guns. Pin.* 1989: *The Forgotten One. Roe Vs Wade* (TV). *Stepfather II.* 1990: *Perry Mason: The Case of the Paris Paradox* (TV). *Blind Fury. Blood Oath/Prisoners of the Sun. Perry Mason: The Case of the Desperate Deception* (TV). *Kaleidoscope/Danielle Steel's Kaleidoscope* (TV). 1991: *The Last to Go. The Rocketeer. Company Business. Shoot First: A Cop's Vengeance* (TV. GB: *Vigilante Cop*). 1992: *My Samurai. Sexual Advances* (TV). *The Cutting Edge. The Good Fight* (TV). *Amityville: A New Generation* (TV). *Deliver Them from Evil: The Taking of Altaview* (TV). *Wild Card* (TV). 1993: *Amityville 1993: The Image of Evil. Born Too Soon* (TV). *The Lipstick Camera. Tombstone.* 1994: *Don't Talk to Strangers* (TV). *Techno-Fear* (later *Techno-Sapiens*).

ORBACH, Jerry 1935–

Tall, dark, dangerous-looking, unsmiling American actor and singer with rutted cheeks and hooded eyes. Best known for most of his career as a star of Broadway musicals, he increased his previously spare film activity from 1985 onwards, to build a gallery of sleek-suited Mafia mobsters and other men of power who could ruin your career with a phone call if you double-crossed them. Such criminal activity was unsurprising in view of his looks. And, after all, his Broadway debut was as Mack the Knife in *The Threepenny Opera*! A big hit as the voice of Lumière in Disney's *Beauty and the Beast*.

1958: *Cop Hater.* 1961: *Mad Dog Coll. 24 Hours in a Woman's Life* (TV). 1964: *John Goldfarb, Please Come Home.* 1971: *The Gang That Couldn't Shoot Straight.* 1972: *A Fan's Notes.* 1974: *Foreplay.* 1976: *The Sentinel.* 1981: *Prince of the City. Underground Aces.* 1983: *An Invasion of Privacy* (TV). 1985: *Brewster's Millions. The Imagemaker. F/X* (GB: *FX: Murder by Illusion*). 1987: *I Love N.Y. Dirty Dancing. Someone to Watch Over Me. Love Among Thieves* (TV). 1989: *Crimes and Misdemeanors. Perry Mason: The Case of the Musical Murder* (TV). 1990: *Dead Women in Lingerie. In Defense of a Married Man* (TV). *Upworld.* 1991: *Kojak: None So Blind* (TV). *Broadway Bound* (TV. GB: cinemas). *Delirious. California Casanova. Delusion. Perry Mason: The Case of the Ruthless Reporter* (TV). *Beauty and the Beast* (voice only). *Toy Soldiers. Out for Justice.* 1992: *Mr Saturday Night. Straight Talk. Universal Soldier.* 1993: *National Lampoon's Loaded Weapon 1. The Cemetery Club. Black Death* (TV). 1994: *The Adventures of a Gnome Called Gnorm.*

OSCAR, Henry
(H.O. Wale) 1891–1969

Light-haired British actor, usually seen in films in meek, wheedling or vindictive 'subservient' roles. His extraordinarily varied and prolific career outside the cinema included touring British camps in World War I, staging numerous plays from the 1930s to the 1950s, being the first actor to receive a BBC Radio contract (1922), writing books, directing in repertory, being an active actors' trade unionist from 1919,

becoming drama director of ENSA in World War II, playing more than 100 TV and theatrical roles and earning a reputation as a painter. An excellent sardonic villain for the cinema when the right part came along.

1932: *After Dark.* 1933: *I Was a Spy.* 1934: *Red Ensign* (US: *Strike!*). *Brides to Be. The Man Who Knew Too Much.* 1935: *Me and Marlborough. The Tunnel* (US: *Transatlantic Tunnel*). *Sexton Blake and the Bearded Doctor. The Case of Gabriel Perry. Father O'Flynn. Night Mail.* 1936: *The Man Behind the Mask. Seven Sinners* (US: *Doomed Cargo*). *Dishonour Bright. Love in Exile. No Escape. Spy of Napoleon. Fire Over England. Sensation.* 1937: *Who Killed John Savage? Dark Journey. The Academy Decides. The Return of the Scarlet Pimpernel.* 1938: *Luck of the Navy* (US: *North Sea Patrol*). *The Terror. Black Limelight.* 1939: *Hell's Cargo* (US: *Dangerous Cargo*). *Dead Man's Shoes. On the Night of the Fire* (US: *The Fugitive*). *The Four Feathers. The Saint in London. Spies of the Air.* 1940: *Two for Danger. The Flying Squad. Tilly of Bloomsbury. Mein Kampf My Crimes.* 1941: *The Seventh Survivor. Hatter's Castle. Atlantic Ferry* (US: *Sons of the Sea*). *Penn of Pennsylvania* (US: *The Courageous Mr Penn*). 1942: *The Day Will Dawn* (US: *The Avengers*). *Squadron Leader X.* 1947: *They Made Me a Fugitive* (US: *I Became a Criminal*). *The Upturned Glass. Mrs Fitzherbert.* 1948: *The Idol of Paris. Bonnie Prince Charlie. House of Darkness. It Happened in Soho. The Greed of William Hart. The Bad Lord Byron.* 1949: *The Man from Yesterday. Which Will You Have?* (US: *Barabbas the Robber*). 1950: *Prelude to Fame. The Black Rose.* 1953: *Martin Luther. Knights of The Round Table.* 1954: **Men at Work. Diplomatic Passport. Beau Brummell. Three Cases of Murder.* 1955: *Portrait of Alison* (US: *Postmark for Danger*). *It's a Great Day.* 1956: *Private's Progress.* 1957: *The Little Hut.* 1958: *The Spaniard's Curse. The Secret Man.* 1959: *Beyond This Place* (US: *Web of Evidence*). 1960: *Oscar Wilde. Brides of Dracula. Foxhole in Cairo.* 1962: *Lawrence of Arabia.* 1963: *The Long Ships.* 1964: *Murder Ahoy.* 1965: *City Under the Sea* (US: *War Gods of the Deep*).

O'SHEA, Milo 1925–
Black-browed, smiling-faced, very dark-haired (now strikingly grey) Irish actor, often

in slightly eccentric roles. On stage in Dublin at 10, he was 'discovered' by John Gielgud, and eventually became a popular British TV star, although efforts to make him a star in films, as opposed to a top character player, never quite gelled. Still busy in the theatre, plus occasional film and TV roles, often in ingratiating, wise, or even smilingly threatening roles.

1951: Talk of a Million (US: You Can't Beat the Irish). 1958: Rooney. 1959: This Other Eden. 1962: Mrs Gibbons' Boys. 1963: Carry On Cabby. 1964: *Down Boy! Never Put It in Writing. 1967: Ulysses. Barbarella. 1968: Romeo and Juliet. 1969: The Adding Machine. 1970: Paddy. The Angel Levine. Loot. 1971: Sacco and Vanzetti. 1972: The Love Ban (originally It's a Two-Foot-Six-Inch-Above-the-Ground World. 1973: The Hebrew Lesson. And No One Could Save Her (TV). Theatre of Blood. Steptoe and Son Ride Again. 1974: Professor Popper's Problem (serial). Digby the Biggest Dog in the World. QB VII (TV). Percy's Progress (US: It's Not the Size That Counts). 1977: Peter Lundy and the Medicine Hat Stallion (TV). 1979: Arabian Adventure. The Pilot. 1980: A Time for Miracles (TV). 1981: Portrait of a Rebel (TV). 1982: The Verdict. 1985: The Purple Rose of Cairo. Wild Boys. 1987: Once a Hero (TV). Angel in Green (TV). Broken Vows (TV). 1988: The Dream Team. 1990: Opportunity Knocks. 1991: Only the Lonely.

OSMOND, Hal 1919–1959
Short, small-nosed, brown-haired, narrow-eyed, wasp-lipped, rat-like, sometimes bespectacled British supporting actor who played cloth-capped criminals, minor crafts-men, small-time safecrackers, caretakers, stoolpigeons and the like. One would have expected more comedy roles in his 87-film career, which was entirely packed into the years 1947 to 1959 before his early death. He scuttled from film to film in the briefly booming British cinema of the 1950s, often appearing for only a few moments.

1947: The Courtneys of Curzon Street (US: The Courtney Affair). 1948: Here Come the Huggetts. Miranda. Once Upon a Dream. Quartet. A Boy, a Girl and a Bike. Vote for Huggett. 1949: It's Not Cricket. Helter Skelter. Diamond City. Marry Me! The Spider and the Fly. Stop Press Girl. 1950: Waterfront (US: Waterfront Women). No Trace. Double Con-

fession. Last Holiday. There is Another Sun (US: Wall of Death). Treasure Island. Your Witness (US: Eye Witness). 1951: Hell is Sold Out. Death of an Angel. The Magic Box. 1952: The Story of Robin Hood and His Merrie Men. The Happy Family (US: Mr Lord Says No). Stolen Face. The Brave Don't Cry. The Gambler and the Lady. The Lost Hours (US: The Big Frame). Top Secret (US: Mr Potts Goes to Moscow). The Oracle (US: The Horse's Mouth). The Net (US: Project M7). 1953: The Steel Key. The Dog and the Diamonds. The Million Pound Note (US: Man with a Million). Hobson's Choice. Love in Pawn. The Sword and the Rose. Rob Roy The Highland Rogue. Three Steps to the Gallows (released 1955. US: White Fire). A Day to Remember. Recoil. You Know What Sailors Are. 1954: Forbidden Cargo. The Crowded Day. The Young Lovers (US: Chance Meeting). One Good Turn. The Gilded Cage. To Dorothy a Son (US: Cash on Delivery). 1955: Portrait of Alison (US: Post-mark for Danger). Tiger by the Tail. Value for Money. Simon and Laura. You Can't Escape. 1956: Bond of Fear. Passport to Treason. Town on Trial! Eyewitness. *Dick Turpin – Highwayman. It's a Wonderful World. The Last Man to Hang? Loser Takes All. Three Men in a Boat. The Big Money (released 1958). 1957: The Depraved. High Flight. Murder Reported. The Vicious Circle (US: The Circle). Just My Luck. Hell Drivers. Stranger in Town. The Truth About Women. 1958: Blood of the Vampire. The Great Van Robbery. The Square Peg. Innocent Meeting. Links of Justice. No Safety Ahead. Tread Softly, Stranger. Carve Her Name with Pride. A Night to Remember. 1959: Crash Drive. The 39 Steps. Top Floor Girl. Upstairs and Downstairs. Jack the Ripper. Web of Suspicion.

OTTIANO, Rafaela 1887–1942
Dark-haired, sharp-faced, pop-eyed Italian actress who came to America and played dangerously hysterical characters. Her menials, from maids to housekeepers, were not to be relied upon, and she was a formidable adversary for Mae West in She Done Him Wrong. She died from intestinal cancer at 55.

1924: The Law and the Lady. 1925: Married? 1932: Washington Masquerade (GB: Mad Masquerade). As You Desire Me. Grand Hotel. 1933: Her Man. Bondage. She Done Him

Wrong. Female. Ann Vickers. 1934: A Lost Lady (GB: Courageous). Mandalay. All Men Are Enemies. The Last Gentleman. Great Expectations. 1935: Lottery Lover. Remember Last Night? Enchanted April. The Florentine Dagger. Curly Top. One Frightened Night. Crime and Punishment. Riffraff. 1936: Anthony Adverse. That Girl from Paris. The Devil-Doll. Mad Holiday. We're Only Human. 1937: Seventh Heaven. Maytime. The League of Frightened Men. 1938: I'll Give a Million. Suez. The Toy Wife (GB: Frou-Frou). 1939: Paris Honeymoon. 1940: Victory. The Long Voyage Home. A Little Bit of Heaven. 1941: Topper Returns. 1942: The Adventures of Martin Eden. I Married an Angel.

OULTON, Brian 1908–1992
Tallish, dark-haired, hesitant, dubious-looking British actor, often as prim-and-proper, easily scandalized characters. Almost entirely a man of the theatre (for which he also wrote and directed) until 1948, he was at first seen in quasi-romantic leads, but soon settled into (mainly comic) character roles for the post-war British cinema. A master of exasperation and despair. Married fellow character player Peggy Thorpe-Bates (1914–1989).

1931: Sally in Our Valley. 1938: This Man is News. Too Many Husbands. 1941: The Prime Minister. 1948: Miranda. It's Not Cricket. Panic at Madame Tussaud's. Warning to Wantons. 1949: The Huggetts Abroad. Helter Skelter. Paper Orchid. 1950: Last Holiday. 1951: Young Wives' Tale. Quo Vadis? 1952: Castle in the Air. 1953: Will Any Gentleman?... The Dog and the Diamonds. The Million Pound Note (US: Man With a Million). 1954: Devil on Horseback. The Crowded Day. Doctor in the House. 1955: The Reluctant Bride (US: Two Grooms for a Bride). The Deep Blue Sea. The Man Who Never Was. Miss Tulip Stays the Night. Private's Progress. 1956: Charley Moon. Brothers in Law. The Good Companions. 1957: Happy Is the Bride! 1958: The Spaniard's Curse. The Silent Enemy. 1959: Carry On Nurse. The Devil's Disciple. The Thirty-Nine Steps. I'm All Right, Jack. 1960: There Was a Crooked Man. The Bulldog Breed. Carry On Constable. A French Mistress. No Kidding (US: Beware of Children). Suspect (US: The Risk). 1961: The Damned (US: These Are the Damned). No Love for

Johnnie. Very Important Person (US: A Coming-Out Party). Raising the Wind (US: Roommates). 1962: Kiss of the Vampire. Hair of the Dog. The Iron Maiden (US: The Swingin' Maiden). Jigsaw. 1964: Carry On Cleo. Devils of Darkness. 1965. The Intelligence Men. 1969: Carry On Camping. Some Will, Some Won't. 1971: On the Buses. Mr Forbush and the Penguins (US: Cry of the Penguins). 1972: Ooh . . . You Are Awful (US: Get Charlie Tully). 1976: Emily. 1982: Gandhi. 1985: Young Sherlock Holmes. 1986: The Canterville Ghost (TV). 1988: Suspicion (TV).

OUSPENSKAYA, Maria 1876–1949
Wizened, beetle-faced, tiny Russian actress who came to America in the early 1930s to set up an acting school in New York. Despite playing a wide range of diminutive dynamos of varying nationalities (she was twice Oscar-nominated, in *Dodsworth* and *Love Affair*), film buffs remember her best as the gypsy woman who teaches poor Lon Chaney the werewolf rhyme in *The Wolf Man*. Tragically burned to death in her Los Angeles apartment.

1915: Sverchok na Pechi/The Cricket on the Hearth. 1916: Nichtozniye/Worthless. 1917: Dr Torpokov. 1918: Zazhivo Pogrebenni/ Buried Alive. 1923: Khveska. 1929: Tanka Traktirshitsa. Protiv Otsa. 1936: Dodsworth. 1937: Conquest (GB: Marie Walewska). 1939: Love Affair. The Rains Came. Judge Hardy and Son. 1940: Dance, Girl, Dance. Dr Ehrlich's Magic Bullet (GB: The Story of Dr Ehrlich's Magic Bullet). The Mortal Storm. Waterloo Bridge. Beyond Tomorrow. The Man I Married. 1941: The Shanghai Gesture. The Wolf Man. Kings Row. 1942: The Mystery of Marie Roget. 1943: Frankenstein Meets the Wolf Man. 1945: Tarzan and the Amazons. 1946: I've Always Loved You. 1947: Wyoming. 1949: A Kiss in the Dark.

OVERMAN, Lynne 1887–1943
Grizzled, flat-faced Hollywood veteran (once a jockey) who, after many years of struggle in the theatre, made a few early sound shorts, and then brought his dry wit and even drier, mulish voice to character roles, usually as friendly, fast-talking types from lower-class background. Enjoyed 10 good film years before his death from a heart attack.

1928: The Perfect Crime. 1929: *Kisses. 1930: *Five Minutes from the Station. *Horseshoes. *A Sure Cure. 1933: *Poor Fish. 1934: *Around the Clock. Broadway Bill (GB: Strictly Confidential). Little Miss Marker (GB: Girl in Pawn). The Great Flirtation. Midnight. You Belong to Me. Enter Madame! She Loves Me Not. 1935: Men Without Names. Rumba. Paris in Spring (GB: Paris Love Song). Two for Tonight. *Lucky Stars. 1936: Three Married Men. Poppy. Yours for the Asking. The Jungle Princess. Collegiate (GB: The Charm School). 1937: *Nobody's Baby. Blonde Trouble. Murder Goes to College. Hotel Haywire. True Confession. Partners in Crime. Don't Tell the Wife. Wild Money. Night Club Scandal. 1938: Hunted Men. The Big Broadcast of 1938. Sons of the Legion. Ride a Crooked Mile (GB: Escape from Yesterday). Persons in Hiding. Her Jungle Love. Spawn of the North. Men With Wings. 1939: Union Pacific. Death of a Champion. 1940: Safari. Edison the Man. Typhoon. North West Mounted Police. 1941: New York Town. Aloma of the South Seas. Caught in the Draft. There's Magic in Music. 1942: The Forest Rangers. Roxie Hart. Star Spangled Rhythm. Reap the Wild Wind. Silver Queen. 1943: Dixie. The Desert Song.

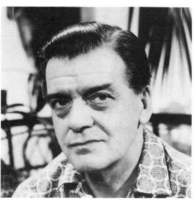

OWEN, Bill
(William Rowbotham) 1914–
Short, dark, pale-faced, bright-eyed British character actor who started in show business as a holiday camp entertainer, turned to acting in films after World War II as forthright cockney types and created a series of real-life people, stamped with the brightness

of his own personality, that almost elevated him to stardom in the mid 1950s. Very much a part of the British cinema of that time: less effective after 1960, although an integral part of the popular TV comedy series *Last of the Summer Wine*. Has also written and directed for the theatre.

1945: †*Song of the People. †The Way to the Stars (US: Johnny in the Clouds). †Perfect Strangers (US: Vacation from Marriage). 1946: †School for Secrets (US: Secret Flight). Daybreak. 1947: †Dancing with Crime. When the Bough Breaks. Holiday Camp. Easy Money. 1948: Trouble in the Air. My Brother's Keeper. The Weaker Sex. Once a Jolly Swagman (US: Maniacs on Wheels). 1949: Trottie True (US: Gay Lady). Diamond City. The Girl Who Couldn't Quite. 1951: Hotel Sahara. 1952: The Story of Robin Hood and his Merrie Men. There Was a Young Lady. 1953: The Square Ring. A Day to Remember. Thought to Kill. 1954: The Rainbow Jacket. Murder in Two Moods (unreleased). 1955: The Ship That Died of Shame (US: PT Raiders). 1956: Not So Dusty. 1957: Davy. 1958: Carve Her Name with Pride. Carry on Sergeant. 1959: Carry on Nurse. The Shakedown. 1961: The Hellfire Club. On the Fiddle (US: Operation Snafu). Carry on Regardless. 1963: Carry on Cabby. 1964: The Secret of Blood Island. 1966: Georgy Girl. The Fighting Prince of Donegal. 1968: Headline Hunters. 1969: Mischief. 1972: Kadoyng. 1973: O Lucky Man! 1974: In Celebration. 1975: Smurfs and the Magic Flute (voice only). 1977: The Comeback. Last of the Summer Wine (TV). 1984: Laughterhouse/ Singleton's Pluck. 1985: Uncle of the Bride (TV).

† As Bill Rowbotham

PAIVA, Nestor 1905–1966
Bald, bushy-browed, scowling American actor, built like a barn door, with square features, staring eyes and inverted Joe E. Brown mouth, mostly in aggressive or temperamental roles. His long radio experience gave the California-born actor an ear for foreign accents that he quickly turned to his advantage after arriving in Hollywood in 1938. Playing Russians, Mexicans, Red Indians, Arabs, South Americans, Spaniards, Italians and half-castes in general, he soon became one of the cinema's

'familiar faces' to whom it was most difficult to add the name.

1938: The Spider's Web (serial). Prison Train. Ride a Crooked Mile (GB: Escape from Yesterday). 1939: Midnight. Another Thin Man. Bachelor Mother. Flying G-Men (serial). The Hunchback of Notre Dame. Beau Geste. The Magnificent Fraud. Union Pacific. 1940: Dark Streets of Cairo. The Devil's Pipeline. The Primrose Path. Arise, My Love. He Stayed for Breakfast. Boom Town. North West Mounted Police. The Marines Fly High. Phantom Raiders. The Sea Hawk. Santa Fé Trail. They Knew What They Wanted. 1941: Flame of New Orleans. Dressed to Kill. Hold Back the Dawn. Hold That Ghost! Tall, Dark and Handsome. Meet Boston Blackie. Pot o' Gold (GB: The Golden Hour). The Kid from Kansas. Johnny Eager. Rise and Shine. Ship Ahoy! Wild Geese Calling. 1942: Broadway. For Me and My Gal (GB: For Me and My Girl). Fly-by-Night. Flying Tigers. The Girl from Alaska. Jail House Blues. The Lady Has Plans. Reap the Wild Wind. Road to Morocco. Pittsburgh. Timber. King of the Mounties (serial). The Hard Way. 1943: Chetniks/Chetniks — The Underground Guerrillas. The Crystal Ball. The Dancing Masters. The Desert Song. Rhythm of the Islands. Background to Danger. The Fallen Sparrow. The Song of Bernadette. Tarzan's Desert Mystery. Tornado. True to Life. 1944: The Falcon in Mexico. Kismet. Music for Millions. The Purple Heart. Shine On, Harvest Moon. Tampico. 1945: Along the Navajo Trail. Cornered. A Medal for Benny. Nob Hill. The Southerner. Salome, Where She Danced. Fear. A Thousand and One Nights. Road to Utopia. The Trouble with Women (released 1947). 1946: Badman's Territory. Humoresque. The Last Crooked Mile. Sensation Hunters. Suspense. The Well-Groomed Bride. 1947: Carnival in Costa Rica. A Likely Story. Angels' Alley. The Lone Wolf in Mexico. Ramrod. Shoot to Kill. Robin Hood of Monterey. Road to Rio. 1948: Adventures of Casanova. Joan of Arc. Alias Nick Beal (GB: The Contact Man). Mr Reckless. Mr Blandings Builds His Dream House. The Paleface. 1949: Bride of Vengeance. Mighty Joe Young. Follow Me Quietly. Oh, You Beautiful Doll. Rope of Sand. The Inspector General/Happytimes. Young Man with a Horn (GB: Young Man of Music). 1950: The Desert Hawk. I Was a Shoplifter. The Great Caruso. 1951: Flame of Stamboul. Double Dynamite. Jim Thorpe — All American (GB: Man of

Bronze). The Lady Pays Off. A Millionaire for Christy. My Favorite Spy. On Dangerous Ground. 1952: Diplomatic Courier. April in Paris. Five Fingers. Phone Call from a Stranger. South Pacific Trail. Mara Maru. The Fabulous Senorita. Viva Zapata! With a Song in My Heart. 1953: The Bandits of Corsica (GB: Return of the Corsican Brothers). Killer Ape. Jivaro (GB: Lost Treasure of the Amazon). Prisoners of the Casbah. Call Me Madam. Casanova's Big Night. 1954: The Cowboy. The Creature from the Black Lagoon. The Desperado. Four Guns to the Border. Thunder Pass. 1955: All That Heaven Allows. Hell on Frisco Bay. New York Confidential. Tarantula! Revenge of the Creature. 1956: Comanche. The Mole People. Ride the High Iron. Scandal Inc. The Wild Party. 1957: The Guns of Fort Petticoat. Les Girls. 10,000 Bedrooms. The Lady Takes a Flyer. 1958: The Deep Six. Outcasts of the City. The Case Against Brooklyn. The Left-Handed Gun. 1959: Alias Jesse James. The Nine Lives of Elfego Baca (TV. GB: cinemas). Vice Raid. Pier Five — Havana. 1960: Can-Can. Frontier Uprising. The Purple Gang. 1961: The Four Horsemen of the Apocalypse. 1962: The Three Stooges in Orbit. The Wild Westerners. Girls! Girls! Girls! California. 1964: Madmen of Mandoras/They Saved Hitler's Brain (shot 1960). Ballad of a Gunfighter. 1965: Jesse James Meets Frankenstein's Daughter. 1966: Let's Kill Uncle. The Spirit is Willing.

PALLETTE, Eugene 1889–1954

Squat, dark, gravel-voiced American actor, who looked like some huge black beetle, but who, for all his girth, was almost always dressed in immaculately cut suits. On stage at 16, he was a busy man in films from 1913 onwards, but especially popular as a character actor in the 1930s, usually as fathers or figures of authority who proved to be neither as dumb nor as grouchy as they looked.

1912: *When the Light Fades. *The Transgression of Manuel. 1913: *The Tattooed Arm. *When Jim Returned. *Broken Nose Bailey. *The Homestead Race. *Suspended Sentence. *The Kiss. *The Light Woman. *Brother Love/Brotherly Love. *Vengeance. *The Only Clue. *The Tomboy's Race. *The Bravest Man. Monroe. *An Accidental Clue. *The Helping Hand. *A Man's Awakening. 1914: *The Peach Brand. *The Beat of the Year. *The

Gunman. *The Sheriff's Prisoner. *The Horse Wrangler. *The Burden. *On the Border. *The Thief and the Book. *Educating His Daughter. *The Reform Candidate. *The Portrait of Anita. *The Stronger Hand. *Texas Bill's Last Ride. *The Atonement. *The Stolen Radium. *A Diamond in the Rough. *A Pair of Cuffs. *The Wheels of Destiny. *The Stolen Oar. *The Bank Burglar's Fate. *Turned Back. *Through the Dark. *The Runaway Freight. *Detective Burton's Triumph. *The Tardy Cannon Ball. *The Kaffir's Skull. *A Woman Scorned. *Who Shot Bud Walton? 1915: The Birth of a Nation. *The Story of a Story. *After 20 Years. *The Highbinders. *The Death Doll. *The Penalty. When Love is Mocked. The Isle of Content. *How Hazel Got Even. *The Spell of the Poppy. *The Emerald Brooch. *The Ever-Living Isles. The Scarlet Lady. The Victim. *The Adventure Hunter. *The Death Dice. 1916: Intolerance. Hell-to-Pay Austin. Gretchen the Greenhorn. Children in the House. Whispering Smith. His Guardian Angel. Going Straight. Sunshine Dad. Runaway Freight. Diamond in the Rough. 1917: *The Purple Scar. Lonesome Chap. The Winning of Sally Temple. Heir of the Ages. Ghost House. The Bond Between. The Marcellini Millions. World Apart. A Man's Man. Each of His Kind. 1918: His Robe of Honor. Madame Who. Tarzan of the Apes. Vivette. The Turn of a Card. Breakers Ahead. No Man's Land. 1919: Be a Little Sport. The Amateur Adventuress. Fair and Warmer. Words and Music By ... 1920: Terror Island. Alias Jimmy Valentine. Parlor, Bedroom and Bath. Twin Beds. 1921: The Three Musketeers. Fine Feathers. 1922: Without Compromise. Two Kinds of Women. 1923: The Ten Commandments. Hell's Hole. A Man's Man (and 1917 film). To the Last Man. North of Hudson Bay. 1924: The Wolf Man. The Cyclone Rider. The Galloping Fish. Wandering Husbands. 1925: The Light of Western Stars. Ranger of the Big Pines. Without Mercy. Wild Horse Mesa. 1926: Mantrap. Desert Valley. Rocking Moon. Whispering Smith (remake). Yankee Señor. The Fighting Edge. The Volga Boatman. Whispering Canyon. 1927: *Many Scrappy Returns. *The Lighter That Failed. *Fluttering Hearts. *Should Men Walk Home? Moulders of Men. Chicago. *Sugar Daddies. *The Second Hundred Years. *Battle of the Century. 1928: *Aching Youths. *Barnum and Ringling Inc. *Don't Be Jealous. *How's Your Stock? Out of the Ruins. The Goodbye Kiss. The Red Mark. Lights of New York. His Private Life. 1929: The Greene Murder Case. The Canary Murder Case. The Studio Murder Mystery. Pointed Heels. The Dummy. The Love Parade. The Virginian. 1930: Follow Thru. *The Dancing Instructor. The Kibitzer (GB: The Busybody). Slightly Scarlet. The Border Legion. Sea Legs. Santa Fé Trail (GB: The Law Rides West). The Benson Murder Case. The Sea God. Let's Go Native. Men are Like That. Paramount on Parade. Playboy of Paris. 1931: Gun Smoke. Fighting Caravans. The Adventures of Huckleberry Finn. Dude Ranch. Girls About Town. It Pays to Advertise. 1932: Tom Brown of Culver. Shanghai Express. Strangers of the Evening. Wild Girl (GB: Salomy Jane). Dancers in the Dark. Thunder Below. The Night Mayor. *Off His Base. *A Hockey Hick (GB: Ice Hockey Hick). *The

Stolen Jools (GB: The Slippery Pearls). The Half-Naked Truth. *The Loud Mouth. *The Pig Boat. 1933: Storm at Daybreak. Made on Broadway (GB: The Girl I Made). Mr Skitch. From Headquarters. Hell Below. *Hip Zip Hooray! Shanghai Madness. The Kennel Murder Case. Phantom Fame. *Meet the Champ. *One Awful Night. 1934: Friends of Mr Sweeney. Caravan. The Dragon Murder Case. One Exciting Adventure. Cross Country Cruise. I've Got Your Number. Strictly Dynamite. *News Hounds. 1935: Baby Face Harrington (GB: Baby Face). Steamboat 'round the Bend. Bordertown. Black Sheep. All the King's Horses. The Ghost Goes West. 1936: The Golden Arrow. My Man Godfrey. Stowaway. Easy to Take. Dishonour Bright. The Luckiest Girl in the World. 1937: Song of the City. Topper. Clarence. One Hundred Men and a Girl. She Had to Eat. The Crime Nobody Saw. 1938: The Adventures of Robin Hood. There Goes My Heart. 1939: First Love. Wife, Husband and Friend. Mr Smith Goes to Washington. 1940: Sandy is a Lady. Young Tom Edison. He Stayed for Breakfast. It's a Date. A Little Bit of Heaven. The Mark of Zorro. 1941: Unfinished Business. Ride, Kelly, Ride. World Premiere. The Bride Came COD. The Lady Eve. Appointment for Love. Swamp Water (GB: The Man Who Came Back). 1942: Almost Married. The Male Animal. Are Husbands Necessary? Tales of Manhattan. The Big Street. Lady in a Jam. The Forest Rangers. Silver Queen. 1943: It Ain't Hay (GB: Money for Jam). The Gang's All Here (GB: The Girls He Left Behind). The Kansan (GB: Wagon Wheels). Slightly Dangerous. Heaven Can Wait. 1944: Pin-Up Girl. In the Meantime, Darling. Heavenly Days. Step Lively. Sensations of 1945. The Laramie Trail. Lake Placid Serenade. 1945: The Cheaters. 1946: Suspense. In Old Sacramento. 1948: Silver River.

PANGBORN, Franklin 1893–1958

Pangborn was the dark-haired American character comedian who always looked as though he had detected a bad smell in the room, and frequently behaved as if whatever he was doing was beneath him. The height of prissiness as hotel manager, banker, dress-shop manager or floorwalker, he had his routine to perfection, and could make audiences laugh even in the midst of a bad film. Unbelievably, in his early theatrical days, he was once typed as a villain.

1926: Chasing Trouble. Exit Smiling. 1927: Getting Gertie's Garter. The Cradle Snatchers. My Friend from India. The Rejuvenation of Aunt Mary. The Night Bride. The Girl in the Pullman. Fingerprints. 1928: On Trial. Blonde for a Night. The Rush Hour. 1929: The Sap. *The Crazy Nut. Watch Out. Lady of the Pavements (GB: Lady of the Night). *Who's the Boss? Masquerade. *Happy Birthday. 1930: Not So Dumb. A Lady Surrenders (GB: Blind Wives). Cheer Up and Smile. Her Man. *The Doctor's Wife. *Poor Aubrey. *The Chumps. *Reno or Bust. 1931: *Hollywood Halfbacks. *Camping Out. A Woman of Experience. *Against the Rules. *Rough House Rhythm. *Torchy Passes the Buck. 1932: A Fool's Advice. *Torchy Raises the Auntie. *Doctor's Orders. *Tee for Two. *Torchy's Two Toots. *Torchy's Busy Day. *The Giddy Age. *Torchy Turns the Trick. *Torchy's Night Cap. The Half-Naked Truth. *Torchy's Vocation. Over the Counter. *What Price, Taxi? *The Candid Camera. *Torchy Rolls His Own. Meet the Mayor (released 1938). *Jimmy's New Yacht. *Lighthouse Love. *The Loudmouth. *Station S.T.A.R. 1932–3: The Singing Boxer. 1933: Professional Sweetheart (GB: Imaginary Sweetheart). International House. Flying Down to Rio. The Important Witness. Design for Living. Headline Shooters (GB: Evidence in Camera). Only Yesterday. *Torchy Turns Turtle. *Torchy's Loud Spooker. *Blue of the Night. *Easy on the Eyes. *Wild Poses. *Dream Stuff. *Sweet Cookie. *Sing Bing Sing. *Art in the Raw. *Torchy's Kitty Coup. Bed of Roses. 1934: Strictly Dynamite. Manhattan Love Song. Many Happy Returns. Stand Up and Cheer. Imitation of Life. That's Gratitude. *Up and Down. Young and Beautiful. Unknown Blonde. King Kelly of the USA (GB: Irish and Proud of It). Cockeyed Cavaliers. College Rhythm. 1935: $1,000 a Minute. Headline Woman (GB: The Woman in the Case). Eight Bells. Flirtation. Tomorrow's Youth. She Couldn't Take It. *The Captain Hits the Ceiling. *Ye Old Saw Mill. 1936: Three Smart Girls. Mr Deeds Goes to Town. Don't Gamble with Love. To Mary – With Love. Hats Off. Doughnuts and Society (GB: Stepping into Society). The Luckiest Girl in the World. My Man Godfrey. The Mandarin Mystery. Tango. 1937: *Bad Housekeeping. *Bridal Griefs. They Wanted to Marry. Step Lively, Jeeves. She Had to Eat. It Happened in Hollywood. High Hat. Easy Living. We Have Our Moments. When Love is Young. Dangerous Number. Hotel Haywire. All Over Town. Stage Door. I'll Take Romance. The Lady Escapes. Swing High, Swing Low. Danger! Love at Work. Turn Off the Moon. Thrill of a Lifetime. A Star Is Born. She's Dangerous. Dangerous Holiday. The Life of the Party. Living on Love. 1938: Rebecca of Sunnybrook Farm. Vivacious Lady. Always Goodbye. Just Around the Corner. Bluebeard's Eighth Wife. Love on Toast. Topper Takes a Trip. The Girl Downstairs. She Married an Artist. It's All Yours. Three Blind Mice. Joy of Living. Carefree. Dr Rhythm. Mad About Music. Four's a Crowd. 1939: Fifth Avenue Girl. Broadway Serenade. 1940: Public Deb No. 1. The Bank Dick (GB: The Bank Detective). Turnabout. The Villain Still Pursued Her. Christmas in July. Spring Parade. Hit Parade of 1941. 1941: Flame of New Orleans. Where

Did You Get That Girl? Bachelor Daddy. Tillie the Toiler. A Girl, a Guy and a Gob (GB: The Navy Steps Out). Never Give a Sucker an Even Break (GB: What a Man!). Week-End for Three. Mr District Attorney in the Carter Case (GB: The Carter Case). Sullivan's Travels. Obliging Young Lady. Sandy Steps Out. 1942: Moonlight Masquerade. George Washington Slept Here. Now, Voyager. Call Out the Marines. Strictly in the Groove. What's Cookin'? (GB: Wake Up and Dream). The Palm Beach Story. 1943: Reveille With Beverly. Honeymoon Lodge. His Butler's Sister. Never a Dull Moment. Stage Door Canteen. Two Weeks to Live. Crazy House. Holy Matrimony. *Slick Chick. The Great Moment. 1944: Hail the Conquering Hero. The Reckless Age. Allergic to Love. My Best Gal. 1945: The Horn Blows at Midnight. *Hollywood Victory Caravan. Hollywood and Vine (GB: Daisy (the Dog) Goes Hollywood). See My Lawyer. Tell It to a Star. You Came Along. 1946: Lover Come Back. Two Guys from Milwaukee (GB: Royal Flush). The Sin of Harold Diddlebock (later and GB: Mad Wednesday). I'll Be Yours. 1947: Calendar Girl. Addio Mimi (GB and US: Her Wonderful Lie). 1948: Romance on the High Seas (GB: It's Magic). 1949: Down Memory Lane. My Dream Is Yours. 1957: The Story of Mankind. Oh, Men! Oh, Women!

PANTOLIANO, Joe 1954–

Small, brown-haired, dark-eyed, rabbitty American actor of considerable versatility, although often in sympathetic roles calling for a gentle core to a tough exterior. An actor at 18, he made a low-key film debut at 20, but achieved the breakthrough to becoming a well-known face through TV sit-com series and, especially, as the tragic Angelo Maggio in the TV mini-series version of From Here to Eternity in 1979. Such mainline films as The Fugitive brought him more to the fore in the 1990s, and he had his first genuine leading role in Golddigger in 1993.

1974: The Godfather Part II. 1978: More Than Friends (TV). 1980: The Idolmaker. Alcatraz: The Whole Shocking Story (TV). 1981: Campsite Massacre/The Final Terror/Three Blind Mice/Carnivore. 1982: Eddie and the Cruisers. Monsignor. 1983: Risky Business. 1984: The Mean Season. 1985: The Goonies. 1986: La Bamba. Running Scared. 1987: Scenes from the Goldmine (TV). Empire of the Sun. The

Squeeze. Destination: America (TV). 1988: Rock 'n' Roll Mom (TV). The 'In' Crowd. Midnight Run. 1989: Backstreet Dreams (released 1990). Nightbreaker. 1990: Short Time. Downtown. El Diablo (cable TV). Zandalee. Tales from the Crypt (TV). The Last of the Finest (GB: Blue Heat). 1991: Robot in the Family. 1992: Used People. 1993: Taking Gary Feldman. Golddigger. Three of Hearts. Me and the Kid (TV). The Fugitive. Calendar Girl. 1994: Baby's Day Out. The Last Word. 1995: Bad Boys. Steal Big, Steal Little.

PARKE, (J.) MacDonald 1891–1960
Rotund, bald, bespectacled, back-slapping American-born actor of Scots-Canadian parentage whose salty tones made him the Walter Brennan-cum-Eugene Pallette of British pictures. He was even better known on TV and radio, winning nationwide popularity in the latter medium in the western series Riders of the Range. In films he played mostly gullible millionaire Americans being sold imaginary assets.

1938: Hey! Hey! USA. 1939: Shipyard Sally. 1941: Hi, Gang! They Flew Alone (US: Wings and the Woman. 1943: Candlelight in Algeria. The Yellow Canary. 1944: English Without Tears (US: Her Man Gilbey). 1947: Teheran (US: The Plot to Kill Roosevelt). Broken Journey. 1948: No Orchids for Miss Blandish. 1949: The Fool and the Princess. 1950: Dangerous Assignment. Night and the City. 1951: A Tale of Five Cities (US: A Tale of Five Women). Saturday Island (US: Island of Desire). 1952: Penny Princess. Babes in Baghdad. The Man Who Watched Trains Go By (US: Paris Express). 1953: Is Your Honeymoon Really Necessary? Innocents in Paris. 1954: The Good Die Young. Out of the Clouds. The Last Moment. The Red Dress. 1955: Summer Madness (US: Summertime). 1956: The March Hare. 1957: Beyond Mombasa. A King in New York. 1958: I Was Monty's Double (US: Monty's Double). 1959: A Touch of Larceny. The Battle of the Sexes. The Mouse That Roared. John Paul Jones. 1960: Never Take Sweets from a Stranger (US: Never Take Candy from a Stranger).

PARNELL, Emory 1894–1979
Bulky American actor with receding brown hair, a big demon imp of a man with a neck that stretched from the point of his jaw to his chest, and just as likely to turn up in a

lunatic comedy part or as a prison warden. He also played a large number of policemen – frequently baffled by the hero on the case. A former vaudevillian, he made scores of Hollywood films before venturing into television in the 1950s, becoming familiar to viewers as the bartender in the long-running western series Lawman. He had originally trained as a concert violinist, but musical ambitions had been forgotten by the time he became a booking agent in the 1920s, followed by a sidestep into character acting around 1930. He died from a heart attack.

1938: Doctor Rhythm. Blondie. Arson Racket Squad. Call of the Yukon. Angels with Dirty Faces. Girls on Probation. I Am the Law. King of Alcatraz (GB: King of the Alcatraz). The Mad Miss Manton. Sweethearts. 1939: At the Circus/The Marx Brothers At the Circus. East Side of Heaven. They Day the Bookies Wept. The House of Fear. I Stole a Million. Little Accident. One Hour to Live. Pacific Liner. Off the Record. The Roaring Twenties. The Secret of Dr Kildare. The Spellbinder. The Star Maker. *Tiny Troubles. Winter Carnival. St Louis Blues. Idiot's Delight. They Shall Have Music (GB: Melody of Youth). Let Freedom Ring. Union Pacific. You Can't Get Away with Murder. Invisible Stripes. 1940: Blondie on a Budget. Foreign Correspondent. If I Had My Way. The Great McGinty (GB: Down Went McGinty). The Monster and the Girl. North West Mounted Police. Out West With the Peppers. Stranger on the Third Floor. Sued for Libel. 1941: *All the World's a Stooge. The Blonde from Singapore (GB: Hot Pearls). The Case of the Black Parrot. Johnny Eager. Kiss the Boys Goodbye. Louisiana Purchase. The Maltese Falcon. Mr and Mrs Smith. The Lady from Cheyenne. So Ends Our Night. Sullivan's Travels. A Shot in the Dark. The Monster and the Girl. Young Tom Edison. Unholy Partners. 1942: Cadets on Parade. Arabian Nights. All Through the Night. I Married a Witch. Highways by Night. London Blackout Murders (GB: Secret Motive). The Major and the Minor. Over My Dead Body. Once Upon a Honeymoon. Obliging Young Lady. Saboteur. Syncopation. Larceny Inc. The Pride of the Yankees. The Remarkable Andrew. Wings for the Eagle. The Hard Way. Kings Row. They All Kissed the Bride. 1943: The Dancing Masters. Government Girl. The Human Comedy. It's a Great Life. Let's Face It. Mission to Moscow. The Outlaw. Mr Lucky. Slightly Dangerous. Du

Barry Was a Lady. This Land is Mine! That Nazty Nuisance. Two Señoritas from Chicago. The Unknown Guest. Young Ideas. You're a Lucky Fellow, Mr Smith. 1944: Andy Hardy's Blonde Trouble. Address Unknown. And Now Tomorrow. The Great Moment. Casanova Brown. The Falcon in Hollywood. Gildersleeve's Ghost. Heavenly Days. The Falcon in Mexico. *Love Your Landlord. *Radio Rampage. *The Kitchen Cynic. *He Forgot to Remember. *Feather Your Nest. *Triple Trouble. The Miracle of Morgan's Creek. A Night of Adventure. Seven Days Ashore. Tall in the Saddle. Once Upon a Time. Wilson. It's in the Bag! (GB: The Fifth Chair). 1945: *Alibi Baby. *The Big Beef. Crime Doctor's Courage (GB: The Doctor's Courage). *You Drive Me Crazy. *What, No Cigarettes? Having Wonderful Crime. Mama Loves Papa. Sing Your Way Home. State Fair. Two O'Clock Courage. What a Blonde. Colonel Effingham's Raid (GB: Man of the Hour). 1946: Abie's Irish Rose. Badman's Territory. Deadline at Dawn. The Falcon's Alibi. It Shouldn't Happen to a Dog. Little Iodine. Deadline for Murder. The Show Off. Summer Holiday (released 1948). Queen of Burlesque. Strange Triangle. 1947: Calendar Girl. Crime Doctor's Gamble (GB: The Doctor's Gamble). Gas House Kids Go West. The Guilt of Janet Ames. Stork Bites Man. Suddenly It's Spring. Violence. 1948: Assigned to Danger. Blonde Ice. Here Comes Trouble. Mr Blandings Builds His Dream House. Song of Idaho. Ma and Pa Kettle. Strike It Rich. Words and Music. You Gotta Stay Happy. 1949: Alaska Patrol. The Beautiful Blonde from Bashful Bend. Ma and Pa Kettle Go to Town (GB: Going to Town). Hellfire. Massacre River. Hideout. Rose of the Yukon. A Woman's Secret. 1950: *Nightclub Daze. Beware of Blondie. Chain Gang. County Fair. Key to the City. Rock Island Trail (GB: Transcontinent Express). To Please a Lady. Unmasked. 1951: All That I Have. Belle le Grand. Boots Malone. *Deal Me In. Ma and Pa Kettle Back on the Farm. My True Story. Footlight Varieties. Honeychile. Trail of Robin Hood. Golden Girl. Let's Go Navy. Showboat. 1952: Dreamboat. *Lost in a Turkish Bath. *Three Chairs for Betty. The Fabulous Señorita. Gobs and Gals (GB: Cruising Casanovas). Ma and Pa Kettle at the Fair. Oklahoma Annie. Has Anybody Seen My Gal. The Lawless Breed. When in Rome. The Yellow-Haired Kid (TV. GB: cinemas). Lost in Alaska. Washington Story (GB: Target for Scandal). Macao. Rancho Notorious. 1953: Call Me Madam. The Band Wagon. Fort Vengeance. Here Come the Girls. Easy to Love. The Girl Who Had Everything. Safari Drums (GB: Bomba and the Safari Drums). Sweethearts on Parade. Shadows of Tombstone. 1954: Battle of Rogue River. Jungle Gents. The Long, Long Trailer. Ma and Pa Kettle At Home. Pride of the Blue Grass (GB: Prince of the Blue Grass). The Rocket Man. Sabrina (GB: Sabrina Fair). 1955: Artists and Models. How to Be Very, Very Popular. The Looters. The Road to Denver. *So You Want to Be a VP. You're Never Too Young. 1956: Pardners. That Certain Feeling. *So You Think the Grass is Greener. *So Your Wife Wants to Work. 1957: The Delicate Delinquent. The Hot Angel. 1958: Man of the West. The Notorious Mr Monks. 1959: Alias Jesse James. A Hole in the

Head. This Earth is Mine! 1961: Ada. The Two Little Bears. 1965: Git! The Bounty Killer. 1971: The Andromeda Strain.

PARSONS, Nicholas 1928–

Tall, cheerful-looking British actor with light, wavy hair who played handsome but sometimes lamebrained types in a few British comedy films before his genial tones and easygoing manner launched him into new careers as straight man for TV comedians, and as quizmaster for radio and TV games shows, notably the perennial *Just a Minute*. Made his film debut at 19 while in repertory in Glasgow after an engineering apprenticeship on Clydebank. Married actress Denise Bryer.

1947: *Master of Bankdam*. 1954: *To Dorothy a Son (US: Cash on Delivery)*. 1955: *Simon and Laura. An Alligator Named Daisy*. 1956: *Eyewitness. The Long Arm (US: The Third Key)*. 1957: *Happy is the Bride!* 1958: *Too Many Crooks. Carlton-Browne of the FO (US: Man in a Cocked Hat)* 1959: *Upstairs and Downstairs*. 1960: *Doctor in Love. Let's Get Married*. 1961: *Carry On Regardless*. 1964: *Every Day's a Holiday (US: Seaside Swingers). Murder Ahoy*. 1966: *The Wrong Box*. 1967: *The Ghost Goes Gear*. 1968: *Don't Raise the Bridge, Lower the River*. 1971: *Danger Point!* 1972: †*Mad Dogs and Cricketers*. 1974: *The Best of Benny Hill*. 1976: *Spy Story*. 1984: †*Relatively Greek*. 1987: *Mr Jolly Lives Next Door*.

† And directed

PATCH, Wally

(Walter Vinnicombe) 1888–1970
Stoutly built, dark-haired (vanishing from a high forehead), massive-headed British cockney portrayer of working-class types from dustmen to foremen with a good few sergeant-majors in between. He was a sandblaster, a bookmaker, a boxing promoter, a dentist, a nightclub proprietor and a music-hall entertainer before coming to films in 1926 and staying for more than 40 years, starring in a few minor comedies to which he often contributed script material, or standing solidly around as a cheery support to the stars.

1926: *Boadicea*. 1927: *The Luck of the Navy. Carry On! The King's Highway. Blighty.*

Shooting Stars. 1928: *The Guns of Loos. Balaclava (US: The Jaws of Hell)*. *Dr Sin Fang (and ensuing series). A Reckless Gamble. You Know What Sailors Are. Warned Off. The Woman in White*. 1929: *Dick Turpin (and ensuing series). High Treason*. 1930: *The Great Game. Kissing Cup's Race. Thread o' Scarlet*. 1931: *The Sport of Kings. Shadows. Tell England (US: The Battle of Gallipoli). Never Trouble Trouble. The Great Gay Road*. 1932: *Castle Sinister. Little Waitress. Illegal. Heroes of the Mine. Here's George*. 1933: *The Crime at Blossoms. Friday the Thirteenth. The Private Life of Henry VIII. The Good Companions. Don Quixote. Britannia of Billingsgate. Orders Is Orders. Tiger Bay. Channel Crossing. Marooned. Sorrell and Son. Trouble. The Scotland Yard Mystery (US: The Living Dead)*. 1934: *The Man I Want. Those Were the Days. Passing Shadows. Music Hall. The Perfect Flaw. What Happened to Harkness. Virginia's Husband. Badger's Green. Crazy People. The Scoop. The Old Curiosity Shop. A Glimpse of Paradise. Borrow a Million. Lost Over London. Once in a New Moon/Once in a Blue Moon*. 1935: *His Majesty and Co. Death on the Set (US: Murder on the Set). Dandy Dick. The Public Life of Henry the Ninth. That's My Wife. Street Song. Off the Dole. Marry the Girl. Half Day Excursion. Where's George? (US: The Hope of His Side). What the Parrot Saw. While Parents Sleep. Old Faithful. Get Off My Foot. A Wife or Two. Ticket of Leave. A Fire Has Been Arranged*. 1936: *On Top of the World. King of the Castle. Excuse My Glove. What the Puppy Said. Prison Breaker. A Touch of the Moon. Not So Dusty. Interrupted Honeymoon. Apron Fools. The Man Who Could Work Miracles. Luck of the Turf. Hail and Farewell. Busman's Holiday. Men Are Not Gods. The Scarab Murder Case. You Must Get Married. Dusty Ermine (US: Hideout in the Alps)*. 1937: *The Inspector. The Price of Folly. Holiday's End. The High Command. The Street Singer. Farewell Again (US: Troopship). Dr Syn. Missing – Believed Married. Night Ride. The Sky's the Limit. Captain's Orders. Owd Bob (US: To the Victor)*. *The Monkeys on the Field. Bank Holiday (US: Three on a Weekend)*. 1938: *Quiet Please. On Velvet. The Lady Vanishes*. *The Prodigal Son. Almost a Honeymoon. Break the News. Alf's Button Afloat. 13 Men and a Gun. A Night Alone. Pygmalion. Inspector Hornleigh. The Ware Case*. 1939: *The Mind of Mr Reeder (US: The Mysterious Mr Reeder). Home from Home.*

Sword of Honour. Poison Pen. Down Our Alley. What Would You Do Chums? The Lion Has Wings. *Hospital Hospitality. Inspector Hornleigh on Holiday (US: Inspector Hornleigh on Leave). Laugh It Off. Return to Yesterday. Just William. Band Waggon*. 1940: *They Came By Night. Henry Steps Out. Contraband (US: Blackout). Charley's (Big-Hearted) Aunt. Pack Up Your Troubles. Night Train to Munich (US: Night Train). Two Smart Men. Old Mother Riley in Business. Gasbags. Neutral Port*. 1941: *Quiet Wedding. Inspector Hornleigh Goes to It (US: Mail Train). Jeannie (US: Girl in Distress). Once a Crook. Facing the Music. Cottage To Let (US: Bombsight Stolen). I Thank You. The Seventh Survivor. Gert and Daisy's Weekend. The Common Touch. Bob's Your Uncle. Banana Ridge. Major Barbara*. 1942: *Let the People Sing. Sabotage at Sea. We'll Smile Again. Unpublished Story. Asking for Trouble. In Which We Serve. Much Too Shy*. 1943: *Death by Design*. *Strange to Relate*. *Women in Bondage. The Life and Death of Colonel Blimp (US: Colonel Blimp). Get Cracking. The Butler's Dilemma*. 1945: *Old Mother Riley at Home. Don Chicago. I Didn't Do It. Dumb Dora Discovers Tobacco*. 1946: *A Matter of Life and Death (US: Stairway to Heaven). Gaiety George (US: Showtime). Appointment with Crime. London Town (US: My Heart Goes Crazy). George in Civvy Street. Wanted for Murder*. 1947: *Green Fingers. The Ghosts of Berkeley Square. Dusty Bates (serial). Brighton Rock (US: Young Scarface)*. 1948: *River Patrol. A Date With a Dream. The Guinea Pig. Calling Paul Temple. The History of Mr Polly*. 1949: *Helter Skelter. The Adventures of Jane. Marry Me! Stop Press Girl*. 1950: *The Twenty Questions Murder Mystery*. 1951: *Salute the Toff*. 1952: *Hammer the Toff. Will Any Gentleman?... Thought to Kill. The Wedding of Lilli Marlene*. 1955: *Josephine and Men. Private's Progress*. 1956: *Not So Dusty (and 1936 film). Suspended Alibi*. 1957: *Morning Call (US: Strange Case of Dr Manning). The Naked Truth (US: Your Past Is Showing!)*. 1959: *Too Many Crooks. I'm All Right, Jack. Operation Cupid. The Challenge (US: It Takes a Thief)*. 1960: *The Millionairess. The Night We Got the Bird*. 1961: *The Damned (US: These Are the Damned). Nothing Barred*. 1962: *Serena. Sparrows Can't Sing. Danger by My Side*. 1963: *A Jolly Bad Fellow (US: They All Died Laughing). The Comedy Man*. 1964: *The Bargee*. 1967: *Poor Cow.*

PATE, Michael 1920–

There can't be many Australian actors who went to Hollywood and played Red Indians. Pate began performing on stage and radio as a child and grew to be dark and handsome in a sullen-looking way, going to the States in 1951 and portraying period villains (often with moustache and beard) as well as Redskins. In 1968, he returned to Australia, where he concentrated on the production side, with the occasional foray into direction. Also wrote screenplays and books (*The Film Actor, The Director's Eye*) and made a TV series, *Hondo* — as an Indian chief.

1940: *40,000 Horsemen*. 1949: *Sons of Matthew (GB and US: The Rugged*

O'Riordans). 1950: Bitter Springs. 1951: Thunder on the Hill (GB: Bonaventure). The Strange Door. Ten Tall Men. 1952: Five Fingers. The Black Castle. Face to Face. Target Hong Kong. Scandal at Scourie. 1953: Julius Caesar. The Desert Rats. Rogue's March. Houdini. The Maze. All the Brothers Were Valiant. Royal African Rifles (GB: Storm Over Africa). El Alamein (GB: Desert Patrol). Hondo. 1954: The Silver Chalice. Secret of the Incas. King Richard and the Crusaders. 1955: A Lawless Street. African Fury (narrator only). The Court Jester. 1956: The Killer Is Loose. The Revolt of Mamie Stover. Congo Crossing. 7th Cavalry. Reprisal! 1957: Something of Value. The Oklahoman. The Tall Stranger. 1958: Desert Hell. Hong Kong Confidential. 1959: Green Mansions. Curse of the Undead. Westbound. 1960: Zorro the Avenger (TV. GB: cinemas). Walk Like a Dragon. 1961: The Canadians. 1962: Tower of London. Sergeants Three. Beauty and the Beast. California. PT109. 1963: Drums of Africa. McLintock! Advance to the Rear (GB: Company of Cowards). 1964: Major Dundee. 1965: Brainstorm. The Great Sioux Massacre. The Singing Nun. 1966: Return of the Gunfighter. Willie and the Yank (TV. GB: cinemas, as Mosby's Marauders). Hondo and the Apaches. 1969: The Little Jungle Boy. 1976: Mad Dog/Mad Dog Morgan. 1981: Duet for Four. Partners. Crazy Times (TV). 1982: The Return of Captain Invincible. 1983: The Wild Duck. 1984: The Camel Boy. 1986: Body Builders. Death of a Soldier. 1987: The Marsupials: The Howling III.

As director:
1978: Tim.

PATINKIN, Mandy
(Mandel Patinkin) 1947–
Heftily built, heavy-headed, dark-haired, handsome in a slightly sly-looking sort of way, this versatile, chameleon-like American actor, singer and entertainer has had a go at most things since success as Che Guevara in the Broadway production of *Evita* brought him belated prominence in the cinema. Romantic heroes, villains, singers, period comedy roles, cameos and even an alien: Patinkin has tried them all. Born in Chicago and educated in Kansas, Patinkin acted in regional theatres before coming to New York, slaving away on TV for years before his name gradually became better known.

Often on stage, he is still a less frequent visitor to films than moviegoers would like. Since 1994, he has been entrenched on television in the hospital series *Chicago Hope*.

1978: The Big Fix. Night of the Juggler (released 1980). 1979: Charleston (TV). French Postcards. Last Embrace. 1981: Ragtime. 1983: Daniel. Yentl. 1985: Maxie. 1986: Sunday in the Park with George. 1987: The Princess Bride. 1988: Alien Nation. The House on Carroll Street. 1990: Dick Tracy. Impromptu. True Colors. 1991: The Doctor. 1993: The Music of Chance. 1994: Squanto: A Warrior's Tale.

PATON, Charles 1886–1950
Strong-featured, pale-eyed, balding, surprised-looking British supporting player who came to films at the very beginnings of sound, following a background in music hall, circuses and concert parties. He often played respected working-class figures – citizens, councillors, small businessmen and the like, although sometimes with a quaint, quizzical quality. After a lifetime of blue-collar service, he was seen in progressively smaller roles towards the end of his career, although he was still busy when he died from a heart attack at 64.

1927: *John Citizen. *John Citizen's Lament. 1928: In Borrowed Plumes. Two of a Trade. 1929: Piccadilly. The Feather. Blackmail. 1930: A Sister to Assist 'Er. The 'W' Plan. 1931: Stepping Stones. The Sleeping Cardinal (US: Sherlock Holmes' Fatal Hour). My Wife's Family. The Great Gay Road. The Lyons Mail.

The Girl in the Night. Glamour. What a Night. The Speckled Band. Contraband Love. The Other Mrs Phipps. Rynox. 1932: The Spare Room. Bachelor's Baby. The Third String. A Letter of Warning. Josser Joins the Navy. The Iron Stair. 1933: This Acting Business. The Love Nest. The Ghost Camera. 1934: Freedom of the Seas. Song at Eventide. The Man Who Changed His Name. Girls Will Be Boys. The Girl in Possession. Once in a New Moon/Once in a Blue Moon. 1935: The Private Secretary. Royal Cavalcade (US: Regal Cavalcade). Music Hath Charms. No Monkey Business. Jury's Evidence. 1936: Public Nuisance No 1. Crime Over London. Men Are Not Gods. Rembrandt. When Knights Were Bold. The Vandergilt Diamond Mystery. The Marriage of Corbal (US: The Prisoner of Corbal). Pal o' Mine. 1937: London Melody (US: Girls in the Street). Missing – Believed Married. Good Morning, Boys (US: Where There's a Will). Over She Goes. Museum Mystery. The Dominant Sex. The Last Chance. Old Mother Riley. 1938: A Sister to Assist 'Er (and 1930 film). Crackerjack (US: The Man With a Hundred Faces). Double or Quits. Mother of Men. Sailing Along. Convict 99. Weddings Are Wonderful. The Ware Case. 1939: Men Without Honour. Old Mother Riley MP. The Saint in London. The Four Just Men (US: The Secret Four). Meet Maxwell Archer (US: Maxwell Archer, Detective). The Body Vanishes. 1940: Under Your Hat. The Girl in the News. Let George Do It. The Briggs Family. 1941: South American George. Pimpernel Smith (US: Mister V). Hi, Gang! Major Barbara. Old Mother Riley's Ghosts. 1942: The Young Mr Pitt. Back Room Boy. It's That Man Again. Went the Day Well? (US: 48 Hours). Uncensored. Old Mother Riley Detective. 1943: The Demi-Paradise (US: Adventure for Two). Theatre Royal. The Adventures of Tartu (US: Tartu). 1944: A Canterbury Tale. Give Us the Moon. He Snoops to Conquer. Fiddlers Three. Strawberry Roan. 1945: Waltz Time. I'll Be Your Sweetheart. Caesar and Cleopatra. 1946: Bedelia. London Town (US: My Heart Goes Crazy). Spring Song (US: Springtime). 1947: Green Fingers. Uncle Silas (US: The Inheritance). 1948: Miranda. Love in Waiting. Man on the Run. Cardboard Cavalier. House of Darkness. 1949: Celia. The Man from Yesterday. The Spider and the Fly. 1950: The Adventurers (US: The Great Adventure). Night and the City. Once a Sinner. Portrait of Clare.

PATRICK, Lee 1906–1982
Long-faced, fair-haired, plain but peppy American actress, hard on the heels of Veda Ann Borg (qv) and Gladys George in the shop-soiled blonde stakes, although not quite in the same mould, being just as likely to turn up as secretary (supremely as girl-Friday Effie in *The Maltese Falcon*, a role she amusingly reprised 34 years later in *The Black Bird*), or confidante. Died from a heart attack.

1929: Strange Cargo. 1937: Danger Patrol. Music for Madame. Hideaway. Border Café. Crashing Hollywood. 1938: Maid's Night Out. Law of the Underworld. Night Spot. Condemned Women. The Sisters. 1939: Fisherman's Wharf. Invisible Stripes. 1940: City for Conquest.

Strange Cargo. Money and the Woman. Father is a Prince. South of Suez. Saturday's Children. Ladies Must Live. 1941: Footsteps in the Dark. The Maltese Falcon. Honeymoon for Three. The Smiling Ghost. Million Dollar Baby. Kisses for Breakfast. The Nurse's Secret. Dangerously They Live. 1942: In This Our Life. George Washington Slept Here. Now, Voyager. Somewhere I'll Find You. A Night to Remember. 1943: Nobody's Darling. Larceny With Music. Jitterbugs. 1944: Gambler's Choice. Mrs Parkington. Faces in the Fog. Moon Over Las Vegas. 1945: See My Lawyer. Keep Your Powder Dry. Mildred Pierce. Over 21. 1946: The Walls Came Tumbling Down. Strange Journey. Wake Up and Dream. 1947: Mother Wore Tights. 1948: Singing Spurs. Inner Sanctum. The Snake Pit. 1949: The Doolins of Oklahoma (GB: The Great Manhunt). 1950: The Lawless (GB: The Dividing Line). The Fuller Brush Girl (GB: The Affairs of Sally). Caged. 1951: Tomorrow Is Another Day. 1953: Take Me to Town. 1954: There's No Business like Show Business. 1958: Auntie Mame. Vertigo. 1959: Pillow Talk. 1960: A Visit to a Small Planet. 1961: Goodbye Again. Summer and Smoke. 1962: A Girl Named Tamiko. 1963: Wives and Lovers. 1964: The Seven Faces of Dr Lao. The New Interns. 1975: The Black Bird.

PATTERSON, Elizabeth 1874–1966
American actress with scruffed-back brown hair, shuffling gait, scrawny neck, dumpy figure and take-it-all-in gaze. She came to Hollywood sound films at 55 to bring her Tennessee accent to portraits of down-

to-earth country spinsters and maiden aunts and continued doing it for another 30 years. Had a rare leading role as Charley Grapewin's worn-out wife in *Tobacco Road*.

1926: The Boy Friend. The Return of Peter Grimm. 1929: South Sea Rose. Timothy's Quest. Words and Music. 1930: The Lone Star Ranger. Harmony at Home. The Big Party. The Cat Creeps. 1931: Tarnished Lady. Husband's Holiday. Heaven on Earth. Daddy Long Legs. The Smiling Lieutenant. Penrod and Sam. 1932: Love Me Tonight. Miss Pinkerton. The Expert. Play Girl. Two Against the World. New Morals for Old. Breach of Promise. So Big. No Man of Her Own. The Conquerors. Jazz Babies. A Bill of Divorcement. Guilty As Hell (GB: Guilty As Charged). Life Begins (GB: The Dawn of Life). They Call It Sin (GB: The Way of Life). Dangerous Brunette. 1933: Doctor Bull. They Just Had to Get Married. Ever in My Heart. Golden Harvest. Dinner at Eight. The Infernal Machine. Hold Your Man. The Story of Temple Drake. The Secret of the Blue Room. 1934: Hide-Out. 1935: Men Without Names. So Red the Rose. Mississippi. Chasing Yesterday. 1936: Timothy's Quest (and 1929 film). The Return of Sophie Lang. Three Cheers for Love. Go West, Young Man. Small Town Girl. Her Master's Voice. Old Hutch. 1937: A Night of Mystery. Hold 'Em Navy. High, Wide and Handsome. Night Club Scandal. 1938: Scandal Street. Bulldog Drummond's Peril. Bluebeard's Eighth Wife. Sing, You Sinners. The Adventures of Tom Sawyer. Sons of the Legion. 1939: The Story of Alexander Graham Bell (GB: The Modern Miracle). Bulldog Drummond's Bride. Our Leading Citizen. Bad Little Angel. The Cat and the Canary. Bulldog Drummond's Secret Police. Remember the Night. 1940: Anne of Windy Poplars (GB: Anne of Windy Willows). Adventure in Diamonds. Michael Shayne, Private Detective. Who Killed Aunt Maggie? Earthbound. 1941: Belle Starr. Kiss the Boys Goodbye. Tobacco Road. The Vanishing Virginian. 1942: Almost Married. Her Cardboard Lover. Beyond the Blue Horizon. My Sister Eileen. Lucky Legs. I Married a Witch. 1943: The Sky's the Limit. 1944: Follow the Boys. Together Again. Hail the Conquering Hero. 1945: Lady on a Train. Colonel Effingham's Raid (GB: Man of the Hour). 1946: The Secret Heart. I've Always Loved You (GB: Concerto). The Shocking Miss Pilgrim. 1947: Welcome, Stranger. Out of the Blue. 1948: Miss Tatlock's Millions. 1949: Little Women. Song of Surrender. Intruder in the Dust. 1950: Bright Leaf. 1951: Katie Did It. 1952: Washington Story (GB: Target for Scandal). 1955: Las Vegas Shakedown. 1957: Mr and Mrs McAdam (TV). Pal Joey. 1958: Portrait of a Murderer (TV). 1959: The Oregon Trail. 1960: Tomorrow (TV). Tall Story.

PATTON, Will 1954–
Slim, strong-jawed, lankly fair-haired American actor with shadowed features that adapt equally well to reliability or treachery. A too-rare visitor to Hollywood films who has been in dozens of Broadway stage productions, Patton has shown up best in sneaky, hateful roles (like Gene Hackman's aide-de-camp in *No Way Out*), although he

also proved interesting in the central role of the low-budget British/West German film *Chinese Boxes*. His creepy characters slid more frequently across our screens in the early 1990s.

1981: The Third Person. 1982: King Blank. 1983: Variety. Silkwood. 1984: Chinese Boxes. 1985: After Hours. Belizaire the Cajun. Desperately Seeking Susan. 1987: No Way Out. A Gathering of Old Men/Murder in the Bayou (TV). Stars and Bars. 1988: Wildfire. 1989: Signs of Life. 1990: Dillinger (TV). Everybody Wins. A Shock to the System. 1991: Dillinger (TV). The Rapture. Cold Heaven. In the Soup. Deadly Desire (cable TV). 1992: In the Deep Woods (TV). Paint Job (GB: The Painted Heart). 1993: Romeo is Bleeding. Taking the Heat. Midnight Edition. 1994: Tollbooth. The Client. The Puppet Masters. Natural Causes. Judicial Consent. 1995: Johns.

PEARCE, Alice 1913–1966
Short, beaky, brown-haired American comic actress with receding chin and protruding lips, who made the most of her caricature of a face to create the unforgettably sinus-ridden Lucy Schmeeler in the stage and film versions of *On the Town*. A popular Broadway and nightclub comedienne following her stage debut in *New Faces of 1943*, she found too little time to provide films with enough gems to follow the toothy and far from juicy Lucy, everyone's idea of the blind date they'd rather not see. She won an Emmy for her running role as Gladys in the TV series *Bewitched*. Died from cancer.

*1949: On the Town. 1952: Belle of New York.
1955: How to Be Very, Very Popular. 1956:
The Opposite Sex. 1962: Lad: a Dog. 1963:
My Six Loves. The Thrill of It All. Tammy and
the Doctor. Beach Party. 1964: The Disorderly
Orderly. Dear Heart. Kiss Me Stupid. 1965:
That Darn Cat! Dear Brigitte . . . Bus Riley's
Back in Town. 1966: The Glass Bottom Boat.*

PEARSON, Richard 1918–
Tubby, worried-looking, often bespectacled
Welsh-born actor with a shock of unruly
wavy fair hair, seen as a range of mild-
mannered professional men during his
infrequent apperances in British films.
Much busier, though, in TV and on the
stage, where he made his debut at London's
Collins's Music Hall when only 18. Almost
a dead ringer for former British foreign
secretary Lord Howe.

*1938: *An Act of Mercy. 1949: A Run for Your
Money. 1950: The Woman in Question (US:
Five Angles on Murder). The Girl is Mine. The
Woman With No Name (US: Her Paneled
Door). The Clouded Yellow. 1951: Scrooge
(US: A Christmas Carol). 1953: The Blue
Parrot. 1954: Dangerous Cargo. Fabian of the
Yard. Svengali. 1958: The Crowning Touch.
Battle of the V1 (US: V1/Unseen Heroes). Sea
Fury. 1959: Life in Danger. Libel. Model for
Murder. 1961: The Man in the Moon. Attempt
to Kill. 1962: Guns of Darkness. 1963: The
Comedy Man. *The King's Breakfast. 1964:
The Yellow Rolls-Royce. One Way Pendulum.
1965: The Legend of Young Dick Turpin. The
Agony and the Ecstasy. 1967: Charlie Bubbles.
How I Won the War. 1968: The Strange
Affair. Inspector Clouseau. 1970: The Rise and
Rise of Michael Rimmer. 1971: Sunday Bloody
Sunday. Macbeth. Catch Me a Spy. 1972:
Pope Joan. 1974: Love Among the Ruins (TV).
1975: Royal Flash. One of Our Dinosaurs is
Missing. 1976: The Blue Bird. It Shouldn't
Happen to a Vet (US: All Things Bright and
Beautiful). 1978: She Fell Among Thieves
(TV). 1979: Tess. 1980: Masada (TV. GB:
cinemas, abridged, as The Antagonists). The
Mirror Crack'd. 1985: Water. Reunion at
Fairborough (TV). 1986: Pirates. Whoops
Apocalypse.*

PENDLETON, Nat 1895–1967
'Playing dumb' made Pendleton one of the
most popular American supporting actors of

the 1930s. Tall, dark and handsome in a
faintly bemused-looking way, Pendleton,
brother of actor Gaylord Pendleton, was in
reality an Olympic wrestling champion and
all-round smart guy with a college degree.
In films, however, he was soon playing dim
hoodlums and other characters with more
brawn than brain to whom the truth dawned
but slowly. When demands for his services
declined in the post-war period, he slipped
away from show business into early retirement. Died from a heart attack.

*1912: The Battle of Gettysburg. 1924: Monsieur
Beaucaire. The Hoosier Schoolmaster (GB: The
Schoolmaster). 1926: Let's Get Married. 1929:
The Laughing Lady. 1930: The Big Pond. The
Big Trail. Last of the Duanes. The Sea Wolf.
Liliom. 1931: The Star Witness. Spirit of
Notre Dame (GB: Vigour of Youth). The Seas
Beneath. Blonde Crazy (GB: Larceny Lane).
Mr Lemon of Orange. The Ruling Voice. Fair
Warning. The Secret Witness/Terror by Night.
Cauliflower Alley. *Pottsville Paluka. 1932:
Taxi! Play Girl. Attorney for the Defense.
Exposure. Hell Fire Austin. Beast of the City.
State's Attorney (GB: Cardigan's Last Case).
The Sign of the Cross. Manhattan Parade. By
Whose Hand? Horse Feathers. Night Club Lady.
Flesh. The Tenderfoot. You Said a Mouthful.
*A Fool's Advice. 1933: College Coach (GB:
Football Coach). Parachute Jumper. Baby Face.
Whistling in the Dark. The White Sister.
Goldie Gets Along. Lady for a Day. Deception.
Penthouse (GB: Crooks in Clover). I'm No
Angel. The Chief (GB: My Old Man's a
Fireman). 1934: Fugitive Lovers. Death on the
Diamond. The Defense Rests. The Cat's Paw.
Manhattan Melodrama. Lazy River. The Thin
Man. The Gay Bride. Sing and Like It. The
Girl from Missouri (GB: 100 Per Cent Pure).
Straight Is the Way. 1935: Reckless. Times
Square Lady. Baby Face Harrington. Murder
in the Fleet. Calm Youself. It's in the Air. Here
Comes the Band. 1936: Trapped by Television
(GB: Caught by Television). Two in a Crowd.
The Garden Murder Case. The Great Ziegfeld.
Sworn Enemy. The Luckiest Girl in the World.
Sing Me a Love Song. 1937: Gangway. Under
Cover of Night. Song of the City. Life Begins in
College (GB: The Joy Parade). 1938: Meet
the Mayor (filmed 1932). Shopworn Angel.
Arsene Lupin Returns. Swing Your Lady. Fast
Company. Young Dr Kildare. The Crowd Roars.
The Chaser. 1939: Calling Dr Kildare. Burn
'Em Up O'Connor. It's a Wonderful World.*

*6,000 Enemies. At the Circus. On Borrowed
Time. Another Thin Man. The Secret of
Dr Kildare. 1940: The Ghost Comes Home.
Northwest Passage. Dr Kildare's Strangest Case.
Phantom Raiders. New Moon. The Golden
Fleecing. Dr Kildare's Crisis. Flight Command.
Dr Kildare Goes Home. 1941: Buck Privates
(GB: Rookies). Dr Kildare's Wedding Day (GB:
Mary Names the Day). Top Sergeant Mulligan.
The Mad Doctor of Market Street. †Dr Kildare's
Victory (GB: The Doctor and the Debutante).
1942: Calling Dr Gillespie. Jail House Blues.
Dr Gillespie's New Assistant. 1943: Swing
Fever. Dr Gillespie's Criminal Case (GB: Crazy
to Kill). 1946: Death Valley. 1947: Buck
Privates Come Home (GB: Rookies Come
Home). Scared to Death.*

† Scene deleted from final release print

PENN, Christopher (or Chris) 1958–
Thick-set, strong-jawed, small-eyed,
brown-haired American actor, a real-life
bright spark whose physical appearance has
often had him playing characters without
too much grey matter on screen. The son of
writer-director Leo Penn and brother of
actor-director Sean Penn, he excelled at
sports from an early age and, indeed, disappeared from screens large and small for
several years in the 1980s while pursuing
activities in athletics, boxing and kick-
boxing. A role *as* a kick-boxer in *Best of the
Best* brought him back to films, and he has
recently been very busy playing a variety
of redneck types both sympathetic and
unsympathetic. Has also written screenplays
and has ambitions to follow his father and
brother into directing.

*1982: Moonlight (TV). Frances. 1983: Rumble
Fish. 1984: The Wild Life. Footloose. All the
Right Moves. 1985: North Beach and Rawhide
(TV). Pale Rider. At Close Range. 1988: Made
in USA. 1989: Best of the Best. Return from the
River Kwai. 1991: Futurekick. Mobsters (GB:
Mobsters The Evil Empire). 1992: Leather
Jackets. Reservoir Dogs. 1993: Best of the
Best 2. True Romance. Josh and S.A.M. Short
Cuts. The Pickle. The Music of Chance.
Beethoven's 2nd. 1994: Luck, Trust & Ketchup.
Imaginary Crimes. Fist of the North Star. 1995:
Under the Hula Moon. Sacred Cargo.
Mulholland Falls.*

PERCIVAL, Lance 1933–

Toothy, fair-haired, languorous-looking, Scots-born satirist, entertainer, revue star, comic actor and light singer. He came to prominence in London cabaret and the trailblazing TV satire programme *That Was the Week That Was*. The cinema generally asked him to play comedy roles rather too broad for his talents, seeing his donkey-like features only in farce. His laconic voice proved most effective telling TV stories (especially for children) or in unseen narration.

1956: Three Men in a Boat. 1961: In the Doghouse. What a Whopper! On the Fiddle (US: Operation Snafu). Raising the Wind (US: Roommates). 1962: Postman's Knock. The Devil's Daffodil. Twice Round the Daffodils Carry On Cruising. 1963: *The Sure Thing (voice only). The VIPs. Hide and Seek. It's All Over Town. 1964: The Yellow Rolls-Royce. 1965: You Must Be Joking! The Big Job. Joey Boy. 1968: Yellow Submarine (voice only). Mrs Brown, You've Got a Lovely Daughter. 1969: Darling Lili. Too Late the Hero. 1970: There's a Girl in My Soup. Concerto per pistola solista (GB: The Weekend Murders). 1971: The Magnificent Six and a ½ (third series). Up Pompeii. Up the Chastity Belt. 1972: Up the Front. Our Miss Fred. 1973: *The Cobblers of Umbridge. 1974: The Boy With Two Heads (serial). 1977: Confessions from a Holiday Camp. 1978: The Water Babies (voice only). Rosie Dixon Night Nurse. 1987: Jekyll and Hyde (TV).

PERRINS, Leslie 1902–1962

Dark-haired, moustachioed, full-faced British actor, a very smooth and professional villain, charming the heroine up the wrong path, and so good at it that the British cinema pigeonholed him in the role and kept him frantically busy throughout the 1930s. From 1940 on, his sharply cultured tones were heard rather more often on radio, several times as police inspectors in longrunning series. A dominant personality; didn't often play comedy.

1928: *Silken Threads. *The Clue of the Second Goblet. *Blake the Lawbreaker. 1930: Immediate Possession. 1931: The Sleeping Cardinal (US: Sherlock Holmes' Fatal Hour). The Rosary. The Calendar (US: Bachelor's Folly). We Dine at Seven. The House of Unrest. 1932: Betrayal. Whiteface. 1933: The Lost Chord. Early to Bed. Just Smith (US: Leave It to

Smith). The Roof. The Pointing Finger. The Scotland Yard Mystery (US: The Living Dead). Lily of Killarney (US: Bride of the Lake). 1934. Lord Edgware Dies. The Man Who Changed His Name. The Lash. Song at Eventide. Gay Love. Open All Night. Womanhood. D'Ye Ken John Peel? (US: Captain Moonlight). 1935: The Rocks of Valpré (US: High Treason). The Shadow of Mike Emerald. The Triumph of Sherlock Holmes. The Village Squire. White Lilac. The Silent Passenger. Lucky Days. Expert's Opinion. Line Engaged. Sunshine Ahead. 1936: They Didn't Know. Tudor Rose (US: Nine Days a Queen). Rhythm in the Air. Southern Roses. The Limping Man. No Escape. Sensation. 1937: The Price of Folly. Bulldog Drummond at Bay. Secret Lives (US: I Married a Spy). The High Command. Dangerous Fingers (US: Wanted by Scotland Yard). 1938: Mr Reeder in Room 13 (US: Mystery of Room 13). Romance à la Carte. The Gables Mystery. No Parking. Calling All Crooks. His Lordship Goes to Press. Luck of the Navy (US: North Sea Patrol). Old Iron. 1939: I Killed the Count (US: Who is Guilty?). The Gang's All Here (US: The Amazing Mr Forrest). All at Sea. Blind Folly. 1940: John Smith Wakes Up. 1941: The Prime Minister. 1942: Suspected Person. Women Aren't Angels. 1944: Heaven Is Round the Corner. 1946: I'll Turn to You. 1947: The Turners of Prospect Road. 1948: Idol of Paris. Man on the Run. It's Hard to Be Good. 1949: A Run for Your Money. 1950: Midnight Episode. 1952: The Lost Hours (US: The Big Frame). 1956: Guilty? 1957: Fortune is a Woman (US: She Played With Fire). 1958: Grip of the Strangler (US: The Haunted Strangler).

PERSOFF, Nehemiah 1920–

Powerful, stockily built, squat-faced Israeliborn actor with dark, fuzzy hair. In America from the age of nine, he worked at one time as a subway electrician, but in post-war years, he enrolled at the Actors' Studio, emerging in the late 1940s and becoming a film regular from the mid-1950s, often in intense, aggressive roles, but later in more routine 'guest star'-type spots as professors, elders and the like.

1948: The Naked City. A Double Life. 1954: On the Waterfront. 1956: The Wild Party. The Harder They Fall. The Wrong Man. 1957: Men in War. Street of Sinners. 1958: The Badlanders. This Angry Age (GB: The Sea

Wall). Never Steal Anything Small. 1959: Al Capone. Some Like It Hot. Green Mansions. Day of the Outlaw. 1961: The Comancheros. The Big Show. 1963: The Hook. A Global Affair. 1964: Fate Is the Hunter. 1965: The Greatest Story Ever Told. 1966: The Dangerous Days of Kiowa Jones (TV. GB: cinemas). Too Many Thieves (TV. GB: cinemas). 1967: The Power. Panic in the City. 1968: The Money Jungle. Escape to Mindanao (TV). Il giorno della civetta (GB: Mafia). The Girl Who Knew Too Much. 1970: Cutter's Trail (TV). Mrs Pollifax—Spy. The People Next Door. Red Sky at Morning. 1972: Lieutenant Schuster's Wife (TV). 1974: The Stranger Within (TV). The Sex Symbol (TV. GB: cinemas). Eric (TV). Psychic Killer. 1976: Deadly Harvest (filmed 1972). Francis Gary Powers: The True Story of the U-2 Spy Incident (TV). Voyage of the Damned. 1978: Stone/Killing Stone (TV). Ziegfeld: The Man and His Women (TV). FDR: The Last Year (TV). The Henderson Monster (TV). 1979: The French Atlantic Affair (TV). The Rebels (TV). BAD Cats (TV). 1980: In Search of Historic Jesus (TV. GB: cinemas, as Jesus). Turnover Smith (TV). 1981: St Helens/Killer Volcano. O'Hara's Wife. 1983: Yentl. Sadat (TV). 1986: An American Tail (voice only). 1988: The Big Knife (TV). The Last Temptation of Christ. 1990: The Dispossessed. 1991: An American Tail 2: Fievel Goes West (voice only).

PERTWEE, Jon 1917–

Tall, long-striding, red-headed (now white), beaky-nosed British comic actor with burbling tones whose chief claim to fame in the post-war years was as a radio voice, especially in the series *Waterlogged Spa* and *The Navy Lark*, sadly not transferring his character in the latter to the film version. He was also popular on television as one of the personalities of *Dr Who*. A sort of minor-key British Danny Kaye, an actor for whom, strangely, Pertwee 'stood in' on the London location scenes of Kaye's *Knock on Wood*. Son of playwright and screen-writer Roland Pertwee, and brother of another, Michael Pertwee. Father of actor Sean Pertwee.

1937: A Yank at Oxford. Dinner at the Ritz. 1939: Young Man's Fancy. The Four Just Men (US: The Secret Four). There Ain't No Justice! 1947: Penny and the Pownall Case. 1948: William Comes to Town. Trouble in the Air. A Piece of Cake. 1949: Murder at the Windmill (US: Murder at the Burlesque). Helter Skelter. Stop Press Girl. Dear Mr Prohack. Miss Pilgrim's Progress. 1950: The Body Said No. Mr Drake's Duck. 1953: Will Any Gentleman . . . ? 1954: The Gay Dog. Knock on Wood (stand-in). 1955: A Yank in Ermine. 1956: It's a Wonderful World. 1958: The Ugly Duckling. 1959: Just Joe. 1960: Not a Hope in Hell. 1961: Nearly a Nasty Accident. 1963: Ladies Who Do. Carry On Cleo. *The Quay to the Tor (narrator only). 1965: You Must be Joking! How to Undress in Public Without Undue Embarrassment. Runaway Railway. Carry On Cowboy. I've Gotta Horse. 1966: Carry On Screaming. A Funny Thing Happened on the Way to the Forum. 1969: Up in the Air. Under the Table You Must Go. 1970: The House That Dripped Blood. There's a Girl in My Soup. 1974: Four Against the Desert. 1975: One of Our Dinosaurs is Missing. 1977: Adventures of a Private Eye. Wombling Free (voice only). No. 1 of the Secret Service. 1978: The Water Babies (voice only). 1983: The Boys in Blue. 1992: Carry On Columbus.

PETRIE, Hay
(David H. Petrie) 1895–1948
Short, scuttling Scottish actor who specialized in eccentric characterizations. In his element as The MacLaggan in *The Ghost Goes West*, although probably his biggest role was as the avaricious Quilp in the 1934 version of Dickens's *The Old Curiosity Shop*. Otherwise cast as an assortment of tiny terrors, from stagedoor-keepers to spies, who could give anyone as good as they got in the verbal stakes.

1930: Suspense. Night Birds. 1931: Gipsy Blood (US: Carmen). Many Waters. 1932: Help Yourself. 1933: The Private Life of Henry VIII. Daughters of Today. Lucky Number. Song of the Plough (US: County Fair). Crime on the Hill. Matinee Idol. Red Wagon. Colonel Blood. 1934: Nell Gwyn. The Old Curiosity Shop. The Queen's Affair (US: Runaway Queen). The Private Life of Don Juan. Blind Justice. 1935: Peg of Old Drury. The Ghost Goes West. Moscow Nights (US: I Stand Condemned). Invitation to the Waltz. I Give My Heart. The Silent Passenger. Koenigsmark. 1936: Men of Yesterday. The House of the Spaniard. Conquest of the Air (released 1940). Hearts of Humanity. Forget-Me-Not (US: Forever Yours). Rembrandt. No Escape. Not Wanted on Voyage (US: Treachery on the High Seas). 1937: Murder in the Stalls. Secret Lives (US: I Married a Spy). Knight Without Armour. 21 Days (released 1940. US: 21 Days Together). 1938: The Last Barricade. Consider Your Verdict. Keep Smiling (US: Smiling Along). The Loves of Madame Du Barry. 1939: Shipyard Sally. The Rebel Son. Ten Days in Paris (US: Missing Ten Days). The Four Feathers. Q Planes (US: Clouds Over Europe). The Spy in Black (US: U-Boat 29). Jamaica Inn. Inquest. Trunk Crime (US: Design for Murder). Spy for a Day. 1940: Contraband (US: Blackout). Spellbound (US: The Spell of Amy Nugent). Convoy. Pastor Hall. Mein Kampf My Crimes. The Thief of Bagdad. Crimes at the Dark House. 1941: *Rush Hour. Quiet Wedding. Freedom Radio (US: A Voice in the Night). Turned Out Nice Again. The Ghost of St Michael's. Cottage to Let (US: Bombsight Stolen). This Was Paris. They Flew Alone (US: Wings and the Woman). 1942: Hard Steel. Those Kids from Town. The Great Mr Handel. One of Our Aircraft is Missing. 1943: Battle for Music. Escape to Danger. The Demi-Paradise (US: Adventure for Two). They Met in the Dark. 1944: A Canterbury Tale. On Approval. Kiss the Bride Goodbye. 1945: The Voice Within. Waltz Time. Night Boat to Dublin. For You Alone. 1946: The Laughing Lady. Great Expectations. Under New Management. The Magic Bow. 1948: The Monkey's Paw. The Red Shoes. The Guinea Pig. The Lucky Mascot/ Brass Monkey. The Fallen Idol. Noose (US: The Silk Noose). The Queen of Spades.

PETTINGELL, Frank 1891–1966
Beefy, phlegmatic, dark-haired British actor who brought his good-humoured north country-men to sound films after 20 years' experience on stage. He made his debut as Will Mossop in the first sound version of *Hobson's Choice* and was thereafter mostly in stout supporting roles, though none more effective than the justice-seeking policeman in the British version of *Gaslight*. Also wrote and adapted a number of historical plays for the theatre.

1931: Hobson's Choice. Jealousy. Frail Women. 1932: In a Monastery Garden. The Crooked Lady. Once Bitten. Double Dealing. Tight Corner. 1933: The Medicine Man. Yes, Madam. The Good Companions. Excess Baggage. That's My Wife. Lucky Number. The Private Life of Henry VIII. This Week of Grace.

A Cuckoo in the Nest. Red Wagon. 1934: Keep It Quiet. Sing As We Go. My Old Dutch. 1935: Say It With Diamonds. The Big Splash. The Right Age to Marry. Where's George? (US: The Hope of His Side). The Last Journey. The Amateur Gentleman. 1936: On Top of the World. Fame. Millions. 1937: It's a Grand Old World. Take My Tip. Spring Handicap. 1938: Queer Cargo (US: Pirates of the Seven Seas). Sailing Along. 1939: Return to Yesterday. 1940: Busman's Honeymoon (US: Haunted Honeymoon). Gaslight (US: Angel Street). 1941: This England. Kipps (US: The Remarkable Mr Kipps). Once a Crook. The Seventh Survivor. Ships With Wings. 1942: The Young Mr Pitt. When We Are Married. The Goose Steps Out. 1943: Get Cracking. The Butler's Dilemma. 1946: Gaiety George (US: Showtime). 1948: No Room at the Inn. Escape. 1951: The Magic Box. 1952: The Card (US: The Promoter). The Crimson Pirate. The Great Game. Meet Me Tonight. 1953: Meet Mr Lucifer. 1955: Value for Money. 1958: Up the Creek. Corridors of Blood. 1962: Term of Trial. The Dock Brief (US: Trial and Error). 1963: Becket.

PHILLPOTTS, Ambrosine 1912–1980
Forthright, forceful, dark-haired British actress who was a formidable stage Lady Macbeth at 19 and made scores of subsequent appearances in the theatre, far too many, alas, to allow this distinctive actress to carve out a film career as well. Often in aristocratic or bitchy roles, or in fact anything with a bit of bite.

1946: This Man Is Mine! 1950: The Franchise Affair. Happy Go Lovely. 1951: Mr Denning Drives North. Angels One Five. 1952: Stolen Face. Father's Doing Fine. 1953: The Captain's Paradise. 1956: Up in the World. 1957: The Truth About Women. 1958: The Reluctant Debutante. The Duke Wore Jeans. Room at the Top. 1959: Operation Bullshine. Expresso Bongo. 1960: Doctor in Love. 1961: Carry On Regardless. 1962: Two and Two Make Six. 1963: Carry On Cabby. 1965: Life at the Top. 1967: Berserk! 1969: Carry On Again, Doctor. 1972: Diamonds on Wheels. Ooh... You Are Awful (US: Get Charlie Tully). 1980: The Wildcats of St Trinian's.

PHIPPS, Nicholas 1913–1980

Tall, dark-haired, heavily moustachioed, wolfish-looking British comedy actor likely to be remembered for his successful screenplays rather than his (nonetheless enjoyable) performances. He wrote or co-wrote many of the Anna Neagle–Michael Wilding romances, as well as the later 'Doctor' films from the books by Richard Gordon. An elegant light comedian in the theatre, both in revue and straight plays. In films, his characters often had an eye for the heroine but rarely got her.

1940: Contraband (US: Blackout). You Will Remember. Old Bill and Son. 1946: Piccadilly Incident. 1947: The Courtneys of Curzon Street (US: The Courtney Affair). 1948: Spring in Park Lane. 1949: Maytime in Mayfair. Elizabeth of Ladymead. Madeleine. 1951: Appointment With Venus (US: Island Rescue). 1953: The Intruder. The Captain's Paradise. 1954: Doctor in the House. Forbidden Cargo. Mad About Men. Out of the Clouds. 1955: Doctor at Sea. All for Mary. Who Done It? 1956: The Iron Petticoat. 1957: Doctor at Large. 1958: Orders to Kill. Rockets Galore (US: Mad Little Island). The Captain's Table. 1959: Upstairs and Downstairs. Don't Panic, Chaps! 1960: The Pure Hell of St Trinian's. Doctor in Love. 1961: No Love for Johnnie. A Pair of Briefs. 1962: The Wild and the Willing. Summer Holiday. The Amorous Prawn. 1963: Doctor in Distress. Heavens Above! 1967: Charlie Bubbles. 1969: Some Girls Do. Monte Carlo or Bust! (US: Those Daring Young Men in Their Jaunty Jalopies). 1970: The Rise and Rise of Michael Rimmer.

PICCOLI, Michel
(Jacques M. Piccoli) 1925–

Long-headed, tall French actor, kindly-looking in a vaguely condescending way, with curly hair disappearing over a high forehead. Of Italian parentage, he was on stage immediately following World War II, and his film career built up gradually from the end of the 1940s. He played largely supporting roles, often as urbane businessmen, but also showed up prominently in films by Luis Buñuel, Claude Chabrol, Louis Malle and other top directors, winning some central roles from the 1960s on, and proving himself an actor of great versatility in subsequent decades, without ever quite becoming an international name. Married actress Juliette Greco (second of three).

*1944: Sortilèges (US: The Bellman). 1948: Le point du jour. 1949: Le parfum de la dame en noir. Sans laisser d'adresse. 1950: *Terreur en Oklahoma. 1951: Torticola contre Frankenberg. *Chicago Digest. 1952: Destinées (GB: Love and the Frenchwoman/Love, Soldiers and Women. US: Daughters of Destiny). 1953: Interdit de séjour. 1954: Tout chante autour de moi. 1955: French Cancan (GB: French Can Can. US: Only the French Can). Les mauvaise rencontres. Ernst Thälmann, Führer seiner Klasse. Marie-Antoinette. 1956: La muerte en este jardin (GB: Evil Eden. US: Death in the Garden). 1957: Rafles sur la ville (GB and US: Sinners of Paris). Nathalie, agent secret (GB and US: The Foxiest Girl in Paris). Sylviane de mes nuits. Les copains du dimanche. Les sorcières de Salem (GB and US: The Witches of Salem). 1958: Tabarin. 1959: La bête à l'affut. La dragée haute. 1960: Le bal des espions. Le vergini di Roma/The Virgins of Rome. 1961: Les rendez-vous. Le chevelure. Climats. 1962: Le Doulos (GB: Finger Man. US: Doulos – The Finger Man). Le jour et l'heure (GB and US: The Day and the Hour). 1963: Le mépris (GB and US: Contempt). Le journal d'une femme de chambre (GB and US: Diary of a Chambermaid). Marie-Soleil. 1964: La chance et l'amour. Masquerade. De l'amour. 1965: Lady L. Compartiment tueurs (GB and US: The Sleeping Car Murders). Le coup de grâce. Les ruses du diable. Les créatures. Is Paris Burning? 1966: La curée (GB and US: The Game is Over). La voleuse. La guerre est finie (GB: The War is Over). 1966: Un homme de trop (GB and US: Shock Troops). Les demoiselles de Rochefort/The Young Girls of*

Rochefort. 1967: Belle de jour. Diabolik (GB: Danger: Diabolik). Mon amour, mon amour. 1968: Benjamin. La voie lactée (GB and US: The Milky Way). La chamade. Dillinger is Dead. La prisonnière. 1969: Topaz. Gli invitati. L'invasion. Les choses de la vie (GB: The Things of Life). 1970: Max et les ferrailleurs. 1971: La poudre d'escampette (US: Touch and Go). Liza/La cagna. La décade prodigieuse (and English-language version: Ten Days' Wonder). L'udienza. 1972: L'attentat (GB: Plot. US: The French Conspiracy). Le charme discret de la bourgeoisie (GB and US: The Discreet Charm of the Bourgeoisie). Themroc. La femme en bleu. 1973: La grande bouffe. Les noces rouges (GB: Red Wedding. US: Wedding in Blood). Touche pas à la femme blanche! Le Far West. Life Size (US: Love Doll). 1974: Le trio infernal. Grandeur nature. Le fantôme de la liberté/The Phantom of Liberty. Vincent, François, Paul et les autres. La faille. 1975: Léonor. La main occulte. Strauberg ist da. 7 morts pour l'ordonnance. 1976: Mado. F ... comme Fairbanks. La dernière femme (GB and US: The Last Woman). René la canne. Des enfants gâtés. La part du feu. 1977: Todo Modo. L'imprécateur. 1978: L'état sauvage (US: The Savage State). La petite fille en velours bleu (US: The Girl in Blue Velvet). Le sucre. Le divorcement. 1979: Giallo Napoletano (France: Melodie meutrière). Le mors aux dents. La vis et la survie. Atlantic City (GB and US: Atlantic City USA). Salto nel vuoto. 1980: Der Preis fuers überleben. La fille prodigue. 1981: Les uns et les autres/Bolero (US: The Ins and the Outs). Une étrange affaire. Le passante du Sans-Souci. Espion, lève-toi! Oltra la porta/Behind the Door. Les yeux, la bouche/Those Lips, Those Eyes. La nuit de Varennes. 1982: Passion. Une chambre en ville. Que les gros salaires lèvent le doigt! Le prix du danger/The Prize of Peril. 1983: Le général de l'armée morte. La diagonale du fou. La passante. 1984: Adieu, Bonaparte. Viva la vie. Péril en la demeure. Le succès à tout prix/Success is the Best Revenge. Partir, revenir. Le matelot 512. 1985: Mon beau frère à tué ma soeur. 1986: Mauvais sang/Bad Blood. La puritaine. Le paltoquet. La rumba. 1987: L'homme voilé. Y'a bon des blancs. Das weite Land. Maladie d'amour. 1988: Blanc de chine/The Chinese Connection. 1989: Le peuple singe. La revolution Française/The French Revolution. Milou en mai (GB: Milou in May. US: May Fools). 1990: Marthe und Ich. Actor. 1991: La belle noiseuse. Le voleur d'enfants/The Colonel's Children. Les equilibristes (US: Walking a Tightrope). 1992: Le bal des casse-pieds. Il segreto del Bosco Vecchio. Archipelago. La vie crevée. 1993: Tirano banderos. Le souper (voice only). Ruptures. La reine Margot. La cavale des fous (US: Loonies at Large). 1994: Al-Mohager/The Emigrant. Les cent et une nuits. L'ange noir.

PICKENS, Slim
(Louis Lindley) 1919–1983

Pickens's rather grand real name certainly hardly suited the beak-nosed, buck-toothed, bright-eyed, no-chinned 'B' western side-kicks he played in the early 1950s, coming to films after years as a rodeo clown. Later put on weight and became a quite formidable

character player, in both comic and dramatic roles. Despite the twangy drawl, he came from California. Died following the removal of a brain tumour.

1946: Smoky. 1950: Rocky Mountain. 1951: Colorado Sundown. 1952: The Last Musketeer. Old Oklahoma Plains. Border Saddlemates. Thunderbirds. South Pacific Trail. The Story of Will Rogers. 1953: Old Overland Trail. Iron Mountain Trail. Down Laredo Way. Shadows of Tombstone. Red River Shore. The Sun Shines Bright. 1954: The Boy from Oklahoma. The Phantom Stallion. The Outcast (GB: The Fortune Hunter). 1955: The Last Command. Santa Fé Passage. 1956: Stranger at My Door. When Gangland Strikes. The Great Locomotive Chase. Gun Brothers. 1957: Gunsight Ridge. 1958: Tonka. The Sheepman. 1959: Escort West. 1960: Chartroose Caboose. 1961: One-Eyed Jacks. A Thunder of Drums. 1963: Savage Sam. Dr Stangelove, or: How I Learned to Stop Worrying and Love the Bomb. Stampede at Bitter Creek (TV. GB: cinemas). Bristle Face (TV). 1965: Major Dundee. Up from the Beach. In Harm's Way. The Glory Guys. 1966: An Eye for an Eye. Stagecoach. 1967: The Flim Flam Man (GB: One Born Every Minute). Rough Night in Jericho. Will Penny. Never a Dull Moment. 1968: Skidoo. 1969: Eighty Steps to Jonah. Desperate Mission (TV. GB: cinemas, as Joaquin Murieta). Operation S.N.A.F.U. 1970: Goodbye to Yesterday (TV). The Ballad of Cable Hogue. Savage Season. The Deserter. 1971: J.C. The Devil and Miss Sarah (TV). Hitched (TV. GB: Westward the Wagon). The Cowboys. Sam Hill: Who Killed the Mysterious Mr Foster? (TV). 1972: Rolling Man (TV). The Honkers. The Getaway. Outdoor Rambling. 1973: Pat Garrett and Billy the Kid. Ginger in the Morning (GB: TV). 1974: Bootleggers. The Gun and the Pulpit (TV). Twice in a Lifetime (TV). The Legend of Earl Durand. Blazing Saddles. Poor Pretty Eddie. The Apple Dumpling Gang. 1975: Sweet Punkin. Rancho DeLuxe. Babe (TV). White Line Fever. 1976: Pony Express Rider. Hawmps. Banjo Hackett (TV). 1977: Mr Billion. The Shadow of Chikara/Wishbone Cutter. The White Buffalo. 1978: The Swarm. Smokey and the Good Time Outlaws (GB: Good Time Outlaws). The Sweet Creek County War. Heartbreak Motel. The Freedom Riders (TV). Undercover With the KKK/My Undercover Years with the Ku Klux Klan (TV). Charlie and the Great Balloon Chase (TV).

1979: Redneck County Rape. The Sacketts (TV). Swan Song (TV). 1941. Beyond the Poseidon Adventure. 1980: Tom Horn. Spirit of the Wind. The Howling. Honeysuckle Rose. The Story of a Cowboy Angel. 1981: High Country Pursuit. This House Possessed (TV). 1982: Christmas Mountain. Pink Motel (GB: Motel). 1983: Nashville Grab (TV).

PIPER, Frederick 1902–1979
Probably one of the most anonymous of those British actors who played men in the street. Dark-haired, medium-built, ferret-faced Piper, a former tea merchant who switched to acting, turned up in dozens of pictures just flashing through a scene—as bus conductors, milkmen. postmen, policemen or neighbours. He also worked in many television series from as far back as 1938, including one called, appropriately, *Down Our Street*. The loss of his hair in later years only accentuated the image of the working man *par excellence*.

1933: The Good Companions. 1935: The 39 Steps. 1936: Jack of All Trades (US: The Two of Us). Crown v Stevens. Sensation! Where There's a Will. Everything is Thunder. Rhodes of Africa (US: Rhodes). Fame. Sabotage (US: The Woman Alone). One Good Turn. The Crimson Circle. 1937: Feather Your Nest. Non-Stop New York. Farewell Again (US: Troopship). Young and Innocent (US: The Girl Was Young). 1938: They Drive By Night. 1939: Jamaica Inn. The Four Just Men (US: The Secret Four). 1940: Spare a Copper. East of Piccadilly (US: The Strangler). 1941: 49th Parallel (US: The Invaders). The Big Blockade. 1942: In Which We Serve. Let the People Sing. 1943: San Demetrio London. Nine Men. The Bells Go Down. 1944: Fiddlers Three. Return of the Vikings. It Happened One Sunday. Champagne Charlie. 1945: Johnny Frenchman. Pink String and Sealing Wax. 1947: Hue and Cry. The October Man. The Loves of Joanna Godden. Master of Bankdam. It Always Rains on Sunday. Penny and the Pownall Case. Easy Money. 1948: Fly Away Peter. My Brother's Keeper. To the Public Danger. Look Before You Love. Escape. Vote for Huggett. It's Not Cricket. 1949: Passport to Pimlico. Don't Ever Leave Me. The History of Mr Polly. The Blue Lamp. 1950: Your Witness (US: Eye Witness). 1951: The Lavender Hill Mob. Home at Seven. Brandy for the Parson. 1952: Hunted (US: The

*Stranger in Between). The Story of Robin Hood and His Merrie Men. Escape Route (US: I'll Get You). Cosh Boy (US: The Slasher). 1954: Conflict of Wings (US: Fuss over Feathers). The Rainbow Jacket. Lease of Life. Devil on Horseback. 1955: Doctor at Sea. 1956: The Man in the Road. The Passionate Stranger (US: A Novel Affair). Suspended Alibi. 1957: Doctor at Large. Second Fiddle. The Birthday Present. Barnacle Bill (US: All at Sea). 1958: Dunkirk. Violent Moment. 1959: A Touch of Larceny. 1960: Dead Lucky. The Day They Robbed the Bank of England. The Monster of Highgate Ponds (completed 1957). 1961: *Evidence in Concrete. The Breaking Point. The Frightened City. What a Carve-Up! (US: Home Sweet Homicide). Very Important Person (US: A Coming-Out Party). The Piper's Tune. Return of a Stranger. Only Two Can Play. 1962: Postman's Knock. 1963: Reach for Glory. Ricochet. Becket. 1964: Catacombs (US: The Woman Who Wouldn't Die). One Way Pendulum. Murder Most Foul. 1965: He Who Rides a Tiger. 1971: Burke and Hare.*

PITHEY, Wensley 1914–1993
Thick-set, brown-haired, often moustachioed South African-born actor in British films, often as working types or hard-headed businessmen, but latterly best-known for his portrayals of Sir Winston Churchill. He began his career in his native country when, at 23, he won a nationwide contest for a radio announcer. He came to Britain in post-war years, and usually tackled roles — sometimes also as policemen or minor figures of authority — that were older than his years. The cinema's demands slackened after 1962, but he continued to be busy in television.

1947: The October Man. The Mark of Cain. 1948: London Belongs to Me (US: Dulcimer Street). Blue Scar. It's Hard to Be Good. Cardboard Cavalier. 1950: Guilt is My Shadow. Your Witness (US: Eye Witness). 1951: Brandy for the Parson. 1952: The Woman's Angle. Lady in the Fog (US: Scotland Yard Inspector). Father's Doing Fine. The Story of Robin Hood and His Merrie Men. 1953: The Titfield Thunderbolt. Isn't Life Wonderful! The Intruder. 1954: The Men of Sherwood Forest. The Diamond (US: Diamond Wizard). The Belles of St Trinian's. 1955: The Dark Avenger (US: The Warriors). You Can't Escape. 1956:

Moby Dick. Tiger in the Smoke. 1957: Kill Me Tomorrow. The Long Haul. Blue Murder at St Trinian's. Doctor at Large. Hell Drivers. 1959: Serious Charge (US: A Touch of Hell). 1960: Make Mine Mink. Snowball. The Pure Hell of St Trinian's. 1961: Seven Seas to Calais. 1962: The Barber of Stamford Hill. The Boys. *The Guilty Party. 1965: The Knack . . . and how to get it. 1968: Oliver! 1969: Oh! What a Lovely War. 1975: One of Our Dinosaurs is Missing. 1979: Ike (TV). 1980: FDR: The Last Year (TV). 1982: Red Monarch. 1987: White Mischief. 1988: The Diamond Trap (TV). 1991: American Friends.

PITTS, ZaSu 1898–1963
Bird-like, dark-haired, slender American actress with thin upper lip and large, dark, darting eyes. At first in vulnerable roles, most notably in Von Stroheim's *Greed*, she later took to comedy in early sound two-reelers with various partners, then played equally vulnerable spinsterish character parts. Died from cancer.

1917: *Tillie of the Nine Lives. *He Had 'Em Buffaloed. *Canning the Cannibal King. *The Battling Bellboy. *O-My the Tent-Mover. *Behind the Map. *Why They Left Home *His Fatal Beauty. *Uneasy Money. *We Have the Papers. *Desert Dilemma. *Behind the Foot-lights. The Little Princess. A Modern Musketeer. Rebecca of Sunnybrook Farm. 1918: Talk of the Town. A Lady's Name. How Could You, Jean? As the Sun Went Down. A Society Sensation. 1919: Better Times. The Other Half. Men, Women and Money. 1920: Poor Relations. Bright Skies. Seeing It Through. Heart of Twenty. 1921: Patsy. 1922: Youth to Youth. For the Defense. Is Matrimony a Failure? A Daughter of Luxury. 1923: Poor Men's Wives. The Girl Who Came Back. Tea – With a Kick. West of the Water Tower. Mary of the Movies. Souls for Sale. Three Wise Fools. 1924: Triumph. Daughters of Today. The Legend of Hollywood. The Fast Set. Greed. The Goldfish. Changing Husbands. Wine of Youth. 1925: The Great Love. Old Shoes. The Business of Love. The Re-Creation of Brian Kent. Thunder Mountain. A Woman's Faith. What Happened to Jones? The Great Divide. Lazybones. Pretty Ladies. Secrets of the Night. Wages for Wives. Mannequin. 1926: Monte Carlo (GB: Dreams of Monte Carlo). Early to Wed. Risky Business. Sunny Side Up. Her Big Night. 1927: Casey at

the Bat. 1928: †Love (GB: Anna Karenina). 13 Washington Square. Buck Privates. The Wedding March. Wife Savers. Sins of the Fathers. *Sunlight. The Honeymoon/Mariage du prince. 1929: Her Private Life. The Argyle Case. The Dummy. Oh, Yeah! (GB: No Brakes). The Locked Door. Paris. This Thing Called Love. The Squall. Twin Beds. 1930: ‡All Quiet on the Western Front. Honey. The Lottery Bride. No, No, Nanette. River's End. The Squealer. The Devil's Holiday. Little Accident. Monte Carlo. Passion Flower. Sin Takes a Holiday. War Nurse. Free Love. 1931: Finn and Hattie. Beyond Victory. Their Mad Moment. Bad Sister. The Big Gamble. Seed. A Woman of Experience. Penrod and Sam. The Guardsman. The Secret Witness. *Let's Do Things. *Catch As Catch Can. *The Pajama Party. *War Mamas. 1932: *Seal Skins. *On the Loose. *Red Noses. *The Old Bull. *Strictly Unreliable. *Show Business. *Alum and Eve. *The Soilers. Shopworn. Steady Company. The Trial of Vivienne Ware. Unexpected Father. Westward Passage. Blondie of the Follies. Make Me a Star. The Crooked Circle. One in a Lifetime. Broken Lullaby (GB: The Man I Killed). Destry Rides Again. Strangers of the Evening. Speak Easily. Is My Face Red? Roar of the Dragon. Vanishing Frontier. Madison Square Gardens. Back Street. They Just Had to Get Married. 1933: Hello, Sister!/Walking Down Broadway. Professional Sweetheart (GB: Imaginary Sweetheart). Love, Honor and Oh, Baby! *Sneak Easily. *Asleep in the Fleet. *Maids à la Mode. *One Track Minds. *The Bargain of the Century. Aggie Appleby, Maker of Men (GB: Cupid in the Rough). Mr Skitch. Out All Night. Her First Mate. Meet the Baron. 1934: Two Alone. The Meanest Gal in Town. Three on a Honeymoon. Mrs Wiggs of the Cabbage Patch. Their Big Moment (GB: Afterwards). Sing and Like It. The Love Birds. Private Scandal. The Gay Bride. Dames. 1935: Hot Tip. Ruggles of Red Gap. The Affairs of Susan. Going Highbrow. She Gets Her Man. Spring Tonic. 1936: Thirteen Hours by Air. The Plot Thickens (GB: The Swinging Pearl Mystery). Sing Me a Love Song. Mad Holiday. 1937: Forty Naughty Girls. 52nd Street. Wanted. Merry Comes to Town. 1939: Naughty But Nice. The Lady's from Kentucky. Mickey the Kid. Nurse Edith Cavell. Eternally Yours. 1940: No, No, Nanette (remake). It All Came True. 1941: Niagara Falls. Broadway Limited. Mexican Spitfire's Baby. Week-End for Three. Miss Polly. 1942: So's Your Aunt Emma/Meet the Mob. Tish. Mexican Spitfire at Sea. The Bashful Bachelor. 1943: Let's Face It. 1946: The Perfect Marriage. Breakfast in Hollywood (GB: The Mad Hatter). 1947: Life with Father. *A Film Goes to Market. 1949: Francis. 1952: Denver and Rio Grande. 1954: Francis Joins the WACs. 1956: Mr Belvedere (TV. GB: cinemas). 1957: This Could be the Night. 1959: The Gazebo. 1961: Teen-Age Millionaire. 1963: The Thrill of It All. It's a Mad, Mad, Mad, Mad World.

† Scenes deleted from final release version.
‡ Silent version only.

PLATT, Edward C. 1916–1974
Neat, sturdy, waspish American actor with greying hair and trim moustache (he looked

skull-like when clean-shaven), a former dance-band vocalist who turned to acting in his thirties. Became a more than useful support—for some, perhaps too useful!—to the stars of minor 'A' budget studio (mainly Universal) films of the 1950s before drifting into television and a long run (as Ed Platt) as the spy chief in the comedy series *Get Smart*. Died from a heart attack.

1953: Stalag 17. 1955: The Shrike. The McConnell Story (GB: Tiger in the Sky). The Private War of Major Benson. Rebel Without a Cause. Cult of the Cobra. Illegal. Sincerely Yours. 1956: Serenade. Written on the Wind. The Proud Ones. Backlash. Storm Center. The Unguarded Moment. The Steel Jungle. The Lieutenant Wore Skirts. The Great Man. Reprisal! Rock, Pretty Baby. 1957: The Tattered Dress. Designing Woman. Omar Khayyam. House of Numbers. The Helen Morgan Story (GB: Both Ends of the Candle). Damn Citizen! 1958: The Gift of Love. Oregon Passage. Summer Love. Last of the Fast Guns. The High Cost of Loving. Gunman's Walk. 1959: North by Northwest. They Came to Cordura. Inside the Mafia. The Rebel Set. Cash McCall. 1960: Pollyanna. 1961: Atlantis, the Lost Continent. The Explosive Generation. The Fiercest Heart. Cape Fear. 1962: Black Zoo. 1963: A Ticklish Affair. 1964: Man from Button Willow (voice only). Bullet for a Badman.

PLIMPTON, Martha 1970–
Fair-haired, scrawny-looking, full-lipped American actress of pixieish prettiness, the daughter of actors Shelley Plimpton and

Keith Carradine. On stage at 8, her face had become familiar in TV commercials by the time she was 11. In her early cinema days, she was often seen as hoydenish, abusive, rebellious teenagers; her versatility is leading her into a good range of adult roles as top supporting player and sometime star.

1981: Rollover. 1984: The River Rat. 1985: The Goonies. 1986: The Mosquito Coast. 1987: Shy People. 1988: Running On Empty. Another Woman. Stars and Bars. 1989: Parenthood. Silence Like Glass. Zwei Frauen. 1990: Stanley & Iris. 1991: Samantha. 1992: Crazy in Love (TV). Inside Monkey Zetterland. *A Blink of Paradise. 1993: Josh and SAM. My Life's in Turn-around. Daybreak. Chantilly Lace (TV). 1994: A House in the Hamptons. The Beans of Egypt, Maine. Mrs Parker and the Vicious Circle. 1995: Beautiful Girls.

PLOWRIGHT, Joan 1929–
Round-faced, calm-looking British actress with dark, curly hair and prominent cheekbones, often seen in passive roles, but rarely outside the theatre until the 1980s. On stage at 21, she quickly attained prominence in London productions, and her name became familiar countrywide after she wed Sir Laurence Olivier (her second marriage) in 1961. They remained married until his death in 1989, by which time Plowright was well launched into a second career as a sterling character actress, nominated for an Academy Award for her performance in *Enchanted April* in 1991.

1956: Moby Dick. 1957: Time Without Pity. 1960: The Entertainer. 1963: Uncle Vanya. 1970: Three Sisters. 1977: Equus. 1982: Britannia Hospital. Brimstone and Treacle. 1983: Wagner. 1985: Revolution. 1988: The Dressmaker. Drowning by Numbers. 1990: Avalon. I Love You to Death. 1991: Enchanted April. 1993: Last Action Hero. Stalin (TV). Dennis the Menace (GB: Dennis). The Clothes in the Wardrobe (TV. US: cinemas, as The Summer House). A Place for Annie (TV). 1994: Widow's Peak. On Promised Land (TV). Hotel Sorrento. A Pin for the Butterfly. A Pyromaniac's Love Story. The Return of the Native (TV). 1995: The Grass Harp. Jane Eyre.

PLUMMER, Amanda 1957–
Thin-faced, brown-haired, grave-looking American actress with narrow top lip, who normally seems to wear little makeup and play people without pretensions. The daughter of actors Tammy Grimes and Christopher Plummer, she made a rather flashy screen debut in *Cattle Annie and Little Britches*, but soon settled down to give thoughtful performances both in leading and supporting roles. The winner of a Tony award for her work as a nun in the 1982 Broadway play *Agnes of God*, she also gave a sensitive performance in a running role as a retarded young woman in the TV series *LA Law*.

1981: Cattle Annie and Little Britches. 1982: The World According to Garp. 1983: Daniel. 1984: The Dollmaker (TV). The Hotel New Hampshire. 1986: Static. Courtship (TV). 1987: Made in Heaven. 1989: Prisoners of Inertia. 1990: Joe Versus the Volcano. 1991: The Fisher King. Kojak: None So Blind (TV). 1992: Freejack. 1993: So I Married an Axe Murderer. Last Light (TV). Needful Things. Whose Child is This? The War for Baby Jessica (TV). 1994: God's Army. Nostradamus. Pulp Fiction. Dead Girl. Butterfly Kiss. Pax. Habitat. 1995: American Perfect Drunks. Martin Eden.

POHLMANN, Eric
(Erich Pohlmann) 1913–1979
Austrian actor who came to Britain in 1938 and, after World War II, became familiar in British crime thrillers as the fat, oily, moustachioed villain with the thick cigar and carnation in lapel, never doing his own dirty work and vying with Ferdy Mayne (*qv*) as the treacherous charming foreigner behind most crooked night-clubs and river-side rackets in the business. Returned to Austria and Germany for a few films towards the end of his days.

1948: Portrait from Life (US: The Girl in the Painting). 1949: Children of Chance. The Third Man. Marry Me! Traveller's Joy (released 1951). 1950: Blackout. Highly Dangerous. Cairo Road. Chance of a Lifetime. State Secret (US: The Great Manhunt). The Clouded Yellow. There Is Another Sun (US: Wall of Death). 1951: The Long Dark Hall. Hell Is Sold Out. His Excellency. 1952: The Woman's Angle. Emergency Call (US: Hundred Hour

Hunt). Penny Princess. Venetian Bird (US: The Assassin). Top Secret (US: Mr Potts Goes to Moscow). Moulin Rouge. The Gambler and the Lady. Monsoon. The Man Who Watched Trains Go By (US: Paris Express). 1953: Blood Orange. The Beggar's Opera. Mogambo. Rob Roy the Highland Rogue. 1954: They Who Dare. Knave of Hearts (US: Lovers, Happy Lovers). Forbidden Cargo. 36 Hours (US: Terror Street). Flame and the Flesh. The Belles of St Trinian's. 1955: A Prize of Gold. The Constant Husband. Gentlemen Marry Brunettes. The Glass Cage (US: The Glass Tomb). The Adventures of Quentin Durward (US: Quentin Durward). Break in the Circle. Dust and Gold. 1956: The Gelignite Gang. Reach for the Sky. Anastasia. Let's Be Happy. Zarak. The High Terrace. Lust for Life. House of Secrets (US: Triple Deception). The Counterfeit Plan. 1957: Interpol (US: Pickup Alley). Fire Down Below. Not Wanted on Voyage. Across the Bridge. Barnacle Bill (US: All at Sea). I Accuse! 1958: The Duke Wore Jeans. Nor the Moon by Night (US: Elephant Gun). The Man Inside. A Tale of Two Cities. Three Crooked Men. Further Up the Creek. The Mark of the Phoenix. Alive and Kicking. Life Is a Circus. 1959: Upstairs and Downstairs. The Navy Lark. The House of the Seven Hawks. Expresso Bongo. John Paul Jones. 1960: Snowball. Sands of the Desert. Surprise Package. The Man Who Couldn't Walk. Visa to Canton (US: Passport to China). No Kidding (US: Beware of Children). The Singer Not the Song. 1961: Curse of the Werewolf. The Kitchen. Village of Daughters. Carry On Regardless. 1962: Mrs Gibbons' Boys. 55 Days at Peking. The Devil's Agent. Das Rätsel der roten Orchidee (GB: The Puzzle of the Red Orchid. US: Secret of the Red Orchid). 1963: Cairo. Shadow of Fear. Dr Syn—Alias the Scarecrow. Hot Enough for June (US: Agent 8¾). Follow the Boys. From Russia with Love (voice only). The Million Dollar Collar. 1964: Carry On Spying. The Sicilians. Night Train to Paris. 1965: Joey Boy. Those Magnificent Men in Their Flying Machines. Where the Spies Are. 1967: Heisses Pflaster Köln (GB: Walk the Hot Streets). 1968: Mit Eichenlaub und Feigenblatt. Inspector Clouseau. The Mini Affair. 1969: Foreign Exchange (TV). 1970: The Horsemen. 1973: Tiffany Jones. 1974: The Return of the Pink Panther. 1976: Auch Mimosen wollen blühen. 1979: Ashanti. Tales from the Vienna Woods.

POLLARD, Michael J.
(M. J. Pollack) 1939–

Diminutive American actor with light, curly (latterly white) hair, cherubic face and demonic smile. An Actors' Studio graduate, he shot to fame as *Bonnie and Clyde*'s accomplice C. W. Moss in 1967 (he was nominated for an Oscar) but, as the leading actor he briefly became, he proved difficult to cast and his films were not too successful. There were too few appearances from him from the early 1970s to the mid 1980s, but he returned in blink-eyed character roles and became fiercely busy until the early 1990s.

1962: Hemingway's Adventures of a Young Man (GB: Adventures of a Young Man). The Stripper (GB: Woman of Summer). Summer Magic. 1966. The Russians Are Coming, the Russians Are Coming. Caprice. 1967: The Wild Angels. Enter Laughing. Bonnie and Clyde. 1968: Hannibal Brooks. The Smugglers (TV). Jigsaw (TV. GB: cinemas, as Jigsaw Murders). 1970: Little Fauss and Big Halsy. 1971: Les pétroleuses/The Legend of Frenchie King. 1972: Dirty Little Billy. 1974: Sunday in the Country. 1977: Between the Lines. 1980: Melvin and Howard. 1982: America (released 1986). 1985: Heated Vengeance. 1986: The American Way. The Patriot. 1987: Roxanne. American Gothic. 1988: Young Werewolves in Love. An American Murder. Scrooged. 1989: The Awakening. Never Cry Devil/Night Visitor. Fast Food. Next of Kin. Un plan d'enfer. Season of Fear. Sleepaway Camp 3: Teenage Wasteland. Stuck With Each Other (TV). Tango & Cash. Why Me? 1990: I Come in Peace. Dick Tracy. Joey Takes a Cab. Working Trash (TV). Enid is Sleeping (GB: Over Her Dead Body). 1991: The Art of Dying. Skeeter. 1992: Split Second. Motorama. Arizona Dream.

POLLOCK, Ellen 1903–

Black-haired, green-eyed British actress (born in Heidelberg, Germany) of long, strong facial features and predatory look. Her relatively few films through the years have tended to cast her as harpies and other women, but in the theatre she has gained a reputation as a formidable interpreter of George Bernard Shaw (she is also a long-time president of the Shaw Society). Ran her own street market antique stall. Her second husband was the painter James Proudfoot.

1928: Moulin Rouge. 1929: Piccadilly. The Informer. 1930: Too Many Crooks. Night Birds. 1931: Midnight. A Gentleman of Paris. My Wife's Family. Let's Love and Laugh (US: Bridegroom for Two). 1932: The First Mrs Fraser. The Last Coupon. Down Our Street. 1933: Heads We Go (US: The Charming Deceiver). Channel Crossing. 1934: Mr Cinders. Lord Edgware Dies. 1935: I Give My Heart. It's a Bet. Royal Cavalcade (GB: Regal Cavalcade). 1936: The Happy Family. Millions. Aren't Men Beasts! 1937: The Street Singer. Non-Stop New York. Splinters in the Air. 1939: *Shadow of Death. Sons of the Sea. 1940: Spare a Copper. 1942: Soldiers Without Uniform. 1944: Kiss the Bride Goodbye. 1945: Don Chicago. 1946: Bedelia. 1948: Warning to Wantons. 1950: Something in the City. To Have and to Hold. 1951: The Galloping Major. 1953: The Fake. 1954: The Golden Link. 1955: The Time of His Life. 1956: Not So Dusty. 1957: The Hypnotist (US: Scotland Yard Dragnet). 1958: The Long Knife. The Gypsy and the Gentleman. 1961: So Evil, So Young. 1963: Master Spy. 1965: Rapture. 1966: Finders Keepers. Who Killed the Cat? 1973: Horror Hospital. 1983: The Wicked Lady. 1985: Florence Nightingale (TV).

POSTLETHWAITE, Pete(r) 1946–

Grim-looking, bony-faced British actor with thinning dark hair. So little known until the late 1980s that he wasn't even listed in books on *British* actors, Postlethwaite gradually moved into prominence by playing villains, then burst from anonymity in 1994 by winning an Academy Award nomination for his moving performance as the wrongfully convicted Giuseppe Conlon in *In the Name of the Father*. Also memorable as the bestial Obadiah Hateswell in TV's costume action series *Sharpe*, Postlethwaite was initially a teacher before enrolling in drama school at 24. Refusing to change his name (he changed his agent instead) he built up a solid reputation in repertory before moving into TV. A long relationship with actress Julie Walters eventually ended and he now lives 'half way up a mountain' with a former BBC drama assistant and their five-year-old son.

1984: A Private Function. 1986: Coast to Coast (TV). 1988: Tumbledown. The Dressmaker. To Kill a Priest. Distant Voices, Still Lives. 1990: Hamlet. 1991: The Grass Arena (TV). A Child from the South. They Never Slept (TV). 1992: Split Second. Waterland. Alien 3. The Last of the Mohicans. 1993: In the Name of the Father. 1995: A Pint o' Bitter. (later On the Line). Suite 16. The Usual Suspects.

POWER, Hartley 1894–1966

Big, bald, explosive, full faced American actor of genial expression. He acted on stage in America, Australia, England and Ireland before settling in England and bringing his booming tones to a handful of films from 1931 on, sometimes as con-man, agent, American officer, impresario or out-and-out crook. Married British actress-singer Betty Paul.

1931: Down River. 1933: Aunt Sally (US: Along Came Sally). Just Smith (US: Leave It to Smith). Friday the Thirteenth. Yes Mr Brown. 1934: Road House. Evergreen. The Camels Are Coming. 1935: Jury's Evidence. 1936: Where There's a Will. Living Dangerously. 1938: The Return of the Frog. Just Like a Woman. 1939: Murder Will Out. A Window in London (US: Lady in Distress). Return to Yesterday. 1941: Atlantic Ferry (US: Sons of the Sea). 1942: Alibi. 1945: The Man from Morocco. The Way to the Stars (US: Johnny in the Clouds). Dead of Night. 1946: A Girl in a Million. 1951: The Armchair Detective. 1952: The Net (US: Project M7). 1953: Roman Holiday. The Million Pound Note (US: Man

With a Million). 1954: To Dorothy a Son (US: Cash on Delivery). 1957: Island in the Sun.

PRICE, Nancy
(Lillian N. Price) 1880–1970

Formidable doyenne British actress with long nose and strong, stern facial features. Especially in the latter half of her long career (first stage appearance 1899), she appeared in dominant and sinister roles in which one could almost see the malevolence flashing from the eyes and the cobwebs trailing behind. In real life, this remarkable woman was a musicologist, painter, author, climber, naturalist, world-wide traveller and quasi-mystic. Her daughter, Joan Maude (Nancy Price married Charles Maude, who predeceased her), was also an actress.

1916: The Lyons Mail. 1921: Belphegor the Mountebank. 1923: Love, Life and Laughter (US: Tip Toes). Comin' thro' the Rye. The Woman Who Obeyed. Bonnie Prince Charlie. 1927: Huntingtower. 1928: His House in Order. The Price of Divorce. 1929: The American Prisoner. The Doctor's Secret. Three Live Ghosts. 1930: The Loves of Robert Burns. 1931: The Speckled Band. 1932: Down Our Street. 1934: The Crucifix. 1939: The Stars Look Down. Dead Man's Shoes. 1942: Secret Mission. 1944: Madonna of the Seven Moons. 1945: I Live in Grosvenor Square (US: A Yank in London). I Know Where I'm Going! 1946: Carnival. 1947: Master of Bankdam. 1948: The Three Weird Sisters. 1950: The Naked Heart (Maria Chapdelaine/The Naked Earth). 1952: Mandy (US: Crash of Silence).

PROCHNOW, Jürgen 1945–

Rather drawn and dangerous-looking German actor with lightish brown hair, good-looking but with small chin and thin lips that rarely break into a smile. His German films were too few in his younger days and, after his breakthrough as the skipper of the doomed submarine in *Das Boot*, he was cast in international roles that made his face more familiar than his name. Forty years earlier, Hollywood would have seized him as a cultured villain in war films and swashbucklers, and indeed he was allowed to flash a mean sword in the disappointingly scripted *Robin Hood*; Prochnow

still awaits a Hollywood role that will allow his penetrating style to register properly.

1971: Zoff. 1973: Zärtlichkeit der Wölfe. 1974: Der Verrohung des Franz Blum (US: The Brutalization of Franz Blum). 1975: Die verlorene Ehre der Katharina Blum (GB and US: The Lost Honour of Katharine Blum). 1976: Shirin's Wedding. 1977: Die Konsequenz. Operation Ganymed. 1978: Einer von uns beiden. 1979: Unter Verschluss. 1980: Soweit das Auge. 1981: Das Boot. 1982: Love is Forever/Comeback. Forbidden (cable TV. Originally for cinemas). Krieg und Frieden/War and Peace. 1983: The Keep. 1984: Dune. 1985: Der Bulle und das Mädchen (US: The Cop and the Girl). 1986: Killing Cars. Murder: By Reason of Insanity (TV). Terminus. 1987: Beverly Hills Cop II. Devil's Paradise. 1988: The Seventh Sign. The Man Inside (released 1990). 1989: The Fourth War. A Dry White Season. 1990: Hurricane Smith. The Skipper/Kill Cruise. 1991: Robin Hood (TV. GB: cinemas). 1992: Red Hot. Body of Evidence. Twin Peaks Fire Walk With Me. 1993: Le musher. Interceptor. Der Fall Lucona. The Last Border. The Fire Next Time (TV). 1994: In the Mouth of Madness. Red Eagle (TV). 1995: Judge Dredd.

PROSKY, Robert 1930–

Round-faced, round-bodied, seemingly ever-smiling, genial, piggy-eyed American actor with a halo of white hair. He belatedly began an acting career after winning an amateur talent contest, which led to a scholarship with the American theatre wing. Remaining a Broadway actor for years

(veteran of 40 stage productions), Prosky's face was practically unknown to film and TV audiences until he took over (on the death of another actor) as the desk sergeant in the long-running TV police series *Hill Street Blues*. When the series ended in 1987, he was seen more frequently in films, his grating tones suiting both stern and benevolent roles. His characters were frequently out of breath, but rarely out of humour.

1980: Just Another Missing Kid (TV). 1981: Thief (later and GB: Violent Streets). The Ordeal of Bill Carney (TV). 1982: Hanky Panky. The Lords of Discipline. Monsignor. 1983: Christine. The Keep. 1984: The Natural. 1985: Into Thin Air (TV). 1987: Big Shots. Outrageous Fortune. Broadcast News. The Murder of Mary Phagan (TV). 1988: Things Change. The Great Outdoors. 1989: Loose Cannons. From the Dead of Night (TV). The Heist (TV). A Walk in the Woods (TV). Home Fires Burning (TV). 1990: Gremlins 2: The New Batch. The Love She Sought (TV. GB: A Green Journey). Green Card. Funny About Love. Dangerous Pursuit. 1991: Age Isn't Everything/Life in the Food Chain. 1992: Far and Away. Hoffa. Teamster Boss: The Jackie Presser Story (TV). Double Edge (TV). 1993: Last Action Hero. Rudy. Mrs Doubtfire. 1994: Miracle on 34th Street. 1995: He Ain't Heavy.

PROUTY, Jed 1879–1956

Mr Jones, of course. The soul of bespectacled benevolence, this small, smily, dark-haired American actor was a song-and-dance vaudevillian for the first 25 years of his career, before descending on Hollywood and, after a false start as a character who stuttered (producers actually thought he had a speech defect), ran up a long line of flustered fathers with small-town values. His tenure as the head of The Jones Family began with *Every Saturday Night*, and ran through 5 years and 17 films, by which time the Joneses had not only been kept up with, but passed by the Hardys. After that, he kept going in homely comedies until slipping into semi-retirement at 64.

1919: Her Game. 1920: Sadie Love. 1921: The Conquest of Canaan. Experience. The Great Adventure. Room and Board. 1922: Kick In. 1923: The Gold Diggers. The Girl of the Golden West. Souls for Sale. 1925: The Coast of Folly. The Knockout. Scarlet Saint. The Unguarded

Hour. One Way Street. 1926: Bred in Old Kentucky. Ella Cinders. Everybody's Acting. Don Juan's Three Nights. Her Second Chance. Miss Nobody. The Mystery Club. Unknown Treasures. 1927: Orchids and Ermine. Smile, Brother, Smile. The Gingham Girl. No Place to Go. The Siren. 1928: Domestic Meddlers. Name the Woman. 1929: The Fall of Eve. His Captive Woman. The Broadway Melody. Girl in the Show. It's a Great Life. Sonny Boy. Why Leave Home? Two Weeks Off. *Imperfect Ladies. 1930: *No Questions Asked. The Florodora Girl (GB: The Gay Nineties). The Devil's Holiday. Paramount on Parade. True to the Navy. 1931: Annabelle's Affairs. Age for Love. Night Nurse. The Secret Call. Strangers May Kiss. Seed. 1932: Business and Pleasure. The Conquerors. Hold 'Em Jail. Manhattan Tower. 1933: The Big Bluff. Morning Glory. Jimmy and Sally. Skyway. 1934: Hollywood Party. I Believed in You. Music in the Air. One Hour Late. Private Scandal. The Life of Vergie Winters. Murder on the Blackboard. 1935: Alibi Ike. Life Begins at 40. Black Sheep. George White's 1935 Scandals. Let 'Em Have It (GB: False Faces). Ah, Wilderness! Navy Wife/Beauty's Daughter. 1936: Back to Nature. Can This Be Dixie? Every Saturday Night. Educating Father. Little Miss Nobody. Special Investigator. Pigskin Parade. Under Your Spell. College Holiday. His Brother's Wife. Happy-Go-Lucky. The Texas Rangers. 1937: Big Business. Happy-Go-Lucky. Borrowing Trouble. The Crime Nobody Saw. Dangerous Holiday. Hot Water. Life Begins in College (GB: The Joy Parade). A Star is Born. Off to the Races. Small Town Boy. Sophie Lang Goes West. 100 Men and a Girl. You Can't Have Everything. 1938: Danger on the Air. Down on the Farm. The Duke of West Point. Everybody's Baby. Keep Smiling. Love on a Budget. Goodbye Broadway. Safety in Numbers. A Trip to Paris. Walking Down Broadway. 1939: *Coat Tales. The Gracie Allen Murder Case. The Jones Family in Hollywood. The Jones Family in Quick Millions. Exile Express. Hollywood Cavalcade. The Jones Family in Grand Canyon. Second Fiddle. Too Busy to Work. 1940: Barnyard Follies. The Lone Wolf Keeps a Date. On Their Own. Remedy for Riches. Young As You Feel. 1941: Bachelor Daddy. Father Steps Out. Obliging Young Lady. City Limits. Go West, Young Lady. Look Who's Laughing. Pot o' Gold (GB: The Golden Hour). Roar of the Press. Unexpected Uncle. 1942: The Affairs of Jimmy Valentine. *Hold 'Em Jail (and 1932 feature). It Happened in Flatbush. Moonlight Masquerade. The Old Homestead. Scattergood Rides High. 1943: Mug Town. 1950: Guilty Bystander.

PUGLIA, Frank

(Franco Puglia) 1892–1975
Sharp-featured, hawk-like, Italian-born actor with receding dark hair, a stern player who looked hard-put to raise a smile in most of his roles as bad guys of sundry nationalities. Equally serious as chiefs of police and the occasional priest, he only rarely turned to comedy, and even played a Japanese diplomat in Blood on the Sun. He had come to America at 13, already experienced in his native Sicily as a member of a travelling light opera group. A year later, he

had joined an Italian theatre company in New York's Bowery area and begun a lifetime of acting. D.W. Griffith brought him to Hollywood to play the 'good' brother in Orphans of the Storm, but he didn't really settle until the early 1930s, working steadily in exotic roles and only easing up when he passed 65. Just before his death, Puglia described himself as a 'lucky nobody'. Most buffs, though, wouldn't agree.

1922: Orphans of the Storm. Fascination. 1924: Isn't Life Wonderful? Romola. 1925: The Beautiful City. 1927: The Man Who Laughs. 1933: The White Sister. 1934: Men in White. Stamboul Quest. Viva Villa! Bordertown. 1935: The Melody Lingers On. Captain Blood. 1936: Bulldog Edition (GB: Lady Reporter). The Devil is a Sissy (GB: The Devil Takes the Count). His Brother's Wife. Fatal Lady. Love on the Run. The Gay Desperado. The Garden of Allah. Wife Vs Secretary. *The Public Pays. 1937: Bulldog Drummond's Revenge. A Doctor's Diary. The Bride Wore Red. The Firefly. Mama Steps Out. King of the Gamblers. Maytime. Song of the City. Lancer Spy. When You're in Love (GB: For You Alone). Seventh Heaven. Thin Ice (GB: Lovely to Look At). You Can't Have Everything. 1938: Barefoot Boy. Dramatic School. I'll Give a Million. Spawn of the North. Rascals. Mannequin. The Shining Hour. Sharpshooters. Tropic Holiday. Yellow Jack. 1939: Balalaika. Code of the Secret Service. In Name Only. Forged Passport. Pirates of the Skies. The Girl and the Gambler. Mystery of the White Room. Lady of the Tropics. In Old Caliente. Mr Smith Goes to Washington. Maisie. Zaza. 1940: The Fatal Hour (GB: Mr Wong at Headquarters). Charlie Chan in Panama. Love, Honor and Oh, Baby! Arise, My Love. No, No, Nanette. Down Argentine Way. The Mark of Zorro. Rangers of Fortune. Meet the Wildcat. 'Til We Meet Again. Torrid Zone. Charlie Chan in the City of Darkness (GB: City of Darkness). 1941: Billy the Kid. Law of the Tropics. The Parson of Panamint. That Night in Rio. 1942: Always in My Heart. Escape from Hong Kong. The Boogie Man Will Get You. Flight Lieutenant. In Old California. Jungle Book. Now, Voyager. Secret Agent of Japan. Who is Hope Schuyler? Casablanca. 1943: Background to Danger. For Whom the Bell Tolls. Action in the North Atlantic. Around the World. Phantom of the Opera. The Iron Major. Pilot No. 5. Mission to Moscow. Princess O'Rourke. Tarzan's Desert Mystery. Ali Baba

and the Forty Thieves. 1944: Brazil. The Story of Dr Wassell. Tall in the Saddle. Passage to Marseille (GB: Passage to Marseilles). Together Again. This is the Life. Dragon Seed. 1945: Roughly Speaking. A Song to Remember. Week-End at the Waldorf. 1946: Without Reservations. 1947: Brute Force. Fiesta. Escape Me Never. The Lost Moment. My Favorite Brunette. Road to Rio. Stallion Road. 1948: Dream Girl. Joan of Arc. 1949: Bagdad. Bride of Vengeance. Colorado Territory. Special Agent. 1950: Black Hand. Captain Carey USA (GB: After Midnight). The Desert Hawk. Federal Agent at Large. Walk Softly, Stranger. 1953: The Bandits of Corsica (GB: Return of the Corsican Brothers). The Caddy. Casanova's Big Night. Steel Lady (GB: The Treasure of Kalifa). Son of Belle Starr. 1954: The Shanghai Story. Jubilee Trail. A Star is Born. 1956: The Burning Hills. The First Texan. Accused of Murder. Serenade. Duel at Apache Wells. 1957: Twenty Million Miles to Earth. 1959: The Black Orchid. Cry Tough. 1962: Girls! Girls! Girls! 1965: The Sword of Ali Baba. 1966: The Spy in the Green Hat (TV. GB: cinemas). 1972: Say Goodbye, Maggie Cole (TV). 1975: Mr Ricco.

PULLMAN, Bill 1954–
Square-jawed, open-faced, very slightly disgruntled-looking American actor who looks a bit like Jeff Daniels, and generally plays losers – rejected suitors, husbands who have the wool pulled over their eyes, victims of conspiracies, the occult or medical disaster: they're all in Pullman's casebook of men who should have stayed at home. He initially thought of a career in building construction, but switched colleges, graduating in theatre arts and becoming a teacher at the University of Montana, leaving at 27 to pursue an acting career. He soon made his mark as mild-mannered, handsome men of low-level achievement and has rarely looked like bringing home the bacon since his debut as the dim-witted extortionist in Ruthless People. He moved into star roles in 1995.

1986: Ruthless People. 1987: Spaceballs. 1988: The Accidental Tourist. The Serpent and the Rainbow. Rocket Gibraltar. 1989: Home Fires Burning (TV). Brain Dead/Paranoia. 1990: Cold Feet. Bright Angel. Sibling Rivalry. 1991: Liebestraum. Going Under. 1992: Newsies (GB: The News Boys). Crazy in Love (TV). Singles. A League of Their Own. Nervous

Ticks. 1993: Sommersby. Sleepless in Seattle. Malice. Mr Jones. 1994: Wyatt Earp. Casper. The Last Seduction. The Favor (completed 1991). 1995: While You Were Sleeping. Mr Wrong.

PURCELL, Noel 1900–1985

Lugubrious, bewhiskered Irish actor, the life and soul of many a British comedy of the forties, fifties and sixties. His tall, shambling figure was seen for many years in Irish stage classics at Dublin theatres before he became a film regular. His characters usually liked a tipple or two, but were nobody's fools even when intoxicated.

1934: Jimmy Boy. 1938: Blarney (US: Ireland's Border Line). 1946: Odd Man Out. 1947: Captain Boycott. 1949: Saints and Sinners. The Blue Lagoon. 1951: Talk of a Million (GB: You Can't Beat the Irish). No Resting Place. Appointment with Venus (US: Island Rescue). Encore. 1952: Father's Doing Fine. The Pickwick Papers. Decameron Nights. The Crimson Pirate. 1953: Grand National Night (US: Wicked Woman). Doctor in the House. 1954: The Seekers (US: Land of Fury). Mad About Men. Svengali. 1955: Doctor at Sea. 1956: Jacqueline. Lust for Life. Moby Dick. 1957: Doctor at Large. The Rising of the Moon. 1958: Merry Andrew. Rooney. The Key. Rockets Galore (US: Mad Little Island). 1959: Tommy the Toreador. *Seven Wonders of Ireland (narrator only). Shake Hands With the Devil. Ferry to Hong Kong. The Three Worlds of Gulliver. 1960: Make Mine Mink. Watch Your Stern. Man in the Moon. The Millionairess. No Kidding (US: Beware of Children). 1961: Double Bunk. Johnny Nobody. 1962: The Iron Maiden (US: The Swingin' Maiden). Nurse on Wheels. Mutiny on the Bounty. 1963: The List of Adrian Messenger. The Ceremony. The Running Man. Zulu. 1964: Lord Jim. 1966: Doctor in Clover. Drop Dead Darling (US: Arrivederci Baby). 1969: Sinful Davey. Where's Jack? The Violent Enemy. 1970: The MacKenzie Break. 1971: Flight of the Doves. 1973: The Mackintosh Man.

PURDELL, Reginald
(R. Grasdorf) 1896–1953

Cheerful, chunky, ebullient, dark-haired British stage and radio comedian, screenplay writer and comic actor, often in 'ordinary

man' roles, occasionally at the head of the cast, more often bolstering the support. Wrote the script for the 1933 version of *Three Men in a Boat* and many other minor film comedies.

1930: The Middle Watch. 1931: Congress Dances. A Night in Montmartre. 1933: My Lucky Star. Strictly in Confidence. Up to the Neck. Crime on the Hill. 1934: On the Air. The Queen's Affair (US: Runaway Queen). Luck of a Sailor. The Old Curiosity Shop. What's in a Name? 1935: Key to Harmony. Royal Cavalcade (GB: Regal Cavalcade). Get Off My Foot. 1936: Crown v Stevens. Debt of Honour. Where's Sally? Hail and Farewell. 1937: Side Street Angel. Ship's Concert. The Dark Stairway. 1938: Quiet Please. The Viper. Simply Terrific. Many Tanks Mr Atkins. 1939: The Missing People. The Middle Watch (and 1930 version). Q Planes (US: Clouds Over Europe). His Brother's Keeper. Pack Up Your Troubles. 1940: Busman's Honeymoon (US: Haunted Honeymoon). Fingers. 1943: Variety Jubilee. Bell Bottom George. We Dive at Dawn. It's in the Bag. The Butler's Dilemma. 1944: Candles at Nine. 2,000 Women. Love Story (US: A Lady Surrenders). 1946: London Town (US: My Heart Goes Crazy). 1947: Brighton Rock (US: Young Scarface). Holiday Camp. Captain Boycott. The Root of All Evil. Man About the House. 1951: Files from Scotland Yard.

As director:
1937: Patricia Gets Her Man.

As co-director:
1937: Don't Get Me Wrong.

PYLE, Denver 1920–

Sharp-featured American actor with Donald Sutherland mouth, in later years buried beneath a bushy beard. Almost entirely cast in westerns (the name may have had something to do with it: he was christened after the capital of the state, Colorado, in which he was born), at first played lean, mean and sneaky characters. But, after his vengeful sheriff in *Bonnie and Clyde*, he got away from all that, helped by a stint in TV's *The Doris Day Show*, and reappeared as benevolent westerners, in harmony with their surroundings. Had his first leading role in 1976 in *Guardian of the Wilderness*.

1947: Devil Ship. The Guilt of Janet Ames. 1948: Where the North Begins. Train to Alcatraz. The Man from Colorado. Marshal of Amarillo. 1949: Hellfire. Flame of Youth. Streets of San Francisco. Too Late for Tears. Red Canyon. 1950: Dynamite Pass. Federal Agent at Large. The Flying Saucer. Singing Guns. Customs Agent. The Old Frontier. Jet Pilot (released 1957). 1951: Rough Riders of Durango. Million Dollar Pursuit. Hills of Utah. 1952: Oklahoma Annie. Desert Passage. The Lusty Men. Fargo. Man from the Black Hills. The Maverick. 1953: Gunsmoke! Texas Bad Man. Vigilante Terror. Canyon Ambush. Rebel City. Topeka. Goldtown Ghost Riders. A Perilous Journey. Ride Clear of Diablo. 1954: The Boy from Oklahoma. Drum Beat. Johnny Guitar. The Forty-Niners. Crime Squad. 1955: To Hell and Back. Rage at Dawn. Run for Cover. Ten Wanted Men. Top Gun. 1956: Please Murder Me. I Killed Wild Bill Hickok. The Naked Hills. 7th Cavalry. Yaqui Drums. 1957: The Lonely Man. Gun Duel in Durango. Destination 60,000. Domino Kid. 1958: The Left-Handed Gun. Fort Massacre. The Party Crashers. China Doll. Good Day for a Hanging. 1959: The Horse Soldiers. King of the Wild Stallions. Cast a Long Shadow. 1960: The Alamo. Home from the Hill. 1962: Bearheart of the Great Northwest (TV). Geronimo. Terrified. This Rugged Land (TV. GB: cinemas). The Man Who Shot Liberty Valance. 1963: Mail Order Bride (GB: West of Montana). 1964: Cheyenne Autumn. The Rounders. 1965: Mara of the Wilderness. Shenandoah. The Great Race. Incident at Phantom Hill. Gunpoint. 1966: Welcome to Hard Times (GB: Killer on a Horse). 1967: Bonnie and Clyde. Tammy and the Millionaire. 1968: Bandolero! Five Card Stud. 1971: Something Big. 1972: Who Fears the Devil?/Legend of Hillbilly John. 1973: Hitched (TV. GB: Westward the Wagon). Cahill, United States Marshal (GB: Cahill). 1974: Sidekicks (TV). Murder or Mercy (TV). The Life and Times of Grizzly Adams (GB: TV). Escape to Witch Mountain. 1975: Death Among Friends (TV). Winterhawk. 1976: Buffalo Bill and the Indians, or: Sitting Bull's History Lesson. Hawmps. Welcome to LA. Guardian of the Wilderness. The Adventures of Frontier Fremont (GB: Spirit of the Wild). 1978: Return from Witch Mountain. 1981: Legend of the Wild. 1987: Discovery Bay. 1994: Maverick. Father and Scout (TV).

QUAID, Randy

(Randall Quaid) 1948–

Tall, strapping American actor with light, curly hair, 'simple' looks and idiot grin. A former stand-up nightclub comic who worked as a cartoonist and painter in his spare time, Quaid was brought to films by Peter Bogdanovich, and was especially well-cast in *The Last Detail*; his moving performance was nominated for an Oscar. His female impersonation in *Breakout* was amusing and clearly relished, but (he's six-feet-five) unlikely to fool anyone. Equally likely these days to be villainous or vacuous. Brother of actor Dennis Quaid.

1967: Targets. 1971: The Last Picture Show. 1972: What's Up Doc? Getting Away from It All (TV). 1973: Paper Moon. The Last Detail. Lolly Madonna XXX (GB: The Lolly Madonna War). 1974: The Apprenticeship of Duddy Kravitz. The Great Niagara (TV). 1975: Breakout. 1976: The Missouri Breaks. Bound for Glory. 1977: The Choirboys. Three Warriors. 1978: Midnight Express. 1979: Foxes. Guyana Tragedy: The Story of Jim Jones (TV). 1980: To Race the Wind (TV). The Raid on Coffeyville/The Last Ride of the Dalton Gang (TV). The Long Riders. 1981: Inside the Third Reich (TV). Of Mice and Men (TV). Heartbeeps. 1983: Cowboy (TV). National Lampoon's Vacation. 1984: The Slugger's Wife. A Streetcar Named Desire (TV). The Wild Life. 1985: Sweet Country. Fool for Love. 1986: The Wraith. 1987: Evil in Clear River (TV). LBJ: The Early Years (TV). Moving. Dear America (voice only). No Man's Land. 1988: Parents. Dead Solid Perfect (TV). Out Cold. Bloodhounds of Broadway. Caddyshack II. 1989: Martians Go Home. National Lampoon's Christmas Vacation (GB: National Lampoon's Winter Holiday). Cold Dog Soup. 1990: Texasville. Days of Thunder. Quick Change. 1991: Picture This. 1992: Frankenstein – The Real Story (TV). 1993: Roommates. Freaked. Murder in the Heartland (cable TV). 1994: The Paper. Major League II. Roommates (TV). Bye Bye Love. The Last Dance. Next Door (TV). Curse of the Starving Class. 1995: Esperanza/Legends of the North.

QUALEN, John

(Johan Oleson, later changed to J.O. Kvalen) 1899–1987

Sad-looking, dark-haired little actor of apologetic demeanour, born in Canada

QUADE, John 1938–

Tiny-eyed, pumpkin faced, squash-nosed, paunchy American actor with scruffy red hair and hostile demeanour. From the start of his briefly prolific film career, he played dirty, smelly, aggressive characters: bikers, redneck thugs and western villains, needing an army of cohorts to bully the hero, but ready to turn tail at a reduction of the odds. Equally ready with a scowl or mocking smile, he encountered Clint Eastwood's heroes several times before his film output slackened in the 1980s.

1972: Bad Company. Goodnight, My Love (TV). Hammer. High Plains Drifter. 1973: The Blue Knight (TV. GB: cinemas, in abridged version). Papillon. The Sting. 1974: The Godchild (TV). Honky Tonk (TV). Mixed Company. Planet Earth (TV). The Swinging Cheerleaders. Rancho de Luxe. The Virginia Hill Story (TV). 1975: Last Hours Before Morning (TV). Mr Ricco. 92 in the Shade. 1976: The Last Hard Men. The Outlaw Josey Wales. Special Delivery. 1977: Escape from Bogen County (TV). Night Terror (TV). Peter Lundy and the Medicine Hat Stallion (TV). 1978: Every Which Way But Loose. Go West, Young Girl! The Ghost of Flight 401 (TV). Vegas (TV). 1980: Any Which Way You Can. Cattle Annie and Little Britches. Power (TV). 1981: Trouble in High Timber Country (TV). 1984: No Man's Land (TV). 1986: La Bamba. Houston: The Legend of Texas (TV). The B.R.A.T. Patrol (TV). 1987: The Highwayman (TV). Tiger Shark. Werewolf (TV). 1988: The Tracker (TV). Dead or Alive. Longarm (TV). 1991: Skeeter.

to Norwegian parents (his father was a minister) and Hollywood's resident Scandinavian (often put-upon, occasionally sinister) from the mid-1930s. After his excellent performance as Axel in *The Long Voyage Home*, his mournful, oval, moustachioed features were seen in several more John Ford films through the years. Also a talented musician: played piano, flute and saxophone. Died from heart failure.

*1931: Street Scene. Arrowsmith. 1933: The Devil's Brother (GB: Fra Diavolo). Hi, Nellie! Counsellor at Law. 1934: Let's Fall in Love. He Was Her Man. No Greater Glory. Private Scandal. Our Daily Bread. Servants' Entrance. Straight is the Way. Upper World. Sing and Like It. 365 Nights in Hollywood. 1935: Black Fury. Charlie Chan in Paris. The Farmer Takes a Wife. Chasing Yesterday. Cheers of the Crowd. The Great Hotel Murder. Doubting Thomas. Man of Iron. One More Spring. Orchids to You. The Silk Hat Kid. Thunder in the Night. The Three Musketeers. 1936: The Country Doctor. Girls' Dormitory. Meet Nero Wolfe. Reunion (GB: Hearts in Reunion). The Road to Glory. Wife versus Secretary. Whipsaw. Ring Around the Moon. 1937: Angel's Holiday. Fifty Roads to Town. Fit for a King. Bad Man from Brimstone. Nothing Sacred. She Had to Eat. Seventh Heaven. 1938: The Chaser. Five of a Kind. Joy of Living. The Mad Miss Manton. Outside the Law. The Texans. 1939: Career. Four Wives. Honeymoon in Bali (GB: Husbands or Lovers). Let Us Live. Mickey the Kid. Stand Up and Fight. Thunder Afloat. 1940: Angels Over Broadway. Babies for Sale. Blondie on a Budget. Brother Orchid. His Girl Friday. The Long Voyage Home. The Grapes of Wrath. Ski Patrol. Knute Rockne – All American (GB: A Modern Hero). Saturday's Children. Youth Will Be Served. On Their Own. 1941: All That Money Can Buy/The Devil and Daniel Webster/Daniel and the Devil. Million Dollar Baby. Model Wife. New Wine (GB: The Great Awakening). Out of the Fog. Shepherd of the Hills. 1942: Arabian Nights. Jungle Book. Larceny Inc. Tortilla Flat. Casablanca. 1943: Swing Shift Maisie (GB: The Girl in Overalls). 1944: An American Romance. Dark Waters. The Impostor. 1945: Adventure. Captain Kidd. *It Happened in Springfield. Roughly Speaking. River Gang (GB: Fairy Tale Murder). 1947: High Conquest. The Fugitive. Song of Scheherezade. Reaching From Heaven. 1948: Alias a Gentleman. Hollow Triumph*

(GB: The Scar). †A Miracle Can Happen (later and GB: On Our Merry Way). My Girl Tisa. Sixteen Fathoms Deep. Criss Cross. 1949: Captain China. The Big Steal. Buccaneer's Girl. 1950: The Jackpot. Woman on the Run. 1951: Belle le Grand. The Flying Missile. Goodbye, My Fancy. 1952: Hans Christian Andersen . . . and the dancer. 1953: Ambush at Tomahawk Gap. Francis Covers the Big Town. I, the Jury. 1954: The High and the Mighty. Passion. The Student Prince. The Other Woman. 1955: At Gunpoint (GB: Gunpoint!). The Sea Chase. Unchained. 1956: Johnny Concho. The Searchers. 1957: The Big Land (GB: Stampeded!). 1958: *So Alone. The Gun Runners. My World Dies Screaming (GB: Terror in the Haunted House). Revolt in the Big House. 1959: Anatomy of a Murder. 1960: Elmer Gantry. Hell Bent for Leather. North to Alaska. 1961: The Comancheros. Two Rode Together. 1962: The Man Who Shot Liberty Valance. 1963: The Prize. 1964: Cheyenne Autumn. The Seven Faces of Dr Lao. Those Calloways. 1965: I'll Take Sweden. A Patch of Blue. The Adventures of Bullwhip Griffin. The Sons of Katie Elder. 1966: A Big Hand for the Little Lady (GB: Big Deal at Dodge City). 1967: P J (GB: New Face in Hell). Firecreek. 1969: Hail, Hero! 1971: Getting Away from It All (TV). 1973: Frasier the Sensuous Lion.

† Scenes deleted from final release print

QUILLAN, Eddie 1907–1990
Bright-eyed, dark-haired, effervescent, not-too-tall American juvenile lead, well at home in collegiate comedies, who later developed into a useful supporting player, at home in both comedy and drama. On stage with his family's vaudeville act at 7, he came to Hollywood at 19 to feature in comedy shorts, but it was in strong drama that he was to get one of his best roles, in 1940's The Grapes of Wrath, in which he was cast as Connie Rivers. He played increasingly smaller roles in post-war years, but kept acting up until the mid 1980s. A lifetime bachelor, he died from cancer.

1922: Up and At 'Em! 1926: *Pass the Dumplings. *A Love Sundae. *Her Actor Friend. 1927: *College Kiddo. *The Bullfighter. *The Plumber's Daughters. *Love in a Police Station. 1928: Show Folks. 1929: The Godless Girl. The Sophomore. Geraldine. Noisy Neighbors. Hot and Bothered. 1930: Night Work. Big Money. *Eddie Cuts In. A Little Bit

of Everything. 1931: *Stout Hearts and Willing Hands. Looking for Trouble. Sweepstakes. Tip Off. The Big Shot (GB: The Optimist). 1932: Girl Crazy. Easy Money. 1933: Strictly Personal. Broadway to Hollywood (GB: Ring Up the Curtain). 1934: Gridiron Flash (GB: Luck of the Game). Hollywood Party. 1935: Mutiny on the Bounty. *Screen Snapshots No. 5. 1936: Fury. The Gentleman from Louisiana. The Mandarin Mystery. 1937: London by Night. Big City. 1938: Swing Sister Swing! The Family Next Door. 1939: The Flying Irishman. Allegheny Uprising (GB: The First Rebel). Made for Each Other. Young Mr Lincoln. 1940: La Conga Nights. Dark Streets of Cairo. The Grapes of Wrath. Hawaiian Nights. Margie. 1941: Dancing on a Dime. Flame of New Orleans. Flying Blind. Six Lessons from Madame La Zonga. Too Many Blondes. Where Did You Get That Girl? 1942: Kid Glove Killer. Priorities on Parade. 1943: Follow the Band. Here Comes Kelly. Hi Ya Sailor! It Ain't Hay (GB: Money for Jam). Melody Parade. 1944: Dark Mountain. Dixie Jamboree. Hi Good Lookin'. The Impostor. Moonlight and Cactus. Mystery of the River Boat (serial). Slightly Terrific. This is the Life. Twilight on the Prairie. 1945: Jungle Queen (serial). Jungle Raiders (serial). Song of the Sarong. 1946: A Guy Could Change. Sensation Hunters. 1948: *Crabbin' in the Cotton. *Parlor, Bedroom and Wrath. 1949: *Let Down Your Aerial. 1950: Sideshow. *House About It. 1951: *He Flew the Shrew. *Fun on the Run. 1952: *A Fool and His Money. *Heebie Gee Gees. *Strop, Look and Listen. 1953: *A-Punting They Did Go. *He Popped His Pistol. 1954: Brigadoon. *Doggie in the Bedroom. 1955: *His Pest Friend. *Nobody's Home. *He Took a Powder. 1956: *Come On Seven. 1961: The Ladies' Man. 1962: Who's Got the Action? 1963: Promises! Promises! Move Over, Darling. Advance to the Rear (GB: Company of Cowards). Take Her, She's Mine. Viva Las Vegas (GB: Love in Las Vegas). Papa's Delicate Condition. Gunfight at Comanche Creek. 1965: Zebra in the Kitchen. The Ghost and Mr Chicken. The Bounty Hunter. 1967: A Guide for the Married Man. Did You Hear the One About the Traveling Saleslady? 1969: Angel in My Pocket. 1971: How to Frame a Figg. 1972: The Judge and Jake Wyler (TV). 1973: She Lives (TV). 1974: Hitchhike! (TV). Melvin Purvis, G-Man (TV. GB: cinemas, as The Legend of Machine-Gun Kelly). 1975: The Strongest Man in the World. 1977: Mad Bull (TV). 1979: The Darker Side of Terror (TV). 1980: For the Love of It (TV). 1981: White Mama (TV). 1984: Highway to Heaven (TV).

QUINN, Tony
(Anthony Quin) 1899–1967
Tall, shuffling, fair-haired (soon grey) Irish actor who, after a long stage career in Ireland (from 1919) and England (from 1927), popped in and out of dozens of British films as briefly glimpsed ushers, guides, drivers, neighbours and manual workers, but occasionally donned a suit and spectacles to look wise. He moved to London (where he died) and became an expert on military history, building up a huge collection of toy soldiers.

1934: Lest We Forget. 1936: Ourselves Alone (US: River of Unrest). 1937: Non-Stop New York. 1939: Just William. The Arsenal Stadium Mystery. 1941: The Saint Meets the Tiger. Penn of Pennsylvania (US: The Courageous Mr Penn). Danny Boy. 1942: Squadron Leader X. Unpublished Story. Thunder Rock. 1943: It's in the Bag. 1944: Welcome Mr Washington. 1946: I See a Dark Stranger (US: The Adventuress). Hungry Hill. 1947: Uneasy Terms. The Imperfect Lady. 1948: Bond Street. 1949: Saints and Sinners. The Strangers Came (US: You Can't Fool an Irishman). Diamond City. Boys in Brown. 1950: Never Say Die/Don't Say Die. 1951: Tom Brown's Schooldays. Talk of a Million (US: You Can't Beat the Irish). The Long Dark Hall. High Treason. The Lavender Hill Mob. 1952: The Gentle Gunman. Song of Paris (US: Bachelor in Paris). Treasure Hunt. The Gift Horse (US: Glory at Sea). 1954: The Beachcomber. 1955: Shadow of a Man. See How They Run. 1956: Secret Tent. Not So Dusty. The Last Man to Hang? Tons of Trouble. Satellite in the Sky. Operation Murder. 1957: The Story of Esther Costello (US: Golden Virgin). The Man Without a Body. Booby Trap. Undercover Girl. The Rising of the Moon. 1958: Life in Emergency Ward 10. Alive and Kicking. 1959: The Great Van Robbery. Trouble With Eve (US: In Trouble With Eve). 1960: Circle of Deception. The Trials of Oscar Wilde. The Unstoppable Man. 1961: The Trunk. The Golden Rabbit. 1962: The Durant Affair. Out of the Fog. The Quare Fellow. 1963: Hide and Seek. 1964: The Runaway. Murder Ahoy. 1965: Rotten to the Core.

R

Six. Information Received. 1962: Jigsaw. Live Now – Pay Later. The Traitors. 1963: The Comedy Man. 1965: Where the Spies Are. 1966: Slave Girls (US: Prehistoric Women). 1967: The Magnificent Six and ½ (first series). 1968: Subterfuge. 1969: The Magic Christian. The Haunted House of Horror. 1970: Toomorrow. Loot. The Rise and Rise of Michael Rimmer. 1971: Dad's Army. Catch Me a Spy. 1980: The Biggest Bank Robbery/A Nightingale Sang in Berkeley Square (made for cinemas but shown only on TV). The Mirror Crack'd.

RAGLAN, Robert 1906–
Heavy-set, dark-haired, moustachioed British actor of flat nose and choleric complexion. Usually to be seen as the trilby-hatted, raincoated police-sergeant or inspector called to the scene of the crime. He once reckoned to have played 27 different policemen of all ranks in one year's television work alone. Latterly seen as military types.

1946: The Courtneys of Curzon Street (US: The Courtney Affair). 1947: Circus Boy. Night Beat. 1952: The Ringer. 1953: The Broken Horseshoe. Gilbert Harding Speaking of Murder. The Good Beginning. Recoil. 1954: The Yellow Robe. Child's Play. 1955: *The Mysterious Bullet. Portrait of Alison (US: Postmark for Danger). Confession (US: The Deadliest Sin). Handcuffs London. Private's Progress. 1956: The Crooked Sky. Brothers in Law. 23 Paces to Baker Street. 1957: The Big Chance. Morning Call (US: The Strange Case of Dr Manning). The One That Got Away. Man from Tangier (US: Thunder Over Tangier). There's Always a Thursday. Count Five and Die. Undercover Girl. Zoo Baby (released 1960). 1958: Gideon's Day (US: Gideon of Scotland Yard). No Safety Ahead. Violent Playground. A Night to Remember. High Jump. Count Five and Die. The Great Van Robbery. Innocent Meeting. Corridors of Blood (released 1961). 1959: Follow a Star. An Honourable Murder. Hidden Homicide. 'Beat' Girl (US: Wild for Kicks). The Child and the Killer. Web of Suspicion. A Woman's Temptation. 1960: Dead Lucky. A Taste of Money. 1961: Two and Two Make

RALPH, Jessie
(Jessica R. Chambers) 1864–1944
One of those 'stately as a galleon' ladies, this dark-haired American actress brought a touch of warmth and dignity to everything she tackled – nurses, governesses, companions and dowagers. At one end of the scale, she was a good fairy in The Blue Bird, then in the same year enjoyed a rare chance to play the harridan as W.C. Fields' mother-in-law in The Bank Dick. Forced to give up acting only after the amputation of a leg in 1941.

1915: Mary's Lamb. 1916: New York. 1921: Such a Little Queen. 1933: Elmer the Great. Child of Manhattan. Cocktail Hour. Ann Carver's Profession. 1934: Nana (GB: Lady of the Boulevards). Coming-Out Party. One Night of Love. We Live Again. Evelyn Prentice. Murder at the Vanities. The Affairs of Cellini. 1935: David Copperfield. Les Misérables. Paris in Spring (GB: Paris Love Song). Enchanted April. Vanessa: Her Love Story. Mark of the Vampire. Jalna. I Live My Life. Metropolitan. Captain Blood. I Found Stella Parish. 1936: The Garden Murder Case. San Francisco. Bunker Bean (GB: His Majesty Bunker Bean). The Unguarded Hour. After the Thin Man. Camille. Little Lord Fauntleroy. Yellow Dust. Walking on Air. 1937: Double Wedding. The Last of Mrs Cheyney. The Good Earth. 1938: Hold That Kiss. Love Is a Headache. Port of Seven Seas. 1939: St Louis Blues. Mickey the Kid. Café Society. Four Girls in White. The Kid from Texas. Drums Along the Mohawk. 1940: Star Dust. The Girl from Avenue A. I Can't Give You Anything But Love, Baby. The Blue Bird. The Bank Dick (GB: The Bank Detective). I Want a Divorce. 1941: The Lady from Cheyenne. They Met in Bombay.

RAMBEAU, Marjorie 1889–1970
Handsome, sunny-dispositioned American actress with light-brown hair, on the stage at 12, a star of silents by 1916. With sound, she came back as a character actress, often as discarded mistresses, but in as many high- as low-society roles in post-war years. She made a few raucous comedies opposite Wallace Beery, rather ironically in the light of the fact that her character in Min and Bill had been killed off by Beery's most famous partner Marie Dressler, and was twice nominated for the Best Supporting Actress Oscar, in The Primrose Path and Torch Song. Her characters were perhaps summed up by the title of her 1931 release Leftover Ladies.

1916: The Dazzling Miss Davison (GB: Who is She?). Motherhood. The Greater Woman. 1917: Mary Moreland. The Mirror. The Debt. 1918: The Common Cause. 1920: The Fortune Teller. 1922: On Her Honor. 1926: Syncopating Sue. 1930: Her Man. Min and Bill. 1931: Son of India. Inspiration. The Easiest Way. Silence. A Tailor-Made Man. Strangers May Kiss. Leftover Ladies (GB: Broken Links). This Modern Age. The Secret Six. Laughing Sinners. Hell Divers. 1933: The Warrior's Husband. Strictly Personal. A Man's Castle. 1934: Ready for Love. A Modern Hero. Palooka (GB: The Great Schnozzle). Grand Canary. 1935: Under Pressure. Dizzy Dames. 1937: First Lady. 1938: Merrily We Live. Woman Against Woman. 1939: Sudden Money. The Rains Came. Heaven With a Barbed-Wire Fence. Laugh It Off (GB: Lady Be Gay). 1940: Santa Fé Marshal. Twenty-Mule Team. The Primrose Path. East of the River. Tugboat Annie Sails Again. 1941: Three Sons o' Guns. Tobacco Road. So Ends Our Night. 1942: Broadway. 1943: In Old Oklahoma (later and GB: War of the Wildcats). 1944: Oh, What a Night! Army Wives. 1945: Salome, Where She Danced. 1948: The Walls of Jericho. 1949: The Lucky Stiff. Abandoned. Any Number Can Play. 1953: Bad for Each Other. Forever Female. Torch Song. 1955: A Man Called Peter. The View from Pompey's Head (GB: Secret Interlude). 1956: Slander. 1957: Man of a Thousand Faces.

RAMSEY, Anne 1928–1988
Square-faced, snub-nosed, brown-haired, chunky American actress, usually in hostile characterizations, whose truculent ugliness

rivalled that of British TV's famous harridan Violet Carson. She first acted in her native Omaha, Nebraska, while still in her teens. Marriage to fellow character player Logan Ramsey (1921–) followed, but she returned to acting in the early 1970s, and belatedly broke through to prominence more than a decade later with her grungy portrayals in *The Goonies* and *Throw Momma from the Train* (she was Momma). A year after making the latter, however, she died from cancer.

1971: *The Sporting Club*. 1972: *The New Centurions* (GB: *Precinct 45 – Los Angeles Police*). *Up the Sandbox*. 1973: *The Third Girl from the Left* (TV). 1974: *The Law* (TV). *For Pete's Sake*. 1975: *Attack on Terror: The FBI Vs the Ku Klux Klan* (TV). 1976: *The Boy in the Plastic Bubble* (TV). *Dawn: Portrait of a Teenage Runaway* (TV). 1977: *Fun With Dick and Jane*. 1978: *The Gift of Love* (TV). *Goin' South*. 1979: *Blind Ambition* (TV). *When You Comin' Back, Red Ryder?* 1980: *Any Which Way You Can*. *The Black Marble*. *White Mama* (TV). *Marilyn: The Untold Story* (TV). 1981: *The Killing of Randy Webster* (TV). *A Small Killing* (TV). 1982: *Marian Rose White* (TV). *National Lampoon's Class Reunion*. 1983: *I Want to Live!* (TV). *Joy Sticks*. 1984: *The Killers* (completed 1981). 1985: *The Goonies*. 1986: *Say Yes*. 1987: *Throw Momma from the Train*. 1988: *Homer and Eddie*. *Another Chance*. 1989: *Good Old Boy* (TV). *Meet the Hollowheads*.

RATOFF, Gregory 1897–1960

Heavy-set, scruffy-looking, big-nosed, brown-haired Russian-born actor with delightfully thick Slavic accent, having come to America in the late 1920s. He was always welcome as arm-waving impresarios and the like, but from the late 1930s, he began to concentrate on direction and became, for a while, one of 20th Century-Fox's leading directors. His returns to acting were infrequent and he died in Switzerland at 63.

1929: *For Sale*. 1932: *Roar of the Dragon*. *Skyscraper Souls*. *Deported*. *Once in a Lifetime*. *Symphony of Six Million* (GB: *Melody of Life*). *Secrets of the French Police*. *Undercover Man*. *What Price Hollywood?* *Thirteen Women*. 1933: *Headline Shooter* (GB: *Evidence in Camera*). *Professional Sweetheart* (GB: *Imaginary*

Sweetheart). *I'm No Angel*. *Sweepings*. *Girl Without a Room*. *Sitting Pretty*. *Broadway Thru a Keyhole*. 1934: *The Forbidden Territory*. *Falling in Love* (US: *Trouble Ahead*). *George White's Scandals*. *The Great Flirtation*. *Let's Fall in Love*. 1935: *Hello Sweetheart/The Butter and Egg Man*. *King of Burlesque*. *Remember Last Night?* 1936: *Here Comes Trouble*. *Sins of Man*. *Under Two Flags*. *Sing, Baby, Sing*. *The Road to Glory*. *Under Your Spell*. 1937: *Top of the Town*. *Seventh Heaven*. *Café Metropole*. 1938: *Sally, Irene and Mary*. *Gateway*. 1940: *The Great Profile*. 1950: *My Daughter Joy* (US: *Operation X*). *All About Eve*. 1952: *O. Henry's Full House* (GB: *Full House*). 1954: *Abdullah's Harem* (GB: *Abdullah the Great*). 1957: *The Sun Also Rises*. 1960: *Once More With Feeling*. *Exodus*. 1961: *The Big Gamble*.

As director:

1933: †*Sins of Man*. 1937: *Lancer Spy*. 1938: *Wife, Husband and Friend*. 1939: *Rose of Washington Square*. *Barricade*. *Day-Time Wife*. *Intermezzo: A Love Story* (GB: *Escape to Happiness*). *Hotel for Women/Elsa Maxwell's Hotel for Women*. 1940: *I Was an Adventuress*. *Public Deb No. 1*. 1941: *Adam Had Four Sons*. *The Men in Her Life*. *The Corsican Brothers*. 1942: *Two Yanks in Trinidad*. *Footlight Serenade*. 1943: *Something to Shout About*. *The Heat's On* (GB: *Tropicana*). 1944: *Song of Russia*. *Irish Eyes Are Smiling*. 1945: *Paris Underground* (GB: *Madame Pimpernel*). *Where Do We Go from Here?* 1946: *Do You Love Me?* 1947: *Carnival in Costa Rica*. *Moss Rose*. 1949: *Black Magic*. *That Dangerous Age* (US: *If This Be Sin*). 1950: *My Daughter Joy* (US: *Operation X*). 1953: *Taxi*. 1954: *Abdullah's Harem* (GB: *Abdullah the Great*). 1960: *Oscar Wilde*.

† Co-directed

RAYMOND, Cyril 1895–1973

Affable, brown-haired, moustachioed British actor of ruddy complexion and solid, pipe-smoking image. An actor since he was 19, he was quietly professional in many 'reliable' roles, such as doctors, police inspectors or family solicitors – but probably most memorably as the 'dull', sit-by-the-fire husband of Celia Johnson in *Brief Encounter*. This beautifully understated performance is one of his best. Retired at 70. Married to actresses Iris Hoey and Gillian Lind.

1916: *The Morals of Weybury/The Hypocrites*. *Disraeli*. 1919: *His Last Defence*. *I Will*. 1920: *The Scarlet Kiss*. *Wuthering Heights*. 1921: *Moth and Rust*. *Single Life*. *Sonia* (US: *The Woman Who Came Back*). 1922: *The Norwood Builder*. *Cocaine*. *While London Sleeps*. *The Faithful Heart*. 1931: *These Charming People*. *The Happy Ending*. *Man of Mayfair*. *The Ghost Train*. *Condemned to Death*. 1932: *The Frightened Lady* (US: *Criminal at Large*). 1933: *The Shadow*. *Mixed Doubles*. *Home Sweet Home*. *Strike It Rich*. *The Lure*. *The Man Outside*. 1934: *Keep It Quiet*. 1935: *King of the Damned*. *The Tunnel* (US: *Transatlantic Tunnel*). 1936: *It's Love Again*. *Accused*. *Tomorrow We Live*. *Thunder in the City*. 1937: *Mad About Money* (US: *He Loved an Actress*). *Stardust*. *Dreaming Lips*. 1938: *Night Alone*. 1939: *The Spy in Black* (US: *U-Boat 29*). *Goodbye Mr Chips!* *Come On George*. 1940: *Saloon Bar*. 1942: *The First of the Few* (US: *Spitfire*). 1945: *Brief Encounter*. 1946: *Men of Two Worlds* (US: *Kisenga*). 1947: *This Was a Woman*. 1948: *Quartet*. *The Jack of Diamonds*. 1951: *Angels One Five*. 1952: *Rough Shoot* (US: *Shoot First*). 1953: *The Heart of the Matter*. 1954: *The Crowded Day*. *Lease of Life*. *The Gay Dog*. 1955: *One Just Man*. 1956: *Charley Moon*. *The Baby and the Battleship*. 1957: *The Safecracker*. 1958: *Dunkirk*. 1960: *No Kidding* (US: *Beware of Children*). 1961: *Carry On Regardless*. 1962: *Don't Talk to Strange Men*. 1964: *Night Train to Paris*.

REDMOND, Liam 1913–

Burly, dark-haired-but-balding, full-faced Irish actor, often in angry or aggressive roles, who divided his time between the English, Irish and American stages, squeezing in nearly 50 film assignments as well. A master of dialect who often didn't sound Irish at all, he's best remembered as the chief saboteur in *High Treason*. Made several trips to Hollywood.

1946: *I See a Dark Stranger* (US: *The Adventuress*). 1947: *Captain Boycott*. 1948: *Daughter of Darkness*. 1949: *Saints and Sinners*. *Sword in the Desert*. *The Twenty Questions Murder Mystery*. 1951: *High Treason*. 1952: *The Gentle Gunman*. *The Cruel Sea*. 1954: *Devil on Horseback*. *Final Appointment*. *The Passing Stranger*. *The Divided Heart*. *Happy Ever After* (US: *Tonight's the Night/O'Leary Night*). *The Glass Cage* (US: *The Glass Tomb*).

1956: *Jacqueline. Yield to the Night (US: Blonde Sinner). 23 Paces to Baker Street. Safari.* 1957: *The Long Haul. Night of the Demon (US: Curse of the Demon).* 1958: *Rooney. Ice-Cold in Alex (US: Desert Attack). Diplomatic Corpse. She Didn't Say No! Alive and Kicking. No Trees in the Street (US: No Tree in the Street).* 1959: *The Boy and the Bridge.* 1960: *Scent of Mystery (GB: Holiday in Spain). Under Ten Flags.* 1961: *The Valiant.* 1962: *Phantom of the Opera. The Playboy of the Western World. Kid Galahad.* 1964: *The Luck of Ginger Coffey.* 1965: *The Ghost and Mr Chicken. The Amorous Adventures of Moll Flanders. The Adventures of Bullwhip Griffin.* 1966: *Tobruk.* 1967: *The 25th Hour. The Last Safari. The Sky Bike.* 1969: *David Copperfield (TV. GB: cinemas).* 1972: *The Alf Garnett Saga (US: Alf 'n' Family).* 1973: *And No One Could Save Her (TV).* 1975: *Barry Lyndon. Philadelphia, Here I Come!*

REED, Pamela 1949–

Dark-haired American actress of pinched attractiveness and careworn eyes, who can play feisty or whingeing with equal confidence. A latecomer to acting, she worked on the Trans-Alaska oil pipeline and ran a day-care centre before taking a drama course and breaking into television in the late 1970s. She soon proved herself a versatile performer, often in determined roles: two of her earliest characters in films were a gunslinging western prostitute and a prehistoric medicine woman. Also showed up strongly as Arnold Schwarzenegger's partner in *Kindergarten Cop*. Film appearances too scattered for the liking of her fans.

1980: *Melvin and Howard. The Long Riders.* 1981: *Eyewitness (GB: The Janitor). Inmates: A Love Story (TV). Until She Talks (TV).* 1982: *Young Doctors in Love.* 1983: *Heart of Steel (TV). I Want to Live (TV). The Right Stuff. The Goodbye People.* 1985: *Scandal Sheet (TV).* 1986: *The Best of Times. The Clan of the Cave Bear.* 1988: *Rachel River. Tanner '88 (TV). Chattahoochee (released 1991).* 1990: *Cadillac Man. Caroline? (TV).* 1991: *Kindergarten Cop. Prime Target.* 1992: *Woman With a Past (TV). Bob Roberts. Passed Away.* 1993: *Born Too Soon (TV).* 1994: *Junior.*

REEVES, (P.) Kynaston 1893–1971

Tall, stork-like, beaky British actor with high forehead disappearing into fuzzy, receding hair; almost always in learned roles: deans, professors, ministers, clerics and the like. After an army career, he turned to the theatre at 27 and ran up a huge list of credits, as well as making over 70 films and appearing frequently on TV. Seemed to become increasingly emaciated in later years, when his gravity was often turned to comic use. The P stood for Philip. The Kynaston came from his mother's maiden name.

1919: *His Last Defence.* 1932: *The Sign of Four. The Lodger (US: The Phantom Fiend).* 1933: *Puppets of Fate (US: Wolves of the Underworld).* 1934: *Broken Melody. The Crimson Candle. Jew Süss (US: Power).* 1935: *Vintage Wine. Dark World.* 1936: *Take a Chance.* 1937: *King of Gamblers. A Romance in Flanders (US: Lost on the Western Front).* 1938: *The Citadel. Sixty Glorious Years (US: Queen of Destiny). Housemaster.* 1939: *The Outsider. Dead Men Are Dangerous. Sons of the Sea. The Stars Look Down. Inspector Hornleigh on Holiday (US: Inspector Hornleigh on Leave).* 1940: *Two for Danger. The Flying Squad.* 1941: *The Prime Minister. This England.* 1942: *The Young Mr Pitt. The Night Invader.* 1943: *They Met in the Dark.* 1944: *Strawberry Roan.* 1945: *The Rake's Progress (US: Notorious Gentleman). The Echo Murders. Murder in Reverse (US: Query).* 1946: *Bedelia. *Family Doctor.* 1947: *This Was a Woman. Vice Versa.* 1948: *The Winslow Boy. Counterblast. The Guinea Pig. The Weaker Sex. Badger's Green. *The Marshall Plan.* 1949: *For Them That Trespass. Madness of the Heart. The Twenty Questions Murder Mystery.* 1950: *Madeleine. Tony Draws a Horse. Blackout. The Mudlark. The Undefeated. Trio.* 1951: *Captain Horatio Hornblower RN (US: Captain Horatio Hornblower). Smart Alec.* 1952: *Top Secret (US: Mr Potts Goes to Moscow). Penny Princess. *Moving House. Song of Paris (US: Bachelor in Paris).* 1953: *Top of the Form. Laxdale Hall (US: Scotch on the Rocks). Four Sided Triangle.* 1954: *Eight O'Clock Walk. Burnt Evidence. The Crowded Day.* 1955: *Touch and Go (US: The Light Touch). Fun at St Fanny's.* 1956: *Guilty? Brothers-in-Law.* 1957: *High Flight. Light Fingers.* 1958: *Fiend Without a Face. Family Doctor (US: RX Murder. And 1946 short). A Question of Adultery. Carlton-Browne of the FO (US: Man in a Cocked Hat).* 1959: *School for Scoundrels.* 1960: *In the Nick. The Trials of Oscar Wilde (US: Man With the Green Carnation). The Night We Got the Bird.* 1961: *Shadow of the Cat. Carry On Regardless. In the Doghouse. Don't Bother to Knock! (US: Why Bother to Knock?).* 1962: *Go to Blazes.* 1963: *Hide and Seek.* 1968: *Hot Millions.* 1969: *Anne of the Thousand Days.* 1970: *The Private Life of Sherlock Holmes.*

REICHER, Frank
(Franz Reichert) 1875–1965

German-born actor in Hollywood whose small chin, high forehead, pointed nose and crow's-feet eyes gave the impression that he was forever leaning intently forward. He had begun his film career as a director of silents, but in sound films concentrated on acting, mostly as professors, doctors, surgeons and small-town officials. Usually in kind or gentle parts, occasionally victims or suspicious figures of authority, he was intensely busy throughout the latter stages of his career.

1921: *Behind Masks. Out of the Depths. Wise Husbands. Idle Hands. Ridin' Pretty.* 1926: *Her Man o' War.* 1928: *Beau Sabreur. The Blue Danube (GB: Honour Above All). Four Sons. The Masks of the Devil. The Masked Angel (GB: Her Love Cottage). *Napoleon's Barber. Sins of the Fathers.* 1929: *Big News. Black Waters. The Changeling. His Captive Woman. Her Private Husband. Mister Antonio. Paris Bound. Strange Cargo.* 1930: *Die Sehnsucht jeder Frau. Girl of the Port. The Grand Parade.* 1931: *Beyond Victory. A Gentleman's Fate. Mata Hari. Suicide Fleet.*

1932: *The Crooked Circle. Scarlet Dawn. A Woman Commands.* 1933: *A Bedtime Story. After Tonight. Captured. Ever in My Heart. Employees' Entrance. King Kong. Jennie Gerhardt. Rasputin and the Empress* (GB: *Rasputin – The Mad Monk). Before Dawn. Topaze. Son of Kong. Hi, Nellie!* 1934: *British Agent. Countess of Monte Cristo. I Am a Thief. Journal of a Crime. The Case of the Howling Dog. The Fountain. Little Man, What Now? Let's Talk It Over. The World Moves On. No Greater Glory. Return of the Terror.* 1935: *Charlie Chan in Egypt. A Dog of Flanders. The Florentine Dagger. The Fighting Marines* (serial). *The Great Impersonation. Kind Lady. Life Returns. The Man Who Broke the Bank at Monte Carlo. The Lone Wolf Returns. Magnificent Obsession. Mills of the Gods. Star of Midnight. Remember Last Night. Rendezvous. Straight from the Heart. The Story of Louis Pasteur.* 1936: *Along Came Love. The Country Doctor. The Ex-Mrs Bradford. Girls' Dormitory. The Gorgeous Hussy. Anthony Adverse. Camille. Sutter's Gold. The Invisible Ray. The Murder of Dr Harrigan. Old Hutch. Star for a Night. Murder on a Bridle Path. 'Til We Meet Again. Second Wife. Stolen Holiday. Under Two Flags.* 1937: *Beg, Borrow or Steal. The Emperor's Candlesticks. Fit for a King. The Life of Emile Zola. Midnight Madonna. Night Key. Lancer Spy. Prescription for Romance. The Great O'Malley. Laughing at Trouble. The Mighty Treve. Espionage. Stage Door. The Road Back/Return of the Hero. On Such a Night. Westbound Limited. Under Cover of Night.* 1938: *City Streets. Letter of Introduction. I'll Give a Million. Of Human Hearts. Prison Nurse. The Storm. Three Comrades. Torchy Gets Her Man. Rascals. Suez.* 1939: *The Escape. Everything Happens at Night. Juarez. The Magnificent Fraud. Nurse Edith Cavell. Mystery of the White Room. Ninotchka. Our Neighbors, the Carters. Never Say Die. Society Smugglers. South of the Border. Unexpected Father* (GB: *Sandy Takes a Bow). Woman Doctor.* 1940: *All This and Heaven Too. Devil's Island. Dr Cyclops. The Lady in Question. The Man I Married. South to Karanga. Sky Murder. Typhoon.* 1941: *Flight from Destiny. Four Mothers. Father Takes a Wife. The Face Behind the Mask. Dangerously They Live. The Nurse's Secret. Shining Victory. One Foot in Heaven. They Dare Not Love. Underground.* 1942: *Beyond the Blue Horizon. The Gay Sisters. I Married an Angel. The Mystery of Marie Roget. Nazi Agent. The Mummy's Tomb. Night Monster* (GB: *House of Mystery). Salute to Courage. Secret Enemies. Scattergood Survives a Murder. To Be or Not to Be.* 1943: *Above Suspicion. Background to Danger. Captain America* (serial). **Plan for Destruction. Mission to Moscow. Hangmen Also Die. The Song of Bernadette. Tornado. Watch on the Rhine. Yanks Ahoy!* 1944: *The Adventures of Mark Twain. The Canterville Ghost. Address Unknown. The Hitler Gang. The Mummy's Ghost. The Big Bonanza. The Conspirators. In Our Time. House of Frankenstein. Scattergood's Ghost. Mrs Parkington.* 1945: *Blonde Ransom. Hotel Berlin. The Jade Mask. A Medal for Benny. *Phantoms Inc. Rhapsody in Blue. The Tiger Woman. Voice of the Whistler.* 1946: *Home in Oklahoma. My Pal Trigger. Sister Kenny. The Shadow Returns. The Strange Mrs*

Gregory. 1947: *Escape Me Never. Mr District Attorney. Monsieur Verdoux. The Secret Life of Walter Mitty. Song of Love. Violence. Yankee Fakir.* 1948: *Carson City Raiders. Fighting Mad* (GB: *Joe Palooka in Fighting Mad). I, Jane Doe.* 1949: *Barbary Pirate. Samson and Delilah.* 1950: *The Arizona Cowboy. Cargo to Capetown. The Happy Years. Kiss Tomorrow Goodbye.* 1951: *The Lady and the Bandit* (GB: *Dick Turpin's Ride). Superman and the Mole Men* (GB: *Superman and the Strange People).*

As director:
1915: *The Chorus Lady. The Case of Becky. The Secret Orchard* (GB: *The Secret Garden). The Secret Sin.* 1916: *For the Defense. The Love Mask. Witchcraft. The Dupe. The Victory of Conscience. Puddin' Head Wilson. Alien Souls. The Black Wolfe.* 1917: *Castles for Two. The Eternal Mother. Lost and Won. Sacrifice. The Inner Shrine. Unconquered. An American Widow.* 1918: *The Claim. The Only Road. Suspense. The Treasure of the Sea. The Prodigal Wife. The Trap.* 1919: *The American Way. The Battler.* 1920: *The Black Circle. Empty Arms.* 1921: *Behind Masks. Idle Hands. Wise Husbands. Out of the Depths.* 1929: *†Paris Bound. †Big News. †Mister Antonio.* 1930: *†The Grand Parade.*

† Co-directed

REID, Beryl 1920–
Purse-lipped, round-faced, light-haired British radio comedienne who amused audiences through three decades with her impersonations of lisping schoolgirls with such names as Marlene and Monica, before unexpectedly becoming a star character actress of considerable impact, mostly in comic roles, but most noticeably with the tragi-comic *The Killing of Sister George*, a film repeat of her stage triumph. Latterly in 'guest star' roles, and the co-author (with Eric Braun) of several autobiographical books. Some sources give date of birth as 1918, but the actress herself insists that it's 1920.

1940: *Spare a Copper.* 1954: *The Belles of St Trinian's.* 1956: *The Extra Day.* 1960: *Two-Way Stretch.* 1962: *The Dock Brief* (US: *Trial and Error).* 1968: *Inspector Clouseau. The Assassination Bureau. Star! The Killing of Sister George.* 1970: *Entertaining Mr Sloane.*

The Beast in the Cellar. 1972: *Dr Phibes Rises Again. Father Dear Father. Psychomania.* 1973: *No Sex Please—We're British.* 1976: *Joseph Andrews.* 1978: *Rosie Dixon Night Nurse. Carry On Emmannuelle.* 1980: **Late Flowering Love.* 1983: *Yellowbeard.* 1985: *The Doctor and the Devils.* 1987: *Didn't You Kill My Brother?* 1990: *Duel of Hearts* (TV).

REID, Carl Benton 1893–1973
Distinguished-looking, authoritative, sometimes moustachioed American actor with long theatrical experience. He came to Hollywood to recreate his stage role of the conniving Oscar Hubbard in *The Little Foxes* and his squatly handsome features remained near the top of Hollywood casts for the next 20 years as doctors, wardens, Cavalry captains, businessmen and lawyers, never overplaying his hand in any guise.

1941: *The Little Foxes.* 1942: *Tennessee Johnson* (GB: *The Man on America's Conscience).* 1943: *The North Star* (later *Armored Attack). Mission to Moscow.* 1949: *The Doctor and the Girl.* 1950: *The Fuller Brush Girl* (GB: *The Affairs of Sally). The Killer That Stalked New York* (GB: *The Frightened City). Stage to Tucson* (GB: *Lost Stage Valley). In a Lonely Place. Convicted. The Flying Missile.* 1951: *The Family Secret. The Great Caruso. Lorna Doone. Smuggler's Gold. Criminal Lawyer. Boots Malone.* 1952: *The Sniper. Carbine Williams. The Brigand. The First Time. The Story of Will Rogers. Indian Uprising.* 1953: *Escape from Fort Bravo. Main Street to Broadway.* 1954: *The Command. Broken Lance. Athena. The Egyptian.* 1955: *One Desire. The Spoilers. Wichita. The Left Hand of God.* 1956: *A Day of Fury. The First Texan. The Last Wagon. Strange Intruder. Battle Hymn.* 1957: *Time Limit. Spoilers of the Forest.* 1958: *Tarzan's Fight for Life. Last of the Fast Guns. The Trap* (GB: *The Baited Trap).* 1960: *The Bramble Bush. The Gallant Hours.* 1962: *Underwater City. Pressure Point.* 1963: *The Ugly American.* 1965: *Madame X.*

REID, Milton 1917–
Massively-built, shaven-headed, India-born ex-wrestler who entered the British entertainment arena in his late thirties and played sadistic villains, mutes, mulattoes, genies, thugs and other exotic characters, mostly of the menacing variety. Just the sort of man to

turn up in James Bond films, he did eventually make one, remaining active in films and (especially) television into his early sixties, still often playing muscular heavies.

1952: Ivanhoe 1953: Star of India. 1954: Knights of the Round Table. 1955: The Adventures of Quentin Durward (US: Quentin Durward). 1957: Undercover Girl. 1958: The Camp on Blood Island. Blood of the Vampire. 1959: Ferry to Hong Kong. Our Man in Havana. Swiss Family Robinson. 1960: Visa to Canton (US: Passport to China). 1961: The Terror of the Tongs. Follow That Man! The Wonders of Aladdin. 1962: Captain Clegg (US: Night Creatures). 1963: Panic. Three Faces of Sin. 1964: Ursus. Spartacus and the Ten Gladiators. 1965: Monster! Cimbro. 1966: Deadlier Than the Male. 1967: Berserk! Great Catherine. Casino Royale. 1968: The Assassination Bureau. 1969: How To Make It (GB: Target: Harry). 1970: The Horsemen. Blood on Satan's Claw (US: Satan's Skin). 1971: Blinker's Spy Spotter. 1972: Dr Phibes Rises Again. 1974: The Return of the Pink Panther. 1977: Come Play With Me. The Spy Who Loved Me. The People That Time Forgot. No 1 of the Secret Service. 1978: Terror. What's Up Superdoc? 1979: Arabian Adventure. Confessions from the David Galaxy Affair. Queen of the Blues.

RELPH, George 1888–1960
Dark, moustachioed, amiable British actor with hound-like face who, unfortunately for filmgoers, decided to spend almost his entire career on stage after film experience in

Hollywood in the early silent days. Now best remembered on film as the vicar in *The Titfield Thunderbolt*. Father of producer and sometime director Michael Relph.

1916: Paying the Price. 1921: Candytuft, I Mean Veronica. The Door That Has No Key. 1939: Too Dangerous to Live. 1944: Give Us the Moon. 1947: Nicholas Nickleby. 1951: I Believe in You. 1953: The Final Test. The Titfield Thunderbolt. 1957: Doctor at Large. Davy. 1959: Ben-Hur.

REMSEN, Bert 1925–
Chunky, chubby-faced, curly-haired American actor, usually in straight-talking roles as editors, sergeants (army and police) and other minor figures of authority. A much-decorated veteran of World War Two (he served as a coxswain on a destroyer), Remsen studied drama post-war, and would almost certainly have built up a much greater list of film and TV acting credits had it not been for a serious accident while making a TV series in 1965: a crane fell on him, breaking his back and leg. Remsen became a casting director, but was able to return to acting five years later and pursue dual careers.

1957: Peyton Place. 1959: Pork Chop Hill. 1960: Tess of the Storm Country. 1962: Moon Pilot. Kid Galahad. 1964: Dead Ringer (GB: Dead Image). 1965: The Lollipop Cover. 1970: Rabbit Run. Brewster McCloud. The Strawberry Statement. 1971: McCabe and Mrs Miller. If Tomorrow Comes (TV). 1972: Fuzz. 1974: Thieves Like Us. Death Squad (TV). California Split. 1975: Nashville. Sweet Hostage (TV). 1976: Buffalo Bill and the Indians. Brink's: The Great Robbery (TV). Baby Blue Marine. Harry and Walter Go to New York. 1977: Tarantulas: The Deadly Cargo (TV). 1978: The Hamster of Happiness (later Second Hand Hearts). The Awakening Land (TV). Uncle Joe Shannon. A Wedding. 1979: Fast Break. Joni. Love for Rent (TV). The Rose. 1980: Carny. Inside Moves. Borderline. 1981: Crazy Times (TV). Flesh and Blood (TV). 1982: Independence Day/Restless. Lookin' to Get Out. Victims (TV). 1983: Hobson's Choice (TV). M.A.D.D: Mothers Against Drunk Drivers (TV). Memorial Day (TV). The Sting II. Policewoman Centerfold (TV). 1984: Places in the Heart. Lies. 1985: Code of Silence. 1986: Eye of the Tiger. 1988: Remote Control. South of Reno.

1989: Miss Firecracker. Night Walk (TV). 1990: Vietnam, Texas. Evil Spirits. Payback. Daddy's Dyin' – Who's Got the Will? Dick Tracy. Jezebel's Kiss. Peacemaker. 1991: Only the Lonely. 1992: Loving Lulu. Made for Each Other (TV). The Player. Lady Killer. Wild Card (TV). 1993: Jack the Bear. There Was a Little Boy (TV). The Adventures of Brisco County Jr (TV). 1994: Secret Sins of the Father (TV). Maverick. Come Die With Me (TV).

REVERE, Anne 1903–1990
Fresh-faced, dark-haired, old-looking American character actress who looked set for a record number of hard-working, worldly-wise mothers and sympathetic if sharp-tongued friends, before the McCarthy blacklistings stopped her career. Academy Award as Elizabeth Taylor's mother in *National Velvet* (plus two more nominations). Died from pneumonia.

1934: Double Door. 1940: The Howards of Virginia (GB: The Tree of Liberty). One Crowded Night. 1941: The Devil Commands. Men of Boys' Town. HM Pulham Esq. Remember the Day. Design for Scandal. The Flame of New Orleans. 1942: The Falcon Takes Over. The Gay Sisters. Meet the Stewarts. Star Spangled Rhythm. The Meanest Man in the World. Are Husbands Necessary? 1943: Old Acquaintance. The Song of Bernadette. Shantytown. 1944: The Keys of the Kingdom. Standing Room Only. Sunday Dinner for a Soldier. The Thin Man Goes Home. Rainbow Island. National Velvet. 1945: Don Juan Quilligan. Fallen Angel. 1946: Dragonwyck. The Shocking Miss Pilgrim. 1947: Gentleman's Agreement. Carnival in Costa Rica. Forever Amber. Body and Soul. 1948: Deep Waters. Secret Beyond the Door. Scudda-Hoo! Scudda-Hay! (GB: Summer Lightning). 1949: You're My Everything. 1950: The Great Missouri Raid. 1951: A Place in the Sun. 1960: Call of the Holy Land (narrator only). 1969: Deadlock (TV). Tell Me That You Love Me, Junie Moon. 1970: Macho Callahan. 1972: Two for the Money (TV). 1976: Birch Interval.

REVILL, Clive 1930–
Fair-haired, barrel-shaped, parrot-like New Zealand-born actor attracting attention with scene-stealing performances in British films from the mid-1960s. Later worked much in America, especially from the late 1970s,

when films, plays and television kept him working hard in both comic and dramatic rôles, in which his slightly off-centre characterizations proved equally effective.

*1953: *The Drayton Case. 1956: Reach for the Sky. 1958: The Horse's Mouth. 1959: The Headless Ghost. 1965: Bunny Lake Is Missing. 1966: Modesty Blaise. Kaleidoscope. A Fine Madness. 1967: The Double Man. Italian Secret Service. Fathom. 1968: Nobody Runs Forever (US: The High Commissioner). The Shoes of the Fisherman. The Assassination Bureau. 1970: The Private Life of Sherlock Holmes. The Buttercup Chain. A Severed Head. Boulevard du rhum (US: Rum Runner). 1972: Avanti! Escape to the Sun. 1973: The Legend of Hell House. Ghost in the Noonday Sun (unreleased). 1974: The Boy With Two Heads (serial. Voice only). The Black Windmill. Galileo. The Little Prince. 1975: One of Our Dinosaurs Is Missing. 1976: The Great Houdinis (TV). 1977: Pinocchio (TV). 1978: Matilda. Once Upon a Brothers Grimm (TV). 1979: TR Sloane of the Secret Service (TV). She's Dressed to Kill (TV. GB: Somebody's Killing the World's Greatest Models). Charlie Muffin (TV). 1980: The Empire Strikes Back (voice only). 1981: Zorro the Gay Blade. The Monkey Mission (TV). 1984: Samson and Delilah (TV). 1986: A Masterpiece of Murder (TV). 1987: The Frog Prince. The Emperor's New Clothes. Rumpelstiltskin. 1989: Mack the Knife. Jake Spanner — Private Eye (TV). 1991: 'Let Him Have It'. 1993: The Sea Wolf (TV). Crime and Punishment.*

REY, Fernando

(F. Casado d'Arambillet) 1915–1994
Kindly-looking in a rather haggard way, this Spanish actor popped up here, there and everywhere over the past 50 years. Every time a British or American company made a film in Spain, it seemed that Rey was in it. He made much international co-production rubbish, but was also associated with Oscar-winning films and regularly hired by Spain's most famous director, Luis Buñuel. As a young man, Rey fought in the Spanish Civil War against the Frangistes and was captured. In the 1940s, he dubbed British and American films into Spanish while building his own screen career. He was particularly grateful for the association with Buñuel—'Something in my cadaverous expression must have caught his eye'—but

probably best-known to international audiences as the smooth mastermind in the 'French Connection' films. Remained busy right up to his death from cancer.

1936: Nuestra natacha. 1939: Los cuatros Robinsons. 1940: La gitanilla. 1944: El rey que rabio. Eugenia de Montijo. 1945: Tierra sedienta. Los ultimos de Filipinas. Misión blanca. 1946: La prodiga. 1947: Locura de amor (US: The Mad Queen). Don Quijote de la Mancha (US: Don Quixote). Reine santa. La princesa de los Ursinos. Fuentovejuno. Noche de reyes. 1948: Si te hubieses casado con amigo. 1949: Du sang à l'aube. Los aventuras de Juan Lucas. 1950: Agustina de Aragon. Mare nostrum. 1951: Cielo negro. Esa pareja feliz/Cet heureux couple. La señora de Fatima. 1952: Bienvenido Mr Marshall! (GB and US: Welcome Mr Marshall!). La laguna negra. 1953: Cómicos. En alcalde de Zalamea. Aeropuerto. Cabaret. Rebeldia. 1954: Tangier Assignment. 1955: Marcelino. Don Juan (GB and US: Pantaloons). Un marido de ida y vuelta. Les aventures de Gil Blas de Santillane. 1956: Faustina. 1957: La venganza/Vengeance. Les bijoutiers du clair de lune (GB: Heaven Fell That Night. US: The Night Heaven Fell). 1958: Culpables. Parque de Madrid. Los habitantes de la casa deshabitada. 1959: Mission in Morocco. The Last Days of Pompeii. Sonatas. Operación Relampage. Las dos y media y renuno. Nacido para la música. 1960: Fabiola. Don Lucio y el hermano pío. A los cinco de la tarde. Teresa de Jesus. 1961: The Revolt of the Slaves. Viridiana. Goliath Against the Giants. 1962: The Savage Guns. Face of Terror. Shéhérazade (GB: Scorching Sands). Rogelia. 1963: The Castilian. El espontanes. Dios eligio sus viajeros. The Running Man. The Ceremony. El diablo también Ilora. 1964: Los palomas. Son of a Gunfighter. El Greco. Echappement libre (US: Backfire). El señor de la salle. La nueva cenicienta. 1965: Cards on the Table. Toto di Arabia. Dos de la Mafia. España insolita. Misión Lisboa. Zampo y yo. 1966: The Desperate Ones. Chimes at Midnight (US: Falstaff). Run Like a Thief. Navajo Joe. Return of the Seven. Don Quijote. Dulcinea del Toboso. Das Vermachtnis des Inka. Los jeuces de la Biblia. 1967: The Viscount. Amor en el aire. Cervantes/Cervantes, The Young Rebel. Attack of the Robots. Más alla de las montañas. 1968: Villa Rides! Guns of the Magnificent Seven. The Immortal Story. 1969: Fellini-Satyricon. Land Raiders. Il prezzo di potere (GB: The Price of Power). Candidate for a

Killing. 1970: La colésa del viente. Tristana. The Adventurers. Muerte de un presidente. Compañeros! 1971: A Town Called Bastard (US: A Town Called Hell). The Light at the Edge of the World. Los frios ojos del miedo. Historia de una traición. The French Connection. 1972: Antony and Cleopatra. La duba. Questa specie d'amore. Le charme discret de la bourgeoisie (GB and US: The Discreet Charm of the Bourgeoisie). Chicas de club. I due volti della paura (GB: The Two Faces of Fear). 1973: La polizia incrimma, la legge assolve (GB: High Crime). La chuté d'un corps. El mejor alcalde, el Rey. White Sister. One Way. 1974: Peña de muerte. Cinco lobitas. Tarots. White Fang (US: Challenge to White Fang). La femme aux bottes rouges. Corruzione al Palazzo di Giustizia. Fatti di gente perbene (GB: Drama of the Rich). Dite-le avecles fleurs. 1975: French Connection II (GB: French Connection No. 2). Pasqualino settebellez (GB and US: Seven Beauties). Il contesto. Cadaveri eccellenti (GB and US: Illustrious Corpses). La grande bourgeoise. Le originia della Mafia. 1976: Jesus of Nazareth (TV). A Matter of Time. Le desert des Tartars/Desert of the Tartars. Voyage of the Damned. Strip-Tease. 1977: Elisa vida mia. L'uomo del 4 piano. Cet obscur objet du désir (GB and US: That Obscure Object of Desire). The Assignment. 1978: El segundo poder. Le dernier amant romantique. 1979: The Crime of Cuenca. Le grand embouteillage. Cabo Blanco. Quintet. Vestire gli ignudi. L'ingorgo. 1980: La dame aux camélias (US: Camille — The True Story). 1981: Confessions of Felix Krull. Casta e pura. Meile di donna/Honey. Tragala, pervò. 1982: Cervasi Jesù. Monsignor. Estrangeira. 1983: Bearn/La sala de las muñecas. 1984: The Hit. Saving Grace. The Black Arrow (cable TV). Nicolo', ou l'enfant trouvé. Un amour interdit. 1985: El caballero del dragon (US: Star Knight). Padre nuestro. Rustlers' Rhapsody. Saving Grace. 1986: Hotel du Paradis. Frankenstein's Aunt. Commando Mengele. Boogie Woogie. 1987: Hard to Be a God. The Issue at Stake. Mi General. The Tunnel. El bosque animado. 1988: Moon Over Parador. Pasodoble. Blackmail. Diario de invierno. El aire de un crimen. 1989: The Betrothed. Naked Tango. 1990: Diceria dell' untore (US: The Plague Sower). The Battle of the Three Kings. 1992: L'Atlantide. 1492 Conquest of Paradise. La sposa di Cristo. Después del sueño. 1993: El cianuro? — Solo o con leche? I leoni del sol. Tirano banderos. 1994: Madre Gilda. Les hirondelles ne meurent pas à Jerusalem. Al oltro lado de tunel.

RHODES, Erik 1906–1990

Pale-faced, frequently moustachioed American musical-comedy actor, handsome in an alarmed-looking sort of way, who played the unsuccessful Italian suitor in a couple of Astaire–Rogers musicals of the 1930s during his brief five-year tenure in Hollywood. After 1939, returned to the stage, his excitable lotharios no longer in demand. Died from pneumonia.

1934: Give Her a Ring. The Gay Divorcee (GB: The Gay Divorce). 1935: A Night at the

Ritz. The Nitwits. Charlie Chan in Paris. Old Man Rhythm. Another Face. Top Hat. 1936: One Rainy Afternoon. Special Investigator. Second Wife. Chatterbox. Two in the Dark. The Smartest Girl in Town. 1937: Criminal Lawyer. Fight for Your Lady. Music for Madame. Beg, Borrow or Steal. Woman Chases Man. 1938: Meet the Girls. Dramatic School. Say It in French. Mysterious Mr Moto. 1939: On Your Toes.

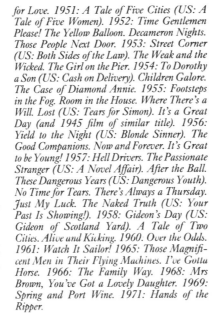

for Love. 1951: A Tale of Five Cities (US: A Tale of Five Women). 1952: Time Gentlemen Please! The Yellow Balloon. Decameron Nights. Those People Next Door. 1953: Street Corner (US: Both Sides of the Law). The Weak and the Wicked. The Girl on the Pier. 1954: To Dorothy a Son (US: Cash on Delivery). Children Galore. The Case of Diamond Annie. 1955: Footsteps in the Fog. Room in the House. Where There's a Will. Lost (US: Tears for Simon). It's a Great Day (and 1945 film of similar title). 1956: Yield to the Night (US: Blonde Sinner). The Good Companions. Now and Forever. It's Great to be Young! 1957: Hell Drivers. The Passionate Stranger (US: A Novel Affair). After the Ball. These Dangerous Years (US: Dangerous Youth). No Time for Tears. There's Always a Thursday. Just My Luck. The Naked Truth (US: Your Past Is Showing!). 1958: Gideon's Day (US: Gideon of Scotland Yard). A Tale of Two Cities. Alive and Kicking. 1960: Over the Odds. 1961: Watch It Sailor! 1965: Those Magnificent Men in Their Flying Machines. I've Gotta Horse. 1966: The Family Way. 1968: Mrs Brown, You've Got a Lovely Daughter. 1969: Spring and Port Wine. 1971: Hands of the Ripper.

and the Hidden Staircase. Mr Moto in Danger Island (GB: Mr Moto on Danger Island). Honeymoon in Bali (GB: Husbands or Lovers). Tell No Tales. Tailspin. Wings of the Navy. Nancy Drew, Trouble Shooter. Daytime Wife. 1940: Kit Carson. The Man Who Wouldn't Talk. The Ghost Comes Home. Remedy for Riches. The Doctor Takes a Wife. The Shop Around the Corner. Oh Johnny, How You Can Love. 1941: Unfinished Business. You're the One. Adam Had Four Sons. Ziegfeld Girl. They Died with Their Boots On. Ice-Capades. Affectionately Yours. You Belong to Me (GB: Good Morning, Doctor). 1942: Whispering Ghosts. Blondie for Victory (GB: Troubles Through Billets). Grand Central Murder. There's One Born Every Minute. 1943: The Man from Music Mountain. 1944: None But the Lonely Heart. Can't Help Singing. Take It Or Leave It. Jam Session. Three is a Family. 1945: Club Havana. A Song for Miss Julie. Anchors Aweigh. The Picture of Dorian Gray. 1946: Bad Bascomb. Bringing Up Father. So Goes My Love (GB: A Genius in the Family). 1947: Winter Wonderland. Jiggs and Maggie in Society. 1948: The Time of Your Life. Jiggs and Maggie in Court. An Act of Murder. 1949: Jackpot Jitters/Jiggs and Maggie in Jackpot Jitters. 1950: Jiggs and Maggie Out West. 1951: As Young As You Feel. The Barefoot Mailman. 1953: Clipped Wings. 1955: The Man With the Gun (GB: The Trouble Shooter). 1964: Bikini Beach. Pajama Party. 1965: The Family Jewels. 1966: Three on a Couch. Fireball 500.

RHODES, Marjorie
(M.R. Wise) 1902–1979

Marjorie Rhodes played the kind of women whose daughter you hoped your son wouldn't marry. One can picture the flowered hat, the print dress and the coverall coat. Her mothers could have lashing tongues or loving natures, but whether from London or her native Yorkshire, they were all thoroughly working class. Occasionally she broke out of the mould to play something like the wardress in Yield to the Night, but generally shabbiness and homeliness prevailed.

1939: Just William. Poison Pen. 1941: Hi Gang! Love on the Dole. The Black Sheep of Whitehall. World of Plenty. 1942: Squadron Leader X. When We Are Married. 1943: Old Mother Riley Detective. Theatre Royal. Escape to Danger. The Butler's Dilemma. 1944: Tawny Pipit. On Approval. It Happened One Sunday. 1945: Great Day. 1946: Land of Promise. School for Secrets (US: Secret Flight). 1947: Uncle Silas (US: The Inheritance). The Silver Darlings. This Was a Woman. 1948: Escape. Enchantment. 1949: Private Angelo. The Cure

RIANO, Renie 1899–1971

Bony-faced, dark haired, big-hipped (but slim), long-jawed American comic actress adept at nosy neighbours and inquisitive busybodies, as well as nursemaids, teachers and governesses who brooked few arguments from their charges. The daughter of stage actress Irene Riano (1871–1940), Renie was on stage with her mother as a toddler, and made her Broadway bow in the musical show, Honey Girl, at 18. After she made herself a reputation as a comedienne, films drew her in from 1937 for character roles. From 1946, she starred in the low-budget 'Jiggs and Maggie' comedies with Joe Yule (qv). But the series was cut short by Yule's early death, and Riano returned to cameos.

1937: Tovarich. My Dear Miss Aldrich. You're a Sweetheart. 1938: Thanks for Everything. Strange Faces. Outside of Paradise. Spring Madness. Four's a Crowd. Nancy Drew, Detective. Men Are Such Fools. The Road to Reno. 1939: Wife, Husband and Friend. The Honeymoon's Over. Nancy Drew, Reporter. Disputed Passage. The Women. Bridal Suite. Nancy Drew

RICHARDS, Addison 1887–1964

Tall, brown-haired, narrow-eyed, solidly-built American actor with peaches and cream complexion and slugger's jaw. Seemingly facially cut out to play villains, he in fact rarely played a bad guy, and stuck to such solid citizens as attorneys, editors, senators, prison wardens and officers in various branches of the US armed forces. There were also some stern but kindly fathers, although he occasionally did prove that he could be a very shuddery villain indeed when he chose. Pursuance of this might have brought him bigger roles, but in most of his films he was well down the credits, surprising for an actor who was associate director of the Pasadena Playhouse before coming to Hollywood. A certain rigidity of expression, though, perhaps kept him from the first rank of character stars. Died from a heart attack.

1933: Lone Cowboy. Riot Squad. 1934: Babbitt. Beyond the Law. 365 Nights in Hollywood. The Case of the Howling Dog. The Girl from Missouri (GB: 100 Per Cent Pure). Gentlemen Are Born. British Agent. Let's Be Ritzy (GB: Millionaire for a Day). A Lost Lady (GB: Courageous). Love Captive. Our Daily Bread (GB: The Miracle of Life). The St Louis Kid (GB: A Perfect Weekend). 1935: Alias Mary Dow. The Crusades. Ceiling Zero. The Eagle's Brood. Freckles. Frisco Kid. Dinky. A Dog of Flanders. Front Page Woman. Home on the Range. Society Doctor. Sweet Music. G Men. Here Comes the Band. Little Big Shot. The White Cockatoo. Only Eight Hours. The Petrified Forest. 1936: Anthony Adverse. The Case of the Velvet Claws. China Clipper. Colleen. Hot Money. Black Legion. Bullets or Ballots. Man Hunt. Jailbreak. The Eagle's Brood. The Law in Her Hands. Public Enemy's Wife (GB: G-Man's Wife). Road Gang (GB: Injustice). Song of the Saddle. Sutter's Gold. Smart Blonde. Trailin' West (GB: On Secret Service). The Walking Dead. God's Country and the Woman. Draegerman Courage (GB: The Cave-In). 1937: The Barrier. Dance, Charlie, Dance. Wine, Women and Horses. Love is On the Air (GB: The Radio Murder Mystery). Her Husband's Secretary. Ready, Willing and Able. Empty Holsters. The Singing Marine. Mr Dodd Takes the Air. White Bondage. 1938: Accidents Will Happen. Alcatraz Island. Boys' Town. The Black Doll. Flight to Fame. The Devil's Party. Gateway. The Last Express. Prison Nurse. Valley of the Giants. 1939: Bad Lands. Exile Express. Andy Hardy Gets Spring Fever. The Gracie Allen Murder Case. I Was a Convict. Burn 'em Up O'Connor. Geronimo. Tell No Tales. When Tomorrow Comes. Nick Carter, Master Detective. The Mystery of the White Room. Inside Information. Off the Record. Espionage Agent. They All Come Out. They Made Her a Spy. Twelve Crowded Hours. Thunder Afloat. Whispering Enemies. 1940: Andy Hardy Meets Debutante. Boom Town. Charlie Chan in Panama. Edison, the Man. Gangs of Chicago. Public Deb No. 1. The Girl from Havana. Island of Doomed Men. The Man from Dakota (GB: Arouse and Beware). The Man from Montreal. The Lone Wolf Strikes. Northwest Passage. Give Us Wings. Arizona. Black Diamonds. Santa Fé Trail. Cherokee Strip (GB: Fighting Marshal). Flight Angels. Flight Command. My Little Chickadee. South to Karanga. Slightly Honorable. Moon Over Burma. Wyoming (GB: Bad Man of Wyoming). 1941: Back in the Saddle. Ball of Fire. Andy Hardy's Private Secretary. Badlands of Dakota. The Great Lie. Dive Bomber. I Wanted Wings. Design for Scandal. Sealed Lips. Her First Beau. Men of Boys' Town. Mutiny in the Arctic. Our Wife. International Squadron. Strawberry Blonde. The Trial of Mary Dugan. Sheriff of Tombstone. Tall, Dark and Handsome. Texas. They Died With Their Boots On. Western Union. 1942: A-Haunting We Will Go. A Close Call for Ellery Queen. Cowboy Serenade (GB: Serenade of the West). The Flying Tigers. Friendly Enemies. The Lady Has Plans. My Favorite Blonde. The Man With Two Lives. The Mystery of Marie Roget. Men of Texas (GB: Men of

Destiny). Pride of the Army. Pacific Rendezvous. Ship Ahoy! Secret Agent of Japan. Seven Days' Leave. Secret Enemies. Pride of the Yankees. Top Sergeant. Ridin' Down the Canyon. Underground Agent. War Dogs. 1943: Air Force. Always a Bridesmaid. Corvette K-225 (GB: The Nelson Touch). A Guy Named Joe. Destroyer. The Mystery of the Thirteenth Guest. Mystery Broadcast. Headin' for God's Country. Secrets of a Co-Ed (GB: Secret Witness). Smart Guy. The Mad Ghoul. Where Are Your Children? The Deerslayer. Salute to the Marines. 1944: Are These Our Parents? (GB: They Are Guilty). The Fighting Seabees. Follow the Boys. Barbary Coast Gent. Bordertown Trail. Grissly's Millions. Moon Over Las Vegas. The Mummy's Curse. Since You Went Away. The Sullivans. A Night of Adventure. Three Men in White. Roger Touhy, Gangster (GB: The Last Gangster). Three Little Sisters. Marriage is a Private Affair. 1945: Bells of Rosarita. Bewitched. The Chicago Kid. Black Market Babies. Divorce. The Adventures of Rusty. Betrayal from the East. Come Out Fighting. Danger Signal. I'll Remember April. Men in Her Diary. Rough, Tough and Ready. *The Last Installment. God is My Co-Pilot. Lady on a Train. The Master Key (serial). Spellbound. Duffy's Tavern. Strange Confession. The Shanghai Cobra. The Tiger Woman. Leave Her to Heaven. 1946: Angel On My Shoulder. Anna and the King of Siam. Courage of Lassie. Criminal Court. Dragonwyck. Don't Gamble With Strangers. The Hoodlum Saint. Step by Step. Renegades. Love Laughs at Andy Hardy. Secrets of a Sorority Girl (GB: Secret of Linda Hamilton). 1947: The Millerson Case. Monsieur Verdoux. Call Northside 777. Reaching from Heaven. 1948: Lulu Belle. The Saxon Charm. A Southern Yankee (GB: My Hero). 1949: Henry — The Rainmaker. Mighty Joe Young. Rustlers. 1950: Davy Crockett — Indian Scout. 1955: Illegal. High Society. Fort Yuma. 1956: The Broken Star. Fury at Gunsight Pass. The Fastest Gun Alive. Everything But the Truth. Reprisal! Walk the Proud Land. When Gangland Strikes. The Ten Commandments. 1957: Gunsight Ridge. Last of the Badmen. 1958: The Saga of Hemp Brown. 1959: The Oregon Trail. 1960: All the Fine Young Cannibals. The Dark at the Top of the Stairs. 1961: The Flight That Disappeared. Frontier Uprising. The Gambler Wore a Gun. 1962: Saintly Sinners. 1963: The Raiders. 1964: For Those Who Think Young.

RICKMAN, Alan 1946–

Light-haired, lizard-lidded, slim-faced, cynical-looking British actor who started life as a graphic designer, but threw it up at 26 to study acting at RADA. Although a classically trained actor whose roots are still in the theatre, Rickman proved on a belated arrival to films to make a superb, cruel, mocking villain, and has played other bad guys since, amid an assortment of alternately languorous and hypnotic roles. A dominant performer with hints of playfulness, detachment and ruthlessness in his characters' makeup, Rickman should have made his film debut five years earlier than he did, but a 1983 project with Dirk Bogarde and

Glenda Jackson was aborted at the last minute.

1988: Die Hard. The January Man. 1990: Quigley Down Under. 1991: Close My Eyes. Truly Madly Deeply. Robin Hood Prince of Thieves. Closet Land. 1992: Bob Roberts. 1993: Lost in the City of Light. Fallen Angels 2 (TV). 1994: Mesmer. 1995: An Awfully Big Adventure. The Poet. Sense and Sensibility.

RIDGELY, John
(J. Rea) 1909–1968
Plum-nosed American actor of set expression, dark hair and strikingly pale blue eyes. Born in Chicago, he was trained in industry but became interested in acting while working in California, and work at the Pasadena Community Playhouse led to a film contract with Warners. Ridgely's tall, faintly menacing figure moved into its best roles there in the 1940s, notably in Hawks's Air Force, and as Eddie Mars, chief menace to Humphrey Bogart, in Hawks's The Big Sleep. Declining to smaller roles, his later acting days were spent in stock and TV. Died from a heart ailment at 58.

1937: Larger Than Life. They Won't Forget. Submarine D-1. Kid Galahad. Hollywood Hotel. 1938: Forbidden Valley. The Invisible Menace. Torchy Gets Her Man. Crime School. Secrets of an Actress. The Patient in Room 18. He Couldn't Say No. Blondes at Work. Torchy Blane in Panama (GB: Trouble in Panama). Little Miss Thoroughbred. White Banners. When Were You Born? Nancy Drew — Detective. Cowboy from Brooklyn (GB: Romance and

Rhythm). My Bill. Going Places. Hard to Get. Broadway Musketeers. Boy Meets Girl. Western Trails. Garden of the Moon. Crime School. 1939: Angels Wash Their Faces. The Cowboy Quarterback. Torchy Runs for Mayor. Nancy Drew and the Hidden Staircase. Kid Nightingale. Dark Victory. Secret Service of the Air. Everybody's Hobby. Indianapolis Speedway (GB: Devil on Wheels). Women in the Wind. Torchy Plays with Dynamite. They Made Me a Criminal. You Can't Get Away with Murder. Nancy Drew, Reporter. King of the Underworld. Private Detective. Wings of the Navy. The Return of Dr X. The Kid from Kokomo (GB: Orphan of the Ring). Smashing the Money Ring. Naughty But Nice. Each Dawn I Die. The Roaring Twenties. Confessions of a Nazi Spy. Invisible Stripes. 1940: River's End. Father Is a Prince. The Man Who Talked Too Much. Three Cheers for the Irish. *Pony Express Days. Castle on the Hudson (GB: Years Without Days). Saturday's Children. Flight Angels. Torrid Zone. Brother Orchid. They Drive by Night (GB: The Road to Frisco). The Letter. The Fighting 69th. 'Til We Meet Again. Knute Rockne—All-American (GB: A Modern Hero). No Time for Comedy. The Lady With Red Hair. A Child Is Born. 1941: The Wagons Roll at Night. Million Dollar Baby. International Squadron. The Great Mr Nobody. The Man Who Came to Dinner. Here Comes Happiness. Strange Alibi. Navy Blues. Highway West. Steel Against the Sky. They Died With Their Boots On. Nine Lives Are Not Enough. The Bride Came COD. 1942: Bullet Scars. Wings for the Eagle. The Big Shot. Secret Enemies. Honeymoon for Three. Dangerously They Live. 1943: Air Force. Northern Pursuit. Arsenic and Old Lace. 1944: Destination Tokyo. Hollywood Canteen. The Doughgirls. 1945: Pride of the Marines (GB: Forever in Love). God Is My Co-Pilot. Danger Signal. 1946: The Big Sleep. My Reputation. Two Guys from Milwaukee (GB: Royal Flush). 1947: High Wall. The Man I Love. That's My Man/Will Tomorrow Ever Come? Nora Prentiss. That Way With Women. Cheyenne. Cry Wolf. Possessed. 1948: Night Winds. Luxury Liner. Sealed Verdict. Trouble Makers. The Iron Curtain. 1949: Command Decision. Once More, My Darling. Border Incident. Task Force. Tucson. South Sea Sinner (GB: East of Java). 1950: Backfire. The Lost Volcano/Bomba and the Lost Volcano. The Petty Girl (GB: Girl of the Year). Rookie Fireman. Saddle Tramp. Edge of Doom (GB: Stronger Than Fear). 1951: The Last Outpost. When the Redskins Rode. Thunder in God's Country. Half Angel. Al Jennings of Oklahoma. The Blue Veil. A Place in the Sun. When Worlds Collide. As You Were. 1952: Room for One More. The Greatest Show on Earth. The Outcasts of Poker Flat. Off Limits (GB: Military Policemen). Fort Osage.

RIDGES, Stanley 1891–1951

One of Hollywood's most underrated players, a tall, heavy-set British-born actor whose dark-brown wig hid thinning, greying hair, but suited his strong features and commanding presence. In America from 1920, he was mainly a stage actor until 1938, coming too late to Hollywood to make the impact he deserved, but offering some startlingly good performances, particularly in the dual role he inherited from Bela Lugosi in Black Friday.

1923: Success. 1930: *Let's Merge. *For Two Cents. 1934: Crime Without Passion. 1935: The Scoundrel. 1936: Sinner Take All. Winterset. 1937: Internes Can't Take Money (GB: You Can't Take Money). 1938: *They're Always Caught. Yellow Jack. There's That Woman Again (GB: What a Woman). The Mad Miss Manton. If I Were King. 1939: Let Us Live! I Stole a Million. Confessions of a Nazi Spy. Union Pacific. Each Dawn I Die. Silver on the Sage. Dust Be My Destiny. Espionage Agent. Nick Carter, Master Detective. 1940: Black Friday. 1941: Mr District Attorney. Sergeant York. They Died With Their Boots On. The Sea Wolf. 1942: To Be or Not To Be. Eyes in the Night. The Big Shot. Eagle Squadron. *Love is a Song. The Lady Is Willing. Air Force. 1943: Tarzan Triumphs. This Is the Army. 1944: The Sign of the Cross (new prologue to 1932 feature). The Story of Dr Wassell. The Master Race. Wilson. 1945: The Suspect. God Is My Co-Pilot. Captain Eddie. The Phantom Speaks. 1946: Mr Ace. Because of Him. Canyon Passage. 1947: Possessed. 1948: An Act of Murder. 1949: You're My Everything. Streets of Laredo. Thelma Jordon (GB: The File on Thelma Jordon). There's a Girl in My Heart. Task Force. 1950: No Way Out. Paid in Full. 1951: The Groom Wore Spurs.

RIGBY, Edward
(E. Coke) 1879–1951

Stocky (almost tubby), dark-haired, knowing-looking British character lead, who, after starting life in farming, led a full stage career before coming to films in his mid-fifties and becoming the British cinema's best-loved old buffer, often in near-star roles, for 18 years. Collarless, waistcoated and cloth-capped, his characters usually looked as if they had just left the factory after a hard day's work. Few were more adept at portraying the common man and, when one critic reviewed Rigby's wartime starring vehicle Salute John Citizen by writing 'There is no doubt at all that it is British', he might have been referring to Rigby himself.

1907: The Man Who Fell by the Way. 1910: The Blue Bird. 1934: Lorna Doone. 1935:

Gay Old Dog. Windfall. No Limit. Queen of Hearts. 1936: Land Without Music (US: Forbidden Music). This Green Hell. Crime Over London. Irish for Luck. Accused. The Heirloom Mystery. 1937: The Fatal Hour. Jump for Glory (US: When Thief Meets Thief). Mr Smith Carries On. The Show Goes On. Under a Cloud. Young and Innocent (US: The Girl Was Young). A Yank at Oxford. 1938: Keep Smiling (US: Smiling Along). The Ware Case. Yellow Sands. Kicking the Moon Around. 1939: Young Man's Fancy. The Four Just Men (US: The Secret Four). There Ain't No Justice. The Proud Valley. Poison Pen. The Stars Look Down. 1940: Convoy. Fingers. The Farmer's Wife. Sailors Don't Care. The Girl in the News. 1941: The Common Touch. Kipps (US: The Remarkable Mr Kipps). Penn of Pennsylvania (US: The Courageous Mr Penn). Major Barbara. 1942: Flying Fortress. Let the People Sing. Salute John Citizen. Went the Day Well? (US: 48 Hours). 1943: Get Cracking. They Met in the Dark. 1944: A Canterbury Tale. Don't Take It to Heart. The Agitator. 1945: I Live in Grosvenor Square (US: A Yank in London). Perfect Strangers (US: Vacation from Marriage). Murder in Reverse. 1946: Piccadilly Incident. Quiet Weekend. The Years Between. Daybreak. 1947: The Loves of Joanna Godden. Temptation Harbour. Easy Money. Green Fingers. The Courtneys of Curzon Street (US: The Courtney Affair). 1948: It's Hard to be Good. The Three Weird Sisters. Rover and Me. Noose (US: The Silk Noose). All Over the Town. 1949: Christopher Columbus. Don't Ever Leave Me. A Run for Your Money. 1950: The Happiest Days of Your Life. Double Confession. Tony Draws a Horse. What the Butler Saw. Into the Blue (US: The Man in the Dinghy). The Mudlark. 1951: Circle of Danger.

RILLA, Walter 1894–1980

Tall, eminent, rather grim-looking German actor with very black eyebrows. In international (mainly British) films from 1934, he played evil, sinister criminals and megalomaniac statesmen. Also directed one film and a number of television plays. His son is the director Wolf Rilla.

1922: Hanneles Himmelfahrt. 1923: Alles für Geld (US: Fortune's Fool). 1924: Der Sprung ins Leben. 1925: The Blackguard. 1926: Der Geiger von Florenz. 1927: Der gefährliche Alter. 1928: Revolutionshochzeit (US: The Last

Night). *Prinzessin Olala* (GB and US: *Princess Olala*). 1929: *Vererbte Triebe. Sajenko der Soviet.* 1930: *Kommt mit mir zum Rendezvous* (US: *Rendezvous*). 1931: *Zirkuz Leben/ Schatten der Manege* (US: *Circus Life*). *Die Männer um Lucie.* 1932: *Namensheirar.* 1933: *Ein Gewisser Herr Gran. La voce del sangue.* 1934: *Lady Windermeres Fächer* (GB and US: *Lady Windermere's Fan*). *The Scarlet Pimpernel.* 1935: *Abdul the Damned.* 1937: *Victoria the Great.* 1938: *Sixty Glorious Years* (US: *Queen of Destiny*). 1939: *At the Villa Rose* (US: *House of Mystery*). *Hell's Cargo. The Gang's All Here* (US: *The Amazing Mr Forrest*). *Black Eyes.* 1943: *The Adventures of Tartu* (US: *Tartu*). *Candlelight in Algeria.* 1944: *Mr Emmanuel.* 1946: *Lisbon Story.* 1948: *It's Hard to Be Good.* 1949: *Golden Salamander.* 1950: *State Secret* (US: *The Great Manhunt*). *My Daughter Joy* (US: *Operation X*). *Shadow of the Eagle.* 1951: *I'll Get You For This* (US: *Lucky Nick Cain*). 1952: *Venetian Bird* (US: *The Assassin*). 1953: *Desperate Moment. Senza bandiera. Star of India.* 1954: *The Green Buddha. Track the Man Down.* 1956: *The Gamma People. Die Bekenntnisse des Hochstaplers Felix Krull* (GB and US: *The Confessions of Felix Krull*). 1958: *The Girl Rosemarie.* 1959: *Scampolo.* 1960: *Song Without End.* 1961: *Der Fälscher von London. The Secret Ways. Cairo* (released 1963). 1962: *Room 13. The Testament of Dr Mabuse. The Wonderful World of the Brothers Grimm.* 1963: *Death Drums Along the River.* 1964: *Der Fall X701* (GB and US: *Frozen Alive*). *Die Todesstrahlen des Dr Mabuse* (US: *Death Rays of Dr Mabuse*). *Kennwort ... Reiter* (US: *The River Line*). *Code 7, Victim 5* (GB: *Victim Five*). 1965: *The Face of Fu Manchu. Die Rechnung — eiskalt serviert. The Four Keys.* 1966: *Martin Soldat.* 1967: *I giorni dell' ira* (GB and US: *Day of Anger*). 1970: *Der Teufel kam aus Akasava/The Devil Came from Akasava.* 1971: *Malpertuis.*

As director:
1951: *Behold the Man.*

RIPPER, Michael 1913–
Bright, jaunty, brown-haired British actor, mostly seen as minor crooks, comedy relief or oppressed little men until the mid-1950s, from which time he gradually became the favourite prey of the screen's monsters, particularly those from the Hammer vaults. As

if aggrieved by all this horror, his own film characters grew less good-tempered as he got older. Drifted away from the cinema and into the theatre in the late 1970s.

1935: *Twice Branded.* 1936: *Prison Breaker. A Touch of the Moon. Not So Dusty. To Catch a Thief. Nothing Like Publicity. Busman's Holiday. The Heirloom Mystery. All That Glitters.* 1937: *Pearls Bring Tears. Farewell to Cinderella. The Strange Adventures of Mr Smith. Fifty Shilling Boxer. Father Steps Out. Why Pick on Me? Racing Romance. Easy Riches.* 1938: *Merely Mr Hawkins. Paid in Error. Luck of the Navy. Romance à la Carte. If I Were Boss. Coming of Age. His Lordship Regrets. Weddings Are Wonderful. His Lordship Goes to Press. You're the Doctor. Miracles Do Happen.* 1939: *Blind Folly.* 1947: *Captain Boycott. The Dark Road.* 1948: *Noose* (US: *The Silk Noose*). *Oliver Twist.* 1949: *The History of Mr Polly. The Adventures of PC 49. The Rocking Horse Winner.* 1950: *The Undefeated. Your Witness* (US: *Eye Witness*). 1951: *Old Mother Riley's Jungle Treasure. A Case for PC 49. Lady Godiva Rides Again.* 1952: *Secret People. Derby Day* (US: *Four Against Fate*). *Treasure Hunt. Alf's Baby. Folly to be Wise. Appointment in London.* 1953: *The Story of Gilbert and Sullivan* (US: *The Great Gilbert and Sullivan*). *The Intruder. Blood Orange.* 1954: *The Rainbow Jacket. The Belles of St Trinian's. A Tale of Three Women. The Sea Shall Not Have Them.* 1955: *Geordie* (US: *Wee Geordie*). *Secret Venture. The Constant Husband. Richard III.* 1984. 1956: *Reach for the Sky. The Green Man.* **A Man on the Beach. Yield to the Night* (US: *Blonde Sinner*). *X the Unknown.* 1957: *The Steel Bayonet. These Dangerous Years* (US: *Dangerous Youth*). *Not Wanted on Voyage. Woman in a Dressing Gown. The One That Got Away. Blue Murder at St Trinian's. The Naked Truth* (US: *Your Past is Showing!*). *Quatermass II* (US: *Enemy from Space*). 1958: *The Changing Years. Up the Creek. The Camp on Blood Island. I Only Arsked! The Revenge of Frankenstein. Further Up the Creek. Girls at Sea.* 1959: *The Man Who Could Cheat Death. Bobbikins. The Ugly Duckling. The Mummy. Sink the Bismarck!* 1960: *Jackpot. The Pure Hell of St Trinian's. Dead Lucky. Macbeth. Circle of Deception. The Brides of Dracula.* 1961: *The Curse of the Werewolf. Petticoat Pirates. A Matter of WHO. The Pirates of Blood River.* 1962: *The Amorous Prawn* (US: *The Amorous Mr Prawn*). *Captain Clegg* (US:

Night Creatures). *The Punch and Judy Man. The Phantom of the Opera. The Prince and the Pauper. Out of the Fog. A Prize of Arms. Two Left Feet.* 1963: *The Scarlet Blade* (US: *The Crimson Blade*). *What a Crazy World. The Devil-Ship Pirates.* 1964: *The Curse of the Mummy's Tomb. Every Day's a Holiday* (US: *Seaside Swingers*). *The Secret of Blood Island.* 1965: *The Spy Who Came in from the Cold. The Plague of the Zombies. Rasputin — The Mad Monk. The Reptile.* 1966: *Where the Bullets Fly. The Great St Trinian's Train Robbery.* 1967: *The Mummy's Shroud. The Deadly Bees. Torture Garden.* 1968: *Inspector Clouseau. The Lost Continent. Dracula Has Risen from the Grave.* 1969: *Moon Zero Two. Mumsy, Nanny, Sonny and Girly.* 1970: *Taste the Blood of Dracula. The Scars of Dracula.* 1972: *The Creeping Flesh. That's Your Funeral.* 1973: *No Sex, Please—We're British. Le pétomane* (released 1979). 1974: *Legend of the Werewolf.* 1977: *The Prince and the Pauper* (US: *Crossed Swords*). 1978: *Sammy's Super T-Shirt.* 1980: *Danger on Dartmoor.* 1985: *No Surrender.* 1992: *Revenge of Billy the Kid.*

RISDON, Elisabeth 1887–1958
Delicately pretty, doe-eyed, light-haired star of British silent films, with the appearance of a startled fawn. She married her director, the American George Loane Tucker, and went with him when he returned to Hollywood in 1917. He died at 49, leaving his 34-year-old widow to continue her acting career. She eventually turned up in Hollywood in the mid-1930s, where she immediately began playing grey-haired mothers, largely creatures whose docile exteriors sometimes concealed backbones of steel, or who exploded into fury when pushed too far. She retired in 1952, and died from a brain haemorrhage six years later, the same year as the death of her second husband, actor Brandon Evans.

1913: *Bridegroom Beware. Maria Marten: Or, The Murder in the Red Barn.* 1914: *The Cup Final Mystery. The Finger of Destiny.* **Inquisitive Ike. The Loss of the Birkenhead. Beautiful Jim* (US: *The Price of Justice*). *The Bells of Rheims. Black-Eyed Susan* (US: *The Battling British*). *It's a Long, Long Way to Tipperary. The Suicide Club.* **The Courage of a Coward.* **The Sound of Her Voice. Her Luck in London. The Idol of Paris.* 1915: **Gilbert Gets Tigeritis.* **There's Good in Everyone. Honeymoon for

Three. Midshipman Easy. London's Yellow Peril. Florence Nightingale. From Shopgirl to Duchess. Her Nameless Child. Another Man's Wife. Grip. The Christian. Home. Charity Ann. Fine Feathers. A Will of Her Own. Love in a Wood. 1916: Driven (US: Desperation). Motherlove (US: Motherly Love). Meg the Lady. Esther. The Morals of Weybury (US: The Hypocrites). The Mother of Dartmoor. The Princess of Happy Chance. The Manxman. A Mother's Influence. 1917: Smith. 1919: *A Star Overnight. 1935: Crime and Punishment. Guard That Girl. 1936: Craig's Wife. The Final Hour. Don't Gamble With Love. Lady of Secrets. The King Steps Out. Theodora Goes Wild. 1937: Dead End. Make Way for Tomorrow. Mountain Justice. They Won't Forget. The Woman I Love. 1938: Cowboy from Brooklyn (GB: Romance and Rhythm). Mannequin. Mad About Music. My Bill. The Affairs of Annabel. Girls on Probation. Tom Sawyer, Detective. 1939: Girl from Mexico. The Great Man Votes. Five Came Back. Full Confession. The Adventures of Huckleberry Finn. Disputed Passage. The Forgotten Woman. The Man Who Dared. Mexican Spitfire. The Roaring Twenties. Sorority House (GB: That Girl from College). I Am Not Afraid. 1940: Abe Lincoln in Illinois (GB: Spirit of the People). The Howards of Virginia (GB: The Tree of Liberty). Honeymoon Deferred. Let's Make Music. Ma, He's Making Eyes at Me. Sing, Dance, Plenty Hot (GB: Melody Girl). The Man Who Wouldn't Talk. Saturday's Children. Mexican Spitfire Out West. Slightly Tempted. 1941: Footlight Fever. High Sierra. Mexican Spitfire's Baby. Mr Dynamite. Nice Girl? 1942. Jail House Blues. The Man Who Returned to Life. The Lady is Willing. Mexican Spitfire at Sea. Are Husbands Necessary? I Live on Danger. Journey for Margaret. Mexican Spitfire Sees a Ghost. Paris Calling. Reap the Wild Wind. Random Harvest. Mexican Spitfire's Elephant. White Cargo. 1943: The Amazing Mrs Holiday. Higher and Higher. Lost Angel. Never a Dull Moment. Mexican Spitfire's Blessed Event. 1944: The Canterville Ghost. Cobra Woman. Blonde Fever. In the Meantime, Darling. Tall in the Saddle. Weird Woman. Grissly's Millions. 1945: The Fighting Guardsman. Mama Loves Papa. A Song for Miss Julie. The Unseen. 1946: Lover Come Back. Roll On, Texas Moon. The Walls Came Tumbling Down. They Made Me a Killer. The Shocking Miss Pilgrim. 1947: The Egg and I. High Wall. Life With Father. Mourning Becomes Electra. The Romance of Rosy Ridge. 1948: Bodyguard. The Bride Goes Wild. Every Girl Should Be Married. Sealed Verdict. 1949: Down Dakota Way. 1950: Bunco Squad. Guilty of Treason (GB: Treason). Hills of Oklahoma. The Milkman. The Secret Fury. Sierra. 1951: Bannerline. It's a Big Country. In Old Amarillo. My True Story. 1952: Scaramouche.

RITTER, Thelma 1905–1969

With a face best described as homely, brown hair scruffed back (you could almost see the curlers), plaintive, nasal tones and a figure usually tied up like a sack of potatoes, Brooklyn's Thelma Ritter, arms akimbo, ruined more than one star's chance of being the thing most remembered from a film.

She was a character comedienne on radio who quickly established herself in top-billed supporting roles in post-war years, being nominated six times for the Best Supporting Actress Oscar between 1950 and 1962 without winning. Died from a heart attack.

1947: Miracle on 34th Street (GB: The Big Heart). Call Northside 777. 1949: A Letter to Three Wives. City Across the River. Father Was a Fullback. 1950: Perfect Strangers (GB: Too Dangerous to Love). All About Eve. I'll Get By. 1951: The Mating Season. The Model and the Marriage Broker. As Young As You Feel. 1952: With a Song in My Heart. 1953: Titanic. Pick Up on South Street. The Farmer Takes a Wife. 1954: Rear Window. 1955: Lucy Gallant. The Late Christopher Bean (TV. GB: cinemas). Daddy Long Legs. 1956: The Proud and Profane. 1959: A Hole in the Head. Pillow Talk. 1961: The Misfits. The Second Time Around. 1962: Bird Man of Alcatraz. How the West Was Won. 1963: A New Kind of Love. For Love or Money. Move Over, Darling. 1965: Boeing-Boeing. 1967: The Incident. 1968: What's So Bad About Feeling Good?

ROBARDS, Jason Sr 1892–1963

Erect, dark-haired, rather sad-looking American actor, father of Jason Robards Jr. He achieved theatrical prominence before coming to Hollywood silents as a leading man. With the advent of sound, he soon slipped into character roles, making dozens for RKO in the 1940s as figures of some authority—with the occasional villain misusing authority thrown in. Died from a heart attack.

1921: The Land of Hope. The Gilded Lily. 1925: Paris. Stella Maris. 1926: The Cohens and the Kellys. The Third Degree. Footloose Widows. Honeymoon Express. 1927: Hearts of Maryland. A Bird in the Hand. Hills of Kentucky. White Flannels. Tracked by the Police. Irish Hearts. Jaws of Steel. Wild Geese. Streets of Shanghai. Polly of the Movies. 1928: Casey Jones. The Death Ship. On Trial. 1929: Gamblers. Isle of Lost Ships. Trial Marriage. Paris (and 1925 film). *A Bird in Hand. Some Mother's Boy. Pain. Flying Marine. 1930: Peacock Alley. Crazy That Way. The Last Dance. Abraham Lincoln. Jazz Cinderella. Lightnin'. *Trifles. Sisters. 1931: Charlie Chan Carries On. Subway Express. Salvation Nell (GB: Men Women Love). Ex-Bad Boy. Caught Plastered. Full of Notions. Law of the Tongs. 1932: Discarded Lovers. Docks of San Francisco. Unholy Love (GB: Deceit). Klondike. The White Eagle. The Pride of the Legion. The Conquerors. Slightly Married. 1933: Strange Adventure. Corruption. Only Yesterday. The Way to Love. Dance Hall Hostess. The Devil's Mate (GB: He Knew Too Much). Ship of Wanted Men. Carnival Lady. Public Stenographer (GB: Private Affairs). 1934: All of Me. *Super Snooper. Broadway Bill (GB: Strictly Confidential). The Merry Widow. Woman Unafraid. Take the Stand (GB: The Great Radio Mystery). The Crimson Romance. One Exciting Adventure. A Woman Condemned. Burn 'Em Up Barnes (GB: Devils on Wheels). 1935: The President Vanishes (GB: Strange Conspiracy). The Last Days of Pompeii. The Fighting Marines (serial). Break of Hearts. Ladies Crave Excitement. The Crusades. The Miracle Rider (serial). 1936: The White Legion. San Francisco. Laughing at Death (GB: Laughing at Trouble). 1937: Sweethearts of the Navy. Damaged Lives. The Firefly. Zorro Rides Again (serial). The Man Who Cried Wolf. 1938: The Adventures of Marco Polo. Clipped Wings. Cipher Bureau. Flight to Fame. Little Tough Guy. 1939: Mystery Plane. The Mad Empress/Juarez and Maximilian (GB: Carlotta. The Mad Empress). Stunt Pilot. Range War. Sky Patrol. Scouts to the Rescue (serial). Zorro's Fighting Legion (serial). Danger Flight (GB: Scouts of the Air). I Stole a Million. 1940: The Fatal Hour (GB: Mr Wong at Headquarters). I Love You Again. 1941: San Antonio Rose. 1942: Joan of Ozark (GB: Queen of Spies). Give Out, Sisters. Silver Queen. 1944: Bermuda Mystery. Sing a Jingle (GB: Lucky Days). Mademoiselle Fifi. The Master Race. Music in Manhattan. 1945: What a Blonde. Betrayal from the East. Isle of the Dead. Ding Dong Williams (GB: Melody Maker). *Let's Go Stepping. *It Shouldn't Happen to a Dog. Man Alive. Wanderer of the Wasteland. The Falcon in San Francisco. Radio Stars on Parade. Johnny Angel. A Game of Death. *What, No Cigarettes? Dick Tracy (GB: Split Face). 1946: The Falcon's Alibi. Bedlam. Step by Step. Vacation in Reno. Criminal Court. Deadline at Dawn. *Twin Husbands. *I'll Take Milk. *I'll Build It Myself. The Falcon's Adventure. *Follow That Music. The Bamboo Blonde. 1947: *Do or Diet. The Farmer's Daughter. Desperate. Dick Tracy's Dilemma (GB: Mark of the Claw). A Likely Story. Riffraff. Seven Keys to Baldpate. Trail Street. Under the Tonto Rim. Thunder Mountain. Wild Horse Mesa.

Born to Kill (GB: Lady of Deceit). 1948: Fighting Father Dunne. Guns of Hate. If You Knew Susie. Mr Blandings Builds His Dream House. Race Street. Return of the Bad Men. Smoky Mountain Melody. Son of God's Country. Variety Time. Impact. Western Heritage. 1949: Alaska Patrol. Haunted Trails. Feudin' Rhythm (GB: Ace Lucky). Post Office Investigator. Riders of the Whistling Pines. Rimfire. South of Death Valley (GB: River of Poison). Horsemen of the Sierras (GB: Remember Me). 1950: The Second Woman (GB: Ellen). Western Pacific Agent (narrator only). 1951: Flying Leathernecks. 1961: Wild in the Country.

ROBINSON, Andrew or Andy 1942–
Whippily built, baby-faced, cold-eyed American actor with fair, curly hair. He hasn't smiled a lot in a film career that began in a big way as the punk who menaced Clint Eastwood throughout *Dirty Harry*, but hasn't quite found his footing in the years that followed. He tends not to appear in run-of-the-mill subjects and has been in some controversial TV movies as well as a wide variety of drama, horror and adventure films.

1970: The Catcher (TV). 1971: Dirty Harry. 1973: Charley Varrick. 1974: The Family Kovack (TV). 1975: A Part Time Wife/A Woman for All Men. The Drowning Pool. Mackintosh and TJ. Someone I Touched (TV). 1976: Lanigan's Rabbi (TV). 1980: The Reward (TV). 1985: Mask. Not My Kid (video). 1986: Cobra. The Verne Miller Story (TV). 1987: Hellraiser. Shoot to Kill (GB: Deadly Pursuit). 1990: Rock Hudson (TV). 1991: Prime Target. Into the Badlands (cable TV). Dead on Target. 1992: Fatal Charm (cable TV). Trancers III: Deth Lives. Telling Secrets (TV). Criminal Behavior (TV). 1994: There Goes My Baby (filmed 1992).

ROBSON, May
(Mary Robison) 1858–1942
One of Australia's most valuable exports to Hollywood: a light-haired, round-as-a-dumpling lady who took to acting when widowed at 25, and soon found herself in demand for strong-willed character roles. She came to Hollywood from the stage for good in 1931 to play very human doyennes from both sides of the tracks, who had a flinty exterior and usually took a firm hand

with the juveniles, but were good for a tear at the end. Had a few leading roles in an appropriate batch of titles: *Lady for a Day, You Can't Buy Everything, Grand Old Girl* and *Granny Get Your Gun*. For her Apple Annie in *Lady for a Day*, she was nominated for an Oscar.

*1915: How Molly Made Good. 1916: A Night Out. 1919: A Broadway Saint. His Bridal Night. The Lost Battalion. 1926: Pals in Paradise. 1927: A Harp in Hock. Rubber Tires. The Angel of Broadway. The King of Kings. Chicago. Turkish Delight. The Rejuvenation of Aunt Mary. 1928: The Blue Danube. 1931: The She-Wolf of Wall Street (later and GB: Mother's Millions). Red-Headed Woman. 1932: Letty Lynton. Strange Interlude (GB: Strange Interval). Little Orphan Annie. Two Against the World. If I Had a Million. *The Engineer's Daughter. 1933: Reunion in Vienna. Dinner at Eight. Broadway to Hollywood (GB: Ring Up the Curtain). Solitaire Man. Dancing Lady. Beauty for Sale (GB: Beauty). One Man's Journey. Alice in Wonderland. Lady for a Day. Men Must Fight. The White Sister. 1934: Straight is the Way. You Can't Buy Everything. Lady by Choice. 1935: Grand Old Girl. Vanessa: Her Love Story. Mills of the Gods. Three Kids and a Queen (GB: The Baxter Millions). Strangers All. Anna Karenina. Reckless. Age of Indiscretion. 1936: The Captain's Kid. Wife vs Secretary. Rainbow on the River. 1937: A Star is Born. Woman in Distress. The Perfect Specimen. Top of the Town. 1938: The Texans. Bringing Up Baby. The Adventures of Tom Sawyer. Four Daughters. 1939: Yes, My Darling Daughter. The Kid from Kokomo (GB: The Orphan of the Ring). Daughters Courageous. That's Right, You're Wrong. Nurse Edith Cavell. Four Wives. They Made Me a Criminal. 1940: The Texas Rangers Ride Again. Irene. Granny Get Your Gun. 1941: Four Mothers. Million Dollar Baby. Playmates. 1942: Joan of Paris.*

ROSE, George 1920–1988
Stocky, fuzzily dark-haired British actor with ready grin, adept at characters whose surface bonhomie dissolved speedily into panic at the first signs of crisis. He turned from farming to acting in his mid-twenties and popped up regularly in British films of the 1950s. After 1961, he was seen mainly in America, principally on the New York stage. Killed in a car crash.

1952: The Pickwick Papers. The Beggar's Opera. 1953: Grand National Night (US: Wicked Wife). The Square Ring. 1954: Devil on Horseback. The Sea Shall Not Have Them. The Good Die Young. Track the Man Down. 1955: John and Julie. The Night My Number Came Up. Port of Escape. 1956: Reach for the Sky. The Last Wagon. The Long Arm (US: The Third Key). The Good Companions. Brothers in Law. Sailor Beware! (US: Panic in the Parlor). 1957: No Time for Tears. The Shiralee. Barnacle Bill (US: All at Sea). 1958: A Tale of Two Cities. Law and Disorder. A Night to Remember. Cat and Mouse/The Desperate Ones. 1959: Jet Storm. The Heart of a Man. The Devil's Disciple. Jack the Ripper. The Flesh and the Fiends (US: Mania). Macbeth. Desert Mice. 1961: No Love for Johnnie. 1964: Hamlet. 1966: Hawaii. 1967: The Pink Jungle. 1969: The Tree. 1971: A New Leaf. 1973: From the Mixed-Up Files of Mrs Basil E Frankweiler (GB: The Hideaways). 1982: The Pirates of Penzance. 1988: Pound Puppies and the Legend of Big Paw (voice only).

ROSENBLOOM, (Slapsie) Maxie
1903–1976
Big, friendly, dark-haired, plug-ugly American boxer and, later, actor. A cross between Mike Mazurki and Dan Seymour (qv), his gnarled features were a legacy of many years in the ring, during which he became light-heavyweight champion of the world in 1932, a title he held for three years. In films, he played dim and sometimes friendly hoodlums and, after he left Warners, where he had some of his best roles, there was a brief attempt to make him and Max

Baer (strangely, another boxer) into a low-budget comedy team. The cumulative effect of batterings in the ring took its toll in later years and he was much in hospital after 1970, dying from Paget's Disease.

1933: Mr Broadway. King for a Night. 1936: Muss 'Em Up (GB: House of Fate). Kelly the Second. 1937: Nothing Sacred. Two Wise Maids. Big City. The Kid Comes Back (GB: Don't Pull Your Punches). 1938: The Amazing Dr Clitterhouse. Gangs of New York. The Crowd Roars. His Exciting Night. Mr Moto's Gamble. Submarine Patrol. 1939: Each Dawn I Die. The Kid from Kokomo (GB: The Orphan of the Ring). Naughty But Nice. Private Detective. 20,000 Men a Year. Women in the Wind. 1940: Grandpa Goes to Town. Passport to Alcatraz. Public Deb No. 1/Elsa Maxwell's Public Deb No. 1. *Sockaroo. 1941: Harvard, Here I Come (GB: Here I Come). Louisiana Purchase. The Stork Pays Off. 1942: The Boogie Man Will Get You. Smart Alecks. To the Shores of Tripoli. The Yanks Are Coming. 1943: Here Comes Kelly. My Son the Hero. Swing Fever. 1944: Allergic to Love. Crazy Knights. Follow the Boys. Ghost Crazy. Irish Eyes Are Smiling. Night Club Girl. Slick Chick. Three of a Kind. 1945: Men in Her Diary. Penthouse Rhythm. Trouble Chasers. 1948: Hazard. 1950: Mr Universe. *Two Roaming Champs. Skipalong Rosenbloom. 1951: *Wine, Women and Bong. *The Champ Steps Out. 1952: *Rootin' Tootin' Tenderfeet. 1955: Abbott and Costello Meet the Keystone Kops. Guys and Dolls. 1956: Hollywood or Bust. 1958: I Married a Monster from Outer Space. 1959: The Beat Generation. 1960: The Bellboy. 1962: †Two Guys Abroad. 1963: Follow the Boys (and 1944 film of same title). 1966: The Spy in the Green Hat (TV. GB: cinemas). Don't Worry, We'll Think of a Title. 1967: Cottonpickin' Chickenpickers. 1969: My Side of the Mountain.

† Unreleased

ROSSINGTON, Norman 1928–
Stocky, bouncy British actor with dark, curly hair. He made his name as one of the bone-idle soldiers in the TV comedy series *The Army Game*, and was thereafter frequently seen in films, almost always as the ebullient but none-too-bright sidekick of the hero, or an inept comic crook. An expert at working-class accents from broad cockney to his native Liverpudlian.

1955: Keep It Clean. 1956: Three Men in a Boat. 1957: The Long Haul. Strangers' Meeting. The One That Got Away. Saint Joan. 1958: A Night to Remember. I Only Arsked! Carry On Sergeant. 1959: Carry On Nurse. The League of Gentlemen. 1960: Doctor in Love. Saturday Night and Sunday Morning. 1961: No Love for Johnnie. Carry On Regardless. 1962: Go to Blazes. Lawrence of Arabia. The Longest Day. Crooks Anonymous. 1963: The Comedy Man. Nurse on Wheels. 1964: A Hard Day's Night. Daylight Robbery. 1965: Cup Fever. Joey Boy. Those Magnificent Men in Their Flying Machines. 1966: The Wrong Box. Double Trouble. Tobruk. 1968: The Charge of the Light Brigade. Negatives. 1969: The Adventures of Gerard. Two Gentlemen Sharing. 1970: The Rise and Rise of Michael Rimmer. *Simon, Simon. The Engagement. 1971: Man in the Wilderness. Young Winston. 1972: Death Line/Raw Meat. Go for a Take. 1973: Digby the Biggest Dog in the World. 1976: Joseph Andrews. 1979: The Prisoner of Zenda. SOS Titanic. 1980: Masada (TV. GB: cinemas (abridged), as The Antagonists). 1982: House of the Long Shadows. 1990: The Krays. 1991: 'Let Him Have It'.

ROSSITER, Leonard 1926–1984
Lugubrious, beaky, dark-haired British player, established on the stage as a straight dramatic actor before a succession of situation comedy television series in the 1970s revealed his talents as a comic star, mostly as complaining charlatans. Through twisted mouth, he played it straight and got the laughs—continuing to win leading roles in the theatre although he did not emerge as a consistent star attraction at the cinema box-office. Died from a heart attack in the interval of a play.

1958: The Two-Headed Spy. 1962: A Kind of Loving. This Sporting Life. 1963: Billy Liar! A Jolly Bad Fellow. 1965: King Rat. 1966: The Wrong Box. Hotel Paradiso. The Witches (US: The Devil's Own). Deadlier Than the Male. The Whisperers. 1967: Deadfall. 1968: 2001: A Space Odyssey. Oliver! Otley. Diamonds for Breakfast. 1973: Luther. Butley. *Le pétomane (released 1979). 1975: Barry Lyndon. 1976: The Pink Panther Strikes Again. Voyage of the Damned. 1978: *The Waterloo Bridge Handicap. 1980: Rising Damp. 1982: Britannia Hospital. Trail of the Pink Panther. 1985: Water.

ROYLE, Selena 1904–1983
Gracious-looking, fair-haired American actress with beautiful light-skinned complexion. After a long stage career, she was drafted into Hollywood in the war years to play mothers. Although she proved she could handle superbly a major role such as the mother of *The Sullivans*, she gained a reputation for being outspoken about anomalies in the film city, and never rose above supporting roles. Married (second) to fellow character player George Renavent (1896–1969), she lived in Mexico after 1955, and later wrote *A Gringa's Guide to Mexican Cooking* there.

1932: The Misleading Lady. 1943: Stage Door Canteen. *Paddy Rollers. 1944: Main Street After Dark. The Sullivans. Mrs Parkington. Thirty Seconds Over Tokyo. 1945: This Man's Navy. The Harvey Girls. 1946: The Green Years. Courage of Lassie. Gallant Journey. No Leave, No Love. Night and Day. Till the End of Time. Summer Holiday (released 1948). 1947: Cass Timberlane. The Romance of Rosy Ridge. Wild Harvest. 1948: Smart Woman. You Were Meant for Me. A Date With Judy. Joan of Arc. Moonrise. 1949: Bad Boy. My Dream Is Yours. You're My Everything. The Heiress. 1950: The Big Hangover. Branded. The Damned Don't Cry. 1951: Come Fill the Cup. He Ran All the Way. 1953: Robot Monster. 1955: Murder Is My Beat.

RUGGLES, Charles 1886–1970
Small, sandy-haired, moustachioed American comic actor, all huffle and snuffle and an amusingly offhand style: a likeable asset to a film whether as support or star, and especially popular as the dapper but hen-pecked husband in a very successful series of comedies with big Mary Boland as his wife. Brother of director Wesley Ruggles. Died from cancer.

1915: Peer Gynt. The Reform Candidate. The Majesty of the Law. 1923: The Heart Raider. 1928: *Wives Etc. 1929: The Lady Lies. Gentlemen of the Press. The Battle of Paris. 1930: *The Hot Air Merchants. *The Family Next Door. Queen High. Roadhouse Nights. Young Man of Manhattan. Charley's Aunt. 1931: The Girl Habit. Honor Among Lovers. Beloved Bachelor. The Smiling Lieutenant. This Is the Night. 1932: Husband's Holiday. Make Me a Star. One Hour with You. 70,000

RUYSDAEL, Basil 1888–1960
Relaxed, wise-looking, brown-haired American actor, often as judges, lawyers and senior officers. A prominent opera singer (he appeared with Caruso) in his younger days, Ruysdael turned first to straight acting, then became a radio announcer in the 1930s. In post-war years, he moved to Hollywood character roles to play out the remainder of his long and varied career.

Witnesses. Evenings for Sale. Madame Butterfly. Love Me Tonight. This Reckless Age. The Night of June 13. Trouble in Paradise. If I Had a Million. 1933: Mama Loves Papa. Murders in the Zoo. Alice in Wonderland. Melody Cruise. Girl Without a Room. Goodbye Love. Terror Aboard. 1934: Murder in the Private Car (GB: Murder on the Runaway Train). Six of a Kind. The Pursuit of Happiness. Friends of Mr Sweeney. Melody in Spring. 1935: No More Ladies. People Will Talk. Ruggles of Red Gap. The Big Broadcast of 1936. 1936: Wives Never Know. Early to Bed. Anything Goes. Mind Your Own Business. Hearts Divided. Yours for the Asking. The Preview Murder Mystery. 1937: Exclusive. Turn off the Moon. 1938: Service De Luxe. Bringing Up Baby. His Exciting Night. Breaking the Ice. 1939: Sudden Money. Yes, My Darling Daughter. Invitation to Happiness. Boy Trouble. Balalaika. Night Work. 1940: Maryland. The Farmer's Daughter. Opened by Mistake. Public Deb No. 1. No Time for Comedy. 1941: Model Wife. The Invisible Woman. The Parson of Panamint. The Perfect Snob. Go West, Young Lady. 1942: Friendly Enemies. 1943: Dixie Dugan. 1944: Our Hearts Were Young and Gay. *The Shining Future. The Doughgirls. Three is a Family. 1945: Bedside Manner. Incendiary Blonde. 1946: The Perfect Marriage. A Stolen Life. Gallant Journey. 1947: It Happened on Fifth Avenue. Ramrod. 1948: Give My Regards to Broadway. 1949: The Loveable Cheat. Look for the Silver Lining. 1958: The Male Animal (TV). Girl on the Subway (TV. GB: cinemas). 1961: All in a Night's Work. The Pleasure of His Company. The Parent Trap. 1963: Son of Flubber. Papa's Delicate Condition. 1964: I'd Rather Be Rich. 1966: The Ugly Dachshund. Follow Me, Boys!

RUMANN, Siegfried or Sig 1884–1967
Truculent, crop-haired, walrus-like German-born actor often seen as eccentric professors, idiot saboteurs and moronic megalomaniacs. He never lost the thick continental accent that was part of his splutteringly excitable personality and helped him make a brilliant and explosive foil for comedians with wild senses of humour, notably The Marx Brothers, Jack Benny and Jerry Lewis. His pop eyes and manic smile were never seen to better advantage than as 'Concentration Camp' Erhardt in *To*

Be or Not To Be. Surname sometimes spelled Ruman. Died from a heart attack.

1929: The Royal Box. 1934: Servants' Entrance. The World Moves On. Black Moon. Marie Galante. 1935: East of Java (GB: Java Seas). Under Pressure. Spring Tonic. The Farmer Takes a Wife. The Wedding Night. A Night at the Opera. 1936: The Beloved Rogue. The Bold Caballero. The Princess Comes Across. I Loved a Soldier. 1937: Seventh Heaven. Midnight Taxi. On the Avenue. Thin Ice (GB: Lovely to Look At). Think Fast, Mr Moto. This Is My Affair (GB: His Affair). Love Under Fire. Lancer Spy. Heidi. Maytime. Thank You, Mr Moto. The Great Hospital Mystery. A Day at the Races. Nothing Sacred. Dead Yesterday. The Bold Caballero (GB: The Bold Cavalier). 1938: I'll Give a Million. Paradise for Three (GB: Romance for Three). Suez. The Great Waltz. The Saint in New York. Girls on Probation. 1939: Ninotchka. Honolulu. Remember? Only Angels Have Wings. Never Say Die. Confessions of a Nazi Spy. 1940: Dr Ehrlich's Magic Bullet (GB: The Story of Dr Ehrlich's Magic Bullet). Outside the 3-Mile Limit (GB: Mutiny on the Seas). Four Sons. I Was an Adventuress. Comrade X. Bitter Sweet. Victory. 1941: So Ends Our Night. Love Crazy. Shining Victory. This Woman Is Mine. The Man Who Lost Himself. World Premiere. That Uncertain Feeling. The Wagons Roll at Night. 1942: Crossroads. Remember Pearl Harbor. Enemy Agents Meet Ellery Queen (GB: The Lido Mystery). To Be or Not To Be. China Girl. Berlin Correspondent. Desperate Journey. 1943: Tarzan Triumphs. They Came To Blow Up America. Sweet Rosie O'Grady. The Song of Bernadette. Government Girl. 1944: The Hitler Gang. It Happened Tomorrow. Summer Storm. House of Frankenstein. 1945: The Dolly Sisters. A Royal Scandal (GB: Czarina). The Men in Her Diary. She Went to the Races. 1946: A Night in Casablanca. Faithful in My Fashion. Night and Day. 1947: Mother Wore Tights. 1948: Give My Regards to Broadway. The Emperor Waltz. If You Knew Susie. 1949: Border Incident. 1950: Father Is a Bachelor. 1951: On the Riviera. 1952: The World in His Arms. O. Henry's Full House (GB: Full House). Ma and Pa Kettle on Vacation (GB: Ma and Pa Kettle Go to Paris). 1953: Houdini. Stalag 17. The Glenn Miller Story. 1954: White Christmas. Living It Up. Three-Ring Circus. 1955: Many Rivers to Cross. Spy Chasers. Carolina Cannonball. 1957: The Wings of

1929: The Cocoanuts. 1934: Dealers in Death (narrator only). 1949: Pinky. Colorado Territory. Come to the Stable. Thelma Jordon (GB: The File on Thelma Jordon). The Doctor and the Girl. Task Force. 1950: One Way Street. Broken Arrow. Gambling House. High Lonesome. The Dungeon. Raton Pass (GB: Canyon Pass). 1951: The Scarf. My Forbidden Past. Half Angel. People Will Talk. Boots Malone. 1952: Hoodlum Empire. Carrie. 1954: The Shanghai Story. Prince Valiant. The Violent Men (GB: Rough Company). Davy Crockett—King of the Wild Frontier. 1955: Pearl of the South Pacific. Blackboard Jungle. Diane. 1956: Jubal. These Wilder Years. 1958: The Last Hurrah. 1959: The Horse Soldiers. 1960: The Story of Ruth.

RYAN, John P. 1938–
Full-faced, frog-eyed, light-haired American actor with distinctive thin mouth and pale eyes. This 'Irish'-style countenance

carried such natural toothy menace that he has often been cast as especially mean and vicious criminals whose calm exteriors barely concealed the explosive violence beneath. But he also did extremely well when given the rare opportunity to play for sympathy – as with the leading role of the father to the monster baby in the *It's Alive* films. Hasn't been seen often enough in mainline films in recent times, most of his movies being of the straight-to-video type.

1967: The Tiger Makes Out. 1968: What's So Bad About Feeling Good? A Lovely Way to Die (GB: A Lovely Way to Go). 1970: Five Easy Pieces. 1972: The Legend of Nigger Charley. Shamus. The King of Marvin Gardens. 1973: Cops and Robbers. Dillinger. It's Alive! 1974: Target Risk (TV). 1975: Death Scream (TV). 1976: The Missouri Breaks. Futureworld. 1977: The Killing Affair (TV). Kill Me If You Can (TV). 1978: It Lives Again! On the Nickel. 1980: The Last Flight of Noah's Ark. 1981: The Postman Always Rings Twice. 1982: One from the Heart. The Escape Artist. 1983: Breathless. The Right Stuff. Rumble Fish. Beam. 1984: The Cotton Club. 1985: Runaway Train. 1986: Avenging Force. Houston: The Legend of Texas (TV). City of Shadows. 1987: Fatal Beauty. Three O'Clock High. Death Wish 4 The Crackdown. Rent-a-Cop. 1988: Paramedics. 1989: Class of 1999. The Abraxas. Eternity. Best of the Best. 1990: Delta Force 2: The Colombian Connection. 1991: Young Commandos. Blood River (TV). Delta Force 3. 1992: Star Time. White Sands. Hoffa. 1993: Young Goodman Brown. Batman: Mask of the Phantasm (voice only). C.I.A. II: Target Alexa. American Cyborg: Steel Warrior. Codename Assassin. 1995: Tall Tale.

SADLER, William 1952–
Fair-haired, pale-eyed, skeleton-faced, thin-lipped, hard-staring American actor who often plays icy villains. Classically trained, Sadler received an MFA in acting from Cornell University before racking up a long list of Broadway credits, culminating in his portrayal of Sgt Toomey in *Biloxi Blues*, which won him a hatful of awards. The cinema, which had barely used his services before the late 1980s, sat up and took notice: he sprang to attention as the fanatical Col Stuart in *Die Hard 2* and showed he could play comedy, too, by stealing all his scenes as the Grim Reaper in *Bill and Ted's Bogus Journey*. Billed as Bill Sadler in several of his film roles.

1981: Ragtime. Charlie and the Great Balloon Chase (TV). 1982: Hanky Panky. 1986: Off Beat. 1987: Project X. 1989: K-9. Tales from the Crypt (TV). 1990: Die Hard 2. Hard to Kill. The Hot Spot. 1991: Tagget. Rush. Dragonfire. 1992: Trespass/The Looters. Bill and Ted's Bogus Journey. 1993: Freaked. Jack Reed: Badge of Honor (TV). 1994: The Shawshank Redemption. Bermuda Grace (TV). Demon Knight. Rebel Highway (TV).

SÄGEBRECHT, Marianne 1945–
Plump, light-haired Austrian actress with amused, doll-like facial features, an unconventional star in German-made international ventures, but a supporting player in most of her few ventures further afield. After a varied early life as laboratory assistant, PA to a neuro-psychiatrist, cabaret manageress and photography editor on a magazine, she conceived and founded Opera Curiosa, a travelling cabaret circus show, which led her into acting. Her career in this medium has been sporadic to say the least, although several of her appearances on film, notably in *Zuckerbaby* and *Bagdad Café*, have been memorable ones.

1980: Herr Kischott (TV). 1983: Die Schaukel (GB and US: The Swing). 1984: Irrsee. 1985: Zuckerbaby (GB and US: Sugarbaby). 1987: Crazy Boys. Bagdad Café. 1988: Moon Over Parador. 1989: Rosalie Goes Shopping. The War of the Roses. 1990: Martha und Ich (GB and US: Martha and I). 1992: La Vida Lactea/ The Milky Life. Run of Hearts. 1993: Dust Devil: The Final Cut. 1994: Erotique. Mona Must Die. 1995: All Men Are Mortal.

SAKALL, S.Z. 'Cuddles'
(Eugene Gero) 1884–1955
Roly-poly Hungarian character actor, seen initially in Hungarian and German silent and early sound films, but remembered only from his Hollywood period as a white-haired, beaming, bespectacled, multi-jowled fractured-English flapper and forehead-mopper, just about everybody's favourite uncle. Died from a heart attack.

1916: †Süszterherceg. †Ujszulott Apa. 1918: †Az Onkéntes Tüzoltó. 1922: †Die Stumme von Portici/The Dumb Girl of Portici. 1926: †Wenn das Herz der Jugend spricht. 1927: †Familientag in Hause Prellstein. †Der fidele Bauer. 1928: †Mary Lou. †Ratschbahn. 1929: †Grosstadtschmetterling. †Wer wird denn weinen, wenn man auseinandergeht. 1930: †Der Hempelmann. †Kan zu mir zum Rendezvous. †Susanne macht Ordnung. †Zweimal Hochzeit. †Zwei Herzen im ¾ Takt. 1931: †Der unbekannte Gast. †Der Zinker. †Die Faschingsee. †Die Frau, von der man spricht. †Die schwebende Jungfrau. †Ich heirate meinen Mann. †Ihr Junge. †Ihre Magestät der Liebe (German version of Her Majesty Love). †Kopfüber ins Glück. †Meine Cousine aus Warschau. †Walzerparadies. 1932: †Eine Stadt steht Kopf. †Glück über Nacht. †Gräfin Mariza. †Ich will nicht wissen, wer du bist. †Kaiserwalzer. †Mädchen zum Heiraten. †Melodie der Liebe (GB: The Right to Happiness). †Muss man sich gleich scheiden lassen. 1933: †Eine Frau wie Du. †Es war einmal ein Musikus. †Grossfürstin Alexandra. †Skandal in Budapest. †Mindent a Nort. †Az Ellopot Szerda. 1934: †Frühlingsstimmen. †Helvet az Oregeknek. 1935: †Harom es Fel Musketas/4½ Musketeers. †Tagebuch der Geliebten. †Baratsagos Arcot Kerek. †Smile, Please. 1936: †Mircha. †Fräulein Lilly. 1937: †The Lilac Domino. 1938: †Les affaires de Maupassant. 1940: It's a Date. Spring Parade. My Love Came Back. Florian. 1941: The Devil and Miss Jones. The Man Who Lost Himself. Ball of Fire. That Night in Rio. 1942: Seven Sweethearts. Yankee Doodle Dandy. Broadway. Casablanca. 1943: Thank Your Lucky Stars. Wintertime. The Human Comedy. 1944: Hollywood Canteen. Shine on Harvest Moon. 1945: The Dolly Sisters. Wonder Man. San Antonio. Christmas in Connecticut. 1946: Cinderella Jones. Never Say Goodbye. The Time, the Place and the Girl. Two Guys from Milwaukee (GB: Royal Flush). 1947: Cynthia

*(GB: The Rich, Full Life). 1948: April Showers. Whiplash. Embraceable You. Romance on the High Seas (GB: It's Magic). 1949: My Dream Is Yours. It's a Great Feeling. Oh, You Beautiful Doll! In the Good Old Summertime. Look for the Silver Lining. 1950: Tea for Two. Montana. The Daughter of Rosie O'Grady. 1951: Sugarfoot. Lullaby of Broadway. Painting the Clouds with Sunshine. It's a Big Country. 1952: *Screen Snapshots No. 205. 1953: Small Town Girl. 1954: The Student Prince.*

† As Szöke Szakall

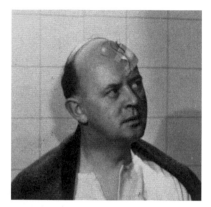

SALEW, John 1897–1961

Versatile, plump-cheeked British actor, dark-haired but bald from an early age, and equally likely to crop up as villain or victim. In fact this chubby supporting player, despite his meek and mild-mannered appearance, was quite often cast as a bad guy. Although one of the most difficult 'familiar faces' to put a name to, Salew nevertheless built up a formidable list of credits after switching from a theatrical to a movie career when the demand for non-serving actors in Britain became acute at the onset of World War II. A weightier actor in his later years, he also made many episodes of television drama series, and was still very busy in both films and TV at the time of his death from a heart attack.

1938: It's in the Air (US: George Takes the Air). Hey! Hey! USA. 1939: They Came by Night. Dead Men Are Dangerous. The Silent Battle (US: Continental Express). A Window in London (US: Lady in Distress). 1940: Sailors Don't Care. The Briggs Family. Neutral Port. 1941: The Saint Meets the Tiger/Meet the Tiger. Inspector Hornleigh Goes to It (US: Mail Train). Once a Crook. Turned Out Nice Again. 1942: The Young Mr Pitt. One of Our Aircraft is Missing. Suspected Person. Next of Kin. Secret Mission. Back Room Boy. The Day Will Dawn (US: The Avengers). Squadron Leader X. Tomorrow We Live (US: At Dawn We Die). 1943: The Bells Go Down. The Adventures of Tartu (US: Tartu). Warn That Man. The Night Invader. We Dive at Dawn. The Hundred Pound Window. Millions Like Us. Time Flies. 1944: Tawny Pipit. The Way Ahead (US: Immortal Battalion). Give Us the Moon. Candles at Nine. Don't Take It to Heart. 1945: Murder in Reverse. The Rake's Progress (US:

*Notorious Gentleman). Bothered by a Beard. 1946: Wanted for Murder. I See a Dark Stranger (US: The Adventuress). Bedelia. Caravan. Beware of Pity. Meet Me at Dawn. A Girl in a Million. 1947: Uncle Silas (US: The Inheritance). Dancing with Crime. Anna Karenina. Nicholas Nickleby. Temptation Harbour. The October Man. It Always Rains on Sunday. My Brother Jonathan. 1948: Counterblast. Noose (US: The Silk Noose). It's Hard to be Good. All Over the Town. The Bad Lord Byron. London Belongs to Me (US: Dulcimer Street). Quartet. Lucky Mascot/ The Brass Monkey. Bond Street. Cardboard Cavalier. 1949: Kind Hearts and Coronets. For Them That Trespass. Marry Me! The Spider and the Fly. No Way Back. Dark Secret. Don't Ever Leave Me. Diamond City. The Blue Lamp. The Twenty Questions Murder Mystery. 1950: *Help Yourself. 1951: Green Grow the Rushes. Hotel Sahara. The Lavender Hill Mob. Night Was Our Friend. Mystery Junction. His Excellency. No Highway (US: No Highway in the Sky). 1952: The Happy Family (US: Mr Lord Says No). 1953: Stryker of the Yard. 1954: Face the Music (US: The Black Glove). Father Brown (US: The Detective). Alive on Saturday (released 1957). Duel in the Jungle. The Red Dress. Lease of Life. 1955: Three Cases of Murder. Dust and Gold. 1956: It's Great to be Young! Rogue's Yarn. Wicked As They Come. The Good Companions. 1957: Night of the Demon (US: Curse of the Demon). 1958: Tread Softly, Stranger. The Gypsy and the Gentleman. Alive and Kicking. Dunkirk. Conscience Bay. 1959: Left, Right and Centre. 1960: The Shakedown. Too Hot to Handle (US: Playgirl After Dark). 1961: The Impersonator. Three on a Spree. *The Never Never Murder.*

SALLIS, Peter 1921–

Dark-haired, diffident, thin-mouthed, often bespectacled British actor; frequently seen in sneaky roles in the early part of his career, he has latterly become more associated with comedy through his participation in the long-running British television series *Last of the Summer Wine*. Started life as a bank clerk, but after some amateur acting in the RAF during World War II, he enrolled at RADA on leaving the service.

1954: Child's Play. 1956: Anastasia. Julie. 1958: The Scapegoat. The Doctor's Dilemma.

*A Night to Remember. 1960: Saturday Night and Sunday Morning. Doctor in Love. 1961: No Love for Johnnie. Curse of the Werewolf. 1962: I Thank a Fool. 1963: Clash by Night. The VIPs. Mouse on the Moon. 1964: The Third Secret. 1965: Rapture. 1967: Charlie Bubbles. 1968: Inadmissible Evidence. 1969: Scream and Scream Again. My Lover, My Son. The Reckoning. 1970: Taste the Blood of Dracula. Wuthering Heights. 1971: The Night Digger. 1973: Frankenstein: The True Story (TV. GB: cinemas in abridged version). 1976: Full Circle (US: The Haunting of Julia). The Incredible Sarah. 1978: Who Is Killing the Great Chefs of Europe? (GB: Too Many Chefs). 1979: Dracula. 1982: Witness for the Prosecution (TV). 1983: Last of the Summer Wine (TV). 1985: Uncle of the Bride (TV). 1993: *The Wrong Trousers (voice only).*

SALMI, Albert 1928–1990

Heavy-set, tow-haired, thick-faced American actor, usually seen in sweaty, forceful roles, and a typical graduate of the Actors' Studio in the 1950s. After war service, Salmi worked for a detective agency, but quit when the agency decided its operatives would carry guns, and enrolled in a drama workshop instead. At first in prestigious supporting roles in films, he later played more routine stuff, including a stint as Barry Newman's 'leg-man' in the popular TV series *Petrocelli*, which gave him a more sympathetic role than the rednecks he often played. Married to actress Peggy Ann Garner (first of two) from 1956 to 1963. Shot himself after killing his estranged wife Roberta.

1956: The Open Door (TV). 1958: The Brothers Karamazov. Man Under Glass (TV). The Bravados. 1959: The Unforgiven. 1960: The Peter Hurkos Story (TV). Wild River. 1964: The Outrage. 1966: The Flim Flam Man (GB: One Born Every Minute). 1967: Hour of the Gun. The Ambushers. 1968: Three Guns for Texas (TV. GB: cinemas). 1969: Four Rode Out. 1970: The Deserter. Lawman. Menace on the Mountain (TV. GB: cinemas). 1971: Escape from the Planet of the Apes. Something Big. 1972: Kung Fu (TV). 1973: Female Artillery (TV). 1974: The Crazy World of Julius Vrooder/Vrooder's Hooch. The Take. A Place Without Parents. Night Games (TV). 1975: Truckin'. The Legend of Earl Durand.

1976: The Manhunter (TV). 1977: Viva Knievel! Black Oak Conspiracy. Empire of the Ants. Moonshine County Express. 1978: Love and Bullets. The Sweet Creek County War. Freedom Riders (TV). The Magnificent Hustle (TV). My Undercover Years with the Ku Klux Klan/Undercover with the KKK (TV). 1979: Steel. Cloud Dancer. Thou Shalt Not Kill (TV). 1980: Key West. Brubaker. Crossing. The Great Cash Giveaway Getaway (TV). Caddyshack. 1981: I'm Dancing As Fast As I Can. The Coming. Dragonslayer. The Guns and the Fury. 1982: Love Child. 1984: Best Kept Secrets. Hard to Hold. 1985: Superstition (made 1981). Arctic Heat. The Witch. 1986: Born American. 1988: Jesse (TV). 1989: B-Men (TV). Breaking In. Billy the Kid (TV).

SAMPSON, Will 1933–1987

Giant-sized American Indian actor (a full-blooded member of the Musgokee tribe) who spent most of his working life as an artist, teacher, gallery owner and self-taught painter. He moved massively into films as Chief Bromden in One Flew Over the Cuckoo's Nest (a performance that won him an Academy Award nomination). But subsequent roles worthy of his talent and stature were always going to be hard to find, and he was seen too seldom before his early death soon after a heart and lung transplant. He founded the American Indian Registry for the Performing Arts and also served as a director on the board of the American Indian Film Institute.

1975: One Flew Over the Cuckoo's Nest. 1976: The Outlaw Josey Wales. Buffalo Bill and the Indians: Or, Sitting Bull's History Lesson. 1977: The Hunted Lady (TV). The White Buffalo. Orca/Orca . . . Killer Whale. Relentless (TV). 1978: Vegas (TV). Standing Tall. 1979: Fish Hawk. 1980: Alcatraz: The Whole Shocking Story (TV). 1984: Insignificance. 1986: Poltergeist II: The Other Side. Firewalker.

SAWYER, Joe
(Joseph Sauers) 1901–1982
Tough-looking, square-faced, fair-haired, large-headed, solidly-built American actor with small eyes and pale complexion. Busy in small roles from the early 1930s, he played top sergeants, taxi-drivers, crooks, sailors and sundry denizens of working-class districts. The scourge of the rookie

serviceman, Sawyer was a sort of B-picture William Bendix who could play straight or comic. He actually teamed with Bendix in a few rough-and-ready comedies of the 1940s, and made eight army comedies with another partner, moon-faced William Tracy, around the same period, as the cartoon-strip characters Doubleday and Ames. He died from cancer of the liver.

1929: †*Campus Sweethearts. 1931: †Surrender. 1932: †Arsene Lupin. †Huddle (GB: Impossible Lover). †Forgotten Commandments. 1933: †College Humor. †Hold Your Man. †Saturday's Millions. †Three-Cornered Moon. †College Coach (GB: Football Coach). †Blood Money. †The Stranger's Return. †Ace of Aces. †Son of a Sailor. 1934: †Death on the Diamond. †Looking for Trouble. †Behond My Wife! †College Rhythm. †The Prescott Kid. †The Band Plays On. †Stamboul Quest. †Jimmy the Gent. †The Case of the Howling Dog. †The Notorious Sophie Lang. †The Westerner. †The Whole Town's Talking (GB: Passport to Fame). 1935: †Broadway Gondolier. †Car 99. †Special Agent. †The Arizonian. †The Informer. I Found Stella Parish. Little Big Shot. Man of Iron. Frisco Kid. Moonlight on the Prairie. The Man on the Flying Trapeze (GB: The Memory Expert). The Revenge Rider. The Petrified Forest. 1936: Big Brown Eyes. And Sudden Death. Murder With Pictures. Crash Donovan. The Leathernecks Have Landed (GB: The Marines Have Landed). Two in a Crowd. Freshman Love (GB: Rhythm on the River). The Country Doctor. The Last Outlaw. The Walking Dead. High Tension. Special Investigator. Pride of the Marines. Black Legion. 1937: Great Guy (GB: Pluck of the Irish). Slim. Midnight Madonna. *Behind the Criminal. A Dangerous Adventure. The Lady Fights Back. They Gave Him a Gun. Navy Blues. Reported Missing. Motor Madness. San Quentin. 1938: Always in Trouble. Tarzan's Revenge. Stolen Heaven. Gambling Ship. Heart of the North. The Storm. Passport Husband. 1939: You Can't Get Away With Murder. The Lady and the Mob. I Stole a Million. Union Pacific. Sabotage (GB: Spies at Work). Inside Information. Confessions of a Nazi Spy. Frontier Marshal. The Roaring Twenties. 1940: The Man from Montreal. The Grapes of Wrath. King of the Lumberjacks. Women Without Names. The Long Voyage Home. Border Legion. Santa Fé Trail. The House Across the Bay. Dark Command. Lucky Cisco Kid. Melody

Ranch. Wildcat Bus. 1941: Tanks a Million. The Lady from Cheyenne. Last of the Duanes. Down in San Diego. Swamp Water (GB: The Man Who Came Back). You're in the Army Now. Sergeant York. Belle Starr. Down Mexico Way. They Died With Their Boots On. 1942: About Face. The McGuerins from Brooklyn. *A Letter from Bataan. Wrecking Crew. Sundown Jim. Hay Foot. Brooklyn Orchid. 1943: Buckskin Frontier (GB: The Iron Road). Fall In. Prairie Chickens. Taxi, Mister. Yanks Ahoy. Let's Face It. Tarzan's Desert Mystery. The Outlaw. Cowboy in Manhattan. Hit the Ice. Tornado. Alaska Highway. Sleepy Lagoon. 1944: Moon Over Las Vegas. Hey, Rookie. Raiders of Ghost City (serial). The Singing Sheriff. South of Dixie. 1945: The Naughty Nineties. High Powered. Brewster's Millions. 1946: Joe Palooka—Champ. Deadline at Dawn. GI War Brides. The Runaround. Gilda. Inside Job. 1947: Big Town After Dark. Christmas Eve. A Double Life. Roses are Red. 1948: Half Past Midnight. If You Knew Susie. Fighting Back. Coroner Creek. The Untamed Breed. Here Comes Trouble. Fighting Father Dunne. 1949: The Gay Amigo. Deputy Marshal. And Baby Makes Three. Curtain Call at Cactus Creek (GB: Take the Stage). Kazan. The Lucky Stiff. The Stagecoach Kid. Tucson. ‡Two Knights in Brooklyn/Two Mugs from Brooklyn. 1950: Blondie's Hero. Operation Haylift. The Travelling Saleswoman. The Flying Missile. 1951: Pride of Maryland. Comin' Round the Mountain. As You Were. 1952: Deadline USA (GB: Deadline). Red Skies of Montana. Indian Uprising. Mr Walkie Talkie. 1953: It Came from Outer Space. 1954: Taza Son of Cochise. Johnny Dark. Riding Shotgun. 1955: The Kettles in the Ozarks. 1956: The Killing. 1960: North to Alaska. 1962: How the West Was Won. 1973: Harry in Your Pocket (GB: Harry Never Holds).

† As Joseph Sauer
‡ Combined GB version of The McGuerins from Brooklyn/Taxi, Mister

SCALES, Prunella 1932–
Small, dumpy, brown-haired, round-faced British actress with disapproving voice and an immense comic talent. She has made lamentably few film appearances in between theatre and TV work, but at least can be seen permanently on video in the highpoint of her career − the husband-haranguing Sybil Fawlty in the classic British TV

comedy series of the late 1970s, *Fawlty Towers*. Also a big hit in another TV series, *Mapp and Lucia*. Married to fellow character star Timothy West (1934–). The actor Samuel West is their son.

1953: Laxdale Hall (US: Scotch on the Rocks). Hobson's Choice. 1954: What Every Woman Wants. The Crowded Day. 1958: Room at the Top. 1962: Waltz of the Toreadors. 1976: Escape from the Dark (US: The Littlest Horse Thieves). 1977: The Hound of the Baskervilles. 1978: The Boys from Brazil. 1983: The Wicked Lady. Wagner (TV). 1987: Consuming Passions. The Lonely Passion of Judith Hearne. 1989: A Chorus of Disapproval. 1991: A Question of Attribution (TV). 1992: Freddie As F.R.O.7 (voice only). My Friend Walter. 1993: Second Best. 1994: Fair Game (TV). Wolf. 1995: An Awfully Big Adventure.

SCHALLERT, William 1922–
Thin, friendly-looking, twinkling-eyed American actor with brushed-across dark hair and wide, if cynical smile – a snip for scientists, judges, and fathers of feisty teen-age girls, following an early career in often harassed roles. The son of a drama editor and a film critic, Schallert began his acting days with a small, exclusive Hollywood theatre group and quickly moved into films in his mid twenties. But the theatre and television (where long-running series roles have several times kept him off cinema screens for years) remain his favourite media. Films too seldom pitched him high enough in the cast list, and he remained one of those faces to which it was almost impossible to put the name. Also a composer, pianist and singer, he married actress Lia Wagger and has four sons.

1947: The Foxes of Harrow. 1949: Mighty Joe Young. The Reckless Moment. 1950: Lonely Hearts Bandits (GB: Lonely Heart Bandits). 1951: Belle le Grand. The Man from Planet X. The People Against O'Hara. The Red Badge of Courage. 1952: Hoodlum Empire. Captive Women (GB: 3000 AD). Flat Top (GB: Eagles of the Fleet). Storm Over Tibet. Sword of Venus (GB: Island of Monte Cristo). Rose of Cimarron. 1953: Port Sinister. Torpedo Alley. Commander Cody, Sky Marshal of The Universe (serial). 1954: Black Tuesday. Gog. The High and the Mighty. Riot in Cell Block 11. Tobor the Great. Them! Shield for Murder. 1955: Hell's Horizon.

Smoke Signal. Top of the World. Annapolis Story (GB: The Blue and the Gold). 1956: Friendly Persuasion. Gunslinger. Raw Edge. Bigger Than Life. 1957: The Girl in the Kremlin. Band of Angels. The Incredible Shrinking Man. The Story of Mankind. The Tattered Dress. Written on the Wind. The Monolith Monsters. Man in the Shadow (GB: Pay the Devil). 1958: Cry Terror! Some Came Running. The Tarnished Angels. 1959: Blue Denim (GB: Blue Jeans). Day of the Outlaw. The Beat Generation. Pillow Talk. 1960: The Gallant Hours. 1962: Paradise Alley (completed 1957). Alcatraz Express (TV). Lonely Are the Brave. Philbert. 1967: Hour of the Gun. In the Heat of the Night. Will Penny. 1968: Speedway. Hawaii Five-O (TV pilot). 1969: Sam Whiskey. Colossus: The Forbin Project. 1970: The Computer Wore Tennis Shoes. Tora! Tora! Tora! 1971: Escape (TV). Man on a String (TV). 1972: The Trial of the Catonsville Nine. 1973: Charley Varrick. Hijack! (TV). Partners in Crime (TV). 1974: Death Sentence (TV). Remember When? (TV). 1975: Promise Him Anything (TV). The Strongest Man in the World. 1976: Dawn: Portrait of a Teenage Runaway (TV). Tunnelvision. 1977: Tail Gunner Joe (TV). 1978: Little Women (TV). 1979: Ike (TV). Blind Ambition (TV). 1980: Hangar 18. 1983: The Twilight Zone (GB: Twilight Zone The Movie). Grace Kelly (TV. GB: The Grace Kelly Story). Through Naked Eyes (TV). 1984: Amazons (TV). Teachers. 1986: Under the Influence (TV). Houston: The Legend of Texas (TV). 1987: Suspect. Inner-Space. 1989: Bring Me the Head of Dobie Gillis (TV). The Incident (TV). 1990: Held Hostage (TV). 1991: Mrs Lambert Remembers Love (TV). House Party 2. 1993: Matinee.

SCHIAVELLI, Vincent 1947–
Ghoulish, tombstone-toothed, rabbit-faced, open-mouthed, lugubrious American actor with wild receding curly hair, who looks like a refugee from The Three Stooges. After dramatic training, he was in films from his early twenties, but scored his first big success on TV as gay set designer Peter Panama in *The Corner Bar* (1972/3), a kind of precursor of *Cheers*. Films remarkably few considering such individual looks, and mostly in unpleasant or outraged roles. Memorable as the subway ghost who teaches Patrick Swayze the rules of the game in *Ghost*, he married the equally distinctive-looking

character actress Allyce Beasley, whose biggest hit to date has been as the daffy secretary in the TV series *Moonlighting*.

1971: Taking Off. 1974: The Great Gatsby. For Pete's Sake. The Happy Hooker. 1975: Angels. One Flew Over the Cuckoo's Nest. Next Stop Greenwich Village. 1976: Taxi Driver. 1977: Un autre homme, une autre chance (GB: Another Man, Another Woman. US: Another Man, Another Chance). An Unmarried Woman. 1979: Butch and Sundance The Early Days. Rescue from Gilligan's Island (TV). 1980: Escape (TV). Nightside (TV). Teen Mothers. White Mama (TV). The Return. The Gong Show Movie. Seed of Innocence. 1981: American Pop (voice only). Chu Chu and the Philly Flash. 1982: Night Shift. Fast Times at Ridgemont High (GB: Fast Times). 1984: Amadeus. The Ratings Game (TV). Kidco. The Adventures of Buckaroo Banzai Across the Eighth Dimension. 1985: Lots of Luck (TV). 1986: Time Out. 1987: Bride of Boogedy (TV). 1988: Homer & Eddie. 1989: Valmont. Waiting for the Light. Cold Feet. Playroom. 1990: Mister Frost. Penny Ante. Ghost. 1991: Love in Venice. Freejack. Ted and Venus. 1992: Batman Returns. Miracle Beach. 1993: The Painted Desert. 1994: Cultivating Charlie. The Whipping Boy (TV). 1995: He Ain't Heavy.

SCHILDKRAUT, Joseph 1895–1964
Dashing, moustachioed, dark-haired Austrian-born actor with flashing smile. Came to Hollywood in the early twenties, and played lithe heroes. Sound films cast him mainly as suave, irritable villains – although there were also some good character roles, and for one of them, Captain Dreyfus in *The Life of Emile Zola*, he won an Academy Award. Died from a heart attack.

1908: The Wandering Jew. 1915: Árpád Szomory. Schlemihl. 1916: Schweigepflich. 1918: Die Leben von Theordore Herzl. 1920: Der Roman der Komtesse Orth. 1922: Orphans of the Storm. 1923: Dust of Desire. 1924: The Song of Love. 1925: The Road to Yesterday. 1926: Young April. Meet the Prince. Shipwrecked. 1927: His Dog. The King of Kings. The Heart Thief. The Forbidden Woman. 1928: The Blue Danube (GB: Honour Above All). Tenth Avenue. 1929: Mississippi Gambler. Show Boat. 1930: Die Sehnsucht jeder Frau. Cock o' the Walk. Night Ride. 1931: Carnival (US: Venetian Nights). The Blue Danube (remake). *1934: Viva Villa! Cleopatra. Sisters Under the Skin. 1935: The Crusades. 1936: The Garden of Allah. 1937: Souls at Sea. Slave Ship. Lady Behave. The Life of Emile Zola. Lancer Spy. 1938: Suez. The Baroness and the Butler. Marie Antoinette. 1939: The Man in the Iron Mask. Idiot's Delight. Lady of the Tropics. Barricade. The Three Musketeers (GB: The Singing Musketeer). Mr Moto Takes a Vacation. The Rains Came. Pack Up Your Troubles (GB: We're in the Army Now). 1940: Rangers of Fortune. The Shop Around the Corner. Phantom Raiders. Meet the Wildcat. 1941: The Parson of Panamint. *The Tell Tale Heart. 1945: Flame of the Barbary Coast. The Cheaters. 1946: Monsieur Beaucaire. The Plainsman and the Lady. 1947: Northwest Outpost (GB: End of the Rainbow). 1948: Gallant Legion. Old Los Angeles. 1959: The Diary of Anne Frank. 1961: King of the Roaring Twenties (GB: The Big Bankroll). 1965: The Greatest Story Ever Told.*

SCHOFIELD, Johnnie 1889–1961

Chunky, chirpy, brown-haired, dark-eyed Londoner with cheery face. From pantomime, revue and musical comedy, he was an assistant director looking to move his career backstage when sound films grabbed him for light supporting roles, of which he would play more than 100 before his retirement in 1954. Many of his appearances are fleeting, but he drove cabs, coaches, ambulances and lorries, served drinks at cafés and nightclubs, attended lifts and played orderlies, workmen, servicemen, stage managers and generally men with their sleeves rolled up. Appropriate that he should have played in *Millions Like Us*; in the same year (1943), he had his only leading role, in *Down Melody Lane*.

1933: Hawleys of High Street. The Pride of the Force. 1934: Josser on the Farm. The Outcast. Lost in the Legion. Doctor's Orders. 1935: Cock o' the North. Jimmy Boy. Father O'Flynn. The Mystery of the Marie Celeste/The Mystery of the Mary Celeste (US: Phantom Ship). A Real Bloke. Sexton Blake and the Bearded Doctor. Variety. 1936: The End of the Road. Once in a Million (US: Weekend Millionaire). Living Dangerously. The Amazing Quest of Ernest Bliss (US: Romance and Riches). Song of Freedom. Men Are Not Gods. Melody of My Heart. One Good Turn. 1937: Victoria the

*Great. Our Fighting Navy (US: Torpedoed!). The Last Adventurers. Rhythm Racketeer. Sam Small Leaves Town. Song of the Road. Talking Feet. Make-Up. 1938: Lassie from Lancashire. Incident in Shanghai. Sixty Glorious Years (US: Queen of Destiny). Mountains o' Mourne. Night Journey. Special Edition. *Receivers. I See Ice. 1939: The Arsenal Stadium Mystery. The Spy in Black (US: U-Boat 29). Down Our Alley. The Middle Watch. 1940: The Briggs Family. Two Smart Men. Contraband (US: Blackout). Gaslight (US: Angel Street). Spare a Copper. Convoy. Let George Do It. 1941: Bob's Your Uncle. Gert and Daisy's Weekend. Sheepdog of the Hills. 1942: The Young Mr Pitt. In Which We Serve. Old Mother Riley Detective. Uncensored. The Day Will Dawn (US: The Avengers). Went the Day Well? (US: 48 Hours). Back Room Boy. The Goose Steps Out. Next of Kin. Squadron Leader X. 1943: The Bells Go Down. The Demi-Paradise (US: Adventure for Two). Theatre Royal. Down Melody Lane. We Dive at Dawn. Millions Like Us. The Gentle Sex. *Welcome to Britain. 1944: Love Story (US: A Lady Surrenders). Fanny By Gaslight (US: Man of Evil). English Without Tears (US: Her Man Gilbey). Give Me the Stars. Tawny Pipit. Waterloo Road. The Way Ahead (US: Immortal Battalion). Welcome Mr Washington. They Came to a City. 1945: The Echo Murders. The Way to the Stars (US: Johnny in the Clouds). The Wicked Lady. The Voice Within. The Rake's Progress (US: Notorious Gentleman). Perfect Strangers (US: Vacation from Marriage). Night Boat to Dublin. 1946: The Shop at Sly Corner (US: The Code of Scotland Yard). This Man is Mine. I See a Dark Stranger (US: The Adventuress). Wanted for Murder. 1947: Captain Boycott. The Mark of Cain. Mine Own Executioner. While I Live. Dancing With Crime. My Brother Jonathan. 1948: Love in Waiting. Mr Perrin and Mr Traill. So Evil My Love. 1949: Adam and Evelyne (US: Adam and Evalyn). The Perfect Woman. The Rocking Horse Winner. Dark Secret. Train of Events. 1950: Blackmailed. Night and the City. The Reluctant Widow. The Second Mate. 1951: Appointment with Venus (US: Island Rescue). The Browning Version. A Case for PC 49. Lady Godiva Rides Again. I Believe in You. White Corridors. 1952: Home at Seven (US: Murder on Monday). The Net (US: Project M7). Something Money Can't Buy. The Voice of Merrill (US: Murder Will Out). 1953: Love In Pawn. Meet Mr Lucifer. The Final Test. The Saint's Return (US: The Saint's Girl Friday). Solution by Phone. Small Town Story. Three Steps to the Gallows (released 1955. US: White Fire). Wheel of Fate. The Fake. The Square Ring. 1954: Carrington VC (US: Court-Martial). Aunt Clara. The Scarlet Web. 1955: See How They Run.*

SCOTT, Terry

(Owen Scott) 1927–1994

Plump, dark-haired British comedian who moved from spluttering schoolboys to indignant adults before success in television series led him to comedy roles in films. These series, mostly in collaboration, included *Great Scott It's Maynard*, *Hugh and I*, *Happy Ever After* and *Terry and June*. Perhaps not quite enough of an actor to

settle down to leading comedy roles in the cinema, he remained largely in cameos. Originally studied to be an accountant. Survived a major brain operation in 1979, as well as cancer of the bladder and a nervous breakdown in the late 1980s, to continue a busy stage and TV career. Died from cancer.

1957: Blue Murder at St Trinian's. 1958: Carry On Sergeant. Too Many Crooks. 1959: The Bridal Path. I'm All Right, Jack. And the Same to You. 1960: The Night We Got the Bird. 1961: Nothing Barred. A Pair of Briefs. Double Bunk. Nearly a Nasty Accident. No, My Darling Daughter! What a Whopper! Mary Had a Little . . . 1963: Father Came Too. 1964: Murder Most Foul. 1965: Gonks Go Beat. 1966: The Great St Trinian's Train Robbery. Doctor in Clover. 1968: A Ghost of a Chance. Carry On Up the Khyber. 1969: Carry On Camping. Carry On Up the Jungle. 1970: Carry On Henry. Carry On Loving. 1972: Carry On Matron. Bless This House. 1982: The Pantomime Dame.

SEDAN, Rolfe

(Edward Sedan) 1896–1982

Stocky, dark-haired, moustachioed, eager-looking American small-part actor with an amused mouth, and a nose and chin that threatened to bump into one another. A considerably bigger star on stage than in films, Sedan played everything from walk-ons and one-liners to prominent featured roles. He was as often seen as lotharios and partygoers in the social swirl as he was as wiseacre waiters, chefs, croupiers or salesmen. He first entered films as a schoolboy extra in 1908. Bitten by the acting bug, he was a stage actor at 17 before beginning a busy film career in his twenties: it stretched from 1919 to 1981, one of the longest on record. Mostly in comedy parts, including innumerable shorts for Hal Roach and others in the 1920s and 1930s. Died from a coronary occlusion.

*1919: Louisiana. 1922: *The Leather Pushers. 1923: Merry Go Round. The Hunchback of Notre Dame. 1924: *Every Man for Himself. Sporting Youth. The Dangerous Blonde. Excitement. Love and Glory. The Mad Whirl. Young Ideas. 1925: *Is Marriage the Bunk? *Looking for Sally. The Merry Widow. The Phantom of the Opera. Smouldering Fires. 1926: *Mighty Like a Moose. *Bromo and Juliet. *Baby Clothes. Beau Geste. Fifth Avenue. Man Trap. My Old Dutch. 1927: Compassion. Flesh and the Devil. The Denver Dude (GB: The Man from Colorado). The Magic Flame. Seventh Heaven. Uncle Tom's Cabin. 1928: The Adorable Cheat. Chinatown Charlie. Celebrity. Man Made Woman. The Chinatown Mystery (serial). Reilly of Rainbow Division. 1929: *Double Whoopee. *Dad's Day. *†Men o' War. The Dance of Life. The Iron Mask. Love and the Devil. Making the Grade. One Hysterical Night. Street Girl. 1930: Children of Pleasure. A Lady's Morals (GB: Jenny Lind). Monte Carlo. Paramount on Parade. Party Girl. Show Girl in Hollywood. Sweethearts and Wives. Sweet Kitty Bellairs. Swing High. What a Widow! 1931: Finn and Hattie. The Spy. Fifty Million Frenchmen. The Galloping Ghost (serial). Just a Gigolo (GB: The Dancing Partner). Monkey Business. The Woman Between (GB: Madame Julie). 1932: The Devil on Deck. Central Park. Evenings for Sale. Grand Hotel. Love Me Tonight. Trouble in Paradise. If I Had a Million. Back Street. The Match King. The Passionate Plumber. 70,000 Witnesses. Winner Take All. Temptation's Workshop/Youth's Highway (GB: Young Blood). 1933: *Arabian Tights. *Luncheon at Twelve. *Mush and Milk. *Sneak Easily. Cocktail Hour. Devil's Mate (GB: He Knew Too Much). The Devil's Brother (GB: Fra Diavolo). Adorable. Design for Living. Laughing at Life. Reunion in Vienna. The Little Giant. Private Detective 62. The Sin of Nora Moran. 42nd Street. Topaze. What! No Beer? The World Gone Mad (GB: The Public Be Hanged). 1934: *Done in Oil. †Evelyn Prentice. Kansas City Princess. Ladies Should Listen. The Man Who Reclaimed His Head. Paris Interlude. Palooka (GB: The Great Schnozzle). The Merry Widow (and French version). Now and Forever. The Thin Man. Wonder Bar. 1935: All the King's Horses. Broadway Gondolier. Charlie Chan in Paris. Broadway Melody of 1936. †Coronado. Here Comes the Band. Lottery Lover. $1,000 a Minute. Paris in Spring (GB: Paris Love Song). Mad Love. A Night at the Opera. Ruggles of Red Gap. Ship Café. A Tale of Two Cities. 1936: *Arbor Day. The Accusing Finger. Anything Goes. Rose-Marie. Smartest Girl in Town. Under Two Flags. 1937: Café Metropole. Double or Nothing. The Firefly. The Girl Said No. Fight for Your Lady. High, Wide and Handsome. Hitting a New High. 100 Men and a Girl. Rhythm in the Clouds. Shall We Dance? The Singing Marine. Souls at Sea.*

*1938: *Headliner No. 1. Adventure in Sahara. I'll Give a Million. Bluebeard's Eighth Wife. A Letter of Introduction. Holiday/Unconventional Linda (GB: Free to Live). A Desperate Adventure. Paradise for Three. Stolen Heaven. Strange Faces. That Certain Age. Topper Takes a Trip. Under the Big Top (GB: The Circus Comes to Town). A Trip to Paris. 1939: Charlie Chan in City of Darkness. Everything Happens at Night. Juarez y Maximilian/The Mad Empress. Ninotchka. She Married a Cop. The Man in the Iron Mask. The Story of Vernon and Irene Castle. The Wizard of Oz. 1940: Florian. Hudson's Bay. Golden Gloves. I Was an Adventuress. Laughing at Danger. Private Affairs. 1941: Angels with Broken Wings. Charley's Aunt. Law of the Tropics. San Antonio Rose. That Uncertain Feeling. 1945: The Horn Blows at Midnight. 1946: The People's Choice. 1949: That Forsyte Woman (GB: The Forsyte Saga). Not Wanted. 1950: Let's Dance. 1951: A Millionaire for Christy. My Favorite Spy. 1952: Something to Love For. April in Paris. 1953: Gentlemen Prefer Blondes. Mississippi Gambler. 1954: Phantom of the Rue Morgue. So This is Paris. 1956: The Birds and the Bees. 1957: Silk Stockings. 1964: Bedtime Story. McHale's Navy. 36 Hours. 1965: The Art of Love. 1967: How I Spent My Summer Vacation (TV). 1969: Wake Me When the War is Over (TV). Darling Lili. 1972: Un homme est mort (GB and US: The Outside Man). 1974: Chinatown. Young Frankenstein. 1975: The Hindenburg. 1977: The World's Greatest Lover. The Happy Hooker Goes to Washington. 1979: The Frisco Kid. †Love at First Bite. 1981: The Unseen.*

† Scenes deleted from final release print.

SESSIONS, Almira 1888–1974

Dark-haired, thin-lipped, beady-eyed, tight-faced, bony, tallish, snoopy-looking gannet-like American actress who sternly disapproved of many a poor Hollywood heroine in the 1940s and would have no doubt done so throughout the previous decade had she come to films earlier. Initially a singer 'until I learned I could make more money singing off-key', she became a comic entertainer before coming to Hollywood in 1940 to play old maids, nurses, charwomen, landladies and meanies who were often figures of fun. Her type-casting was perhaps summed up by her appearance as the President of the Anti-Vice League in Mae West's *The Heat's On*.

*1940: Chad Hanna. Jennie. Little Nellie Kelly. 1941: Ringside Maisie. Blondie in Society (GB: Henpecked). Blossoms in the Dust. Obliging Young Lady. She Knew All the Answers. Sun Valley Serenade. Three Girls About Town. Sullivan's Travels. 1942: Blondie for Victory (GB: Troubles Through Billets). Nightmare. My Sister Eileen. I Married an Angel. The Ox-Bow Incident (GB: Strange Incident). 1943: Happy Go Lucky. Madame Curie. The Heat's On (GB: Copacabana). My Kingdom for a Cook. Presenting Lily Mars. Assignment in Brittany. Slightly Dangerous. *Seeing Nellie Home. 1944: Bathing Beauty. Dixie Jamboree. Henry Aldrich's Little Secret (GB: Henry's Little Secret). The Miracle of Morgan's Creek. Can't Help Singing. I Love a Soldier. The Doughgirls. Maisie Goes to Reno (GB: You Can't Do That to Me). San Diego, I Love You. 1945: Fear. State Fair. Nob Hill. The Southerner. She Wouldn't Say Yes. Two O'Clock Courage. The Woman Who Came Back. 1946: Cross My Heart. Do You Love Me? (GB: Doll Face). The Diary of a Chambermaid. Night and Day. The Missing Lady. It's a Wonderful Life! 1947: The Bishop's Wife. The Tender Years. For the Love of Rusty. Love and Learn. Merton of the Movies. Monsieur Verdoux. Cass Timberlane. I Wonder Who's Kissing Her Now. 1948: Apartment for Peggy. Arthur Takes Over. The Bride Goes Wild. Good Sam. Julia Misbehaves. Family Honeymoon. On Our Merry Way/A Miracle Can Happen. 1949: Ladies of the Chorus. The Fountainhead. Night Unto Night. Take Me Out to the Ball Game (GB: Everybody's Cheering). Roseanna McCoy. 1950: Black Hand. The Blazing Sun. Fancy Pants. Montana. Harvey. Kill the Umpire. Humphrey Takes a Chance. Please Believe Me. The Old Frontier. Summer Stock (GB: If You Feel Like Singing). 1951: *Hollywood Honeymoon. Here Comes the Groom. The Lemon Drop Kid. Valentino. A Millionaire for Christy. 1952: Oklahoma Annie. Jack and the Beanstalk. Wagons West. 1953: The Affairs of Dobie Gillis. Paris Model. Code Two. The Sun Shines Bright. Ride, Vaquero! Sweethearts on Parade. 1954: Forever Female. Hell's Outpost. The Rocket Man. 1955: It's Always Fair Weather. The Prodigal. Rebel Without a Cause. 1956: Calling Homicide. The Scarlet Hour. 1957: Loving You. 1958: The Female Animal. Andy Hardy Comes Home. 1961: Summer and Smoke. 1962: Paradise Alley (completed 1957). 1963: Under the Yum Yum Tree. 1966: Last of the Secret Agents? 1967: Firecreek. 1968: The Boston Strangler. Rosemary's Baby. 1969: The Over-the-Hill Gang (TV). . . . tick . . . tick . . . tick. 1970: Watermelon Man. 1971: Willard. 1972: Everything You Always Wanted to Know About Sex* *But Were Afraid to Ask.*

SETON, Sir Bruce 1909–1969

Tall, sour-looking, narrow-eyed, dark-haired (greying in his forties) British actor who had a military career before switching to show business and becoming a dancer in the Drury Lane Theatre chorus. As a speciality dancer in partnership with Betty Astell (later a queen of British 'quota quickies') he broke into films, mixing straight dramas with small-scale musicals. He was relegated to minor roles in post-war years, but his career received an enormous boost with his long-running portrayal of a real-life detective in TV's *Fabian of the Yard* series. Returned to lesser roles in the latter stages of his career. Married to actresses Tamara Desni and Antoinette Cellier. Never used his (hereditary) title in films.

1935: Blue Smoke. Flame in the Heather. The Shadow of Mike Emerald. Sweeney Todd the Demon Barber of Fleet Street. The Vandergilt Diamond Mystery. 1936: Melody of My Heart. *The Beauty Doctor. Wedding Group (US: Wrath of Jealousy). Jack of All Trades (US: The Two of Us). The Man Who Changed His Mind. *Cocktail. Annie Laurie. The End of the Road. Café Colette (US: Danger in Paris). Love from a Stranger. 1937: Racing Romance. Song of the Road. Fifty Shilling Boxer. Father Steps Out. The Green Cockatoo (US: Four Dark Hours). 1938: If I Were Boss. Weddings Are Wonderful. You're the Doctor. Miracles Do Happen. 1939: Old Mother Riley Joins Up. The Middle Watch. Lucky to Me. 1946: The Curse of the Wraydons. 1948: The Story of Shirley Yorke. Scott of the Antarctic. Look Before You Love. Whisky Galore! (US: Tight Little Island). Bonnie Prince Charlie. Bond Street. 1949: The Blue Lamp. 1950: Portrait of Clare. Paul Temple's Triumph. Take Me to Paris. Blackmailed. Seven Days to Noon. 1951: White Corridors. High Treason. Worm's Eye View. 1952: The Second Mrs Tanqueray. Emergency Call (US: Hundred Hour Hunt). Rough Shoot (US: Shoot First). The Cruel Sea. 1954: Doctor in the House. Eight O'Clock Walk. Delayed Action. Fabian of the Yard. 1955: Man of the Moment. Handcuffs, London. 1956: Break-away. West of Suez (GB: Fighting Wildcats). 1957: There's Always a Thursday. Morning Call (US: The Strange Case of Dr Manning). The Crooked Sky. Zoo Baby (released 1960). Undercover Girl. 1958: Violent Moment. Hidden Homicide. 1959: Make Mine a Million. John Paul Jones. Life in Danger. Strictly Confidential. Operation Cupid. Trouble With Eve (US: In Trouble With Eve). The League of Gentlemen. 1960: Carry On Constable. Just Joe. Greyfriars Bobby. 1961: The Frightened City. Gorgo. Freedom to Die. The Valiant. 1962: Ambush in Leopard Street. Dead Man's Evidence. The Prince and the Pauper. The Pot Carriers. 1963: Dr Syn Alias the Scarecrow. 1965: The Legend of Young Dick Turpin.

SEYLER, Athene 1889–1990
Light-haired, charmingly pug-faced, plump British actress, second only to Dame Margaret Rutherford in endearing qualities, and seen in her heyday as maiden aunts and loveable old dears from all walks of life. Played quite prominent film roles into her early seventies, having made her stage debut in 1908. Although no-one seemed more at home among the raspberry jam and Royal Doulton teacups, she could also convincingly play pioneer ladies of indomitable spirit. Married (second; first husband died) fellow character player Nicholas Hannen (1880–1972). Prodigiously busy throughout her long life, she never took holidays. 'My work,' she said, 'was my holiday to me, I enjoyed it so much. I had a smashing time.'

1921: The Adventures of Mr Pickwick. 1923: This Freedom. 1931: The Perfect Lady. 1932: Tell Me Tonight (US: Be Mine Tonight). 1933: Early to Bed. 1934: Blossom Time (US: April Romance). The Rocks of Valpré (US: High Treason). The Private Life of Don Juan. 1935: Scrooge. Royal Cavalcade (US: Regal Cavalcade). Drake of England (US: Drake the Pirate). Moscow Nights (US: I Stand Condemned). D'Ye Ken John Peel? (US: Captain Moonlight). 1936: Irish for Luck. It's Love Again. The Mill on the Floss. Sensation. Southern Roses. 1937: The Sky's the Limit. The Lilac Domino. Non Stop New York. 1938: Sailing Along. Jane Steps Out. The Citadel. The Ware Case. 1939: The Saint in London. Young Man's Fancy. 1940: Tilly of Bloomsbury. The House of the Arrow (US: Castle of Crimes). 1941: Quiet Wedding. 1943: Dear Octopus (US: The Randolph Family). 1947: Jassy. Nicholas Nickleby. 1948: The First Gentleman (US: Affairs of a Rogue). 1949: The Queen of Spades. 1951: The Franchise Affair. Young Wives' Tale. No Highway (US: No Highway in the Sky). Secret People. 1952: Treasure Hunt. Made in Heaven. The Pickwick Papers. 1953: The Beggar's Opera. The Weak and the Wicked. 1954: For Better, For Worse (US: Cocktails in the Kitchen). 1955: As Long As They're Happy. 1956: Yield to the Night (US: Blonde Sinner). 1957: Campbell's Kingdom. Doctor at Large. How to Murder a Rich Uncle. Night of the Demon (US: Scream of the Demon). Happy is the Bride! 1958: The Inn of the Sixth Happiness. A Tale of Two Cities. 1960: Make Mine Mink. A French Mistress. Passport to China (GB: Visa to Canton). The Girl on the Boat. 1961: Francis

of Assisi. Two and Two Make Six. 1962: I Thank a Fool. The Devil Never Sleeps (US: Satan Never Sleeps). 1963: Nurse on Wheels.

SEYMOUR, Anne 1909–1988
Knowing-looking, tough-but-tender, light-haired American actress with droll tones and no-nonsense manner who, after long theatrical experience and very few films, came to Hollywood in the late 1950s and dispensed wit and wisdom in some brittle comedies and dramas, mainly in the 1957–1968 period, outside which she was much more often seen in the theatre and on TV. Ideally cast as a lady judge or intelligent administrator, she was often seen in 'social conscience' TV movies from 1974 on. Died from heart failure.

1931: Aloha (GB: No Greater Love). 1944: The Rainbow (dubbed US version of Russian film). 1949: All the King's Men. 1951: The Whistle at Eaton Falls (GB: Richer Than the Earth). 1957: Four Boys and a Gun. Desire Under the Elms. Man on Fire. 1958: The Gift of Love. Handle With Care. 1959: Home from the Hill. 1960: All the Fine Young Cannibals. The Subterraneans. Pollyanna. Sunrise at Campobello. 1961: Misty. 1962: This Rugged Land (TV. GB: cinemas). 1964: Good Neighbor Sam. Stage to Thunder Rock. Where Love Has Gone. 1965: Blindfold. Mirage. 1966: How to Succeed in Business Without Really Trying. Waco. 1967: Fitzwilly (GB: Fitzwilly Strikes Back). 1968: Stay Away Joe. 1972: The Man. 1973: So Long Blue Boy. Tenafly (TV). 1974: A Tree Grows in Brooklyn (TV). A Cry in the Wilderness (TV). 1975: The Gemini Affair. The Last Survivors (TV). Hearts of the West (GB: Hollywood Cowboy). 1976: Dawn: Portrait of a Teenage Runaway (TV). 1977: James at 15 (TV). 1980: The Miracle Worker (TV). Angel on My Shoulder (TV). 1981: Charlie and the Great Balloon Chase. 1982: Life of the Party: The Story of Beatrice (TV). Triumphs of a Man Called Horse. 1984: Gemini Affair II – A Diary. Trancers. 1985: Future Cop. 1986: The Leftovers (TV). 1988: Big Top Pee-wee. 1989: Field of Dreams.

SEYMOUR, Dan 1912–1993
Dark, plump, crunch-faced, blue-jowled Seymour was one of the slimiest Hollywood villains of the 1940s, his 'inverted' mouth

twisting frequently into a scowl, as he contemplated committing some new and more painful mayhem on the hero, most notably Humphrey Bogart and his associates in *To Have and Have Not*. Although only 32 at the time of this film, Seymour, a former nightclub entertainer, always looked around (a very round) 40. Occasionally relaxed and played a comic hoodlum instead; was too little seen after the end of the 1950s. Died following a stroke.

*1941: *Crazy Like a Fox. *The Whistler and his Dog. 1942: Cairo. Road to Morocco. Bombs Over Burma. The Talk of the Town. Casablanca. 1943: Tahiti Honey. Rhythm of the Islands. Klondike Kate. Mug Town. Tiger Fangs. 1944: †Rainbow Island. Kismet. It's in the Bag! (GB: The Fifth Chair). To Have and Have Not. 1945: The Spanish Main. San Antonio. Confidential Agent. 1946: A Night in Casablanca. Cloak and Dagger. 1947: Slave Girl. Hard Boiled Mahoney. The Searching Wind. Philo Vance's Gamble. Intrigue. 1948: Highway 13. Johnny Belinda. Unfaithfully Yours. Key Largo. 1949: Trail of the Yukon. 1950: Joe Palooka in the Squared Circle (GB: The Squared Circle). Abbott and Costello in the Foreign Legion. Young Man with a Horn (GB: Young Man of Music). 1951: The Blue Veil. 1952: Rancho Notorious. Mara Maru. Glory Alley. Face to Face. 1953: The System. Second Chance. Tangier Incident. The Big Heat. 1954: Moonfleet. Human Desire. 1955: While the City Sleeps. Abbott and Costello Meet the Mummy. 1956: Beyond a Reasonable Doubt. 1957: The Buster Keaton Story. The Sad Sack. Undersea Girl. 1959: The Return of the Fly. Watusi. 1973: Unholy Rollers. The Way We Were. 1974: Escape to Witch Mountain. Center Fold Girls (GB: Centrefold Girls).*

† Scenes deleted from final release print

SHAUGHNESSY, Mickey

(Joseph Shaughnessy) 1920–1985
Bullet-headed, snub-nosed, button-eyed, crop-haired, fast-talking, aggressive American actor, built like a little tank. After war service, he became a nightclub singer, then mixed comedy with the singing. Became a well-known film face as the serviceman who has his swear-words 'fluffed out' on the soundtrack in *Don't Go Near the Water*. Disappeared into television after 1970. Died from lung cancer.

1952: The Marrying Kind. Last of the Comanches (GB: The Sabre and the Arrow). 1953: From Here to Eternity. 1955: The Burglar. Conquest of Space. 1956: Don't Go Near the Water. 1957: Slaughter on 10th Avenue. Designing Woman. Until They Sail. Jailhouse Rock. 1958: The Sheepman. Gunman's Walk. A Nice Little Bank That Should Be Robbed (GB: How to Rob a Bank). 1959: Don't Give Up the Ship. Edge of Eternity. The Hangman. 1960: The Adventures of Huckleberry Finn. Sex Kittens Go to College. North to Alaska. College Confidential. Dondi. 1961: King of the Roaring Twenties (GB: The Big Bankroll). Pocketful of Miracles. 1962: How the West Was Won. 1963: A Global Affair. 1964: A House Is Not a Home. 1967: Never a Dull Moment. A Boy Called Nuthin' (TV). 1969: My Dog, the Thief. 1970: The Boatniks. 1985: Hellfire.

SHAW, Denis 1921–1971

Bulky British actor with a shock of dark wavy hair whose simian features consigned him to 'heavy' roles in more ways than one, although his portrayal of a judo-throwing Interpol detective in one minor thriller was engaging enough to make one regret the lack of a follow-up. But his slit eyes and outsize frame moved back into greasy-villain roles. Died from a heart attack at 49.

*1952: Girdle of Gold. The Long Memory. 1953: House of Blackmail. *The Candlelight Murder. The Case of Soho Red. 1954: Forbidden Cargo. Beau Brummell. The Seekers (US: Land of Fury). The Colditz Story. 1955:*

Keep It Clean. The Prisoner. Who Done It? 1956: Port Afrique. The Weapon. Stars in Your Eyes. 1957: Seven Thunders (US: The Beasts of Marseilles). The Flesh is Weak. The Depraved. 1958: Blood of the Vampire. A Woman Possessed. Soap Box Derby. Moment of Indiscretion. Links of Justice. The Great Van Robbery. 1959: Passport to Shame (US: Room 43). Innocent Meeting. The Bandit of Zhobe. No Safety Ahead. Jack the Ripper. The Mummy. Trouble With Eve (US: In Trouble With Eve). The Man Who Could Cheat Death. The Night We Dropped a Clanger. Naked Fury. 1960: The Criminal (US: The Concrete Jungle). Beyond the Curtain. The Misfits. The Two Faces of Dr Jekyll (US: House of Fright). The Night We Got the Bird. Make Mine Mink. 1961: Ticket to Paradise. Curse of the Werewolf. The Hellfire Club. A Weekend With Lulu. Nothing Barred. The Pirates of Blood River. Carry On Regardless. 1962: The Day of the Triffids. Invitation to Murder (completed 1959). 1964: The Runaway. 1966: The Deadly Affair. 1967: The Viking Queen. The Magnificent Six and a ½ (first series). 1969: The File of the Golden Goose. The Magnificent Six and ½ (second series).

SHAWN, Wallace 1943–

Small, pinkly bald, gremlin-like, troubled-looking American cameo player. The son of William Shawn, for 35 years editor of *The New Yorker*, Shawn made his name, following education at Harvard and Oxford, as a writer and playwright. He was drawn into acting in his mid thirties through taking a role in one of his own plays and, after his performance as Diane Keaton's waspish ex-husband in Woody Allen's *Manhattan*, quickly came into demand for small but telling featured roles in films, where he pops up, like some sardonic and malignant spirit, some two or three times a year, between continued success writing Broadway plays. Bids fair to become the Oscar Levant of his generation.

1979: Manhattan. All That Jazz. Starting Over. 1980: Atlantic City USA (GB and US: Atlantic City). Simon. 1981: My Dinner With André. A Little Sex. 1982: The First Time. 1983: Lovesick. Saigon — Year of the Cat (TV). Strange Invaders. Deal of the Century. Crackers. 1984: The Bostonians. The Hotel New Hampshire. Micki + Maude. 1985: Heaven Help Us (GB: Catholic Boys). 1986: Head Office. 1987: Nice Girls Don't Explode.

The Bedroom Window. Prick Up Your Ears. The Princess Bride. Radio Days. 1988: The Moderns. 1989: Scenes from the Class Struggle in Beverly Hills. She's Out of Control. We're No Angels. 1991: Mom and Dad Save the World. Shadows and Fog. Nickel and Dime. 1992: 00 Kid. Unbecoming Age. 1993: The Diary of the Hurdy Gurdy Man. The Meteor Man. The Cemetery Club. The Magic Bubble. 1994: Mrs Parker and the Vicious Circle. Vanya on 42nd Street. The Wife. 1995: Clueless. Canadian Bacon. House Arrest. A Goofy Movie (voice only).

SHAYNE, Tamara
See Tamiroff, Akim

SHEPLEY, Michael
(M. Shepley-Smith) 1907–1961
Brown-haired, solidly built, moustachioed, myopically peering British actor who played amiable buffoons through three decades of films; the sort of chap you'd expect to find asleep at the club behind his newspaper. It comes as no surprise to learn that his principal interest outside show-business was cricket.

1931: Black Coffee. 1933: A Shot in the Dark. 1934: Are You a Mason? Bella Donna. Tangled Evidence. Lord Edgware Dies. The Green Pack. Open All Night. 1935: Lazybones. Vintage Wine. The Rocks of Valpré (US: High Treason). The Ace of Spades. The Lad. Squibs. Jubilee Window. Private Secretary. The Triumph of Sherlock Holmes. That's My Uncle. 1936: In the Soup. Dishonour Bright. 1937: Beauty and the Barge. 1938: Crackerjack (US: The Man With a Hundred Faces). Housemaster. It's in the Air (US: George Takes the Air). 1939: Goodbye Mr Chips! 1940: Contraband (US: Blackout). 1941: Quiet Wedding. 1942: The Great Mr Handel. Women Aren't Angels. 1943: The Demi-Paradise (US: Adventure for Two). 1944: Henry V. 1945: A Place of One's Own. I Live in Grosvenor Square (US: A Yank in London). 1947: Nicholas Nickleby. Mine Own Executioner. 1949: Helter Skelter. Maytime in Mayfair. Elizabeth of Ladymead. 1951: Mr Denning Drives North. Secret People. 1952: Home at Seven (US: Murder on Monday). 1953: You Know What Sailors Are. 1954: Trouble in the Glen. Happy Ever After (US: Tonight's the Night/O'Leary Night). Out of the Clouds. 1955: Where There's a Will. An

Alligator Named Daisy. Doctor at Sea. 1956: My Teenage Daughter (US: Teenage Bad Girl). Dry Rot. The Passionate Stranger (US: A Novel Affair). 1957: Not Wanted on Voyage. 1958: Gideon's Day (US: Gideon of Scotland Yard). 1960: Just Joe. 1961: Don't Bother to Knock! (US: Why Bother to Knock?). Double Bunk.

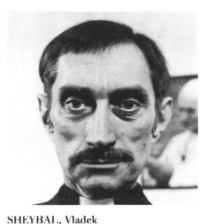

SHEYBAL, Vladek
(Wladyslaw Sheybal) 1923–1992
Polish actor with dark hair and pinched, cunning-looking features. Twice escaped from concentration camps during World War Two then, after one memorable film appearance in Poland, came to England and became a TV director. He returned to acting in 1963 and was seen occasionally in British and international films, usually in eccentric or menacing roles. Married/divorced Polish actress Irena Aklarovna.

1957: †Kanal. 1963: From Russia With Love. 1965: Return from the Ashes. 1967: Casino Royale. Billion Dollar Brain. 1968: The Limbo Line. Deadfall (shown 1967). Mosquito Squadron. 1969: Doppelgänger (US: Journey to the Far Side of the Sun). Women in Love. Leo the Last. 1970. The Last Valley. The Music Lovers. Puppet on a Chain. 1971: *The Spy's Wife. The Boy Friend. 1972: Innocent Bystanders. Scorpio. 1973: Pilatus und andere. Un baccio di una morte. 1974: S*P*Y*S. QB VII (TV). 1975: Bordella. The Wind and the Lion. The Sellout. 1976: Gulliver's Travels (voice only). Hamlet. 1977: Exorcist II The Heretic (voice only). 1979: The Lady Vanishes. Avalanche Express. 1980: Shōgun (TV. GB: cinemas, in abbreviated version). The Apple (GB: Star Rock). 1982: Funny Money. 1983: Memed My Hawk. Where is Parsifal? (released 1985). The Jigsaw Man. 1984: Red Dawn. 1989: Champagne Charlie (TV). 1990: Strike It Rich/Loser Take All. 1992: Double X — The Name of the Game.

† As Wladyslaw Sheybal

SHIELDS, Arthur 1895–1970
Light-haired, wistful-looking Irish actor, recognizably the brother of character superstar Barry Fitzgerald. Shields (the real family name) played much smaller roles than his brother after their arrival in Hollywood in the 1930s, but nonetheless etched some sharp studies. Often seen in rimless spectacles, usually dispensing wisdom to those

more headstrong than himself. Died from emphysema.

1918: Rafferty's Rise. 1936: The Plough and the Stars. 1939: Drums along the Mohawk. 1940: The Long Voyage Home. Little Nellie Kelly. 1941: How Green Was My Valley. The Gay Falcon. Lady Scarface. Confirm or Deny. 1942: Pacific Rendezvous. Dr Gillespie's New Assistant. Gentleman Jim. This Above All. Broadway. Nightmare. Random Harvest. The Black Swan. 1943: Lassie Come Home. The Man from Down Under. Madame Curie. Above Suspicion. 1944: The Keys of the Kingdom. The Sign of the Cross (new prologue to 1932 feature). The White Cliffs of Dover. Youth Runs Wild. National Velvet. 1945: *Phantoms Inc. Too Young to Know. The Corn Is Green. The Valley of Decision. The Picture of Dorian Gray. Roughly Speaking. 1946: Three Strangers. Gallant Journey. Never Say Goodbye. The Verdict. The Shocking Miss Pilgrim. 1947: Easy Come, Easy Go. Seven Keys to Baldpate. The Fabulous Dorseys. 1948: Fighting Father Dunne. Tap Roots. My Own True Love. 1949: Red Light. Challenge to Lassie. The Fighting O'Flynn. She Wore a Yellow Ribbon. 1950: Tarzan and the Slave Girl. 1951: Sealed Cargo. Apache Drums. Blue Blood. The People Against O'Hara. A Wonderful Life. The River. The Barefoot Mailman. 1952: The Quiet Man. Scandal at Scourie. 1953: South Sea Woman. Main Street to Broadway. 1954: Pride of the Blue Grass (GB: Prince of the Blue Grass). World for Ransom. River of No Return. 1955: Lady Godiva (GB: Lady Godiva of Coventry). 1956: The King and Four Queens. 1957: Daughter of Dr Jekyll. 1958: Enchanted Island. 1959: Night of the Quarter Moon. 1960: For the Love of Mike (GB: None But the Brave). 1961: King of the Roaring Twenties (GB: The Big Bankroll). 1962: The Pigeon That Took Rome.

SHINE, Bill
(Wilfred Shine Jr) 1911–
Tall, light-haired, sleepy-eyed, thin British supporting actor with handlebar moustache; you were prepared for the upper-crust accent before it came and he fitted in well as well-meaning but addle-brained officer or aristocrat. He was also seen as the hero's friend or slightly inefficient official. The son of actor Wilfred Shine, who appeared in early British sound films, Bill (billed as Billy until 1940) made his first appearance on

stage at six, playing a stork. Hobbies: ridin', fishin' and racin' (what about the shootin'?). Splendidly cast in one film as 'Flying Officer Prang'.

1929: High Seas. The Flying Scotsman. Under the Greenwood Tree. 1930: The Last Hour. The Yellow Mask. Harmony Heaven. 1931: These Charming People. Money for Nothing. Many Waters. 1932: Verdict of the Sea. The Man from Toronto. 1934: My Old Dutch. Waltzes from Vienna (US: Strauss's Great Waltz). The Scarlet Pimpernel. 1935: Blue Smoke. It Happened in Paris. Late Extra. Music Hath Charms. Old Roses. 1936: Highland Flying. You Must Get Married. Rembrandt. Take a Chance. Find the Lady. Servants All. Gaolbreak. To Catch a Thief. Sensation! 1937: The Strange Adventures of Mr Smith. Farewell Again (US: Troopship). Young and Innocent (US: The Girl Was Young). The Last Adventurers. The Green Cockatoo (US: Four Dark Hours). Over the Moon (released 1940). The Compulsory Wife. The Squeaker (US: Murder on Diamond Row). Cotton Queen. Dinner at the Ritz. There Was a Young Man. First Night. *Agony Column. 1938: The Villiers Diamond. Second Thoughts. You're the Doctor. They Drive By Night. The Terror. His Lordship Goes to Press. 1939: The Face at the Window. 1940: Let George Do It. Three Silent Men. Crooks' Tour. 1941: Inspector Hornleigh Goes to It (US: Mail Train). Turned Out Nice Again. *As You Are. 1944: Champagne Charlie. Fiddlers Three. 1945: Perfect Strangers (US: Vacation from Marriage). For You Alone. 1946: Wanted for Murder. 1947: Captain Boycott. Vice Versa. 1948: The Red Shoes. The Winslow Boy. The Small Voice (US: Hideout). Another Shore. 1949: Passport to Pimlico. Private Angelo. Under Capricorn. The Chiltern Hundreds (US: The Amazing Mr Beecham). 1950: Something in the City. The Woman With No Name (US: Her Paneled Door). Old Mother Riley's Jungle Treasure. 1951: Talk of a Million (US: You Can't Beat the Irish). Scarlet Thread. 1952: Love's a Luxury (US: The Caretaker's Daughter). The Woman's Angle. Never Look Back. Hot Ice. No Haunt for a Gentleman. Mother Riley Meets the Vampire (US: Vampire Over London). There Was a Young Lady. 1953: Melba. Innocents in Paris. The Blakes Slept Here. The Clue of the Missing Ape. 1954: Knave of Hearts (US: Lovers, Happy Lovers). Father Brown (US: The Detective). Duel in the Jungle. Devil on Horse-

back. Happy Ever After (US: Tonight's the Night/O'Leary Night). 1955: As Long As They're Happy. An Alligator Named Daisy. The Adventures of Quentin Durward (US: Quentin Durward). The Gold Express. The Deep Blue Sea. Richard III. Raising a Riot. Where There's a Will. John and Julie. 1956: Bond of Fear. Not So Dusty. Women Without Men (US: Blonde Bait). The Last Man to Hang? 1957: The Tommy Steele Story (US: Rock Around the World). High Flight. The House in the Woods. Blue Murder at St Trinian's. 1958: Diplomatic Corpse. The Man Inside. 1959: Libel! Make Mine a Million. Left, Right and Centre. Jack the Ripper. The Boy and the Bridge. The Challenge. Trouble With Eve (US: In Trouble With Eve). 1960: The Pure Hell of St Trinian's. 1961: Double Bunk. 1963: The Rescue Squad. 1964: The Yellow Rolls-Royce. 1965: Joey Boy. 1966: The Great St Trinian's Train Robbery. Bindle (One of Them Days). 1967: *Ouch! The Sky Bike. 1971: Burke and Hare. Not Tonight Darling! 1983: The Jigsaw Man. 1985: The McGuffin (TV). 1987: A Very Peculiar Practice (TV).

SHOWALTER, Max 1917–
Fair-haired, pale-eyed American actor who changed his name to Casey Adams when with 20th Century-Fox in 1952 and played glib charmers and light romantic leads. He reverted to his real name during 1962, but has preferred to concentrate on his secondary career as a composer of background scores for the theatre and cinema. He also composed the title song for Vicki, in which he had one of his best roles.

1949: Always Leave Them Laughing. 1952: With a Song in My Heart. †What Price Glory? †My Wife's Best Friend. 1953: †Niagara. †Destination Gobi. †Dangerous Crossing. †Vicki. 1954: †Night People. †Naked Alibi. †Down Three Dark Streets. 1955: †The Return of Jack Slade (GB: Texas Rose). 1956: †Never Say Goodbye. †The Indestructible Man. †Bus Stop. 1957: †Dragoon Wells Massacre. †The Monster That Challenged the World. †Designing Woman. 1958: †The Female Animal. †Voice in the Mirror. †The Naked and the Dead. 1959: †It Happened to Jane. 1960: †Elmer Gantry. 1961: †Return to Peyton Place. †Summer and Smoke. †The Music Man. 1962: †Bon Voyage! Smog. 1963: My Six Loves. Move Over, Darling. 1964: Fate Is the Hunter. Sex and the

Single Girl. 1965: How to Murder Your Wife. Lord Love a Duck. 1969: A Talent for Loving. 1970: The Moonshine War. 1971: The Anderson Tapes. 1972: Bonnie's Kids. 1978: Sergeant Pepper's Lonely Hearts Club Band. 1979: '10'. 1981: A Gun in the House (TV). 1984: Racing With the Moon. Sixteen Candles.

† As Casey Adams

SHULL, Richard B. 1929–
Chubby, po-faced American actor with a shock of dark (now greying) wavy hair, often seen as benign blunderers, who has coughed and spluttered his way through far too few film and TV roles since making the move from stage management and directing and becoming a full-time actor in 1971 in his early forties. At his busiest in the 1970s, Shull has recently made some welcome reappearances as elderly duffers and non-threatening types, but been given too little screen time for his own delicate brand of fun.

1971: The Anderson Tapes. B.S. I Love You. 1972: Klute. Such Good Friends. 1973: Hail to the Chief! Slither. Sssssss (GB: Sssnake). 1974: Cockfighter/Born to Kill. The Fortune. 1975: The Black Bird. Hearts of the West (GB: Hollywood Cowboy). 1976: The Big Bus. 1977: The Pack/The Long Dark Night. 1978: Ziegfeld: The Man and His Women (TV). Dreamer. Wholly Moses! 1981: Heartbeeps. 1983: Lovesick. Spring Break. 1984: Splash. Unfaithfully Yours. Garbo Talks. 1986: Seize the Day (originally for TV). Spot Marks the X (TV). 1990: Tune in Tomorrow (GB: Aunt Julia and the Scriptwriter). 1992: HouseSitter. 1993: Love or Money (GB: The Concierge). 1994: Trapped in Paradise.

SIKKING, James B. 1934–
Tall, dark, dour American actor with a passing resemblance to Roy Scheider. Playing officers, detectives and businessmen, he seemed to escape the public eye until pitched into the limelight with his running role as Hunter in the popular TV series Hill Street Blues. Sometimes bespectacled in recent years, he continues to achieve a good range of roles, and one also suspects a dry sense of comedy. The 'B' stands for Barrie (named after his parents' favourite author).

1955: Five Guns West. 1956: The Revolt of

Mamie Stover. 1963: The Strangler. The Carpetbaggers. 1964: The Americanization of Emily. 1965: Von Ryan's Express. 1967: Point Blank. 1969: Charro! Daddy's Gone a-Hunting. 1971: The Night God Screamed (GB: Scream). Chandler. 1972: The Astronaut (TV). Man on a String (TV). Brother on the Run. The Magnificent Seven Ride! Boots Turner. Family Flight (TV). Scorpio. The New Centurions (GB: Precinct 45 — Los Angeles Police). 1973: The Alpha Caper (TV. GB: cinemas, as Inside Job). Coffee, Tea or Me? (TV). 1974: The FBI versus Alvin Karpis, Public Enemy Number One (TV). The Terminal Man. 1977: Capricorn One. Young Joe, the Forgotten Kennedy (TV). Kill Me If You Can (TV). The Last Hurrah (TV). 1978: A Woman Called Moses (TV). 1979: The Electric Horseman. 1980: Ordinary People. Trouble in the High Timber Country (TV). The Competition. 1981: Outland. 1983: The Star Chamber. 1984: Up the Creek. Star Trek III The Search for Spock. 1985: Morons from Outer Space. First Steps (TV). 1986: Soul Man. 1987: Police Story: The Freeway Killings (TV). Bay Coven (TV. GB: Bay Cove). 1988: Too Good to be True (TV). 1989: Ollie Hopnoodle's Haven of Bliss (TV). Narrow Margin. The Final Days (TV). Desperado: Badlands Justice (TV). 1991: Final Approach. Doing Time on Maple Drive (TV). 1993: The Pelican Brief. 1994: Strong City. Dead Badge. 1995: In Pursuit of Honor (TV).

SILVA, Henry 1928—

Cold-eyed, impassive, scowling, slightly oriental-looking, dark-haired American actor (of Puerto Rican parentage) who often plays emotionless killers. If you saw Silva coming down a street towards you, the odds are that you would cross to the other side. An attempt to install him in leading roles in the early sixties was not successful and, although he has continued with bad guys, they have often been too silly for him to make an impact. Much in Italy from the mid-sixties, he later made many obscure action films of the 'straight to video' variety.

1952: Viva Zapata! 1956: Crowded Paradise. 1957: A Hatful of Rain. The Tall T. 1958: The Law and Jake Wade. The Bravados. Ride a Crooked Trail. 1959: Green Mansions. The Jayhawkers. 1960: Cinderfella. Ocean's Eleven. 1962: Sergeants Three. The Manchurian Candidate. 1963: A Gathering of Eagles.

Johnny Cool. 1964: The Secret Invasion. 1965: The Reward. The Return of Mr Moto. Je vous salue Mafia (US: Hail Mafia). 1966: Matchless. The Plainsman. Un fiume di dollari (GB: The Hills Run Red). 1967: Assassination. Never a Dull Moment. 1968: Quella carogna dell' Ispettore Sterling (US: Blood Money). 1969: Probabilità zero. Drive Hard, Drive Fast (TV). 1970: The Animals (GB: Five Savage Men). 1971: Black Noon (TV). Man and Boy. 1972: The Falling Man. La 'mala' ordina (GB: Manhunt in Milan). L'insolent. Les hommes. 1973: Il boss (GB: Murder Inferno). Zinksarge für die Goldjungen. 1974: Cry of a Prostitute. Milano odia: la polizia non puo' sparare (US: Almost Human). The Kidnap of Mary Lou. 1975: L'uomo della strada fa giustizia. Zanna Bianca alla riscossa/Challenge to White Fang. 1976: Shoot. Eviolenti. 1977: Fox Bat. Contract on Cherry Street (TV). 1978: Love and Bullets. 1979: Buck Rogers in the 25th Century (TV. GB: cinemas). 1980: Thirst. Virus. Alligator. 1981: Sharky's Machine. Trapped. 1982: Wrong is Right (GB: The Man With the Deadly Lens). Megaforce. 1983: Happy (TV). Chained Heat. Violent Breed. Cannonball Run II. 1984: Crossfire. Man Hunt Warning (US: The Manhunt). 1985: Escape from the Bronx. Lust in the Dust. Code of Silence. 1986: Robur. Allan Quatermain and the Lost City of Gold. Amazon Women on the Moon. 1987: Above the Law. Bulletproof. 1988: Trained to Kill. Fists of Steel. 1989: The Hard Way. White Cobra Express. Cy-Warrior. 1990: Critical Action. Dick Tracy. 1991: The Last Match. 1992: Three Days to a Kill. The Harvest. South Beach. 1993: Possessed by the Night. 1995: Drifting School.

SILVER, Ron

(R. Zimelman) 1946—

Hook-nosed, moon-faced, intense-looking, sometimes bearded, dark-haired American actor, cast an extrovert in his earlier days, but latterly in more withdrawn complex roles, in a mixture of leads and top supporting roles. Education in America and China was followed by stints as teacher and social worker before 'I dwindled into being an actor'. In the later 1980s, he stuck to the theatre, returning to films after a break of several years with his reputation enhanced. One of Hollywood's great activists, Silver is often seen in politically correct roles that concern human rights. Became president of Actors' Equity in 1991.

1971: The French Connection. 1976: Tunnelvision. The Return of the World's Greatest Detective (TV). 1977: Semi-Tough. 1978: Betrayal (TV). Murder at the Mardi Gras (TV). 1979: Dear Detective (TV). 1981: Word of Honor (TV). 1982: Best Friends. The Entity. Silent Rage. 1983: Lovesick. Silkwood. 1984: Garbo Talks. The Goodbye People. Romancing the Stone. Oh, God! You Devil. 1985: Eat and Run. 1986: Trapped in Silence (TV). 1988: A Father's Revenge (TV). 1989: Enemies, A Love Story. Blue Steel. 1990: Fellow Traveller. Forgotten Prisoners. Reversal of Fortune. 1991: Married To It. 1992: Mr Saturday Night. Live Wire. 1993: Lifepod (TV). The Good Policeman. Blind Side (cable TV). 1994: Time Cop. 1995: Deadly Takeover.

As director:
1993: Lifepod (TV).

SILVERHEELS, Jay

(Harold J. Smith) 1917—1980

One of the few American Indian actors to play 'normal' acting roles as well, round-faced, cheerful-looking Silverheels, the son of a Canadian Mohawk chief, came to films as an extra and stuntman in 1938, in the days when he was a budding boxing and lacrosse star in real life. His best film roles came after his television success as Tonto in the long-running (1949—57) western series *The Lone Ranger*. In later years, he combined acting with a career in harness-racing, but died at 63 as a result of complications from an attack of pneumonia.

1939: Geronimo. 1940: The Sea Hawk. Too Many Girls. 1941: Western Union. 1942:

Valley of the Sun. 1943: Good Morning, Judge. Northern Pursuit. The Girl from Monterey. Daredevils of the West (serial). 1945: †Song of the Sarong. 1946: †Singin' in the Corn (GB: Give and Take). †Canyon Passage. 1947: †The Last Round-Up. †Unconquered. †Vacation Days. †Gas House Kids Go West. Captain from Castile. Northwest Outpost (GB: End of the Rainbow). 1948: Indian Agent. The Feathered Serpent. Key Largo. Fury at Furnace Creek. The Prairie. Singing Spurs. Yellow Sky. Family Honeymoon. 1949: Will James' Sand (GB: Sand). Trail of the Yukon. For Those Who Dare. Lust for Gold. Laramie. The Cowboy and the Indians. Song of India. 1950: Broken Arrow. 1951: Red Mountain. The Wild Blue Yonder (GB: Thunder Across the Pacific). 1952: Brave Warrior. The Battle at Apache Pass. Yankee Buccaneer. The Will Rogers Story (GB: The Story of Will Rogers). The Pathfinder. Last of the Comanches (GB: The Sabre and the Arrow). 1953: War Arrow. Jack McCall — Desperado. The Nebraskan. 1954: The Black Dakotas. Masterson of Kansas. Drums Across the River. Four Guns to the Border. Saskatchewan (GB: O'Rourke of the Royal Mounted). 1955: The Vanishing American. 1956: Walk the Proud Land. The Lone Ranger. 1958: Return to Warbow. The Lone Ranger and the Lost City of Gold. 1959: Alias Jesse James. 1962: Geronimo's Revenge (TV. GB: cinemas). 1964: Indian Paint. 1969: Smith! True Grit. The Phynx. 1972: Santee. 1973: One Little Indian. The Man Who Loved Cat Dancing.

† As Silverheels Smith

SIM, Gerald 1925–
Light-haired British actor with friendly, open face, often cast in inoffensive, well-meaning roles, such as probation officers, social workers or helpful civil servants. He was unsuccessful in getting a foothold in films as a young man but, after an effective appearance in *The Angry Silence*, he was seen in almost all of the subsequent films made by its co-producers, Bryan Forbes and Sir Richard Attenborough. Still around in patrician roles.

1947: Fame is the Spur. 1950: Trio. Seven Days to Noon. Desparate Journey. 1955: Josephine and Men. 1959: The Angry Silence. 1960: Cone of Silence (US: Trouble in the Sky). 1961: Whistle Down the Wind. The Painted Smile. Only Two Can Play. 1962:

Flat Two. The Amorous Prawn (US: The Amorous Mr Prawn). The Wrong Arm of the Law. The L-Shaped Room. 1963: I Could Go On Singing (shown 1962). West 11. Heavens Above! 1964: The Pumpkin Eater. Seance on a Wet Afternoon. 1965: King Rat. 1966: The Murder Game. The Whisperers. 1967: Our Mother's House. Nobody Runs Forever (US: The High Commissioner). 1969: Mischief. The Madwoman of Chaillot. Oh! What a Lovely War. The Last Grenade (US: Grigsby). 1970: Ryan's Daughter. The Man Who Haunted Himself. Doctor in Trouble. The Raging Moon (US: Long Ago Tomorrow). 1971: Dr Jekyll and Sister Hyde. Young Winston. 1972: Dr Phibes Rises Again. Frenzy. Kadoyng. 1973: No Sex, Please — We're British. 1976: The Slipper and the Rose. 1977: A Bridge Too Far. 1978: Death on the Nile. 1982: Gandhi. 1987: Cry Freedom. 1988: Number One Gun. 1992: Patriot Games. Chaplin. 1993: Shadowlands.

SIMS, Joan
(Irene J. Sims) 1930–
Cheery-looking, fair-haired British actress with distinctive light voice and pinched lips. Almost entirely in comedy parts, at first as curvaceous, man-hungry cockneys, sometimes with assumed upper-class accents, and later, with added weight, a key member of the 'Carry On' comedy team, usually playing nagging wives. Vanished from the cinema with the demise of that series.

1953: Will Any Gentleman?... The Square Ring. Colonel March Investigates. Trouble in Store. Meet Mr Lucifer. 1954: Doctor in the House. What Every Woman Wants. The Young Lovers (US: Chance Meeting). The Belles of St Trinian's. To Dorothy a Son (US: Cash on Delivery). The Sea Shall Not Have Them. 1955: As Long As They're Happy. Doctor at Sea. Lost (US: Tears for Simon). 1956: Keep It Clean. The Silken Affair. Stars in Your Eyes. Dry Rot. 1957: Just My Luck. Davy. Carry On Admiral (US: The Ship Was Loaded). No Time for Tears. The Naked Truth (US: Your Past is Showing). 1958: The Captain's Table. 1959: Passport to Shame (US: Room 43). Carry On Nurse. Life in Emergency Ward 10. Carry On Teacher. Upstairs and Downstairs. Please Turn Over. 1960: Carry On Constable. Doctor in Love. Watch Your Stern. His and Hers. 1961: Carry On Regardless. Mr Topaze (US: I Like Money). No, My Darling Daughter!

A Pair of Briefs. 1962: Twice Round the Daffodils. The Iron Maiden (US: The Swingin' Maiden). Nurse on Wheels. 1963: Strictly for the Birds. 1964: Carry On Cleo. 1965: The Big Job. San Ferry Ann. Carry On Cowboy. Doctor in Clover. 1966: Carry On Screaming. Don't Lose Your Head. 1967: Follow That Camel. Carry On Doctor. 1968: Carry On Up the Khyber. 1969: Carry On Camping. Carry On Again, Doctor. Carry On Up the Jungle. 1970: Doctor in Trouble. Carry On Loving. Carry on Henry. 1971: The Magnificent Seven Deadly Sins. Carry On at Your Convenience. 1972: Carry On Matron. The Alf Garnett Saga. Carry On Abroad. Not Now Darling. 1973: Carry On Girls. Don't Just Lie There, Say Something. 1974: Carry On Dick. Love Among the Ruins (TV). 1975: Carry On Behind. One of Our Dinosaurs is Missing. 1976: Carry on England. 1978: Carry On Emmannuelle. 1990: The Fool.

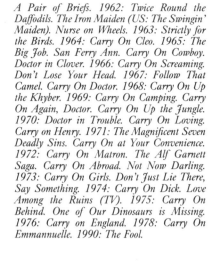

SINGER, Campbell 1909–1976
Dark-haired, lively, moustachioed British actor whose oval features could easily express such disparate emotions as hopefulness, friendliness, grouchiness and resolution. He was generally cast as hard workers — police sergeants, railwaymen, labourers or forces types. Born in London, he was raised in South Africa, where he made his stage debut in 1928 before returning to England in the early 1930s. A busy employee of the British cinema (usually lending a friendly hand to the hero) from 1947 to 1962; after that he devoted his talents mainly to television. Mainly in minor parts, but had a good leading role in *The Young and the Guilty*.

1938: Premiere (US: One Night in Paris). 1947: The Woman in the Hall. Take My Life. Jim the Penman. 1948: Dick Barton — Special Agent. Operation Diamond. Woman Hater. 1949: Rover and Me. The Spider and the Fly. The Blue Lamp. Hangman's Wharf. 1950: Dick Barton at Bay. Cage of Gold. Pool of London. Blackout. Quiet Woman. 1951: The Man With the Twisted Lip. A Case for PC 49. 1952: Emergency Call (US: Hundred Hour Hunt). The Happy Family (US: Mr Lord Says No). Lady in the Fog (US: Scotland Yard Inspector. Home at Seven (US: Murder on Monday). The Yellow Balloon. The Ringer. Appointment in London. The Titfield Thunder-

bolt. Time Bomb (US: Terror on a Train). 1953: Street Corner (US: Both Sides of the Law). The Girl on the Pier. The Intruder. 1954: Forbidden Cargo. Conflict of Wings (US: Fuss Over Feathers). To Dorothy a Son (US: Cash on Delivery). 1955: Simba. †As Long As They're Happy. 1956: Ramsbottom Rides Again. Reach for the Sky. Town on Trial! 1957: Davy. 1958: The Young and the Guilty. No Trees in the Street (US: No Tree in the Street). The Square Peg. 1960: The Hands of Orlac. The Trials of Oscar Wilde (US: The Man With the Green Carnation). Sands of the Desert. 1961: No, My Darling Daughter! 1962: On the Beat. The Devil's Daffodil (US: The Daffodil Killer). The Wild and the Willing. The Fast Lady. Flat Two. The Pot Carriers. 1964: Go Kart Go! 1966: †The Collector.

† Scenes deleted from final release print

SKIPWORTH, Alison
(née Groom) 1863–1952
Brown-haired, heavy-featured, slightly menacing British actress, a heavyweight who looked built for stern dramatics, but more often scored in comedy. Married to the artist Frank Markam Skipworth, she didn't become an actress until she was 30 and went to America two years later, gradually becoming a solid player on Broadway. In Hollywood from 1930, she never looked her real age, and people were amazed to find she was 75 when she finally retired. More than a match for W.C. Fields and even Mae West, she had a couple of vehicles of her own (A Lady's Profession, Madame Racketeer) as well as taking the Sydney Greenstreet role in Satan Met a Lady, the second version of The Maltese Falcon!

1920: 39 East. 1921: Handcuffs or Kisses. 1930: Du Barry, Woman of Passion (GB: Du Barry). Oh! For a Man. Outward Bound. Raffles. Strictly Unconventional. 1931: Devotion. The Virtuous Husband (GB: What Wives Don't Want). The Road to Singapore. Tonight or Never. Night Angel. Sinners in the Sun. 1932: High Pressure. Madame Racketeer (GB: The Sporting Widow). Unexpected Father. Night After Night. If I Had a Million. 1933: Tonight Is Ours. He Learned About Women. A Lady's Profession. Song of Songs. Tillie and Gus. Midnight Club. Alice in Wonderland. 1934: Six of a Kind. Wharf Angel. The Notorious Sophie Lang. Here in My Heart.

Shoot the Works (GB: Thank Your Stars). Coming-Out Party. The Captain Hates the Sea. 1935: Shanghai. The Devil Is a Woman. The Casino Murder Case. Becky Sharp. The Girl from 10th Avenue (GB: Men On Her Mind). Doubting Thomas. Dangerous. 1936: Hitch Hike Lady (GB: Eventful Journey). The Princess Comes Across. Satan Met a Lady. The Gorgeous Hussy. Two in a Crowd. White Hunter. Stolen Holiday. 1937: Two Wise Maids. 1938: King of the Newsboys. Wide Open Faces. Ladies in Distress.

SLATER, John
(B. John Slater) 1916–1975
Dark-haired British actor of thin lips and shadowed aspect — from the narrowness of his projecting features — who usually found himself cast as down-to-earth working types. Sometimes he would don a scowl and play a crook. His beetle brows were much in evidence in British films from 1941 to 1957 (although his career was temporarily slowed when he was injured in an air crash in 1946), after which he was mainly on stage and TV. Also for many years the narrator of the Mining Review documentary shorts. He suffered from ill-health later in his career, although he did become popular as Sgt Stone in TV's Z Cars. Died from a heart attack.

1938: †Alf's Button Afloat. 1941: †Love on the Dole. †The Patient Vanishes (later This Man is Dangerous). †The Harvest Shall Come. Gert and Daisy's Weekend. Hatter's Castle. Jeannie (US: Girl in Distress). The Saint Meets the Tiger. *Shunter Black's Night Off (narrator only). Pimpernel Smith (US: Mister V). Facing the Music. The Common Touch. Penn of Pennsylvania (US: The Courageous Mr Penn). They Flew Alone (US: Wings and the Woman). 1942: The Young Mr Pitt. Uncensored. Went the Day Well? (US: 48 Hours). The Day Will Dawn (US: The Avengers). 1943: We Dive at Dawn. Candlelight in Algeria. The Adventures of Tartu (US: Tartu). Undercover (US: Underground Guerrillas). Deadlock. Millions Like Us. The Hundred Pound Window. 1944: A Canterbury Tale. *Unity is Strength. For Those in Peril. 1945: I Live in Grosvenor Square (US: A Yank in London). Murder in Reverse. The Seventh Veil. 1946: Othello. 1947: Teheran (US: The Plot to Kill Roosevelt). It Always Rains on Sunday. 1948: Against the

Wind. Noose (US: The Silk Noose). Escape. 1949: Passport to Pimlico. 1950: Prelude to Fame. 1951: The Third Visitor. 1952: The Ringer. Faithful City. The Long Memory. *Dark London (narrator only). Appointment in London. 1953: The Flanagan Boy (US: Bad Blonde). The Million Pound Note (US: Man With a Million). Strange Stories (narrator only). Star of India. 1955: Dollars for Sale. Johnny You're Wanted. *Puzzle Corner No.17. *Puzzle Corner No.18. 1956: *Do You Remember? 1957: The Devil's Pass. Violent Playground. 1960: The Night We Got the Bird. 1961: Three on a Spree. Nothing Barred. 1962: *The Wrestling Game (narrator only). *Pig Tales (narrator only). 1963: A Place to Go. 1966: The Yellow Hat. *Germany Today (narrator only).

† As B. John Slater

SLEZAK, Walter 1902–1983
Tubby, moustachioed Austrian actor, just as likely to be affable or menacing (but probably most memorable as the German on Hitchcock's Lifeboat) and a welcome part of any film. He had two bursts of intense film activity, in Germany from 1924 to 1928 and in Hollywood from 1942 to 1954, having been in America since the early 1930s. Otherwise mostly on stage. Also a writer and humorist. Slezak, the son of an opera star, was no mean singer himself. Retired in 1972, but in 1983 committed suicide by shooting himself.

1921: Sodom and Gomorrah. 1924: Mein Leopold. Michael. 1925: Die gefundene Braut. Grüss mir das blonde Kind am Rhein. O alte Burschenherrlichkeit. Sumpf und Moral. 1926: Aus des Rheinlands Schicksalstagen. Das war in Heidelberg in blauer Sommernacht. Junges Blut. Marccos tollste Wette. Der Seekadett. Wie bleibe ich jung und schön. 1927: Der Fahnenträger von Sedan. Die grosse Rause. Liebe geht seltsame Wege. Die Lorelei. 1928: Das Hannerl vom Rolandsbogen. Einen Jux will er sich machen. Ledige Mütter. Addio. Glovinezza. 1930: Eros in Ketten. 1932: Spione am Savoy Hotel. 1942: Once Upon a Honeymoon. 1943: This Land Is Mine. The Fallen Sparrow. 1944: Step Lively. Lifeboat. Till We Meet Again. And Now Tomorrow. The Princess and the Pirate. 1945: The Spanish Main. Salome, Where She Danced. Cornered. 1947: Born to Kill (GB: Lady of Deceit). Riffraff. Sinbad the Sailor. 1948: The

Pirate. 1949: The Inspector General. 1950: The Yellow Cab Man. Spy Hunt (GB: Panther's Moon). Abbott and Costello in the Foreign Legion. 1951: Bedtime for Bonzo. People Will Talk. 1953: Confidentially Connie. White Witch Doctor. Call Me Madam. 1954: The Steel Cage. 1956: The Last Patriarch (TV). Deadlier Than the Male. 1957: Ten Thousand Bedrooms. 1958: The Gentleman from Seventh Avenue (TV). 1959: The Miracle. 1961: Come September. 1962: The Wonderful World of the Brothers Grimm. 1964: Emil and the Detectives. Wonderful Life (US: Swingers' Paradise). 1965: 24 Hours to Kill. Der Kongress amüsiert sich. A Very Special Favor. 1966: Coppelius. 1967: The Caper of the Golden Bulls (GB: Carnival of Thieves). 1968: Legend of Robin Hood (TV). Heidi Comes Home (US: Heidi). 1971: Black Beauty. Treasure Island. 1972: The Mysterious House of Dr C.

SLOANE, Everett 1909–1965

Small, hard-hitting American actor with receding gingery hair and weasel-like face, often bespectacled. Made his initial impact in films with Orson Welles, his Mercury Theatre colleague, then rather faded away before *The Big Knife* and *Patterns* deservedly restored him to prominence among in-demand character stars. But in 1965 he committed suicide with sleeping pills.

1941: Citizen Kane. 1942: Journey into Fear. 1945: We Accuse (narrator only). 1948: The Lady from Shanghai. 1949: Prince of Foxes. 1950: The Men. The Enforcer (GB: Murder Inc.). The Prince Who Was a Thief. 1951: Sirocco. The Desert Fox (GB: Rommel—Desert Fox). Bird of Paradise. The Blue Veil. The Sellout. 1952: Way of a Gaucho. 1955: The Big Knife. 1956: Patterns (GB: Patterns of Power). Child of the Regiment (TV). Lust for Life. Somebody Up There Likes Me. Massacre at Sand Creek (TV). 1958: Marjorie Morningstar. The Gun Runners. 1959: The Sounds of Eden (TV). 1960: Home from the Hill. Alas, Babylon (TV). 1961: By Love Possessed. 1962: Brushfire! 1963: The Man from the Diner's Club. 1964: Ready for the People. The Disorderly Orderly. The Patsy.

SLOANE, Olive 1896–1963

British actress who should have gone to Hollywood, where frowzy blondes of the

type she portrayed so expertly were much more in demand. As it was, she stayed in the British cinema (and theatre) and had to be content with a couple of decent film roles in the early 1950s. Began as a child entertainer, singer and clog dancer, making a few silent films as a leading lady before coming back to sound films in her late thirties.

1921: Greatheart. The Door That Has No Key. 1922: Lonesome Farm. Trapped by the Mormons. 1923: Rogues of the Turf. The Dream of Eugene Aram. 1925: Money Isn't Everything. 1933: The Good Companions. Soldiers of the King (US: The Woman in Command). Lily of Killarney (US: Bride of the Lake). 1934: Sing As We Go. Faces. Brides To Be. Music Hall. 1935: Key to Harmony. Alibi Inn. Squibs. The Private Secretary. 1936: In the Soup. The Howard Case. Café Colette (US: Danger in Paris). 1937: Overcoat Sam. Dreaming Lips. Mad About Money/Stardust (US: He Loved an Actress). 1938: Consider Your Verdict. Make-Up. Make It Three. 1939: Inquest. 1941: The Tower of Terror. 1942: Thunder Rock. Those Kids from Town. Let the People Sing. 1943: The Dummy Talks. 1945: They Knew Mr Knight. The Voice Within. 1946: Send for Paul Temple. 1947: Bank Holiday Luck. 1948: The Guinea Pig. Counterblast. 1949: Under Capricorn. 1950: Waterfront (US: Waterfront Women). Seven Days to Noon. Once a Sinner. The Franchise Affair. 1952: Tall Headlines. Curtain Up! My Wife's Lodger. 1953: Alf's Baby. Meet Mr Lucifer. The Weak and the Wicked. 1954: The Golden Link. 1955: A Prize of Gold. 1956: The Man in the Road. The Last Man to Hang? Brothers in Law. 1959: Serious Charge (US: A Touch of Hell). Wrong Number. Your Money or Your Wife. The Price of Silence. 1960: The House in Marsh Road. 1963: Heavens Above!

SMITH, Sir C. Aubrey
(Charles A. Smith) 1863–1948

Tall, craggy, stately, aristocratic-looking English actor with bristling moustache and untamed eyebrows. Went to Hollywood in 1931, and became the doyen of the English colony there, organizing their cricket in between a hectic acting life. Died (from pneumonia) with his boots on at 85, his last film still to be shown. Known to his friends as 'Round-the-Corner Smith', from the way he bowled at cricket. Knighted in 1944.

*1915: Builder of Bridges. John Glayde's Honor. Jaffery. 1916: The Witching Hour. 1918: Red Pottage. 1920: The Face at the Window. Castles in Spain. *The Bump. The Shuttle of Life. 1922: Flames of Passion. The Bohemian Girl. 1923: The Temptation of Carlton Earlye. 1924: The Unwanted. The Rejected Woman. 1930: Birds of Prey (US: The Perfect Alibi). Such Is the Law. 1931: Contraband Love. Bachelor Father. Trader Horn. Daybreak. Never the Twain Shall Meet. Just a Gigolo (GB: The Dancing Partner). Man in Possession. Guilty Hands. Son of India. Phantom of Paris. Surrender. 1932: But the Flesh is Weak. Polly of the Circus. Trouble in Paradise. They Just Had to Get Married. Tarzan the Ape Man. Love Me Tonight. No More Orchids. 1933: The Barbarian (GB: A Night in Cairo). Luxury Liner. The Monkey's Paw. Bombshell (GB: Blonde Bombshell). Secrets. Adorable. Morning Glory. Queen Christina. 1934: Curtain at Eight. The House of Rothschild. Cleopatra. One More River (GB: Over the River). The Firebird. Gambling Lady. Bulldog Drummond Strikes Back. Madame Du Barry. Caravan. We Live Again. Riptide. The Scarlet Empress. 1935: The Florentine Dagger. The Right to Live (GB: The Sacred Flame). Clive of India. Jalna. The Tunnel (US: Transatlantic Tunnel). Lives of a Bengal Lancer. The Gilded Lily. China Seas. The Crusades. 1936: *The Story of Papworth. The Garden of Allah. Little Lord Fauntleroy. Romeo and Juliet. Lloyds of London. 1937: Wee Willie Winkie. The Hurricane. The Prisoner of Zenda. Thoroughbreds Don't Cry. 1938: Sixty Glorious Years (US: Queen of Destiny). Four Men and a Prayer. Kidnapped. 1939: The Four Feathers. The Sun Never Sets. East Side of Heaven. The Under-Pup. Another Thin Man. Eternally Yours. Five Came Back. Balalaika. 1940: A Bill of Divorcement. Rebecca. Beyond Tomorrow. City of Chance. Waterloo Bridge. A Little Bit of Heaven. 1941: Maisie Was a Lady. Dr Jekyll and Mr Hyde. Free and Easy. 1943: Two Tickets to London. Forever and a Day. Flesh and Fantasy. Madame Curie. 1944: They Shall Have Faith (GB: The Right to Live). Secrets of Scotland Yard. The White Cliffs of Dover. The Adventures of Mark Twain. Sensations of 1945. 1945: And Then There Were None (GB: Ten Little Niggers). Scotland Yard Investigator. 1946: Cluny Brown. Rendezvous With Annie. 1947: Unconquered. High Conquest. An Ideal Husband. 1949: Little Women.*

SMITH, Charlie Martin

(latterly Charles Martin Smith) 1953–
Baby-faced, earnest-looking, sometimes bespectacled and occasionally bearded American supporting actor of small, slight stature and wild, thinning, light-brown hair, blinking his way into film and TV movie roles while still at college. A must for guys who got pushed around because of his lack of height and meek demeanour, Smith shot to prominence as one of the boys in *American Graffiti*. Good follow-up roles proved surprisingly hard to find, although he has achieved a decent range in those he has taken, with one or two offbeat leading parts thrown in. He turned director in 1986, but still looked a more useful asset in front of the cameras.

1972: Go Ask Alice (TV). The Rookies (TV). The Culpepper Cattle Co. Fuzz. 1973: Pat Garrett and Billy the Kid. American Graffiti. 1974: The Spikes Gang. 1975: Rafferty and the Gold Dust Twins. 1976: Law of the Land (TV). The Deputies (TV). No Deposit, No Return. 1977: The Hazing (later The Campus Corpse). 1978: The Buddy Holly Story. 1979. Cotton Candy (TV). More American Graffiti/ The Party's Over/Purple Haze. 1980: Herbie Goes Bananas. 1983: Never Cry Wolf. 1984: Starman. 1986: Trick or Treat. 1987: The Untouchables. 1988: The Experts. 1990: The Hot Spot. 1991: 50/50. 1992: Deep Cover. 1993: And the Band Played On. 1994: Perfect Alibi. Speechless. I Love Trouble. Roswell (TV). 1995: He Ain't Heavy.

As director:
1986: Trick or Treat. 1989: Boris and Natasha in Our Boy Badenov. 1991: 50/50 (released 1993).

SMITH, Cyril

(C. Bruce-Smith) 1892–1963
Shortish, dark-haired, dark-eyed, bulge-nosed, slightly-built, crestfallen-looking Scottish-born actor in British films from silent times. He shuffled his way through dozens of working-class types and penny-ante crooks without finding the limelight until towards the end of his life, when he repeated on film his stage success as Pa Hornett in *Sailor Beware!* – the henpecked husband to end them all. He also worked in America (mainly on stage) between 1921 and 1930.

1908: The Great Fire of London. 1914: Old St Paul's. 1919: Pallard the Punter. 1920: Walls of Prejudice. *Sweep. *On the Reserve. *Cupid's Carnival. *Run! Run! *A Broken Contract. *Cousin Ebenezer. *Souvenirs. *A Little Bet. *A Pair of Gloves. *Home Influence. *The Lightning Liver Cure. The Fordington Twins. 1921: The Way of a Man. Class and No Class. 1923: Fires of Fate. 1924: The Desert Sheik. 1930: His First Car. 1932: The Mayor's Nest. The Maid of the Mountains. The Innocents of Chicago (US: Why Saps Leave Home). 1933: The Good Companions. Friday the Thirteenth. Channel Crossing. The Roof. I Was a Spy. The Black Abbot. 1934: Waltzes from Vienna (US: Strauss's Great Waltz). It's a Cop! Evensong. The Iron Duke. Wild Boy. Evergreen. 1935: Me and Marlborough. Music Hath Charms. The Last Journey. Hello Sweetheart. Key to Harmony. Mr What's His Name. Lend Me Your Wife. Brown on Resolution (later For Ever England. US: Born for Glory). Bulldog Jack (US: Alias Bulldog Drummond). The Tunnel (US: Transatlantic Tunnel). 1936: Pot Luck. Jack of All Trades (US: The Two of Us). OHMS (US: You're in the Army Now). 1937: Storm in a Teacup. Dark Journey. The Frog. 1938: No Parking. The Challenge. The Return of the Frog. St Martin's Lane (US: Sidewalks of London). 1939: Sword of Honour. Traitor Spy (US: The Torso Murder Mystery). 1940: Law and Disorder. The Flying Squad. 1941: This England. They Flew Alone (US: Wings and the Woman). 1942: One of Our Aircraft is Missing. 1943: When We Are Married. 1944: One Exciting Night (US: You Can't Do Without Love). Meet Sexton Blake. Fanny by Gaslight. 1945: The Echo Murders. The Agitator. Don Chicago. Murder in Reverse. 1946: School for Secrets (US: Secret Flight). This Man is Mine! Appointment with Crime. 1947: Vice Versa. So Well Remembered. They Made Me a Fugitive (US: I Became a Criminal). 1948: Escape. No Room at the Inn. It's Hard to be Good. The History of Mr Polly. 1949: Conspirator. The Rocking Horse Winner. Madness of the Heart. The Interrupted Journey. 1950: The Body Said No! Old Mother Riley Headmistress. The Dark Man. 1951: No Highway (US: No Highway in the Sky). Calling Bulldog Drummond. Green Grow the Rushes. Mystery Junction. The Third Visitor. Night Was Our Friend. Judgment Deferred. 1952: Stolen Face. Mother Riley Meets the Vampire (US: Vampire Over London). The Lost Hours (US: The Big Frame). Women of Twilight (US: Twilight Women). Hindle

Wakes (US: Holiday Week). 1953: Innocents in Paris. Wheel of Fate. 1954: Burnt Evidence. The Angel Who Pawned Her Harp. *The Strange Case of Blondie. Svengali. The Brain Machine. 1955: John and Julie. Value for Money. *The Silent Witness. Who Done It? 1956: Sailor Beware! (US: Panic in the Parlor). 1959: The Rough and the Smooth (US: Portrait of a Sinner). 1960: Light Up the Sky. 1961: Watch It Sailor! Over the Odds. On the Fiddle (US: Operation Snafu). 1962: She Knows Y'Know.

SMITH, William 1931–

Tall, big-built, ever-smiling American actor, often seen in humorous action roles. Billed in his earliest roles as Bill Smith, he played many parts on television from 1951, but few for the cinema, and it was a TV series, *Laredo*, about three brawling Texas Rangers, than gave him his biggest popular hit. From 1970, he started to pile up an enormous number of thriller and adventure film credits, many in the kind of stuff that would later be going straight to video. The best-recalled part of his later times is probably as battler Jack Wilson, taking on Clint Eastwood in the bare-knuckle brawl in *Any Which Way You Can*. Still around in formula action stuff, looking as tough and happy-go-lucky as ever.

1951: Saturday's Hero (GB: Idols in the Dust). 1952: Sudden Fear. 1961: Atlantis, The Lost Continent. 1963: Mail Order Bride (GB: West of Montana). 1967: Three Guns for Texas (TV). 1968: Backtrack (TV). The Manhunter (TV). 1969: Run, Angel, Run! The Over-the-Hill Gang (TV). 1970: Angels Die Hard! C.C. and Company. Darker Than Amber. Crowhaven Farm (TV). The Losers. 1971: Chrome and Hot Leather. The Runaways. Summertree. 1972: Camper John. Hammer. Piranha Piranha. Grave of the Vampire/Seed of Terror. The Thing With Two Heads. Slaughter. 1973: Invasion of the Bee Girls. The Deadly Trackers. The Last American Hero. A Taste of Hell. Sweet Jesus, Preacher Man. 1974: Black Samson. Crackle of Death. Boss Nigger (GB: The Black Bounty Killer). The Rockford Files (TV). The Sex Symbol (TV). Policewoman (TV). 1975: Dr Minx. The Swingin' Barmaids. Mrs R: Death Among Friends (TV). Tiger Cage. The Ultimate Warrior. 1976: Gentle Savage (revised version of Camper John). The Hollywood Man. Scorchy. 1977: Blood and Guts/Heavy Thunder. Twilight's Last

Gleaming. Death Threat. 1978: Fast Company. Gas Pump Girls. 1979: Seven. The Frisco Kid. The Rebels (TV). Wild Times (TV). 1980: Any Which Way You Can. 1981: The Cop Killers. Conan the Barbarian. 1982: Tales of the Apple Dumpling Gang (TV). 1983: The Outsiders. Rumble Fish. 1984: Red Dawn. The Jerk Too (TV). 1985: Fever Pitch. The Mean Season. 1986: Eye of the Tiger. 1987: Bulletproof. Commando Squad. Moon in Scorpio. 1988: Hell Comes to Frogtown. Evil Altar. Hell on the Battleground. Maniac Cop. Platoon Leader. Jungle Assault/Jungle Patrol. The Kill Machine (and co-directed). Red Nights. Memorial Valley Massacre. B.O.R.N. Emperor of the Bronx. Action USA. Empire of Ash. Terror in Beverly Hills. The Peace Officer. 1989: Forgotten Heroes. Deadly Breed. L.A. Vice. Rapid Fire. Supercarrier. The Last Battle (TV). Slowburn. 1990: East L.A. Warriors. Empire of Ash 3. Instant Karma. Cartel. The Last Riders. The Final Sanction. Spirit of the Eagle. 1991: Highway Warrior. Cybernator. Vaya con Dios. 1992: Tuesday Never Comes. Merchant of Evil. 1993: Covert Action: Operation Red Star. 1994: Taken Alive. Maverick.

SOFAER, Abraham 1896–1988
Dark-haired, long-faced Burmese actor of austere aspect, often in sinister (sometimes bearded) roles. A teacher in Rangoon, then London, he turned to acting in his mid-twenties, his sombre tones and commanding presence soon getting him into important, often foreign-slanted roles. Also a respected Shakespearian and a popular voice on radio. British film roles were pretty scattered after the mid-1930s and, after 1955, he lived and worked in Hollywood, where his last film appearance was as a Red Indian! Died from congestive heart failure.

1931: Dreyfus (US: The Dreyfus Case). The House Opposite. Stamboul. 1932: The Flag Lieutenant. The Flying Squad. Insult. 1933: Ask Beccles. Karma. High Finance. Little Miss Nobody. Long Live the King. The Wandering Jew. Trouble. 1934: Nell Gwyn. Oh No Doctor! The Admiral's Secret. The Private Life of Don Juan. 1935: Abdul the Damned. 1936: The House of the Spaniard. Rembrandt. Things to Come. 1940: Crooks' Tour. 1941: Freedom Radio (US: A Voice in the Night). 1946: A Matter of Life and Death (US: Stairway to Heaven). Dual Alibi. 1947: The Ghosts of

Berkeley Square. 1948: Calling Paul Temple. 1949: The Green Promise (GB: Raging Waters). Christopher Columbus. 1950: Cairo Road. Pandora and the Flying Dutchman. 1951: Quo Vadis? Judgment Deferred. 1953: His Majesty O'Keefe. 1954: Elephant Walk. The Naked Jungle. Out of the Clouds. 1955: Yacht on the High Sea (TV. GB: cinemas). 1956: Bhowani Junction. The First Texan. 1957: Omar Khayyam. The Story of Mankind. 1958: The Sad Sack. 1961: King of Kings. Song Without End. 1962: Taras Bulba. 1963: Twice-Told Tales. Captain Sindbad. Four for Texas. 1965: The Greatest Story Ever Told. 1967: Journey to the Center of Time. 1968: Head. 1969: Justine. Che! 1970: Chisum.

SOKOLOFF, Vladimir
(V. Sokolov) 1889–1962
Impassive, diminutive, brown-haired Russian actor with snaky eyes and (often) goatee beard. He usually played the evil brains behind the muscle, but occasionally got a more sympathetic role. Sokoloff portrayed almost as many nationalities as J. Carrol Naish (qv), following his arrival in Hollywood late in 1936 after a career in German and French films. Continued acting until his death from a stroke.

1926: Die Abenteuer eines Zehnmarkscheines (US: Uneasy Money). Napoléon. Die Liebe der Jeanne Ney (GB and US: The Love of Jeanne Ney). Der Sohn der Hoger (US: Out of the Mist). 1928: Die weisse Sonate. 1929: Das Schiff der verlorenen Menschen. Sensation in Wintergarten. 1930: Liebling der Götter/Der grosse Tenor (US: Darling of the Gods). Moral im Mitternacht. Abschied. Westfront 1914. Die heilige Flamme. Das Flotenkonzert. L'opéra de quat-sous. 1931: Niemandsland (US: Hell on Earth). Kismet. Die Dreigroschenoper (GB: The Threepenny Opera. US: The Beggar's Opera). 1932: Die Herrin von Atlantis (and French-language version). Teilnehmer antwortet nicht. Gehetzte Menschen/Steckbrief Z. Strafsache von Geldern. 1933: Dans les rues (US: Song of the Street). Du haut en bas. Don Quichotte. 1934: Le lac aux dames. Le secret de Waronzeff. Napoléon Bonaparte (revised version of 1926 film with sound added). 1935: Mayerling. 1936: Mister Flow (US: Compliments of Mr Flow). Sous les jeux d'accident. Les bas-fonds (GB and US: The Lower Depths). La vie est à nous. 1937: The Life of Emile Zola.

Conquest (GB: Marie Walewska). West of Shanghai. Tovarich. Expensive Husbands. Beg, Borrow or Steal. The Prisoner of Zenda. 1938: Alcatraz Island. Arsène Lupin Returns. Spawn of the North. Blockade. Ride a Crooked Mile. The Amazing Dr Clitterhouse. 1939: Juarez. The Real Glory. 1940: Comrade X. 1941: Love Crazy. 1942: Crossroads. Road to Morocco. 1943: Mission to Moscow. Song of Russia. Mr Lucky. For Whom the Bell Tolls. 1944: Passage to Marseille (GB: Passage to Marseilles). Till We Meet Again. The Conspirators. 1945: The Blonde from Brooklyn. Paris Underground (GB: Madame Pimpernel). Back to Bataan. A Royal Scandal (GB: Czarina). Scarlet Street. 1946: Two Smart People. Cloak and Dagger. Thieves' Holiday (later and GB: A Scandal in Paris). 1948: To the Ends of the Earth. 1950: The Baron of Arizona. 1952: Macao. 1956: While the City Sleeps. Istanbul. 1957: Sabu and the Magic Ring. I Was a Teenage Werewolf. The Monster from Green Hell. 1958: Twilight for the Gods. 1960: Man on a String (GB: Confessions of a Counterspy). Beyond the Time Barrier. The Magnificent Seven. Cimarron. 1961: Mr Sardonicus (GB: Sardonicus). The Judas Goat (TV. GB: cinemas). Escape from Zahrain. 1962: Taras Bulba.

SOLON, Ewen 1921–1985
Brown-haired, foxy-looking New Zealand actor with fine-boned face, slightly menacing smile, gravel tones and dark complexion, in roles of gradually increasing importance in the British cinema until swallowed up for several years by his part as Lucas in TV's highly successful Maigret series, which began in 1961 and ran for several seasons. He was little seen in film parts after that, occasionally popping up, with less hair, in more fragile roles.

1948: Esther Waters. London Belongs to Me (US: Dulcimer Street). 1949: Vengeance is Mine. 1950: The Naked Heart (Maria Chapdelaine/The Naked Earth). Highly Dangerous. The Dark Man. The Rossiter Case. 1951: Valley of Eagles. Assassin for Hire. Mystery Junction. 1952: The Card (US: The Promoter). Hunted (US: The Stranger in Between). The Story of Robin Hood and His Merrie Men. Crow Hollow. Ghost Ship. 1953: The Sword and the Rose. Rob Roy the Highland Rogue. 1954: *Night Plane to Amsterdam. The

End of the Road. The Young Lovers (US: Chance Meeting). The Dam Busters. 1955: As Long As They're Happy. *The Stateless Man. *Murder Anonymous. The Dark Avenger (US: The Warriors). Jumping for Joy. Lost (US: Tears for Simon). Who Done It? 1956: Behind the Headlines. 1984. The Big Money (released 1958). 1957: The Long Haul. Robbery Under Arms. The Devil's Pass. The Flesh is Weak. Yangtse Incident (US: Battle Hell/Escape of the Amethyst). The Story of Esther Costello (US: Golden Virgin). Murder Reported. There's Always a Thursday. Account Rendered. Black Ice. Mark of the Hawk/Accused. 1958: The Silent Enemy. 1959: The Hound of the Baskervilles. The White Trap. The Stranglers of Bombay. Jack the Ripper. 1960: Tarzan the Magnificent. The Sundowners. 1961: The Terror of the Tongs. Curse of the Werewolf. 1962: Mystery Submarine (US: Decoy). 1963: The Cracksman. 1966: The Sandwich Man. *Infamous Conduct. 1976: The Message (US: Mohammed Messenger of God). 1979: The Spaceman and King Arthur (US: Unidentified Flying Oddball). The Biggest Bank Robbery/A Nightingale Sang in Berkeley Square (made for cinemas but shown only on TV). 1980: Lion of the Desert/Omar Mukhtar Lion of the Desert. 1982: Nutcracker. 1983: The Wicked Lady. 1984: Master of the Game (feature version of TV mini-series).

SONDERGAARD, Gale
(Edith Sondergaard) 1899–1985
Tall, dark, stern-looking American actress who, after winning an Academy Award in her first feature, *Anthony Adverse* (she was nominated again for *Anna and the King of Siam*), went on to corner the market, with Dame Judith Anderson (*qv*), in sinister housekeepers, domineering mothers and femmes very fatale. Career wrecked by the McCarthy witch-hunts (her second husband, writer-director Herbert Biberman, was one of the 'Hollywood 10').

1936: Anthony Adverse. 1937: The Life of Emile Zola. Maid of Salem. Seventh Heaven. 1938: Lord Jeff (GB: The Boy from Barnardo's). Dramatic School. 1939: Juarez. Never Say Die. The Cat and the Canary. *Sons of Liberty. 1940: The Llano Kid. The Mark of Zorro. The Blue Bird. The Letter. 1941: The Black Cat. Paris Calling. 1942: Enemy Agents Meet Ellery Queen (GB: The Lido Mystery). My Favorite

Blonde. A Night To Remember. 1943: Isle of Forgotten Sins. Appointment in Berlin. The Strange Death of Adolf Hitler. Sherlock Holmes and Spider Woman (GB: Spider Woman). 1944: Follow the Boys. Christmas Holiday. The Invisible Man's Revenge. Enter Arsène Lupin. The Climax. Gypsy Wildcat. 1946: Anna and the King of Siam. Spider Woman Strikes Back. The Time of Their Lives. A Night in Paradise. 1947: Road to Rio. Pirates of Monterey. 1949: East Side, West Side. 1969: Slaves. 1970: Comeback (later copyrighted 1973 as Savage Intruder). 1973: The Cat Creature (TV). 1976: The Return of a Man Called Horse. Pleasantville. 1977: Hollywood on Trial. 1980: Echoes.

SORVINO, Paul 1939–
Chunky, chubby-cheeked, cheerful-looking American actor with a mop of dark hair. An unusual kind of star, he nonetheless found some interesting leading roles in the 1970s and 1980s, mixing them with high-ranking supports. A frustrated Mario Lanza who took singing lessons for 18 years, Sorvino worked in advertising until breaking into TV commercials at 30. Better roles came fairly quickly and he has also directed with distinction on Broadway; his greatest acting success on stage was in *That Championship Season*, a role he repeated (to less effect) on film. Recently in pungent cameos. Father of actress Mira Sorvino.

1970: Where's Poppa? 1971: The Panic in Needle Park. Made for Each Other. Cry Uncle (GB: Super Dick). 1972: Dealing, or: the Berkeley-to-Boston-Forty-Bricks-Lost-Bag Blues. A Touch of Class. 1973: Day of the Dolphin. 1974: Tell Me Where It Hurts (TV). It Couldn't Happen to a Nicer Guy (TV). The Gambler. Shoot It Black Shoot It Blue. 1975: Bert d'Angelo (TV). I Will . . . I Will For Now. 1977: Oh God! 1978: Slow Dancing in the Big City. Bloodbrothers. The Brink's Job. 1979: Lost and Found. The Silence of Daniel Lang (TV). Dummy (TV). 1980: Cruising. 1981: Reds. I the Jury. A Question of Honor (TV). 1982: Off the Line. Melanie (released 1985). That Championship Season. 1983: Off the Wall. 1984: Intent to Kill (TV. GB: With Intent to Kill.) My Other's Secret Life (TV). Turk 182! 1985: The Stuff. A Fine Mess. Surviving (TV). Chiller (TV). 1986: Vasectomy, a Delicate Matter. Betrayed by Innocence (TV). Very Close Quarters. 1990: Goodfellas.

DMZ. Dick Tracy. 1991: The Rocketeer. Life in the Food Chain/Age Isn't Everything. Don't Touch My Daughter (TV). Nightmare (TV). 1993: Dead Wrong. The Firm. Backstreet Justice. 1994: Parallel Lives. (TV). Without Consent (TV). Trapped and Deceived (TV). 1995: Oh No, Not Her! Nixon.

SPARKS, Ned
(Edward Sparkman) 1883–1957
Thin, dark-haired, fast-talking, darting-eyed Canadian actor who once sold patent medicines in a carnival and, when into Hollywood sound films, harangued his audiences with the same unique style that had once held customers in thrall. With his incisive nasal tones, he became one of filmdom's most imitated actors and, in between a legion of reporters, press agents and con-men, all of whom seemed to live life on a nervous edge, he made a marvellous caterpillar in the 1933 *Alice in Wonderland*. Died from a blocked intestine.

1915: Little Miss Brown. 1919: A Virtuous Vamp. 1920: In Search of a Sinner. Good References. Nothing But the Truth. 1922: A Wide-Open Town. The Bond Boy. 1925: Bright Lights. His Supreme Moment. Faint Perfume. The Boomerang. Seven Keys to Baldpate. The Only Thing. Soul Mates. 1926: Mike. Love's Blindness. The Hidden Way. Oh, What a Night! Money Talks. When the Wife's Away. The Auction Block (GB: Lock, Stock and Barrel). 1927: Alias the Deacon. The Small Bachelor. The Secret Studio. Alias the Lone Wolf. 1928: The Big Noise (GB: Nine Days' Wonder). The Magnificent Flirt. On to Reno. 1929: The Canary Murder Case. Strange Cargo. Nothing But the Truth. Street Girl. 1930: The Fall Guy (GB: Trust Your Wife). Love Comes Along. Double Crossroads. The Devil's Holiday. Conspiracy. Leathernecking (GB: Present Arms). 1931: The Iron Man. Corsair. *Big Dame Hunting. *Wide Open Spaces. The Secret Call. Kept Husbands. 1932: The Miracle Man. Big City Blues. Blessed Event. The Crusader. 1933: 42nd Street. Lady for a Day. Too Much Harmony. Gold Diggers of 1933. Alice in Wonderland. The Kennel Murder Case. Going Hollywood. Secrets. Hi, Nellie! 1934: Servants' Entrance. Operator 13 (GB: Spy 13). Marie Galante. Private Scandal. Sing and Like It. Down to Their Last Yacht (GB: Hawaiian Nights). Imitation of Life. 1935: George White's

Scandals of 1935. Sweet Adeline. Sweet Music. 1936: Collegiate (GB: The Charm School). The Bride Walks Out. One in a Million. Two's Company. 1937: Wake Up and Live. This Way, Please. 1938: Hawaii Calls. 1939: The Star Maker. 1941: For Beauty's Sake. 1943: Stage Door Canteen. 1947: Magic Town.

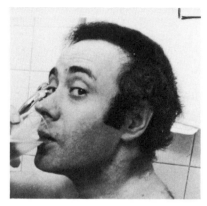

SPINETTI, Victor 1932–
Dark, slim Welsh-born actor (of Italian father) with distinctive crinkly, very short receding hair, Bob Hope nose and pained expression. Usually seen in comic cameo roles in British films, often as head waiters, TV directors, impresarios or avant-garde friends, much given to arm-waving, sarcasm and panic. He came to the fore in London revue but film roles, on the whole, provided him with too little subtlety, and he has preferred television and the theatre.

1958: Behind the Mask. 1959: Expresso Bongo. 1961: The Gentle Terror. 1962: Sparrows Can't Sing. 1963: Stolen Hours. The Horse Without a Head. Becket. 1964: *I Think They Call Him John (narrator only). The Wild Affair. A Hard Day's Night. 1965: Help! 1966: The Taming of the Shrew. The Biggest Bundle of Them All. 1968: Can Hieronymous Merkin Ever Forget Mercy Humppe and Find True Happiness? 1969: A Promise of Bed. Start the Revolution Without Me. 1971: Unman, Wittering and Zigo. Under Milk Wood. 1972: The 500-Pound Jerk (TV. GB: The Strong Man). 1973: Digby the Biggest Dog in the World. 1974: The Little Prince. Return of the Pink Panther. The Great McGonagall. 1975: Dick Deadeye (voice only). 1976: Emily. Voyage of the Damned. 1977: The Rise and Rise of Casanova/Casanova & Co. Hardcore (US: Fiona). 1986: Under the Cherry Moon. 1987: The Attic: The Hiding of Anne Frank (TV). 1990: The Krays. Romeo-Juliet (voice only).

SQUIRE, Ronald
(R. Squirl) 1886–1958
Bald, burly, affable British actor with beaming smile and splendid moustache. He found himself billed above the title in middle age, following many years on stage as actor, producer and director, having started his long career with seaside concert parties. Continued to be popular in film roles up to his death.

1916: Whoso Is Without Sin. 1934: The Unfinished Symphony. Wild Boy. Forbidden Territory. 1935: Come Out of the Pantry. 1936: Love in Exile. Dusty Ermine (US: Hideout in the Alps). 1937: Action for Slander. 1941: Freedom Radio (US: A Voice in the Night). Major Barbara. 1943: The Flemish Farm. 1944: Don't Take It to Heart. 1945: Journey Together. 1946: While the Sun Shines. 1948: The First Gentleman (US: Affairs of a Rogue). Woman Hater. 1949: The Rocking Horse Winner. 1951: No Highway (GB: No Highway in the Sky). Encore. 1952: It Started in Paradise. My Cousin Rachel. Laxdale Hall (US: Scotch on the Rocks). 1953: Always a Bride. The Million Pound Note (US: Man With a Million). 1954: The Man Who Loved Redheads (narrator only). 1955: Raising a Riot. Josephine and Men. Footsteps in the Fog. 1956: Now and Forever. The Silken Affair. Around the World in 80 Days. 1957: Seawife. Island in the Sun. 1958: The Sheriff of Fractured Jaw. Law and Disorder. The Inn of the Sixth Happiness. 1959: Count Your Blessings.

STANDER, Lionel 1908–1994
Fuzzy-haired, gravel-voiced New Yorker much in demand for comic gangsters and other side-of-the-mouth types before the McCarthy blacklist halted his career in 1948. After a spell as a Wall Street broker, he played many character roles in Britain and Italy before going back to Hollywood and finding a secure slot with the five-season-long TV series Hart to Hart. Six times married, he had six daughters. Died from lung cancer.

1926: Men of Steel. 1935: *The Old Grey Mayor. The Gay Deception. The Scoundrel. Hooray for Love. If You Could Only Cook. Page Miss Glory. We're in the Money. I Live My Life. 1936: Meet Nero Wolfe. The Music Goes Round. The Milky Way. They Met in a Taxi. Mr Deeds Goes to Town. More than a Secretary. Soak the Rich. 1937: The Last Gangster. The League of Frightened Men. A Star Is Born. 1938: The Crowd Roars. No Time To Marry. Professor Beware! 1939: Ice Follies of 1939. What a Life. 1941: The Bride Wore Crutches. 1943: Tahiti Honey. Guadalcanal Diary. Hangmen Also Die. 1945: A Boy, a Girl and a Dog (GB: Lucky). The Big Show-Off. 1946: Specter of the Rose. The Kid from Brooklyn. Gentleman Joe Palooka. In Old Sacramento. The Sin of Harold Diddlebock (later and GB: Mad Wednesday). 1947: Call Northside 777. 1948: Unfaithfully Yours. Trouble Makers. 1951: St Benny the Dip (GB: Escape If You Can). 1961: Blast of Silence (narrator only). 1963: The Moving Finger. 1965: The Loved One. Promise Her Anything. 1966: Cul-de-Sac. 1967: Al di la della legge/Beyond the Law. 1968: The Gates to Paradise. A Dandy in Aspic. Sette volte sette. Once Upon a Time in the West. H2S. Die letzte Rechnung zählst du selbst. 1969: Casanova. La collina degli stivali (US: Boot Hill). Zenabel. 1970: Room 17. Mir hat es immer Spass gemacht. How Did a Nice a Girl Like You Get into This? ... 1971: Treasure Island. The Gang That Couldn't Shoot Straight. Le président aime les femmes (US: The Senator Likes Women). Per grazia ricevuta (US: The Cross-Eyed Saint). 1972: La dove volano le pallotole. Milano calibro 9 (GB: The Contract). Pulp. Don Camillo e i Giovani d'Oggi. Siamo tutti in libertà provvisoria. Tutti fratelli nel West ... per parte di padre. 1973: Crescete e moltiplicatevi. Mordi e fuggi (US: Bite and Run). The Black Hand. Paolo il caldo/The Sensual Man/Sensuous Sicilian (GB: The Con Men). Piazzi pulita (GB: Pete, Pearl and the Pole). Partirono preti, tornarono curati. 1975: The Black Bird. San Pasquale Baillone, protettore delle donne (GB: Sex for Sale). Giubbe rosse. ... e io lo dico a Zorro. 1976: The Cassandra Crossing. 1977: New York, New York. 1978: Matilda. Cyclone. The Big Rip-Off (US: The Squeeze). 1979: 1941. Hart to Hart (TV). 1986: The Transformers (voice only). 1988: Wicked Stepmother. 1989: Cookie. 1990: Joey Takes a Cab. 1994: The Last Good Time.

STANTON, Harry Dean 1926–
Considered by many to be the best Hollywood character actor of recent times, Stanton found that his dark, lean and hungry-looking features confined him for many years to psychos, vicious villains and (often mean-tempered) 'countrified' characters. Nobody's idea of a native New Yorker or Californian, Stanton was born in Kentucky and took up acting after wartime service with the US Navy. For years he toured with a children's theatre company before beginning to pick up film and television work in the late 1950s. In recent times, his shadowed unsmiling face has belatedly appeared with success in demanding lead roles, and he has even tried comedy. Billed as Dean Stanton until 1968.

1956: *The Wrong Man. The Tomahawk Trail.* 1957: *Revolt at Fort Laramie.* 1958: *The Proud Rebel.* 1959: *Pork Chop Hill. A Dog's Best Friend.* 1960: *The Adventures of Huckleberry Finn.* 1961: *Hero's Island.* 1962: *How the West Was Won.* 1963: *The Man from the Diner's Club.* 1965: *Ride in the Whirlwind.* 1966: *The Hostage. The Dangerous Days of Kiowa Jones (TV. GB: cinemas).* 1967: *A Time for Killing (GB: The Long Ride Home). Cool Hand Luke.* 1968: *Day of the Evil Gun. The Mini-Skirt Mob.* 1970: *Rebel Rousers (completed 1967). The Intruders (TV). Kelly's Heroes.* 1971: *Two-Lane Blacktop.* 1972: *Count Your Bullets/Face to the Wind/Apache Massacre (GB: Naked Revenge). Cisco Pike. Pat Garrett and Billy the Kid.* 1973: *Dillinger. Where the Lilies Bloom.* 1974: *Born to Kill (later and GB: Cockfighter). Another Day at the Races (GB: Win, Place or Steal). Rancho de Luxe. The Godfather Part II. Zandy's Bride.* 1975: *Farewell, My Lovely. Rafferty and the Gold-Dust Twins. 92 in the Shade.* 1976: *The Missouri Breaks.* 1977: *Straight Time. Renaldo and Clara.* 1978: *Flatbed Annie and Sweetiepie: Lady Truckers (TV. GB: Girls of the Road).* 1979: *Alien. The Rose. Death Watch/Le mort en direct. Wise Blood.* 1980: *Private Benjamin. The Black Marble. The Oldest Living Graduate (TV).* 1981: *Escape from New York.* 1982: *Tough Enough/Tough Dreams. One from the Heart. Young Doctors in Love.* 1983: *I Want to Live! (TV). Christine.* 1984: *Uforia 84 (filmed 1980). Paris, Texas. Red Dawn. Repo Man.* 1985: *The Bear. One Magic Christmas. The Care Bears Movie (voice only). Fool for Love.* 1986: *Pretty in Pink. Slam Dance.* 1987: *Stars and Bars.* 1988: *Mr North. Dream a Little Dream.* 1989: *Monster Maker. Twister.* 1990: *Motion and Emotion. Wild at Heart. The Fourth War.* 1991: *Stranger in the House. Payoff.* 1992: *Man Trouble. Twin Peaks Fire Walk With Me. Hotel Room (TV). Hostages (TV).* 1994: *Blue Tiger. Against the Wall (cable TV). A Hundred and One Nights.* 1995: *Never Talk to Strangers.*

STAPLETON, Maureen 1925–
Dumpy but dynamic American actress, equally successful at being lonely or companionable, snobbish or down-to-earth, aggressive or vulnerable. Despite motherly looks, she played a wide variety of roles from her 1946 Broadway debut onwards, making occasional but memorable forays into films. After being three times nominated

for the best supporting actress Oscar (in *Lonelyhearts, Airport,* and *Interiors*), she finally won it for *Reds*. More recent roles, though, have given her fewer opportunities to shine.

1959: *For Whom the Bell Tolls (TV). Lonelyhearts.* 1960: *The Fugitive Kind.* 1961: *A View from the Bridge.* 1963: *Bye Bye Birdie.* 1967: *Among the Paths to Eden (TV).* 1969: *Airport. Trilogy.* 1970: *Cold Turkey. Plaza Suite.* 1971: *Summer of '42 (voice only).* 1974: *Tell Me Where It Hurts (TV).* 1975: *Queen of the Stardust Ballroom (TV).* 1976: *Cat on a Hot Tin Roof (TV).* 1977: *The Gathering (TV).* 1978: *Interiors.* 1979: *Arthur Miller on Home Ground. Letters from Frank (TV). Lost and Found. The Runner Stumbles.* 1981: *The Fan. Reds. On the Right Track.* 1982: *Little Gloria: Happy at Last (TV).* 1984: *America and Lewis Hine (voice only). Johnny Dangerously.* 1985: *Cocoon. The Cosmic Eye. Private Sessions (TV). The Money Pit.* 1986: *Heartburn.* 1987: *Stars and Bars. Nuts. Hello Actors Studio. Sweet Lorraine. Made in Heaven.* 1988: *Cocoon The Return. Liberace: Behind the Music (TV). Doin' Time on Planet Earth.* 1989: *Twister. B.L. Stryker: Auntie Sue (TV).* 1991: *Last Wish (TV).* 1992: *Passed Away. Miss Rose White (TV).* 1993: *Trading Mom.* 1994: *The Last Good Time.*

STARK, Graham 1922–
Dapper, dark-haired British comedian, scriptwriter, sometime director and general contributor of comic cameos, with Mr Punch-like facial features which made him

look as if he was always about to laugh. A minor member of The Goons who gradually assumed greater familiarity and importance, he built up his early experience with a mixture of straight and comic film roles and funny voices in radio comedy. Attempts to direct comedy were less successful and he returned to the front of the camera. With photography, he has had more luck, having had exhibitions of his work. In the cinema, he has continued to crop up in increasingly broad comic vignettes.

1939: *The Spy in Black (US: U-Boat 29).* 1952: *Emergency Call (US: Hundred Hour Hunt). Down Among the Z Men.* 1953: **The Super Secret Service. Forces' Sweetheart. Flannelfoot.* 1954: *Johnny on the Spot. The Sea Shall Not Have Them.* 1955: **Song of Norway.* 1956: *They Never Learn.* 1959: *Inn for Trouble. Sink the Bismarck!* 1960: **The Running, Jumping and Standing Still Film. The Millionairess.* 1961: *Dentist on the Job (US: Get On With It!). Watch It Sailor! She'll Have to Go (US: Maid for Murder). A Weekend with Lulu. Double Bunk. Only Two Can Play. On the Fiddle (US: Operation Snafu). Village of Daughters. A Pair of Briefs.* 1962: *Operation Snatch. The Wrong Arm of the Law. Lancelot and Guinevere (US: Sword of Lancelot).* 1963: *The Mouse on the Moon. Ladies Who Do. Strictly for the Birds. The Pink Panther. Becket.* 1964: *Guns at Batasi. A Shot in the Dark. Go Kart Go!* 1965: *Runaway Railway. San Ferry Ann. Those Magnificent Men in Their Flying Machines. You Must Be Joking!* 1966: *Alfie. Finders Keepers. The Wrong Box.* 1967: *Casino Royale. The Plank. Jules Verne's Rocket to the Moon (US: Those Fantastic Flying Fools). Ghost of a Chance.* 1968: *Salt and Pepper.* 1969: *The Picasso Summer. Start the Revolution Without Me. The Magic Christian.* 1970: **Simon Simon. Scramble. Doctor in Trouble. Rhubarb. A Day at the Beach.* 1971: *The Magnificent Seven Deadly Sins.* 1972: *Hide and Seek.* 1973: **The Laughing Girl Murder. *Le Pétomane (released 1979). Secrets of a Door-to-Door Salesman.* 1974: *Where's Johnny? Return of the Pink Panther.* 1975: *I'm Not Feeling Myself Tonight. The Remarkable Rocket (voice only).* 1976: *Gulliver's Travels (voice only). The Pink Panther Strikes Again. Virginity/Come una rosa al naso.* 1977: *The Prince and the Pauper (US: Crossed Swords). Hardcore (US: Fiona). What's Up Nurse? Chimpmates (second series). Let's Get Laid.* 1978: *Revenge of the Pink Panther.* 1979: *There Goes the Bride. The Prisoner of Zenda.* 1980: *Hawk the Slayer. The Sea Wolves.* 1982: *Trail of the Pink Panther. Victor/Victoria.* 1983: *Superman III. Curse of the Pink Panther. Bloodbath at the House of Death.* 1986: *Neat and Tidy (TV).* 1987: *Jane and the Lost City. Blind Date.* 1993: *Son of the Pink Panther.*

As director:
1970: **Simon Simon.* 1971: *The Magnificent Seven Deadly Sins.*

STEELE, Bob
(Robert Bradbury Jr) 1906–1988
Dark-haired American cowboy star of slight stature but whirlwind acting style. His smile turned so readily to a distinctive scowl that

he was soon seen in the occasional double-shaded role, after starting as a teenager in films directed by his father, Robert North Bradbury, a western specialist, and developing into a two-fisted star of 'B' westerns and minor action films. As the 1930s ebbed, he won some interesting character roles, such as Curley in *Of Mice and Men* and Canino in the 1946 version of *The Big Sleep*, and went over to character acting altogether in post-war years. In some ways, his career pattern was similar to that of Tim Holt, another small-scale cowboy hero, although Steele's role grew very minor as his career drew towards its close. Still thought by some western buffs to have had the fastest draw of all B-movie cowboys.

As Bob Bradbury Jr:
1920: *The Adventures of Bob and Bill (series).
1921: *Trapping the Bobcat. *Outwitting the Timber Wolf. *The Fox. *Trailing the Coyote. *The Fox. *Civet Cat. *The American Badger. *The Skunk. *A Day in the Wilds. *Trapping the Weasel. 1922: *Mysterious Tracks. *Capturing the Canadian Lynx. *The Opossum. *Trapping a Raccoon. *Capturing a Koala Bear. *Secret Trails. 1926: The Border Sheriff. The Fighting Doctor. The College Boob. Daniel Boone Thru the Wilderness. With Buffalo Bill on the U.P. Trail. With Sitting Bull at the Spirit Lake Massacre. Davy Crockett at the Fall of the Alamo.

As Bob Steele:
1927: The Bandit's Son. The Mojave Kid. 1928: Breed of the Sunsets. Captain Careless. Drifting Sands. Man in the Rough. Lightning Speed. Come and Get It! Headin' for Danger. Riding Renegade. Crooks' Caution. Trail of Courage. Crooks Can't Win. Spirit of Youth. 1929: The Amazing Vagabond. The Cowboy and the Outlaw. The Invaders. Laughing at Death. 1930: Breezy Bill. Headin' North. Hunted Men. Land of Missing Men. The Man from Nowhere. The Oklahoma Sheriff. Near the Rainbow's End. Oklahoma Cyclone. Texas Cowboy. Western Honor. 1931: Law of the West. At the Ridge. Nevada Buckaroo. Near the Trail's End. The Ridin' Fool. The Sunrise Trail. 1932: Fighting Fool. Hidden Valley. The Man from Hell's Edges. The Fighting Champ. Near the Trail's End. Riders of the Desert. Son of Oklahoma. South of Santa Fé. Texas Buddies. Young Blood. 1933: Breed of the Border. Gal-

loping Romeo. California Trail. The Gallant Fool. Mystery Squadron (serial). Rangers' Code. Trailin' North. 1934: Brand of Hate. Demon for Trouble. No Man's Range. 1935: Alias John Law. Big Calibre. Kid Courageous. Powdersmoke Range. Rider of the Law. The Ridin' Fool (remake of 1931 film). Smokey Smith. Tombstone Terror. Western Justice. 1936: Arizona Gunfighter. Brand of Outlaws. Cavalry. Last of the Warrens. The Law Rides. The Kid Ranger. Sundown Saunders. Trail of Terror. 1937: Border Phantom. The Colorado Kid. The Gun Ranger. Lightnin' Crandall. Gun Lords of Stirrup Basin. Doomed at Sundown. The Red Rope. Ridin' the Lone Trail. The Trusted Outlaw. 1938: Durango Valley Raiders. The Feud Maker. Desert Patrol. Paroled to Die. Thunder in the Desert. 1939: El Diablo Rides. Mesquite Buckaroo. Feud on the Range. Pinto Canyon. Pal from Texas. Riders of the Sage. Smokey Trails. Of Mice and Men. Wild Horse Valley. 1940: Billy the Kid in Texas. Billy the Kid Outlawed. Billy the Kid's Gun Justice. The Carson City Kid. City for Conquest. Lone Star Raiders. Trail Blazers. Under Texas Skies. 1941: Billy the Kid's Fighting Pals. Billy the Kid in Sante Fé. Billy the Kid's Range War. The Great Train Robbery. Pals of the Pecos. Prairie Pioneers. Gangs of Sonora. Gauchos of Eldorado. Outlaws of Cherokee Trail. Saddlemates. West of Cimarron. 1942: Code of the Outlaw. The Phantom Plainsmen. Raiders of the Range. Valley of Hunted Men. Westward Ho! 1943: Blocked Trail. Death Valley Rangers. Revenge of the Zombies (GB: The Corpse Vanished). Riders of the Rio Grande. Sante Fé Scouts. Shadows on the Sage. Thundering Trails. 1944: Arizona Whirlwind. Marked Trails. The Outlaw Trail. Sonora Stagecoach. Trigger Law. The Utah Kid. Westward Bound. 1945: The Navajo Kid. Northwest Trail. Wildfire. 1946: Ambush Trail. The Big Sleep. Rio Grande Raiders. Sheriff of Redwood Valley. Six Gun Man. Thunder Town. 1947: Bandits of Dark Canyon. Cheyenne. Exposed. Killer McCoy. Six Guns for Hire. Twilight on the Rio Grande. 1949: South of St Louis. 1950: The Savage Horde. The Enforcer (GB: Murder Inc). 1951: Cattle Drive. Fort Worth. Silver Canyon. 1952: Bugles in the Afternoon. The Lion and the Horse. Rose of Cimarron. 1953: Column South. Island in the Sky. San Antone. Savage Frontier. 1954: Drums Across the River. The Outcast (GB: The Fortune Hunter). 1955: The Fighting Chance. The Spoilers. 1956: Gun for a Coward. Last of the Desperadoes. Pardners. The Steel Jungle. 1957: Band of Angels. Decision at Sundown. Duel at Apache Wells. The Parson and the Outlaw. 1958: The Bonnie Parker Story. Giant from the Unknown. Once Upon a Horse. 1959: Atomic Submarine. Pork Chop Hill. Rio Bravo. 1960: Hell Bent for Leather. 1961: The Comancheros. Six Black Horses. 1962: The Wild Westerners. 1963: Showdown. Four for Texas. He Rides Tall. McLintock! 1964: Bullet for a Badman. Taggart! Cheyenne Autumn. Major Dundee. 1965: Outlaw Trail. The Bounty Killer. Requiem for a Gunfighter. Shenandoah. Town Tamer. 1967: Hang 'Em High. 1969: The Great Bank Robbery. 1970: Rio Lobo. 1971: Skin Game. Something Big. 1972: Nightmare Honeymoon. 1973: Charley Varrick.

STEPANEK, Karel 1899−1980
Crafty-looking, thin-mouthed Czech actor. In German films through the thirties, he fled to England with the outbreak of World War II and quickly became that country's answer to Eduardo Ciannelli (qv). He was not too keen on playing Nazis, but was inevitably seen as villainous foreigners of one kind or another. Later made a few films in Hollywood.

1928: †Ein Lieb, ein Dieb, ein Warenhaus. 1931: †Berlin−Alexanderplatz. 1932: †Fünf von der Jazzband. †Hallo Hallo! Hier Spricht Berlin. †Spione im Savoy-Hotel. 1933: †Ein Lied Für Dich. †Walzerkrieg. 1934: †Hermine und die sieben Aufrechten. 1935: †Aussenseiter. †Die Werft zum grauen Hecht. 1936: †Die Fledermaus. †Signal in der Nacht. 1938: †Es leuchten die Sterne. †Narren im Schnee. †War es dem in dreiter Stock? 1939: †Jede Frau hat ein süsses Geheimnis. †Der Florentiner Hut/The Italian Straw Hat. †Die kluge Schwiegermutter. †Drei Väter um Anna. †Hotel Sacher. †Alles Schwindel. 1942: Our Film. Secret Mission. Tomorrow We Live (US: At Dawn We Die). 1943: Escape to Danger. They Met in the Dark. 1946: The Captive Heart. 1947: Broken Journey. 1948: Counterblast (US: The Devil's Plot). The Fallen Idol. 1949: Conspirator. Give Us This Day (US: Salt to the Devil). The Third Man. Golden Arrow (US: The Gay Adventure. Released 1952). 1950: State Secret (US: The Great Manhunt). Cairo Road. 1951: No Highway (US: No Highway in the Sky). The Third Visitor. 1952: Walk East on Beacon! (GB: Crime of the Century). Affair in Trinidad. 1953: City Beneath the Sea. Never Let Me Go. Rough Shoot (GB: Shoot First). 1954: Dangerous Cargo. A Tale of Three Women. 1955: Secret Venture. A Prize of Gold. Man of the Moment. Cockleshell Heroes. 1956: The Man in the Road. Anastasia. 1957: West of Suez (US: Fighting Wildcats). The Traitor (US: The Accused). 1959: Our Man in Havana. Sink the Bismarck! 1960: Schachnovelle (GB: Three Moves to Freedom. US: The Royal Game). I Aim at the Stars. 1961: *Johann Sebastian Bach. 1962: Neunzig Minuten nach Mitternacht (US: Terror After Midnight). 1963: The Devil Doll. 1965: Licensed to Kill (US: The Second Best Secret Agent in the Whole Wide World). Operation Crossbow (US: The Great Spy Mission). Sperrbezirk. The Heroes of Telemark. 1966: The Frozen Dead. Der Mörderclub von

Brooklyn. 1968: The File of the Golden Goose.
1969: Before Winter Comes. The Games.

† As Karl Stepanek

STEPHENSON, Henry
(H.S. Garroway) 1871–1956
Tall, elegant, moustachioed, jut-jawed British actor with firm gaze, a key member of Hollywood's prominent British community of the 1930s. Long in America, after considerable experience on the London and New York stages, he was often cast in lordly roles, as historical figures or the hero's aristocratic friend. Born in Grenada.

1917: The Spreading Dawn. 1919: A Society
Exile. 1920: Tower of Jewels. 1921: The Black
Panther's Cub. 1925: Men and Women. Wild,
Wild Susan. 1932: Red-Headed Woman.
Cynara. The Animal Kingdom (GB: The
Woman in His House). Guilty As Hell (GB:
Guilty as Charged). A Bill of Divorcement.
1933: Little Women. Tomorrow at Seven.
Queen Christina. Blind Adventure. Double
Harness. My Lips Betray. If I Were Free. 1934:
One More River (GB: Over the River). Man of
Two Worlds. Outcast Lady (GB: A Woman of
the World). Stingaree. The Richest Girl in the
World. Thirty Day Princess. What Every
Woman Knows. The Mystery of Mr X. She
Loves Me Not. All Men Are Enemies. 1935:
The Flame Within. Vanessa: Her Love Story.
O'Shaughnessy's Boy. Mutiny on the Bounty.
The Night Is Young. Rendezvous. Reckless. The
Perfect Gentleman. Captain Blood. 1936: Little
Lord Fauntleroy. Half Angel. Walking on Air.
Hearts Divided. Beloved Enemy. Give Me Your
Heart. The Charge of the Light Brigade. 1937:
The Prince and the Pauper. When You're in
Love (GB: For You Alone). The Emperor's
Candlesticks. Conquest (GB: Marie Walewska).
Wise Girl. 1938: Marie Antoinette. The Young
in Heart. Dramatic School. Suez. The Baroness
and the Butler. 1939: The Private Lives of
Elizabeth and Essex. Tarzan Finds a Son! The
Adventures of Sherlock Holmes. 1940: Spring
Parade. It's a Date. Little Old New York.
Down Argentine Way. 1941: The Lady from
Louisiana. The Man Who Lost Himself. 1942:
Rings On Her Fingers. This Above All. Half
Way to Shanghai. 1943: The Man Trap. Mr
Lucky. 1944: Secrets of Scotland Yard. The
Hour Before the Dawn. The Reckless Age. Two
Girls and a Sailor. 1945: Tarzan and the
Amazons. 1946: The Green Years. Her Sister's

Secret. The Return of Monte Cristo (GB: Monte
Cristo's Revenge). Heartbeat. Night and Day.
The Locket. Of Human Bondage. 1947: The
Homestretch. Dark Delusion (GB: Cynthia's
Secret). Ivy. Time Out of Mind. Song of Love.
1948: Julia Misbehaves. Enchantment. Oliver
Twist. 1949: Challenge to Lassie.

STERN, Daniel 1957–
Very tall, stringy, slyly smiling American actor with dark, curly hair, a multi-talented performer who hasn't quite found a niche in films, although he became much better known after his appearance as one of the two burglars in the *Home Alone* comedies. Starting his film career as one of the cycling youths in *Breaking Away*, he has since appeared equally in comedy and drama (and with and without a beard). Towards the end of the 1980s, he revealed additional ambitions in writing and directing, helming several episodes of the TV series *The Wonder Years*, for which he also provided the narration. He directed his first film in 1993 and supplied the screenplay for *The Tenants* the following year.

1979: Breaking Away. Starting Over. 1980: It's
My Turn. A Small Circle of Friends. One-Trick
Pony. Stardust Memories. 1981: I'm Dancing
As Fast As I Can. Honky Tonk Freeway. 1982:
Diner. 1983: Blue Thunder. Get Crazy.
*1984: C.H.U.D. *Frankenweenie. 1985: Key*
Exchange. 1986: The Boss's Wife. Hannah and
Her Sisters. 1987: Born in East L.A. 1988:
D.O.A. The Milagro Beanfield War. Weekend
War (TV). 1989: Leviathan. Friends, Lovers
& Lunatics. Little Monsters. Coupe de Ville
(released 1992). Crazy Horse. 1990: My Blue
Heaven. Home Alone. The Court-Martial of
Jackie Robinson (TV). 1991: City Slickers.
1992: Home Alone 2: Lost in New York. 1993:
Rookie of the Year (and directed). 1994: City
Slickers: The Legend of Curly's Gold. Pee Wee
Football. 1995: Tenderfoots.

STEVENS, Onslow
(O. Stevenson) 1902–1977
Dark, serious-looking, taciturn, long-faced American actor, the son of Houseley Stevenson (*qv*). In occasional leads, few of which have survived in the memory, save perhaps his mad scientist in *House of Dracula*, but more often phlegmatic character parts as sobersides lawyers, prison officers, police-

men and politicians. Directed many plays in the theatre, but never a film. Murdered by persons unknown in a convalescent home.

1932: Once in a Lifetime. Okay America (GB:
Penalty of Fame). Heroes of the West (serial).
Radio Patrol. Jungle Mystery (serial). The
Golden West. Born to Fight. 1933: Peg o'
My Heart. Nagana. Secret of the Blue Room.
Counsellor at Law. Only Yesterday. Grand
Exit. Yellow Dust. 1934: Bombay Mail. This
Side of Heaven. House of Danger. The Crosby
Case (GB: The Crosby Murder Case). In Love
With Life (GB: Re-Union). Life Returns.
Affairs of a Gentleman. The Vanishing Shadow
(serial). I'll Tell the World. I Can't Escape.
1935: The Three Musketeers. A Notorious
Gentleman. Born to Gamble. F Man. Bridge of
Sighs. Three on a Trail. Forced Landing. 1936:
Under Two Flags. Straight from the Shoulder.
Murder With Pictures. Easy Money. 1937: You
Can't Buy Luck. Flight from Glory. There Goes
the Groom. 1939: Those High Gray Walls
(GB: The Gates to Alcatraz). When Tomorrow
Comes. 1940: Mystery Sea Raider. Who Killed
Aunt Maggie? The Man Who Wouldn't Talk.
1941: The Monster and the Girl. Go West,
Young Lady. 1942: Sunset Serenade. 1943:
Appointment in Berlin. Idaho. Hands Across the
Border. 1945: House of Dracula. 1946: Angel
on My Shoulder. Canyon Passage. OSS. 1948:
The Gallant Blade. The Night Has a Thousand
Eyes. The Creeper. Walk a Crooked Mile. 1949:
Red, Hot and Blue. Bomba the Jungle Boy.
1950: Mark of the Gorilla. State Penitentiary.
Revenue Agent. Motor Patrol. Lonely Hearts
Bandits (GB: Lonely Heart Bandits). 1951:
Lorna Doone. One Too Many (GB: Killer With
a Label). All That I Have. The Hills of Utah.
The Family Secret. Sirocco. Sealed Cargo. 1952:
The Magnificent Adventure. The San Francisco
Story. 1953: A Lion Is in the Streets. The
Charge at Feather River. 1954: Fangs of the
Wild. Them! They Rode West. 1955: New York
Confidential. 1956: Tribute to a Bad Man.
Outside the Law. Kelly and Me. 1958: The
Buccaneer. Tarawa Beachhead. Lonelyhearts.
The Party Crashers. 1960: All the Fine Young
Cannibals. 1962: The Couch. Geronimo's
Revenge (TV. GB: cinemas).

STEVENS, Ronnie 1925–
Breezy, light-haired British light comedian who came to films from revue success and proved a polished foil and semi-straight man in a number of British comedies from the

early 1950s. After the 1960s he was much busier in the theatre and on TV.

1952: Top Secret (US: Mr Potts Goes to Moscow). Made in Heaven. 1953: Love in Pawn. 1954: The Scarlet Web. For Better, For Worse (US: Cocktails in the Kitchen). The Embezzler. 1955: The Narrowing Circle. Value for Money. An Alligator Named Daisy. As Long As They're Happy. The Hornet's Nest. 1957: Doctor at Large. 1958: Bachelor of Hearts. I Was Monty's Double (US: Monty's Double). Danger Within (US: Breakout). 1959: I'm All Right, Jack. 1960: Doctor in Love. Dentist in the Chair. 1961: Dentist on the Job (US: A Coming-Out Party). Nearly a Nasty Accident. A Pair of Briefs. 1962: It's Trad Dad. On the Beat. Carry On Cruising. 1963: Doctor in Distress. 1964: A Home of Your Own. 1965: San Ferry Ann. Those Magnificent Men in Their Flying Machines. 1966: Doctor in Clover. The Sandwich Man. Give a Dog a Bone. 1967: Smashing Time. 1969: Some Girls Do. Goodbye, Mr Chips. 1979: SOS Titanic. 1980: Twelfth Night. 1982: Captain Stirrick. 1985: Morons from Outer Space. 1989: Killing Dad. 1990: Secret Weapon (TV). 1991: Blame It on the Bellboy.

STEVENSON, Houseley 1879–1953
Bony, sharp-featured British-born actor who made no films anywhere until he was pushing 60, but enjoyed a hectic few postwar Hollywood years up to his death playing cantankerous old codgers, often unshaven, hollow-cheeked westerners. Father of actors Onslow Stevens (*qv*) and Houseley Stevenson Jr.

1936: Law in Her Hands. Isle of Fury. 1937: Once a Doctor. 1942: Native Land. 1943: Happy Land. 1945: Dakota. 1946: Little Miss Big (GB: The Baxter Millions). Somewhere in the Night. Without Reservations. 1947: The Brasher Doubloon (GB: The High Window). Dark Passage. Thunder in the Valley (GB: Bob, Son of Battle). Ramrod. The Ghost and Mrs Muir. Forever Amber. Time Out of Mind. Four Faces West (GB: They Passed This Way). 1948: The Challenge. Smart Woman. The Paleface. Secret Beyond the Door. Casbah. Kidnapped. Joan of Arc. Moonrise. Apartment for Peggy. 1949: Colorado Territory. Leave It to Henry. Bride of Vengeance. Calamity Jane and Sam Bass. Knock on Any Door. The Lady Gambles. Masked Raiders. Sorrowful Jones. You Gotta Stay Happy. Take One False Step. The Walking Hills. The Gal Who Took the West. All the King's Men. 1950: Edge of Doom (GB: Stronger than Fear). Sierra. The Gunfighter. The Sun Sets at Dawn. 1951: All That I Have. Cave of Outlaws. Hollywood Story. The Secret of Convict Lake. As Young As You Feel. Darling, How Could You? (GB: Rendezvous). 1952: The Atomic City. The Wild North. Oklahoma Annie.

STEWART, Paul
(P. Sternberg) 1908–1986
Cold-eyed, heavy-eyebrowed American actor of set, rather menacing features; a leading member of Orson Welles' Mercury Theatre group who only gradually became a Hollywood film regular, in villainous (often callously so) roles. Stewart went grey early, and in any case always looked older than his years. After 1955, he directed a large number of productions and episodes for television, as well as continuing a sporadic acting career. Died following a heart attack.

1941: Citizen Kane. Johnny Eager. 1942: The World at War (narrator only). 1943: Government Girl. Mr Lucky. 1949: The Window. Illegal Entry. Easy Living. Champion. Twelve O'Clock High. 1950: Walk Softly, Stranger. Edge of Doom (GB: Stronger than Fear). 1951: Appointment With Danger (completed 1949). 1952: Carbine Williams. Deadline USA (GB: Deadline). Loan Shark. We're Not Married. The Bad and the Beautiful. 1953: The Juggler. The Joe Louis Story. 1954: Deep in My Heart. Prisoner-of-War. 1955: Chicago Syndicate. Kiss Me Deadly. Hell on Frisco Bay. The
Cobweb. *1956: The Wild Party. Confession (TV). 1957: Top Secret Affair (GB: Their Secret Affair). 1958: King Creole. 1962: A Child Is Waiting. 1965: The Greatest Story Ever Told. 1967: In Cold Blood. 1969: How to Commit Marriage. Jigsaw. 1973: F for Fake. 1974: The Day of the Locust. Murph the Surf (GB: Love a Little, Steal a Lot). 1975: Bite the Bullet. 1976: W. C. Fields and Me. 1977: Opening Night. 1978: The Revenge of the Pink Panther. The Nativity (TV). 1981: SOB. Nobody's Perfect. 1982: Tempest. 1983: Emergency Room (TV). 1985: Seduced (TV).*

As director:
1956: Lady in Fear (TV. GB: cinemas).

STOCK, Nigel 1919–1986
Light-haired, pugnacious British actor (born in Malta) who lived up to his name by being stocky and square-built. Mostly on stage (where he first performed as a boy of 12), he gave a number of determined screen performances that were often better than those billed above him. Also a first-class Dr Watson in TV 'Sherlock Holmes' series featuring Douglas Wilmer and Peter Cushing. Died from a heart attack.

*1937: Lancashire Luck. 1938: Break the News! Luck of the Navy (GB: North Sea Patrol). 1939: Goodbye Mr Chips! Sons of the Sea. 1944: *Victory Wedding. 1947: It Always Rains on Sunday. Brighton Rock. 1951: The Lady With a Lamp. 1952: Derby Day (US: Four Against Fate). 1953: Malta Story. 1954: Aunt Clara. The Dam Busters. 1955: The Night My Number Came Up. 1956: *The Gentle Corsican (narrator only). Eyewitness. Battle of the River Plate (US: Pursuit of the Graf Spee). 1958: The Silent Enemy. 1960: Never Let Go. 1961: Victim. 1962: The Password Is Courage. HMS Defiant (US: Damn the Defiant!). 1963: The Great Escape. To Have and to Hold. Nothing But the Best. 1964: Weekend à Zuydcoote/Weekend at Dunkirk. The High Bright Sun (US: McGuire Go Home!). 1966: The Night of the Generals. 1968: The Lost Continent. The Lion in Winter. 1970: Cromwell. 1973: Bequest to the Nation (US: The Nelson Affair). 1975: Russian Roulette. Operation Daybreak. 1977: *When I'm Rich (voice only). 1979: A Man Called Intrepid (TV). 1980: The Mirror Crack'd. 1982: Red Monarch (TV, but first shown in* cinemas). 1983: Yellowbeard. 1985: Young Sherlock Holmes. 1986: Blood Hunt (TV).

STONE, George E.
(Georgy Stein) 1903–1967

Small (5 ft 3½ in) Polish-born actor with dark hair and droopy moustache, who could be furtive or forlorn and whose Brooklynese gangsters were alternately vicious or broadly comic. He was The Sewer Rat in *Seventh Heaven* and The Runt in the Boston Blackie films — two 'monickers' that summed up his screen characters. A close friend of author Damon Runyon, he played Runyon's Society Max in *Guys and Dolls*. Died following a stroke. Acting since childhood.

1914: *Kid Regan's Hands. 1915: *The Baby. *The Rivals. *The Little Cupids. *Little Dick's First Case/Little Dick's First Adventure. *The Straw Man. *Her Filmland Hero. *Pirates Bold. *Dirty Face Dan. *The Ash Can. *The Kid Magicians. *A Ten Cent Adventure. *The Runaways. *The Doll-House Mystery. Let Katy Do It. Martha's Vindication. 1916: The Children in the House. The Patriot. Children of the Feud. Going Straight. Gretchen the Greenhorn. The Little Schoolma'am. 1917: Jim Bludso. Sudden Jim. 1918: 'Till I Come Back to You. Six Shooter Andy. The Gypsy Trail. Ali Baba and the Forty Thieves. The Scoffer. 1919: The Poppy Girl's Husband. The Jungle Trail. The Speed Maniac. 1920: Just Pals. Fighting Creesy. Rio Grande. 1921: Penny of Top Hill Trail. Jackie. Desperate Trails. White and Unmarried. The Whistle. 1923: The Fourth Musketeer. 1927: Seventh Heaven. Brass Knuckles. 1928: San Francisco Nights (GB: Divorce). Turn Back the Hours (GB: The Badge of Courage). Clothes Make the Woman. State Street Sadie (GB: The Girl from State Street). Walking Back. Beautiful But Dumb. The Racket. Tenderloin. 1929: The Redeeming Sin. Skin Deep. Weary River. Naughty Baby (GB: Reckless Rosie). The Girl in the Glass Cage. Two Men and a Maid. Melody Lane. 1930: The Medicine Man. *The Bearded Lady. Under a Texas Moon. Little Caesar. The Stronger Sex. *So This is Paris Green. 1931: *The Stolen Jools (GB: The Slippery Pearls). The Front Page. Five Star Final. Cimarron. The Spider. Sob Sister (GB: The Blonde Reporter). 1932: The Last Mile. Taxi! File No. 113. The Woman from Monte Carlo. The World and the Flesh. The Phantom of Crestwood. 1933: 42nd Street.

King for a Night. Vampire Bat. Sailor Be Good. Song of the Eagle (GB: The Beer Baron). Emergency Call. The Big Brain (GB: Enemies of Society). Sing, Sinner, Sing. Penthouse (GB: Crooks in Clover). Ladies Must Love. He Couldn't Take It. 1934: The Return of the Terror. Viva Villa! The Dragon Murder Case. Embarrassing Moments. One Hour Late. Frontier Marshal. Secret of the Chateau. 1935: Make a Million. Hold 'Em Yale (GB: Uniform Lovers). Moonlight on the Prairie. Frisco Kid. Public Hero No. 1. Million Dollar Baby. 1936: Freshman Love (GB: Rhythm on the River). King of Hockey (GB: King of the Ice Rink). Jailbreak. Polo Joe. Boulder Dam. Rhythm on the Range. Man Hunt. Anthony Adverse. Bullets or Ballots. Here Comes Carter (GB: The Voice of Scandal). The Captain's Kid. Don't Get Me Wrong. 1937: Clothes and the Woman. Back in Circulation. The Adventurous Blonde/Torchy Blane the Adventurous Blonde. 1938: Alcatraz Island. A Slight Case of Murder. Over the Wall. Mr Moto's Gamble. You and Me. The Long Shot. Submarine Patrol. 1939: You Can't Get Away With Murder. The Night of Nights. The Housekeeper's Daughter. 1940: Island of Doomed Men. I Take This Woman. North West Mounted Police. Slightly Tempted. Cherokee Strip (GB: Fighting Marshal). Road Show. 1941: Broadway Limited. Last of the Duanes. The Face Behind the Mask (GB: Behind the Mask). Confessions of Boston Blackie (GB: Confessions). 1942: The Affairs of Jimmy Valentine. The Lone Star Ranger. Little Tokyo USA. Boston Blackie Goes Hollywood (GB: Blackie Goes Hollywood). The Devil With Hitler. Alias Boston Blackie. 1943: After Midnight With Boston Blackie (GB: After Midnight). The Chance of a Lifetime. 1944: Strangers in the Night. Timber Queen. My Buddy. One Mysterious Night. Roger Touhy, Gangster (GB: The Last Gangster). 1945: Boston Blackie Booked on Suspicion (GB: Booked on Suspicion). Boston Blackie's Rendezvous (GB: Blackie's Rendezvous). Scared Stiff. Nob Hill. Midnight Manhunt. 1946: One Exciting Week. Shock. Doll Face (GB: Come Back to Me). Boston Blackie and the Law (GB: Blackie and the Law). A Close Call for Boston Blackie (GB: Lady of Mystery). The Phantom Thief. Suspense. Sentimental Journey. Abie's Irish Rose. 1947: Daisy Kenyon. 1948: Trapped by Boston Blackie. The Untamed Breed. 1949: Dancing in the Dark. 1952: Bloodhounds of Broadway. A Girl in Every Port. 1953: The Robe. Pickup on South Street. Combat Squad. 1954: The Treasure of Bengal (GB: Jungle Boy. US: Jungle Hell). The Miami Story. The Steel Cage. Broken Lance. Three-Ring Circus. Woman's World. 1955: Guys and Dolls. The Man With the Golden Arm. 1956: Slightly Scarlet. The Conqueror. 1957: The Story of Mankind. Sierra Stranger. Baby-Face Nelson. Calypso Heat Wave. The Tijuana Story. 1958: Some Came Running. 1959: Some Like It Hot. Alias Jesse James. Night of the Quarter Moon. 1960: Ocean's Eleven. 1961: Pocketful of Miracles.

STONE, Harold J. 1911–

Heavy-set, thick-lipped, intense American actor with black, curly hair. Trained at the Actors' Studio, he became briefly very

popular in the mid-1950s with personable performances that earned him marquee billing and saw him as high as third on the cast list. After this initial surge, however, he was more often seen on Broadway and television, although he has continued to appear from time to time in (smaller) roles in films.

1956: Slander. The Harder They Fall. Somebody Up There Likes Me. The Wrong Man. 1957: House of Numbers. The Garment Jungle. Man Afraid. The Invisible Boy. 1959: These Thousand Hills. Stampede at Bitter Creek. 1960: Spartacus. 1961: The Chapman Report. 1962: Recoil (TV. GB: cinemas). 1963: Showdown. 'X'—The Man With the X-Ray Eyes (GB: The Man With the X-Ray Eyes). 1965: Girl Happy. The Greatest Story Ever Told. 1967: The St Valentine's Day Massacre. The Big Mouth. 1970: Breakout (TV). Which Way to the Front? (GB: Ja! Ja! Mein General, But Which Way to the Front?). 1971: The Seven Minutes. 1972: Pickup on 101 (GB: Echoes of the Road). 1975: The Legend of Valentino (TV). The Wild McCulloughs. 1977: Mitchell. 1981: Hardly Working.

STONE, Lewis 1879–1953

Lean, straight-backed American actor, a leading man of silents with occasional forays into silky villainy. His slightly sinister personality became a concerned one as the sound years wore on, and he became totally identified with his running role as the wise *paterfamilias*, Judge Hardy, in the Andy Hardy series. Nominated for an Academy Award on *The Patriot*. Died from a heart attack when trying to chase vandals from his property.

1915: *The Man Who Found Out.* 1916: *Honor's Altar. According to the Code. The Havoc.* 1918: *Inside the Lines.* 1919: *Man of Bronze. Man's Desire. Johnny Get Your Gun.* 1920: *Held by the Enemy. Milestones. Nomads of the North. The River's End. The Concert.* 1921: *The Golden Snare. The Child Thou Gavest Me. Beau Revel. Pilgrims of the Night. Don't Neglect your Wife.* 1922: *A Fool There Was. The Dangerous Age. Trifling Women. The Rosary. The Prisoner of Zenda.* 1923: *Scaramouche. You Can't Fool Your Wife. The World's Applause.* 1924: *Why Men Leave Home. The Stranger. Cytherea. Inez from Hollywood. Husbands and Lovers.* 1925: *The Lost World. Confessions of a Queen. Cheaper to Marry. The Lady Who Lied. What Fools Men. The Talker. Fine Clothes.* 1926: *Old Loves and New. The Girl from Montmartre. Don Juan's Three Nights. Midnight Lovers. Too Much Money. The Blonde Saint.* 1927: *The Notorious Lady. An Affair of the Follies. The Prince of Head Waiters. Lonesome Ladies. The Private Life of Helen of Troy.* 1928: *Freedom of the Press. Foreign Legion. The Patriot. Inspiration.* 1929: *The Trial of Mary Dugan. A Woman of Affairs. Madame X. Wild Orchids. Wonder of Women. The Circle.* 1930: *Romance. Strictly Unconventional. Their Own Desire. The Office Wife. The Big House. Passion Flower. Father's Son.* 1931: *Inspiration. My Past. The Sin of Madelon Claudet (GB: The Lullaby). Always Goodbye. Phantom of Paris. The Bargain. The Secret Six. Mata Hari. Stolen Heaven. Strictly Dishonorable.* 1932: *Night Court (GB: Justice for Sale). Grand Hotel. The Wet Parade. Letty Lynton. Divorce in the Family. Unashamed. New Morals for Old. Red-Headed Woman. The Mask of Fu Manchu. The Son-Daughter. Strange Interlude.* 1933: *Looking Forward (GB: Service). The White Sister. Queen Christina. Bureau of Missing Persons. Men Must Fight.* 1934: *Treasure Island. The Mystery of Mr X. You Can't Buy Everything. The Girl from Missouri (GB: 100 Per Cent Pure).* 1935: *David Copperfield. Vanessa, Her Love Story. China Seas. Shipmates Forever. West Point of the Air. Public Hero Number One. Woman Wanted.* 1936: *The Unguarded Hour. Small Town Girl. Suzy. Three Godfathers. Sworn Enemy. Don't Turn 'Em Loose.* 1937: *The Man Who Cried Wolf. Outcast. The Thirteenth Chair. You're Only Young Once.* 1938: *Stolen Heaven. Bad Man of Brimstone. Judge Hardy's Children. The Chaser. Out West with the Hardys. Yellow Jack. Love Finds Andy Hardy.* 1939: *Joe and Ethel Turp Call on the President. The Hardys Ride High. Ice Follies of 1939. Andy Hardy Gets Spring Fever. Judge Hardy and Son.* 1940: *Sporting Blood. Andy Hardy Meets Debutante.* 1941: *Andy Hardy's Private Secretary. The Bugle Sounds. Life Begins for Andy Hardy.* 1942: *The Courtship of Andy Hardy. Andy Hardy's Double Life.* 1943: **Plan for Destruction (narrator only).* 1944: *Andy Hardy's Blonde Trouble.* 1946: *The Hoodlum Saint. Love Laughs at Andy Hardy. Three Wise Fools.* 1948: *State of the Union (GB: The World and His Wife). The Sun Comes Up.* 1949: *Any Number Can Play.* 1950: *Key to the City. Stars in My Crown. Grounds for Marriage.* 1951: *Angels in the Outfield (GB: Angels and the Pirates). Bannerline. The Unknown Man. It's a Big Country. Night into Morning.* 1952: *Just This Once. Talk about a Stranger. Scaramouche. The Prisoner of Zenda.* 1953: *All the Brothers Were Valiant.*

STONE, Marianne 1924–
Dark-haired, dark-eyed, ultra-slim British actress whose rather downcast looks got her cast, after beginnings as a leading lady, in serious, scarf-over-the-head roles; landladies, working wives and slum mums. After scores of such roles, she tackled more comedy in the 1970s, by which time she had become Britain's most prolific supporting actress of the post-war period. Long married to show business columnist Peter Noble. Other sources give year of birth as 1923 and 1925.

1947: *Brighton Rock (US: Young Scarface). Escape Dangerous. When the Bough Breaks.* 1948: *The Idol of Paris. It's Hard to be Good.* 1949: *A Boy, a Girl and a Bike. Adam and Evelyne (US: Adam and Evalyn). A Run for Your Money. Miss Pilgrim's Progress. Marry Me!* 1950: *The Clouded Yellow. Blackmailed. Seven Days to Noon. Mr Drake's Duck.* 1951: *High Treason. The Magic Box. Appointment With Venus (US: Island Rescue). Home to Danger. Angels One Five.* 1952: *The Pickwick Papers. The Net (US: Project M7). Venetian Bird (US: The Assassin). Time Gentlemen Please!* 1953: *A Day to Remember. The Runaway Bus. Spaceways. The Weak and the Wicked. You Know What Sailors Are.* 1954: *The Dog and the Diamonds. The Brain Machine. The Good Die Young. Beautiful Stranger (US: Twist of Fate). 36 Hours (US: Terror Street). Dance Little Lady. Mad About Men.* 1955: *Man of the Moment. Portrait of Alison (US: Postmark for Danger). Barbados Quest. Simon and Laura. Fun at St Fanny's. Lost (US: Tears for Simon). Cloak Without Dagger (US: Operation Conspiracy). The Quatermass Experiment (US: The Creeping Unknown). Private's Progress.* 1956: **Person Unknown. Charley Moon. Passport to Treason. Yield to the Night (US: Blonde Sinner). The Long Arm (US: The Third Key). A Touch of the Sun. The High Terrace. Eyewitness. Bond of Fear. Tiger in the Smoke. The Good Companions. The Intimate Stranger (US: Finger of Guilt). Brothers in Law.* 1957: **The Tyburn Case. Quatermass II (US: Enemy from Space).* Man from Tangier (US: Thunder Over Tangier). High Tide at Noon. Time Lock. Hell Drivers. Woman in a Dressing Gown. Just My Luck. 1958: *The Golden Disc (US: The Inbetween Age). Innocent Sinners. A Night to Remember. Carve Her Name with Pride. At the Stroke of Nine. A Cry from the Streets. *Man With a Dog. No Trees in the Street (US: No Tree in the Street). Carlton-Browne of the FO (US: Man in a Cocked Hat).* 1959: **The Ghost Train Murder. The 39 Steps. Jet Storm. Carry On Nurse. Tiger Bay. Jack the Ripper. Operation Bullshine. I'm All Right, Jack. The Man Who Liked Funerals. Please Turn Over. Horrors of the Black Museum. Don Quixote (unfinished. Voice only). Follow a Star. The Heart of a Man. The Angry Silence.* 1960: *The Big Day. Never Let Go. Doctor in Love.* 1961: *Double Bunk. Five Golden Hours. Two and Two Make Six. Watch It Sailor! Lolita. The Frightened City. On the Fiddle (US: Operation Snafu). The Day the Earth Caught Fire.* 1962: *Crooks Anonymous. Gaolbreak. The Wild and the Willing. Night of the Prowler. Jigsaw. The Wrong Arm of the Law. The Fast Lady. Paranoiac. Play It Cool.* 1963: *Doctor in Distress. A Stitch in Time. The Cool Mikado. Return to Sender. The Marked One. Echo of Diana. Carry On Jack (US: Carry On Venus). The Hi-Jackers. Heavens Above! The Victors. Blind Corner. West 11. The World 10 Times Over (US: Pussycat Alley). Ladies Who Do. Stolen Hours. Nothing But the Best.* 1964: *Troubled Waters. A Hard Day's Night. Hysteria. Rattle of a Simple Man. The Beauty Jungle (US: Contest Girl). We Shall See. The Curse of the Mummy's Tomb. The Intelligence Men. Act of Murder. Witchcraft. Devils of Darkness.* 1965: *Catch Us If You Can (US: Having a Wild Weekend). You Must Be Joking! Traitor's Gate. The Night Caller (US: Blood Beast from Outer Space). Strangler's Web.* 1966: *The Wrong Box. The Spy With a Cold Nose. Eye of the Devil. Deadlier Than the Male. Carry On Screaming. The Sandwich Man. A Countess from Hong Kong. Don't Lose Your Head. The Long Duel. To Sir with Love.* 1967: *The Jokers. Carry On Doctor. The Man Outside. Here We Go Round the Mulberry Bush.* 1968: *Twisted Nerve. Crooks and Coronets (US: Sophy's Place). The Best House in London. The Bliss of Mrs Blossom. The Games.* 1969: *Lock Up Your Daughters! All the Right Noises. Oh! What a Lovely War.* 1970: *Doctor in Trouble. Scrooge. The Raging Moon (US: Long Ago Tomorrow). Assault. Countess Dracula. Every Home Should Have One (US: Think Dirty). The Firechasers. Hoverbug. There's a Girl in My Soup.* 1971: *Mr Forbush and the Penguins (US: Cry of the Penguins). Carry On at Your Convenience. Whoever Slew Auntie Roo? (US: Who Slew Auntie Roo?). Danny Jones. All Coppers Are . . .* 1972: *Carry On Matron. Tower of Evil (US: Horror of Snape Island). Bless This House. The Cherry Picker. The Creeping Flesh. The Love Ban (originally It's a Two-Foot-Six-Inch-Above-the-Ground World) Baxter! (US: The Boy).* 1973: *Penny Gold. Vault of Horror. Carry On Girls. Mistress Pamela. Craze.* 1974: *Carry On Dick. Dead of Night (TV). Confessions of a Window Cleaner. Percy's Progress.* 1975: *That Lucky Touch. Carry On Behind. I'm Not Feeling Myself Tonight.* 1976: *The Incredible Sarah. The*

Chiffy Kids (series). 1977: Confessions from a Holiday Camp. The Great Snail Race. 1978: Sammy's Super T-Shirt. What's Up Superdoc? The Class of Miss MacMichael. 1979: The Human Factor. A Man Called Intrepid (TV). 1980: Dangerous Davies The Last Detective (TV). Little Lord Fauntleroy (TV. GB: cinemas). 1981: Beyond the Fog. 1982: Funny Money. 1983: The Wicked Lady. The Zany Adventures of Robin Hood (TV). 1984: Always/Deja Vu. 1986: Terry on the Fence.

STONE, Milburn 1904–1980

Stocky, moustachioed American actor with dark wavy hair who alternated as hero and villain of low-budget action films and serials, then moved into character roles as bankers, crooks, wardens, doctors and officers. He found a permanent home on television with the role of the grouchy Doc Adams in *Gunsmoke*, a role in which the quizzical Stone features were seen from 1955 to 1972. Died from a heart attack.

1935: The Fighting Marines (serial). Ladies Crave Excitement. Rendezvous. The Three Mesquiteers. 1936: The Milky Way. Rose Bowl (GB: O'Riley's Luck). Banjo on My Knee. China Clipper. The Princess Comes Across. Two in a Crowd. Murder With Pictures. 1937: A Doctor's Diary. Atlantic Flight. Federal Bullets. Wings Over Honolulu. Blazing Barriers. Music for Madame. Swing It, Professor. Youth on Parole. The Thirteenth Man. The Man in Blue. Port of Missing Girls. Mr Boggs Steps Out. You Can't Beat Love. They Gave Him a Gun. 1938: Wives Under Suspicion. The Storm. Sinners in Paradise. Crime School. Paroled from the Big House. California Frontier. 1939: Mystery Plane/Sky Pilot. King of the Turf. Society Smugglers. Fighting Mad. Blind Alley. Young Mr Lincoln. Tail Spin. Tropic Fury. Stunt Pilot. Spirit of Culver (GB: Man's Heritage). Blackwell's Island. When Tomorrow Comes. Sky Patrol. Made for Each Other. Danger Flight. Nick Carter, Master Detective. Crashing Through. Charlie McCarthy, Detective. The Big Guy. 1940: Chasing Trouble. Enemy Agent (GB: Secret Enemy). Johnny Apollo. An Angel from Texas. Framed. *Buyer Beware. Give Us Wings. Lillian Russell. Colorado. The Great Plane Robbery. 1941: The Phantom Cowboy. The Great Train Robbery. Death Valley Outlaws. 1942: Reap the Wild Wind. Eyes in the Night. Rubber Racketeers.

Invisible Agent. Frisco Lil. Police Bullets. Pacific Rendezvous. 1943: Keep 'em Slugging. You Can't Beat the Law. Get Going. Sherlock Holmes Faces Death. Captive Wild Woman. Corvette K-225 (GB: The Nelson Touch). Silent Witness (GB: Attorney for the Defence). Gung Ho! The Mad Ghoul. 1944: The Imposter. Hi, Good Looking. Hat Check Honey. Moon Over Las Vegas. Jungle Woman. Phantom Lady. Twilight on the Prairie. The Great Alaskan Mystery (serial). 1945: The Master Key (serial). The Beautiful Cheat (GB: What a Woman!). The Daltons Ride Again. The Frozen Ghost. I'll Remember April. On Stage, Everybody. She Gets Her Man. Strange Confession. Swing Out, Sister. The Royal Mounted Rides Again (serial). 1946: Danger Woman. Inside Job. Smooth As Silk. Little Miss Big (GB: Baxter's Millions). Spider Woman Strikes Back. Strange Conquest. Her Adventurous Night. 1947: Cass Timberlane. Killer Dill. The Michigan Kid. Headin' for Heaven. Buck Privates Come Home (GB: Rookies Come Home). 1948: Train to Alcatraz. The Judge (GB: The Gamblers). 1949: The Green Promise (GB: Raging Waters). Calamity Jane and Sam Bass. Sky Dragon. 1950: No Man of Her Own. The Fireball. Snow Dog. Branded. 1951: Behind Southern Lines (TV). Operation Pacific. The Racket. Road Block. Flying Leathernecks. 1952: The Atomic City. The Savage. 1953: The Sun Shines Bright. Invaders from Mars. Second Chance. Arrowhead. Pickup on South Street. 1954: The Siege at Red River. Black Tuesday. The Long Gray Line. 1955: White Feather. Smoke Signal. The Private War of Major Benson. 1957: Drango. 1972: The World of Sport Fishing (documentary).

STRANGE, Glenn

(George G. Strange) 1899–1973
Massive American actor with square, solid, often moustachioed features that betrayed his part-Cherokee ancestry. A promising heavyweight boxer until he developed trouble with his hands, Strange tried ranching and rodeo riding (he was even once a deputy sheriff) before drifting into show business as one of the Arizona Wranglers group on radio, playing fiddle, composing songs and joining in the chorus. After playing dozens of minor heavies in low-budget westerns, Strange won a small slice of screen fame with three portrayals of the Frankenstein monster in the 1940s. He died from cancer.

1931: Border Law. The Deadline. Hard Hombre. The Fighting Marshal. The Range Feud. Wild Horse. The Guilty Generation. 1932: Hurricane Express (serial). McKenna of the Mounted. *His Royal Shyness. Ride Him, Cowboy. The Cowboy Counsellor. 1933: Somewhere in Sonora. The Sundown Rider. The Thrill Hunter. The Whirlwind. 1934: The Law of the Wild (serial). The Star Packer (GB: He Wore a Star). 1935: Border Vengeance. Cyclone of the Saddle. His Fighting Blood. The Gallant Defender. Lawless Range. Moonlight on the Prairie. Hard Rock Harrigan. The Law of the 45s (GB: The Mysterious Mr Sheffield). The New Frontier. Stormy. Suicide Squad. Westward Ho! 1936: Avenging Waters. The Cattle Thief. Flash Gordon (serial). The California Mail. Conflict. Guns of the Pecos. The Fugitive Sheriff (GB: Law and Order). The Lonely Trail. Sunset of Power. Trailin' West (GB: On Secret Service). Song of the Gringo (GB: The Old Corral). 1937: Adventure's End. Arizona Days. Blazing Sixes. The Californian (GB: Beyond the Law). Cherokee Strip (GB: Strange Laws). The Devil's Saddle Legion. Danger Valley. Courage of the West. Empty Holsters. God's Country and the Man. Land Beyond the Law. The Singing Outlaw. *The Sunday Round-Up. Trouble in Texas. Stars Over Arizona. A Tenderfoot Goes West. 1938: Black Bandit. Border Wolves. Forbidden Valley. California Frontier. Call of the Rockies. The Frontiersman. Ghost Town Riders. Guilty Trails. Gun Packer. Gunsmoke Trail. The Mexicali Kid. Honor of the West. In Old Mexico. Pride of the West. Sunset Trail. The Mysterious Rider. The Spy Ring. The Last Stand. Prairie Justice. Prison Break. The Painted Trail. Whirlwind Horseman. State Police. Six-Shootin' Sheriff. 1939: Across the Plains. Blue Montana Skies. Days of Jesse James. *Cupid Rides the Range. Flying G-Men (serial). The Fighting Gringo. Arizona Legion. The Llano Kid. Law of the Pampas. Range War. The Lone Ranger Rides Again (serial). The Night Riders. The Phantom Stage. Oklahoma Terror. Rough Riders' Round Up. *Ride, Cowboy, Ride. Overland Mail. 1940: The Cowboy from Sundown. Covered Wagon Trails. Dark Command. Land of the Six-Guns. Pioneer Days. San Francisco Docks. Rhythm of the Rio Grande. Pals of the Silver Sage. Stage to Chino. Triple Justice. Wagon Train. *Bar Buckaroos. *Teddy, the Rough Rider. Three Men from Texas. The Fargo Kid. Wyoming (GB: Bad Man of Wyoming). Drums of the Desert. 1941: Arizona Cyclone. Come On, Danger! Billy the Kid Wanted. Forbidden Trails. The Bandit Trail. The Driftin' Kid. Dude Cowboy. In Old Colorado. Lone Star Law Men. Riders of Death Valley (serial). Badlands of Dakota. *Westward Ho-Hum. The Kid's Last Ride. Saddlemates. *California or Bust. Billy the Kid's Round Up. Wide Open Town. Fugitive Valley. 1942: Down Texas Way. The Ghost of Frankenstein. Army Surgeon. Billy the Kid Trapped. Boot Hill Bandits. Juke Girl. Little Joe, the Wrangler. The Lone Rider and the Bandit. Billy the Kid's Smoking Guns (GB: Smoking Guns). Bandit Ranger. The Mad Monster. The Mummy's Tomb. Stagecoach Buckaroo. Romance on the Range. Raiders of the West. Sunset on the Desert. Rolling Down the Great Divide. Western Mail. Prairie Gunsmoke. Overland Stagecoach.

Texas Trouble Shooters. Sundown Jim. 1943: Arizona Trail. Black Market Rustlers (GB: Land and the Law). The Black Raven. Bullets and Saddles (GB: Vengeance in the Saddle). Action in the North Atlantic. Death Valley Rangers. The Desperadoes. False Colors. The Lone Rider in Border Roundup (GB: Border Roundup). Cattle Stampede. Mission to Moscow. Haunted Ranch. The Kid Rides Again. The Kansan (GB: Wagon Wheels). The Return of the Rangers. Western Cyclone. Wild Horse Stampede. The Woman of the Town. 1944: Alaska. Can't Help Singing. The Contender. Forty Thieves. Knickerbocker Holiday. Harmony Trail (GB: White Stallion). The Monster Maker. Renegades of the Rio Grande (GB: Bank Robbery). Sonora Stagecoach. The Silver City Kid. Trail to Gunsight. San Antonio Kid. Valley of Vengeance (GB: Vengeance). House of Frankenstein. 1945: Bad Men of the Border. Blazing the Western Trail (GB: Who Killed Waring?). House of Dracula. Saratoga Trunk. 1946: Beauty and the Bandit. Devil's Playground. Up Goes Maisie (GB: Up She Goes). 1947: Brute Force. The Fabulous Texan. Frontier Fighters (shortened version of 1943's Western Cyclone). Sea of Grass. Northwest Outpost (GB: End of the Rainbow). The Wistful Widow of Wagon Gap (GB: The Wistful Widow). Sinbad the Sailor. Heaven Only Knows. Wyoming. Four Faces West (GB: They Passed This Way). 1948: Red Rider. Abbott and Costello Meet Frankenstein (GB: Abbott and Costello Meet the Ghosts). California Firebrand. The Far Frontier. The Gallant Legion. A Southern Yankee (GB: My Hero). Silver Trails. Montana Belle (released 1952). 1949: The Gal Who Took the West. Master Minds. Rimfire. Roll, Thunder, Roll. 1950: Comanche Territory. Double Crossbones. Surrender. 1951: Comin' Round the Mountain. The Red Badge of Courage. Callaway Went Thataway (GB: The Star Said No). Texas Carnival. Vengeance Valley. 1952: The Lusty Men. I Dream of Jeanie. The Lawless Breed. Wagons West. 1953: Escape from Fort Bravo. The Great Sioux Uprising. All the Brothers Were Valiant. Calamity Jane. Devil's Canyon. Born to the Saddle. Veils of Bagdad. 1954: Jubilee Trail. Gypsy Colt. Treasure of Ruby Hills. 1955: The Kentuckian. The Road to Denver. The Vanishing American. 1956: Backlash. Beau James. The Fastest Gun Alive. 1957: The Halliday Brand. Last Stagecoach West. Gunfire at Indian Gap. Jailhouse Rock. 1958: Quantrill's Raiders. Terror in a Texas Town. 1959: Alias Jesse James. Last Train from Gun Hill. The Jayhawkers.

STRATHAIRN, David 1953–

Slim, dour, dark, hollow-eyed, laconic-looking American actor with shadowed face: a real expert at blending into the background. Strathairn has had a number of starring and co-starring parts as well as supporting roles, but it's doubtful if the general cinemagoer would recognize either the name or the face of the modern cinema's Mr Cellophane. Strangely for such a sober-sides on screen, the San Francisco-born Strathairn is a graduate of the Ringling Brothers Clown College in Florida. But there has been little to laugh at in his gallery of sympathetic film portraits, several of them

for writer-director John Sayles, who often casts Strathairn as a man of the earth. He eventually did get to play a bad guy in 1995's Dolores Claiborne.

1980: Return of the Secaucus 7. 1982: When Nature Calls. 1983: Enormous Changes at the Last Minute. Silkwood. Lovesick. 1984: Iceman. The Brother from Another Planet. 1985: At Close Range. 1987: Matewan. Stars and Bars. 1988: Dominick and Eugene (GB: Nicky and Gino). Eight Men Out. Call Me. 1989: The Feud. Day One (TV). 1990: Memphis Belle. Judgment. Son of the Morning Star (TV). 1991: City of Hope. Without Warning: The James Brady Story (TV). 1992: O Pioneers! (TV). Big Girls Don't Cry ... They Get Even (GB: Stepkids). Sneakers. Bob Roberts. A League of Their Own. Passion Fish. 1993: The Firm. The American Clock (TV). A Dangerous Woman. Lost in Yonkers. 1994: The River Wild. 1995: Losing Isaiah. Dolores Claiborne. Stand off.

STRAUSS, Robert 1913–1975

This gloweringly round-faced, dark-haired, solid-featured American actor was near the top of the character tree following his stage and film performances as Animal in Stalag 17, for the latter of which he was nominated for an Academy Award. But he slid steadily down the cast after that, revealing a certain monotony of performance, and ended up in some fairly bizarre exploitation films before his early death from complications following a stroke.

1937: Marked Woman. 1942: Native Land. 1950: The Sleeping City. 1951: Sailor Beware.

1952: The Redhead from Wyoming. Jumping Jacks. 1953: Stalag 17. Act of Love. Money from Home. Here Come the Girls. 1954: The Atomic Kid. The Bridges at Toko-Ri. 1955: The Seven-Year Itch. The Man With the Golden Arm. 1956: Attack! 1958: Frontier Gun. I, Mobster. 1959: Li'l Abner. The 4-D Man (GB: The Evil Force). Inside the Mafia. 1960: Wake Me When It's Over. September Storm. 1961: The Last Time I Saw Archie. Dondi. The George Raft Story (GB: Spin of a Coin). Twenty Plus Two (GB: It Started in Tokyo). 1962: Girls! Girls! Girls! 1963: The Wheeler Dealers (GB: Separate Beds). The Thrill of It All. 1964: Stage to Thunder Rock. 1965: Harlow (Carol Lynley version). That Funny Feeling. The Family Jewels. Frankie and Johnny. 1966: Fort Utah. Movie Star, American Style, or: LSD, I Hate You. 1971: Dagmar's Hot Pants Inc. 1975: The Noah.

STRITCH, Elaine 1925–

Round-faced, corncrake-voiced American singer, actress and light comedienne with fluffy blonde hair and aggressive style. Little seen in films, but after a stage debut at 20 and extensive Broadway experience, a tremendous success both in brassy musicals on stage and comedy series on television, notably the British two-hander Two's Company, in harness with Donald Sinden, from 1976 to 1980. Noted for her power-house singing and comic timing, Stritch came back to films and TV movies in her sixties in a few elderly but still abrasive cameos.

1956: The Scarlet Hour. Three Violent People. 1957: A Farewell to Arms. 1958: The Perfect Furlough (GB: Strictly for Pleasure). 1959: Kiss Her Goodbye. 1965: Who Killed Teddy Bear? 1968: Too Many Thieves (originally for TV). 1970: The Sidelong Glances of a Pigeon Kicker/Pigeons. *Original Cast Album: Company. 1975: The Spiral Staircase. 1977: Providence. 1988: September. Cocoon The Return. 1990: Cadillac Man. Sparks: The Price of Passion (TV). The Secret Life of Archie's Wife (TV).

STRODE, Woody/Woodrow 1914–1995

Strapping (6 ft 5 in), muscly, often shaven-headed black American actor with granite-carved features. A former professional footballer and all-round athlete, it took

Strode a long time to prove himself a good actor as well, but he took the chance in the title role of John Ford's *Sergeant Rutledge*, and went on to a series of hard action-men in continental westerns and adventure films. Even as a grizzled veteran, he was still acting in small featured roles. Died from lung cancer on New Year's Day.

1941: Sundown. 1942: Star Spangled Rhythm. 1943: No Time for Love. 1951: Bride of the Gorilla. Lion Hunters (GB: Bomba and the Lion Hunters). 1952: Bomba and the African Treasure. Caribbean (GB: Caribbean Gold). 1953: City Beneath the Sea. 1954: The Gambler from Natchez. Demetrius and the Gladiators. Jungle Gents. 1955: Son of Sinbad. 1956: The Ten Commandments. 1958: The Buccaneer. Tarzan's Fight for Life. 1959: Pork Chop Hill. 1960: Spartacus. The Last Voyage. Sergeant Rutledge. 1961: Two Rode Together. The Sins of Rachel Cade. 1962: The Man Who Shot Liberty Valance. 1963: Tarzan's Three Challenges. 1965: Genghis Khan. 7 Women. 1966: The Professionals. Daniel Boone – Frontier Trail Rider (TV. GB: cinemas). 1967: Tarzan's Deadly Silence (TV. GB: cinemas). 1968: Shalako. Once Upon a Time in the West. Seduto all sua destra (GB: Out of Darkness. US: Black Jesus). 1969: King Gun (later The Gatling Gun). Che! Ciak Mull, l'uomo della vendetta (GB: The Unholy Four). La collina degli stivali (US: Boot Hill). 1970: Breakout (TV). The Deserter. 1971: The Last Rebel. 1972: La 'mala' ordina (GB: Manhunt in Milan. US: The Italian Connection). Black Rodeo (narrator only). The Revengers. 1973: Key West (TV). 1974: Colpo in canna (GB: Stick 'em Up, Darlings!). 1975: Winterhawk. Oil: The Billion Dollar Fire. We Are No Angels. 1976: Loaded Guns. Keoma (GB: The Violent Breed). 1977: Kingdom of the Spiders. 1979: Jaguar Lives. Ravagers. Kill Castro!/Cuba Crossing. Sweet Dirty Tony/The Mercenaries. 1981: Kampuchea Express (US: Angkor-Cambodia Express). 1982: Vigilante. 1983: The Black Stallion Returns. The Final Executioner/The Last Warrior. The Violent Breed and 1976 film. 1984: Lust in the Dust. The Cotton Club. Jungle Warriors. 1985: Scream (filmed 1981). 1986: On Fire (TV). 1987: A Gathering of Old Men/Murder on the Bayou (TV). 1989: The Bronx Executioner. 1991: Super Brother. 1992: Storyville (completed 1991). Return of the HMS Bounty. 1993: Posse. 1995: The Quick & the Dead.

STROUD, Don 1937–
Pugnacious, strongly built, fair-haired American actor who only came to films and television at 30, but was quickly in demand, mostly as wild eyed, violent types, although he could handle quieter roles extremely effectively. He seemed about to become a star at the beginning of the 1970s, but did not quite make it, returning to playing characters destined to be troublemakers beneath a barely calm surface.

1967: The Ballad of Josie. Games. Banning. Journey to Shiloh. 1968: Madigan. What's So Bad About Feeling Good? Coogan's Bluff. Something for a Lonely Man (TV). 1969: Bloody Mama. ... tick ... tick ... tick. Explosion. 1970: Angel Unchained. Breakout (TV). 1971: The DA: Conspiracy to Kill (TV). Von Richthofen and Brown (GB: The Red Baron). 1972: The Daughters of Joshua Cabe (TV). The Deadly Dream (TV). Rolling Man (TV). Joe Kidd. 1973: The Elevator (TV). Scalawag. The Nightmare Step (TV). Slaughter's Big Rip Off. 1974: Murph the Surf (GB: Live a Little, Steal a Lot). 1975: The Killer Inside Me. The Return of Joe Forrester (TV). 1976: The Hollywood Man. The House by the Lake (GB: Death Weekend). High Risk (TV). Death Threat. 1977: Sudden Death. The Choirboys. 1978: Katie: Portrait of a Centerfold (TV). The Buddy Holly Story. 1979: The Amityville Horror. Supertrain (TV. GB: Express to Terror). Search and Destroy. 1981: The Night the Lights Went Out in Georgia. Striking Back. 1983: Murder Me, Murder You (TV). I Want to Live (TV). 1984: Sweet Sixteen. 1985: Gidget's Summer Reunion (TV). 1986: The Return of Mike Hammer (TV). Armed and Dangerous. 1987: Two to Tango. 1988: Black Forest. 1989: Licence to Kill. Down the Drain. Murder Takes All (TV). Twisted Justice. 1990: Cartel. Mob Boss. Street War. The King of the Kickboxers. 1991: Hell Comes to Frogtown II. Prime Target. The Divine Enforcer. 1992: The Roller Blade Seven. The Roller Blade Seven, Part 2. 1993: Doc Holliday: The Man and the Legend. 1994: Of Unknown Origin. 1995: Dillinger and Capone.

SULLIVAN, Francis L. 1903–1956
Heavyweight British actor with stern, forbidding face, the epitome of pompous portliness. Almost always cast as either prosecuting counsels or villains, he had made his name in Shakespeare (1921–

1931) before bringing his massive presence and withering gaze to the cinema. Also filmed in Hollywood, especially towards the end of his life — but mostly in unworthy roles. Played the same role (Jaggers) in both 1934 and 1946 versions of *Great Expectations*. The L stood for Loftus.

*1932: When London Sleeps. The Missing Rembrandt. The Chinese Puzzle. 1933: The Right to Live. The Stickpin. Called Back. FP1. The Fire Raisers. The Wandering Jew. Red Wagon. 1934: Chu Chin Chow. Cheating Cheaters. Jew Süss (US: Power). Princess Charming. What Happened Then? The Return of Bulldog Drummond. Great Expectations. 1935: The Mystery of Edwin Drood. Her Last Affaire. Strange Wives. 1936: Spy of Napoleon. The Interrupted Honeymoon. The Limping Man. A Woman Alone (US: Two Who Dared). 1937: Fine Feathers. Dinner at The Ritz. Action for Slander. Non-Stop New York. 21 Days (released 1940. US: 21 Days Together). 1938: The Drum (US: Drums). The Gables Mystery. *First at the Post. Kate Plus Ten. Climbing High. The Ware Case. The Citadel. 1939: The Four Just Men (US: The Secret Four). Young Man's Fancy. 1940: The Briggs Family. 1941: Pimpernel Smith (US: Mister V). 1942: †The Foreman Went to France (US: Somewhere in France). The Day Will Dawn (US: The Avengers). Lady from Lisbon. 1943: The Butler's Dilemma. 1944: Fiddlers Three. 1945: Caesar and Cleopatra. 1946: The Laughing Lady. Great Expectations (re-make). 1947: The Man Within (US: The Smugglers). Take My Life. Broken Journey. 1948: Oliver Twist. The Winslow Boy. Joan of Arc. 1949: Christopher Columbus. The Red Danube. 1950: Night and the City. 1951: My Favorite Spy. Behave Yourself! 1952: Caribbean (GB: Caribbean Gold). 1953: Sangaree. Plunder of the Sun. Ali Baba Nights. 1954: Drums of Tahiti. 1955: Hell's Island. The Prodigal.*

† As François Sully

SUMMERFIELD, Eleanor 1921–
Blonde, blue-eyed British actress with soar-away eyebrows and shopgirl looks. After winning a gold medal at the Royal Academy of Dramatic Art, she began her film career in straight roles, sometimes minor leads. It soon became evident, however, that her personality was more suited to bright and chatty comedy roles, and she was often the

woman you couldn't get away from. A vivacious real-life personality, she was popular for years on radio panel games, especially *Many a Slip*. Married actor Leonard Sachs.

1947: Take My Life. 1948: London Belongs to Me (US: Dulcimer Street). The Weaker Sex. The Story of Shirley Yorke. Man on the Run. All Over the Town. 1949: No Way Back. 1951: The Third Visitor. Laughter in Paradise. Scrooge (GB: A Christmas Carol). 1952: Mandy (US: Crash of Silence). Top Secret (US: Mr Potts Goes to Moscow). The Last Page (US: Manbait). Isn't Life Wonderful! 1953: Street Corner (US: Both Sides of the Law). 1954: Face the Music (US: The Black Glove). Final Appointment. 1955: Murder by Proxy (completed 1953. US: Blackout). Lost (US: Tears for Simon). 1956: It's Great to be Young! Odongo. No Road Back. 1958: Gideon's Day (US: Gideon of Scotland Yard). A Cry from the Streets. 1960: Dentist in the Chair. The Millionairess. 1961: Spare the Rod. Don't Bother to Knock! (US: Why Bother to Knock?). Petticoat Pirates. On the Fiddle (US: Operation Snafu). 1962: On the Beat. Guns of Darkness. 1963: The Running Man. 1965: The Yellow Hat. 1969: Foreign Exchange (TV). The Spy Killer (TV). Some Will, Some Won't. 1981: The Watcher in the Woods. Island of Adventure.

SUMMERVILLE, Slim
(George Summerville) 1892–1946
Very tall, gangling, brown-haired, big-nosed, sleepy-eyed American comedy actor with a clown's smile that made him look as if he never had any teeth and an unmistakeable

slow, drawling voice — assets that set him up for a lifetime of countrified characterizations. After directing dozens of silent comedy shorts and starring in some early sound two-reel frolics, he proved an amiable foil for such distinctively different scene-stealers as ZaSu Pitts (they made nine films together) and Shirley Temple. Died following a stroke.

*1914: *A Rowboat Romance. *Gentlemen of Nerve. *The Knock-Out. *Mabel's Busy Day. Tillie's Punctured Romance. *Laughing Gas. *Cursed by His Beauty. *Dough and Dynamite. *Ambrose's First Falsehood. *Fatty and the Heiress. *Soldiers of Misfortune. *Mabel's Latest Prank. *He Loves the Ladies/He Loved the Ladies. *The Anglers. *High Spots on Broadway. *Stout Hearts But Weak Knees. *How Heroes Are Made. *The Noise of Bombs. *The Plumber. *Wild West Love. *Gussie the Golfer. 1915: *Caught in the Act. *Her Winning Punch. *Other People's Wives/The Home Breakers. *Their Social Splash. *Gussie's Day of Rest. *The Bitter Sweets. *The Great Vacuum Robbery. *Her Painted Hero. *A Game Old Knight. *Beating Hearts and Carpets. Those College Girls. *His Bitter Half. *A Bird's a Bird. *A Lucky Leap. *A Human Hound's Triumph. *Crossed Love and Swords. *Merely a Married Man. *A Rascal's Wolfish Way. *A Home Breaking Hound. 1916: *Bucking Society. *His Bread and Butter. *Her Busted Trust. *The Three Slims. *Cinders of Love. 1917: *A Dog Catcher's Love. *Villa of the Movies. *The Winning Punch (and 1915 film of similar title). *Are Waitresses Safe? *Her Fame and Shame. *His Precious Life. *A Pullman Bride. *Mary's Little Lobster. *Roping Her Romeo. *Hold That Line. *It Pays to Exercise. *High Diver's Last Kiss. *Ten Nights Without a Barroom. 1918: *The Beloved Rogue. The Kitchen Lady. 1919: *Footballs and Frauds. 1920: *Hold Me Tight. *Pretty Baby. *Training for Husbands. 1921: Skirts. 1923: *The Rivals. *Easy Work. 1924: *William Tell. *Why Wait. *Easy Money. *Keep Healthy. *Ship Ahoy. *Green Grocers. *Politics. *Miners Over Twenty-One. *The Cry Baby. *Hello, Frisco. *Case Dismissed. *My Little Brother. 1926: The Texas Steer. The Texas Streak. 1927: *Red Suspenders. *Oh What a Kick. *Why Mules Leave Home. The Denver Dude. The Beloved Rogue (remake). Hey Hey Cowboy. Painted Ponies. The Chinese Parrot. The Wreck of the Hesperus. 1928: Riding for Fame. 1929: King of the Rodeo. The Shannons of Broadway. The Last Warning. Strong Boy. Tiger Rose. 1930: Under Montana Skies. *Voice of Hollywood No. 2. One Hysterical Night. The King of Jazz. Her Man. See America Thirst. Troopers Three. All Quiet on the Western Front. Little Accident. The Spoilers. Free Love. *Hello Russia! *Parlez-vous. *We! We! Marie. 1931: Reckless Living. Heaven on Earth. Many a Slip. Bad Sister. The Front Page. Lasca of the Rio Grande. *Arabian Knights. *Bless the Ladies. *Let's Play. *Royal Bluff. *Parisian Gaieties. *Sarge's Playmates. *Here's Luck. 1932: Tom Brown of Culver. Unexpected Father. They Just Had to Get Married. Airmail. Racing Youth. *Eyes Have It. *In the Bag. *Kid Glove Kisses. 1933: Love, Honor and Oh! Baby. Her First*

Mate. Out All Night. Early to Bed. Meet the Princess. *Sea Soldier's Sweeties. 1934: Their Big Moment (GB: Afterwards). The Love Birds. Horseplay. 1935: Way Down East. Life Begins at 40. The Farmer Takes a Wife. 1936: The Country Doctor. Captain January. Pepper. Reunion (GB: Hearts in Reunion). Can This Be Dixie? White Fang. 1937: The Road Back/Return of the Hero. Off to the Races. Fifty Roads to Town. Love is News. 1938: Up the River. Kentucky Moonshine (GB: Three Men and a Girl). Five of a Kind. Rebecca of Sunnybrook Farm. Submarine Patrol. 1939: Charlie Chan in Reno. Jesse James. Winner Takes All. Henry Goes Arizona (GB: Spats to Spurs). 1940: Anne of Windy Poplars (GB: Anne of Windy Willows). Gold Rush Maisie. 1941: Miss Polly. Puddin' Head (GB: Judy Goes to Town). Niagara Falls. Highway West. Tobacco Road. Western Union. 1942: The Valley of Vanishing Men (serial). *Garden of Eatin'. 1944: I'm from Arkansas. Bride by Mistake. Swing in the Saddle (GB: Swing and Sway). *Bachelor Daze. 1945: Sing Me a Song of Texas (GB: Fortune Hunter). 1946: The Hoodlum Saint.*

As director (all shorts):
1920: †Hold Me Tight. 1921: Pardon Me. One Moment Please. 1922: Hold the Line. Ranch Romeos. The Eskimo. High and Dry. The Barnstormer. 1923: The Cyclist. The Five Fifteen. The Artist. The Riding Master. Rough Sailing. Unreal News Reel. Wet and Weary. 1924: Why Wait? Unreal News Reel No. 3. Green Grocers. Her Ball and Chain. Hello, 'Frisco! Keep Healthy. The Orphan. The Pinhead. Ship Ahoy! The Very Bad Man. Case Dismissed. Politics. Miners Over Twenty-One. The Cry Baby. Unreal News Reel No. 4. A Free Ride. In the Air. Taking the Heir. Tiddly Winks. 1925: When Dumb Bells Ring. Absent Minded. All Out. Back to Nature. All Tied Up. Faint Heart. Happy Go Lucky. Kick Me Again. 1926: The Village Cut Up. Wanted a Bride. Badly Broke. A Bedtime Story. Business Women. Don't Be a Dummy. A Dumb Friend. Hearts for Rent. The Honeymoon Quickstep. Oprey House Tonight. Papa's Mama. A Perfect Lie. A Swell Affair. Switching Sleepers. Tune Up! Too Much Sleep. 1927: Hop Along. Jailhouse Blues. In Again, Out Again. Meet the Husband. The Midnight Bum. A Run for His Money. 1929: Don't Say Ain't. Who's the Boss?

† Co-directed.

SUMNER, Geoffrey 1908–1989
Round-faced, dark-haired, ruddy-cheeked, pop-eyed, pipe-smoking British comedy actor with thick, short moustache and 'I say, old boy' voice. He began his career as a newsreel commentator, then switched to acting, portraying mainly pompous army officers and affable asses, notably in TV's *The Army Game*. From 1958 to 1962, he became a producer/writer/reporter on documentary films; he was also managing director of the company that made them. In private life he enjoyed the rural life on a farm; he died at his retirement home in the Channel Islands.

1938: Murder in Soho (US: Murder in the Night). Premiere (US: One Night in Paris). Too Many Husbands. 1939: She Couldn't Say

*No. The Gang's All Here (US: The Amazing Mr Forrest). 1940: Law and Disorder. For Freedom. 1946: While the Sun Shines. 1947: Mine Own Executioner. Easy Money. 1949: The Perfect Woman. Helter Skelter. Traveller's Joy (released 1951). Dark Secret. 1950: The Dark Man. 1951: A Tale of Five Cities (US: A Tale of Five Women). Appointment with Venus (US: Island Rescue). 1952: Top Secret (US: Mr Potts Goes to Moscow). The Happy Family (US: Mr Lord Says No). 1953: Always a Bride. The Dog and the Diamonds. Those People Next Door. 1954: Doctor in the House. Five Days (US: Paid to Kill). 1955: The Flying Eye. 1956: The Silken Affair. 1958: I Only Arsked! 1962: Band of Thieves. 1964: *All in Good Time. 1966: Cul-de-Sac. 1972: That's Your Funeral. 1975: Side by Side. 1979: There Goes the Bride.*

SUNDBERG, Clinton 1906–1987

Po-faced American actor with sleek dark hair who played fusspots, worriers and assiduous assistants. He began his career as a teacher, but turned to acting and in 1946 was put under contract by MGM as a supporting player, turning in effective cameos for them for the next eight years, but almost entirely on television after leaving the studio. His best role was probably on loan-out to Universal-International as the right-hand man of the title detective in *The Fat Man*. Died from a heart attack.

1946: The Mighty McGurk. Love Laughs at Andy Hardy. Undercurrent. 1947: Living in a

Big Way. The Song of Love. Song of the Thin Man. Desire Me. Undercover Maisie (GB: Undercover Girl). The Hucksters. Good News. 1948: The Kissing Bandit. Good Sam. Easter Parade. Mr Peabody and the Mermaid. A Date With Judy. Words and Music. Command Decision. 1949: Big Jack. In the Good Old Summertime. The Barkleys of Broadway. 1950: Annie Get Your Gun. Key to the City. Father is a Bachelor. Duchess of Idaho. The Toast of New Orleans. Two Weeks With Love. Mrs O'Malley and Mr Malone. 1951: On the Riviera. The Fat Man. As Young as You Feel. 1952: The Belle of New York. 1953: The Girl Next Door. Main Street to Broadway. Sweethearts on Parade. The Caddy. 1956: The Birds and the Bees. 1961: Bachelor in Paradise. 1962: The Wonderful World of the Brothers Grimm. How the West Was Won. 1967: Hotel. 1968: Shadow Over Elveron (TV).

SUTTON, Dudley 1933–

British actor with a mass of tight, fair curls and impish, puck-like face beneath. He tended to play smiling neurotics in his younger days but, with the passing years, his villains became scruffier and less menacing. Can still occasionally be nasty to great effect, but has chosen to go for raffish comedy in the long-running TV series *Lovejoy*.

1961: Go to Blazes. 1962: The Boys. 1963: The Leather Boys. 1965: Rotten to the Core. 1969: Crossplot. 1970: The Walking Stick. One More Time. A Town Called Bastard (US: A Town Called Hell). 1971: The Devils. Mr Forbush and the Penguins (US: Cry of the Penguins). 1972: Diamonds on Wheels. 1973: Paganini Strikes Again. 1974: The Stud. 1975: Cry Terror. Great Expectations (TV. GB: cinemas). 1976: The Pink Panther Strikes Again. Virginity/Come una rosa al naso. One Hour to Zero. 1977: Fellini's Casanova. Valentino. The Prince and the Pauper (US: Crossed Swords). No. 1 of the Secret Service. 1978: The Big Sleep. The Playbirds. 1979: The London Connection (US: TV, as the Omega Connection). 1980: George and Mildred. The Island. 1982: Brimstone and Treacle. 1983: Those Glory, Glory Days (originally TV). 1984: The House (TV). 1985: Lamb. A State of Emergency. 1986: Caravaggio. 1991: Edward II. 1992: Orlando.

SUTTON, Grady 1908–

Tall, dark-haired, damply plump, dumpling-cheeked, shyly smiling American actor who played faintly effete suitors doomed not to get the girl, or victims of verbal venom. His small features could explode into a marvellous array of surprised, outraged or anguished expressions, and he remained well in demand for cameos and amusing supporting parts from the beginning of sound until the end of the 1940s, when he became heavily (!) involved in television. Notable quailing from the acid tongue of W. C. Fields, he was still occasionally glimpsed in cinema and TV up to the 1980s.

*1925: The Mad Whirl. Skinner's Dress Suit. The Freshman. 1926: The Boy Friend. 1928: The Sophomore. 1929: Tanned Legs. 1930: *Doctor's Orders. Bigger and Better. Wild Company. Let's Go Native. Hit the Deck. *Blood and Thunder. *Ladies Last. 1931: *Love Fever. *Air Tight. *High Gear. *Call a Cop! *The Kick-Off! *Mama Loves Papa. 1932: *Boys Will Be Boys. *You're Telling Me. *Family Troubles. *Who, Me? Movie Crazy. *Love Pains. The Knockout. *Too Many Women. *Wild Babies. This Reckless Age. Are These Our Children?/Age of Consent. Hot Saturday. Pack Up Your Troubles. 1933: The Story of Temple Drake. College Humor. *The Big Fibber. *Don't Play Bridge with your Wife. *See you Tonight. *Husband's Reunion. *Uncle Jack. *The Pharmacist. *Sweet Cookie. Ace of Aces. *Flirting in the Park. *Walking Back Home. The Sweetheart of Sigma Chi (GB: Girl of My Dreams). Only Yesterday. 1934: *The Undie-World. *Rough Necking. *Contented Calves. *Hunger Pains. Bachelor Bait. Gridiron Flash (GB: Luck of the Game). 1935: Stone of Silver Creek. Laddie. *A Night at the Biltmore Bowl. *Pickled Peppers. Alice Adams. The Man on the Flying Trapeze (GB: The Memory Expert). Dr Socrates. 1936: Palm Springs (GB: Palm Springs Affair). King of the Royal Mounted. She's Dangerous. The Singing Kid. Valiant is the Word for Carrie. Pigskin Parade (GB: The Harmony Parade). My Man Godfrey. 1937: Waikiki Wedding. Stage Door. We Have Our Moments. Dangerous Holiday. Love Takes Flight. Turn Off the Moon. Behind the Mike. Two Minutes to Play. 1938: Vivacious Lady. Having Wonderful Time. Alexander's Ragtime Band. Joy of Living. Hard to Get. Three Loves Has Nancy. The Mad Miss Manton. 1939: You Can't Cheat an Honest Man. It's a*

Wonderful World. In Name Only. Naughty But Nice. Blind Alley. Blondie Meets the Boss. They Made Her a Spy. Angels Wash Their Faces. Three Sons. Three Smart Girls Grow Up. The Flying Irishman. 1940: Anne of Windy Poplars (GB: Anne of Windy Willows). Lucky Partners. Sky Murder. Torrid Zone. Too Many Girls. The Bank Dick (GB: The Bank Detective). City of Chance. We Who Are Young. Millionaire Playboy. He Stayed for Breakfast. Millionaires in Prison. 1941: She Knew All the Answers. Blondie in Society. Father Takes a Wife. Four Jacks and a Jill. Penny Serenade. Bedtime Story. Flying Blind. Doctors Don't Tell. You Belong to Me (GB: Good Morning, Doctor). Three Girls About Town. 1942: Whispering Ghosts. Dudes Are Pretty People. The Affairs of Martha (GB: Once Upon a Thursday). The Bashful Bachelor. Somewhere I'll Find You. 1943: The More the Merrier. A Lady Takes a Chance. What a Woman! (GB: The Beautiful Cheat). The Great Moment. 1944: Johnny Doesn't Live Here Anymore. Week-End Pass. Nine Girls. Allergic to Love. Goin' to Town. Since You Went Away. Hi, Beautiful (GB: Pass to Romance). Casanova Brown. Guest Wife. 1945: Grissly's Millions. A Royal Scandal (GB: Czarina). Three's a Crowd. On Stage, Everybody. Her Lucky Night. Captain Eddie. The Stork Club. She Went to the Races. A Bell for Adano. Anchors Aweigh. Pillow to Post. Brewster's Millions. 1946: Ziegfeld Follies (completed 1944). The Fabulous Suzanne. My Dog Shep. Hit the Hay. It's Great to be Young. Nobody Lives Forever. Idea Girl. The Plainsman and the Lady. The Magnificent Rogue. Partners in Time. The Show Off. Susie Steps Out. Dragonwyck. Two Sisters from Boston. No Leave, No Love. Dead Reckoning. 1947: Beat the Band. Philo Vance's Gamble. Love and Learn. My Wild Irish Rose. Always Together. 1948: Romance on the High Seas (GB: It's Magic). Jiggs and Maggie in Court. Last of the Wild Horses. My Dear Secretary. 1949: Grand Canyon. Air Hostess. 1954: Living It Up. A Star is Born. White Christmas. 1961: Madison Avenue. The Chapman Report. 1962: Jumbo/Billy Rose's Jumbo. 1963: Come Blow Your Horn. 1964: My Fair Lady. 1965: Tickle Me. The Chase. The Bounty Killer. Paradise, Hawaiian Style. 1968: I Love You, Alice B. Toklas. Something for a Lonely Man (TV). 1969: The Great Bank Robbery. 1970: Suppose They Gave a War and Nobody Came. Myra Breckinridge. Dirty Dingus Magee. 1971: Support Your Local Gunfighter. 1979: Rock 'n' Roll High School.

SYDNEY, Basil

(B.S. Nugent) 1894–1968

Heavily-built, testy-looking British actor, seen as narrow-eyed villains, senior civil servants, domineering fathers and the like, with a few leading roles thrown in, especially in the early thirties. At a twitch, he could turn his affable smile into a thin-lipped sneer. Married (third) to forties' star Joyce Howard (1922–). He made his film debut in Hollywood in the screen version of a stage success.

1920: Romance (GB: Red-Hot Romance). 1932: The Midshipmaid (US: Midshipmaid Gob). 1934: The Third Clue. Dirty Work.

1935: The Tunnel (US: Transatlantic Tunnel). The Riverside Murder. White Lilac. The Amateur Gentleman. 1936: Accused. Blind Man's Bluff. Talk of the Devil. Crime over London. Rhodes of Africa (US: Rhodes). 1939: The Four Just Men (US: The Secret Four). Shadowed Eyes (US: Dr Zander). 1940: The Farmer's Wife. Spring Meeting. 1941: Ships with Wings. The Big Blockade. The Black Sheep of Whitehall. 1942: The Next of Kin. Went the Day Well? (US: 48 Hours). 1945: Caesar and Cleopatra. 1947: Meet Me at Dawn. The Man Within (US: The Smugglers). Jassy. 1948: Hamlet. 1950: The Angel with the Trumpet. Treasure Island. 1951: The Magic Box. 1952: Ivanhoe. 1953: Salome. Three's Company. Hell Below Zero. Star of India. 1954: Simba. The Dam Busters. 1956: Around the World in 80 Days. 1957: Seawife. Island in the Sun. Man from Tangier (US: Thunder over Tangier). 1958: A Question of Adultery. 1959: John Paul Jones. The Devil's Disciple. The Three Worlds of Gulliver. 1960: The Hands of Orlac. A Story of David.

TAFLER, Sydney 1916–1979

British actor with receding dark hair and 'working-class' looks. In occasional star roles in early 1950s' thrillers, he was more likely to turn up, cigarette dangling from his mouth, as smooth-talking sharpsters or thieves. On stage from the age of 20, he became an indelible part of the British cinema scene, as probably the character you'd least want to buy a second-hand car from. Married to actress Joy Shelton (1922–) from 1944. Died from cancer.

1939: The Gang's All Here (US: The Amazing Mr Forrest). 1942: The Young Mr Pitt. 1943: The Bells Go Down. 1946: I See a Dark Stranger (US: The Adventuress). 1947: The Little Ballerina. It Always Rains on Sunday. 1948: London Belongs to Me (US: Dulcimer Street). The Monkey's Paw. Calling Paul Temple. Uneasy Terms. No Room at the Inn. 1949: Passport to Pimlico. 1950: Dance Hall. Once a Sinner. 1951: Assassin for Hire. The Lavender Hill Mob. The Galloping Major. Scarlet Thread. Hotel Sahara. Chelsea Story. Mystery Junction. Blind Man's Bluff. There is Another Sun (US: Wall of Death). 1952: Secret People. Emergency Call (US: Hundred Hour Hunt). Wide Boy. Venetian Bird (US: The Assassin). Time Gentleman Please! The Oracle (US: The Horse's Mouth). There Was a Young Lady. 1953: The Floating Dutchman. Operation Diplomat. Johnny on the Run. The Square Ring. The Saint's Return (US: The Saint's Girl Friday). 1954: The Crowded Day. The Sea Shall Not Have Them. A Kid for Two Farthings. The Glass Cage (US: The Glass Tomb). 1955: Dial 999 (US: The Way Out). The Woman for Joe. Cockleshell Heroes. 1956: Guilty? Reach for the Sky. The Long Arm (US: The Third Key). Fire Maidens from Outer Space. The Counterfeit Plan. Booby Trap. 1957: Interpol (US: Pickup Alley). The Surgeon's Knife. 1958: Carve Her Name With Pride. The Bank Raiders. 1959: Too Many Crooks. Tommy the Toreador. The Crowning Touch. Follow a Star. Sink the Bismarck! Bottoms Up! 1960: Make Mine Mink. Let's Get Married. Light Up the Sky. No Kidding (US: Beware of Children). The Bulldog Breed. 1961: Five Golden Hours. A Weekend With Lulu. Carry On Regardless. 1964: The Seventh Dawn. 1965: Runaway Railway. Promise Her Anything. 1966: Alfie. The Sandwich Man. 1967: Berserk! 1969: The Birthday Party. 1970: The Adventurers. 1971: Danger Point. 1977: The Spy Who Loved Me.

TALBOT, Lyle

(Lysle Henderson) 1902–1987

Square-faced, wide-mouthed, heavy-set, dark-haired American actor, a second-rank leading man of the 1930s who later appeared as villains in mostly minor westerns and thrillers. He seems to have been content to play anything; certainly he kept very busy for three decades. Began his career as a teenage magician; later founded his own repertory

company before heading for Hollywood when sound came in. A cross between Lon Chaney Jr and Richard Arlen.

1930. *The Nightingale. 1931: *The Clyde Mystery. 1932: The Purchase Price. Big City Blues. Three on a Match. Miss Pinkerton. Stranger in Town. Klondike. Love is a Racket. No More Orchids. Unholy Love (GB: Deceit). The Thirteenth Guest. 20,000 Years in Sing Sing. 1933: Ladies They Talk About. 42nd Street. College Coach (GB: Football Coach). The Life of Jimmy Dolan (GB: The Kid's Last Fight). Parachute Jumper. A Shriek in the Night. Girl Missing. Mary Stevens MD. She Had to Say Yes. Havana Widows. 1934: The Dragon Murder Case. Mandalay. A Lost Lady. Fog Over Frisco. One Night of Love. Registered Nurse. Return of the Terror. Murder in the Clouds. Heat Lightning. 1935: While the Patient Slept. Party Wire. Page Miss Glory. Chinatown Squad. The Case of the Lucky Legs. Red Hot Tires (GB: Racing Luck). Oil for the Lamps of China. It Happened in New York. Our Little Girl. Broadway Hostess. 1936: Murder by an Aristocrat. Trapped by Television (GB: Caught by Television). The Law in Her Hands. Mind Your Own Business. The Singing Kid. Boulder Dam. Go West, Young Man. 1937: Second Honeymoon. Three Legionnaires. The Affairs of Cappy Ricks. Westbound Limited. What Price Vengeance? (GB: Vengeance). 1938: Get-a-Way. Change of Heart. I Stand Accused. Call of the Yukon. One Wild Night. The Arkansas Traveler. 1939: They Asked for It. Forged Passport. Second Fiddle. Torture Ship. 1940: A Miracle on Main Street. He Married His Wife. Parole Fixer. 1941: A Night for Crime. 1942: They Raid by Night. She's in the Army. Mexican Spitfire's Elephant. 1943: Man of Courage. 1944: One Body Too Many. Dixie Jamboree. Are These Our Parents? (GB: They Are Guilty). Up in Arms. The Falcon Out West. Mystery of the River Boat (serial). Gambler's Choice. Sensations of 1945. 1945: Trail to Gunsight. 1946: Murder is My Business. Strange Impersonation. Gun Town. Song of Arizona. Chick Carter, Detective (serial). Shep Comes Home. 1947: Danger Street. The Vigilante (serial). 1948: Appointment with Murder. Joe Palooka in Winner Take All (GB: Winner Take All). Quick on the Trigger (GB: Condemned in Error). The Vicious Circle. Parole Inc. The Devil's Cargo. Highway 13. Thunder in the Pines. 1949: Wild Weed (GB: The Devil's Weed). Sky Dragon. Fighting Fools.

Mississippi Rhythm. Batman and Robin (serial). Joe Palooka in the Big Fight. The Mutineers. Ringside. 1950: Border Rangers. Atom Man versus Superman (serial). Cherokee Uprising. Everybody's Dancing. Revenue Agent. Lucky Losers. Federal Man. Tall Timber (GB: Big Timber). The Jackpot. Champagne for Caesar. Triple Trouble. 1951: Abilene Trail. The Man from Sonora. Jungle Manhunt. Purple Heart Diary (GB: No Time for Tears). Colorado Ambush. Oklahoma Justice. Fury of the Congo. Fingerprints Don't Lie. Texas Lawman. Hurricane Island. Gold Raiders (GB: Stooges Go West). Varieties on Parade. Blue Blood. 1952: The Old West. Sea Tiger. With a Song in My Heart. Son of Geronimo (serial). Kansas Territory. Montana Incident. Outlaw Women. Desperadoes' Outpost. The Daltons' Women. Six-Gun Decision (TV. GB: cinemas). Feudin' Fools. African Treasure (GB: Bomba and the African Treasure). Texas City. Untamed Women. Wyoming Roundup. Mesa of Lost Women (completed 1949. Voice only). 1953: Down Among the Sheltering Palms (completed 1951). White Lightning. Trail Blazers. Tumbleweed. Star of Texas. Commander Cody, Sky Marshal of the Universe (serial). 1954: Tobor the Great. Captain Kidd and the Slave Girl. The Desperado. The Hidden Face. Jail Bait. There's No Business Like Show Business. *So You Want to Be Your Own Boss. Two Guns and a Badge. The Steel Cage. Trader Tom of the China Seas (serial). Gunfighters of the Northwest (serial). 1955: Jail Busters. Stories of the Century No.1 – Quantrill and His Raiders. Sudden Danger. 1956: Calling Homicide. The Great Man. 1957: She Shoulda Said No. 1958: Hot Angel. The Notorious Mr Monks. Plan 9 from Outer Space. High School Confidential. 1959: City of Fear. 1960: Sunrise at Campobello.

TALMAN, William 1915–1968
Tall, cold-eyed, unsmiling American actor with crinkly blond-auburn hair who switched from writing (and playing pro. tennis) to acting, and was building up a nice line in film villainy when sidetracked into television where, from 1957 to 1965, he was internationally known as the DA who lost every case to Perry Mason in the last reel. Married/divorced actress Barbara Read, who died at 45 in 1963, five years before Talman's own death from cancer.

1949: I Married a Communist (GB: The Woman on Pier 13). Red, Hot and Blue. The Kid from Texas (GB: Texas Kid—Outlaw). 1950: Armored Car Robbery. 1951: The Racket. 1952: One Minute to Zero. 1953: The Hitch-Hiker. City That Never Sleeps. 1955: Big House, USA. Smoke Signal. Crashout. 1956: The Man Is Armed. Two Gun Lady. Uranium Boom. 1957: The Persuader. Hell on Devil's Island. 1967: The Ballad of Josie.

TAMIROFF, Akim 1898–1972
One can still see Tamiroff in that white trilby, moustache glistening with sweat, white handkerchief mopping the brow, cooking up some new double-deal. Nearly all the characters created by this Russian-born actor (in America since the early twenties) were disreputable, whether in filthy sweat-shirt or lurking beneath semi-respectable clothes. Small, round and beetle-like, he was invaluable to any film. Academy Award nominations for The General Died at Dawn and For Whom the Bell Tolls. Married Russian-American actress Tamara Shayne (1897–1983), a fellow character player who portrayed Larry Parks's mother in the two Al Jolson biopics.

1932: Okay America (GB: Penalty of Fame). 1933: Storm at Daybreak. Gabriel Over the White House. Professional Sweetheart (GB: Imaginary Sweetheart). Fugitive Lovers. Queen Christina. The Devil's in Love. 1934: The Great Flirtation. Wonder Bar. Now and Forever. The Merry Widow (and French version). Here is My Heart. The Winning Ticket. Sadie McKee. Whom the Gods Destroy. Chained. The Captain Hates the Sea. Lives of a Bengal Lancer. The Scarlet Empress. Murder in the Private Car (GB: Murder on the Runaway Train). 1935: Black Fury. Rumba. Paris in Spring (GB: Paris Love Song). The Gay Deception. Two Fisted. Naughty Marietta. Go into Your Dance (GB: Casino de Paree). China Seas. The Last Outpost. The Big Broadcast of 1936. Reckless. Black Sheep. 1936: The Story of Louis Pasteur. Anthony Adverse. Woman Trap. The Jungle Princess. The General Died at Dawn. Desire. 1937: King of Gamblers. Her Husband Lies. High, Wide and Handsome. The Soldier and the Lady (GB: Michael Strogoff). The Great Gambini. This Way Please. 1938: Dangerous to Know. Spawn of the North. Ride a Crooked Mile (GB: Escape from Yesterday).

The Buccaneer. Paris Honeymoon. 1939: The Magnificent Fraud. King of Chinatown. Disputed Passage. Union Pacific. Honeymoon in Bali (GB: Husbands or Lovers). Geronimo. 1940: The Great McGinty (GB: Down Went McGinty). The Way of All Flesh. Texas Rangers Ride Again. Northwest Mounted Police. Untamed. 1941: New York Town. The Corsican Brothers. 1942: Tortilla Flat. Are Husbands Necessary? 1943: His Butler's Sister. Five Graves to Cairo. For Whom the Bell Tolls. 1944: The Miracle of Morgan's Creek. Dragon Seed. The Bridge of San Luis Rey. Can't Help Singing. 1945: Pardon My Past. 1946: A Scandal in Paris. 1947: The Gangster. Fiesta. 1948: Relentless. My Girl Tisa. Tenth Avenue Angel. 1949: Black Magic. Outpost in Morocco. 1953: Desert Legion. You Know What Sailors Are. 1954: Cartouche. They Who Dare. 1955: La vedova (US: The Widow). The Black Forest. Confidential Report (US: Mr Arkadin). 1956: The Black Sleep. Anastasia. 1957: The Miracle Worker (TV). Yangtse Incident (US: Battle Hell). †Don Quixote. 1958: Touch of Evil. Me and the Colonel. 1959: Desert Desperadoes/ The Sinner. 1960: Les bacchantes/Le baccanti. Ocean's Eleven. 1961: Romanoff and Juliet. I briganti italiani/Seduction of the South. With Fire and Sword. Il giudizio universale (US: The Last Judgment). Ursus e la ragazza tartara (GB: The Savage Hordes. US: Tartar Invasion). La moglie di mio marito. 1962: The Reluctant Saint. A Queen for Caesar. The Trial. 1963: The Black Tulip. Panic Button. 1964: La bambole (GB: Four Kinds of Love). Topkapi. Spirit Elf. The Fabulous Adventures of Marco Polo (GB: Marco the Magnificent). 1965: Lord Jim. Marie-Chantal contre le docteur Kah. The Liquidator. The Blue Panther. Par un beau matin d'été (US: Crime on a Summer Morning). 1966: Alphaville. Lt. Robin Crusoe U.S.N. After the Fox. I nostri mariti. Adultery Italian Style. Hotel Paradiso. The Vulture. Every Man's Woman/A Rose for Everyone. 1967: Great Catherine. 1968: Justine and Juliet/Marquis de Sade: Justine. Tenderly (GB and US: The Girl Who Couldn't Say No). 1969: The Great Bank Robbery. Sabra. Then Came Bronson (TV: GB: cinemas).

† Unfinished.

TANDY, Jessica 1909–1994

Petite, whippy, dark-haired, slightly devious-looking British-born actress, in America since 1940. A powerful character star, she was often seen in crafty or neurotic roles, but remained largely a stage actress, although she renewed her interest in the cinema in the 1980s, playing generally more sympathetic roles, and winning an Academy Award in 1990 for *Driving Miss Daisy*. Her second husband (since 1942) was the Canadian actor Hume Cronyn (qv); their daughter, Tandy Cronyn, is also an actress. Jessica Tandy's first husband (1932–1942) was the British star Jack Hawkins. Died from ovarian cancer.

1932: The Indiscretions of Eve. 1938: Murder in the Family. 1944: The Seventh Cross. 1945: The Valley of Decision. 1946: The Green Years. Dragonwyck. 1947: Forever Amber. A Woman's Vengeance. 1950: September Affair. 1951: The Desert Fox (GB: Rommel – Desert Fox). 1958:

The Light in the Forest. 1959: The Moon and Sixpence (TV). 1962: Hemingway's Adventures of a Young Man (GB: Adventures of a Young Man). 1963: The Birds. 1973: Butley. 1981: Honky Tonk Freeway. 1982: Still of the Night. Best Friends. 1983: The World According to Garp. 1984: The Bostonians. 1985: Cocoon. 1987: Batteries Not Included. Foxfire (TV). 1988: The House on Carroll Street. Cocoon The Return. 1989: Driving Miss Daisy. 1991: Fried Green Tomatoes (GB: Fried Green Tomatoes at the Whistle Stop Café). The Story Lady (TV). 1992: Used People. 1994: Camilla. To Dance With the White Dog (TV). Nobody's Fool.

TAPLEY, Colin 1911–

Tall, good-looking, light-haired, pale-eyed, often moustachioed New Zealand actor of rather stiff demeanour and reassuring air. He played strong, silent types in Hollywood from 1934 after winning a contract in a Paramount talent contest. He never became a star personality and, following war service, came to Britain to make his career from 1950. Here he began in semi-star roles, but soon regressed to lesser stuff, and dropped out of the profession in his late fifties.

1934: Double Door. Limehouse Blues. Come On Marines! Murder at the Vanities. The Pursuit of Happiness. Search for Beauty. 1935: The Black Room. Becky Sharp. The Crusades. The Lives of a Bengal Lancer. The Last Outpost. Peter Ibbetson. My Marriage. Without Regret. 1936: Early to Bed. The Return of Sophie Lang. Too Many Parents. The Preview Murder Mystery. The Sky Parade. Till We Meet Again.

Thank You, Jeeves. 1937: The Crime Nobody Saw. Hotel Haywire. King of Gamblers. Booloo. Night of Mystery. Bulldog Drummond Escapes. Maid of Salem. Souls at Sea. 1938: If I Were King. Storm Over Bengal. Wild Money. 1939: The Light That Failed. 1940: Women in War. North West Mounted Police. 1941: Arizona. 1949: Samson and Delilah. 1951: Cloudburst. Angels One Five. 1952: Wings of Danger (US: Dead on Course). Wide Boy. 1953: Strange Stories. The Steel Key. Noose for a Lady. Three Steps to the Gallows (released 1955. US: White Fire). 1954: The Diamond (US: Diamond Wizard). *Late Night Final. The Dam Busters. Little Red Monkey (US: The Case of the Little Red Monkey). 1955: Barbados Quest (US: Murder on Approval). 1957: Stranger in Town. The Safecracker. Rogue's Yarn. 1958: Blood of the Vampire. High Jump. 1959: Innocent Meeting. Man Accused. An Honourable Murder. Night Train for Inverness. 1960: Compelled. 1961: So Evil, So Young. Strongroom. In the Dog-house. 1962: Emergency. The Lamp in Assassin Mews. Gang War. Paranoiac. 1963: Shadow of Fear. 1968: Fraulein Doktor.

TAYLOR, Dub

(Walter Taylor) 1907–1994

Shortish, dumpy, wisp-haired American supporting actor with happily apologetic air, a former saxophonist given his first acting chance by director Frank Capra, who used him several times in featured roles over the years. In the 1940s, Taylor became a 'B' western sidekick, a sort of poor man's Smiley Burnette (qv), to such stars as Bill Elliott, Russell Hayden, Charles Starrett and singing cowboy Jimmy Wakely. More recently, he was seen playing old-timers in westerns and hillbilly capers, and remained active into his late eighties. Died from a heart attack.

1938: You Can't Take It with You. 1939: Mr Smith Goes to Washington. Taming of the West. 1940: One Man's Law. The Return of Wild Bill (GB: False Evidence). Beyond the Sacramento (GB: Power of Justice). The Wildcat of Tucson (GB: Promise Fulfilled). Pioneers of the Frontier (GB: The Anchor). Prairie Schooners (GB: Through the Storm). The Man from Tumbleweeds. 1941: The Son of Davy Crockett (GB: Blue Clay). Across the Sierras (GB: Welcome Stranger). North from the Lone Star. Hands across the Rockies. King of Dodge

City. *The Return of Daniel Boone* (GB: *The Mayor's Nest*). *Roaring Frontiers.* 1942: *The Lone Prairie* (GB: *Inside Information*). *A Tornado in the Saddle* (GB: *Ambushed*). 1943: *What's Buzzin' Cousin?* *Silver City Raiders* (GB: *Legal Larceny*). *Saddles and Sagebrush* (GB: *The Pay-Off*). *The Vigilantes Ride* (GB: *Hunted*). *Cowboy in the Clouds.* *Riders of the Northwest Mounted.* 1944: *Cowboy Canteen* (GB: *Close Harmony*). *Wyoming Hurricane* (GB: *Proved Guilty*). *Marshal of Gunsmoke. Cowboy from Lonesome River* (GB: *Signed Judgment*). *Saddle Leather Law* (GB: *The Poisoner*). *Sundown Valley.* *The Last Horseman. Hidden Valley Outlaws. Cyclone Prairie Rangers.* 1945: *Both Barrels Blazing* (GB: *The Yellow Streak*). *Sagebrush Heroes. Lawless Empire* (GB: *Power of Possession*). *Blazing the Western Trail* (GB: *Who Killed Waring?*). *Rough Ridin' Justice* (GB: *Decoy*). *Rustlers of the Badlands* (GB: *By Whose Hand?*). *Outlaws of the Rockies* (GB: *A Roving Rogue*). *Texas Panhandle.* 1946: *Frontier Gun Law* (GB: *Menacing Shadows*). 1947: †*Ridin' Down the Trail.* 1948: †*Song of the Drifter.* †*Oklahoma Blues.* †*Partners of the Sunset.* †*Range Renegades.* †*Silver Trails.* †*The Rangers Ride.* †*Outlaw Brand.* †*Courtin' Trouble.* †*Cowboy Cavalier.* 1949: †*Gun Runner.* †*Gun Law Justice.* †*Across the Rio Grande.* †*Brand of Fear.* †*Roaring Westward.* †*Lawless Code.* 1950: *Riding High.* 1952: *The Will Rogers Story* (GB: *The Story of Will Rogers*). *Woman of the North Country.* *Lure of the Wilderness.* 1953: ††*Crime Wave* (GB: *The City is Dark*). *The Charge at Feather River.* 1954: *A Star is Born.* *The Bounty Hunter.* *Dragnet.* *Riding Shotgun.* *Them!* 1955: *Tall Man Riding.* *I Died a Thousand Times.* 1956: *You Can't Run Away from It.* *The Fastest Gun Alive.* 1958: *No Time for Sergeants.* *Street of Darkness.* *Auntie Mame.* *Hot Rod Gang* (GB: *Fury Unleashed*). 1959: *A Hole in the Head.* 1960: *Home from the Hill.* 1961: *Parrish.* *Pocketful of Miracles.* *Sweet Bird of Youth.* 1962: *The Moonussers* (TV. GB: *cinemas*). *Black Gold.* 1963: *Spencer's Mountain.* 1964: *Major Dundee.* 1965: *The Hallelujah Trail.* *The Adventures of Bullwhip Griffin.* *The Cincinnati Kid.* 1967: *Don't Make Waves.* *Bonnie and Clyde.* *The Shakiest Gun in the West.* 1968: *Three Guns for Texas* (TV). *Bandolero!* *Something for a Lonely Man.* *The Money Jungle.* 1969: *The Reivers.* *Ride a Northbound Horse* (TV. GB: *cinemas*). *Death of a Gunfighter.* *The Wild Bunch.* *God Bless You, Uncle Sam.* *The Undefeated.* ... *tick* ... *tick* ... *tick.* *The Liberation of L.B. Jones.* 1970: *A Man Called Horse.* *El Condor.* *The Wild Country.* 1971: *Support Your Local Gunfighter.* *Evel Knievel.* *Wild in the Sky.* *Sam Hill: Who Killed the Mysterious Mr Foster?* (TV). 1972: *Man and Boy.* *The Delphi Bureau* (TV). *Menace on the Mountain.* *Junior Bonner.* *The Getaway.* 1973: *Brock's Last Case* (TV). *Shoot-Out in a One-Dog Town* (TV). *Tom Sawyer.* *This is a Hijack!* *Pat Garrett and Billy the Kid.* 1974: *Honky Tonk* (TV). *The Winds of Autumn* (released 1976). *Thunderbolt and Lightfoot.* *Run Run Joe.* *Bank Shot.* *The Fortune.* 1975: *Flash and the Firecat.* *The Daughters of Joshua Cabe Return* (TV). *Country Blue.* *Poor Pretty Eddie. Hearts of the West* (GB: *Hollywood Cowboy*). 1976: *Gator.* *Treasure of Matecumbe.* *Doc*

Hooker's Bunch. *Burnt Offerings.* *The Creature from Black Lake.* *Pony Express Rider.* *The Great Smokey Roadblock/The Last of the Cowboys.* 1977: *The Rescuers* (voice only). *Moonshine County Express.* 1978: *Beartooth. Heartbreak Motel.* *They Went That-a-Way and That-a-Way.* *Wolf Lake/The Honor Guard.* 1979: *Redneck County Rape.* *1941.* 1980: *Used Cars.* 1981: *Return to Boggy Creek.* 1982: *Soggy Bottom USA.* 1983: *Cannonball Run II.* 1984: *The Outlaws* (TV). 1986: *The Best of Times.* 1987: *Once Upon a Texas Train* (TV). 1990: *My Heroes Have Always Been Cowboys. Back to the Future Part III.* 1991: *Souvenirs/ Falling from Grace.* *Conagher* (TV). 1993: *Johnny Bago* (TV). 1994: *Maverick.*

† As Dub 'Cannonball' Taylor
†† As Walter Dub Taylor

TAYLOR, Vaughn 1910–1983
Slight, balding American actor with pencil moustache, alligator smile and waspish delivery of a line, just as likely to turn up as an avuncular adviser or a crooked attorney. Mainly on stage after a couple of films as a young man, he became a semi-regular in films from the 1950s, returning to Broadway in between Hollywood assignments. Forced to retire in the mid 1970s with crippling spinal deterioration, he died from a cerebral haemorrhage.

1932: *Lawyer Man.* 1933: *Picture Snatcher.* 1951: *Up Front.* *Francis Goes to the Races.* *Meet Danny Wilson.* 1952: *Hoodlum Empire.* *Back at the Front* (GB: *Willie and Joe in Tokyo*). 1953: *It Should Happen to You.* 1957: *This Could Be the Night.* *Jailhouse Rock.* *Decision at Sundown.* *Cowboy.* *Screaming Mimi.* 1958: *The Young Lions.* *Cat on a Hot Tin Roof.* *Gunsmoke in Tucson.* *Andy Hardy Comes Home.* *Party Girl.* *The Lineup.* 1959: *Blue Denim* (GB: *Blue Jeans*). *Warlock.* 1960: *The Wizard of Baghdad.* *The Plunderers.* *The Gallant Hours.* *Psycho.* 1962: *FBI Code 98.* *Diamond Head.* 1963: *The Carpetbaggers. Twilight of Honor* (GB: *The Charge is Murder*). *The Wheeler Dealers* (GB: *Separate Beds*). 1964: *The Unsinkable Molly Brown.* 1965: *Dark Intruder.* *Zebra in the Kitchen.* 1966: *The Russians Are Coming, the Russians Are Coming.* *The Professionals.* 1967: *In Cold Blood.* *The Last Challenge* (GB: *The Pistolero of Red River*). *The Power.* 1968: *Fever Heat.* *The Shakiest Gun in the West.* 1969: *My Dog*

The Thief. *Set This Town on Fire* (TV. Not shown until 1973). 1970: *The Ballad of Cable Hogue.* 1971: *Million Dollar Duck.* *They Call It Murder* (TV). 1973: *Brock's Last Case* (TV). 1974: *Winterkill* (TV). 1975: *Eleanor and Franklin* (TV). *The Daughters of Joshua Cabe Return* (TV). 1976: *The Gumball Rally.*

TEAL, Ray 1902–1976
Solidly-built, moustachioed, bullet-headed, pointed-nosed American 'western' actor with thinning brown hair and perpetual frown. Teal played saxophone in dance bands for 20 years, then drifted into films and ended up as the screen's best-known sheriff, whose friendly smile was often a mask for graft and corruption. He was largely lost to the long-running TV western series *Bonanza* after 1961, in which he played – the sheriff.

1937: *Radio Patrol* (serial). *Zorro Rides Again* (serial). *Sweetheart of the Navy.* 1938: *Western Jamboree.* 1939: *Edison the Man.* 1940: *The Adventures of Red Ryder* (serial). *Cherokee Strip* (GB: *Fighting Marshal*). *Strange Cargo.* *Kitty Foyle.* *I Love You Again.* *New Moon.* *Northwest Passage.* *Florian.* *Prairie Schooners* (GB: *Through the Storm*). *Third Finger, Left Hand.* *The Trail Blazers.* *Pony Post.* 1941: *Bad Men of Missouri.* *Billy the Kid.* *The Bugle Sounds. Honky Tonk.* *Shadow of the Thin Man.* *They Met in Bombay.* *Sergeant York.* *They Died with Their Boots On.* *Outlaws of the Panhandle* (GB: *Faro Jack*). *Wild Bill Hickok Rides. Ziegfeld Girl.* *Woman of the Year.* 1942: *Apache Trail.* *The Big Shot.* *Calling Dr Gillespie. Fingers at the Window.* *Juke Girl.* *Nazi Agent. Prairie Chickens.* *Northwest Rangers.* *Captain Midnight* (serial). *Tarzan's New York Adventure.* *Secret Enemies.* *Tennessee Johnson* (GB: *The Man on America's Conscience*). 1943: *Chance of a Lifetime.* *Lost Angel.* *A Gentle Gangster.* *Madame Curie.* *North Star* (later *Armored Attack*). *She Has What It Takes.* *Song of Russia.* *Thousands Cheer.* *Whistling in Brooklyn.* *Slightly Dangerous.* *The Youngest Profession.* *Dangerous Blondes.* 1944: *An American Romance.* *Barbary Coast Gent.* *Maisie Goes to Reno* (GB: *You Can't Do That to Me*). *Hollywood Canteen.* *The Princess and the Pirate. None Shall Escape.* *Nothing But Trouble. Strange Affair.* *A Wing and a Prayer.* *Slightly Dangerous.* *The Thin Man Goes Home. Once Upon a Time.* *Raiders of Ghost City*

(serial). *Mr Co-Ed. *The Home Front. Ziegfeld Follies (released 1946). 1945: Circumstantial Evidence. The Clock. Anchors Aweigh. The Fighting Guardsman. Captain Kidd. Along Came Jones. Gentle Annie. Adventure. Back to Bataan. The Harvey Girls. Keep Your Powder Dry. *A Gun in His Hand. Strange Voyage. Snafu (GB: Welcome Home). Shady Lady. Sudan. Wonder Man. 1946: Blondie Knows Best. Blonde Alibi. The Best Years of Our Lives. Decoy. Deadline for Murder. Dangerous Business. The Bandit of Sherwood Forest. Canyon Passage. A Letter for Evie. The Missing Lady. Dead Reckoning. Pursued. Till the Clouds Roll By. Love Laughs at Andy Hardy. The Runaround. Three Wise Fools. 1947: Brute Force. Cheyenne. Desert Fury. Driftwood. Deep Valley. Louisiana. My Favorite Brunette. High Wall. Road to Rio. Roses Are Red. The Fabulous Texan. Northwest Outpost (GB: End of the Rainbow). The Long Night. The Sea of Grass. The Swordsman. Unconquered. Undercover Maisie (GB: Undercover Girl). The Michigan Kid. Ramrod. 1948: An Act of Murder. Bad Boy. The Countess of Monte Cristo. The Black Arrow (GB: The Black Arrow Strikes). Black Bart (GB: Black Bart – Highwayman). Daredevils of the Clouds. Hazard. Fury at Furnace Creek. The Mating of Millie. The Miracle of the Bells. I Wouldn't Be in Your Shoes. The Man from Colorado. One Sunday Afternoon. Raw Deal. Road House. The Snake Pit. Walk a Crooked Mile. Joan of Arc. Tenth Avenue Angel. Whispering Smith. Montana Belle (released 1952). 1949: Ambush. Blondie Hits the Jackpot (GB: Hitting the Jackpot). The Great Gatsby. Gun Crazy/Deadly is the Female. Kazan. It Happens Every Spring. Mr Soft Touch (GB: House of Settlement). Oh, You Beautiful Doll. Once More, My Darling. Rusty's Birthday. Scene of the Crime. Streets of Laredo. Samson and Delilah. The Kid from Texas (GB: Texas Kid – Outlaw). 1950: The Asphalt Jungle. Convicted. Davy Crockett – Indian Scout. The Great Missouri Raid. Edge of Doom (GB: Stronger Than Fear). Harbor of Missing Men. The Men. No Way Out. The Petty Girl (GB: Girl of the Year). Our Very Own. The Redhead and the Cowboy. Southside 1–1000 (GB: Forgery). When You're Smiling. Winchester '73. Where Danger Lives. 1951: The Big Carnival (later and GB: Ace in the Hole). Along the Great Divide. Fort Worth. Lorna Doone. Tomorrow is Another Day. The Secret of Convict Lake. Flaming Feather. Distant Drums. 1952: The Captive City. Carrie. Hangman's Knot. Jumping Jacks. The Lion and the Horse. Cattle Town. The Turning Point. The Wild North. 1953: Ambush at Tomahawk Gap. The Wild One. 1954: About Mrs Leslie. The Command. Lucky Me. Rogue Cop. 1955: Apache Ambush. The Desperate Hours. The Indian Fighter. The Man from Bitter Ridge. Rage at Dawn. Run for Cover. 1956: The Burning Hills. Canyon River. Decision (TV. GB: cinemas). The Young Guns. 1957: Band of Angels. Decision at Sundown. Phantom Stagecoach. The Wayward Girl. The Guns of Fort Petticoat. The Oklahoman. Girl on the Run. The Tall Stranger. Utah Blaine. 1958: Gunman's Walk. Saddle the Wind. 1960: Home from the Hill. Inherit the Wind. One-Eyed Jacks. 1961: Ada. Judgment at Nuremberg. Posse from Hell. 1962: A Girl Named Tamiko. 1963: Cattle King (GB: Guns of Wyoming). 1964: Bullet for a Badman. Taggart. 1970: The Liberation of L.B. Jones. Chisum. 1974: The Hanged Man (TV).

TESSIER, Robert 1934–1990
Shaven-headed American actor whose round, but precisely etched features made him look like a menacing version of the Man in the Moon, and betrayed his Algonquin Indian/French parentage. He broke into films as a stuntman in the early 1960s, but his distinctive features were soon appearing in leeringly threatening roles, most notably as the bareknuckle boxer Charles Bronson takes on in *Hard Times*. Less often seen in films after 1982, though there were a few more tough guys to come in the late 1980s in video-aimed action films. Died from cancer.

1967: Born Losers. 1968: The Glory Stompers. 1969: The Babysitter. Five the Hard Way. 1971: The Velvet Vampire. Cry Blood, Apache. The Hard Ride. The Jesus Trip. 1973: How Come Nobody's On Our Side? (released 1975). 1974: The Longest Yard (GB: The Mean Machine). 1975: Hard Times (GB: The Streetfighter). Doc Savage, The Man of Bronze (GB: Doc Savage). 1976: Breakheart Pass. 1977: The Deep. Un autre homme, un autre chance (GB: Another Man, Another Woman. US: Another Man, Another Chance). Last of the Mohicans (TV). Starcrash. 1978: Hooper. The Deerslayer (TV). 1979: Steel. The Villain (GB: Cactus Jack). The Billion Dollar Threat (TV). 1981: The Cannonball Run. 1982: Double Exposure. The Sword and the Sorcerer. 1983: The Lost Empire. 1984: The Fix. 1986: No Safe Haven (released 1989). 1988: One Man Force. 1989: C.O.P.S. Nightwish.

THATCHER, Heather 1895–1987
Sparkling, long-nosed, blue-eyed blonde British musical comedy star of the theatre who led a sporadic career in home-grown features, then went to Hollywood in the 1930s and came into demand for eccentric characterizations lent strength and animation by her off-centre features and stylish delivery. Returned to Britain in the late 1940s to round out her career with a few sharply witty character roles.

1915: The Prisoner of Zenda. 1916: Altar Chains. 1918: The Key of the World. 1919: Pallard the Punter. The First Men in the Moon.

The Green Terror. 1920: *A Little Bet. *Home Influence. *A Pair of Gloves. The Little Hour of Peter Wells. 1925: *Stage Stars Off Stage. 1926: The Flag Lieutenant. *Gaumont Mirror No. 2. 1929: The Plaything. *Express Love. Comets. 1930: A Warm Corner. 1931: Stepping Stones. 1932: But the Flesh Is Weak. 1933: Loyalties. It's a Boy! 1934: The Private Life of Don Juan. 1935: The Dictator (US: The Loves of a Dictator). 1937: Tovarich. The Thirteenth Chair. Mama Steps Out. 1938: Fools for Scandal. If I Were King. 1939: Girls' School. Beau Geste. 1940: Scotland Yard. 1941: Man Hunt. 1942: We Were Dancing. Son of Fury. The Moon and Sixpence. This Above All. The Undying Monster (GB: The Hammond Mystery). 1943: Journey for Margaret. Flesh and Fantasy. Above Suspicion. 1944: Gaslight (GB: The Murder in Thornton Square). The Conspirators. 1948: Anna Karenina. 1949: Trottie True (US: Gay Lady). Dear Mr Prohack. 1951: Encore. 1952: The Hour of 13. Father's Doing Fine. 1953: Will Any Gentleman ...? 1954: Duel in the Jungle. 1955: The Deep Blue Sea. Josephine and Men.

THATCHER, Torin
(Torren Thatcher) 1905–1981
Tall, burly, dark-haired, strong-looking, India-born actor, in British films off and on for 20 years before going to Hollywood, where he played villains in westerns, swashbucklers, comedies and thrillers, without ever quite making star billing. Began his career as a schoolmaster (and enthusiastic amateur boxer) before going on the stage. Retired at the end of 1969. Died from cancer.

1932: But the Flesh Is Weak. 1933: General John Regan. Red Wagon. 1934: Irish Hearts (US: Norah O'Neale). 1935: Drake of England (US: Drake the Pirate). School for Stars. 1936: Sabotage (US: The Woman Alone). Well Done Henry. Crime Over London. The Man Who Could Work Miracles. 1937: The Return of the Scarlet Pimpernel. Young and Innocent (US: The Girl Was Young). Dark Journey. Knight Without Armour. 1938: Climbing High. St Martin's Lane (US: Sidewalks of London). 1939: Old Mother Riley MP. The Spy in Black (US: U-Boat 29). The Lion Has Wings. Too Dangerous to Live. 1940: Let George Do It. Law and Disorder. Night Train to Munich (US: Night Train). Gasbags. Contraband (US: Blackout). The Case of the Frightened Lady (US: The Frightened Lady). Saloon Bar. 1941: Major Barbara. 1942: Next of Kin. Saboteur. 1946: The Captive Heart. I See a Dark Stranger (US: The Adventuress). Great Expectations. 1947: Jassy. The End of the River. The Man Within (US: The Smugglers). When the Bough Breaks. 1948: Bonnie Prince Charlie. The Fallen Idol. Lost Illusion. 1949: Which Will You Have? (US: Barabbas the Robber). 1950: The Black Rose. 1952: Affair in Trinidad. The Snows of Kilimanjaro. The Crimson Pirate. Blackbeard the Pirate. 1953: The Desert Rats. Houdini. The Robe. 1954: Knock on Wood. Bengal Brigade (GB: Bengal Rifles). The Black Shield of Falworth. Helen of Troy. 1955: Lady Godiva (GB: Lady Godiva of Coventry). Love Is a Many-Splendored Thing. Diane. Yacht on the High Sea (TV. GB: cinemas). 1957: Istanbul. Witness for the Prosecution. Band of Angels. So Soon to Die (TV). Darby's Rangers (GB: The Young Invaders). 1958: The 7th Voyage of Sinbad. 1959: The Miracle. 1961: Jack the Giant Killer. The Canadians. 1962: Mutiny on the Bounty. The Sweet and the Bitter. 1963: Decision at Midnight. Drums of Africa. 1964: From Hell to Borneo. 1965: The Sandpiper. 1966: Hawaii. 1967: The King's Pirate. 1968: Dr Jekyll and Mr Hyde (TV). 1976: Brenda Starr/Brenda Starr — Girl Reporter (TV).

THESIGER, Ernest 1879–1961

Eccentric British character actor, as emaciated as he was animated, who carved out some memorably grotesque and sometimes quite frightening figures, most notably his Dr Praetorius, the scientist who kept miniature beings in bottles, in *Bride of Frankenstein*. Later in more routine roles in post-war Britain, although each had the distinctive Thesiger touch. Began his career as an artist, but took to the stage at 30.

1916: *The Real Thing at Last. 1918: Nelson. The Life Story of David Lloyd George. 1919: A Little Bit of Fluff. 1921: The Adventures of Mr Pickwick. The Bachelor Club. †Number Thirteen. 1928: Weekend Wives. 1929: The Vagabond Queen. 1930: *Ashes. 1932: The Old Dark House. 1933: The Only Girl (US: Heart Song). The Ghoul. 1934: My Heart Is Calling. The Night of the Party. 1935: Bride of Frankenstein. 1936: The Man Who Could Work Miracles. 1938: The Ware Case. They Drive by Night. Lightning Conductor. 1943: The Lamp Still Burns. My Learned Friend. 1944: Don't Take It to Heart. Henry V. 1945:

A Place of One's Own. Caesar and Cleopatra. 1946: Beware of Pity. 1947: The Man Within (US: The Smugglers). Jassy. The Ghosts of Berkeley Square. 1948: The Winslow Boy. Portrait from Life (US: The Girl in the Painting). The Bad Lord Byron. Quartet. The Brass Monkey/Lucky Mascot. 1950: Last Holiday. Midnight Episode. 1951: The Man in the White Suit. Laughter in Paradise. Scrooge (US: A Christmas Carol). The Magic Box. The Woman's Angle. 1953: Thought to Kill. Meet Mr Lucifer. The Robe. The Million Pound Note (US: Man With a Million). 1954: Father Brown (US: The Detective). Make Me an Offer. 1955: Value for Money. An Alligator Named Daisy. The Adventures of Quentin Durward (US: Quentin Durward). Who Done It? 1956: Three Men in a Boat. 1957: Doctor at Large. 1958: The Truth About Women. The Horse's Mouth. 1959: Battle of the Sexes. 1960: Sons and Lovers. 1961: The Roman Spring of Mrs Stone.

† Unfinished.

THORNTON, Frank 1921–

Erect, dark-haired, sometimes moustachioed British actor, whose expression of impending outrage or horror came in useful in comedy after he had proved himself as a distinguished Shakespearian actor without quite making his mark in films. In the 1970s, he became a nationally known figure in Britain with his portrayal of Captain Peacock in the long-running TV comedy programme *Are You Being Served?* He also starred in the spin-off film.

1953: *The Silent Witness. 1954: Radio Cab

Murder. 1955: Cloak Without Dagger (US: Operation Conspiracy). Johnny You're Wanted. Portrait of Alison (US: Postmark for Danger). Stock Car. 1958: Battle of the V1 (US: V1/ Unseen Heroes). The Great Van Robbery. 1960: The Tell Tale Heart. 1961: The Impersonator. Tarnished Heroes. Victim. 1962: It's Trad, Dad! (US: Ring-a-Ding Rhythm). The Dock Brief (US: Trial and Error). Doomsday at Eleven. 1963: The Comedy Man. The Mouse on the Moon. 1964: The Tomb of Ligeia. A Hard Day's Night. The Wild Affair. 1965: The Big Job. *The Ride of the Valkyrie. The Murder Game. The Early Bird. Gonks Go Beat. 1966: Carry On Screaming. A Funny Thing Happened on the Way to the Forum. Red, White and Zero. 1967: Danny the Dragon. 30 is a Dangerous Age, Cynthia. 1968: A Flea in Her Ear. The Assassination Bureau. The Bliss of Mrs Blossom. Crooks and Coronets (US: Sophie's Place). 1969: The Bed Sitting Room. The Magic Christian. Till Death Us Do Part. Some Will, Some Won't. 1970: The Private Life of Sherlock Holmes. All the Way Up. The Rise and Rise of Michael Rimmer. 1971: Up the Chastity Belt. 1972: Our Miss Fred. Bless This House. That's Your Funeral. 1973: No Sex, Please — We're British. Digby the Biggest Dog in the World. Steptoe and Son Ride Again. Keep It Up, Jack! 1974: The Three Musketeers (The Queen's Diamonds). Vampira (US: Old Dracula). 1975: Spanish Fly. Side by Side. The Bawdy Adventures of Tom Jones. 1977: Are You Being Served? 1980: The Taming of the Shrew (TV). 1989: The B.F.G. (voice only).

THORPE-BATES, Peggy
See OULTON Brian

THUNDERCLOUD, Chief
(Victor Daniels) 1889–1955
Despite his 'white man's name', this stern-faced native American actor with slit eyes and lined forehead was a full-blooded Cherokee Indian, the oldest of nine children. Going through spells as a miner, boxer, ranchhand and rodeo performer, he ended up in Hollywood as a stuntman in westerns, also doing extra work and bit parts. His first high-profile success came in his late forties when he portrayed Tonto in a couple of Lone Ranger serials. After that he played the title role in *Geronimo*, and even showed a talent for comedy as a bumbling Sitting Bull in *Buffalo Bill*. He retired from films in 1952, and died from cancer three years later.

1930: The Big Trail. 1935: Fighting Pioneers. Wagon Trail. The Singing Vagabond. Annie Oakley. The Farmer Takes a Wife. Rustlers' Paradise. 1936: Custer's Last Stand (serial). The Plainsman. Ramona. Ride, Ranger, Ride. Silly Billies. 1937: Renfrew of the Royal Mounted. 1938: Flaming Frontiers (serial). The Lone Ranger (serial). Renfrew on the Great White Trail (GB: On the Great White Trail). The Great Adventures of Wild Bill Hickok (serial). 1939: The Lone Ranger Rides Again (serial). Geronimo. Union Pacific. 1940: Hudson's Bay. Murder on the Yukon. Northwest Mounted Police. Typhoon. Wyoming (GB: Bad Man of Wyoming). Young Buffalo Bill. 1941: Law and Disorder. The Silver Stallion. Western Union. 1942: King of the Stallions. My Gal Sal. Shut My Big Mouth. 1944: Black Arrow (serial). Buffalo Bill. The Falcon Out West. The Fighting Seabees. Outlaw Trail. Sonora Stagecoach. 1946: Badman's Territory. Renegade Girl. Romance of the West. 1947: The Senator Was Indiscreet (GB: Mr Ashton Was Indiscreet). Unconquered. 1948: Blazing Across the Pecos (GB: Under Arrest). 1949: Ambush. Call of the Forest. 1950: Colt 45. I Killed Geronimo. Davy Crockett – Indian Scout. A Ticket to Tomahawk. The Traveling Saleswoman. 1951: Santa Fé. 1952: Buffalo Bill in Tomahawk Territory. The Half-Breed. The Snows of Kilimanjaro.

TIGHE, Kevin 1944–

Fair-haired, round-faced, bull-necked American actor with wolfish smile, who looks born to play characters called Tug or Dutch who speak round a cigar. He began as a charismatic leading man in the TV series *Emergency!* Tighe played one of two young paramedics in the series, which ran from 1972 to 1978. After a role in the 1979 miniseries, *The Rebels*, Tighe vanished from screens large or small and built a career on the stage. Director John Sayles brought him into cinema roles in his early forties, and featured him in several of his offbeat films, as Tighe (pronounced 'Tie') built a new image as arrogant bullies or treacherously affable men of power. Has been acting since he was 10.

1971: Emergency! (TV). 1987: Matewan. 1988: Eight Men Out. 1989: K-9. Lost Angels (GB: The Road Home). Road House. 1990: Bright Angel. Perry Mason: The Case of the

Defiant Daughter (TV). Tales from the Crypt (cable TV). Another 48 Hrs. 1991: City of Hope. Face of a Stranger. 1992: School Ties. Skeeters. Newsies (GB: The News Boys). 1993: Better Off Dead (TV). I Love a Man in Uniform. Geronimo: An American Legend. What's Eating Gilbert Grape. 1994: William Putch: A Life in the Theater. Caught in the Act (TV).

TILLY, Jennifer 1958–

Long-faced, lithe, tallish American actress with dark, darting eyes and distinctive, little-girl voice, which has led her to play bimbos, mistresses and sympathetic sex symbols. Born in Canada, she followed her sister Meg (1960–) into the series *Hill Street Blues* on TV (she portrayed a gangster's moll who is eventually shot dead) and thence to films, where she has played largely attention-grabbing supporting roles; but an Academy Award nomination for *Bullets over Broadway* gave her career fresh impetus.

1984: No Small Affair. 1985: Moving Violations. 1986: Inside Out. 1987: He's My Girl. 1988: High Spirits. Rented Lips. Johnny Be Good. Remote Control. 1989: Let It Ride. The Fabulous Baker Boys. Far from Home. 1991: Scorchers. 1992: The Webbers/The Webbers' 15 Minutes. Agaguk/Shadow of the Wolf. 1993: Made in America. 1994: Heads (TV). The Getaway. Double Cross. Bullets Over Broadway. 1995: Bird of Prey. Embrace of the Vampire. From the Edge. Man With a Gun. Bound. House Arrest.

TOBEY, Kenneth 1919–

Tall, craggy American actor with wavy copper-coloured hair. After stage work and small film roles, he became a doughty fighter of monsters from the deep (or outer space) in the 1950s, but was otherwise confined to the minor roles he still plays today. The following list would undoubtedly be much longer but for his participation in the long-running TV series *Whirlybirds* in the late 1950s and early 1960s. Sometimes billed as Ken Tobey.

1947: Dangerous Venture. This Time for Keeps. 1948: He Walked By Night. 1949: The Doctor and the Girl. The File on Thelma Jordon/ Thelma Jordon. Free for All. The Great Sinner. I Was a Male War Bride (GB: You Can't Sleep Here). The Stratton Story. Twelve O'Clock High. Task Force. 1950: Kiss Tomorrow Good-

bye. The Gunfighter. My Friend Irma Goes West. Right Cross. When Willie Comes Marching Home. The Flying Missile. 1951: Rawhide/Desperate Siege. The Thing . . . from Another World. 1952: Angel Face. 1953: The Beast from 20,000 Fathoms. The Bigamist. Fighter Attack. 1954: Ring of Fear. Down Three Dark Streets. The Steel Cage. Davy Crockett – King of the Wild Frontier. 1955: Rage at Dawn. It Came from Beneath the Sea. 1956: Davy Crockett and the River Pirates. The Great Locomotive Chase. The Search for Bridey Murphy. The Man in the Gray Flannel Suit. The Steel Jungle. Gunfight at the OK Corral. 1957: Jet Pilot (completed 1950). The Vampire. The Wings of Eagles. 1958: Cry Terror! 1960: Seven Ways from Sundown. 1961: X-15. 1962: Six-Gun Law (TV. GB: cinemas). 1963: Stark Fear. 1966: A Man Called Adam. 1967: A Time for Killing (GB: The Long Ride Home). 40 Guns to Apache Pass. 1969: Marlowe. Don't Push, I'll Charge When I'm Ready (TV). 1970: Breakout (TV). 1971: Terror in the Sky (TV). Billy Jack. 1972: The Crooked Hearts (TV). Fireball Forward (TV). Ben. The Candidate. Rage. 1973: Coffee, Tea or Me? (TV). The Alpha Caper (TV. GB: cinemas, as Inside Job). Homebodies. Walking Tall. 1974: Death Squad (TV). Dirty Mary, Crazy Larry. 1976: Baby Blue Marine. W C Fields and Me. 1977: MacArthur The Rebel General. 1978: Wild and Wooly (TV). Nowhere to Run (TV). 1979: Hero at Large. 1980: Airplane! The Murder That Wouldn't Die (TV). The Howling. 1981: The Creature Wasn't Nice. 1983: Strange Invaders. 1984: The Last Starfighter. 1985: The Lost Empire. 1987: InnerSpace. 1988: Big Top Pee-wee. 1989: Ghostwriter. 1990: Gremlins 2: The New Batch. 1992: Honey, I Blew Up the Kid. Single White Female. 1993: Body Shot.

TOBIAS, George 1901–1980

Tall, lumpy, small-eyed, affable-looking American supporting actor whose homely pan decorated Warner films for most of the 1940s, mostly as the hero's loyal, but not-too-bright sidekick, but sometimes in juicier and more interesting roles. Hung around in films as a freelance for a few years afterwards, but was mostly seen on television after 1958. Died from cancer.

1939: They All Came Out. Maisie. The Hunchback of Notre Dame. Balalaika. Ninotchka. 1940: The Man Who Talked Too Much. Music

in My Heart. Saturday's Children. City for Conquest. Calling All Husbands. River's End. Torrid Zone. The Fighting 69th. They Drive By Night (GB: The Road to Frisco). South of Suez. East of the River. 1941: The Strawberry Blonde. The Bride Came C.O.D. Affectionately Yours. You're in the Army Now. Sergeant York. Out of the Fog. 1942: Wings for the Eagle. My Sister Eileen. Yankee Doodle Dandy. Juke Girl. Captains of the Clouds. 1943: Mission to Moscow. Thank Your Lucky Stars. This Is the Army. Air Force. 1944: Make Your Own Bed. The Mask of Dimitrios. Passage to Marseille. Between Two Worlds. 1945: Mildred Pierce. Objective Burma! 1946: Her Kind of Man. Nobody Lives Forever. Gallant Bess. 1947: My Wild Irish Rose. Sinbad the Sailor. 1948: The Adventures of Casanova. The Judge Steps Out (GB: Indian Summer). 1949: Everybody Does It. The Set-Up. 1950: Southside 1–1000 (GB: Forgery). 1951: Rawhide. Mark of the Renegade. The Tanks Are Coming. The Magic Carpet. Ten Tall Men. 1952: Desert Pursuit. 1953: The Glenn Miller Story. 1955: The Seven Little Foys. 1957: The Tattered Dress. Silk Stockings. 1958: Marjorie Morningstar. 1963: A New Kind of Love. Nightmare in the Sun. 1964: Bullet for a Badman. 1966: The Glass Bottom Boat. 1969: The Phynx.

TOBOLOWSKY, Stephen 1951–

Tall, dark, bald, bespectacled, lugubrious-looking (but often affably threatening), fish-like American actor playing oily slimeballs in the cinema of the 1980s and 1990s. Texas-born, Tobolowsky made his film debut while still at university studying

theatre; he later wrote and directed for that medium before embarking on film character roles in earnest in 1986, often being seen as an obnoxiously hearty friend, unctuous businessman, or groping boss. A sometime director, he also co-wrote the 1986 film True Stories.

1972: Keep My Grave Open/The House Where Hell Froze Over (released 1980). 1983: Swing Shift. 1984: The Philadelphia Experiment. 1986: Nobody's Fool. 1987: Spaceballs. 1988: Mississippi Burning. Checking Out. 1989: Roe Vs Wade (TV). Breaking In. Great Balls of Fire. In Country. *To the Moon, Alice. 1990: Wedlock. Welcome Home, Roxy Carmichael. The Grifters. Tagget (TV). Bird on a Wire. Last Flight Out (TV). Funny About Love. 1991: Deadlock (TV). The Marla Hanson Story (TV). Where the Day Takes You. Thelma & Louise. 1992: Memoirs of an Invisible Man. Basic Instinct. Single White Female. Sneakers. Hero (GB: Accidental Hero). Roadside Prophets. 1993: Groundhog Day. Calendar Girl. The Pickle. Josh and S.A.M. 1994: My Father, the Hero. Radioland Murders. Murder in the First. 1995: Dr Jekyll and Ms Hyde.

As director:
1988: Two Idiots in Hollywood.

TOLKAN, James 1931–

Shaven-headed, vindictive-looking, ferret-like American actor with mean, menacing presence on screen. A stage actor for the bulk of his early career, Tolkan has made six times as many films since 1980 as before it. As well as a whole jailblock full of street-wise and sometimes galaxy-wise bad guys, he also became well known as the smart-mouthed, incredulous Detective Lubic in the Back to the Future films. His stage career struggled along for many years until a lucky break – Robert Duvall's hip – propelled him from understudy to leading role in a Broadway play.

1969: Stiletto. 1971: They Might Be Giants. 1973: The Friends of Eddie Coyle. Serpico. 1975: Love and Death. 1981: Wolfen. Prince of the City. 1982: Hanky Panky. Author! Author! 1983: WarGames. Nightmares. 1984: The River. Iceman. 1985: Turk 182! Back to the Future. 1986: Little Spies (TV). Top Gun. Armed and Dangerous. Off Beat. 1987: Masters of the Universe. Split Decisions/Kid Gloves. Made in Heaven. 1988: A Leap of Faith (TV).

Viper. Weekend War (TV). 1989: Second Sight. Family Business. Ministry of Vengeance. The Case of the Hillside Stranglers (TV). Back to the Future Part II. 1990: Dick Tracy. Back to the Future Part III. Sunset Beat (TV). Opportunity Knocks. 1991: Autobahn (US: Trabbi Goes to Hollywood). Hangfire. Problem Child 2. 1992: Bloodfist IV – Die Trying. Sketch Artist. The Hat Squad (TV). 1993: Boiling Point. A Question of Faith (TV). 1994: Beyond Betrayal (TV). 1995: Sketch Artist II: Hands That See.

TOMBES, Andrew 1889–1976

Bald American actor, a great gnome of a man whose upper lip was almost non-existent, dwarfed by a distance between nose and mouth that give him an aspect of Macchiavellian glee. Tombes once wanted to be an acrobat and was a star baseball player in his twenties. But, following World War I, he became a vaudeville and musical-comedy entertainer – then, with the approach of middle-age, moved into film character roles in which he was equally likely to be genial or grasping as undertaker, insurance man, agent, school governor or policeman, giving many of his characters a faintly zany slant.

1933: The Bowery. 1934: Moulin Rouge. Born to Be Bad. 1935: Doubting Thomas. Here Comes Cookie (GB: The Plot Thickens). Music is Magic. Thanks a Million. 1936: King of Burlesque. The Devil is a Sissy (GB: The Devil Takes the Count). Hot Money. The Country Beyond. Here Comes Trouble. Stage Struck. Ticket to Paradise. It Had to Happen. 1937: Big City. Meet the Boy Friend. Charlie Chan at the Olympics. Turn Off the Moon. Easy Living. Sing and Be Happy. The Holy Terror. Borrowing Trouble. Checkers. Fair Warning. Riding on Air. Time Out for Romance. 45 Fathers. 1938: Sally, Irene and Mary. Battle of Broadway. Everybody Sing. Romance on the Run. Vacation from Love. A Desperate Adventure (GB: It Happened in Paris). Always in Trouble. Five of a Kind. One Wild Night. Thanks for Everything. 1939: What a Life. Nick Carter – Master Detective. Too Busy to Work. Boy Trouble. 1940: Captain Caution. Wolf of New York. Money to Burn. Village Barn Dance. Third Finger, Left Hand. Dr Kildare Goes Home. In Old Missouri. Charter Pilot. 1941: Sis Hopkins. Meet the Chump. Melody for Three. Wild Man of Borneo. Lady Scarface. World Premiere.

Birth of the Blues. Don't Get Personal. A Girl, a Guy and a Gob (GB: The Navy Steps Out). A Dangerous Game. Mountain Moonlight. Louisiana Purchase. Bedtime Story. Meet John Doe. Texas. The Obliging Young Lady. The Last of the Duanes. Caught in the Draft. Down Mexico Way. Double Date. Hellzapoppin. 1942: Blondie Goes to College. Larceny Inc. My Gal Sal. They All Kissed the Bride. Road to Morocco. Between Us Girls. Hi-Ya Chum (GB: Everything Happens to Us). Don't Get Personal. A Close Call for Ellery Queen (GB: A Close Call). The Meanest Man in the World. 1943: Coney Island. Hi Diddle Diddle. I Dood It (GB: By Hook or By Crook). His Butler's Sister. A Stranger in Town. Swing Fever. Let's Face It. Riding High (GB: Melody Inn). DuBarry Was a Lady. San Fernando Valley. Crazy House. Reveille With Beverly. Honeymoon Lodge. Phantom Lady. My Kingdom for a Cook. It Ain't Hay (GB: Money for Jam). It's a Great Life. The Mad Ghoul. 1944: Lake Placid Serenade. Goin' to Town. Murder in the Blue Room. Night Club Gal. Bathing Beauty. Show Business. Something for the Boys. Can't Help Singing. Reckless Age. The Singing Sheriff. Week-end Pass. 1945: Don't Fence Me In. Frontier Gal (GB: The Bride Wasn't Willing). G I Honeymoon. Rhapsody in Blue. You Came Along. Bring on the Girls. Incendiary Blonde. Patrick the Great. Badman's Territory. Sing While You Dance. 1946: Two Sisters from Boston. 1947: Hoppy's Holiday. Beat the Band. Copacabana. The Devil Thumbs a Ride. My Wild Irish Rose. The Fabulous Dorseys. Christmas Eve. 1948: Two Guys from Texas (GB: Two Texas Knights). 1949: Oh! You Beautiful Doll. 1950: Joe Palooka in Humphrey Takes a Chance (GB: Humphrey Takes a Chance). The Jackpot. 1951: A Wonderful Life. Belle le Grand. 1952: Oklahoma Annie. I Dream of Jeanie. 1955: How to Be Very, Very Popular.

TOMELTY, Joseph 1910–
Thick-set Irish actor with a bush of silver hair. He played whimsical roles in British films from 1952 to 1960, mostly as helpful old codgers in shabby waistcoats and rolled-up sleeves. Apart from this period, however, he remained largely on the stages of theatres in Ireland. Began his career as a playwright.

1946: Odd Man Out. 1952: Treasure Hunt. You're Only Young Twice! The Oracle (US:

The Horse's Mouth). The Sound Barrier (US: Breaking the Second Barrier). The Gentle Gunman. 1953: Meet Mr Lucifer. Melba. Front Page Story. Hell Below Zero. 1954: Devil Girl from Mars. The Young Lovers. The Death of Michael Turbin. Happy Ever After (US: Tonight's the Night/O'Leary Night). Hobson's Choice. Simba. A Prize of Gold. A Kid for Two Farthings. 1955: Timeslip. Bedevilled. John and Julie. 1956: Moby Dick. 1958: A Night to Remember. Life Is a Circus. Tread Softly, Stranger. The Captain's Table. 1959: Upstairs and Downstairs. Hell Is a City. 1960: The Day They Robbed the Bank of England. 1962: Lancelot and Guinevere. 1964: The Black Torment.

TOOMEY, Regis 1901–1991
Slight, pleasant, pale-eyed, light-haired, fast-talking American actor, in on sound films from the outset, and popular in minor leads in the 1930s, usually as breezy, clean-cut juveniles. Later played reporters, tail-gunners, cab-drivers and other eager-beaver types, sometimes the second-line good guy who bit the dust, but only rarely on the wrong side of the law. Enjoyed new popularity in the 1960s as one of Gene Barry's sidekicks in the long-running TV show Burke's Law.

1929: Rich People. Wheel of Life. Alibi. Illusion. 1930: The Light of Western Stars. Crazy That Way. Framed. A Man from Wyoming. Good Intentions. Street of Chance. Shadow of the Law. 1931: Finn and Hattie. Perfect Alibi. Graft. Scandal Sheet. 24 Hours (GB: The Hours Between). Touchdown (GB: Playing the Game). Murder by the Clock. The Finger Points. Kick In. Other Men's Women. Under 18. Sky Bride. 1932: Shopworn. They Never Come Back. The Crowd Roars. A Strange Adventure. The Midnight Patrol. The Penal Code. 1933: Laughing at Life. State Trooper. Picture Brides. Soldiers of the Storm. She Had to Say Yes. Big Time or Bust (GB: Heaven Bound). 1934: Red Morning. What's Your Racket? Redhead. She Had to Choose. Murder on the Blackboard. 1935: One Frightened Night. G Men. Reckless Roads. Shadow of Doubt. Skull and Crown. Manhattan Moon (GB: Sing Me a Love Song). The Great God Gold. 1936: Bulldog Edition (GB: Lady Reporter). *Sweethearts and Flowers. Shadows of the Orient. 1937: The Big City. Midnight Taxi. Back in Circulation. Sub-

marine D-1. 1938: His Exciting Night. Hunted Men. Illegal Traffic. The Invisible Menace. 1939: Smashing the Spy Ring. Street of Missing Men. Wings of the Navy. Indianapolis Speedway (GB: Devil on Wheels). Hidden Power. The Phantom Creeps (serial). Society Smugglers. Pirates of the Skies. The Mysterious Miss X. Confessions of a Nazi Spy. Trapped in the Sky. Union Pacific. Thunder Afloat. His Girl Friday. 1940: Northwest Passage. Till We Meet Again. Northwest Mounted Police. Arizona. 1941: The Devil and Miss Jones. A Shot in the Dark. Law of the Tropics. Meet John Doe. The Lone Wolf Takes a Chance. They Died with Their Boots On. Reaching for the Sun. The Nurse's Secret. Dive Bomber. You're in the Army Now. 1942: The Forest Rangers. Bullet Scars. Tennessee Johnson (GB: The Man on America's Conscience). I Was Framed. 1943: Adventures of the Flying Cadets (serial). Jack London. Destroyer. Phantom Lady. 1944: Song of the Open Road. The Doughgirls. Dark Mountain. Follow the Boys. Raiders of Ghost City (serial). When the Lights Go On Again. Murder in the Blue Room. 1945: Follow That Woman. Spellbound. Betrayal from the East. Out of the Night (GB: Strange Illusion). 1946: Mysterious Intruder. Her Sister's Secret. The Big Sleep. Child of Divorce. Sister Kenny. The Big Fix. 1947: High Tide. The Guilty. The Thirteenth Hour. Magic Town. Reaching from Heaven. The Bishop's Wife. 1948: I Wouldn't Be in Your Shoes. Raw Deal. Station West. The Boy with Green Hair. 1949: The Girl from Jones Beach. The Devil's Henchman. Mighty Joe Young. Come to the Stable. Beyond the Forest. 1950: Undercover Girl. Again, Pioneers. Mrs O'Malley and Mr Malone. Tomahawk (GB: Battle of Powder River). Dynamite Pass. Frenchie. 1951: The Tall Target. Navy Bound. Show Boat. Cause for Alarm. The People Against O'Hara. Cry Danger. 1952: Just For You. My Six Convicts. My Pal Gus. The Battle at Apache Pass. Never Wave at a WAC (GB: The Private Wore Skirts). Take the High Ground. 1953: The Nebraskan. Island in the Sky. It Happens Every Thursday. Son of Belle Starr. 1954: Drums Across the River. The High and the Mighty. The Human Jungle. 1955: Top Gun. Guys and Dolls. 1956: Great Day in the Morning. Dakota Incident. Three for Jamie Dawn. Men Against Speed (TV. GB: cinemas). 1957: Curfew Breakers. The Still Trumpet (TV). 1958: Sing, Boy, Sing. Joy Ride. 1959: Warlock. The Hangman. Guns of the Timberland. 1961: The Last Sunset. Voyage to the Bottom of the Sea. King of the Roaring Twenties (GB: The Big Bankroll). 1963: Man's Favorite Sport? 1966: Night of the Grizzly. 1967: Gunn. 1969: Change of Habit. 1970: Cover Me Babe. 1972: The Carey Treatment. 1974: The Phantom of Hollywood (TV). God Damn Dr Shagetz/God Bless Dr Shagetz. 1975: Won Ton Ton, the Dog Who Saved Hollywood. 1979: Chomps. 1987: Evil Town.

TOWB, Harry 1925–
Roughly-spoken, tough-looking Irish portrayer of aggressive characters in British films. His sleepy-eyed, jut-lipped, tousle-headed features were mostly seen as thugs and lower ranks, but mellowed as the years went by. Has kept very busy in television

and the theatre; still popped up occasionally in films until the mid 1980s.

1950: Quiet Woman. 1951: Reluctant Heroes. 1952: Gift Horse (US: Glory at Sea). Escape by Night. 13 East Street. 1953: John Wesley. 1954: The Night of the Full Moon. The Sleeping Tiger. Knave of Hearts (US: Lovers, Happy Lovers). A Prize of Gold. 1955: Above Us the Waves. The Case of the Split Ticket. The Time of His Life. 1956: Eyewitness. Doublecross. The March Hare. 1957: Stranger in Town. The End of the Road. 1958: Murder at Site Three. 1959: The Thirty-Nine Steps. 1960: Crossroads to Crime. 1961: All Night Long. 1963: The Scarlet Blade (US: The Crimson Blade). 1966: The Blue Max. 1967: 30 is a Dangerous Age, Cynthia. 1968: Prudence and the Pill. The Bliss of Mrs Blossom. All Neat in Black Stockings. 1969: Patton (GB: Patton — Lust for Glory). 1971: Carry On at Your Convenience. 1972: Some Kind of Hero. 1973: Digby The Biggest Dog in the World. 1974: Sex Play/The Bunny Caper. The Girl from Petrovka. 1975: Barry Lyndon. 1978: Rosie Dixon Night Nurse. 1983: Lassiter. 1986: Lamb.

TOWNLEY, Toke 1912–1984
With his clown's face and high forehead topped by a frizz of hair, Townley was impossible to miss in a film. The son of a vicar, this British actor was working as a clerk in a factory when he became interested in amateur dramatics and, at 32, decided to throw his job up to go on a stage tour. Turning professional, he quickly found regular employment in small roles, often as country bumpkins and slow-witted menials. Lost to the cinema after 1972, when he became a regular in the long-running TV series *Emmerdale Farm*, in which he played Sam Pearson, a role which, the frizz of hair now disappeared, he played until his death from a heart attack.

1951: Lady Godiva Rides Again. 1952: Treasure Hunt. Meet Me Tonight. Time Gentlemen Please! Down Among the Z Men. Cosh Boy (US: The Slasher). 1953: Innocents in Paris. Turn the Key Softly. The Broken Horseshoe. Meet Mr Lucifer. The Runaway Bus. 1954: Fast and Loose. The Men of Sherwood Forest. Bang! You're Dead (US: Game of Danger). 1955: The Blue Peter (US: Navy Heroes). John and Julie. Doctor at Sea. The Quatermass Experiment (US: The Creeping Unknown). 1956: Three Men in a Boat. Now and Forever. 1957: The Admirable Crichton (US: Paradise Lagoon). Carry On Admiral (US: The Ship Was Loaded). Barnacle Bill (US: All at Sea). 1958: Law and Disorder. A Cry from the Streets. 1959: Look Back in Anger. Our Man in Havana. Libel. Third Man on the Mountain. 1960: The World of Suzie Wong. Piccadilly Third Stop. 1961: Go to Blazes. 1962: HMS Defiant (US: Damn the Defiant!). The Fast Lady. The Prince and the Pauper. 1963: Doctor in Distress. 1964: The Chalk Garden. 1965: The Legend of Young Dick Turpin. 1969: Oh! What a Lovely War. 1970: The Scars of Dracula. 1973: Clouds of Witness (TV). 1977: Chimpmates.

TRAVERS, Henry
(T. Heagerty) 1874–1965
British-born actor, in America from the turn of the century, whose long, thin mouth only added to his benign expression. Came to films when almost 60 and specialized in wisdom and whimsicality, combining both in memorable fashion as Clarence the Angel in Capra's *It's a Wonderful Life!* Died from complications following arteriosclerosis. Oscar nomination for *Mrs Miniver*.

1933: Reunion in Vienna. My Weakness. Another Language. The Invisible Man. 1934: Ready for Love. The Party's Over. Death Takes a Holiday. Born to be Bad. 1935: Escapade. Maybe It's Love. Captain Hurricane. Four Hours to Kill. After Office Hours. Pursuit. Seven Keys to Baldpate. 1936: Too Many

Parents. 1938: The Sisters. 1939: Dodge City. Remember? Dark Victory. You Can't Get Away with Murder. On Borrowed Time. Stanley and Livingstone. The Rains Came. 1940: Edison the Man. Wyoming (GB: Bad Man of Wyoming) The Primrose Path. Anne of Windy Poplars (GB: Anne of Windy Willows). 1941: A Girl, a Guy and a Gob (GB: The Navy Steps Out). Ball of Fire. I'll Wait for You. High Sierra. The Bad Man (GB: Two-Gun Cupid). 1942: Pierre of the Plains. Random Harvest. Mrs Miniver. The Moon is Down. 1943: Madame Curie. Shadow of a Doubt. 1944: The Very Thought of You. Dragon Seed. None Shall Escape. 1945: The Bells of St Mary's. Thrill of a Romance. The Naughty Nineties. 1946: The Yearling. It's a Wonderful Life! Gallant Journey. 1947: The Flame. 1948: Beyond Glory. 1949: The Girl from Jones Beach. The Accused.

TREACHER, Arthur
(A. Veary) 1894–1975
Tall, dark-haired, long-faced, rather disdainful British actor who came to America in 1926 and in the next decade became Hollywood's perfect butler, complete with upper-crust voice and unflappable manner. He actually played P.G. Wodehouse's Jeeves twice but from 1940 was less busy, and began to devote more time to television and outside interests, having built up a chain of up-market fish-and-chip shops in America at the time of his death from a heart ailment.

*1929: The Battle of Paris. 1933: Alice in Wonderland. 1934: Fashions of 1934/ Fashions. Madame Du Barry. Riptide. *When Do We Eat? The Key. Gambling Lady. Desirable. Here Comes the Groom. The Captain Hates the Sea. Forsaking All Others. Hollywood Party. Viva Villa! Student Tour. Bordertown. 1935: David Copperfield. The Nitwits. No More Ladies. Orchids to You. The Woman in Red. Magnificent Obsession. Cardinal Richelieu. I Live My Life. Bright Lights (GB: Funny Face). Personal Maid's Secret. Curly Top. Let's Live Tonight. Remember Last Night? The Daring Young Man. Splendor. A Midsummer Night's Dream. Go Into Your Dance (GB: Casino de Paree). Vanessa: Her Love Story. The Winning Ticket. 1936: Mister Cinderella. Hitch Hike Lady (GB: Eventful Journey). Stowaway. The Case Against Mrs Ames. Hearts Divided. Under Your Spell. Anything Goes. Satan Met a*

Lady. Thank You, Jeeves. Hard Luck Dame. 1937: You Can't Have Everything. Thin Ice (GB: Lovely to Look At). She Had to Eat. Heidi. Step Lively, Jeeves. 1938: Mad About Music. My Lucky Star. Up the River. Always in Trouble. 1939: Bridal Suite. The Little Princess. Barricade. 1940: Irene. Brother Rat and a Baby (GB: Baby Be Good). 1942: Star Spangled Rhythm. 1943: Forever and a Day. The Amazing Mrs Holliday. 1944: Chip Off the Old Block. In Society. National Velvet. 1945: Delightfully Dangerous. Swing Out, Sister. That's the Spirit. 1947: Slave Girl. Fun on a Weekend. 1948: The Countess of Monte Cristo. 1949: That Midnight Kiss. 1950: Love That Brute. 1964: Mary Poppins.

TREVOR, Austin
(A.T. Schilsky) 1897–1978
Neat, latterly moustachioed, tiny-mouthed, Irish-born, Swiss-educated actor in British films who made his stage debut in America and, after World War I service, played with the Rhine Army Dramatic Company in Cologne. This cosmopolitan upbringing led to his becoming a formidable interpreter of foreign accents and, with the coming of sound, he was much in demand for the portrayal of continental detectives, including A.E.W. Mason's Inspector Hanaud and Agatha Christie's Hercule Poirot, his meticulous acting style rounding off the characterization. Later seen as affable aristocrats in more routine roles.

1930: Escape. At the Villa Rose (US: Mystery at the Villa Rose). The 'W' Plan. The Man from Chicago. 1931: Alibi. A Night in Montmartre. Black Coffee. 1932: The Chinese Puzzle. The Crooked Lady. A Safe Proposition. 1933: On Secret Service (US: Secret Agent). 1934: The Broken Melody. Lord Edgware Dies. Death at Broadcasting House. 1935: Inside the Room. Royal Cavalcade (US: Regal Cavalcade). Mimi. The Silent Passenger. 1936: As You Like It. La vie parisienne. Spy 77. The Beloved Vagabond. Dusty Ermine (US: Hideout in the Alps). Rembrandt. Sabotage (US: The Woman Alone). Le vagabond bien-aimé. Thunder in the City. 1937: Dark Journey. Knight Without Armour. 1939: Goodbye Mr Chips! The Lion Has Wings. 1940: The Briggs Family. Law and Disorder. Under Your Hat. Night Train to Munich (US: Night Train). 1941: The Seventh Survivor. The Big Blockade. 1942: The Young

Mr Pitt. 1944: Heaven is Round the Corner. Champagne Charlie. 1946: Lisbon Story. 1947: Anna Karenina. 1948: Bonnie Prince Charlie. The Red Shoes. 1950: So Long at the Fair. 1954: Father Brown (US: The Detective). To Paris with Love. 1956: Tons of Trouble. 1957: Dangerous Exile. The Naked Truth (US: Your Past is Showing!). Seven Waves Away (US: Abandon Ship!). 1959: Horrors of the Black Museum. Carlton-Browne of the FO (US: Man in a Cocked Hat). 1961: Konga. The Day the Earth Caught Fire. The Court Martial of Major Keller. 1962: Never Back Losers. 1965: The Alphabet Murders.

TRIESAULT, Ivan 1898–1980
Brown-haired Estonian actor with strained, lined features and darting eyes. He came to America in 1920 to pursue his career as a ballet dancer and mime artist, but became interested in acting and, with the call for foreign types in Hollywood films of the war years, was drawn to the film capital from 1941. Although appearing with some irregularity in films, he became a prolific performer on TV, at first as Slavic menaces, but in later years as scientists and professors. Died from heart failure.

1941: The Girl from Leningrad. Out of the Fog. 1943: Mission to Moscow. Song of Russia. Cry of the Werewolf. Days of Glory. The Strange Death of Adolf Hitler. The Black Parachute. 1944: The Mummy's Ghost. In Our Time. Uncertain Glory. The Hitler Gang. The Story of Dr Wassell. 1945: A Song to Remember. Counter-Attack (GB: One Against Seven). Escape in the Fog. 1946: Crime Doctor's Manhunt. Escape Me Never. Notorious. The Return of Monte Cristo (GB: Monte Cristo's Revenge). 1947: The Crimson Key. Golden Earrings. 1948: To the Ends of the Earth. The Woman from Tangier. 1949: Captain Carey USA (GB: After Midnight). Battleground. DOA. Johnny Allegro (GB: Hounded). Home in San Antone. 1950: Jet Pilot (released 1957). Kim. Spy Hunt (GB: Panther's Moon). 1951: The Desert Fox (GB: Rommel − Desert Fox). The Lady and the Bandit (GB: Dick Turpin's Ride). My Favorite Spy. My True Story. 1952: The Bad and the Beautiful. Five Fingers. Scandal at Scourie. Ma and Pa Kettle on Vacation (GB: Ma and Pa Kettle Go to Paris). 1953: Desert Legion. Back to God's Country. How to Marry a Millionaire. Young Bess. 1954: Border River.

Charge of the Lancers. The Gambler from Natchez. Her Twelve Men. 1955: The Girl in the Red Velvet Swing. 1957: The Buster Keaton Story. Silk Stockings. Top Secret Affair (GB: Their Secret Affair). 1958: Fraulein. Me and the Colonel. The Young Lions. 1959: The Amazing Transparent Man. 1960: Cimarron. 1961: Barabbas. It Happened in Athens. 1962: Escapade in Florence. The 300 Spartans. 1963: The Prize. Viva Las Vegas (GB: Love in Las Vegas). 1965: Von Ryan's Express. Morituri (GB: The Saboteur − Code Name Morituri). 1966: Batman. 1967: Search for the Evil One. How to Succeed in Business Without Really Trying.

TROUGHTON, Patrick 1920–1987
Squat, stern-looking, dark-haired British actor who, after acting training in America, war service at sea and theatrical experience with the Old Vic, scurried from role to role on radio and TV in the post-war years. He never really settled in films, but became nationally known on British television as one of the portrayers of science-fiction time traveller Dr Who. Died from a heart attack.

1948: Hamlet. Escape. Cardboard Cavalier. Badger's Green. 1950: Treasure Island. The Franchise Affair. Chance of a Lifetime. The Woman with No Name (US: Her Paneled Door). Waterfront (US: Waterfront Women). 1951: White Corridors. 1954: The Black Knight. 1955: Richard III. 1957: The Curse of Frankenstein. The Moonraker. 1962: The Phantom of the Opera. 1963: Jason and the Argonauts. 1964: The Black Torment. The Gorgon. 1966: The Viking Queen. 1967: Witchfinder-General (US: The Conqueror Worm). 1970: Scars of Dracula. 1972: Doomwatch. 1973: Frankenstein and the Monster from Hell. 1976: The Omen. 1977: Sinbad and the Eye of the Tiger. 1978: A Hitch in Time.

TRUBSHAWE, Michael 1905–1985
Gangling, very tall, dark-haired British actor whose rather gloomy features were lightened by the addition of a huge handlebar moustache. A close friend of David Niven since their days together in the British Army of the late 1920s, he drifted into acting following Niven's joke of trying to mention the name Trubshawe in all his films. The real Trubshawe soon became established as

hearty officer types and played around 40 film roles before his retirement in 1970.

1950: They Were Not Divided. Dance Hall. 1951: The Lavender Hill Mob. Encore. The Magic Box. Brandy for the Parson. 1952: The Card (US: The Promoter). Meet Me Tonight (US: Tonight at 8:30). Something Money Can't Buy. The Titfield Thunderbolt. 1954: Orders Are Orders. The Rainbow Jacket. 1955: You Lucky People. Private's Progress. 1956: The Passionate Stranger (US: A Novel Affair). 23 Paces to Baker Street. Around the World in 80 Days. 1957: The Rising of the Moon. Doctor at Large. I Accuse! 1958: Gideon's Day (US: Gideon of Scotland Yard). Law and Disorder. 1960: Scent of Mystery (GB: Holiday in Spain). 1961: The Guns of Navarone. The Best of Enemies. 1962: Operation Snatch. Reach for Glory. 1963: The Mouse on the Moon. The Pink Panther. 1964: A Hard Day's Night. The Runaway. 1965: Those Magnificent Men in their Flying Machines. The Amorous Adventures of Moll Flanders. 1966: The Sandwich Man. The Spy with a Cold Nose. 1967: Bedazzled. 1968: Salt and Pepper. A Dandy in Aspic. 1969: Monte Carlo or Bust. Battle of Britain. The Magic Christian. 1970: The Rise and Rise of Michael Rimmer.

TRUMAN, Ralph 1900–1977
Tall, dark-haired, genial-looking, often moustachioed British actor with distinctive long, oval face, a superstar of radio who never quite made the same impact in films, although seen as a good variety of solid, reliable types. Once estimated to have made

more than 5,000 broadcasts since his radio debut in 1925, he married fellow radio player Ellis Powell, who for many years played Mrs Dale in the long-running British radio soap *Mrs Dale's Diary*.

1930: City of Song (US: Farewell to Love). 1931: The Bells. 1932: Partners Please. Called Back. 1933: The Shadow. 1934: Catherine the Great. The Perfect Flaw. 1935: That's My Uncle. The Lad. The Case of Gabriel Perry (Wild Justice). Three Witnesses. Captain Bill. Death on the Set (US: Murder on the Set). Late Extra. The Silent Passenger. Jubilee Window. Lieutenant Daring RN. Mr Cohen Takes a Walk. Father O'Flynn. 1936: The Crimson Circle. East Meets West. The Marriage of Corbal (US: The Prisoner of Corbal). The Gay Adventure. Fire Over England. Dusty Ermine (US: Hideout in the Alps). 1937: Under the Red Robe. It's a Grand Old World. Change for a Sovereign. Dinner at the Ritz. South Riding. Silver Blaze (US: Murder at the Baskervilles). Secret Lives (US: I Married a Spy). The Lilac Domino. 1938: The Challenge. Just Like a Woman. Many Tanks Mr Atkins. The Drum (US: Drums). 1939: The Outsider. The Saint in London. Dead Man's Shoes. Black Eyes. 1941: The Seventh Survivor. 1942: Sabotage at Sea. 1943: The Butler's Dilemma. 1944: Henry V. 1946: Beware of Pity. Lisbon Story. The Laughing Lady. Woman to Woman. 1947: Mrs Fitzherbert. The Man Within (US: The Smugglers). 1948: Eureka Stockade (US: Massacre Hill). Oliver Twist. Mr Perrin and Mr Traill. 1949: Christopher Columbus. The Interrupted Journey. 1950: Treasure Island. The Reluctant Widow. 1951: Quo Vadis? 1952: La carrozza d'oro (GB and US: The Golden Coach). Ivanhoe. 1953: Androcles and the Lion. Malta Story. The Master of Ballantrae. 1954: Beau Brummell. Knights of the Round Table. 1955: The Night My Number Came Up. The Ship That Died of Shame (US: PT Raiders). 1956: The Man Who Knew Too Much. The Long Arm (US: The Third Key). The Black Tent. Wicked As They Come. The Silken Affair. Tons of Trouble. The Good Companions. 1957: Yangtse Incident (US: Battle Hell/Escape of the Amethyst). 1958: The Spaniard's Curse. 1959: Ben-Hur. Beyond This Place (US: Web of Evidence). 1960: Exodus. Under Ten Flags. 1961: El Cid. 1971: Nicholas and Alexandra. 1972: Lady Caroline Lamb.

TULLY, Tom 1896–1982
Big, beefy, brown-haired American actor with a face that looked as though he had gone many rounds in the ring rather than had a career as a reporter, served in the US Navy and made a name for himself on Broadway. He came to films in the war years in tough-but-tender roles that suited his volcanic features and gruffly kindly personality. Nominated for an Oscar in *The Caine Mutiny*, after which he did have one leading role, as the prison warden, opposite Sylvia Sidney, in *Behind the High Wall*. Very busy on TV until the end of the 1960s, when he slowed his work rate.

1938: Carefree. 1943: Mission to Moscow. Northern Pursuit. Destination Tokyo. 1944: Secret Command. The Sign of the Cross (new

prologue to 1932 feature). The Town Went Wild. I'll Be Seeing You. 1945: The Unseen. Kiss and Tell. Adventure. 1946: The Virginian. Lady in the Lake. Till the End of Time. 1947: Intrigue. Killer McCoy. Scudda Hoo! Scudda Hay! (GB: Summer Lightning). 1948: Blood on the Moon. June Bride. Rachel and the Stranger. 1949: The Lady Takes a Sailor. A Kiss for Corliss. Illegal Entry. 1950: Where the Sidewalk Ends. Branded. Tomahawk (GB: The Battle of Powder River). 1951: The Lady and the Bandit (GB: Dick Turpin's Ride). Texas Carnival. Love is Better than Ever (GB: The Light Fantastic). Return of the Texan. 1952: Lure of the Wilderness. The Turning Point. Ruby Gentry. 1953: Trouble Along the Way. Sea of Lost Ships. The Moon is Blue. The Jazz Singer. 1954: Arrow in the Dust. The Caine Mutiny. 1955: Love Me or Leave Me. Soldier of Fortune. 1956: Behind the High Wall. 1958: Ten North Frederick. 1960: The Wackiest Ship in the Army. 1963: The Carpetbaggers. 1965: McHale's Navy Joins the Air Force. 1968: Coogan's Bluff. 1969: Any Second Now (TV). 1973: Charley Varrick. Hijack! (TV). 1980: In the Child's Best Interest (TV. Released 1986 as A Child's Cry). 1981: Madame X (TV). 1983: Porky's II: The Next Day.

TURNBULL, John 1880–1956
Burly, bull-headed, light-haired, sometimes moustachioed Scottish actor in stalwart roles. He played schoolmasters, statesmen, policemen and officers for years, finally getting his first leading role at 67 in his fourth-last film. He was a medical student and a purser before deciding on an acting

career, also dabbling in stage direction and producing ENSA shows for the troops during World War II. A lifelong cricket fanatic, he was a Lords Taverners and MCC member and long-time president of the Stage Cricket Club.

1913: The Good Samaritan. The Star and Crescent. 1930: Tons of Money. 1931: 77 Park Lane. Rodney Steps In. Keepers of Youth. The Man at Six (US: The Gables Mystery). Lloyd of the CID (serial US: Detective Lloyd). The Wickham Mystery. 1932: Murder on the Second Floor. A Voice Said Goodnight. The Midshipmaid (US: Midshipmaid Gob). Puppets of Fate (US: Wolves of the Underworld). The Iron Stair. 1933: The Man Outside. The Medicine Man. The Umbrella. Ask Beccles. The Private Life of Henry VIII. The Black Abbot. The Shadow. The Lady is Willing. 1934: Music Hall. The Case for the Crown. Badger's Green. Lord Edgware Dies. What Happened to Harkness. Passing Shadows. Warn London! The Girl in the Flat. It's a Cop! Tangled Evidence. The Night of the Party. The Scarlet Pimpernel. Once in a New Moon. 1935: The 39 Steps. The Small Man. The Lad. A Real Bloke. Sexton Blake and the Bearded Doctor. Radio Pirates. Black Mask. Line Engaged. Music Hath Charms. The Passing of the Third Floor Back. 1936: Rhodes of Africa (US: Rhodes). The Limping Man. Conquest of the Air (released 1940). Tudor Rose (US: Nine Days a Queen). Rembrandt. His Lordship (US: Man of Affaires). Shipmates o' Mine. Where There's a Will. Hearts of Humanity. The Amazing Quest of Ernest Bliss (US: Romance and Riches). 1937: Sunset in Vienna. It's a Grand Old World. Song of the Road. Make Up. Silver Blaze (US: Murder at the Baskervilles). Talking Feet. Saturday Night Revue. Who Killed Fen Markham?/The Angelus. Death Croons the Blues. 1938: The Gaunt Stranger. The Terror. Stepping Toes. Star of the Circus (US: Hidden Menace). Night Alone. Strange Boarders. 1939: Inspector Hornleigh on Holiday (US: Inspector Hornleigh on Vacation). Return to Yesterday. Dead Men Are Dangerous. Spies of the Air. 1940: Under Your Hat. Three Silent Men. Spare a Copper. 1941: The Common Touch. Old Mother Riley's Circus. 1942: Hard Steel. 1943: There's a Future in It. The Shipbuilders. 1944: Don't Take It to Heart. Fanny by Gaslight (US: Man of Evil). 1945: A Place of One's Own. 1946: Daybreak. 1947: The Hangman Waits. So Well Remembered. 1949: The Man from Yesterday. 1950: The Happiest Days of Your Life.

TURTURRO, John 1957–

Narrow-headed, dark-eyed, Italianate-style actor with a shock of dark hair who, with the odd exception, has tended to play dour roles since award-winning performances in the theatre propelled him into films. Blue-collar ghetto workers proved his stock-in-trade, mostly in stories with adult themes and language, and he was a useful part of the company in dark films by Spike Lee, the Coen Brothers and others. Leading roles in *Barton Fink* and *Mac* (the latter of which he also directed) brought him critical and festival praises, but proved less positive performers at the box-office. The overall grim

seriousness of his characters began to lighten in the mid 1990s.

1980: Raging Bull. 1984: Exterminator II. The Flamingo Kid. 1985: Desperately Seeking Susan. To Live and Die in LA. 1986: The Color of Money. Hannah and Her Sisters. Gung Ho. Off Beat. 1987: The Sicilian. Five Corners. 1989: Do the Right Thing. Backtrack (GB: Catchfire). 1990: Miller's Crossing. Mo' Better Blues. State of Grace. Men of Respect. 1991: Barton Fink. Jungle Fever. 1992: Mac (and directed). Brain Donors. 1993: Fearless. The Search for James C Hoyt. 1994: Quiz Show. Being Human. Search and Destroy. Unstrung Heroes. 1995: Clockers. Grace of My Heart. Nixon.

TYNER, Charles 1925–

No doubt he has a full set of molars and wouldn't hurt a fly but this dark, taciturn, 'countrified' American actor looked toothless and dangerous. With his familiar big black floppy hat, unkempt clothes and wad of chewing tobacco, he was just as likely to shoot the hero (or worse) before asking questions, and the only surprise about his brief flowering in the cinema was that he didn't turn up in *Deliverance*. Brought by Paul Newman from Broadway for a typically sadistic role in *Cool Hand Luke*, he was less effective outside this image, and has been mainly back in the theatre since 1977.

1964: Lilith. 1967: Cool Hand Luke. 1968: The Stalking Moon. 1969: The Reivers. Gaily, Gaily (GB: Chicago, Chicago). 1970: The Moonshine War. The Cheyenne Social Club. Monte Walsh. The Traveling Executioner.

1971: Lawman. Sarge: The Badge or the Cross (TV). The Cowboys. Sometimes a Great Notion (GB: Never Give an Inch). 1972: Harold and Maude. Bad Company. Fuzz. Jeremiah Johnson. 1973: The Emperor of the North Pole (GB: Emperor of the North). The Stone Killer. 1974: Winterkill (TV). The Longest Yard (GB: The Mean Machine). The Midnight Man. The Greatest Gift (TV). 1976: Family Plot. The Young Pioneers (TV). 1977: Pete's Dragon. Peter Lundy and the Medicine Hat Stallion (TV). 1978: Lassie: The New Beginning (TV). The Awakening Land (TV). 1979: The Incredible Journey of Dr Meg Laurel (TV). 1981: Evilspeak. A Matter of Life and Death (TV). 1985: Deadly Messages (TV). Hamburger – The Motion Picture. 1987: Best Seller. Pulse. 1988: Planes, Trains and Automobiles. I'll Be Home for Christmas (TV). 1990: Enid is Sleeping (later and GB: Over Her Dead Body).

U

URECAL, Minerva
(M. Holzer) 1894–1966

Formidable, square-jawed, hook-nosed, raucous-voiced American actress with damped-down brown hair, a cross between Marjorie Main and Hope Emerson (both *qv*) and usually seen in roles calling for explosive emotional reaction of one kind or another, often cruelty or indignation, but sometimes turned to good comedy effect. Her character names – Death Watch Mary in *Oh, Doctor*, and Hatchet-Faced Woman in *The Doughgirls* – give a good impression of what to expect of this radio-trained player of Scottish ancestry, whose stage name was sort-of-an-anagram from Eureka, California, her birthplace. In the late fifties, she actually got her own television series, *The Adventures of Tugboat Annie*. She died from a heart attack.

*1933: Meet the Baron. 1934: Sadie McKee. Student Tour. Straight is the Way. You Can't Buy Everything. 1935: Biography of a Bachelor Girl. Bonnie Scotland. The Man on the Flying Trapeze (GB: The Memory Expert). *His Bridal Sweet. Here Comes the Band. 1936: Fury. God's Country and the Woman. *Vocalising. Bulldog Edition (GB: The Lady Reporter). Love on a Bet. The Three Godfathers/Miracle in the Sand. 1937: Behind the Mike. Ever Since Eve. Exiled to Shanghai. The Go Getter. Her*

*Husband's Secretary. Life Begins With Love. Love in a Bungalow. Mountain Justice. Oh, Doctor. Charlie Chan at the Olympics. Live, Love and Learn. Portia on Trial (GB: The Trial of Portia Merriman). She Loved a Fireman. 1938: Air Devils. Dramatic School. City Streets. The Devil's Party. Frontier Scout. In Old Chicago. Lady in the Morgue (GB: Case of the Missing Blonde). Prison Nurse. Start Cheering. Thanks for Everything. Wives Under Suspicion. ††Blondes at Work. 1939: Dancing Co-Ed (GB: Every Other Inch a Lady). Destry Rides Again. Golden Boy. Four Girls in White. Little Accident. *Maid to Order. No Place to Go. Second Fiddle. Sabotage (GB: Spies at Work). Should Husbands Work? She Married a Cop. S.O.S. Tidal Wave (GB: Tidal Wave). Unexpected Father (GB: Sandy Takes a Bow). Golden Boy. Missing Evidence. You Can't Cheat an Honest Man. 1940: Boys of the City/The Ghost Creeps. No, No, Nanette. The Sagebrush Family Trails West. Wildcat Bus. You Can't Fool Your Wife. San Francisco Docks. 1941: Accent on Love. Arkansas Judge (GB: False Witness). Billy the Kid. Bowery Blitzkrieg (GB: Stand and Deliver). The Cowboy and the Blonde. Dressed to Kill. Lady for a Night. A Man Betrayed (GB: Citadel of Crime) Marry the Boss's Daughter. Man at Large. Golden Hoofs. Moon Over Her Shoulder. Murder Among Friends. Murder by Invitation. Never Give a Sucker an Even Break (GB: What a Man!). Sailors on Leave. Six Lessons from Madame La Zonga. Skylark. The Trial of Mary Dugan. They Died With Their Boots On. The Wild Man of Borneo. 1942: Beyond the Blue Horizon. The Corpse Vanishes (GB: The Case of the Missing Brides). Almost Married. The Daring Young Man (GB: Lock Your Doors). Henry and Dizzy. In Old California. My Favorite Blonde. Henry Aldrich, Editor. The Living Ghost. Man in the Trunk. Quiet Please Murder. The Powers Girl (GB: Hello! Beautiful). Riding Through Nevada. Sons of the Pioneers. Sweater Girl. That Other Woman. A Tragedy at Midnight. 1943: The Ape Man. Dangerous Blondes. Ghosts on the Loose. Hit the Ice. Keep 'Em Slugging. Kid Dynamite. Klondike Kate. My Kingdom for a Cook. So This is Washington. *Pitchin' in the Kitchen. *You Dear Boy. The Song of Bernadette. Shadow of a Doubt. White Savage (GB: White Captive). Wagon Tracks West. Here Comes Elmer. A Stranger in Town. Dixie Dugan. Dangerous Blondes. 1944: And Now Tomorrow. Block Busters. The Bridge of San Luis Rey. The*

*Doughgirls. County Fair. Crazy Knights/Ghost Crazy. *Bachelor Daze. Irish Eyes Are Smiling. It Happened Tomorrow. Louisiana Hayride. Kismet. Mr Skeffington. Moonlight and Cactus. Music in Manhattan. Man from Frisco. Mark of the Whistler. One Mysterious Night. When Strangers Marry/Betrayed. 1945: *Alibi Baby. A Bell for Adano. The Bells of St Mary's. Crime Doctor's Manhunt. George White's Scandals. The Kid Sister. A Medal for Benny. Mr Muggs Rides Again. Out of This World. Sensation Hunters. State Fair. Who's Guilty? (serial). Men in Her Diary. Wanderer of the Wasteland. Colonel Effingham's Raid (GB: Man of the Hour). Salty O'Rourke. 1946: *Andy Plays Hookey. The Bride Wore Boots. California. Crime Doctor's Manhunt. The Dark Corner. Little Miss Big (GB: The Baxter Millions). No Leave, No Love. Rainbow Over Texas. Sensation Hunters. Sioux City Sue. The Trap (GB: Murder at Malibu Beach). Swell Guy. The Virginian. Wake Up and Dream. Without Reservations. The Well-Groomed Bride. 1947: Apache Rose. Blaze of Noon. Bowery Buckaroos. Cynthia (GB: The Rich, Full Life). *Hired Husband. The Lost Moment. Saddle Pals. The Secret Life of Walter Mitty. Ladies' Man. The Devil Thumbs a Ride. Undercover Maisie (GB: Undercover Girl). Heartaches. 1948: April Showers. Carson City Raiders. Family Honeymoon. Fury at Furnace Creek. Good Sam. Marshal of Amarillo. The Night Has a Thousand Eyes. The Noose Hangs High. Joan of Arc. Secret Service Investigator. Sitting Pretty. Sundown at Santa Fe. The Snake Pit. The Strange Mrs Crane. 1949: Big Jack. Holiday in Havana. The Lovable Cheat. Master Minds. Outcasts of the Trail. Down to the Sea in Ships. Scene of the Crime. Song of Surrender. Take One False Step. The Traveling Saleswoman. Side Street. 1950: The Arizona Cowboy. *A Slip and a Miss. *His Baiting Beauty. Harvey. The Jackpot. Mister 880. Quicksand. My Blue Heaven. The Milkman. 1951: *Blonde Atom Bomb. The Great Caruso. Mask of the Avenger. Stop That Cab. Texans Never Cry. *The Awful Sleuth. Dear Brat. The Raging Tide. 1952: Aaron Slick from Punkin Crick (GB: Marshmallow Moon). Harem Girl. Gobs and Gals (GB: Cruising Casanovas). Fearless Fagan. Lost in Alaska. Anything Can Happen. Oklahoma Annie. †Two Gun Marshal. (TV). *Happy Go Wacky. 1953: By the Light of the Silvery Moon. Niagara. She's Back on Broadway. The Woman They Almost Lynched. 1955: A Man Alone. *So You Want to Be a VP. *So You Want to Build a Model Railroad. Miracle in the Rain. Double Jeopardy. Marty. Sudden Danger. 1956: Crashing Las Vegas. Death of a Scoundrel. 1957: Footsteps in the Night. 1960: The Adventures of Huckleberry Finn. 1962: Mr Hobbs Takes a Vacation. 1964: The 7 Faces of Dr Lao. 1965: That Funny Feeling.*

† Shown in cinemas outside US

†† Scenes deleted from final release print

VALK, Frederick
(Fritz Valk) 1901–1956

Imposing, hugely headed, brown-haired Czechoslovakian actor with a mouth like a gaping wound, a menacing figure in British films after his flight from Germany in the late 1930s. A favourite for Nazi roles at the onset of the 1940s, he is best remembered as the sceptical Dr Van Straaten from Ealing's chiller compendium *Dead of Night*. Briefly in international roles in his last years.

1939: Traitor Spy (US: The Torso Murder Mystery). 1940: Neutral Port. Gasbags. Night Train to Munich (US: Night Train). 1941: This Man is Dangerous/The Patient Vanishes. Dangerous Moonlight (US: Suicide Squadron). 1942: The Young Mr Pitt. Thunder Rock. 1944: Hotel Reserve. 1945: Dead of Night. Latin Quarter (US: Frenzy) 1947: Mrs Fitzherbert. 1948: Saraband for Dead Lovers (US: Saraband). 1949: Dear Mr Prohack. 1951: The Magic Box. Outcast of the Islands. 1952: Top Secret (US: Mr Potts Goes to Moscow). 1953: Never Let Me Go. The Flanagan Boy (US: Bad Blonde). Albert RN (US: Break to Freedom). 1954: The Colditz Story. Secret Venture. 1955: I Am a Camera. Double Jeopardy. 1956: Magic Fire. Wicked As They Come (US: Portrait in Smoke). Zarak.

VAN EYCK, Peter
(Götz von Eick) 1911–1969

If there had been a competition for the title 'The Devil's Imp', German-born Van Eyck would almost certainly have won. Very

blond, brown-eyed, square-faced and Teutonic-looking, he went to America in the mid-thirties as a musician, but his features so eminently qualified him for playing Nazis that it was not surprising he broke into Hollywood films in the early forties. In post-war years he was busy in America, Germany and Britain, without ever becoming a star, usually as a cold-eyed, tight-lipped but plausible menace.

1942: †Hitler's Children The Moon is Down. 1943: Edge of Darkness. Action in the North Atlantic. Five Graves to Cairo. 1944: Address Unknown. The Imposter. The Hitler Gang. 1949: Hello, Fräulein. 1950: Opfer des Herzens. Export in Blond. Königskinder. Epilog. Furioso. 1951: The Desert Fox (GB: Rommel – Desert Fox). Die Dritte von rechts. Au coeur de la Casbah. 1953: Alerte au sud. Le salaire de la peur (GB and US: The Wages of Fear). Single-Handed (US: Sailor of the King). Die letzte Etappe. Das unsichtbare Netz. La chair et le diable/Flesh and the Devil. 1954: Night People. The Blue Camellia. Le grand jeu. 1955: A Bullet for Joey. Sophie et le crime (US: The Girl on the Third Floor). Tarzan's Hidden Jungle. Jump into Hell. Confidential Report (US: Mr Arkadin). Der Cornet. 1956: Le feu au poudre. Fric-Frac en dentelles. Attack! The Rawhide Years. Run for the Sun. 1957: Der sechste Mann. Der gläserne Turm/The Glass Tower. Retour de manivelle (GB and US: There's Always a Price-Tag). Tous peuvent me tuer/Anyone Can Kill Me. Dr Crippen Lives. 1958: Lockvogel der Nacht. The Snorkel. The Girl Rosemarie. Schmutziger Engel (GB: Dirty Angel). Du gehörst mir. Schwarze Nylons – heisse Nächte (US: Indecent). 1959: The Rest is Silence. Rommel ruft Kairo. Verbrechen nach Schulschuss (US: The Young Go Wild). Sweetheart of the Gods. Labyrinth. Abschied von den Wolken (GB: Rebel Flight to Cuba). Geheimaktion schwartze Kapelle (GB and US: Black Chapel). 1960: The 1,000 Eyes of Dr Mabuse. Foxhole in Cairo. 1961: Legge di guerra. Die Stunde, die du glücklich bist. La fête espagnole (US: No Time for Ecstasy). On Friday at 11 (US: World in My Pocket). Unter Ausschluss der Öffentlichkeit. 1962: Finden sie, dass Constanze sich richtig verhält? Kriegsgesetz. Vengeance (US: The Brain). The Devil's Agent. The Longest Day. Station Six – Sahara. 1963: Ein Alibi zerbricht. And So to Bed. Scotland Yard jagt Dr Mabuse. Verführung am Meer (GB: Island of Desire. US: Seduction by the

Sea). The River Line. 1964: I misteri della giungla nera (GB: The Mystery of Thug Island. US: Mysteries of the Black Jungle). Kennwort: Reiher. 1965: La guerre secrète (GB and US: The Dirty Game). Duell vor Sonnenuntergang. Die Herren. Spione unter sich. Die Todestrahlen des Dr Mabuse, The Spy Who Came in from the Cold. 1966: Der Chef schickt seinen besten Mann (GB and US: Requiem for a Secret Agent). 1967: Assignment to Kill. Million Dollar Man. Karriere. Sechs Pistolen jagen Professor Z. 1968: Shalako. The Bridge at Remagen. Heidi Comes Home (US: Heidi). 1969: Tevye and His Seven Daughters. Code Name Red Roses.

† As Goetz Van Eyck

VAN FLEET, Jo 1919–

Incisive, fiercely dominant blonde American stage actress of waspishly attractive features who made her name by playing women older than herself. Almost entirely a stage personality, she stopped off in Hollywood just long enough to win an Academy Award for her first screen role — as James Dean's mother (at 35) in *East of Eden*.

1954: East of Eden. 1955: The Rose Tattoo. I'll Cry Tomorrow. Heidi (TV). 1956: The King and Four Queens. Gunfight at the OK Corral. 1958: This Angry Age/The Sea Wall. 1960: Wild River. 1967: Cool Hand Luke. 1968: I Love You, Alice B Toklas. 1969: 80 Steps to Jonah. 1971: The Gang That Couldn't Shoot Straight. 1973: The Family Rico (TV). 1973: Satan's School for Girls (TV). 1976: The Tenant. 1979: Power (TV). 1986: Seize the Day (originally for TV).

VAN SLOAN, Edward 1881–1964

Eagle-nosed, hawk-eyed, fair-haired American actor (once a commercial artist) who came to films with the beginning of sound, and spent much of his time in the cinema as the voice of science and reason, meddling with a motley of monsters and sporting a variety of guttural accents. Retired in 1948. Best remembered for his portrayal of the dogged Van Helsing in the 1930 *Dracula*.

1916: Slander. 1930: Dracula. 1931: Frankenstein. 1932: Play Girl. The Infernal Machine. Man Wanted. Thunder Below. The Last Mile. Manhattan Parade. Billion Dollar

Scandal. Behind the Mask. Forgotten Commandments. The Mummy. The Death Kiss. 1933: Silk Express. Trick for Trick. The Deluge. Infernal Machine. The World Gone Mad (GB: The Public Be Hanged). The Working Man. It's Great to be Alive. 1934: Murder on the Campus (GB: On the Stroke of Nine). Death Takes a Holiday. The Scarlet Empress. Manhattan Melodrama. The Crosby Case (GB: The Crosby Murder Case). The Man Who Reclaimed His Head. The Life of Vergie Winters. I'll Fix It. 1935: The Woman in Red. Grand Old Girl. The Last Days of Pompeii. The Black Room. Mills of the Gods. A Shot in the Dark. Air Hawks. Grand Exit. 1936: The Story of Louis Pasteur. Fatal Lady. Dracula's Daughter. Sins of Man. Road Gang (GB: Injustice). 1937: The Man Who Found Himself. 1938: Danger on the Air. Penitentiary. Storm over Bengal. 1939: The Phantom Creeps (serial). Honeymoon in Bali (GB: Husbands or Lovers). 1940: Abe Lincoln in Illinois (GB: Spirit of the People). The Secret Seven. The Doctor Takes a Wife. Before I Hang. 1941: The Monster and the Girl. Virginia. Love Crazy. 1942: Valley of Hunted Men. A Man's World. 1943: Submarine Alert. Mission to Moscow. Riders of the Rio Grande. End of the Road. The Masked Marvel (serial). Captain America (serial). Hitler's Children. The Song of Bernadette. 1944: The Conspirators. Wing and a Prayer. 1945: I'll Remember April. 1946: The Mask of Diijon. Betty Co-Ed (GB: The Melting Pot). 1948: A Foreign Affair. Sealed Verdict.

VAN ZANDT, Phil(ip) 1904–1958

Squat, burly, florid, dark-haired, moustachioed Dutch actor, much given to fake smiles. He came to America in the late 1920s and had practically lost his accent by the time he started making Hollywood films in 1939. Often a sinister villain, especially in the war years; he played many broad comedy roles, too, several of them in shorts with The Three Stooges. He died from an overdose of barbiturates at 53.

1939: Those High Gray Walls (GB: The Gates of Alcatraz). 1940: The Lady in Question. *Boobs in Arms. 1941: City of Missing Girls. Citizen Kane. Invisible Woman. New York Town. Paris Calling. In Old Colorado. Ride On Vaquero. So Ends Our Night. 1942: All Through the Night. Calling Dr Gillespie. Commandos Strike at Dawn. Desperate Journey. Invisible Agent. Maisie Gets Her Man

(GB: She Gets Her Man). Nazi Agent. The Daring Young Man. Northwest Rangers. Reunion/Reunion in France (GB: Mademoiselle France). Sherlock Holmes and the Secret Weapon. Wake Island. The Hard Way. 1943: Air Raid Wardens. Above Suspicion. Always a Bridesmaid. The Deerslayer. Hangmen Also Die. Hostages. None Shall Escape. Old Acquaintance. Hit Parade of 1943. Tarzan Triumphs. Murder on the Waterfront. A Guy Named Joe. Tarzan's Desert Mystery. 1944: America's Children. The Big Noise. The Black Parachute. Call of the Jungle. The Conspirators. Dragon Seed. The Hitler Gang. Swing Hostess. Shine On, Harvest Moon. The Story of Dr Wassell. Till We Meet Again. The Unwritten Code. House of Frankenstein. 1945: Boston Blackie's Rendezvous (GB: Blackie's Rendezvous). Counter-Attack (GB: One Against Seven). I Love a Bandleader (GB: Memory for Two). Outlaws of the Rockies (GB: A Roving Rogue). Sudan. A Thousand and One Nights. 1946: Below the Deadline. California. Decoy. Don't Gamble With Strangers. The Avalanche. Gilda. Monsieur Beaucaire. A Night in Casablanca. *Pardon My Terror. The Bandit of Sherwood Forest. Joe Palooka, Champ. Somewhere in the Night. Night and Day. 1947: Last Frontier Uprising. Slave Girl. Life With Father. 1948: Alias Nick Beal (GB: The Contact Man). April Showers. Embraceable You. The Big Clock. The Loves of Carmen. The Night Has a Thousand Eyes. The Lady from Shanghai. *Mummy's Dummies. *Squareheads of the Round Table. The Saxon Charm. The Shanghai Chest. The Vicious Circle. Walk a Crooked Mile. The Street With No Name. *Fiddlers Three. 1949: The Blonde Bandit. The Lady Gambles. The Lone Wolf and His Lady. *Fuelin' Around. Red, Hot and Blue. Tension. 1950: Between Midnight and Dawn. Copper Canyon. Cyrano de Bergerac. *Dopey Dicks. The Flame and the Arrow. Indian Territory. The Petty Girl (GB: Girl of the Year). A Lady Without Passport. *One Shivery Night. The Jackpot. Where Danger Lives. 1951: The Desert Fox (GB: Rommel − Desert Fox). Ghost Chasers. His Kind of Woman. *Three Arabian Nuts. Mask of the Avenger. Submarine Command. Two-Dollar Bettor (GB: Beginner's Luck). Target Unknown. Ten Tall Men. 1952: At Sword's Point (GB: Sons of the Musketeers. Completed 1949). The Iron Mistress. Because of You. The Pride of St Louis. Son of Ali Baba. Thief of Damascus. Viva Zapata! Yukon Gold. Macao. 1953: *Love's a-Poppin'. *So You Want to be a Musician. *So You Want a

Television Set. *Spooks. *So You Want to be an Heir. Clipped Wings. Captain John Smith and Pocahontas (GB: Burning Arrows). *Down the Hatch. The Girl Who Had Everything. Prisoners of the Casbah. Ride Vaquero! (and 1941 film of similar title) A Perilous Journey. Two Sailors and a Girl. Knock On Wood. 1954: The Adventures of Hajji Baba. Gog. The High and the Mighty. Three-Ring Circus. Dragon's Gold. Yankee Pasha. Playgirl. *So You Want to Go to a Nightclub. *Musty Musketeers. *Knutzy Knights. *Scotched in Scotland. The Big Combo. 1955: *So You Want to be a Gladiator. *So You Want to be a VP. *Bedlam in Paradise. I Cover the Underworld. Untamed. *G I Dood It. To Catch a Thief. 1956: *Army Daze. *Hot Stuff. Around the World in 80 Days. Our Miss Brooks. Uranium Boom. The Pride and the Passion. 1957: *Outer Space Jitters. The Crooked Circle. The 27th Day. Man of a Thousand Faces. The Lonely Man. Shoot-Out at Medicine Bend. 1958: *Fifi Blows Her Top.

VARCONI, Victor

(Mihaly Varkonyi) 1891−1976
Brown-haired, smoothly handsome Hungarian matinée idol of silent days in Hungary, Germany and then Hollywood. With the coming of sound, his lips tightened and he took on a more sinister look as suave continentals who often proved to be on the other side of the fence from that they first pretended. Died from a heart attack.

1913: Sarga csiko/The Yellow Colt. Marta. 1914: Bank bán. Tetemrahivas. 1915: Talkoas. A tanitono. Havasi Magdolna. 1916: Baccarat. Hotel Imperial. A riporter kiraly. Magia. 1918: Szent Peter esernyoje. Sapho. A skorpio. '99'. Varazskeringo. 1919: Jenseits von Gott und Rose. 1921: Die sonne Asiens. 1922: Herrin der Meere. Eine versunkene Welt (Herrin der Meere II). Sodom und Gomorra. 1924: The Dancers. Poisoned Paradise. Changing Husbands. Triumph. Feet of Clay. Worldly Goods. 1925: L'uomo più allegro di Vienna. 1926: Die Warshauer Zitadelle. The Last Days of Pompeii. The Volga Boatman. For Wives Only. Silken Shackles. 1927: The King of Kings. The Angel of Broadway. Fighting Love. The Forbidden Woman. Chicago. The Little Adventuress. 1928: Sinners' Parade. Tenth Avenue (GB: Hell's Kitchen). 1929: The Divine Lady. Eternal Love. Kult ciala. 1930: Captain Thunder.

1931: Doctors' Wives. Safe in Hell. Men in Her Life. The Black Camel. 1932: The Doomed Battalion. The Rebel (and German version). 1933: The Song You Gave Me. 1935: A Feather in Her Hat. Mister Dynamite. Roberta. 1936: Dancing Pirate. The Plainsman. 1937: Trouble in Morocco. Big City. Men in Exile. 1938: King of the Newsboys. Suez. Submarine Patrol. 1939: Mr Moto Takes a Vacation. The Story of Vernon and Irene Castle. Disputed Passage. Everything Happens at Night. 1940: The Sea Hawk. *Pound Foolish. Strange Cargo. 1941: Federal Fugitives. Forced Landing. 1942: My Favorite Blonde. Reap the Wild Wind. They Raid by Night. 1943: For Whom the Bell Tolls. 1944: The Story of Dr Wassell. The Hitler Gang. 1945: Scotland Yard Investigator. 1947: Unconquered. Where There's Life. Pirates of Monterey. 1949: Samson and Delilah. 1950: Once a Gentleman (TV). 1951: My Favorite Spy. 1953: The Roman Kid (TV). 1957: The Man Who Turned to Stone. 1959: Atomic Submarine.

VARDEN, Norma 1898−1989
Tall, dignified, blonde British actress, attractive in a supercilious, look-down-her-nose kind of way, who began her career as a concert pianist. She became a butt for the gags of the Aldwych farceurs on stage, much as Margaret Dumont with the Marx Brothers, and moved with them into films in 1932. She went to Hollywood in 1939 and played largely sniffy aristocrats there until her retirement at 70. Died from heart failure.

1932: A Night Like This. 1933: Turkey Time. Happy. 1934: Evergreen. The Iron Duke. 1935: The Student's Romance. Foreign Affaires. Boys Will Be Boys. Music Hath Charms. Stormy Weather. Get Off My Foot. 1936: East Meets West. The Amazing Quest of Ernest Bliss (US: Rags to Riches). Where There's a Will. Fire Over England. Windbag the Sailor. 1937: The Lilac Domino. Wanted! The Strange Adventures of Mr Smith. Make Up. Rhythm Racketeer. 1938: You're the Doctor. Everything Happens to Me. Fools for Scandal. 1939: Home from Home. Shipyard Sally. 1940: Waterloo Bridge. The Earl of Chicago. 1941: The Mad Doctor (GB: A Date With Destiny). Glamour Boy (GB: Hearts in Springtime). Road to Zanzibar. Scotland Yard. 1942: Random Harvest. Flying With Music. The Glass Key. The Major and the Minor. We Were Dancing. Casablanca. 1943:

Dixie. The Good Fellows. My Kingdom for a Cook. Sherlock Holmes Faces Death. Slightly Dangerous. What a Woman! (GB: The Beautiful Cheat). 1944: Mademoiselle Fifi. National Velvet. The White Cliffs of Dover. 1945: Bring On the Girls. Hold That Blonde. The Cheaters. Girls of the Big House. Those Endearing Young Charms. The Trouble With Women (released 1947). 1946: The Searching Wind. The Green Years. 1947: Forever Amber. Ivy. Millie's Daughter. The Senator Was Indiscreet (GB: Mr Ashton Was Indiscreet). Thunder in the Valley (GB: Bob, Son of Battle). Where There's Life. 1948: The Amazing Mr X (GB: The Spiritualist). Let's Live a Little. My Own True Love. Hollow Triumph (GB: The Scar). 1949: Adventure in Baltimore (GB: Bachelor Bait). The Secret Garden. 1950: Fancy Pants. All About Eve. 1951: Strangers on a Train. Thunder on the Hill (GB: Bonaventure). 1952: Les Miserables. Something to Live For. Washington Story (GB: Target for Scandal). 1953: Loose in London. Elephant Walk. Gentlemen Prefer Blondes. Young Bess. 1954: The Silver Chalice. Three Coins in the Fountain. Superman and Scotland Yard (TV. GB: cinemas). 1955: Jupiter's Darling. 1956: The Birds and the Bees. 1957: Witness for the Prosecution. 1958: The Buccaneer. In the Money. 1962: Rome Adventure (GB: Lovers Must Learn). Island of Love. Five Minutes to Live. 1963: 13 Frightened Girls! Kisses for My President. 1965: A Very Special Favor. The Sound of Music. 1966: Door-to-Door Maniac. 1967: Doctor Dolittle. 1968: Istanbul Express (TV. GB: cinemas). The Impossible Years.

Inspector Hornleigh on Holiday (US: Inspector Hornleigh on Leave). 1941: Kipps (US: The Remarkable Mr Kipps). South American George. *Rush Hour. Hatter's Castle. 1942: Secret Mission. Talk About Jacqueline. Squadron Leader X. 1943: Millions Like Us. We Dive at Dawn. The Bells Go Down. The Man in Grey. *There's a Future in It. I'll Walk Beside You. Welcome to Britain. 1944: Bees in Paradise. Welcome Mr Washington. Love Story (US: A Lady Surrenders). *Victory Wedding. Waterloo Road. 1945: The Wicked Lady. The Agitator. The Seventh Veil. Great Day. Johnny Frenchman. 1946: Send for Paul Temple. Bedelia. 1947: The Upturned Glass. So Well Remembered. Jassy. Holiday Camp. The Little Ballerina. Master of Bankdam. My Brother Jonathan. 1948: No Room at the Inn. Good Time Girl. My Brother's Keeper. *The Marshall Plan. 1949: Marry Me! Adam and Evelyne (US: Adam and Evalyn). 1950: Paul Temple's Triumph. She Shall Have Murder. Gone to Earth (US: revised version: The Wild Heart). 1951: Out of True. 1952: Hindle Wakes (US: Holiday Week). 1953: Melba. Death Goes to School. 1954: Bang! You're Dead (US: Game of Danger). The Black Rider. 1955: Jumping for Joy. 1956: The Feminine Touch (US: The Gentle Touch). Tiger in the Smoke. The Good Companions. 1957: Sea Wife. Hell Drivers. The Surgeon's Knife. 1958: Room at the Top. Bachelor of Hearts. 1959: The Rough and the Smooth (US: Portrait of a Sinner). Horrors of the Black Museum. 1960: *Identity Unknown. 1961: Echo of Barbara. 1962: Night Without Pity.

Agent. 1963: The Horse Without a Head. The Victors. 1964: Smokescreen. 1965: Fanatic (US: Die, Die, My Darling). Rotten to the Core. 1967: The Man Outside. The Naked Runner. A Twist of Sand. 1968: The Bofors Gun. Hammerhead. 1969: Taste of Excitement. Alfred the Great. 1970: Eyewitness (US: Sudden Terror). 1971: Straw Dogs. The Pied Piper. 1972: Savage Messiah. Madigan: The Lisbon Beat (TV). 1973: The Mackintosh Man. *The Return. The Blockhouse. Massacre in Rome. The Seaweed Children/Malachi's Cove. 1974: Symptoms. 11 Harrowhouse. 1975: Intimate Reflections. 1976: Queen of Diamonds. 1977: Valentino. 1979: Porridge. Zulu Dawn. 1981: Time Bandits. The French Lieutenant's Woman. The Missionary. 1982: Coming Out of the Ice. 1984: The Razor's Edge. Forbidden. 1986: Haunted Honeymoon. Monte Carlo (TV). Coast to Coast (TV). 1988: The Bourne Alternative (TV). 1989: Mountains of the Moon. King of the Wind. 1991: Prisoners of Honor. 1993: The Remains of the Day. 1994: Heart of Darkness (TV). Oliver's Travels (TV). Fatherland (TV).

VENESS, Amy 1876–1960
Fair-haired, pleasantly plump British actress with rosy cheeks and beaming face. Her housekeepers were always well-scrubbed and usually ready with a cheery word of advice. She was middle-aged when she came to sound film roles; but stayed for 25 years, having begun her long stage career in the chorus of a George Edwardes musical show in the 1890s.

1919: The Brat. 1931: Murder on the Second Floor. My Wife's Family. Hobson's Choice. Money for Nothing. 1932: Pyjamas Preferred. The Marriage Bond. Flat No. 9. Let Me Explain, Dear. Self-Made Lady. Tonight's the Night. 1933: Hawleys of High Street. Their Night Out. A Southern Maid. The Love Nest. Red Wagon. 1934: The Old Curiosity Shop. Brewster's Millions. Lorna Doone. 1935: Play Up the Band. Royal Cavalcade (US: Regal Cavalcade). Drake of England (US: Drake the Pirate). Joy Ride. Did I Betray? 1936: King of Hearts. The Beloved Vagabond. Windbag the Sailor. Skylarks. The Mill on the Floss. Aren't Men Beasts! Crime Over London. 1937: Who Killed Fen Markham?/The Angelus. The Show Goes On. 1938: Thistledown. Yellow Sands. 1939: Just William. Flying Fifty-five. 1940:

VARLEY, Beatrice 1896–1969
Careworn-looking, grey-eyed, brown-haired British actress whose low eyebrows, down-turned mouth and narrow, wrinkled forehead consigned her for years to downtrodden women who, one felt, had perhaps come from slightly better stock than those who ill-treated them. Also played maids, housekeepers and glum aunts and was certainly memorable in one film, Hatter's Castle, as the cancer and husband-ridden Mrs Brodie, a role that set the pattern for her career.

1936: Tomorrow We Live. 1937: Oh, Mr Porter! Spring Handicap. Young and Innocent (US: The Girl Was Young). 1939: Poison Pen.

VAUGHAN, Peter (P. Ohm) 1923–
Heavily jawed British actor of massive menace with very thin lips and small eyes set deep inside a large head topped by close-cropped brown hair. A useful leading actor in his younger days, he was quite busily employed by the British cinema until the mid 1970s, when he became the powerful leading figure in some successful television series. Still around in elderly seedy cameos. He was formerly married to the actress Billie Whitelaw.

1959: The 39 Steps. Sapphire. Follow That Horse! 1960: Make Mine Mink. Village of the Damned. 1961: Two Living, One Dead. The Court Martial of Major Keller. 1962: I Thank a Fool. The Punch and Judy Man. The Devil's

John Smith Wakes Up. 1941: This England. The Saint Meets the Tiger. 1943: Millions Like Us. The Silver Fleet. The Man in Grey. 1944: Fanny by Gaslight (US: Man of Evil). Madonna of the Seven Moons. This Happy Breed. Don't Take It to Heart. The World Owes Me a Living. 1945: Don Chicago. They Were Sisters. 1946: Carnival. 1947: Master of Bankdam. The Turners of Prospect Road. The Woman in the Hall. Blanche Fury. 1948: Bond Street. My Brother's Keeper. Good Time Girl. Oliver Twist. Here Come the Huggetts. A Boy, a Girl and a Bike. Vote for Huggett. 1949: Madeleine. The Huggetts Abroad. 1950: The Woman With No Name (US: Her Paneled Door). Chance of a Lifetime. The Astonished Heart. Portrait of Clare. Tom Brown's Schooldays. 1951: The Magic Box. Captain Horatio Hornblower RN (US: Captain Horatio Hornblower). Angels One Five. 1954: Doctor in the House. 1955: The Woman for Joe.

VERNO, Jerry 1895–1975
Chirpy British cockney, slightly built, who moved from music-hall comedian to minor leading roles in early low-budget British comedy-musicals, then settled down as a 'second banana' through the 1930s. His film career became distinctly spotty after 1940, although he continued to be busy in the theatre, appearing in pantomimes, musicals and straight drama, ending on the New York stage in the mid-1960s. Also well-known as the voice of 'Shorty' in the long-running (1941–52) radio series Taxi. Began his career as a boy singer in 1907.

1931: Two Crowded Hours. My Friend the King. The Beggar Student. 1932: Hotel Splendide. His Lordship. His Wife's Mother. There Goes the Bride. 1934: The Life of the Party. 1935: Lieutenant Daring RN. The 39 Steps. Royal Cavalcade (US: Regal Cavalcade). 1936: Ourselves Alone. Broken Blossoms. Gypsy Melody. Pagliacci. Sweeney Todd the Demon Barber of Fleet Street. Annie Laurie. Sensation! 1937: Farewell Again (US: Troopship). River of Unrest. Non-Stop New York. Young and Innocent (US: The Girl Was Young). 1938: Queer Cargo (US: Pirates of the Seven Seas). Oh, Boy! The Gables Mystery. Mountains o' Mourne. Old Mother Riley in Paris. Anything to Declare? Just Like a Woman. St Martin's Lane (US: Sidewalks of London). *Take Cover. 1939: A Girl Must Live. The Chinese

Bungalow. 1940: The Girl in the News. 1941: The Common Touch. 1945: Bothered by a Beard. 1948: My Brother's Keeper. The Red Shoes. 1949: Dear Mr Prohack. The Perfect Woman. 1954: The Belles of St Trinian's. 1957: After the Ball. 1961: Watch It, Sailor! 1963: A Place to Go. 1966: The Plague of the Zombies.

VERNON, John 1932–
Heavy-headed, light-eyed, soft-voiced Canadian actor, who has played a rare old melange of movie roles since he provided the voice of Big Brother in the original 1984 soon after completing his studies at RADA in London. He has combined prestigious Italian, Yugoslav and Canadian films with chores for Hitchcock, Don Siegel and Clint Eastwood and a considerable slice of Hollywood rubbish. Despite his good looks, films have often seen him as a frazzle-nerved villain; he has also adapted a slightly over-the-top style easily to comedy.

1956: 1984 (voice only). 1964: Nobody Waved Goodbye. 1967: Point Blank. 1969: Trial Run (TV). Justine. Tell Them Willie Boy is Here. Topaz. 1971: Escape (TV). One More Train to Rob. Dirty Harry. 1972: Journey. Cool Million (TV). Fear is the Key. 1973: Charley Varrick. 'W'. Hunter (TV). 1974: The Questor Tapes (TV). The Virginia Hill Story (TV). Sweet Movie. Mousey (TV. GB: cinemas, as Cat and Mouse). The Black Windmill. 1975: Angela (released 1978). Brannigan. The Imposter (TV). The Swiss Family Robinson (TV). Barbary Coast (TV). Matt Helm (TV). 1976: The Outlaw Josey Wales. 1977: The Uncanny. Golden Rendezvous. Una giornata particolare (GB and US: A Special Day). Mary Jane Harper Cried Last Night (TV). 1978: National Lampoon's Animal House. 1979: It Rained All Night the Day I Left. The Sacketts (TV). Crunch (completed 1975). 1980: Fantastica. Herbie Goes Bananas. 1981: Heavy Metal (voice only). Kinky Coaches and the Pom Pom Pussy-cats. 1982: Curtains. Airplane II The Sequel. 1983: Chained Heat. 1984: Angela (completed 1977). Savage Streets. Jungle Warriors. Le sang des autres (TV). 1985: Fraternity Vacation. Doin' Time. 1987: Blue Monkey. Night Stick/ Calhoun. Ernest Goes to Camp. Double Exposure. Dixie Lanes. 1988: Deadly Stranger. Border Heat. Killer Klowns from Outer Space. War of the Worlds (TV). 1989: Mob Story. B-Men (TV). War Bus Commando. Bail Out.

I'm Gonna Git You, Sucka! 1990: Terminal Exposure. Object of Desire. 1992: The Naked Truth. Wojeck: Out of the Fire (TV). 1993: Cockroach Hotel. Sodbusters. 1994: Hostage for a Day. Class Act. 1995: Malicious.

VERNON, Richard 1925–
Tall, distinguished-looking, husky-voiced, moustachioed British actor of somewhat shambling gait and harassed air, often seen as magistrates, officers or (faintly seedy) aristocrats. Films have generally taken second place to his successes on television (especially the series Upstairs, Downstairs, Edward the Seventh and The Duchess of Duke Street) and in the theatre. Has always tended to look somewhat older than his years.

1936: Conquest of the Air (released 1940). 1949: Stop Press Girl. 1958: Indiscreet. 1959: SOS Pacific. The Navy Lark. The Siege of Pinchgut (US: Four Desperate Men). Sapphire. 1960: Village of the Damned. Clue of the Twisted Candle. Foxhole in Cairo. 1962: We Joined the Navy! The Share-Out. Reach for Glory. Cash on Demand. 1963: The Servant. Hot Enough for June (US: Agent 8¾). Accidental Death. Just for Fun. 1964: The Yellow Rolls Royce. Goldfinger. A Hard Day's Night. Allez France! (US: The Counterfeit Constable). The Tomb of Ligeia. 1965: The Intelligence Men. The Secret of My Success. The Early Bird. 1969: One Brief Summer. Destiny of a Spy/ The Gaunt Woman (TV). Goodbye Mr Chips. 1970: Song of Norway. 1971: She'll Follow You Anywhere. 1973: The Satanic Rites of Dracula. 1976: The Pink Panther Strikes Again. 1978: Sammy's Super T-Shirt. 1979: The Human Factor. 1980: Oh Heavenly Dog. 1981: Evil Under the Sun. 1982: La Traviata (voice only). Witness for the Prosecution (TV). Gandhi. 1985: Lady Jane. Paradise Postponed. 1987: A Month in the Country. 1992: A Masculine Ending (TV).

VICTOR, Charles
(C.V. Harvey) 1896–1965
Stubby, brown-haired British actor with crooked eyebrows, plum nose and battered, homely features; even his smile held a hint of a scowl. So it's surprising to find that this portrayer of down-to-earth Londoners was a dancer in his early days (1917–1929) before turning to straight dramatic acting.

From the early 1950s he supplemented his cinematic gallery with numerous stage portraits of Alfred Doolittle in *Pygmalion* and *My Fair Lady* and then took several minor leading character roles in films in the Eliot Makeham/Edmund Gwenn tradition of downtrodden little men seeking their own salvation. Also perfectly cast as the grumbling Inspector Teal in *The Saint's Return*. Hollywood credits from *Motor Patrol* (1950) to *40 Pounds of Trouble* (1962) would seem to belong to an American player of the same name.

1935: *The 39 Steps. Me and Marlborough.* 1936: *Conquest of the Air* (released 1940). *Where There's a Will. Windbag the Sailor.* 1937: *The Academy Decides. Song of the Road.* 1938: *Stepping Toes.* 1939: *Hell's Cargo* (US: *Dangerous Cargo*). *Laugh It Off. Where's That Fire? Dr O'Dowd.* 1940: *Contraband* (US: *Blackout*). *Old Mother Riley in Society. You Will Remember. East of Piccadilly* (US: *The Strangler*). *Old Mother Riley in Business.* 1941: *Major Barbara. The Prime Minister. 49th Parallel* (US: *The Invaders*). *Love on the Dole. Ships With Wings.* *Rush Hour. The Common Touch. This England. Atlantic Ferry* (US: *Sons of the Sea*). *He Found a Star. The Saint Meets the Tiger.* *You're Telling Me. Love on the Dole. Breach of Promise* (US: *Adventure in Blackmail*). *They Flew Alone* (US: *Wings and the Woman*). 1942: *Seven Days' Leave. Those Kids from Town. The Missing Million. The Foreman Went to France. The Peterville Diamond. Lady from Lisbon. Squadron Leader X.* 1943: *Undercover* (US: *Underground Guerrillas*). *The Silver Fleet. When We Are Married. Escape to Danger. Rhythm Serenade. My Learned Friend. The Shipbuilders. They Met in the Dark. San Demetrio, London. The Bells Go Down.* 1944: *Soldier, Sailor. It Happened One Sunday.* 1945: *The Man from Morocco. The Way to the Stars* (US: *Johnny in the Clouds*). *I Live in Grosvenor Square* (US: *A Yank in London*). *Caesar and Cleopatra. The Rake's Progress* (US: *Notorious Gentleman*). 1946: *Woman to Woman. Gaiety George* (US: *Showtime*). *While the Sun Shines. This Man is Mine! The Magic Bow. Meet Me at Dawn.* 1947: *While I Live. Green Fingers. Broken Journey. Temptation Harbour.* 1948: *The Calendar. Vote for Huggett. Fools Rush In.* 1949: *Landfall. The Cure for Love.* 1950: *Waterfront* (US: *Waterfront Women*). *The Elusive Pimpernel* (US:

The Fighting Pimpernel). *The Woman in Question* (US: *Five Angles on Murder*). 1951: *The Magic Box. Calling Bulldog Drummond. The Galloping Major. Encore.* 1952: *Something Money Can't Buy. Made in Heaven. The Frightened Man. The Ringer. Appointment in London. Those People Next Door.* 1953: *Street Corner* (US: *Both Sides of the Law*). *The Girl on the Pier. Meet Mr Lucifer. The Love Lottery. The Saint's Return* (US: *The Saint's Girl Friday*). 1954: *Fast and Loose. The Rainbow Jacket. For Better, For Worse* (US: *Cocktails in the Kitchen*). *The Embezzler.* 1955: *Police Dog. Value for Money. An Alligator Named Daisy. Dial 999* (US: *The Way Out*). *Now and Forever.* 1956: *The Extra Day. Charley Moon. Eyewitness. Tiger in the Smoke. Home and Away. The Prince and the Showgirl.* 1957: *There's Always a Thursday. After the Ball.* 1966: *The Wrong Box.*

VIGRAN, Herb (or Herbert) 1910–
Jolly, round-faced, beetle-browed American actor from Indiana, with receding dark hair and non-existent top lip. After heading for Hollywood straight from university, he got a role as a radio operator in *Happy Landing* (1934) and, perhaps inspired, switched to radio where his became a familiar voice before he returned to films in 1940, and has been scrambling for screen space ever since, as benign bartenders, perplexed policemen and hearty colleagues. Perhaps best remembered as the all-too-affable mobile home salesman who sold Lucille Ball and Desi Arnaz *The Long, Long Trailer*, he has enhanced his income considerably in more recent times with work for TV commercials, both before the camera and with voiceovers. Not surprising work for one of filmland's fastest talkers.

1934: *Happy Landing* (GB: *The Air Patrol*). *The Morning After.* 1935: *Vagabond Lady.* 1936: *Death from a Distance.* 1940: *Stranger on the Third Floor. Cross-Country Romance. It All Came True.* 1941: *Murder by Invitation. Million Dollar Baby. Reg'lar Fellers.* *Who's a Dummy?* 1942: *Pardon My Sarong. The Great Gildersleeve. Secrets of a Co-Ed* (GB: *Silent Witness*). *Rings on Her Fingers. Secret Enemies. Secrets of the Underground.* 1943: *Dr Gillespie's Criminal Case* (GB: *Crazy to Kill*). *It Ain't Hay* (GB: *Money for Jam*). *Ghost Ship. Sweet Rosie O'Grady.* 1945: *Her Adventurous Night.*

1946: *Joe Palooka, Champ. One Exciting Week.* 1947: *Monsieur Verdoux. Joe Palooka in The Knockout.* 1948: *All My Sons. Hazard. Joe Palooka in Fighting Mad. Joe Palooka in Winner Take All* (GB: *Winner Take All*). *The Noose Hangs High. Texas, Brooklyn and Heaven* (GB: *The Girl from Texas*). *The Judge* (GB: *The Gamblers*) 1949: *Side Street. House of Strangers. Tell It to the Judge.* 1950: *And Baby Makes Three. Mister 880. Let's Dance. Mrs O'Malley and Mr Malone.* 1951: *Bedtime for Bonzo. The Racket. Half Angel. Night into Morning. Iron Man. Three Guys Named Mike. Abbott and Costello Meet the Invisible Man.* 1952: *Just for You. Just Across the Street. Somebody Loves Me. The Rose Bowl Story. Oklahoma Annie.* 1953: *The Band Wagon. Let's Do It Again. Susan Slept Here. The Girl Next Door.* 1954: *The Long, Long Trailer. Lucky Me. Dragnet. White Christmas.* *So You're Taking in a Roomer. 20,000 Leagues Under the Sea.* 1955: *Good Morning, Miss Dove. I Died a Thousand Times. Illegal. Not As a Stranger. Last of the Desperados. Hell on Frisco Bay.* 1956: *Calling Homicide. A Cry in the Night. Our Miss Brooks. That Certain Feeling. These Wilder Years. You Can't Run Away from It. Three for Jamie Dawn.* 1957: *Gunsight Ridge. The Midnight Story* (GB: *Appointment With a Shadow*) *Public Pigeon Number One. The Vampire. A Hatful of Rain.* 1958: *The Plunderers of Painted Flats. The Case Against Brooklyn.* 1959: *Go, Johnny, Go!* 1961: *The Errand Boy.* 1962: *Period of Adjustment.* 1964: *The Brass Bottle. The Candidate. Send Me No Flowers. The Unsinkable Molly Brown.* 1965: *That Funny Feeling.* 1967: *Blackbeard's Ghost.* 1968: *Did You Hear the One About the Traveling Saleslady? Support Your Local Sheriff!* 1970: *Which Way to the Front?* (GB: *Ja! Ja! Mein General! But Which Way to the Front?*). *The Barefoot Executive.* 1971: *Vanished* (TV). *Support Your Local Gunfighter. Emergency!* (TV). 1972: *Cancel My Reservation.* 1973: *Charlotte's Web* (voice only). *Herbie Rides Again. Chase* (TV). 1974: *How to Seduce a Woman. Benji. Murph the Surf* (GB: *Live a Little, Steal a Lot*). 1975: *Babe* (TV). 1976: *Hawmps. The Loneliest Runner* (TV). *The Shaggy DA.* 1977: *Testimony of Two Men* (TV). *Kill Me If You Can* (TV). 1981: *First Monday in October.* 1982: *I Was a Mail Order Bride* (TV).

VILLIERS, James 1930–
Tall, dark, long-nosed, full-lipped, snootylooking British actor with plummy uppercrust voice, long typecast in sardonic, snobby, arrogant or obnoxious role, since a West End debut in his early twenties in a stage production of *Toad of Toad Hall*. The theatre has remained his most gainful employer, despite a cluster of film roles in the 1960s. Villiers also plays villains, both sinister and slightly comic and began to move into a more interesting range of characters after reaching early middle age.

1954: *Late Night Final.* 1958: *Carry On Sergeant.* 1960: *The Entertainer.* 1961: *Clue of the New Pin. The Damned* (US: *These Are the Damned*). *Petticoat Pirates.* 1962: *Operation Snatch. Eva* (GB: *Eve*). 1963: *Bomb in the High Street* (first registered 1961). *Murder*

at the Gallop. Nothing But the Best. Father Came Too. Girl in the Headlines (US: The Model Murder Case). 1964: King and Country. Daylight Robbery. 1965: The Alphabet Murders/The ABC Murders. Repulsion. You Must Be Joking! The Nanny. 1966: The Wrong Box. 1967: Half a Sixpence. 1968: Otley. The Touchables. 1969: A Nice Girl Like Me. Some Girls Do. 1970: Blood from the Mummy's Tomb. 1971: Follow Me (US: The Public Eye). The Ruling Class. 1972: The Amazing Mr Blunden. Asylum. 1973: Ghost in the Noonday Sun (unreleased). 1975: The Double Kill (TV). 1976: Joseph Andrews. Seven Nights in Japan. 1977: Spectre (TV). 1979: The Music Machine. Saint Jack. 1981: For Your Eyes Only. 1982: The Scarlet Pimpernel (TV). 1983: Mantrap. 1984: Under the Volcano. Honour, Profit and Pleasure. 1988: Scandal. 1989: Mountains of the Moon. 1990: King Ralph. 1991. 'Let Him Have It'. 1995: E=MC².

Man. Jewel Robbery. Two Against the World. The Crash. I Am a Fugitive from a Chain Gang. Second-Hand Wife (GB: The Illegal Divorce). 1933: As Husbands Go. The Power and the Glory. Midnight Club. Little Giant. Grand Slam. The Kennel Murder Case. 1934: The Gift of Gab. Broadway Bill (GB: Strictly Confidential). Let's Try Again. The Life of Vergie Winters. The Captain Hates the Sea. 1935: The Wedding Night. A Notorious Gentleman. Private Worlds. Age of Indiscretion. The Tunnel (US: Transatlantic Tunnel). King of the Damned. 1936: Love in Exile. Reunion (GB: Hearts in Reunion). 1937: Vogues of 1938. Live, Love and Learn. 1939: In Name Only. 1940: The Bowery Boy. Curtain Call. Enemy Agent (GB: Secret Enemy). Married and in Love. Torrid Zone. Beyond Tomorrow. 1941: Nothing But the Truth. 1944: Chip Off the Old Block. The Lady and the Monster. The Thin Man Goes Home. Are These Our Parents? (GB: They Are Guilty).

and *Mystery Train*, both films for director Jim Jarmusch, and his unsettling demeanour has led filmmakers to keep calling on his services between singing and composing assignments. Not to be confused with actor Tom (sometimes Thomas G) Waites, who has also made appearances in films, including *On the Yard* and *Blue Jean Cop*.

1978: Paradise Alley. 1982: Poetry in Motion. 1983: The Outsiders. Rumble Fish. 1984: The Cotton Club. 1986: Down by Law. 1987: Candy Mountain. Ironweed. 1988: Big Time. 1989: Cold Feet. Bearskin: An Urban Fairytale. Mystery Train (voice only). 1990: The Two Jakes. 1991: Queens Logic. The Fisher King. At Play in the Fields of the Lord. 1992: Deadfall. 1993: Bram Stoker's Dracula. Short Cuts. 1994: Luck, Trust & Ketchup.

WAKEFIELD, Hugh 1888–1971
Light-haired, moustachioed, tall, dandified British actor, often in monocled, aristocratic or regal roles. He began on stage as a boy actor of 10 and continued his career unbroken in the theatre and cinema until his retirement in 1954. Films saw the most of him in the 1930s, when he played character leads and roguish rakes in some light-hearted entertainments.

1930: City of Song (US: Farewell to Love). 1931: The Sport of Kings. The Man They Could Not Arrest. 1932: Aren't We All? Life Goes On. Women Who Play. 1933: The Crime at Blossom's. King of the Ritz. The Fortunate Fool. 1934: Luck of a Sailor. My Heart Is Calling. Lady in Danger. The Man Who Knew Too Much. 1935: Marry the Girl. 18 Minutes. No Monkey Business. Runaway Ladies. 1936: The Improper Duchess. The Crimson Circle. Forget-Me-Not (US: Forever Yours). The Interrupted Honeymoon. It's You I Want. The Limping Man. Dreams Come True. 1937: The Live Wire. The Street Singer. Death Croons the Blues. 1938: Make It Three. 1945: Journey Together. Blithe Spirit. 1948: One Night With You. 1951: No Highway (US: No Highway in the Sky). 1952: Love's a Luxury (US: The Caretaker's Daughter). 1953: The Million Pound Note (US: Man With a Million).

VINSON, Helen (H. Rulfs) 1907–
Tall, attractive American actress with fluffy blonde hair, mean lips and long, pencilled eyebrows. In Hollywood from 1932, she quickly became the 'other woman' *par excellence*, although she fought against the typecasting and in the mid-1930s went to Britain in search of a wider range of leading roles. She left films in the post-war years to concentrate on a stage career. Briefly (second of three husbands) married to British tennis star Fred Perry in 1935.

*1930: *A Sure Cure. It's a Deal. 1932: They Call It Sin (GB: The Way of Life). Lawyer*

WAITS, Tom 1949–
Tall, thin, horse-faced, small-nosed, croaky-voiced American singer and songwriter with brown, wavy hair whose slightly disreputable persona has led him into film roles playing flaky, often down-at-heel, sometimes violent types: the human insect you'd least like to find under that stone. Waits proved himself a fascinating black comedy player in such films as *Down by Law*

WALBURN, Raymond 1887–1969
Round-faced, brown-haired, moustachioed, pop-eyed American actor, a favourite comic

character star of the 1930s and 1940s, often seen as phony military types and jovial confidence tricksters, and constantly surprised at the pricking of his own pomposity or bogusness. Excelled in the low-budget 'Henry' comedies of the late 1940s and early 1950s. A most likeable rogue.

1916: *The Scarlet Runner* (serial). 1929: *The Laughing Lady*. 1934: *Lady by Choice. The Great Flirtation. Broadway Bill* (GB: *Strictly Confidential*). *The Defense Rests. Jealousy. The Count of Monte Cristo.* 1935: *Mills of the Gods. Thanks a Million. It's a Small World. She Married Her Boss. Society Doctor. Death Flies East. I'll Love You Always. Welcome Home. Redheads on Parade.* 1936: *The Lone Wolf Returns. The Great Ziegfeld. They Met in a Taxi. The King Steps Out. Craig's Wife. Mr Deeds Goes to Town. Absolute Quiet. Three Wise Guys. Mr Cinderella. Born to Dance.* 1937: *High, Wide and Handsome. Breezing Home. Thin Ice* (GB: *Lovely to Look At*). *Murder in Greenwich Village. Let's Get Married. It Can't Last Forever. Broadway Melody of 1938.* 1938: *The Battle of Broadway. Sweethearts. Professor Beware! Gateway. Start Cheering. The Under-Pup. Let Freedom Ring. It Could Happen to You. Heaven With a Barbed-Wire Fence. Eternally Yours.* 1940: *Flowing Gold. Dark Command. Christmas in July. San Francisco Docks. Millionaires in Prison. Third Finger, Left Hand.* 1941: *Bachelor Daddy. Kiss the Boys Goodbye. Rise and Shine. Louisiana Purchase. Puddin' Head* (GB: *Judy Goes to Town*). *Confirm or Deny.* 1942: *The Man in the Trunk.* 1943: *Let's Face It. Dixie. Lady Bodyguard. The Desperadoes. Dixie Dugan.* 1944: *Heavenly Days. And the Angels Sing. Music in Manhattan. Hail the Conquering Hero.* 1945: *I'll Tell the World. The Cheaters. Honeymoon Ahead.* 1946: *Breakfast in Hollywood* (GB: *The Mad Hatter*). *Rendezvous With Annie. The Plainsman and the Lady. Lover Come Back. The Affairs of Geraldine. The Sin of Harold Diddlebock* (later and GB: *Mad Wednesday*). 1948: *State of the Union* (GB: *The World and His Wife*). 1949: *Leave It to Henry. Red, Hot and Blue. Riding High. Henry the Rainmaker.* 1950: *Key to the City. Father Makes Good. Short Grass. Father's Wild Game.* 1951: *Excuse My Dust. Father Takes the Air. Golden Girl.* 1953: *She Couldn't Say No* (GB: *Beautiful But Dangerous*). 1955: *The Spoilers.*

WALSH, J.T. 1947–

Full-faced, brown-haired, well-scrubbed, sarcastic-looking American actor with untrustworthy smile. He often plays pushy figures of authority with feet of clay. Born in San Francisco, but raised in Europe, Walsh threw up a sales career at 30 to start acting with an off-Broadway theatre company. One of Hollywood's busiest and most familiar character players from the late 1980s on, often in top featured roles, his parts as straight arrows can be counted on the fingers of one hand, and treachery and double-dealing have remained his stocks-in-trade.

1981: *Little Gloria – Happy at Last* (TV). *Today's FBI* (TV). 1983: *Eddie Macon's Run. Jacobo Timmerman/Prisoner Without a Name – Cell Without a Number* (TV). 1984: *Hard Choices* (released 1986). 1985: *On the Edge. Right to Kill?* (TV). *Power.* 1986: *Hannah and Her Sisters.* 1987: *Tin Men. Good Morning, Vietnam. House of Games.* 1988: *Things Change. Tequila Sunrise. The Big Picture.* 1989: *Dad. Un plan d'enfer. Why Me? Defenseless* (released 1991). *Wired.* 1990: *Crazy People. The Grifters. Misery. Narrow Margin. The Russia House.* 1991: *Backdraft. Iron Maze. True Identity.* 1992: *In the Shadow of a Killer* (TV). *A Few Good Men. The Prom. Sniper. Hoffa. Red Rock West.* 1993: *National Lampoon's Loaded Weapon 1. The American Clock* (TV). *Needful Things. Morning Glory.* 1994: *The Client. The Last Seduction. Blue Chips. Miracle on 34th Street. Silent Fall.* 1995: *The Low Life. Sacred Cargo. Outbreak. Nixon.*

WALSH, M. Emmet 1935–

Bulky, open-mouthed American supporting player with large face and thinning gingery hair, a kind of more serious Stateside equivalent of Britain's Roy Kinnear (*qv*). Despite graduating from college with a degree in business administration, Walsh was drawn to acting, although he found himself consistently cast in minor beastly roles, such as bullying sheriffs and interfering officials, following his arrival in Hollywood in 1968. Boosted to better parts after his excellent portrayal of the seedy, amoral private eye in *Blood Simple*, he now alternates between big-city cops and wheezy rurals.

1969: *Midnight Cowboy. Stiletto. End of the Road. Alice's Restaurant.* 1970: *Loving. The Traveling Executioner. Cold Turkey. Little Big*

Man. 1971: *They Might Be Giants. Escape from the Planet of the Apes.* 1972: *Get to Know Your Rabbit. What's Up, Doc?* 1973: *Kid Blue/Dime Box. Serpico.* 1974: *The Gambler. Sara T: Portrait of a Teenage Alcoholic* (TV). 1975: *The Prisoner of Second Avenue. At Long Last Love. Crime Club* (TV). 1976: *Bound for Glory. Mikey and Nicky. Nickelodeon. The Invasion of Johnson County* (TV). 1977: *Straight Time. Slap Shot. Airport '77. Red Alert* (TV). *Superdome* (TV). 1978: *A Question of Guilt* (TV). 1979: *Dear Detective* (TV). *Mrs R's Daughter* (TV). *No Other Love* (TV). *The Gift* (TV). *The Jerk. The Fish That Saved Pittsburgh.* 1980: *Brubaker. Raise the Titanic. Ordinary People. Hellinger's Law* (TV). *High Noon Part Two* (TV). *City in Fear/Panic on Page One* (TV). 1981: *Back Roads. Reds. Fast-Walking. Skag/The Wildcatters* (TV). 1982: *The Escape Artist. Cannery Row. Blade Runner.* 1983: *Silkwood. Scandalous. Night Partners* (TV). 1984: *The Pope of Greenwich Village. Blood Simple. Missing in Action. Grandview USA. Courage* (GB: *TV*, as *Raw Courage*). 1985: *Fletch. Con Sawyer and Hucklemary Finn* (TV). 1986: *Critters. Wildcats. The Deliberate Stranger* (TV). *Hero in the Family* (TV). *Raising Arizona. The Best of Times. Resting Place* (TV). *Back to School.* 1987: *Broken Vows* (TV). *The Abduction of Kari Swenson* (TV). *No Man's Land. Harry and the Hendersons* (GB: *Bigfoot and the Hendersons*). 1988: *Clean and Sober. War Party. Red Scorpion. The Milagro Beanfield War. The Mighty Quinn. Sunset.* 1989: *Sundown: The Vampire in Retreat. Thunderground. Catch Me If You Can. Chattahoochee.* 1990: *Love and Lies* (TV. GB: *True Betrayal*). *Narrow Margin. The Fourth Story* (cable TV). *Flash* (TV). 1992: *Killer Image. Equinox. White Sands. Wild Card* (TV). *The Naked Truth.* 1993: *The Music of Chance. Cockroach Hotel. Bitter Harvest. Wilder Napalm. Free Willy. Four Eyes and Six Guns* (TV). 1994: *The Glass Shield. Sleepless. Camp Nowhere. Relative Fear/The Child. Dead Badge. Willy 2: The Adventure Home.*

WALSTON, Ray 1917–

Slight, energetic American actor whose film roles have been few but almost always ripe and juicy. A theatre player until the early 1950s, the light-haired, fizzy Walston was older than he looked and began to appear like a wizened hobgoblin with the advent of the 1970s. Also very popular as the extra-terrestrial visitor in TV's long-running

My Favorite Martian. Still around in spiky cameos.

1957: Kiss Them for Me. 1958: Damn Yankees (GB: What Lola Wants). South Pacific. Shadows Tremble (TV). 1959: Say One for Me. 1960: The Apartment. Portrait in Black. Tall Story. 1962: Convicts Four (GB: Reprieve!). 1963: Who's Minding the Store? Wives and Lovers. 1964: Kiss Me, Stupid. 1967: Caprice. 1969: Paint Your Wagon. 1970: Viva Max! 1973: The Sting. 1976: Silver Streak. 1977: The Happy Hooker Goes to Washington. 1978: Institute for Revenge (TV). The Fall of the House of Usher (shown 1982). 1980: Popeye. 1981: Galaxy of Terror. O'Hara's Wife. 1982: Fast Times at Ridgemont High (GB: Fast Times). The Kid With the Broken Halo (TV). 1983: Private School. This Girl for Hire (TV). The Jerk, Too (TV). 1984: Johnny Dangerously. For Love or Money (TV). O C and Stiggs (released 1987). 1985: Amos (TV). 1986: RAD. Ask Max (TV). 1987: From the Hip. 1988: Crash Course. (TV). Blood Relations. Red River (TV). Fine Gold/Oro fino. Paramedics. A Man of Passion. Saturday the 14th Strikes Back. 1989: Blood Salvage. Ski Patrol. 1990: Popcorn. Space Case. Angel of Death (TV). 1991. One Special Victory (TV). 1992: The Player. Of Mice and Men. 1995: House Arrest.

WALTERS, Hal 1891–1940

Hook-nosed, smudge-eyebrowed, dark-haired British comedian and comic actor, a whippersnapper of a man fond of loud suits and an ideal foil for Max Miller (and other British comedians) in crazy, rough-edged comedies of the 1930s. After running up more than 60 films in nine years, mostly as men on the make, Walters was killed by a bomb in a wartime air raid.

*1931: Tonight's the Night – Pass It On. 1932: Come into My Parlour. Old Spanish Customers. *On the Air. Verdict of the Sea. Little Fella. The River House Ghost. *Women Are That Way. 1933: Great Stuff. Yes, Madam. Going Straight. That's My Wife. Long Live the King. I'll Stick to You. Enemy of the Police. Strike It Rich. Marooned. 1934: The Man I Want. Bagged. Open All Night. The Perfect Flaw. Virginia's Husband. Crazy People. Big Business. Widows Might. 1935: Department Store. Death on the Set (US: Murder on the Set). A Fire Has Been Arranged. The Right Age to Marry. Blue Smoke. Can You Hear Me, Mother? Don't*

*Rush Me! 1936: The Interrupted Honeymoon. Where There's a Will. Apron Fools. Educated Evans. They Didn't Know. 1937: The Vulture. Pearls Bring Tears. Song of the Forge. Beauty and the Barge. Non-Stop New York. The Strange Adventures of Mr Smith. Keep Fit. Little Miss Somebody. Television Talent. 1938: Crackerjack (US: The Man With a Hundred Faces). The Viper. Double or Quits. Meet Mr Penny. Thank Evans. Everything Happens to Me. Ghost Tales Retold (series). 1939: The Four Feathers. Good Old Days. *Pandamonium. Hoots Mon! Spies of the Air. 1940: They Came by Night. That's the Ticket.*

WALTERS, Thorley 1913–1991

Brown-haired British actor with square face and trim moustache, angry-looking in an ineffectual way, often seen in British comedy films as aggressive buffoons or ministerial bunglers. The son of a priest, he began in Shakespearian roles and essayed the occasional light leading role in films. But he was seen in increasingly comic and light-hearted parts on stage, and his cinema career as a featured player took off in the mid-1950s with his association with the Boulting Brothers and Launder-Gilliat teams, as he frowned alternately in suspicion and bemusement at the misfortunes that befell him.

1934: The Love Test. His Majesty and Co. Once in a New Moon. 1937: The Reverse Be My Lot. 1939: Trunk Crime (US: Design for Murder). Secret Journey (US: Among Human Wolves). 1940: Gentleman of Venture (US: It Happened to One Man). 1944: Medal for the

General. 1945: Waltz Time. They Were Sisters. 1955: Josephine and Men. Who Done It? Private's Progress. 1956: You Can't Escape. The Baby and the Battleship. The Passionate Stranger (US: A Novel Affair). 1957: Second Fiddle. The Birthday Present. Blue Murder at St Trinian's. Happy Is the Bride! The Truth About Women. 1958: A Lady Mislaid. Carlton-Browne of the FO (US: Man in a Cocked Hat). 1959: Don't Panic Chaps! 1960: Two Way Stretch. Suspect (US: The Risk). A French Mistress. The Pure Hell of St Trinian's. 1961: Invasion Quartet. Petticoat Pirates. Murder She Said. 1962: The Phantom of the Opera. 1963: Sherlock Holmes und das Halsband des Todes (GB and US: Sherlock Holmes and the Deadly Necklace). Ring of Spies. Heavens Above! 1964: The Earth Dies Screaming. A Home of Your Own. 1965: Joey Boy. Rotten to the Core. A Study in Terror (US: Fog). The Psychopath. 1966: Dracula Prince of Darkness. The Family Way. The Wrong Box. 1967: Frankenstein Created Woman. 1968: Twisted Nerve. Crooks and Coronets (US: Sophie's Place). The Last Shot You Hear. 1969: Oh! What a Lovely War. Frankenstein Must Be Destroyed. 1970: Bartleby. The Man Who Haunted Himself. Trog. There's a Girl in My Soup. 1971: Vampire Circus. Mr Forbush and the Penguins (US: Cry of the Penguins). Young Winston. 1973: Death in Small Doses (TV). Soft Beds, Hard Battles (US: Undercovers Hero). 1975: The Adventure of Sherlock Holmes' Smarter Brother. 1977: The People That Time Forgot. 1980: The Wildcats of St Trinian's. 1982: Soft Targets (TV). 1983: The Sign of Four. 1984: The Little Drummer Girl. 1988: The Richest Man in the World (TV).

WANAMAKER, Sam

(Samuel Watenmaker) 1919–1993
Cheerful-looking, close-cropped, chunkily built, brown-haired American actor who was also a director and producer from his early pre-war days. After war service, he broke into films, but soon fled the McCarthy blacklist to end up in Britain, where he made the bulk of his career for the next 15 years. A distinguished figure in the theatre, Wanamaker never achieved the same impact in the cinema, where he moved gradually from incorruptible to sneakier roles. Even his efforts at directing films were less noteworthy than those for the stage. Father of actress Zoë Wanamaker. Died of cancer.

1948: My Girl Tisa. 1949: Give Us This Day (US: Salt to the Devil). 1951: Mr Denning Drives North. 1955: The Secret. 1959: Battle of the Sexes (narrator only). 1960: The Criminal (US: The Concrete Jungle). 1962: Taras Bulba. 1963: Man in the Middle. 1965: Those Magnificent Men in Their Flying Machines. The Spy Who Came in from the Cold. 1967: The Day the Fish Came Out. Warning Shot. Danger Route. 1973: Mousey (TV. GB: cinemas, as Cat and Mouse). 1974: The Law (TV). 1975: The Sellout. The Spiral Staircase. 1976: Voyage of the Damned. 1977: Billy Jack Goes to Washington. 1978: Death on the Nile. 1979: From Hell to Victory. 1980: The Competition. Private Benjamin. 1981: Our Family Business (TV). 1982: I Was a Male Order Bride (TV). 1984: Irreconcilable Differences. Heartsounds (TV). The Ghost Writer (TV). The Aviator. 1986: Raw Deal. 1987: Superman IV: The Quest for Peace. Baby Boom. Sadie and Son (TV). Judgment in Berlin. 1988: Secret Ingredient. 1990: Running Against Time (cable TV). Cognac. 1991: Guilty by Suspicion. Pure Luck.

As director:
1969: The File of the Golden Goose. 1970: The Executioner. 1971: Catlow. 1977: Sinbad and the Eye of the Tiger. 1979: Charlie Muffin (TV).

WARD, Michael
(George Ward) 1909–
Thin, long-faced British actor and pianist with disdainful looks and light crinkly hair, often in fey or sourpuss roles and a master of flappability. The son of a clergyman, he was briefly a teacher before years of slog trying to break into films were eventually rewarded. Usually impeccably dressed, his characters were inevitably targets for 'idiot' comedians, especially Norman Wisdom, with whom he appeared five times. He played a number of straight roles, but comedy gradually took over his career. Once took three years off acting and became a qualified statistician.

1947: The First Gentlemen (US: Affairs of a Rogue). An Ideal Husband. 1948: Once a Jolly Swagman (US: Maniacs on Wheels). Calling Paul Temple. Sleeping Car to Trieste. The Queen of Spades. 1949: Hi Jinks in Society. Trottie True (US: Gay Lady). Stop Press Girl. Saraband for Dead Lovers (US: Saraband).

Helter Skelter. Marry Me! 1950: What the Butler Saw. So Long at the Fair. Tony Draws a Horse. Trio. Pool of London. No Trace. Lilli Marlene. Tom Brown's Schooldays. 1951: Cheer the Brave. Chelsea Story. Calling Bulldog Drummond. High Treason. The House in the Square (US: I'll Never Forget You). Appointment With Venus (US: Island Rescue). The Galloping Major. Whispering Smith Hits London (US: Whispering Smith Versus Scotland Yard). 1952: Tall Headlines. The Happy Family (US: Mr Lord Says No). The Frightened Man. 13 East Street. Emergency Call (US: Hundred Hour Hunt). Song of Paris (US: Bachelor in Paris). Tread Softly. 1953: The Fake. Street Corner (US: Both Sides of the Law). Trouble in Store. The Love Lottery. *A Body Like Mine. 1955: Man of the Moment. Josephine and Men. Lost (US: Tears for Simon). Jumping for Joy. Private's Progress. 1956: The Intimate Stranger (US: Finger of Guilt). Dry Rot. Up in the World. Brothers in Law. 1957: Just My Luck. 1958: Carlton-Browne of the FO (US: Man in a Cocked Hat). 1959: The Ugly Duckling. I'm All Right, Jack. The Rough and the Smooth (US: Portrait of a Sinner). Follow a Star. 1960: Doctor in Love. 1961: Mary Had a Little... A Pair of Briefs. Carry On Regardless. 1963: Father Came Too. Carry On Cabby. 1964: Carry On Cleo. 1965: The Big Job. 1966: Carry On Screaming. Don't Lose Your Head. Where the Bullets Fly. 1967: *Ouch! Smashing Time. 1973: Frankenstein and the Monster from Hell. 1974: Man About the House. *The Walker. 1978: Revenge of the Pink Panther.

WARDEN, Jack 1920–
Ginger-haired, ruddy-complexioned, ebullient American actor whose forceful personality and barking tones first brought him to the fore as one of the jurors in *Twelve Angry Men*. He was a top featured player after that, often third or fourth on the cast list, but rarely the villain. More recently he has taken to playing eccentrics, sometimes apoplectic senior officials. He was unlucky in the 1970s when two good TV 'pilots' failed to lead to successful series. Nominated for Oscars in *Shampoo* and *Heaven Can Wait*.

1950: The Asphalt Jungle. USS Teakettle (later You're in the Navy Now). 1951: The Frogmen. The Man With My Face. 1952: Red Ball Express. 1953: From Here to Eternity. 1956:

Edge of the City (GB: A Man Is Ten Feet Tall). 1957: Twelve Angry Men. The Bachelor Party. Darby's Rangers (GB: The Young Invaders). 1958: Run Silent, Run Deep. 1959: The Sound and the Fury. That Kind of Woman. 1960: Wake Me When It's Over. The Lawbreakers (TV. GB: cinemas). 1961: Escape from Zahrain. 1963: Donovan's Reef. 1964: The Thin Red Line. 1965: Mirage. 1966: Blindfold. Fame Is the Name of the Game (TV). 1968: Bye Bye Braverman. 1970: The Sporting Club. Wheeler and Murdoch (TV). 1971: Man on a String (TV). Summertree. Brian's Song (TV). Who Is Harry Kellerman and Why Is He Saying These Terrible Things About Me? Welcome to the Club. The Face of Fear (TV). 1972: Lt Schuster's Wife (TV). 1973: Remember When? (TV). What's a Nice Girl Like You? ... (TV). The Man Who Loved Cat Dancing. Billy Two Hats. 1974: The Godchild (TV). The Apprenticeship of Duddy Kravitz. 1975: Journey from Darkness (TV). Shampoo. Jigsaw John (TV). 1976: Raid on Entebbe (TV. GB: cinemas). All the President's Men. †Voyage of the Damned. 1977: The White Buffalo. 1978: Death on the Nile. Heaven Can Wait. The Champ. 1979: ... and Justice for All. Beyond the Poseidon Adventure. Being There. Dreamer. Topper (TV). 1980: Used Cars. A Private Battle (TV). Chu Chu and the Philly Flash. Carbon Copy. 1981: So Fine. The Great Muppet Caper. 1982: The Verdict. 1983: Helen and Teacher. Hobson's Choice (TV). Crackers. 1984: The Aviator. 1987: Still Crazy Like a Fox (TV). The Three Kings (TV). September. 1988: The Presidio. Dead Solid Perfect (TV). 1990: Everybody Wins. Problem Child. 1991: Problem Child 2. 1992: Passed Away. Night and the City. Toys. 1993: Guilty As Sin. 1994: Bullets Over Broadway. 1995: While You Were Sleeping. Things to Do in Denver When You're Dead.

† Scenes deleted from final release print

WARNER, H.B. (Henry Byron Warner-Lickford) 1875–1958
Tall, skeletal, dignified, light-haired, moustachioed British actor who went to Hollywood in 1914 and spent more than 40 years in films playing men whose opinion had to be respected, even when, as was often the case, they were under pressure. After hitting the limelight with his portrait of Jesus in the 1927 version of *King of Kings*, he kept acting almost to the end of his long

life. Nominated for an Academy Award for his performance in the 1937 version of *Lost Horizon*.

1900: English Nell. 1914: The Ghost Breaker. Your Ghost and Mine. Lost Paradise. 1915: The Beggar of Cawnpore. The Raiders. 1916: The Vagabond Prince. The Market of Vain Desire. The House of 1,000 Candles. Shell 43. A Wife's Sacrifice. 1917: Wrath. The Danger Trail. The Seven Deadly Sins. God's Man. 1919: The Man Who Turned White. A Fugitive from Matrimony. Uncharted Channels. For a Woman's Honor. The Pagan God. Maruja. 1920: Gray Wolf's Ghost. Haunting Shadows. Once a Plumber. Dice of Destiny. The White Dove. One Hour Before Dawn. Felix O'Day. Below the Deadline. 1921: When We Were Twenty-One. 1923: Zaza. 1924: Is Love Everything? The Lone Fighter. The Dark Swan. 1926: The Temptress. Silence. Whispering Smith. 1927: King of Kings. French Dressing (GB: Lessons for Wives). Sorrell and Son. 1928: Conquest. The Romance of a Rogue. The Naughty Duchess. Man-Made Women. 1929: The Doctor's Secret. The Divine Lady. The Gamblers. The Show of Shows. The Green Goddess. The Trial of Mary Dugan. The Argyle Case. Stark Mad. Tiger Rose. 1930: The Second Floor Mystery. Wedding Rings. On Your Back. The Princess and the Plumber. The Furies. Wild Company. Liliom. 1931: Woman of Experience. Expensive Women. Five Star Final. The Reckless Hour. 1932: A Woman Commands. The Menace. Charlie Chan's Chance. The Crusader. The Son-Daughter. Tom Brown of Culver. Cross Examination. Unholy Love (GB: Deceit). The Phantom of Crestwood. 1933: Sorrell and Son (GB remake). Supernatural. Jennie Gerhardt. Justice Takes a Holiday. Christopher Bean (GB: The Late Christopher Bean). 1934: Night Alarm. Grand Canary. Behold My Wife. In Old Santa Fé. 1935: Born to Gamble. A Tale of Two Cities. 1936: Moonlight Murder. The Garden Murder Case. Blackmailer. Rose of the Rancho. Mr Deeds Goes to Town. Along Came Love. 1937: Our Fighting Navy (US: Torpedoed!). Victoria the Great. Lost Horizon. 1938: The Toy Wife (GB: Frou Frou). The Adventures of Marco Polo. Bulldog Drummond in Africa. You Can't Take It With You. Girl of the Golden West. Kidnapped. Army Girl (GB: The Last of the Cavalry). 1939: Arrest Bulldog Drummond! The Rains Came. Bulldog Drummond's Secret Police. The Gracie Allen Murder Case. Bulldog Drummond's Bride. Nurse Edith Cavell. Mr Smith Goes to Washington. Let Freedom Ring. 1940: New Moon. 1941: All That Money Can Buy/ The Devil and Daniel Webster. Ellery Queen and the Perfect Crime (GB: The Perfect Crime). City of Missing Girls. Topper Returns. The Corsican Brothers. South of Tahiti (GB: White Savage). 1942: Crossroads. A Yank in Libya. Boss of Big Town. Hitler's Children. 1943: Woman in Bondage. 1944: Faces in the Fog. Action in Arabia. Enemy of Women. 1945: Captain Tugboat Annie. Rogues' Gallery. 1946: Gentleman Joe Palooka. Strange Impersonation. It's a Wonderful Life! 1947: Driftwood. The High Wall. Bulldog Drummond Strikes Back. 1948: The Prince of Thieves. The Judge Steps Out (GB: Indian Summer). 1949: El Paso. Hellfire. 1950: Sunset Boulevard. Night

and the City. 1951: The First Legion. Journey into Light. Savage Drums. Here Comes the Groom. 1956: The Ten Commandments. 1957: Darby's Rangers (GB: The Young Invaders).

WARREN, C. Denier 1889–1971
Tubby, balding, frequently bespectacled American-born comedy actor in British films — often cast as explosive and excitable Americans, in spite of the fact that he lived mainly in Britain from the age of eight. Busy in character roles through the major part of the 1930s, he then devoted himself to writing and appearing in the popular wartime 'Kentucky Minstrels' programmes on radio. Still popped up occasionally in films after that, but semi-retired after 1961. Often billed in his earlier films without the 'C', which stood for Charles.

1932: Let Me Explain, Dear. 1933: Channel Crossing. Counsel's Opinion. No Funny Business. Prince of Arcadia. 1934: The Great Defender. Two Hearts in Waltztime. Music Hall. Kentucky Minstrels. 1935: Radio Parade of 1935 (US: Radio Parade). Royal Cavalcade (US: Regal Cavalcade). Marry the Girl. A Fire Has Been Arranged. The Clairvoyant. Heat Wave. The Small Man. A Real Bloke. Temptation. Be Careful, Mr Smith. Charing Cross Road. Heart's Desire. Birds of a Feather. 1936: A Star Fell from Heaven. They Didn't Know. The Big Noise. It's in the Bag. Spy of Napoleon. The Beloved Vagabond. Everybody Dance. You Must Get Married. Café Colette (US: Danger in Paris). 1937: Good Morning, Boys (US: Where There's a Will). Over She Goes. Cotton Queen. Song of the Forge. Rose of Tralee. Keep Fit. A Romance in Flanders (US: Lost on the Western Front). Change for a Sovereign. Little Miss Somebody. Who Killed John Savage? Melody and Romance. Captain's Orders. Second Best Bed. 1938: Make It Three. Strange Boarders. Kicking the Moon Around (US: The Playboy). Break the News. Old Mother Riley in Paris. My Irish Molly (US: Little Miss Molly). The Challenge. Take Off That Hat. It's in the Air (US: George Takes the Air). 1939: Trouble Brewing. The Body Vanishes. Come On George. Trouble for Two. Me and My Pal. A Gentleman's Gentleman. Secret Journey (US: Among Human Wolves). 1942: We'll Smile Again. 1943: The Hundred Pound Window. The Shipbuilders. 1944: Twilight Hour. Kiss the Bride Goodbye. Candles at Nine. 1945: Don Chicago. 1949: Old Mother Riley's New Venture. 1950:

Old Mother Riley. Headmistress. The Dragon of Pendragon Castle. Night and the City. 1953: Alf's Baby. House of Blackmail. 1955: Handcuffs, London. 1957: A King in New York. 1960: Bluebeard's Ten Honeymoons. A Taste of Money. Escort for Hire. 1961: Return of a Stranger. So Evil, So Young. The Silent Invasion. Lolita. Two Wives at One Wedding. The Treasure of Monte Cristo (US: The Secret of Monte Cristo). 1969: The Adding Machine.

WARREN, Kenneth J. 1926–1973
Burly, balding (later shaven-headed), slit-eyed, pugnacious Australian actor in British films, frequently playing aggressive, tough-guy roles, or even objectionable bullies. In private life an enthusiastic gourmet cook and talented painter. He made his name in stage productions of *Summer of the Seventeenth Doll*, and stayed in Britain from 1958 after being in the Australian production of the play there.

*1958: I Was Monty's Double (US: Monty's Double). 1959: The Siege of Pinchgut (US: Four Desperate Men). 1960: The Criminal (US: The Concrete Jungle). Danger Tomorrow. Circus of Horrors. Dr Blood's Coffin. 1961: On the Fiddle (US: Operation Snafu). Strip Tease Murder. Part Time Wife. *The Grand Junction Case. 1962: The Boys. 1963: Life for Ruth (US: Walk in the Shadow). The Small World of Sammy Lee. The Informers. *The Invisible Asset. 1965: A High Wind in Jamaica. 1966: The 25th Hour. 1967: The Double Man. 1968: Decline and Fall . . . of a Birdwatcher! 1969: The Spy Killer (TV). 1970: Leo the Last. I, Monster. The Revolutionary. 1971: Demons of the Mind. 1972: The Creeping Flesh. 1973: Digby the Biggest Dog in the World. 1974: S*P*Y*S.*

WARWICK, John
(J. Beattie) 1905–1972
Australian actor with fuzzy brown hair and vindictive eyes who starred in and produced films in his native country before coming to Britain in 1936. Here the shiftiness in his makeup seemed to pigeonhole him as a natural successor to Donald Calthrop (*qv*) and he played an equal number of good and bad guys before war service disrupted the pattern of his career. In post-war years, he was seen in much smaller roles, often as

policemen, before returning to Australia in the mid-1960s, dying there from a heart attack.

1933: In the Wake of the Bounty. The Squatter's Daughter. 1934: The Silence of Dean Maitland. 1935: Down on the Farm. 1936: Orphan of the Wilderness. Find the Lady. 1937: Lucky Jade. Double Alibi. Catch as Catch Can. When the Poppies Bloom Again. 21 Days (released 1940. US: 21 Days Together). Passenger to London. The Ticket-of-Leave Man. Riding High. A Yank at Oxford. 1938: John Halifax—Gentleman. This Man Is News. Bad Boy. 1939: Me and My Pal. Dead Men Are Dangerous. The Mind of Mr Reeder (US: The Mysterious Mr Reeder). The Face at the Window. Flying Fifty-Five. All at Sea. 1940: The Case of the Frightened Lady (US: The Frightened Lady). Spare a Copper. 1941: Danny Boy. My Wife's Family. The Saint's Vacation. 1942: The Missing Million. The Day Will Dawn. Talk About Jacqueline. 1946: Woman to Woman. 1947: Dancing With Crime. Teheran (US: The Plot to Kill Roosevelt). While I Live. 1950: The Franchise Affair. Pool of London. 1951: The Lavender Hill Mob. 1952: Never Look Back. Circumstantial Evidence. Escape Route (US: I'll Get You). 1953: Thought to Kill. The Accused. Street Corner (US: Both Sides of the Law). Trouble in Store. 1954: Up to His Neck. The Red Dress. Bang! You're Dead (US: Game of Danger). Dangerous Voyage. 1955: Contraband Spain. One Just Man. *The Mysterious Bullet. 1956: Town on Trial! The Long Arm (US: The Third Key). 1957: *The Tyburn Case. Just My Luck. 1958: *Print of Death. *The Crossroad Gallows. Law and Disorder. The Square Peg. Dunkirk. Gideon's Day (US: Gideon of Scotland Yard). 1959: The Desperate Man. Horrors of the Black Museum. Murder at Site Three. 1961: The Fourth Square. Go to Blazes. 1969: Adam's Woman. 1971: Demonstrator.

WARWICK, Robert
(R. Taylor Bien) 1878–1964
Solidly built, dark-haired, stiff-backed, banana-nosed, authoritative, rarely smiling American actor who starred in a string of early silents after a distinguished Broadway career, then returned to Hollywood in middle age to play concerned fathers, judges, bankers, society swells and aides-de-camp and an assortment of executive figures who twiddled with their pocket watches while deciding the fates of employees. Early ambitions to sing in opera remained unfulfilled despite musical training in Paris. Twice married and divorced, Warwick outlived both his ex-wives and appeared in films past the age of 80.

1914: The Dollar Mark. Across the Pacific. Man of the Hour. 1915: The Face in the Moonlight. Alias Jimmy Valentine. Stolen Voice. Sins of Society. 1916: All Man. Friday the 13th. Human Driftwood. The Heart of a Hero. Sudden Riches. 1917: The Argyle Case. The Family Honor. The Mad Lover. Hell Hath No Fury. The Silent Master. The False Friend. A Modern Othello. A Girl's Folly. The Man Who Forgot. 1918: An Accidental Honeymoon. 1919: Told in the Hills. An Adventure in Hearts. In Mizzoura. The Secret Service. 1920: The City of Masks. The Tree of Knowledge. The Fourteenth Man. Jack Straw. Thou Art the Man. Hunting Trouble. 1924: The Spitfire. 1929: Unmasked. 1930: The Royal Bed (GB: The Queen's Husband). 1931: A Holy Terror. Not Exactly Gentlemen. Three Rogues. Your Number's Up. 1932: The Dark Horse. Doctor X. Afraid to Talk. The Girl from Calgary. I Am a Fugitive from a Chain Gang. The Rich Are Always With Us. The Silver Dollar. So Big. Unashamed. The Woman from Monte Carlo. Secrets of Wu Sin. 1933: Charlie Chan's Greatest Case. The Three Musketeers (serial). Fighting With Kit Carson (serial). Frisco Jenny. Female. The Power and the Glory. Ladies They Talk About. Whispering Shadows (serial). Pilgrimage. 1934: Cleopatra. The Dragon Murder Case. Jimmy the Gent. School for Girls. 1935: Code of the Mounted. Hop-a-Long Cassidy. Murder Man. Night Life of the Gods. Anna Karenina. The Farmer Takes a Wife. A Shot in the Dark. A Tale of Two Cities. Fighting Marines (serial). The Little Colonel. Whipsaw. *A Thrill for Thelma. 1936: Bulldog Edition (GB: Lady Reporter). The Bold Caballero. The Bride Walks Out. Bars of Hate. Adventure in Manhattan (GB: Manhattan Madness). Can This Be Dixie? *Behind the Headlines. Charlie Chan at the Race Track. Ace Drummond (serial). In His Steps (later Sins of the Children). Mary of Scotland. The Vigilantes Are Coming (serial). The Return of Jimmy Valentine. Sutter's Gold. Timber War. Tough Guy. Romeo and Juliet. White Legion. 1937: The Awful Truth. Conquest (GB: Marie Walewska). Counsel for Crime. High Hat. Let Them Live. The Life of Emile Zola. The Road Back/Return of the Hero. The Prince and the Pauper. The Trigger Trio. The Bold Caballero (GB: The Bold Cavalier). Jungle Menace (serial). 1938: Army Girl (GB: The Last of the Cavalry). The Adventures of Robin Hood. Blockade. Come On, Leathernecks. Annabel Takes a Tour. Gangster's Boy. Going Places. Law of the Plains. The Spy Ring. Squadron of Honor. 1939: Almost a Gentleman. In Old Monterey. Juarez. The Magnificent Fraud. The Private Lives of Elizabeth and Essex. Konga, the Wild Stallion (GB: Konga). 1940: Devil's Island. The Earl of Chicago. The Great McGinty (GB: Down Went McGinty). On the Spot. Christmas in July. New Moon. The Sea Hawk. A Dispatch from Reuter's (GB: This Man Reuter). Murder in the Air. 1941: I Was a Prisoner on Devil's Island. The Lady Eve. Louisiana Purchase. Sullivan's Travels. A Woman's Face. 1942: Cadets on Parade. Eagle Squadron. The Fleet's In. I Married a Witch. Secret Enemies. Tennessee Johnson (GB: The Man on America's Conscience). The Palm Beach Story. 1943: Dixie. The Deerslayer. Petticoat Larceny. Two Tickets to London. In Old Oklahoma/War of the Wildcats. 1944: Bowery to Broadway. Hail the Conquering Hero. Kismet. Man from Frisco. The Princess and the Pirate. Secret Command. 1945: Sudan. 1946: Criminal Court. The Falcon's Adventure. 1947: Gentleman's Agreement. Unconquered. Pirates of Monterey. 1948: Fury at Furnace Creek. Gun Smugglers. The Three Musketeers. Million Dollar Weekend. Adventures of Don Juan (GB: The New Adventures of Don Juan). Impact. 1949: Francis. A Woman's Secret. 1950: In a Lonely Place. Tarzan and the Slave Girl. Vendetta. 1951: Mark of the Renegade. Sugarfoot. The Sword of Monte Cristo. 1952: Against All Flags. 1953: Jamaica Run. Mississippi Gambler. Salome. 1954: Passion. Silver Lode. 1955: Chief Crazy Horse (US: Valley of Fury). Escape to Burma. Lady Godiva (GB: Lady Godiva of Coventry). 1956: Walk the Proud Land. While the City Sleeps. 1957: Shoot-Out at Medicine Bend. 1958: The Buccaneer. 1959: It Started With a Kiss. Night of the Quarter Moon.

WASHBOURNE, Mona 1903–1988
Brown-haired, round-faced, dumpy, likeable British actress who played 'dear old things' from her forties, mostly on stage but with a good sprinkling of films thrown in, with characters that could be forthright or querulous. Her two most striking film performances — in *Night Must Fall*, as the pathetic Mrs Bramson, and in *Stevie*, as the 'lion aunt' (the latter winning her a British Oscar) — were both from plays. Originally trained as a concert pianist, she was married to fellow character player Basil Dignam (*qv*).

1948: Once Upon a Dream. The Winslow Boy. 1949: Maytime in Mayfair. Adam and Evelyne (US: Adam and Evelyn). 1950: Double Confession. Dark Interval. 1952: The Gambler and the Lady. Wide Boy. 1953: Johnny on the Run. Star of My Night. The Million Pound Note (US: Man With a Million). 1954: Adventure in the Hopfields. Betrayed. Child's Play. Doctor in the House. To Dorothy a Son (US: Cash on Delivery). The Yellow Robe. 1955: Cast a Dark Shadow. Lost (US: Tears for Simon). Triple Blackmail. John and Julie. Count of Twelve.

The Diamond Expert. 1956: It's Great to be Young. Loser Takes All. Alias John Preston. Yield to the Night (US: Blonde Sinner). 1957: The Good Companions. Stranger in Town. Three Sundays to Live. Son of a Stranger. 1958: A Cry from the Streets. Dunkirk. 1959: Count Your Blessings. Libel! 1960: Brides of Dracula. No Love for Johnnie. 1963: Billy Liar. Night Must Fall. 1964: My Fair Lady. Ferry 'Cross the Mersey. One Way Pendulum. 1965: The Third Day. The Collector. 1967: Mrs Brown, You've Got a Lovely Daughter. Casino Royale. Two a Penny. If . . . 1969: The Games. The Bed Sitting Room. 1970: Fragment of Fear. 1971: What Became of Jack and Jill? (US: Romeo and Juliet '71). 1973: O Lucky Man! 1974: Mister Quilp. The Driver's Seat/ Identikit. 1976: The Blue Bird. 1978: Stevie. 1979: The London Affair/The London Connection (US: The Omega Connection). 1982: Charles and Diana, a Royal Love Story (TV). 1984: December Flower (TV).

WATERS, Russell 1908–

Stocky, inoffensive-looking, brown-haired, Scottish-born actor with high sloping forehead and breezy air. He made a start in British films in his twenties as the hapless hero of director Richard Massingham's highly rated comedy shorts of the 1930s. After war service, Waters settled down to play dozens of mildly authoritative, not-to-be-feared official figures and kept busy on television as well.

*1934: *Tell Me If It Hurts. 1936: *And So to Work. 1937: *The Daily Round. 1947: The*

*Woman in the Hall. 1948: *What a Life! Once a Jolly Swagman (US: Maniacs on Wheels). London Belongs to Me (US: Dulcimer Street). Obsession (US: The Hidden Room). The Blue Lagoon. 1949: Dear Mr Prohack. Don't Ever Leave Me. The Chiltern Hundreds (US: The Amazing Mr Beecham). Marry Me! Stop Press Girl. Helter Skelter. 1950: Chance of a Lifetime. *The Cure. State Secret (US: The Great Manhunt). Madeleine. The Happiest Days of Your Life. The Wooden Horse. The Magnet. Seven Days to Noon. Pool of London. 1951: The Browning Version. Mr Denning Drives North. Captain Horatio Hornblower RN (US: Captain Horatio Hornblower). Outcast of the Islands. Calling Bulldog Drummond. Green Grow the Rushes. The Man in the White Suit. Lady Godiva Rides Again. Death of an Angel. Saturday Island (US: Island of Desire). Angels One Five. 1952: Castle in the Air. The Brave Don't Cry. The Ringer. You're Only Young Twice! The Long Memory. Miss Robin Hood. Isn't Life Wonderful! The Story of Robin Hood and His Merrie Men. The Cruel Sea. 1953: Turn the Key Softly. Rob Roy the Highland Rogue. The 'Maggie' (US: High and Dry). Street Corner (US: Both Sides of the Law). The Sword and the Rose. Grand National Night (US: Wicked Wife). 1954: The Sleeping Tiger. Lease of Life. The Young Lovers (US: Chance Meeting). Adventure in the Hopfields. The Passing Stranger. The Love Match. The Case of the Pearl Payroll. 1955: John and Julie. Third Party Risk (US: The Deadly Game). The Case of the Pennsylvania Gun. Now and Forever. 1956: It's Great to be Young. Reach for the Sky. Man in the Sky (US: Decision Against Time). 1957: The Little Hut. Interpol (US: Pick-Up Alley). Let's Be Happy. 1958: Dunkirk. A Night to Remember. Next to No Time! The Key. The Horse's Mouth. 1959: Yesterday's Enemy. Left, Right and Centre. The Bridal Path. 1960: The Man in the Moon. Danger Tomorrow. Marriage of Convenience. 1961: Bomb in the High Street (released 1963). 1962: Flat Two. The Punch and Judy Man. Reach for Glory. The Amorous Prawn (US: The Amorous Mr Prawn). Waltz of the Toreadors. The Longest Day. Play It Cool! The War Lover. 1963: I Could Go On Singing (shown 1962). The Flood. Crooks in Cloisters. Heavens Above! 1965: The Heroes of Telemark. The Legend of Young Dick Turpin. 1966: The Family Way. The Trygon Factor. 1967: The Devil Rides Out (US: The Devil's Bride). 1968: Twisted Nerve. Headline Hunters. 1971: Kidnapped. 1972: Endless Night. That's Your Funeral. 1973: The Wicker Man. 1979: Black Jack.*

WATKIN, Pierre 1887–1960

Silver-haired, pale-eyed, patrician-looking American supporting actor of ruddy complexion and erect bearing. After coming to Hollywood in his late forties, the Iowa-born actor was cast for the next 25 years as men of some standing, usually in smart suits and breast-pocket handkerchiefs. Often a district attorney or faintly ineffectual government official, he could also play figures of authority whose geniality sometimes hid an iron fist in a velvet glove. The relatively minor nature of these roles enabled him to turn out close to 20 films a year for most of his Hollywood career.

1935: Dangerous. 1936: China Clipper. Bunker Bean (GB: His Majesty Bunker Bean). Forgotten Faces. Counterfeit. The Gentleman from Louisiana. Love Letters of a Star. It Had to Happen. Mr Deeds Goes to Town. Nobody's Fool. Swing Time. Sitting on the Moon. Under Your Spell. Country Gentlemen. Larceny on the Air. 1937: Waikiki Wedding. The Singing Marine. Bill Cracks Down (GB: Men of Steel). Breakfast for Two. The Californian (GB: Beyond the Law). Confession. Daughter of Shanghai (GB: Daughter of the Orient). Ever Since Eve. Devil's Playground. Green Light. The Hit Parade. Dangerous Number. The Go-Getter. Internes Can't Take Money (GB: You Can't Take Money). The Last Gangster. The Man Who Cried Wolf. Rosalie. The Life of Emile Zola. Marked Woman. Married Before Breakfast. Paradise Isle. Michael O'Halloran. Breezing Home. Sea Devils. She's Dangerous. Stage Door. Reported Missing. Mountain Justice. 1938: Midnight Intruder. The Chaser. Arsene Lupin Returns. Dangerous to Know. Girls on Probation. Illegal Traffic. Girls' School. King of Alcatraz (GB: King of the Alcatraz). The Lady Objects. The Mad Miss Manton. Boy Meets Girl. Mr Doodle Kicks Off. Mr Moto's Gamble. There's Always a Woman. State Police. Tip-Off Girls. You Can't Take It With You. Young Dr Kildare. There's That Woman Again. 1939: The Covered Trailer. First Offenders. Adventures of Jane Arden. Death of a Champion. Geronimo. King of the Underworld. The Great Victor Herbert. Mr Smith Goes to Washington. The Mysterious Miss X. King of Chinatown. Off the Record. Outside These Walls. Risky Business. Secret Service of the Air. Spirit of Culver (GB: Man's Heritage). Society Lawyer. They Made Her a Spy. Wall Street Cowboy. Wings of the Navy. Everything's On Ice. The Jones Family in Hollywood. 1940: Dr Kildare's Crisis. Captain Caution. The Earl of Chicago. Father is a Prince. Out West With the Peppers. Golden Gloves. I Love You Again. No Time for Comedy. Hired Wife. Five Little Peppers in Trouble. Queen of the Mob. Road to Singapore. Rhythm on the River. The Bank Dick (GB: The Bank Detective). Sailor's Lady. Street of Memories. Yesterday's Heroes. Mystery Sea Raider. Knute Rockne – All American (GB: A Modern Hero). 1941: A Man Betrayed (GB: Citadel of Crime). Adventure in Washington (GB: Female Correspondent). Buy Me That Town. Cheers for Miss Bishop. Cracked Nuts. Ellery Queen and the Murder Ring (GB: The Murder Ring). Father

Takes a Wife. For Beauty's Sake. Jesse James at Bay. Lydia. Bedtime Story. The Green Hornet Strikes Again (serial). Great Guns. Life Begins for Andy Hardy. Lady for a Night. Meet John Doe. Life With Henry. Nevada City. Naval Academy. Petticoat Politics. Obliging Young Lady. She Knew All the Answers. The Trial of Mary Dugan. Unfinished Business. Ice-Capades Revue (GB: Rhythm Hits the Ice). 1942: Nazi Agent. Panama Hattie. Secrets of the Underground. Stand By All Networks! The Adventures of Martin Eden. Heart of the Rio Grande. The Magnificent Dope. The Pride of the Yankees. We Were Dancing. Whistling in Dixie. Yokel Boy (GB: Hitting the Headlines). Dr Kildare's Wedding Day (GB: Mary Names the Day). Cinderella Swings It. 1943: The Iron Major. Destination Tokyo. Thousands Cheer. The Chance of a Lifetime. Du Barry Was a Lady. Destroyer. Jack London. Mission to Moscow. Old Acquaintance. Crazy House. Riding High (GB: Melody Inn). Swing Shift Maisie (GB: The Girl in Overalls). They Came to Blow Up America. This is the Army. What a Woman (GB: The Beautiful Cheat). Week-End Pass. It Ain't Hay (GB: Money for Jam). 1944: Once Upon a Time. Atlantic City. Bermuda Mystery. Dead Man's Eyes. The Great Mike. Jungle Woman. End of the Road. Ladies of Washington. Oh, What a Night. South of Dixie. Shadow of Suspicion. Meet Miss Bobby Socks. Song of the Range. Wing and a Prayer. 1945: Incendiary Blonde. The Stork Club. Divorce. Thrill of a Romance. Here Come the Co-Eds. Allotment Wives (GB: Woman in the Case). Adventure. Dakota. Docks of New York. Follow That Woman. Captain Tugboat Annie. I'll Tell the World. I Love a Bandleader (GB: Memory for Two). Keep Your Powder Dry. Mr Muggs Rides Again. Roughly Speaking. The Phantom Speaks. Out of the Night/Strange Illusion. I'll Remember April. Over 21. Three's a Crowd. Honeymoon Ahead. She Gets Her Man. Apology for Murder. 1946: Magnificent Doll. The Plainsman and the Lady. The Jolson Story. Behind the Mask. Claudia and David. G I War Brides. I Ring Doorbells. Little Giant (GB: On the Carpet). Miss Susie Slagle's (completed 1944). The Madonna's Secret. Murder is My Business. High School Hero. The Missing Lady. Her Sister's Secret. The Kid from Brooklyn. Secrets of a Sorority Girl (GB: Secret of Linda Hamilton). The Shadow Returns. Shock. Sioux City Sue (Watkin was actually born in Sioux City!). Two Years Before the Mast. So Goes My Love (GB: A Genius in the Family). Swamp Fire. The Shocking Miss Pilgrim. 1947: Brick Bradford (serial). Monsieur Verdoux. Jack Armstrong (serial). Hard-Boiled Mahoney. Her Husband's Affair. The Red Stallion. Song of Love. The Fabulous Texan. Glamour Girl. The Secret Life of Walter Mitty. The Web. Violence. The Wild Frontier. 1948: The Counterfeiters. BF's Daughter (GB: Polly Fulton). Superman (serial). A Southern Yankee (GB: My Hero). Fighting Back. Daredevils of the Clouds. Incident. Don't Trust Your Husband/An Innocent Affair. The Gentleman from Nowhere. The Hunted. Mary Lou. Siren of Atlantis. State of the Union (GB: The World and His Wife). The Strange Mrs Crane. The Shanghai Chest. Trapped by Boston Blackie. 1949: Slightly French. The Fountainhead. Alaska Patrol. Flamingo Road. Neptune's Daughter. Siren of

Atlantis. Make Believe Ballroom. Samson and Delilah. Hold That Baby. Frontier Outpost. Knock on Any Door. The Story of Seabiscuit (GB: Pride of Kentucky). Miss Mink of 1949. Tulsa. Zamba (GB: Zamba the Gorilla). 1950: Emergency Wedding (GB: Jealousy). Key to the City. Three Little Words. Blue Grass of Kentucky. The Big Hangover. Atom Man vs Superman (serial). Last of the Buccaneers. Nancy Goes to Rio. Over the Border. Radar Secret Service. Redwood Forest Trail. Rock Island Trail (GB: Transcontinent Express). Southside 1–1000 (GB: Forgery). Sunset in the West. The Second Face. Two Lost Worlds. 1951: Belle le Grand. In Old Amarillo. Scandal Sheet (GB: The Dark Page). 1952: Hold That Line. Lovely to Look At. Thundering Caravans. A Yank in Indo China (GB: Hidden Secret). 1953: Canadian Mounties vs Atomic Invaders (serial). Count the Hours (GB: Every Minute Counts). The Stranger Wore a Gun. 1954: About Mrs Leslie. Johnny Dark. 1955: Lay That Rifle Down. The Big Bluff. The Creature With the Atom Brain. The Eternal Sea. Sudden Danger. Rin Tin Tin: Hero of the West (TV. GB: cinemas). 1956: Don't Knock the Rock. The Maverick Queen. Thunder Over Arizona. Shake, Rattle and Rock. 1957: Beginning of the End. Pal Joey. Spook Chasers. 1958: High School Confidential! Marjorie Morningstar. 1959: The Flying Fontaines.

WATLING, Jack 1923–
Fair-haired, round-faced, boyish-looking British actor, in films as a teenager. Despite experience on the Shakespeare stage, he found himself cast in post-war years as slightly shady, trilby-tilted types from working-class backgrounds. From 1952 to 1964 he was the hero of many low-budget light thrillers and comedies. Several of his children later took up acting careers, although none with quite the same success.

1938: Sixty Glorious Years (US: Queen of Destiny). The Housemaster. 1939: Goodbye Mr Chips! 1941: Ships with Wings. Major Barbara. 1942: The Young Mr Pitt. The Day Will Dawn (US: the Avengers). 1943: The Demi-Paradise (US: Adventure for Two). We Dive at Dawn. 1944: The Way Ahead (US: Immortal Battalion). 1945: Journey Together. 1947: The Courtneys of Curzon Street (US: The Courtney Affair). Easy Money. 1948: The Winslow Boy. Quartet. 1949: Maria Chapdelaine/The Naked Heart. Under Capricorn.

1950: Once a Sinner. 1951: White Corridors. 1952: Private Information. Father's Doing Fine. 1953: Flannelfoot. Meet Mr Lucifer. 1954: A Tale of Three Women. Dangerous Cargo. Trouble in the Glen. The Golden Link. The Sea Shall Not Have Them. 1955: *The Imperfect Gentleman. Windfall. A Time to Kill. Confidential Report (US: Mr Arkadin). 1956: Reach for the Sky. That Woman Opposite (US: City After Midnight). 1957: The Birthday Present. The Admirable Crichton (US: Paradise Lagoon). 1958: Gideon's Day (US: Gideon of Scotland Yard). A Night to Remember. Chain of Events. The Solitary Child. Links of Justice. 1959: Sink the Bismarck! 1960: The Queen's Guards. 1961: Nearly a Nasty Accident. Three on a Spree. Mary Had a Little . . . Nothing Barred. 1962: Flat Two. 1964: Who Was Maddox? 1965: The Nanny. 1971: Follow Me (US: The Public Eye). 1972: Father Dear Father. 1974: 11 Harrowhouse.

WATSON, Jack 1921–
Craggy, rugged-looking, ginger-haired Londoner who so firmly established himself as a character actor in the 1960s (sergeant-majors and similarly gruff types) that few now remember that he was also a brisk and funny music-hall comedian and monologuist for 15 years, in succession to his comedian father Nosmo King, to whom he was stooge in his first variety experience. He played very sporadic post-war film roles, but it was a part in TV's Z Cars that launched his second career in earnest. In private life an outdoor sports fanatic for many years.

1945: *Pathé Radio Music Hall. 1948: The Small Back Room (US: Hour of Glory). 1951: Captain Horatio Hornblower RN (US: Captain Horatio Hornblower). 1953: Blood Orange. 1954: Dangerous Cargo. 1955: Barbados Quest. 1956: Booby Trap. 1957: The Steel Bayonet. 1958: A Cry from the Streets. 1960: The Man Who Was Nobody. Peeping Tom. The Queen's Guards. 1961: Konga. 1962: Time to Remember. Fate Takes a Hand. Out of the Fog. On the Beat. This Sporting Life. 1963: Five to One. Master Spy. 1964: The Gorgon. 1965: The Hill. The Night Caller (US: Blood Beast from Outer Space). 1966: The Idol. Grand Prix. Tobruk. 1967: The Strange Affair. 1968: The Devil's Brigade. Decline and Fall . . . of a Birdwatcher! 1969: Midas Run (GB: A Run on Gold). 1970: Every Home Should Have One

(US: *Think Dirty*). *The Mackenzie Break.*
1971: *Von Richthofen and Brown* (GB: *The
Red Baron*). *Kidnapped.* 1972: *Tower of Evil*
(US: *Horror of Snape Island*). 1973: *From
Beyond the Grave.* 1974: *The Four Musketeers*
(*The Revenge of Milady*). *Juggernaut. 11
Harrowhouse.* 1975: *Brannigan.* 1976:
Treasure Island. 1977: *The Wild Geese. Purple
Taxi/Taxi mauve.* 1978: *Schizo.* 1979: *North
Sea Hijack* (US: *ffolkes*). 1980: *The Sea
Wolves. Masada* (TV. GB: abridged for cinemas
as *The Antagonists*). 1983: *Tangier.*

WATSON, Lucile 1879–1962

Pixie-like, fair-haired, sharp-nosed, bright-
eyed, often dominant Canadian actress who
played character roles in Hollywood from
1934 after long stage experience in New
York dating back to 1900. Often assuming
British or foreign accents, the veteran actress
was, as befitted her Broadway experience,
an expert at taking centre stage from less
experienced principals. After making her
last Hollywood film in 1951, she returned to
the stage and made occasional appearances
in TV drama up to her death.

1916: *The Girl With the Green Eyes.* 1934:
What Every Woman Knows. *Men in Black.*
1935: *The Bishop Misbehaves* (GB: *The
Bishop's Misadventures*). 1936: *The Garden of
Allah. A Woman Rebels.* 1937: *Three Smart
Girls.* 1938: *The Young in Heart. Sweethearts.*
1939: *Made for Each Other. The Women.*
1940: *Florian. Waterloo Bridge.* 1941: *Mr and
Mrs Smith. Footsteps in the Dark. Rage in
Heaven. The Great Lie. Model Wife.* 1943:
Watch on the Rhine. 1944: *The Thin Man
Goes Home. Uncertain Glory. Till We Meet
Again.* 1946: *Song of the South. Tomorrow is
Forever. Never Say Goodbye. My Reputation.
The Razor's Edge.* 1947: *Ivy.* 1948: *The
Emperor Waltz. That Wonderful Urge. Julia
Misbehaves.* 1949: *Little Women. Everybody
Does It.* 1950: *Harriet Craig. Let's Dance.*
1951: *My Forbidden Past.*

WATSON, Wylie

(John Wylie Robertson) 1889–1966
Small, slightly built, dark-haired, moustachioed Scottish actor who played wily,
henpecked or mealy-mouthed little men. A
member of a family variety act, he started
his career before the turn of the century, as
a boy vocalist singing 15 times a day in a

waxworks. He is said to have made his film
debut in a 1928 Hollywood film while on a
trip to America, but became a British film
regular after his role as Mr Memory in
Hitchcock's 1935 version of *The 39 Steps.*
Went to Australia in the early 1950s.

1932: *For the Love of Mike.* 1933: *Leave It to
Me. Hawleys of High Street.* 1934: *Road House.*
1935: *The 39 Steps. Black Mask.* 1936: *Radio
Lover.* 1937: *Please Teacher. Why Pick On
Me? Paradise for Two* (US: *The Gaiety Girls*).
1938: *Queer Cargo* (US: *Pirates of the Seven
Seas*). *Yes, Madam?* 1939: *Jamaica Inn.
She Couldn't Say No.* 1940: *Pack Up Your
Troubles. 'Bulldog' Sees It Through.* 1941:
*Danny Boy. *From the Far Corners. My Wife's
Family. The Saint Meets the Tiger. *Mr
Proudfoot Shows a Light.* 1943. *The Lamp
Still Burns. The Flemish Farm.* 1944: *Tawny
Pipit. Kiss the Bride Goodbye. Waterloo Road.
Don't Take It to Heart. Strawberry Roan. The
World Owes Me a Living.* 1945: *Don Chicago.
Waltz Time. Murder in Reverse. The Trojan
Brothers.* 1946: *The Years Between. A Girl in
a Million.* 1947: *Brighton Rock* (US: *Young
Scarface*). *Fame Is the Spur. Temptation Har-
bour. My Brother Jonathan.* 1948: *London
Belongs to Me* (US: *Dulcimer Street*). *No Room
at the Inn. Things Happen at Night. Whisky
Galore!* (US: *Tight Little Island*). *The History
of Mr Polly.* 1949: *Train of Events.* 1950:
Your Witness (US: *Eye Witness*). *Morning
Departure* (US: *Operation Disaster*). *Shadow
of the Past. The Magnet. Happy Go Lovely.*
1960: *The Sundowners.*

WATTIS, Richard 1912–1975

Bespectacled, heron-like British supporting
actor whose neat light-brown hair concealed
an unexpected bald patch at the back and
whose thin, elongated lips could open wide
and screw themselves into expressions of
Donald Duck-like outrage, while the plain-
tively light, upper-class Wattis tones com-
plained of some new affront. He was the
happy butt of many British comedians, often
as salesmen, butlers, solicitors and teachers.
Died from a heart attack.

1937: *A Yank at Oxford.* 1949: *Marry Me!
Kind Hearts and Coronets. Helter Skelter. Stop
Press Girl. The Chiltern Hundreds* (US: *The
Amazing Mr Beecham*). 1950: *The Happiest
Days of Your Life. The Clouded Yellow. Your
Witness* (US: *Eye Witness*). 1951: *Appointment
with Venus* (US: *Island Rescue*). *Lady Godiva*

Rides Again. 1952: *Song of Paris* (US: *Bachelor
in Paris*). *The Happy Family* (US: *Mr Lord
Says No*). *Mother Riley Meets the Vampire*
(US: *Vampire Over London*). *Made in Heaven.
The Importance of Being Earnest. Stolen Face.
Derby Day* (US: *Four Against Fate*). *Penny
Princess. Top Secret* (US: *Mr Potts Goes to
Moscow*). *Appointment in London.* 1953: *The
Intruder. The Final Test. Background* (US:
Edge of Divorce). *Top of the Form. Innocents in
Paris. Colonel March Investigates. Small Town
Story. Blood Orange. Park Plaza 605* (US:
Norman Conquest). 1954: *The Belles of St
Trinian's. Doctor in the House. Lease of Life.
Hobson's Choice. The Crowded Day. The
Colditz Story.* 1955: *Escapade. As Long As
They're Happy. Man of the Moment. See How
They Run. The Time of His Life. I Am a
Camera. A Yank in Ermine. An Alligator
Named Daisy. Simon and Laura. Jumping for
Joy. The Man Who Never Was.* 1956: *The
Silken Affair. Around the World in 80 Days.
The Man Who Knew Too Much. Eyewitness.
It's a Wonderful World. The Green Man. The
Iron Petticoat.* 1957: *The Prince and the Show-
girl. The Abominable Snowman. Second Fiddle.
Barnacle Bill* (US: *All at Sea*). *High Flight.
The Little Hut. Blue Murder at St Trinian's.*
1958: *The Inn of the Sixth Happiness. The
Captain's Table. Ten Seconds to Hell.* 1959:
*The Ugly Duckling. Libel. Left, Right and
Centre. Your Money or Your Wife. Follow a
Star. Follow That Horse!* 1961: *Very Important
Person* (US: *A Coming Out Party*). *Dentist on
the Job* (US: *Get On With It!*). *Nearly a Nasty
Accident.* 1962: *Play It Cool. I Thank a Fool.
Bon Voyage! The Longest Day. Come Fly With
Me.* 1963: *The VIPs.* 1964: *Carry On Spying.*
1965: *The Amorous Adventures of Moll
Flanders). The Battle of the Villa Fiorita. The
Legend of Young Dick Turpin. Up Jumped a
Swagman. You Must Be Joking! Bunny Lake is
Missing. The Alphabet Murders/The ABC
Murders. Operation Crossbow* (US: *The Great
Spy Mission*). *The Liquidator.* 1966: *The Great
St Trinian's Train Robbery.* 1967: *Casino
Royale.* 1968: *Wonderwall. Chitty Chitty Bang
Bang.* 1969: *Monte Carlo or Bust* (US: *Those
Daring Young Men in Their Jaunty Jalopies*).
1970: *Games That Lovers Play. Egghead's
Robot.* 1971: *Tam Lin/The Devil's Widow.
The Troublesome Double.* 1972: *Sex and the
Other Woman. That's Your Funeral. Diamonds
on Wheels.* 1973: *Take Me High* (US: *Hot
Property*). 1974: *Confessions of a Window
Cleaner.*

WEBBER, Robert 1924–1989

Smooth, handsome (a kind of cross between Richard Arlen and Bruce Cabot), dark-haired American actor who started as a leading man, but seemed to prefer character roles, often turning up as plausible charmers or executives with feet of clay. He began acting in the US Marines during his war service, but didn't settle in films until the mid-1960s. Said he liked playing 'the antagonist' and later also showed a penchant for fairly broad comedy.

1951: Highway 301. 1957: Twelve Angry Men. 1962: The Nun and the Sergeant. 1963: The Stripper (GB: Woman of Summer). Hysteria. 1965: The Sandpiper. The Third Day. Tecnida di un omicidio (GB: No Tears for a Killer. US: Hired Killer). 1966: Dead Heat on a Merry-Go-Round. Harper (GB: The Moving Target). The Silencers. 1967: Don't Make Waves. The Dirty Dozen. 1968: Manon 70. The Big Bounce. 1970: The Great White Hope. The Movie Murderer (TV). Hauser's Memory (TV). 1971: Thief (TV). $ (GB: The Heist). 1972: Cutter. 1973: Piedone à Hong Kong. Death and the Maiden (TV). Double Indemnity (TV). 1974: Bring Me the Head of Alfredo Garcia. Murder or Mercy (TV). 1975: Death Stalk. 1976: Passi di morte perduti nel buio. Madame Claude (US: The French Woman). Midway (GB: Battle of Midway). 1977: Casey's Shadow. L'imprecateur. The Choirboys. 1978: Revenge of the Pink Panther. Gardenia. 1979: '10'. Streets of LA (TV). Tenspeed and Brown-shoe (TV). Courage fuyons. 1980: Les séducteurs/Sunday Lovers. Private Benjamin. 1981: S.O.B. 1982: Don't Go to Sleep. Not Just Another Affair (TV). The Man with the Deadly Lens/Wrong is Right. Starflight One (TV. GB: cinemas). Who Dares Wins (US: The Final Option). 1983: Cocaine: One Man's Seduction (TV). Shooting Stars (TV). 1984: No Man's Land (TV). Getting Physical (TV). 1985: Wild Geese II. Half Nelson (TV). In Like Flynn (TV). 1986: Assassin (TV). 1987: Nuts.

WEIDLER, Virginia 1927–1968

Not many screen children really qualify as character players, but bumpy-nosed Virginia Weidler was definitely one of them. The dark-haired California tot had homely, inquisitive features, could sing a bit (her mother was an opera singer) and was usually seen as the kid told to scram because she

bothered the adults. One director went on record as saying she would never really get anywhere as a juvenile because 'all she can do is act'. He was right. Despite spells at Paramount and MGM, the 'little horror' was washed up at 18. She married happily, but died from a heart attack at 41.

1931: Surrender. 1933: After Tonight. 1934: Long Lost Father. Stamboul Quest. Mrs Wiggs of the Cabbage Patch. 1935: Freckles. Laddie. *Lucky Stars. The Big Broadcast of 1936. Peter Ibbetson. 1936: Trouble for Two (GB: The Suicide Club). *Lucky Starlets. Timothy's Quest. Girl of the Ozarks. The Big Broadcast of 1937. 1937: Maid of Salem. Souls at Sea. The Outcasts of Poker Flat. 1938: Scandal Street. Out West With the Hardys. Love Is a Headache. Mother Carey's Chickens. Men With Wings. Too Hot to Handle. 1939: Fixer Dugan. The Lone Wolf Spy Hunt (GB: The Lone Wolf's Daughter). The Under-Pup. Bad Little Angel. The Women. The Great Man Votes. The Spellbinder. The Rookie Cop (GB: Swift Vengeance). Henry Goes Arizona (GB: Spats to Spurs). 1940: All This and Heaven Too. Gold Rush Maisie. The Philadelphia Story. 1941: Young Tom Edison. I'll Wait for You. Barnacle Bill. Keeping Company. Babes on Broadway. 1942: The Affairs of Martha (GB: Once Upon a Thursday). This Time for Keeps. Born to Sing. 1943: The Youngest Profession. Best Foot Forward.

WEIR, Molly 1920–

One of the best-known voices on British radio for more than 40 years belongs to this diminutive Scots woman with the dimpled cheeks and mile-wide grin who, in more recent times, also made her mark in TV commercials. Despite a 1944 film debut, she has rarely ventured into films, but has become a 'home' expert on cookery, gardening and knitting and a popular public speaker, as well as somehow finding time to write seven amusing volumes of autobiography. Her distinctive Glaswegian tones became nationally famous in the 1940s and 1950s as Tattie in ITMA and Aggie in Life With the Lyons — two long-running British radio shows.

1944: 2,000 Women. *Birthday. 1948: *It Began on the Clyde! 1949: Madeleine. Floodtide. 1950: Something in the City. 1951: Flesh and Blood. Cheer the Brave. 1952: Miss Robin

Hood. 1953: Forces' Sweetheart. Small Town Story. *The Silent Witness. Life With the Lyons (US: Family Affair). 1954: The Diamond (US: Diamond Wizard). The Lyons in Paris. 1955: John and Julie. Value for Money. 1957: Let's Be Happy. 1959: The Bridal Path. 1960: The Hands of Orlac. 1961: Carry On Regardless. What a Whopper! 1968: The Prime of Miss Jean Brodie. 1970: Scrooge. 1971: Hands of the Ripper. The Magnificent Six and a ½ (third series). 1972: Bless This House. 1973: Assassin. 1975: One of Our Dinosaurs is Missing. 1978: Mr Selkie.

WELDEN, Ben

(Benjamin Weinblatt) 1901–

Short, stockily-built, round-faced, wary-looking American-born actor with receding dark hair, popular in early British films as tough-talking gangsters and sharpsters, even getting a leading role or two. He went to Hollywood in 1936 and stayed, although, after a good start as Humphrey Bogart's henchman in Kid Galahad, he declined to fairly minor mobster roles, often of the dim variety.

1929: The Hole in the Wall. 1930: The Man from Chicago. Big Business. 1931: Who Killed Doc Robin? 77 Park Lane (US: Gambling Den). 1932: The Missing Rembrandt. Tin Gods. His Lordship (US: Man of Affaires). The Innocents of Chicago (US: Why Saps Leave Home). Born Lucky. Puppets of Fate (US: Wolves of the Underworld). 1933: Home Sweet Home. Send 'Em Back Half Dead. The Medicine Man. Mr Quincey of Monte Carlo. Their Night

Out. His Grace Gives Notice. Pride of the Force. General John Regan. This is the Life. Mannequin. The River Wolves. 1934: Aunt Sally (US: Along Came Sally). The Black Abbot. The Man Who Changed His Name. Gay Love. The Medium. 1935: Death on the Set (US: Murder on the Set). Annie, Leave the Room! Royal Cavalcade (US: Regal Cavalcade). The Big Splash. Admirals All. Come Out of the Pantry. The Mystery of the Marie Celeste/The Mystery of the Mary Celeste (US: Phantom Ship). The Triumph of Sherlock Holmes. Trust the Navy. Alibi Inn. 1936: The Man Who Could Work Miracles. The Avenging Hand. Hot News. The Improper Duchess. She Knew What She Wanted. 1937: The Great Barrier (US: Silent Barriers). Another Dawn. Back in Circulation. Alcatraz Island. Confession. The Duke Comes Back (GB: The Call of the Ring). Kid Galahad. The Great Garrick. Love is On the Air (GB: The Radio Murder Mystery). The Missing Witness/Missing Witnesses. The Last Gangster. Love and Hisses. The King and the Chorus Girl (GB: Romance is Sacred). Maytime. Marked Woman. Westbound Mail. That Certain Woman. Varsity Show. 1938: Always Goodbye. City Girl. Federal Man Hunt (GB: Flight from Justice). Crime Ring. *What Price Safety? Happy Landing. Little Miss Broadway. Mystery House. Little Orphan Annie. The Night Hawk. Smashing the Rackets. Prison Nurse. The Saint in New York. Straight, Place and Show (US: They're Off!). Tenth Avenue Kid. 1939: The Earl of Chicago. Fugitive at Large. Hollywood Cavalcade. Boys' Reformatory. I Was a Convict. The Lone Wolf Spy Hunt (GB: The Lone Wolf's Daughter). The Roaring Twenties. Sergeant Madden. The Star Maker. Rose of Washington Square. Stand Up and Fight. 1940: City for Conquest. Tear Gas Squad. Passport to Alcatraz (GB: Alien Sabotage). Outside the 3-Mile Limit (GB: Mutiny on the Seas). Strange Cargo. South of Pago Pago. Wolf of New York. 1941: *At the Stroke of 12. I'll Wait for You. Mr District Attorney. Men of Boys' Town. Right to the Heart/Knockout. Manpower. Out of the Fog. Strange Alibi. Nine Lives Are Not Enough. 1942: All Through the Night. A Close Call for Ellery Queen (GB: A Close Call). Bullet Scars. Dangerously They Live. Highways by Night. Maisie Gets Her Man (GB: She Gets Her Man). Stand By for Action! (GB: Cargo of Innocents). 1943: Appointment With Murder. Here Comes Elmer! Dr Gillespie's Criminal Case (GB: Crazy to Kill). Secrets of the Underground. 1944: The Fighting Seabees. Shadows in the Night. It's in the Bag! (GB: The Fifth Chair). 1945: Angel on My Shoulder. Circumstantial Evidence. Bells of Rosarita. Follow That Woman. The Missing Corpse. 1946: Anna and the King of Siam. The Big Sleep. Dangerous Business. Mr Hex (GB: Pride of the Bowery). The Last Crooked Mile. 1947: Fiesta. Heading for Heaven. Here Comes Trouble. The Man I Love. Killer Dill. The Pretender. Sinbad the Sailor. Too Many Winners. 1948: Appointment With Murder (and 1943 film). The Dude Goes West. Jinx Money. Lady at Midnight. My Dear Secretary. The Noose Hangs High. Smart Girls Don't Talk. A Song is Born. The Vicious Circle. Impact. Trapped by Boston Blackie. 1949: Fighting Fools. Mary Ryan, Detective. Riders in the Sky. Search for Danger. Sorrowful Jones.

Tough Assignment. 1950: Buccaneer's Girl. The Desert Hawk. On the Isle of Samoa. 1951: *The Awful Sleuth. *Woo Woo Blues. The Lemon Drop Kid. My True Story. Tales of Robin Hood. 1952: Deadline – U.S.A. (GB: Deadline). Night Stage to Galveston. 1953: All Ashore. Thunder Bay. The Veils of Bagdad. 1954: Killers from Space. The Steel Cage. 1955: The Benny Goodman Story. Ma and Pa Kettle at Waikiki. The Adventures of Captain Africa (serial). 1956: Superman Flies Again (TV. GB: cinemas). Hidden Guns. Hollywood or Bust. 1957: Spook Chasers. Night Passage.

WELSH, John 1905–1985
Tall, lean, austere, balding, slightly aloof-looking Irish actor, often cast as people of breeding and authority, sometimes with feet of clay. After years of theatrical experience at the Gate Theatre, Dublin, he moved to London, entering the theatre there in 1950 and films two years later. Much television work followed (and a spell with the Royal Shakespeare Company), often playing decaying aristocrats. He died from cancer.

1952: Isn't Life Wonderful! 1953: The Case of Soho Red. The Clue of the Missing Ape. 1954: Diplomatic Passport. Mask of Dust (US: Race for Life). Track the Man Down. An Inspector Calls. The Divided Heart. 1955: Contraband Spain. Confession (US: The Deadliest Sin). The Dark Avenger (US: The Warriors). Lost (US: Tears for Simon). The Man Who Never Was. 1956: The Long Arm (US: The Third Key). The Man in the Road. Women Without Men (US: Blonde Bait). The Secret Place. Brothers in Law. 1957: Lucky Jim. The Counterfeit Plan. Man in the Shadow. The Long Haul. The Surgeon's Knife. The Safe-cracker. The Birthday Present. The Man Who Wouldn't Talk. 1958: Dunkirk. Indiscreet. She Didn't Say No. Behind the Mask. The Revenge of Frankenstein. Next to No Time! Room at the Top. Nowhere to Go. 1959: The Rough and the Smooth (US: Portrait of a Sinner). Bobbikins. The Night We Dropped a Clanger (US: Make Mine a Double). Operation Bullshine. Follow That Horse! 1960: Konga. The Trials of Oscar Wilde (US: The Man With the Green Carnation). Beyond the Curtain. Snowball. 1961: Circle of Deception. Francis of Assisi. The Mark. *The Square Mile Murder. Johnny Nobody. The Wild and the Willing. Go to Blazes. 1962: Playboy of the Western World. Number Six.

The Quare Fellow. The Inspector (US: Lisa). Out of the Fog. 1963: Life for Ruth (US: Walk in the Shadow). Nightmare. 1964: Dead End Creek. 1965: Rasputin – The Mad Monk. 1967: Attack on the Iron Coast. 1968: Subterfuge. 1970: The Man Who Haunted Himself. Cromwell. 1971: The Pied Piper. 1973: Yellow Dog. A Story of Tutenkhamun (TV. US: cinemas). 1978: The Thirty-Nine Steps. 1981: From a Far Country. 1983: Krull.

WENGRAF, John
(Johannes Wenngraft) 1897–1974
Scraggy, dark-haired, bush-browed Viennese-born actor with unusually long space between nose and lip; it gave him lowering looks which he would adapt equally to the kindly or sinister. He was almost entirely a stage actor before flight from the Nazis took him first to Britain, then to Hollywood. Inevitably at first cast as Nazis himself, he later played more than a fair share of professors and ambivalent advisers.

1922: Homo sum. 1940: †Night Train to Munich (US: Night Train). †Convoy. †Sailors Three (US: Three Cockeyed Sailors). 1911: *†All Hands. 1942: Lucky Jordan. 1943: Mission to Moscow. Paris After Dark (GB: The Night Is Ending). Sahara. Song of Russia. 1944: The Seventh Cross. Till We Meet Again. U-Boat Prisoner (GB: Dangerous Mists). The Thin Man Goes Home. Strange Affair. 1945: Week-End at the Waldorf. 1946: Tomorrow is Forever. The Razor's Edge. 1947: T-Men. 1948: Sofia. 1949: The Loveable Cheat. 1951: Belle le Grand. 1952: Five Fingers. Tropic Zone. 1953: The Desert Rats. Flight to Tangier. The French Line. Call Me Madam. 1954: Hell and High Water. The Gambler from Natchez. Paris Playboys. Gog. 1955: The Racers (GB: Such Men Are Dangerous). 1956: Never Say Goodbye. The Pride and the Passion. 1957: Valerie. Oh Men! Oh Women! The Disembodied. 1958: The Return of Dracula (GB: The Fantastic Disappearing Man). 1960: Portrait in Black. 12 to the Moon. 1961: Judgment at Nuremberg. Hitler. 1963: The Prize. 1965: Ship of Fools.

† As Hans Wengraf

WESSON, Dick 1919–1979
Toothy, mule-faced, crew-cut American nightclub comedian, often in endearingly panicky roles in his brief (10-film) contract

years with Warner Brothers, during which his most successful part was as Francis Fryer in *Calamity Jane*. He provided likeable comedy relief in other films, and it was a surprise when he returned to radio, TV and nightclub work in the mid-1950s. Cropped up a couple of times on screen in 1977, looking the same as 20 years before; but then, within three weeks of his 60th birthday, Wesson shot himself. Not to be confused with thick-set American supporting actor Dick Wessel (1910–1965), in dozens of films from 1934 on. Father of actress Eileen Wesson (1948–).

1949: Destination Moon. 1950: Breakthrough. 1951: Inside the Walls of Folsom Prison. Sunny Side of the Street. Starlift. Force of Arms. Jim Thorpe—All American (GB: Man of Bronze). 1952: About Face. The Man Behind the Gun. 1953: The Desert Song. Calamity Jane. 1954: The Charge at Feather River. 1955: Paris Follies of 1956. 1961: The Errand Boy. 1976: A Star is Dead (TV). 1977: Dog and Cat (TV). Rollercoaster.

WEST, Lockwood 1905–1989
Balding, sharp-eyed, crane-like (but solidly built) British actor with friendly air; equally likely to turn up in amiable or ghoulish roles. Once employed by a north of England collieries' association, he determined to become an actor, and made his debut on the London stage in 1931, appearing almost exclusively in the theatre until the late 1940s, when his fish-eye lens features began to

crop up in the occasional film. Father of actor Timothy West (1934–). Died from cancer.

1937: The Gap. 1948: A Song for Tomorrow. 1949: For Them That Trespass. No Place for Jennifer. Celia. 1950: Mr Drake's Duck. Last Holiday. 1951: High Treason. 1952: Hammer the Toff. The Oracle (US: The Horse's Mouth). 1953: Single-Handed (US: Sailor of the King). 1954: Seagulls Over Sorrento (US: Crest of the Wave). Lilacs in the Spring (US: Let's Make Up). 1955: Touch and Go (US: The Light Touch). Private's Progress. 1957: Accused/ Mark of the Hawk. The Birthday Present. 1959: The Man Who Could Cheat Death. 1960: Tunes of Glory. 1961: Strongroom. 1963: The Leather Boys. The Running Man. 1965: Game for Three Losers. Life at the Top. Rotten to the Core. 1967: Bedazzled. Up the Junction. 1968: A Dandy in Aspic. 1969: One Brief Summer. 1970: Jane Eyre (TV. GB: cinemas). Loot. 1973: Clouds of Witness (TV). The Satanic Rites of Dracula (US: Count Dracula and His Vampire Bride). 1983: The Dresser. 1984: The Shooting Party. 1985: Young Sherlock Holmes.

WESTERFIELD, James 1912–1971
Big, beaming Jim Westerfield was the perfect screen incarnation of the slightly comic, frequently nonplussed New York cop. One can still see him taking off the peaked cap and scratching the balding head. There was a lot of this Tennessee-born actor at 6ft 1in and 200 lbs-plus, and much of the big face seemed to be teeth and eyebrows. Westerfield may have looked thick-skulled, but it was far from the truth. As a man of the theatre—the reason he didn't make more films—he was at various times set designer, producer and director and won two New York Drama Critics' awards for his acting. Died from a heart attack.

1940: The Howards of Virginia (GB: The Tree of Liberty). 1941: Highway West. 1942: The Magnificent Ambersons. The Spirit of Stanford (GB: Fighting Spirit). Timber. 1943: Around the World. 1944: Since You Went Away. 1946: The Chase. Undercurrent. O.S.S. 1950: Side Street. 1951: The Whistle at Eaton Falls (GB: Richer Than the Earth). 1954: The Human Jungle. Three Hours to Kill. On the Waterfront. The Violent Men (GB: Rough Company). 1955: Chief Crazy Horse (GB: Valley of Fury). The Cobweb. The Scarlet Coat. The Man With the

Gun (GB: The Trouble Shooter). Lucy Gallant. 1956: Away All Boats. 1957: Jungle Heat. Three Brave Men. Decision at Sundown. 1958: Cowboy. The Proud Rebel. 1959: The Hangman. The Shaggy Dog. The Gunfight at Dodge City. The Scarface Mob (TV. GB: cinemas). 1960: Wild River. The Plunderers. 1961: The Absent-Minded Professor. Homicidal. 1962: Birdman of Alcatraz. 1963: Son of Flubber. Man's Favorite Sport? 1964: Bikini Beach. 1965: The Sons of Katie Elder. That Funny Feeling. 1966: Dead Heat on a Merry-Go-Round. Scalplock (TV. GB: cinemas). 1967: Hang 'Em High. 1968: Blue. Now You See It, Now You Don't (TV). A Man Called Gannon. Burn! (GB: Queimada!). 1969: Smith! The Love God? True Grit. Set This Town on Fire (TV. Shown 1973). 1971: Dead Aim. 1973: Stacey and Her Gangbusters (completed 1971).

WESTMAN, Nydia 1902–1970
Fair-haired, palely attractive, stocky little American actress who had spinsters-on-the-shelf down to a T, and could make them comic, pathetic, twittering or fey. From theatrical parents, she made her Broadway debut at 16, alternating plays with films from the early 1930s. Left films in the late 1940s, but came back years later for a few old maids. Died from cancer.

1932: Strange Justice. Manhattan Tower. 1933: Bondage. The Way to Love. Little Women. The Cradle Song. King of the Jungle. From Hell to Heaven. 1934: Success at Any Price. Two Alone. Ladies Should Listen. Manhattan Love Song. The Trumpet Blows. One Night of Love. 1935: Dressed to Thrill. A Feather in Her Hat. Captain Hurricane. Sweet Adeline. 1936: Rose Bowl (GB: O'Riley's Luck). The Gorgeous Hussy. Craig's Wife. The Invisible Ray. Pennies from Heaven. Three Live Ghosts. 1937: Bulldog Drummond's Revenge. When Love is Young. 1938: The Goldwyn Follies. The First Hundred Years. Bulldog Drummond's Peril. 1939: When Tomorrow Comes. The Cat and the Canary. 1940: Hullabaloo. Forty Little Mothers. 1941: The Bad Man (GB: Two-Gun Cupid). The Chocolate Soldier. 1942: They All Kissed the Bride. The Remarkable Andrew. 1943: Hers to Hold. Princess O'Rourke. 1944: Her Primitive Man. 1947: The Late George Apley. 1948: The Velvet Touch. 1962: Don't Knock the Twist. 1963: For Love or Money. 1965: The Chase. 1966: The Ghost and Mr

Chicken. The Swinger. 1967: The Reluctant Astronaut. 1968: The Horse in the Gray Flannel Suit. 1969: Silent Night, Lonely Night (TV). 1970: Flap (GB: The Last Warrior). Rabbit Run.

WESTON, Jack (J. Weinstein) 1925–
Tubby, balding American actor sometimes seen as not-too-serious crooks or bungling, would-be helpful friends. He had a hard struggle to establish himself near the top of the supporting actors' league, taking menial work while fighting for a foothold in TV (which began to happen from the early 1950s) and films, to which he has remained only an occasional, but distinctive visitor. Married to actress Marge Redmond; he lists his hobbies as acting, films and lying down.

1958: Stage Struck. I Want to Live! 1959: Imitation of Life. 1960: Please Don't Eat the Daisies. 1961: The Honeymoon Machine. All in a Night's Work. 1962: It's Only Money. 1963: Palm Springs Weekend. The Incredible Mr Limpet. 1965: Mirage. The Cincinnati Kid. 1966: Code Name: Heraclitus (TV). Fame is the Name of the Game (TV). 1967: Wait Until Dark. I Love a Mystery (TV. Shown 1973). 1968: Now You See It, Now You Don't (TV). The Thomas Crown Affair. The Counterfeit Killer (TV. GB: cinemas). 1969: The April Fools. Cactus Flower. 1971: A New Leaf. 1972: Fuzz. 1973: Deliver Us from Evil (TV). Marco. 1976: Gator. The Ritz. 1979: Cuba. 1980: Can't Stop the Music. 1981: The Four Seasons. 1983: High Road to China. 1985: The Long Shot. 1987: Ishtar. RAD. Dirty Dancing. 1988: Short Circuit 2.

WHEATLEY, Alan 1907–1991
Supercilious, dark-haired (soon greying), shifty-eyed British actor with neat moustache and cutting, upper-class tones. Often the smooth villain whose surface coolness (and hair) was dishevelled by the hero before the end. An industrial psychologist who gradually veered away into acting, he was a newsreader for BBC radio in World War II. Gained greatest national fame in the 1950s as the Sheriff of Nottingham in the popular TV series *Robin Hood*. Died from a heart attack.

1936: Conquest of the Air (released 1940). 1945: Caesar and Cleopatra. The Rake's

Progress (US: Notorious Gentleman). 1946: Spring Song (US: Springtime). Appointment with Crime. 1947: Brighton Rock (US: Young Scarface). Jassy. End of the River. 1948: Calling Paul Temple. Counterblast. Corridor of Mirrors. Sleeping Car to Trieste. It's Not Cricket. 1949: For Them That Trespass. 1951: Home to Danger. Whispering Smith Hits London (US: Whispering Smith versus Scotland Yard). 1952: The Gift Horse (US: Glory at Sea). The Pickwick Papers. 1953: Spaceways. Small Town Story. The Limping Man. 1954: The House across the Lake (US: Heatwave). *Elizabethan Express (narrator only). The Diamond (US: Diamond Wizard). Delayed Action. 1955: Simon and Laura. 1958: The Duke Wore Jeans. 1959: Inn for Trouble. 1961: Shadow of the Cat. Checkmate. *Frederic Chopin. 1962: Tomorrow at Ten. 1963: Clash by Night. A Jolly Bad Fellow (US: They All Died Laughing).

WHILEY, Manning 1915–1975
British actor with dark hair and complexion, usually in neurotic or villainous roles. Despite something of a *tour de force* in the leading role of his second film, *Trunk Crime*, he soon slipped into routinely bad-tempered parts, and had faded from the show-business scene by the early 1950s.

1938: Consider Your Verdict. 1939: Trunk Crime (US: Design for Murder). The Four Just Men (US: The Secret Four). Inspector Hornleigh on Holiday (US: Inspector Hornleigh on Leave). 1940: Contraband (US: Blackout). Gasbags. Pastor Hall. The Flying Squad. Saloon Bar. *Miss Grant Goes to the Door. Pack Up Your Troubles. Sailors Three (US: Three

Cockeyed Sailors). Old Bill and Son. 1941: Freedom Radio (US: A Voice in the Night). *Mr Proudfoot Shows a Light. Pimpernel Smith (US: Mister V). The Ghost of St Michael's. The Saint's Vacation. Penn of Pennsylvania (US: The Courageous Mr Penn). 1943: Bell Bottom George. The Dummy Talks. 1944: Meet Sexton Blake. 1945: The Seventh Veil. For You Alone. 1946: The Shop at Sly Corner (US: The Code of Scotland Yard). 1947: Teheran (US: The Plot to Kill Roosevelt). Uncle Silas (US: The Inheritance). 1949: Children of Chance. 1952: Little Big Shot.

WHITAKER, Forest 1961–
Bulky, bubbly, round-faced black actor who has played his fair share of humbling and guileless innocents but also essayed a good variety of other roles, even attempting foreign accents with varying degrees of success. A former football star, Whitaker's first love was music, but he switched to drama while at university and was handed his first acting jobs at 21. Mainly in co-starring or top supporting roles, although he was an amusing centre to the mayhem in *A Rage in Harlem*, and won a Cannes Festival best actor award for his portrayal of jazz legend Charlie Parker in *Bird*. Has also dabbled in production and direction.

1982: Fast Times at Ridgemont High (GB: Fast Times). Tag – The Assassination Game. 1983: The Grand Baby. 1985: Vision Quest. 1986: Platoon. The Color of Money. 1987: Good Morning, Vietnam. Hands of a Stranger (TV). StakeOut. Bloodsport. 1988: Bird. 1989: Men at Work. Johnny Handsome. 1990: Downtown. Criminal Justice (TV). 1991: A Rage in Harlem. Article 99. Diary of a Hitman. 1992: The Crying Game. Consenting Adults. 1993: Lush Life. Body Snatchers. Last Light (TV). 1994: Bank Robber. Blown Away. Jason's Lyric. The Gold Cup. Prêt-à-Porter (US: Ready to Wear). Smoke. The Enemy Within. 1995: Species.

As director:
1933: Strapped. 1994: The Number Four. 1995: Waiting to Exhale.

WHITE, Jesse 1918–
Pug-faced, plug-ugly, beaky-nosed, brown-haired, cigar-chewing, stoutly built American actor who might have stepped straight from the pages of Damon Runyon.

His characters usually spoke out the side of their mouth, wore a pin-striped suit and were on the make. One can just imagine White at his earlier occupations of selling the latest cosmetics and beauty aids, before he tried cracking gags in nightclubs for a living and ended up as a legitimate actor on the Broadway stage by 1942. Hollywood gave him a few post-war roles, and, after he repeated his stage success supporting James Stewart in *Harvey*, he settled in as a character player, a favourite for taxi-drivers but an eye-catching performer in anything. Under-used by the cinema in more recent times.

1947: Kiss of Death. Gentleman's Agreement. 1948: Texas, Brooklyn and Heaven (GB: The Girl from Texas). 1950: Harvey. 1951: Death of a Salesman. Katie Did It. Bedtime for Bonzo. Francis Goes to the Races. Callaway Went Thataway (GB: The Star Said No!). The Raging Tide. 1952: The Girl in White (GB: So Bright the Flame). Million Dollar Mermaid (GB: The One Piece Bathing Suit). 1953: Gunsmoke. Forever Female. Champ for a Day. 1954: Hell's Half Acre. Witness to Murder. 1955: Not As a Stranger. The Girl Rush. 1956: The Come On. The Bad Seed. Back from Eternity. The Hefferan Family (TV. GB: cinemas). He Laughed Last. 1957: Designing Woman. God is My Partner. 1958: Country Music Holiday. Marjorie Morningstar. 1959: The Rise and Fall of Legs Diamond. 1960: The Big Night. Three Blondes in His Life. 1961: Tomboy and the Champ. A Fever in the Blood. On the Double. The Right Approach. Sail a Crooked Ship. 1962: It's Only Money. 1963: The Yellow Canary. It's a Mad, Mad, Mad, Mad World. 1964: Pajama Party. A House is Not a Home. Looking for Love. 1965: Dear Brigitte . . . 1966: The Spirit is Willing. The Ghost in the Invisible Bikini. 1967: The Reluctant Astronaut. 1970: Togetherness. 1971: Bless the Beasts and Children. 1973: The Brothers O'Toole. 1975: Las Vegas Lady. Return to Campus. Won Ton Ton, the Dog Who Saved Hollywood. 1976: New Girl in Town. Nashville Girl. 1978: The Cat from Outer Space. 1986: Monster in the Closet. 1993: Matinee.

WHITMORE, James 1921–

Solidly-built American actor with homely, philosophical face and crinkly sandy hair. Utterly reliable in performance, he was sort of a supporting players' Spencer Tracy. A

solid bulwark to MGM films of the early 1950s, Whitmore was usually to be found in sincere dramatic roles, but could also be delightfully comic, as demonstrated by his singing/clowning partnership with Keenan Wynn (*qv*) in *Kiss Me, Kate!* When films failed to make the most of him, he toured America with one-man shows. Twice nominated for an Oscar, in *Battleground* and *Give 'Em Hell Harry*.

1949: The Undercover Man. Battleground. 1950: The Asphalt Jungle. Please Believe Me. The Outriders. Mrs O'Malley and Mr Malone. The Next Voice You Hear. 1951: Across the Wide Missouri. The Red Badge of Courage (narrator only). Shadow in the Sky. 1952: Because You're Mine. Above and Beyond. 1953: The Girl Who Had Everything. Kiss Me, Kate! All the Brothers Were Valiant. The Great Diamond Robbery. 1954: The Command. Them! 1955: The McConnell Story (GB: Tiger in the Sky). Battle Cry. The Last Frontier. Oklahoma! 1956: The Eddy Duchin Story. Crime in the Streets. 1957: Deep Water (TV. GB: cinemas). The Young Don't Cry. Galvanized Yankee (TV). 1958: The Deep Six. The Restless Years (GB: The Wonderful Years). Free Week-End (TV). 1959: Face of Fire. Who Was That Lady? Dark December (TV). The Sounds of Eden (TV). 1964: The Tenderfoot (TV. GB: cinemas). Black Like Me. 1967: Chuka. Nobody's Perfect. Waterhole No. 3 (GB: Waterhole 3). Planet of the Apes. 1968: Madigan. The Split. 1969: Guns of the Magnificent Seven. 1970: Tora! Tora! Tora! 1971: If Tomorrow Comes (TV). 1972: Chato's Land. The Lost World of Libra. 1973: The Harrad Experiment. High Crime/Calling Crime Command. 1974: Where the Red Fern Grows. The Challenge (TV. GB: cinemas. Filmed 1968). Venditore di palloncini (GB: Last Moments. US: The Last Circus Show). 1975: I Will Fight No More Forever (TV). Give 'Em Hell Harry. 1977: The Serpent's Egg. 1978: Bully. A Force of One. 1980: The First Deadly Sin. Mark, I Love You (TV). The Rage (TV). 1981: The Killing of Randy Webster (TV). 1984: Purple Hearts: A Vietnam Love Story (TV). 1985: The Adventures of Mark Twain (voice only). Sky High (TV). 1986: All My Sons (TV). 1987: Nuts. 1989: Old Explorers. Glory! Glory! (cable TV). 1994: The Shawshank Redemption.

WHITNEY, Peter
(P. Engle) 1916–1972

Chunky, powerful, full-faced, dark-haired American actor, often seen as men of inbred violence from the wrong side of the tracks. As far as producers were concerned he was nearly always 'in the ranks' and his best roles in an in-and-out film career proved to be as twins in *Murder He Says* and as Anthony Quinn's adversary in *Man from Del Rio*. Died from a heart attack.

1941: Nine Lives Are Not Enough. Blues in the Night. Underground. 1942: Rio Rita. Valley of the Sun. Busses Roar. Spy Ship. Whistling in Dixie. Reunion/Reunion in France (GB: Mademoiselle France). 1943: Action in the North Atlantic. Destination Tokyo. 1944: Mr Skeffington. 1945: Murder He Says. Hotel Berlin. Bring on the Girls. 1946: The Notorious Lone Wolf. Blonde Alibi. The Brute Man. Canyon Passage. Three Strangers. 1947: The Gangster. Northwest Outpost (GB: End of the Rainbow). Violence. 1948: The Iron Curtain. 1953: The Great Sioux Uprising. The Big Heat. All the Brothers Were Valiant. 1954: Superman's Peril (TV. GB: cinemas). Day of Triumph. The Black Dakotas. Gorilla at Large. 1955: The Sea Chase. The Last Frontier. 1956: Man from Del Rio. Great Day in the Morning. The Cruel Tower. 1957: The Domino Kid. 1958: Buchanan Rides Alone. 1962: The Wonderful World of the Brothers Grimm. 1965: The Sword of Ali Baba. 1967: In the Heat of the Night. Chubasco. 1969: The Great Bank Robbery. 1970: The Ballad of Cable Hogue.

WHITTY, Dame May 1865–1948

Small, neat, plump-cheeked, brown-haired British actress who, after a distinguished stage career, made her first Hollywood film at 72, and largely stayed there for the last 11 years of her life, exuding kindliness, resourcefulness and British common sense. Most memorable as the disappearing Miss Fray in Hitchcock's *The Lady Vanishes*. Created Dame in 1918. Academy Award nominations for *Night Must Fall* and *Mrs Miniver*.

1914: Enoch Arden. 1915: The Little Minister. 1920: Col. Newcome the Perfect Gentleman. 1937: Night Must Fall. Conquest (GB: Marie Walewska). The Thirteenth Chair. 1938: I Met My Love Again. The Lady Vanishes. 1939: Return to Yesterday. 1940: Raffles. A Bill of Divorcement. 1941: Suspicion. One Night in

Lisbon. 1942: Thunder Birds. Mrs Miniver. Crash Dive. 1943: The Constant Nymph. Slightly Dangerous. Forever and a Day. Lassie Come Home. Stage Door Canteen. Madame Curie. Devotion (released 1946). 1944: The White Cliffs of Dover. Gaslight (GB: The Murder in Thornton Square). 1945: My Name is Julia Ross. 1947: This Time for Keeps. Green Dolphin Street. If Winter Comes. 1948: The Sign of the Ram. The Return of October (GB: Date with Destiny).

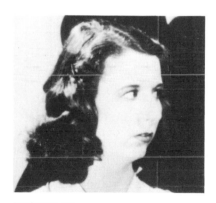

WICKES, Mary

(M. Wickenhauser) 1912–

Tallish, beaky, angular, chestnut-haired, bony-fingered American actress with the look of a startled but aggressive bird, and an increasingly goose-like voice. She became an actress straight from majoring in political science at college, and soon started stage and film careers, often playing people looking after other people, or busybodies, or do-gooders, and, arms akimbo, stood no nonsense from any of her elderly or variously eccentric charges. The original Mary Poppins in a TV production of 1949, she continued her career into her eighties in the TV series *The Father Dowling Mysteries* and as confrontational nuns in the *Sister Act* films.

*1938: Too Much Johnson (unreleased). 1939: *Seeing Red. 1941: Andy Hardy's Private Secretary. The Man Who Came to Dinner. 1942: Private Buckaroo. Now, Voyager. Blondie's Blessed Event (GB: A Bundle of Trouble). Who Done It? The Mayor of 44th Street. 1943: My Kingdom for a Cook. Rhythm of the Islands. Happy Land. How's About It?*

Higher and Higher. 1948: The Decision of Christopher Blake. June Bride. 1949: Anna Lucasta. 1950: The Petty Girl (GB: Girl of the Year). Ma and Pa Kettle at Home. 1951: On Moonlight Bay. I'll See You in My Dreams. 1952: The Will Rogers Story (GB: The Story of Will Rogers). Young Man with Ideas. Bloodhounds of Broadway. 1953: By the Light of the Silvery Moon. Half a Hero. The Actress. 1954: Destry. Ma and Pa Kettle at Home. White Christmas. 1955: Good Morning, Miss Dove. 1956: Dance with Me, Henry. 1957: Don't Go Near the Water. 1959: It Happened to Jane. 1960: Cimarron. 1961: The Sins of Rachel Cade. 101 Dalmatians (voice only). The Music Man. 1964: Fate is the Hunter. Dear Heart. 1965: How to Murder Your Wife. The Trouble with Angels. 1966: The Spirit is Willing. 1967: Where Angels Go ... Trouble Follows. 1969: The Monk (TV). 1971: Napoleon and Samantha. 1973: Snowball Express. 1979: Willa (TV). 1980: Touched by Love. 1987: Fatal Confession (TV). 1989: The Missing Body Mystery (TV). 1990: Postcards from the Edge. 1992: Sister Act. 1993: Sister Act 2: Back in the Habit. 1994: Little Women. 1996: The Hunchback of Notre Dame (voice only).

WIEST, Dianne 1948–

Dark-haired, sleepy-eyed American actress of sensual mouth and lemon-sour prettiness, a dab hand at protective parents (surprisingly, since she has never married) and women under repression. The Missouri-born daughter of an army colonel, Wiest switched from ballet to acting early in her career, and had built up a formidable repertory of classical roles (many of them Shakespearian) on stage before trying her hand at films in her early thirties. Her distinctive looks and ability to manipulate an audience's emotions quickly gained her acceptance among filmgoers. She won an Academy Award for her role in *Hannah and Her Sisters* and was nominated again for *Parenthood*. Often seen in films made by Woody Allen, she has also directed for the stage. She won a second Oscar for Allen's Bullets Over Broadway.

1980: It's My Turn. 1981: The Wall (TV). I'm Dancing As Fast As I Can. 1982: Independence Day/Restless. 1984: Footloose. Falling in Love. 1985: The Purple Rose of Cairo. 1986: Hannah and Her Sisters. 1987: Radio Days. The Lost Boys. September. 1988: Bright Lights,

Big City. 1989: Cookie. Parenthood. 1990: Edward Scissorhands. 1991: Little Man Tate. 1993: Yesterday. 1994: Cops and Robbersons. The Scout. Bullets Over Broadway. 1995: Drunks. Birds of a Feather.

WILHOITE, Kathleen 1964–

Angular, raw-boned, strong-chinned, dark-haired, antelope-like American actress with distinctive husky voice. A strong singer too, she joined an all-girl group while still at high school, then played her first movie role – the film was so bad she probably wished she hadn't bothered – while still in her first year at the University of Southern California studying drama. Generally seen thereafter as tough types who don't mince words, or independent-minded friends destined not to get the hero. She has said 'I tend to do well playing assertive, acerbic ladies' and her leading roles in *Murphy's Law* and *Dream Demon* bear witness to that; otherwise she has been confined to top supporting assigments in which she often proves more interesting than the heroine.

1983: Private School. Quarterback Princess (TV). Flight 90: Disaster on the Potomac (TV). 1984: Single Bars, Single Women (TV). 1985: Not My Kid (TV). 1986: Ratboy. Murphy's Law. 1987: The Morning After. Angel Heart. Witchboard (formerly Ouija). Brenda Starr (released 1989). Campus Man. Under Cover. 1988: Crossing Delancey. 1989: Everybody Wins. Road House. 1990: Bad Influence. 1992: Live! From Death Row (TV). Lorenzo's Oil. 1993: Fire in the Sky. Broken Promises (TV). 1994: The Color of Night. Erotic Tales.

WILKE, Robert J. 1911–1989

Tall, broad-shouldered, light-haired, agile American actor with curling lips, icy eyes and taut features. A former stuntman, Wilke looked ill-at-ease in a suit and, often seen in serials, was almost always cast as western villains. He made dozens of these minor 'oaters' and almost 200 films, most of them in the period 1944–1958, before proving, towards the end of his career, that he could handle *bona-fide* character roles as well. He also made the occasional foray into horror, most notably as *The Catman of Paris*. Also billed variously as Robert Wilkie, Bob Wilkie, Robert Wilke and Bob Wilke.

1936: San Francisco. 1937: SOS Coastguard (serial). San Quentin. 1938: Come On Rangers! The Fighting Devil Dogs (serial). Under Western Stars. 1939: Daredevils of the Red Circle (serial). In Old Monterey. Rough Riders' Round-Up. 1940: The Adventures of Red Ryder (serial). King of the Royal Mounted (serial). 1941: Dick Tracy vs Crime Inc (serial). King of the Texas Rangers (serial). Honeymoon for Three. 1942: Spy Smasher (serial). 1943: The Masked Marvel (serial). California Joe. 1944: Captain America (serial). Beneath Western Skies. Bordertown Trail. Code of the Prairie. Call of the Rockies. The Big Bonanza. Cheyenne Wildcat. The Cowboy and the Señorita. Firebrands of Arizona. Haunted Harbor (serial). Hidden Valley Outlaws. Marshal of Reno. Sheriff of Sundown. Stagecoach to Monterey. Zorro's Black Whip (serial). The Tiger Woman (serial). The San Antonio Kid. Sheriff of Las Vegas. Vigilantes of Dodge City. Yellow Rose of Texas. 1945: Bandits of the Badlands. Bells of Rosarita. Corpus Christi Bandits. The Great Stagecoach Robbery. The Lone Texas Ranger. The Man from Oklahoma. The Purple Monster Strikes (serial). Rough Riders of Cheyenne. Sunset in El Dorado. Sheriff of Cimarron. Santa Fé Saddlemates. Trail of the Badlands. The Topeka Terror. The Trail of Kit Carson. 1946: Badman's Territory. The Catman of Paris. The Crimson Ghost (serial). Daughter of Don Q (serial). Haunted Harbor (feature version of 1944 serial). The El Paso Kid. The Inner Circle. King of the Texas Rangers (feature version of 1941 serial). The Phantom Rider (serial). Out California Way. Roaring Rangers (GB: False Hero). Passkey to Danger. Dick Tracy vs Crime Inc (feature version of 1941 serial). Traffic in Crime. Do You Love Me. White Tie and Tails. Rendezvous with Annie. 1947: The Black Widow (serial). Buck Privates Come Home (GB: Rookies Come Home). Blackmail. G-Men Never Forget (serial). The Last Days of Boot Hill. Law of the Canyon (GB: The Price of Crime). The Michigan Kid. The Pilgrim Lady. Twilight on the Rio Grande. The Vigilantes Return. The Web of Danger. West of Dodge City (GB: The Sea Wall). 1948: Carson City Raiders. Desperadoes of Dodge City. Dangers of the Canadian Mounted (serial). A Southern Yankee (GB: My Hero). Sundown in Santa Fé. River Lady. Daredevils of the Clouds. Six Gun Law. Out of the Storm. Trail to Laredo (GB: Sign of the Dagger). The Wreck of the Hesperus. West of Sonora. 1949: *Coyote Canyon. Federal Agents v Underworld Inc (serial). Ghost of

Zorro (serial). Death Valley Gunfighter. Frontier Outpost. Laramie. The Kid from Texas (GB: Texas Kid − Outlaw). Flaming Fury. San Antone Ambush. The Traveling Saleswoman. The Wyoming Bandit. 1950: Across the Badlands (GB: The Challenge). The Blonde Bandit. The James Brothers of Missouri (serial). The Desert Hawk. Kill the Umpire! Mule Train. Outcast of Black Mesa (GB: The Clue). Twilight in the Sierras. 1951: Beyond the Purple Hills. Best of the Badmen. Cyclone Fury. Gunplay. Hot Lead. Overland Telegraph. Pistol Harvest. Saddle Legion. Vengeance Valley. 1952: Carbine Williams. Shane. High Noon. The Las Vegas Story. Frontier Outpost. Laramie Mountains (GB: Mountain Desperadoes). Hellgate. Fargo. Road Agent. The Maverick. Cattle Town. Wyoming Roundup. 1953: From Here to Eternity. Powder River. War Paint. Arrowhead. Cow Country. 1954: Black Widow. 20,000 Leagues Under the Sea. The Lone Gun. Son of Sinbad. The Far Country. Two Guns and a Badge. 1955: Strange Lady in Town. Wichita. Smoke Signal. Shotgun. The Rawhide Years. 1956: The Lone Ranger. Backlash. Raw Edge. Canyon River. Gun the Man Down. Written on the Wind. Mountain Fortress (TV. GB: cinemas). 1957: The Tarnished Angels. Night Passage. Hot Summer Night. 1958: Man of the West. Return to Warbow. 1959: Never Steal Anything Small. 1960: The Magnificent Seven. Texas John Slaughter. Spartacus. 1961: A Blueprint for Robbery. The Long Rope. 1963: The Gun Hawk. 1964: Fate is the Hunter. Shock Treatment. 1965: The Hallelujah Trail. 1966: Smoky. 1967: Tony Rome. 1968: Joaquin Murieta (released only on TV, in 1975, as Desperate Mission). 1970: The Cheyenne Social Club. A Gunfight. 1971: They Call It Murder (TV). The Resurrection of Zachary Wheeler. 1972: Santee. The Rookies (TV). 1973: The Boy Who Cried Werewolf. 1978: Days of Heaven. Wild and Wooly (TV). The Sweet Creek County War/Good Time Outlaws. 1979: The Great Monkey Rip-Off. 1981: Stripes.

WILLES, Jean
(J. Donahue) 1922−1989

Tall, dark, strongly-built American actress of handsome looks and forceful style − sometimes blonde but just as formidable. After years in comedy shorts, she had a couple of minor leading roles in the 1950s, but was usually seen either as a saloon girl or as an officer in the forces, and never broke into the upper echelon of roles that her ability seemed to warrant. No doubt a match for the professional wrestler she married in real life (changing her billing to her married name in 1947).

1943: †So Proudly We Hail! 1944: †Here Come the Waves. 1945: †Salty O'Rourke. †You Came Along. 1946: †It's Great to be Young. †Sing While You Dance. †*Monkey Business-men. †*Ain't Love Cuckoo? †*Slappily Married. 1947: †The Mating of Millie. †*Scooper Dooper. †Down to Earth. †*Bride and Gloom. *Hectic Honeymoon. 1948: The Winner's Circle. 1949: Chinatown at Midnight. *Let Down Your Aerial. 1950: *A Snitch in Time. *A Slip and a Miss. *His Baiting Beauty. *Hold That Monkey. *House About It. The

Fuller Brush Girl (GB: The Affairs of Sally). *Foy meets Girl. Emergency Wedding (GB: Jealousy). Kill the Umpire! The Petty Girl (GB: Girl of the Year). Revenue Agent. A Woman of Distinction. *Marinated Mariner. 1951: The Awful Sleuth. *Blonde Atom Bomb. *The Champ Steps Out. *Don't Throw That Knife. *Foy Meets Girl. *Hula-La-La. *He Flew the Shrew. *Wine, Women and Bong. 1952: *A Fool and His Honey. *Rootin' Tootin' Tenderfeet. The First Time. Gobs and Gals (GB: Cruising Casanovas). Jungle Jim in the Forbidden land. The Sniper. A Yank in Indo-China (GB: Hidden Secret). Son of Paleface. 1953: All Ashore. Abbott and Costello Go to Mars. From Here to Eternity. Run for the Hills. 1954: Bowery to Bagdad. Masterson of Kansas. 1955: *Gypped in the Penthouse. *His Pest Friend. *He Took a Powder. *Nobody's Home. Bobby Ware is Missing. Five Against the House. Count Three and Pray. 1956: Invasion of the Body Snatchers. The King and Four Queens. The Lieutenant Wore Skirts. The Man Who Turned to Stone. The Revolt of Mamie Stover. Toward the Unknown (GB: Brink of Hell). 1957: Hear Me Good. Hell on Devil's Island. The Tijuana Story. 1958: Desire Under the Elms. No Time for Sergeants. 1959: The FBI Story. These Thousand Hills. 1960: The Crowded Sky. Elmer Gantry. Ocean's 11. 1961: By Love Possessed. 1962: Gun Street. Gypsy. 1964: McHale's Navy. 1970: The Cheyenne Social Club. 1975: Bite the Bullet.

† As Jean Donahue

WILLIAMS, Guinn 'Big Boy'
1899−1962

Big, hunkish, light-haired, small-eyed American actor, a former baseball pro in his youth, who began in tiny roles, won feature billing in a series of 1920s westerns then, with the coming of sound, settled down to more than 20 years of being the big, loyal, but not-too-bright friend of the hero, mostly in vigorous action pictures. He died from uraemic poisoning.

1919: *Soapsuds and Sapheads. Water, Water, Everywhere. Almost a Husband. Jubilo. 1920: Jes' Call Me Jim. Cupid the Cowpuncher. 1921: Western Firebrands. The Jack Rider. The Vengeance Trail. Doubling for Romeo. 1922: Trail of Hate. Blaze Away. The Freshie (GB: Life Begins at 17). The Roping Fool. The Cowboy King. Across the Border. Rounding Up the Law. 1923: $1,000 Reward. Cyclone Jones.

Riders at Night. End of the Rope. 1924: The Avenger. The Eagle's Claw. Rodeo Stevens. 1925: The Big Stunt. Black Cyclone. Fangs of Wolfheart. Riders of the Sandstorm. Sporting West. Wolfheart's Revenge. Bad Man from Bodie. Courage of Wolfheart (GB: Lone Bandit). Red Blood and Blue. Rose of the Desert. Whistling Jim. 1926: Brown of Harvard. The Desert's Toll. 1927: Arizona Bound. The Down Grade. Babe Comes Home. Backstage. Slide, Kelly, Slide (GB: They All Cheered for Kelly). The Woman Who Did Not Care. The College Widow. Quarantined Rivals. Lightning. Snowbound. 1928: Ladies' Night in a Turkish Bath (GB: Ladies' Night). Beggars of Life. Burning Daylight. Lucky Star. Vamping Venus. My Man. 1929: From Headquarters. The Forward Pass. Noah's Ark. 1930: College Lovers. The Big Fight. City Girl. The Bad Man. Liliom. 1931: Bachelor Father. The Great Meadow. The Phantom. *Catch As Catch Can. *War Mamas. 1932: 70,000 Witnesses. Polly of the Circus. The Devil is Driving. Ladies of the Jury. Drifting Souls. Heritage of the Desert. You Said a Mouthful. 1933: Mystery Squadron (serial). The Phantom Broadcast (GB: Phantom of the Air). Laughing at Life. Man of the Forest. College Coach (GB: Football Coach). 1934: Half a Sinner. Rafter Romance. *The Undie-World. The Cheaters. Flirtation Walk. Thunder over Texas. Palooka (GB: The Great Schnozzle). Our Daily Bread. Romance in the Rain. Here Comes the Navy. Silver Streak. 1935: Private Worlds. One in a Million. Village Tale. Gun Play. Danger Trail. The Law of the .45s (GB: The Mysterious Mr Sheffield). Miss Pacific Fleet. Cowboy Holiday. The Glass Key. Society Fever. Powdersmoke Range. Big Boy Rides Again. The Littlest Rebel. 1936: The Big Game. Muss 'Em Up (GB: House of Fate). End of the Trail. Career Woman. The Vigilantes Are Coming (serial). *The Champ's a Chump. Grand Jury. Kelly the Second. North of Nome (GB: Alaska Bound). 1937: A Star is Born. You Only Live Once. The Singing Marine. She's No Lady. My Dear Miss Aldrich. Bad Man from Brimstone. Girls Can Play. Don't Tell the Wife. Dangerous Holiday. Big City. Wise Girl. 1938: Down in Arkansaw. Everybody's Doing It. Professor, Beware. I Demand Payment. Flying Fists. Army Girl (GB: The Last of the Cavalry). You and Me. Hold That Co-Ed (GB: Hold That Gal). The Marines Are Here. Crashin' Through Danger. 1939: 6,000 Enemies. Pardon Our Nerve. Fugitive at Large. Mutiny on the Blackhawk. Bad Lands. Dodge

City. Blackmail. Street of Missing Men. Legion of Lost Flyers. 1940: Virginia City. The Fighting 69th. Santa Fé Trail. Dulcy. Castle on the Hudson (GB: Years Without Days). Money and the Woman. *Pleased to Mitt You. Alias the Deacon. Wagons Westward. 1941: Billy the Kid. Six Lessons from Madame La Zonga. Swamp Water (GB: The Man Who Came Back). Riders of Death Valley (serial). Country Fair. You'll Never Get Rich. The Bugle Sounds. 1942: American Empire (GB: My Son Alone). Mr Wise Guy. Lure of the Islands. Between Us Girls. Silver Queen. 1943: Buckskin Frontier (GB: The Iron Road). The Desperadoes. Hands Across the Border. Minesweeper. 1944: Swing in the Saddle (GB: Swing and Sway). Belle of the Yukon. The Cowboy and the Señorita. Nevada. Thirty Seconds Over Tokyo. Cowboy Canteen (GB: Close Harmony). 1945: The Man Who Walked Alone. Rhythm Roundup (GB: Honest John). Sing Me a Song of Texas (GB: Fortune Hunter). Song of the Prairie (GB: Sentiment and Song). 1946: Throw a Saddle on a Star. Cowboy Blues (GB: Beneath the Starry Skies). That Texas Jamboree (GB: Medicine Man). Singing on the Trail (GB: Lookin' for Someone). 1947: King of the Wild Horses (GB: King of the Wild). Singin' in the Corn (GB: Give and Take). Road to the Big House. Over the Santa Fé Trail (GB: No Escape). 1948: Bad Men of Tombstone. Station West. Smoky Mountain Melody. 1949: Brimstone. 1950: Hoedown. Rocky Mountain. 1951: Al Jennings of Oklahoma. Man in the Saddle (GB: The Outcast). 1952: Springfield Rifle. Hangman's Knot. 1954. Southwest Passage (GB: Camels West). Massacre Canyon. The Outlaw's Daughter. 1956: Hidden Guns. Man from Del Rio. 1957: The Hired Gun. 1959: Five Bold Women. 1960: Home from the Hill. The Alamo. 1961: The Comancheros.

WILLIAMS, John 1903–1983
Tall, stately, sandy-haired, moustachioed British actor who never lost his essential Englishness despite living almost entirely in America from 1924. His film appearances are minor apart from his famous running role as Inspector Hubbard in *Dial M for Murder*, which he played on stage, in film and on television. He began on stage as a boy of 13, playing John in *Peter Pan*; during World War II he served with the RAF and made a few movies in England. The John Williams who appears in 1935's *Emil and the Detectives* (US: *Emil*) is not the same actor.

1919: Edge o' Beyond. 1942: The Goose Steps Out. The Foreman Went to France (US: Somewhere in France). Next of Kin. 1944: He Snoops to Conquer. 1947: A Woman's Vengeance. The Paradine Case. 1949: Blue Scar. The Dancing Years. 1950: Kind Lady. 1951: The Lady and the Bandit (GB: Dick Turpin's Ride). Thunder in the East (released 1953). 1952: 24 Hours of a Woman's Life (US: Affair in Monte Carlo). 1954: Dial M for Murder. The Student Prince. Sabrina (GB: Sabrina Fair). 1955: To Catch a Thief. 1956: D-Day the Sixth of June. The Solid Gold Cadillac. 1957: Will Success Spoil Rock Hunter? (GB: Oh! For a Man!). Island in the Sun. Witness for the Prosecution. 1959: The Young Philadelphians (GB: The City Jungle). Dossier (TV. GB: cinemas). 1960: Midnight Lace. Visit to a Small Planet. 1965: Harlow (Carol Lynley version). Dear Brigitte . . . 1966: The Last of the Secret Agents? 1967: Double Trouble. The Secret War of Harry Frigg. 1968: A Flea in Her Ear. 1972: The Hound of the Baskervilles (TV. GB: cinemas). 1973: Dagger of the Mind (TV. GB: cinemas). 1974: Lost in the Stars. 1976: No Deposit, No Return. 1978: Hot Lead and Cold Feet. The Swarm.

WILLIAMS, Rhys 1897–1969
Barrel-shaped Welsh-born actor with small facial features beneath a bald head, with two bushes of black hair at the sides. He never lost the Welsh lilt in his voice despite being in America since boyhood. He was a stage player until going to Hollywood in 1941 to work as a dialogue coach and technical adviser on *How Green Was My Valley*. Director John Ford asked him to play a role in the film and Hollywood found it had an efficient and likeable new character player in its hands. Williams stayed there for the remainder of his career, playing preachers, doctors and other anxious-looking professional men.

1941: How Green Was My Valley. 1942: This Above All. Remember Pearl Harbor. Mrs Miniver. Cairo. Eagle Squadron. Underground Agent. Gentleman Jim. Random Harvest. 1943: No Time for Love. 1945: The Corn is Green. The Bells of St Mary's. You Came Along. Blood on the Sun. The Spiral Staircase. The Trouble with Women (released 1947). 1946: The Imperfect Lady (GB: Mrs Loring's Secret). Cross My Heart. So Goes My Love (GB: A Genius in the Family). Easy Come, Easy Go. The Strange

Woman. Voice of the Whistler. 1947: The Farmer's Daughter. Moss Rose. If Winter Comes. 1948: Hills of Home (GB: Master of Lassie). The Black Arrow (GB: The Black Arrow Strikes). Tenth Avenue Angel. 1949: Bad Boy. The Crooked Way. Tokyo Joe. The Inspector General. Fighting Man of the Plains. 1950: Devil's Doorway. Kiss Tomorrow Goodbye. California Passage. The Showdown. Tyrant of the Sea. 1951: Lightning Strikes Twice. One Too Many (GB: Killer with a Label). The Son of Dr Jekyll. The Sword of Monte Cristo. Never Trust a Gambler. The Law and the Lady. The Light Touch. Million Dollar Pursuit. 1952: Okinawa. Mutiny. Carbine Williams. Plymouth Adventure. Les Misérables. The World in his Arms. Scandal at Scourie. 1953: Julius Caesar. Bad for Each Other. 1954: Johnny Guitar. Man in the Attic. The Black Shield of Falworth. Crime Squad. There's No Business Like Show Business. 1955: Battle Cry. How to Be Very, Very Popular. Many Rivers to Cross. The Scarlet Coat. Mohawk. The King's Thief. The Kentuckian. 1956: Nightmare. The Fastest Gun Alive. The Desperadoes Are in Town. The Boss. 1957: Raintree County. The Restless Breed. Lure of the Swamp. 1958: Merry Andrew. 1960: Midnight Lace. 1965: The Sons of Katie Elder. Our Man Flint. 1969: Skullduggery.

WILLMAN, Noel 1918–1988

Soft-spoken, short-haired Irish actor, often in roles of quietly chilling menace. On stage in London at 20, he appeared in a few British films in post-war years, floating through the more sinister ones like some ethereal death's head moth. A certain lack of warmth may have limited these appearances, but he was kept working hard in the theatre, directing as well as acting. Died from a heart attack.

1952: The Pickwick Papers. Androcles and the Lion. 1953: The Net (US: Project M7). Malta Story. 1954: Beau Brummell. 1955: The Dark Avenger (US: The Warriors). 1956: The Man Who Knew Too Much. 1957: Seven Waves Away (US: Abandon Ship!). Across the Bridge. 1958: Carve Her Name with Pride. 1960: Cone of Silence (US: Trouble in the Sky). The Criminal (US: The Concrete Jungle). Never Let Go. The Girl on the Boat. 1961: Two Living, One Dead. 1962: Kiss of the Vampire (US: Kiss of Evil). 1965: Doctor Zhivago. The

Reptile. 1968: The Vengeance of She. 1974: The Odessa File. 1976: 21 Hours at Munich (TV. GB: cinemas).

WILLS, Chill 1903–1978

Amiable, scrape-voiced, frog-faced American actor who played mainly folksy western roles. He began as an equally wheezy country-and-western singer (with his group, the Avalon Boys; they formed a memorable background to Laurel and Hardy's soft-shoe number in *Way Out West*), but graduated to small acting roles in the late 1930s and remained a popular, colourful support. Almost never a villain. Later the voice of Francis the Talking Mule in Universal-International's comedy series. Nominated for an Oscar in *The Alamo*.

*1933: Bar 20 Rides Again. 1936: *At Sea Ashore. Anything Goes. Nobody's Baby. The Call of the Prairie. 1937: Hideaway Girl. Way Out West. 1938: Lawless Valley. 1939: Racketeers of the Range. Arizona Legion. Allegheny Uprising (GB: The First Rebel). Sorority House (GB: That Girl from College). Timber Stampede. The Days the Bookies Wept. Trouble in Sundown. 1940: The Westerner. Boom Town. Sky Murder. Wyoming (GB: Bad Man of Wyoming). Tugboat Annie Sails Again. 1941: Billy the Kid. Western Union. The Bugle Sounds. Belle Starr. Honky Tonk. The Bad Man (GB: Two Gun Cupid). 1942: Apache Trail. Tarzan's New York Adventure. Stand by for Action! (GB: Cargo of Innocents). The Omaha Trail. Her Cardboard Lover. 1943: Best Foot Forward. A Stranger in Town. 1944: See Here, Private Hargrove. Rationing. *The Immortal Blacksmith. Barbary Coast Gent. Sunday Dinner for a Soldier. Meet Me in St Louis. I'll Be Seeing You. 1945: What Next, Corporal Hargrove? Leave Her to Heaven. The Harvey Girls. 1946: The Yearling. Gallant Bess. 1947: Heartaches. High Barbaree. 1948: The Sainted Sisters. *It Can't Be Done. That Wonderful Urge. Family Honeymoon. Raw Deal. The Saxon Charm. Northwest Stampede. 1949: Tulsa. *The Grass is Always Greener. *Trailin' West. Loaded Pistols. Red Canyon. Francis (voice only). The Sundowners (GB: Thunder in the Dust). 1950: Rio Grande. Rock Island Trail (GB: Transcontinent Express). Stella. High Lonesome. 1951: Cattle Drive. The Sea Hornet. Oh! Susanna. Francis Goes to the Races (voice only). 1952: Bronco Buster. Francis Goes to West Point (voice only). Ride*

the Man Down. 1953: City That Never Sleeps. The Man from the Alamo. Small Town Girl. Francis Covers the Big Town (voice only). Tumbleweed. 1954: Francis Joins the WACs. Ricochet Romance. 1955: Hell's Outpost. Timberjack. Francis in the Navy (voice only). 1956: Santiago (GB: The Gun Runner). Giant. Kentucky Rifle. Francis in the Haunted House (voice only). Gun for a Coward. 1957: Gun Glory. 1958: From Hell to Texas (GB: Manhunt). 1959: The Sad Horse. 1960: The Alamo. Tomorrow (TV). 1961: Gold of the Seven Saints. Where the Boys Are. The Little Shepherd of Kingdom Come. The Deadly Companions. 1962: Young Guns of Texas. 1963: The Wheeler Dealers (GB: Separate Beds). McLintock! The Cardinal. 1964: The Rounders. 1966: Fireball 500. 1969: The Over-the-Hill Gang (TV). 1970: The Liberation of L B Jones. The Over-the-Hill Gang Rides Again (TV). 1971: The Steagle. 1973: Pat Garrett and Billy the Kid. Guns of a Stranger. 1975: Big Daddy. 1977: Poco — Little Dog Lost. Mr Billion.

WILSON, Dooley

(Arthur D. Wilson) 1894–1953

Small black actor and entertainer with sad eyes but massive smile. A singing drummer and nightclub owner in his early years, he took up acting in 1930, won praise for the leading role in the stage production of *Cabin in the Sky*, and then brought his warm personality to films, most notably as Sam, the pianist in Rick's Café Americain in *Casablanca*. Ironically, this was easily his best-remembered role; in real life, he could not play a note, and was dubbed for the film.

1939: Keep Punching. 1941: Take a Letter, Darling (GB: The Green-Eyed Woman). 1942: Cairo. A Night in New Orleans. Casablanca. My Favorite Blonde. 1943: Stormy Weather. Two Tickets to London. Higher and Higher. 1944: Seven Days Ashore. 1948: Triple Threat. Racing Luck. 1949: Free for All. Knock on Any Door. Come to the Stable. 1950: No Man of Her Own. Father is a Bachelor. 1951: Passage West (GB: High Venture).

WILSON, Ian 1901–*

Small, scurrying, dark-haired, bespectacled British actor with disapproving mouth, the archetypal fussy little man or petty official of the British cinema through five decades,

often in one-scene roles. He was to be spotted in most of the films from the Boulting Brothers, for whom his appearances seemed to be something of a good luck charm. He was also part of the Norman Wisdom comedies and the early 'Carry On' capers.

1922: A Master of Craft. 1923: Through Fire and Water. 1924. *After Dark. *The Cavern Spider. 1925: *A Mercenary Motive. 1926: The Fighting Gladiator. *Windsor Castle. 1927: Shooting Stars. 1928: *Double Dealing. What Next? 1929: The Broken Melody. 1930: Bed and Breakfast. The Dizzy Limit. 1931: Splinters in the Navy. 1932: Heroes of the Mine. Double Dealing (and 1928 short). Little Waitress. *The Bailiffs. 1933: *Oh For a Plumber! Facing the Music. Lucky Blaze. 1934: The Unholy Quest. The Broken Rosary. The Merry Men of Sherwood. The Love Test. Those Were the Days. Song at Eventide. Love, Life and Laughter. 1935: Father O'Flynn. Birds of a Feather. Play Up the Band. The City of Beautiful Nonsense. *Polly's Two Fathers. Joy Ride. 1936: Melody of My Heart. Pal o' Mine. Apron Fools. 1937: Song of the Forge. The Vicar of Bray. 1940: Let George Do It. 1941: Quiet Wedding. 1943: The Demi-Paradise (US: Adventure for Two). The Dummy Talks. We Dive at Dawn. My Learned Friend. 1944: Don't Take It to Heart. 1947: Vice Versa. 1948: My Sister and I. Bond Street. It's Hard to be Good. Trottie True (US: Gay Lady). 1949: The History of Mr Polly. 1950: Seven Days to Noon. The Lady Craves Excitement. 1951: The Magic Box. Whispering Smith Hits London (US: Whispering Smith versus Scotland Yard). 1952: The Last Page (US: Manbait). Miss Robin Hood. Mother Riley Meets the Vampire (US: Vampire Over London). Treasure Hunt. Meet Me Tonight. Top Secret (US: Mr Potts Goes to Moscow). Hindle Wakes (US: Holiday Week). 1953: The Saint's Return (US: The Saint's Girl Friday). The Flanagan Boy (US: Bad Blonde). The Million Pound Note (US: Man With a Million). The Floating Dutchman. Trouble in Store. Single-Handed (US: Sailor of the King). 1954: *The Strange Case of Blondie. The Brain Machine. Radio Cab Murder. Seagulls Over Sorrento (US: Crest of the Wave). Time is My Enemy. One Good Turn. The Glass Cage (US: The Glass Tomb). 1955: Man of the Moment. See How They Run. One Way Out. Jumping for Joy. Private's Progress. Portrait of Alison (US:

Postmark for Danger). Value for Money. 1956: Brothers in Law. The Big Money (released 1958). The Good Companions. My Wife's Family. Up in the World. 1957: Kill Me Tomorrow. Hell Drivers. The Key Man. Just My Luck. Lucky Jim. Happy is the Bride! How to Murder a Rich Uncle. Morning Call (US: The Strange Case of Dr Manning). 1958: Carlton-Browne of the FO (US: Man in a Cocked Hat). Family Doctor (US: RX Murder). The Square Peg. Hidden Homicide. 1959: Idle on Parade (US: Idol on Parade). The Ugly Duckling. I'm All Right, Jack. Top Floor Girl. A Woman's Temptation. Suddenly Last Summer. 1960: Suspect (US: The Risk). Feet of Clay. Carry On Constable. Two-Way Stretch. A French Mistress. 1961: Raising the Wind (US: Roommates). Carry On Regardless. Two and Two Make Six. 1962: Phantom of the Opera. Carry On Cruising. Postman's Knock. The Iron Maiden (US: The Swingin' Maiden). The Day of the Triffids. 1963: Carry On Cabby. Heavens Above! 1964: The Runaway. Carry On Jack (US: Carry On Venus). Carry On Cleo. 1965: Help! Rotten to the Core. San Ferry Ann. 1966: The Sandwich Man. 1967: *Ouch! The Plank. Tell Me Lies. 1973: The Wicker Man.

* Believed deceased, but date of death uncertain.

WILSON, Richard 1936–

Slimly-built, balding, sour-faced, mongoose-like Scottish-born portrayer of grumps and grouches, sometimes in high office, who achieved complete anonymity for 25 years, only to burst into the spotlight in his fifties as the star of the TV comedy series One Foot in the Grave, which he followed with other small-screen successes. In his mid twenties, he switched from working as a laboratory technician to enrolling as a drama student at RADA. Films few, but stage work much and varied, and many TV series from Dr Finlay's Casebook in the early 1960s to the present day. He has also directed several plays on stage and TV.

1964: John Goldfarb, Please Come Home. 1972: The Trouble with 2 B. 1983: Those Glory Glory Days (originally for TV). 1984: A Passage to India. 1986: Foreign Body. Whoops Apocalypse. 1987: Prick Up Your Ears. 1989: How to Get Ahead in Advertising. A Dry White Season. 1990: Fellow Traveller. 1991: Kremlin Farewell. 1992: Carry On Columbus. 1993: Soft Top, Hard Shoulder.

WINNINGER, Charles
(Karl Winninger) 1884–1969
Chubby, loveable, round-faced, usually moustachioed American character actor and entertainer, from a family of vaudevillians with whose act he stayed for many years, on and off, until films claimed him as a regular after his role as Cap'n Andy in the 1936 Show Boat. He was a top-featured attraction after that until the early fifties, almost equalling his earlier success when he played the father of the family in the 1945 version of State Fair.

1915: The Doomed Groom. 1924: Pied Piper Malone. 1926: The Canadian. Summer Bachelors. 1930: Soup to Nuts. 1931: Flying High (GB: Happy Landing). Bad Sister. The Sin of Madelon Claudet (GB: The Lullaby). Fighting Caravans. Children of Dreams. Night Nurse. God's Gift to Women (GB: Too Many Women). *Chip Shots. Gun Smoke. 1932: Husband's Holiday. 1934: Social Register. 1936: White Fang. Show Boat. 1937: Woman Chases Man. Three Smart Girls. Café Metropole. The Go-Getter. You're a Sweetheart. Nothing Sacred. You Can't Have Everything. Every Day's a Holiday. 1938: Hard to Get. Goodbye Broadway. 1939: Babes in Arms. Destry Rides Again. Barricade. Three Smart Girls Grow Up. 1940: Beyond Tomorrow. If I Had My Way. My Love Came Back. Little Nellie Kelly. 1941: The Get-Away. When Ladies Meet. Ziegfeld Girl. My Life with Caroline. Pot o' Gold (GB: The Golden Hour). 1942: Friendly Enemies. 1943: Coney Island. A Lady Takes a Chance. Hers to Hold. Flesh and Fantasy. 1944: Sunday Dinner for a Soldier. Broadway Rhythm. Belle of the Yukon. 1945: State Fair. She Wouldn't Say Yes. 1946: Lover Come Back. 1947: Living in a Big Way. Something in the Wind. 1948: The Inside Story. Give My Regards to Broadway. 1950: Father is a Bachelor. 1953: The Sun Shines Bright. Torpedo Alley. Champ for a Day. A Perilous Journey. 1955: Las Vegas Shakedown. 1960: Raymie. 1963: The Miracle of Santa's White Reindeer.

WINTERS, Roland 1904–1989
Bulkily-built, florid-featured, moustachioed American actor with light, crinkly hair. In Hollywood, he played mostly minor figures of authority with gruff good humour, plus a three-year stint as the cinema's third, last and, to be honest, least charismatic Charlie

Chan — although he was hardly ideal casting as the oriental sleuth. With his Chan chore over, Winters looked more relaxed playing his sometimes oily wheeler-dealers and father figures.

1946: 13 Rue Madeleine. 1947: The Chinese Ring. The Red Hornet. 1948: The Return of October (GB: Date with Destiny). Mystery of the Golden Eye. Kidnapped. Cry of the City. The Feathered Serpent. Docks of New Orleans. The Shanghai Chest. 1949: Once More, My Darling. Tuna Clipper. Sky Dragon. A Dangerous Profession. Abbott and Costello Meet the Killer, Boris Karloff. Malaya (GB: East of the Rising Sun). Captain Carey, USA (GB: After Midnight). 1950: Guilty of Treason (GB: Treason). The West Point Story (GB: Fine and Dandy). Killer Shark. Convicted. Between Midnight and Dawn. The Underworld Story. To Please a Lady. Raton Pass (GB: Canyon Pass). 1951: Follow the Sun. Inside Straight. Sierra Passage. 1952: She's Working Her Way Through College. 1953: So Big. 1956: Bigger Than Life. 1957: Jet Pilot (filmed 1950). Top Secret Affair (GB: Their Secret Affair). 1959: Never Steal Anything Small. Cash McCall. 1961: Everything's Ducky. Blue Hawaii. 1962: Follow That Dream. 1970: Loving. 1973: Miracle on 34th Street (TV). 1978: The Dain Curse (TV). 1979: You Can't Go Home Again (TV).

WINWOOD, Estelle
(E. Goodwin) 1882–1984
Angular, twittering, bird-like, amazingly long-lived British-born actress, who com-

pleted a remarkable 80 years on stage (she made her theatrical debut at 16) and played a leading role in a film at the age of 94. Largely in America from 1916, with occasional returns to the London stage. Her film appearances were far too few, but almost all memorable as she click-clacked, like knitting needles on legs, through one eccentric characterization after another. Married character actor Arthur Chesney (1882–1949).

1931: The Night Angel. 1933: The House of Trent. 1937: Quality Street. 1954: The Glass Slipper. 1956: The Swan. 23 Paces to Baker Street. 1957: This Happy Feeling. 1958: Alive and Kicking. Darby O'Gill and the Little People. 1960: Sergeant Rutledge. 1961: The Misfits. 1962: The Cabinet of Caligari. The Notorious Landlady. 1964: Dead Ringer (GB: Dead Image). 1967: Games. Camelot. 1968: The Producers. 1969: Jenny. 1976: Murder by Death.

WISEMAN, Joseph 1918–
Dark-haired, cruel-looking Canadian actor with sharply defined features who has been providing uncompromising and humourless villainy for more than 40 years. His crook in Detective Story and title character from Dr No were only two of some memorably etched portraits. But his bad men became less rooted in reality with the passing years, and he has done most of his best work in the theatre.

1950: With These Hands. 1951: Detective Story. 1952: Viva Zapata! Les Misérables. 1953: Champ for a Day. 1954: The Silver Chalice. 1955: Melba (narrator only). The Prodigal. 1957: Three Brave Men. Eliahu (narrator only). The Garment Jungle. 1959: The Unforgiven. 1962: The Happy Thieves. Dr No. 1967: The Outsider (TV). The Counterfeit Killer. 1968: Bye Bye Braverman. The Night They Raided Minsky's. 1969: The Mask of Sheba (TV). Stiletto. 1971: Lawman. 1972: Pursuit (TV). The Valachi Papers. 1973: QB VII (TV). The Suicide Club (TV). 1974: The Apprenticeship of Duddy Kravitz. Men of the Dragon (TV). 1976: Journey into Fear (GB: TV, as BurnOut). 1977: Murder at the World Series (TV). Homage to Chagall (narrator only). Jaguar Lives. 1979: Buck Rogers in the 25th Century (TV. GB: cinemas). 1980: Masada (TV. GB: cinemas, in abridged version, as The Antagonists). 1984:

The Ghost Writer (TV). 1986: Seize the Day (originally for TV). 1988: Lady Mobster (TV).

WITHERS, Grant
(Granville G. Withers) 1904–1959
Thick-set, aggressively handsome, dark-haired American tough-guy actor who gave up a career as a reporter to become the rugged lead of minor action films and romantic dramas in the 1920s and 1930s. After 1935 he was mainly seen taking leading roles in serials, or secondary roles in tough outdoor dramas. Rarely looking at home on screen in collar and tie, Withers was in real life five times married and divorced, including actresses Loretta Young (second 1930–1) and Estelita Rodriguez (fifth 1953–8). Committed suicide with sleeping pills.

1926: *The Lady of Lyons N.Y. The Gentle Cyclone. 1927: The Final Extra. College. Upstream. In a Moment of Temptation. 1928: Golden Shackles. The Road to Ruin. Bringing Up Father. Tillie's Punctured Romance. 1929: Saturday's Children. Hearts in Exile. Greyhound Limited. Tiger Rose. The Madonna of Avenue A. The Show of Shows. The Time, the Place and the Girl. In the Headlines. So Long, Letty. 1930: Broken Dishes. Back Pay. The Second Story Murder (later and GB: The Second Floor Mystery). Scarlet Pages. Soldiers and Women. The Other Tomorrow. Dancing Sweeties. Sinners' Holiday. 1931: First Aid (GB: In Strange Company). Too Young to Marry. Swanee River. Other Men's Women/The Steel Highway. 1932: Gambling Sex. Red-Haired Alibi. 1933: Secrets of Wu Sin. 1934: The Red Rider (serial). Tailspin Tommy (serial). Goin' to Town. 1935: Rip Roaring Riley (GB: The Mystery of Diamond Island). Hold 'Em Yale (GB: Uniform Lovers). Waterfront Lady. Storm Over the Andes. Fighting Marines (serial). Ship Café. Valley of Wanted Men. Skybound. Society Fever. 1936: Border Flight. *Three on a Limb. Lady, Be Careful. The Sky Parade. Let's Sing Again. Arizona Raiders. 1937: Jungle Jim (serial). Bill Cracks Down (GB: Men of Steel). Hollywood Roundup. Radio Patrol (serial). Paradise Express. 1938: Held for Ransom. Telephone Operator. The Secret of Treasure Island (serial). Touchdown Army (GB: Generals of Tomorrow). Mr Wong, Detective. Three Loves Has Nancy. 1939: Navy Secrets. Irish Luck

(GB: Amateur Detective). Mr Wong in Chinatown. Boys' Reformatory. Mutiny in the Big House. Mystery of Mr Wong. Daughter of the Tong. Lure of the Wasteland. 1940: Mexican Spitfire. Son of the Navy. The Fatal Hour (GB: Mr Wong at Headquarters). Men Against the Sky. Mexican Spitfire Out West. On the Spot. Doomed to Die (GB: The Mystery of the Wentworth Castle). Let's Make Music. Phantom of Chinatown. Tomboy. 1941: Country Fair. Billy the Kid. Father Takes a Wife. The Bugle Sounds. The Get-Away. H M Pulham Esq. The Masked Rider. The People vs Dr Kildare (GB: My Life is Yours). Swamp Water (GB: The Man Who Came Back). Parachute Battalion. You'll Never Get Rich. Woman of the Year. No Hands on the Clock. *Your Last Act. 1942: Apache Trail. Between Us Girls. Butch Minds the Baby. Lure of the Islands. Panama Hattie. Ship Ahoy. Northwest Rangers. Tennessee Johnson (GB: The Man on America's Conscience). 1943: Captive Wild Woman. Dr Gillespie's Criminal Case (GB: Crazy to Kill). Gildersleeve's Bad Day. A Lady Takes a Chance. Petticoat Larceny. No Time for Love. In Old Oklahoma (later and GB: War of the Wildcats). 1944: Cowboy Canteen (GB: Close Harmony). The Cowboy and the Señorita. The Girl Who Dared. Goodnight, Sweetheart. The Fighting Seabees. Three Men in White. The Yellow Rose of Texas. Roger Touhy, Gangster (GB: The Last Gangster). Silent Partner. 1945: Bells of Rosarita. Bring on the Girls. China's Little Devils. Dakota. Dangerous Partners. Road to Alcatraz. Utah. The Vampire's Ghost. 1946: Cowboy Blues (GB: Beneath the Starry Skies). Affairs of Geraldine. In Old Sacramento. My Darling Clementine. Singing on the Trail (GB: Lookin' for Someone). Singin' in the Corn (GB: Give and Take). That Texas Jamboree (GB: Medicine Man). Throw a Saddle on a Star. 1947: Blackmail. Gunfighters (GB: The Assassin). The Ghost Goes Wild. King of the Wild Horses. Over the Santa Fé Trail. The Trespasser. Tycoon. Wyoming. 1948: Angel in Exile. Bad Men of Tombstone. Daredevils of the Clouds. Fort Apache. Gallant Legion. Homicide for Three (GB: An Interrupted Honeymoon). Old Los Angeles. Station West. The Plunderers. Sons of Adventure. Wake of the Red Witch. Nighttime in Nevada. 1949: Brimstone. The Duke of Chicago. The Fighting Kentuckian. The Last Bandit. Hellfire. 1950: Bells of Coronado. Rio Grande. Rock Island Trail (GB: Transcontinent Express). The Savage Horde. Trigger Jr. Tripoli. Hoedown. Hit Parade of 1951. Rocky Mountain. 1951: Al Jennings of Oklahoma. Belle le Grand. Man in the Saddle (GB: The Outcast). Million Dollar Pursuit. The Sea Hornet. Spoilers of the Plains. Utah Wagon Train. 1952: Captive of Billy the Kid. Hangman's Knot. Hoodlum Empire. Leadville Gunslinger. Oklahoma Annie. Springfield Rifle. Tropical Heatwave. Woman of the North Country. 1953: Champ for a Day. Fair Wind to Java. Iron Mountain Trail. The Sun Shines Bright. Tropic Zone. 1954: Jubilee Trail. Massacre Canyon. The Outlaw's Daughter. Southwest Passage (GB: Camels West). 1955: Lady Godiva (GB: Lady Godiva of Coventry). Run for Cover. 1956: Hidden Guns. The White Squaw. Man from Del Rio. 1957: The Hired Gun. Hell's Crossroads. The Last Stagecoach West. 1958: I, Mobster.

WITHERSPOON, Cora 1890–1957

An apt name for the brown-haired, solidly built, disdainful-looking, New Orleans-born American actress who was an expert at withering looks. Of all her shrews, harridans and disapproving matrons, the best-remembered is probably her portrayal of W.C. Fields' wife in The Bank Dick, although it was ironically immediately after this that she found her career struggling, for the first time since she began on the New York stage at the age of 17 by playing a 70-year-old woman.

1931: The Night Angel. Peach o' Reno. 1932: Ladies of the Jury. 1933: *The Way of All Freshmen. 1934: Gambling. Midnight. 1935: Frankie and Johnnie. 1936: Libeled Lady. Piccadilly Jim. 1937: Beg, Borrow or Steal. The Big Shot. Dangerous Number. Madame X. The Lady Escapes. On the Avenue. Personal Property. Quality Street. 1938: He Couldn't Say No. Just Around the Corner. Marie Antoinette. Port of Seven Seas. Professor, Beware! Three Loves Has Nancy. 1939: Dark Victory. Dodge City. The Flying Irishman. For Love or Money. Woman Doctor. The Women. 1940: The Bank Dick (GB: The Bank Detective). Charlie Chan's Murder Cruise. I Was an Adventuress. 1943: Follies Girl. 1945: Colonel Effingham's Raid (GB: Man of the Hour). Over 21. This Love of Ours. She Wouldn't Say Yes. 1946: Dangerous Business. She Wrote the Book. I've Always Loved You. Young Widow. 1947: Down to Earth. 1951: The Mating Season. 1952: The First Time. Just for You. 1953: It Should Happen to You.

WOLFE, Ian 1896–1992

Slight, gaunt, mean-looking American actor with light, thinning hair and vindictive mouth, who might have been born to play landlords who foreclose the mortgage and throw the heroine out in the snow. His characters, although mostly minor, frequently carried a quiet menace that sent a shiver down the spine. He came to films in his late thirties (after prestigious Broadway experience) and was almost always seen thereafter in humourless supporting roles. Making up for his late start in Hollywood, Wolfe was still acting over 50 years and 150 films later, taking a major role in his 93rd year and still gleefully playing cameos up to his death.

1934: The Fountain. The Barretts of Wimpole Street. The Mighty Barnum. 1935: Clive of India. The Raven. Mad Love (GB: Hands of Orlac). Mutiny on the Bounty. $1,000 a Minute. 1936: The Leavenworth Case. Romeo and Juliet. The Last of the Mohicans. The Bold Caballero. 1937: The Prince and the Pauper. The Firefly. The Devil is Driving. Maytime. The Emperor's Candlesticks. The League of Frightened Men. Conquest (GB: Marie Walewska). The Bold Caballero (GB: The Bold Cavalier). 1938: Orphans of the Street. Blondie. Marie Antoinette. Arsene Lupin Returns. You Can't Take It With You. 1939: Fast and Loose. Society Lawyer. On Borrowed Time. Tell No Tales. Blondie Brings Up Baby. The Return of Dr X. The Great Commandment. Allegheny Uprising (GB: The First Rebel). 1940: Son of Monte Cristo. Earthbound. We Who Are Young. Hudson's Bay. The Earl of Chicago. Abe Lincoln in Illinois (GB: Spirit of the People). Foreign Correspondent. 1941: The Trial of Mary Dugan. Love Crazy. The Great Commandment. Paris Calling. Bombs Over Burma. 1942: Secret Agent of Japan. We Were Dancing. Eagle Squadron. Mrs Miniver. Now, Voyager. Random Harvest. Nightmare. The Moon Is Down. *Keep 'Em Sailing. Saboteur. *Famous Boners. 1943: Government Girl. Sherlock Holmes in Washington. Flesh and Fantasy. Sherlock Holmes Faces Death. Corvette K-225 (GB: The Nelson Touch). The Falcon in Danger. Holy Matrimony. The Iron Major. The Falcon and the Co-Eds. The Song of Bernadette. 1944: The Impostor. Seven Days Ashore. The Invisible Man's Revenge. Are These Our Parents? (GB: They Are Guilty). Her Primitive Man. Once Upon a Time. Babes on Swing Street. In Society. Mystery of the River Boat (serial). The Reckless Age. Pearl of Death. The White Cliffs of Dover. The Merry Monahans. The Scarlet Claw. Murder in the Blue Room. 1945: Zombies on Broadway (GB: Loonies on Broadway). The Brighton Strangler. Counter-Attack (GB: One Against Seven). Blonde Ransom. Love Letters. Confidential Agent. The Fighting Guardsman. Tomorrow is Forever. A Song to Remember. This Love of Ours. Confidential Agent. 1946: Three Strangers. The Notorious Lone Wolf. The Searching Wind. The Bandit of Sherwood Forest. Gentleman Joe Palooka. Without Reservations. Dressed to Kill (GB: Sherlock Holmes and the Secret Code). Pursued. Tomorrow is Forever. The Verdict. The Falcon's Adventure. Bedlam. California. 1947: That Way With Women. †Unexpected Guest. Dishonored Lady.

Wild Harvest. The Marauders. They Live by Night (released 1949). If Winter Comes. 1948: The Twisted Road. Mr Blandings Builds His Dream House. Johnny Belinda. Julia Misbehaves. Angel in Exile. The Judge Steps Out (GB: Indian Summer). Silver River. Three Daring Daughters (GB: The Birds and the Bees). 1949: Bride of Vengeance. The Younger Brothers. Homicide. They Live by Night. Manhandled. Colorado Territory. Joe Palooka in The Counterpunch. 1950: Please Believe Me. Emergency Wedding (GB: Jealousy). No Way Out. Copper Canyon. The Petty Girl (GB: Girl of the Year). The Magnificent Yankee (GB: The Man with Thirty Sons). 1951: The Great Caruso. On Dangerous Ground. Mask of the Avenger. A Place in the Sun. Here Comes the Groom. 1952: The Captive City. Les Misérables. Captain Pirate (GB: Captain Blood, Fugitive). Something for the Birds. Scandal at Scourie. 1953: 99 River Street. Houdini. Julius Caesar. The Actress. Young Bess. 1954: Her Twelve Men. About Mrs Leslie. Seven Brides for Seven Brothers. The Steel Cage. The Silver Chalice. 1955: The King's Thief. Moonfleet. Rebel Without a Cause. Sincerely Yours. The Court Martial of Billy Mitchell (GB: One Man Mutiny). Diane. 1956: Gaby. 1957: Witness for the Prosecution. 1960: Pollyanna. The Lost World. 1961: All in a Night's Work. 1962: The Wonderful World of the Brothers Grimm. 1963: Diary of a Madman. 1964: One Man's Way. 1967: Games. 1971: THX 1138. 1972: The Devil's Daughter (TV). 1973: Homebodies. 1974: The Fortune. The Terminal Man. 1975: The New Original Wonder Woman (TV). Mr Sycamore. 1976: Dynasty (TV). 1978: Seniors. Mean Dog Blues. 1979: The Frisco Kid. 1980: Up the Academy. Trouble in the High Timber Country (TV). 1981: Reds. 1982: Jinxed. Mae West (TV). 1985: Creator. 1987: LBJ: The Early Years (TV). 1988: Checking Out. 1990: Dick Tracy.

† Scenes deleted from final release print

WOODARD, Alfre 1953–

If this slim, elegant, full-lipped, challenging-looking black American actress seems to have been everywhere in the last dozen years or so, that probably owes much to her involvement in such high-profile TV series as *Hill Street Blues*, *St Elsewhere* and *L.A. Law*, for her appearances in films have actually been (far too) few. People have had trouble with both her names since she grew

up in Tulsa, Oklahoma: appropriately, though, her film debut was in *Remember My Name*. The face and talent, though have proved more memorable: she was nominated for an Academy Award in *Cross Creek*, a role that triggered an upswing in her career.

1978: Remember My Name. 1979: Health. 1981: The Ambush Murders (TV). Freedom (TV). 1983: Cross Creek. 1984: The Killing Floor (TV). Sweet Revenge (TV). Go Tell It on the Mountain. Trial of the Moke (TV). 1986: Extremities. Unnatural Causes: The Agent Orange Story (TV). 1988: Scrooged. The Child Saver (TV). 1989: Mandela (TV). A Mother's Courage: The Mary Thomas Story (TV). Miss Firecracker. 1990: A Show of Force. 1991: Grand Canyon. 1992: Passion Fish. The Gun in Betty Lou's Handbag. 1993: Bopha! Heart and Souls. Rich in Love. 1994: Crooklyn. Blue Chips. Race to Freedom: The Underground Railroad (TV). 1995: Follow Me Home. How to Make an American Quilt. The Piano Lesson (TV).

WOODBRIDGE, George 1907–1973

Big, jovial British actor with ruddy, countryman's complexion (he came from Devon), always likely to be one of the locals you saw in film taverns, whether pulling pints, swapping stories, scared of the vampire or just having a drink after a day's farming. He also played policemen – most notably the sergeant in the 'Stryker of the Yard' featurettes of the 1950s.

1937: Young and Innocent (US: The Girl Was Young). 1940: Mein Kampf My Crimes. 1941: The Saint Meets the Tiger. The Black Sheep of Whitehall. The Tower of Terror. The Big Blockade. 1942: The Day Will Dawn (US: The Avengers). 1943: Escape to Danger. The Life and Death of Colonel Blimp (US: Colonel Blimp). 1945: A Diary for Timothy. 1946: Green for Danger. I See a Dark Stranger (US: The Adventuress). 1947: The October Man. Temptation Harbour. Blanche Fury. My Brother Jonathan. 1948: Bonnie Prince Charlie. Escape. The Queen of Spades. The Fallen Idol. The Red Shoes. The Bad Lord Byron. Silent Dust. 1949: Children of Chance. 1950: The Naked Heart (Maria Chapdelaine/The Naked Earth). Double Confession. Trio. The Black Rose. 1951: Cloudburst. 1952: Isn't Life Wonderful! The Crimson Pirate. Murder in the Cathedral. 1953: The Story of Gilbert and Sullivan (US: The Great Gilbert and Sullivan). Stryker of the

*Yard. The Flanagan Boy (US: Bad Blonde). The Bosun's Mate. The Case of Express Delivery. The Case of Soho Red. The Case of Canary Jones. The Case of Gracie Budd. The Case of the Black Falcon. The Case of the Last Dance. The Case of the Marriage Bureau. 1954: The Night of the Full Moon. Companions in Crime. The Case of the Second Shot. Conflict of Wings (US: Fuss Over Feathers). The Case of the Bogus Count. The Green Buddha. The Case of Diamond Annie. An Inspector Calls. The Case of Uncle Henry. For Better, For Worse (US: Cocktails in the Kitchen). The Case of the Pearl Payroll. Mad About Men. Third Party Risk (US: The Deadly Game). 1955: The Constant Husband. An Alligator Named Daisy. Richard III. Passage Home. A Yank in Ermine. Lost (US: Tears for Simon). 1956: Eyewitness. Three Men in a Boat. The Passionate Stranger (US: A Novel Affair). Now and Forever. 1957: Day of Grace. High Flight. A King in New York. The Moonraker. 1958: The Revenge of Frankenstein. A Tale of Two Cities. Dracula (US: The Horror of Dracula). Son of Robin Hood. 1959: The Siege of Pinchgut (US: Four Desperate Men). Breakout. The Mummy. Jack the Ripper. The Flesh and the Fiends (US: Mania). 1960: Two-Way Stretch. Brides of Dracula. 1961: Curse of the Werewolf. Only Two Can Play. The Piper's Tune. What a Carve-Up! (US: No Place Like Homicide). Raising the Wind (US: Roommates). 1962: Out of the Fog. The Iron Maiden (US: The Swingin' Maiden). The Amorous Prawn. 1963: Nurse on Wheels. Carry On Jack (US: Carry On Venus). Heavens Above! The Scarlet Blade. 1964: Dead End Creek. 1965: Dracula – Prince of Darkness. 1966: The Reptile. 1967: The Magnificent Six and a $\frac{1}{2}$ (first series). 1969: *Bachelor of Arts (US: Durti Weekend). Where's Jack? Take a Girl Like You. 1970: David Copperfield (TV. GB: cinemas. Shown 1969). All the Way Up. 1971: Up Pompeii. 1972: Doomwatch. Along the Way. Diamonds on Wheels.*

WORDEN, Hank
(Norton Worden) 1901–1992

Skinny, dark-haired, balding, sometimes moustachioed portrayer of tall bedraggled westerners for more than 50 years, at first as sidekicks in B movies, but later often seen in the films of John Wayne and/or John Ford, where he might be the townsman leaning on the corral or sitting in a rocking chair outside the saloon. A genuine cowboy and rough rider, Worden and his roommate Tex Ritter (who became a star singing cowboy) were picked from the rodeo circuit in 1930 to play cowhands in the Broadway show *Green Grow the Lilies*. Films followed from 1936 and he even outran his old friend Wayne by appearing in them over a 55-year period. Once memorably described as a 'purveyor of scrawny simpletons', he played a recurring role in TV's *Twin Peaks* in the early 1990s. Surname pronounced Werden.

1936: *Ghost Town Gold. The Plainsman.* 1937: †*Hittin' the Trail.* †*The Mystery of the Hooded Horsemen.* †*Riders of the Rockies (GB: Rocky Mountain Riders).* ‡*Sing, Cowboy, Sing.* †*Tex Rides With the Boy Scouts. Moonlight on the Range.* 1938: *Frontier Town. Ghost Town Riders. The Singing Outlaw. The Stranger from Arizona. Rollin' Plains. Western Trails. Where the Buffalo Roam.* 1939: *The Cowboy and the Lady. Chip of the Flying U.* **Cupid Rides the Range. The Night Riders. Oklahoma Frontier. Rollin' Westward. Sundown on the Prairie. Timber Stampede.* 1940: *Cross Country Romance. Gaucho Serenade.* **Molly Cures a Cowboy. Northwest Passage. Riders of Pasco Basin. Winners of the West (serial).* 1941: *Border Vigilantes. Robbers of the Range.* **Mud About Moonshine.* 1942: *Code of the Outlaw. Cowboy Serenade (GB: Serenade of the West). Range Busters (completed 1940). Riding the Wind.* 1943: *Black Market Rustlers (GB: Land and the Law). Canyon City. A Lady Takes a Chance. Tenting Tonight on the Old Camp Ground. Wild Horse Stampede.* 1944: *Lumberjack. Prairie Raiders. Wyoming Hurricane (GB: Proved Guilty).* 1945: *Bud Abbott and Lou Costello in Hollywood. The Bullfighters.* 1946: *Duel in the Sun. Frontier Gun Law (GB: Menacing Shadows). The Lawless Breed. Undercurrent. The Shocking Miss Pilgrim.* 1947: *Angel and the Badman. The Man from Texas. Prairie Express. The High Wall. Sea of Grass. Slippy McGee. The Secret Life of Walter Mitty.* 1948: *Fort Apache. Feudin', Fussin' and a-Fightin'. Lightnin' in the Forest. Hazard. Angel in Exile. Red River. The Sainted Sisters. Tap Roots. 3 Godfathers. Yellow Sky.* 1949: *The Fighting Kentuckian. Roseanna McCoy. Hellfire. Red Canyon. Curtain Call at Cactus Creek (GB: Take the Stage). Streets of Laredo.* 1950: *Father is a Bachelor. Frenchie. Wagonmaster. When Willie Comes Marching Home.* 1951: *Joe Palooka in Triple Cross (GB: The Triple Cross). The Man With a Cloak. Sugarfoot/Swirl of Glory.* 1952: *Apache War Smoke. The Big Sky. Boots Malone. The Quiet Man. Woman of the North Country.* 1953: *Crime Wave (GB: The City is Dark).* 1954: *Ma and Pa Kettle at Home. The Outcast (GB: The Fortune Hunter).* 1955: *The Indian Fighter. Davy Crockett and the River Pirates. The Road to Denver.* 1956: *Accused of Murder. Meet Me in Las Vegas (GB: Viva Las Vegas!). The Quiet Gun. The Searchers. The Truth (TV).* 1957: *The Buckskin Lady. Forty Guns. Dragoon Wells Massacre. Spoilers of the Forest.* 1958: *Bullwhip! The Notorious Mr Monks. Toughest Gun in Tombstone.* 1959: *The Horse Soldiers.* 1960: *The Alamo. Sergeant Rutledge. One-Eyed Jacks.* 1961: *The Music Man.* 1963: *McLintock!* 1965: *Big Daddy.* 1967: *Good Times. Hondo*

and the Apaches. The President's Analyst. 1969: *True Grit.* 1970: *Chisum. Rio Lobo.* 1971: *Big Jake. Black Noon (TV). Bedknobs and Broomsticks.* 1973: *Cahill, United States Marshal (GB: Cahill).* 1974: *The Hanged Man (TV).* 1975: *Sky Heist (TV).* 1976: *The Legend of Frank Woods.* 1977: *Smokey and the Bandit. Which Way is Up?* 1978: *Big Wednesday. Every Which Way But Loose. Sergeant Pepper's Lonely Hearts Club Band. They Went That-a-Way and That-a-Way.* 1980: *Bronco Billy.* 1982: *Hammett.* 1984: *The Ice Pirates.* 1985: *Scream (filmed 1981). Runaway Train.* 1990: *Almost an Angel.*

† As Heber Snow
‡ As Henry Snow

WRIGHT, Will 1891 1962
Tall, slightly stooping, long-faced American supporting actor with a slick of dark hair and a hangdog look. Quite unmistakeable in appearance, but rarely rose above minor roles; a happy exception was his seedy apartment house detective in *The Blue Dahlia*. His credits are sometimes confused with those of a younger actor, William Wright, but the films given here should all belong to the correct actor! Died from cancer.

1936: *China Clipper.* 1939: *Silver on the Sage.* 1940: *Blondie Plays Cupid.* 1941: *Rookies on Parade.* **The Tell Tale Heart. Honky Tonk. Cracked Nuts. Shadow of the Thin Man. Blossoms in the Dust. Maisie Was a Lady. Nothing But the Truth. World Premiere. Richest Man in Town.* 1942: *The Postman Didn't Ring. True to the Army. Shut My Big Mouth. Lucky Legs. Tennessee Johnson (GB: The Man on America's Conscience). Parachute Nurse. A Gentleman After Dark. Wildcat. Night in New Orleans. Sweetheart of the Fleet. Saboteur. The Daring Young Man. The Major and the Minor. Tales of Manhattan.* **A Letter from Bataan. The Meanest Man in the World.* 1943: *Murder in Times Square. In Old Oklahoma (later and GB: War of the Wildcats). Cowboy in Manhattan. Sleepy Lagoon. Reveille with Beverly. Saddles and Sagebrush (GB: The Pay Off). So Proudly We Hail! Here Comes Elmer.* 1944: *The Navy Way. Practically Yours. One Mysterious Night. The Town Went Wild. Wilson.* 1945: *Eadie Was a Lady. Eve Knew Her Apples. State Fair. Salome, Where She Danced. Road to Utopia. Grissly's Millions. Scarlet Street. The Strange Affair of Uncle*

Harry/Uncle Harry. Rhapsody in Blue. Gun Smoke. Bewitched. You Came Along. 1946: *Lover Come Back. The Blue Dahlia. Without Reservations. Johnny Comes Flying Home. One Exciting Week. The Inner Circle. The Madonna's Secret. Rendezvous with Annie. Hot Cargo. The Hoodlum Saint. The Jolson Story. Blue Skies. Nocturne. Down Missouri Way. California.* 1947: *Along the Oregon Trail. Blaze of Noon. Mother Wore Tights. Cynthia (GB: The Rich, Full Life). Keeper of the Bees. Wild Harvest. The Trouble with Women. They Live by Night (released 1949).* 1948: *An Act of Murder. So This is New York. Station West. Mr Blandings Builds His Dream House. The Inside Story. Disaster. Black Eagle. Act of Violence. Relentless. Green Grass of Wyoming. The Walls of Jericho. Whispering Smith.* **California's Golden Beginning (narrator only).* 1949: *Lust for Gold. Little Women. Big Jack. Adam's Rib. Miss Grant Takes Richmond (GB: Innocence Is Bliss). Mrs Mike. Impact. Brimstone. All the King's Men.* 1950: *Dallas. No Way Out. The Savage Horde. Sunset in the West. Mister 880. The House by the River. A Ticket to Tomahawk.* 1951: *Excuse My Dust. My Forbidden Past. Vengeance Valley. Young Man With Ideas. The Tall Target. People Will Talk.* 1952: *Holiday for Sinners. The Las Vegas Story. Paula (GB: The Silent Voice). O. Henry's Full House (GB: Full House). Lydia Bailey. The Happy Time. Lure of the Wilderness.* 1953: *Niagara. The Last Posse. The Wild One.* 1954: *River of No Return. The Raid. Johnny Guitar.* 1955: *The Tall Men. The Kentuckian. The Man with the Golden Arm. The Court Martial of Billy Mitchell (GB: One Man Mutiny). Not As a Stranger.* 1956: *These Wilder Years.* 1957: *The Iron Sheriff. Johnny Tremain. The Wayward Bus. Jeanne Eagels.* 1958: *The Missouri Traveler. Quantrill's Raiders. Gunman's Walk.* 1959: *Alias Jesse James. The 30-Foot Bride of Candy Rock.* 1961: *The Deadly Companions. Twenty Plus Two (GB: It Started in Tokyo). Cape Fear.* 1964: *Fail Safe.*

WYCHERLY, Margaret 1881–1956
Hawk-faced, eager-eyed, sharp-nosed, dark-haired British-born actress who played only one really memorable film role — James Cagney's possessive mother in *White Heat*. After a London stage debut at 17, she came to America in the early years of the 20th century and stayed to chalk up numerous

Broadway appearances before making a few film appearances as well, mainly in the 1940s. Usually played mothers, aunts, or grasping relatives. Several filmographies credit her with an appearance in *Richard III* (1955), but she isn't listed in the longest available cast. Academy Award nominee for *Sergeant York*.

*1915: The Fight. 1929: The Thirteenth Chair. 1934: Midnight. 1938: *Wanderlust. 1940: Victory. 1941: Sergeant York. 1942: Cross-roads. Keeper of the Flame. Random Harvest. 1943: Assignment in Brittany. Hangmen Also Die. The Moon is Down. 1944: Experiment Perilous. 1945: Johnny Angel. The Enchanted Cottage. 1946: The Yearling. 1947: Forever Amber. Something in the Wind. 1948: The Loves of Carmen. 1949: White Heat. 1951: The Man with a Cloak. 1953: The President's Lady. That Man from Tangier.*

WYNN, Ed
(Isaiah Edwin Leopold, later legally changed) 1886–1966
Dark-haired, inimitably Jewish (although he married a Catholic), bespectacled American comedian, known in his wildly successful, baggy-panted vaudeville days as 'The Perfect Fool'. His early film sound comedies were not successful, but he returned to Hollywood in his seventies with his gurgling voice intact and found himself in demand to play eccentric old gentlemen, especially in Walt Disney productions. Father of Keenan Wynn (qv). Nominated for an Oscar in *The Diary of Anne Frank*. Died from cancer.

*1912: *Exposed by the Dictograph. 1927: Rubber Heels. 1930: Follow the Leader. 1933: The Chief (GB: My Old Man's a Fireman). 1943: Stage Door Canteen. 1951: Alice in Wonderland (voice only). 1956: The Great Man. Requiem for a Heavyweight (TV). 1957: The Great American Hoax (TV). 1958: Marjorie Morningstar. 1959: The Diary of Anne Frank. Miracle on 34th Street (TV). 1960: The Absent-Minded Professor. Cinderfella. 1961: Babes in Toyland. 1962: The Golden Horseshoe Revue. 1963: Son of Flubber. 1964: Those Calloways. Mary Poppins. The Patsy. 1965: That Darn Cat! Dear Brigitte . . . The Greatest Story Ever Told. 1966: The Daydreamer (voice only). 1967: The Gnome-Mobile. Warning Shot.*

WYNN, Keenan
(Francis K. Wynn) 1916–1986
Dark-haired, often moustachioed American actor with faintly dejected air, rough-edged voice and energetic character. At his best during his long association with MGM, specifically from 1945 to 1955, he provided more useful back-up for the stars than some of them could handle, notably in comedy. He might well have been nominated for an Oscar for his best performances, in *Holiday for Sinners* and *Kiss Me, Kate!*, although later portrayals were more extravagant and less enjoyable. Son of Ed Wynn (qv); father of screenwriter Tracy Keenan Wynn. Died from cancer.

1934: Chained (as stunt double). 1942: For Me and My Gal (GB: For Me and My Girl). Somewhere I'll Find You. Northwest Rangers. 1943: Lost Angel. 1944: Marriage is a Private Affair. See Here, Private Hargrove. Since You Went Away. Ziegfeld Follies (released 1946). 1945: What Next, Corporal Hargrove? Between Two Women. Without Love. Week-End at the Waldorf. The Clock (GB: Under the Clock). 1946: The Thrill of Brazil. The Cockeyed Miracle (GB: Mr Griggs Returns). Easy to Wed. No Leave, No Love. 1947: Song of the Thin Man. The Hucksters. 1948: My Dear Secretary. BF's Daughter (GB: Polly Fulton). The Three Musketeers. 1949: Neptune's Daughter. That Midnight Kiss. 1950: Love That Brute. Annie Get Your Gun. Royal Wedding (GB: Wedding Bells). Three Little Words. 1951: Texas Carnival. Kind Lady. It's a Big Country. Angels in the Outfield (GB: Angels and the Pirates). The Belle of New York. 1952: Skirts Ahoy. Phone Call from a Stranger. Fearless Fagan. Sky Full of Moon. Desperate Search. Holiday for Sinners. 1953: All the Brothers Were Valiant. Battle Circus. Code Two. Kiss Me, Kate! 1954: Men of the Fighting Lady. Tennessee Champ. The Long, Long Trailer. The Glass Slipper. 1955: The Marauders. Running Wild. Shack Out on 101. 1956: The Naked Hills. The Man in the Gray Flannel Suit. Johnny Concho. Requiem for a Heavyweight (TV). 1957: Joe Butterfly. The Great Man. The Last Tycoon (TV). Don't Go Near the Water. The Fuzzy Pink Nightgown. The Troublemakers (TV). 1958: Touch of Evil. A Time to Love and a Time to Die. The Deep Six. No Time at All (TV). The Perfect Furlough (GB: Strictly for Pleasure). 1959: A Hole in the Head. The Scarface Mob (originally TV). That

Kind of Woman. 1960: The Crowded Sky. The Absent-Minded Professor. 1961: The Power and the Glory (TV. GB: cinemas). Il re di poggioreale. King of the Roaring Twenties (GB: The Big Bankroll). 1963: The Bay of St Michel (US: Pattern for Plunder). Son of Flubber. Dr Strangelove, or: How I Learned to Stop Worrying and Love the Bomb. Man in the Middle. Nightmare in the Sun. 1964: Stage to Thunder Rock. Honeymoon Hotel. The Americanization of Emily. The Patsy. Bikini Beach. 1965: The Great Race. Promise Her Anything. 1966: Around the World Under the Sea. Night of the Grizzly. Stagecoach. Welcome to Hard Times (GB: Killer on a Horse). Run Like a Thief. 1967: Warning Shot. Point Blank. The War Wagon. 1968: Spara, Gringo, spara (GB: and US: The Longest Hunt). Finian's Rainbow. Blood Holiday. Once Upon a Time in the West. 1969: Smith! McKenna's Gold. The Young Lawyers (TV). The Monitors. 80 Steps to Jonah. 1970: Viva Max! Loving. Assault on the Wayne (TV). The House on Greenapple Road (TV). Battle at Gannon's Ridge (TV). The Animals (GB: Five Savage Men). 1971: L'uomo dagli occhi di ghiaccio. Terror in the Sky (TV). BJ Presents. Pretty Maids All in a Row. The Falling Man. 1972: Padella calibro 38/Panhandle Calibre 38 (released 1975). Assignment Munich (TV). The Artist. Wild in the Sky. Cancel My Reservation. The Mechanic (later Killer of Killers). 1973: Snowball Express. Hijack (TV). Hit Lady (TV). Hollywood Knight. Night Train to Terror. Herbie Rides Again. 1974: The Legend of Earl Durand. The Internecine Project. 1975: Target Risk (TV). A Woman for All Men/A Part Time Wife. The Devil's Rain. The Man Who Would Not Die. Nashville. He Is My Brother. The Killer Inside Me. 1976: The Lindbergh Kidnapping Case (TV). Twenty Shades of Pink (TV). The Shaggy DA. High Velocity. The Quest (TV). 1977: Orca . . . Killer Whale. The Thoroughbreds (later Treasure Seekers). Kino, the Padre on Horseback. Sex and the Married Woman (TV). Laserblast. 1978: Coach. The Dark. Piranha. The Bushido Blade (released 1982). Touch of the Sun. 1979: Monster. The Billion Dollar Threat (TV. GB: cinemas). Supertrain (TV. Later: Express to Terror). The Clonus Horror. Just Tell Me What You Want. The Glove (released 1981). Sunburn. 1980: Mom, the Wolfman and Me (TV). The Monkey Mission (TV). 1981: A Piano for Mrs Cimino (TV). The Capture of Grizzly Adams (TV). The Last Unicorn (voice only). 1982: Wavelength. Best Friends. Hysterical. 1983: Boomerang. Return of the Man from UNCLE (TV). 1984: Prime Risk. Call to Glory (TV). 1985: Black Moon Rising. Tales from the Darkside. The Last Precinct (TV). Mirrors (TV). 1986: Hyper Sapien: People from Another Star. Vasectomy, a Delicate Matter.

Father? Squibs. 18 Minutes. Jubilee Window. Full Circle. The Deputy Drummer. Handle With Care. 1936: Queen of Hearts. Faithful. The Man in the Mirror. In the Soup. What the Puppy Said. Gypsy Melody. No Escape/No Exit. Fame. 1937: Beauty and the Barge. Merry Comes to Town (US: Merry Comes to Stay). The Compulsory Wife. The Biter Bit/Calling All Ma's. French Leave. You Live and Learn. 1938: You're the Doctor. Prison Without Bars. 1939: The Face at the Window. French Without Tears. 1940: Crimes at the Dark House. Two Smart Men. George and Margaret. The Second Mr Bush. Henry Steps Out. 1942: Tomorrow We Live (US: At Dawn We Die). 1943: Thursday's Child. It's in the Bag. 1944: *The Two Fathers.

Beverly Hills Brats. 1989: Medium Rare. Last Exit to Brooklyn. Wait Until Spring, Bandini. The Unsinkable Shecky Moscowitz. 1990: Diving In. Backstreet Dreams/Backstreet Strays. Trouble in the Night. A Family Matter/Vendetta (cable TV). Club Fed. Bright Angel. Betsy's Wedding. Rocky V. 1991: Americano Rosso. The Final Contract (TV). Columbo: Undercover (TV). 1993: Behind the Truth (TV. GB: Double Deception). Il caso bianco Berlino. 1994: Excessive Force. 1995: Monastery. Opposite Corners. The North Star.

† As John Harris

YARDE, Margaret 1878–1944

Formidable, dark-haired, big-eyebrowed British actress who had many years of theatrical experience behind her – she started as a chorus girl at 16 – before she came to British films to play mothers, land-ladies and nagging wives. This Kathleen Harrison of her day moved from the chorus to begin the main part of her career as an opera singer – then turned to straight acting with the accent on comedy. Had it not been for her relatively early death, she would doubtless have gone on blustering into post-war British films as garrulous grans.

1913: A Cigarette Maker's Romance. 1922: The Unwanted Bride. 1923: *Falstaff the Tavern Knight. *Madame Recamier – or The Price of Virtue. 1925: *The Weakness of Men. *Red Lips. *Sables of Death. *Hearts Trump Diamonds. *Heel Taps. The Only Way. *The Leading Man. *Caught in the Web. 1926: London. 1929: The Crooked Billet. 1930: Night Birds. 1931: Michael and Mary. Let's Love and Laugh (US: Bridegroom for Two). Third Time Lucky. Uneasy Virtue. The Woman Between (US: The Woman Decides). 1932: Down Our Street. The Sign of Four. The Man from Toronto. 1933: The Good Companions. A Shot in the Dark. I Lived With You. Tiger Bay. Matinee Idol. Enemy of the Police. Trouble in Store. 1934: Nine Forty-Five. Father and Son. Sing As We Go. A Glimpse of Paradise. The Broken Rosary. Guest of Honour (US: The Man from Blankley's). 1935: Scrooge. That's My Uncle. Widows Might. It Happened in Paris. The Crouching Beast. Who's Your

YOUNG, Burt 1940–

Fat-lipped, bulbous-eyed, round-faced, stockily-built aggressive little American actor with rapidly disappearing dark curly hair. An ex-prizefighter who also writes screenplays, he has mostly appeared in streetwise roles (notably as the brother of Talia Shire in the *Rocky* films) where, between tiptilted trilby and grubby collar, he seemed more at home with modern scatological dialogue than most. Nominated for a best supporting Oscar in *Rocky*, his profile has been lower since the boxing series ended.

1970: †Carnival of Blood. 1971: Born to Win. The Gang That Couldn't Shoot Straight. 1972: Across 110th Street. 1973: Cinderella Liberty. The Connection (TV). 1974: The Great Niagara (TV). Chinatown. Murph the Surf (GB: Live a Little, Steal a Lot). The Gambler. 1975: Hustling (TV). The Killer Elite. 1976: Harry and Walter Go to New York. Rocky. Serpico: The Deadly Game (TV). Woman of the Year (TV). 1977: Twilight's Last Gleaming. The Choirboys. 1978: Convoy. Daddy, I Don't Like It Like This (TV). 1979: Rocky II. Uncle Joe Shannon. 1980: Blood Beach (filmed 1978). Murder Can Hurt You! (TV). Lookin' to Get Out (released 1982). 1981: All the Marbles . . . (GB: The California Dolls). 1982: Rocky III. Amityville II The Possession. 1983: Over the Brooklyn Bridge. Once Upon a Time in America. 1984: The Pope of Greenwich Village. 1985: A Summer to Remember (TV). Rocky IV. 1986: The Right Hand Man. Back to School. 1987: Blood Red. 1988:

YOUNG, Roland 1887–1953

Huffly-snuffly, apologetic, moustachioed British-born actor with a wisp of brown hair, who was almost always beautifully bewildered, and deservedly became a star character actor, his best run coming from 1935 to 1941, years in which he played the ghost-beset banker Topper three times. For the first of the series, Young was nominated for an Oscar.

1922: Sherlock Holmes (GB: Moriarty). 1923: Fog Bound. Grit. 1929: The Unholy Night. Her Private Life. 1930: Madam Satan. Wise Girl. New Moon. The Bishop Murder Case. 1931: The Squaw Man (GB: The White Man). The Prodigal. The Sin of Madelon Claudet (GB: The Lullaby). The Guardsman. Don't Bet on Women. Annabelle's Affairs. Pagan Lady. This is the Night. 1932: Wedding Rehearsal. A Woman Commands. Street of Women. Lovers Courageous. One Hour with You. 1933: Pleasure Cruise. They Just Had to Get Married. His Double Life. A Lady's Profession. Blind Adventure. 1934: Here is My Heart. 1935: David Copperfield. Ruggles of Red Gap. 1936: The Man Who Could Work Miracles. Gypsy. The Unguarded Hour. One Rainy Afternoon. Give Me Your Heart (GB: Sweet Aloes). 1937: King Solomon's Mines. Call It a Day. Ali Baba Goes to Town. Topper. 1938: Sailing Along. The Young in Heart. 1939: The Night of Nights. Topper Takes a Trip. Here I Am, a Stranger. Yes, My Darling Daughter. 1940: Star Dust. He Married His Wife. Dulcy. The Philadelphia Story. Irene. Private Affairs. No, No, Nanette. 1941: Two-Faced Woman. Topper Returns. The Flame of New Orleans. 1942: Tales of Manhattan. The Lady Has Plans. They All Kissed the Bride. 1943: Forever and a Day. 1944: Standing Room Only. 1945: And Then There Were None (GB: Ten Little Niggers).

1948: Bond Street. You Gotta Stay Happy. 1949: The Great Lover. 1950: Let's Dance. 1951: St Benny the Dip (GB: Escape If You Can). 1953: That Man from Tangier.

YULE, Joe
(Ninnian J. Yule Jr) 1888–1950

Short, stumpy, snub-nosed, red-haired, mischievous-looking Scottish comedian who came to America as a young man, became a music-hall, burlesque and vaudeville comedian, and found his fame eclipsed by that of his son, Ninnian Joe Jr, who grew up to be Mickey Rooney. When Rooney became a world star, he brought his father to MGM, where Yule played small supporting roles as a comic character actor, before starring in the low-budget Jiggs and Maggie comedies of the late 1940s, a series brought to a premature conclusion by Yule's death from a heart attack at 61.

1938: A Christmas Carol. Four Girls in White. Idiot's Delight. 1939: Judge Hardy and Son. Sudden Money. Fast and Furious. They All Come Out. The Secret of Dr Kildare. 1940: Florian. Forty Little Mothers. Broadway Melody of 1940. Strike Up the Band. New Moon. Go West/Marx Brothers Go West. Boom Town. Third Finger, Left Hand. Phantom Raiders. 1941: Come Live With Me. Billy the Kid. Married Bachelor. I'll Wait for You. Babes on Broadway. Shadow of the Thin Man. Maisie Was a Lady. The Trial of Mary Dugan. Wild Man of Borneo. The Get-Away. Woman of the Year. Kathleen. The Big Store. 1942: Grand Central Murder. The Omaha Trail. For Me and My Gal (GB: For Me and My Girl). Calling Doctor Gillespie. Jackass Mail. Born to Sing. Nazi Agent. Panama Hattie. 1943: Presenting Lily Mars. I Dood It (GB: By Hook or By Crook). Swing Shift Maisie (GB: The Girl in Overalls). Air Raid Wardens. Three Hearts for Julia. 1944: Two Girls and a Sailor. Nothing But Trouble. Kismet. Lost Angel. Barbary Coast Gent. Bathing Beauty. The Seventh Cross. The Thin Man Goes Home. 1945: The Picture of Dorian Gray. 1946: The Mighty McGurk. Murder in the Music Hall. Bringing Up Father. 1947: Jiggs and Maggie in Society. 1948: Jiggs and Maggie in Court. 1949: Jackpot Jitters/Jiggs and Maggie in Jackpot Jitters. 1950: Jiggs and Maggie Out West.

YURKA, Blanche
(B. Jurka) 1887–1974

Strong Hollywood actress of Bohemian parentage (brought to America in infancy), with inimitably mellow voice and hollow-set eyes. A former opera singer, she made her name on the Broadway stage in the early 1920s, and became a Hollywood character actress with her memorably brooding Madame DeFarge ('I was the 67th actress to test for the part') in *A Tale of Two Cities*. At one time married to actor Ian Keith (I.K. Ross, 1899–1960), she died from arteriosclerosis.

*1918: *She's Everywhere. 1935: A Tale of Two Cities. 1940: Queen of the Mob. City for Conquest. Escape. 1941: Ellery Queen and the Murder Ring (GB: The Murder Ring). 1942: Pacific Rendezvous. A Night to Remember. Lady for a Night. Keeper of the Flame. 1943: Hitler's Madman. The Song of Bernadette. Tonight We Raid Calais. 1944: One Body Too Many. The Bridge of San Luis Rey. Cry of the Werewolf. 1945: The Southerner. 1946: 13 Rue Madeleine. 1947: The Flame. 1950: The Furies. 1951: At Sword's Point (GB: Sons of the Musketeers). 1953: Taxi. 1959: Thunder in the Sun.*

ZERBE, Anthony 1936–

Solidly built American actor with thick brown wavy hair, square face, raised eyebrows, quizzical expression and slight scowl, faintly reminiscent of Britain's Victor Maddern (*qv*). Hitchhiking to New York to become an actor, he broke into television

from 1965 and films from 1967. At first he was (frequently) seen in violent or bigoted roles; he estimates that in one early year he killed or was killed 119 times, mostly on TV, a medium in which his long-running role as the police lieutenant in the *Harry O* series gave him the chance to pitch a quieter, more laconic note. Not much seen in the 1990s.

1967: Cool Hand Luke. Will Penny. 1969: The Molly Maguires. The Liberation of L B Jones. 1970: Cotton Comes to Harlem. They Call Me MISTER Tibbs! 1971: The Omega Man. The Priest Killer (TV). 1972: The Life and Times of Judge Roy Bean. The Strange Vengeance of Rosalie. The Hound of the Baskervilles (TV). 1973: Snatched (TV). She Lives (TV). The Laughing Policeman (GB: An Investigation of Murder). Papillon. 1974: The Parallax View. The Healers (TV). 1975: Farewell, My Lovely. Rooster Cogburn. 1976: The Secret of the Pond (TV). 1977: In the Glitter Palace (TV). The Turning Point. 1978: Child of Glass (TV). Who'll Stop the Rain? (GB: Dog Soldiers). Attack of the Phantoms/KISS Meets the Phantom of the Park (TV). 1979: The Chisholms (TV). 1980: The First Deadly Sin. Attica: The Story of a Prison Riot (TV). The Seduction of Miss Leona (TV). 1982: Rascals and Robbers: The Secret Adventures of Tom Sawyer and Huck Finn (TV). Soggy Bottom USA. A Question of Honor (TV). 1983: The Dead Zone. The Return of the Man from UNCLE (TV). 1986: PI Private Investigations. One Police Plaza (TV). Opposing Force/Hell Camp. 1987: Independence (TV). Steel Dawn. 1988: Baja Oklahoma. Licence Revoked. 1989: Columbo Goes to the Guillotine (TV). Listen to Me. 1990: Onassis: The Richest Man in the World (TV).

BIBLIOGRAPHY

Of the many magazines used in the compilation of this book, listings, reviews and casts published by the following between 1925 and 1995 have proved especially useful:

Film, Film Dope, Film in Review, Films and Filming, Hollywood Reporter, Monthly Film Bulletin, The Movie, New York Times, Picturegoer, Picture Show, Sight and Sound and *Variety.*

My thanks go also to the authors of the following books which provided so many of the fragments that went towards building up what I hope are mounds of information.

AARONSON, Charles S. (and others, eds). *International Motion Picture Almanac.* 1933−1984. Quigley Publications, dates as given.

ADAMS, Les, and RAINEY, Buck. *Shoot-em-Ups.* Arlington House, 1980.

BARBOUR, Alan G. *Cliffhanger, a Pictorial History of the Motion Picture Serial.* A & W Publishers/BCW Publishing, 1977.

BAXTER, John. *The Hollywood Exiles.* Macdonald and Jane's, 1976.

BLUM, Daniel. *A Pictorial History of the Silent Screen.* Spring, Books, 1953.

BLUM, Daniel. *A Pictorial History of the Talkies.* Spring Books, 1958. (Revised) Grosset and Dunlap, 1970.

BODEEN, DeWitt. *From Hollywood.* Barnes, 1976.

BODEEN, DeWitt. *More from Hollywood.* Barnes/Tantivy, 1977.

BROWN, Geoff. *Launder and Gilliat.* British Film Institute, 1977.

BROWNLOW, Kevin. *The War, the West and the Wilderness.* Secker and Warburg, 1978.

CAMERON, Ian and Elisabeth. *Heavies.* Studio Vista, 1967.

CAMERON, Ian and Elisabeth. *Broads.* Studio Vista, 1969.

CAMERON-WILSON, James. *Young Hollywood.* B.T. Batsford Ltd, 1994.

COPYRIGHT Entries, 1912−1960. Washington DC: Copyright Office of the Library of Congress.

CORNEAU, Ernest N. *The Hall of Fame of Western Film Stars.* Christopher Publishing, 1969.

COWIE, Peter, ed. *International Film Guide.* 1948 through 1994. Tantivy Press, dates as given.

DIMMITT, Richard Bertrand. *An Actor Guide to the Talkies* (two vols). The Scarecrow Press, 1968.

EISNER, Lotte. *Fritz Lang.* Secker and Warburg, 1976.

EVERSON, William K. *The Bad Guys.* Citadel, 1964.

EYLES, Allen. *The Western.* Barnes/Tantivy, 1975.

FILMLEXICON *degli autori e delle opera* (six vols). Bianco e Nero, 1958, 1962.

FITZGERALD, Michael V. *Universal Pictures.* Arlington House, 1977.

GERTNER, Richard, (and others, eds). *International Television Almanac,* 1929 through 1994. Quigley Publishing Company, dates as given.

GIFFORD, Denis. *Catalogue of British Films, 1895−1970.* David and Charles, 1971.

GIFFORD, Denis. *The Illustrated Who's Who in British Films.* B.T. Batsford, 1978.

HALLIWELL, Leslie. *The Filmgoer's Companion* (nine editions). MacGibbon and Kee/Hart−Davis−MacGibbon/ Grarada Publishing. Dates various, 1965−1987.

HERBERT, Ian, (and others, eds). *Who's Who in the Theatre* (17 editions), Pitman Publishing. Dates various, 1929−1984.

JONES, Ken D., MCCLURE, Arthur F. and TWOMEY, Alfred E. *Character People,* Citadel Press, 1976.

JONES, Ken D., MCCLURE, Arthur F. and TWOMEY, Alfred E. *More Character People.* Citadel Press 1984.

KATZ, Ephraim. *The International Film Encyclopedia.* Macmillan, 1980 and 1994 (two editions).

KULIK, Karol. *Alexander Korda.* W.H. Allen, 1975.

LAMPARSKI, Richard. *Whatever Became Of. . .?* (ten volumes). Crown Publishing, various dates, 1967 through 1986.

LAMPRECHT, Gerhardt. *Deutsche Stummfilm* (nine volumes). Deutsche Kinemathek, 1967.

LOW, Rachael. *The History of the British Film* (six volumes to date; Vol 1 written with Roger Manvell). Unwin Brothers/ George Allen and Unwin. Various dates, 1948−1979.

MALTIN, Leonard, and others. *The Real Stars* (two volumes). Signet Books, 1969 and 1972.

MALTIN, Leonard, and BANN, Richard W. *Our Gang.* Crown Publishing, 1977.

MARILL, Alvin H. *Motion Pictures Made for Television 1964−1986.* Baseline, 1987.

MARTIN, Mick and PORTER, Marsha. *Video Movie Guide 1995.* Ballatine Books, 1994.

MCCLURE, Arthur F, and JONES, Ken D. *Heroes, Heavies and Sagebrush.* Barnes, 1972.

MEYERS, Warren B. *Who Is That?* Production Design Associates, 1967.

NASH, Jay Robert, and ROSS, Stanley Ralph. *The Motion Picture Guide* (nine volumes). CineBooks, 1985.

NOBLE, Peter, and others ed. *International Film and TV Yearbook.* 1946 through 1984. British and American Film

Press/Holdings Ltd/Screen International EMAP, dates as given.

OLIVIERO, Jeffrey. *Motion Picture Players' Credits*. McFarland, 1991.

PALMER, Scott. *British Film Actors' Credits 1895–1987*. McFarland, 1988.

PALMER, Scott. *A Who's Who of British Film Actors*. The Scarecrow Press, 1981.

PARISH, James Robert. *Actors' Television Credits, 1950–1972*. The Scarecrow Press, 1973.

PARISH, James Robert. *Film Actors' Guide – Western Europe*. The Scarecrow Press, 1977.

PARISH, James Robert. *Hollywood Character Actors*. Arlington House, 1978.

PARISH, James Robert, and BOWERS, Ronald L. *The MGM Stock Company*, Ian Allan, 1973.

PARISH, James Robert, and DECARL, Lennard. *Hollywood Players: The Forties*. Arlington House, 1976.

PARISH, James Robert, and LEONARD, William T. *Hollywood Players – The Thirties*. Arlington House, 1976.

PARISH, James Robert, and STANKE, Don E. *The Leading Ladies*. Rainbow Books, 1979.

PERRY, George. *Forever Ealing*. Pavilion/Michael Joseph, 1981.

PERRY, George. *Hitchcock*. Macmillan, 1975.

PICKARD, Roy. *The Oscar Movies* (two editions). Muller, 1977 and 1982.

PICTURE SHOW *Who's Who on the Screen*. The Amalgamated Press, 1956.

PICTUREGOER *British Film and TV Who's Who*. Published with magazine, Odhams Press, 1953.

PICTUREGOER *Hollywood Who's Who*. Published with magazine. Odhams Press, 1953.

QUINLAN, David. *British Sound Films: The Studio Years 1928– 1959*. B.T. Batsford, 1984.

RAGAN, David. *Who's Who in Hollywood 1900–1976*. Arlington House, 1976.

READE, Eric. *The Australian Screen*. Lansdowne Press/BCW Publishing, 1975.

ROTHEL, David. *The Singing Cowboys*. Barnes, 1978.

ROUD, Richard, ed. *Cinema: a Critical Dictionary* (two volumes). Secker and Warburg, 1980.

SILVER, Alain, and WARD, Elizabeth, eds. *Film Noir*. Secker and Warburg, 1980.

SPEED, F. Maurice, and CAMERON-WILSON, James. *Film Review*. Various editions. 1947–1994. MacDonald and Co/W.H. Allen.

THOMAS, Tony. *Cads and Cavaliers*. Barnes, 1973.

THOMAS, Tony. *The Films of the Forties*. Citadel Press, 1975.

TRUITT, Evelyn Mack. *Who Was Who on Screen* (three editions). R.R. Bowker Co, 1973, 1977 and 1984.

TV Feature Film *Source Book*, 1994 edition. Broadcast Information Bureau, date as given.

TWOMEY, Alfred E. and MCCLURE, Arthur, F. *The Versatiles*. Barnes, 1969.

VERMILYE, Jerry. *The Great British Films*. Citadel Press, 1978.

WEAVER, John T. *Forty Years of Screen Credits* (two volumes). The Scarecrow Press, 1970.

WEAVER, John T. and JOHNSON, A. Collins. *Twenty Years of Silents*. The Scarecrow Press, 1971.

WEAVER, Tom. *Poverty Row Horrors!* McFarlane, 1994.

WILLIAMS, Mark. *Road Movies*. Proteus, 1978.

WILLIS, John. *Screen World* (42 editions, to 1994). Muller.

WITCOMBE, R.T. *The New Italian Cinema*. Secker and Warburg, 1982.

YOUNG, Jordan R. *Reel Characters*. The Moonstone Press, 1986.

ZIEROLD, Norman J. *The Child Stars*. MacDonald, 1965.